FIELDING TRAVEL GUIDES

FIELDING'S BUDGET EUROPE

Fielding Titles

Fielding's Amazon
Fielding's Australia
Fielding's Bahamas
Fielding's Belgium
Fielding's Bermuda
Fielding's Borneo
Fielding's Brazil
Fielding's Britain
Fielding's Budget Europe
Fielding's Caribbean
Fielding's Europe
Fielding's Far East
Fielding's France
Fielding's Guide to the World's Most Dangerous Places
Fielding's Guide to the World's Great Voyages
Fielding's Guide to Kenya's Best Hotels, Lodges & Homestays
Fielding's Guide to the World's Most Romantic Places
Fielding's Hawaii
Fielding's Holland
Fielding's Italy
Fielding's London Agenda
Fielding's Los Angeles Agenda
Fielding's Malaysia and Singapore
Fielding's Mexico
Fielding's New York Agenda
Fielding's New Zealand
Fielding's Paris Agenda
Fielding's Portugal
Fielding's Scandinavia
Fielding's Seychelles
Fielding's Southeast Asia
Fielding's Spain
Fielding's Vacation Places Rated
Fielding's Vietnam
Fielding's Worldwide Cruises

FIELDING'S BUDGET EUROPE

Fun and Adventure on a Budget! The Fielding Guide to Great Times, Great Buys and Discovery in 18 Countries

Joseph & Judith Raff

Fielding Worldwide, Inc.
308 South Catalina Avenue
Redondo Beach, California 90277 U.S.A.

Fielding's Budget Europe

Published by Fielding Worldwide, Inc.

FIELDING WORLDWIDE INC.

PUBLISHER AND CEO **Robert Young Pelton**
PUBLISHING DIRECTOR **Paul T. Snapp**
PUBLISHING DIRECTOR **Larry E. Hart**
PROJECT DIRECTOR **Tony E. Hulette**
ACCOUNT EXCUTIVE **Beverly Riess**
ACCOUNT SERVICES MANAGER **Christy Harp**

EDITORS

Linda Charlton **Kathy Knoles**

PRODUCTION

Gini Martin **Chris Snyder**
Craig South

COVER DESIGNED BY **Digital Artists, Inc.**
COVER PHOTOGRAPHERS — Front Cover **Guy March/FPG**
Bob Krist/Tony Stone Images
Sylvain Grandadam/Tony Stone Images
Julie Houck/Westlight
Robert Young Pelton/Westlight
Back Cover **Julie Houck/Westlight**

Inquiries should be addressed to: Fielding Worldwide, Inc., 308 South Catalina Ave., Redondo Beach, California 90277 U.S.A., Telephone (310) 372-4474, Facsimile (310) 376-8064, 8:30 a.m.–5:30 p.m. Pacific Standard Time.

ISBN 1-56952-058-5

Library of Congress Catalog Card Number

94-068352

Printed in the United States of America

Letter from the Publisher

In 1946, Temple Fielding began the first of what would be a remarkable new series of well-written, highly personalized guide books for independent travelers. Temple's opinionated, witty, and oft-imitated books have now guided travelers for almost a half-century. More important to some was Fielding's humorous and direct method of steering travelers away from the dull and the insipid. Today, Fielding Travel Guides are still written by experienced travelers for experienced travelers. Our authors carry on Fielding's reputation for creating travel experiences that deliver insight with a sense of discovery and style.

Tired of sleeping in railway stations and eating off push carts? Fielding's *Budget Europe* is for travelers who not only want to save money but experience more! See the real Europe without traveling like a pauper. Only long-time European resident Joseph Raff can show you how. Fielding's *Budget Europe* is your discount ticket to more fun for your dollar—and more laughs for your lira.

In 1995, the concept of independent travel has never been bigger. Our policy of *brutal honesty* and a highly personal point of view has never changed; it just seems the travel world has caught up with us.

Enjoy your European adventure with Joseph Raff and Fielding.

RYP

Robert Young Pelton

Publisher and CEO

Fielding Worldwide, Inc.

CURRENCY CONVERSION CHART

Country	US $		Local Equivalent
AUSTRIA	$1	=	10.55 schillings
	$9.48	=	100 schillings
BELGIUM	$1.00	=	30.84 francs
	$3.24	=	100 francs
DENMARK	$1	=	5.85 kroner
	$17.09	=	100 kroner
ENGLAND	$1	=	.612 pounds
	$163.40	=	100 pounds
FINLAND	$1	=	4.54 markka
	$22.03	=	100 markka
FRANCE	$1	=	5.13 francs
	$19.49	=	100 francs
GERMANY	$1	=	1.50 marks
	$66.67	=	100 marks
GREECE	$1	=	230 drachmas
	$ 4.35	=	1000 drachmas
IRELAND	$1	=	.62 punts
	$161.29	=	100 punts
(Note: There is no longer parity between English and Irish currency.)			
ITALY	$1	=	1531 lire
	$6.53	=	10,000 lire
LUXEMBOURG uses BELGIAN francs.			
LIECHTENSTEIN uses SWISS francs.			
NETHERLANDS	$1	=	1.68 guldens
	$59.52	=	100 guldens
NORWAY	$1	=	6.51 kroner
	$15.36	=	100 kroner
MONACO uses FRENCH francs.			
PORTUGAL	$1	=	153 escudos
	$6.54	=	1000 escudos
SPAIN	$1	=	125 pesetas
	$8	=	1000 pesetas
SCOTLAND uses ENGLISH pounds.			

CURRENCY CONVERSION CHART			
Country	US $		Local Equivalent
SWEDEN	$1	=	7.06 kronor
	$14.16	=	100 kronor
SWITZERLAND	$1	=	1.25francs
	$80	=	100 francs

These were the exchange rates as of Nov. 18, 1994.

Judith Raff

Judith shares with Joe the demanding research schedule that goes into the preparation of the Fielding Britain and European guides. Her specialty is the evaluation of merchandise and current fashions for the Selective Shopping Guide, but still she is involved totally in the gathering, weighing, and reporting on every major field of activity covered in the Fielding guides to Europe and Britain.

Born in Philadelphia, she was educated at Connecticut College for Women, the University of North Carolina, and New York University. When there is time for leisure, it is usually answered through downhill skiing, golf, or sailing.

Joseph Raff

For many years Joe and his wife, Judith, have lived in Europe and crisscrossed their beat annually by car, train, boat, and plane to report on the latest trends and developments for readers of the Fielding guides.

Born in New York, Joe was graduated from the University of North Carolina at Chapel Hill, studied at Harvard, Ohio, and Indiana Universities, and then reported for the *Associated Press* and *Sports Illustrated* before moving overseas to edit the *Rome Daily American.* Since 1961 he has worked on the Fielding guides to Britian and Europe.

Travel writing for the Fielding publications requires almost six months of road work each year. Between times Joe is an avid sailor, an ardent golfer, and an Alpine skier. He lives on Mallorca.

Fielding Rating Icons

The Fielding Rating Icons are highly personal and awarded to help the besieged traveler choose from among the dizzying array of activities, attractions, hotels, restaurants and sights. The awarding of an icon denotes unusual or exceptional qualities in the relevant category.

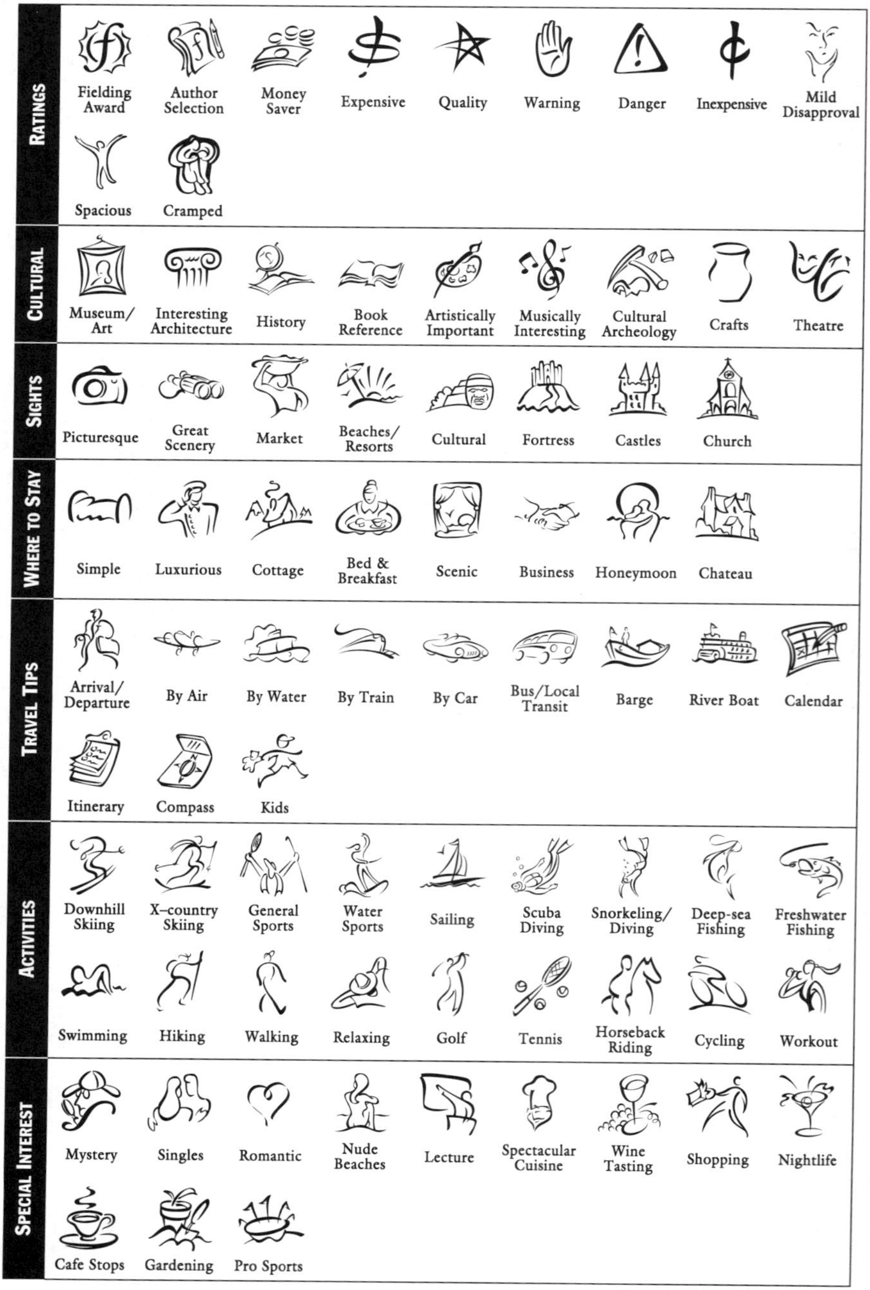

TABLE OF CONTENTS

LIST OF MAPS

INTRODUCTION

FOR STARTERS

Before you even think about how to obtain the biggest bargain in transatlantic fares, you might as well consider your destination—and how you can afford it. No matter how expensive the goal, there are numerous techniques for obtaining it for a better price. The coming pages will help you once you actually set foot on foreign soil and even guide you in those preparations. Still, the object of all travel is to have a good time while gaining new experiences. In other words, it shouldn't be too restrictive based on budget alone. If you choose a country which is inherently costly and your worries are constant, you are likely to come away disenchanted—or broke. Or both. Let's explore ways around both of those problems, first in general and then nation by nation.

The Europe you will experience in 1995 is making an effort to become united, but even within the United States, with a single currency and more than 200 years of bonding, there are regions that are dramatically more costly than others. The Europe we write about here boasts a fledgling "Community" which contains about a dozen independent states—and rising—with perhaps another dozen in various stages of application or admission. This unity movement has had a major influence across the map of Europe. All states maintain their own currencies, but the larger institutions frequently invest in a basket of mixed funds to provide stability and credibility to the world markets. This is the ECU currency designation you are likely to come across in your European reading. All these separate states perpetuate individual economies, jealously guarding their areas of profit while reluctantly contributing to the shaky union which is still a dream away. Now this simply means that you will be selecting your destination(s) from a menu of approximately 20 very distinctive nations that are trying to live harmoniously in some vague economic sisterhood.

If one were forced to make a generalization (not advised), you could probably say that southern Europe is cheaper than northern Europe. Furthermore, within the boundaries of each nation you can assume that metropolitan Europe is far more expensive than rural Europe. The same argument, however, does not apply if you try to compare, for example, the cost of living in a Swiss alpine resort with that of central Athens.

On a regional basis, let's look at the choices. Scandinavia is universally considered to be the most costly of all. Sweden, Norway, and (to a lesser degree) Denmark offer sweeping hotel rate reductions—as much as 50 percent in many cases—during the summer months when there are fewer business travelers on the ground. Finland, though not a Scandinavian country technically, follows this same custom. All of these countries offer tourist discount programs for food, transportation and entertainment during this period, too. Comestibles, traditionally thunderingly high in the Norseland restaurants, can be had in other surroundings. Oslo, as one example, has built almost an entire outdoor city down by the harbor. Helsinki offers a magnificent waterfront market, an Eden of the North, plus an exciting, lip-smacking covered market right next door, in case it's raining. You can get your nutrition from wonderful street kiosks and outdoor stands in sylvan deerparks or by midtown lakes, in thriving open-air markets or at the colorful wharfsides where there is an abundance of delicious herrings, crackling grilled sausages, inventive sandwiches, salads and gleaming dippers of berries which you only find in the arctic realms. Eating this way is an adventure every mealtime and not crushingly expensive. The absolute budget-buster in all of the North is drink. Alcohol (beer included) is handled by the various governments and taxed until each victim issues an exquisite squeal. Many meals, with only modest imbibing by normal U.S. standards, can cost more for the liquids in your glass than for the solids on your plate. Austerity is the only survival course if your thirst is great. Fruit juice is a meek alternative, but it's cheaper and of great variety.

Switzerland, the little land of big big bankers and their super-rich depositors, is not in the European Community, so, therefore, it does not receive some of the benefits of agricultural control which exist, for example, in France, Germany and Benelux. Nevertheless, there are a few Swiss left who are not millionaires—and they survive very nicely, as you can, if you know how and where to buy. The Helvetians have such a well developed sense of tidyness, cleanliness and perfection that you can feel pillow-puff comfort—even pampered—in the most modest and inexpensive pension or boarding house. The food will be hearty, not fancy, and it will be delivered with a smile. Usually, it will be characterized by the region in which it is cooked—and all the cantons are different. The working-class cafés offer huge meals at realistic prices; you can also specify one serving, or, empty the entire platter if you are famished; you will be charged accordingly. Switzerland is a place where you can go to a supermarket in the morning and collect a hamper for the day's picnic at truly bargain prices. The Migros chain is represented in almost every town and village; it is superb for variety and value. Heading up into the Alps with your pack filled will be among the most glorious memories you will take home with you—and at very little cost to your budget. So don't be intimidated by myth that Switzerland is impossibly expensive.

Germany, too, has a reputation for high cost. But colossal beer halls exist everywhere and they serve giant hocks of pork or steaming wedges of boiled beef, rich bread by the bushel, luscious baked apples or puddings and an ever-tootling ooompah band for free entertainment, all for a pittance. Remember, too, there are two parts to the new Germany and in the eastern districts your money will go farther than in the west. (Moreover, there's much less to buy in the east so far.) Austria has fewer beer halls, but there is magic in a wine garden at springtime or full summer. In my clearly prejudiced opinion, the Austrians seem to have a greater mandate on flavor. Its brotherhood with Hungary years ago has rendered a fascinating culinary influence. Here, as in Switzerland, the boarding house (pension) is the soul of warm-hearted hospitality, flower-filled window boxes to greet your nostrils every morning, and music, music, music—in the streets, in the bars, or in the magnificent concert halls and operas. Every hamlet has its own well-regarded bandstand in the center of the public common. It's open to all—the birds, the squirrels and you.

From the mountains to the Lowlands, the Netherlands on the surface gives most visitors the shivers for cost. But go to the ultra-cozy "brown cafes" which are ubiquitous and you will be fed no worse than a *doge* or a duke, drink lovely wines or floods of distinctive new beers, nibble cheese, and engage in the fun-loving pub life that so captivated the Dutch genre painters of the 17th century. You (and your liver) can spend many convival hours here after a full morning of sightseeing with very little damage to your budget or your constitution. Since it rains so much in Holland, I'd opine that the "brown cafe" has done more to keep the Dutch citizenry dry than has the umbrella. And it's far more chummy. These fair-minded people know they live on what is perhaps the most expensive parcel of Europe—much of it reclaimed from the sea—so they provide numerous hostels, sleep-inns, tent cities, student centers, concerts, or low-cost and free pastimes for the visitors to their country.

Belgium, Luxembourg, and Liechtenstein are smaller gems so you will probably see them quickly and their cost will be relatively painless. The first, of course is the largest so allocate more time to the glorious ancient cities of Brussels, Bruges and Ghent. They are enchanting and should not be missed no matter what the outlay. Monaco is not really for the economizer, but it can be viewed as part of your romp around France or in your rovings across the north of Italy. Incidentally, Italy, once a cheap destination, is now in dubious flux. A lot of the value you receive (apart from the wondrous art and culture) will depend on the wild fluctuations of the *lira*, so if you guess right and choose your moment, it can provide unforgettable experiences for a reasonable sum. France has a relatively stable economy and heaps of variety for the traveler. In general, it can never be considered low in cost. Strangely, however, in the matter of dining, almost all French meals automatically come with bread, vegetables and a salad included in the singular tab whereas, in Italy, every pea in the plate and each morsel you swallow seems to have its own separate price tag. Remember that when ordering.

Spain is still a good buy. While lodgings can be poor for the lofty tariffs, you can certainly save on food and drink. The same goes for Portugal, Greece and Ireland.

Britain offers a bit of everything. You can dine very well, but for sleeping you may have to spend more than you wish. If England suffers at all, it suffers from being vastly popular all year-round. Never mind. What you see and experience is the splendid reward and that will stay with you for many a decade and bring you back many times again. Since transportation absorbs such a significant sum from your budget, it is especially important in the British Isles to look for bargains in this sector. The individual chapters to come will provide tips on how to achieve these and other savings. This has just been a cursory overview to help you pick the right country from a basketful of blossoms. If you can afford it, go to several. Make your transatlantic passage work for you by taking in as much as you can in the same journey. Save the "in depth" trip for another year.

By the way, many of the islands have economies which differ considerably from their mainland mommies. Because they may be small and not self-sufficient in agriculture, food prices tend to be high due to the built-in transportation costs. To level things out a bit, accommodations are often cheaper and the hospitality is genuine.

MONEY

Your funds should be broken down in three ways: U.S. currency (as an emergency measure only), dollar traveler's checks, and personal checks on your hometown bank. Credit cards, of course, are almost a necessity today.

For cash transfers, ask your bank about the **Swift** cable service, which is so fast and efficient there is nothing to match it; in minutes, not days, it can and does forward funds to travelers in any part of the world.

Leftover European change is a wasteful problem. Surplus bills can normally be exchanged in the next country, but people will turn up their noses at your foreign change. Get rid of all coins (except souvenirs) before crossing any border.

PASSPORTS

Guard your passport more carefully than your wallet; losing it can make European officials surly and stubborn. (If you can't find yours, get in touch with the nearest U.S. consulate immediately; it will assist you with new documentation.)

For about a year now U.S. citizens have been issued new green passports instead of the blue one of old. Also, they incorporate a sneak-proof optical device similar to a hologram, special inks, and graphics to deter counterfeiters. If you have an older blue one, it can be used until the expiration date. Passports are valid for 10 years for persons 18 years or older and cost $65; for those under 18, it's $40 and is valid for five years. In addition, there's a $10 fee for applicants who are required to apply in person. However, that sum is waived for applicants whose latest passport was issued within the past 12 years, who were 18 or over when it was issued, and who are able to submit that passport with their new application. If you meet these requirements, you are eligible to apply by mail and should obtain Form DSP-82, "Application for Passport by Mail," which may be sent to one of the passport agencies mentioned below. Applicants who can't qualify under the rules above must apply in person.

Have two identical photos (2"x2" and snapped within the last 6 months) ready to adorn the document. These must have a plain or off-white background. For your first passport, you must present in person a completed Form DSP-11, "Passport Application," at one of the agencies located in Boston, Chicago, Honolulu, Houston, Los Angeles, Miami, New Orleans, New York, Philadelphia, San Francisco, Seattle, Stamford, and Washington, D.C., or at one of the several thousand federal or state courts or U.S. post offices that accept passport applications. Be sure you can prove you are a U.S. citizen (birth or naturalization certificate) as well as have proof of identity (driver's license). Forms are available for any of those items. Persons already abroad should go to any American consulate.

As a precaution against loss or theft, have two photocopies made of your passport identification page. Leave one at home and carry the other with you but separate from your passport.

MEDICAL ADVICE

Immunization isn't required for European travelers. They have good public health officials, fine doctors, and the latest drugs in Europe; many of the last appear on pharmacy shelves years before they are put up for sale in North America—even when they may be produced by U.S. manufacturers. (Europeans often test their products quicker than the F.D.A.)

Though shots are not required in Europe, information on foreign immunization laws for countries further afield can be obtained from the U.S. Public Health Service. Check your phone book under U.S. Government, Department of Health and Human Services. Also helpful is an organization called International Association for Medical Assistance to Travellers. IAMAT (736 Center St., Lewiston, NY 14092) can provide the names of English-speaking doctors in many foreign nations. I have had occasion to meet and use a few of its colleagues and feel the service is worthwhile. If you are moving on to hotter lands than Europe, be sure to read IAMAT's information on malaria prevention, still a major health problem in some areas.

Here are some tips on staying in shape. Naturally, everyone is cautious about the drinking water in questionable places; this should include the water for brushing your teeth and ice cubes. Raw vegetables and fruits also require attention if your stay is to be a short one; avoid homemade mayonnaise in hot climates. If you are making a longer visit, it might be better, according to some medical opinion, to go ahead and live as the locals do unless the area suffers from extreme pollution. Beer is drinkable almost everywhere, but wines are more suspect.

Turista is likely to lurk anywhere; nonprescription Polymagma or Pepto-Bismol are useful health aids in liquid or tablet form. We are also hearing good reports about Hoffmann-La Roche's Bactrim tablet. Diarrhea can cause loss of salts and fluids, so take lots of sugar in hot tea; it apparently enhances the absorption of salt. Imodium (also in liquid or capsule form) is useful, fast-acting, and seems to be effective in keeping people on the tourist trails and worry-free.

Motion sickness has many combatants in tablet form, some of which produce drowsiness, so it may be a tradeoff as to whether you would prefer to be alert and queasy. Meclizine (generic), Antivert, Dramamine, and Bonine taken anywhere from a half- to one hour before the motion begins are often effective. At the onset of nausea, lozenges, suppositories, or injections of Phenergan, Compazine, or Tigan are indicated. CIBA's Transderm V (scopolamine) is a novel approach to relief. It's a dime-size adhesive patch that can be worn behind the ear or elsewhere on the body; the skin absorbs protective chemicals for up to three days—an easy way to wear, instead of swallow, your medication.

AIDS? Well, Europe suffers from it too. The causes are the same as elsewhere in the world and the precautions, of course, should be the same as those employed in the U.S.

For the handicapped traveler, the American Automobile Association (AAA) distributes a guide. Another organization, **Society for the Advancement of Travel for the Handicapped**, offers further aid; it is located at *26 Court St., Brooklyn, NY 11242*; ☎ *(212) 858-5483.*

Medic Alert Foundation renders an invaluable nonprofit service to travelers who suffer from any hidden medical problem. It furnishes lifesaving emblems of 10-karat gold-filled, sterling silver, or stainless steel to be worn around the neck or wrist. Should the patient be unable to talk, medical personnel or law-enforcement officials are instantly informed of dangers inherent in standard treatment. The tag carries such warnings as "diabetic," "allergic to penicillin," "taking anticoagulants," "wearing contact lenses," "neck breather," or whatever difficulty. It also bears the telephone number of the Medic Alert headquarters in California to which anyone may call (Collect) from anywhere in the world at any hour of day or night for additional file material about the individual case. (The price of the emblem includes a lifetime membership to the organization.) This laudable project is the charitable mission of Marion Collins, M.D., who almost lost his teenage daughter when she was given an antitetanus injection following an automobile accident (a preventive that would be administered routinely if the physician were not warned). If you'll pardon our paraphrase, no traveler should ever be caught alive without one of these emblems. The organization also features an electric unit worn around the neck or wrist that alerts a telephonic standby facility if the wearer suffers a medical crisis. For more information about this splendid organization (donations are tax deductible), write to **Medic Alert Foundation International**, *P.O. Box 1009, Turlock, CA 95381-1009.*

U.S. CONSULATE

If you should encounter serious trouble on your trip—anything from a lost passport to an arrest to the death of a companion to a spectrum of other deep crises—communicate immediately with the nearest American consular office. They are, however, proscribed from extending loans to travelers in financial distress. Although they will give restricted aid in a dispute that could lead to legal or police action, furnish a list of reputable local lawyers, and try to prevent discrimination under foreign law, regulations prohibit them from participating on a direct level. If a citizen is arrested, they will visit him or her in detention, notify relatives and friends, provide a roster of attorneys, and attempt to obtain relief if conditions are inhumane or unhealthy. Here are some of their other duties: assistance in finding appropriate medical services, including English-speaking physicians;

guidance on how to inform the local police about stolen funds or inform the issuing authorities about missing traveler's checks; full extension of notary facilities; help in locating missing Americans; protection of U.S. voyagers and residents during civil unrest or in natural disasters.

It may be useful to leave behind at home the following direct Washington telephone numbers of the office of Special Consular Services:

- To find missing wanderers about whom there is special concern or to transmit emergency messages: ☎ *202-647-5225.*
- To transmit funds to your destitute ones on foreign soil when commercial banking facilities are unavailable or to arrange medical evacuation: ☎ *202-632-9706* or *202-632-3529.*
- For questions about members of your clan who have been arrested and how to get money to them: ☎ *202-632-8089* or *202-632-7823.*
- For help when an American dies abroad ☎ *202-632-1423* or *202-632- 2172.*
- For civil judicial inquiries and assistance: ☎ *202-632-2400.*
- Night and weekend emergency number for all of the above: ☎ *202-655-4000.* Ask for the Duty Officer.

The **Overseas Citizens Services** (☎ *202-632-5225*) is a general helpmate for troubled travelers. Don't ask these officials to do the work of travel agencies, information bureaus, or banks; search for missing luggage; settle disputes with hotel managers or shopkeepers; help get work permits; or find jobs.

CUSTOMS OFFICIALS

At gateways, be pleasant and cooperative, but don't get chatty. Their sole interest is to get rid of you.

Hold your passport casually in hand—don't flaunt it—so that the inspector can identify you.

The **U.S. Customs** personnel have the legal right to examine every piece of luggage carried by every traveler; under the spot-check system, however, you may be snagged or you may be breezed by without an inquisitive glance. To save time if you are inspected, carry all your European purchases in one bag. Cheating? That's like trying to sneak daybreak past a rooster.

Anyone **out of the States for more than 48 hours** may bring in $400 in retail value of merchandise without paying a cent—figure on retail rather than wholesale value. Next $1000 in value is taxable at only 10%. To be eligible, the goods must accompany you personally on your return. The only other modification worth noting is that your free importation of wines and spirits is limited to one quart per person 21 years or over.

The regulations continue to be loaded with hidden assets that work to your advantage. Here are a few. Each individual is given the maximum amount. You may pool with any member of your family. Even infants-in-arms are granted exactly the same exemption. You may send an unlimited number of under $50 gifts from abroad to U.S. friends (more about this below), and Customs will pass them without charge.European prices are often low enough so that you can slap down duty on most of your purchases and still save money. (Your U.S. or Canadian merchant must pay exactly the same duties you pay, plus high brokerage fees, transportation, and agency profit margins—before adding his own markup. By the time you buy it from him, therefore, it's going to be fatally higher than if you'd bought it yourself at the source and paid duty.)

Gifts costing less than $50 may be mailed from abroad on a duty-free basis, with no effect on your exemptions. Alcohol, tobacco, and perfume are ineligible, although many bottles of the last have been known to pass through. No one person may receive more than one gift in one day; plainly mark the package "Unsolicited Gift—Value Under $50."

Finally, it is illegal to bring back meats, fruits, plants, soil, or any agricultural products without special permission; all goods made from endangered species of animals; absinthe; liqueur-filled chocolates; firearms; ammunition; wildlife; lottery tickets; and, of course, narcotics. For details, write to: **Quarantines, U.S. Department of Agriculture**, *Federal Center Building, Hyattsville, MD 20782.*

On the European side, cigarettes are usually what the officials look for first—if they look at all. Above the prescribed number, there's a handsome duty to be paid. Most countries allow 400 cigarettes on entry. But the majority wink at a reasonable excess for personal consumption. Stuff as many packages as you can into your clothing pockets.

MAIL

For the period that you are traveling, ask your family and friends to send messages directly to your foreign hotels. In addition to the normal directions, a line should be written on the envelope requesting "Hold for arrival on such-and-such date." (Incidentally, tell your family and friends to write out the month. To a European 9/11/95 means Nov. 9, not Sept. 11.) This almost always works when you have firm reservations. However, most houses recommended in this volume will hold your letters even if they've never communicated with you.

International postal service today is plainly wretched. Switzerland is the best; Italy and Greece are the worst. If you are writing for reservations or expecting mail from home, count on approximately three weeks for delivery. Post all letters Air Mail and the more important ones should be marked Express or Special Delivery.

FOR THE CAMPER

Europe is chockablock with efficient camping equipment in all price ranges. You'll save headaches by buying most of the things you'll need after your arrival.

Tents are available in profusion. All sizes, colors, materials, and prices.

Sleeping bag? Camping equipment stores exist everywhere, but really useful low-cost sleeping bags often can be found at shopping centers. We recently bought two for $75 in a supermarket in Spain; at a neighboring sporting goods shop, similar tack was selling for $140 apiece.

If you plan to **backpack**, buy your pack before you go; North Americans currently manufacture the most efficient designs. But try on several (preferably preloaded to whatever weight you'll be toting) before deciding which one you choose. The pack should be magnesium- or aluminum-framed for spinal support; it also should have strong, fully adjustable straps, and be a "high," rather than the "wide" type (unless you don't mind getting trapped in bus exits, guillotined by elevator doors, and jostled in crowds).

Hikers who plan to cover most of their great leaps forward by commercial transportation may prefer the soft, frameless type of pack. These are available throughout the Continent, and they're easier to toss on train luggage racks or to stack in odd corners.

Hiking boots can be unbeatable buys abroad (especially in Austria, Spain, Italy, and Switzerland). They should not only be light and leather-lined, but extend to just above the ankle. We recently bought a pair for each of us in St. Moritz; excellent quality for about $40 each.

Jogging shoes are available everywhere at prices similar to U.S. levels. Again, supermarkets offer the best bargains; they are usually selling their own brands instead of famous international names.

Cooking utensils, dishes, etc.? Purchase them cheaply on the Continent—but not in Spain or Portugal where they are costly and the selection is poor.

FOR THE BACKPACKER

Backpacks (see above) entail a dramatic tradeoff of paraphernalia for mobility. But you should use them only under three conditions: hostel-hopping, camping, or splitting a pad or cabin. The occasional hotelier listed in this book will balk if he sees your possessions hanging on your back. That happens pretty rarely today. However, we suggest that you take a bunk-size bed sheet, because hostels insist that you use a clean one; if you don't supply it, you have to rent it, which adds up. In many youth hostels you can purchase a paper sheet (about $3.50), which is of surprisingly fine quality and resembles soft linen in its tactile properties; these can last up to three nights—if you're a light sleeper. A combination lock makes good sense for your locker; petty thievery is rampant. Scout-type eating utensils (knife-fork-spoon kit, collapsible drinking cup, corkscrew-bottle/can opener, pocket knife) are your tickets to grocery store shelves, which provide cheaper food than restaurants, of course. Picture postcards of your town (take about 50) make inexpensive and effective "thank you" gifts. Multiple vitamins are a healthy idea for anyone dining mostly on junk foods, particularly for a month or more.

YOUR TRAVEL ARRANGEMENTS

Overall, you have three choices: as a front-runner, as a trailblazer, or as a member of an escorted tour.

As a **front-runner**, you'd accept the challenges—and the overwhelming advantages—of nailing down every possible routing, rate, transportation booking, and hotel reservation before your departure from America. If you already know Europe well, you'll probably have a wonderful holiday.

As a **trailblazer**, you would make the usual plane reservations, but you will let everything else ride until you touch down on foreign soil. In the winter, early spring, or late fall, you can usually get away with it. But in summer, it can be difficult. At sleep-inns, the earliest arrivals usually plunk down on the most convenient plots of indoor real estate while latecomers are sent to the park benches. Reservations don't exist in these shelters. The season in London, Paris, Amsterdam, Rome, Vienna, and other capitals will start by Easter. The first-line budget accommodations are snapped up early.

As a **member of an escorted tour**, you don't even have to know that Paris is in France or that the Matterhorn isn't a tuba. If you're a stranger to the Continent, or if you're lonely, lazy, gregarious, fun-loving, or shy—any of 10-dozen reasons—here might be the perfect answer for your requirements. Parties run from 15 to 30. When you sign up, one lump sum must be paid in advance. This usually takes care of the entire trip except your tips, wines, liquors, laundry, gifts, snacks, and other extras.

Scores of organizations specialize in this field of orthodox travel. If you pick the right operator, you probably can see more of Europe under better conditions for less money than you could possibly do by flip-flopping from one costly address to another. Obviously, it's all a matter of choosing the right firm and making sure that they book you with the right tour company.

Now, what about a **travel agent**? First, no agency can possibly afford to service all of the individual needs of an economy traveler. While he or she would probably be happy to arrange all your air, sea, and rail tickets—at no cost to you—the expense of booking you into the smaller, less expensive hotels or pensions would vastly overweigh his balance sheet. The hours involved in drawing up your itinerary and room-request letters, the airmail postage to 10, 17, or 24 foreign points, and the tariffs on last-minute cables simply would not be covered by the small commission the agent would receive on each low-cost reservation. In all fairness, if you're a front-runner, make your lodging arrangements on your own.

Do-it-yourselfers? Here are a few hints on the best way to make hotel reservations. Be specific. In some countries a bath is a bath; it may not include a john as well. If you prefer a shower to a tub, say so; usually it is even cheaper. Be sure to indicate your date of arrival and date of departure. Should you omit the latter, you may be bounced out to make room for a more specific booking. Save all confirmation letters. You may have to show some of them when some grumpy desk clerk has "no record" of your reservation or somehow has you down for a higher-priced room than the one you ordered. If you've written to a certain hostelry and receive notice from the local tourist office booking you into a different house, don't fret. This merely means your first choice was filled and your request was passed on to some local authority who found you a similar establishment at a comparable rate. If you don't like the substitute, you may either not confirm it, or write to the organization expressing some other preference.

AIRWAY BARGAINS

If you read any newspaper or Sunday travel supplement you hardly need guidance to buy scheduled fare tickets across the Atlantic. Scheduled fare is the highest you can pay in any class category. For that you buy flexibility. You can cancel, rejoin or postpone with little or no penalty. APEX reduces that ridiculous astronomic sum somewhat, but as the letters stand for "advance purchase," you must know well ahead of departure when you want to go, pay for your passage in full, and stick rigidly to your flight plan. If you can take off on short notice, one of the best fly-buys of all will remain the standby rate for scheduled services. But each season fewer carriers offer last-minute bargains.

In order to link up with domestic airports that service foreign destinations, take advantage of low fares sometimes offered under temporary promotional names which are different from the "frequent flyer" programs or "air passes." A later trend (but not always a cheaper one) is the urge to merge, which domestic services are realizing with foreign carriers. The alliances try to effect, more or less, continuous handling by one company from departure point to destination. There is a certain convenience in this continuity, but I doubt if it will result in substantially lower prices unless the carriers are in the midst of an air-fare war. In the few seasons of use that I have flown it, I have not observed any benefit except the effort to produce relatively seamless connections. Moreover, I've noticed an unfortunate erosion of quality, usually from the domestic carrier and very often from the foreign partner as well.

Some airline reservation clerks can be self-serving louts by not offering all the options for connecting flights. As we are coming into an epoch of more and more interactive systems through which bookings may be made directly by the traveling public, a policy such as this could soon result in a lot of unemployed desk personnel. In spite of today's more regulated "deregulation" (or possibly because of it), their computers are "fixed" to favor certain routes, dates, and similar details so that you may feel you are forced to book with that primary carrier. If you have a good agent and insist on knowing all of the possibilities, you can significantly enhance your travel program.

Internationally, low-season cut-rate passage between London and New York can sometimes be picked up for as little as $275 one way or $375 between Great Britain and Los Angeles. (Eastbound passage—that is, going to Europe—is about 35 percent higher.) If there's a price war (usually off season or during times of international crisis), these figures may decline. I've seen bucketshop (also called consolidator) notices for transoceanic or transcontinental flights for as low as $102! It's also a bit cheaper to fly on weekdays than on weekends. Under the APEX plan the ticket must be purchased 21 days before departure and the passenger must spend from 7 to 180 days abroad—and you specify the flight and dates. Standard excursion outlays require 14 to 60 days at your destination. An APEX link between NY and London ranges between $479 and $749 roundtrip (seasonal variations); with Los Angeles as your starting point, it will cost between $665 and $865. Some carriers are now trying to cut your overall vacation expenses through "independent packaging." The air ticket remains unchanged but they can realize savings for you in hotels (up to 50 percent off), car rentals (also big advertised cuts but often bumped up to make the discounts seem more generous), and other ground arrangements.

The whole picture is nothing more than an unmitigated crazy-quilt of fares which favor the airline (usually), secondarily the contracted agent which in a real sense works for the airline, and which can favor you only if you know your way around the fare tables. On a recent check, for example, a Swiss friend of mine spent nearly $1000 to fly round-trip (Club class) to London and return—a nothing distance it is, too. In the same week I flew from the British capital to Zurich and back, same class, same everything, and shelled out just a shade over half that amount. Vienna–London is the same story, with British Airways offering a fare that's dramatically lower than Austrian Airlines' return loop out of Vienna. I can provide endless examples, but to boil it down to the nubbins, you should buy most of your tickets from the cheaper end of the circuit and combine destinations so that you gain from back-to-back purchases. This could mean even taking a one-way fare to a cheaper destination in order to obtain a more thrifty combination for ongoing flights. A fare-minded (fair-minded?) travel agent operating in your behalf can work all this out with a little bit of diligence. But since agents operate on commissions from the airlines, it is not easy to find ones who will sacrifice from their own income to serve you better. In this respect your only leverage is being a steady customer who threatens to take the business elsewhere unless you get the occasional good deal. An alternative, of course, is to do the homework yourself and make your own bookings. That way the savings could be significant. It is a complicated business, however, and I don't recommend it to everyone.

SAVINGS AT GROUND ZERO

Saving francs, pounds, or D-marks can be an important wrinkle in your travel budget when it comes to something as basic as transportation. There's no need to be pound-foolish just to conform. When you arrive at most international gateways you are stuck far out at a strange airport, so you often fall for the easiest solution for getting into town—the taxi. Well, sadly, that is one of the best ways to become a first-class spendthrift. Moreover, riding in this style will not necessarily guarantee that you will arrive in mid-city any faster than by other more economical methods. I recently took the train from Gatwick Airport into London. It took less time than by taxi and I covered the rather longish distance in a jiffy—at a cost that was roughly twenty times less than the hackey's fare. I had the choice, too, of being deposited at either Victoria Station or The City. From Heathrow Airport, for example, the subway ride in costs about $4.50 while a taxi would take up to $35 (without tip) to cover a similar short distance. Paris, Munich, Frankfurt, Zurich, Geneva, Barcelona and many other hubs now help the tourist with rail connections to and from the air terminals. As a guideline, here are some of the more noteworthy airport rail services sprinkled around Europe, with the distances and times from the cities.

Airport	Distance to Town	Frequency
Amsterdam	**15 km**	**every 7 mins**
Berlin Schonefled	**18 km**	**every 20 mins**
Berlin Tempelhof	**5 km**	**regular subway**
Brussels	**12 km**	**every 20 mins**
Düsseldorf	**8 km**	**every 20 mins**

Airport	Distance to Town	Frequency
Florence-Pisa	84 km	hourly
Frankfurt	10 km	every 10 mins
Geneva	4 km	every 10 mins
London Gatwick	43 km	every 6 mins
London Heathrow	25 km	regular subway
London Stansted	55 km	every 30 mins
Munich	37 km	every 20 mins
Paris CDG	26 km	every 15 mins
Paris Orly	16 km	every 15 mins
Rome	32 km	every 30 mins
Stuttgart	20 km	every 15 mins
Zurich	12 km	every 12 mins

Of course, all cities offer bus connections to and from airports. These are reasonably priced, too, but often slowed down by traffic snarls.

THOSE JET-LAG MISERIES

You can avoid them, according to master traveler Stephen Forsyth, who has made a career of helping and advising globe-spanners. I've applied the Forsyth technique to myself on numerous long-distance flights and while I, frankly, don't like giving up that extra cocktail or celebratory mood which frequently seems to accompany big trips (and which is encouraged by the airlines to somehow justify their numbing prices), I follow his advice—sometimes. Here are some sage excerpts from the Forsyth Library;

The Day Before: Be calm. Get all details out of the way. No matter what time you fly tomorrow, try to avoid crises, conflicts, or agitation on flight day or the day before. Eat a full balanced dinner high in carbohydrates, like pasta. Go light on wine, liquor, and caffeine. Go to bed at the normal time and plan to get up as you normally would.

Flight Day: You are not going to eat food, pastry, snacks or candy, take any nonpresciption drugs, drink coffee or tea (caffeinated or decaffeinated) or drink any liquor, including beer or wine. Drink lots of fruit juices, vegetable juices and water. No carbonated drinks. Take Vitamin C. This will be a shorter day than normal because you are flying east. From Chicago to London, for example, crosses six time zones, thus reducing the 24-hour day to 18. Because of the sensible diet, your body clock will be on "hold" waiting for you to restart it. You may be tired, but you won't be run-down. You probably won't be famished either, just moderately hungry. Accept only juices and water. No food trays. Set your watch to the time of your destination and think in that direction. Get comfortable; that's important. See the movie, listen to music, relax. Sleep if you can; use a pillow and blanket.

Arrival Day: Cabin lights come on. Everyone else wants to go on sleeping, but you get up and head first to the lavatory. Wash as much as you can and even change your clothes—socks and underwear, too. This gives you a New Day feeling and helps you reset your clock psychologically. Now you can eat your normal morning meal. Don't compare your time right now to what it is back home. Think right now or forward. If the airline meal was insufficient have another breakfast at your hotel. The extra bonus of food won't hurt you because you are conditioned to another time zone.

Homeward Bound and Flying West: Moderation is the only tonic. You can repeat the eastward process this time probably with less or no sleep. Remember, this will be a longer day—by six additional hours. But once home, you will be sleeping easily.

Well, Mr. Forsyth, I thank you for the wise advice. I also know from my experience that it works for me. How many of us apply it remains to be seen.

STUDENT FLIGHTS

Many campuses organize their own charter flights, so check your student union for any plans they might have. In addition, the CIEE (see "Student Travel") continues to offer a large range of bargains.

You can often save money by flying one carrier transatlantic to the closest European gateway, and continuing from there on the **SATA** (Student Air Travel Association) network, which also extends to Asia, the Middle East, and Africa. Fares run from 1/3 to 2/3 less than do those of regular carriers. Though flights are offered year-round, they are naturally more frequent in high season (book as early as possible for these), departing daily from major hubs such as London, Paris, or Rome. Fares and schedules change too frequently for us to advise you properly here, so contact the CIEE/SOFA for their list of flights. Bookings may be made through CIEE/SOFA or from a list of ticket offices that they will send you free.

Check at time of booking for data on whether meals or refreshments are served aboard.

Some "student" flights allow students to be accompanied by non-student spouses, children, or group leaders.

Don't forget to be prepared for the airport departure taxes. Many student flights wing out from smaller terminals (Le Bourget in Paris, for example, rather than Charles de Gaulle or Orly). This can soften the bite.

BAGGAGE SIZE

Economy-class travelers are permitted two bags and one carry-on, one with dimensions that total no more than 62 inches, and both bags totaling a maximum of 106 inches; the largest should weigh no more than 70 lbs. (While bags are always weighed, I have never in my entire life of air travel seen anyone measure a suitcase before acceptance.) Tight security restrictions today limit carry-ons to only one item per person. Beyond this you are charged by the piece according to a scale of flat amounts determined by the distance you are flying. Some bulky sports equipment (golf bags, skis, etc.) is hauled free when the gear is considered the largest piece.

LOST BAGGAGE

About one percent of the world's personal cargo (15 million pieces) will be misplaced this year. Approximately 90 percent of that luggage is recovered by the owner within 24 hours of loss. While airlines permit seven days for notification, you should report your loss while you are still at the airport. If you are with a tour, then speak to your group leader. Some airlines, when they know they cannot retrieve the pieces quickly, provide emergency overnight kits; others hand out modest sums of money for basic necessities.

A "property irregularity" form must be filled in describing your loss. If you put some identification inside your suitcase, it will help tremendously should the outside tag have been ripped off. You are required nowadays to have your personal luggage tag on every piece. (All airlines, incidentally, have keys to every sort of luggage; rest assured that Customs also will be having a look inside.) If it finds your bag, the carrier will deliver it to you promptly.

After a week has passed and your baggage still hasn't been located, you should begin the process of extracting a settlement. Our experience has been that you won't get anything near the value of your carryall or wardrobe (not to mention valuables such as cameras or jewelry, which should have been among hand luggage anyway). The best protection, in other words, is your own insurance policy.

BOUNCING

(Artistically labeled "involuntary boarding denial" by the airlines. Also called "bumping.") Not infrequently the airlines book more people onto their flights than they have seats for. If you show up with your ticket and are told that there is no more space for you, then you've been bounced.

What to do? Know your "fly-rights" and use them.

Provided you hold a confirmed reservation plus a properly validated ticket on a regularly scheduled flight and have shown up on time, the airline must deliver you to your overseas destination by other means within four hours of your planned arrival time. If unable to do so, it is required to give you at least partial compensation, depending upon the distance, of not less than $37.50 (or the one-way fare) or more than $200, plus free passage on the next available flight. If they don't get you to your destination within two hours of the scheduled time, their apology must be doubled, to a maximum of $400 plus overnight expenses. This is in addition to the price of your original ticket, which you can turn in for a 100 percent refund. Moreover, you must be paid this "denied boarding compensation" (DBC) within 24 hours; if you aren't, you have 90 days in which to file a claim. So if you get the bounce, insist that you be given the printed regulation on the subject as well as the necessary forms you must fill out to collect this penalty. This applies, of course, only within the U.S., before or after international flights. European carriers within the community are following the U.S. example and a lost ride might cost the carrier from $100 to $700 (if the departure is from an EC terminus). Community law provides $180 DBC for short flights and $352 for hauls over 3500 kms. This can be halved if your delay is no more than two or four hours respectively. SAS employs a voucher system with a spread of $100 to $300 depending upon the delay or inconvenience. European airlines on their own home territory vary dramatically on how they handle such delicate matters. SAS, BA and KLM are as thoughtful as US airlines in crisis situations. You might have to demand your DBC from Iberia or Alitalia, and outside of Europe you might not receive any compensation whatsoever. (Remember that Switzerland and Austria are not yet EC members, but they do have understanding airlines.) If you display defiance plus a knowledge of the intimidations at your disposal, it's probable that any wise airline official will break into a righteous sweat and come to your aid.

AIRPORTS

New York, Newark, Boston, Chicago, Los Angeles, San Francisco, Washington, Minneapolis-St. Paul, Denver, Kansas City, St. Louis, Cleveland, Pittsburgh, Houston, Detroit, Philadelphia, Miami, Tampa, Orlando, Atlanta, New Orleans, Dallas-Fort Worth, Seattle, Portland, Toronto, and Montreal are, of course, the major North American stations for transatlantic air traffic. You can fly direct from any of these without changing planes—but not all airlines go from all these points. Additional gateways are being discussed now by the authorities.

The special bus hookup from the Grand Central Station to John F. Kennedy Airport gets you there on time, come hell or highway congestion. Travel time to the International Terminal is normally 60 minutes, depending on traffic. Ask your travel agent about the Gray Line bus connection to LaGuardia ($13), JFK ($16), or Newark ($18). On a weekend when traffic is light and there are at least three people in your party, it can work out cheaper to take a taxi, but naturally this depends on your starting point in Manhattan; ask a driver to give you an estimate.

You can also take the 75-minute, low-cost transit run linking midtown with Kennedy Airport. Board either the E or F subway train in Manhattan, and switch to the Q-10 Bus at Union Turnpike Station.

Upon arrival in Europe, as already mentioned, public transportation is always available into the gateway city or to continental rail networks. In nations where there are special services or special problems, we have tried to cover them in the individual country chapters

IN EUROPE

METRIC MEASUREMENT

The metric system is used in every European country, except the United Kingdom and Ireland, which are already converting to some continental standards; frequently the English use both systems on wearables and similar products.

Here are a few simple translations.

A **kilometer** is roughly 6/10ths of a mile. Multiply by 6, knock off one decimal point place, and you've got it in miles.

A **kilo** or kilogram (potatoes and onions) is 2.2 pounds.

A **meter** (dress material) and a **liter** (gasoline, beer) are both roughly 11/10ths—one of a yard, the other of a quart. (There are about 2-1/2 centimeters to 1 inch.)

A **gram** (airmail letters) is very tiny. There are about 28 ounce.

Here are some conversions that can come in handy. Since sizes are not standardized, this is a rough yardstick. Try on the items whenever possible.

APPROXIMATE CLOTHING SIZES (American-Continental)

Women's Clothing						
American	6	8	10	12	14	16
Continental:						
France	36	38	40	42	44	46
Italy	38	40	42	44	46	48
Rest of Europe	34	36	38	40	42	44

APPROXIMATE CLOTHING SIZES (American-Continental)						
Women's Shoes						
American	4	5	6	7	8	9
Continental	35	36	37	38	39	40
Men's Sweaters						
American	S	M	L	XL		
Continental	48	50	52	54		
Men's Shoes						
American	8	8-1/2	9-1/2	10-1/2	11-1/2	
Continental	41	42	43	44	45	

APPROXIMATE CLOTHING SIZES (American-British)										
Women's Clothing										
American	8	10	12	14	16					
British	10	12	14	16	18					
Women's Shoes										
American	4	5	6	7	8	9				
British	2-1/2	3-1/2	4-1/2	5-1/2	6-1/2	7-1/2				
Men's Sweaters										
American	S	M	L	XL						
British	38	40	42	44						
Men's Shoes										
American	8	8-1/2	9	9-1/2	10	10-1/2	11	11-1/2	12	13
British	7	7-1/2	8	8-1/2	9	9-1/2	10	10-1/2	11	12

(In the past, both men's and women's shoe sizes in England have run 1-1/2 to two sizes smaller than those in the U.S., but English manufacturers often print both, as well as continental sizes inside the shoe or on the exterior instep.)

Glove and hosiery sizes are fairly standard almost everywhere.

Last, to change Celsius **temperatures** into Fahrenheit, the classic method is to take 9/5ths of the Celsius temperature (the reading on European thermometers) and add 32. A much easier way is to double the Celsius reading, deduct 10%, and add the same 32. Example: Let's imagine that the mercury says 15°. Twice 15 is 30, and 10% of 30 is 3. Taking 3 from 30 leaves 27. Add 32 to 27, and you'll have the Yankee version of 59°. In print the process looks complicated–but in practice it's so simple that any traveler can do it in his head.

SIGHTSEEING SUGGESTIONS

Plan your schedule so that your day breaks into two or three different and unrelated parts. Eight hours of unrelieved sightseeing, shopping, or exploring on foot are too much at one clip; what starts as fun soon becomes heavy legwork. A sensible itinerary, for example, would cover the museums and cultural interests in the morning, take you to an open-air restaurant for lunch, and send you out refreshed for afternoon browsing.

The city maps we've provided are merely for your general orientation. Official tourist bureaus of the cities you visit often will sell detailed ones for only a few cents. Others are often included in *What's On* publications and similar inexpensive tip sheets. The most palatial and expensive hotels offer free ones to their patrons.

TRAINS

One of the fattest transport bargains in Europe is the **Eurailpass.** This is a railroad ticket that entitles any *resident* of North, Central, or South America to roam where he wishes, when he wishes, on any mainland train (not the U.K., which has its own **ThriftRail** and **Britrail Youth** plan) without further payment except for routine sleeper or *couchette* supplements. It comes in packages ranging from 21 days to up to three months of railroading. Children under 12 are charged halffare; those under four are free. Including Trans-Europe Expresses (TEE) and all other extrafare runs, it is valid on the national railways and many private trains, steamers, and ferry crossings in the following 18 nations: Austria, Belgium, Denmark, Finland, France, Germany, Greece, Holland, Hungary, Ireland, Italy, Luxembourg, Netherlands, Norway, Portugal, Spain, Sweden, and Switzerland, as well as on sea crossings that link Ireland into the continental system. (BritRail includes English Channel crossings.) You may choose its continuous usage period during six months following its purchase. Anyone under 26 (the limitation to students has been dropped) may opt for the **Eurail Youthpass**, which offers one month of unlimited roving in all of the same carriers in *second class* for a lower flat sum plus the option of bumping it up to two months. Among its other alluring financial benefits are substantial savings on hotel bills by either dozing, sitting up, spending these nights in an inexpensive *couchette* or, for slightly more, taking a tourist sleeper. Neither of these arrangements includes reservation fees (strongly urged always and compulsory for berths), meals, refreshments or, with the latter, fees and supplements required to board certain trains. Both cards are personal and nontransferable, with the penalty of confiscation if another bearer is caught showing them. Your passport must always be produced when requested by conductors, gatemen, and other authorized personnel. Neither is refundable if lost or stolen. If you are traveling off-season (October 1 to March 31) ask about the **Saverpass**, which knocks off about 25% of the 15-day rate and applies only to couples or larger groups. There's also a **Flexipass** for any 5-day use over a 15-day span, another scheme for any 9-day use over a 21-day span, and yet another for any 14-day use over a 30-day span. The **Youth Flexipass** is a great moneysaver for any 15-day use over a two-month span.

VITAL: *You must buy your pass before heading for Europe because it is not sold abroad. To secure confirmed reservations booked through U.S. agencies is tricky unless application is made long in advance.* For further inquiries, see your travel agent or write to Eurailpass at Trains, *P.O. Box M, Staten Island, NY 10305.*

RUNNING TIME

Intercity and **EuroCity** trains are the top-grade sizzlers all over Europe. Both first- and second-class are being equalized in terms of air conditioning, modern styling, and other basics. (The main difference today is in the size and comfort of the seats.) Average running speed is about 80 miles per hour; Paris-Brussels is only two hours, 22 minutes (87 mph average! Compare that with 3-1/2 hours by air from midcity to midcity). and Paris-Zurich is only 6 hours. Dining facilities are always on hand. Punctuality is assured.

SLEEPING CARS

Wagons-Lits offer three first-class and two second-class categories. First class consists of regular one-berth or two-berth accommodations, plus Specials for shorter runs (20 small single compartments per car). Second class offers the T-2 arrangement with 18 double-decked twin units per car, which are supplementing the older three-berth facilities. Germany and France have the second-class couchette—a minimum- priced six-seat (or six-berth) compartment in which passengers may lie down without undressing.

Check the **date of expiration** on your round-trip ticket. On some short rides, they expire within 24 hours.

Enroute, the standard fixed **meal** at the standard fixed price generally runs between $9 and $13. Your own picnic—assembled before boarding—will not only save you money on the longer treks, but also taste a lot better than the relatively expensive snacks sold by platform vendors in the stations or by salesmen in the aisles.

MOTORING

Gasoline prices in Europe are roughly double those in the U.S., and in a few places they are three times as much.

Americans are permitted to drive in any nation in Eastern or Western Europe except Albania.

Don't glance at the map and casually announce, "We're going to make 350 miles on secondary roads tomorrow!"—because in most cases you're not, anywhere in Europe, unless you're prepared for total exhaustion. The most important routes run north and south; you'll usually have to thread your way going east and west. Very few superhighways or thruways—as we know them at home—exist, except in Austria, Holland, Denmark, Germany, Belgium, and the new links in Italy. France is rampant with "Who's chicken?" speedways equipped with a center "suicide" lane. Speed limits everywhere have been lowered in order to conserve fuel, but still when you hit the open road in Europe, you can put the pedal down and legally glide along at slightly more than 75 mph (130 kph is the turnpike limit in many countries, but powerful cars are often cruising at 160 kph). Germany is trying to save its forests, so in some regions it is imposing strict low limits to discover if pollution is reduced through cutting exhaust fumes. A few nations (Switzerland, as an example) are moving rapidly toward use of unleaded gasoline for environmental benefits.

Third-Party Insurance (Public Liability and Property Damage, often called the "green card") is compulsory throughout most of Europe. Rates vary if you're buying your car abroad. Ask AAA about insurance and be sure to get complete coverage—fire, theft, damage to yourself, the works—wherever you go on the Continent. If there's any kind of accident, no matter how trivial, you'll be up to your neck in gendarmes, red tape, and A.D. 1066 legal procedures—and it's the devil to prove that the other fellow is wrong when you have to shout him down in his mother tongue. The insurance companies have their people in all principal cities—so let them handle the snarls.

If there isn't any AAA office in your immediate neighborhood, write to **AAA Insurance Services**, *1000 AAA Drive, Heathrow, FL 32746-5063.* The Foreign Motoring Insurance Section is very helpful. Or if you should need assistance on the other side of the water, contact their official branches—AAA World-Wide Travel in Paris (*9 rue de la Paix*), in London (*32 Grosvenor Sq.*), or in Rome (*84 via Veneto*).

Left-hand traffic? Only in Great Britain and Ireland. In all other countries, you'll cruise on the same side as you do at home.

In most European countries, those in the front seats are required to buckle their safety harnesses; in many places, this means only for highway driving, but a few sticklers (Switzerland, for example) enforce the edict full time and on Sundays.

CAR HIRE

In general, we recommend that you wait until you've crossed the Atlantic, instead of setting up advance reservations in North America unless car rental comes as part of your overseas package. Here is our reasoning:

Every good-size city on the Continent has scads of excellent self-drive rentals. Even many of the big chains make use of a string of independent local operators. What you're driving isn't an AAA or

Hertz or Avis car; in all too many cases, it's actually a Schmidt or DuPres or Angelotti car, booked by the American company for you under an arrangement between these principals.

While we have no special quarrel with this setup, we'd personally prefer the privilege of selecting our own local operator, examining what we are paying for before agreeing to take it, and making our own deal.

On the first point, the caliber of local operators selected by these and other U.S. agencies varies considerably. Moreover, once you book with any American company, you get the vehicle they give you, and that's that.

On the second point, no single local outfit can stock every kind of car. Before leaving home, you might think you want a Ford or Rover, but after comparative shopping, that Volvo or Fiat might be far closer to your personal taste. Remember, too, that gasoline prices are more than double the back-home tariff, and since this outlay comes from your pocket, you may prefer an economical four-cylinder job such as a Ford Fiesta or one of the new thirstless little Opels.

On the third point, prices are supposed to be standard—but they aren't. If you do your own talking, particularly in off-season, you can end up with quotations that are substantially under the "official" prices that you must pay in the U.S. Older people also can receive discounts, as can travel agents, certain service personnel, and members of some clubs or groups. Also, do the booking yourself instead of leaving it to your hotel porter; you can save an immediate 20 percent by doing your own dialing. Very often, weekend rentals are half the price of midweek hiring.

STUDENT TRAVEL

Kalhovd/Telemark

Whether you are going abroad to study or just to have fun, your student status entitles you to an extraordinary number of bargains plus sources of aid and information. Active student travel offices operate in almost every corner of the globe; in Western Europe, increasingly well-organized national student travel agencies usually have offices in the capital, with branches in large cities and university towns. Many offer welcome centers, publications on student facilities and other services. Their addresses (and often some of their publications) may be obtained from the national tourist offices of the countries you'll be visiting. In the "Suggestions for Students" sections of the country chapters to follow, we'll also be listing many of their addresses and facilities.

STUDYING ABROAD

Nearly every college from Ivy Leaguers to little old Wachchova U. offers foreign scholarships. High schools have also joined in to some degree. In addition, classroom lectures are scheduled in many European lands.

Programs—often for credit—generally fall into these categories:

- Summer, trimester, semester, or full year at European universities or institutes.
- Summer seminar, a project within a single country or regional grouping.
- Independent travel from one to four months, led by a professor.
- Foreign apprenticeships arranged by U.S. universities as part of a "sabbatical year" from normal classroom routine.
- Summer-long combinations of study, travel, and work.
- High school language seminars crammed between lengthy excursions.

IDENTITY CARD

Apart from your passport you'll also need an **International Student Identity Card**. All full-time graduate students and undergraduates are eligible. (High school students and other nonuniversity students are issued an International Scholar Identity Card.) Armed with an ISIC, you can eat, sleep, wheel and deal at vastly reduced rates.

CIEE/SOFA (Council on International Educational Exchange/ Student Overseas Flights for Americans) *Student Travel Services* (*205 E. 42nd St., New York, NY 10017*, with retail/information counter attention at *777 U.N. Plaza*) is probably the best place to get these cards. Return their application form plus: (a) proof that you are currently a full-time student (taking at least 12 credits) in the fall or spring term (summer school is not acceptable) at an accredited school, (b) one passport-size photo (1-1/2"x2"), and (c) a check or money order for $10, which includes ISIC travel insurance. The cards are valid for 15 months beginning on Oct. 1. (If you show up in person, the entrance to the building is around the corner on E. 44th St.)

Incidentally, there's a 1500-room center that is a student union, budget hotel and college dorm called **William Sloane House** where you can bunk on your way to and from Europe. Rates at about $40 per single or $55 per twin; location *356 W. 34th St., NY 10001*; telephone reservations ☎ *(212) 760-5860*; open year-round with office hours 9-5 weekdays and 11 a.m. to 3 p.m. May 17 to July 26. Special weekly prices available. You'll need your ID card.

A few campus and other organizations are also authorized to issue the ISIC, but because some sharpies have been selling forgeries and imitations (sometimes for $10 or more!), be sure yours is issued by either the CIEE or a CIEE-approved source.

With this card you can receive discounts from five-66 percent on a variety of important items, depending upon the largesse of the individual host countries. Reductions fall into these broad categories: (1) lodging (student hotels and hostels covered later); (2) dining; (3) entertainment (scores upon scores of theaters, concert halls and movie houses); (4) sightseeing (museums and art galleries in many lands; archaeological sites); and (5) transportation (European network of scheduled charter flights, student flights from Europe to Asia or Africa, plus ship and rail connections).

TRAINS

Eurail Youthpass is the economy version of the Eurailpass (see "In Europe"). For a very reasonable outlay, you can wander at will in second-class compartments in over 16 continental countries for two solid months, provided you're under the age of 26. *This must be bought before your departure overseas.*

Fare reductions are also extended by several **national student groups** on special trains. For these seats, tickets are sold on a point-to-point basis, and an ISIC is usually required. The sole disadvantage of these student trains, so far as we can see, is that they usually run only once or twice a week in high season. Routes, fares and schedules are available from national student travel offices abroad; reservations may be made, but only after your arrival on foreign soil.

MOTOR SCOOTERS

A buyer's—not renter's—market. In a few centers where foreign visitors have descended en masse, scooter hire is catching on. But the rental cost for a scooter or other motorized two-wheeler is very often nearly the same as for an inexpensive car. The warm countries, naturally, offer the best opportunities. In the more temperate nations, however, you might have trouble finding one by the day or week. Due partly to the exploding demand for inexpensive transportation, the major dealers are concentrating on volume sales. Since most European manufacturers now maintain U.S. branches, consult the office of your choice before departure for information on factory-pickup plans, which are legion. Further details on local rental or purchase will be found in each chapter.

Not only is it wise to wear a **protective helmet**, but in many countries it's **obligatory**.

STUDENT HOSTELS

These usually offer school-operated hotels and university residence halls. Speaking broadly, you'll find the candles burning late, a fellow collegian receptionist to greet you, chambermaids to clean your room—and sometimes even a kitchen staff to serve in the dining room or cafeteria. The overnight levies range from around $8 to $22, with the average this year at $15.

Check-in time? Better register before 3 p.m.—unless, of course, you've already written ahead to specify your arrival time. Since one-night occupancy is so common, you'd also better tell the reception desk the precise duration of your stay. Otherwise, you might be asked to move out before you had intended to go.

In the "Suggestions for Students" sections of the chapters that follow, we have evaluated many student lodgings.

INFORMATION SOURCES

UNESCO (*Unipub, P.O. Box 433, New York, NY 10016,* or *9 place Fontenoy, Paris VII*) publishes *Study Abroad*, an international directory to full year study programs.

More helpful might be the **Institute of International Education** (*809 United Nations Plaza, New York, NY 10017*), which guides educational exchange programs sponsored by governments, universities, and foundations. IIE not only publishes directories to international study, but will send material geared to your needs if you'll write them explaining your field of interest and scholastic level, your language skills and country preferences, and whether you are interested in summer, semester, or longer study.

CIEE/SOFA *Student Travel Services* (mentioned above) offers the excellent free *Student Travel Catalogue* covering its vast skein of activities (which include group tours, study programs, insurance, transport on ships, planes, buses, and trains, car leasing, plus advice and information on almost every aspect of international travel, study, and work opportunities abroad). For students aged 18 to 30 who can fulfill certain qualifications, they also can arrange work permits and/or jobs. Much of this information has been collated into their *A Student Guide to Work, Study and Travel Abroad.* The latest edition is available in many bookstores and from CIEE, which also sells by mail a number of useful pamphlets and paperback guides that are unavailable or hard to find in bookshops.

The American Institute for Foreign Study may be able to answer some of your questions on its toll-free ☎ *800-243-4567.* The working day is nine-to-five.

AUSTRIA

Here, at the geographic epicenter of Europe, is the vital and promising link between east and west. Enterprising traders from the U.S.A., Japan, and Germany already are setting up their office branches in Vienna for the anticipated business traffic through this corridor—hoping to be more important than Brussels once the Eastern economy gets stoked up. Austria was created only as late as 1918, carved by political whittlers out of the German-speaking provinces of the old Austro-Hungarian monarchy.

Two thousand years ago, its eastern Alps were home to Celtic tribes. Three centuries later, the Romans set their imperialistic sights on the same Alps—and by 14 B.C. had subjugated all the territory south of the Danube. This river of Strauss waltz fame then marked the frontier of the Roman occupation.

Today Austria's invading legions are funseekers. They come, they ski, and they consort. In the capital you will see opportunists jostling for position to greet the surging waves of commerce from the eastern states.

From 1438 to 1804 the title of Holy Roman Emperor was donned, with one exception, only by Austrian sovereigns. Then came the (singular) Austrian and the (tandem) Austro-Hungarian dominance. And from empire to empire, the nation's volatile history continued in a topsy-turvy vein—a tale of royal infighting, shifting alliances, and elastic borders.

Wars, rebellions, intrigues, and uprisings continually reshaped the national identity until 1945 when the country finally gelled into a confederation of nine *Bundeslander* (states): Vienna, Lower Austria,

Burgenland, Upper Austria, Salzburg, Styria, Carinthia, Tyrol, and Vorarlberg.

At the same time its people—a curious but willing assemblage of East, West, North, and South Europeans—joined hands across their provincial borders to become citizens, linked by the German language and the Catholic faith.

Climatically, Austria is middle-of-the-road. There are no great swings of temperature. Much of the country is over 1000 meters high, so up in these climes the thermometer frequently plays tag with Jack Frost—even in spring and autumn. For the rest, Austria keeps its cool, rarely becoming uncomfortably hot.

Its people, too, are of a temperate nature, graceful as their music and prone—perhaps because of their geography and history—to being natural diplomats. They are a hospitable, reserved yet friendly lot. But find them a bit into their *schnaps* or *gluhwine* and they're likely to be unabashedly jovial. Red-cheeked, rosy, and robust, they can't resist tucking into a good time. Besides commanding one of Europe's choicest morsels of scenic and cultural real estate, Austria wisely views itself as the commercial and social bridge between two mighty geopolitical realms, a potentially key figure in Eurasia's complex jigsaw puzzle.

TIPS ON AUSTRIA

FOOD

For hungry wanderers who might be unfamiliar with local terms for standard dishes, here are translations for some of the linguistic mouthfuls that you may encounter:

Backhendl: A very young, milk-fed chicken, breaded and deep-fried.

Bauernschmaus: A "farmer's plate" of savory sausage, pork, sauerkraut, and dumplings. Beer is its happiest companion.

Griessnockerlsuppe: A hard-wheat dumpling beef broth.

Gulyassuppe: A long-simmering Hungarian Goulash soup.

Leberknodlsuppe: A liver-dumpling brew of just-right potency.

Naturschnitzel: An unbreaded veal cutlet.

Nockerln: A bite-size dumpling often steeped in Polish sauce.

Palatschinken: A thin, unrolled but sugared, U.S. Sunday-morning flapjack. They also come in other forms and with 2432 toppings or sauces.

Tafelspitz: Boiled beef with chive sauce, potatoes, apples, and horseradish.

Wiener Koch: A vanilla souffle.

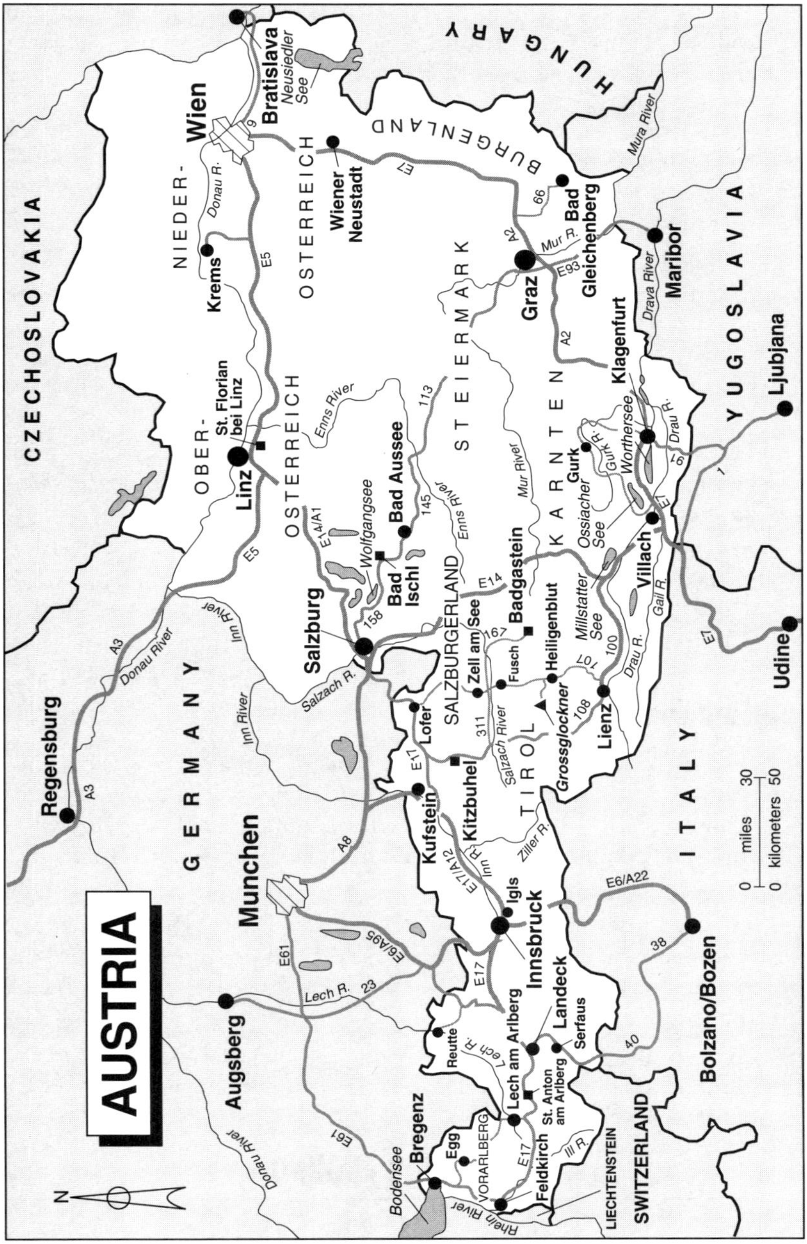
AUSTRIA
CZECHOSLOVAKIA
GERMANY
HUNGARY
YUGOSLAVIA
ITALY
SWITZERLAND
LIECHTENSTEIN
NIEDER-
OSTERREICH
OBER-
OSTERREICH
STEIERMARK
BURGENLAND
KARNTEN
SALZBURGERLAND
TIROL
VORARLBERG
Wien
Bratislava
Neusiedler See
Wiener Neustadt
Krems
St. Florian bei Linz
Linz
Bad Aussee
Wolfgangsee
Bad Ischl
Salzburg
Badgastein
Zell am See
Fusch
Heiligenblut
Grossglockner
Lofer
Kitzbuhel
Kufstein
Igls
Innsbruck
Landeck
Serfaus
St. Anton am Arlberg
Lech am Arlberg
Reutte
Bregenz
Egg
Feldkirch
Bodensee
Graz
Bad Gleichenberg
Maribor
Klagenfurt
Gurk
Worthersee
Ossiacher See
Villach
Millstatter See
Lienz
Ljubjana
Udine
Bolzano/Bozen
Regensburg
Munchen
Augsberg
Donau R.
Donau River
Enns River
Mur River
Mur R.
Mura River
Drava River
Drau R.
Gail R.
Gurk R.
Inn River
Inn R.
Salzach R.
Salzach River
Ziller R.
Lech R.
Ill R.
Rhein River
E5
E7
E14
E14/A1
E17
E17/A12
E93
E6/A95
E6/A22
E61
A2
A3
A8
9
66
113
145
158
167
311
108
107
100
91
1
23
38
40
0 30 miles
0 50 kilometers

Wiener Schnitzel: A breaded veal cutlet served with sliced lemon on the side. The garnished version adds capers and filets of anchovies on a curled round of lemon. If you order it *Schnitzel a la Holstein*, you will get Naturschnitzel with a fried egg on top (with the anchovies crisscrossed and the capers sprinkled around the yolk.)

DRINKS

Wines are very carefully policed since the scandalous revelations of diethyleneglycol found in some pressings. Most bottlers have always maintained ethical standards. Prices average from $9 to $23 per bottle and from $2 to $3.50 for a fourth of a liter.

While Klosterneuburger is perhaps the best white wine, if you stick to Gumpoldskirchner (available in most places), you'll probably be pleased. Other dependable and sound labels are Kremser, Duernsteiner, Hohenwarther, Nussberger, and Wachauer (Danube). An excellent red is Voslauer; the reds from Baden also are most often superb.

Of the beers, Gosser Brau is a rich brew made in Styria. It's full bodied and fine; choice of light or dark. Schwechater is tops in Vienna. Price: about $2 per glass.

Imported potables are relatively expensive. Strictly for nickel-plated gullets, there's a local rum that puts life in the afternoon tea, a "club whisky" that will lift the hat right off your head, and a schnapps that you'll find still delicately flaked with enamel from the bathtub. (In fairness, most of the latter are fine in quality, but pack the wallop of a Titan missile.) If you have about $6 to spend and can take it like W. C. Fields, there's also the local plum brandy or slivovitz. Enzian is another brandy, distilled from the roots of the tall yellow (not blue) gentian. Speaking personally, I'd much prefer a delicious snooker of Viennese coffee. Bowle is a refreshing summer punch made of white wine, champagne, or curacao, and fresh fruits; served from a bowl at about $2.50 per glass.

If you order a dry martini, be sure always to specify Beefeater (cheaper) or Gordon's as its base. As there is no home-bred gin, the low-grade imported English stock (which is used extensively) is best applied to arrest baldness.

Soft drinks, Coca-Cola, at perhaps $1.45 per glass, is mighty steep. Lemonade and other locally bottled citrus beverages are priced at the same level.

GETTING AROUND

TRAINS

The Austrian Federal Railways offers an hourly or two-hourly intercity service linking the capital with Salzburg, Graz, Innsbruck, and Villach. *The Wiener Walzer Express* (sleeping cars available) and the

Transalpin Express (daylight passage with new carriages) have cut the running times between Vienna-Zurich to about 9 hours.

These are very comfortable. So also are the famed *Arlberg Express, Romulus Express, Vienna-Ostend Express, Mozart Express, Tirolerland, Erzherzog Johann, Wiener Walzer, Johann Strauss,* and most of the other orange-colored international stars. The majority offer sleepers (singles at luxury prices to 6-bed economy couchette cars) and dining facilities; all serve drinks. The modern autorail cars are good, too.

Fares are not excessive. Children up to 6 years travel as honored guests of the Republic and to age 15 receive a 50% reduction, as do elders (women of 60 and above, men at 65). You'll need an official identity card to qualify; it costs AS200. Then there are unlimited-travel bargains that vary with seasons and locations. Ask a travel agent to give you the details.

On Austria's railways, expect glorious scenery, efficient equipment, courteous attendants—and exactly 1,000,001 curves per mile.

MOTORING

The 9-mile Arlberg Tunnel is a time-saver! In summer, when other routes and passes are open, the toll drops considerably. The Salzburg-Vienna autobahn is wonderful. The expressway over the Brenner Pass between Innsbruck and Italy also is tops for convenience and speed. The 6-lane highway from Vienna southward reaches Gloggnitz; another span runs between Innsbruck and Kufstein. In high season, where there's no autobahn, you can find yourself frustrated by traffic congestion.

CAR HIRE

Agencies galore. In the capital, **Avis** (*Opernring 1; ☎ 5873595*), **Hertz** (*Karntnering 17; ☎ 5128677*), and **ARAC-Autovermietung** (*Mollardgasse 15; ☎ 5971675*) continue to uphold their reputations for integrity and reliability. Hertz was outstanding in Salzburg for my latest VW rental. Because of high import duties and high taxes, the basic rates start in the stratosphere—and they climb from there. Thus, you would be wise to weigh this system against those of alternate modes of transport.

AUTHOR'S OBSERVATION

In winter the two auto clubs, OAMTC and ARBO rent snow chains if you need them.

MOTORSCOOTER OR MOTORBIKE RENTAL

Try the Modo Guzzi motorbikes at **Rainer Kraftfahrzeughandel** (*Simmeringer Hauptstr. 279; ☎ 766531/0*). If you want a plain **bicycle**, more than 130 Austrian rail stations have them available from early April until late Oct. for very modest rentals.

SIGHTSEEING

MUSIC

Music is the constant heartbeat and throb of all Austrians. *Vienna's* summer festival runs from late June to mid-Sept.; *Salzburg's* from late July to end of Aug.; *Graz's* from mid-Sept. through Oct.; *Bregenz's* from July into Aug. For specifics ask the Austrian National Tourist Office or your travel agent. Many smaller and fine festivals exist elsewhere and throughout the seasons.

BIRDWATCHING

Birdwatching your bailiwick? Try *Lake Neusiedl* in May or Oct.

ARTS AND CRAFTS

Interested in **icon painting**? Bookbinding? Woodcarving? *Geras* is the place. About 100 km northwest of Vienna, it offers **over 100 arts and crafts courses** all year round.

FITNESS

Those with a fitness fetish might want to try a **biotraining** vacation at **Health Center Lanser Hof** or at **Baden** near Vienna. A 14-day package at the former (full board) costs $700; a 7-day package at the latter (half board) costs about $200.

LANGUAGE STUDY

Pack your participles and head for the universities at *Klessheim, Salzburg* or *Vienna*. A 6-week course price is $1600, while the cost for 4 weeks' tuition and accommodation runs close to $850.

FARM LIVING

Why not hitch up your *lederhosen* and go *bauernhof*-hopping? It's cheap, rustic, and colorful. For as little as $9.50 a day per person, you can have your butter and churn it, too. These neat-as-a-pin bed-and-breakfast accommodations often offer an ample morning's repast: homemade bread, smoked ham, farm-fresh butter. If you feel like milking the cows or lending a hand with the harvest, you're welcome; if not, just consider it your hof away from home. How to book your hayloft? Request regional *Urlaub Am Bauernhof* brochures from the Austrian National Tourist Office, then contact your selected family directly.

LOCAL RACKETS

Commercial brokers and concierges collect a 20% commission on opera, concert, and other performance tickets, on top of which they may add their own tip and perhaps delivery charges. It disturbs my sense of ethics to think that so much of what I might spend to hear a great artist who has cultivated his or her virtuosity over a lifetime could go into the pocket of someone who peddles a ticket day after day on a routine basis. Thus, to save schillings and to get a decent location, go to the box office and buy them for yourself. I generally pick up late tickets at reasonable prices at the Tourist Information desk on the subway level beneath the opera plaza. You can also order tickets to the Staatsoper or Volksoper on your credit card via a long-distance phone call. The number is ☎ *43-1-513-1513*; phone office hours Central European Time (six days before performances) or mornings on Sat. and Sun.

SPORTS

SKIING

Be it downhill or cross-country, this is Austria's trademark sport. Snow begins to fall in mid-Nov. and the skiing remains generally good through spring. Nearly all lifts continue to function through Easter, and some afterwards. To find out the conditions while still in the States, dial the **Austrian Snow Phone** (☎ *212-697-8295*) any day of the wintry week for the recorded round-the-clock report. The Austrian National Tourist Office can help you nail down all alpine arrangements.

MOUNTAINEERING

Prefer climbing up the slopes to skiing down them? The calf building opportunities are endless. Mountaineering schools exist in **Innsbruck** (*Kaiser-Josef Str. 3* and at the nearby village of *Natters*) and **Salzburg** (*Neutorgasse 42*), as well as elsewhere, but all are rather costly. Minimum rates run about $85 a day. For outdoor life and hiking at lower economic altitudes, places such as *Seefeld* and *Lech* offer daily excursions, breakfast included, at $140 or so for a week-long package. At *Muehlviertel* you can toss your pack on a truck and waddle along light as a duck feather. Cost is about $200 for 7 days of escorted touring.

AUTHOR'S OBSERVATION

For parents who wish to be more independent, many ski resorts and mountaineering schools offer all-day, supervised activities for young children.

WATERSPORTS

With the spring thaw, a skier's thoughts may likewise turn to water. On *Lake Constance* at *Lochau* (*Bahnhofstrasse 16*), a week's **sailing** course costs about $200; a **windsurfing** course, about $85. Or how about a kayak course? There's a white-water thriller offered at *Lammertal* in the savage, alpine, pretty-as-a-postcard *Berchtesgaden* (Germany) area. Cost of the 5-day course: about $170.

FLY FISHING

Angling for brook, gold, or rainbow trout and numerous other feisty and flavorful species is possible throughout Austria. Contact the local tourist offices for specific details.

HORSES

The bangtails race every weekend from late March to late July in the *Vienna Freudenau*. The Derby, early in June, offers the fattest purse.

Should you prefer to mount your own steed, there are **riding** courses at *Ampflwang*, between the Danube and the Salzkammergut District. Seven days, full pension, run anywhere from $200 to $800. Already skilled in the saddle and eager to trot through the Tyrol on your own? Local tourist offices can supply rental information.

WHERE TO GO

ARLBERG

This pass between the Alps and the Rhine Valley threads into the Vorarlberg, Austria's most petite province, which offers the nation's most electric thrills to sports and nature buffs. Alpine skiers have been known to hock their progeny in order to schuss along the slopes of *Lech*, *Zurs*, *St. Anton*, *Stuben*, and *St. Christoph. Lech* has the widest range of accommodations, runs through the trees as well as on open slopes, and has a zinging nightlife. *Petersboden* is a solid bet for headquartering in *Oberlech*, but down in the valley we'd pick the *Berghof* or the more expensive *Arlberg*; the *Alphorn* is an excellent bargain stopover. *Zurs* is in the upper crust of social snow-balling; lacking woodlands, it's scenically dull to us. *St. Anton* is the train-highway-ski-lift intersection of the region, as well as the jovial junction for the robust youth trade. *Nassereinerhof* is a reliable medium-price *gasthof* here. *Valluga* is also outstanding. The chillier characteristics of *Stuben* simply don't lure us, but the skiing is excellent. The *Post*, *Mondschein*, and *Arlberg* are fine stops here.

BREGENZ

The summer music and dance festival in this Celto-Roman town is bewitching for its magnificent addition of a floating stage to the watersports of *Lake Constance*; it usually functions from late July through most of August, mixing drama with opera and symphonic productions. Low-cost shelter is available at the *Adler*, *Central*, the *Deutschmann*, and the *Messmer*, with costlier digs at the *Post am See*. Excursionists find it within easy driving distance of the *Arlberg*, *Flexen*, and *Hochtannberg Passes*.

DANUBE CRUISE

If you are Vienna-bound and distressed by the scramble of train or bus connections, here's a relaxed way to arrive—except at peak season when nearly every mode of transportation is strained to capacity. Route yourself only as far as the railway hub of Linz, and disembark. The *Stadt Wien, the Stadt Passau, the Austria, the Schoenbrunn*, *Wachau*, and the *Theodor Koerner* may be boarded at 9 a.m. It's delightful to have a light brunch in the city, to climb aboard for the smooth glide through the pastoral countryside, and then to dock at the capital at 8 p.m. Ample restaurant and bar facilities afloat; moderate prices; more beguiling than the Rhine excursion, because it's not so cut and dried. If your starting point for this little adventure is Vienna, you may entrain to the docks in *Melk* (penultimate stop) in time for a 4:40 p.m. boarding. Check schedules carefully because the above route goes about 4 times a month while the longer Grein-Vienna circuit is daily. If you are motoring along the Danube through the wine-rich *Wachau* Valley and Strauss's *Wienerwald*, don't miss the excavated Roman city of *Carnuntum*, the classical museum at *Deutsch Altenburg* or the fortified border town of *Hainburg*.

GRAZ

It's a university town whose Old City center is in excellent preserve, some say the best in Europe. The **Opera** has recently been restored to the glories of its 1898 origins, providing performances three or four times each week from Sept. through June. Try to see the **Landeszeughaus**, an armory with more than 30,000 medieval suits and historical weapons, the **Eggenburg Palace** and, if it doesn't spook you, the **Imperial Mausoleum**, which, by the way, is not always open to the public. Graz is an alluring springboard for exploring the enchanted realm of *Styria.* The **Erzherzog Johann** is a fair stop in the upper-moderate price bracket. **Zum Alten Fassl** is more economical and very good, as are the **Gasthof Zum Kreuz** and the **Pension Iris**. Many nice, cheap guesthouses dot the surrounding hills. Just west of town is the castle enclave of **Piber** where the celebrated Lipizzaner stallions are bred; these are the glorious white stars of the equestrian world, which perform at the Spanish Riding School in Vienna.

INNSBRUCK

This handsome valley town reaching up the mountain flanks is the capital of Tyrol. You'll probably want to visit the Old City, the **Hofkirche** (court chapel) with 28 heroic-sized bronze statues, **Ambras Castle**, and the famous **Golden Roof**. The site of two Winter Olympics, Innsbruck is surrounded by ski slopes. Extensive accommodations are available in every price bracket, and there is nature galore for campers. **Gasthof Ferrarihof** is a student shelter. (There are a half dozen more in and around town.). The **Happ** is a happy *gasthof*; so are the **Mozart**, the **Leipziger Hof**, and the **Koreth**. From here are rewarding jaunts to **Seefeld** (resort stop with famous casino), the **Ziller Valley**, **Obergurgl**, **Solden** (tiny and rustic), and the dramatic peak of the **Zugspitze**. (Reached by cable car, it marks the boundary with Germany and seems to be the ground floor of heaven.) Don't miss the village of **Igls**, 10 minutes up the valley from Innsbruck. Also in the highlands, some adventurous Iowans discovered the cozy **Sport Pension** and the **Hotel Delevo** in **Hungerburg** which they recommended to other travelers.

TRAVEL BARGAIN

Anyone staying in Innsbruck for at least 3 days automatically becomes a member of *Club Innsbruck*. The membership card, issued at your accommodation, entitles you to a welcome drink at the Monday evening Tourist Office presentation at the **Disco-Pascha**; free rides on the **Innsbruck Mountain Bus**; participation in the Innsbruck mountaineering program (including free mountain guides); a 50% reduction on admission to the **Museum of Tirolean Folk Art**, the **Ferdinandeum State Museum of Tirol**, and the **Hofkirche**; approximately 20% off on cable car and lift fees; and 10% reductions on tennis-court fees at **Igls Congress Center**, on greens fees at Rinn and the 9-hole "**Sperberegg**," on panorama flights over the Central Alps, and on admission to the alpine animal zoo.

KITZBUHEL

Here's the stuff of winter sport dreams in season; lively, youthful, and a good value for the pocket. The area has every kind of ski slope; experts consider it second only to the Arlberg resorts. A reasonably priced tuck-in is the **Hotel Montana**, where the people are extra-cordial. For a bit more, the **Toni Sailer Haus** is a drawing card for sporting types; in the same range is the **Fyra Vindar** with breakfast only.

Eggerwirt is a reliable guest house. Excursions to the **Kitzbuheler Horn** and **Fieberbrunn** to partake of the health springs and local festivals are pleasant postscripts to the winter's pastimes.

LINZ

This rather commercial town is world-famous for the delicious Linzer tart or torte, a cake or cookie with a raspberry heart. The young Brucknerhaus Concert Hall is busy, especially in autumn when the festival is piping. If you've got a baroque turn of mind for such as the **Bruckner organ**, then the nearby **Monastery of St. Florian** should pull out all of your stops. The fabulous Bruckner Music Festival is in the fall (usually in Sept.). There's also a castle museum of Austrian folk art, but we'd say the town's best use is as a springboard for visiting the lakelands of *Salzkammergut*. For overnighting, try the **Zum Schwarzen Baren**, the **Wolfinger**, or the **Nibelungenhof**.

SALZBURG

Surrounded by scenic mountains, this captivating city is in a gleaming medieval chalice filled with antique architecture and some of the world's most enchanting music—one could scarcely expect less of the birthplace of Mozart. Concerts and opera are Salzburg's stock in tourist trade, and during the annual Music Festival in July and August, the culture here is so thick you could cut it with a halberd. There's also the Mozart Week in late January, as well as the yearly Easter Festival, another musical classics spree in Oct.-Nov., plus a performance somewhere in the city perhaps 200 nights per year.

WHERE TO STAY

Elefant • *Sigmund Haffner Gasse 4*; ☎ *843397*. 40 rooms that go back to A.D. 1200; an inviting Stube on the ground floor for dining.

Blaue Gans • *Getreidegasse 43;* ☎ *841317*. Cozy and well situated in midtown.

Haus Gassner • *Moosstrasse 126B;* ☎ *843467*. Modest but very hospitable.

Kernstock • *Karolingerstrasse 29;* ☎ *827469*. Offers an apartment plus 4 rooms in a private chalet-style house. If you phone from the station or airport, Mrs. Elfriede Kernstock will pick you up in her car for no charge. She's also helpful in guidance suggestions and she speaks English.

Zum Touristen • *Linzer Gasse 43-45;* ☎ *71401*. Good space for about 50 touristen.

Gasthaus Austria • *Linzer Gasse #76;* ☎ *72313*. About half the size of Zum Touristen but plenty of heart.

Blobergerhof • *Hammerauerstrasse 4;* ☎ *830227*. A gastehaus with real homespun warmth; the Nussbaumer-Keuschnigg family care for their clients and provide a lot for your money. You'll probably fall in love with it as soon as you see the blossoms cascading over the balconies and window boxes.

Auerhahn • *Bahnhofstrasse 15;* ☎ *51052*. Offers a dozen clean rooms.

Trimerstuberl • *Bergstrasse 6;* ☎ *74776*. Excellent value here.

Weisse Taube • *Kaigasse 9;* ☎ *842404*. Well situated; costly but nice.

Doktorschloessl • *Glasserstrasse 7;* ☎ *23088*. Fair-size pension; half the units with private bath; well appointed.

Eva Maria • *Sinnhubstrasse 25;* ☎ *845960*. A smaller pension with ample warmth and kind staff.

Schlosswirt • *Anif.* A huge country manse; fine if you've got wheels; otherwise, the taxi fare can be pulverizing.

YOUTH HOSTELS

Seven in the town and near region. Go to the City Tourist Center at *Auerspergasse 7* for information or to the main station or *Mozartplatz 5*. I've inspected most of them and they are fully reliable. You might also ask about the numerous and delightful **Camping Grounds** in summer and the **Jugendgastehaus** (*J. Preis Allee 18;* ☎ *842674*).

WHERE TO EAT

Bosna Grill • *Griesgasse 19.* Situated in an alley, this is the cheapest for a marvelous pair of slavic wursts; stand as you eat. Delicious hot dog kiosk.

Hagenauerstuben • *In Mozarts Geburtshaus.* Has roots going back to 1372, with food a little bit more modern. Delicatessen plus cafeteria. Top quality but not high prices. The most historic spot in town.

Herzl • *Next to Goldener Hirsch.* A romantic, wood-lined tavern with true regional cooking, meats, cheeses, and grostl plus beer and wine.

Goldene Ente • *Goldgasse 10.* More formal; reliable cookery.

Nordsee • *Getreidegasse 27.* The place to go for fishy fast food.

Peterskeller • *The* spot for Old World atmosphere; the wines are wonderful too and not expensive.

Schlosswirt • If you've got transportation, a terrific buy for cookery and the entire experience of going.

WHERE TO DRINK

Augustinerbraustuberl • A mammoth beer hall with a chestnut-tree garden. Good for a hoot.

Peterskeller • Basically for wine, but in one room you can order a beer, so ask first. In summer, most of the drinking is done under the cathedral arches outside.

WHAT TO SEE AND DO

Among the many classic attractions are **Mozart's birthplace** (closed Sun.), the **Mozart Museum**, and the enchanting **Salzburg Marionette Theater** (closed Sun.)—probably the best-known company of its kind on the boards today and a joy for adults as well as kids. Rubbing elbows with the Vienna State Opera House is **the Salzburg Festspielhaus**. Adjacent to the old building, this supermodern 7-unit structure contains 2340 seats—none more than 115 feet from that beauty spot on the contralto's chin! Equally interesting, the **Palace Concerts** scheduled over most of the year. And don't forget the **cable car**, 5 miles out, which zips up 6170 feet of Alps in 8 minutes, for a commendably modest price per dizzy head. About 9 miles south of town there's the popular **Hallein Salt Mine**. Take the cableway up the **Durrnberg**, slip into floppy coveralls and whoooosh down the sliding boards à la playland for a brief walk through the excavations. Over at **Werfen**, supercool underground moles may join a 2-hour guided tour of the spectacular **Giant Ice Caves**, which are sufficiently thawed to view from May to early Oct. Other nearby targets: **St. Gilgen**, **Wolfgangsee**, the **Salzkammergut** lake district, Franz Joseph's summer haven of **Bad Ischl**, and **Gmunden**, a winning lakeside pottery village where many of the studios welcome kibitzers. A somewhat longer but breathtakingly lovely loop should tuck in the storybook **Zell am See** as well as a glacier-high ride among the edelweiss to the 12,460-foot **Grossglockner**.

WHERE TO SHOP

CANDLES

Peter Nagy (*Getreidegasse*, across from the Goldener Hirsch Hotel) is almost a wax museum. Beautiful bouquets; Christmas and ceremonial candles; floral patterns, figures and novelty pieces in burgundy, green, beige; some honey and herb candles and scented ones. It's a Saxon waxen wonderland!

COUNTRY FASHIONS AND SPORTING GOODS

Sport und Waffen E. Dschulnigg KG (*Griesgasse 8*) and **Cosi's by Dschulnigg** (*Griesgasse 6*) has everything for field and stream, town and country, man and woman, elders and children—all in a splendid Austrian motif. The outdoor world of fashion reaches its zenith here. **Alois Wenger u. Co.** (*Getreidegasse 29*) is aimed more at what Salzburgers call *trachten,* or distinctive costume of the region. These include dirndls for daytime or evening, sport jackets for men and women, for informal or formal occasions, and a blizzard of accessories.

CRYSTAL AND PORCELAIN

Sigrist (*Griesgasse 13*) has been the foremost purveyor of these home and gift items since early in the last century. Though the names displayed are of prestigious manufacturers, the prices are very reasonable for many selections.

GLASS SPECIALIST

Fritz-Reiner Kreis (*Sigmund-Haffner-Gasse 14*) tinkles with a crystalline realm of glass, bells, trinkets, marriage and baptism presentations. Initialing can usually be done in a jiffy. Convenient shipping facilities for special orders.

HANDICRAFTS

Salzburger Heimatwerk (*Residenzpl. 9*) is one you will probably visit anyway because it's built into the famous Glockenspiel Tower. It is a monument to the skills of regional artisans, who work in silk, wool, wood, dried flowers, glass, leather, and ceramics. The prices are incredibly low for such delightful and delicate creations. You could fill your Christmas sacks for years here and save bundles.

JEWELRY

Lahrm (*Universitatsplatz 16*) is the more economically priced purveyor of distinctive Lahrm collections, many of them in the antique style that suits Austrian outerwear. He specializes in hearts but, of course, the range is extensive. **Anton Koppenwallner** (*Klampferergasse 2*) focuses chiefly on items to be worn with trachten. It is so definitive that when you see it you must have it.

MARKET

Grunmarkt (*Universitatsplatz-Wiener Philarmoniker-Gasse*) is in high gear every morning, Mon.-Sat. All the flavor of this jewel-of-a-city rolled into one.

RECORDINGS

Both **Sound of Music** (*Judengasse 17*) and **EMI-Columbia Austria** (*Universitatsplatz 15*) supply grooves and tapes of Austrian music. Their libraries are vast and a few samples make wonderful keepsakes of your trip, especially late recordings from the Salzburg Festivals.

REGIONAL CERAMICS

Guglhupf (*Franz-Josefs-Kai 5*) is a joyful haven for the colorful breakfast sets, dinnerware, candelabra, and dollops for the happy home. There is also a splendid collection of Gmunder creations from upper Austria. A fun place.

VIENNA

Like Salzburg, Vienna is a city of music. It long ago attracted such composing titans as Mozart, Haydn, Schubert, Gluck, and Beethoven, thus establishing itself as the world's heavyweight music capital.

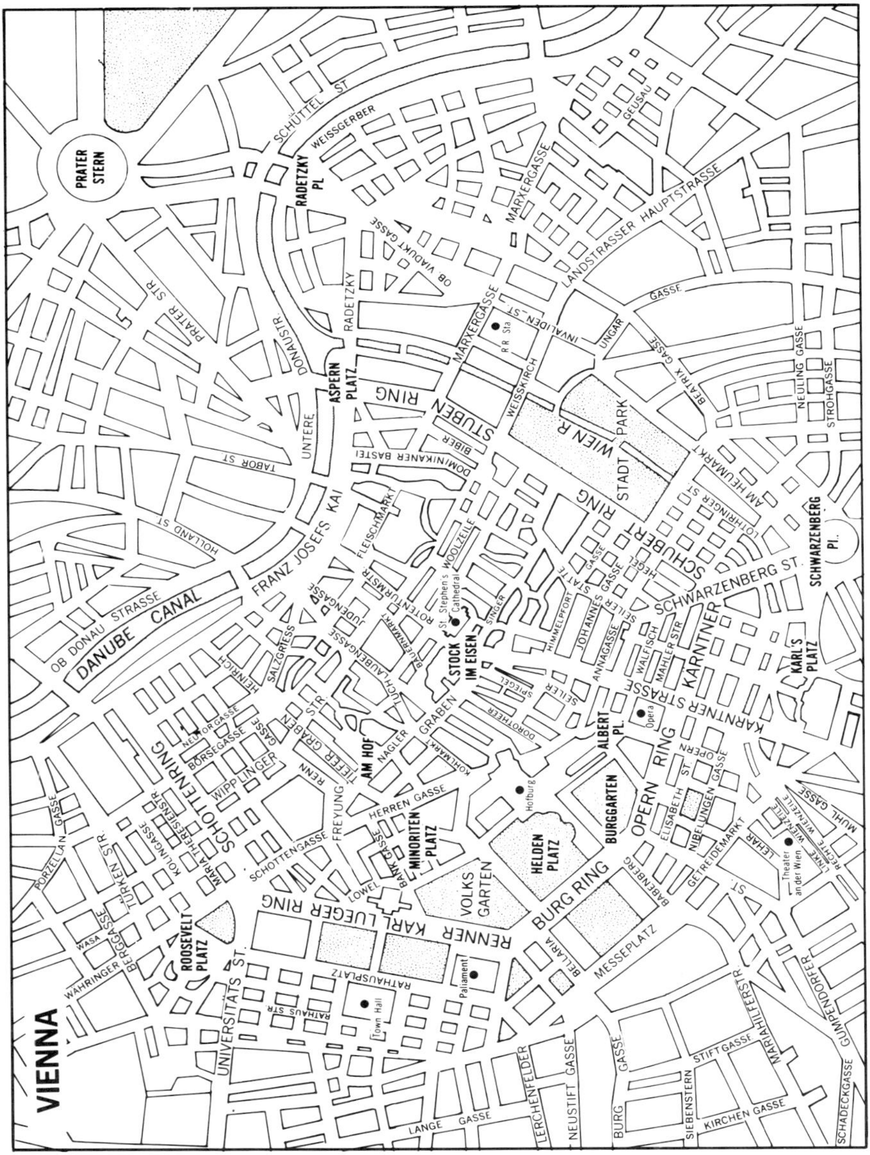
VIENNA
PRATER STERN
SCHÜTTEL ST
WEISSGERBER
RADETZKY PL
GEUSAU
MARXERGASSE
LANDSTRASSER HAUPTSTRASSE
OB. VIADUKT GASSE
RADETZKY
PRATER STR
DONAUSTR.
UNTERE
ASPERN PLATZ
STUBEN RING
R.R. Sta.
INVALIDEN ST.
WEISSKIRCH
UNGAR
GASSE
BEATRIX GASSE
NEULING GASSE
STROHGASSE
WIEN R.
STADT PARK
PARK RING
BIBER
DOMINIKANER BASTEI
TABOR ST
FLEISCHMARKT
FRANZ JOSEFS KAI
HOLLAND ST
WOLLZEILE
SCHUBERT RING
AM HEUMARKT
LOTHRINGER ST.
SCHWARZENBERG PL.
SCHWARZENBERG ST.
HEGEL
SEILER
STATTE
GASSE
JOHANNES GASSE
HIMMELPFORT
ANNAGASSE
WALFISCH
MAHLER STR
KARNTNER
KARNTNER STRASSE
KARL'S PLATZ
OB DONAU STRASSE
DANUBE CANAL
ROTENTURMSTR
JUDENGASSE
SALZGRIESS
ROTENTURM
St. Stephen's Cathedral
SINGER
STOCK IM EISEN
SPIEGEL
SEILER
DOROTHEER
LAUBENGASSE
BAUERNMARKT
TUCH
HEINRICH
NEUTORGASSE
BÖRSEGASSE
GASSE
SCHOTTENRING
WIPPLINGER
TIEFER GRABEN
STR
AM HOF
NAGLER
GRABEN
KOHLMARKT
ALBERT PL.
Opera
OPERN RING
OPERN GASSE
ST.
ELISABETH
NIBELUNGEN
GETREIDEMARKT
Hofburg
BURGGARTEN
RENN
FREYUNG
HERREN GASSE
MINORITEN PLATZ
BANK GASSE
HELDEN PLATZ
MUHL GASSE
RECHTE WIENZEILE
LINKE WIENZEILE
LEHAR
Theater an der Wien
PORZELLAN GASSE
TÜRKEN STR.
KOLINGASSE
MARIA THERESIENSTR.
SCHOTTENGASSE
LOWEL
VOLKS GARTEN
BURG RING
BABENBERG
ST.
WASA
BERGGASSE
ROOSEVELT PLATZ
RENNER KARL LUEGER RING
BELLARIA
MESSEPLATZ
WÄHRINGER
UNIVERSITÄTS ST.
RATHAUSPLATZ
Parliament
RATHAUS STR
Town Hall
GUMPENDORFER
MARIAHILFERSTR.
LERCHENFELDER
NEUSTIFT GASSE
BURG GASSE
SIEBENSTERN
STIFTGASSE
KIRCHEN GASSE
LANGE GASSE
SCHADECKGASSE

Under the resilient Hapsburg dynasty, which spanned six centuries, Vienna commanded an empire that blossomed from the Balkans across Europe and the Atlantic to Spanish America. Though today Vienna commands a country smaller than Maine, its ego is clearly heir to the Hapsburg era: It prefers white tie and tails to T-shirts, and the opera to most everything else. Straitlaced and gracefully aloof, it has a penchant for **schlag**-topped pastries with Viennese coffee at the appointed afternoon hour. Vienna does, however, frequently let its long-hair tradition down—and nowhere as freely as at the **Heuriger** in Grinzing or in the "Bermuda Triangle" in midcity.

DIRECTORY

U.S. Embassy • *Boltzmanngasse 16*; ☎ *315511.*

American Express • *Karntner S tr. 21-23*; ☎ *51540/0.*

Ambulance service • ☎ *144.*

English-Speaking Dentist • Dr. Georg Weinlaender, *9, Boltzmanngasse 12*; ☎ *340598.*

Police • Fremdenpolizei, *9, Wasagasse 20*; ☎ *313-4400.*

Favorite Pawnshop • Dorotheum, *Dorotheergasse 17*; ☎ *51560/0.*

HOW TO GET AROUND

Vienna provides fast and relatively modern **streetcars** and **buses**. The system is easy once you learn the hang of it. First, picture the Ringstrasse as your guideline. Outside, there are a dozen tram lines at your fingertips. Inside, you can roll within a matter of minutes to such attractions as the Spanish Riding School (*Hofburg*), St. Stephen's (*Karntner Str.-Rotenturm Str.*), the Kunsthistorisches Museum (*Maria Theresien Platz*), and a score of others.

For Schonbrunn Palace, take trams #52, #58, or hop on the subway U4; for Belvedere Palace, tram D at the Opera; for Auersperg Palace (only a 2-minute walk from the Ring, near the Parliament Building), tram #46 at Burg Ring and Bellaria Strasse.

FARES

You'll pay the equivalent of about US$2 (AS20) on most one-way runs, including transfers. You can further economize by buying tickets in advance (blocks of 5 at AS75 per unit). If it is offered this season, the **24-Hour Vienna Ticket** can haul you over 500 km of underground and metropolitan rails plus all of the bus routes in and around the city for the moderate sum of AS45. A 72-hour ducat costs AS115. Be sure to check at transportation centers for these money savers.

SUBWAYS AND TRAINS

They are called Schnellbahn, and U-bahn—and they go in every direction, with more stops being added every year. Familiarize yourself with these fast, efficient, low-cost systems and you will save a bundle.

AIRPORT RUNS

The town terminal is in the Hilton Hotel. The airport is a long way out, so taxi rates are lethal (about $40 for the circuit). Buses are around AS60 per body (less than half that for children). A microbus feeder service that will pick you up at your hotel costs around $22 per person.

WHERE TO STAY

With an exception or two, the very small houses are the choicest. Since it would be a waste of your time to delineate the myriad of 6-room, 3-room, 8-room, 4-room possibilities—the limited capacities of which leave hopelessly little flexibility in bookings—your best bet would be to consult either the headquarters of the **Austrian National Tourist Office** in Vienna (*Margaretenstrasse 1*; ☎ *5872000*) or its U.S. branch (*500 Fifth Ave., New York, NY 10110*).

In Vienna, the Tourist Office branches at the railroad stations and the airport can reserve rooms for you; there's another run by the Vienna City Tourist Board (*Karntner Str. 38*); the central facility is at Obere Augartenstr (*40*; ☎ *211140*; FAX *216-8492*).

The word *pension* in the names of Austrian lodgings does not necessarily mean that you must purchase a meal package. In Viennese parlance, this usually indicates that the establishment is relatively small, probably occupying a floor or two of a larger building.

LEAST $

Schweizer Pension Solderer • *Heinrichsgasse 2;* ☎ *5338156.* About $50 with basin or $65 with bath or shower; single, about $33. Breakfast included. One of the best in this category.

Pension Reimer • *Kirchengasse 18 (near the Mariahilfer Church);* ☎ *936162.* Double with shower, $52; $43 without. All-dry singles, $30-ish. Triples for $55 or quads in the $65 range best-buys. Breakfast extra; kitchen facilities for light snacks. Babysitting service. From the West Station, trams #52 or #58 or bus #13 from the South Station. If this is full, **Lindenhof**, (*around the corner*) is said to be a worthy alternative.

Hedwig Gally (Mrs.) • *25/10 Arnsteingasse;* ☎ *892-9073.* Located in the area of Westbahnhof, a 10-minute walk from Schonbrunn Palace. Simple cooking facilities; very willing hostess. Single about $23; twin with shower, nudging $44.

Pension Zipser • *Lange Gasse 49;* ☎ *420228.* $40-or-so per person with full facilities. Breakfast and surcharges included.

The Monopol • *Prinz Eugen Str. 68;* ☎ *5058526.* Almost adjoins the South and East Railway Stations. Undistinguished mien; fair service. Singles without vistas have drawn some reader complaints.

Irmgard Lauria • *Kaiser Str. 77;* ☎ *934152.* Both rooms and hostess come recommended by a bombardment of enthusiastic letters from readers. Cleanliness, comfort, and kindness are all underscored; all rooms with color TV, kettle, toaster, and plates; corridor showers free; in family-style units, rates run close to $23 per person. Furnishings in Biedermeier style. You can have a reasonable meal at the nearby Café Journal, on the same street at #56.

Altwienerhof • *Herklotzgasse 6 (near Westbahnhof);* ☎ *837145.* Recommended; excellent singles with shower; variable prices throughout. Superior restaurant and service. Reserve ahead, especially in summer.

Haus Dobling • *Gymnasium Str. 85;* ☎ *347631.* A far-north-of-center dormitory for students in winter, open to travelers other times. Clean, convenient, and worth the price: Twin rate, including breakfast, $45. All rooms boast private baths.

Don Bosco Turmherberge (Youth Hostel) • *Lechner Str. 12;* ☎ *7131494.* 50-bed dormitory. You don't have to be a student, but you do have to be male. First night: about $8.50; each night thereafter: circa $7. No meals (not even breakfast). Opens in March and closes when the potbelly stove can no longer cut the ice—usually November.

Kolpingfamilie Wien Meidling • *Bendlgasse 10-12; ☎ 835487.* Again, men only. Barely recommended.

YOUTH HOSTELS

Apart from the facilities already mentioned, you have the following: **Brigittenau** (*F.-Engels Platz 24; ☎ 338294*); **Jugendherberge Neubau** *(Myrthengasse 7 Wein; ☎ 936316)*; **Ruthensteiner** (*R.-Hamerlinggasse 24; ☎ 834693*); and **Stadt Wien Hutteldorf-Hacking** (*Schlossberggasse 8; ☎ 8770263*).

MORE $$

In this mid-range category, you may expect to pay from $40 to $55 each in twin accommodations this year—occasionally with bath, but far more often with extra-charge, down-the-hall privileges only. Decent lodgings at this level are rare.

Regina • *Rooseveltplatz 15; ☎ 427681.* 127 clean, good-size rooms, all with private plumbing.

Pension Aclon • *Dorotheergasse 6-8; ☎ 5127949/0.* Coin-operated elevator to thirdfloor entrance; 25 amiably dated rooms; singles usually far less fetching than doubles, though some are being refreshed. Directress Frau Michelmayer is very kind.

Royal • *Singer Str. 3 (beside the Dom); ☎ 51568.* Spectacular views from the roof terrace. Royal comfort; cordial staff.

Graben • *Dorotheergasse 3; ☎ 5121531.* Operated by the same interests as the Regina and Royal; upholds the same high standards.

Pension Nossek • *Graben 17; ☎ 5337041.* In the heart of Vienna's main shopping area. Spacious 16-table restaurant. 17 singles, none with bath; commodious doubles with partitioned sinks (cots if required); 3 apartments for multiple accommodation. For night owls this house provides frontdoor keys without charge. Good.

Rathaus • *Lange Gasse 13 (near, you guessed it, the Rathaus); ☎ 434302.* 60 kips in 34 chambers on 4 levels; 60% with bath or toilet. No frills; substantial value.

Jagdschloss Arabella • *Jagdschlossgasse 79; ☎ 8043508.* A pleasant terrace restaurant and private swimming pool; 48 rooms with bath or shower. A good investment.

Cottage • *Hasenauer Str. 12; ☎ 312571-0.* 20 minutes by bus or tram from downtown. Small dining room. Units with bath at $60 per night. Adequate.

Hotel Wandl • *Petersplatz 9; ☎ 53455-0.* 137 dark but spacious rooms. Caters to singles, mates, families, or entire tribes.

Graf Stadion • *Buchfeldgasse 5 (near the Josefstadt Theatre); ☎ 425284.* 45 ho-hum chambers at high-level tariffs.

President • *Wallgasse 23; ☎ 59990.* 77 rooms; smartly furnished. Summer breakfast garden; Nordic-style dining salon. Preferred to the Strudlhof, next.

Strudlhof • *Pasteurgasse 1; ☎ 312522.* Well appointed, modern, economically priced.

Schweizerhof • *Bauernmarkt 22; ☎ 5331931.* 40 units. Excellent location under the famous Anker Clock.

EVEN MORE $$$

Pension Elite • *Wipplinger Str. 32;* ☎ *5332518.* Lives up to its name. 30 baroque bedchambers—#24 wins top bid; 22 units with private plumbing. Costly, but soothing.

Hotel Schneider • *Getreidermarkt 5;* ☎ *588380.* 42 lodgings; 50% bath-or-shower ratio; 2 large 4- to 5-person apartments. Between $55 and $70 on a perperson basis, including breakfast and extras. Rates high but without the charm of the Elite.

Terminus • *Fillgradergasse 4;* ☎ *5877386.* Prices have been rising steadily, but the quality is here for a very modest address. The management is especially kind and comforts assured.

Hotel Atlanta • *Wahringer Str. 33-35;* ☎ *421230.* 57 rooms: 44 with shower, 13 with tub. Some singles with comfortable sofas.

Hotel Tyrol • *Mariahilfer Str. 15;* ☎ *5875415.* On a busy shopping street outside the "Ring." Some twin beds on a foot-to-foot arrangement; #25 a spacious corner unit with 2 easy chairs and a coffee table. OK.

Andreas • *Schlosselgasse 11;* ☎ *423488.* 40 recommendable rooms.

Falstaff • *Mullnergasse 5;* ☎ *349127.* On a par with the Andreas.

Hohe Warte • *Steinfeldgasse 7;* ☎ *373212.* Suburban and tranquil. Medium-size twins with garden panorama and modern plumbing; singles with double doors and green-tile baths; triples available. All rates include breakfast and surcharges.

Hotel Wimberger • *Neubaugurtel 34-38;* ☎ *937636.* Should be totally renewed by the time of your arrival. Very likely the prices also will have a higher gloss.

Atrium • *Burggasse 118;* ☎ *933114.* On 2 upper floors of a modern, terraced apartment house. 13 twin rooms; all with bath or shower and toilet; cooperative staff.

An Der Wien • *Keisslergasse 24 (less than a mile from the Tourist Information booth on the Salzburg-Vienna highway);* ☎ *942114.* 55 sparkling rooms. Ask directions. Very good if you can find it.

CAMPING

A garrison of fine sites ring the city. Two of the choicer grounds are **Wien-West I** (*Huttelberg Str. 40;* ☎ *941449*), open June through Sept., and **Wien-West II** (*Huttelberg Str. 80;* ☎ *942314*), operating year round. Both are perhaps 4 miles from the center. Or, if you've just cleared the Italian border, **Wien-Sud** (*Breitenfurter Str. 267;* ☎ *869218*), also 4 miles out, is handier for pitching your tent.

Aktiv Neue Donau (*Am Kleehaufel;* ☎ *942314*). **Rodaun** (*An der Au. 2;* ☎ *884154*), south of town, and **Camping Schloss Laxenburg** (*Erholungszentrum;* ☎ *02236/71333*) are also recommended. Operative from midMarch to late Oct. or even earlier and later if the weather is nice; charges at all about $4 or so per person, plus a similar fee for your auto.

Most of the above are connected to the center by bus lines; some have pools, bungalows for rent and even boating, bathing, and riding facilities. For full details, check with the Austrian National Tourist Office or the Vienna Tourist Board (*Obere Augarten Str. 40, A-1025 Vienna;* ☎ *211-140*).

SUGGESTIONS FOR STUDENTS

Try to plan your visit for July, Aug., or Sept., because these are the key months when the University of Vienna's shutdown opens all kinds of doors for foreign travelers.

SPECIAL LODGINGS

The **Student Union Hotels** (*Fuhrichgasse 10* for reservations in any) belong to the official Osterreichische Studenten-Foerderungs-Stiftung, which translates as Austrian Foundation for the Furtherance of Students. Overnight tariffs are in the $10 range; although this is high, their amenities are the best of their class in the city.

The **International Student House** (*Seilerstatte 30; ☎ 5128463*), within the Ring, is 2 blocks from Stadt Park and the Kursalon. Plain bedrooms with uplifting bright touches; bed and breakfast only; $20 single and $30 double without bath, including breakfast, service, and taxes. This one is operative from July to Sept.

The **University Student Aid Association** (*Asylverein der Wiener Universitat, Porzellangasse 30; ☎ 347282*) is across from Liechtenstein Park. Old-style trappings; no I.D. required; $12 per person for the first night and about $10.50 thereafter for a dormitory bed, a shower, and breakfast.

The **Roman Catholic Student Dorm** (*Ebendorfer Str. 8; ☎ 408-35870*), and the 2 branches of the **Studentenunterstutzungsverei Akademiker-hilfe**—enough syllables?—(*Pfeilgasse 4-6 for men and No. 1a for women*). The installation at No. 3a is completely modern, and has its own cafeteria.

DINING

The cafeteria of the prestigious **Vienna Technische Hochschule** (*Wiedner Haupt Str. 8-10*, south of the *Ringstrasse*) is famous for its steaming $2.25 lunches; mostly male clientele. So are the patrons at the **cafeteria** on Universitatsstrasse, 1 block behind the university, which is a great deal more modern and which also stuffs 3000 mouths simultaneously. Both are loaded with foreign scholars. We also hear good words about the **Katholische Hoch-schulmensa** (*Ebendorfer Str. 8*), which dips out low-cost meals to scholars. Excellent values.

LOW-COST TOURING

The **Austrian Committee for International Educational Exchange** (OKISTA, *Turkenstr. 4, Vienna A-1090*; ☎ *347526*; FAX *74571*) dispenses vouchers for a variety of charter flights, rail connections, and bus excursions, not to mention the other helpful services and guidance it renders through offices in other Austrian cities. It is state supported and smoothly operated—so successful, in fact, that it has opened a capital branch called **Osterreichische Studentenreisen** (*Reichsrat Str. 12, Vienna A-1010*). For anything you need, ask here and be sure to pick up **OKISTA**'s splendid 36-page Student Guide to Austria; it's a goldmine for travelers of any age or status. Other sources include the **Student Travel Bureau** (*Schreyvogelgasse 3*; ☎ *5333589*) or the **Foreign Student Office** (mainly for the administration of academic affairs) at the University (*Osterreichischer Auslandsstudentendienst*; ☎ *423150*).

WHERE TO EAT

U.S.-style breakfast averages $5 or so. Lunch or dinner in the flossier establishments can easily run from $18 to $30. In pensions and hotels, your continental eye-opener is almost always included in your hotel bill. If breakfast is not provided in the overall charge, beware of the extraordinary levies that sometimes are added. A good bet are the *gasthaus* (inn) and the *beisel* (pub) where your noon or evening fare should fall within the $5 to $9 range, without beverages. And don't hesitate, either, to venture into the plethora of Vienna's foreign-based kitchens. You'll find Polish, Turkish, Hungarian, German, quasi-American, Italian, Middle Eastern, Oriental, and others.

LEAST $

Leupold • *Schottengasse 7 (near Rooseveltplatz).* 10-table verandah attracts sun-lovers in summer and students from the nearby university in winter. Bustling atmosphere; telescoped labyrinth of drinking and dining rooms; extended tavern-style keller (higher-priced). Trio of set menus at around $8, $11, and $13 for superb value. (Though the medium tab comes in rather high for this category, it's mentioned first because of the rewards in quality.)

Wiener Winzerhaus • *Rotenturm Str. 17.* A Polish establishment offering 2 rooms; try the smaller nook to the rear and the beef roulade. Fast, efficient service. Music and dancing in the evening.

Zobinger Weinstube • *Drahtgasse 2 (neighboring the Am Hof Platz).* Informal; tranquil sidewalk terrace. You can catch up on the current Viennese theater scene from the poster-filled wall on one side. Solid regional fare. Lowenbrau on draft. Pleasant, unhurried attention. About $11 should do it.

Gosser Brau • *Near the Opera.* This 500-seat bierkeller caters to pre- and after-theater crowd.

Augustiner Keller • *Augustiner Str. 1 (under the sharp corner of the Albertina Museum).* Presents a limited menu: chicken, chicken, salad, and wine, red or white. Arched brick ceiling; heavy timbered tables. Half-chicken Grillhuhn, $9; half-chicken Backhuhn, $10; salad, $3. Lunch only.

Wienerwald • *Mariahilfer Str. 156.* Held in high regard among locals. Small garden; adjoining bar. Specialty: grilled fowl. Not too expensive.

Gosser Bierklinik • *Steindlgasse.* Pleasant and full of regional flavor.

Ofenloch • *Kurrentgasse 8; ☎ 5338844.* One of the city's oldest ghetto taverns with oodles of heavy dark atmosphere, close quarters, joviality, bare wooden tables, and full breadbaskets; you can even request a mulling iron for your wine. Excellent wursts, Rindsroulade, and hashes. Better reserve; closed Sun. and holidays. Marvelous for color and honest local fare.

Csardasfurstin • *Schwarzenberg Str. 2; ☎ 5129246.* Rough-and-tumble atmosphere often draws a noisy and merry crowd. Lively music. Bustling service. The food was born Hungarian, but is Viennese-educated. Gemutlichkeit makes up for the routine fare, which rings up about $10 per platter.

Bukarest • *Brauner Str. 7; ☎ 5123763.* A wonderful Romanian tavern. Long tunnel room under aged vaults; woven rugs on the walls. Delicious lowpriced Slavic specialties; an ample Balkan plate for 2 about $20. Excellent *Cevapcici* (well spiced), *Gulyas* (tops), *Shiskebab Ciorba Tavaneasca* (rich meat soup), pepper salad, Ajvar (tomatoes and peppers blended) and desserts of pancakes, baklava, and a delicate regional strudel called *Gibanica.* Don't miss it. If you do miss it or it's full, at #5 on the same street, **Ilona's** does similar cooking in the homemade vernacular.

Paulusstube • *Walfischgasse 7 (1 minute from the Opera).* A midtown transplant of Grinzing Heuriger. Handsome facade; shabby but comfortable interior; strolling musicians.

CAFETERIA OR CONVENTIONAL FARE

Wild • *Neuer Markt 10.* A foodstore with a delicatessen capability, a few shelves for stand-up snacks, and casements where you can choose your dainty and eat it there. The quality is fabulous. Drinks also available.

Pizzaland • *Petersplatz 3 (near the Peterskirche).*

Rondo Grill • *Opernpassage (in the subterranean passage outside the Staatsoper).*

Stadtbahnbogen • *Josefstadter Str. 84 (east of Parliament).*

Anker Treff Zum Nestroy • *Brauner Str. 4.* A midtown, low-cost sandwich palace with a fine finish in its delightful applestrudel.

CHAINS

Stadtkeller • *Singerstr. 6.* Espresso counter for streetside snacks. Come early for fresh rolls with continental breakfast; lunch and dinner from $6 or so. Open from 10 a.m. to 9 p.m.

Naschmarkt • *Headquarters at Mariahilfer str. 85.* Most useful ones: *Schottengasse 1; and Schwarzenbergplatz 16.* All are spacious, brightly lit, spartanly furnished, and reasonably priced. Absolute cleanliness. Teeming at noontime; addled but kindly personnel. Hours vary from branch to branch.

Wienerwald • *15 outlets;* Most convenient ones: *Bellaria Str. 12; Annagasse 3; Westbahn Str. 14; Fasangasse 33; Mariahilfer Str. 156* (mentioned earlier because of its central location and nice little garden); *Thalia Str. 92; Grinzing-Cobenzlgasse 7.* Sample fare includes Brathendl or Backhendl (about $7 per 1/2-chicken), onion soup or goulash for $3.50.

MORE $$

Wiener Rathauskeller • *Rathausplatz (in City Hall).* A perfect blue-ribbon choice. Its mammoth cellar offers a quartet of colorful possibilities: the Rittersaal, under enormous painted arches and stained glass windows, the Ziehrer Stuberl, in gold leaf and dark woods, the Gruner Saal, the least attractive, and the Grinzinger Keller, with music from 7:30 p.m. to 1 a.m. Vast range of prices and selections.

Zum Batzenhausl • *Dr. Karl Lueger Ring 12 (east of the Rathaus Park).* A leading light in the inner city. Postage-stamp terrace; quartet of tiny tables beneath a green and white canopy; stolid alpine interior replete with 7 beer barrels, heavy rafters, and antlers; 12 or so tables in 2 or so rooms; several booths. Casual, cordial service. Satisfactory traditional cookery. Maximum main-course items about $8, but never on Sun.

Balkan Grill • *Brunnengasse 13 (about 15 minutes from the center).* Main restaurant and warm-weather dining pavilion that opens onto a garden illuminated by lamps suspended from the trees. Waiters in Bosnian costumes; strolling musicians. Start with a Barack (apricot brandy); order the Serbian hors d'oeuvres, then the Shishkebab a la Jenghiz Khan (in the $7 range for small orders, or almost triple this for a giant 3-person skewer). Finally, you'll be given a serving of Turkish paste with your demitasse; tuck the piece between your molars and cheek in the Balkan way to sip your coffee mumps-style. Your full repast should average about $22. Evenings only, from 6:30 p.m. to 1 a.m.; closed Sun.

Donauturm • Vienna's rotating restaurant in the 820-foot sightseeing tower. Improved cuisine and a broader selection make it worthwhile. If you don't want to pay the meal prices, enjoy the view from the bar one level below the top.

D'Rauchkuchl • *Schwegler Str. 37.* Bills itself as "Vienna's Only Medieval Restaurant"; baroque decor cunningly conceived; cuisine perked up notably.

Eckel • *Sieveringer Str. 46.* Best fish catch in the 19th District. Not too costly.

LIGHT BITES

Pastries and light bites? Emperor of the legendary Konditoreien (confection shops, for want of a better word) is wonderful old and ultracostly **Demel** (*Kohlmarkt 14*). Foreigners and locals have been waddling in and out happily since A.D. 1813. This spot is a sightseeing fixture even if you don't tuck into the calories. Other outstanding examples are **Lehmann** (*Graben 1*), **Sluka** (*Rathausplatz 8*), and **Heiner** (*Wollzeile 9 or Karntner Str. 21*). **Hawelka** (*Dorotheergasse 6*) is possibly the city's oldest coffee house, a gathering hub for artists and writers.

For a similar but more commercial and lower price operation, pop in at one of the ubiquitous **Aida** shops. There are now 20 spread across the city. All guarantee tiptop freshness that only a volume operation can turn out at such low-down tariffs. Really terrific values.

NIGHTLIFE

Great variety—from pale copies of a Latin Quarter, to cozy drop-in spots, to cabaret-and-strip, to out-and-out sex at its rawest and most commercial. Drinks are $5-and-up in most of those places. Admission fees are usually $2 per person.

You might enjoy wandering casually through the "*Bermuda Triangle*," so called because if you stroll into this quarter of narrow lanes, you could simply vanish forever. It's safe—have no fears—and it's fun. There are taverns, wine bars, and cafes, sometimes called *Beisel.* Visit **Salzamt** on *Ruprechtsplatz*, the **Alt Wien** and the **Oswald & Kalb** on *Backerstrasse*, the **Roter Engel** on *Rabensteig*, or any of the joints along *Rotenturmstrasse.* If you navigate among the shoals between St. Stephen's Dom and the Danube Canal, you'll experience a journey to the mists of a Viennese night.

Queen Anne • *Johannesgasse 12.* The best of the discos for many locals as well as for foreign visitors. Prices are not too high and the crowd is fun.

Wurlitzer • *Schwarzenbergplatz 10.* Just what you think, a shrine for boogie and jukebox antics. Entry via Papa's Tapas any night but Mon.

Amerlingbeisl • *Stiftgasse 8.* Top of the trends for young people; best of a summer's eve when the focus is outside in the court.

Die Tenne • *Annagasse 3.* A spacious log cabin. Milling clientele jammed to its roof beams; ceiling festooned with oxen yokes, corncobs, a spinning jenny, 7 cartwheel chandeliers, and a sled; waitresses in dirndls; dance partners almost always available; speedy service at 2 tiers of tables or a 9-stool, high-rise bar; dollar admission good for the first drink. The live music begins at 11 p.m. with a third-rate, 1/4-hour show; go at 11:15. Mildly diverting, but not special.

The Chattanooga • *Graben 29A.* A snack bar during the day, hitches on dancing at 8 p.m. It hits a full head of steam about midnight.

The Scotch-Bar • *Parkring 10, in the cellar of Scotch Cafe.* Successfully blends such unlikely ingredients as sailing regalia, clan tartans, and Tyrolean festoonery. Ground-level bar with portholes and lanterns; twin subterranean chambers for dancing and drinking; competitive prices. A small side room features comfortable black-leather banquettes, bagpipes, and the heraldry of such old-line Viennese families as the MacMacs, the MacPikes, and the MacKnausaras. *The music is by MacWurlitzer.*

The Schaukelpferd Bar • *"Rocking Horse," Kegelgasse 30.* Warmer, stucco walls, wood beams, and fireplace; routine tab for Scottish moonshine; nice for cuddlers.

The Atrium • *Schwarzenbergplatz 10.* Lures a student following. Pipes and girders overhead resembling an Erector Set gone wild; tables with batteneddown tray-boxes so your libations won't spill should the cabin begin to tip; escape difficult from its narrow-beamed booths. There's a minimum fee until 12:30 a.m.; thereafter it's free.

For light snacks, beer, and small talk, you might enjoy **Zwolf Apostel-Keller** (*Sonnenfelsgasse 3*), **Urbanikeller** (*Am Hof 12*), or the **Piaris-tenkeller** (*Piaristengasse 45*) with its live zither melodies. All 3 are amiable.

Give a wide berth to the nightspots in the 2nd and 20th Districts—the island between the Danube Canal and the river.

WINE GARDENS

Vienna is famous for its *Heurigen*—the "new wine" or "fresh-wine" gardens. The most celebrated (and touristic) are in *Grinzing*, 15 to 25 minutes from the center. You can take a trolley-car out and save money, but be sure to check the departure time back for the city. Look for the garland of pine twigs and vine leaves over the door. Until recently you could bring your own cold meat, butter, cheese, and bread if you wished. Now, many *Heurigen* are full-blown restaurants or have their own buffets, and the custom of bringing your own vittles has been restricted to the smallest establishments. Try their old-time specialty, *Backhendl*. Typical, sound examples of the larger meccas are **Altes Presshaus**, *Coblenzlgasse 15*, the oldest in Grinzing; don't miss the cellar; the family-corner-tavern-style **Reinprecht** a few steps down the street, **Hauermandl**, **Maly**, **Bachhengl**, **Weinbottich**, the amiable **Rode's "Altes Haus**," where we again had a delicious meal, and, over in **Sievering**, the popular **Backhendlstation Martinkovits**. Out at **Nussdorf**, the **Hollerl Maria** has a good name; in *Neustift*, **Zeiler** draws a young crowd and **Emminger** an older one. *Heiligenstadt* also has several choices. **Perchtoldsdorf** is famous for its "*Brodl*" wine served in taverns along Brunnergasse. **Stammersdorf** is noteworthy for its wine gardens in the old style. In general, Grinzing is the most expensive. Even though it has long and boldly capitalized itself as a tourist attraction, it remains essentially a charming suburb for after-dark romancers and camaraderie. All are shut down intermittently, whenever the barrels run out; usually only light buffet and wine, with no spirits or beer.

WHAT TO SEE AND DO

Take in the **Ringstrasse** (The Ring) and, for tradition only, a glimpse of the not-so-blue **Danube**. The former is the world-famous boulevard that encircles the heart of the Old City; most points of interest are within walking distance and Hofburg Palace probably is your best springboard for excursions by foot. The town may be viewed most conveniently and sweepingly from the summit of the **Donauturm** ("Danube Tower"), an 820-foot TV-radio mast with a rotating restaurant. (Forget the food; go to the bar, 1 level below.) Then you might try: the *ne plus ultra* of this capital of music, the **Opera House** (which allots 200 seats per performance to local travel agents for foreign visitors; sometimes the information kiosk in the Opera underpass has a few reasonably priced tickets, and this stand is open longer hours than the vending office in the Opera itself). The eye-popping **Spanish Riding School** (precision horse-training rehearsals every weekday morning except Mon. and none during July-Aug.; 1/2-hour Sat. and Sun. morning shows and the full-dress Wed. evening performance during high season; early Mar. to end-June and early Sept. to mid-Dec. only); is very often a sellout, so be sure to confirm performance times and availability as soon as you arrive. Don't miss the **Theater an der Wien** (musicals), the venerable and impressive **St. Stephen's Cathedral** (organ concert on Wed. at 7 p.m.), **Schonbrunn Palace** (ancient summer castle of the double-eagle monarchy, in the theater of which there are performances in July and Aug. by the Vienna Kammeroper; in summer there are guided evening tours plus chamber music), and the **Clock Museums** (*Schulhof 2* in the First District and Geyermullerschlossl at *Potzleinsdorfer Str. 102* in the Eighteenth; more than 3000 specimens on silent exhibit, without a single cuckoo in the lot). Not to be overlooked are the **Music and Light Around Belvedere Palace** spectacle (held at this famed baroque structure that has played such an important role in the nation's history—sad to say, only a short introduction in English), the **Auersperg Palace**, which Richard Strauss immortalized in *Der Rosenkavalier*, the splendid Brueghel collection and other *rarae aves* in the **Kunsthistorisches Museum** (Museum of Fine Arts), and the **Beethoven Memorial House** (*Probusgasse 6*), where the master lived in 1802. The former home of Johann Strauss recently was opened to the public, too; it is at *Praterstr. 54*, halfway between St. Stephen's and the giant Ferris wheel. Plenty of first-rate art galleries, other museums, and other Baedeker attractions in and around this center. If you should be in the city from about the end of May to the middle of June, don't miss the **Vienna Festival**, with its plethora of operas, operettas, concerts, and recitals.

Schubert's birthplace • *Nussdorfer Str. 54*. This is now a small museum.

Freud's apartment • *Berggasse 19*. The original furnishings have been restored—but the famous couch is at his daughter's home in London.

GOTTA GO

The opulent lavatory by Adolf Loos (why the British still call their bathrooms *loos*) has been restored in all its *Jugendstil* glory on the Graben pedestrian street. The cost for revamping the *art nouveau* subterranean toilet was close to $1 million. Next, the city renovated Loos' 1908 **American Bar** nearby. You can also see the **House Without Eyebrows** (*Michaelerplatz 3*), which is flushed with Loos' graphics, a restoration of Vienna's earliest functional architecture.

FARTHER AFIELD

Run out to **Burgenland** on a sunny day and lunch at the **Nikolaus-Zeche** in **Purbach**. It's about an hour's drive from Vienna, on the Hungarian border, and near lapping Neusiedler Lake. Closer to town and formerly a royal hunting ground, is **Lainz Game Park**, a lovely parcel of the **Vienna Woods**. There are some 500 deer, numerous boar, wild sheep and other critters roaming around the stately **Hermes Villa**, built for Empress Elizabeth. Take tram #62 from the Opera or bus #60B from *Hermes Strasse*.

CONCERTS

By around 4 p.m. most of the musicians have already tuned up for the 2-hour session to come, and you can enjoy them alfresco in this nostalgic city for the price of a cup of coffee and a pastry. Here are some of the favorite gathering spots in or around the capital: **Palais Auersperg** (Wintergarden), **Kursalon im Stadtpark**, and **Cafe Im-**

perial (in the hotel all year round); check locally for the days of the week when the music men are tootling.

AMUSEMENT PARK

The **Prater** is as vast as it is historic. Within 6 sq. m. is a sports center, flat-race and trotting courses, exhibition ground, trade fair, and you-name-it—all in the shadow of what must be Europe's tallest Ferris wheel. Tram #1 and subway U1 reach it from the Ring. Watch your change carefully at snack bars and local taverns.

MOVIES

Burg Kino, smack on the *Ring* near the Opera, **Top Kino** on *Gumpendorfer Str.*, **Stadtkino** on *Schwarzenbergpl.*, and **De France Kino** specialize in original-language versions of films; consult the paper or tip sheets.

MARKETS

The **Naschmarkt** is a splendid place to do your incidental food shopping. Strewn around it are inexpensive open stands for light bites and coffee. The location is handily on the Wienzeile near the Opera and the Theater an der Wien. Every Sat., Vienna's Flea Market is held here. Closed Sunday.

PUBLICATIONS

Program of Events is issued by the Vienna Tourist Board. The 3-language *Wiener Wochenspiegel* is a private sheet that is on sale all over town. *Vienna Life* and *Danube Weekly* are lively on entertainment subjects and general lore. All are reliable.

For sightseeing information, go to the **Vienna Tourist Board** branches at *Western Station* (Westbahnhof), the *Southern Station* (Sudbahnhof), or Vienna Airport. In addition, during the summer season, you may apply at Purkersdorf, *Highway #1*, or Inzersdorf, *Highway #17*, or Praterkai station for the Danube steamers. Posted conspicuously here and on the autobahns west and south leading to the capital are booths in which official hostesses will answer your queries. There is also an office at Karntnerstrasse 38.

WHERE TO SHOP

Vienna offers some of the nation's top shopping values. Because it is the capital, generally it has the greatest variety and the highest quality. Pedestrian malls are lined with benches, trees, and lights. These include *Karntner Str.*, *Graben*, *Stephansplatz*, *Kohlmarkt*, *Schonlaterngasse*, and *Naglergasse*. They are a delight for idle browsing. The busy *Mariahilfer Str.* tends to draw more local consumers than tourists—less flair in merchandise.

CAKES

The Imperial Torte produced by the famous Imperial Hotel is a taste treat that can travel home with you or be air mailed. It's delicious and far better in my view than the darker chocolate versions that almost every baker has copied. Shelf life is a month or longer and you can even freeze them for serving to guests much later. Two sizes: small (about a pound) and large (just over 2 lbs.). The hotel can package and airmail for you or charge it all to a credit card.

DIRNDLS, REGIONAL CLOTHING

Trachten Tostmann (*Schottengasse*) has fine regional costumes, folklore items, and general decorative notions. **Lanz** (*Karntner Str. 10*) is internationally famous.

ENAMEL JEWELRY

Michaela Frey Team (*Gumpendorfer Str. 81*, ☎ *5971160*) is easily reached by taking Bus #57A from the Ring and getting off at the Hofmuhlgasse stop. From there it is only a short walk to the headquarters of this world-renowned firm. The bracelets, rings, lockets, brooches, and earrings gleam in fashionable colors; skilled workers demonstrate their techniques. There's a wonderful children's line too. Starting prices amazingly reasonable for this traditional and unique Viennese handicraft.

HANDICRAFTS

Osterreichische Werkstatten (*Karntner Str. 6*) offers tremendous variety with items in bone, horn, wood, cork, textiles, glass, candles, felt, dried flowers, brass, pewter, and even varnished bread dough; superb quality; highest level of taste used in selection of merchandise.

PETIT-POINT

Maria Stransky (*Hofburgpassage 2*) is eminently honest and dependable. Close to the Hofburg (Imperial Palace); a shopping foray here is the perfect adjunct to sightseeing. Ingrid Vytlacil will give detailed explanations as to how the beautiful articles are made. There are eyeglass cases, brooches, pendants, pictures, mats, runners, bags, and purses galore. Charming little place cards with a petit-point corner start at about $2 and bookmarks are only $3.50; pill boxes and compacts are also moderately priced. Naturally, the handbags, with 1600 stitches per inch, are another story. There are even finer quality pieces by experts at 2500 and 3000 stitches per inch!

PORCELAIN

Lobmeyr (*Karntner Str. 26*) is the place for Herend from Hungary. The Spanish Riding School figurines of famous **Wiener Porzellanfabrik Augarten** (3 outlets: *Stock-Im-Eisenplatz 3, Mariahilfer Str. 99, Schloss Augarten*) are magnificent.

BEST SOUVENIR

The special 50- or 100-schilling commemorative coins that are minted annually to honor some selected occasion or outstanding event—handsome mementos that soon become collectors' items. Check with any national bank.

Don't forget the intriguing **Dorotheum Auction** (*Dorotheergasse 11*; ☎ *515600*). Open most of the year; everything tagged with a starting price set by neutral experts. If you hit it right, it is Paris's Flea Market 1000 times enhanced.

HOURS

Generally 8 or 9 a.m. to 6:30 p.m., Sat. 9 a.m. to noon or 1 p.m. On the first Sat. of each month the hours are 9 a.m. to 5 p.m. Food shops and tobacconists often stretch their days by almost an hour at either end.

NOTE

Now you can get a big portion of your shopping outlay refunded. If you've spent a minimum of 1000 schillings in a store, just fill out a form and back will come your Value-Added Tax (VAT), which starts at 10% but nips you for 20% in most cases. After Customs has stamped your U34 form (which all merchants can provide) you may collect your rebate when leaving the country, which could amount to as much as 16.6% after service charges are deducted. For complete coverage of Austria's shopping possibilities, consult our latest companion edition, *Fielding's Selective Shopping Guide to Europe*.

FOR MORE INFORMATION ON AUSTRIA

USA • **Austrian National Tourist Office**, *500 Fifth Ave., Suite 2009-22, New York, NY 10110,* ☎ *(212) 944-6880; 11601 Wilshire Blvd., Suite 2480, Los Angeles, CA 90025,* ☎ *(310) 477-3332.*

CANADA • Check listings in Montreal, Toronto and Vancouver.

INSIDER TIP

*(1) Routine holiday questions in Vienna are handled by the official Tourist Information Office (*Osterreich Werbung *at* Margaretenstrasse 1, 1040 Vienna; ☎ 5872000*). The knowledgeable co-managers are Dr. Klaus Lukas and Dkfm. Frank Kubler.*

(2) There are 9 Provincial Tourist Offices (locally called Landesfremdenverkehrsamter.

(3) Winter Sports: See "Tips on Austria."

BELGIUM

Dinant's clifftop Citadel

Belgium is seldom the first choice of first-time visitors to Europe, but experienced travelers are aware of the natural beauty and the spectacularly preserved tradition and folklore that make this tiny but go-ahead country especially fascinating. Nudging up to France, Germany, and the Netherlands, and with scarcely 40 miles of sandy coastline of its own, it's a veritable hub of activity. It also hosts the European Common Market, NATO, and the Atomic Energy Commission; as a constitutional monarchy, it combines a unique fairy-tale history with a thoroughly contemporary lifestyle. The Flemings (about 5.6 million of them) speak—and almost insist on—Flemish (which resembles Dutch—if you are eating hot potatoes); the nation's 3.2 million Walloons *parle* French. Both usually also know English. Brussels, a city of one million presumed bilingual Belgians, is more or less a neutral zone.

About the size of Maryland, Belgium bristles with castles, museums, rustic country inns, and superb restaurants that easily challenge the finest of France. There's a bewildering variety of natural color. The sweet-smelling forests and dark hills of the rugged Ardennes beckon to the backpacker, while in the summer, the flatlands (especially around Ghent) are carpeted with a fantasy of flowers—azaleas, begonias and orchids, which are grown here and marketed worldwide. Belgian flower growers even vie with the neighboring Dutch.

But Belgium's greatest charm must surely lie in its extraordinary medieval imagery. The characteristic houses along the Quai des Herbes (or Graslei) in Ghent sport ornate Gothic frontages whose faded ocher brickwork glows golden in the late afternoon. This city's grand cathedral houses Jan van Eyck's famous *Adoration of the Mystic Lamb*, and its museum displays works by Brueghel, Rubens, and Tintoretto.

It's only a hop and a skip from Ghent to Bruges, world famous for its delicate lace. Once one of Europe's busiest ports, located on the River Zwin, Bruges was a great commercial center, attracting not only tradesmen, but architects, goldsmiths, artists, and sculptors. Curiously though, this thriving river silted up, leaving Bruges high and dry. But its watery tradition remains, and its enchanting network of canals can serve as your sightseeing lanes should you step aboard one of the tiny boats that nose around the flowered walls of this quiet, dignified city, sometimes called "The Venice of the North." Flemish architecture and the stately swans evoke a haunting atmosphere of the Middle Ages. Its Procession of the Holy Blood, held on Ascension Day in May, is one of Belgium's many colorful festivals, this one dating from the time of the Crusades. Slightly farther south, in the town of Ypres, restored after World War I, you can catch the triannual Festival of Cats in early May. (Pet lovers may prefer to avoid this freakish carnival in which toy cats are tossed from the belfry in imitation of a time when live felines were hurled to rid the town of evil spirits.) Farther south at Binche you'll be dodging flying oranges, said to represent Peruvian gold brought to Belgium by the Spanish in the 16th century, when they dominated this plucky little country.

After all this excitement, you can get away from it all along the short but varied coastline. Enjoy deliciously fresh seafood at Ostend, a sedate watering place favored mainly by hardy North Sea yachtsmen. Sample the sandy reaches of Knokke-Heist, where the chilly sea-bathing is only for the dedicated enthusiast, as is the Cartoon Festival, which is held there every summer. A few miles north of

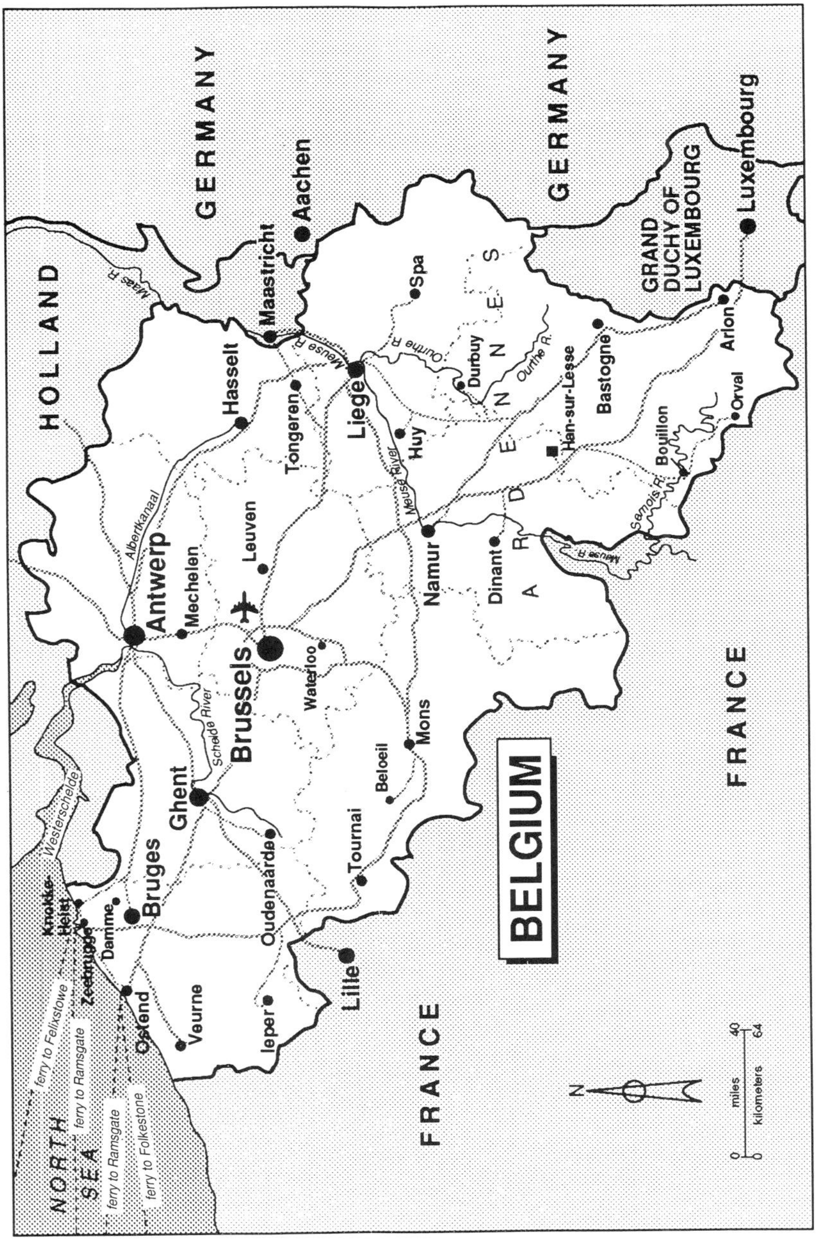
BELGIUM
HOLLAND
GERMANY
GERMANY
FRANCE
FRANCE
GRAND DUCHY OF LUXEMBOURG
NORTH SEA
ARDENNES
Maas R.
Meuse R.
Meuse River
Ourthe R.
Semois R.
Scheldt River
Westerschelde
Albertkanaal
Antwerp
Brussels
Ghent
Bruges
Liege
Namur
Mechelen
Leuven
Hasselt
Tongeren
Maastricht
Aachen
Spa
Durbuy
Huy
Han-sur-Lesse
Bastogne
Arlon
Orval
Bouillon
Dinant
Waterloo
Mons
Beloeil
Tournai
Oudenaarde
Lille
Ieper
Veurne
Ostend
Zeebrugge
Damme
Knokke-Heist
Luxembourg
ferry to Felixstowe
ferry to Ramsgate
ferry to Ramsgate
ferry to Folkestone
N
miles
kilometers
0
40
0
64

Knokke, at Zwin, near the Dutch border, you'll discover a wildlife sanctuary set among the dunes and salt marshes, an ornithological must, especially at the migrating seasons in October and March, when impressive flights pass overhead.

From Antwerp to Zeebrugge, Belgium is a celebration of the senses.

TIPS ON BELGIUM

FOOD

It's marvelous! The price is often high but then so is the quality. In simpler places, costs can be surprisingly low, especially now that government-supervised Tourist Menus appear around the nation. At these establishments, you'll enjoy a 3-course meal for $11, or $15 tops—service and taxes included but not beverages. For the list of participants, ask the Belgian National Tourist Office or look for the decal of a "T" in an oval ring that members display.

Belgians, born by the shore, are fond of seafood; indeed, you might think their diets are mussel-bound because everywhere you dine you hear the clang of black shells on white porcelain. Sauces have much in common with those of the French; nevertheless, every region (which are about 5 miles apart) boasts its own specialty—from green eels to steamed hops to pheasant stew. If you travel around, be sure to investigate the local dishes because they are highly inventive and usually delicious.

Street stands abound and the snacks are just as delicious as the wafting aromas predict. The ones that always tempt us are the thick toasted waffles (*gaufre*) or the cones of French fries (*pommes frites*), topped with mayonnaise. (The typical Belgian is so fond of his frites that he eats over 220 pounds of potatoes per year, a third above the European average.) Buy a stout rawhide belt before you go strolling down a Belgian boulevard because the nibbles along the *rue* are tantalizing—and cheap.

DRINKS

Trappist beer is unique. It comes in two types: Double and the hard-to-find Triple. Both are different from anything brewed anywhere else—vaguely Coca-Cola overtones, believe it or not, which 50 percent of the first-timers loathe and 50 percent are wild about: an interesting curiosity. Other national labels (Stella Artois, Maes, Jupiter, Gueuze-Lambic) each has a distinctive character, infinitely superior to that bottled froggy water sold in France. A favorite in Brussels is Gueuze; sipped naturally, it will put a permanent pucker on your lips. Many locals add sugar; I suggest at least 328 heaping tablespoons per glass. The locals also savor Kriek-Lambic, a cherry blend found only in the oldest taverns. If you like beer, there are scores of "boutique" breweries to explore, but you'll have to find out about them from fellow tipplers or from local tourist offices. Some pubs purvey literally hundreds of brews, and I know of one (see "Antwerp") with more than a thousand!

GETTING AROUND

TRAINS

Fares are on a par with those in other European lands. The 1-day excursion plan, called Un Beau Jour and routed to the sea or to the Ardennes, is a blessing if you want to cover as much landscape as possible for as little as possible. Other variations include a 5-day, all inclusive, bargain-priced billet. There's a line joining Bruges-Heist-Knokke.

BUSES

Comfortable, but fairly costly. Only the tour coach variety makes extensive excursions outside the capital. Samples: half-day run to Laeken, Waterloo, and the Atomium (World's Fair site), whole-day jaunts through Holland to Ghent and Bruges. If these targets interest you, pack a lunch. For offbeat trekking, the railways offer a better deal.

CAR HIRE

Self-drive autos are readily available from such familiar giants as **Hertz** and **Avis**, whose rates are downright stiff.

SIGHTSEEING

The nationwide spring, summer, and fall **flower festivals** are thought by many to out-blossom those in Holland. **Le Long Fond**, in the Brussels suburb of La Hulpe (*Chaussée de Bruxelles 117*; ☎ *02-571634*) is one of the biggest orchid-growing centers in Europe; it welcomes visitors. The king's greenhouses at the **royal palace** at **Laeken** also are open to view on selected days in May, and the begonia fields at **Lochristi**, near Ghent, bloom white, yellow, and red during all of August. Ask for details at the Tourisme BBB in Brussels.

LOCAL RACKETS

The places to be careful are the boozier after-dark haunts. While this is a common risk throughout the world, Brussels has for so long been a second home to businessmen, diplomats, and other well-funded expense-accounters that saloonkeepers and B-girls seem to have learned (and employed) every trick in the nighttime trade. Tabulate your checks carefully, remembering the price stated on the drinks list. If the light is too dim for reading the sums, ask for a flashlight; all places have them, so if there's a pause in finding a light, you'll know they are "correcting" your bill.

SPORTS

WATERSPORTS

Swimming, waterskiing, and kayaking are the major offerings. Ask the **BTO** (*61 rue Marche-aux-Herbes in the capital*; ☎ *5040300*) for details on **Hofstade** and **Nieuport** boating and skiing arrangements.

WINTER SPORTS

Plenty of skating, some skiing (only so-so) in the **Ardennes** (many sites for cross-country and about a dozen for downhill).

PIGEON RACING

A national mania. Turn on your radio any Sunday morning to hear voices chanting the release times of the birds.

WHERE TO GO

ANTWERP

It recently served as the "European City of Culture," an exercise, certainly, in understatement. Although it's 54 miles from the smell of salt water, here is one of the world's busiest ports. The Scheldt River is the key; 45,000 barges and 17,000 ocean ships tie up to its 50 miles of docks every year; its Berendrecht Lock is the biggest on the globe. Diamond-cutting studios line the streets of this bustling metropolis. There are 17 museums (it was home to Rubens, Van Dyck and Jordaens), a jillion art galleries, Rubens' mansion (a *must* for any visitor), rococo fountains, a 16th-century printing house (Plantin Moretus), a fantastic zoo, and the overwhelming majesty of the Gothic **Our Lady Cathedral**, largest in the country and now without scaffolding for the first time in more than six decades. Two of our favorite spots for repeat visits are the private home that was given to the city with its fabulous art collection, the **Mayer van den Bergh Museum** (with Brueghel's *Mad Meg*) and the enchanting sculpture display at **Middelheim Park**. Though now becoming more commercial (a 6-lane, 2000-foot-long tunnel under the river has greatly helped accessibility), Antwerp remains a cultural trove for wanderers in the Lowlands. Nightly there is much more action in the Grand' Place than oohing and aahing at its magnificent architecture. It is less animated, of course, than the capital, but moving up swiftly and spiritedly. For overnighting, there is the **New International Youth Pension** (*Provincistraat 256*) near the station. It functions year-round and qualifies as a professional moneysaver. There's a youth hostel called **Boomerang** (*Volkstraat 58*) that provides superb value for young people. If these are full, try **Op Sinjoorke** (*Eric Sasselaan*) or **Square Sleep-Inn** (*Bolivarplaats 1*). **Rubenshof** (*Amerikalei 15*; ☎ *383031*) is more ornate and so are the prices. The **Theater** and the **Scandic Crown** are substantial, charging lofty tabs, as do most conventional hotels in this gemtown. **Novotel** is basic, clean, but more for motorists. For dining, **Ciro's** (*Amenkulei*) is in the area of the Palace of Justice and is well known for its Steak Ciro, which comes with chips and salad. **Quinten Matsys** (*Moriaanstraat 17*) was born in 1590 and has never changed its occupation as a tavern—Antwerp's oldest. **De Groote Witte Arend** (*Reyndersstraat 18*) still bears the imprint of its convent origins. Piped classical music, Trappist beers, cheese, pate, cakes, and other nibbles at the benches and refectory tables or in its sunny open courtyard. **Kulminator** (*Vleminckveld*) is the city's leading pub, featuring 550 varieties of beer presented in their proper glasses at the precise temperature required. If you are enthused by the overwhelming choice, try the "brew of the week" at a cut-rate price. Snacks available; summer garden in back. As for nightlife, the best hunting grounds are in the market square, the cathedral area, Stadswaag (for the young), and Central Station (pretty roar). **Steve's Club**, near the Hotel de Keyser, is fun and recommendable.

BASTOGNE

This is the principal center in the Ardennes, surrounded by an enchanted forest on the eastern flank of the nation. See the splendid **Mardasson Monument**, dedicated to the American troops lost in the Battle of the Bulge. The rose-colored **Lebrun** is satisfactory for a night or two.

BINCHE

Maximilian started it all back in the 16th century—a **carnival** that is worth a 500-mile detour from any European itinerary. Beneath the 27 towers of the town's medieval ramparts, the *gilles* sport color-blazed Inca Indian-style costumes and 4- to-5-foot-tall ostrich-plume headdresses during the wild merriment of the festival. On climax day, 500 participants "dance" the Grand Parade. Wear jeans or old clothes plus a size-44 pucker because the crowd will kiss you, hit you painlessly with air-filled skin bags, and throw dwarf oranges at you. About an hour's drive from Brussels; ask the Belgian Tourist Bureau for the exact date (just before Lent), which varies yearly. A thriller.

BRUGES

This medieval city, less than an hour from the capital, is the favorite excursion point. If you're in Belgium on Ascension Day in May, don't miss the world-famous Procession of the Holy Blood here. The **marketplace**, **Carillon**, **Town Hall**, **Notre Dame**, and **St. Saviour** churches, and **Cloth Hall**, as well as the **Groeninge** and **Memling museums**, are among Bruges' leading targets; so is the **Gruuthuse**, with exhibits of furniture, lace, and armaments of the Middle Ages; so are simple and beautiful walks along the canals. Don't resist the temptation to do as every other tourist and board one of the tiny boats that poke among the willows and walls of the town—just about one of the most romantic settings on Planet Earth. The ancient architecture is intact; no one can build a new chicken coop unless it adheres to Flemish style. Handmade lace and delightful little local pastries catch many a visitor's eye. If you pause overnight, the **Barge** (*Bargeweg*; ☎ *331150*) offers 23 staterooms with shower and W.C. in a reproduction of an antique wooden ship. Prices are down on the gunwales and the rewards are high. The **Central** (*Market 30*; ☎ *331805*) only can boast 8 accommodations, but it is located smack on the central market. **Keizershof** (*Oostmeers 126*; ☎ *338728*) is about the same size; it is near the station. **Hans Memling** (*Kuipersstraat 18*; ☎ *332096*) is an explosion of 17 rooms very handy to the City Theatre. **Ter Duinen** (*Langerei 52*; ☎ *330437*) is a snug little 3-story white house on a canal within walking distance of all the important sights. The breakfast room, with open hearth, looks out on the water. Very nice textiles and some units with open beams. A giant asset is the friendly Bossu couple (Marc and Lieve) who run everything here. A warmhearted home. Other choices are the **Notre-Dame** (*Mariastraat 3*; ☎ *333193*) and, of course, the youth hostel called **Europa-Jeugdherberg** (*Ruzettelaan 143*; ☎ *352679*), which has a capacity for 208 men or women in dormitory shelter. There is also a sleep-in called **Snuffel** (*Ezel* or donkey, *straat 49*; ☎ *333133*) with very basic amenities; bed and breakfast only. When hunger strikes **'t Voermanshuys** (*Oude Burg 14*), behind the belfry, sizzles up grills that are delicious. We are also fond of **Heer Halewyn** (*Walplein 10*) as well as **Malpertuus** (*Eiermarkt 6*); the latter puts its accent on Belgian specialties. For quality dining

Pandreitje does the best. Two breathtakingly situated spots to keep in mind are the canalside **Bourgoensch Cruyce**, with its terrace for drinks and lovely vistas, and the neighboring **Bourgoensch Hof**, which opens onto the same waterway and the same romantic patio. The prices at both are above average due to the splendid location; in any case, the rewards are high. Philip Traen, the chef-patron of the former, runs the **Oud Huis Amsterdam** (*Spiegelrei 3*), an excellent inn (though rated as a high-grade hotel) with atmosphere oozing from every ancient pore. Have a look.

BRUSSELS

The real nucleus of Belgian activity is its capital, a cosmopolitan city that discloses a harmonic coexistence of old and new. Approaching on a supermodern network of auto routes, thruways, overpasses, and traffic tunnels, the motorist arrives in the undisturbed Old World atmosphere of the Grand' Place, a 17th-century market square as ornate as anything this side of Bangkok. Its baroque architecture of gold-trimmed guildhalls, its carved-wood frontages and cobblestone streets stand in sharp contrast to the surrounding commercial districts whose up-to-the-minute high-price phalanxes rattle with the hustle and bustle of the computer age.

Every visitor pays a call on the *Manneken Pis*, a wee Belgian cherub who has become the nation's most endearing and enduring citizen. Roam around on foot through lanes and ornate plazas to the 13th-century *Cathedral of St. Michel* with its amazing stained glass windows. (Tours are available by phoning ☎ *32-2-2196834* or *2178345*.) Pass through the fascinating *rue des Bouchers*, where artists and artisans display their wares on the sidewalk while buskers and troubadours perform street theater, passing around the hat for a few francs. Here are lively luncheries and elegant restaurants serving seafood specialties. Enjoy opera, ballet, and concerts at the *Theatre Royal de Monnaie*, the *Palais des Beaux Arts*, or the mysterious, pint-size **marionette theater**, a spectacle for kids and geriatrics alike. It's a town for all seasons—and all ages.

DIRECTORY

T.I.B. • The city's official source of information for the traveler. It's located *in Town Hall in the Grand' Place*. ☎ *5138940.*

U.S. Embassy • *blvd. du Regent 27*; ☎ *5133830.*

American Express • *place Louise.*

Laundromat • Quick Shop, *rue Haute.*

Barber and Hairdresser • J. Dessange, *1 Marche aux Herbes*, and Laris *rue Nardi aux Ponlets.*

Dry Cleaning and Pressing • 5a Sec, *7 Marche aux Herbes.*

Suit Rental • Evening 21, *rue de la Fourche 21*; ☎ *5116352.*

Doctor on Duty • ☎ *4791818.*

Dentist on Duty • ☎ *4261026.*

Police • Division Centrale, *rue Marche au Charbon 30*; ☎ *5132840*; emergency number ☎ *101*, which is traced back to your telephone automatically and immediately whether or not you utter a sound.

Favorite Pawnshop • Mont de Piete, *rue St. Ghislain 23*; ☎ *5121383.*

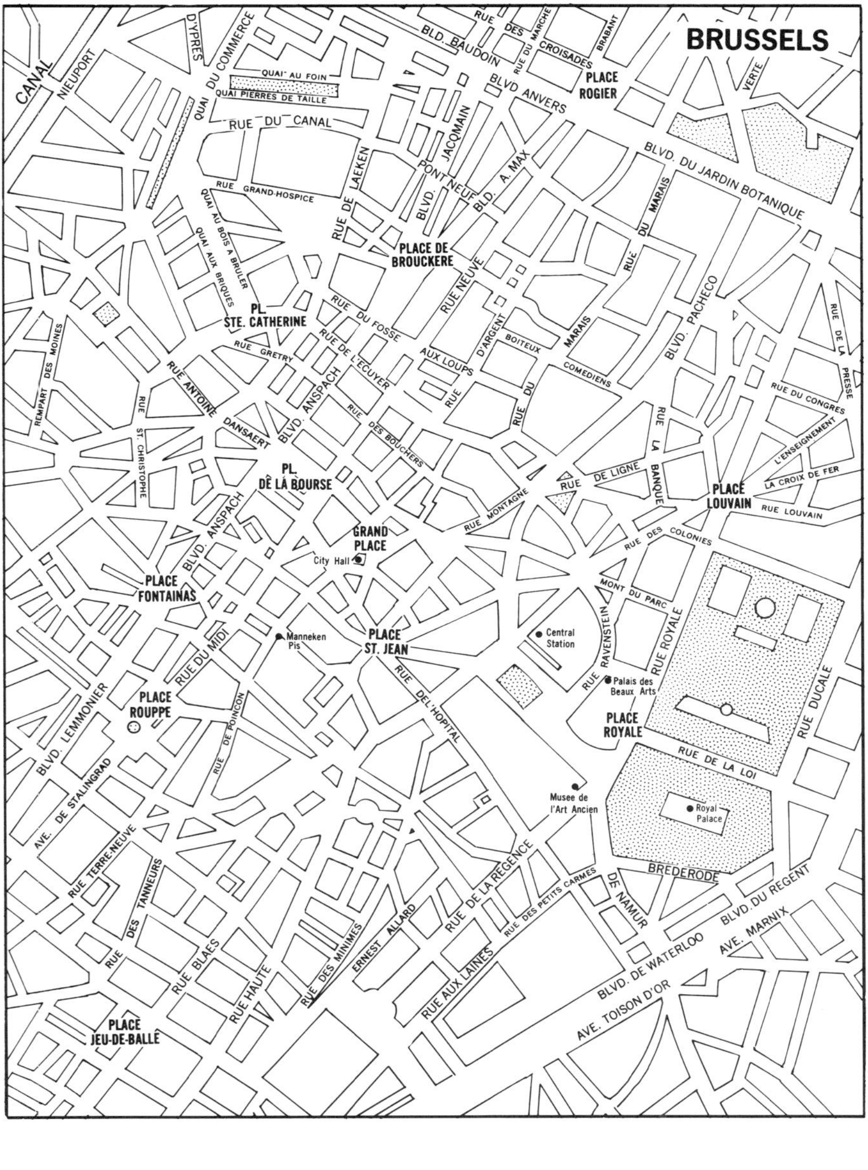
BRUSSELS
CANAL
NIEUPORT
D'YPRES
QUAI DU COMMERCE
QUAI AU FOIN
QUAI PIERRES DE TAILLE
RUE DU CANAL
BLD. BAUDOIN
RUE DES CROISADES
RUE DU MARCHE
BRABANT
PLACE ROGIER
BLVD ANVERS
VERTE
BLVD. JACQMAIN
PONT NEUF
BLVD. A. MAX
BLVD. DU JARDIN BOTANIQUE
RUE DE LAEKEN
RUE GRAND-HOSPICE
QUAI AU BOIS A BRULER
QUAI AUX BRIQUES
PLACE DE BROUCKERE
RUE DU MARAIS
BLVD. PACHECO
RUE NEUVE
PL. STE. CATHERINE
RUE DU FOSSE
RUE DE LA PRESSE
RUE D'ARGENT
BOITEUX
RUE AUX LOUPS
COMEDIENS
RAMPART DES MOINES
RUE GRETRY
RUE DE L'ECUYER
RUE DU CONGRES
RUE ANTOINE DANSAERT
BLVD. ANSPACH
RUE ST. CHRISTOPHE
RUE DES BOUCHERS
RUE DU
RUE LA BANQUE
L'ENSEIGNEMENT
PL. DE LA BOURSE
RUE DE LIGNE
LA CROIX DE FER
PLACE LOUVAIN
RUE MONTAGNE
RUE LOUVAIN
GRAND PLACE
RUE DES COLONIES
City Hall
PLACE FONTAINAS
MONT DU PARC
Manneken Pis
PLACE ST. JEAN
Central Station
RUE RAVENSTEIN
RUE ROYALE
RUE DU MIDI
RUE DE L'HOPITAL
Palais des Beaux Arts
BLVD. LEMMONIER
PLACE ROUPPE
RUE DE POINCON
PLACE ROYALE
RUE DUCALE
RUE DE LA LOI
AVE. DE STALINGRAD
Musee de l'Art Ancien
Royal Palace
RUE TERRE-NEUVE
RUE DES TANNEURS
RUE DE LA REGENCE
BREDERODE
RUE DES PETITS CARMES
DE NAMUR
BLVD. DU REGENT
RUE BLAES
RUE ERNEST ALLARD
RUE DES MINIMES
RUE HAUTE
RUE AUX LAINES
BLVD. DE WATERLOO
AVE. MARNIX
AVE. TOISON D'OR
PLACE JEU-DE-BALLE

HOW TO GET AROUND

If your visit to Brussels is a long one, pick up a tourist card at the capital's Tourist Information Board in Town Hall. This entitles you to unlimited low-cost tram and bus travel. Several other sources sell them, such as the three train stations and the information bureau of the Metro. Ask for a transit map while you're there, and you'll have the city in the palm of your hand.

The subway system ranks as one of Europe's proudest. The existing circuits are almost unbelievable to American moles who have been accustomed to danger, heat, discomfort, and filth. The marble-clad stations sparkle like hospital corridors; the seats are upholstered and not cut by knives or adorned with chewing gum; the floors are carpeted; and the quiet, clean atmosphere is filled with piped music. A 40 BF Metro ride could cost multiples of that by taxi on a weekend night, so go underground whenever you can. For 160 BF you can purchase a **Tourist Ticket**, which provides open-ended one-day transportation aboard any tram, bus, or subway in the city. If you are an M.I.T. grad, you might be able to comprehend the map that describes the operative segments and transfer points.

AIRPORT-TO-CITY

There's a special train with frequent departures between 5 a.m. and 11 p.m. Board it in the basement of the main airport building. In 20 minutes, it will deposit you at the Central Station or North Station. The cost? Only 70 BF. Compare that with the preposterous 750 BF for a taxi ride over the same distance—which would have been even higher on a weekend or at night.

WHERE TO STAY

AUTHOR'S OBSERVATION

Brussels is a crowded city; unless you confirm your reservations long in advance, you're likely to shell out plenty for markedly inferior accommodations.

LEAST $

George V • *rue 't Kint 23;* ☎ *5135093.* More economical for twins (around 1500 BF together) than for singles. Very clean and well managed.

Du Congres • *rue du Congres 42-44;* ☎ *2171890.* Receives many groups but you benefit from the volume price structure. Nice restaurant, too.

Sabina • *rue du Nord 78;* ☎ *2182637.* One of the best buys for the category, especially for singles, but doubles offer good value as well.

Opera • *rue Gretry 53;* ☎ *2194343.* Very good rates for singles and a twin sum of roughly 2000 BF tops.

Mirabeau • *place Fontainas 18-20;* ☎ *5111972.* Even more economical and very well outfitted for creature comforts. A reliable stop at reasonable tabs.

Ste. Catherine • *place St. Catherine;* ☎ *5137620.* A mid-city address that is modern, fresh, and becoming rather costly (what isn't?). Total of 234 rooms in a triangular pattern so that baths (showers) are on the outer periphery. Modular plastic furnishings; clever bed foldouts for expanding capacity; self-serve luggage carts; doubles about 3000 BF including breakfast.

Vieille Lanterne • *29 Lievevrouwbroedersstraat;* ☎ *5127494.* Also recommended. Space usually available; exceptionally clean.

YOUTH HOSTELS

Auberge de Jeunesse Bruegel • *rue du St. Esprit 2;* ☎ *5110436.* Fresh faced and fantastic. 100 rooms right in the middle of town. Ultramodern singles and doubles at Stone-Age prices. Dining salon, TV lounge, piped music. Great value.

Chab • *rue Traversiere 8;* ☎ *2170158.* Chab is near subway and bus stops as well as the North Train Station; single to 4-bedrooms as well as dorms; luggage storage; restaurant; bikes for rent. Thoughtfully put together and priced attractively.

Sleep Well • *rue de la Blanchisserie 27;* ☎ *2185050.* Nearby, open year-round, and does not require a membership card. About 100 kips at 280 to 430 BF, including breakfast and shower (if you want one). A useful alternative.

Auberge de Jeunesse Jacques Brel • *rue de la Sablonniere 30;* ☎ *2180187.* Recommended for reliability and cleanliness. Very busy with multinational travelers.

MORE $$

Marie-Jose • rue *de Commerce 73 (3 blocks east of the Palais de la Nation and the Brussels Park);* ☎ *5120842.* With 17 bedchambers; some skylighted atelier nooks; other units with small sitting cubicles, many bright and comfortable; all with excellent floral-tiled baths or showers. TV lounge with antique fireplace. Set meals. Generally recommended.

Van Belle • *chaussee de Mons 39-43 (off the boulevard Raymond Poincare);* ☎ *5213516.* Very convenient location. (Bus #46 from the Stock Exchange runs direct.) Cozy bar, dining salon, small lounge with piano and color TV; 54 doubles, 18 singles, and 8 triples. Restaurant menu $14 or so. Friendly, well-maintained family operation.

A la Grande Cloche • *place Rouppe 10-12;* ☎ *5126140.* An old-timer on a busy square. Sparsely appointed but neat wallpapered cells; 14 private baths, none with W.C. Old-fashioned dining room in wrought iron and stained glass.

La Madeleine • *rue de la Montagne 22-24 (midtown near the Air Terminal);* ☎ *5132973.* Ranks low among the leaders due to cramped quarters; 14 doubles with full tubs and telephone showers at about 3500 BF; 14 singles with stall showers; foam-rubber mattresses; ample shelf space.

L'Agenda • *rue de Florence 6 (a quiet street off the fashionable Ave. Louise);* ☎ *5390031.* Great money-saver because all its 40 bedrooms and 2 suites come with complete kitchen, minibar, color TV, and lots of cheer. Breakfast salon. A honey. Also try **La Legende**. *33 rue de l'Etuve;* ☎ *5128290.*

EVEN MORE $$$

Albert I • *place Rogier 20;* ☎ *2172125.* Commands one of the prime locations in town. A fine old and noble period piece that has been wonderfully restored.

President Nord • *boulevard Adolphe Max 107;* ☎ *2190060.* Pleasant English bar and snack room. All accommodations with traditional furnishings, floral-tile baths, direct-dial telephones, radio with shortwave bands, TV on request, and shoe boxes for nightly shining; several commodious corner rooms—#706 a favorite. Breakfasts of fresh orange juice, meat, cheese, and the normal beverages at no extra charge. Clean and bright.

President Centre • *rue Royale 160 (halfway between the Park and Botanical Garden);* ☎ *2190065.* The Nord's running mate. In many ways even nicer.

Bedford • *rue du Midi 135;* ☎ *5127840.* 220 ample chambers with built-in furniture and silent valets; all with bath or shower; those ending in "10" with curtained-off sitting alcoves. Loners with bath pegged from 3000 BF; doubles at about 4000 BF. Breakfast included. Standard meal in the dining salon about $11. Very good.

New Siru • *place Rogier;* ☎ *2177760.* Totally revamped and sparkling; superb gourmet restaurant called Le Couvert, not cheap but outstanding value. Wall-to-wall carpets; telephones; the most spacious rooms end in "8."

Arenberg • *rue d'Assaut 15;* ☎ *5110770.* A fresh, 160-room hostelry that appears to be owned by a zealous rug-weaver—even the walls of the phone booths are carpeted! Large proportion of twin units; restaurant tending toward the commercial, but still recommended.

Arlequin • *rue de la Fourche 17;* ☎ *514 16 15.* It is new and proud. The architecture is cleverly done in contemporary style. Prices per twin around 2200 BF including breakfast.

Palace • *3 rue Gineste 1210 adjoining place Rogier, plus a parkside entrance;* ☎ *2176200.* This is an old deluxe hotel that had faded and now has been restored with middle-budget and tour groups as its target audience. The building is grand, even if the prices are not.

Manos • *Chaussée de Charleroi 100-104;* ☎ *5379682.* In a quiet neighborhood not far from the Ramada Inn. Tandem travelers can expect to spend about 3000 BF per night including breakfast.

CAMPING

Here are some of the top tent cities near the capital. Their rates generally are in line with other Common Market trailer parks and suburban pull-offs. The minutes refer to normal driving time to the center of Brussels: **Grimbergen** (*Veldkantst. 64*; ☎ *2692597*), 25 min; **Heverlee** (*Kampingweg*; ☎ *238668*), 30 min; and **Huldenberg Holiday Park** (*Dreef 16*; ☎ *6876782*). If you need more data, ask the Belgian National Tourist Office for its countrywide 32-page booklet called *Camping*, which lists almost 200 sites.

SUGGESTIONS FOR STUDENTS

The previously mentioned **Auberge de Jeunesse Jacques Brel** is the student stomping grounds. You can enter and slip under the covers from 10 p.m. onwards.

Don't forget **Chab**, mentioned earlier. **Maison Internationale** (*Chaussée de Wavre 205*; ☎ *6488529*) comes on with indoor (hence *"maison,"* I reckon) as well as outdoor camping possibilities; very low rates. Take bus 95/96, or from Central Station bus 37, to the first stop after Luxembourg Sq. Pitch your tent near place du Luxembourg. Open all year (7 a.m. to 12:30 a.m.) **Acotra World** (*rue de la Madeleine 51*; ☎ *5128607* or *5125540*) is satisfactory, too. This nonprofit organization is expanding its services rapidly; you may wish to check at its Welcome Desk at the airport.

STUDENT AND YOUTH AID

Plenty. Far and away the best place to go with woe is **Infor-Jeunes** (*rue du Marche-aux-Herbes 27*,) ☎ *5123274*, and *Gare du Midi*. These sympathetic folk will field almost any problem you can think of; they even provide free medical service, and *you don't have to give your name.* Open 10 a.m. to 7 p.m. and 12 to 7 p.m. on Sat. There are IJ offices all over Belgium, by the way, including ones in Antwerp, Liege, Ghent, Mons, and Namur. **SOS-Jeunes** (*27 rue Mercelis;* ☎ *5128020*) is open 24 hours a day to help young people in distress. Travel tips, living with Belgian families, emergency pads, crib sheets for your Flemish Fluency Exam? You'll find these and more at **International Student Information Service** (*rue Belliard 61*), **University of Brussels Information Office** (*ave. Franklin Roosevelt 50;* ☎ *6490030*) or, at the same premises **Centre International Culturel et Social de l'Universite** and the above-mentioned Acotra office, which is hitched up to an amusing tour-by-bus service; more details from the TIB office in Town Hall (☎ *5138940*). Don't be surprised if your host announces, "That's the royal palace. If the flag of Belgium is flying over it, it means the king is in residence. If you see a foreign flag, it means we've been invaded again."

WHERE TO EAT

LEAST $

City 2 • *On a pedestrian mall across from the Sheraton Hotel.* A widespread shopping complex with enormous self-service possibilities. The mood is upbeat, but the prices are down. Browse and nosh.

Falstaff • *Bourse.* Gives you a front-row seat overlooking some of the world's loveliest architecture expressed in art nouveau. (Brussels can boast the best anywhere.) A full lunch for about $5, and quite substantial.

Chez Pierrot Astrid • *rue de la Presse 21;* ☎ *2173831.* A favorite of diplomats, artists, and politicians. Friendly, relaxed air reminiscent of a Greenwich Village hideaway. After cooking each order, owner-chef Pierrot Bracke often comes out to chat with customers. Quality food; menu begins at close to 1000 BF; good wines. Closed July 15 to Aug. 15.

Petite rue des Bouchers • Along this *rue* (emphasize the word *petite* when asking directions) are many delightful bistros. It's only a few steps from the Grand' Place. Fine choices include **La Petite Rue** (*#12*), **Le Grand Bi** (*#2*), **Le Bigorneau** (*#4*), and **Le Trouvere** (*#9-11-13*), plus other more expensive candidates that are very appealing. Take a stroll and choose among them.

Le Savarin • *#7.* Its wine "cellar" is upstairs! A happy maison where the food vies for praise with the attentive waiters and upbeat ambience. Fixed price meals at 800 BF; above average for the outlay.

Chez Leon • *#18 rue des Bouchers and #20 blvd. du Centenaire.* Specializes in steamed mussels; in season, it processes one ton each of Moules Marinieres and Moules Casseroles per weekend! A plate of 50 will set you back $9; four dining rooms upstairs. Fascinating menu with color photos showing the nine ways in which the house bivalve is prepared; large choice of other dishes, too. Menu of the day starting at 600 BF.

Western Steak • *place de Brouckere 15.* 12-ounce sirloins with French-fried or baked potatoes and a beverage for about $10. Self-service.

TAVERNS

In local parlance, pubs are called Estaminets. Enthusiastically recommended are: **La Becasse** (*rue Tabora 11*), **A l'Image de Notre-Dame** (*rue du Marche aux Herbes 6; up a narrow alley and typical of Flemish country architecture*), **Toone** and **À la Mort Subite** (the last means Sudden Death, but don't fret—try their wonderful omelets instead). **Cafe Henri** has a tasty range of cheeses and beers. **Falstaff** (*rue Henri Maus*), and **Bierodrome** (*place F. Cocq*), both are terrific for suds and snacks.

SNACKS

Manneken • *rue au Beurre 42-44.* A few steps off the Grand' Place, with counter service or at tables. Pick your delicatessen choices from one block of casements and order marvelous waffles or crepes from the next bank. The salads, shrimp, sandwich spreads, salamis, and pâtés are mouth-melting.

The Edwardian Drug Opera • *rue Gretry 51.* Spreads over three floors in the heart of the downtown shopping district. Costs on the high side, but somebody must pay for that outstandingly lush decor.

Wittamer • *In the Grand Sablon.* One of the world's greatest pastry shops. Their prices are nearly as fat as your waistline will be. But don't miss it if you have a sweet tooth.

Manneken #1 • *rue au Beurre 42.* Provides takeout orders of sandwiches, cold cuts, and the like. Also a small restaurant and crepes stand to the rear. Low cost, sound quality.

City Garden • *At the beginning of avenue Louise.* An attractive region of shops and dining spots overlooking a park. **Passage 44**, above City 2, offers further choices in the same vein.

Cafe de la Grand' Place *(also known as* **Roi d'Espagne***)* • Don't miss this medieval-style, 2-tier inn. Central gas flame hearth and a view of the famous square. Beer and coffee are the mainstays of its student clientele; also sandwiches and snacks.

Le Paon • *Grand' Place 35.* Serves delicious Flemish carbonnades; also try the lapin à la biere.

La Chaloupe d'Or • *Grand' Place 25.* We're not nearly as fond of the gold-plated (and priced). A chicken sandwich, a ham sandwich, a beer, and an orangeade came to $18!

Last, don't forget those wonderful Belgian waffles sold at street-side windows labeled GAUFRERIE; there's a good one at 57 rue des Fripiers. Cost: about $1.25.

LATE-NIGHT BITES

Le Pimms *and* **J&B Grill** • *rue du Baudet 2 and next door.* These places fill cups until about 3 a.m. Though in the high-rent district (not far from the Hilton), prices are reasonable.

BRUNCH

Cafe Henry • *blvd. de Waterloo 8.* Does a splendid brunch, plus music, piano, beer, and cheer.

DEPARTMENT STORE DINING

Breakfast, lunch, or an early supper may be had at **Innovation** (*rue Neuve*). Try the 3rd-stage Selfinno. Also good (*on the same street*) is **Sarma**.

MORE $$

Vincent • *rue des Dominicains 8 (just off the rue des Bouchers in the Old Town).* Tempting window display of beef and fish. Entry via kitchen. Split personality—one maritime, the other auberge—both jocular. On last visit the entrecote was football-size, with salad, beer, coffee, and dessert; the bill for two came to roughly $35.

Francois • *Quai aux Briques 9.* Seafood specialties in a two-story house. Starter of mussels on an iced platter (counted 20), a meal in itself; then the Turbot Dug-lere was huge; fried shrimps were a disappointment. Popular with locals. Not too costly.

Le Marmiton • *rue des Bouchers 43a.* A rustic personality and solid fare (try lamb) or delicate offerings (try *timbale du pecheur*); both excellent.

Chez Lagaffe • *rue d l'Epee 4-6.* A specialist in sea products such as salmon in dill and lime and other tempters of the deep.

L'Eperon D'Or • *rue des Eperonniers 8 (a block east of the Grand' Place);* ☎ *5125239.* Displays a lot of brass—both in its decor and through its tabs. Ardennes ham, Chateaubriand, and cheese will set you back about $29.

Hippopotamus • *rue Capitaine Crespel 2.* Specializes in made-to-measure steaks—any size, any style, any sauce. Very reliable; very cheerful surroundings; very recommendable if you're a red meat addict. Moreover, the prices are commendable.

NIGHTLIFE

The capital is riddled with out-and-out clip joints—bare-bosom floor shows, large orchestras, predatory B-girls, and champagne at $40 to $90 per bottle.

Some spots require that you become a "member" before you're permitted beyond the front door. This "membership" can be had for perhaps $2. The ones below should be pretty reliable and proper.

JAZZ

Bierodrome • *place Fernand Coq.* A red-hot number on the nightscape.

Fashion Club • Offers modern sounds for young ears bent on a disco trend.

Chez Lagaffe • *rue de l'Epee 4-6.* In the same sound stream and quite popular at night.

BARS FOR FUN

La Grande Porte • *rue Notre-Seigneur 9.* Lively.

La Fleur en Papier Doree • *rue des Alexiens.* A tiny, ultra-cozy and curious place. A coal stove dominates the front room; old prints, letters, and memorabilia dot the ancient tavern walls. Go here to fall in love over coffee and enchanted spirits.

Le Cerf • *Grand' Place 20.* A private club, but you can get in if you try; pretentious and expensive, though.

WHAT TO SEE AND DO

In a one-day walk around the capital, its possible to see the history of Belgian civilization; things are relatively close together.

First is the **Grand' Place**, most of it's gilded buildings were rebuilt in the 17th century. The fantastic assembly of filigreed roofs, statues, and gables is dominated by the **Town Hall**, with its stately, commanding belfry. Visit the magnificent interior on a tour. In the same area is the eye-popping **City Museum**—and if you don't take your quaff at one of the engaging outdoor cafes on the plaza, you can see how it's made at the **Brewers' Museum** (*Grand' Place 10*). During good weather, a Sunday morning open bird market dispenses an incredible number of oddments on its cobbled pavement; autos have been banned. From April to September on four nights per week there is a **sound and light** program.

There's an eye-popping **art nouveau** bus tour of this city that nurtured master architect Victor Horta. Take a camera.

The **Royal Palace** displays rare tapestries, Napoleonic furniture, and priceless porcelain, as well as Good King Baudouin's marble Staircase of Honor and the huge Throne Room. Open all of August, while the sovereigns preside over the royal summer residence.

Manneken Pis (*corner of rue du Chene and rue de l'Etuve*) is the famous bronze statue of the boy doing you-know-what; one story goes that a king wanted to immortalize his son in the last position he saw him in just before the youngster was accidentally killed. Another is that he was lost—and the searchers found him in that particular pose. He has been stolen four times; a brand-new little squirt was created from the original mold after his latest kidnapping. A Tokyo newspaper and an Indian prince are among the 80 parties who have donated costumes (numbering over 500) to cover his nakedness—all of which may be viewed at the Maison du Roi. His miniature in various forms of dress is one of Belgium's most popular souvenirs.

For thrilling Flemish art, go to the **Musee de l'Art Ancien** (*rue de la Regence 3*). Open 10 a.m. to noon and 1 to 5 p.m. every day except Monday; splendid array of Brueghels, Van Dycks, Rubenses, several fine Bosches (his best are in Madrid's Prado), plus scads of brilliant minor artists. Here's the finest low-cost treat in town. It is attached to the splendid new and imaginatively conceived **Museum of Modern Art** (also free). This displays one of Europe's finest collections in a marvelous subterranean setting aided by cleverly built light wells. You might also enjoy seeing the 18th- and 19th-century noble ensembles of furniture and household items at the **Royal Museums of Art and History**. Other tastes may prefer the architecture at the **Horta Museum** or Mother Nature's works at the **National Botanical Gardens**.

Plenty of cathedrals (Belgium is almost entirely Catholic), including **St. Michel**. Other standbys are the **King's Palace**, the **Courts of Justice**, **Petit Sablon**, **Chateau de Laeken**, **Musee Instrumental**, **Theatre Royal de la Monnaie** (T.R.M. for short) with its wonderful winter concerts with artists of international renown—plus the pleasant boulevards lined with once-elegant 18th-century residences.

Most excursions are available thrice daily in summer and once daily in the cold months; ask your hotel porter or desk clerk for details—or go to boulevard Adolphe Max, where the major companies are.

How about puppets? **The Theatre de Toone** (*Petite rue des Bouchers*; ☎ *5117137*). From noon on; staff can tell you in what language the day's performance will be. World famous, the marionette shows begin at 8:30 p.m.; there are benches for seats; the fun is for all ages; at intermission, custom calls for drinks, open-faced cheese sandwiches, and fruit pies in its colorful hearthside bar.

CONCERTS

During the winter months there's one every Wednesday at 12:40 p.m. at the **Musee d'Art Ancien** (*rue de la Regence 3*). A low-priced buffet lunch is available.

THEME PARK

The **Atomium** is highly diverting. This giant three-dimensional structure represents an iron crystal molecule magnified 200 million times; it was built for Belgium's '58 World's Fair and still draws tourists as if it were a sightseeing breeder plant. As for sylvan parks surrounding the city, the following are lovely: **Bois de la Cambre**, **Tervuren** (with its Royal Central Africa Museum), and **Huizingen** (swimming pool plus a small zoo).

MOVIES

Since they come in original-language versions, look for the English-language titles. Interesting films can be seen at the **Musee de Cinema** (*rue Baron Horta, near Beaux-Arts*); shows take place at 5:30 and 10:30 p.m.

MARKETS

The **Flea Market** convenes daily from 7 a.m.-2 p.m. in the place du Jeu-de-Balle. The **Dog Market** is only on Sun. mornings until 2 p.m. at Anderlecht at the same time as **birds** and **flowers** are being purveyed in the Grand' Place. The **fruit** and **vegetable** market is from 7 a.m. to 5 p.m. in the area near St. Catherine Church. The **antique market** and book sales flourish all day Sat. and Sun. until 1 p.m. in the Grand Sablon.

PUBLICATIONS

What's On gives the scoop each week in English. It's available at the Tourist Board and nearly all central kiosks and hotels.

WHERE TO SHOP

The shops that circle the Grand' Place stock souvenirs, including miniatures of the Manneken Pis. Neither his looks nor his price rates very high. The Grand Sablon district is the mecca for antique hunters. An outdoor sale is held here under tents all day on Sat. and till 1 p.m. on Sunday. The local Flea Market is underway at the *Jeu de Balle daily 7 a.m. to 2 p.m.* Upmarket boutiques (the big names from Paris) center around *Porte Namur, place Stephanie, and ave. Louise.* Popular-priced stores are more often found in the lower town around *blvd. Adolf Max and rue Neuve.*

Lace is the biggest bargain—and it's a racketeer's jungle. *Go alone and unheralded,* because kickbacks are not uncommon.

F. Rubbrecht is in the eye of the needlework trade; the selection is vast and laces of all qualities are purveyed. The site alone at *23 Grand' Place* is one of the most historic under the Belgian flag.

BAKED GOODS

Dandoy (*rue au Beurre 31 and rue Charles Buls, both just off the Grand' Place*) features crisp, rich spice cookies called *speculoos,* which are molded in various sizes and make tasty gifts. Another specialty is a sweet rusk called *pain à la grecque.* They ship all over the map.

CHOCOLATES AND SWEETS

There's the well-known **Godiva** (*Grand' Place 22*), but don't forget other names such as **Neuhaus**, **Mary**, **Nihoul**, **Corne**, and **Wittamer** (*Grand Sablon*). **Leonidas** is a fine brand and good value.

CRYSTAL AND PORCELAIN

Buss (*Marche aux Herbes 84-86*) is one of the finest purveyors of Belgium's pride—Val St. Lambert. The price differential between here and the States is so significant and worth considering. Savings of up to 40 percent on other top names, too.

DEPARTMENT STORES AND SHOPPING ARCADES

The rue Neuve, now a pedestrian thoroughfare, boasts **Innovation** and the **City II** center. You'll find covered galleries (since 1846, an integral part of the shopping scene) everywhere. **Galerie St. Hubert** is one of the best. What a boon in bad weather.

MINERALS AND FOSSILS

La Geode (*rue Marche-aux-Herbes 53*) is the local pacesetter in this field.

Shopping hours are generally 9:30 a.m. to 6 p.m. (Fri. until 8 p.m.)

AUTHOR'S OBSERVATION

V.A.T. is set at 20 percent. This is automatically deducted from all purchases shipped. However, you must spend a minimum of 7000 BF in each store on goods you wish to hand carry out of the country.

DAMME

Reposing dramatically on the western polders (reclaimed dammed-off land), for centuries it has served as the outer harbor for Bruges. **Our Lady Tower** is visible for miles across the flats. The **Burgundian mansions** and the **Town Hall** also should be on your local checklist. One romantic way to arrive is by boat from Bruges via the waters of one of the loveliest canals in the Lowlands.

GHENT

In the 16th century the most powerful city next to Paris, it's also where Charles V was born and brought up. Gothic and baroque styles abound, most of them now gleaming after their recent steam cleaning. In the **St. Bavo Cathedral**, a wondrous example of the former, hangs *The Adoration of the Mystic Lamb*, the world famous masterpiece by the Van Eyck brothers and one of the finest primitive Flemish paintings in existence. Many waterways traverse the inner town and flow toward the old port of the Graslei. Guild houses recall the trade, the power, and the spirit of medieval enterprise. The **Meat Hall**, the **Korenlei**, with its elegant facades, and the old **Fish Hall** are all nearby. **Town Hall**, partly Gothic, partly Renaissance, is a pearl of architecture. The 800-year-old **Castle of the Counts** rises in the town center. These are but a few examples of the monuments, castles, churches, abbeys, beguinages, and museums that you can experience. By now you're probably thirsty, so try either **Dulle Griet** (*Vrydagmarkt*) or **Druppelkot** (*Groentenmarkt*) for a pick-up; the first is a fabulous beer shop and the second purveys *jenever* (gin). For overnighting, the **Condor** and **Eden** are quite good, while the **Gravensteen** has more flair—more cost, too.

KNOKKE-HEIST

This is the most famous seaside resort in Belgium. Cold sea bathing; tepid casino; one very expensive, very fine hotel, **La Reserve**, and scads of low-to-medium-priced accommodations. There are loads of attractive boarding houses one street back of the coastal thoroughfare. If you are a birdwatcher, rent a bike and ride over to **Zwin**, also on the coast; it's one of Europe's greatest sanctuaries for feathered creatures.

LAARNE

The chief drawing card here is the grandiose fortress, which contains the biggest silver collection in Europe. If you've been poised, finger on camera shutter to shoot a real moated castle, fire away! An interesting short stopover.

LIEGE

Embraced by the Meuse basin, which long ago inspired the masters of Mosan art, today it has become a student center and an industrial town. It is third in population in the nation. The legendary FN-Browning small arms plant, plus 20 smaller competitors (obtain entrance to some through the local Tourist Office) have made the city an armament hub since the Middle Ages. The panorama from the **Cointe** is particularly beguiling. Liege folk have been known for generations for their especially friendly hospitality. Don't miss the **Batte Sunday Market**—a flea market *par excel-*

lence—which runs full blast from 9 a.m. till noon. P.S. For families: About 25 m north (beyond Hasselt and into the Limburg province), you'll find **Bokrijk**—an open-air museum, a rebuilt Kempen village, playgrounds, a deer park, and a nice rustic stable for meals. Open 10 a.m. to 6 p.m., April through October. A diverting brush with nature and Flemish culture. Stay at the **Cygne d'Argent** or the **Couronne** if you're looking for European atmosphere, the **Ramada Inn** if you're homesick; the last, incidentally, has a good kitchen.

NAMUR

The sweeping vista from the cable-car platform atop the **Citadel** is breathtaking. A toy-like train chugs up the same hill. Aside from this monument, the major cultural attractions are the treasury in the **House of the Sisters of Our Lady**, **St. Aubin's Cathedral** with its historic paintings, the **Croix Mansion**, and the Roman and Merovingian works in the **Archaeological Museum**.

OSTEND

Here's a salty town for salty types. The seafood here is among the best anywhere. Can't single out any other special reason for desiring to return—just *like* the place!

WATERLOO

If you wish to see fields, turf, and an unusually ugly memorial pyramid, here they are. They've never raised one tingle of historical excitement, nostalgia, or pastoral reverence in us—only yawns.

ZEEBRUGGE

Here is the nation's number one fishing harbor and second port. While I happen to prefer Ostend, countless serious sea dogs probably disagree. It's an excursion point only or an embarcation zone, so overnighting is not suggested.

FOR MORE INFORMATION ON BELGIUM

USA • Belgian National Tourist Office, *745 Fifth Ave., New York, NY 10151*; ☎ *(212) 758-8130.*

BRUSSELS • BBB (**Belgium**, **Brussels**, **Brabant**), *61 rue du Marche-aux-Herbes*; ☎ *5040300.*

INSIDER TIP

(1) To move around cheaply, pick up a low-cost Tourist Card at the BBB headquarters. This entitles you to a day of unlimited tram and bus travel.

(2) The youth center called "Welcome to Brussels" sponsors an English-speaking guide service so that local citizens can improve their language facilities while promoting good relations with foreigners. Volunteers of all ages.

(3) The Director of Press and Public Relations, Jacques van Gampelaere (Flemish), can answer any question or point you in the right direction. The French director is M. Pierre Coenegrachts. The staff is one of the finest in Europe. The U.S. counterpart is Ms. Frederique Raeymaekers.

DENMARK

Frederiksborg Castle

Here in the smallest and most southerly of Scandinavian realms, the ancient and the new come into harmonious confluence. The rugged monarchy that started with Gorm the Old was born early in the 10th century; it matured into one of the most modern, socially conscious countries in the democratic world. Denmark is a land of laughter, banter, and progress. The terrors of Harald Blue-tooth or the melancholy of Prince Hamlet are no more; only legends remain—and castles, plenty of castles. Design and fashion occupy prominent roles. Even the most mundane kitchen utensil—if it is Danish—has special flair, a newer concept, a unique color, or some twist that makes you stare again at the item and admire it. Look, for example, what Bang & Olufsen does in the audio realm. Exciting, fresh arts and crafts are to be seen everywhere. Considering the population of merely 5 million souls, it is amazing to find so many museums throughout the tiny nation. Viking relics play counterpoint to 20th-century glasswork, canvases, sculpture, pottery, textiles, and other crafts. Having been such mariners as well as conquerers in the past, Danes traditionally are collectors. Their slim, plundering ships returned to Europe with "souvenirs" from the Far East. The runic stones at Jelling tell part of the story (if your runic is up-to-date), but it is certainly more fun to absorb history through the numerous festivals that pepper the Danish summer months. Frolicsome Viking Games take place in Frederikssund and Jels in late June and early July. Aarhus celebrates the Nordic legacy in jovial summer fetes. In July many young people recapture the past by hunkering in the huts and ateliers of the Hjerl Hede Outdoor Museum as well as at Lejre Research Center near Roskilde on Zealand.

Naturally, the May-to-September time frame is the most rewarding period for touring this composite of 500 islands, storybook hamlets, quiet rills, moors, dunes, and forests. Ferries now ply the routes of the earlier longboats. Bonfires mark the sites of all-night lawn parties instead of serving as beacons for warriors. The cheerful "skaal", toasted with ice-chilled akvavit, has replaced the "skull" of some vanquished enemy. Parks are abundant. Food is delicious. (Much of it can be found at inexpensive street stands.) There are fortresses and palaces for tireless sightseers. Copenhagen's famous Tivoli Park—with copies to be seen as far away as Japan—entertains lovers and fun lovers as no other amusement magnet on earth. A planetarium is the pride of the capital skyline. The Little Mermaid continues to welcome voyagers through the nation's maritime gateway—simultaneously as real, as whimsical, and as touching as a tale from Mr. Andersen's very own pen. Her greeting is as warm and sincere as any Dane's.

TIPS ON DENMARK

FOOD

Denmark sets a splendid table. Usually it's an expensive one, too, since only nature's finest ingredients are found on it. Street stands, however, do purvey snack items at reasonable prices, and to make up for costly items such as tiny savory shrimp, salmon, roast beef, and excellent dairy products, a plethora of ethnic restaurants offer affordable options that may ease some of the sting. High quality and good taste seem to be two enemies that consort to keep native Danish food prices so lofty.

Meal hours: about the same as in Small Town, U.S.A. Most Danes habitually lunch around noon, dine somewhere around 7 p.m., and

DENMARK
Skagen
Hirtshals
40
Frederikshavn
Saeby
13
E45
Goteborg
SWEDEN
11
Aalborg
Mariager
KATTEGAT
Skive
Randers
E45
11
Silkeborg
Arhus
15
JUTLAND
Horsens
Vejle
Helsingborg
Helsingor
Hillerod
Copenhagen
23
Roskilde
Malmo
Koge
Esbjerg
E20
Odense
E20
FUNEN
ZEALAND
E20
E47
Naevstad
BORNHOLM
Ribe
NORTH SEA
E45
11
9
Svendborg
LANGELAND
To Bornholm
MON
9
FALSTER
E47
LOLLAND
AERO
5
Flensburg
BALTIC SEA
E45
N
5
Hamburg
0 miles 30
0 kilometers 50
GERMANY

end their evening with a pre-bedtime snack. Don't be surprised if, in summer, your hotel or restaurant switches to light-bite-and-beer service before the sun goes down. Sophisticated restaurants, of course, follow continental standards, but kitchen labor demands still require that evening service usually terminates before 10 p.m.

DRINK

Beer, beer, beer—everywhere you turn. Although Carlsberg and Tuborg merged commercially, they continue to produce their own formulae. The products of the smaller Wiibroe Brewery up in Elsinore or of the Faxe people are also fine. If you don't like the stronger "Export" (Gold or Silver Cap) grade, there are at least 7 or 8 types to choose from; the dry, pale "Green" Tuborg or "Hof" Carlsberg (never exported) and the Carlsberg bock-style are perennial favorites.

Akvavit (schnapps) is the national "hard" drink. King of akvavits is the Aalborg brand, which for some tastes surpasses all Swedish and Norwegian types. Chase it with beer, as the Danes do—but treat it with proper respect.

Peter Heering, formerly called (and still widely thought of as) Cherry Heering, is marvelous. It has been a Danish national institution since the first Peter Heering mixed the formula in 1818. On only one of the country's 500 islands—Zealand—can be found the dark, rich cherries with their special flavor. Be sure that the beverage is served ice cold.

Another Danish liqueur specialty has been produced from black currants infused with fine West Indian rums. The generic name is *Solbaerrom*—and the brand to be *certain* to ask for is Bestle. Here's a delectable accompaniment to cheese, hot pancakes, apple dumplings, and other sweets. Serve it chilled.

Genuine absinthe is sold over the counter or by the drink in Denmark—one of the few countries in the world that still permit it.

Soft drinks? The Carlsberg-Tuborg factories are again tops for their variety of citrus and other beverages. Jolly Cola is a country cousin (Danish, of course) of Coca-Cola. Grape tonics and *aeblemost* (apple cider) are among other nonalcoholic offerings.

At bars, government taxes on spirits and wines make the prices alone enough to produce a mile-high hangover. It is a rude shock to toast your arrival in Denmark—only to be jolted by $6 per drink for a portion scarcely bigger than a thimble.

GETTING AROUND

TRAINS AND FERRIES

Pride of the Danes is the crack trains that fan out from Copenhagen to the major cities. There are also the modern **Intercity** express wagons that connect the main towns of Jutland and Funen with Copenhagen and Zealand every hour. One superb and scenic route is the England-bound dasher that runs between the capital and Esbjerg (port for England). The service and facilities are excellent—but make your reservations ahead of time as trains are crowded. Fares are still a bargain. There are several ticketing options that can bring you significant savings; these depend on the length of your stay, the size of your tribe, and other factors. Be sure to inquire at the information kiosk.

Most local excursions, however, are made by boat, car, or bus, the short-hop conveyances in Denmark.

There is a handy rail-and-super-highway seam from Copenhagen to the southern tip of the archipelago. A train-and-car ferry handles the 1-hour, 11-m route between Denmark and the West German island of Fehmarn. Smart drivers get advance reservations for their auto, giving them priority when the piggyback train ferries are loaded. From here, a bridge joins the mainland.

The 500 islands of this maritime nation are linked by clean, attractive ferries. Across the Kattegat new vessels sail between Aarhus-Kalundborg, Frederiks-havn-Oslo, Frederikshavn-Larvik, Frederikshavn-Goteborg, Hirtshals-Kristiansand, Ebeltoft-Sjaellands Odde, and Grenaa-Varberg. German connections include Puttgarden-Rodby and Kiel-Bagenkop. The overnight ferry between Esbjerg and the British coast was extremely comfortable on our recent voyage.

CAR HIRE

Hertz (*Kastrup Airport*; ☎ *33-127700, Ved Vesterport 3 in Copenhagen*, and outlets in most of the larger provincial cities) is number one in the Danish car-hire field. Its fleet of 500 vehicles includes Mercedes, Consuls, Datsuns, Volvos, Opels, Tauruses, and Volkswagens. **Avis** (*Kampmannsgade 1, and at the Air Terminal*; ☎ *33-152299*) has competitive rates and good cars, too.

CAR PURCHASE

Many foreign manufacturers have franchised their own local dealers to represent them. Since prices, insurance premiums, and U.S. specifications (if you plan to ship your auto home) are subject to change without notice, we urge that you double-check all arrangements upon arrival.

In Copenhagen **Kemwell Pitzner Auto** (*Trommesalen 4*; ☎ *33-111234*) offers 12 major European marques from Austins to Volvos, and **Jorgen Fischer** (*Tagensvej 116*; ☎ *33-834414*) operates the local Saab salesroom.

BIKES

See **Kobenhavns Cyclebors** (*main rail station, Copenhagen*) for a conventional two-wheeler. Motorized versions have been dropped due to severe insurance codes. Another spoke to consider is **Danwheel** (*Colbjornsensgade 3*, also in the capital).

SPORTS

The nation flexes its muscles with glee and can help you do the same through a multitude of pastimes and in scores of resort locales. The sources for obtaining brochures are the Danish Tourist board or the tourist information hub, both mentioned at the beginning of this chapter.

BICYCLING

Generally gentle hills make for minimal pedal-pushing and maximum enjoyment. For bike rental in Copenhagen, see directly above; **Danish State Railways (DSB)** also arranges rentals: in the Copenhagen area at the **Klampenborg**, **Lyngby**, **Hillerod**, and **Noestved** stations; in **Falster** at Nykobing F1 station. Cost? About $4.50 a day. Local tourist offices also assist with bike rentals.

HIKING

Walking tours of Denmark march on all year long. Ask the tourist office of the **Danish Motoring Organization (FDM)** for the Danish State Forest Service pamphlet series *Walks in Danish Forests.* Further information is in *Kalenderen*, published by Dansk Gangforbund.

One of the most popular trails follows the old Military Road in **Central Jutland**. Contact Viborg Tourist Office.

WATERSPORTS

Windsurfing sites are at **North Jutland**, **Esbjerg**, **Zealand**, **Barnholm**, **Funen**, **Falster**, and the **Limfjorden** area. Some offer 2- to 7-day courses for $125 to $325.

Waterskiing is best at Lake Furesoen in **Holte**. Any local travel agency can put you on the end of a towline.

SIGHTSEEING

VIKING VACATION

Go the Viking route. A multitude of amusing highly publicized events include annual plays at **Frederikssund** (mid-June/July) and **Jels** (early July): Danes in ancient dress supported by a cast of horses and goats. A "typical" banquet follows.

CASTLES AND MANOR HOUSES

There are hundreds to see; most are in the eastern parts of **Jutland** and at **Funen**, **Zealand**, and **Lolland**. Ask for detailed data at the Danish Tourist Board (*H.C. Andersens Blvd. 22—opposite City Hall—DK-1553 Copenhagen V;* ☎ *33-111325*).

WEAVING, HERBAL DYING, SPINNING

A week's inclusive inn-plus-instruction-plus-food costs about 1450DK; specify your language preference. Again, use the Grindsted address or (*Skive-egnens Turistkontor, Østerbro 7, DK-7800, Skive*), or Sydthy Turistkontor, (*Jernbanegade 2, DK-7760, Hurup*).

FARMHOUSE HOLIDAY

Farm accommodation prices are fixed throughout Denmark and modern facilities are guaranteed. Adults, about $35 per night, full board; children under 12 at half price; infants even less. Minimum stay 3 days. Write directly to the regional tourist offices for information or to the Danish Tourist Board, which has a list of about 30 "Dandatanumbers" pertaining to specific districts.

HOME EXCHANGE

You can make arrangements through the Tourist Office at Aarhus and through Dansk Boligbytte, (*Hesselvang 20, DK 2700, Hellerup ☎ 31-610405*).

KEEP FIT

Sports and all forms of huffing and puffing can be had through Idraetscentret Oure, at Idraetsvej, (*5883 Oure ☎ 62-281156*). Duration is 7 to 28 days; accommodation in a double room.

LOCAL RACKETS

We've run across only one. Watch for the substitution of inferior spirits for Scotch whisky—at Scotch prices—in some cheap spots.

WHERE TO GO

AALBORG

Far to the north (on the Jutland Peninsula at the base of the Limfjorden), this town, with its ancient houses dating back to the 16th century, is the magnet of many industrial fairs; it is also the birthplace of Danish *akvavit*, the national hard drink.

The only European Fourth of July celebration on a grand scale is held every year at **Rebild**, a national park founded in 1912 by Danish-Americans. Thousands gather to hear distinguished speakers, see other VIPs, and watch the fireworks displays at Aalborg. If you're within shooting distance of Denmark around this historic date, it would be high treason to miss it! For more Americana, you'll find a Lincoln-style log cabin in the Hills of Rebild. Aalborg has its own **Tivoliland** for youngsters of any age, an excellent **Zoo**, and a panoramic **Viewing Tower** for more highlife pastime. The 16th-century cottages at Ground Zero add further charm. The **Chagall** (*Vesterbro 36*; *☎ 98126933*), the **Park** (*Boulevarden 41*; *☎ 98-123133*), and the **Prinsens Hotel** in Aalborg (*Prinsensgade 14-16*; *☎ 98-133733*) provide fair value for low prices.

For snacks, try the **Duus Vinkjaelder**, a wine cellar in Jens Bang's House. For more complete dining, go to the **Fyrtojet**, which has a lovely outdoor lunch in summer. **Regensen** is best for beefeaters (steak sizzling on a metal platter).

AARHUS

A vacation city, a university city, and second in importance after Copenhagen, this is a port with commercial overtones. It boasts a unique open-air museum—a complete medieval town rebuilt with original bricks and timber. Nearby are several castles. Ample shelter can be found at the family-style **Missions Hotel Ansgar** (*Banegårdspladsen 14 ☎ 86124122*) or the neighboring **Ritz** (*Banegårdpladsen 12*; *☎ 86134444*), which is more costly, as you may have guessed from the name.

BILLUND

Here is the headquarters of Legoland, a genuine toyland created by one of the world's biggest toy manufacturers. If you have children, or if you yourself are under 95 years of age (actually, adults like it as much as kids do), be sure to make a visit. There's also a trotting course nearby.

COPENHAGEN

The name of the city means Merchant's Harbor—and so it was and is. Today the harbor is also a busy tourist lane right into the heart of the metropolis. Ferries and sleek hydrofoils deposit incoming visitors within walking distance of the central attractions of one of Scandinavia's most beguiling capitals. And beside the watery approach sits the city's official hostess, the Little Mermaid. She sets a certain tone for all of your days in Denmark—a kind of whimsy and leitmotif captured first by Hans Christian Andersen in the 19th century and which now has seeped into the Danish culture from island to islet.

Copenhagen is a walking city. The old port is a contradiction in terms because it is called Nyhavn, or New Port. It used to be bawdy and rollicking with street action and bordellos to serve the maritime crews. While it isn't as prim as a lawn party today, it is still a colorful district that is gradually becoming fashionable—a mutation common to many formerly roughhouse neighborhoods. Nyhavn is absolutely safe and shouldn't be missed. The main pedestrian mall of town—the name changes several times along its length—has trees and benches, little parks, and friendly esplanades where, on a sunny day, young people sing to guitar music, an organ-grinder passes, the Royal Guards march by in splendid regalia, and there are hundreds of interesting stores for endless window-shopping. Tivoli, of course, is a must; all of Copenhagen goes and so do newcomers. There is something of interest for everyone, with pastimes and restaurants for every budget. Palaces, museums, monuments all exist here, but Copenhagen's best feature is the air of welcome and fun that is everywhere.

As a living demonstration of that hospitality, the city sells the reasonably priced **Copenhagen Card**, which provides free unlimited travel on bus and rail services, no-cost entry to 55 museums and sights, discounts galore, and a booklet that describes and displays photographs of many prize attractions. The Tourist Information office (*Bernstorffsgade 1*), most hotels, and the SAS passenger service at the airport can issue the cards and fill you in on the favors in store.

DIRECTORY

U.S. Embassy • *Dag Hammarskjolds Alle 24;* ☎ *31-423144.*

American Express • *Amagertorv 18;* ☎ *33-122301.*

Laundromat • Quick Vask; branches everywhere.

Dry Cleaning and Pressing • Kobenhavns Toj-& Hattepresse A/S. *Vester Farimagsgade 3;* ☎ *33-124545.*

Suit Rental • Amorin, *Vesterbrogade 45, 2nd floor;* ☎ *31-212021.*

Main Post Office • *Tietgensgade 35-39, 1704 Copenhagen V.*

Police • Politigarden, *Polititorvet;* ☎ *33-141448;* Emergency calls: ☎ *112.*

HOW TO GET AROUND

TAXIS

They are good; the tip is included in the meter reading. Many drivers speak English, but it's wise to jot down your destination in advance. Just pop into the nearest restaurant or hotel, and anyone there will be happy to telephone for one to pick you up on the spot—usually free of charge.

BUSES AND TRAINS

Buses and trains operate on a zone basis with fares also calculated on the number of transfers you make during a certain time period.

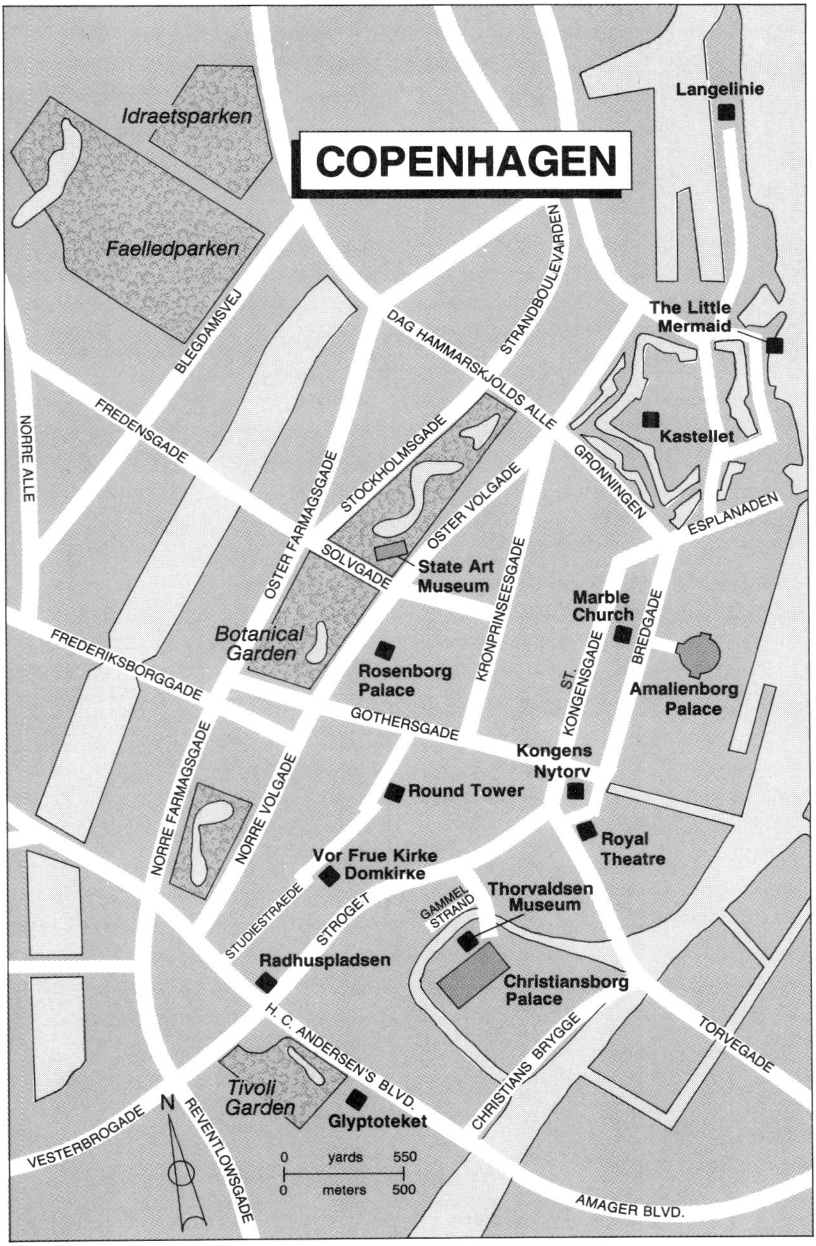
COPENHAGEN
Idraetsparken
Faelledparken
Langelinie
The Little Mermaid
Kastellet
BLEGDAMSVEJ
DAG HAMMARSKJOLDS ALLE
STRANDBOULEVARDEN
NORRE ALLE
FREDENSGADE
STOCKHOLMSGADE
OSTER VOLGADE
GRONNINGEN
ESPLANADEN
OSTER FARMAGSGADE
SOLVGADE
State Art Museum
KRONPRINSEESGADE
Marble Church
BREDGADE
Botanical Garden
FREDERIKSBORGGADE
Rosenborg Palace
ST. KONGENSGADE
Amalienborg Palace
GOTHERSGADE
Kongens Nytorv
NORRE FARMAGSGADE
NORRE VOLGADE
Round Tower
Royal Theatre
Vor Frue Kirke Domkirke
Thorvaldsen Museum
GAMMEL STRAND
STUDIESTRAEDE
STROGET
Radhuspladsen
Christiansborg Palace
H. C. ANDERSEN'S BLVD.
CHRISTIANS BRYGGE
TORVEGADE
Tivoli Garden
Glyptoteket
VESTERBROGADE
N
REVENTLOWSGADE
0 yards 550
0 meters 500
AMAGER BLVD.

AIRPORT RUNS

Taxi fare averages about $15 one-way. By SAS bus it's about $10, and by city #32, the tariff is $1.50.

MOTORISTS TO COPENHAGEN

The fastest, shortest, and most pleasant route is via Puttgarden, over the bridge to Fehmarn Island (also Germany), then by ferry to Rodby Havn (southern tip of Danish Lolland). Because the sea gap here narrows to 11 miles, there are many more sailings than on the Travemunde-Gedser schedule. Fares are so reasonable that the gasoline alone on the Jutland alternate would cost you more.

WHERE TO STAY

The Danish Tourist Board (*Danmarks Turistrad*), with a network of 15 foreign branches, is considered by many experts to be the most efficient official bureau in tourism today. Its Tourist Information headquarters is at *Bernstorffsgade 1*. It does not undertake practical arrangements such as booking hotel rooms. However, you may apply by post to **Hotelbooking Kobenhavn** (*Bernstorffsgade, DK-1571, Copenhagen V*; ☎ *32-122880*). If you can't get a hotel reservation, try the previously mentioned Hotelbooking Office *after* you arrive. It has registered the cream of the crop from thousands of private homes it has inspected in the capital. It, too, will not handle reservations by mail. Cost? Roughly $3 per voyager. Prices in these simple but excellent accommodations start at about $16 per person. VAT and service (but not breakfast) are usually included in the prices quoted.

LEAST $

Absalon • *Helgolandsgade 15;* ☎ *31-242211.* Vast restructuring; 260 rooms and 167 baths that have been given a thorough fluff-up; the entire establishment now glistens. Basic dining facilities and attractive prices.

Selandia • *Helgolandsgade 12;* ☎ *31-314610.* Centrally located near the main depot. 81 dissimilar rooms—smaller doubles with wardrobes from DK 525 best bet; largest double is the #108 corner unit; 13 family rooms at DK 1000 with breakfast.

YOUTH HOSTELS

See "Suggestions for Students" below.

MORE $$

At this level, keys can be scarce during high season, so you'll be far safer if you make your reservations long in advance. As we pointed out above, private housing is an alternative, with plenty of satisfactory rooms on tap.

During the winter months, however, a number of Copenhagen's deluxe or first-class hotels have inaugurated the policy of slashing their rates dramatically. Be sure to inquire if you arrive after autumn because the savings can be significant.

Komfort Hotel • *Longangsstraede 27 (near Town Hall Sq.);* ☎ *33-126570.* Well-appointed rooms; bathless singles at DK 620; doubles top at DK 910. Inexpensive 3-course dinners and cold sandwiches. One of the best buys.

Hotel Danmark • *Vester Voldgade 89;* ☎ *33-114806.* 85 beds with prices between 850 DK-925.

Osterport • *Oslo Plads 5;* ☎ *33-112266.* 170 units; prime twins, DK 890 (some at DK 840) and singles DK 750. All-you-can-eat gourmet lunch modestly priced for the quality. All-around great value. Take the S train; it's the third stop from the main station.

City • *Peder Skramsgade 24;* ☎ *33-130666.* 85 rooms; 1/2-block from Swedish hydrofoils pier; solidly comfortable singles at DK750; doubles from DK 850 to 1125 .

Ibsens • *Vendersgade 23;* ☎ *33-131913.* 50 properly outfitted rooms; no private baths. Singles DK 320 and doubles DK 400-950, including breakfast. Noisy location but convenient.

Savoy • *Vesterbrogade 34;* ☎ *31-314073.* Spotless maintenance of a fully renovated older hotel; lots of traditional charm preserved; petite garden; color TV and minibar; 67 units with bath. A jump upward in category—and an appropriate bump in prices (DK 830-990).

If you don't mind traveling 20 minutes to **Gentofte**, you might like to reside in the home of Anna and Tage Petersen (*Gentoftegade 7, 2820 Gentofte;* ☎ *31-658271*), where two can stay and enjoy a substantial breakfast for $50 per day or $32 per single. There's a nearby laundromat, a takeout Chinese eatery, all sorts of grocery and delicatessen possibilities, a lake with swans and ducks—tailor-made for budgeteering picnic buffs. The S train runs out here and, if you have a Eurailpass, it is honored for the free commute. The Petersens live 2 minutes by foot from the station. This suburb is charming and the people are delightful. You'd better telephone before going out, however.

EVEN MORE $$$

If you're lucky, you might pay under $100 for a double in this first-class grouping.

Neptun • *St. Annae Plads 18 (beside the Norwegian ferry dock);* ☎ *33-138900.* Central sightseeing location; also within walking distance of the major shopping lanes; totally renovated and more appealing than ever, but you'll pay for this refresher course in higher rates than before.

Vestersoehus • *Vestersoegade 58;* ☎ *33-113870.* Charming. Centrally located and lakeside. 44 rooms; doubles at about DK 660-1050 (20% off in winter). Scenic and comfortable.

Cosmopole • *Colbjornsensgade 11 (near the train depot);* ☎ *31-213333.* Clean units, most with bath; singles, a high DK 695; standard doubles DK 610-900; 4 wide-gauge corner twins; #306 a favorite.

Excelsior • *Colbjornsensgade 4;* ☎ *31-245085.* Location a bit noisy. 100 rooms. Including lavish breakfast, DK 575-1000 per unit.

Christian IV • *Dronningens Tvaergade 45;* ☎ *33-321044.* A freshet of Nordic taste. White with blue awnings; comfortable Danish furnishings; handy location facing Rosenborg Castle and the King's Gardens. Good investment.

Wittrup Motel • *Roskildevej 251 (20 minutes out along Highway A1 toward Roskilde);* ☎ *42-649551.* Convenient for motorists. 48 doubles at $65; 8 singles at $55; all with shower and toilet. Utilitarian.

CAMPING

You'll find the groundwork already smoothed out by the Danish Tourist Board, which now lists 8 approved sites. Top entries: the **Naerum** (*Ravnebakken;* ☎ *42-801957*), 10 miles out, which is open from early May to mid-Sept; the **Bellahoj** (*Hvidkildevej 64;* ☎ *31-101150*), central, but jammed from late June to Aug.; and the huge **Absalon Camping** (*Korsdalsvej, Rodovre;* ☎ *31-410600*, and not to be confused with the aforementioned hotel), can handle several hundred simultaneous tenters and caravaners all year. If you need more guidance for sites here or in North

Sealand, for youth hostels, dormitories, or low-cost kips anywhere in the land, ask the officials at Tourist Information near the Town Hall for the appropriate booklet. The Danes not only provide the facts, but they present them in a way that makes travel irresistible.

SUGGESTIONS FOR STUDENTS

University Quarter is in the middle of the Copenhagen campus. Studiestraede and Vestergade are twin arteries to its heartland, which is also bounded by Norregade (west), Krystalgade (northwest), Kobmagergade (northeast), and Skindergade (east).

DORMITORIES

Kobenhavns Vandrerhjem • *Herbergvejen 8;* ☎ *31-289715.* A youth hostel located about 3 miles from the center, providing 308 beds in 33 dorms; sheets are required but you can rent them locally. Open year-round except Dec.; check in before 10 a.m. or after 1 p.m., but not later than 5 p.m.; closing time is 1:30 a.m.; membership is required.

Copenhagen Hostel • *Sjaellandsbroen 55 Amager;* ☎ *32-522908.* Serves the same function, membership is required. Low rates; cafeteria; take bus #46 to Bella Center, closed in Jan.

Lyngby Vandrerhjem • *Radvad 1, Lyngby;* ☎ *42-803074.* Located about 8 m. out and offers similar facilities plus some fancy rooms.

Vesterbro Ungdomsgard • *Absalonsgade 8; buses #6, 28 or 27;* ☎ *31-312070.* Rents beds and linens for modest sums per night, including breakfast; small cafeteria; functions May 5 to August 31.

At peak season **Sleep-Ins** blink awake to relieve some of the pressure, so if you're stuck, check at **Use It** (☎ *33-156518*) or go to **Osterbro Skojtehal** (*per Henrik Lings Alle 6*), where from late June to late Aug., it can provide bed and breakfast.

DINING AND YAKKING

Napoli • *Kobmagergade 63;* ☎ *33-121962.* Near the Round Tower, serves Spanish-Italian lunches and dinners for quite reasonable prices. Mediterranean wines also are on tap.

PERSONAL OR TRAVEL PROBLEMS

Danmarks Internationale Studenterkomite • *Skindergade 28,* ☎ *33-110044.* This office can outrassle almost any of your difficulties. If they are more complex, the police, embassy, or the tourist office are all known for their sympathy and understanding.

The following Danish agencies specialize in school and youth travel: **GFL Rejsebureau A/S** (*Vesterbro 48, DK 9100 Aalborg;* ☎ *98-127022*), **Benns Rejser** (*Norregade 51, DK-7500 Holstebro;* ☎ *97-426800*), **Skolerejsebureauet Dansk Skole-og Ungdomsrejse Service** (*Amagertorv 19, 1. sal, DK 1160 Copenhagen K;* ☎ *33-116060*) **Danmark's Vandrehjem Rejseafdeling** (*Vesterbrogade 39, DK-1620 Copenhagen V;* ☎ *31-313612*).

WHERE TO EAT

The food is generally excellent but expensive by back-home standards. Apart from restaurants, the street stands have delectable light bites of sausages, frankfurters, and open sandwiches. Fish is usually a good buy; so is chicken. Drinking beer instead of wine will realize substantial savings.

LEAST $

Kransekagehuset • *In Pistol Street.* Literally a "cake house," but also a lively meeting place for Danes-of-the-moment. Order *kransekage* (almost marzipan) with tea, coffee, or chocolate—and in summer you can have it outside in this delightful enclave of the Middle Ages.

Crazy Time • *In the same vicinity.* A knockout for buffet-style nibbles. You can have a fine salad, pasta, meat, and wine for under 100 DK.

Bacchullus • *Gronnegade, off Pistol Street.* One of the most delightful parts of the Old Town. Attractive and nourishing.

DSB Railway Station • Twin restaurants for serious economizing. On one side, a cafeteria with excellent open sandwiches, drinks, and some hot dishes. The adjacent hall features a gargantuan cold buffet—1001 taste delights for 70 DK at lunch and DK 23, 95, or 125 for the dinner spread (which begins as early as 5 p.m.). Simpler buffet for DK 90. Open 11:30 a.m. to 11 p.m.

DSB Grill • *At the corner of this same building.* More of a conventional diner. Solid Scandinavian fare of meats and fowl. Affordable prices.

Cafe Nytorv • *Radhusstraede 2 (above a corner of the Stroget shopping mall).* A glittering assortment on the smorrebrod spread. Very commendable.

Spinderokken • *Trommesalen 5.* Old-fashioned trappings; 87-entry menu. Cozy and appealing in every way.

Cafe du Nord • This is a street cafe at the entrance to the main pedestrian mall where, in summer, you can enjoy pancakes, piroques, salads, mousses, sea fare, sandwiches, and splendid ice cream under huge parasols outside. The interior is fresh and clean too. Fun for people-watching.

Chico's Cantina • *Borgergade 2.* Serves genuine Danish enchiladas, tacos, frijoles, and like dishes of the far north. Actually, the Mexican selections are vast, good and predictably low in price compared to Scandinavian fare. There are also many set-meal choices that pack in a lot of calories for little dough.

Bolten's • *Old Town.* This is a 17th- and 18th-century cul de sac in the center of Copenhagen where you can snack or dine outdoors or inside the restored ancient ochre-toned buildings. Often there are concerts in the courtyard beneath the gaily tiled roofs and gables. Within the enclave are half a dozen more cafes, bars, or refreshment sites, including a theatre cafe. A pleasant catalogue of humanity passes by all through the day.

Josty • *Pilealle 14A.* Indoor-outdoor converted mansion. Medium tabs. Medium-to-poor service. Medium-to-good cooking. Open every day all year. Skittle alley and surrounding woods for romping children.

71 Nyhavn Hotel • *71 Nyhavn.* Splendid value in a warm, tavernlike atmosphere. Some platters cafeteria-style. Maritime theme beside the port. Great cheese selection.

Frederiksberg Radhuskaelder • *Smallegade 1 (in the Frederiksberg Town Hall).* One of the few Danish *ratskellers.* Substantial fare; pork especially tasty and well presented.

Axelborg Bodega • *Axelborg Street.* Smoky, informal atmosphere. Patrons toss dice for drinks. Menu features half-chickens or fish dishes. Vast selection of sandwiches.

Groften • *Tivoli Gardens (next to the Pantomime Theater—winter entrance on Vesterbrogade).* A fascinating location. Here you can combine 3 open-faced sandwiches (herring, meat, and cheese) for a $10 lunch; a 2-course dinner is around $14. A novelty worth seeing.

Copenhagen Zoo Restaurant • A potpourri of picnic tables, snack bars, cafeterias, and interior dining. All prices, all tastes, all excellent.

LIGHT BITES

Croissant'en • *Ostergade 61.* A marvel—we don't see how they can do it. Delicious croissants or other pastries with lip-smacking fillers, hot or cold. An excellent snack that bites back for only a dollar or less. Also, the location on the main walking street is very convenient.

Cheval Blanc • *Mikkelbryggersgade 6 (behind the Palace Hotel).* Specializes in light nibbles, open sandwiches, and grills. Counter in front, plus a lineup of bleached-wood tables; popular, shiny, easy, and inexpensive.

SMORREBROD

It refers to a bread-spread: open-faced sandwiches blessed with cheese, herring, liverwurst, shrimp, fish, roast beef, fowl, or many other delights, and garnished with berries, sweet pickles, fried onion crisps, or horseradish. Numerous places serve this delicacy (usually at lunch with beer and snaps), but the two most noteworthy are **Slotskoloeren** or **Hos Kik** (*4 Fortunstraede*) and **Ida Davidsen** (*70 Store Kongensgade*).

STREET STANDS

One successful mass-production outfit has outposts at many strategic corners. Plunk down $1 in ore, and one of those succulent sausages on a fresh Danish roll is all yours; local custom dictates that your mustard is dolloped upon the accompanying waxed paper.

MORE $$

Kanalen • *Wilders Plads 2; ☎ 1-951330.* Ultra-Scandinavian, on a lovely waterway in the old port area. Small menu plus à la carte at lunch; more extensive choice in evenings. Recommended on all counts, but especially for the scenery.

Gammel Dok • *Strandgade 27-B.* In the same area and within an ancient warehouse with 3-story-high ceilings. The waterside district is clean and safe, unlike docklands elsewhere. Traditional Danish food; not costly for the agreeable rewards.

El Gaucho Argentinsk • *Rosenborggade 7; ☎ 33-126120.* You guessed it—excellent steaks. Frequented by thrifty families.

Pasta Basta • *Valkendorfsgade 22, near Stroget; ☎ 33-112131.* Clever in its presentation of cold pastas, salads, and mix-n-match foodstuffs on its buffet; a cooked meal of other choices also available. Bleached-wood floors; Danish furniture; Bunsen burners for table illumination. Fresh and fun.

Abelone • *Magstraede 16; ☎ 33-152735.* Dishes up recipes from the dawn of the Danish kingdom (perhaps four centuries ago). Danish wags wonder that Denmark still exists if their ancestors cooked that way. But you may find it oddly engaging as a culinary curiosity.

Stedet • *13 Lavendelstraede;* ☎ *33-156625.* Serves lunch and a buffet in the finest Danish tradition. Holiday closure.

Vesuvio • *4 Radhuspladsen.* Try a low-cost pizza when the herring and wildfowl wear thin.

EVEN MORE $$$

Bof & Ost • *Grabrodretorv 13;* ☎ *33-119911.* Appealing cellar atmosphere; friendly; grills among the best in town. One of the more enduring restaurants in the capital.

Peder Oxe • ☎ *33-110077.* 18th-century building. Spotlight on the salad bar and meats. Under the same management as the Bof & Ost and also on the Copenhagen hit parade.

Gilleleje • *Nyhavn 10;* ☎ *33-125858.* Strong marine motif. Midday munching from noon to 3 p.m.; cozy at dinner. Fish and fowl lead the choices. The above trio of restaurants are closed Sun.

Fyrskib 71 • More sea oriented, being a century-old lightship with deck dining in summer. It's in the midst of the harbor activity at Nyhavn. Try the poached haddock and know Scandinavia at its best.

Bronnum • *Kgs. Nytorv;* ☎ *33-930365.* Focus on game, lamb, and creatures of the deep. A well-regarded house with good values.

Els • *Store Strandstraede (next to the Royal Theatre),* ☎ *33-141341.* Satisfying rewards from a limited selection. Lovely arches and wall decorations preserved from the 19th century; candle and chandelier atmosphere; 3-course set menu; a romantic corner that oozes intimacy. Stays open well after the theater curtain falls.

NIGHTLIFE

Tivoli has already been mentioned; it is one of Europe's greatest fun spots and is not to be missed. Across from the main entrance on Axeltorv, there's the **Scala** complex in a double-feature with the **Palace Theatre.** This spread is loaded with ethnic restaurants, bars, nightlife, and shops which stay open 'til all hours. We recently counted more than 30 dining, snacking, drinking or dancing stops—all apart from the hectic whirl of Tivoli itself. The one thing you won't find on either side of the street is boredom.

Vin og Olgod • *Skindergade 45;* ☎ *33-132625.* On the site of the A.D. 1200 Town Hall, throbs with very special, very Danish zest. We love it. Capacity for 400 on 3 different levels; separate segment successively devoted to an English Pub, a Portuguese Bodega, a Ratskeller, a Grill-Rotisserie, and a mammoth Main Hall. Emphasis on drinking, snacking, and musical revelry; more adults than teen types; jackets required for gentlemen; oompah band; songbooks at each place setting; locked-arms singing; "dancing" on the benches and tables whenever the spirit moves. Entrance fee low from Mon. through Thurs. but doubling on Fri. and Sat.; very reasonable prices; active daily from 8 p.m. to 2 a.m. or later and from 8 p.m. on Sat. Closed on Sun. Packed with authentic Copenhagen color that you won't want to miss.

Woodstock • *Vestergade 12;* ☎ *33-112071.* Recalls the mood and music of the sixties. Open as early as 9 p.m. but more in tune long after midnight.

Vognporten • *In "Huset", Magstraede 14;* ☎ *33-120471.* Offers theater, jazz, cabaret, song, films, food, drink, you-name-it-they've-got-it. A real entertainment mill that's kind of slaphappy but fun.

Musketererne • *In the Bolten's complex;* ☎ *33-112507.* Specializes in notes (both blue and red-hot) imported from Mississippi mud flats and Louisiana back streets. Closed on the Lord's day and Monday, too.

Radhusarkaden • *Radhuspladsen, next to the Copenhagen Corner restaurant.* The place to meet fast-lane traffic for your nightwork. There are bars, snacks, and more elaborate calories, but the real function here is getting set up for the hours ahead. Very lively and useful.

Montmartre • *Norregade 41;* ☎ *33-136966.* Whips up evenings of jazz and whimsy. We're glad to note the born-again spirit of this old stomper. Inactive Sun. and Mon.

Radhuskroen • *Longangsstraede 21;* ☎ *33-116453.* Practices folk traditions, with afternoon sessions too.

Purple Door • *Fiolstraede 28;* ☎ *33-136628.* You'll enjoy beat, rock, and folk renditions on Thurs. and Sat. nights.

Galathea • *Radhusstraede 9;* ☎ *33-116627.* An intimate little bar; cozy, jolly, and popular; routine tabs; recommended.

Red Pimpernel • *H. C. Andersens Blvd. 7;* ☎ *33-122032.* Marches in with students and young marrieds; cheek-to-cheek ballads; medium tariffs. Good but not a rave.

Lauritz Betjent • *Ved Stranden 16;* ☎ *33-120301.* The name means "Officer Lawrence," and he does his thing without conventions of any sort. Free and easy 11 p.m. to 5 a.m.

Sweet Dreams • *Allegade 8;* ☎ *31-212042.* Provides a chummy English-tavern atmosphere, sometimes with live music. It's worth popping in.

Hviids Vinstue • *Kongens Nytory 19.* Noteworthy for its commerce in singles. Friendly and relaxed.

Faergekroen • *In Tivoli Gardens.* Offers something called *stemning* every night of the week. You figure it out!

WHAT TO SEE AND DO

Tivoli should be your priority stop. It's incomparable. The setting and decor are magnificent; the location is in the center of Copenhagen. Admission is 30 DK for an all-day ticket for adults, while children pay half-price; for ridiculously small change, you can hear a 54-piece symphony orchestra and Europe's greatest soloists in the stunning Concert Hall. Don't miss the Tivoli Boy Guard marching band strutting its stuff on weekends at 6:30 and 8:30 p.m. The Pantomime Theater offers a program of classical pantomime at 7:45 p.m. and high-spirited ballet at 10 p.m. each night except Sun. (*Open from late April to mid-Sept.*)

Behind Tivoli is the renowned **Glyptothek**, outstanding art galleries built on millions of mugs of beer. Many years ago, the public-spirited Carlsberg brewery endowed a National Foundation for development and furtherance of Danish painting, sculpture, literature, and fine art. Glyptothek is one of the results, and it is a joy to the soul. The **Royal Museum of Fine Arts** (*Solvgade*) is a thing of beauty, too. Both close on Mondays.

The **Little Mermaid**, Denmark's most beloved and most photographed lassie, looks as fresh as she did at her unveiling in 1913. She sits and muses at Langelinie Quay, in the port area—possibly in a reverie over the $750,000 she generates annually in souvenir, T-shirt, ashtray, and postcard revenues.

Then there's **Rosenborg Palace**, with crown jewels (in the cellar and on view from 10 a.m. to 4 p.m. in summer; in winter open from 11 a.m. to 3 p.m.) and private collections of art, clothing, furniture, and paraphernalia used by Danish kings through many centuries.

And don't forget the **zoo**, with more than 700 species (2000 head) of wild animals on 30 well-planned acres of choice ground. This vies with the Royal Hotel as the highest point in Copenhagen; from the big platform you can see Sweden on a clear day; excellent restaurants; lots of fun.

At least 8 metropolitan and 6 suburban or rural **sightseeing tours** are now sponsored and operated by all the top travel agencies. Within the capital, their durations vary from 1-1/2 to 2-3/4 hours; their prices start at about $10. Depending upon the time of your visit, they cover the local castles, jewels, arts, crafts, gardens, harbors, and just about everything of cultural or historic interest. Half-day to whole-day tours available at higher tariffs. The provincial excursions strike out for points as distant as Odense. Starting point for all is the statue of the Lure Horn Blowers in Town Hall Square.

Incidentally, if you like walking, the **Copenhagen on Foot** circuit can be greatly rewarding. Duration is 2 hours and prices are quite low. Pick up a program at the Tourist Information Office.

For covering Copenhagen by boat, Copenhagen at night, the Carlsberg or Tuborg breweries (free samples!), North or South Zealand (Zealand is also known as Seeland or Sjaelland), or a half-dozen other local options, either your hotel concierge or the staff of Tourist Information can give you the most up-to-date advice. They know all of the agencies and what's best at what season.

CONCERTS

Tivoli Concert Hall has programs most of the year, even though the park itself closes in winter. Consult the local newspaper or tip sheets (see "Publications") for what's on when you are in town.

MOVIES

They are presented in their original versions with Danish subtitles. Numerous late-release American and British films appear at the leading cinemas. Along Vesterbrogade and Istedgade (*behind the Main Station*) there are diamond-hard, porn and blue-film, screening rooms, usually associated with adjoining sex shops. Most shows run continuously through the business hours of the day.

MARKETS

Buy vegetables and flowers in Israels Plads.

FOOLIN' AROUND

The **Eksperimentarium** is an audience-participation enterprise to help young and old understand how things work—things like jumbo jets, weather satellites, energy sources, the environment, human health, and natural sciences. Open every day; take Bus #6 from the center and #21 and #23 from Hellerup Station; also the S-train to Hellerup or Svanemollen. It's on Tuborg Havnevej, Hellerup.

PUBLICATIONS

Copenhagen This Week is so helpful that you shouldn't be without one. You should find it at any newsstand and in many hotels.

EXCURSION

On a fine summer day you might take a trip to **Rungstedlund** at **Rungsted**, 15 miles north of Copenhagen. It was the home of Karen Blixen (*Out of Africa*), who wrote under the name of Isak Dinesen. Now the house and gardens form a museum; open daily May 15-Sept. 30 and daily except Tues., Oct. 1-April 30.

WHERE TO SHOP

With perhaps the finest shopping on the Continent, Denmark offers outstandingly tasteful, soothing prices nearly everywhere.

DEPARTMENT STORE

Even most of the souvenirs are superb in this land. Gigantic **Magasin du Nord** (*Kongens Nytorv*) is possibly the most popular target for them and for candles, linens, and more expensive bric-a-brac.

GLASSWARE

Skandinavisk Glas (*Ny Ostergade 3*) specializes in crystal from most of the top European factories, but with a special emphasis on the Orrefors and Kosta Boda output plus examples from Holmegaard. This last name, pride of Denmark, has its own showcase. **Holmegaard** (*Ostergade 15*) sells this brand exclusively.

HOBBY SHOPS

In the **Panduro** chain the most convenient link for do-it-yourselfers is at *Norre Voldgade 21*.

HOME FURNISHINGS

Illums Bolighus is the closest we've found in Europe to being the dream shop of any hostess or host. *Bolighus* means Home House. Everything from furniture to glass, ceramics, tableware, curtains, candles, and party items is here. There is a Mini-Illums branch in Tivoli.

PAPERBACK REPRINTS, LITHOGRAPHS, FINE ART REPRODUCTIONS

Boghallen in Politikens Hus (one block up *Town Hall Square*) is loaded with these, plus a copious selection of Stateside books and magazines. Also at **G.E.C. Gad** (*Pedestrian Mall*) and **Arnold Busck** (*Kobmagergade* near *Runderarn*).

PEWTER

Tin-Centret (*Ny Ostergade 2*)—the Pewter Centre—has the largest selection in Scandinavia. Proprietor Arne Lovendahl has assembled a comprehensive array of classic forms and designs as well as modern interpretations from more than a dozen nations. Wide price range, too, for every pocketbook.

PIPES

W. O. Larsen (*Amagertorv 9*) is the king of this distinctive Danish art. All models are handwrought; there's a vast selection of tobacco blends; take time to see the splendid museum of pipes. A landmark for 130 years.

PORCELAIN

Royal Copenhagen (*Amagertorv 6*) is as much an institution as the Little Mermaid. Prices are, of course, startlingly lower here than in the United States. Figurines and dinnerware are great buys, but even an inexpensive egg-shaped paperweight captures the essence of their artistry. **Frosig** (*Norrebrogade 9*) is a small, crowded center for "seconds" and replacement pieces of all leading porcelain factories.

SWEATERS

The **Sweater Market** (*15 Frederiksberggade*) offers more than 20,000 items. Whether you take your purchase with you or ship it home, the staff handles everything here to make it easy for you.

WATCHES

Through a curious trade exchange, Denmark can sell Swiss watches for the same price or even lower than Switzerland. That's true! If you are in the market for one, don't fail to visit **Ole Mathiesen** (*Ostergade 8*) who stocks all the top Swiss brands.

Finally, Copenhagen Airport is becoming the most go-getting duty-free operation in Europe—and very attractive as a replica of the capital's main pedestrian mall. It stocks choice liquors and U.S. cigarettes plus a bounty of forget-me-not items for the outward bound. Anyone may purchase up to the limits prescribed by the Customs at his destination, merely by producing his ticket and Aircraft Boarding Card as identification.

STORE HOURS

Mon.-Fri. usually 10 a.m.–6 p.m; Sat. 10 a.m. to 1 p.m. or 10 a.m. to 5 p.m. on the first Sat. of every month; no noon closings; Fri. many stay open until 7 p.m. and department stores don't close till 8 p.m. Merchants along the pedestrian streets even work weekend afternoons in July and Aug.

SHOPPING ZONES

Stroget, the 3/4-mile walking street is the target—with the **Radhuspladsen** at one end and **Kongens Nytorv** at the other. Parallel to it on either side are other good hunting grounds. **Scala**, on Axeltorv facing Tivoli, is a zesty shopping and leisure complex. And don't forget the **Copenhagen Airport Duty Free Shops** where the nation's top products are represented and sold at tax-reduced prices. Go early and save a bundle.

AUTHOR'S OBSERVATION

There is a rebate of 20% against the MOMS tax (which is actually a whopping 25%) for exported merchandise totaling DK 600 or more per store. Be sure to instruct the shopkeeper to ship all applicable purchases either directly to your home or to your Danish point of departure (airport, dock, or other). If you're flying out, you can obtain your rebate right at the airport, but get the correct forms for this and allow yourself plenty of time.

ELSINORE (HELSINGOR IN DANISH)

One of the wealthiest towns of medieval times, it remains one of the best preserved in Europe today through the generosity and shrewdness of its energetic citizens. It is 28 m north of the capital, one hour by train. You can easily spend a full day visiting Hamlet's home, **Kronborg Castle**, and the **Danish Maritime Museum**. Other sights may include the **Technical Museum**, **Marienlyst Palace**, and the **Our Lady Carmelite Monastery**, or you may try bathing on **Julebaek** beach (br-r-r-r-r). For lingerers the two hotels in the center are adequate, and the sprinkling of boarding houses are snappy-clean and filled with Danish hospitality. Actually, the capital is not so far away, so unless you arrive late in the day (and days here are long in summer) you can easily be back in Copenhagen for nightwork.

ESBJERG

Far over on the western flank of Jutland, this is the sea-link port for ships plying to England. The 1250-passenger, 470-car ferry M.S. *Dana Anglia*, as well as the much larger boats *Tor Scandinavia* and *Tor Britannia*, sails regularly between this harbor and Harwich (for Newcastle in summer). *DFDS Seaways* flys the house flag. An airport offers flights to the capital as well as to other Scandinavian locals and to the U.K.

FREDERIKSHAVN

The few tourists who trek up to this northern extremity are usually to-ing and fro-ing to other points in Scandinavia. But it is rewarding to pause here. The fresh **Centrum** and the **Turisthotellet** are economy stops, but for longer stays, the **Jutlandia** affords more comfort. The **Park** and the **Mariehønen** will cost more and offer good value. **Lisboa** is a motel. If you are cold-blooded, the luxury-class **Frederikshavn** could warm you up. The subtropical enclave surrounds a swimming pool complex that eliminates the outside chill factor.

FREDERIKSSUND

No late June or early July visitor should dream of missing the world-famous **Viking plays** at Viking Town, 24 m northwest of Copenhagen. Here is what might be called the Scandinavian Oberammergau, minus religious aspects and plus Hellzapoppin'. Each summer there's a different authentic tale: *Roar and Helge*, *Uffe the Meek*, or *Starkad the Mighty*. All the actors—150 to 200 persons—are townsfolk with either a lot or a little ham in their souls. The play takes place in the open air, on a beautiful stage. While these sagas always have a highly dramatic content, the big fighting scenes always give the audience the best thrill (castles are burned down, scoundrels are murdered, and the good always seem to survive). After the performance, everybody gathers in Valhalla, a Viking Guild Hall, where roast chicken and beer are offered, and a group of Vikings entertain in various languages. Ask the Danish Tourist Board for further details.

HORNBAEK

This seaside resort, as well as nearby **Dronningmolle**, are both about 1-1/2 hours by train from Copenhagen. Lovely beach-and-dunes landscape plus the **Rudolph Tegner Museum** and **Sculpture Park**. Southeast of here is **Humlebaek** (on the return pike to Copenhagen), where the fabulous **Louisiana Museum** and park are located. Despite the entrance fee, this creation was opened as a noncommercial locus for the best in Danish avantgarde paintings, sculpture, graphic arts, crafts, and design. Everything possible has been done to maintain an atmosphere of natural beauty and of privacy; there are no petty regulations and no uniformed guards; good coffee shop. A delight to the eyes and to the spirit.

ODENSE

Hans Christian Andersen lived in this third city of Denmark—one of the oldest towns in Scandinavia. (In 1988 it lit its 1000th birthday candle.) The storyteller's top hat and his trunk, lovingly preserved, rate as high with local burghers as the Holy Grail. In this major port on the island of **Fyn**, rich in industry, you may also find King Canute's famous monument in the market square and the A.D. 1090 crypt containing the ashes of some of Denmark's greatest kings. The town has a splendid railway museum, even displaying royal coaches from 1880 and 1900. The modern **Scandic** is a good buy for overnighting. The **Motel Odense** (*Hunderupgrade 2;* ☎ *66-114213*) is a mile from the center.

RIBE

Another ancient city that is a paragraph out of the Middle Ages. It is not too easily reached unless you are cycling or motoring in the Jutland area. If you do get to this district, plan to pause here.

ROSKILDE

Only 1/2-hour from the capital by train, this town offers its wonderful **Viking Ship Museum**, the **Cathedral** and its **Royal Tombs**, walks through the **Ledreborg Castle** estate, and prehistoric dwellings at Lejre. Very handy and very nice. As accommodation is on the high side here, either bunk in Copenhagen and see the sights by day or go to the local tourist office and get space at a private home or country inn.

VEJLE

Vejle is an important port facing Fyn from a deep fjord on Jutland. For wanderers it is chiefly a springboard rather than a place to linger. If you're stuck, the **Park** (*Orla Lehmanns Gade 5*) isn't expensive; the **Munkebjerg** is, but we think it's worth the difference for merely a night. The latter is welded to a lovely wooded mountain on the outskirts; the vistas are heavenly and the food is good, too.

FOR MORE INFORMATION ON DENMARK

USA • **Danish Tourist Board**, *655 3rd Ave., 18th floor, New York, NY 10017;* ☎ *(212) 949-2333.* **Scandinavian Tourist Board** (Denmark-Sweden), *150 North Michigan Ave., Suite 2110, Chicago, IL 60601;* ☎ *(312) 726-1120; 8929 Wilshire Blvd., Beverly Hills, CA 90211;* ☎ *(310) 854-1549.*

CANADA • *P.O. Box 115, Sta. N. Toronto, Ont. M8V 3S4,* ☎ *(416) 823-9620.*

INSIDER TIP

(1) For the usual tourist guidance, ☎ 33-111325. *If you can't get a hotel reservation,* ☎ 4533-122880 *or write* **Hotelbooking**, (Copenhagen, DK 1570), *ahead of your arrival.*

(2) SAS offers the very same service at Kastrup Airport. Offered are inexpensive, simple, but excellent accommodations.

(3) The National Tourist Office network of 13 foreign branches runs as smoothly as a quartz watch. The 139 domestic offices are autonomous and supply information to tourists as well.

(4) Students seeking inexpensive shelter should write **Danmark's Vandrehjem** (Vesterbrogade 39, DK-1620 Copenhagen V) *for tips.* **Tourist Information** (Bernstorffsgade 1) *in Copenhagen is a font of aid; so is* **Use It** (Radhusstraede 13, DK-1204 Copenhagen K) (☎ 33-156518).

ENGLAND

This is a pageant, a show to satisfy your greatest expectations. At every turn, nostalgia parades with fresh revelation. The wraith of Dickens still occupies an intimate mews in central London. There are reminders everywhere of Shakespeare, Bacon, Spencer, Hardy, Marlowe, Byron, Wordsworth, and other legendary figures of England's finest literary hours. The quiet landscape remains pure Constable. Inns, cottages, pubs, gardens, castles, and dungeons all conspire to recall a colorful, lusty past. And just as naturally, there's a very modern side, too, with comfort, grace, and convenience.

To wander through Albion's winding byways is a constant delight, packed with surprises as you roam the rolling hills or meander through her green and mellowed dales—a sudden confrontation with the fearsome Cerne Abbas Man, a naked giant engraved into the chalky soil by prehistoric masons; your first sighting of Stonehenge, earliest of time machines silhouetted against the great sky rolling above the flat expanse of Salisbury Plain; the exhilarating view from Glastonbury Tor, that curious man-made mound, haunt of Druids since King Arthur's days.

But there's more to the English countryside than ancient history. The connoisseur unearths his musty *Olde Curiosity Shoppes*, and the epicure can follow the scent to a genuine pub-made steak-andkidney pie in a friendly hostelry tucked away in a sleepy medieval hamlet. For the sportsman, there are miles of golf courses, rod-bending fish—trout or salmon—in a multitude of rivers and streams, deep-sea fishing and brisk sailing on every coast, or even hang gliding high above a filigree of pocket-size fields.

You can reach any part of England by British Rail or by the efficient Express Coachways, whose vehicles are clean and comfortable, and whose fares are often less than half what you'd pay on the train. Or rent a car, if your budget can stand it, and travel the back routes. Why not skipper a canal boat by the week and take the whole family cruising through Britain's infinite network of picturesque canals? Used formerly for transporting goods by horse-drawn barge, they're now employed as a pleasure complex. This has to be the cheapest and most novel means of seeing both town and country while avoiding traffic jams.

Merrie England is the acknowledged center of drama, music, and the performing arts. Every metropolis has its theaters and art centers offering a nonstop range of entertainment.

You'll see top classical theater at unbelievably low prices, music-hall romps for even less, and hear performances from rock to baroque. Established landmarks such as Stratford-on-Avon or London's West End present the widest variety of major productions. You'll find pleasures to suit every pocket. Whether you're standing under Big Ben or the steeple of some village green, you'll find that Old England and New England are so close to us and to our interwoven cultures that it's scarcely a tick of the clock between King John and Elton John.

TIPS ON ENGLAND

ACCOMMODATIONS

Between June and October in London and more than 2-dozen other university towns across England and Scotland, vacant student facilities are available to families and loners at $15 to $18 per night, including breakfast. Multiroom apartments also are rentable during this limited period for $135 to $175 per week. For any type of booking—student or otherwise—one of the best £5 investments you can make is in **TABS**—the Telephone Accommodation Booking Service run by the London Tourist Board (☎ *071-8248844*), and the staff can set you up in the capital or advise you for the rest of Britain via any of the numerous **Tourist Information Centres** around the realm. Another good start is the free BTA booklet called *London Accommodation for Budget Travellers.* Two other invaluable sources that list low-cost stops across England and Wales are *Britain Youth Accommodation*, available through the BTA and the meticulous, well-mapped Youth Hostel Association. Handbook, which can be obtained by writing YHA Services Ltd. (*29 John Adam St., W.C.2, also in London*). The latter is especially suited to the needs of bikers, campers, caravaners, and other adventurers.

An enterprising organization called **MinOtels** (*11 Palmeira Mansions, Church Road, Hove, East Sussex BN3 2GA, England*) has about

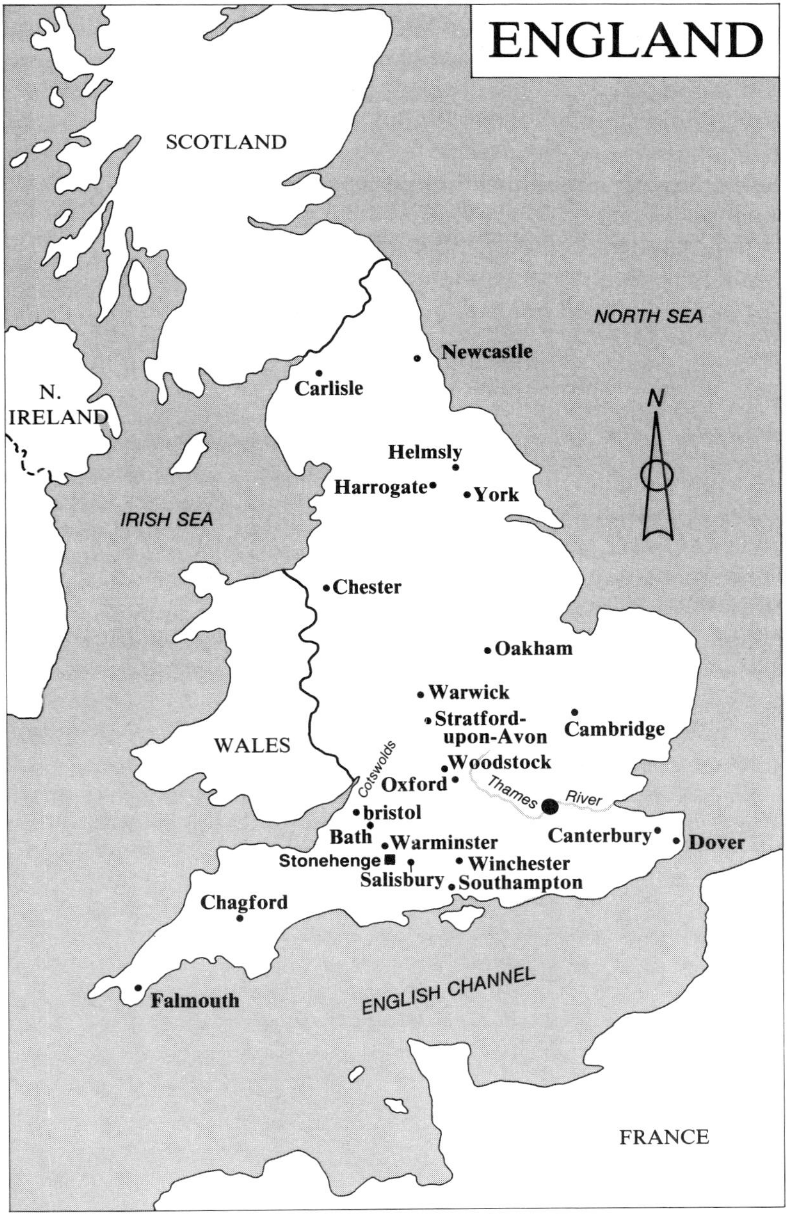
ENGLAND
SCOTLAND
NORTH SEA
N.
IRELAND
IRISH SEA
WALES
Newcastle
Carlisle
N
Helmsly
Harrogate
York
Chester
Oakham
Warwick
Stratford-
upon-Avon
Cambridge
Cotswolds
Woodstock
Oxford
Thames
River
bristol
Bath
Warminster
Canterbury
Dover
Stonehenge
Winchester
Salisbury
Southampton
Chagford
Falmouth
ENGLISH CHANNEL
FRANCE

175 members in its independent budget confederation, which spreads throughout the British Isles and Ireland (also in France, Switzerland, and Italy). Prices are reasonable, quality is reliable, and reservations are quickly facilitated through the network. Write them for a brochure.

A similar confederation called **Wolsey Lodges** (*17 Chapel St., Bildeston, Suffolk* ☎ *0449-741297*) has more than 140 splendid homes throughout the nation in which lovely double accommodations usually run about $70 per night. The brochure is as inviting as the people who have put it together. They can also make provisional bookings for you. An organization called **Bed & Breakfast (GB)** offers many more homes, farms, or hotels at very low rates and operates its own round-the-clock hotline and faxline. **Inter-Hotels** has about 80 members in the London area and elsewhere in Britain. Ask about both of these at the BTA kiosks already mentioned, or by phone you can reach B&B at ☎ (*0491*) *578803* (FAX *410806*) and Inter-Hotels at ☎ (*071*) *373-3241*.

Something even more unusual? Then how about a **boating holiday** on the canals of Britain? You can board an easy-to-handle "narrowboat" (an elongated bargelike houseboat) or small cruiser for prices that will set you hunting for your Topsiders. Rentals are usually for a week or a fortnight and the per-berth rate generally runs close to $200 per person for 7 days afloat! Details and bookings through: **Boat Enquiries Ltd.** (*7 Walton Well Rd., Oxford OX2 6ED*; ☎ *0865-511161*). Ask them for their 60-page booklet called *Boating Holidays.* One line that has been receiving boatloads of praise is **UK Waterway Holidays**; their range includes cruises through history, into ghostly corners of England, to cricket pitches (no running aground), and along canals where you'll meet British fowl and wildlife, flora and Morris dancers. It moors at *Penn Place, Rickmansworth, Herts. W.D. 3 1E.U.*

FOOD

Many of your best values will be found in foreign-style kitchens and some of the so-called workmen's cafes. Wine bars and pubs offer a plenitude of low-cost choices that are very British in flavor and traditionalism. Certain national items have always been good: roasts, grills, Scotch salmon, Yorkshire ham, Stilton cheese, bacon, and quite a few others. The "foody's" taste for trendy French cuisine has pushed prices skyward in this sector, so try to dine more on English cookery if you are economizing. If you are not totally a beefeater, the answer may lie in visiting a few fish-and-chips spots (see later under "London").

Meal hours are fixed. Breakfast used to be heavy, but it is now comparatively light; lunch, seldom taken before 1 o'clock, is substantial;

a cup of tea at 4:30 p.m. is a sacred ritual in every walk of life; dinner, between 7 p.m. and 8:30 p.m., is the biggest repast of all.

English oysters are superb but wickedly expensive.

In case you're baffled by the difference between these so typical look-alikes, steak-and-kidney *pie* is made with pastry crust, while steak-and-kidney *pudding* ("pud" to the locals) is made with suet dough topping.

Double-check the prices of all exotic delicacies. Many are flown in from distant points; if your maitre d' suggests "that nice piece of melon," it might come from Israel, and it might cost $6. A portion of asparagus is liable to be $8!

SOUL FOOD

A dozen British cathedrals now offer an opportunity for you to break bread with them. Prices are blessedly modest, products are fresh, and all cooking is done on the premises. Try the Norman mood at the Monks' Dormitory in Durham or the architecturally splendid setting at the cloister at Wells. St. Albans offers a historic Chapter House. London has Southwark and more can be enjoyed on your pilgrimage to York, Lincoln, Coventry, or Gloucester. Further alms extended at Liverpool, Ely, Guilford, and Chichester.

DRINKS

Beer, gin, rum, and liquors are plentiful. English wine is rare—an act of charity provided by nature. British sparkling wine, however, is bubbling up in volume as well as in popularity. (The champagne clans of Reims are not losing too much sleep over it just yet.) Scotch is costly. You'll pay from £1.50 for a "small" (understatement of the year) and from £2.25 for a "large" (junior-size) portion. The bottle price is correspondingly high (close to £10) for most proprietary brands. Scotch in Britain is somewhat weaker than exports available in America.

British brews vary in strength and fullness of flavor from pale ale to light ale, lager (which comes closest to the beer North Americans know), mild, bitter, brown ale, and the strongest of them all, stout. English drinkers like to mix these basic types to suit their individual preferences. Burton, a rich, sweetish, brown libation, is available from Sept. to June only. Brewers generally are lowering the alcohol content of their products in order to hold the line on costs. Usually the volume per measured serving remains linked to the pint.

To the English, ice used to be that strange substance upon which the fishmonger chilled halibut; there were said to be no more than 114 pieces in all of London at any one time. Now that so many visiting Americans have insisted that whisky requires the stuff, a publican might go along by dropping one small cube—or two, at the most—into your drink. British lager is generally the only type of beer that will be served chilled; the rest usually come out at taproom temperature.

Don't drive a car if you have consumed even as little as 2 pints of beer! Under the stringent provisions of the Road Safety Act, the vehicle operator doesn't have to be drunk to face fines of from $20 to $200, 4 months in jail (or both), and loss of his or her license for one year. Suspects are required to take a roadside "Breathalyser" test.

London may be the world tea-sipping capital. Two gourmet dispensers are the **Ceylon Tea Centre** (*Regent St.*), which serves 4 different, relatively milder types, and the **India Tea Centre** (*343 Oxford St.*), where there is a choice of no less than 10 different brews—including some served on ice.

PUBS

The celebrated Public House—"pub" for short—has been the heartbeat of England. In the old-timers there are no jukeboxes, no bustling bartenders, no feeling of haste. It's a social center, a place to relax and talk, to play a game of darts for a brace of pints, and sometimes to dine informally on the staples of English cooking.

The traditional pubs are divided into 2 parts. On one side, you'll find the Public Bar—plain, utilitarian, for drinkers who want no nonsense. On the other side, with a separate entrance, is the Saloon Bar—better decorated, more comfortable, the one you'll probably head for. Prices are usually a trifle higher in the latter.

Then, of course, there are 3 styles of classic pub: City Tavern (spirits and wine featured above draught beers), Gin Palace (typically Victorian if authentic), and Alehouse (plain, ancient, and historic). London also has 2 Dickensian pubs that serve nothing but apple or pear cider—with no resemblances to the brew Grandma pours on Thanksgiving. If you try a pint of "scrumpy," you'll ask for a second—but don't risk more than two because their hangovers are notorious.

SIGHTSEEING

Before you leave North America, inquire about the **Great British Heritage Pass**, which will admit you to historic sites that are in the care of the British Government, including castles, museums, galleries, estates, and gardens. Operating in a similar fashion is the **National Trust** through which part of your overall fee goes toward maintaining these beautiful and valuable heirlooms of history. Details are available from the **British Tourist Authority**. (See your travel agent or the **BTA**; once in London, the place to go is *12 Regent St.* at *Victoria Station Forecourt.*)

Bus tours: A top-quality program is produced by **Grey-Green Coaches Ltd.**, which operates 2- to 8-day tours in England, Scotland, Wales, Ireland, as well as continental circuits in France, Holland, Germany, and Belgium. The prices are remarkably low. Here are some examples: a fantastic 3-day whirl that includes the *Cotswolds*, *Wye Valley*, and *Malverns* from $220; another of *Devon* and *Cornwall* for approximately the same price; a 5-day romp around the *Cornish Coast* and *Lands End* for about $330, and a glorious swing over to the *Isle of Skye* and the *Western Highlands* for about $410. Some jaunts, such as the 2-day *Heart of England* loop, go for as little as $120 and they are amply worth the outlay. Write for fully detailed, photo-filled color brochures that give the full story. The address is 53-55 Stanford Hill, London N16 5TD (☎ *81-8008010*). BTA can also fill you in on 37 regions that are covered by bus, some of the routes employing double-deck and opentop vehicles. Exciting, convivial programs at very low rates.

GETTING AROUND

TRAINS

Most main lines radiate from London. Service generally is only routine. The faster ones can hit 125 mph on some few stretches. The proudest pacesetters include the famous **Yorkshire**, **Tyne-Tees**, and **Blue Pullmans**, most with air conditioning. Other favorites are the **Flying Scotsman** (393 miles between London and Edinburgh in 350 minutes), the **Cornish Riviera Express**, and the Norwich-bound **East Anglian**.

If you plan to do a lot of roving in the U.K., the **BritRail Pass** offers the best bargain reductions (discounts on rail and steamer services to Ireland and the Channel Islands; further cuts available for children). Go to the British Railways offices in New York, Los Angeles, Chicago, or Toronto for this booking as it is not on sale within the U.K. To qualify for their **Youth Pass** (for 1- to 4-week duration and cheaper than the standard version), you've got to be between 14 and 22. A Senior Citizens' benefit as well as a children's reduction spans the extremes of the age scale. Britain is also in the previously described Eurailpass network. Where you will *not* save money, however, is in the dining car, a scene of high prices and grim cooking. To facilitate your program, start at the **British Travel Centre**, *the Rail division, 12 Regent St.*

The "open-plan saloon carriage" is most common, although a few "compartment" type coaches are still in use. There are 2 classes with smoking and nonsmoking sections. Seats are often bookable in advance on the main circuits.

Take the trains for long distances, but unless you seek much greater speed the buses are best for excursions. The fares are lower by about half, and the nation has an extensive grid of bus routes. Outside the capital and the cities, these become "motor coaches." For the most part, you'll find them comfortable. Air conditioning has been introduced by many firms.

MOTORING

The British road system is appallingly behind the times. Britain has a piddling 800 miles or so of fast turnpikes. To ramble through England's colorful by-lanes is a joy—but to get to them via the choked main arteries is an exasperation.

GASOLINE

The British gallon is nearly a fifth larger than the U.S. gallon. The price, at this writing, is nearly twice as much as you pay at your neighborhood pump.

CAR HIRE

I have had very good luck with a company called **British Car Rental**, which is a subsidiary of The Rover Group and a major bank, so reliability is assured. They are big on stock and especially good for vans and station wagons (known as "estate cars" to the Brits). ☎ *203-716166* or FAX *203-716175.* In London, **Avis** (Texaco Garage, *68 North Row, W.1;*☎ *629 7811*) offers a variety of models at standard tariffs. **Europcar** (*Davis House, Wilton Rd., S.W. 1*; ☎ *834 8484*) is also outstanding.

FERRIES

Car-ferrying across the English Channel is popular. In peak season there are about 120 trips a day linking Britain with France or the Belgian headlands at Ostend. A drive-on-and-off car-ferry goes between Newhaven and Dieppe (103 miles from Paris)—ideal for motorists pointing for southwestern France, Spain, or Portugal. There's also a fine service between Harwich and Esbjerg, Denmark. The Dover-Calais sailing is better suited to the cost-conscious motorist or walk-on tourist. Hovercrafts zip summer passengers from Ramsgate to Calais in about 40 minutes (conventional vessels take almost 3 times longer); fares are approximately the same as on the slower ferries. British Rail's Seaspeed operates the world's 3 biggest hovercrafts from Dover, Calais, and Boulogne. Each carries 400 passengers and 60 cars. In high season, there are at least 18 crossings each way daily. The Jetfoil plies the waters between London's Tower Bridge and Ostend six times a day, making the trip in 3-1/2 hours.

MOTORCYCLES AND SCOOTERS

Not many are generally available for rent. But in London, **Rent-A-Scooter Ltd.** (*59 Albert Embankment, S.E.1* ☎ *624 8491*) hires out Lambrettas and motorized bicycles ("Mopeds" in Britain) on a 7-day basis or at a daily rate. **Comerfords Ltd.**, Portsmouth Rd., Thames Ditton, Surrey (☎ *81-3985531*) *sells* both scooters and cycles. Out at Haywards Heath (50 minutes by train from London), David Milne tells us he rents Suzukis and Hondas (500 cc.). Drop a line to him at **Cycletour** (*36 Meadow Dr., Lindfield, Haywards Heath, W. Sussex*).

BICYCLES

Two-wheelers of all sizes and complexities are racked up at **On yer Bike** (*52 Tooley St., S.E.1*; ☎ *4071309*). The fold-away type is a useful twist since you can pack it into a car and drive to where you would like to cycle. Even 10-speed models are on hand. Rates are geared down, too. An associated company now sells new bikes as well as used ones retired from the rental agency.

SHOPPING

Differences in sizes: British women's clothes are 1 size larger than North American. Women's shoes: 1-1/2 sizes smaller. Men's trousers: 1 size larger. Men's shoes: 1-1/2 sizes smaller. Men's suits, shirts, collars, and any measurements given in inches such as bust sizes: same. Most British clothing items are also sized by the metric system.

Money-Saving Personal Export Scheme: Upon presenting their passports, overseas visitors may buy clothes and most other goods free of the Purchase Tax. Retailers are now permitted to make over-the-counter sales to them on this basis, provided that the buyers carry all of these items and the accompanying documents in their hand baggage, produce them for inspection by the Departure Customs, and export them within a 3-month period. Goods shipped are, of course, free of V.A.T., too. In this case, the export price you pay will have had the 17.5% tax already discounted, thus avoiding the paperwork. Merchants are under no obligation whatsoever to offer this service. If they do, legally they may deduct a sum from the rebate to cover their costs. Since a large number of the leading establishments do subscribe, however, please be sure to inquire whenever you shop within a sufficiently substantial range.

There are alternative programs that are less fuss. Companies such as U.K. Tax Free Shopping will handle the rebate. Participating stores will display stickers showing they are associated. Vouchers have been simplified and can be issued for anywhere from £50 to £150, depending on the store. (Selfridges requires that you spend at least £75, while Harrods doubles that, just to give you two examples.) You'll get back 14.89% of the tax; however, calculate that you must pay between £5.50 and £6 in handling charges in these emporiums, so the actual rebate is reduced even more. It's still worth the effort. Once stamped by Customs all the forms can be returned in one envelope to the company and the refund is made quickly by one check to the purchaser's home address in his own currency or put on his credit card.

An even better bet might be the Europe Tax-Free Shopping Service operating at all four Heathrow Airport terminals. Immediate rebates are available upon presentation of your shopping receipts. Ask for more details about this one locally. It seems these refunds are valid for purchases made throughout Europe, too. If it's the case, you've cut through even more red tape.

Shopping hours 9 a.m. to 6 p.m. Mon. through Fri.; 9 a.m. to 1 p.m. for some stores on Sat.; a number of department stores, especially in London, stay open until 8 p.m. on Wed. and Thurs. You might find a lot more open on Sun. too, since bans were lifted on this point, but check it out locally.

LOCAL RACKETS

Whenever you cash a traveler's check in a hotel, inquire *first* about the hotel's percentage on the transaction. If it's too big a bite (which it frequently is!), you'll save a chunk by going to the nearest bank.

Don't make international telephone calls from your hotel because of the appalling house charges that most of them levy; go to the Central Exchange or a neighborhood one instead. An increasing number are joining **Teleplan**, a moneysaving program developed by the telephone companies, but until more hotels are members your best bet will be at the exchange.

SPORTS

CYCLING

Why not wheel among the abbeys and stately homes of North Yorkshire? A year-round 8-day itinerary costs about $130 per person, including 6 days' cycle hire, 7 nights' bed and breakfast, and VAT. Contact Freedom of Ryedale Holidays, *23A Market Place, Helmsley, Yorkshire YO6 5BJ*; ☎ *(0439) 70775.*

For a bit more, you can arrange a week of one-night stands or circulate from a central cycling point. Both biped and motorized mounts available. Price includes baggage movement, tour guide, and bed-and-breakfast accommodation (dinner optional); discount for children. Contact Bike Hike, *2nd Floor, Pearl Ass. House, 1 Yarm Lane, Stockton on Tees, Cleveland*; ☎ *(0642) 603847.*

MOUNTAINEERING

Three or five day mountaincraft course at about $55 and $70 per person includes full-board and youth-hostel accommodation. Contact Blencathra Centre, Threlkeld, Keswick, Cumbria CA12 4SG; ☎ *(059 683) 601.*

Or learn basic mountain skills in **Capel Curig**, Wales. One-week course Mar.-Dec. runs about $75 inclusive. Information from Booking Department, *Plas y Brenin, Capel Curig, Betws-y-Coed, Gwynedd, Wales LL24 OET*; ☎ *(06904) 214.*

HIKING

Over 20 one- or 2-week graded walks offered from about $80 per walk. Tariff covers youth hostel accommodation, half-board, and VAT. Contact Youth Hostels Association Adventure Holidays,

Trevelyan House, *St. Albans, Hertfordshire AL1 2DY*; ☎ *(56) 55215.* There's an especially good walk on the **Ridgeway**, a prehistoric route that runs 75 miles west of London to the Berkshire Downs overlooking the Vale of White Horse. **Court Hill Hostel** is composed of 5 wood-beamed barns carefully reassembled at midpoint along this footpath of early man. You'll find an amphitheater, barbecue, a great log stove, and prices you won't believe. Cyclists also can pedal in.

HORSES

From Easter through Oct. you can take the route of the poets by ponying through the **Lake District**. Cost? Half-day treks from about $31, bed-and-breakfast about $27, and dinner about $8.

From Apr. to mid-Sept. you can pony trek in Wales. One week is about $130, covering full-board farmhouse accommodation (hotel optional), guide, and VAT. Insurance minimally extra but mandatory. Contact Galleon World Travel Association Ltd. *1, Galleon House, King Street, Maidstone, Kent ME14 1EG*; ☎ *(0622) 63411.*

For more pence, try your horsemanship in the **New Forest**; 10 hours riding with instruction at about $42; sleep and half-board per day comes to about $22. Contact New Park Manor, *Lyndhurst Road, Brockenhurst, New Forest, Hampshire SO4 7QH*; ☎ *(059 02) 3467.*

WATERSPORTS

Go surfing off the coast of **Cornwall** from May to Sept. and then dry off in self-contained cabins. Superbargain prices begin at about $35 per week per person covering tuition, self-catering accommodation, surfboards, and wetsuits. Bring your own towels. Contact Skewjack Surf Village, *Sennen, Porthcurno, Cornwall*; ☎ *(073 687) 287.*

1-1/2 days' windsurfing instruction and 1/2-day's soloing run from $75, including 2 nights' accommodation, half-board, service, and VAT. Where? Red House Hotel, *Barton-on-Sea, Hampshire BH25 7HJ*; ☎ *(0425) 610119.*

A one-week white-water, lake, and sea-canoeing and kayak course skims along from Apr. to Oct. in Wales. Fee? About $85, including full-board accommodation. For contact information see Plas y Brenin mountaineering listing.

HANG GLIDING

Two to six day courses at all levels (no pun intended) from about $90 to $175, including equipment and VAT. Accommodation roughly $18 a night. Contact Birdman Flight Training School, *Mildenhall, Marlborough, Wiltshire*; ☎ *(0672) 52909.*

A one-week course in Wales starts at about $150 to include equipment, 6-nights' bed-and-breakfast lodging in a shared twin (about $35 extra to solo), lunches, and VAT. Mar.-Oct. Contact Welsh

Hang Gliding Centre, *New Road, Crickhowell, Powys, Wales*; ☎ *(0873) 810019.*

SPECIAL-INTEREST HOLIDAYS

BEER FESTIVALS

These countrywide celebrations are held in tents or on college campuses from May to Oct. The City Hall, Truro is on tap in early Aug. for the Cornish Real Beer Festival, the East London "knees-up" at Leyton Marshes is in mid-Aug., and the Bedford Beer Festival brews in early Oct. For details on these and others, pick up the latest copy of *What's Brewing*.

HOT-AIR BALLOONING

Up and away for a weekend in **Berkshire**. Price: from $140 per person, including tuition, full-board accommodation, and VAT. Contact Country House Hotel, *Elcot Park, near Newbury, Berkshire*; ☎ *(04885) 276/421.*

ORNITHOLOGY

There's **birdwatching** for weekends in **Devon** from Mar. to Sept. About $75 per person will get you a reservation and guide, 3-nights' accommodation, and full board, with service and VAT included. Contact Coombe Cross Hotel, *Bovey Tracey, Devon TQ13 9EY*; ☎ *(0626) 832476.*

A 12-day course in the ancient art of **falconry** has a base price of about $150; dwelling at the local inn about $14 per person per night, Nov. to Feb. Contact Birds of Prey and Falconry Centre, *Newent, Gloucestershire GL18 1JJ*; ☎ *(0531) 820286.*

HAUNTING HOLIDAYS

Be the guest of the ghost of Ruthin Castle. Bed and breakfast (and optional boos) at about $35 per person; reduction for children. If your telepathy is out of order, communicate by post or phone Ruthin Castle, *Ruthin, Clwyd, North Wales, LL15 2NW*; ☎ *(082 42) 2664.*

Or walk the way of York's best-known ghosts for an evening or a weekend. Half-board weekend costs about $70 per person. Spiritual contact can be made through Enrichment Travel Ltd., *7A St. Sampsons Square, York YO2 4BB*; ☎ *(0904) 52232.*

FARMHOUSE HOLIDAYS

From about $65 per person per week, including full board and VAT; self-catering cottages from $50; reductions for children. Further details from Country Farm Holidays, *The Place, Ham Lane, Powick, Hereford and Worcester WR2 4RA*; ☎ *(0905) 830899.*

HOME EXCHANGE

Contact Home Rooms Ltd., *7 Provost Rd., London NW3 4ST*; ☎ *(01) 722-8973.*

CATCHALL HOLIDAY

Family adventure holidays for everyone from 10-year-old Tommy to Grandpa Joe. Nature courses, canoeing, backpacking, caving, you-name-it. Contact YMCA National Centre, *Lakeside, Ulverston, Cumbria LA12 8Bd*; ☎ Newly Bridge *(0448) 31758.*

WHERE TO GO

BATH

Bath is now probably second only to London as a place of interest for visitors to England. The theater is outstanding; it's easy to reach; most importantly, it's lovely. Since this city takes its name from the fact that Romans used it as a spa, many historic corners still exist for archaeology buffs. (**The Pump Room** is not a chic hideaway but the center of those Latin waterworks.) For more modern tastes there is the A.D. 1499 **Abbey**; then for the dedicated avant garde there are the **Crescents**, 18th-century rings of houses on lovely streets; there's also Jane Austen's house. Band concerts often are presented in the **Parade Gardens**. This rich town is virtually a museum of all periods of architecture. Strangely enough, one of the finest museums of Americana is here, too—better than anything we've seen in the New World. Pleasant overnighting at the refashioned Georgian **Arden Hotel** (*73 Great Pulteney St.*), **The Belmont** (*7 Belmont on Lansdown Rd.*), or the **Henry Guest House** (*6 Henry St.*). For dining try **Sweeney Todd's** (*Milsom St.*) for ribs, veal, and even pizza; the potted palms evoke an oasis effect.

BRISTOL

Athough this port should be known to any devotee of fine sherries, it is also revered for its **university**, its great **cathedral**, the **Cabot Tower**, and the handsome **Norman structures** that decorate the town from the docks up to the modern city. It has grown so busy, however, that as a tourist, we'd prefer to base in nearby Bath. If you insist, the **Ladbroke Dragonara** (modern) and the **Grand** (traditional) are reliable medium-priced hotels in the center.

BROADWAY

This lovely Olde England country town is a pleasant and convenient springboard for excursions into the enchanting **Cotswolds**. **Stratford-upon-Avon** is only 15 miles away; **Warwick Castle** is only 25 miles distant; also nearby are **Kenilworth Castle**, **Banbury**, **Sulgrave Manor** (ancestral home of George Washington, where you'll find the original Stars and Stripes), **Blenheim Palace** (Churchill was born here), and **Worcester**. If you have wheels, investigate such fairy-tale hamlets as **Upper and Lower Slaughter**, **Bourton-on-the-Water**, **Moreton-in-Marsh**, **Stow-on-the-Wold**, **Chipping Campden**, and **Burford**. Then, if you wish to run further afield, try to include **Sutton Benger** and the captivating townlet of **Castle Combe**, often called the most charming village in England. Try to visit the last on a weekday, because on sunny Saturdays and Sundays it is *mobbed.* All of these hamlets are peppered with cozy, low-cost boardinghouses that are amply comfortable. Except for Stratford, each of the abovenamed villages contains only one street (which is usually the main road through). If you want to overnight, try to arrive by 4 p.m., cruise that main lane, and choose your snuggery. There may be one 10-room hotel, but that will be only marginally better than the bed & breakfast guest-houses. Broadway's best stops for value are the **Broadway**, **Dormy House**, and **Collin House**.

CAMBRIDGE

A town of scholars; quaint shops; punters dotting the gray river in spring; venerable stonemasonry at every turning. **British Railways** will take you there and back on a low-cost "day return" ticket. It's only 56 miles from London. If you wish to bunk, however, try **Arundel House** or **Gonville**. **University Arms** is useful, too, if you don't mind the higher prices.

GLYNDEBOURNE

This suburb, partly Tudor and located about a mile north of the town of Glynde, is renowned throughout the music world for its summer opera performances. It's best enjoyed as an excursion point from London, and during the summer music festival, special trains are hitched up to arrive on time and return visitors to the capital the same evening. The **Opera House** and its gardens provide a backdrop for one of the transcending social events in English society. Spectators in formal attire ingest picnic suppers from hampers while seated on the auditorium grounds. Unless you have tickets (they are hideously difficult to obtain), don't waste time by running out with the vain hope of snagging them there; with almost never an exception, they are sold out months in advance. The surrounding southeastern district of England, however, is a wonderland of history and recreation. Just pick up a regional map and wander along the coast or along the shores of the Stour, the Medway, the Wey or the Ouse Rivers. You won't be disappointed.

HAMPTON COURT

This home of Cardinal Wolsey and Henry VIII can easily be visited on a London bus excursion that also includes **Windsor Castle**. The loop, one of the lowest in cost for its length, is also one of the most awe-inspiring "standard" sightseeing circuits anywhere in the land. But before setting out for Windsor, be certain to check whether it is open; Court activities normally close the State Apartments during April and substantial portions of March, May, and June.

LIVERPOOL

Here's England's 3rd city. The focus traditionally has been on docks, freighters, and railway switchyards, but with prosperity comes vanity, and increasing attention is being given to touristic matters. This is reflected in the carefully renovated **Albert Dock** complex with its imposing **Maritime Museum** and the **Beatles Experience**. If you happen to be here and yearn for some Old World scenery and aesthetics, hop over to nearby **Chester** and stroll along the ancient walls, the River Dee, and among its half-timbered houses and inns. I would pick Chester as the place to overnight and then the unspeakably ancient **Ye Olde King's Head**, which also combines a tavern in its midst.

LONDON

The Celts called it *Lyndin*, meaning "waterside fortress," but the Latinized version was *Londinium*. History inevitably weaves itself into the 20th-century tableau—a patchwork that features Westminster Abbey and Mary Quant, Hyde Park and the Hard Rock Cafe, Crown Jewels, and mod rags! It's unquestionably the most mercurial metropolis in Europe.

In 1775, Samuel Johnson reflected, "The full tide of human existence passed me, today at Charing Cross."

Given enough idleness, you might enjoy a similar experience. For all its Big-Ben tradition and stern palace guards, London is vital, smiling, vibrant, and trendy. Like Naples, much of its life takes place on the streets, not only in stiff private clubs or storied oaken salons. About 12 feet below today's asphalt surface rests the capital created by Romans of the first century.

DIRECTORY

U.S. Embassy • *24 Grosvenor Sq., W.1*; ☎ *499-9000.*

American Express • *6 Haymarket, S.W.1*; ☎ *930-4411.*

Barber • The Clip Joint, *46 Maddox St., W.1*; ☎ *629-2753.*

Hairdresser • Robert Fielding of Regent Street, *Main office 12A Golden Sq. W.1R*; ☎ *437-1215.* Call the central number to learn which of its 12 branches is nearest you.

Dry Cleaning and Pressing • Sketchley, 43 locations; see the telephone directory.

Laundromat • Coin Laundries Ltd., *157 Old Brompton Rd., S.W.5.*

Suit Rental • Moss Bros. *Regent St., W.1*; ☎ *240-4567.*

Doctor or Dentist • University College Hospital (*Gower St., W.1*) and Middlesex Hospital (*Mortimer St., W.1*) maintain 24-hour casualty services. Around-the-clock dental assistance is available through Emergency Dental Service (☎ *584-1008*); minimum charge about $23.

Fire, Police, Ambulance, any Major Emergency • ☎ *999.*

Tourist Offices • Tourist Information Centre, *Victoria Station, Forecourt S.W.1.*, ☎ *71-730-3488.*

Favorite Pawnshops • Messrs. A. E. & D. A. Thomson Ltd. (*158 Portobello Rd., Notting Hill; W.11*) and Messrs. T. M. Sutton Ltd. (*156 Victoria St., S.W.1*).

HOW TO GET AROUND

It's easy and inexpensive to travel between London's Heathrow Airport and Piccadilly on the subway. The frequent runs connect the two points in 47 minutes.

It costs very little to ride one of the world's best-planned carrier systems. Just go to your travel agent before you leave home and ask about Travelcards issued in 1-, 3-, 4-, or 7-day versions; these allow you to travel when you like, and as often as you like, to and from most of the main tourist sights, shopping areas, and places of entertainment. They are valid on both the bus and underground networks; children ride for less than half-price. No long lines for ticket purchase and no fussing with unfamiliar money, but you can buy the cards at the underground kiosks, too. A great buy!

The big red double-deck buses are legendary. William Gladstone said "The best way to see London is from the top of a bus." It's still true. London Transport has also begun experimental runs with 16-passenger minibuses, but they're nowhere near the fun of their big brothers. When the conductor arrives, pay according to your destination. If you're not sure where you're going to step off, you can usually arrange with him to remit the difference after leaving your seat.

There's a breed of smaller vehicle called the **Hop-a-Bus**, specifically created for sightseers and shoppers; just hop aboard for 50p and go anywhere on the circuit. The C-1, C-2, and C-3 routes go to the most popular attractions.

When waiting at a bus stop, the fair-minded Britons form a line, so that everyone will board in turn (unlike on the Underground, where it's every man for himself).

WARNING: Your most frequently used numbered buses will begin disappearing toward midnight. For night owls, however, London Transport lays on a few late-late runs that have their own sets of numerals and distinctive routes. Grab a cab if you can afford it (you can now legally share a taxi with another fare); if not, a lengthy conver-

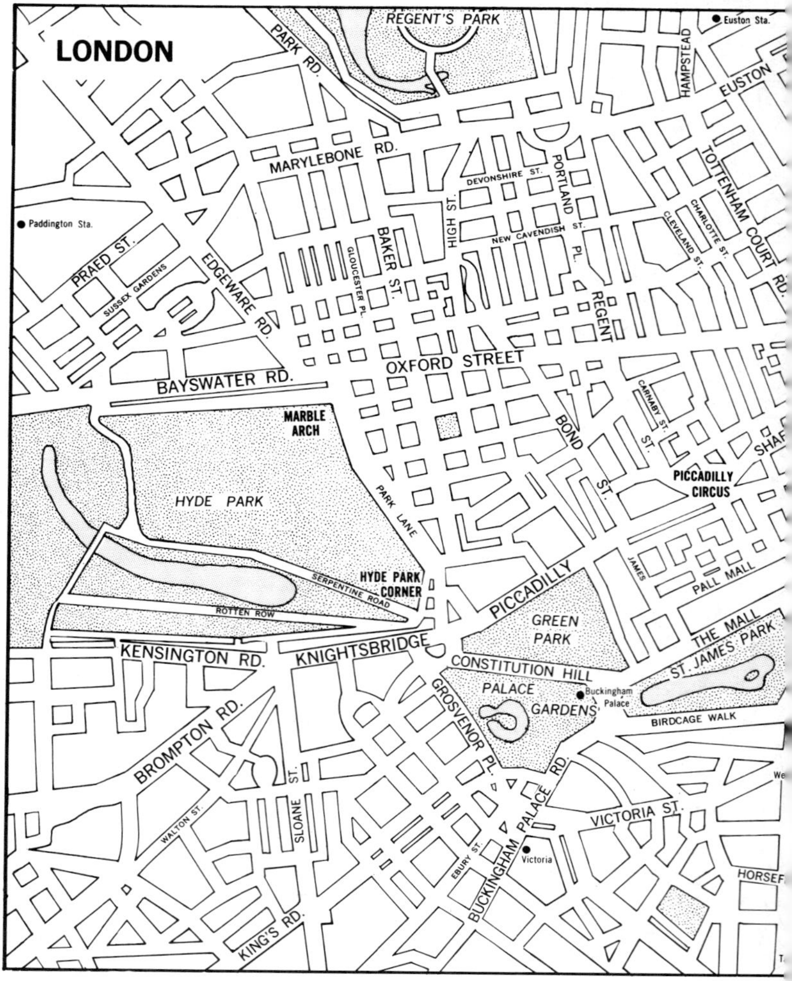
LONDON
REGENT'S PARK
Euston Sta.
PARK RD.
HAMPSTEAD
EUSTON
MARYLEBONE RD.
DEVONSHIRE ST.
PORTLAND PL.
TOTTENHAM COURT RD.
CHARLOTTE ST.
CLEVELAND ST.
Paddington Sta.
HIGH ST.
NEW CAVENDISH ST.
BAKER ST.
GLOUCESTER PL.
PRAED ST.
SUSSEX GARDENS
EDGEWARE RD.
REGENT
OXFORD STREET
BAYSWATER RD.
MARBLE ARCH
BOND ST.
CARNABY ST.
PICCADILLY CIRCUS
HYDE PARK
PARK LANE
JAMES
PALL MALL
HYDE PARK CORNER
SERPENTINE ROAD
ROTTEN ROW
PICCADILLY
GREEN PARK
THE MALL
ST. JAMES PARK
KENSINGTON RD.
KNIGHTSBRIDGE
CONSTITUTION HILL
PALACE GARDENS
Buckingham Palace
GROSVENOR PL.
BIRDCAGE WALK
BROMPTON RD.
ST.
SLOANE
BUCKINGHAM PALACE RD.
VICTORIA ST.
WALTON ST.
EBURY ST.
Victoria
HORSEF
KING'S RD.

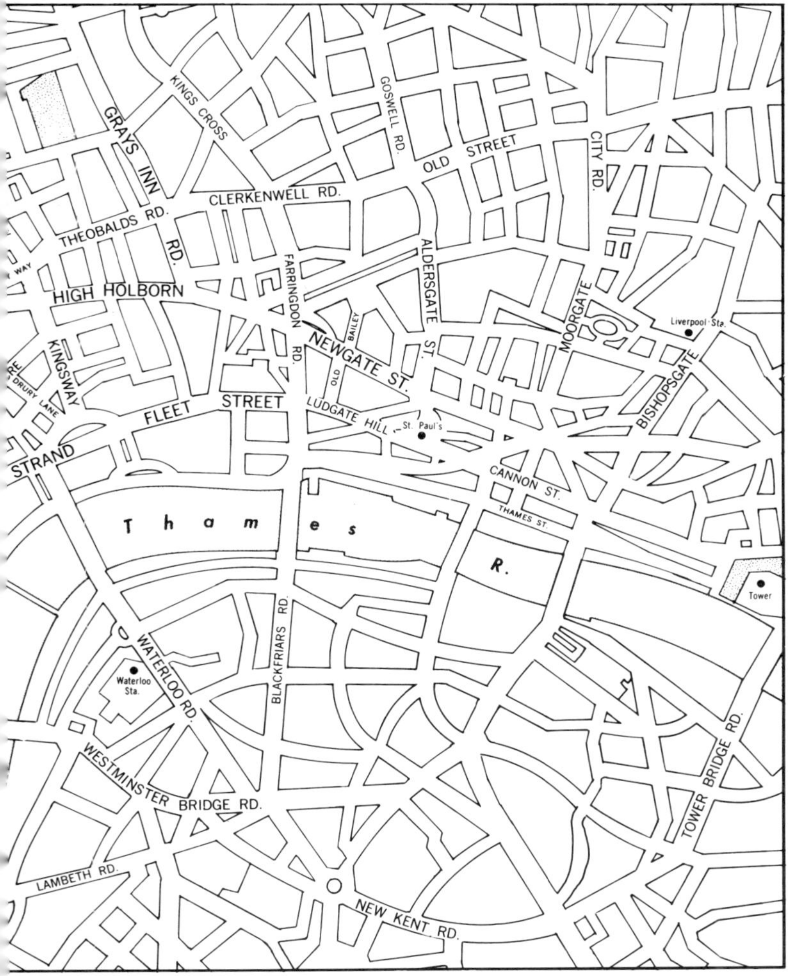
KINGS CROSS
GRAYS INN RD.
GOSWELL RD.
OLD STREET
CITY RD.
CLERKENWELL RD.
THEOBALDS RD.
FARRINGDON RD.
ALDERSGATE ST.
MOORGATE
HIGH HOLBORN
Liverpool Sta.
OLD BAILEY
NEWGATE ST.
KINGSWAY
DRURY LANE
BISHOPSGATE
FLEET STREET
LUDGATE HILL
St. Paul's
STRAND
CANNON ST.
THAMES ST.
Thames R.
Tower
WATERLOO RD.
Waterloo Sta.
BLACKFRIARS RD.
WESTMINSTER BRIDGE RD.
TOWER BRIDGE RD.
LAMBETH RD.
NEW KENT RD.

sation with the conductor may be necessary to determine if his vehicle might pass somewhere not *too* far from your destination.

Underground routes: The London "tubes" are wonderful—almost always clean, and always much, much faster than taxis or buses over any appreciable distance. Tickets are by zones you cover: Outside of the morning and afternoon rush peaks, seats are nearly always available. A map is indispensable. They are available free at the **Transport Enquiry Offices** at *Piccadilly Circus*, or any station ticket office. For **Buckingham Palace**, the tube stations are *St. James's Park* or *Green Park*; for **Westminster Abbey** and **Parliament**, it's *Westminster*; the **Tate Gallery** is *Pimlico*; the **National Gallery** is *Charing Cross*; the **British Museum** is *Tottenham Court Road*; **St. Paul's Cathedral** and **Old Bailey** are *St. Paul's*; **Tower of London** is *Tower Hill*; **Madame Tussaud's** is *Baker Street*; **Speakers' Corner** in *Hyde Park* is *Marble Arch*; the **Stock Exchange** is *Bank*; **Dickens' House** is *Russell Square*; **Johnson's House** is *Blackfriars*. It's almost impossible to get lost in this well-marked network. Warning: Don't count on a late tube-train home, because all routes shut down between about midnight and 5 a.m. If you're a late-night rider (this is when the rare muggings are beginning to occur), sit in either the front car or the rear car, where guards are posted. Should you be stuck with no trains running, check the yellow pages of the phone directory for all-night taxi services.

WHERE TO STAY

LEAST $

The first thing to do is to write to the **London Tourist Board** 6 weeks or so ahead of your arrival requesting accommodation; otherwise, go to the office at Victoria Station Forecourt, between 9 a.m. and 7 p.m. or the Heathrow Tourist Information Centre when you arrive. In standard hotels and pensions (not hostels) rates start at around $26 and up per person; children under 12 usually are charged half rate if they share the adults' bedchamber. Student shelter begins around $11 per night. Information on private homes, tenting, student digs, hostels, and schools also is available.

Driscoll House • *172 New Kent Rd., S.E.1; ☎ (71) 703-4175, FAX: 703-8013.* Operated since 1973 for people of all nations from 18 to 70 years of age. Expect to pay about £130 per week with partial board. Priority given to Americans. Many travelers are very pleased here.

Central Club • *16-22 Great Russell St.; ☎ (71) 636-7512.* Handy location; snacks available; pool and gym; hairdresser; space for 172 guests; 25 public baths. Rates begin at £15.

Passfield Hall • *1 Endsleigh Pl.; ☎ (71) 387-7743.* Not far from Euston Station; nicely reformed Georgian establishment with space for about 200; rates £16–£22 for bed and breakfast. Functions March–April and July until Sept.

John Adams Hall • *15-23 Endsleigh St.; ☎ (71) 387-4086.* Similar to the above and in the same street; full board for a week £153–185. Same opening period but also from Dec.–Jan.

Lords • *20-22 Leinster Sq.; ☎ (71) 229-8877.* In the Bayswater area; residents bar; a fair number of units with private bath.

College House • *13 Cromwell Rd., S.W.7; ☎ (71) 589-1275.* A Royal College of art collage *open from July 17 to Sept. 26*; no meals.

Wilbraham • *Wilbraham Place (convenient to Sloane Square).* A sure value if only for its central location. Superb but a bit more costly than the previous entries.

Stanley House • *19-21 Belgrave Rd., S.W.1;* ☎ *(71) 834-5042, FAX: 834-8439.* Fair for the low prices; a 30-room, well-sited sleep-in.

Cranley Gardens Hotel • *33 Cranley Gardens, S.W.7,* ☎ *71-373-3232, FAX: 373-7944.* Well-regarded by readers for many years. Solid value.

Alison House Hotel • *82 Ebury St., S.W.1,* ☎ *71-730-9529, FAX: 730-5494.* Ditto for this one. Extensive updatings make it better than ever.

Annandale House • *39 Sloane Gardens, S.W.1.* Friendly and most agreeable for the accoutrements.

Holland House • *Holland Park, Kensington area, W.8;* ☎ *(71) 937-0791.* The best site. Roughly $15 enrolls you as a member; $10 a bunk; $2.50 for breakfast or packed lunch; $5 per supper.

Also see "Suggestions for Students" further along.

AUTHOR'S OBSERVATION

The British Tourist Authority now offers a brochure listing 4-score-ormore hotels in four conveniently central areas at tariffs ranging from around £9.50 to £25 per person per night, including continental breakfast, service, and tax. Write BTA, 40 W. 57th St., New York, N.Y. 10019 requesting London Accommodation for Budget Travellers.

MORE $$

Sloane Hall • *6 Sloane Gardens, Sloane Square, S.W.1;* ☎ *(71) 730-9206.* 2-dozen rooms in a terrific location; 6 twins with private bath. Including breakfast, per-person rate averages £21 for normal units, about £16 in the family quarters, and £23 with private bath. Kindly staff.

Kerwin • *20 St. George's Dr., S.W.1;* ☎ *(71) 834-8351.* Clean chambers with small bunks and telephone; no W.C. 3 solos start at £14.50; doubles at £27 (corner stalls #7, #15, and #28 recommended); 2 trios for around £27. Not grand, but cheerful.

Apollo • *18-22 Lexham Gardens, W.8;* ☎ *(71) 373-3236.* Central heating; bar; TV lounge. Breakfast. Best for singles.

Atlas • *24-30 Lexham Gardens W.8;* ☎ *(71) 373-7873.* Same street, same management. More or less same facilities, but with evening restaurant and many private baths.

Arden • *112-116 Lexham Gardens;* ☎ *(71) 373-7788.* Same street, same management. Highly agreeable tariff schedule.

Reynolds • *41-42 Stanhope Gardens, S.W.7 (1 block south of the Cromwell Road);* ☎ *(71) 373-2393.* Often occupied exclusively by students at the American University, so be sure to reserve in advance. No private baths, but plenty of hot and cold water in the washbasins of the 21 doubles, 5 singles, 4 triples, and 2 quads.

Strutton Park • *45 Palace Ct., W.2.;* ☎ *(71) 727-5074.* Occupies a Victorian house in Bayswater. Single with shower at £16 (tax, service, and breakfast included); double about £30. Basement restaurant.

Howard Winchester • *19 Argyle Square, W.C.1 (near the King's Cross station); ☎ (71) 837-9146.* 27 expandable pair-ups at all-inclusive £26-or-so; 3 oneperson kips. Reduction for children. Some rooms warmed by fireplaces, others by electric hearths. Clean and friendly.

Edward Leer • *30 Seymour St., Marble Arch, W.1.* Recommended by Australian readers who praise its cleanliness and comfort as well as the ample breakfasts. It's just off Oxford St. and handy to many midtown sites.

Sandringham • *3 Holford Rd., N.W.3; ☎ (71) 435-1569.* Long ride from center; winsome view of Hampstead Heath and Parliament Hill. Spacious, inviting chambers at about £15 per person for the 6 singles and 9 doubles—plus a 10% surcharge. Clean and commendable.

Dormers • *1 Talbot Sq., W.2 (practically in Paddington Station); ☎ (71) 723-1726.* Fresh and quiet. 22 comfy kips with radios and intercoms around £17 per person in combinations of 1, 2, or 3.

Grenville House • *4 Guilford St., W.C.1 (near Russell Sq.); ☎ (71) 405-9470.* Offers shelter, but little else. Facilities uneven. Tabs run £16 per head, including breakfast.

Thanet • *8 Bedford Pl., W.C.1 (one block east of the British Museum off Russell Sq.); ☎ (71) 636-2869.* Convenient for museum buffs; so-so maintenance.

Lonsdale • *Next door.* Fresher and more pleasant for only slightly more. A very good buy on a dignified street.

Clifton • *7 St. Chad's St., W.C.1. (around the corner from the King's Cross intersection); ☎ (71) 837-4452.* 5 triples (£24 range) and 4 smallish doubles (£23 range); 7 private baths. Passable.

Wysall Lodge • *5 Hemstal Rd., N.W.6 (a short amble from the West Hampstead underground); ☎ (71) 624-5731.* Alluring prices for 7-day-minimum boarders. 12 rooms; 2 showers; coin-operated heaters. About £16 a day for singles, £25 for doubles.

Langley • *18 Argyle Sq., W.C.1; ☎ (71) 837-5816.* Neighborhood not the best, but accommodation fair; £17 per snoozer.

Tyne Hotel • *17 Argyle Sq., W.C.1.* Next door to the Langley and run by the same family. Strange, but at similar tariffs, it falls short of its harness mate.

Carlton • Nearby, but not recommended. This entire area—near Euston, King's Cross, and St. Pancras stations—not advised for lone females after dark.

NAT Hotel • *145 Cromwell Rd.; ☎ (71) 373-5066.* Bright, winning; with cozy accommodations. Sauna; bar with guitarist.

Sherbrooke • *59 Queens Gate, S.W.7; ☎ (71) 584-8800.* 18 chambers seem rawboned. Considering proximity to Museum of Natural History (across street), perhaps that's appropriate.

Dilston House • *116 Sussex Gardens, W.2; ☎ (71) 723-8717.* No baths or W.C.s in its 20 crannies. 7 are family affairs with twin beds, double beds, and bunk beds.

Harley House • *16 Bernard St., W.C.1; ☎ (71) 837-5184.* Simple and well-scrubbed. Twin with bath about £16. Recommended.

Gower House • *57 Gower St., W.C.1;* ☎ *(71) 636-4685.* Run very properly.

Mount Pleasant • *53 Calthorpe St., W.C.1;* ☎ *(71) 837-9781.* 435-bunk colossus. Singles average £17.

Armsden • *32 Philbeach Gardens, S.W.5 (in Earls Court);* ☎ *(71) 370-2159.* Singles about the same as above; doubles perhaps £22 in high season.

Oasis • *13 Norfolk Sq. Off Hyde Park, W.2;* ☎ *(71) 723-5442.* Tiny bedrooms for £13.

Lancashire • *24-28 Norfolk Sq.;* ☎ *(71) 723-2189.* 55 bed-and-breakfast bunks at roughly £12.

Northumberland • *9-11 Euston Rd., N.W.1;* ☎ *(71) 837-2786.* £17 singles and £24 doubles.

Tudor House • *17-18 Bernard St., W.C.1;* ☎ *(71) 837-1691.* Not fancy but okay.

George • *58-60 Cartwright Gardens, W.C.1;* ☎ *(71) 387-1528.* Per person rate of a lofty £23; hygienic surroundings.

Europe • *131-137 Cromwell Rd., S.W.7;* ☎ *(71) 370-2336.* A wide assortment among its 100 rooms.

Hansel & Gretel • *64-76 Belgrave Rd., S.W.1. 100 rooms in 7 houses,* ☎ *71-828-1806.* Good breakfasts; always busy.

Hobbs • *80-86 Belgrave Rd., S.W.1.* Links 150 units under 5 separate roofs.

Dawson House • *72 Canfield Gardens, N.W.6;* ☎ *(71) 624-0079.* Satisfies many readers.

Lynton House • *108 Ebury St., S.W.1.* Very good area, but facilities not recommended.

Regent House • *28 Bloomsbury St., W.C.1.* Likewise.

EVEN MORE $$$

At this level of innkeeping, a double runs $60 to $97; singles range from $50 to $78.

Dolphin Square • *Chichester St., S.W.1;* ☎ *(71) 834-9134.* Pound-for-pound the best value in London. 1050 privately leased apartments in a quadrangle of houses. Rodney House accommodates 150 by the day, week, or month. Shops; restaurant; indoor pool; 2 bars; 8 squash courts; travel-bureau-cum-theater-ticket agency; saunas. Some sample tariffs, subject to change before your arrival: 3-room apartments £95 or so per night (or tops about £500 per week); 2-room apartments £86 per night (base tab of about £380 on a 7-day basis); 1-room £55 by the day, £290 per week (lowering to about £280 or so per week for a minimum one-month stay). All with fully equipped kitchenettes. Extra cots and TV available.

Royal Scot • *100 King's Cross Rd., W.C.1;* ☎ *(71) 278-2434.* Large; caters to tours. Borders Islington, so ideal for antiquaries. Mini-apartments with tea- and coffee-making equipment, bath and shower; 3 bars; restaurant. Single rate: £37; twins at £75; suites (some with canopy bed and color TV): £85, plus taxes. Superb value.

Royal National • *Bedford Way, W.C.1;* ☎ *(71) 637-2488.* Similar in size and personality. Near theater district. All units with bed consoles for TV and radio; phones. Also a good buy.

Elizabeth • *37 Eccleston Sq., S.W.1. (on the fringe of Belgravia);* ☎ *828-6812/3.* Sedately faces park and garden once enjoyed by neighbor W. Churchill. Single-to-family units all tasteful. Tennis court available.

Coburg • *129 Bayswater Rd., W.2;* ☎ *(71) 229-3654.* Warm and inviting 120-room inn. Good connections to West End via the Queensway and Bayswater stations. Units with bath have TVs. Some traffic noise, so light sleepers should book in the back.

Hospitality Inn • *104-05 Bayswater Rd., W.2;* ☎ *(71) 262-4461.* Scans Kensington Gardens and Hyde Park. 175 rooms; air conditioning parkside; TV.

Park House • *47 Egerton Gardens, S.W.3;* ☎ *(71) 589-0715.* In Knightsbridge, a shopper's dream. Mostly twin accommodations with bath and color TV. Turned-down beds and other niceties give it special appeal.

Royal Trafalgar • *Whitcomb St., W.C.2 (around the corner from Leicester Sq.);* ☎ *(71) 930-4477.* Prime site for sightseers. Angus Steak House branch and Battle of Trafalgar Pub excellent. 108 functional but worn billets.

Fielding • *4 Broad Ct., Bow St., W.C.2 (very near Covent Garden Opera House);* ☎ *(71) 836-8305.* Each of the 26 units in this 300-year-old house is different. As example, #24 a duplex with cozy sitting room 1 flight down. Not in any way related to this guidebook.

Bailey's Hotel • *Gloucester Rd., S.W.7 (near Gloucester Road tube station).* Ancient landmark in Kensington. 143 Old-World spacious bedrooms; about 60% with bath or shower. Though costly, worth it to travelers seeking its special type of ambiance.

Goring • *Beeston Pl., S.W.1 (near Buckingham Palace, Victoria Station, and the Air Terminal);* ☎ *(71) 834-8211.* Resembles Bailey's in feeling. All chambers centrally heated; modern plumbing, radios, and phones. Again, very good.

Concorde • *50 Great Cumberland Place, W.2.* Quiet site handy to Marble Arch and Oxford St. All 28 bedchambers with bath or shower and W.C.

Beverley Towers • *106-108 Belgrave Rd., S.W.1.* 33 rooms with radio and phone. Singles beginning at £18, doubles from £27, both plus service and taxes. Breakfast only. Cheerful.

Kingshill • *55 Westbourne Terrace, W.2 (near Paddington Station, Lancaster Gate, and Hyde Park).* Elegant street with Late Regency facades; 145 worn roomettes, all with private plumbing and TV.

Averard • *10 Lancaster Gate, W.2 ;* ☎ *(71) 723-8877.* 60 smallish rooms with private baths and showers. Singles from £24, doubles for £36. Tranquil and suitable.

Clarendon Court • *Edgware Rd., Maida Vale, W.9;* ☎ *(71) 286-8080.* 180 rooms in a redbrick Victorian structure. Pleasant neighborhood; bus stop at door. Centrally heated.

Royal Eagle • *26-30 Craven Rd., W.2; ☎ (71) 723-3262.* 85 nests only 3 blocks from Hyde Park. Full plumbing, phone, radio, and central heating. #421 a cheery aerie-for-2.

Green Park • *Half Moon St., W.1; ☎ (71) 629-7522.* 175 units across from Green Park and 15 minutes from Soho. Barber, sauna. Generally ample and well-cared for; singles and studio doubles offer more space than twins.

Ambassador • *12 Lancaster Gate, W.2; ☎ (71) 262-7361.* Small rooms with central heating, bath, radio, and phone. Dependents under 12 free if they bunk with their parents.

Barkston • *Barkston Gardens, Earls Court, S.W.5; ☎ (71) 373-7851.* 71 spacious, livable accommodations, all with TV and bath. Stiffish costs, but relaxing.

Durand • *109 Warwick Rd., S.W.5; ☎ (71) 370-4474.* 18 abodes include 8 family rooms with private showers; 4 public baths; widely varying accommodations. Nearby tennis court.

Town House • *46-48 West Cromwell Rd., S.W.5; ☎ (71) 373-4546.* Its 29 well-furnished bedchambers have drawn enthusiastic reader responses.

Sorbonne • *39 Cromwell Rd., S.W.7; ☎ (71) 589-6636.* Small, super-clean Kensington-area hostelry. 9 private bathrooms among 6 singles, 7 doubles, and 6 triples. Units fairly large.

Vanderbilt • *76 Cromwell Rd., S.W.7; ☎ (71) 584-0491.* 91 rooms near museums and shopping streets. Clean but old-fashioned; baths with hand showers. Staff efficient and hospitable.

Georgian House • *87 Gloucester Pl., W.1; ☎ (71) 935-2211.* 17 units on a noisy thoroughfare, all with bath-shower, W.C., and basin. Rich billings include a hearty English breakfast. A honey.

London Ryan • *Gwynne Pl., King's Cross Rd., W.C.1; ☎ (71) 278-2480.* 5 minutes from King's Cross Station. Family units among its 215 billets with bath, central heating, phone, radio, and TV; £48 per twin.

Lancaster Gate • *106 Lancaster Gate, W.2; ☎ (71) 402-5111.* Fronts Bayswater Road and Kensington Gardens. Theater-ticket agency in diminutive lobby. All units with phone, radio, and bath.

White House • *Albany St., N.W.1; ☎ (71) 387-1200.* Some of its 587 rooms seem Danish: narrow beds, small sitting area, pair of chairs, small TV table, tiny baths. Sound but costly.

Swallow International • *Cromwell Rd., S.W.5.* A cool complement of 425 rooms. Somewhat ill-kept.

Willett • *32 Sloane Gardens, S.W.1; ☎ (71) 730-0634.* Singles start around £20; doubles approximately £30; nice location in midcity.

Caring • *24 Craven Hill Gardens, W.2; ☎ (71) 262-8708.* Same price scale.

Rutland Court • *21-23 Draycott Pl., S.W.3 (near Sloane Square); ☎ (71) 589-9691.* Simple and comfortable; quiet, conservative mien at fine location.

Glendower • *9 Glendower Pl, S.W.7; ☎ (71) 589-4462.* Adequate but not special. Doubles seem overpriced.

Eden House • *111 Old Church St., S.W.3;* ☎ *(71) 352-3403.* 15 rooms. Better for families than singles.

Clive • *Primrose Hill Rd., N.W.3;* ☎ *(71) 586-2233.* Modernistic and amply comfortable; pleasing for its residential rather than metropolitan surroundings.

Centre • ☎ *(81) 759-2400.* Heathrow's low-slung, likeable entry. 300 rooms; 60 kitchen-equipped "flatlets" with full bath, triple-glaze windows, radio, phone, alarm clock, and adjustable air cooling.

Post House • ☎ *(81) 759-2323.* 600 rooms for do-it-yourselfers, from key pickup to lugging luggage. Youngsters to age 16 gratis when accompanied by parents.

CAMPING

Tent City is at *East Acton, W3-7DP* (*Old Oak Common Lane*; ☎ (*81*) *743-5708*) where a tented hostel is raised every summer in a spacious park that can accommodate almost 500 hardies. Well organized; a bunk costs roughly (no pun) £5. Then you might try **Crystal Palace Camping Site** (*6 miles from the center, S.E.19,* ☎ *778-7155*); a restful ride aboard the #2B bus from Victoria Station; showers and shops service both trailers and tenters at nominal fees. Operative the calendar 'round, but always jammed in summer. **Abbey Wood**, a likely alternative. Lay the foundation by popping into or calling either the **Camping Club of Great Britain & Ireland** (*11 Lower Grosvenor Pl., S.W.1*; ☎ (*71*) *828-1012*) or the **Caravan Club Ltd.** (*E. Grinstead House, E. Grinstead, E. Sussex*; ☎ *0342 26944*), and by procuring from the **British Tourist Authority** the booklet *Caravan and Camping Sites,* which includes a map and a list for England, the Channel Isles, Wales, Scotland, and Northern Ireland), and from the **Forestry Commission** (*25 Savile Row, London, W.1*) the booklet *Camping in the Forest Parks.*

SUGGESTIONS FOR STUDENTS

Three areas teem with students, both foreign and domestic. Bloomsbury is closest to the center; its magnets are the University of London, the British Museum, and the lecture halls scattered between Russell Square and Baker Street. The South Kensington colony clusters around the Imperial College, the City and Guilds College, and the Royal College of Art and Music; its key streets are Cromwell and Exhibition roads, and Queens Gate. The third is in the suburban area of Hampstead Heath.

SPECIAL LODGINGS

See "Tips on England" earlier in this chapter for comments on **dormitory** living. **Halliday Hall** at King's College (*64-67 Clapham Common*) is a good place to begin. It faces the open grassy spread of the southern facade and counts more than 200 beds and 100 private baths. Ask for Mrs. Fennell at ☎ (*71*) *351-6011* or phone directly ☎ (*81*) *673-2032.* Mrs. Fennell can also fill you in on the 250-bunk **Queen Elizabeth Hall** near *Kensington High St.* The **Nomad Travellers Club** (*168 Sussex Gardens, W.2*; ☎ *723-4287*) offers a battery of services for London bivouackers and those going beyond the city lines—including car rentals, theater bookings, employment agencies, minibus forays to Istanbul and Marrakech, and all-points air charter. Headquarters of these strategic operations are in 2 hostels and 2 hotels; the former accommodate overnighters dorm-style with no private latrines or showers from £6 a night; the latter offer bunks that trade at £8 to £13. The command post is fitted with a snack bar, "Grub Inn" mess hall, publike cocktail corner, and discotheque; a 3-month or a 1-year fee is mandatory.

Gayfere Hostel • *8 Gayfere St., S.W.1;* ☎ *(71) 222-6894.* Perfectly sited near the Houses of Parliament. This one supplies dormitory bunks or mattresses on the floor for an outlay of £6 in winter and £8 in the warm months. TV lounge; no central heating; no meals provided; kitchen and laundry available; student credentials required (age 17 to 25). If you're really stuck for a place to stay, the **Accommodation Service of the London Tourist Board** (*Forecourt at Victoria Station, near platform 15*) has been set up especially for your assistance. You can also call on the **Centrepoint Soho Emergency Center** (*57 Dean St., W.1*; maximum age here for guests is 19 years).

STUDENT AID

Pop in at the **International Students House** (*229 Great Portland St., W.1*; ☎ *(71) 636-9471*), where Miss Mary Travelyan will almost surely know the answers. She's the former adviser to overseas students at the University of London.

WHERE TO EAT

LEAST $

Upstairs/Downstairs • *Basil St. (just a few paces from Harrods).* Downstairs counter and wine bar; make your selection, pay, get a chit, retrieve your food. Delicious dish of the day about £2; other good selections at £1.50; wine by bottle or glass. Upstairs more airy; huge all-you-can-eat salad board (your choice for £2); cafeteria-style service; £3.50 for full lunch. Both open noon to 3 p.m. and 5:30 p.m. to 11; closed Sun.

San Martino • *Walton St.* Amazing lunches for £6; 3-course dinner £7. Extremely courteous, sprightly service. Spaghetti Martino served in a paper bag with seafood additives. Highly recommended. Closed Sun.

Granary • *39 Albermarle St., W.1.* Serve-yourself counter-style. At least a half dozen types of quiches. Wonderful midday stop. Open till 7 p.m.; closes Sat. 2:30 p.m. and all day Sun.

Hungry Horse • *196 Fulham Rd., S.W.10.* Spirited stable of fun. Generous and delicious roast beef dinner approximately £10—and that's nearly the most expensive choice on the menu.

Tandoori • *153 Fulham Rd., S.W.3;* ☎ *589-7617 or 37A Curzon St., W.1;* ☎ *629-0600.* Named for the chicken dish it prepares fantastically by baking it in an Indian oven that produces extremely dry high temperatures. Or try Chicken Taeki, bathed in a barbecue sauce. Excellent drinks. Extremely reasonable prices.

Rowley's • *113 Jermyn St., W.1;* ☎ *930-2707 Branch: 38 Beauchamp Place, S.W.3;* ☎ *589-4856.* Great, provided you enjoy its lone specialty—grilled entrecote in Cafe de Paris sauce, served with French fries, salad, a rich dessert, and wine poured from magnums (charge depends on how much you drink). Feast for 2 will absorb £19.

Troubador • *265 Old Brompton Rd. (south of Earl's Court Square), S.W.5.* Popular with resident French. "American" menu (omelettes, steaks, spaghetti, stuffed peppers, dew-fresh green salads, bread, and butter). Not one combination totaled more than £8. Good value.

Old Chesterfield • *Shepherd St., W.1;* ☎ *493-9640.* Slightly shabby; crab-filled avocado ($6.50) and cold ham with salad ($7), tasty but skimpily proportioned. Open Mon. to Sat. from noon to 2:20 and 6:30 to 10:15 p.m.

Pimlico's Bistro • *22 Charlwood St., S.W.1 (near Dolphin Square);* ☎ *828-3303.* Pert; pleasing in price. Ample menu with imagination. Superb minestrone and barbecued spareribs; good service. Different and engaging.

La Cucaracha • *12-13 Greek St.;* ☎ *734-2253.* Soho's answer to South of the Border. Delicious margaritas are a great accompaniment to the mariachi band. Lunch and dinner Mon. through Fri.; evenings-only Sat.; closed Sun.

Foxtrot Oscar • *79 Hospital Rd., S.W.3;* ☎ *352-7179.* An intimate English tavern. Try the salmon for a treat. First-rate quality and a splendid value. Name is aviation parlance for the initials F.O.—just jovial impudence.

The Widow Applebaum's • *46 S. Molton St. (on a pedestrian mall off Oxford St.).* Delicatessen with pastrami, corned (salt) beef, and similar cold-cut staples at about £3 per sandwich.

Gatsby's • *Just across from The Widow.* Not so kosher, but conventional light meals substantial, prices low, and atmosphere subtle. In the same house where William Blake resided (he often noshed with Applebaum).

Creperie • *Down the mall and in an alley on the same side as The Widow A's.* Enormous selection of buckwheat crepes. Apple-and-calvados was a petit package of pure culinary bliss. Other items available but stick to lowcost house specialties.

Le Reve • *330 King's Rd., S.W.3;* ☎ *352-8572.* Chelsea perch for swingers on a budget. Most cuisine born on other side of the Channel; didn't travel too well.

Le Chef • *41 Connaught St., W.2;* ☎ *262-5945.* Also does it the French way. Piped soft music; plate-of-the-day and a reliable open wine came to $16; reasonable for this high-rent Bayswater district.

Fanny's Bistro • *51 Maddox St., W.1.* Intimate rewarding choice in tranquil setting; invites hand-holding. Risotto with mushrooms, trout, and chicken in cream sauce are best.

Grumbles • *35 Churton St., S.W.1 (off Vauxhall Bridge Rd., 7 blocks from the Tate Gallery);* ☎ *834-0149.* Semi-suburban, so generally tourist-free; $16 suppers. Wide selection; indifferent preparation at times. Good service. Shuttered on Sun.

The Museum Tavern • *49 Great Russell St., W.C.1 (opposite the British Museum).* Collects sandwich-hungry culture-vultures. Cut-price lunches in an animated atmosphere. Good beer.

Romano Santi • *50 Greek St., W.1 (near Soho Sq.).* Touch of the Tiber in decor—but look at the address. Skillet work mainly "Continental"—which means, of course, Frenchish. Try the fish. Lunch in £7 range; fixed-price plates slightly less. Amiable, but geographically mixed up.

Cafe Italien • *19 Charlotte St., W.1;* ☎ *636-4174.* Similar style cuisine with an added touch of grace in the execution; 1930-ish mood. Wine list backing the menu diptych, a fascinating journey to yesteryear's vintages.

Green Parrot • *146 Southampton Row, W.C.1 (in the Russell Sq. environs).* Plain, quiet, red-and-white checkered-tablecloth mien. Low-cost 3-course meals. About £8 à la carte. Bar.

Hard Rock Cafe • *150 Old Park Lane, W.1;* ☎ *629-0382.* A smash-hit hangout for the young, but hardly for the impoverished. Loud taped music; burgers; American beers; grilled steaks; chili; hot fudge sundaes; apple pie à la mode. Dinner for 2 with house wine about £20, which makes it one of the world's more expensive hamburger joints. The built-in chic bumps up the price tags. Open noon till after midnight daily.

Planet Hollywood • *Trocadero Centre, near Leicester Square.* "Square" is not the operative word at this Piccadilly headquarters for mood and food. The explosive music decimates the decibel system. Outside you are told you'll have to wait in line—a hype because the flow is swift. Inside, you are pawed over by "smile police" in baseball caps who slaver over you with unctuous concern. Above, movie snippets are projected onto the silver screens to keep you entertained at every possible level. In that din of dizzy dingdongs, a hamburger will cost ten big bucks.

HEALTH FOOD

Cranks • *Marshall St., near Regent St.* One of the finest vegetarian establishments found anywhere. Buffet service with selection of compost-grown veggies, salads, soups, and savories; unrefined, nonchemical ingredients; live yogurts and yogurt drinks; juice bar; adjoining takeaway shop. Open Mon. to Fri. 10 a.m. to 5 p.m. and to 4 p.m. on Sat.

Dairy Centre • *Nearby on North Row.* Sells the obvious. It is in partnership with the adjacent **Eden Wine Bar**. Excellent selections in both; sandwiches as big as dinner plates and good.

FISH-AND-CHIPS

This is one of the best budget meals going. Chips, as you probably know, is the anglicism for lightly fried potatoes, sometimes in the form of french fries and occasionally appearing as hash browns. Hundreds of counters dot the townscape, chiefly in working districts where the clients often walk away from the stalls bearing cones of wax paper filled with these ingredients and topped with tartar sauce or ketchup. The better kiosks feature haddock, plaice, cod, and the poor cousins of sole. Cheaper dens often utilize dogfish, skate, and shavings of ray. Here are a few choices.

The Rock and Sole Plaice • *47 Endell St., W.C.2.* Obviously puts its menu into its title. If you are in the Covent Garden area, it is handy and agreeable.

Sweetings • *39 Queen Victoria St., E.C.4.* Realizes that even habitues of the banking district still must economize occasionally. It is amusing to see sartorially perfect executives with copies of the Financial Times daintily digesting their chippies in absolute aplomb. Evidently, this "joint" is a bit more upmarket than most.

Upper Street Fish Shop • *324 Upper St., N.1.* Handy to the antique grazing lands of Islington and Camden Passage. An ideal excursion: Browse among the whatnot stalls on Saturday morning and take lunch here.

Sea Shell • *49-51 Lisson Grove, N.W.1.* Offers top-quality sole from the Dover coast as well as more modest wigglers. The variety is in full flood at every meal. Don't miss the fish cakes.

WEST INDIAN

Afric-Carib • *1 Stroud Green Rd.; ☎ 263-7440.* A low-down (cellar), low-cost haven for (chiefly) Nigerian cookery. It's near Finsbury Park and worth the sampling.

Calabash • *Africa Centre, 38 King St.;* ☎ *836-1976.* In the exciting Covent Garden complex. Even the beer and wine come from Africa.

Brixtonian • *11 Dorrell Place;* ☎ *978-8870.* Has a bar that is the talk of Brixton, if not all of London. Expect to pay about £20 for a fixed-price meal. Though costly, it will be memorable.

CHAINS

Strand Hotels group • *Regent Palace, Strand Palace, and Cumberland.* Offers "Carveries"; all you can eat for perhaps £12. After the appetizer, tuck into at least 6 choice hot or cold roasts. Appetizing presentation; coffee included. Excellent value.

ORIENTAL

Mandarin • *197C Kensington High St., W.8;* ☎ *937-5854.* For authentic Malaysian-Chinese cooking, generally more piquant than Cantonese fare. Marvelous Laksa soup, practically a meal in itself.

Poons' & Co. • *27 Lisle St., W.C.2;* ☎ *437-1528.* Forthright and simple in Soho's China row. Generally superb; wonton soup tasted as if meat filling had been smoked. House delicacies: tangy wind-dried duck, sausage, and beef. Place itself is a dump, but people kind, selection vast, prices low, and quality high.

Tokyo • *U Swallow St., W.1.* Presents beef teriyaki, shrimp Tempura, warmed sake, and perfectly gracious Oriental courtesy. No wonder 95% of the clientele is from Japan. Splendid.

Dumpling Inn • *15A Gerrard St., W.1;* ☎ *437-2567.* In heart of Soho's Chinatown. No bigger than a Peking dumpling itself: 7 tables plus a microcounter. Black and white murals of Venice, that famous capital of the Orient.

Gallery Rendezvous • *53-55 Beak St., W.1;* ☎ *734-0445.* A posher pagoda near Golden Sq., under the same ownership. Outstanding gastronomy.

Mei May • *22-24 Rupert St.;* ☎ *437-8742.* In the theater district; a cheapy with excellent kitchening. Among some 153 items on the menu are ducks' web (bland), scallops in butter (pure yum-yum), Mandarin rice gruel (uncommon offering in the Occident), and chicken's blood curd (an acquired taste you might never acquire).

ITALIAN

Portofino • *Camden Passage, the antique district.* A favorite. Excellent cuisine, reasonable prices, fun atmosphere. Remote-from-midcity location but fine if you are antique hunting.

Pasta Prego • *100 Kew Rd. and la Beauchamp Pl.* Creates marvelous, light, fresh farinaceous platters for about $4 per serving. About a dozen choices. The Beauchamp Place-mats are more inviting than Kew-pads.

New Maple Grill • *Victoria Station area–304 Vauxhall Bridge Rd., S.W.1* and the next-door **Continental**. Both disappointing.

Trattoria del Fungo • *Directly across from the Victoria Station.* Much more satisfactory, especially splendid minestrone.

Alvaro Pizza E Pasta • *39 Charing Cross Rd., W.C.2; 73 Kings Rd., S.W.3; and at Haymarket.* All superb entries.

Pizzaland • *206 Earls Court Rd., S.W. 5.* Pizza in 18 reasonably priced varieties. Pastas, too.

Buon Appetito • *23 Conduit St., W.1.* Clean, simple, and inexpensive.

SCANDINAVIAN

Hungry Viking • *44 Ossington St.* Charming candlelit nookery. Tempting cold buffet table. About £11 for all you can put away.

Norway Food Centre • *166 Brompton Rd..* Performs similarly; more expansive surroundings.

RUSSIAN

Borshtch 'N' Tears • *46 Beauchamp Pl., S.W.3.* Chicken Kiev and kulibiak (salmon in baked pastry) are recommendable. The area is fun. Figure on £10 per head.

ICE CREAM

Dayvilles • *Parlors dot the town.* Delightfully mellow dairy products.

Bernigra • *59 Tottenham Ct. Rd., near the Goodge station.* 16 prize-winning flavors. A cone outside costs half as much as in restaurant, which by the way, is only passable.

SNACKS

Pasta Mania • *27 Wardour St., W. 1.* It's all you can pasta for £3—if you're voracious for something farinaceous.

Wimpy • Though not a favorite, this is the most mammoth restaurateur in the U.K.; 306 shops in London and as many nationwide. Routine in every way, as are the American counterparts in this global bunfest.

AUTHOR'S OBSERVATION

Standup counter inside Woolworth's entrance sells hot meat-filled pastries, franks, and other light bites very cheaply. Good value, too.

PUBS

George • *77 Borough High St., S.E.1 (south of London Bridge Rd.).* A South Bank landmark close to the original Globe Theatre. Wooden tables, benches, and armchairs. Menu spotlighting sausage and mash, fried onions, baked potatoes, meat pies, and sandwiches. One of the best, especially if you catch one of the Sat. summer Shakespearean productions held in the courtyard.

Dickens Inn • *St. Katherine's Way (near the Tower of London).* Quay area stirs merrily with life aboard several Thames barges and scores of recreation boats. Restaurant upstairs in ancient warehouse moved on wheels to this colorful site.

Captain's Cabin • *About a 100 yards away.* Excellent salads and light refreshments.

Beefeater • *Also neighboring.* Chiefly for dining and a touristic cabaret evening.

Ship • *116 Wardour St., W.1.* Anonymous in daylight; go about midevening. Who's-Hot clientele of city's top musicians on their breaks from nearby music halls. Drink and listen; don't eat.

Admiral Codrington • *17 Mossop St., S.W.3.* Busy with Guards officers, debs, journalists; copper-topped bar; deft publicans drawing the pints. Among the best pub food in London.

19 Restaurant • A next-door neighbor and tip-top alternate.

Prospect of Whitby • *57 Wapping Wall, E.1.* Thames-side bedlam. Melange of collegians and longshoremen. Nondescript fittings; river view. So-so food. Bring your lustiest limericks for the evensong. Brassy and fun.

George and Vulture • *3 Castle Ct., E.C.3.* Rough-and-ready chophouse, claims to be oldest tavern (A.D. 1175). Open grill. Stockbrokers joust for seats during lunch-only sitting. Medium prices for good, no-nonsense cookery. Go before 1 p.m. or after 1:45 p.m.

Spaniards Inn • *1 Spaniards Rd., N.W.3.* THE Hampstead Heath rendezvous for pub dining. Bar chatter with genial gentry on either side of counter. Mahogany-rich trappings. Amiable.

Sherlock Holmes • *10 Northumberland St., W.C.2.* Charing Cross chancellery for Conan Doyle doters. Best known of Whitbread Brewery's so-called museum taverns. Among the downstairs memorabilia: "pawprints" of the "Hound of the Baskervilles" and "Lestrade's" handcuffs; upstairs dining room backed by glassed-off "replica" of the famous sleuth's living room at "221B Baker St."

Dirty Dick's • *202-204 Bishopsgate, E.C.2 (east of the Bank of England).* Cobwebs and sawdust. The "squalor" took its cue from Nathaniel Bentley, 18th-century dandy whose betrothed died on their engagement day and resolved, in her memory, to leave everything untouched, even by the whisk of a broom. His vow has been all too well observed.

Hoop and Grapes • *47 Aldgate High St., E.C.3 (in the Aldgate area).* Claims to be the capital's oldest pub (not "tavern," to which George and Vulture lays title). Substantial lunches and dinners in the £8 range. Impressive anachronism.

Anchor • *1 Bankside, S.E.1 (near Shakespeare memorial in Southwark).* Pleasant, albeit remote, riverside setting once beckoned smugglers. Bar animated; noontime fare about £5; dinners £8 or so; operative till 10 p.m. Can be fun; area eerily deserted on weekends.

Bull and Bush • *North End Way, N.W.3.* Sends Keats and Shelley devotees into orbit.

Grenadier • *18 Wilton Row, S.W.1.* Trades on rumors duke of Wellington sipped here during Napoleonic Wars, and that famous grenadier was plugged to death for cheating at cards.

Shakespeare's Head • *Carnaby St., W.1.* Fire-warmed hearth in winter; cream-laced cookery for Falstaffian prices. Seafood the main calling.

Flask • *77 Highgate West Hill, N.6.* Brought the first malt and hops to Hampstead Wells.

Henekey's • *22 High Holborn, W.C.* A long bar terminating in a triangular fireplace.

Albert • *52 Victoria St., S.W.1.* An all-you-can-eat, fixed-price main course plus an array of 8 starters, rich "puds" (desserts) and side dishes. Also offers an English breakfast that won't bankrupt the budget—juices, cereals, eggs, bacon, sausages ("bangers" in English parlance), and mushrooms for about £4.

Ye Olde Cheshire Cheese • *145 Fleet St., E.C.4.* Famous and, alas, touristic. Enshrines the scarred table over which Samuel Johnson and Boswell conducted celebrated dialogues. Period knick-knackery. Roasts, meat pies, and puddings; routine salads; £9.50 for average meals.

Pub-Crawler's Spree • Arranged in no particular order (which is how you'll probably feel at the end of this jaunt): **Angel** (*101 Bermondsey Wall, East Rotherhithe*), a high-priced hideaway in Bermondsey with historical pretensions; **The Nag's Head** (*10 James St., W.C.2*), a Covent Garden inn that is marginally "in" with the theatrical set; **Salisbury** (*90 St. Martin's Lane, W.C.2*), in which Dylan Thomas often orated; **Castle** (*34 Cowcross St., E.C.1*), where the gooseberries are plucked from the neighboring central markets off Farringdon Rd.; **The Square Rigger** (*King William St., E.C.4*), another Southwark bulwark with whaling-ship motif; **King's Head and Eight Bells** (*50 Cheyne Walk, S.W.3*), a Chelsea riverboat anchored near the Albert Bridge; **Jack Straw's Castle** (*North End Way, Hampstead, N.W.3*), an attractively restored retreat across Golders Hill Park from Leg of Mutton Pond; and **The Royal Oak** (*73 St. James Lane, N.10*), a long putt from the Highgate Golf Course.

WINE BARS

Gradually these are beginning to supplant the pubs of yore—a welcome gesture since pubs have lost so much of their ancient flavor. These colorful oases serve quiches, goulash, cold meats, pâtés and cheeses, generally in the range of $5 per platter or less. You choose from tiers of buffet items attractively arranged and pay for your sins individually. Since the eye-appeal is so intense—if you're like me—you'll usually select far too much on the first go-round. An overwhelming variety of wine is on hand from £1.25 per glass; fortified pressings also on tap. In most cases they function from 11:30 a.m. till 3 p.m. and 5:30 p.m. till 11 p.m.; some remain open later and on Sun.

The Wine Bar • *Villiers St., W.C. 2.* Literally a hole in the wall. Some candlelit tables in deep cozy gloom. Snatch one first, then choose meal from the excellent spread near entrance. Delightful and different at about £8 for 2, including palatable wine.

Ebury • *139 Ebury St., S.W.1.* Occupies ground floor of a converted early Victorian house. Excellent salads. Nice feature: tables can be reserved.

Cork & Bottle • *44-46 Cranbourn St., W.C.2.* Entry through garden gate to 2 adjoining cellars. A good candidate for a pretheater nip. In same chain with **Shampers**. *4 Kingly St., W.1*; and **Bubbles** *41 N. Audley St., W.1*, All with fabulous food displays; piped music; house wine about £1.50 per glass.

The Penguin • *7 Cheval Place, S.W.7.* Popular but rather austere. Young crowd goes.

Fino's Wine Cellar • *123 Mount St., W.1.* Very "in" with the advertising world.

Wilfred • This is a wine barge; she's moored twixt Waterloo and Blackfriars bridges. Galley service about $12 for grub and $6 for grog.

AUTHOR'S OBSERVATION

Covent Garden offers a selection of inexpensive and jolly dining experiences in its Central Market Building. Among them: a Courage pub, Peelers English-style brasserie, a Danwich sandwich shop, a Breton creperie, and a wine bar. Open Sun., too.

MORE $$

Punter's Pie • *183 Lavender Hill.* Draws mobs to its Battersea portals. The prices for such quality are the reason why: a bottle of wine and four 2-course meals came to about £40. Try the Fish Pie as a change from the more frequently ordered Shepherd's Pie (which was also good).

The English House • *3 Milner St., S.W.3.* Very highly decorated in Victoriana; could be suffocating to some, prissy to others, lovely to yet another taste dimension. Historic English cuisine. A masterpiece in its way. Closed Sun.

Poissonnerie de l'Avenue • *82 Sloane Ave, W.3.* A king among Europe's seafood restaurants; surprisingly reasonable prices. Club-like with chummy counter service and, of course, numerous tables. Getting a seat is a problem; lunchtime is easier than evening.

La Chanterelle • *119 Old Brompton Rd., S.W.7; ☎ 373-5522.* Ritzy corner location yet fair in price. Couple of tables inside cozy hedgerow; warm interior with polished wood, beveled glass, wine racks in long narrow room; creative new dishes plus staples; fixed price menu at £9. Refined, intimate, and fun.

Au Jardin des Gourmets • *5 Greek St., W.1; ☎ 437-1816.* Known to the inner circle of the theatrical world. Outstanding French cookery. Superior wines. Tab with wine about £16 per person.

D'Artagnan • *19 Blandford St., W.1H.; ☎ 935-1023.* Bills itself as a producer of "la cuisine bourgeoise." Indeed, the common man eats well (judging from the menu): *Terrine chaud de Boudroie et d'Homard Thermidor, Petits Pacquets de Sole aux Fonds d'Artichauts,* or roast saddle of venison with beets and hazelnuts. Wonderful choices by the chef-patron who switched from psychology, medicine, and computer science to skilletry.

Tiddy Dols Eating House • *2 Hertford St., W.1 (in Shepherd Market); ☎ 499-2357.* Named after a legendary gingerbread man; 9 contiguous Mayfair houses with several salons, bars, and a minstrels' gallery. Live entertainment 7 to 11 p.m., dancing 11 p.m. to 3 a.m. Highly promoted renditions of traditional English dishes, possibly as corny as Iowa in July.

Daphne's • *112 Draycott Ave., S.W.3; ☎ 589-4257.* Bountiful French fare; escargots, entrecote, veal, and souffles are staples; fish platters also available. Pink napery and theatrical prints on walls. Evenings only.

Boucha's • *3 North End Parade.* One of the most reliable soldiers of the Earl's Court district. It's also a lot of fun and the food choices are amusingly eccentric. Different.

Smollensky's Balloon • *1 Dover St., W1X; ☎ 491-1199.* Also quirky in a fun-loving way, ideal for tavern types of the late 20th century. While it is close to the Ritz, the prices aren't. One big advantage: it's open 7 days a week.

Brinkley's • *47 Hollywood Rd., S.W.10; ☎ 351-1683.* Emerging area of smart boutiques, wine and cheese bars; crowd of Sloane Rangers—the See-And-Be-Seen Set; attractive long room in 3 sectors; summer garden. If you are interested in the food, you've missed the point. **Jake's**, a few doors away, is simpler; cuisine's better. Both about £16 per person with wine.

Sheekey's • *28-31 St. Martin's Court, W.C.2.* Perfect for theatergoers. Opens early and service until 10:45 p.m. Familial air. Try steamed turbot (this life will offer none better).

White Tower • *1 Percy St., W.1.* North-of-Soho Greek standby. Two floors (and sometimes a 3rd) eternally busy. Superb service. Wonderful dolmades, stuffed eggplant, moussaka, and other authentic Levantine delights.

NIGHTLIFE

Either make the pub rounds for casual cheer during the early evening, or visit the jazz joints after midnight. In summer, **Trafalgar Square** frequently is alive with international folk dancing and singing of commendable quality. (Other nations or regions send their performing groups on the road at this time to spur tourism to their own regions.) It's all free, of course.

Scores of the membership clubs offer extremely attractive dining, wining, and dancing facilities—but the prices can be murderous. These establishments are organized on a "private" basis to skirt the liquor laws. British citizens must pay nominal annual "dues" of perhaps £1 to £5, but overseas travelers with valid foreign passports are often issued a special card, which admits them free or at a reduced charge. Some levy no initiation fees, but recoup the difference through other guises.

Limelight • *136 Shaftsbury Ave., W.1.* Has a church fixation, born-again night hawks in the congregation, and resurrection fever. Possibly a bit weird, but for those who like the unheavenly sounds it's the gospel tonight. The £7 entry fee might make nondisciples feel like telling St. Peter at the gate to go elsewhere.

Ronnie Scott's Jazz Club • *47 Frith St., W.1.* In uppercase Soho. Since entrance is also pretty stiff, you'll drop around £8 before you taste your first drink. Subterranean chamber jammed with debs and celebs; steaks, chops, and Italian specialties; light suppers also available. The resident musicians, including your host, improvise; outsiders sometimes headline the show; open until 3 a.m.

Barbarella • *428 Fulham Rd., S.W.6 and 43 Thurloe St., S.W.7.* Features Italian decor, good music, and a wide variety of drinks. The mood will absorb about £30 per twosome for a nightful. More luxurious than the price suggests.

Tiberio • *22 Queen St., W.1.* Offers Italian cookery and decor; entrance through a below-stairs tiled bar to the gracious vaulted dining room. Very fine skillet work and service to match; lunch from noon to 3 p.m.; dinner from 7 p.m. to 2 a.m.; supper dancing from 11:30 p.m. to 2 a.m. daily; closed Sun. A hot little swinger, but very expensive.

Palookaville • *13a St. James St., W.C.2,* and **Prohibition**. *9 Hanover St., W.1.* Both come on with a speakeasiness that combines jazz with inexpensive booze (which was not mixed in a local bathtub).

Elysee • *13 Percy St., off Tottenham Court Rd., W.1; ☎ 636-4804.* A happy corner-of-Athens-in-London. Enormously amusing when it gets rolling (late); merry Greek patronage. Small ground floor bar in front; about 15 tables and dance floor in back; 2 musicians, plus small cabaret (regional singers). Capping the evening is Proprietor George's balancing act, where up to 7 water glasses are stacked on his head while he scrambles on and off a table in hilarious acrobathos. Only Greek à la carte choices as foodstuffs. Summer roof garden for nearly 100 munchers, some of whom spontaneously leap up to provide impromptu entertainment. Noisy, cheerful, and decidedly brash—but good fun if you hit it right. Operative noon to 3 p.m. for lunch and 6:30 p.m. to 1 a.m. for dinner.

DISCOTHEQUES

Notorious for their flash-in-the-pan success, here are the current hotspots.

Hippodrome • *Charing Cross Rd. and Cranborn St., W.C.2.* Massive and impressive in its state-of-the-artful electronics, lasers, hydraulics, and smoke machines. Different music nightly; Gay day is Monday.

Electric Ballroom • *184 Camden High St., N.W.1.* Plugs in cable and live music, jazz, and all manner of funky fun.

St. Moritz Club • *159 Wardour St., W.1.* Combines fondue and frolic. Popular among younger French, Swiss, and Germans; 2 bars dispensing until 3 a.m.; your Raclette, cheese fondue, or Fondue Bourguignonne served at barrel-top tables; ceilings so low that you'll have to limbo in and out. While the undistinguished band is spelled by Teutonic jukebox hits, the beat is still Hometown, U.S.A. Nonmembers pay a minimum of perhaps £2 when they show their passports; regulars must shell out a small fee every 6 months. Go late-ish.

Finally, a few voguish and thus more volatile contenders: The **Speakeasy** (*48 Margaret St.*) playing host for groups, offers very good disks and tapes. **Tiffany's** (*22 Shaftesbury Ave., W.1*) is popular, too. You can have breakfast at this Tiffany's come 11 p.m. for £4 or so. Next comes the **Raffles** (*287 King's Rd.*) with a library complex, open hearth with crackling fires, and Old English decor. Ask about temporary membership if entry becomes difficult. **Samantha's** (*3 New Burlington St.*) is a typical scene for cooling it. Nicely, too. Admission £3.

GAMBLING

Law requires visitors to register 48 hours in advance at the clubs where they wish to gamble.

Victoria Sporting Club • *150-162 Edgware Rd., W.2.* The best choice, might be termed "a gambling factory." It is the biggest establishment of its type in the British Isles or Europe. First-floor tables for dice, blackjack, roulette, chemin de fer, and 7-card stud poker; 2nd-floor array of poker, bridge, gin rummy, backgammon, and *kaluki* (13-card rummy); 2 one-armed bandits; restaurant service from lunch to breakfast. Not chic or elegant—but you can win or lose as little as you please and nobody will give a hoot. In addition, you won't be clipped—a threat in many other places that accept nickel-and-dime wagers. The casino in the cellar of the **Ritz Hotel** is very different indeed. It evokes a French salon dignity aided by well-dressed attendants and lovely female croupiers in burgundy velvet gowns. It asks a mere £25 for a year's membership—quite a low token fee for such high-class gaming. Low minimum bets. It's, well . . . the Ritz.

Cafe des Artistes • *266 Fulham Rd., S.W. 10.* Corners some of Chelsea's more excitable elements. Coal-chute style entrance near Redcliff Gardens; coffee bar; 2 dance floors; alcove with tables, couches, and candlelight; miserable ventilation; soft drinks only; hand-stamped entry fee at about £2.

Marquee Club • *90 Wardour St., W.1.* Managed by the same London promoters who first pushed the Rolling Stones; bulging with revelers; too dense to dance, but many try it; no alcohol; modest cover charge; 7:30 p.m. onward. An amusing hunting ground for the younger set.

WHAT TO SEE AND DO

SHAKESPEARE'S GLOBE THEATRE

This year's highly deserving recipient of the **Fielding Travel Award**. It is the realization of a lifelong dream nurtured by the distinguished thespian Sam Wanamaker. The American Actor-Director searched out the Thamesside site of the Globe of 1599 and amiably returned the wraith of The Bard to the original boards. The complex is faithfully—and delightfully—Elizabethan. Productions are presented largely as they were during Shakespeare's lifetime, but with the benefit of modern technology in the mounting of the shows. You won't find such theatre anywhere else in the world, and the Wanamaker effort brilliantly adds to the cavalcade of knowledge and appreciation of the brightest hours for the English language.

Tickets available at theatrical agencies or directly through Shakespeare's Globe, *1 Bear Gardens, Bankside, Liberty-of-the-Clink, Southwark, London*; ☎ *071-6200202*; FAX: *071-9287968*. Handy underground stations are *Mansion House* or *London Bridge*.

For a basic general survey, the **Original London Transport Sightseeing Tour** offers the most for the least. This 2-hour, 20-mile bus excursion glides past 28 of the capital's most famous landmarks, including Cleopatra's Needle, Trafalgar Square, Marble Arch, Hyde Park, Piccadilly Circus, and Westminster Abbey. High-season departures are made from Marble Arch, Victoria Underground Station, Baker St. Station, and Piccadilly Circus almost hourly from 10 a.m. to 9 p.m.; in winter they cease at 4 p.m.

WALKING TOURS

With only a modest expenditure of energy and practically no money, you can see most of the London sightseeing scene through organized walking tours; these cover not only the major targets but the minor ones, the offbeat ones, and the droll. Most take about 90 minutes and cost in the neighborhood of £4 for the expert guide service. A pub tour or something of that sort would not include the price of drinks. Here's a sampler of some of the popular circuits: "In the Footsteps of Sherlock Holmes," "1660s: Great Fire and Great Plague," "Ghosts of the City," "SPQR—Roman Londinium," "1888: East End Murders—Jack the Ripper," "Legal and Illegal London—Inns of Court," "A Journey Through Tudor London." Incidentally, for the pub tour, children under 14 are not admitted to these establishments, those between 14 and 15 must be accompanied by an adult, and no one under 18 may imbibe. You can make your selection from any of the following companies with confidence: Streets of London (☎ *81-346-9255*), City Walks (☎ *71-7006931*) and London Walks (☎ *71-6243948*). There's also a Hampstead specialist who can show you residences of artists, writers, and celebrities in this attractive residential district; phone Footloose in London, ☎ *435-0259*.

The **River Thames** makes its way through the port, 3000 acres of wharves and docks. The "City" (*Wall Street*), Westminster (*Capitol Hill*), the West End (*Times Square and Fifth Avenue*), Soho and Chelsea (*Greenwich Village*), Mayfair (*Park Avenue*), and many other districts split the metropolis into its components. Good fun is the 50-minute **boat ride** from Westminster Pier, Tower of London, or Charing Cross to lovely outlying nautical **Greenwich**, to the **Docklands** or to the **Thames Barrier** (☎ *71-7304812*). These operate at 20-minute intervals year-round and the round-trip prices are about £5 for adults and £3 for children. You can board and inspect the original **Cutty Sark** (in drydock), visit the **Gypsy Moth**, idle through the charming streets—and if you've packed a picnic, take your lunch beside the viewful Wolfe Statue in **Greenwich Park** (designed by Charles II). Or you can straddle the

Greenwich Meridian, which bisects the path a few yards north of the gates to the seventeenth-century **Royal Observatory**. After lunch (almost everything is within walking distance), take in the **National Maritime Museum**. At your option, you can return to London on the deck of a riverboat or on a double-decker bus. A splendid excursion; highest recommendation.

Mudlarking. The Thames provides other pastimes for those with boots—scavenging for treasure! If you've got Wellingtons, low tide is the time to burrow (especially at inward curves) for coins, battle relics, marine artifacts, and whatnots from the ages. Best locations are on the south bank near London Bridge and downstream of Vauxhall, Blackfriars, and Kew Bridges. The Port Authority (☎ *71-476-6900*) can tell you the times of ebb and flow.

Windsor Castle. Mentioned under our earlier listing for "Hampton Court"; try not to miss it.

Changing of the Guard. Unfortunately the famous ceremony no longer takes place daily at Buckingham Palace at 11:30 a.m. The Undersecretary of the Army states that for an uncertain period due to the U.K. economy the event will occur every other day. But it's still a daily ceremony for the Horse Guards. You can try to see them by going about halfway down Whitehall (*the Government-building-lined street just south of Trafalgar Square*) at 11 a.m. on weekdays, or an hour earlier on Sunday.

Buckingham Palace itself has become a revenue reaper. This is the official royal residence of Queen Elizabeth II, and the royal flag flies above the roof when the queen is at home. In August and September (when she's away), the 600-room landmark will admit up to 7,000 visitors a day, but not, of course, into the private apartments. While the salons are only somewhat more ornate than the lobbies of some continental hotels, the Picture Gallery is stunning. Tour agents have snatched up their allotments of tickets for years ahead but you can still purchase one (or a maximum of four) at a booth in nearby St. James's Park. The price is £8 per adult with reductions for the young and the elderly. The line (*queue, that is*) will be forming along The Mall. Other information can be obtained by telephoning (☎ *071-9304832.*)

Westminster Abbey (*Parliament Sq.*) is past the nine-century mark. Within its marble floors and crypts rest so many historical figures that it is perhaps the English-speaking world's most famous shrine. It is open daily except during special services; the closing time of the main structure usually extends from 6 p.m. to 8 p.m. on Wed. from Mar. to Oct.; there's a small gate rate for visiting the **Royal Chapels**; conducted tour around $5. The "Poet's Corner" is a favorite of most travelers.

The **Houses of Commons and Lords** are across the street in the Palace of Westminster, the seat of Parliament. Look to the towers to see if they are in session; a flag by day and a light by night (above Big Ben) are the signals. Saturday is visitors' day. To witness a debate from the Strangers' Galleries of either House daily, wait at St. Stephen's Entrance for admission.

The **Tate Gallery** (*Millbank, S.W.1*) and the **National Gallery** (*Trafalgar Sq., W.C.2*) hold the nation's finest art treasures. The former, near Vauxhall Bridge, excites young moderns more than it does traditionalists. Its collection of English painters from the 17th to the 20th centuries is supplemented by Continentals (Seurat, Van Gogh, Rouault, Picasso, Chagall, Renoir, and Braque), as well as by an assortment of Americans (Pollack and de Kooning, among others). The trove of Turners (the bequest contains 300 oils and an evergreen variegation of 19,000 watercolors) resides in the adjoining Thames-side **Clore Gallery**, which is ideal for the artist who loved that river so mightily. Henry Moore's doughnut sculptures, plus his famed London Blitz sketchings, also draw attention. The National Gallery displays priceless gems of every major European school. El Greco's "Agony in the Garden," Gainsborough's "The Painter's Daughters," Holbein's "The Ambassadors," Da Vinci's "The Madonna of the Rocks," Michelangelo's "The Entombment," Rubens' "The Judgment of Paris," and Titian's "Bacchus and Ariadne"—these are only a few examples. You may browse from 10 a.m. to 6 p.m. daily, except Sun., when the opening hour is 2 p.m. The **Wallace Collection** (*Manchester Sq. near Oxford St.*), while less widely known, is also extraordinarily fine.

The **British Museum** (*Great Russell St., W.C.1*) is so massive that it challenges you to spend at least 3 or 4 days among its fabulous archaeological, historical, and literary wealth. Entrance from 10 a.m. to 5 p.m. Mon.-Sat. and 2:30 p.m. to 6 p.m. on Sun. Those in a hurry usually beeline for the Elgin Marbles, the Rosetta Stone, the Magna Carta, and the Egyptian Sphinxes; a new 7-gallery basement has been unearthed for classical sculpture; the reading room that spawned part of Karl Marx's utopian works is also popular for a peek. The **Victoria and Albert Museum** (*Cromwell Rd., S.W.7*) offers a melange of works from various periods and cultures, Oriental being among the more noteworthy of the latter. The gallery for the famous Medieval Treasury (near the main entrance) has been refurbished and is superb. It has similar hours to the B.M. Get off at the S. Kensington underground station. The **Museum of London** begins with the Roman occupation of Londinium and traces the city's genealogy up to the era of pop stars and the BBC. Entrance is free. The new **Design Museum** in the Docklands is fresh, petulant, and one of Britain's more joyful blends of idolatry and iconoclasm. It's possibly the most evocative peek at industry and culture to be experienced under one English roof.

Barbican Centre is London's costly arts complex. The **London Symphony** calls it home. While the **Royal Shakespeare Theatre** took to the boards here, the new focus is on the previously mentioned **Globe Theatre** at Southwark. There are galleries, 3 cinemas, exhibition halls, a library, 2 restaurants, conference rooms, an artificial lake, and even a rooftop greenhouse with full-grown trees. On Aldersgate Street, opposite the Barbican Underground, the **Royal Britain** permanent exhibit has opened recently. It traces the royal family in their finest (and worst) hours of history. Entrance: £5.

St. Paul's Cathedral crowns Ludgate Hill (and London's landscape) as Sir Christopher Wren's finest architectural feat. Most wanderers prefer the brilliant dome to the chilly nave; Wren, Wellington, and Nelson are among the greats buried in the Crypt. Open 8 a.m. to 6 p.m. from Easter through Sept. 30; closed 2 hours earlier during other months; small admission charge to the crypt and 3 galleries. Don't miss the "Whispering Gallery!" Admission weekdays of £2 (1/2-price for children and seniors); no fees for prayers or on Sundays.

The overwhelming sublimity of the little **Chapels Royal** is virtually a secret to foreign visitors. The reason? Unless the tourist dresses conservatively and is quiet and mannerly, he or she is not wanted by the vicars and the congregations. As further illustration, cameras are banned. These beautiful places of worship are tucked away in a number of the most famous and most historic monuments of the United Kingdom. All are sponsored by the Crown. Many date back to the 11th or 12th century. The Sunday services normally start at 11 a.m. The choirs are limited in number but magnificent in voice. Should you wish to attend, you'll find a listing of the locations and the hours in Saturday's better-grade London newspapers.

Tower of London. Within this 11th-century castle of William the Conqueror is the repository of the Crown Jewels, the world's most forbidding chapel (St. Peter's), Sir Walter Raleigh's prison cell for 12 years, the death ground of the tragic Little Princes, and the execution row on which Anne Boleyn, Lady Jane Grey, and numerous other political victims met their fate. The hours are from 9:30 a.m. to 4 p.m. in winter, extending to 5 p.m. in summer; Sun. (high season only) from 2 p.m. till 5 p.m. Tickets combining all sectors for adults about $7; children less than half-price.

Madame Tussaud's (*Marylebone Rd.*), with its Grand Hall, displays dummies (some lifelike, some not), of nearly every major headliner in this century, as well as scores of earlier notables. Its eerie Chamber of Horrors, in the tomb-style cellar, is tailor-made to bring years of nightmares. Admission about £4.50; children under 16, £2; Royal Ticket pegged at another £1 or so adds a visit to the London Planetarium, too; operative 10 a.m. to 5:30 p.m. on weekdays and 10 a.m. to 6:30 p.m. on weekends.

Hyde Park's 363 well-trimmed acres are a delight to bench-warmers of all ages. The renowned Speakers' Corner, near Marble Arch, is the Mad Hatter merry-go-round for debaters who are permitted to blow off steam on any subject short of obscenity. Fanatics from all over the world rant, rave, and spout their philosophies here on Sunday. Bring a lunch or stop for a bite at the nearby park food kiosk. It's especially amusing if you're a fearless, witty heckler.

Hyde Park Serpentine has attracted paddlers, sailors, and lovers in summer for 2-1/2 centuries.

Famed **Old Bailey** (*Newgate St.*) dispenses English criminal justice in open session. It is the fount of much of America's jurisprudence. Worth a visit if you're a barracks lawyer, a veteran juror, or just plain snoopy about other people's malfeasances. The gavel sounds from 10 a.m. to 1 p.m. and from 2 to 4 p.m., Mon. through Fri.

Literary nostalgics like **Dickens' House** (*48 Doughty St., east of Russell Sq., W.C.1*), open Mon. through Sat. from 10 a.m. to 5 p.m., and **Dr. Johnson's House** (*17 Gough Sq. off Fleet St., E.C.4*), which can be toured from 11 a.m. to 5 p.m. except Sun. and holidays.

The **London Stock Exchange** (*Tower Block, Old Broad St., E.C.2*) blends Albion reserve with Madison Avenue verve. Bright young misses will answer your financial questions weekdays from 10 a.m. to 3:15 p.m. during the free guided tour; rather dull films wrap up the package.

CANAL CRUISES

"Jason's Trip," the midtown canal cruise from Argonaut Gallery (*60 Blomfield Rd., W.9; ☎ 071-286-3428*) to the Camden Town locks is good sport. For £4.50 you'll glide through Regent's Park, its world-famous Zoological Gardens, and other points, in a 90-minute loop. Book WELL in advance, get a confirmation that your boat will sail, and hope for good weather. As an alternate, you can sail from Westminster Pier upstream to Kew, Richmond, and Hampton Court in almost 4 hours (each way). If the ride up covers more water than you care for, your ticket also will enable you to hop the train home. The same company operates evening cruises; launchings at 7:30 p.m.; there's a regular daily jaunt to Tower Bridge. The *Jennie Wren* (☎ *071-485-4433*) plies between Camden Town and Little Venice; similar low rates and good value.

A Week on a Barge. *The Captain Webb*, a hotel-barge, offers London and Thames cruising featuring 6-day jaunts with full sightseeing programs. The vessel is shoulder-high in fun, frolic, and gastronomy. Prices are not at all painful when you consider the novel means of covering the ground, water, and skyscape of England. Phone **Another Britain** and ask for Gaynor Waterman—and how's that for an apt handle? (☎ *0836-202408.*)

THEATER

London has 50-plus theaters. Nurtured by Shakespeare and Jonson, needled by Wilde and Shaw, and up-ended by Osborne and Pinter, they display the greatest talent and variety in the world. Tickets £6 to perhaps £20 and a bit more for musicals; seats usually (not always) plentiful; box offices usually open at 10 a.m. Should you purchase ducats through an agent, you'll pay about 20% more per booking, so if you are buying for a family of 5 you can thus save on the overall bill by going directly to the theater. For half-price tickets, TKTS Booth (*Leicester Sq., W.C.2*), is the place. Same day's sales for West End matinees from noon-2 p.m. and from 2:30 p.m.-6 p.m. for evening shows. Fee of £1 tacked on to your reduced tariff. **Theatreline** (☎ *0836-430959/60*) charges a whack for booking information, so don't try it unless you are desperate. I've already mentioned the exciting new **Globe Theatre** at Southwark. The **National Theatre** (*South Bank*) is a sensation. It contains the 900-seat **Lyttelton**, the 1150-seat **Olivier**, and the small, experimental **Cottesloe** theaters beneath one roof. The least expensive seats go on sale at the box office at 8:30 a.m. on the day of any performance.

CONCERTS

The **Royal Festival Hall** (*South Bank, S.E.1*) is the most noteworthy. It provides a dramatic, handsome backdrop for the orchestra—a tableau dominated by copper, silver, and gilded organ pipes. If you feel like dining, there is an adjoining restaurant midstream in the Thames with candle illumination and vast plate-glass windows overlooking the sparkling riverscape. For lower-cost refreshment, there is a cafeteria downstairs plus snack bars off the lobby. The acoustically splendid **Royal Albert Hall** (*Kensington, S.W.7*) should also be in your notebook. In addition, a lot has been happening lately at the **Queen Elizabeth II Hall** (*South Bank*), which accommodates smaller groups. The **Royal Opera House** is in (*Covent Garden*); **Sadlers Wells** produces lighter works as well as ballet, plus **Gilbert & Sullivan** productions through the D'Oyly Carte Opera Co.; **English National Opera** performs at the Coliseum (*St. Martin's Lane, W.C.2*); **Holland Park** is the place for alfresco chords when the Kensington skies are at their kindest.

PARKS

The **Kew Gardens** botanical display would thrill Luther Burbank himself. The capital is full of scenic parks, the most famous of which are **Hyde**, **Regents**, **Kensington**, **St. James's**, and a little further out, **Hampstead Heath**. All of them are infinitely safer for strollers than New York's Central Park.

MARKETS

Covent Garden, the historic comestibles' nexus, moved some years back to more spacious grounds where traffic can maneuver more easily. A kaleidoscope of restaurants, bars, and shops abound where beans and begonias were hawked. As mentioned before, the Opera House remains. (See section further along under "Where to Shop.")

PUBLICATIONS

Pick up the weekly magazine *What's On In London*. We think it's infinitely useful and the best. *Time Out* is also a sound bet. *Rolling Stone* offers clues to the popmusic scene.

WHERE TO SHOP

Before you buy so much as a box of matches, head straight to either the **Design Centre** (*28 Haymarket, S.W.1*), the **Crafts Council Gallery** (*12 Waterloo Pl., Regent St.*), or **Contemporary Applied Arts** (*43 Earlham St., Covent Garden, W.C.2*) This trio offer samples, pictures, and information on thousands of British products. Free admission; frequent exhibitions, many items for sale.

ANTIQUE MARKETS

The largest variety at decent prices is found in the permanent indoor installations. Here the dealers know their business, and the competition is keen. The 2 most venerable ones are the **Chelsea Antique Market** (*253 King's Rd.*) and the **Antique Supermarket** (*3 Barrett St.*). Each contains at least 100 stalls. Much of their merchandise costs less than $100. **Antiquarius** (*135 King's Rd.*) is newer, more trendy, and generally more expensive.

The open-air street markets are a real lark. The **Portobello Road** market (Notting Hill Gate tube station) with its famous **Collectors' Corner**, Islington's **Angel Market** (both Saturdays only), and Islington's **Camden Passage** (Wednesday and Saturday mornings) are currently the hottest bets among hunters In The Know; the last, founded when 12 friends got together, has blossomed into an important little unit. While historic **Petticoat Lane** (Sunday mornings only until 2 p.m.) is often characterized as the old clothes exchange of London (*Liverpool St.*, Aldgate, Aldgate East tube stations), it is worth a dawn visit for its **Cutler Street Silver Market**; while there, the stalls on neighboring **Cheshire Street** should be explored. Finally, the **Bermondsey Market** (*Bermondsey Sq.*) just south of Tower Bridge (Friday mornings) is a lodestone for dealers rather than for visitors; often-dazzling fresh shipments from the country are put up for sale here at ridiculously low tariffs. The catch is that to be successful you must be on the scene around 5 a.m.

Fulham Road and **King's Road**, Chelsea, are for those who can afford sentimentality in the more costly bracket. More than 50 shops in the refashioned **Covent Garden** complex are open until 8 p.m. six days a week, but many are pricey, too.

BOOKS

Foyle (*113-119 Charing Cross Rd., W.C.2*) is a treat—the largest bookstore on earth, with more than 4-million volumes, 30 miles of shelves, and an inventory that makes it almost a private Library of Congress. For out-of-print works, try **Sheppard** (*255 Royal College St.*) in Camden Town, N.W.1. It stocks about 40,000 tomes and encourages browsing.

CASHMERES AND TARTANS

The Scotch House (headquarters at corner of *Knightsbridge* and *Brompton Rd., 84-86 and 191 Regent St.*) has them all licked. Over 300 tartan patterns, Highland accessories, tweeds, sweaters galore, and ready-to-wear clothing.

ODD CUPS AND SAUCERS, UNUSUAL ASHTRAYS, DIFFERENT SERVING PLATES

Reject China (*33 Beauchamp Pl.*) buys unwanted pieces from the factories and offers them with reasonable price tags (at least 50% off). Some items are visibly chipped, nicked, or cracked; many others contain hairline or invisible flaws that only the manufacturer's monitors or similar experts can pick up. Wide variety; unbelievably low tariffs for such an elegant shopping street.

DEPARTMENT STORES

Famous **Harrods** (*Knightsbridge, S.W.1*) has long been the pacesetter in the expensive bracket; economy shoppers can almost always do better elsewhere. **Selfridges** (*Oxford St.*), while several pegs down the ladder in prestige and price tags, also isn't the best bet for those who guard their budgets. Our favorites for s-t-r-e-t-c-h-i-n-g our pounds in solid general merchandise are the **Marks & Spencer** chain (the most convenient "Marks & Sparks" location is at *485 Oxford St.*) and **Peter Jones** (*Sloane Sq.*). Their stocks are versatile and inexpensive. Unfortunately, however, neither accepts credit cards. Toddle along the rest of Oxford Street, and you'll usually find inferior things.

King's Road can be great fun. Just wander along this lengthy artery, window-shopping its flock of way-out boutiques.

Army and Navy Stores (*Victoria St., S.W.1*) is a massive emporium that is yet another British institution. It defies the usual department-store description, because under one roof it also houses a bank, a supermarket, and a liquor store. Lap robes, Wedgwood collections, leather goods, antique jewelry, and kitchen equipment are only a few of its choices. The overall quality and the savings are fair enough, but the stylings—to us, at least—are not impressive. Convenient, however, for a myriad of purposes.

ENAMELS

Halcyon Days (*14 Brook St., Mayfair, W.1* and *4 Royal Exchange, Cornhill, E.C.3*) stocks contemporary renderings of this 18th-century art form that start under $100.

ENGLISH FLOWER PERFUMES AND TOILETRIES

The 264-year-old **J. Floris** (*89 Jermyn St., S.W.1*), perfumers to the Court of St. James, is unrivaled in this specialty. Galaxy of exquisite scents (Edwardian Bouquet, Florissa, Malmaison, Sandalwood, Lily of the Valley, Rose Geranium and many more); unique anywhere in the world for you (male or female) or for decently priced presents.

IRISH SPECIALTIES

The Irish Shop (*11 Duke St.*) purveys the best of the Emerald Isle: Aran sweaters, Claddagh rings, Celtic jewelry, Waterford crystal, Belleek china, linen, and tweeds. Terrific prices.

PIPES AND SMOKING SUPPLIES

Dunhill (*30 Duke St., St. James's, S.W.1*) should need no introduction. Many small, novel, and intriguing gifts are available. **G. Smith and Sons** (*74 Charing Cross Rd.*) is a mecca for snuff takers; more than 22 blends available.

RAINWEAR

Burberrys (*18 Haymarket* and *165 Regent St.*) is more famous than English rain. Prices are far lower, too, than for those trade-name greats on our side of the Atlantic.

SOUVENIRS

For souvenir items, the **Old Curiosity Shop** (*13-14 Portsmouth St., W.C.2*) couldn't be more touristy. This one is loaded to the scuppers with "antique" china, pottery, glass, silver, pewter, plaques, playing cards, silhouettes—as our British friends say, "the lot." You ask for it and they'll find it, because the gent who runs this place isn't about to lose a single customer. Open, naturally, 7 days a week.

AUTHOR'S OBSERVATION

Finally, don't bother with purchases other than tobacco and spirits at the Heathrow Airport Duty Free Shop. You won't realize any savings over midcity prices for cashmeres, woolens, jewelry, or electronics equipment; in fact, most tabs that we compared were marginally higher in cost; moreover, the selections were scanty. So relax and travel light.

MANCHESTER

Here is the nation's leading textile spinner and 4th city—a metropolis that's hell-bent on going modern while retaining remnants of its powerful heritage. Although under its clangor it's a principal hub of political, literary, scientific, and musical advancement, most outlanders find it too commercial, unless they are willing to dig deeper into its feisty past. A lot of its muscle is on display at the **Museum of Science and Industry**; the glamorous side can be seen on a tour of **Granada Studios**.

OXFORD

It's thought to be a half-century older than rival Cambridge, but even the most wizened inhabitant isn't certain of its exact age. It's about 63 miles from London and offers **Blackwell's** world-renowned university bookshop; the animated zeal of young scholars and busy-busy townspeople, each pursuing their own courses; the high-pitched moments of **St. Giles' Fair** (first Mon. and Tues. of Sept.). **London Coastal Coaches, Ltd.** (*Victoria Coach Station, Buckingham Palace Rd.*) offers a round trip for about $18. By rail is much faster. Most visitors agree it's not as scenically attractive as more tranquil Cambridge even though it is a bit more ancient. The **Old Parsonage** is an atmospheric, expanded inn, and **Eastgate Hotel** is more formal but still intimate in concept.

PORTSMOUTH

For salty types, few delights beat a trip to the 18th-century "**Dockyard**," where you can walk the deck of Nelson's magnificent Victory, step back in time to Queen Victoria's Navy with a visit to HMS *Warrior*, or view Henry VIII's famous flagship, the *Mary Rose*. Just across the Solent can be found the **Isle of Wight** with its famous yachting center of **Cowes**. Inland from Portsmouth running west you'll find **Southampton** and **Bournemouth**, with its sandy beaches and subtropical gardens. To the east are **Brighton**, **Eastbourne**, and **Hastings**, the last with plenty of historic scenery from the great battles of yore. The area has an abundance of bed-and-breakfast establishments, especially along the shore road. Your choice really depends on where you want to stop.

STONEHENGE

Since there are no accommodations here, you'll probably headquarter in **Salisbury** if you take more than the one-day excursion from London. While in this town, all outlanders should pay homage to the 13th-century **Cathedral** and perhaps the **Salisbury and South Wiltshire Museum** (The Close). Buses run from Salisbury to **Amesbury** and Stonehenge.

On Midsummer Night, when the early Celtic Druid priests are supposed to "return," the surrounding fields are dotted with sleeping bags. As a result of mindless vandalism, the compound itself has been fenced in, but there is still plenty to see from the fringes. Recently a nearby road was diverted to another route and a visitors' center was created in a less obstructive locality. The revision cost about $18 million.

STRATFORD-UPON-AVON

Here, of course, is the Shakespeare Country's honorary capital. Try to arrive on a day when the **Royal Shakespeare Theatre** is performing; it functions from Mar. to Jan. For a bus shuttle which leaves London at 1:30 p.m., takes in a show, and departs for the capital again at 11:15 p.m., ☎ *(71) 379-1564* in the U.K. or ☎ *800-223-6108* in the U.S.A. They can give you the details and reserve tickets. You may also take in Oxford on another London Coastal Coaches excursion, but this one allows you about enough time in both places to tie your shoelaces. Overcrowded and overcommercial in high season. For overnighting, **Mrs. Peggy Rose** (*52 Banbury Rd.*; ☎ *67094*) takes paying guests in a perfectly maintained house in a nice residential district. Breakfast before an open fire on a chilly morn; twin rates of about £20. **Ravenhurst** is a good conventional hotel **Stratheden** has plenty of old-world charm and reasonable prices. For other accommodation or the lowdown on 2 youth hostels, check with the local tourist office (*20 Chapel St.*). See also "Broadway".

WINCHESTER

The medieval **Cathedral** boasts 7 richly carved chapels plus the bones of such diverse notables as Saxon kings, Danish kings, Izaak Walton, and Jane Austen. The town itself—from St. Gile's Hill to High Street to Kingsgate to City Cross—is a charmer, riddled with history, and replete with memories of literary greatness, architectural antiquity, and beauty. Stay at the **Southgate** or the **Royal**. The **Wessex**, edging the cathedral, is costly but worth a splurge if your budget can stand it for one night. Many dining possibilities for snacks and tea; the **Elizabethan** and **The Old Chesil Rectory** are noteworthy in the more-expensive-but-memorable category.

WINDERMERE

This entry makes the biggest splash in the Lake District. Pretty it is, but stodgy too—and on the way to becoming spoiled by the caravans of tourists who engulf its venerable dignity during high season. The summer is short so there's a sort of honky-tonk frenzy in the make-it-fast approach. Plenty of bed and breakfast guesthouses. Thousands of hikers, campers, and climbers use it as a base camp. Nearby lakeside targets include **Keswick**, **Derwent Water**, **Ambleside**, **Grasmere**, and the **Borrowdale Fells**. The Lake District National Park Information Service in Bowness will happily furnish the name and address of every fish in the lake, the shrines of the Romantic poets, Peter Rabbit's hutch, campsites, walking tours—the lot!

YORK

As a fulcrum of English history, the walls of this Ouse River fortress recall the Roman occupation. **Coppergate** is a recreation of a Viking street when the center was called Jorvik and it was on the trade route between Nordic kingdoms and the Middle East. It has almost as many churches as Norwich, including Europe's largest one, **York Minster**, more than 9 centuries old and now fully repaired after a severe lightning strike. **All Saint's** is famous for its glass and towers. There's the imposing site of **Clifford's Tower** or **York Castle**. Also here are the **Old Debtor's Prison**, (with its Castle Museum and reconstructed streets within the building), the Jacobean timbers of **Sir Thomas Herbert's House**, the **Black Swan Inn**, and one of the world's leading universities. For a bed-and-breakfast stop, try **Parkview Guest House** on Grovenor Place, a friendly spot. **Mayfield** on Scarcroft Rd. is also said to be inexpensive and reliable. You'll find rambling, undulating streets with names such as Whip Ma Whop Ma Gate, the Shambles, and Jubbergate. Almost everything significant that transpired within the tableau of English origins is reflected in the buildings or surrounding dales of York.

FOR MORE INFORMATION ON ENGLAND

USA • British Tourist Authority, *40 W. 57th St., New York, NY 10019,* ☎ *(212) 581-4700;*

CANADA • *94 Cumberland St., Suite 600, Toronto, Ontario M5R,* ☎ *(416) 925-6326.*

INSIDER TIP

If you pop over to Victoria Station Forecourt, 12 Regent St. off Piccadilly Circus, or the Heathrow Travel Centre, you'll find a veritable font of courtesy and assistance from the BTA. London Regional Transport operates further travel loci for information at Heathrow III, and Euston and Charing Cross stations.

FINLAND

Turku

Both geographically as well as politically, Finland teeters on a line that is east of Scandinavia and west of Russia. It is perfectly poised to serve as a window to the east. I have recently returned from St. Petersburg via the Helsinki route leading through the ancient Swedish port of Vyborg and the once-Finnish province of Karelia. While it was fascinating, it is not yet a journey that a budget traveler should consider. There are not enough options in accommodation or good low-cost dining to provide the basics. Indeed, in almost every category of tourism into Russia, the modality is group travel—and even that is unstable and relatively expensive. Plan to go, but wait a few more seasons.

The quality-of-life quotient is high all over Finland, so the traveler who likes his holiday fare as pure as the shimmering waters and as fresh as the arctic air will rejoice over this least-spoiled of European destinations. Among its irresistible offerings: a countryside over two-thirds quilted by forests; exactly 187,888 gleaming lakes often linked by short channels into miles-long chains; roughly 180,000 rock-dotted islands; and finally an amorphous area called Lapland, where frontiers are fluid, and vast herds of reindeer roam the frosted fells.

Possibly as long ago as the beginning of the Christian era, the earliest Finns came over the Urals in the east. The Lapps, aboriginally on the scene, played the persecuted "Indian" to their "cowboy" and by the 8th century had fled to the arctic north where they still preserve their language and a goodly portion of their culture. (The cap of present-day Finland, Sweden, and Norway, crowned by the Arctic Circle, comprises the central axis of Lapland.)

For four uneventful centuries, the Finns sailed along under their own steam; but continual raids on the Swedish coast eventually prompted a conquering response from that nation in the 12th century. Sandwiched between Sweden and Russia, Finland was often doomed to antagonistic crossfire. The 1809 upshot for Finland was status as a semi-independent czarist state held in political escrow as a grand duchy.

Finland won independence in 1917 by taking advantage of World War I, as well as the Russian Revolution, and incurring a brief civil war. But its underdog days proved far from over. In 1939 and 1941 it was again pitted against Russia and, in defeat, forced to cede sizable tracts of land to its number-one nemesis. Finland has in fact had 42 wars with Russia—and has lost them all. No wonder it habitually stretches a conciliatory hand across its eastern neighbor's fence.

After World War II, Finland sensibly switched focus from foreign affairs to home economics, succeeding in raising its standard of living to one of the highest in Europe.

Weaned on long, formidable winters and quickie three-month summers, the Finns are a rugged, hard-working, never-say-die people. (You'll hear the word *sisu* for valiance or endurance used all the time there.) To the natives this country is "Suomi," the realm basking in the Midnight Sun or radiant under the Northern Lights.

TIPS ON FINLAND

FOOD

The Suomis take their table seriously. Although they show a healthy respect for hearty, solid, no-nonsense sustenance, its preparation is interesting and its presentation is almost always attractive. The spine of their sturdy piscatorial diet is made up of sprats, white

FINLAND
Barents Sea
NORWAY
SWEDEN
USSR
0 miles 100
0 kilometers 160
Utsjoki
Inari
Ivalo
Enontekio
Vuotso
Lokka
Kemijarvi
Rovaniemi
Arctic Circle
Kuusamo
Tornio
Kemi
Oulu
Nurmes
Lieksa
Kuopio
Joensuu
Gulf of Bothnia
Vaasa
Savonlinna
Mikkeli
Imatra
Lappeenranta
Tampere
Pori
Heinola
Lahti
Hameenlina
Kotka
Porvoo/Borga
Leningrad
Naantali
Turku
Helsinki
Gulf of Finland
Aland Islands
Stockholm
N

fish, pike, bream, flounder, and salmon, which may swim to your table grilled, pickled, fried, boiled, salted, smoked, baked, poached, creamed, stuffed, in batter or vulcanized. While beef is not so traditional, it is becoming fashionable—a welcome relief, too, from Poron Kieli, or reindeer tongue (usually dried in the smokehouse and suitable for half-soling hunting boots).

If you don't mind one expensive but unique treat, try not to miss the glorious mid-July through Sept. *rapuja* (the minisize freshwater crayfish which the Swedes know as kraftor). The waiter will studiously tie you in a paper bib from your chin to your pelvis; suck every drop from this dill-seasoned-and-decorated crustacean.

The Finnish interpretation of smorgasbord is called *voileipapoyta*, or *pitopoyta* for short(er). As with all such North Country festive boards, always eat your herring first, other cold fish next, then cold meats, and finally tackle the hot preparations—all on separate plates, of course. It is gastronomic heresy to mix sea and land on the same platter.

Try specialties such as Sillisalaatti (herring salad), smoked Poronliha (reindeer), Kesakeitto (fresh vegetable soup with milk), or such hot dishes as Kalakukko (fish and pork pie with salt-baked potatoes—and if you want your tonsils to last 7450 years after you're interred, just eat the skin of those spuds), Karjalanpiirakka (piping-hot Karelian rice-and-potato pastries), Maksalaatikko (liver pudding), Lanttulaatikko (turnip casserole), Punajuuri Salaattia (beetroot salad), and Paistetut Sienet (fried wild mushrooms). The citizenry normally washes these down with Piima (sour milk) or Kalja (nonalcoholic beer); personally, whenever we stare at these 2 beverages, other ideas seem to flow with startling freedom.

Wild game? The most popular candidates include grouse, wild duck, ptarmigan (try it roasted as Riekkopaisti—yum YUM!), and venison.

For dessert, there are luscious fruit soups made from wild or cultivated berries—lingonberry, cloudberry (marvelous but pulverizing in cost), brambleberry, bilberry (similar to our huckleberry), and others. These also garnish pancakes. For your cheese plate, experiment with Romadur or the local interpretation of Camembert.

AUTHOR'S OBSERVATION

In Finland, make your midday meal the main one. At dinner time, and depending on the restaurant, the very same dish will double (or more) in price.

DRINKS

The Finns, as a group, are just about the wettest Wets or the driest Drys that we've ever encountered.

Prohibition was tried and abolished. In its place, the State formed the alcohol monopoly, "Alkoholiliike" ("Alko" for short), to centralize control of all intoxicating beverages and to hard-sell the advantages of beer and wine. Its stocks are large and well chosen; its prices range from moderate to steep, depending on the promotional priority of the product (Scotch is around $40). In Helsinki alone, Alko boasts about 25 retail outlets. If you like your weekend tipple, remember that these are open on weekdays from 10 a.m. to 5 or 6 p.m., plus 9 a.m. to 2 p.m. on Sat., except from May 1 to Sept. 30.

Restaurants may begin serving beer from 9 a.m. and more potent liquids from 11 a.m. For teetotalers there are a sizable number of arid hotels run by the powerful YMCA. Cafes and many restaurants are not granted licenses. They may be called "bars," but their purpose is to serve snacks.

Jaloviina (the generic term for schnapps) is the Finns' favorite hard liquor. There are 7 major types. Poytaviina and Viljavoakuna, both distilled wood alcohol, are cheap—and STRONG. Tahkaviina is made from grain and flavored with malt. It is costlier and less combustible. Koskenkorva is what might be termed the "standard" schnapps of the land, with a flavor reminiscent of Denmark's Aalborg. Finally, Alko's export product, called "Finlandia Vodka," has met with fantastic success. It offers a far smoother, cleaner, less pungent taste than any of the others. There is only one brand made, which sells for about $30 a bottle. (Within the country, the so-called Dry Vodka is the exact same product, but it sells for $18 in the Alko shops.)

Whiskey is beloved by the more cosmopolitan inhabitants—but on a per capita basis, Finns drink more cognac than do the citizens of any other nation. For some screwball reason, soda water is sometimes as expensive as the amber in your glass.

Finland boasts 12 major breweries. Helsinki's kingpin is Koff, but you may also quaff at least 14 other brands in the capital. Only 3 types of beer are vatted. Pilsner, the lightest, guarantees less than 2.2% alcohol. The most popular "3rd Class" (named for a taxation gimmick), goes for about a buck a bottle. Strongest and best is "A" ("Atomic"), the export variety. It's a few cents extra, but worth the difference.

On the nonalcoholic side, you'll find the coolers stocked with all the standard fruit juices, plus lingonberry and cranberry beverages.

GETTING AROUND

TRAINS

Fair to excellent. Here's a bonus: Finland belongs to the **Eurail pass** network, which also incorporates ferry passage on Silja Line ships. The **Finnish State Railways**' trackage is a surprisingly small 3700 miles. About 25% of the haulage is electric.

There is a supplement (15 FM) for express trains which includes a seat designated for you. IC trains (service from the capital to Vaasa, Jyvaskyla and Imatra) have an obligatory seat reservation charge of 25 FM in Second Class (60 FM in First).

The railways offer the **Tourist Ticket System** (Finnrail-train-bus-boat) and **unlimited rail travel** for set sums within the country with a **Finnrail Pass**. Ask your travel agent about these bargains.

AIRLINE

Finnair may again offer its low-fare Holiday Ticket, which provides unlimited flying over a 15-day period. Ask your travel agent about this bargain.

CARS AND MOTORING

Highways are superb, and traffic almost doesn't exist. But in winter, trains, planes, or ships carry most of the passenger load over greater distances. (And winter is long in Finland.) Service stations are plentiful. High-test gasoline is very expensive.

Finland does not manufacture any passenger automobile of its own, but it does have a license agreement with Saab, although Volvos are more common. Importation taxes are lethal on any new car price.

Never sip even a 2.2% beer before you slip behind the wheel. If a blood test reveals even a trace of alcohol (exactly 0.5%), it could mean jail for 6 months. The punishment automatically carries the "hard labor" provision.

Car hire: Dependable agencies are **Hertz** (*Hernesaarenranta 11*; ☎ *6221100*), **Avis** (*Fredrikinkatu 67*; ☎ *441155*), and **Inter-Rent Europcar** (*Hitsaajankatu 7C*; ☎ *7556133*), all in Helsinki.

SPORTS

SKIING

The Finns, having developed the requisite aerodynamic techniques, have practically given today's definition to the term "ski-jumping." One of the most popular winter sports centers is **Lahti**. Special weekend hotel rates (room and meals) are offered in the season.

Finland's flatness makes it best for cross-country skiing. There are several ski centers in Finland. The annual Finlandia Ski Race is a 47-mile competition usually held in February. For details: **Finnish Tour-**

ist Board, *655 Third Ave., New York, NY 10017*; ☎ *(212) 949-2333.* For registration and hotel, write **Area Travel Agency Ltd.**, Incoming Department, *KaisaniemenKatu 13-A, SF-00100 Helsinki*; ☎ *(9) 0-18551.*

Other cross-country races open to all are the Arctic Circle Ski Race, Rovaniemi, Lapland, in March and the Kuusamo Ski Race in April; both cover 39 miles.

CYCLING

There are 4- to 6-day packages on **Aland Island**, about $165 to $350 per person, including bike, youth-hostel or private accommodation, breakfast, map, and guidebook. Contact **Alands Resor Ab**, *Storagatan 8-9, 22100 Mariehamn*; ☎ *(9) 28-28040.*

In **Western Uusimaa**, the coastal area west of Helsinki, they'll offer you three scheduled cycling forays of 32, 55 and 73 miles. These routes start from Ekenas (Tammisaari) or Karis (Karjaa) and take you through old countryside roads, but also include parts of the Lohja-Hanko (Hango) main artery. For further details: **Ekenas City Tourist** Office, *Skillnadsgatan 16, 10600 Ekenas*; ☎ *(9) 11-14 600/149.*

Or how about the 100-mile Border River Keep-Fit Bicycle Tour in western Lapland? Contact **Tornio City Tourist Office**, *Lukiokatu 10, 95400 Tornio*; ☎ *(9) 698-40048*, or *432441.*

Just plain old bike hire? Available at some hotels, camping sites, and most youth hostels, as well as at selected tourist information offices. Fees about $3.50 to $20 a day or reduced rates by the week. This is a good investment since the countryside is so level you can pedal almost anywhere easily.

HIKING

Best months are June to September Leave the alpine boots and climbing gear behind; bring thick-soled rubber boots and a measure of stamina. Maps available from Akateeminen Kirjakauppa, Pohjoisesplanadi St.

WATERSPORTS

Have a Helsinki swim at either Seurasaari Beach (in the far west end), Munkkiniemi Beach (northwest of the downtown district), Hietaranta Plunge (near the center), Pihlajasaari Beach, or the Olympic Swimming Stadium (near the separate Olympic Stadium where world contests were held in 1952).

The waterskiing tariff pushes a dollar a minute, including equipment. Some of Finland's 40 Water-Ski Association clubs arrange 4- to 5-day courses at about $75. **Finnish Water-Ski Association**, *SVUL Radiokatu 12, 00240, Helsinki*; ☎ *(9) 01581.*

Elementary windsurfing courses all over the country run about $80; weekend rentals run about the same. **Finnish Yachting Association**, **Windsurfing Department**, *Radiokatu 12, 0024 Helsinki*; ☎ *(9) 0-1582350.*

Enormous fishing possibilities in a land of 60,000 lakes (not to mention rivers and streams). Inland catches include pike, perch, whitefish, trout, bream, and roach. Wide sea range, too. Licenses at postal bank offices and post offices for about $8.

CANOEING

Best bets: the archipelago off the southwestern coast, the coast of Uusimaa province, the Aland Islands, and the lake regions where the waters are channel-linked. Saimaa has almost 1300 miles of marked channels. Eastern and northeastern Finland offer rapids. Charts of coastal waters and larger inland waterways available from **Karttakeskus Espa** (Map Service of the National Board of Survey), *Etela esplanadi 4, 00130 Helsinki 13*; ☎ *9 (0)-1543168.*

Finnish Canoe Association's member clubs arrange guided tours and hire 1- and 2-seater fiberglass kayaks for $15 to $30 a day.

HORSES

Most of Finland's approximately 130 riding clubs have a riding school. For details: **Finnish Equestrian Federation**, *Radiokatu 12, 00240 Helsinki*; ☎ *(9) 0-1582315.*

SHOPPING

Hours: Weekdays, 9 a.m. to 5 p.m. (department stores till 8 p.m.); Sat., 9 a.m. to 2 p.m. Along the Esplanade, especially in summer, a few shops open from noon to 4 p.m. on specific Sundays. Check locally for exact details. Stores under the Helsinki railway station function weekdays from 10 a.m.–10 p.m. and on Sun. from noon–10 p.m.

THINGS NOT TO BUY

Cigarettes not locally manufactured under Finnish control are terribly costly. All tobacco is very expensive in the Nordic countries. Leather goods and an increasing supply of junky craft items are largely imported. Finnish work is better.

WHERE TO GO

AULANKO

Here is *the* glittering sapphire in the bracelet of western lakes, 3 miles from Sibelius' birthplace of **Hameenlinna**. Justifiably, it's a lodestar for the holiday-minded—accessible by car (slightly over an hour by highway from Helsinki), by train, or by the Silver Line water coach that glides between Hameenlinna and Tampere. Come here for golfing, tennis, boating, swimming, waterskiing, horseback riding, broiling your hide in its log-cabin sauna, sightseeing from the top of its 100-foot granite needle, or just communing with some of the most glorious natural scenery in the northlands. Ski lift and downhill slope add to the winter facilities. The 216-room **Hotel Aulanko** boasts a balcony for each accommodation, private baths for 191 units, a restaurant for 700 clients, a bar, a sauna, and a resident orchestra. It is relatively expensive. **Aulangon Heikkila** affords more modest shelter. There's a daily lake cruise on the Silver

Line route in summer for the restless—restaurant aboard—which touches other nearby beauty ports.

HANKO

This sleepy seacoast town draws many wayfarers to savor its southern summer charms. The sandy beach, watersports, and tennis are its major attractions for outdoor types.

HELSINKI

The Swedes founded this city in 1550 and called it "Helsingfors," still their name for it; in 1812 the Russians capitalized it. However, since an independent Finland is a 20th-century phenomenon, Helsinki was not really of capital importance until the turn of the century.

Still the only town in the country really worthy of being called "large," it is a young upstart in the Old World. Its most striking feature is its architecture: 19th-century neoclassical with bold overtones of Finnish Modern Renaissance. This "White City of the North" offers nothing ancient for the antiquary, its oldest monument dating from the mid-18th century.

Contrary to what you might think, Helsinki did not earn its "white city" nickname by being an ice-bound port from January to May; rather it rates the epithet because most of its elegant buildings are fashioned of light-colored Finnish granite.

The **Helsinki Card** provides bargains at more than 100 attractions, free travel on city-wide transportation, and tips galore on how to save money. It even includes cut-rate accommodations and a 64-page booklet outlining the various economies to be discovered. The card costs about $18 in its one-day adult version ($10 for youngsters between 7 and 16); two-and-three-day Cards also can be purchased at the airport, at travel agencies, tourist offices and many hotels.

DIRECTORY

U.S. Embassy • *Itainen Puistotie 14;* ☎ *171931.*

American Express • Travek Travel Bureau, *Aleksanterink 21;* ☎ *661453.*

Laundromat: • Suomen Pesu, *Porvoonk. 3.*

Barber and Hairdresser • Stockmann's Department Store, *Mannerheimintie 1.*

Dry Cleaning and Pressing • Americano, *Koskelantie 21* or Lindstrom, *Mikonkatu 8.*

Suit Rental • Juhla-Asu, *Fabianinkatu 13.*

English-Speaking Doctor • Dial ☎ *008.*

English-Speaking Dentist • Dial ☎ *736166.*

Main Post Office • *Mannerheimintie 11.*

Police • Central Station, *Pasilanraitio 13,* ☎ *10022; Emergency,* ☎ *112.*

Favorite Pawnshop • *Pursimiehenkatu 7.*

Tourist Information • Dial ☎ *9700-8058.*

News in English • Dial ☎ *040.*

HOW TO GET AROUND

Don't hail an airport cab; the price can be lethal. Instead, hop on a bus shuttle that normally runs every half-hour between the tarmac and the town terminus behind the

Intercontinental Hotel; service is stepped up to every 10 minutes during extra-busy periods. Within the city use Eliel Saarinen's railway station as your home base. From it, the #3T streetcar will propel you to just about everywhere, including the South Harbor, the Swedish Theatre, the University, the Olympic Stadium, and the Linnanmaki Amusement Park. Beach-bounders board the #24 bus for Seurasaari, the #4 streetcar for Munkkiniemi, and the boat (departure from Kaivopuisto) for Uunisaari. Single trips on bus, tram, or metro are 9 FM for an adult (5 FM for the young'uns). A 10-trip ducat costs 70 FM; 25 FM for children. There's also a Tourist Ticket for unlimited travel that is a great money saver. Ask at City Transport offices.

WHERE TO STAY

LEAST $

Before leaving the States, consult the **Finnish Tourist Board** for moment-by-moment developments. Upon arrival make the rounds of the student dormitories that serve budget shelter during summer vacation; or ask the **Hotel Booking Center** (*Helsinki Station*) about hostels. If you plan to travel over the country, the **Finncheque** system applies to 240 upper-level hotels. The price is only 165 FM for a double with breakfast and service. Inquire about these through your travel agent or the FTB.

YOUTH HOSTELS

They're everywhere. One of the best sources of information is the Finnish Youth Hostel Assoc. *(Yrjonkatu 38B, 00100, Helsinki 10)*. Once in the capital, go to Stadionin Retkeilymaja *(Olympic Stadium; ☎ 496071)*; this one is open all year. In summer, you can visit Academica Youth Hostel *(Hietaniemenkatu 14; ☎ 4020206)*. For a pamphlet on them—simply too many to cover here—contact the Finnish Tourist Board offices.

Forays into the hinterland? An indispensable aid is the pamphlet *Budget Accommodation*, which you can obtain free from the Finnish Tourist Board in New York or from any of the network's 11 continental branches (Amsterdam, Hamburg, London, Milan, Munich, Madrid, Paris, Copenhagen, Oslo, Stockholm, and Zurich). More than 350 entries.

MORE $$

Anna • *Annankatu 1; ☎ 648011.* Operated by the Evangelical Lutheran Church; 19 singles at $93; 30 doubles at $126; service included. Quirks: no visitors after 10 p.m.; residents' curfew at 11 p.m.; no alcohol permitted on premises.

Kesa-Dipoli • *Otaniemi (20 minutes by metropolitan bus from midcity); ☎ 435811.* Both a summer and a year-round division—the latter being the newest, boasting over 200 seafront rooms with bath or shower, a restaurant, pool, tennis, jogging track, squash courts and saunas. Top price for a twin about $95 inclusive in the new sector. Singles at $75. The older sector, much less, filled with students in winter, but its 600 beds available to foreigners in high season. Functional but inconveniently sited.

Matkustajakoti Lonnrot • *Lonnrotinkatu 16; ☎ 6932590.* Handy setting, but a bit grim. The Saturday night stampede to the one-and-only public bathroom might possibly have been topped by the 1878 cattle drive into Dodge City.

EVEN MORE $$$

Hotelli Helka • *Pohjoinen Rautatiekatu 23; ☎ 440581.* Centrally located and carefully managed; restaurant with beer and wine license. Spotless doubles starting at $133, loners about 30% less; extra beds about $20 each.

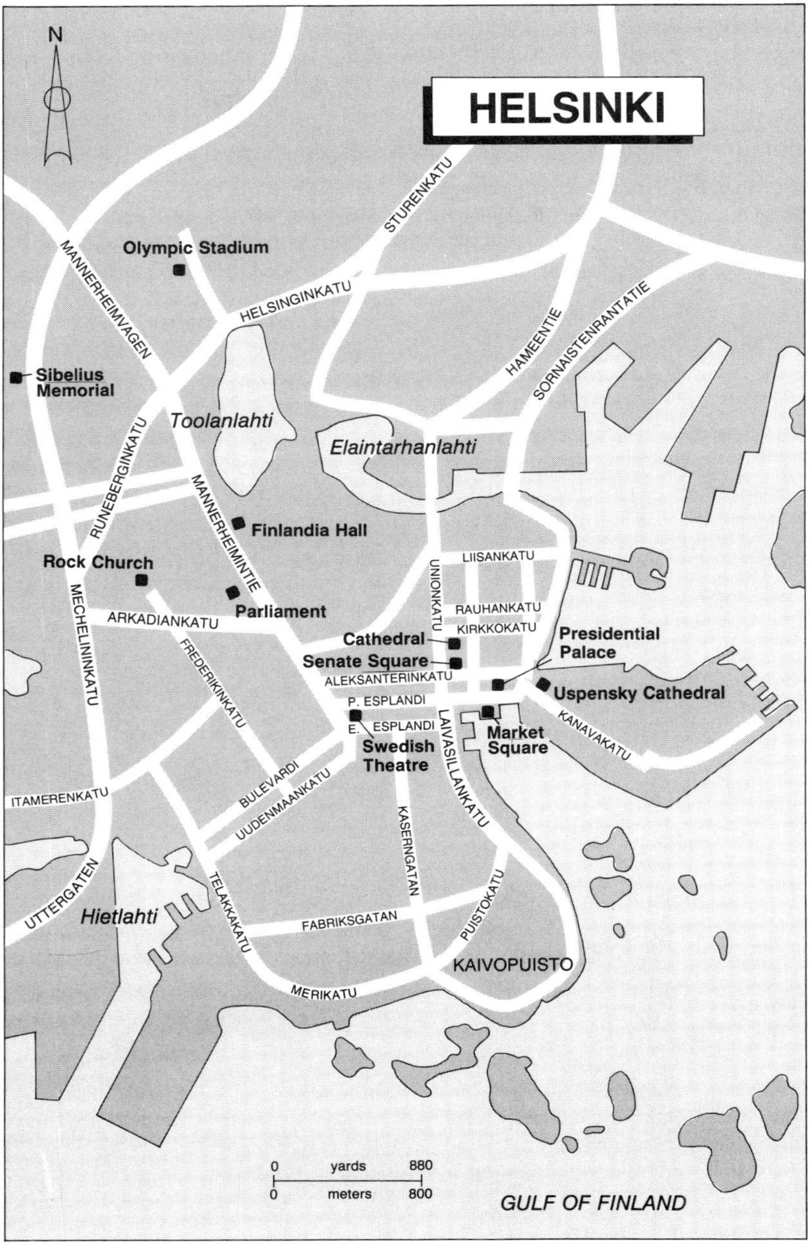
HELSINKI
N
STURENKATU
Olympic Stadium
MANNERHEIMVAGEN
HELSINGINKATU
HAMEENTIE
SORNAISTENRANTATIE
Sibelius Memorial
Toolanlahti
Elaintarhanlahti
RUNEBERGINKATU
MANNERHEIMINTIE
Finlandia Hall
Rock Church
LIISANKATU
UNIONKATU
RAUHANKATU
MECHELININKATU
Parliament
ARKADIANKATU
KIRKKOKATU
Cathedral
Presidential Palace
FREDERIKINKATU
Senate Square
ALEKSANTERINKATU
Uspensky Cathedral
P. ESPLANDI
E. ESPLANDI
LAIVASILLANKATU
Market Square
KANAVAKATU
Swedish Theatre
BULEVARDI
ITAMERENKATU
UUDENMAANKATU
KASERNGATAN
UTTERGATEN
TELAKKAKATU
PUISTOKATU
Hietlahti
FABRIKSGATAN
KAIVOPUISTO
MERIKATU
0 yards 880
0 meters 800
GULF OF FINLAND

Academica • *Hietaniemenkatu 14;* ☎ *4020206.* Singles with basin $50, with full bath $75; doubles $133 to $155, breakfast and service included. Okay for the prices; June 1 through Aug. 31 only.

Marttahotelli • *Uudenmaankatu 24;* ☎ *646211.* Most chambers medium-size. Light bites in the lunchroom from 11 a.m. to 5 p.m. No alcohol; appealing. Singles $88 and doubles $111; service and breakfast included.

Ursula • *Paasivuorenkatu 1;* ☎ *750311.* 46 clean bedrooms, about half offering private plumbing. Maximum singles for $88; doubles, $110.

Klaus Kurki • *Bulevardi 2-4,* ☎ *618911.* 49 singles $160; 84 spacious doubles with bath $205, including service; sauna at $18 per hotshot; room service until 11 p.m. Freshly renovated throughout and very good indeed.

Hospiz • *Vuorikatu 17B;* ☎ *173441.* 164 rooms; gimpy singles $75, better ones $115; twins at $150 with bath; service included.

Cumulus Kaisaniemi • *Kaisaniemenkatu 7 (only 300 yards from the station);* ☎ *172881.* Too noisy for light sleepers. 58 cubicles, all with showers.

CAMPING

Rastila • ☎ *316551.* About 7.5 miles east of town, and a good summer site. Piped hot water; electric and gas cooking; sauna; restaurant; groceries on sale; boats for hire; cottages plus facilities for trailers.

SUGGESTIONS FOR STUDENTS

The eye of the local student cyclone is the university and its immediate environs. The same applies to the 2 schools of economics in Toolo and to the Technical School in Otaniemi.

Use the **Finnish Student Travel Service** (FSTS)—**Travela** (*Mannerheimintie 5C,* ☎ *624101*) for all assistance and up-to-the-minute information on accommodations, eating, clubs, and travel. This is the central headquarters for all facts about the various student unions.

WHERE TO EAT

LEAST $

Covered Market • This assemblage of wonderfully carved, painted stalls has everything: meat sandwiches, sausages, smoked reindeer, rice pies—hot or cold—for about 10 FM to 15 FM per serving. You can walk around the scores of booths until you find your fancy, buy a drink, and either perch on a stool or picnic outside on the piers of the bustling, scenic Open Market. Hours: 8 a.m. to 5 p.m. weekdays and to 2 p.m. Saturdays.

Kellarikrouvi • *Pohj Makasiinikatu 6;* ☎ *179021.* $11 menu offered from 11 a.m. to 2 p.m., but operative from 9 a.m. to midnight; Sun. from noon. Littleto-no English spoken. Most first-timers love it.

Happy Days • *Pohjoisesplanadi 2;* ☎ *624023.* A fun place for meeting young people. The food's not too important.

Academica • *Hietaniemenk 14.* Popular among students and exclusively for them. Lunch or dinner about $12.

SNACK BARS

Chain operations in a coffeeshop vein include **Carrolls** and **McDonald's** (specializing in you-know-what), and **Fazzeria** (again with several outlets and doing short-order drugstore cooking). **Fazer** pastry and cafeteria shops also are ubiquitous in midtown; they have beer, cafeteria selections, and full menu choices for economical prices.

PIZZAS

Pizzeria Dennis • *Fredrikinkatu 36.* Stokes up a worthy oven.

Pizza Hut • *City Centrum.* As much fun for its kitsch as it is for its kitchen. Animated and appealing.

At one of the numerous railroad station kiosks, order one of those *lihapiirakkas*—a hot doughnut packed with meat and rice. It's as heavy as a barbell, but surprisingly delicious—a meal in itself. Other easy-to-swallow (physically and financially) items also are on tap.

AUTHOR'S OBSERVATION

Both baari (bars serving only beer and light meals) and kahvila (cafeterias) are good lunch stops where meals cost between $5.50 and $11. The latter cater to the hearty appetites of Finnish workers.

MORE $$

Orfeus • *Eerikinkatu 2;* ☎ *640378.* Intimate subsurface den 2 blocks from the bustle of Mannerheimintie and Aleksanterinkatu. Music after dark. Á la carte only.

Palace Gourmet • *Etelaranta 10;* ☎ *171114.* Second-floor grill; super chicken-on-spit. Upper-floor dining area with French cuisine and fine view plus piano music. American bar on 11th floor, also viewful.

Torni • *Yrionkatu 26;* ☎ *131131.* Several eggs in one hotel basket. Cantonese cuisine on 12th floor. Seafood on the 13th. Groundfloor **Parrilla Torni** with paella valenciana and suckling pig. **Ritarisali** for Finnish finger-lick'n and game.

SUMMER SPOTS

The schooner **Margona** is moored at the main quai of the Market. **Klippan** is a marvelous 19th-century house on a tiny island (regular transport from the Market). **Sarkanlinna** is facing Kaivopuisto (reached from Cafe Ursula quai); long window-lined seasider that couldn't be more romantic.

NIGHTLIFE

Frequently the restaurants and the nightlife are synonymous here, since the majority of Suomi dining spots would constitute nightclubs in most other lands. Most after-dark places are very expensive.

Underground • *Eerikinkatu 3*; and **La Havanna**, *Erottajankatu 7.* Two of the leaders on the nightscape. They are lively and pull in a frisky young clientele. As discos go, both are pretty reasonable in price.

Vanha Maestr • *Fredrikinkatu 51;* ☎ *644303.* Dutifully opens its doors for those with an urge to dance from 2 p.m. onwards on Mon.-Sat.; On Sunday it rests at 9 p.m., and on this day, and Wednesday it is chiefly for women.

WHAT TO SEE AND DO

First, drop in on the **City Tourist Office** *(Pohjoisesplanadi 19,* ☎ *1693757)*, close to the harbor, for pamphlets, brochures, and suggestions on adventuring through Finland's capital by bus, boat, tram or private car.

If you are a museum buff, then you've arrived in Walhalla, because there are 66 of 'em in the immediate area, probably more per capita than in any capital in the world.

Obtain the 1-, 2-, or 3-day low-cost Helsinki Card providing free entry to about 50 museums and sights plus unlimited travel on the city's public transportation systems. You might like the 1-1/2-hour tours by bus which operate daily in summer, always carry English-speaking guides, and cover just about every standard attraction. The CTO can furnish all the details. So can the **Helsinki Tourist Association** *(Lonnrotinkatu 7; ☎ 645225).*

A number of **boat excursions** are available. They include the fascinating shorty out to **Suomenlinna**, in ancient times considered second only to Gibraltar as a seagirt stronghold. (In winter, if the freeze is solid enough, you can walk on the sea out to the gates.) However, if you wish to go-it-alone, "water taxis" in all sizes are available by the hour or day. Go to the marketplace and take your pick. Built into the fortress are three restaurants: Walhalla (very expensive, but worthwhile as a splurge), an inexpensive cafe in the ramparts with a viewful outdoor terrace for fine days, and, quite naturally, an authentic Finnish pizzeria. A visit can occupy half a day or more, so you'll probably need a meal.

An outstanding target is the Helsinki **zoo** situated on Korkeasaari ("High Island"), a 1/4-hour ferry ride or reachable via the new Mustikkamaa Bridge. This ancient landmark, with its natural "cat" area isolated by sunken pits, is one of Finland's biggest drawing cards.

The special #3T **tram tour** makes a figure 8 through the heart of the metropolis. Cost for this swing is 9 FM. No guides are supplied, but special pamphlets, printed in several languages, are issued. A good place to start and to finish is the Open Market.

Seurasaari, across an island bridge and 15 minutes from the center, offers a fascinating collection of authentic Finnish country houses from various provinces, some of them many centuries old. All have been scouted out on their original sites, disassembled log by log and nail by nail, and reassembled. Guides are dressed in an assortment of regional costumes. Folk dancing is featured in season. Here's the best place of all in which to spend the Midsummer Eve holiday.

Pick up a brochure of the **Walking Tours**. They cover such routes as the Old Town, the Diplomatic Trail, Inner Bay, and Ships and Shore.

The **Mannerheim Museum** *(Kalliolinnantie 14)*, near the U.S. Embassy, presents a massive collection of artifacts gathered by the revered Marshal Carl Gustav Mannerheim, who led his nation's troops in five wars. Open 11 a.m. to 3 p.m. Fri., Sat., and to 4 p.m. Sun.

If you are a fan of unusual architecture, be sure to see the flat-domed rock and glass **Temppelaukio Church**. The interior is hewn into native stone.

The **CTO** publishes various excellent booklets and leaflets which will give you all other listings, hours, admission charges, and other details of interest.

CONCERTS

Finlandia Hall is the building; lakeside Hesperia Park is the place. Alvar Aalto is the architect. They don't only play Sibelius. Recitals, jazz, pop events, as well as symphony performances, regularly exercise the acoustics of this marble and granite tone poem.

HELSINKI FESTIVAL

A cup of culture that overflows annually with ballet, theater, opera, jazz, pop music, cinema, and literature. For details, contact Helsinki Festival, *Unioninkatu 28, SF-00100 Helsinki 10; ☎ (90) 659688.*

AMUSEMENT PARK

Linnanmaki is the best-liked magnet for merrymakers. The highest point (270 feet) of the city might be likened to, in a much more modest way, a Tivoli. It offers the biggest roller coaster in Europe, lots of other rides, variety shows—something for just about everybody. Open May 5 to Sept. 6.

MOVIES

Original-language films subtitled in Finnish and Swedish play on Helsinki's 52 screens; program changes are frequent and extremely current.

MARKETS

To find the **Open Market**, just follow the Esplanade down to the base of the harbor. Fish, flowers, fruits, and vegetables shine on bayside counters. You can wander for a long time soaking up the vibrant sounds, pungent smells, and colorful displays provided by this tent city of stalls, bins, wandering vendors, and chatter. Best from 7 a.m. till 10 a.m. From Easter to late autumn, a couple of coffee tents function at waterside where meat patties, pastries, doughnuts, and other regional snacks and confections are on sale for very little money. We've seen them even in midwinter, when Finland joins Asia by ice. Somehow food tastes better in the fresh air—a filling, inexpensive substitute for a full meal in a restaurant. The **Evening Market** functions at the same locale from 3:30 p.m. to 8 p.m. with less emphasis on food and more on fur hats from Lappish camps, fleece-lined slippers, vests, knitted whatnots, leather, whalebone, and similar nordic notions. It functions from mid-May to late August and is one of the best shows in town.

PUBLICATIONS

Your best bet is the free, 4-language publication *Helsinki This Week*. Your hotel porter or desk clerk should have a stack of copies prominently displayed—but if he hasn't, ask him to send out for one. News in English is reported in *Hufvudstadsbladet* (just try that one at your friendly corner kiosk), or *Aamulehti*.

WHERE TO SHOP

We've already mentioned the Open Market and the Evening Market. Go there first for unusual gift items.

CRYSTAL, PORCELAIN AND CERAMICS

Hackman Shop • *Pohjoisesplanadi 25*. This is the stunning showcase for legendary Arabia company. It is very crowded, but the sales staff handle all queries and orders with ease. Out at the factory *(Hameentie 135)*, a long but rewarding bus ride from midtown, there is an Exhibition Gallery where items in its changing shows are for sale, a fascinating museum displaying famous designs going back a century, and, best of all, a seconds shop to which knowledgeable Finns head. Call the Head Guide *(☎ 790211)* for more details.

DEPARTMENT STORE

Stockmann • *Aleksanterinkatu 52B*. Helsinki's Macy's-Gimbel's-Filene's-Bullocks rolled into one. Not fancy, but just about everything basic is on tap here, including a good souvenir section.

Senaatin Tori *(in the historic Senate Square)* is a conglomerate of about 40 shops plus several restaurants. **Forum** *(Mannerheimintie 20)* and **Kluuvi** *(Aleksanterinkatu 9)* are two additional shopping complexes. There's a little world under the Central Station, too, usually open till 10 p.m. and good in a pinch.

FASHION

Marimekko • *Pohjoisesplanadi 31*. One of the top names of the North.

JEWELRY

It's a toss-up between **Kalevala Koru** *(Unioninkatu 25)* and **Kaunis Koru** *(Senaatin-Tori)* for interesting stocks of spectrolites and other semiprecious stones mined only above Finland's Arctic Circle; prices relatively so low that they're difficult to believe; in addition, the former specializes in ancient Finnish designs in silver and bronze and other handicrafts.

SAUNAWARE

Sauna Soppi-Shop • *Aleksanterinkatu 28, in the Senaatin Tori.* The hottest spot in town for all elements of this Finnish lore. Interesting gift ideas, too.

WOODEN ARTICLES

Aarikka • *Pohjoisesplanadi 27.* You'll find jewelry, games, children's toys, tableware and decorations, ornaments of all kinds and discover myriad present possibilities.

AUTHOR'S OBSERVATION

All goods costing more than 100 FM and going back to the States have 11% deducted from their purchase price. The refund is made at all departure points when a check covering the tax (which has been provided by the store where the article was purchased) is presented along with the merchandise. This applies even if a credit card was used for payment.

HVITTRASK

The former home and studio of Saarinen, Lindgren, and Gesellius is a captivating cache for architecture buffs. It represents one of the early (and graciously successful) attempts to blend structure into landscape. Near the stone-and-log complex there's a superb free swimming beach; also a good restaurant. Connections by bus (platform 62) and taxi are best. The nearest train depots are **Luoma** (a mile walk) and **Masala** (where there's a taxi rank).

JYVASKYLA

This nucleus of central Finland, an ancient cultural community that is now industrialized by big neighboring pulp, paper, and engineering works, is a departure station for expeditions in all directions. Many structures of this unusually eye-appealing town were blueprinted by Alvar Aalto. When needled by a local newspaperman, the professor replied, "My second best building is your Museum, right here at Jyvaskyla. My best I haven't designed yet."

KUOPIO

The touristic capital of the **Eastern Lake District** is the jumping-off point for the renowned lake excursions which ripple out in various directions. Dominating the settlement is a big hill crowned by a tower with a revolving restaurant. Try to visit this center, if you can, and see the daily open market. The town museum also is worth a look. Incidentally, the natives of Kuopio speak such a difficult dialect that not even the other Finns can understand it.

The curious, unique, and legendary **Greek Orthodox church** (with its museum back in the city) and the Valamo monastery near Kuopio (in Heinavesi) are worth a special journey.

LAHTI

A 65-mile inland ride from the capital, this busy center was a market crossroads for hundreds of years. At the turn of the century it sprang into a mushrooming parish which now supports 100,000 inhabitants and industrial dynamism. Because of its youth, and consequent adaptability, architecturally it is a Design for Tomorrow. Many visitors call it "the most American city in Finland." Lahti, proud of the huge Mallasjuoma Brewery, also brags it is the biggest furniture-making center on the Continent.

OULU

Situated on the west coast about 400 miles due north of Helsinki, this city is the shopping, trading, medical, and educational matrix for thousands of square miles of the nation's midriff. This dominant rail and road junction stands on a group of islands at the mouth of the Oulujoki River; its wild rapids have been tamed by mammoth hydroelectric turbines. The first island contains the very modern, swiftly expanding new city, the second a stadium and sports center, and the third a carefully planned community for public entertainment. There are 2 big pulp mills to break the flat, stark skyline; leather is also a local moneymaker. There's a famous quip that the buildings of its recently founded university are spread out so haphazardly that the Dean of Architecture once stepped out for a cup of coffee and was never seen again. This town of around 97,000 draws mainly business traffic.

PORI

Normally businesslike, it changes radically in July when its Jazz Festival is going full-tilt. At that time quite a few foreigners arrive for the music and jubilee. Peaking an isosceles triangle roughly 70 miles above the base formed by Tampere and Turku, Pori is a West Coast port that services the wealthy farming country surrounding it. The textiles produced here are the brightest jewels in its crown; pulp, paper, and engineering works less significant.

PORVOO

On sunny days an excursion here is popular. The steamer J. L. Runeberg departs on Wednesdays, Fridays, and weekends in June and July or Wednesdays and Fridays in August at 10 a.m. from the Helsinki Market Square. If you don't eat aboard enroute, you may save your appetite for the **Vanha Laamanni** in the heart of the lovely Old Town *(Vuorik 17; ☎ 915130455)* or the Haikko Hotel at the stop before.

ROVANIEMI

Teetering perhaps 5 miles below the Arctic Circle and euphemistically called the "Gateway to Lapland," here's an end-of-the-line—the railway line but not the airline. "Gateway?" Yes—except that you must still traverse a 200-mile corridor before reaching the home tundra of the Lapps and their reindeer, an unworthy journey unless you plan to forge onward to the Far Northern settlements of **Pallastunturi** or **Ivalo**. But zip up to Rovaniemi on any of Finnair's easy flights, because it's colorful, unusual, and beautiful, with 2 first-class hotels and a limited number of simple but comfortable budget accommodations for which reservations should be made in advance. Perhaps you'll see Santa at work or at rest. Local Finns gave Mr. Claus a home, a restaurant, a gift (sic) shop, and a post office so that the busy Norseman may offer greater hospitality to visitors of this chilly clime.

SAVONLINNA

Here's another jewel in the eastern diadem of the nation that can be incorporated easily into the lake circuit and medium-range routes north from the capital. Most visitors head straight for the medieval castle of **Olavinlinna**, where in July there is a well-staged Opera Festival that draws patrons from all over the North. As with Kuopio and scads of other Finnish gems, cameras were invented for it.

TAMPERE

This 2nd city of the nation is 109 miles northwest of Helsinki and almost completely encompassed by lakes. This so-called Pittsburgh of Finland keeps the majority of its 170,000 citizens out of mischief in its steel, paper, pulp, linen, and textile factories, plus its university. Despite so much heavy industry, it is a green city replete with parks. Apart from having 4 women to every 3 men, Tampere's next proudest boast is a 1000-seat outdoor auditorium that revolves somewhat less rapidly than a merry-go-round; it spins in season only. The Sarkanniemi Recreation Center is a stellar attraction with an amusement park, children's zoo, observation tower (with the revolving Nasinneula Restaurant airborne 375 feet up), aquarium, and planetarium. Visited each year by many thousands of foreign tourists. Under "Helsinki" we've described the special discount card that the capital offers to visitors. The same sort of program exists for Tampere, so be sure to have a look at the money-saving opportunities that are available here.

TAPIOLA

This unique fragment of organic history, only 6 miles from the capital in the city of **Espoo**, might stagger you. It is probably the finest modern planned community in the world today. In 1954, when the Housing Foundation, a private nonprofit organization, commenced the development of 670 virgin acres of lovely sea vistas ringed by birches and dense pine forests, it selected 12 of Finland's top architects to design it. This still-unfinished masterpiece is broken down into 3 independent neighborhoods, each with its own shopping centers and schools. Here is a 21st-century projection of city planning unparalleled elsewhere.

TURKU

Due west of Helsinki, this thriving metropolis of 162,000 is the land's cultural hub, 14th-century capital, original seat of its tradition-rich A.D. 1640 university, a castle site of the Middle Ages, and a paramount passenger port for Sweden. Its long and spirited competition with Tampere as the nation's 2nd center is lost by a paltry 5000 souls. Shipbuilding, foodstuffs, textiles, and ceramics lead its commerce. The **Handicraft Museum**, one of the few building complexes to survive the great fire of 1827, is especially worth visiting. Not yet much of a tourist magnet.

FOR MORE INFORMATION ON FINLAND

USA • Finnish Tourist Board, *655 Third Ave., New York, NY 10017;* ☎ *(212) 949-2333.*

INSIDER TIP

(1) Once you've arrived, **Finland Travel Bureau**, Kaivokatu 10, Helsinki, *is the master organization. You may also utilize the assistance of the* **Finnish Tourist Board** *at* Etelaesplanadi.

(2) There's an extensive network of offices throughout Europe where you can find additional aid. Check **Finnish Tourist Board** *listings in London, Paris, Copenhagen, Oslo, Stockholm, Madrid, Amsterdam, Zurich, Hamburg, Milan, and Munich.*

(3) There's a live-wire staff at the **City Tourist Office** *in the capital* (Pohjoisesplanadi 19*) who can be of enormous on-the-scene assistance.*

(4) Most municipalities provide their own information facilities.

(5) The **Helsinki Card** *is described under "Helsinki"; a similar one applies to Tampere.*

(6) A recent devaluation of the Finn Mark will bring you great savings across the board.

(7) Most hotels drop their rates by 50% from the middle of June to the middle of August. Always request a reduction.

FRANCE

Hotel de Ville

For the wise traveler, France is always a desired destination. The variety is endless, and today you will find that you receive more for your *franc* than you may get for your converted dollar in many other nations. It's a question of value—and since the French continue to demand it for themselves, you as a visitor also become a beneficiary of this enduring standard.

Where to begin?

Many start with Paris; frenetic, cosmopolitan, with something for everyone. From this dynamic hub of age-old culture and contemporary chic (if not hauteur), you can radiate out to the land of the valiant Normans—the sea-chilled but handsome Atlantic coast; to the lyrical wine-rich Rhone valley, or the other vinelands of Burgundy—so filled with history—of Bordeaux and Champagne; to the nearby Chateaux country with its fairyland magic. Or if you have a car (or bicycle), follow the "Fleche Verte" ("Green Arrow" that looks more like a Roman broadsword) route to the Basque domain along a network of fine back roads through forests and farmland and charming medieval towns with gaunt greystone fortifications and ancient monuments.

The Pyreneean chain is reached via hairpin bends with verdant vistas; it has a rustic, forgotten-country charm all its own. The Côte d'Azur glitters as a genuine playland of international sunbelt habitues, yet despite its gilt-edged appearance there are many ways to enjoy it on an economy basis; moreover, the hilltowns were cradles of Impressionism where many artists lived and where numerous museums have been dedicated to their creativity. Move westward to the winningly bizarre St. Tropez and into the wildly romantic Camargue, where reedy Mediterranean bayous cloak herds of wild horses and flocks of exotic flamingos and marsh fowl.

If it's alpine scenery you crave, the Lyon-Grenoble-Chambery triad offers the combination of superb winter skiing and summer hiking from its many famous resorts. Albertville and the Courchevel complex was the scene of the recent Winter Olympics.

Between all the huffing and puffing of travel, the legendary French cuisine serves as three delightful landmarks in each day—from fresh croissant and cafe au lait at breakfast to your cognac nightcap.

TIPS ON FRANCE

FOOD

Fantastic fare whether you pay a mint or a sou. If you are moving around a lot, pick up a budget guide titled "Relais Routiers." It lists approximately 4000 hotels and restaurants where the prerequisite is that they serve a simple abundant meal for $9 or less. A sampling of about 3 dozen of these entries revealed them to be especially gratifying in the provinces, though they were certainly adequate in or near large centers as well.

If the letters "s.g." or "a.s." are printed instead of the usual mathematical amount, ask for the price of a portion. The letters "s.g." stand for *selon grosseur* and usually refers to lobster or fish, which is sold by weight or size; "a.s." applies to more seasonal items such as melon, asparagus, strawberries, and the like.

To get the full menu, ask for the *carte*; to save money, ask for the "Tourist Menu" ("Menu Touristique") or the regular "Menu." This is the fixed-price meal—usually appetizer or soup, main course, and cheese, fruit, or dessert—that is always much cheaper than if you

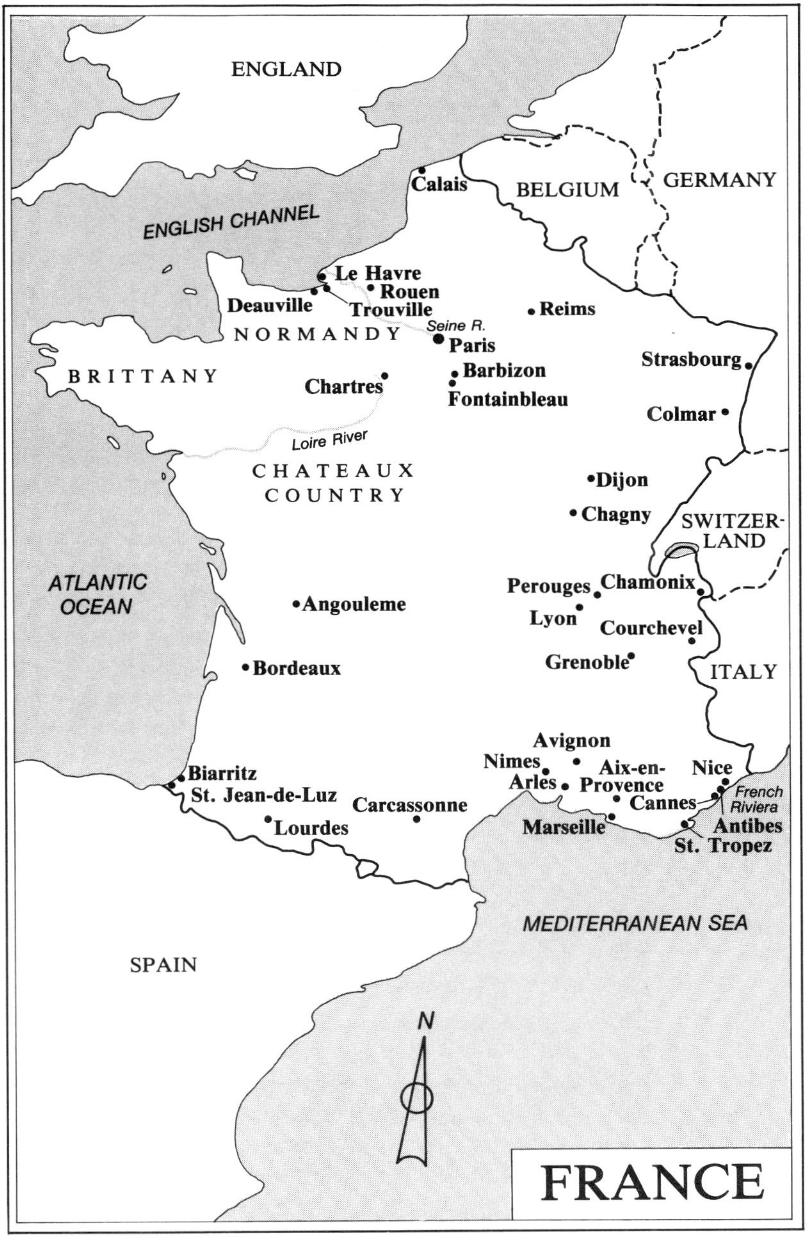
ENGLAND
BELGIUM
GERMANY
ENGLISH CHANNEL
Calais
Le Havre
Rouen
Deauville
Trouville
Reims
Seine R.
NORMANDY
Paris
BRITTANY
Chartres
Barbizon
Fontainbleau
Strasbourg
Colmar
Loire River
CHATEAUX COUNTRY
Dijon
Chagny
SWITZER-LAND
ATLANTIC OCEAN
Perouges
Chamonix
Angouleme
Lyon
Courchevel
Grenoble
Bordeaux
ITALY
Avignon
Nimes
Aix-en-Provence
Nice
Arles
Biarritz
St. Jean-de-Luz
Carcassonne
Cannes
French Riviera
Lourdes
Marseille
Antibes
St. Tropez
MEDITERRANEAN SEA
SPAIN
N
FRANCE

were to order the same items on an á la carte basis. Naturally, the restaurateur will never fail to hand you the latter list first.

You'll probably have to ask repeatedly for ice water. It is not customary for the French to drink tap water (for so many decades it was considered impure). Today many Frenchmen drink mineral water, either alone or to dilute their wine. You may care to order Evian for noncarbonated, Perrier for the most bubbles, and Vichy for fewer bubbles and a slightly salty flavor. There are international brands; many fine regional ones exist, too.

Meats, including lamb and liver, most often are served rare. Specify "*saignant*" when you want them "rare," "*a point*" when you want them "medium," "*bien cuit*" for "well done" or "*très cuit*" for "extra well done."

PRICES

It is more important to speak about values. In France you certainly dine well, and with a certain amount of care, you also can dine inexpensively.

NOTE FOR SMOKERS

It is now official: a non-smoking zone must be provided in restaurants. If, however, a friend of the house smokes, he or she will be given the best window table and non-puffing strangers are likely to be bumping elbows with the swinging doors to the kitchen. It is a law that may look strict on paper, but in spirit it's as evanescent as, well, smoke.

DRINKS

For everyday table wine, the *vin ordinaire* generally sells for about $6 per carafe in restaurants everywhere. Don't expect greatness, but it is usually satisfactory.

Among the lower-priced red wines, Beaujolais is usually an excellent bet. It should be ordered young; sometimes (especially in the south) it is served chilled. If not too wickedly expensive, get either Brouilly (which has been around for ages but becoming fashionable now and with a consequent rise in price), Moulin-a-Vent, Julienas, Morgon, or Fleurie (the subnames on the label). Other old standbys (perhaps higher in price) include Bordeaux such as St.-Julien, St.Emilion, Medoc, Pomerol, and St.-Estephe.

Among white wines, Sancerre can be a stunningly fine buy either from a bottle or a carafe. Chablis is very tricky, due to minuscule supplies of sound types. If you like your wines dry, Pouilly Blanc Fume, Pouilly-Fuisse, or Muscadet are splendid. What passes for Chavignol in many places today is a horrid counterfeit. But Traminer, from Alsace, still has an affinity for a good filet of sole.

Order Vouvray or *vin mousseux* (sparkling wine) if you want to save money. The champagne name is patented, and these varieties originate outside the legal district. Hence, they provide a similar experience at a much lower cost.

Most of the beer is frightful—bitter, watery, with an aftertaste of kidney-fed pollywogs; at least it's cheap. Fortunately, some Alsatian brews are fine and the better Dutch and Scandinavian beers are available at reasonable prices. Always ask for "be-air," because "beer" to the French waiter means "Byrrh," the brand name of a popular red vermouth-type aperitif.

Whereas it used to be scornful to drink water at a French table, many health-conscious consumers (especially at lunchtime) forego wine for mineral water or fruit juice. Incidentally, in France the popular brand of bubbling water, Perrier, is almost never sipped with a meal. It is offered as an *aperitif* beforehand or after the meal for refreshment, while another brand (usually a still water) is served with the food.

GETTING AROUND

TRAINS

The **French National Railroads** (SNCF) are among the best and fastest in the world; you've probably read about the TGV (*Train a Grande Vitesse*), which hit 320 mph on a test run and usually streaks along at close to 170 mph on ordinary passages. East-west local service is poor at times, but north-south trunk lines are generally very good.

And while the speed is stunning—you can zip from Paris to Lille in one hour—it can also take another hour to buy the blasted ticket! The problem is in SNCF's convoluted database, so for the time being be sure to reserve well in advance or use a travel agent with lots of patience.

Before, porters were almost impossible to snag in the Paris stations. On several recent occasions the ones snagged seemed to be either louts or drunks. The same has been true on several encounters with some of the baggage personnel at both Paris airports.

If you plan much pan-European train-travel, take advantage of the savings offered by the Eurailpass; if you are only going to France and the U.K., a combined program has been provided by the two nations. The SNCF offers its own **France Railpass**, which is a great money-saver if you plan to travel only in Gaul. The validity extends over fixed periods but not necessarily over consecutive days. For example, a 4-day ticket may be used over 15 days. There are 9- and 16-day versions, also to apply within a month. These include benefits such as Paris airport transport, car rental, and admission to certain tourist attractions. Ask, too, about the **Rail and Drive Pass**, which provides an auto (3 or 6 days within 15 days or a month respective) and train travel (4 and 9 days within the same time frames). An Avis car can be waiting for you at more than 200 rail depots. The prices are very reasonable. In North America you can obtain all of the details from **Rail Europe**, *230 Westchester Ave., White Plains N.Y. 10604*; ☎ *(914) 682-2999.*

Children under 4 ride free; those under 12 receive sizable reductions. Stopovers are permitted, and groups of 10 or more are given 30 percent to 40 percent reductions. For excursions from Paris, 1-day Sunday tickets and 3-day weekend tickets for destinations within roughly 50 miles of the capital come at a 30 percent to 50 percent bargain.

Fixed meals at about $14 are served; they are unspectacular in quality. You may obtain reservations for 1st, 2nd, or 3rd sitting before departure on the platform in front of the restaurant car, or from the roving steward aboard. You may also be seated without prior arrangement after all reservation holders have been accommodated.

There are 3 ways to sleep: in the coach, in the couchette, and in the *wagon-lit.* The coach is for the adaptable traveler who can sleep in a semi-seated position. The couchette offers 6 bunks per unit for a supplement; you may stretch out but not undress. The *wagon-lit* is the Pullman of Europe; you'll pay for your railroad ticket, your berth, your reservation, and your service tax. Very expensive!

Tickets are collected *after* you get off the train. Don't mistakenly throw yours away, or you may pay double.

PLANES

Air Inter, serving 30 French cities, probably again will be offering its cut-rate **Visit France**, good for 14 days of flying within the network; savings range from 30 percent to 47 percent; fair fleet equipment; clients usually fly during slack hours. There are also money-saving fly-drive packages.

BARGES

You can enjoy *la belle France* afloat from the deck or cabin of a **river barge**. Rates include accommodation, food, and wine; cruise duration usually is about a week. Write to **Continental Waterways** (*127 Albert Bridge Rd., London, S.W. 11*), which also provides a chug through British canals. In the USA they are represented by Abercrombie & Kent. Full information is also contained in a French Tourist Office newsletter under the chapter Ballooning & Waterway Tour Operations.

BUSES

If it is in operation again this year, the **Relais Bus Pass** can save you tanks of francs on 15-, 21-, 30-, or 60-day jaunting. You also receive a free map and a guidebook. For details, write to **Federation Inter Jeunes France Europe**, *218 rue St. Jacques, Paris 75005.*

GASOLINE

Wickedly expensive; expect to pay at least double what you do back home.

ROADS

Good surfaces mostly; many excellent high-speed turnpikes; perhaps 400 more miles of 3-lane killers; superb 2-laners, perhaps the finest in Europe. If you are in no hurry, always take an indirect route via the narrow county roads; they are maintained perfectly and traffic usually is light except when farmers are going to or from their fields just after dawn and at dusk. On these the signposting is generally atrocious, so always buy a detailed map if you're following the byways—especially in the Chateaux District.

A speed limit of 90 kilometers (54 miles) per hour is imposed on all "ordinary" thoroughfares (generally one lane each direction). A 110-kilometer (67 mph) maximum is set for the larger national highways of two lanes in either direction (which constitute most of the balance) and a 130-kilometer (78 mph) limit on the superhighways. In urban and village areas, the 50-kilometer (30 mph) restraint has just been brought down a notch (formerly 60 kph); local mayors can further reduce this speed limit, but they may not increase it. Big trucks are prohibited from rolling on Sundays between 6 a.m. and 10 p.m. Crash helmets are compulsory for motorcyclists. Other checks include massive turnpike surveillance by helicopter and plainclothesmen in unmarked cars, breath analyses and blood tests to assess driver sobriety, and the foundation of the "Commission for the Immediate Suspension of Drivers' Licenses"—a nationwide body empowered to fine violators on the spot (without a court hearing), to confiscate their permits, and to make them *walk* to the nearest garage or town.

Don't park your rented auto in the wrong area in Paris, Marseille, or Nice (to name a few centers), or it will be carted away. The haulage will be charged to you. If you find yourself in one of the many "Blue Zones" (1-hour limit), you must set the time of arrival and of departure on your own parking *disque*, which can be obtained at auto clubs, police stations, rental agencies, and gas pumps. Warning: Once you've set it, don't cheat by resetting it for more time at the same location. It means a $10 or $20 penalty. Officials are putting dragons' teeth into the motoring laws nowadays; heavy fines are not uncommon for parking offenses.

For minor infractions, you may be able to get off cheaper by paying within 8 days. Tobacco shops are supposed to sell special stamps that cost less than the normal fine. Mail these in to the local police department, and you've bought redemption.

CAR HIRE

There are lots of agents and lots of cars of every size and type. **Avis** (*in Paris at 16 pl. Vendome; Metro: Opera;* ☎ *40730896*) can arrange dropoffs in many other countries. This one and **Hertz** are always front-and-center at the airports.

BICYCLES

Rail stations in 241 French cities have bicycles for use locally (a few dollars per day including insurance; deposit required). The price even pays for transport of the bike to your next stopover. If you bring your own, the French National Railroads will haul it as baggage for a very low sum to anywhere in the nation.

MOTORCYCLES AND SCOOTERS

Rentals are rugged—if not impossible—to arrange here. Several dealers, however, *sell* vehicles under a guaranteed repurchase plan, but they habitually end up with the profit end of the stick. In Paris, the **French Federation of Camping and Caravans** (*66 rue Rene-Boulanger; Metro*: Republique; ☎ *42688179*) supplies lists of dealers on request.

SPORTS

SKIING

How about doing it in shorts or in a bikini? The French **Alps** in summer is the place. For courses, either summer or winter, ask the French Government Tourist Office for the new *French Alps Discovery Guide* or contact any of the following: Office of Tourism, *38750 Alpe-d'Huez*; ☎ *76803541*; the Office of Tourism, Deux-Alpes Loisirs, *38860 Les Deux-Alpes*; ☎ *76792200*; the Office of Tourism, SAP-La Plagne, *73210 Aime*; ☎ *79090201*; the Office of Tourism, STGM, ValClaret, *73320 Tignes*; ☎ *79061555*; the STVI, *73150 Val d'Isere*; ☎ *79061083*; and the Office of Tourism, *SETAM-73440 Val-Thorens*; ☎ *79000808*. Winter skiing is superb, but we find it more expensive than in Switzerland; lodging is often more costly. Val d'Isere is tops for serious skiing. In **Les Trois Vallees** (Courchevel, Meribel, and Thorens—recently promoted to four valleys with the inclusion of Les Menuires), Thorens is probably the best buy, while Courchevel 1850 is the most expensive. (The "1850" refers to its altitude in meters; usually the higher the resort, the more lofty the prices.) This district, with Albertville as residential and administrative headquarters, has smartened up considerably since it played host for the Winter Olympics.

HORSES

There are six flat and two trotting tracks in or near Paris. Biggest days Thursdays and Sundays in mild weather (closed August). **Longchamp** and **Auteuil** are the favorites.

SIGHTSEEING

TOURING BY TRAIN

Heading for the Riviera this summer? Take the Alpazur train and savor the Alpine and Provençal scenery enroute. Beginning May 23, shuttles daily between **Grenoble** and **Nice** (both ways). Special stewardesses describe the regional history and culture along the way; also colorful folkloric shows. Snacks and beverages available. About $55 first class; $45 second class. Eurailpass, Eurail Youthpass, and France Vacances travelers hop aboard for about $12.50.

ART AND ARCHITECTURE

France's excellent provincial museums often go unnoticed. The one in **Colmar** is famous for its altarpiece; in **Castres** for Goya's formidable "The Junta of the Philippines"; in **Rouen** for Ingres's "La Belle Zelie." The Matisse Museum at **Cimiez** is just a few yards from where Matisse lived and worked. Students of 19th- and 20th-century works enjoy the Museum of Modern Art in **Troyes**. For more traditional tastes, the Musee Bonnat in **Bayonne** offers Rubens, Goya, Puvish de Chavannes, and Degas. **Orleans** has a Beaux Arts trove containing Gauguin, Courbet, Boucher, Rodin, Maillol, Zadkine—a skein from the 16th-20th centuries; it's north of the cathedral on place Ste. Croix. For a blend of architecture, painting, and sculpture it's the Musee des Augustins in **Toulouse**. The Museum of the New World in **La Rochelle** focuses on Americana from the French perspective.

The **Riviera** is a festival of museum and cultural activity. Apart from its 25 miles of beaches it offers nearly 200 museums and galleries. In my estimation the crown jewel is **St. Paul de Vence**, with its open-air sculpture gardens and corridors of Impressionist art at the hillside **Maeght Foundation**. The Miro and Calder creations seem to dominate the exterior with a treasury of paintings inside by Bonnard, Braque, Dubuffet, Kandinsky, Leger, Matisse, and Chagall. There's also **Matisse's Chapel** at nearby **Vence** (open Tuesdays and Thursdays only) and the stunning and freshly renovated **Fernand Leger Museum** at **Biot** with more than 300 works by the artist. Of special interest are the ceramics. **Nice**, of course, is an attraction in itself, but it boasts the heavily endowed **Museum of Modern and Contemporary Art**. At **Vallauris** you'll find the major ceramics exhibits at the **National Picasso Museum**, home to the monumental War and Peace mural. **Antibes** also boasts a Picasso collection at **Chateau Grimaldi**. Cagnes-sur-Mer displays some extraordinary Renoir gems plus the **Museum of Modern Mediterranean Art**. The **Ile-de-France** at **St. Jean-Cap Ferrat** contains many Renoirs, Monets, and Sisleys. At **Menton**, have a look at the town museum as well as the town hall where works of Jean Cocteau—a myth in his own time along the Côte d'Azur—are on display. Antibes, Cannes, Nice, and a host of villages along this sunny shore are thick with contemporary collections.

WINE TASTING

Throughout the year **L'Académie du Vin** offers 3-, 6-, and 10-session courses ranging in price from about $75 to $160. For full details contact them at *25 rue Royale (Cite Berryer) 75008 Paris*; ☎ *42650982*.

FRANCE FOR THE JEWISH TRAVELER

This newly expanded, 40-page brochure features facets of French Jewish life plus a multitude of ethnic and cultural tips. Published jointly by the French Government Tourist Office, Air France, and the French National Railroads, it includes historic sights, synagogues, kosher restaurants and nosheries. Attention centers on Paris, Lyon, Bordeaux, Bayonne, the Loire, Marseille, Aix-en-Provence, Avignon, Cavaillon, and Carpentras. Available free if you go to the French Government Tourist Office (Paris or New York) or from the Public Information Center, 610 Fifth Ave., New York, NY.

PACKAGE TOURS

The French Government Tourist Office offers the 28-page *France Packages and Tours* summarizing programs ranging from barge, balloon, and biking tours, to Paris show tours and day-trips to the Ile de France. Students and bargain-seekers will find many low-cost offerings. It also lists information on home and villa rentals. Then there is the slick, fat magazine, previously mentioned, called *France Discovery Guide* (put out by the same FGTO) that cleverly assembles tours and fine photos into a lovely montage of temptations. It is designed for all budgets. There's also the *Welcome Center* booklet, which is a mine of tips and suggestions and, once you have both feet on French soil, there's a toll-free phone number called "*numero vert*" (☎ *05-201-202*) that will give you the green light to follow scads of pastimes. It answers Monday through Saturday from 8:30 a.m. to 8 p.m. from May through October. Finally, AT&T may again issue its *Fun Book* with coupons for scores of free drinks, admission to exhibits, and guided tours. Ask about all of these and cash in on some tremendous rewards.

SHOPPING

Store hours are completely screwy: the plush jewelers, dressmakers, hatmakers, and chichi operators stay open on Saturday but are closed Monday a.m. The hairdressers do work on Monday. The food stores are open all day Saturday and some do business on Sunday morning, but many are closed Monday. The department stores are open Monday-Saturday from 9:30 a.m. to 6:30 p.m. Some of the big fellows work right through lunch—but the vast majority operate only from 9 a.m. to 12 or 12:30 p.m., and from 2 p.m. to 6 or 6:30 p.m. Boutiques and specialty shops generally open at 10 a.m. and close between 7–7:30 p.m. Phew!

VAT REFUNDS

A TVA (**Taxe de Valeur Ajoutee** or referred to universally as VAT) customs refund is available to all nonresident travelers who will be leaving the country within 3 months. A minimum purchase of 2000 French francs in any one store qualifies the buyer for this windfall, which may be anywhere from 13 percent to 22 percent. Be sure to carry your passport; ask the salesperson for a Fiche de Douane; fill in the forms; decide how you want to obtain the bonus, mailed to your home, or credited to your credit card account directly. The credit refund is best because your bank is likely to take a large chomp out of any foreign check they cash for you. Follow all instructions offered by the shop and be sure to have your forms validated by French Customs officers at your point of departure, or all will be in vain. Two useful tips: if you're taking the refund at the airport allow an extra hour and a half because lines can be long, and pack your purchases in carry on luggage because you may be requested to show them.

THINGS NOT TO BUY

Very cheap clothing is often shoddy, but usually it will reflect the fashion stylings of the moment.

On the Riviera our enthusiasm for some of the much-touted perfumes of this region, notably Grasse, is very much on the dim side. They're not the same as the Big Name brands. These local varieties might do the job because they're cheap, they're pretty, and nobody can deny that they're French. However, the sales practices impress us as being slippery, misleading, and vile.

LOCAL RACKETS

Petty thievery is common in France. Don't leave any valuables in your hotel room. (We've even heard of locked suitcases being opened in hotel rooms or the pins in the back hinges removed so that a bag can be rifled without touching the locks.)

As mentioned, be careful in the Metros. Be especially alert getting off a train when the closing doors press others close to you and your wallet or purse.

Don't change any money on the streets. When *anyone offers you extra francs to the dollar, you can be certain* that you're about to be duped.

Sidewalk photographers in the tourist areas are a plague. They'll demand up to $8 for *one* Polaroid candid print.

To register an official squawk for any offense, the nation's complaint bureau is in the **French Government Tourist Office** (Service de Reclamations) *on rue de l'Ingenieur Robert Keller in Paris.*

WHERE TO GO

ARLES

The Rhone created it; the Romans polished it; the Gauls made it their capital; the kings of Burgundy called it home. It is a sunny hop from here down to historic **Aigues-Mortes**, to **Les Stes.-Mariesde-la-Mer**, and to the wilderness preserved in France's blustery **Camargue**. You can park at **Camping City** or the **Auberge de Jeunesse** for very little or at the **Moderne** for about $22 per night. The **Select** and **Jules Cesar** are much more expensive. Radiating north of Arles are **Nimes** and **Les Baux**.

AVIGNON

The popes chose it as their favorite home-away-from-home for more than a century (the 14th chiefly), and it's still lovely. If you are an incurable photographer aim your viewfinder at the Gothic churches of *St. Pierre*, *St. Agricol*, and **Notre Dame des Doms**. You can tour the **Palais des Papes** and have the city's history capsulized in the guide's 40-minute spiel. Strolling around the ramparts is free and a marvelous experience. The view from the top of the city is worth an hour's pause in your day, perhaps even the spot for a picnic. Local architecture reflects how real estate changed hands often among the former monarchs, generals, pontiffs, Babylonians, and mayors. A cultural schism and a great one. For overnighting, **St. Roch** and **Le Mignon** are good economy stops; **Le Danieli** and **Blauvac** offer a bit more comfort; **Primotel** is often the choice of motorists and so is the **Formule 1**, part of a good new chain. **Europe**, one of the most expensive, is known for its good kitchen.

BAYONNE

It's been a long time in growing. As one example, this city's famous **cathedral** was begun in 1213 and completed just about the time that Columbus was packing for his first voyage west. Somehow, it still looks unfinished. The busy port has hosted or cannonaded fleets from virtually all of the important maritime realms, many of which left behind characteristics of their respective heritages. Not far away you'll find . . .

BIARRITZ

Which is a swanky beach resort with palatial hotels, two casinos, sleek industrialists with well-oiled hides, and tanned mademoiselles whose demands on the textile crafts are piffling when they attire for fun in the sun. Expensive? Wow!

BORDEAUX

What was once a sleepy, decaying, and forgotten port is now abristle with activity and spirit. The city has awakened; the Old Town has been polished anew; architecture has been restored and cleaned; pedestrian malls have been zippered into the most scenic zones; shopping areas have been given zest and perk. While the Roman ruins remain an attraction for tourists, Bordeaux shines best in its raiments of the 18th century; it is often said to be the most handsome of any city in Europe. Reasonable accommodation (at rates below those of other major centers) can be found at the elegantly styled **Grand Hotel Francais** (a Best Western member), the **Quatresoeurs** bordering the Opera, and the **Royal Medoc**. For budgets try the **Onestar Hotel** in the train station, the **Notre Dame** in the Chartrons district, or the **Continental** in the center. For dining **La Tupina** does cooking in the fashion of a talented French housewife. Gardens, museums, and an infinite variety of walks should heighten your appetite for the excellent and not too costly local cuisine.

CANNES

Here is the gemstone in the costly Mediterranean bracelet known either as the Riviera or the Côte d'Azur—blue sea, golden sand, and red figures (at the bottom of each bill). It is affordable, however, if you know where to dwell, dine, and dawdle.

La Croisette, its palm-lined beach boulevard always a symbol of its discreet upper-class charm, buzzes with a voluptuous procession of glamour and fashion trends. The traffic—two-legged, four-wheeled, two-wheeled, and nautical—is intense; the atmosphere, torrid. Well-ordered beaches glisten with wall-to-wall sun-burnished skin since human barbecue is ritually practiced throughout the warm months. Every spring Cannes hosts the International Film Festival, a period when visitors seem to

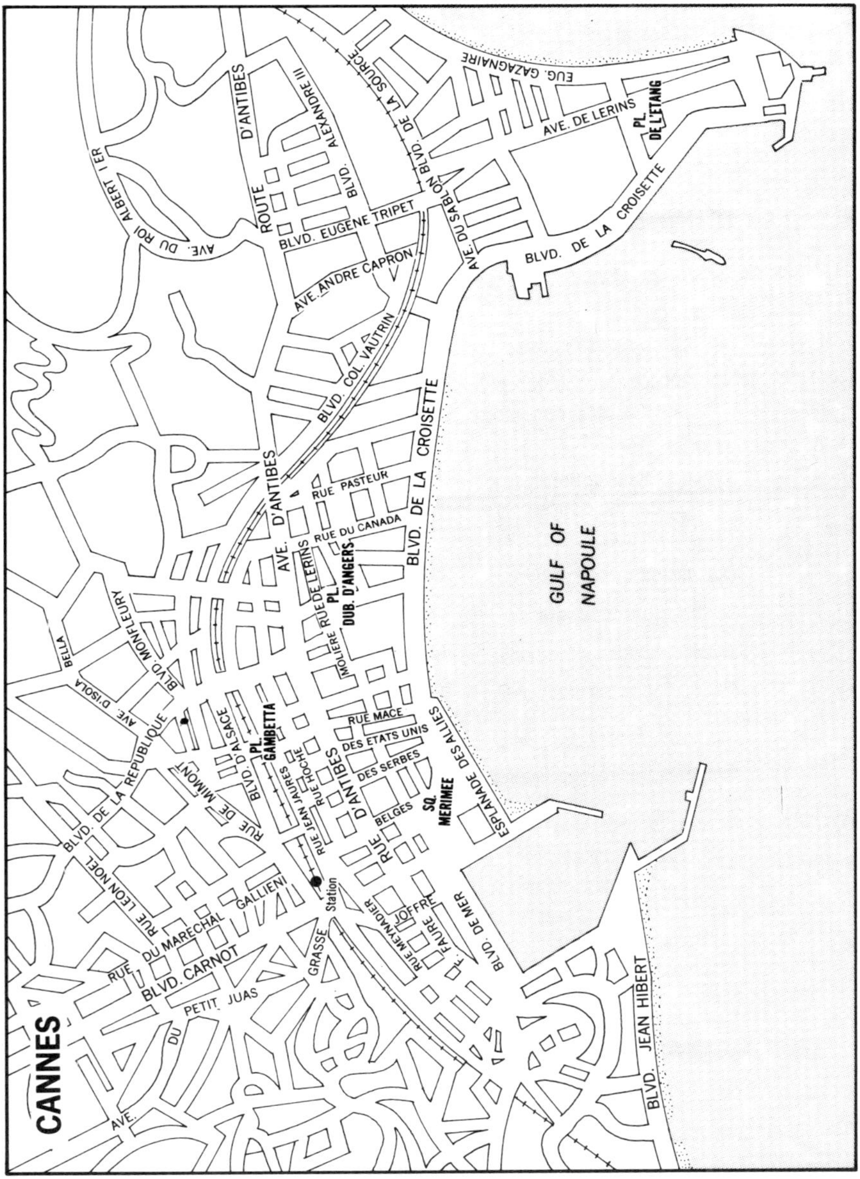
CANNES
GULF OF NAPOULE
BLVD. DE LA CROISETTE
AVE. D'ANTIBES
ROUTE D'ANTIBES
BLVD. ALEXANDRE III
BLVD. DE LA SOURCE
EUG. GAZAGNAIRE
AVE. DE LERINS
PL. DE L'ETANG
AVE. DU SABLON
BLVD. EUGENE TRIPET
AVE. DU ROI ALBERT I ER
AVE. ANDRE CAPRON
BLVD. COL. VAUTRIN
RUE PASTEUR
RUE DU CANADA
RUE DE LERINS
PL. DUB. D'ANGERS
MOLIERE
BLVD. MONFLEURY
BELLA
AVE. D'ISOLA
BLVD. DE LA REPUBLIQUE
RUE DE MIMONT
BLVD. D'ALSACE
PL. GAMBETTA
RUE JEAN JAURES
RUE HOCHE
RUE MACE
DES ETATS UNIS
DES SERBES
RUE D'ANTIBES
BELGES
SQ. MERIMEE
ESPLANADE DES ALLIES
RUE LEON NOEL
GALLIENI
Station
RUE DU MARECHAL
BLVD. CARNOT
GRASSE
RUE MEYNADIER
JOFFRE
FAURE
L.
BLVD. DE MER
AVE. DU PETIT JUAS
BLVD. JEAN HIBERT

reach for the outer limits of bizarre behavior. Unless you have confirmed reservations, avoid it during this manic spell. **Le Suquet**, the old quarter, with twisting lanes and ancient stonework, contrasts sharply with life in the fast lane. Take your choice: unbridled hedonism by the seashore or subtle antiquity among the ruins. Or both, perhaps.

DIRECTORY

U.S. Consulate in Nice • *3 rue du Docteur Barety;* ☎ *93-888955.*

American Express • *boulevard de la Croisette;* ☎ *93-391588.*

Laundromat • Lavoself, *rue Merimee*, corner *rue Rebuffel*, and Washmatic *36 rue G. Clemenceau.*

Barber and Hairdresser • Starlett, *18 rue d'Antibes*, for both men and ladies—and expensive, as they all are.

Dry Cleaning and Pressing • Pressing Europeen, *131 rue d'Antibes.*

English-Speaking Doctor • Dr. Vedrenne, *38 boulevard d'Alsace;* ☎ *93-392220.* Sunny Bank is an English-American hospital (not a tax shelter) at *88 avenue Petit-Juas,* ☎ *93-390198.*

English-Speaking Dentists • Dr. Saint-Paul, *7 square Merimee;* ☎ *93-392127*, Dr. Meyer, *27 boulevard de la Croisette;* ☎ *395221*, and Dr. Collin, *18 rue Latour-Maubourg;* ☎ *93-382129.*

Information Center • Syndicat d'Initiative, *Palais La Croisette;* ☎ *93-991977.*

Police • Central Station, *13 route de Grasse;* ☎ *93-391078.*

Favorite Pawnshop • Credit Municipal, *2 rue Bivouac.*

HOW TO GET AROUND

TAXI

Fares come close to being a swindle. Walk where you can, or use the city **buses** (a "carnet" of 20 tickets is a good buy). If you're bound for any point along the Croisette, minibuses roll until 8:30 p.m. The bus link between Cannes and the Nice Airport is about $10. Inquire at the terminal.

TRAINS

Since coastal distances are relatively short, fares are inexpensive. The 18-mile 1-way ride to Nice, for example, costs only $8 second-class or $13 first-class. You'll save time, too. For information on the national network, consult the transportation section at the beginning of this chapter.

MOTORING

From June 20 to September 20, when the vacation recess of France's schools coincides with high season, the logjam is catastrophic. Bottlenecks at the Italian frontier can be so severe on Sundays and holidays that as many as 300 automobiles stack up at the control points; at the rate of one car per 30 seconds, this can mean a 2-1/2 hour wait before clearance. The best times to cross are between 11 a.m. and 6 p.m., or before 9 a.m. and after 8 p.m. Around 3:30 a.m. isn't too bad, either.

WHERE TO STAY

In low season, hotels of all categories reduce their rates as much as 50 percent. In high season, however, lodgings are extremely tight and can be expensive. Advance reservations are a necessity then, because nearly all of the less costly houses are woefully limited in space.

With the possible exception of the first 2 entries under "Even More $$$" below, we found no *beach-side* hostelries suitable for low-cost travelers this year. But if you eschew the sands in favor of bunking a few blocks inland, you'll have a decent chance to find what you're after.

For last-minute accommodations, try either the **Syndicat d'Initiative de Cannes** (*rue Pasteur, adjoining the Miramar Hotel*) or the Welcome Information Service branch in the railroad terminal.

Cultural Note: Along this coast youth hostels and campgrounds have installed condom vending machines. In hotels *don't swallow the packet on the bedside table* until you examine it. The area is bristling with prophylactics—some free, some dispensed—as a voluntary program to control AIDS. France has the most people in Europe afflicted with the HIV virus.

LEAST $

Touring • *11 rue Hoche; ☎ 93383440.* Total of 30 spotless rooms with colorful bedspreads; $25 to $36 per person, depending on what's available. Breakfast about $3.50. Pleasing.

Le Florian • *8 rue Commandant-Andre; ☎ 93392482.* About 20 rooms with showers; all clean, abundantly furnished and with cretonne spreads.

Mimont • *39 rue de Mimont (near the station); ☎ 93395164.* Most units with shower. Clean and comfortable singles at $21; duals at $25; higher with private plumbing. Breakfast $4.50.

MORE $$

Wagram • *140 rue d'Antibes; ☎ 93945553.* Top choice. All 25 chambers renewed quite recently and on a continuing cycle; extra-pleasant #12 on 4th floor. Full-pension policy in summer, but for some reason you can get a 2-meal tariff in August.

Royal • *28 rue Commandat-Andre; ☎ 93991051.* Offers less than name implies; nonetheless, pretty good; 20 spacious chambers, mostly with showers (there are several full baths).

Hotel Les Dauphins Verts • *9 rue J.-Dollfus (within strolling distance of the Old Port and Plage du Midi); ☎ 93394582.* A converted mansion housing 15 units; half with bath and others with shower.

Moliere • *5 rue Moliere; ☎ 93381616.* In the nexus of the town; 12 bedrooms, 7 with shower or bath; 3 garden quartets. Most chambers narrow, but spotless. Cheerful breakfast nook. Reserve far ahead.

Bivouac • *29 rue Bivouac-Napoleon; ☎ 93396217.* Retreat for 2 troopers $24; $31 buys a shower; #21 fair as a bivouac.

Le Cheval Blanc • *3 rue Guy de Maupassant; ☎ 93398860.* Very agreeable, but you'll need a car.

EVEN MORE $$$

Belle Plage • *6 rue Jean-Dollfus; ☎ 93390812.* 150 yards across parklet from the Plage du Midi, it features courtyard gardens, ample parking, and chipper bedrooms with seaview balconies; approximately $40 to $50 each buys a double and bath with breakfast only. Nearby they also run the **Residence Veles** and **Villa Esterel**.

Corona • *55 rue d'Antibes;* ☎ *93396985.* Also town center; 20 sparkling units all with hot and cold water, fresh carpeting, and cheerful wallpaper. Front with baths; rear with showers. Recommendable.

Athenee • *6 rue Lecerf;* ☎ *93386954.* Another good buy. Modern, bright ambience; 5 of 16 rooms face a tiny breakfast terrace (no other meals).

Saint-Yves • *49 boulevard d'Alsace;* ☎ *93386529.* A converted old mansion nestled among noise-deadening gardens. Prices run between $42 and $62 for 2, including service, taxes, and breakfast; some with private plumbing; triples for about $75.

CAMPING

Mandelieu • A skip and a hop inland, offers about a dozen acceptable sites. Closer in, the **Bellevue** is in the La Bocca precincts (*avenue Maurice-Chevalier;* ☎ *93392897*). Bus #2 goes almost to your tent flaps.

WHERE TO EAT

LEAST $

L'Esterel • *5 square Merimee.* Bills itself as a tearoom, but steaks seem to be the specialty, accompanied by small carafes of wine and followed by chilled desserts. Space-age appointments, with down-to-earth prices.

Vesuvio • *65 boulevard de la Croisette.* Pizza and other Italian specialties. Lively promenade location; rustic interior. Nearly always packed.

Lion d'Or • *53 boulevard de la Republique;* ☎ *93397426.* Friendly mien; predominantly local clientele; super-clean. A meal of crudites, chicken, fruit, wine, and tip totaled $12. Reserve in advance. Very rewarding.

CAFETERIAS

Two suggestions: **Restaurama Côte d'Azur**, *facing Maritime Terminal*, with the American self-service concept. Bustling; counter offering the works for about $12; delightful harbor panorama. **Splendid**, *fronting the Railway Station* with generous portions at low prices.

SNACKS

La Socca • *rue Menadier.* A couple of blocks inland from the Mediterranean, scores with 2 *piccolo* rooms in *trattoria* motif. Most items $3.50 to $5; a la carte dinners perhaps $13. Jet-propelled service.

La Ferme la Mascotte • *place Gambetta.* For hardy fare. Run by the cheerful Corsican lady who opened La Socca. A champ with many Cannois.

MORE $$

Laurent • *16 rue Mace;* ☎ *93393256.* A "little museum of the table" decorated with antique cutlery. Tranquil setting; delicious skilletry; warm welcome. Enjoyable.

Le Coq Hardi • *6 rue de la Rampe (near Quai St.-Pierre);* ☎ *93391991.* Strong on chickens. Unelaborate milieu; more-or-less $17 per person. Try to snag a corner table in the sidewalk extension for harbor views.

Le Dauphin • *1 rue Bivouac-Napoleon;* ☎ *93392273.* Spanish cuisine. Service often frenetic, forgetful, yet terribly kind.

La Toque Blanche • *3 rue Lafontaine;* ☎ *93386195.* Also with slaphappy service, but OK in the gustatory department.

NIGHTLIFE

Mixed drinks are lethally expensive in every nightspot. Beer or wine are cheaper—but not much. One blessing is that few places will charge an admission fee or will hold you to a minimum consumption.

La Chunga • *Across from the Hotel Martinez.* A jovial nightclub-cum-restaurant, with the former dominant. Simple dishes, but more than satisfactory if you're in a festive mood; strolling Mexican guitarists play requests. Very amusing.

Speakeasy • *22 rue Mace.* This place had a rock band hammering it out at one end of the cavern; orange parachutes shuddering menacingly over the dance floor; bar, opposite, libating expensive whiskies. Push the button at the door to gain entrance.

Le Menhir • *"Club de l'Etrier," in the Casino des Felurs, 5-7 rue des Belges.* Two flights below the roulette tables. Gracious atmosphere ornamented by local sophisticates (many in black tie); tropical decor; smooth Latin beats; spacious dance floor; red-canopied bar. Operative the yearround. Pleasant and not too costly.

St. James • *13 rue Bivouac Napoleon; ☎ 93392618.* St. James starts perking at 10 nightly; Sunday matinee from 4 p.m. to 8 p.m. Striptease plus dressier acts; paper favors; drinks relatively inexpensive; no cover or minimum.

BARS FOR FUN

The **Blue Bar**, which holds up one wall of the Palais des Festivals, is number one. Down the scale are **Cosy Night**, *rue Emile-Negrin*, and **Jimmy's**, *rue du Grand-Hotel.* **Slow Club**, *28 rue Commandant-Andre*, is said to be in the fast lane.

NIGHTCAP AT A SENSIBLE PRICE

Try the **Bar Majestic** (not in the Hotel Majestic). It is on the corner of *rue Tony-Allard* and *rue Moliere*, behind the Grand Hotel; you'll probably save 50 percent over any upholstered tavern in town.

WHAT TO SEE AND DO

Relax. If you're like 99.99996 percent of Cannes holidaymakers, you'll probably want to loll in the sun and scan the scenery. All-nude human barbecues are far from unknown here. Salty types will be attracted by the glittering international fleet moored in the two yacht basins.

Culturally, there are several choices. Nearly everyone visits the 10th-century **Castrum Canois**, with the Museum of Mediterranean Civilization in its dungeon. The night view is especially captivating. Then come the **Lerins**, a short run out, where the 5th-century Cistercian Monastery served as St. Patrick's springboard for evangelizing Europe, the **Royal Fort** on Ile Ste.Marguerite, containing the cell that has inspired stories, plays, and movies by the ream and reel (once occupied, they say, by the Man in the Iron Mask), and **Super-Cannes**, with its spectacular vista of the commerical port, the sea, the boulevard de la Croisette, the yacht harbors, and all of Cannes. Take the Observatory bus from the terminal.

Art enthusiasts absolutely must make an excursion up to St.-Paulde-Vence to thrill at the modern paintings and sculpture at the **Maeght Foundation**. Entrance rather steep but a bargain at any price on a nice day; a stroll through these peaceful gardens and this richly endowed private museum offers a special bounty to lovers of Impressionist and post-Impressionist masterworks. It's worth a half day at a minimum, but can easily occupy a whole one.

The *Syndicat d'Initiative de Cannes* or the Welcome Information Service branch in the railroad station can give you the late scoop on events. For anything from yachting to hiking trails, ask the city **Sports Office** (*64 blvd. de la Croisette*; ☎ *93382964*).

CHAMONIX AND SKI CENTERS

This beautiful ski station on the shoulder of **Mont Blanc** is probably the most popular in France—with ample reason. For all levels of enthusiasts, the skiing is usually superb. There are plenty of accommodations, the food is always noteworthy, and at times when the dollar is strong and the franc is weak, it can be a treat to make some cuts on French slopes. With St. Moritz, Gstaad, and a handful of other contenders, it encompasses 2 or 3 of the most fashionable gathering places of the sport; in naboberies such as **Megeve** the elite spend more time dressing (and, of course, undressing) than they do among the snowflakes. As you're probably not going to lug skis 2500 miles or more just to concentrate upon sartorial preening, such stops as **Grenoble**, **Val d'Isere** (serious legwork here), **l'Alpe d'Huez**, **Cour-chevel**, **Tignes**, and **Flaine**, as well as the satellite hamlets that so frequently border these favorites, are recommended. The lesser known stations of **St. Gervais**, **Les Houches**, **La Plagne**, and **Sallanches** are not bad if you don't mind participating in the growth pains normal to budding resorts. Please also see "Sports" for additional ski tips.

DEAUVILLE-TROUVILLE

They're *tete-à-tete* coastal retreats patronized mainly by France's Beautiful and/or Sporting People. The former is the far more elegant and opulent choice of casino buffs, horse-race enthusiasts, and gourmets. The latter is *petit bourgeois* and hence much more relaxed; it has an enjoyable port area with plenty of color and boating activity. The funky cafes are in this district. Stay in Trouville to save money. **La France** is reasonably priced; **La Plage**, facing the Casino, has a better kitchen.

LOURDES

In 1858, 14-year-old Bernadette Soubirous knelt by Massabielle Rock in Lourdes and received the first of her 18 visions. Since then, what is probably the second most famous Catholic shrine in existence has sprung up around the site. More than 1 million pilgrims congregate annually at the grotto where the Virgin Mary started the waters flowing during Bernadette's ninth vision.

Transportation to Lourdes has never been easy because of its off-trail setting near the Spanish border. You may make the 555-mile journey from Paris by rail in 9-1/4 hours, or you may fly in high season via Air France, Aer Lingus, or a number of other regular and charter carriers. In winter, the best connection is from Paris. Flights arrive at Ossun International Airport, about 4 miles out of town.

Unfortunately, the atmosphere of Lourdes is sickeningly commercial. As an example, we saw a sign reading "Visitez Les Grottes de Bethlehem." It was hanging over a Jolly Roger pinball machine in the Snack Bar Parisien. Shoppers gush through the Maison Catholique and the Palais du Rosare—the local market centers of claptrap—to purchase such items as crybaby Jesus dolls and "l'Apparition" plastic hip-flasks for carrying away the local holy water. (A jigger-type screw-cap on the latter, however, suggests it may also be used for other curatives.) This sort of thing is a shock to the devout. Nevertheless, for sincerely religious travelers of any faith, Lourdes can be a deeply moving experience, despite the commercial shoddiness.

There are approximately 420 hotels in and around the city. Though some are on the expensive side, their quality ranges from low-mediocre to downright-miserable. In most, full pension (room *and* meals) is either obligatory or pushed as hard as they can push it. Since the restaurants sampled here were all poor, however, this practice isn't quite as outrageous as it would be in centers with higher gastronomic standards. And, since they know they've got you hooked, you usually must pay *full menu prices for the first 3 days.* After that you qualify for the reduced half- or full-pension rates. Of the ones we know, **Hostellerie de l'Astazou** has a nice atmosphere and the **Windsor** provides good value in shelter and food. The big hotels are the **De la Grotte**, **Ambassadeurs**, and **Imperial**.

LYON

This capital of gastronomy was formed by the junction of 2 rivers (Rhone and Saone) and 2 worlds (central and northern Europe). This apex between the Alps and Burgundy is a busy vale and now France's second city. Renowned for its silks and its stupendous dining establishments; mediocre hotels, by metropolitan standards; heavy industry; Sport Palace, containing one of Europe's largest enclosed tracks; huge convention center to keynote its commercial tone; some Roman antiquities, chateaux, cultural attractions, but a way station rather than a primary target for most U.S. travelers. If you plan to overnight, the **Campanile Pardieux** is only 550 meters from the main station. It offers 170 accommodations and a betterthan-average restaurant for 150 diners. Of course, Lyon is often visited for its cuisine and **Chez Rose** can provide a splendid meal at a reasonable price. **Leon de Lyon** is also typical and moderate in cost.

MARSEILLE

This is the oldest city of France and third in importance. New excavations date it back to Grecian times, when it was called "Massalia." Here is the nation's chief port, with heavy Italian influence, superb restaurants, **Chateau d'If** (Monte Cristo's famous island prison, an interesting 30-minute boat ride away), monuments such as **l'Abbaye de St. Victor** and the **Basilica of Notre-Dame de la Garde**, plenty of color, new construction, and a frenetic atmosphere. The ancient harbor town is brightening to make its bid as the principal anchorage for tourists in southern France. You don't get much for your money here; for shelter, the **Novotel**, the **Bompard**, the **Rome et St.-Pierre**, and the **Castellane** are acceptable and not too costly. Have a seafood feast at **Au Pescadou** at Place Castellane, where the entire front is lined with shellfish bins.

LE-MONT-ST.-MICHEL

Exquisite—If you can somehow manage to tune out the teeming hordes of rubberneckers whose bus convoys seem as endless as a march of ants. Should you overnight, do your sightseeing before the migrations descend; then your rapture will be enhanced tenfold. *Danger! Stay off its surrounding beaches and flats whenever the tide is coming in.* Then push on to **Caen**, **Bayeux**, or, most spellbinding of all, the **Normandy Beachheads** of World War II. To us, Omaha at **St.-Laurent-sur-Mer** offers the greatest sense of reverence and interest; La Pointe du Hoc here has been left intact since its cliff was scaled and its stronghold stormed by U.S. Army Rangers—the most vivid combat reminder along the entire coast. Utah, where legions fought and fell on sands and dunes, is a bust as an excursion. Fascinating **Arromanches-les-Bains** is the customary jump-off point for the British beachheads of Gold, Juno, and Sword, with **Musee du Debarquement** (loosely translated as "Invasion Museum") in this center a magnet that would be a crime for any visitor, young or old, to miss. In Mont-St.Michel stay at the cozy **Mere Poulard**. It also offers a very good kitchen. **Du Guesclin** is nice in the costlier realm. There are many boarding houses in the village where you can rent a room for $26 or so, but get there early because the Mont begins to fill up with tours around 11 a.m. All of the above serve superior food, so don't fear a demipension plan. **Terrasses** is also exceptional for dining, but it has no bedrooms. On the outskirts of the causeway leading to the island, a bedroom community has burgeoned to accommodate the bus tours that overnight here. If you can't find space within the cathedral village, perhaps you can book into one of these peripheral dorms.

MONTIGNAC

Last year this town of 3200 drew more than 10 times that number to see its replica of the Lascaux Cave that painstakingly duplicates the 17,000-year-old wall paintings of the original cave just 600 feet away (the "Sistine Chapel of prehistory"). There are many striking similarities and a few disappointing differences that chiefly experts can discern. The latter probably won't offend the untrained eye. Entrance fee is $4.50.

NICE

While Cannes has a more intimate panache, Nice is often more satisfactory for the more urban types. The famous **Carnival** and the **Battle of Flowers** draw armies of spectators from all over the globe. Don't block off much time for the city itself—but if you do breeze in, look at the "Cannes" section for shared points of interest up in the neighboring foothills of the **Alpes-Maritimes** or along the shore. Nice is jammed with 15 museums, the latest being the important **Museum of Modern and Contemporary Art** facing the National Drama Center. It is composed of 4 towers linked by glass-lined passages. The collection offers about 400 works dating back to the Sixties, mostly of French and American artists. You should also visit the **Chateau St. Helene** on Fabron Hill, where 600 pieces of *naive* art are on display. In the town, **Matisse** (museum reopened after renovations), **Cheret** (Impressionists galore), and **Chagall** usually attract the most viewers. Money-saving digs can be found at **Auberge de Jeunesse**, about 2 miles from the center. In town, the **Victor Hugo** and **Auber** are low in cost; the **Harvey** is pleasant and quiet on its *rue Massena* side. **Georges** provides luxury amenities at medium prices. One of the best dining choices is **Manoir Normand**, *32 rue de France*, with an excellent 3-course meal with vegetables for about $20. Nice people here, too.

NIMES

Shades of Rome! The **amphitheater**, the **Maison Carree**, the **Temple of Diana**, the gardens, the museums, and the downtown architecture are far bolder reflections of their Latin origins than of their Frankish beginnings. There is much to see, so plan a day or two in the area. All around the amphitheater and on the radiating streets there are boarding houses and small hotels. The problem will be in finding space, so start looking early on the day of arrival.

ORLEANS

The **Jeanne d'Arc Museum** is the lodestone that draws most outlanders to this city. But this rock of French civilization crackles with additional cultural attractions. If you are interested in history but not fanatically so, it can be seen on an ambitious 1-day loop from the capital. If you prefer to stay overnight, the **Central** and **Mar-**

guerite are simple; the **St.-Jean** and **St.-Aignan** are more comfortable; the **Orleans** is fine but much more expensive. None has restaurant facilities.

PARIS

It's an enormous sprawling city, wrapped around the beautifully winding Seine, a skyline speared by cathedral spires, broad and bustling tree-lined boulevards, funky art-movie houses, scores of museums, a plethora of great and little restaurants, open markets and more world-famous landmarks than at which you could click a Kodak. Like every metropolis, it has its traffic madness at rush hour. But Paris is also blessed with the Metro—clean, modern subways that glide on silent rubber wheels and whisk you quickly and cheaply to any cranny of town. And if you get tired of that, hop on a Batobus, a floating public transport vessel that pauses at many of the major sights along the river.

Some love Paris in the springtime, some love Paris in the fall, but in the summer even devout Parisians leave the city if they can to vacation during the official paid-holiday term. (There are so many civil servants that "official" is an operative word in the national economy as well as on every household's calendar.) However, if you prefer to sightsee in the capital in a more casual, easygoing way, June to September would be the time for you. Either way, any season, Left Bank or Right, Paris is a captivating City of Light.

DIRECTORY

U.S. Embassy • *2 avenue Gabriel, Metro: Concorde;* ☎ *42657460.*

American Express • *11 rue Scribe, Metro: Opera;* ☎ *47427500.*

Self-Service Laundromat • *In the square of the Metro Station Edgar-Quinet.*

Dry Cleaning and Pressing • Jacfil, *27 rue Gay-Lussac, Metro: Luxembourg.*

Suit Rental • Charles Vachet, *17 rue Rodier, Metro: Anvers,* ☎ *48783417.*

Barber • Louis Coiffeur, *132 rue Courcelles, Metro: Pereire;* ☎ *49243412.*

Hairdresser • Joffo, *8 boulevard de la Madeleine, Metro: Opera;* ☎ *40733084, with a branch at 102 rue St.-Lazare, Metro: Trinite or St.-Lazare;* ☎ *48742571.* Less central but also well recommended is La Coiffure, *3 avenue Mozart, Metro: Muette;* ☎ *2882630.*

American Library • *10 rue Camou, Metro: Ecole Militaire.*

Used Books in English • Shakespeare and Company, *37 rue de la Bucherie, Metro: St.-Michel.*

Late Money Exchange • Gare des Invalides, *Esplanade des Invalides, Metro: Invalides; 6 a.m. to midnight*; Orly and Le Bourget airports.

All-Night Post Offices • *103 rue de Grenelle, Metro: Solferino;* ☎ *44682140, and place de la Bourse, Metro: Bourse;* ☎ *GUT 1662.*

Lost and Found • Bureau des Objets Trouves *36 rue des Morillons, Metro: Convention,* ☎ *2508100.*

English-Speaking Doctors and Dentists • American Hospital, *63 boulevard Victor-Hugo, Neuilly, Metro: Champerret, then buses #83, #163, or #164 to boulevard du Chateau;* ☎ *47475300.* Two fine dentists are Doctors Jerome and Guy Joly, *2 rue Parrot, XIIe.*

Ambulance • *3 avenue Victoria;* ☎ *48872750.*

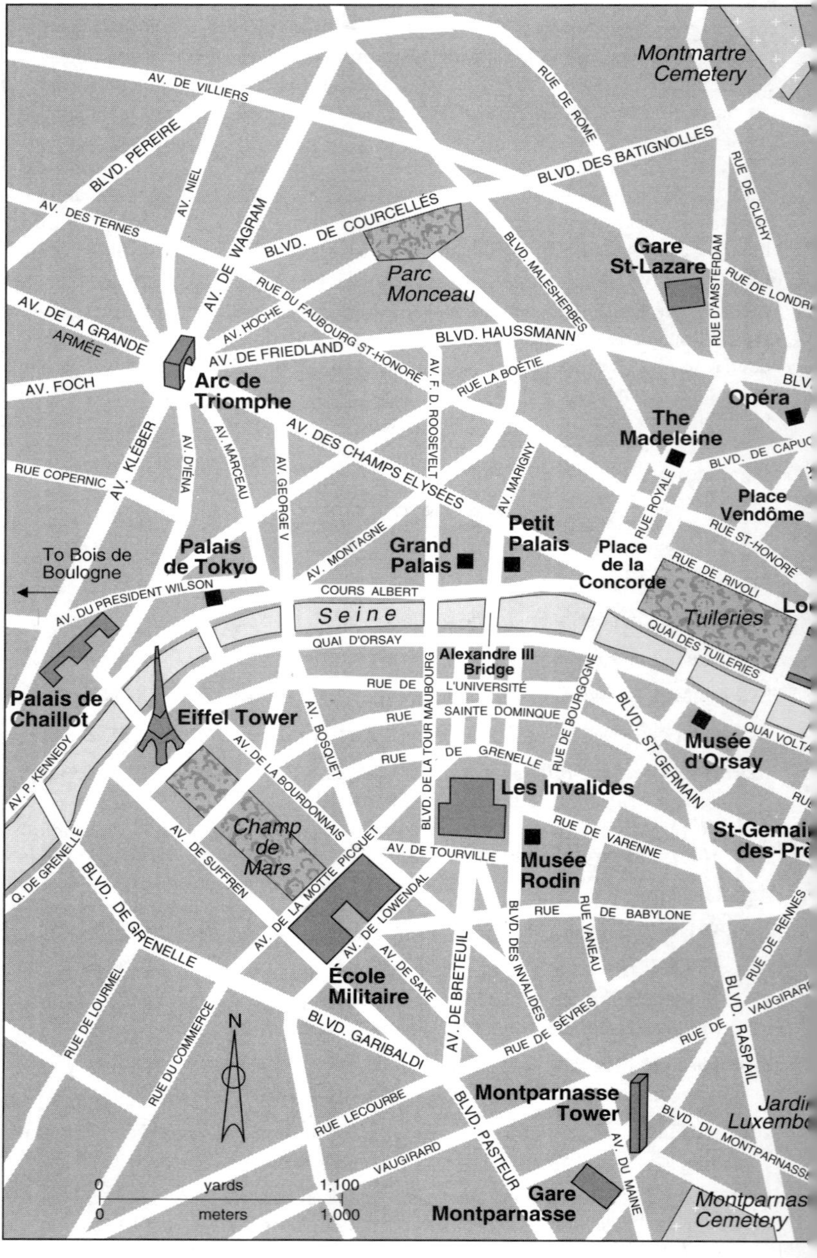
Montmartre Cemetery
Parc Monceau
Gare St-Lazare
Arc de Triomphe
Opéra
The Madeleine
Place Vendôme
Grand Palais
Petit Palais
Place de la Concorde
Palais de Tokyo
To Bois de Boulogne
Seine
Tuileries
Alexandre III Bridge
Palais de Chaillot
Eiffel Tower
Musée d'Orsay
Les Invalides
Champ de Mars
Musée Rodin
École Militaire
Montparnasse Tower
Gare Montparnasse
Montparnasse Cemetery
N
yards 0 1,100
meters 0 1,000

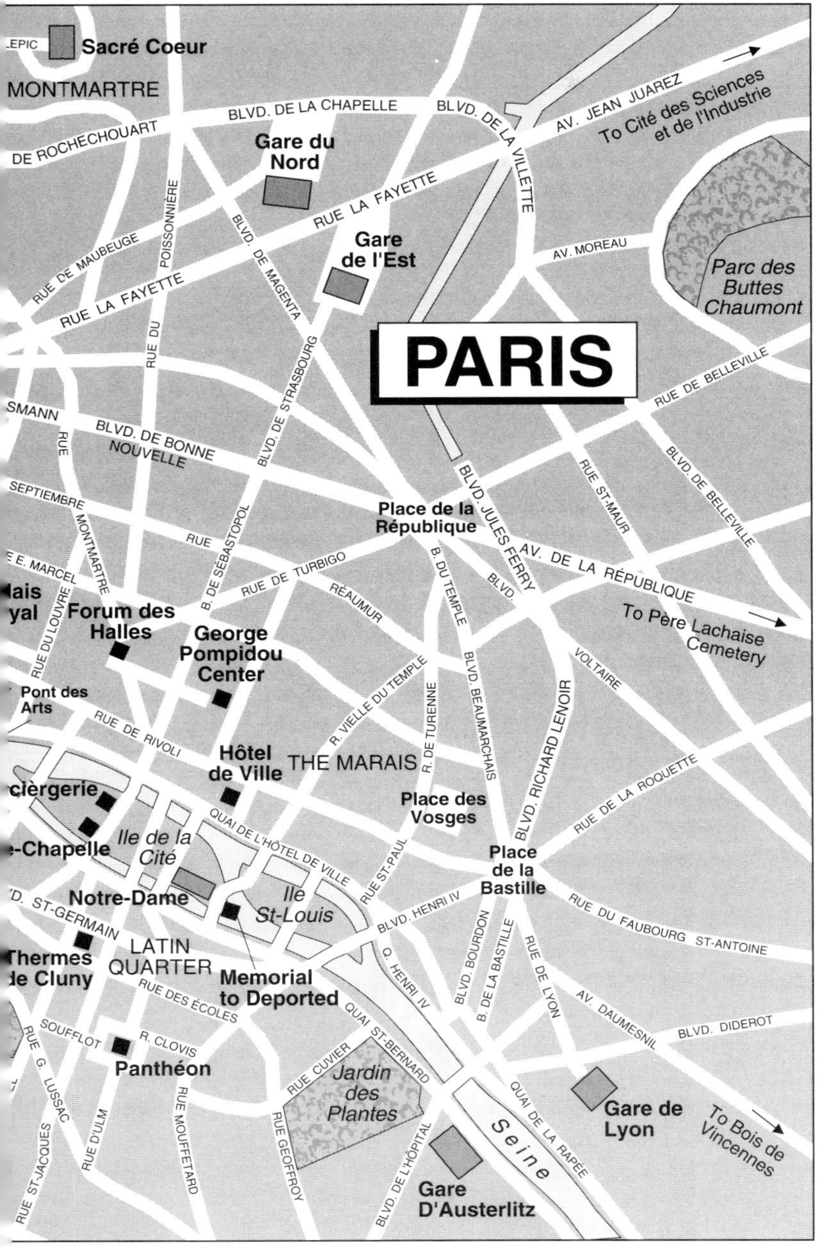
PARIS
Sacré Coeur
MONTMARTRE
BLVD. DE LA CHAPELLE
DE ROCHECHOUART
BLVD. DE LA VILLETTE
AV. JEAN JUAREZ
To Cité des Sciences et de l'Industrie
Gare du Nord
RUE LA FAYETTE
Gare de l'Est
BLVD. DE MAGENTA
RUE POISSONNIÈRE
RUE DE MAUBEUGE
AV. MOREAU
Parc des Buttes Chaumont
BLVD. DE STRASBOURG
RUE DE BELLEVILLE
BLVD. DE BONNE NOUVELLE
BLVD. DE BELLEVILLE
RUE ST-MAUR
Place de la République
BLVD. JULES FERRY
AV. DE LA RÉPUBLIQUE
To Père Lachaise Cemetery
B. DE SÉBASTOPOL
RUE DE TURBIGO
RÉAUMUR
B. DU TEMPLE
RUE MONTMARTRE
RUE DU LOUVRE
Forum des Halles
George Pompidou Center
R. VIELLE DU TEMPLE
R. DE TURENNE
BLVD. BEAUMARCHAIS
BLVD. RICHARD LENOIR
VOLTAIRE
Pont des Arts
RUE DE RIVOLI
Hôtel de Ville
THE MARAIS
RUE DE LA ROQUETTE
Place des Vosges
QUAI DE L'HÔTEL DE VILLE
Ile de la Cité
Place de la Bastille
RUE ST-PAUL
Notre-Dame
Ile St-Louis
RUE DU FAUBOURG ST-ANTOINE
BLVD. HENRI IV
BLVD. BOURDON
B. DE LA BASTILLE
RUE DE LYON
LATIN QUARTER
Memorial to Deported
Q. HENRI IV
AV. DAUMESNIL
BLVD. DIDEROT
RUE DES ÉCOLES
QUAI ST-BERNARD
SOUFFLOT
R. CLOVIS
Panthéon
RUE CUVIER
Jardin des Plantes
QUAI DE LA RAPÉE
Gare de Lyon
To Bois de Vincennes
RUE G. LUSSAC
RUE MOUFFETARD
RUE GEOFFROY
Seine
RUE D'ULM
RUE ST-JACQUES
BLVD. DE L'HÔPITAL
Gare D'Austerlitz

Police • Headquarters *9 boulevard du Palais, Metro: Cite, ☎ 43264420 or 43260630.*

Emergency • ☎ *17.*

Favorite Pawnship • Credit Municipal, Mont de Piete, known in slang as Ma Tante, *62 rue PierreCharron, Metro: Franklin D. Roosevelt; ☎ 43597917.*

HOW TO GET AROUND

You'll pay through the *nez* if you taxi in from either Orly or Le Bourget airports. Seasoned travelers take the bus (every 20 minutes); this 30- to 50-minute shuttle to or from Invalides Terminal costs about $8. Le Bourget's circuit includes a pause at Place Pereire (Metro: Pereire). On either, a sympathetic driver might drop you off at some interim point on request—if you're carrying hand luggage only. To and from Orly and Charles DeGaulle Airports, there are frequent rail connections with the city. The fare is about $6.50. Incidentally, Charles DeGaulle is now in two parts: I and II, so be sure you know beforehand which is your destination.

WATER BUS

Try it. As an experiment in reducing traffic congestion in town, the Seine now has a floating transportation system. The stops correspond to major touristic sites as well as to important commercial nuclei between the Eiffel Tower and Town Hall. Each of the vessels carries 150 passengers at 45-minute intervals. Key docks are at Hotel de Ville, Pont d'Iena (Eiffel Tower), Notre Dame, the Louvre, and the Musee d'Orsay.

SUBWAY

The Metro is gratifyingly simple for any stranger to master. Each station displays maps of the network; the more elaborate push-button charts will outline your route with colored light bulbs. You will need to know only 3 things: the station nearest your destination, your transfer point (correspondance) where your 2 different-colored routes intersect, and the name of the final station on the line for your "direction." Since rumors of subterranean muggings and robberies are beginning to circulate, it might be a good idea to stick with the crowds, especially at night.

All service stops between 1:15 a.m. and 5:30 a.m. A 10-ticket book ("carnet") costs about $8; it may be used on almost all buses, too—and there are 50 major bus routes crisscrossing the city. Various plans are named Formule Une, Paris Sesame, and the kilometer-packed Carte Orange. The **Paris Transportation Company** (RATP) offers a special "**Tourist Ticket**" valid for 2 ($9), 4 ($12), or 7 ($19) consecutive days on all subways, metropolitan buses, and certain suburban carriers. In order to establish your eligibility, you must show your passport at any of the RATP offices (53 bis, quai des Grands-Augustins is one) or before your U.S. departure at the **French National Railroads**, *610 Fifth Ave., New York, NY 10020.*

BUSES

Within Paris's 20 arrondissements, they're cheap, viewful, and remarkably punctual. Ride the Metro if you're in a rush. Take a bus to see this beautiful city. Many of these old-style-but-modernized vehicles sport open-air rear platforms for overflow passengers and smokers. One of the most cherished old classics is the run on #63, which meanders from the Bois de Boulogne along the quais of the Seine and the boulevard St. Germain. Fares add up if you're constantly on the go, so it's wise to buy the carnet of tickets that's right for your style of romp.

MOTORING

During daylight hours you must leave your car on the odd-numbered side of the street during the first 15 days of the month, and on the even-numbered side during the last 15 days.

WHERE TO STAY

Under the government's official rating system, all hostelries considered worthy of receiving foreign visitors are classed as *Hotels de Tourisme*. These are broken down into 5 categories: Deluxe, 4-star, 3-star, 2-star, and 1-star. The same applies to the *Relais de Tourisme* (suburban stops) and *Motels de Tourisme* (on major highways). Price controls cover only the lowest 4 groups. In order to qualify, every physical plant must conform to the standards of the rating for which it has applied—the ratio of private bathrooms to bedrooms, adequate breakfast rooms with the specified number of seats, toilets separated by individual doors, and scores of similar ukases. This supervision applies to lodging charges only; in *pension* (meal) arrangements, the sky is the limit.

Don't forget that you must always pay 10 percent to 15 percent extra for service charge (*majoration*) and taxes. The exact amount depends upon the location and category, *so be certain this total has been included in the quotation before you sign the register.*

One caution to keep in mind is that when you eat your breakfast in your room (most visitors follow this Continental tradition), items such as fruit juice, cereal, eggs, or sausages are not included in the house quotation for the standard coffee or tea complete. They cost like the devil and add up fast.

The **Office de Tourisme de Paris** (*127 Champs-Elysees*) can help in finding emergency lodgings for a very nominal fee. Reservations are guaranteed for only a single night (this avoids competition with the travel agencies). You'll find its branch offices at the major railway stations; the central phone number is ☎ *47236172.*

Away from the capital you may prefer to live in a **farmhouse**. If so, write to **Gite de France**, (*35 rue Godot de Mauroy, 75009 Paris*; ☎ *33-1-4742 2020*) which can send you prices, locations, and other particulars on renting an abode in rural Gaul. An enriching, low-cost experience for adventurous types. Otherwise, while you are *en route*, keep your eyes open for **Formule Une**, a rapidly expanding chain of good, solid hotels and motels all over the nation. They are simple, clean, and almost everywhere. You'll save lots of money and enjoy the stops.

Two publications that may help you with solid, clean low-cost accommodation are *Logis de France* (family-run hotels, but it excludes Paris) and *French Country Welcome*, which concentrates on *gites etapes* or bed-and-breakfast stops. Both are excellent guides.

LEAST $

Doubles without bath should range between $20 and $30 per person; singles should run perhaps from $22 to $27; breakfast (when available) should be about $4. Avoid lodgings in the 9th and 18th *arrondissements*—not the most agreeable for vacationers.

Low-cost accommodations vouchers are available through **Campus Holidays USA Inc**. Purchased in minimum quantities of 3 nights, they can be exchanged in Paris for attractive dwelling space. Cost for one night per person is as low as $16 for a shared room with bath on the same floor to $33 for a single with private bath. Contact this organization at *P.O. Box 881, Upper Montclair, NJ 07043*; ☎ *(201) 744-8724* or toll-free ☎ *(800) 526-2915*.

St. Roch • *25 rue St. Roch Ie (Metro: Pyramides or Opera);* ☎ *42601791*. Petite but pleasant, well-tended rooms. Breakfast, but no other meals. The staff is friendly and can point you in the direction of many attractions within walking distance.

Washington Opera • *50 rue de Richelieu Ie (Metro: Palais-Royal);* ☎ *42966806*. A very good district, but after receiving severe criticisms about the house and its services, I checked it closely on a very recent visit and found nothing grossly amiss. Get your agreement in writing and go with caution.

Familia • *11 rue des Ecoles Ve (Metro: Maubert-Mutualite);* ☎ *43545527*. Well-groomed bedchambers; intimate, friendly breakfast nook.

Marigny • *11 rue de l'Arcade 8*. Handy to the Madeleine; quite satisfactory with singles at close to $35.

Lafayette • *198 rue Lafayette Xe (Metro: Louis-Blanc);* ☎ *46074479*. Rather dark and solemn in parts but numerous updatings now going on; extra-cordial staff. Shower on first floor and WCs on each level.

Paris Est, **Paris Nord** • *Station hotels in the 10th arrondissement. Both functional.* Only recommended in an emergency.

University-Hotel • *160 rue Saint-Jacques Ve (Metro: Luxembourg);* ☎ *43547679*. A block from the Pantheon. C-plus for physical amenities; Z-minus for reception and hospitality.

Saint-Severin • *40 rue St.-Severin Ve (Metro: St.-Michel);* ☎ *46340570*. I like the district; good comfort for a reasonable price. Again quite recommendable.

Star • *2 place Boulnois (Metro: Ternes);* ☎ *43805802*. Walk one block down *avenue des Ternes* from the Metro, turn right on *rue Poncelet*, then swing left on *rue Bayen*. Here *place Boulnois* angles off to the right, about midblock. Marketplace entrance. Adequate-to-good facilities. Fair value.

Raspail • *203 boulevard Raspail XIVe (Metro: Vavin);* ☎ *43206286*. Broods over Montparnasse, near the Dome and Select cafes. Clean rooms. For boulevard view, book #38 (a triple with bidet-sink partitions). Recommended.

Hotel des Balcons • *3 rue Casimir-Delavigne VIe (Metro: Odeon);* ☎ *46347850*. Very inexpensive for couples (running to about $55 in the best units); singles with bath or shower at $38; 58 rooms; good breakfast for $4.75. Above-average maintenance. Delightful decor, rich in art nouveau.

Home Latin • *17 rue du Sommerard Ve (Metro: Maubert-Mutualite);* ☎ *43262521*. A favorite among Sorbonne students; 14 doubles at $33; 2 never vacant singles at $30. A fair shake for the money—if you can get in.

Esmeralda and **Henri IV** • *4 rue St. Julien-le-Pauvre;* ☎ *43541920; Ile de la Cite*. Remarkable cheap hotels that have developed cult followings; almost always booked. Reservations required. The former is near Notre Dame Cathedral.

YOUTH HOSTELS

Check first with the **Centre d' Information et de Documentation Jeunesse** *(101 quai Branly; Metro: Bir Hakeim;* ☎ *45664020)*, which is about 150 yards from the Eiffel Tower. Open every day except Sunday from 9 a.m. to 7 p.m. You can also consult the **Paris Tourist Office** *(127 Champs-Elysees, ☎ 47236172)* from 9 a.m. to midnight. They have all of the details on hostels right there. **Maison Internationale des Jeunes pour la Culture et la Paix** *(9 rue Victor-Masse, Metro: Pigalle; ☎ 48785468)* is within reasonable distance of most of the sights, but perilously close to Pigalle's seamy tendrils. The **YWCA Hostel** *(26 rue d'Anjou, Metro: Madeleine; ☎ 42650957)* close to the British Embassy, usually has limited space, but you'll find a tradition of helping wayfarers to locate other accommodations when necessary.

Centre Quaker International • *114 rue de Vaugirard; Metro: Falguiere; ☎ 42223530.* This place will receive you with typical Quaker cordiality.

Maison des Jeunes Hommes • *15 rue Crespin-du-Gast; Metro: Menilmontant; ☎ 46334430.* This Salvation-Army-sponsored place shelters under-21 wanderers in a house 2 blocks from the avenue de la Republique, near the Pere Lachaise cemetery.

MORE $$

Numerous values in this category, which provides single units for $24-$32 and doubles for roughly $38-$60. Many bargains and nice surprises.

Berthier La Tour and **Brochant La Tour** • *Both at 163 bis avenue de Clichy XVIIe; Metro: Brochant; ☎ 42284040.* Two giant tower hotels sponsored by French railroads. Colorful, clean, extremely well done. Rates at Berthier approximately $35 per single, $48 per double; at Brochant, approximately $36 and $45; pay before you occupy your room. Cafeteria with inexpensive tasty food. Le Village restaurant, Bar Oasis; snacks and drinks available in corridor dispensers. No room service; baggage carts for luggage. The idea is to reduce costs by reducing complexity so that the customer is not surprised by extra fees on departure. No shortage of charm throughout this vast 650-room minicity.

Arcade Paris Cambronne • *Corner rue Cambronne and rue Croix Nivert, Metro: either street; ☎ 45673520.* All 530 rooms with bath and shower. Handy subway connections; quick ride into midcity. Singles $44, doubles $51. Moderate by Paris standards and quite reasonable for such a 2-star hotel.

St. Thomas d'Aquin • *3 rue du Pre-aux-Clercs VIIe, Metro: Bac; ☎ 42610122.* A top choice. Smart-looking lounge and breakfast nook. Deep-carpeted chambers; beds often set into cozy oaken alcoves. Quiet situation. Excellent comfort and taste.

Perreyve • *63 rue Madame, Metro: RER; ☎ 45483501.* Occupies traditional building near the Luxembourg Gardens and St. Germain des Pres, a district that appeals to repeat customers; 30 accommodations. Many extra touches. The value is there.

Marsollier Opera • *13 rue Marsollier IIe, Metro: Opera; ☎ 42966814.* Nice situation on quiet street. Excellent breakfast room. Small baths; extensive comfort; dual rates nearly $48 per night.

Welcome • *5 impasse Royer-Collard Ve, Metro: Luxembourg; ☎ 43540963.* Beautiful upstairs salon and breakfast room with polished table and flowers; 30 lovely carpeted bedrooms, 10 with bath and 17 with shower. Very nice.

Grand Hotel des Gobelins • *57 blvd. St.-Marcel, Metro: Gobelins; ☎ 43317989.* A 2-minute walk from the Latin Quarter, near the Austerlitz station. All units with private bath and color TV. Twin rate about $40. A good bet if you like this district.

Splendid • *29 avenue de Tourville VIIe, Metro: Ecole Militaire; ☎ 45512477.* Close to Invalides; 50 rooms; groups discouraged. Clean, colorless chambers. Solid but rather dated. There seems to be another **Splendid** (*1 bis avenue Carnot; ☎ 47664141*), near the Etoile. Judging only from its category, could be expensive.

Lindbergh • *5 rue Chomel VIIe Metro: Sevres-Babylone; ☎ 45483553.* Most of its 25 rooms with shower; #34, a triple, faces its own courtyard and is tranquil. Quite good.

California • *32 rue des Ecoles Ve, Metro: Card.-Lemoine; ☎ 46341290.* Spacious bedchambers; carpets; elevator. Rates a bit high, but it is a quality house.

De l'Elysee • *12 rue Saussaies VIIIel, Metro: Ch.-Elysees; ☎ 42652925.* We liked room number #21, a double with a nonworking fireplace; 33 more from which to choose.

Elysees Mermoz • *30 rue Jean-Mermoz VIIIe, Metro: F.D. Roosevelt; ☎ 42257530.* Conveniently near Rond-Point and exclusive Faubourg St.Honore. Comfortable bedchambers. Doubles $53 inclusive; triples $65. Location tops in Paris.

St. Germain des Pres • *36 rue Bonaparte VIe, Metro: St.-Sulpice; ☎ 43260019.* Once house of philosopher Auguste Comte; 28 rooms; some good; some require a philosophical attitude.

Square Monge Bernardins • *42 rue des Bernardins Ve, Metro: Maubert-Mutualite; ☎ 40334908.* Quiet situation; outclasses many of its fellows in the Latin Quarter. Some units with fireplaces; almost none with private WCs. All boast comfortable beds and telephones. Twins go for about $46; add $5.50 for a shower. Breakfast, service, taxes extra.

St. Jacques • *35 rue des Ecoles Ve, Metro: Maubert-Mutualite; ☎ 43268253.* Often swings with young Americans. Cafeteria for breakfast only; 40 old-fashioned, carpeted units. From $33–50 for twins, $31 for singles, including all tithings and *petit dejeuner.* A real value.

Arromanches • *6 rue Chateaubriand VIIIe, Metro: George V; ☎ 45637424.* Across the river and into the money trees of the Right Bank. The differing decor of its bedchambers gives it a rare personal touch.

Avenir • *52 rue Gay-Lussac Ve, Metro: St. Placide; ☎ 40337660.* Quiet area; 35 accommodations, 12 with bath or shower. If you land in its improved rooms, you might like it.

Regent's • *44 rue Madame VIe, Metro: St.-Sulpice; ☎ 45480281.* Of 36 rooms, 50 percent face greenery, 3 open onto miniterraces, 14 have private tubs, 2 have showers, and most have WC. Feeling reckless? #32, at roughly $40, offers generous space and extra comfort. Others considerably less, falling to a base of $31 for a single *with* breakfast.

Claude-Bernard • *43 rue des Ecoles Ve, Metro: Maubert-Mutualite; ☎ 43263252.* Mixture of pluses and minuses. Many North Americans, some in lengthy residence. Tariffs vary sharply according to comfort standards. All chambers clean and neat.

Grand Hotel Moderne • *33 rue des Ecoles Ve, Metro: Maubert-Mutualite;* ☎ *43543778.* Roughly $47 for doubles; 45 rooms, all crisply fresh, with telephone; 10 come with full bath, and 19 with shower.

Grand Hotel du Levant • *18 rue de la Harpe Ve, Metro: St.-Michel;* ☎ *46341100.* Offers 50 bedrooms to devotees of Notre Dame's architecture and sidewalk cafe sitting. Charges same for double or single occupancy. Full bath $51; shower $45; without bath $30, inclusive of service, taxes, a modicum of charm. *Cafe complet* nook downstairs. Try for #26, #27, #35, #36, #46, or #52.

St. Romain • *7 rue St.-Roch Ie, Metro: Tuileries;* ☎ *42603170.* Well scrubbed and well located; 2 beds and a tub rent from $33 to $48.

Viator and **Nouvel** • *1 rue Parrot XIIe, Metro: Gare de Lyon;* ☎ *43431100 and 24 avenue Bel Air Metro: Nations;* ☎ *43430181.* Both in 12th arrondissement, not heavily populated by tourists. The first is near rail terminus; the second near zoo. Both adequate.

Royal Cardinal • *1 rue des Ecoles Ve Metro: Card.-Lemoine;* ☎ *43268364.* Never gone through it personally, but friends who have stayed here recommend it.

Le Royal • *212 boulevard Raspail XIV;* ☎ *43206920.* With a noisy address, runs chaud et froid. If you draw one of its few brighter chambers in the rear, you might be satisfied with the $38-per-person outlay. P.S. There are a lot of "Royal" hotels in Paris and some are very expensive (Royal Alma, as one example), so be sure you have the full name and proper address.

Deux-Continents • *25 rue Jacob VIe, Metro: St.-Germain-des-Pres;* ☎ *43267246.* A solid value located in the antique district. Clean. All units with bath. Very good.

Grand Hotel d'Harcourt • *3 blvd. St.-Michel Ve, Metro: St.-Michel;* ☎ *43265235.* Less cheerful.

Academie • *32 rue des Saints-Peres VIe;* ☎ *45483622.* Also on a sclerotic artery. OK.

Saint Pierre • *4 rue d'Ecole de Medecine.* Not very big, but comfortable.

France • *22 rue d'Antin.* Be careful because there are several of this name or similar. Check the address.

Solferimo • *91 rue de Lille.* One of our oldest recommendations and still going well.

Baltimore • *88 avenue Kleber.* A handy location with good public transport.

Des Nations • *29 rue des Ecoles.* Many favorable reports and always busy.

Franklin et Bresil • *19 rue Buffault.* Pleasant personality; run by nice people.

EVEN MORE $$$

Madeleine-Plaza • *33 place de la Madeleine VIIIe, Metro: Madeleine;* ☎ *42652063.* Almost at back door of famous church; 50 glistening rooms; $83 buys double with bath, service, taxes, breakfast; several run over $100. Singles begin in the $45 range. Top 2 levels the calmest, presenting views over rooftops. No restaurant; modern bar-snack lounge. A firm recommendation.

Alexander • *102 avenue Victor Hugo XVIe, Metro: Victor Hugo;* ☎ *45536465.* Elegant, airy 70-unit sanctum on fashionable, but bustling tree-lined street; 10-minute stroll from Arc de Triomphe. Sitting and breakfast rooms done in French period furniture; single or twin beds; large bathrooms: 40 tubs; 30 showers. Plenty of light.

Chomel • *15 rue Chomel, Metro: Sevres-Babylon;* ☎ *45485552.* This place is pleasantly situated on the Left Bank between blvd. Raspail and Bon Marche. About two dozen smart, air-fresh rooms; the atmosphere is cheerful, the tone discreet.

St. Louis • *75 rue St. Louis-en-l'Isle IVe, Metro: Pont Marie;* ☎ *46340480.* Charming accommodations recently updated; 25 smallish chambers made glad with fresher stylings. Many feel happy on island while some feel displaced from the midcity activities. Personally, I love it and recommend it.

Lutece • *65 rue St. Louis-en-l'Isle IVe, Metro: Pont Marie;* ☎ *43262352.* Attractive alternative. Expect to pay from $65 per twinsome.

Hotel des Deux-Iles • *Same street at #59, Metro: Pont Marie;* ☎ *43261335.* A sister of the above Lutece and oozes with equal charm. Intimate cellar lounge under stone arches; hearth; library and TV room. Superb accommodation and style.

Lido • *4 passage de la Madeleine VIIIe, Metro: Madeleine;* ☎ *42662737.* Off rue Tronchet; 29 ample-size modern units; no dining room; varying decor, all with toilet and most with either shower or tub with telephone-type hose. Comfortable mattresses.

Fremiet • *6 avenue Fremiet XVIe, Metro: Passy;* ☎ *45245206.* Quietly sited off avenue du President Kennedy, facing Eiffel Tower across Seine. No dining or public areas; 32 large, old-fashioned, but lovingly maintained bedchambers, each with bath or shower; 6 suites; 6 well-scrubbed 1-person attic nooks; favor #75 and several other rear units with Tower views. Twins with plumbing starting in the $58 region; snazzy, showered 7th-floor singles at perhaps $46.

Scandinavia • *27 rue de Tournon VIe, Metro: Mabillon or Odeon;* ☎ *43296720.* Historic Left Bank inn built during reign of Louis XIII. Authentic period furnishings and paintings. Very useful snack bar; 22 pods, all with bath, beamed ceilings, velvet curtains, and bits of medieval lore; most with double beds. All-inclusive tariffs of about $70 per twin; 20 percent less for singles. So popular, reservations must be made in advance.

Hotel de Castille • *37 rue CambonIe, Metro: Concorde;* ☎ *42615520. Off rue de Rivoli*; owned by the Ritz. Pleasant dining salon with fireplace. Nondescript sitting room. Ancient, open-cage elevator. Most of 55 units are large; a few gigantic.

Campanile • *4 blvd. Berthier.* A newcomer with 250 bedrooms; the restaurant can seat almost half the occupancy of the hotel. But even being so large, the food and value are noteworthy.

Novotel • *La Defense.* Operates one of its giant chain candidates (270 rooms, 6 suites within 17 floors) in an attractive residential part of town. These are cool but efficient hotels and often popular motels along the autoroutes. The Grill is appealing, as is the Bar River Seine.

Hotel de Morny • *4 rue de Liege;* ☎ *42854792.* Antiquity melded nicely with modernity. Sauna. Very agreeable.

Tuileries • *10 rue St. Hyacinthe;* ☎ *42610417.* Reformed 18th-century mansion near the Opera. Also recommended.

Printemps • *1 rue de l'Isly;* ☎ *42941212.* In the heart of the shopping district. Handy and worthy.

D'Angleterre-Champs Elysees • *91 rue de la Boetie VIIIe, Metro: Franklin Roosevelt;* ☎ *43593545.* On one of Paris's busiest streets. Modern lounge. Contemporary furnishings in 40 bedchambers; baths or showers with mosaic tiles. Nearby parking. Quite pleasant.

Grand Hotel de Malte • *63 rue de Richelieu IIe, Metro: Bourse;* ☎ *42965806.* Space for about 130, all with bath or shower; 10 suites; a few duplex apartments with spiral staircases. Noisy but convenient situation.

Saint-Simon • *14 rue St.-Simon VIIe, Metro: Bac;* ☎ *45483566.* Quiet locale near busy boulevard St.Germaine and boulevard Raspail. Old World ambience. French and English-style sitting rooms.

Regence-Etoile • *24 avenue Carnot XVIIe, Metro: Etoile;* ☎ *4380 7560.* Close to Arc de Triomphe; 40 tiny, cheerful, polished quarters; 40 tubs or showers. Top twin rate of almost $67. Hospitable people here.

Tivoli-Etoile • *7 rue Brey;* ☎ *42671268.* A sturdy and peaceful contender in the same district; 30 units with shower or bath.

London • *32 blvd. des Italiens;* ☎ *48245464.* Near the Opera so handy to many sites; 50 rooms with bath and shower; special rates in July and August. As the name implies, English is spoken.

Cecilia • *11 avenue MacMahon XVIIe, Metro: Etoile;* ☎ *43803210.* Especially cordial for families. Lounge, dining corner, and bar. Spacious bedrooms with smattering of chandeliers, fireplaces, and separate wardrobes. Clean bathrooms. Costly, but good.

Colbert • *7 rue Hotel-Colbert;* ☎ *43258565.* On same bank, only a totter across the bridge from Notre Dame. Style of a private home two centuries ago and properly managed by M. Canteloup. A steep but worthy price spread from $95-122 per double.

Trocadero • *21 rue St. Didier,* ☎ *45530182.* A Best Western member with lots of personality and numerous updatings. Very stylish and convenient. Twins close to $87.

Sevigne • *6 rue de Belloy XVIe, Metro: Trocadero;* ☎ *4720 8890.* High-rent district; 30 bedchambers. Full accoutrements including bath or shower, TV, radio, carpeting, desk-vanities, and French, double) beds; balconies on 5th floor; extra space in #43 and #53; twin rate pushing $92, comprising service, taxes, and a breakfast tray.

Kleber • ☎ *47238022.* Nearby hostelry offering 23 additional attractive accommodations.

Derby • *5 avenue Duquesne VIIe, Metro: S.F.-Xavier;* ☎ *47051205.* Trots out 38 conventional rooms, 8 apartments, and 4 kitchenettes. Only breakfast available. Fairly good.

L'Aiglon • *232 boulevard Raspail XIVe, Metro: Vavin;* ☎ *43208242.* Suitable for motorists, self-styled chefs, and family broods. Garage and good streetside parking at this Left Banker; 55 excellently maintained, modish rooms. Standard doubles with bath from $73; $15 more for kitchenette; some suites at about $85.

Montana Tuileries • *12 rue St.-Roch, Metro: Tuileries or Pyramides;* ☎ *42603510.* Well-sited and clean, but otherwise not outstanding.

Massena • *16 rue Tronchet.* The location is convenient and the comforts are reasonable.

Tronchet • *22 rue Tronchet.* An old campaigner and a fine one.

Sydney-Opera • *50 rue des Mathurins, around the corner.* All routine; rather high-priced to compete with those above.

Arc-Elysee and **Eiffel-Elysee** • *45 rue Washington VIIIe, Metro: St. Philippe du Roule;* ☎ *45636933, and 3 blvd. de Grenelle, Metro: Grenelle;* ☎ *45781481.* Sister operations and quite good; 27 rooms the former; 50 rooms the latter. At either, ask for quieter back accommodations.

CAMPING

The **Touring Club de France** (*65 avenue de la Grande-Armee, Metro: Argentine;* ☎ *45534210*) operates a low-cost camping site on the far-western edge of the Bois de Boulogne. It is about 100 yards from the eastern end of the Pont de Suresnes—and a chore to find. The easiest way to get there during the high season is to go out to the Neuilly Metro stop and then wait for one of the camp's 2 small buses to pull up at the corner of rue de Longchamp and avenue de Neuilly. This every-15-minute shuttle is in motion as late as 10:30 p.m. You'll need a membership card—but this can usually be arranged after you've claimed your plot of ground. Lilliputian city with small supermarket that peddles everything from Ajax to paperbacks on Zen; large, frequently scoured shower facilities; snack bar and vending machines; multilingual office staff whose patience seems to wane painfully often; rates of about $15 per head. Since auto-less guests win preference when the compound nears capacity, it's wiser to arrive on foot. The casual, relaxed clientele who lounge and play cards here can be just the right tonic after a hard day of cobblestone-pounding in the city.

SUGGESTIONS FOR STUDENTS

Collegians cluster along parts of these 4 main boulevards: St.Michel ("Boul'Mich"), St.Germain, Raspail, and Montparnasse. Satellite districts also spin out from the Pantheon and hover along the eastern edge of the Luxembourg Gardens. In the Latin Quarter street stands abound for *croque monsieurs* (toasted ham-and-cheese creations), crepes, North African kebabs and pastries, Vietnamese delicacies, and exotica from almost everywhere and anywhere *except* the *Latin* lands. The Cite Universitaire, another constellation, is in a southern precinct. St.Germain-des-Pres has now become so chic that few students can afford it.

For general information and starters, check with **Accueil de France** (*127 av. des Champs-Elysees;* ☎ *47236172*) or the **American Student Advisory Service** (*261 blvd. Raspail;* ☎ *43352150*). Also helpful for study plans is the **Council on International Educational Exchange** (*49 rue Pierre-Charron;* ☎ *43592369*).

OVERNIGHTS

Accueil des Jeunes en France (*12 rue des Barres;* ☎ *42727209*) and **Canadian House** (*31 blvd. Jourdan;* ☎ *45896759*) offer low-cost shelter and convivial companionship of other adventurers. The **Foundation des Etats-Unis** (*15 blvd. Jourdan,*

Metro: Cite Universitaire; ☎ *45893579*) maintains facilities here. About 20 other institutional relatives are scattered through this suburb. During the winter, they serve as dormitories. Visiting scholars are welcomed between July 1 and September 30. Since short-notice billeting is frowned upon, the best way to set things up is to request reservations by airmail as far as possible in advance. A single (no doubles) goes for about $280 a month; a minimum 2-month stay is required. If your plans change, a minimum of 30 days' notice will rescue the 20 percent cancellation fee.

La Maison des Clubs UNESCO • *43 rue de la Glaciere, 13e, Metro: Glaciere;* ☎ *43360063* and ☎ *47079857.* Provides chummy shelter for about 100 students. The rates are low and accommodation is satisfactory if your budget is limited.

Dutch Students' Hostel • *12-14 rue de Vaugirard, Metro: Carrefour d'Odeon;* ☎ *43265078.* Strings together $8 four-person rooms with a community bar and TV. No breakfast is served. Collegians of every country swarm to this beehive; there might even be a social program going for your own nationality. Either write ahead, specifying your gender, to the **Netherlands Office for Foreign Student Relations** (*Rapenburg 6, Leiden, Holland*) or camp on their doorstep. Operative July 1 to September 1.

Federation de la Seine des Oeuvres Laiques • *12 rue de la Victoire, Metro: Notre-Dame-de-Lorette or Le Peletier;* ☎ *45261230.* This group operates a hostel in the southern part of the city for schoolaffiliated groups. Admission is a pain in the pajamas. First you check in at the Federation office. Later you lug your effects to the dormitory at 14 rue du General Humbert, parallel to boulevard Brune (Metro: Porte de Vanves). Open all year, with 4-to-20-capacity bunk rooms, collective baths, and central heating. A small inscription fee is charged. If you're 17 or younger, it's only about $2.75 per night; older folks, about $2.25. The $1.50 breakfast is mandatory. Other meals run perhaps $2.50; beverages extra.

Foyer Internationale d'Accueil de Paris • *30 rue Cabanis, Metro: Glaciere.* Better known by the initials F.I.A.P., is modern, clean, and inexpensive.

Auberge de la Jeunesse de Paris • *Central d'Accueil Leo-Lagrange, 3 boulevard Kellermann;* ☎ *45880070.* A bit dreary but quite low in cost; lounges; self-service restaurant; reservation hours from 7 a.m. to midnight; 4-8-bed units at $7.50 per sleeper, breakfast included; lunch and dinner about $3.50; similar price for a sheet rental. Patrons must deposit 50 percent when they book and pay the remaining 50 percent after arrival.

WOMEN ONLY

Here's a melange: the **Foyer International des Etudiantes** (*93 boulevard St. Michel, Metro: Luxembourg or Odeon;*☎ *46334963*), overlooking the Luxembourg Gardens, with spotless singles and doubles, a dining hall (closed in summer), and a sun roof at reasonable vacation rates; 5-night minimum; the **Foyer International Carrefour** (*41 rue des Bernardins, Metro: Maubert-Mutualite;* ☎ *46332080*), a July-August sanctuary between Notre Dame and the boulevard St.Germain; the **Foyer International La Vigie** (*3 rue des Carmes, Metro: Maubert-Mutualite;* ☎ *46331390*), a clean but cramped cloister that closes during August and **Foyer La Vigie** (*7 rue Poulletier, on Ile St Louis;* ☎ *46333398*); the **Maison des Etudiantes** (*214 blvd. Raspail, Metro: Raspail or Vavin;* ☎ *46336130*); the **Union Chretienne des Jeunes Filles** (*66 rue Orfila, Metro: Gambetta or Pelleport;*

☎ *46368280*); and the well-scoured and tranquil **La Maison** (*36 rue du Montparnasse, Metro: Montparnasse-Bienvenue*; ☎ *2222850*), 3 doors from the Foyer des Artistes et Intellectuels.

The **Cercle Concordia** (*41 rue Tournefort, Metro: Monge*; ☎ *43317516*) and the **Reid Hall** (*4 rue de Chevreuse, Metro: Vavin*; ☎ *43266465*) also provide adequate if not opulent rooms and dining facilities for female students.

The **Paris Universite Club** (*39 avenue de l'Observatoire, Metro: Port-Royal*; ☎ *43269709*) and the **Etrangers** (*14 rue Monsieur-le-Prince, Metro: Odeon*; ☎ *43263716*) are hostels that welcome scholars of both genders.

FINALLY, FOR MEN ONLY:

Oranam (*155 bis rue de Rennes, Metro: St. Placide*; ☎ *45489410*), a Montparnasse favorite of Alliance Francaise students; the **Foyer de l'Entr'aide Universitaire Francaise** (*19 rue de la Victoire, Metro: NotreDame-de-Lorette or Le Peletier*, ☎ *48789682*), a basic but bustling abode near the Folies Bergere; the **Maison des Mines et des Ponts et Chaussees** (*272 rue St.-Jacques, Metro: Luxembourg or Port-Royal*; ☎ *40337725*), in which the Bureau of Mines and the Department of Roads and Bridges offer summer lodgings for foreign students.

The **Office du Tourisme Universitaire** (*137 boulevard St.-Michel, Metro: Port-Royal*; ☎ *43266097* or *43251161*) fills bunks with warm bodies in its placement service for the Latin Quarter. And when it's time to push onward, this same tireless group can arrange your low-cost travel to other parts of Europe.

The **Bureau des Spectacles du COPAR** (*39 avenue de l'Observatoire, Metro: Port-Royal*; ☎ *43260749*) offers tickets to restaurants, theaters, and nightclubs that carry discounts for collegians. You'll need your identity card, plus a minuscule fee for each admission.

The **American Center for Students and Artists** (*261 boulevard Raspail, Metro: Raspail*; ☎ *40339992*) crams its bulletin board with valuable jottings that range from bargains to requests for baby-sitters.

The **Student International Center** (*93 boulevard St.Michel, Metro: Luxembourg* ☎ *46334963*), and the aforementioned Paris Universite Club are other clearinghouses.

WHERE TO EAT

If you're an August visitor to the capital, check beforehand to make certain the place of your choice is open. Hundreds of dining spots put up their shutters during the 31 days of this official "paid vacation" peak. During the rest of the year, many Parisian restaurants close for one day in the early part of the week, usually Monday; most rest on Sunday.

LEAST $

Bistros are the rage in Paris due to their vastly improved quality and the reasonable values they offer. The decor often borrows extensively from the Belle Epoque, with forests of curlicue wood, panels of leaded stained glass, morning-glory lamps, smoked mirrors, bentwood chairs, marble-topped-wrought-iron tables, and other beautifully rendered facsimiles of the era. Three of the handiest entries are the modernized and excellent **Le Bistro de la Gare** (*73 Champs Elysees*), the neighboring **L'Assiette au Boeuf**, and the **Bistro de la Gare**—another one—(*59 boulevard du Montparnasse*). You can also trust any of the **Bistro Romain** group, which are proliferating nowadays. A meal at these can be had for from $17–30.

Le Gros Minet • *1 rue des Prouvaires (near the garden and esplanade that was Les Halles);* ☎ *42330262.* Another interesting candidate. Ask proprietor to show you his cave dating back to 1660. For $18–21 you will be regaled with enormous pans and casseroles of terrine, rillette, and salad; set meal includes a flank steak (*onglet*) with sauteed onions or several other choices of entree. Outstanding.

Bofinger • *5-7 rue de la Bastille, Metro: Bastille;* ☎ *42728783.* Designed in the classic mood of this century's birth with high ceilings, floral sconces, dark wood, and polished glass; potted palms and talented pots from the kitchen. Try souffle of sole au crabe and beef tartare; bar in front; shellfish counter at entrance; waiters in black bowties. A fine experience.

Pied de Cochon • *6 rue Coquilliere (also the Les Halles district).* An unimpressive old standby. (If Parisian soul food begins to Gaul, your western tastes might prefer Tex-Mex chuckwagon grub, available at the nearby **Papa Maya**. Exactly why you came to France, ain't it, pahdner?)

Les Gourmets des Ternes • *Boulevard Courcelles 87 (near the Etoile);* ☎ *42274304.* For steaks, no serious beefeater should miss it. On menu's stampede of meats, don't fail to sample the house's enormous special cut (very tender). More expensive than the others, but well worth it. Closed Saturday and Sunday.

The born-again, still famous **Le Drouot** *(103 rue de Richelieu IIe)*, and **Chartier** *(7 Faubourg Montmartre IXe)*, and **Le Commerce** *(51 rue du Commerce XVe).* Trio of excellent restaurants with quality and soothing prices operated by the same organization. Orders and tabulations made on your paper table mat. Always jammed. Also good is **L'Assiette** *(181 rue du Chateau)*, where the marinated duck is superb. **Astier** *(44 rue Jean-Pierre Timbaud)*, is noteworthy for the rabbit in a smooth mustard sauce. **L'Insulaire** on the restaurant-lined Gregoue de Louis, provides a most affordable fixed price meal consisting of onion soup gratinee, an entree choice, and a selection from desserts.

La Cour St. Germain • *rue Marbeuf 19 (branch 156 boulevard St.-Germain).* Fresh and attractive. Meat and salad combos for about $11. Felt amply rewarded for that sum.

Bar des Pyrenees • *9 rue de l'Ancienne Comedie, Metro: Odeon.* Domineering "Maitre" called "Madame" amuses guests by bellowing at her harried short-order chef. She'll get you "Un steak complet!" (with deep-fry potatoes and roll) and "Un rouge!" (red wine) for about $7.50. Try for lunch or Sunday brunch. Closed Tuesday.

Au Printemps • *65 boulevard Haussmann, Metro: Havre-Caumartin.* Offers 7 quick-meal areas within the Nouveau Magasin department store. Here are only the ones you'll find on the top floor: a cavernous dining chamber cut into enclaves for an elaborate $9.50 full-course meal, a $4.50 *repas rapide* with hors d'oeuvres, main dish, dessert, and wine, a tea-sandwich-pastry section, and one of the best soda fountains on the continent; a cafeteria with a hot entree line priced to sell; a gallery of vending machines that clock out light bites; and a stoolbanked snack bar. Spotless and a bargain for all. **Galeries Lafayette** also provides top-quality, low-cost dining possibilities.

Guen Mai • *2 bis rue de l'Abbaye, Metro: St.-Germain-des-Pres.* Dishes up the curious combination of Japanese food and bastardized couscous with chicken from $5.50.

A la Bonne Crepe • *11 rue Gregoire-de-Tours, Metro: Odeon.* Low, low *prix fixe* menu incorporates pancake specialties and cider.

La Cigale • *11 bis rue Chomel, Metro: Sevre-Babylone; ☎ 45488787.* Pate and hors d'oeuvres ranging up to $3.50; grills with vegetables from $8.50. Cuisine quite good. Very pleasant as a French neighborhood restaurant.

Au Gourmet de l'Isle • *42 rue St.-Louis-en-l'Isle IVe, ☎ 43267927.* A.k.a. "Chez Bourdeau." The guinea hen with lentils, sweetbreads, Charbonee (pork in red wine with carrots and onions) all splendid. A full meal about $18. Closed Monday at noon and all day Thursday, plus all of August. A little honey.

Le Sergent Recreteur • *41 rue St.-Louis-en-l'Isle IVe.* Far more decorative appeal. Food also very good, but set meal begins at $13. Open from 7:30 p.m.

ITALIAN EATERIES

Several in the St.Germain-des-Pres environs serve reasonably good pasta and other peninsular specialties.

Pizza Vesuvio • *145 boulevard St. Germain, corner of rue des Ciseaux.* Features a singing chef whose voice, while wretched, is still better than his pasta; $9 menu.

Pizza Borsalino • *32 rue des Mathurins.* Sports a pizza oven in its window; plat du jour $6.50; large menu $9.50. Very appetizing and worthy.

La Table d'Italie • *69 rue de Seine Vie.* A grocery store that has grown into a snackery. Supplies many items (e.g., pasta dishes) that are sold at steeper prices in fancier Parisian settings.

Pizza Pino • *Champs-Elysees, corner of rue de Marignan.* A 2-story pasta palace to avoid. Stunningly high prices for undistinguished fare at one of the costliest locales in Paris. Miserable, care-nothing service by smart-aleck waiters.

CAFETERIAS

Restaurant Self-Service Elysees • *67 rue Pierre-Charron off the Champs-Elysees, Metro: Franklin D. Roosevelt.* So good you usually have to join the line in the upstairs lobby. Fast but unfrenzied service. Modest selection; above-average preparation. Open 11 a.m.–9:30 p.m. Most recent soup-to-nuts outlay: $7.50.

Cafeteria Marbeuf • *5 rue Marbeuf, Metro: Alma-Marceau.* Offers well-prepared dishes in self-service line. Mobbed at lunch. Candlelit evening setting perfect for a tete-a-tete. The neighboring **Cour de St. Germain** is more of a sitdown establishment for lingering. The prices are rock-bottom and the area is fun.

Latin-Cluny Self Service • *98 boulevard St.-Germain, Metro: St. Michel.* Frequented by Sorbonne cliques. Named for the quarter and museum across the boulevard; assemble a $9.50 meal from glittering deck of hors d'oeuvres, entrees, wines, and desserts. Lunch less busy than evenings.

SNACKS

In the region of the Beaubourg and the Picasso Museum, graze along the rue des Rosiers for falafel palaces, Mexican diners, Vietnamese stands, and levantine nooks. **Orientale Express** at #44 is okay; **Boucherie Chabat** is tops for blinis and pirojkis. Nearby,

Chez Marianne • *rue des Hospitalieres St. Gervais.* Offers a community table, solid fare, and low tabs.

Le Pub Renault • *53 avenue des Champs-Elysees, Metro: George V,* behind Renault showroom. Packed from lunchtime onward. Auto decor and motorcar museum. Menu emphasizes American-type sandwiches and ice cream specialties.

Chez Aron Fils de Tunis • *19 boulevard Montmartre.* Spotlights ultrasweet fritters from Africa called "Beignet."

Les Ecuries Washington • *5 rue Washington.* Flips crepes or plain old honey-capped flapjacks, at $3 per serving, tops.

Au Manneken Pis • *3 rue Ancienne Comedie.* A hole-in-the-wall off boulevard St. Germain, with similar fare at lower prices.

La Boutique de Sandwich • *Just off the Champs-Elysees, on rue du Colisee.* Builds them in 30 different styles.

Pop-Inn • *71 Champs.* Does a good job for quick repasts; burger wrapper suggests filler is 100 percent beef; bet you can't tell whether it's animal, vegetable, or mineral. Nevertheless, I tried one and found it at least better than some U.S. exports.

Piccadilly • *10 rue Cambon.* Presents a lovely midday display of fast foods and pastry. The values are extraordinary—and woefully, so woefully, tempting.

Feuille de ble • *12 rue de Bellechasse.* Very near to the Musee d'Orsay and ideal for a light bite or sandwich. Incidentally, the museum offers 2 restaurants; one for full meals; the other for snacks. The second isn't bad.

Bazaar • *Corner rue St. Benoit and rue Guillaume-Apollinaire.* This place can feed 600 mouths at a time automat-style. Sells everything from hot cross buns to packaged stockings.

CHAINS

Hippopotamus • A splendid linkage that's now all over town. Excellent quality, especially in meats. Light bites to full meals. One of the city's best values and all are decorated blithely in cheerful spring tones.

Oh, Poivrier! • Also ubiquitous in Paris, with limited, high-grade, small-selection plates at reasonable outlays. Even smoked salmon, salad, and sorbet go for about $16. The chain has created a trim-line atmosphere of modern luxury where you can sit and converse—and nosh, of course. Try *2 blvd. Haussmann, 60 rue Pierre-Charron, 2 av. du Maine* for starters.

La Tchaika • *9 rue de l'Eperon;* ☎ *43544702.* A cross between restaurant and tea salon. Good, honest, fresh food in Russian vein. About $15 per person. Open 11:30 a.m. to 10:30 p.m. Closed Sunday, Monday, and August.

Hard Rock Cafe • Unveiled another pebble recently, this one on Blvd. Montmartre, which is similar to the stoneworks of New York, London, Berlin and other quarrys. These are big on theme, loud music, big burgers and big, big prices. While they started as youthful haunts, they now cater more to the yuppie following, which can afford them.

DO-IT-YOURSELF

Inno supermarkets are pleasure domes for bread-wine-and-thou. Everything labeled and price-tagged. One caveat: Forget their supercharged snack bars.

STREET STANDS

Morilo displays tempters from 85¢–$1.25 as you emerge from the St. Denis metro station. Also has takeaway service.

The street vendor at **49 rue Mazarine** (*near the intersection of rue Dauphine, rue Buci, and rue St. Andre-des-Arts*) takes pride in his hot dogs and crisp French fries.

Boulevard St. Michel can be a crepe carnival. Stands here sell them coated with butter, honey, jelly, Cointreau, Grand Marnier, rum, cheese, or chestnut cream; from 60¢–$1.25. Grilled cheese sandwiches also available.

WINE BARS

They're all the rage in Paris, offering wine by the glass, cheese and charcuterie (cold cuts).

Bistrot a Vin *at La Defense*, the vast office and apartment complex west of the city, was the first English-style wine bar. Next appeared **Willy's** in *rue des Petits-Champs near Place des Victoires*. Both cater to a youngish, mostly French crowd. A recent addition in the same vin vein is the **Blue Fox** in the Cite Berryer, an alley of shops off rue Royale, just up the block from Maxim's. Try the hockey-puck-size foie and its lip-smacking sauce or the pastry shell with leeks. Duck is traditional. Since it has English management, many Brits and Yanks sip here and dine at the neighboring **Le Moulin du Village**, where the mood is as winning as the cuisine.

Among the French variations on this theme is **L'Ecluse**, the best, with 4 strategic locations. Specializes in Bordeaux and the food to go with it. Sells a lot of foie gras with the sweet Sauternes. Our favorite is the darkly woody and romantic site at *15 place Madeleine*, a study in art nouveau; other locales, equally recommendable, at *15 quai des Grands Augustins*, *64 rue Francois Ier*, and *2 rue du General H. Bertier*. Working-class wine bars include **Le Rubis** just a few blocks from the Place Vendome; jammed at lunch. A large glass of simple Beaujolais about 85¢. Offers homemade rillettes, good sandwiches, omelets, andouillettes, and a variety of hot dishes. Similar but with more wine and more massive omelets is **Caves Melac** near the Place de Nation. **Au Sauvignon** (*80 rue des St. Peres*) is about as big as a button mushroom, but its following is massive. Cheese, bread, wine, and animated conversation have been the order of the day for generations. We love it for the assured discomfort and flavor of France.

Le Duc de Richelieu in rue de Richelieu, is another good downtown entry. Fleurie is the chief drink; fairly extensive menu. A few other good decanters: **Aux Auvergnats** (*100 boulevard Voltaire*); **Ma Bourgogne** (*19 place des Vosges*); **Le Relais Beaujolais** (*3 rue Milton*) and **Le Sancerre** (*22 avenue Rapp*).

TEA ROOM

Toraya, rue St. Florentin, is Japanese with delicate pastries to add to the aesthetic treats.

STUDENTS

Collegiate cuisine? No fewer than 30 special restaurants throughout the capital. Tickets may be purchased in each one. Unfortunately, the cookery standards in most are dreadful. You might do better in the little places in the Latin Quarter. The **Office du Tourisme Universitaire** (*137 boulevard St.-Michel, Metro: Port-Royal; ☎ 43266097*) provides student tourists with a list of all addresses. About $4 per sitting (50¢ more than French students are charged). A terrific bargain if filling up your stomach is your only concern.

Restaurant du Grand Palais and **Restaurant de la Faculte de Droit** (*rue d'Assas*) are said to be the best of the cluster, but you will need a French student card for entry.

The Cite Universitaire • *19 boulevard Jourdan, Metro: Cite Universitaire,* ☎ *43319095.* operates the largest of the cafeterias; don't expect palace cookery, however. Should you arrive in Paris too late to check in at the OTU, merely present your International Student Identification Card. Most often its operators will furnish your meal first and ask questions later.

The Alliance Francaise cafeteria • *101 blvd. Raspail, Metro: Notre-Damedes-Champs or St. Placide.* In the Montparnasse environs, offers 3-4 course lunches and dinners in a cafeteria above its snack bar. Take the stairs in the lobby at the far end of the courtyard. Starched uniform service in spotless surroundings; no more than 4 or 5 main dishes; price scale that rarely pushes beyond $6. A great spot for meeting new people.

MORE $$

Le Souffle • *36 rue du Mont Thabor (a block from Place Vendome and close to the Tuileries Garden);* ☎ *42602719.* As popular as ever—and with very good reason. Sit *only* in the front room because clients in the back seem to be somewhat neglected. Superb Pilaff St. Jacques, but the *piece de resistance* is M. Faure's *enormous* Souffle Grand Marnier. A meal for 2 about $40, including wine and service. Open from 12–3 p.m. and from 7–10 p.m.; closed Sunday.

Le Montagnard • *24 rue des Canettes, Metro: Mabillon or Sulpice.* Pine-paneled replica of Swiss lodge. Meats with 5 sauces, but many return for huge fondue (cheese at $7, beef at $11). Other choices include Crepes Montagnard (stuffed with seafood and covered with hot cheese) and Brochette Montagnard (4 kinds of spitted meat, baked potato, and courgette). Open 7 p.m. to 1 a.m.; closed Monday.

La Petite Chaise • *36-38 rue de Grenelle, Metro: Bac or Sevre-Babylone.* Perhaps 135 paces off boulevard Raspail. Claims to be Paris's oldest restaurant (1680, and not to be confused with the age of Le Procope Cafe discussed further along). Fixed price for Terrine du Chef, Poulet Mentonaise, fruit salad, and carafe of wine came to $16; coffee and service extra. About 10 main dishes. Open all week and all year.

Restaurant des Beaux-Arts • *11 rue Bonaparte, Metro: St. Germain-des-Pres.* Across from eastern gate of the famed Ecole des Beaux-Arts. File-cabinet bar harks back to its former career as public library. No fewer than 16 hors d'oeuvres and salads. Massive options, including a steaming Coq au Vin and a hefty Grenadin de Veau a l'Italienne; long index of cheeses and desserts. Open noon to 3 p.m. and 7 to 10 p.m.; closed Sunday evenings, Monday, and August.

L'Epicerie • *1 rue St. Benoit, Metro: St. Germain-des-Pres.* Close to St. Germain-des-Pres church. Variety of specialties (partial to the Cassoulet). Chatty and informal; younger patronage predominant. Meals about $17. A find for the price.

Le Berthoud • *1 rue Vallette, Metro: Maubert.* Usually packed with happy diners. Fascinating, inexpensive egg dishes swimming in pools of melted butter or cream, or both; worthy Moujak (Russian tasties); heaps of salad; wee sausages to large steaks for moderate outlays; ultra rich desserts. Really fun. Closed Sunday.

Les Balkans • *3 rue de la Harpe, Metro: St.-Michel; and 33 rue St. Jacques, Metro: Maubert-Mutualite.* Despite uneven cookery and ragged service, draws platoons of Gallic repeaters. Two items usually dependable: shishkebab and goulash. Closed Wednesday.

Lascaud • *7 rue de Mondovi, Metro: Concorde.* On a side street off *rue de Rivoli, west end of Tuileries.* Noontime clientele ranges from chalk-cheeked models to red-faced government ministers. Choose from meal-of-the-day or tempting specialties; Poulet au Riz Sauce Supreme, rice-and-veal plate, duckling in orange sauce or olives. Most entrees $11 or so.

Saint-Antoine • *1 place du Louvre, Metro: Louvre.* At east end of museum. Small and friendly. Try homemade cherry pie (watch out for the pits). Closed Monday from mid-Oct. to Dec. 1.

Ti-Jos • *35 rue St. George IXe and 333 rue de Vaugirard 15.* Bills itself a creperie. Choose from blackboard chalked with substantial selections ($11 top). Noisy and lively. Closed Thursday.

Aux Deux Dragons and **Tai Sam Yuen** • *24 rue Monsieur-le-Prince VIe Metro: Odeon, and 22 rue du Sommerard Metro: Maubert-Mutualite.* The former, a minute's walk south of boulevard St. Germain, offers quiet surroundings and excellent Chinese fare. You can eat decently for $12 and handsomely for $15. Closed Wednesday. The latter with top-notch service and Vietnamese kitchen. Area has many oriental restaurants.

La Chope des Vosges • Along with the previously mentioned wine bar called **Ma Bourgogne** *neighbors on place des Vosges, Metro: Chemin Vert.* Offer bountiful fixed menus. Both are worthy.

La Coupole • *102 boulevard Montparnasse.* Former Hemingway haunt now expensively refashioned and brightened. Still a target for working-class Big Night Out-ers; still living in the lost generation but with a recent facelifting. If you must go, figure about $24 per person, plus wine.

Vagenende • *142 boulevard St.-Germain.* Sometimes called "La Belle Epoque." Stuffed with enough period pieces to launch its own private flea market. Average fare; lamb chops that might bounce if dropped. Amusing, if you're in that *fin de siecle* mood.

Corsaire Basque • *15 rue l'Arc-de-Triomphe, Metro: Etoile.* Country atmosphere in a cottage setting. Daily specials. Crazy about the grilled sardines, piperade, and ham. Figure about $9–11.

KOSHER-STYLE FOOD

Goldenberg's • *69 avenue de Wagram, Metro: Ternes.* Can provide borscht, bagels, pastrami, gefilte fish for reasonable shekels. Open all week.

EVEN MORE $$$

Julien • *16 rue de Faubourg-Saint-Denis; ☎ 47701206.* Maxim's at Macy's prices; will transport you back to turn of the century; memorable lunch or dinner. Be sure to check your bill and your change carefully. Closes 9 p.m. and Sunday.

Highly recommended, as are others in this same group and of a similar mood: **Flo**, **Terminus Nord**, **Le Vaudeville**. Upper-class brasseries.

La Mediterranee • *2 place de l'Odeon, Metro: Odeon;* ☎ *43264675.* Maplike tablecloths; Mediterranean secrets; large menu; great charm. Small terrace. Genuine Provencale bouillabaisse and savory sole; crackly-crisp Salade Nicoise. Maximum of $36-or-so should do it. Honest, popular, and definitely recommended. Open every day.

Marc Annibal de Coconnas • *2 bis place des Vosges, Metro: Chemin Vert;* ☎ *42725816.* Agreeably situated in ancient flower market that Louis XII later converted into his own personal pavilion. Long, narrow room with 20 wooden tables. Indifferent service. Special attention to pates. Try the Poule au Pot. Closed Tuesday.

Dominique • *19 rue Brea, Metro: Vavin;* ☎ *43270880.* At counters near entrance you can eat nobly for about $20, including choice of soup, plat du jour, cheese, and dessert. For special treats try blintzes, borscht a la creme, or Shashlik Karsky. Intimate dining in rear or upstairs will run about $26 for 3 courses and wine.

Chez Isidore • *13 rue d'Artois, Metro: St. Philippe-du-Roule;* ☎ *42250110.* Also called "Artois." Has the grace of age. Small bar. Fireplace in the dining room. House specialties: Gratin du Jambon, charcuteries, Coq au Vin, and sole. A la carte dishes from $7-11. For dessert, try its excellent eclairs. Bookings advisable, especially after 9 p.m. Closed Sunday and from July 14 to Sept. 1.

Le Coupe Choux • *9-11 rue de Lanneau, Metro: Maubert-Mutualite.* Nestles in 17th-century structure on tiny lane adjoining College de France. Open year-round, but warm-weather months best. Large fireplace.

Chez Georges • *34 rue Mazarine, Metro: Odeon.* Small and arty. Very modest. Food fair. Closed Monday and August. Amusing.

L'Auberge Basque • *51 rue de Verneuil, Metro: Solferino or Bac.* Located on a narrow street between boulevard St. Germain and Gare d'Orsay. Intimate atmosphere. About $21 for choice of full-course dinners from day's menu (posted outside); extra for wine (specify ordinaire), coffee, and service. Open every day from 12:30 to 3 p.m. and 7 to 10 p.m. Closed August. Don't go without reservation. Spanish and Basque guitar music for later diners. Memorable.

Le Procope • *13 rue de l'Ancienne Comedie, Metro: Odeon.* A few steps off boulevard St. Germain. Lays claim to being one of the world's oldest cafes (founded 1686). Ben Franklin is numbered (and enshrined) among its notable guests. Don't allow the impatient maitre to rush you because there's at least one menu trap that you'll want to see: $23 fixed-price meal comes in half-price version tucked so unobtrusively into one corner that it is almost invisible. The steak au poivre rates attention. Prefer to order a la carte? You might get away for about $32. Closed Monday.

La Cigogne Gourmand • *17 rue Duphot, Metro: Madeleine.* Opened as port wine-drinking emporium in 1919, but 4 years later converted into present delightful self. Subdued chamber with Portuguese tiles. Open noon to 3 p.m. and 7 to 10 p.m. Closed Sunday.

Androuet's Cheese Shop • *41 rue d'Amsterdam (near Gare St. Lazare) Metro: Liege.* Restaurant adjoining offers a cheesy assortment of dishes and samples.

La Ferme St. Hubert • *21 rue Vignon, in the Eighth District.* Another (and less costly) cheesery with a dining adjunct. The variety is fabulous.

Au Pactole • *44 boulevard St.-Germain, Metro: Odeon.* Enclosed sidewalk terrace; 7 tables inside. Set menus the star attractions: 4-course one for $27, and 5-plate spread with more choices for $34 or so.

Au Petit Riche • *25 rue le Peletier.* Turns back pages of time to before century began. Go early. Closed August as well as Sunday and holidays.

Au Beaujolais • *19 quai de la Tournelle, Metro: Maubert-Mutualite.* About as much atmosphere as a pilot's ready room. Tantalizing menu. Always reserve. Tough to beat for pure and simple eating. Open noon to 2:30 p.m. and 7:30 to 9:30 p.m. Closed Monday and throughout August.

Chei Rene • *14 boulevard St. Germain (around the corner from the above).* Similar personality. Even noisier (if possible); same price scale. Should be able to stuff yourself crosseyed for about $28. Closed Sunday.

NIGHTLIFE

The **Lido** (*78 avenue Champs-Elysees, Metro: George V*), the **Moulin Rouge** (*82 boulevard de Clichy, Metro: Blanche*), the **Folies Bergere** (*32 rue Richer, Metro: Cadet*), and **Paradis Latin** (*28 rue Cardinal Lemoine*) pump out shockingly expensive production-belt entertainment tailored toward endless busloads of tourists. In case you are interested:

The **Lido** extravaganza, probably the most smashing in its history, stuns the customers with its streamlined ensemble of at least 50 dancers, showgirls, seminudes, and headline international acts. But it also levies the cost of a good dinner for two for either a half-bottle of so-called champagne or 2 drinks per person; guests who sit through both 11 p.m. and 1:15 a.m. performances (they are identical) are walloped with double these figures; the cuisine is indifferent and costly. About 9 p.m. is the best time to go.

The almost equally renowned **Moulin Rouge**, immortalized by Toulouse-Lautrec and later known for its can-can, is run by the Lido and charges similar tariffs. Huge, tiered, theaterlike hall; bar atop the pyramid; lavish show. Here again the TV "spectacular," with mammary glands the feature—and enough feathers and chiffon to bury the Gare du Nord. Two 3-hour shows; institutional meal.

Some concierges will offer tickets to both of the above landmarks at "all-inclusive" prices. They will be valid—BUT the intimation that they will entitle you to "all the champagne you can drink" is a swindle. While you do receive a gratis half bottle, the rest is on you.

The **Folies Bergere** also shows plenty of leg and bosom. If you're affluent, either reserve your seats through your hometown travel agent before departure, or go to the Theater Desk at American Express at exactly 5 p.m. on performance day and hope for cancellations (which are frequent). You possibly can buy a standing-room billet for about $10. Tickets are around $37 for orchestra seats and only slightly less for mezzanine perches. Sold out nearly the year-round.

Paradis Latin whomps up a scarlet and gilded atmosphere in which flamboyant productions keep eyes darting with the avidity of a Davis Cup final. The huge dinner and show should denude your budget of at least $66 and possibly $93 if you get the least bit reckless—and that's per person! Costumes, feathers, acrobats, sparklers, stereo gimmicks—all you'd expect. If you don't dine here you can anticipate a beverage zap of close to $38. Lavish and lively.

Cheaper than those above: This first quartet of clubs are all near each other on either side of the Boul' Mich' near the St. Michel Metro:

Caveau de la Huchette • *5 rue de la Huchette, 1 block south of the Seine.* Hewn out behind a nondescript entrance. Specialties are soft talk and quiet sipping; cellar rollicking with a Gallic Dixieland combo; dance floor and stag line always sardined; beverages or seats seldom available down here. This arrangement keeps the staircase crowded with 2-way traffic; about $5.50 to enter. Open from 9:30 p.m. to 2 a.m. except on Saturday, when the lights dim at 3 a.m.

Le Chat Qui Peche • *4 rue de la Huchette.* Just across the alley, turns on French-style jazz, including some locally popular American musicians who often perform in the sets. No charge in the 3-room street-level perch where the sounds are piped up from below; $6 in the "live" portion; about $3 for a beer; double for a stronger quaff. Closed Wednesday.

Le Cameleon • *57 rue St.-Andres-des-Arts.* Another grotto, asks a $3.50 minimum. The shrewdest ploy here is to snag a table and fill up your glass between 9 p.m. and 10 p.m., when libations run from about $2.25 for a beer and about $5 for whiskey; after 10 p.m., the tabs rise astronomically for the first drink, but retreat 50 percent for the refills. Good music sometimes. Closed Tuesday.

Le Kilt • *4 rue Jean-Mermoz, Metro: Franklin D. Roosevelt.* Appropriately decorated with kilts and Highland portraits; couples most prefer the upper dance arena for le cheek to cheek; draw your free soda or tonic water from the centrally located well; "suggested" minimum of about $7, plus tip.

Le Slow Club • *130 rue de Rivoli, Metro: Louvre or Chatelet.* Features dancing in an underground cavern; sometimes there's a Dixieland combo. Pay $5.50 at the entrance, order a couple of $4 drinks, and you'll march with the saints. Closed Sunday and Monday.

Le Riverbop • *67 rue St. Andre-des-Arts, Metro: St. Michel.* Situated in a basement off the carrefour Buci; animated atmosphere; Dixieland; benches only (no tables); docking fee of $4. A journalist recently wrote, "Just breathing for one set is like smoking a pack of cigarettes." They air the place out on Sunday and Monday.

Au Lapin Agile • *22 rue des Saules, Metro: Abbesses.* In the heart of Montmartre, near the place du Tertre. This famed old-timer has been immortalized by Utrillo and is where Picasso once fired a shot in the air to demonstrate his joy over the sale of a picture; it has rung since before the turn of the century with folk songs and the spoutings of would-be (and to-be) poets. Venerable musicians; low ceilings with cloud banks of tobacco smoke; 9 large, shared tables; usually filled for keeps by 10:30 p.m. or so. Closed Monday. An institution.

Caveau des Oubliettes • *1 rue St. Julien-le-Pauvre.* Translates as "The Secret Dungeon." The specialty here is songs of the earth. From the over-rapt audience, would-be canaries often spring forth to perform. A seat and a beer run in the painful $11 range.

Trois Mailletz • *56 rue Galande, Metro: Maubert-Mutualite.* Dispenses the jazz classics at another cellar in an alley off St. Julien-le-Pauvre. If you're over 4 feet tall, watch your noggin going down the twisting stairs. The sophisticated talent matches the verve of its listeners. Entry is $4, and drinks are about $6.50 (cheaper at the bar). Jammed. Closed Monday.

DANCING

The Palace • *8 rue Faubourg Montmartre.* The big news, a French version of New York's Studio 54 with mad getups and lots of go-go.

Balajo • *9 rue de Lappe.* Offers afternoon dancing, mostly by locals with other local wives. At night the pace is more pulsey, but still there's a lingering note of naughty romance.

Le Touquet • *1 bis rue Jean-Mermoz, Metro: Franklin D. Roosevelt.* Near Club Ecossais. Street-level site; translucent glass door; entrance drink-ticket counter where you're challenged to a guess-your-capacity game ($4.50 minimum); "alcoholics" sign directing traffic to the bar at the rear. Many singles here, too.

JAZZ

The rue de Lappe, just northeast of Place de la Bastille, is becoming a haunt for jazz clubs such as the **Chapelle des Lombards** and **Balajo**. Half a century ago it was alive with music halls; then decay set in; and now it is being reborn as an artists' quarter. Accordion tunes and cancans are replaced by salsas, javas, tangos, and even waltzes. It's not the Champs just yet, but here's a colorful and historic district that is groping for a new identity.

Barbary Coast • *Formerly Jacky's Farwest Saloon, 11 rue Jules-Chaplain, Metro: Vavin.* Located in Montparnasse. Its California owner sometimes moseys into his corral in full Hopalong Cassidy rig; the chaps behind the bar usually wear Levis. Western decor; hot discs and an occasional live *chanteur*; entrance scale ranging between $2.25 and $4, depending on the night of the week; the first swig of red-eye included in the admission. Many Americans.

Le Trou Madame • *3 passage de la Petite Boucherie, Metro: St. Germain-des-Pres.* Between the rue de l'Abbaye and boulevard St. Germain. Tapes and discs spinning till 6 a.m.; about a $5 minimum to dance. Good but not special.

Le Musette • *23 rue de Lappe, Metro: Bastille.* Across the river in a low-rent district, is an Apache parlor. Warm and intimate mien; occasional singers; many singles among its young and old patrons; very expensive.

BARS FOR FUN

Le Calavados • *40 avenue Pierre-Ier-de-Serbie.* A sophisticated Right Bank day and latenight haven for the almost-chic international set. (It is open until 6 a.m.!) Air-conditioned; snack bar; lunch or candlelight dining or supping upstairs; piano and guitar music; expensive. The best bet is to listen at the bar, where beer is about $3.50. Then, if the crowd isn't right at the moment, duck out. Conservative dress is advised. An intimate, relaxed, often fun-filled landmark.

La Bombarde • *14 rue Xavier Privas, Metro: St.-Michel.* Supplies a dark interior in which red coach lamps glow feebly. Good jazz platters (not rock, and not too loud); drinks from about $3. Although there's a downstairs cave, most new friendships are sealed at the bar.

Caveau de la Bolee

25 rue de l'Hirondelle, Metro: St. Michel. A sunken vault near the west end of place St. Michel. Hard-to-find entrance; doorway so low that you must duck; minute arched cellar crammed with benches, red-checked tables, and humanity; informal entertainment consisting of dirty jokes in French, an accordion player, and records; so much audience participation that they're likely to wisecrack about you as you enter; drinks about $10 and dinner with show around $40. Closed Sunday and during August.

L'Abbaye • *6 bis rue de l'Abbaye, Metro: St. Germain-des-Pres.* So pleasant and easygoing that it is usually jammed, but always with room for 1 or 2 more; legitimate drinks at perhaps $5.50-or-so, unabashedly clannish.

Rhumerie Martiniquaise and **Le Temps Perdu** (*the first on, and the latter near boulevard St. Germain*) are both agreeable low-cost bars. The latter is particularly popular among the undergraduate and postgraduate groups.

If your French is good, you may enjoy **La Boheme** in Montmartre (*2 pl. du Tertre; Metro: Abbesses*), where the songs are sexy and funny.

PUBS—YES—PUBS

They're proliferating in Merry Olde Paree. Two of the best are **The Red Lion**, *73 Champs Elysees, Metro: George V*, and the **Bedford Arms**, *rue Princesse, Metro: Mabillon*, both dedicated to the fine old Gallic tradition of lager, darts, and jellied eels. The former dispenses, from an open window at the end of the bar, uncommonly large portions of hot and cold "snacks," including grilled steak and "chips," mushroom pie, and sausages and mashed potatoes. We like the atmosphere. The latter offers Guinness at about $2.75 per half pint. **Sir Winston Churchill**, *5 rue de Presbourg, Metro: Etoile*, looks authentic, but is staffed entirely by French waiters. A stand near the door hawks packages of corn flakes, lemon chip cookies, jam, custard, and what-have-you. The ale is tapped cold enough to turn a true publican's nose to Union Jack blue. A $15 tourist menu, including veal-and-ham pie, chicken, a fruit tart, and coffee, was better than expected, but it was like dining at a movie set.

BEDTIME SNACKS

L'Echaude

21 rue de l'Echaude, Metro: St. Germain-des-Pres. A split-level entry near boulevard St. Germain. Narrow stepdown entrance; French colonial posters lining the walls; 10 well-attended tables sprawled in an "L" around the high-stooled bar; serious clientele; delicious cheese omelets and soups, plus full meals; decent prices. Open all night except Sunday and during August.

Still up and still hungry? If you are in this district, amble over to the ever-busy and tiny **rue de la Harpe**. To name only a few spots, the **Patisserie de Sud**, with submarine sandwiches and numerous Tunisian tantalizers; the around-the-corner **Pisteria**, with snacks hot from the grill; the **Djerba**, with tables, whomping up middling Middle Easternisms; **La Vieille Athenas**, with Greek and Armenian selections. Next door there's a tidy Chinese chop-stickery and beside that is a Balkan house. There are more, too, but space here is limited. Wander on your own through this area day or night; it's fascinating, fun, and fattening.

WHAT TO SEE AND DO

MUSEUM PASS

Here's a splendid way to see a lot for a little: 65 francs for a 1-day pass; 130 francs for 3 consecutive days and 180 francs for 5 days. At normal fees only two visits would pay for your card, but this entitles you to see **65 museums and monuments** such as the following: African and Oceanian Arts, Porcelain (Sevres), Cluny, Delacroix, Ennery, Fontainebleau Palace, Louvre, Orsay, Picasso, Home of Napoleon and Josephine, Rodin's House, Museum of Modern Art, Catacombs, Pompidou Center, Crypt of Notre-Dame and Towers, Postal Museum, Cinema Museum, The Mint and The Sewers. You can obtain the pass at underground kiosks, at the museums themselves or at the Paris Tourist Office. Travel agencies also often sell it in the USA and in Europe.

EIFFEL TOWER & THE CLASSIC PARIS

This year the vast **American Center** will open at new digs in Bercy Park, close to the Bastille. The project is aimed at the artistic linkage between the two nations, so there will be lots of exhibits, dance, theater, and films, plus a bookstore, and dining and snack facilities. Check when you arrive to find out what's on. Certainly it will be a good place to meet others.

The **Eiffel Tower**, of course, is a must for first-timers, by day or night. A popular restaurant-cafe has been added on the first platform, plus 27 shops and an audiovisual museum. An excellent but expensive restaurant on the second story also is operative. The hydraulic elevators that produced such problems, especially during icy periods when the fluid froze, are now replaced with electric equipment. (One of the original ones, however, is being preserved for viewing by visitors.) While for a dollar or a little more, you can climb the staircase to the first and second levels, the elevator ride to the first, second, and third floors costs 8, 18, and 26 francs respectively. Hours from Nov. 1 to Mar. 31 are 10:30 a.m. till 11 p.m. From Apr. 1 to May 31: 10 a.m. to 11 p.m. on weekdays and a half-hour earlier on Saturday and Sunday. Here is quite an inspiring face-lift for a Tinker Toy that was only intended as a temporary structure for the Paris World's Fair of 1889!

For further initial bearings, sail under the 18 graceful bridges that span the Seine. Tops on this ferry-go-round is the floodlit view of **Notre Dame**. But you'll also catch glimpses of the spires of **Sainte Chapelle**, with stained glass windows that make it one of the most beautiful churches; the sculptured walls of the **Louvre Museum's** southern wing; the terraces of the **Tuileries Gardens**, which are being given new life and will flower fuller in a few more seasons; **Place de la Concorde**, jammed with autos and flags near the spot where Louis XVI and Queen Marie-Antoinette were guillotined; **Napoleon's Tomb** (Church of the Dome), where the Emperor's body lies in a nest of 6 airtight coffins; the brilliant gardens and fountains of the **Palais de Chaillot**; and **Conciergerie**, the prison during the Reign of Terror. As transportation, take your choice between the **BateauxMouches** and the Vedettes Paris-Tour Eiffel fleet. The former cast off morning through evening from a Right-Bank wharf between Pont des Invalides and Pont de l'Alma; they offer 1-, 1-1/4-, and 2-1/2-hour rides for about $5.50-12. (A dollar cheaper before noon.) The latter, which dock near the Eiffel Tower, feature 90-minute trips for close to $4.50, with departures every 20 minutes. We prefer the B-M fleet because the viewing is better from the larger windows. Snack dispensers are situated on the loading pier if you are in a rush and hungry. Newly added to these waterway routes is the Bat-O-Bus, a taxi service afloat; rates roughly $5 pier-to-pier.

Also available is a half-day cruise on the Seine taking in the Canal St. Martin. The 35-seat catamaran *La Patache Eautobus* leaves at 9 a.m. from Quai Anatole France (Metro: Solferino) daily, except Monday and holidays; $13 adults; half for children 6-12.

Climb aboard one of the Cityrama doubledecker buses (*2 rue du 29 Juillet, Metro: Tuileries*). You'll cover miles of ground, with closeups of **Arc de Triomphe**,

Napoleon's tribute to his armies and to himself; **Place de la Bastille**, where a solitary column marks the dungeon so infamous during the Revolution; **Champs-Elysees**, a glittering aorta of marquees, marquis, and mocca; **Sacre-Coeur**, the onion-domed church crowning the plateau of Montmartre; **Pantheon**, the temple of fame enshrining French heroes from the Revolution to the Resistance; the **Sorbonne**, the 730-year-old seat of French learning; and **UNESCO**, with its frescoes by Picasso and Tamayo, Calder's mobile, and Noguchi's Japanese garden. Hourly takeoffs on this line, 9 a.m. through 5 p.m.; language tape controlled by the driver, with 5-inch hearing discs in each seat; attractive hostesses; refreshment stops where you might spend more than you ever have for just a Coke and a plain cookie. Despite its commercialism, this one rates an A for area covered.

Another old reliable is **Paris Vision**, more than half a century old and still with good vision. This company roams all over the **city** as well as to **Versailles**, **Chartres**, **Fontainebleau**, and, ranging farther, to **Mont St. Michel**, the Chateaux Country, and other destinations that can keep you roadbound for up to 3 days; it also runs local night tours. The loops return to *214 rue de Rivoli* or *1 rue Auber*; any major travel agent can book you aboard.

THE LOUVRE

Apart from the exhibition halls, there's a panoramic sightseeing terrace on the roof of one wing. As if you hadn't already guessed, the glass pyramid utilized as an entrance is one of the most controversial issues in Gaul since the introduction of the New Franc. Now the colossal alabaster Assyrian bulls—five of them weighing in at a mere 25 tons each—have been moved to the **Cour de Zhorsabad** (previously called Cour du Louvre). Islamic and Oriental art occupy the refashioned Richelieu wing. Open 10 a.m. to 5 p.m. except Tuesday; guided tours starting at 10:30 a.m. and 3 p.m. except on Sunday; illuminated Friday night. (Try to see it at this its finest hour.) Free admission on Sunday.

Other familiar museums: the wonderfully presented **Musee d'Orsay**, a resurrected rail station, contains the jewels of French impressionism while the **Jeu de Paume** and the **Orangerie** (*Tuileries Garden, Metro: Concorde*), which once contained the primary thrust of the vast Louvre collection, are able to exhibit select morsels in the limited space they offer; the aesthetically hideous **Centre National d'Art et de Culture Georges-Pompidou**, popularly known as **Beaubourg** (exciting exhibitions, architecturally bizarre, and incorporating the former Musee d'Art Moderne); the **Rodin** (*77 rue de Varenne, Metro: Varenne*), a chapel and mansion in a garden showcase of the sculptor's works, including "The Thinker" and "Gates of Hell"; and the spectacular **Picasso** (Hotel Sale, in the Marais) with 229 paintings (many collected by the Spaniard or given to him by other artists), 137 sculptures, collages, ceramics, and about 3000 other pieces.

But all too many visitors miss these less famous museums: the **Carnavalet**, which views Parisian life and the birth and growth of the city, the **Opera** (*rue Auber entrance, Metro: Opera*), heaped with busts, costumes, and scene sketches from this music center; the **Military** (*Esplanade des Invalides, Metro: Invalides*), with its pictorial and artifactual dossier of major French campaigns; the **Cluny** (*24 rue du Sommerard, Metro: St. Michel*), encompassing 22,000 pieces of medieval arts and crafts in a Gothic edifice; and the recently founded **Archaeology Museum** in digs under the plaza in front of Notre Dame, with 3rd-century ramparts, a Gallo-Roman furnace, remnants of a Merovingian cathedral (it appears to be a popular site for churchgoers) and many more relics of antiquity.

Photography enthusiasts undoubtedly would be fascinated with the 8000 cameras, lenses, and other shutterbug equipment at the **French Museum of Photography** at *78 rue de Paris in Bievres* (7 miles from the capital). If you can't get out there, try the more modest but interesting shop in Montmartre run by Guy Bomet and called **Aux Fontaines de Niepce et Daguerre** (*20 rue Andre del Sarte, 18e*). Both are noteworthy for devotees of the art.

Wacky gallery hours are still a way of life. As one example, the watchmen and guards stay home over Easter and Easter Monday—and then add their customary Tuesday fadeout. Many institutions open and close irregularly during the day. So check before you plunge—and reserve your sorties for Sundays, when tariffs are usually either banished or at half price.

A brush with necrology? The world's largest repository of human bones—from an estimated 4 to 5 million souls—has been unearthed in 2700 feet of catacombs near the **Place Denfert-Rochereau** in Montparnasse. Visitors are issued candles.

Back outdoors, wandering will get you everywhere. It will give you the feel of old Montmartre at sunset, the ancient Marais section in ferment, the **Ile St. Louis's** stunning courtyards in bloom, and Montparnasse's revelry in action.

La Pernoderie, southeast of Paris in the suburb of Creteil (*120, avenue du Marechal Foch*; ☎ *48999145*) shows what goes into the making of Pernod. Free visit with tasting session for a phone call. The 14th-century cellars of the **Musee du Vin**, a cork's turn from the Eiffel Tower *on rue des Eaux*, traces French wine-making history and includes a tasting. **Les Ateliers Hermes**, (*24, Faubourg St. Honore*; ☎ *42652160*) reveals the history and creation of the leather goods of the same name. Free by appointment. **La Parfumerie Fragonard** (*9, rue Scribe*) details the French perfume process. Open every day but Sunday. No entry fee.

CONCERTS

Now that the massive organ at **Notre Dame** has been refurbished (after years of revision), you may hear concerts free on Sundays at 5:30 p.m. Possibly one of the most interesting places to hear music is at the **Espace de Projection** in the Beaubourg, where the hall itself can be tuned as an instrument. Its capacity is small (maximum: 400), but it represents a major step in the acoustics field. Even though classical music in France seems to have suffered a dry spell over recent seasons, we have heard some excellent performances at the **Salle Pleyel**. One of the most prestigious halls for Gallic talent, it also hosts scores of the great orchestras and virtuosos of other lands. In early summer, try the **Marais Festival**. The social zenith is the **Festival d'Automne** (approx. Sept. 10 to Dec. 1), which marks the reopening of the dance, music, and theater seasons. During the rich winter period, as well as in its fringes, there are the famed **Paris Opera** and the **Opera Comique.** Add to that the productions of the **Colonne, Lamoureux** and **Conservatoire** orchestras, plus **Les Amis de la Musique de Chambre**, plus choir recitals in the great cathedrals and abbeys of Paris, plus those of the surrounding countryside—and when you're done, you'll have a weary but happy set of eardrums. Tickets for most of these events can be obtained through **Les Semaines Musicales** (*252 Faubourg-St. Honore*), or for young enthusiasts who seek them on a seasonal basis from **Les Jeunesses Musicales de France** (*45 rue La Boetie*).

PARKS

Nearly the whole city. For woodlands and lakes, retreat to the **Bois de Boulogne** or the extremely central **Tuileries**. While both are lovely by day, both can be dangerous after dusk. The former has rowboats and bikes for rent near the Porte Dauphine metro exit. Closer to the Sablons station, there's the Acclimatization Garden, which youngsters enjoy because of the driving course, distorting mirrors, and mild exposure to this wildlife science.

MOVIES

Most of the big bijoux palaces along the Champs-Elysees and its tributaries reel them out in their original language versions for at least one performance every day. If you don't speak French, check the tip sheets or newspapers for the times. Classic films are rerun at the **Cinematheque Francaise** (*Palais de Chaillot, Metro: Trocadero, and 29 rue d'Ulm, Metro: Luxembourg*). The cost is $2 for double- or triple-feature showings of the world's finest movies, including many all-time American favorites. Afternoon and evening presentations (consult the International Herald Tribune for listings).

MARKETS

The partially condemned **Flea Market** ("Marche aux Puces," *porte de Clignancourt*) is still mobbed by distrait tourists. Its prices are now awful. Open Saturday, Sunday, and Monday only—and the best time to buy is Saturday morning. **Marche St. Pierre**, the textiles and remnants market (*rue Charles-Nodier, foot of Sacre-Coeur Church*) is a maze of stalls that work during the ordinary business hours (see below). The **Dog Market** (*15e at 106 rue Brancion*) parades canines from 2-4 p.m. on Sunday. The **Bird Market** is open on Sunday too, in the then-deserted **Flower Market** on Ile de la Cite. The **Stamp Market** (*along avenue Gabriel, between avenues Matignon and Marigny*) is open on Thursday and Sunday. Dicker your head off in all of these.

PUBLICATIONS

Many of the hotels stock a Cue-type magazine called *Allo Paris*; *Une Semaine de Paris-Pariscope* is similar. And, of course, Paris is home of the famous and excellent *International Herald Tribune*, virtually every English-speaking overseas traveler's lifeline to current events. It is published daily but not Sunday.

EXCURSIONS

Targets worth hitting include: **Versailles**, 13 miles southwest, the palace of Louis XIV, expanded for viewing a recently opened wing of 21 rooms; summer hours 9 a.m. to 7 p.m.; closed Monday; **Fontainebleau**, 38 miles southeast, a hunting ground that became a palace-away-from-home for 6 kings and an emperor; **Vaux-le-Vicomte**, 2 miles from Melun and vaguely in the same region as the above, a spectacular chateau with immaculate furnishings, splendid manicured gardens, and ways to see the inner workings of aristocratic French life in its heyday; **Malmaison**, 10 miles west, where Napoleon and Josephine lived a blissful pre-Empire idyll; **St.-Germain-en-Laye**, 15 miles west, the royal resort enfolded by Europe's most sloth-provoking forest; **Vincennes**, 7 miles east, which contains France's biggest dungeon, one of its busiest racetracks, and the capital's zoo (also reachable by Metro); **Chantilly**, 25 miles north, with its elegant castle and beautiful racetrack; **Chartres**, 60 miles southwest, and the rural pedestal of one of the world's great cathedrals; and **Giverny**, where Claude Monet studied and painted the gardens he designed, are open to the public after years of renovation and reconstitution. On view is the farmhouse, its rooms restored to their original appearance, and the gardens with their willows, the wisteria-hung Japanese bridge, the original boat painted in 1887, and a vast array of flowers. Open Apr. 1-Nov. 1, from 10 a.m.-noon, and 2-6 p.m. daily except Monday. Admission to the gardens roughly $5, to the house $3. Access is easy: from Gare St. Lazare by train to Vernon for $11 or so round trip. Giverny is only a short taxi ride away. And should you wish to rove farther afield, the RATP bus tour company runs multiday circuits from late April to the end of October to the Loire Valley Chateau Country, to Normandy, to the D-Day beachheads, and to many other favorite attractions. **Euro-Disneyland** lies *20 miles east of Paris at Villiers-sur-Marne.* A high-speed train zips right to the Toon Town portals; otherwise there are bus links. Prices are 225 F. for adults, 150 F. for children 3 to 9. These are one-day "passports," but they offer 2- and 3-day versions at 425 FF and 565 FF respectively. For details phone ☎ *(33-1) 6474-4303* (Paris) or in the USA ☎ *(407) 8244321.*

BIKING

It's a cheap way to see a lot. In the capital, **Paris Velo Rent-a-Bike** (*2 rue du Fer a Moulin Ve*) and **Market Moto** (*19 place du Marche St. Honore Ie*) offer pedals at $21 per week; some motorbikes and sterner iron also are for rent at higher tabs. Also refer to our national transportation subsection toward the beginning of this chapter.

TENNIS

Enthusiasts can get information, but not games, at the **Federation Francaise de Lawn Tennis** (*15 rue de Teheran, Metro: Miromesnil;* ☎ *45220241*).

SWIMMING

In the capital, cool off at either the **Piscine Molitor** (*avenue de la Porte-Molitor*) or at the **Stade Francaise** (*Boulogne-sur-Seine*), one of the nicest in the metropolis.

WHERE TO SHOP

ART PRINTS

As you'd expect, here's a lithographic fountainhead for some of Europe's finest reproductions. The stocks at the **Louvre** are the widest; prices start around $3 and climb steeply. The galleries near St. Germain-des-Pres and St. Sulpice offer limited-run paintings at exceptional values, in the $10 to $20 spectrum. *Always insist on being given a bill for Customs reference.* There are export restrictions on various works of art—and here they're tough, even though most prints fall under the "free" classification. As would be expected, some of the intellectual giants at the airports or frontier stations scarcely know the difference between Renoir, Renault, and Raincoat—thus setting things up for a possible delay.

ARCHITECTURE IN MINIATURE

Galerie Architecture Miniature Gault (*206 rue de Rivoli and 5 bis rue Norvins up in Montmartre*) is the showcase for ceramic houses, street scenes, churches, ports and such scenes of Europe created by Jean-Pierre Gault. They make superb gifts (starting at 45 F.) and are becoming valuable to collectors. Gault's ceramics come with a certificate of authenticity.

BAKERY PRODUCTS

Poilane (*8 rue du Cherche-Midi*) has had its ovens going for 100 years. Paris gourmets line up after 4 p.m. to snatch some freshly made bread, butter cookies, and devastatingly delicious apple tarts. An unforgettable experience.

BOOKS

Galignani (*224 rue de Rivoli*) has one of the best stocks in Europe—in English as well as in other tongues. For your own collection or for special presents, don't miss it.

CHEESE

La Ferme Saint Hubert (*21 rue Vignon*) has at least 180 types. If you don't want to pack it away in your luggage, you can pack it away in their adjoining restaurant of the same name.

CRYSTAL AND PORCELAIN

Rue de Paradis is the lodestone. It abounds with shops and factory outlets where savings can run anywhere from 30-50 percent against U.S. prices. **Baccarat** (#30) is a favorite of ours.

DEPARTMENT STORES

Au Printemps tops our list, followed by **Au Bon Marche**, and **Galeries Lafayette**. All are good—and all are close together. **Aux Trois Quartiers**, a neighbor, was revamped and functions as a shopping mall with individual boutiques. **Au Printemps-Nation**, a 5-story branch of the first, opened on Paris's eastern edge, for suburban shoppers.

FASHION TRENDS

The cutting edge of this field is located in the **place Victoire** (2e). The boutiques carry all the styles that will appear next year in other capitals of the world. Another district for viewing premarket apparel is the **Saint-Germain-des-Pres quarter** (6e). Most of this stock is forbiddingly expensive, but for tips on how to buy at up to 50% discounts, refer to our 1994 edition of *Fielding's Selective Shopping Guide to Europe*. And remember, at the sales that usually take place in January and July, you'll be able to pick up some great bargains.

FAIENCE

Quimper Faience (*84 rue St.-Martin*) takes its name from its Brittany origins. (See the factory store if you visit Locronan in Brittany.) Wonderful plates, dining sets, and decorative pieces that bring cheer to any home. Very reasonable, too.

GOURMET ITEMS

Hediard (*21 place de la Madeleine*) has been bringing delicacies and exotica to this land of refined palates for more than a century. You are bound to find something to tickle your taste buds or take home as a gift.

Markets are covered under "What to See and Do."

MOOD MAKERS

The French usually do it aromatically. **Jean Laporte L'Artisan Parfumeur** (*22 rue Vignon and 24 bd. Raspail*) has a novel way to add fragrance and that special ambience to your home. The secret is a porous ring that sits like a crown atop a lamp bulb. The light heats the drops of perfumed oil, which you sprinkle on the ring; soon the scent permeates the atmosphere. There are color-keyed flower and fruit aromas.

PERFUME

Paris means perfume—the best in the world—but it also means Be Careful. The retail end of this industry can be a jungle, with enormous price variations. Today's leaders are: Balmain, Cacharel, Capucci, Caron, Cartier, Carven, Chanel, Chloe, Jean Desprez, Dior, Givenchy, Gres, Hermes, Lagerfeld, Lanvin, Guy Laroche, Missoni, Morabito, Paloma Picasso, Patou, Paco Rabanne, Oscar de la Renta, Nina Ricci, Rochas, Sonia Rykiel, Jean-Louis Scherrer, Valentino, Van Cleef & Arpels, and Yves Saint Laurent. Brand leaders for men are: Azzaro, Bogart, Givenchy, Gucci, Halston and Lanvin. Guerlain is the only producer that insists on selling direct to the Paris public (4 shops in the city).

Remember, also, that most (not all) of the above leaders are "restricted brands" in the U.S. Customs. Whenever this applies, your importation into the States is limited to 1 bottle of the same type per person (in a few types, the 3 oz. size is standard). Have your husband, boyfriend, or child declare the excess! Direct-mail shipment to the United States is sometimes prohibited. Be sure to check these restrictions before you buy, because excess amounts are automatically confiscated. If you select wisely and well, you'll go home with France's greatest shopping bargain. Big official discounts (and sometimes unofficial ones!) are extended with shipment to embarkation point, and/or with large orders. **Sagil** (*242 rue de Rivoli*) is a shop with a very large stock, a solid reputation, a knowledgeable staff ready to assist you, and offers discounts no matter what the amount of your purchase. Manufacturers are constantly adding and deleting fragrances from their lines. Do a little homework before you arrive in France by sampling scents and noting retail prices at home, then you'll really be aware of savings you're getting—even certain American designer perfumes that are made in France can cost less.

TEAS

Christian Constant (*26 rue du Bac*) has his caddies filled with an exotic range. It makes a perfect gift—pleasing both neophyte and specialist—and it's so packable. When you need a tea break you can enjoy a cup right on the spot along with delicious pecan or pumpkin tarts. House-made chocolates are also here for the slim and needy.

REIMS

This was, is, and will probably always be the only capital of true champagne on the globe. A tour through one of the caves here or in the surrounding area (easily arranged and free) is practically guaranteed to put bubbles in anyone's day. Historically it's a wow, too. Starting in A.D. 496 with the coronation of King Choldwig, sovereigns of Gaul chose to be crowned here. As a result, over the past 1-1/2 millennia the contractors have been busy building attractions. It's loaded—as are so many of the crusaders who limit their visits to the fantastic wine cellars. See the Chagall windows in the Cathedral, the slace Royale of Louis V's time, the Benedictine Basilica of St. Remi, and the Salle de Guerre, where Germany formally surrendered in 1945. In early summer Reims goes to its own fair and in July (usually) it hosts the French Grand Prix of racing cars.

There are about 30 champagne producers here and in neighboring Epernay. Most hospitable is **Mumm**, *34 rue du Champs de Mars.* Lots of tiny hotels in the center but why not drive to Laon, overlooking the entire district and dine or overnight at **La Banniere de France**? The walled town itself is bewitching.

ROUEN

This former Celtic seat of power is another old-timer. Pick your century and you'll probably find it represented—except maybe the 20th! While it is an undeniable draw for its cathedral and other treasures of antiquity, if you've got your own transportation and should be tiring of past glories, why not drive into the surrounding countryside and be hypnotized by its Norman spell? There is a pagan charm in this particular landscape that even the south porch of **St. Ouen** can't beat. For overnighting, the **Astrid** has no restaurant, but it is pleasant. The **Poste** is more expensive and more luxurious.

ST.-JEAN-DE-LUZ

Here is one of the major springboards to the **Basque country**. The scenery is so grandiose that we wonder what the chairman of the Swiss National Tourist Office thinks privately when he sees it. The area is enchanting and compact, the list of "must sees" not too demanding, and the people, food, and culture unique. As for St.-Jean itself, look for overnight space in the boarding houses radiating from the port and the main square. The **Donibane** is nice if you have a car, and the **Madison** is excellent in the center of town.

ST. TROPEZ

HOW TO GET AROUND

Within the town, walk wherever you go, because distances are rarely challenging. If you're traveling by rail, you may transfer to the local S.N.C.F. (French National Railroad) trunk line at either Toulon or St. Raphael. Bus-bound wayfarers find daily links between St. Tropez and Marseille, Toulon, Nice, plus several other intermediate villages and fringeland beaches such as nearby Port Grimaud.

WHAT TO SEE AND DO

When you're not doing a full-length bake job on the beaches (the best are Tahiti, Moorea, Clubs 55 and 77, and Salins), there are 3 other main attractions. First, the **Musee de l'Annonciade** (*place Georges Grammont*) exhibits one of the Cote d'Azur's better small-scale modern art collections. While its selections are few, all are choice; Signac, Rouault, Matisse, Vlaminck, Braque, Segonzac, and others are represented. Open any day except Tuesday; small entry fee; open 10 a.m.-noon, plus 3-7 p.m. in summer, and 2-6 p.m. in winter; closed November. A coup for this tiny resort.

The 2 finest lookout points for miles around are from the ancient **Citadelle**, which stands sentry over the little parapet-lined Musee de la Marine, and from the **Mole du Portalet**, the finger jetty that protects the entrance to the port.

If you have a car, **Cannes** and its surrounding targets are only 45-60 minutes away (details are covered under Cannes, above). A shorter jaunt, to nearby **St.-Raphael** and **Frejus-Plage**, recalls to old-timers the St. Tropez of 1937. These toy villages nestle behind or to the side of a lovely crescent beach about 3/4-miles long. Limited appeal, however. **Toulon**, perhaps 1 hour to the west, features the Tour Fondue at the tip of a lonely peninsula, jutting into the sapphire Mediterranean waters. From here, dreamers muse wistfully at the Hyeres Island.

STRASBOURG

The tall red sandstone **Cathedral of Notre-Dame** dates from the 11th century; for art lovers, the **medieval sculptures** are exceptional; the paintings at the **Palais Rohan** are, too. Top sights further include the 15th-century **Maison Kammerzell** (Alsatian restaurant of the same name), the island enclave of **Petite France** (only a 15-minute walk along the riverbank from the 17th-century *Old Town*, with its typical huddle of black-and-white houses), the **Orangerie**, the covered bridges, and, of course, the **Gutenberg Monument**. Alsatian food is splendid. Try *baekenhoffen*, chicken, trout (or anything) cooked in Riesling, *flammekusch, foie gras, choucroute*, or woodcock (in season). Sample these and the pressings of the *Bas-Rhin* in the many *weinstubes* and cafes of the city and neighboring villages. A representative one is the **Tire Bouchon** in the shadow of Notre Dame. **Maison des Tanneurs** at Petite France is for bigger feasts, but also very regional in flavor—and more costly, of course. Personally, we prefer visiting Strasbourg while overnighting in the inns of the surrounding hamlets, where the prices are much lower.

TOURS

Here's the unofficial capital of the **Chateaux Country**. Renaissance France flourished at the peak of its elegance in this region. Because of its serene beauties and proximity to Paris, kings, courtiers, and courtesans relaxed here in dazzling luxury. Strongholds were built, aristocracy thrived, and culture was unfettered. To this day, linguistic scholars point out, the nation's purest French is spoken in the Loire Valley.

The tumbrels of the Reign of Terror swept away the actors of this historic drama, but little of their glorious handwork was despoiled. Still preserved are 46 great castles or mansions in which the flower of the nobility and their friends or mistresses lived, walked, banqueted, gossiped, and played. To tourists from many lands, these sites remain the most fascinating of their continental wanderings.

From June to the end of September, six chateaux are further embellished with *Son et Lumiere* programs. At least 2 dozen others are floodlit nightly or on weekends for nocturnal excursionists. However, the presentations (except at Chenonceaux) are given in French.

First off the bat, don't rush. Even to begin to savor its charms, you'll need 3-5 days; a week will pay dividends.

Second, it would be helpful to read up as much as possible in advance of your arrival. Michelin's *Chateaux de la Loire* (available in French or English) offers the greatest detail of any publication found; suggested trips from 1-5 days are outlined. *Chateaux of the Loire*, distributed by England's Automobile Association (Fanum House, New Coventry St., London W.1), strings together a 450-mile itinerary. Michelin's sectional map No. 64 is indispensable to the motorist.

Your key base should be Tours or its vicinity, because this central point is less than 25 miles from most of the principal chateaux. As an orientation exercise, you may wish to begin with the new **Historial du Touraine**, the restored chateau (in Tours) of Charles VII and Louis XI; now it's a wax museum displaying 33 scenes of Loire *histoire*.

Candidates for the 4 most interesting structures in this cluster are Chenonceaux, Amboise, Azay-le-Rideau, and Villandry. Cheverny is in a special category.

Chenonceaux, a breathtakingly graceful castle, straddles the Cher River. Beautiful formal gardens. Within the trussed-arch building are tapestries and other 17th century treasures. Although finishing touches weren't applied until 1634, Diane de Poitiers, beloved mistress of Henri II, occupied it nearly 100 years earlier. Many visitors vote this one their favorite.

Amboise, the burial place of Leonardo da Vinci, is smaller and less spectacular–but hardly less rewarding. Here you may also visit the illuminated terraces, the chapel, and the gardens, as well as the house nearby where Da Vinci lived: **Chateau du Clos' Luce**. **Azayle-Rideau**, charmingly sited over the Indre River and surrounded by groves, is now a Fine Arts Museum; from the French point of view, this one is possibly the most dramatic of all. **Villandry** is noted for its magnificent 3-tier gardens, as well as for its history; the top level has a 7500-square-yard lake, the middle level formal horticulture, and the bottom level a grandly conceived layout of vegetables!

Cheverny is one of the most perfectly conceived and best preserved edifices in the region. It is thriving as an occupied homestead under the aegis of the Marquis de Vibraye. Only a half dozen rooms open to the public, but these are exquisite; fabulous Hunting Museum dating back through centuries of royal hunts. Don't miss this imposing beauty with its tonsure of precisely maintained gardens and parkland.

Others of note include **Chambord** (largest; enormous grounds but bereft of furnishings and cold inside; Sound and Light programs at night; 40 miles north of Tours), **Langeais** (privately owned and lived in; a beautifully preserved interior; no Sound and Light; 15 miles), and **Loches** (so medieval that it's an Olympus for antiquarians and a bore to travelers with no architectural interests; 15 miles). One of the most exciting from the theatrical point of view is **Chateau du Lude** (32 miles), with

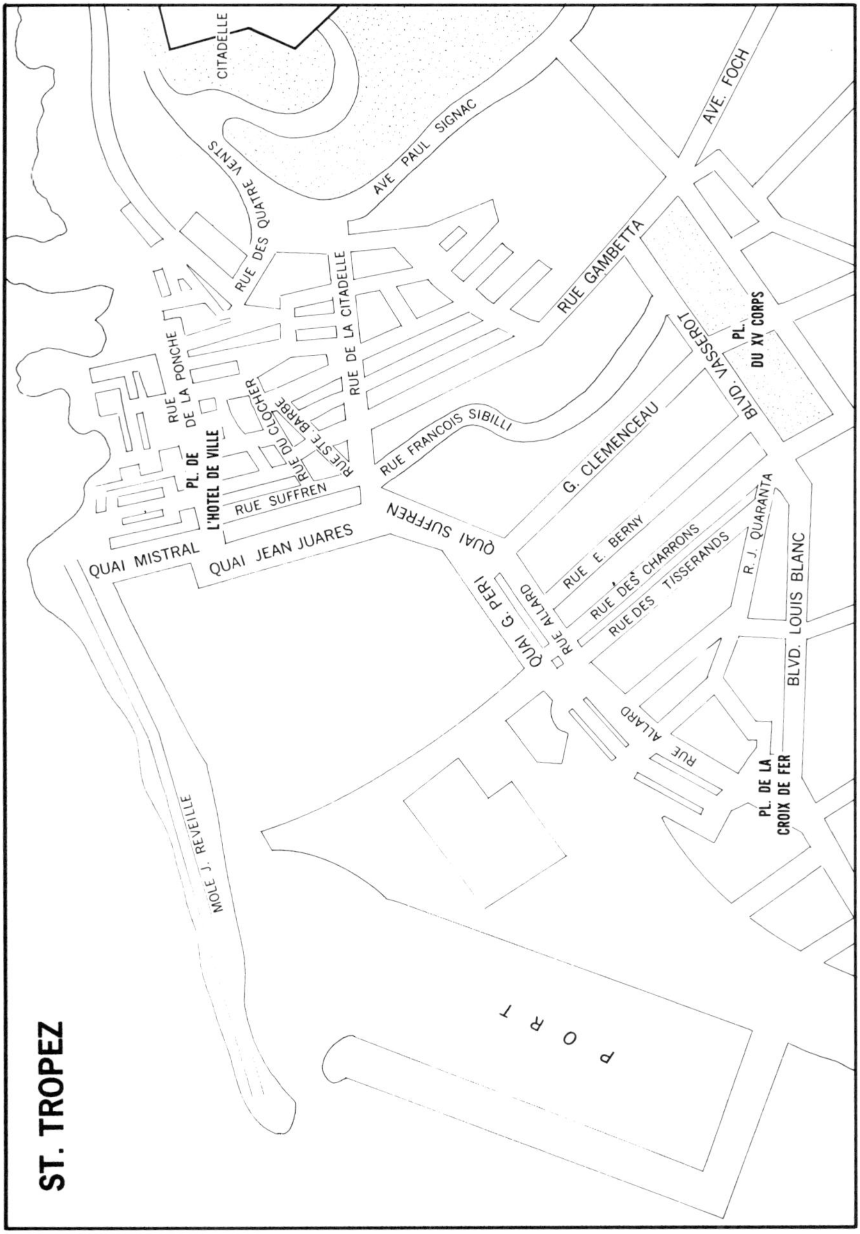
ST. TROPEZ
CITADELLE
RUE DES QUATRE VENTS
AVE PAUL SIGNAC
AVE. FOCH
RUE GAMBETTA
RUE DE LA PONCHE
RUE DE LA CITADELLE
RUE DU CLOCHER
RUE STE BARBE
PL. DE L'HOTEL DE VILLE
RUE FRANCOIS SIBILLI
RUE SUFFREN
QUAI MISTRAL
QUAI JEAN JUARES
QUAI SUFFREN
BLVD. VASSEROT
PL. DU XV CORPS
G. CLEMENCEAU
RUE E. BERNY
RUE DES CHARRONS
RUE DES TISSERANDS
R. J. QUARANTA
BLVD. LOUIS BLANC
QUAI G. PERI
RUE ALLARD
RUE ALLARD
PL. DE LA CROIX DE FER
MOLE J. REVEILLE
PORT

a twice-weekly pageant—in season—of 400 characters in costume, prancing horses, boats, dancers, and singers. This one once captured the nation's Prize for Tourism. The oration is in French, bien sur!

From Tours you can visit **Chenonceaux** (19 miles) and **Amboise** (16 miles) in one evening. Buses leave the Syndicat d'Initiative at 8:15 or 9 p.m. and return at midnight; the all-inclusive excursion is $17-or-so per person. Scads of additional bus departures to your choice of other chateaux available both daytimes and evenings at the Tours railway station; costs vary from $4.50 to $8, plus the entrance fees.

Spot- and floodlighting are employed on various occasions at chateaux in the following places: Ainay-le-Vieil; Bourges (the Mansion of Jacques-Coeur and the Cathedral of St.-Etienne here); Chateaubriant; Chateauneuf-sur-Loire; Culan; La Ferte-St.-Aubin; Fontevrault; Gien; Nantes; Sully-sur-Loire; Tours (with musical program); Valencay.

The chateaux that must be seen by daylight are Beauregard, Chaumont, Cheverny, Chinon, Cinq-Mars-la-Pile, Langeais, Lavardin, Luynes, Menars, Meung-sur-Loire, Montgeoffroy, Moncontour, Montoire, Montreuil-Bellay, Montsoreau, Ponce, Romorantin, St. Aignan-sur-Cher, Saumur, Talcy, Usse, Ile-de-France, Villandry. Courtanvaux, the recently inherited castle of the Duke of Fezensac, scion of the oldest family in France, is a 500-year-old, 112-room estate open to the general public at Besse-sur-Braye, between Tours and Le Mans.

One *must* stop for newcomers—the earlier, the better!—is the **Tours Syndicat d'Initiative**, an ultramodern, round, glass-bound facility on place de la Gare. It is linked by telex to Cannes, Nice, Paris, and 11 other centers, in case your later reservations have gone awry; it will change your money when the banks are closed (Sunday, Monday, and after 6 p.m.); it offers brochures by the yard and regional information by the bushel. From mid-March-mid-October, it is open from 9 a.m. to 9 p.m. (10 p.m. on weekends), with a lunch hour closing between 1 and 2 p.m. They can tell you of all the accommodations available in any of the campsites or villages you plan to visit. For the city of Tours itself, there's the low-cost **Auberge Jeunesse** in the Parc de Grandmont, 2 miles out; **Le Vieux Manoir** asks about $32 for twin occupancy; the **Metropole** is okay; the **Alliance** is large and appealing, but tours roll in constantly; **Central**, in the city proper, is quite nice as a base for Tours-ing. Restaurants in this city are either glorified snack bars or more expensive than they need be since so many package trippers dine in the local hotels on a travel plan. Try to get out of Tours, however, to see the truer beauty of the Chateaux Country.

WHERE TO SHOP

The prices are so high they're comical—a printed cotton T-shirt for $45, denim wrangler suit for $375, crafty necklaces and swinger ware of cheap beads, kerchiefs, belts, or whatever can be stuck together under the guise of novelty, for $15 to $38. Apart from a few ultra-chic operations tied to Paris landmarks, the average St. Tropez store sells shamefully shoddy apparel and gift items.

WHERE TO STAY

Advance reservations are mandatory everywhere during the warm months; most hotels are closed in winter.

LEAST $

Lou Cagnard • *avenue P. Roussel;* ☎ *94970424*. Converted home with 19 ample accommodations. Busy-street location; quietest units overlooking rear garden.

Shower and basin in the rooms, WCs apart. Service-and-taxincluded tariffs of $43 for a *grand lit;* $10 more for 2-bed nests.

Les Lauriers • *rue du Temple;* ☎ *94970488.* Shelter for 17; $27 each in twin beds, $1.25 or so less for pillowmates in double beds.

Les Chimeres • *Half-mile west on Route N98A;* ☎ *94970290.* Far too high in its twins ($36 range) to recommend to couples. Small garden and parking. Tidy well-priced singles with shiny tubs.

Syndicat d'Initiative • *Tourist Office, quai Jean Jaures;* ☎ *94974521.* Through this organization you can find space in the $12 to $24 range in the excellent network of private homes opened to visitors. Might be anything from simple quarters to kitchen-equipped studios to small apartments.

MORE $$

Sube et Continental • *quai Suffren;* ☎ *94970002.* A good one dockside. Bigger and supposedly posher "Hotels" are much more costly, but not much better. Mid-village site near the rue de la Citadelle; handsome harbor view. Spacious dining salon with cheery fireplace; 18 wide-angle rooms, each with 3 beds and balcony; 7 arthritic baths. Widely varying rates from $35-$58 per person.

Mediterranee • *boulevard Louis Blanc (just off place Croix-de-Fer);* ☎ *94970044.* Borders busy, noisy Route N98A. Convivial dining chamber; 14 compact bedrooms, most with baths or showers. Closed October and November, plus January-Mar. 30.

Colombier • *impasse des Conquetes;* ☎ *94970531.* A quiet dozen bedchambers. No restaurant. Rates about $46 per medium-size double with shower and breakfast. Operative from mid-March to mid-September.

CAMPING

Kon-Tiki *(plage de Pampelonne;* ☎ *94971717),* a 3.5-mile run from the center, provides the Mediterranean for its courtyard; **Tournels** (*route du Phare de Camarat;* ☎ *94977004*) and **Canoubiers** (*route des Salins*) are more isolated. The last is open from June to September. **Kon-Tiki** accepts campers from Easter to September.

Finally, an outfit called **Yotel de Cogolin** (*83 Cogolin-Plage;* ☎ *94438444*) will rent you a haystack-shaped, umbrella-topped bungalow, spacious enough for up to three for around $23 a night, depending on the month, or from $33 to $44 or so with full pension. They'll also supply tent, trailer and car space near, but not on, the beach for about $4 a night. Modern sanitary facilities and a 200-seat snack center are on the premises.

WHERE TO EAT

LEAST $

La Belle Isnarde • *40 bis rue Allard (near the port).* Typical of St.-Tropezienne mood. Vague tourist-trap aura. Surprisingly good Blue Plate offerings start at around $14. Sometimes frenetic service. Closed part-time in winter.

O Sympa • *place du Musee (near the casino).* Offers small sidewalk enclave and frenzied dining at 10 interior tables. Bustling, inexpensive, and popular.

Le Bistrot du Port • *(Across the street).* Colorful, but can be wickedly expensive; in this sense it's very traditional for St. Trop.

SNACK BARS

Le Gorille • *On the quay.* Routine during normal hours. But for that predawn breakfast or early-morning nightcap, it is the "in" spot.

Bretonne • *quai F. Mistral,* and **Grand Marnier**, *rue des Ramparts.* Produce delicious fruit crepes. Other variations available, too. Very good and very cheap.

Pizzeria Bruno • *rue Sybille.* Serves slices in two whitewashed rooms braided with garlic and dotted with seemingly uninterested waiters.

MORE $$

L'Escale • *quai Jean-Jaures;* ☎ *94970063.* Still the top spot on most recent visit. Resorty ambience; bustling with sidewalk skippers from the straits of the Seine, the Rhine, and the Thames. Above average fixedprice meal consisting of soup, a main dish, cheese, and fruit at perhaps $31. Likeable. Open mid-March to late October and the Yule fortnight.

Le Girelier • *Same quai;* ☎ *94970387.* Similar atmosphere; big portions; set menus in the $27 bracket (wine extra). Slightly down the scale. Adequate, but no rave.

Cafe des Arts • *place du XVe Corps;* ☎ *94970225.* Fairly good.

La Rascasse • *On the port; Tel: 94970447.* Active in season and typical of the local touristic lore, often shoeless.

L'Aventure • *Nearby,* ☎ *94970407.* Not much of an adventure, but a laugh most nights.

Da Lolo • *Dockside.* Unusually attractive rustic ambience. Many gays at times. Oh-so-theatrical preparation of spit-grilled lamb by the "chef." Nearly everything sampled floated in a greasy (though rather savory) sauce. Last time paid nearly $60 for two without tip.

La Fregate • *52 rue Allard;* ☎ *94970402.* Hardworking galley away from the harbor. Full meal available for about $27 (including better-than-average wine). Open all year. Recommended.

NIGHTLIFE

In season, nightlife in St. Tropez becomes formal when the customer wears shoes.

Senequier • *On the port.* The chic bar where the cognoscenti sit all evening (and all day, too) in comfortable chairs, sipping and watching the passing scene. While the site is ideal, the prices are outlandish. Order only from a menu with the written rates.

L'Esquinade • *rue du Four.* A hot, noisy cluster of 3 cellars; music provided by the latest tapes and records. Drinks about $9; often alive, depending on the presence of the yachting set.

Caves du Roy • Still a social perch for night hawks and **Le Pigeonnier** chirps gay-ly for its own feathering.

La Voom-Voom • *rue Allard.* Draws a crowd that comes for garden breezes, soft talk, and smooth dance melodies. Drinks in line with other local nightspots; good service; not unique, but likeable.

Le Stereo Club • *6 rue de Puits, near Chateau Suffren.* Geared for French punk; if you're 25, you'll feel 85.

Yeti • *rue Fr. Sibilli.* Draws an uninhibited throng of liberated young people. Nobody's a fanatic about sexual preferences.

Papagayo • *quai de l'Epi.* Offers an orchestra from June to September and phono in the fringe weeks; limp decor; no show. Drinks are in the big-fat-$9 range. Ho hum.

FOR MORE INFORMATION ON FRANCE

USA • **French Government Tourist Office**, *610 Fifth Ave., New York, NY 10020, ☎ (212) 757-1125; 645 N. Michigan Ave., Chicago, IL, ☎ (312) 337-6301; 2305 Cedar Springs Rd., Dallas, TX 75201, ☎ (214) 720-4010/11; 9454 Wilshire Blvd., Beverly Hills, Los Angeles, CA 90212, ☎ (310) 271-2358.*

CANADA • *30 St. Patrick St., Suite 700, Toronto, Ont. M5T3A3, ☎ (416) 593-4723; 1981 Ave., McGill College, Montreal H3A 2W9, ☎ (514) 288-4264.* As a shortcut in obtaining information by phone see the third item in "Special Remarks" (directly below) concerning "France On Call."

INSIDER TIP

*(1) The City of Paris has its own Information Bureau (*127 ave. Champs-Elysees*) linked by telex to similar centers in other French hubs. At your service are an exchange office, accredited representatives of touring agencies, and hotel reservations facilities.*

(2) Additional locations for aid in Paris are at the Palais de Congres, Invalides, Gare du Nord, Gare de l'Est, and Gare de Lyon.

(3) Before you leave, try the hotline "France On Call" (☎ 1-900-990-0040*). It can provide loads of travel information (at 50¢ per minute) from 9 a.m. to 5 p.m. Monday-Friday all year around. In peak seasons, all calls to local centers are referred back to this "900" service, so you can save time by phoning this one first.*

GERMANY

Hohlenzollern

Culture, of course, is Germany's potent, everlasting heritage, whether recalled in the wistful *Lorelei*, the sonorous choruses of grand opera or the flashing piano moods of Bach. Painters, writers, architects...their genius is visible everywhere. Economic commitment is heavily directed toward the East today, but the people at the grassroots have not lost their capacity to dream more often of *Rhinegold* than of *feingold*. Whether you are meandering along the Tauber beside the medieval "Romantic Road" or listening to the melody of a concertina at a North Sea port, you'll find there's a pervading air of *gemutlichkeit* among the fun-loving people of this ancient and modern land. All too often, first-time travelers neglect to include the restful vistas of its lakes, of the ice-capped Alps, or the historic coastal havens that are dark and lovely with antiquity. Instead, most newcomers take in only the pulsing and glittering metropolises; the experienced wanderer combines a diverting mixture of both. And in the newly expanded nation there is so much more to see. Eastern cities will soon be flowering again, although early predictions about recovery were overzealous. On the Elbe, for example, you can now cruise the entire length, from Hamburg to Bad Schandau—almost 400 miles of waterway, which pass such "lost" gems as Wittenberg, Magdeburg and historic Meissen.

As a modern republic, Germany went into business only in 1949, having struggled to unify itself since before the Hapsburgs. The popes hindered its nationhood. The Prussians ejected the Austrians. Bismarck consolidated things for a while. And then its darkest hours began to fall over the land as well as over the rest of Europe. Today Germany is resolutely positive again in rebuilding an old brotherhood.

You'll want to see richly forested Bavaria in the south and fall into its jovial, easygoing ways. The eastern alpine tableau soars up to 9000 breathtaking feet, providing a snow-chilled source for some of the most legendary rivers on the Continent. You might sleep in any of five dozen castles—go *schloss*-hopping by the shores of the Rhine, Moselle, Main and Weser.

In the north there are the salty reminders of the mighty days of the Hanseatic League; modernists might prefer the briny slap and dash of Olympic sloops at Kiel. Magnificent woodlands are in every sector, not just in the Black Forest. Festivals star the calendar—from Wagner to punk rock, from book fairs to toy shows, from films to furnishings; Germany is never at rest.

TIPS ON ENJOYING GERMANY

FOOD

Germany can provide possibly the best value for money of any table-top in Europe. That may sound questionable when applied to a country noted for its overheated economy generally. But tradition here calls for solid nutrition at reasonable prices available to almost everyone. You just have to know where to look and how to order. There are numerous beer halls, street stands and institutional establishments that serve hearty platters for a surprisingly small number of marks. But at the same time there are scores of attractive small, family-type establishments in every city where your bill for an outright feast should be in the vicinity of $8.50. In the atmospheric country inns, you can enjoy a 3-course meal for $5.

Avoid specialties such as Prague ham and similar foods that have been processed in a special or time-consuming way. Still, you can order a fine plate of *rippchen* (smoked pork) for almost the same cost

GERMANY
N
NORTH SEA
BALTIC SEA
Kiel
Lubeck
Bremerhaven
Hamburg
Bremen
Hanover
Berlin
Potsdam
Rhine R.
GERMANY
Dusseldorf
Cologne
Leipzig
Meissen
Aachen
Bonn
Dresden
Wiesbaden
Frankfurt am Main
Bayreuth
Wurzburg
CZECHOSLOVAKIA
Rhine R.
Heidelberg
Nurnberg
Rothenberg
Baden-Baden
FRANCE
Stuttgart
Romantic Road
Augsburg
Constance
Munich
Oberammergau
AUSTRIA
Garmisch-Partenkirchen
SWITZERLAND

as a plain chop because it is so universally popular. And, naturally, you shouldn't fall into the lobster trap! When the bill comes for your 1- or 2-lb. serving, it's liable to read $45 or more, since crustaceans are rare in these waters and usually come from far away. Most of the oyster crop is imported, too, at prices that chill the soul. If you're seafood-hungry, stick to home-caught fish only, which are plentiful and fine.

Coffee and tea are higher than in America. There are at least 7 different brews and strengths of coffee, ranging from the insipid, prune juice-colored Mokka, through the popular Kaffee Hag (caffeine-free), to the Italian-style Espresso. "Filter," sometimes known as "Karlsbader Kaffee" from the machine in which it's made, is closest to American style; Double Mokka is grainy and strong.

National custom dictates that tables be shared by 2 or more parties if the tavern is crowded. Often you'll find yourself sitting with strangers—most of the time in a courteous but remote relationship. They'll generally confine their conversation to their own group.

DRINKS

Most connoisseurs (if they weren't born in Burgundy, Bordeaux, or Champagne) agree that Germany makes the finest white wines of the world. With typical Teutonic attention to detail, every bottle of character bears its full pedigree on the label—type, year, district, grower, shipper and often even the condition of the grape at the picking ("*Spatlese*" for fully ripe, "*Beerenauslese*" for overripe, etc.) "*Riesling*" is a generic term for any wine of the Riesling grape, as opposed to the Sylvan grape. Moselle, Rhine, Ahr, Franconia, Palatinate and others are named for their specific districts or valleys, although technically they could be called Rieslings. *Steinwein* is crisp, bordering on sharpness. If your stomach can take the edge, you'll probably enjoy the flavor. Hock, derived from "*Hochheimer*," is erroneously used by many Britons as an appellation for all Rhines and similar types; the vineyards for this are actually on the north bank of the Main.

As for the popular *Liebfraumilch*, there are 2 good bottles of this for 10 bad ones, because this banner covers *all* of the output of the Rheinhessen region. Ask for Oppenheimer Schlossberg, Niersteiner Domthal, or Nackenheimer Rotenberg for delicious examples.

Not quite as costly are Deidesheimer Kieselberg Riesling Auslese, Berncasteler Doctor and Piesporter Lay. Jesuitengarten Riesling Auslese is a Palatinate variety that is available at about $3 per 3-glass carafe. You'll find dozens of delicious, substantial choices from $3.50-$5 per bottle.

Somewhere along the gastronomy trail, the French nurtured the idea that dry white wines are fashionable—possibly because the neighboring Germans produce tons of fuller, more fruity varieties.

To some degree, they even convinced the Germans, but now there is a trend toward rich white beverages with low acid content. Try these ordinary mellow pressings and judge for yourself. The prices are equally easy on the digestion.

German "champagne," called "*Sekt*," is sparkling usually wine from modest vineyards; the biggest producer, Henkell of Wiesbaden, squeezes only French grapes into its bottles. Selected labels of the *brut* types have an urbane and noble character. Mumm Dry (no relative of the French brand of the same name) is an excellent candidate for your white; Henkell-Rosee is a delightful pink.

German beer is as appetizing as ever—and, in the average stop, it's $1.70 per large mug. Bavaria's 1600 breweries produce one-fourth of the world's supply. The choice is vast. There are *Helles* (light), *Dunkles* (dark), *Weisse* (a Bavarian extra-light type that is served all over the country), Berliner Weisse (a Berlin wheatmalt specialty, which is light and lemony). The bock beer season is in May.

GETTING AROUND

TRAINS

The German Federal Railways equal or surpass almost any other system in Europe today. Trains are punctual, clean and comfortable; DB diners are efficient and inexpensive; electric locomotives on some of the Intercity routes now scoot along at the same speeds as France's better known rockets. Air-conditioned dining cars are attached to almost all of these trains today; on some routes rolling minibars come to you with snacks and beverages.

DB has a plan for cyclists in which you can rent bikes (from April 1 to Oct. 31) at very low daily rates, turn them in at any of some 400 stations and pump another two-wheeler elsewhere on the railroad's grid. It's too detailed to outline here, but pick up a DB brochure if you want to entrain and pedal.

Although fares are set up so that short hops are costlier and long hauls cheaper, tariffs are more than reasonable by U.S. standards. You can save even more by using the Eurailpass.

Besides being cheaper, second class, while usually quite crowded, is very agreeable. The mountain divisions, including the funiculars in the Bavarian Alps and the Black Forest, should not be overlooked as you plan your trip because the scenery they offer is glorious.

Buy your international railway tickets and railway agency coupons *outside* Germany to save money. The **Flexipass** covers many travel options. There are special programs for families, twosomes and individuals. Substantial reductions are available and you can also incorporate ferry connections and boat rides into your overall scheme. There are even plans to include weekend jaunts, hotel or pension

overnights, free admission to museums, zoos, or even to health spas. Ask the **German Tourist Offices** in the U.S. or your travel agent. Be specific about the **German Rail Tourist Pass** for unlimited travel of 5, 10, or 15 days; they don't have to be consecutive. (Valid also for bus along the Romantic Road or on the Rhine for day trips.)

The **Junior Pass** is a must if you plan to travel a lot. It is valid for a year and permits unlimited travel for half the normal price.

Also *wunderbar* is the **Wunder Card**: 9 days of unlimited coach-class travel for around $150, 16 days for close to $200 (first class slightly more). It features free bike rentals, discounts on river steamer voyages and reduced fares on round trips to Berlin.

Senior passengers (above 60) have also been given a splendid break. The **Senior Pass** ("*Senioren*") entitles the holder to 50% reductions for a year. Pass-A costs 75 DM and is valid on Mon. through Sat., except for Fri.; Pass-B, good throughout the week, is 110 DM; an RES-Stamp costs 20 DM more, but it entitles holders of both passes to reductions of 30% to 50% in 18 European countries. Bring your passport as proof of your seniority.

If you are an old-fashioned railroader, there are quite a few (100 at last count) narrow-gauge steam engines and cars that operate over antique (but safe) runs. One 1899 chuffer, for example, huffs and puffs over a 5-mile route in 35 minutes. Frankfurt has a circuit that operates through the old factories sector of town. For a timetable, send 4 DM to Verlag Uhle & Kleimann, Postfach 1543, D-4990, Lubbecke 1, Germany. Perhaps your travel agent also can shine his lantern on the subject.

AUTHOR'S OBSERVATION

There's a small surcharge on some expresses (such as on the Intercity loops). For short journeys, it is often better to hop a slower train; the time differential is small, but you are more likely to find a seat. A score of depots feature free self-service hand carts; pile on your effects and roll them to the taxi or tram platforms.

AIRLINES

Ask **Lufthansa** about the **YES ticket**. It stands for "Young Europe Special" and if it operates again this year it applies to under-25s and full-time students under 27. For about $75 per flight, the plan covers 85 cities in 31 countries. Big savings.

BUSES

Most long-haul buses, particularly in the sightseeing districts, are modern. Many offer adjustable chairs, public-address systems, radio loudspeakers and wall-to-wall windows. The **German Federal Railways** and the **German Touring Company** run good ones. The last is linked to the **Europabus** system touching more than 200 cities over a

62,000-mile network. Their "*Castle Route*" is one of the most engaging. Your travel agent can book you a window seat. Dozens of readers have sent rave reports about the motorcoach tours of the Bavarian Alps, the Allgau Alps, the Black Forest roads and other scenic high spots. Some of them even go down to Salzburg and the Tyrol in Austria. These tours are astonishingly cheap; the buses are excellent, service is frequent and the routes are glorious.

DRIVING

The 2 most important German automobile clubs, **ADAC** and **AvD**, offer tour information in most cities. In the ports of Hamburg and Bremerhaven and at a number of key crossings on the frontiers, they and the **German Tourist Association** have set up special bureaus to help foreign visitors plan their trips. No charge. In the Alps, the ADAC rents snow chains; your small deposit is refunded when you return them.

German roads are either wonderful or frustrating—no middle ground. The *autobahn* network is fabulous for speed (100 mph is commonplace) and comfort, but there are very few of these in the former eastern sector. All labor is banned on these main lines during the summer—so as not to impede tourist traffic. Privatization is being debated, so if the legislation passes, tolls will be exacted from motorists. Turnpikes stretch from Belgium to the Czech border and from the Baltic to Switzerland. A Ruhr bypass to Holland detours Germany's most congested area. A few spans of *autobahnen* have lowered speed limits in an experimental effort to reduce air pollution and possibly help save forests; these zones are signposted clearly.

Some main or secondary thoroughfares are sometimes a driver's nightmare. Although paved and in excellent repair, the poor ones are narrow, winding, slippery when wet and loaded with monstrous trailer-trucks. Take an autobahn whenever you can, even if it sends you 50 or 100 extra miles—or enjoy by-lanes in noncommercial districts where the truckers seldom go.

If you bring in your own car, *only you* may drive it. If your spouse or anyone else is caught behind the wheel, you might be socked for the total customs value of the vehicle, plus taxes. To be on the safe side, issue a written authorization to anyone who drives your vehicle.

Stiff penalties for law violators are in effect. Speeding fines are very high; drunken driving may easily draw imprisonment plus a fine of up to $2500. Traffic control is by helicopter on almost all *autobahnen*, particularly the busy ones.

CAR HIRE

Our first vote goes to **Auto-Sixt** (*Seitzstrasse 9-11*; ☎ *223333*), the Munich-headquartered firm that has given us splendid service. See the "Munich" section for more details on this fine independent. **Avis** has its West German base in Frankfurt; a telephone switchboard connects all 3 branches in the city, including the central office (*Eschersheimer Landstrasse 55*; (☎ *15370*).

Warning: Rental rates are high. This is one surefire way to pound your budget into a fine-powdered memory. Be *certain* to total all extra charges (insurance, gasoline, pickup or delivery fees, etc.) These expenses add up quickly—even with the reduced figures for periods of 14 days or more.

Motor homes can be rented on a weekly basis for around $400 shared among 4 people. Write to **interRent**, *Tangstedter Landstr. 81, D-2000 Hamburg 62*; (☎ *040-52018-1*).

SPORTS

CYCLING

An 8-day Bavarian tour starts at around $300. Contact **Kurhotel Furst Bismarck**, *Euerdorfer Str. 4-6, Postfach 1260, D-8730, Bad Kissingen*; ☎ *(0971) 12 77.* Or cycle the sites of the lower Rhine: 1-week with half- board accommodation about $120. Contact **Reiseburo Geldener Reiset- reff**, *Issumer Strasse 74, D-4170 Geldern*; ☎ *(0 28 31) 77 57.* As mentioned, between Apr. and Oct. the Federal German Railways offer bike hire at approximately 400 of their stations priced at about $5 a day; if you travel by train or railway bus and use this service, you'll be entitled to half fare.

RIDING

Schleswig-Holstein and the **Luneburger Heath** specialize in riding vacations. Group lessons usually run about $15, individual ones about $20. A free catalog of riding schools entitled *Reiten in der Freizeit* (Riding in Your Free Time) is available from **Deutsche Reitschule**, *D-4410 Warendorf.* Additional information is available at various tourist offices.

A weekend or week of riding, plus instruction, in the Pfalz costs $85 and $240, respectively, including bed and breakfast. Contact **Reiterbetrieb Rexhof**, *D-6701 Altrip;* ☎ *(0 62 36) 20 89/38 19.*

For approximately $1000 you can ride a horse and study German, too. For information on this 29-day riding and language program: **Goethe Institut**, *Postfach 201009, D-8000 Munchen 2*; ☎ *(089) 59 99-1.*

HIKING

Harz Mountain routes (1 and 2 weeks) are offered in Sept. and Oct.; minimum booking 4 days; at other times write **Harzer Verkehrsverband**, *Postfach 1669, D-3380 Goslar 1*; ☎ *(05321) 20031.*

For 3 different hassle-free, week-long hikes in the Black Forest (luggage is transported for you from hotel to hotel), contact the following offices: **Kurverwaltung**, *D-7290 Freudenstadt*; **Kurverwaltung**, *D-7740 Triberg*; and **Kurverwaltung**, *D-7820 Titisee-Neustadt.* Similar all-inclusive 3-6-day journeys go for $65-130 through

Verkehrs-und Informationsamt, *Postfach 1320, D-6750 Kaiserslautern*; ☎ *(0631) 852316.*

Bavaria also offers two interesting excursions: 5 days on the King Ludwig-of-Bavaria Way for $140, including bed and breakfast. Contact **Arbeitsgemeinschaft**, **Fernwanderwege im Voralpenland**, *von Kuhlmannstr. 15, D-8910 Landsberg/Lech;* ☎ *(08191) 47177* and a 32-mile "Walking Tour for Gourmets" in northern Bavaria for about $380, including 5 nights with full-board and lodging; option of doing the same route on horseback or with cross-country skis in winter. Write **Pflaum's Posthotel**, *8570 Pegnitz.*

MOUNTAINEERING

For about $200 you can climb through a 6-day basic training course from June to Sept.: **Bergfuhrerburo**, *Haupstrasse 6, D-8980 Oberstdorf;* ☎ *(0 83 22) 27 37.* Information on other centers available from **Verband Deutscher Ski-und Bergfuhrer**, *Lindenstrasse 16, 8980 Oberstdorf.*

WATERSPORTS

1-, 2- and 3-week sailing courses available from Apr.-Sept. for $130-400, including bed-and-breakfast plus accommodation. For further details contact **HTS-Hessen Touristik Service**, *Abraham Lincoln Strasse 38-42, D-6200 Wiesbaden*; ☎ *(0 61 21) 77 42 34.*

Six windsurfing days on Lake Constance run from $150 to $210, depending on the type of accommodation. This includes lessons, equipment, wet suit and breakfast. Contact **Verkehrsverein Lindau**, *Postfach 1325, D-8990 Lindau*; ☎ *0 83 92) 50 22.*

FRESHWATER FISHING

A permit is required for freshwater fishing, none for North Sea and Baltic Coast casting. Both state and local permits are mandatory: $5 daily, $17 weekly and about $22 monthly. Local tourist offices will provide details. For about $140 you can reel in a week of fishing in the Black Forest, Apr.-Sept., including double room and half board: **Herrenalber Reiseburo**, *Im Stadthaus, D-7506 Bad Herrenalb*; ☎ *(0 70 83) 4553.*

HANG-GLIDING

A 6-day course costs about $230 with accommodation options beginning at $95: **Westdeutsche Drachenflugschule, Elmar Muller**, *Am Rad 20, D-5788 Winterberg/Hochsauerlan*; ☎ *(0 29 81) 29 07.*

You can combine gliding and language instruction through the Goethe Institute. For the address, see the listing under "Riding."

TENNIS

A week of group instruction in the Pfalz will set you back about $300, including bed and breakfast: **Kurverwaltung Bad Bergzabern Kurtalstrasse 25**, *D-6748 Bad Bergzaber*; ☎ *(0 63 43) 88 11.*

SIGHTSEEING

CRUISING

"Cruises in the Heart of Europe" is the catchall for 1- to 5-or-more- day Rhine trips from Holland to Switzerland or vice versa. Prices are high but there's lots of variety. Contact German Rhine Line, Frankenwerft 15, D-5000 Koln.

For a week's cruise on the Weser with lodging in picturesque cities along the way, contact **Oberweser Dampfschiffahrt**, *D-3250 Hameln.*

WINE

During May, June, Sept. and Oct., the Rhineland-Palatinate Tourist Office arranges hiking (perhaps staggering) tours for oenophiles. The Moselle region offers 3-day wine seminars with full board from close to $130. Contact **Mittelmosel-Verkehrsamt**, *Kreisstandehaus, D-5550 Bernkastel-Kues;* ☎ *(0 65 31) 30 75.*

In Sept. and Oct., the Pfalz offers a week-long seminar, including full board, for about $250. Contact **Zentrale fur Tourismus**, *D-6740 Landau;* ☎ *(0 63 41) 1 42 94.*

WOODCARVING

A 7-day whittle in the Black Forest runs about $155 including half board (sic). Reiseburo address listed under "Water Sports."

Or carve yourself a holiday in the Westerwald for around $180: **Fremdenverkehrsverein Westerwald**, *Kirchstrasse 48 A, D-5430 Montabaur;* ☎ *(0 26 02) 24 24 or 30 01.*

POTTERY

For a 3-day potter plus bed and breakfast at about $85, write **Kurgeschaftsstelle Clausthal-Zellerfeld**, *Bahnhofstrasse 5a, D-3392 Clausthal-Zellerfeld;* ☎ *(0 53 23) 70 24.* A week's instruction in the Westerwald comes to about $135. For contact info, see listing directly above.

HERBAL COOKERY

There's a 2-day course available in the Eifel Mountains in June and July. About $90 covers room, full board and chef: **Verkehrsamt, Kyllweg 1**, *D-5530 Gerolstein;* ☎ *(0 65 91) 1 32 17.*

HOME EXCHANGE

Write **Holiday Service**, *Fischbach 108, 8640 Kronach;* ☎ *(09261) 2 03 63.*

TRAILER CAMPING

Deutscher Camping Club, *Mandlstrasse 28, 8000 Munchen 40;* ☎ *(089) 33 40 21.*

HEALTH HOLIDAYS

Contact **Deutscher Baderverband**, *Schumannstr. 111, 5300 Bonn 1;* ☎ *(0228) 21 10 88.*

ARCHAEOLOGY

Write to **Deutsches Archaologisches Institut**, *Postfach, 1000 Berlin 33;* ☎ *(030) 83 20 41.*

ARCHITECTURE

Contact **Bund Deutscher Architekten**, *Ippendorfer Allee 14b, 5300 Bonn 1*; ☎ *(0228) 63 13 81.*

WHERE TO GO

AACHEN

Also called **Aix-la-Chapelle**, Aachen has many traces of the Roman occupation and of Charlemagne's most glorious years; he finally expired here. The historic artifacts pertaining to the emperor and the following generations of religious and political power are concentrated within a five-minute walk in any direction of the dominating Cathedral in midcity, itself worth a full morning for sightseeing. The nation's kings chose it as their coronation capital from A.D. 814 to the 16th century. For eons, its waters have drawn visitors who suffer from rheumatism. Though there are several boarding houses, hotel accommodation is somewhat limited (and expensive); hence, I suggest seeing Aachen as a full day's excursion from some other overnight headquarter. If you must overnight, try either the **Frankenberg** or the **Danica**, the latter with breakfast only. The **Marx** also is a pleasant budget choice; or ☎ *(0241) 1802950* and the local tourist information office can suggest many more in all price levels.

AUGSBURG

Augsburg too, has a Roman bloodline. It got going back in the 15th century when a merchant family named Fugger began to wheel and deal furiously throughout Europe. Today 2 of the most popular sightseeing attractions are the **Fugger House** and the **Fuggerei** (said to be the oldest social settlement in the world). The Fuggers and the Welsers financed European kings and emperors in their exploits. Maximilianstrasse is magnificently lined with fine old homes. Make a point of seeing **Schaezler Palace** and its **Rococo Hall** and the **Golden Hall** of the **City Hall.** Though any self- respecting Salzburger would be loath to admit it, **Mozart Museum** is so important that no culture lover should pass through Augsburg without visiting it or the famous **Rotes Tor** ("Red Door"), which has long associations with grand opera. The city also has a **Brecht Museum** honoring the local family. For a wide variety of accommodations in every price range check with the **Information Office**, *Bahnhofstr. 7*; ☎ *(0821) 50207-0.*

BADEN-BADEN

The Black Forest fringes this quiet sylvan retreat; golf courses and race tracks skirt its flanks; an Old World casino glistens at night. Among its most powerful magnets are the **Lichtentaler Allee**, **Roman Irish baths** and **ruins, Caracalla Therme** and thermal ablutions. The giant **Convention Center** on Augustaplatz is another big hit—this time with groupies. The socalled **Grand Week** of big-time horse racing (late Aug. to early Sept.) is internationally known; the **Spring Meeting** each Maytime is also festive. The pace is sedate; the grace is immense; the ribbon is decidedly blue. Visit it on a day excursion because living costs are rather lofty. The **Römerhof** is a reasonable overnight stop, but it will provide only bed and breakfast.

BAYREUTH

The romantic poet Jean Paul died in this baroque capital of Upper Franconia. Franz Liszt expired in Villa Wahnfried. Its most famous citizen, Richard Wagner, is buried here. So are dozens upon dozens of less-celebrated, creative personalities. But

Wagner, at least, lives on—during July and Aug., anyway—when its magic **Music Festival** draws thousands of devotees from all over the globe. You can visit the Opera mornings and afternoons (but not Monday) and have a lunch in the romantic gardens. A tour of this charming town should be augmented by visits to a couple of nearby *Schlosser*—the rococo **Eremitage** and **Fantaisie**. A **Youth Hostel** accommodates 150 in 1-, 2-, 4-, or 6-person units; there is a dining salon, plus a discotheque, club room, TV and bowling.

BERLIN

What a place to be at this moment! The focus, of course, is on the burgeoning sociological readjustments which you can witness first-hand. With the Wall parted, you can also see the physical changes. The capital of Germany—Bonn's ministries are rapidly moving over to Berlin—boasts perhaps the most active cultural life of all. The musical and graphics fields have always been leading forces; now the cinematic renaissance is augmenting its theatrical proclivities. Not as charming or graceful as Paris or Rome—but hard-edged and daring in its lines. Steel, glass and brilliantly patterned concrete are everywhere in (former) West Berlin. East of the back-broken Wall, there has been some shoring up of the cityscape. Architecturally the prewar buildings are in reasonable exterior preserve and are really more graceful than the tawdry, neon-draped structures that grew up on the western flank. For starters, go to the "**Museum Island**" in the daytime and to the low-cost and superb State Opera in the evenings. Stand in awe within the resurrected walls of the **Dom** (Cathedral), one of Europe's finest architectural triumphs. Stroll along the broodingly attractive *Unter den Linden* (the showcase boulevard of Old Berlin) and you will get a feeling of the rebirth of a great metropolis.

DIRECTORY

U.S. Consulate • *Clayallee 170* for written requests; ☎ *8324087.*

American Express • *Kurfurstendamm 11*; ☎ *8827575.*

Laundromat • Wash-Center, *Uhlandstr. 52.*

Barber and Hairdresser • Kramer, *Kurfurstendamm 171*; ☎ *8815289*, for both sexes; Arno Coiffeur, *Kurturstendamm 53*; ☎ *8811723*, for ladies.

Suit Rental • Runge, *Bismarkstr. 99*; ☎ *3121187.*

English-Speaking Doctor • Dr. Engert, *Hotel Intercontinental, Budapester Str. 2-18*; ☎ *26020*; request guidance from the hotel concierge.

Police • Polizeiprasidium Berlin, *Tempelhofer Damm 1*; ☎ *6991.*

Favorite Pawnshop • Leihhaus Inh. Neisch, *Momm-senstr. 28*; ☎ *3244147.*

HOW TO GET AROUND

BUSES

Two rapid transit routes crisscross all sectors: the **U-Bahn** (underground) and the **S-Bahn** (surface). Remember the first letters "U" and "S," as reminders. Fares are amazingly low; the *Touristen Karte* will give you the most for your money. It's valid for 24 hours of travel on virtually all buses, S-bahn runs and subway lines within the city. Other ticket structures are outlined on the back of a folder called the *Schnellbahnnetz*, which you might prefer to study before investing. You may purchase these tickets at **Berlin Public Transport** ("BVG," *U-Bahn Kleistpark 8*), at the Zoo Station on the Hardenbergplatz, or at the Tourist Information Office at Tegel Airport. The sights? Easy by this underground complex or by bus. Here are the biggest attractions

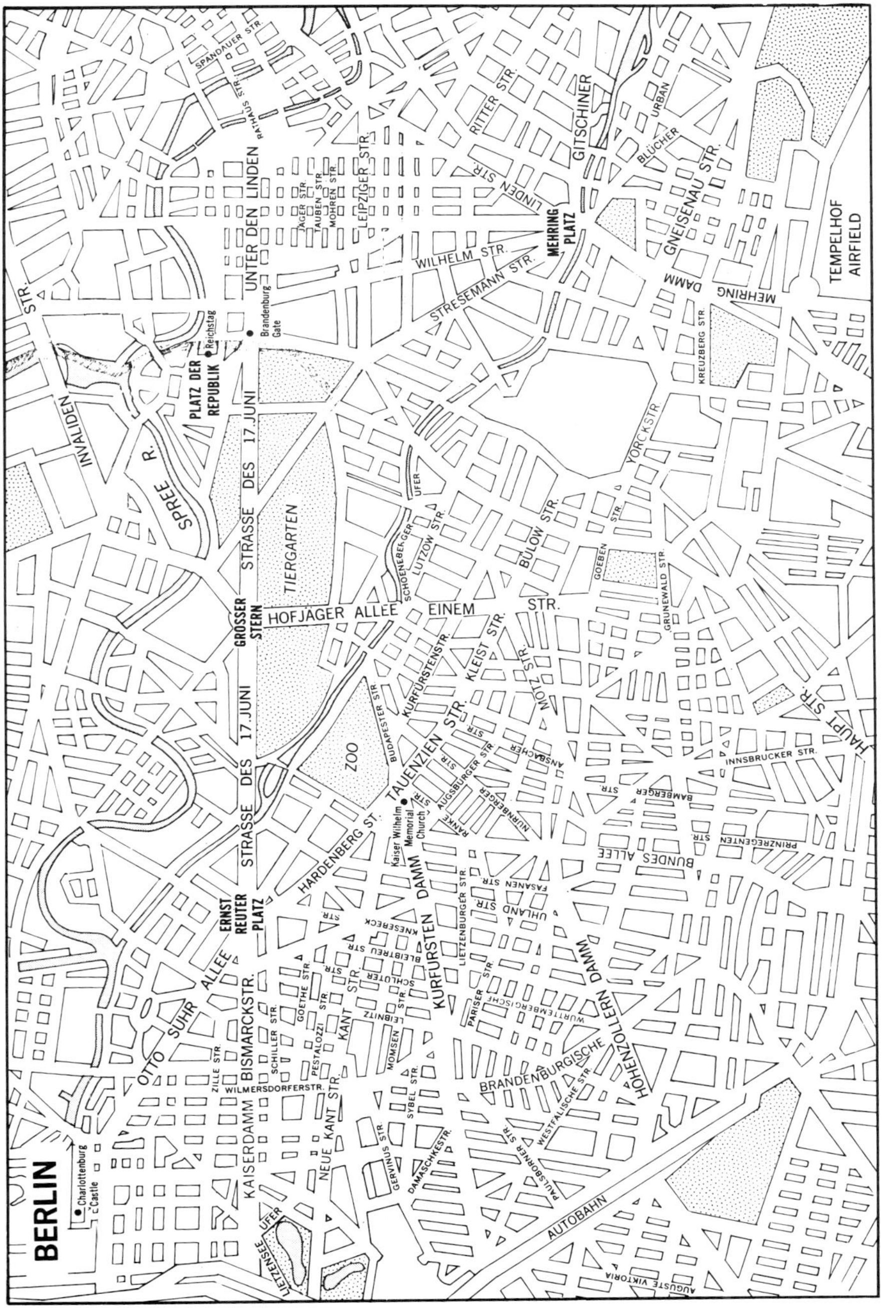
BERLIN
Charlottenburg Castle
SPANDAUER STR.
RATHAUS STR.
UNTER DEN LINDEN
JÄGER STR.
TAUBEN STR.
MOHREN STR.
LEIPZIGER STR.
RITTER STR.
GITSCHINER
URBAN
BLÜCHER
LINDEN STR.
GNEISENAU STR.
TEMPELHOF AIRFIELD
MEHRING PLATZ
WILHELM STR.
STRESEMANN STR.
MEHRING DAMM
INVALIDEN STR.
Reichstag
Brandenburg Gate
PLATZ DER REPUBLIK
KREUZBERG STR.
YORCKSTR.
SPREE R.
STRASSE DES 17. JUNI
TIERGARTEN
UFER
SCHOENEBERGER
LUTZOW STR.
BULOW STR.
GOEBEN STR.
GRUNEWALD STR.
GROSSER STERN
HOFJÄGER ALLEE
EINEM STR.
KURFÜRSTENSTR.
KLEIST STR.
MOTZ STR.
BUDAPESTER STR.
ZOO
TAUENZIEN STR.
HAUPT STR.
INNSBRUCKER STR.
ANSBACHER STR.
AUGSBURGER STR.
BAMBERGER STR.
PRINZREGENTEN STR.
BUNDES ALLEE
Kaiser Wilhelm Memorial Church
HARDENBERG ST.
RANKE STR.
NURNBERGER STR.
FASANEN STR.
UHLAND STR.
ERNST REUTER PLATZ
KNESEBECK
LIETZENBURGER STR.
BLEIBTREU STR.
KURFÜRSTEN DAMM
OTTO SUHR ALLEE
BISMARCKSTR.
SCHLÜTER STR.
GOETHE STR.
PESTALOZZI STR.
SCHILLER STR.
KANT STR.
LEIBNITZ
MOMSEN
PARISER STR.
WÜRTTEMBERGISCHE STR.
HOHENZOLLERN DAMM
BRANDENBURGISCHE
ZILLE STR.
WILMERSDORFERSTR.
NEUE KANT STR.
SYBEL STR.
WESTFÄLISCHE STR.
KAISERDAMM
GERVINUS STR.
DAMASCHKESTR.
PAULSBORNER STR.
AUTOBAHN
LIETZENSEE UFER
AUGUSTE VIKTORIA

and their nearest stations: The National Gallery and Berliner Philharmonic concert hall—accessible by Bus #129; International Congress Center via bus #149; Brandenburg Gate by bus #100 from Zoo Station; Academy of Arts and Hansa Quarter—from the Hansa station; Charlottenburg Castle—from Sophie-Charlotte-Platz, or on Bus #145; Olympic Stadium and Ernst-Reuter- Platz—each with station of its own; Kaiser-Wilhelm Memorial Church and Berlin Zoo—from Zoo Station; Dahlem Museum—from Dahlem-Dorf station, Freedom Bell (in the Schoneberg Town Hall)—from Rathaus in Schoneberg.

TRAINS

German Federal Railways offer flat-rate round trips to Berlin, which include second-class travel on express trains, 2 nights in a hotel or pension with breakfast and a sightseeing tour. Buses are also possible and they're modern. If you have a Eurailpass or similar scheme all of Germany is to be included, but you'd better check first.

CAR HIRE

Here it's really silly to rent one. All of the sightseeing points are accessible by subway, bus, or motorcoach in less than 45 minutes. *Hertz* has licensed a local agency to bear its name (*Budapester Str. 39*; ☎ *2611053*); its rates are identical to those in cities of the Federal Republic.

RENT-A-BIKE

There are seven major stations and since Berlin is flat, bicycle sightseeing is a fine way to travel cheaply all around. Here are some names and addresses: **Am S. Bahnhof Grunewald** at *Schmetterlingsplatz* (☎ *811-5829*); *Tegel* at *Campestrasse 11* (☎ *434-6666*); **Wohlfahrt** at *Kopernikusstrasse 19* (☎ *588-5612*); **Rent-A-Bike** at *Greifswalden Str. 9* (☎ *439- 0373*); **Raderwerk** at *Kortestr.* 14 (☎ *691-8590*). Most require a deposit of $50-$100 D.M.

WHERE TO STAY

Tremendous building renovation programs currently are underway. Good accommodation is becoming even better. In winter some of Berlin's hotels offer reductions from high-season rates.

LEAST $

Havelhaus • *Imchen Allee 33-35;* ☎ *3655800.* In Kladow, 20 minutes out. Bills itself as full-pension, but accepts bed and breakfast clients. Bungalows for longer visits.

Uhlandstr. 3 • (☎ *3135498*) and at **Winklerstr. 11** (☎ *8922422*); Both are apartment stays, near the Kurfurstendamm. Very good and quite useful for saving deutsche marks.

PENSIONS

For basic comfort at low prices, the following are recommended:

Bialas • *Carmerstr. 16*; ☎ *3125025.*

DeLuxe • *Lietzenburgerstr. 76*; ☎ *882- 1828.*

Uhlietz • *Lietzenburgerstr. 77*; ☎ *883-6177.*

Elton • *Pariserstr. 9*; ☎ *8836155.*

Centrum • *Kanstr. 31*; ☎ *316153.*

Nurnberger Eck • *Nurnbergerstr. 24-A*; ☎ *245371.*

Grunau • S-bahn Grunau then tram #86 for 2 stops toward Kopenick to *Dahmestr. 6*; ☎ *6814422.*

Hansablick • *Flotowstr. 6, Tiergarten;* ☎ *3914048.*

Pariser Eck • *Pariserstr. 19;* ☎ *8812145*).

Postillion • *Gasteinerstr. 8;* ☎ *875232.* All run about $22 for singles and up to $38 for twins; bath about $2.

Stadt Tilsit • *Stuttgarter Platz 9;* ☎ *323- 1027.*

YOUTH HOSTELS

Deutsches Jugendherbergswerk Landesverband Berlin • *Tempelhofer Ufer 32;* ☎ *262-3024.* Rules now allow smoking (though perhaps only in a smoking room); curfews at midnight. Request your reservation by letter in advance or in person on the day of check-in . They'll check your credentials, confirm your reservation and point you in the right direction. About $10 per person per night will get you a bunk and breakfast. The office is open 10 a.m. to 3 p.m. Mon., Wed. and Fri.; Tues. and Thurs. hours, 2-5:30 p.m. Closed on weekends—in which case try the

Youth Guest House • *3 Kluckstr;* ☎ *261-1097.* Sleeps 450 pink cheeked youths; Bus #29 from midcity. Others are at *Hermsdorfer Damm 48-50* (☎ *4041610*), Bus #15 or U-Bhf Tegel; and *Kronprinzessinnenweg 27* (☎ *8032034*), S-Bahn Nikolassee.

MORE $$

Bogota • *Schluterstr. 45;* ☎ *8815001.* A long-time favorite, in Colombian motif. A 3-minute stroll from the Europa-Center. Many showers but few tubs. Singles listed at $36 and doubles at $44 or so.

Cortina • *Kantstr. 140;* ☎ *3139059.* Commodious bedrooms—with breakfast for 2 from $36 or $43; singles from $31. Administered by amiable couple. Limited capacity, so book early.

Atlanta • *Kurfurstendamm 66;* ☎ *8834071.* Awash with many tours funneled into 23 tiny chambers, 6 with private shower. Per-person rate approaching $40.

Charlottenburger Hof • *Stuttgarter Platz 14;* ☎ *3244819.* Accommodates 50; no private plumbing. Cozy atmosphere. Well-worn but clean.

Pension Molthan • *Lietzenburger Str. 76 (off the Kurfurstendamm at Uhlandstrasse);* ☎ *8821828.* Tops for family-plan wayfarers. 8 convertible triples at about $40 (extra bed, $4), with enough elbowroom for an army of toddlers; standard doubles $42; singles $28 or so. Clean and fairly priced. Reserve well in advance.

Leibniz-Eck • *Kurfurstendamm 62;* ☎ *8835055.* On last visit swarmed with Americans. A mere 22 beds, 13 showers. Most units plain.

Pension Iris • *Uhlandstr. 33;* ☎ *881577012.* Chambers in 12 motifs. The Contemporary Room, a triple, is most attractive. From $25 to $28, including breakfast.

City • *Kurfurstendamm 173-174;* ☎ *8812001.* Admirably maintained 40-room house. Doubles about $53; singles $31; breakfast included. Above average.

Fasanenhaus • *Fasanenstr. 73;* ☎ *8816713.* Fifteen rooms, a couple with private shower; ample breakfasts to start your day right. Good investment.

Funk • *Fasanenstr. 69;* ☎ *8827193.* Alas, it still appears to be in one. Fine location; student discounts.

Regina • *Kurfurstendamm 37;* ☎ *8815031.* Excellent site; 46 spacious bedrooms, nearly half with private bath or shower. Around $57 for doubles; perhaps $29 for singles. Reservations should be made in writing.

Funkturm • *Wundstr. 72 (in Charlottenburg);* ☎ *3221081.* Tranquil setting near the 455-foot radio tower; 40 capacity, including several suites; 4 private tubs. Okay for a short stay.

EVEN MORE $$$

Sylter Hof • *Kurfurstenstr. 114-116;* ☎ *21200.* 130 units in a stylish setting. Expensive decor with a Frenchy flair. Singles average $47; doubles $74.

Meineke • *Meinekestrasse 10;* ☎ *88281165.* Intimately sophisticated chambers. A double approaches $73, but you get top value.

Penta • *Nurnbergerstrasse 65;* ☎ *240011.* A 425-room hotel administered by airlines. Ultracentral. Superior grade accommodation, decor and service.

Seehof • *(Charlottenburg) Lietzensee Ufer 11;* ☎ *320020.* A haul from the center. Restaurant, terrace, bar and swimming pool facing the lovely Lietzensee. Rustically appealing.

Hamburg • *Landgrafenstr. 4;* ☎ *269161.* Another bright entry. Bath or shower for each of its 240 rooms (150 singles). Efficient service. Lower floors the cheapest.

Alsterhof • *Augsburger Str. 5 (near KaDeWe department store);* ☎ *219960.* 140 rooms, all with bath or shower, tiny though they be. Good.

Berlin • *Kurfurstenstr. 62;* ☎ *269291.* 430 beds; all rooms with bath or shower. Modest doubles at about $82. Reputation exceeds its merits.

Plaza • *Knesebeckstr. 63;* ☎ *884130.* Private plumbing in all 140 bedchambers. Lots of group traffic, so it's better in off season.

Studio • *Kaiserdamm 80-81;* ☎ *302081.* Ten minutes out by car, adjoining the TV station near the Exposition Grounds. Breakfast room and lounge and 80 studio-type units with bath or shower. Rear section quiet.

Am Tauentzien • *Tauentzienstr. 8 (practically in the shadow of Europa Center);* ☎ *2623061.* About 3 dozen rooms with bath and shower, most with terrace. #205 an exceptionally large twin. Modern, clean. Splendid value.

Panorama • *Lewishamstr. 1;* ☎ *3233051.* The same size, but less flair. Shower, W.C. and telephone with each room. Adequate comfort. Friendly bar.

Excelsior • *Hardenbergstrasse 14;* ☎ *3199110.* Minutes by foot from the Bahnhof and just a couple of blocks off the Ku-damm. Restaurant excellent; 325 fine units often filled by tours.

Savigny • *Brandenburgische Str. 21;* ☎ *881300.* Large and hospitable; double rate $38–49. Avoid front units if you are a light sleeper.

APARTMENT LIVING

Stossensee • *Glockenturmstr 30;* ☎ *305101140.* Functional but uninspired abodes by lake of the same name. Sports facilities and supermarket nearby. All units decorated in "Middle Mundane". Minimum stay 2 weeks; 40% discount for a month or more. Bus #94 to the center.

CAMPING

Haselhorst is now the top choice. It can be reached by subway (*Haselhorst Station; Pulvermuhlenweg;* ☎ *3345955*). It's open all year. Another is

Kohlhasenbruck • (*Neue Kreis Str.; ☎ 8051737*) with 30 thousand square yards of sand along the little Griebnitz See, an offshoot of the Havel. The East German border, marked by black-and-white buoys, cuts the lake in half. April-Sept. only.

Kladow • (*Krampnitzer Weg 111-117; ☎ 3652797*) is bigger. Motorists should follow Heerstrasse from the center, turning left on Potsdamer Chaussee. Frontage on the Gross Glienicker See; similar buoys are in midlake; similar costs and facilities. Open all year.

SUGGESTIONS FOR STUDENTS

Dahlem (Free University) and Charlottenburg (Technical University) share the allegiance of Berlin's 100,000 collegians. Although several dormitories have been erected (see below), these areas are dead after school hours.

The Berlin Tourist Office will make hotel reservations for students. If you should write—do it 6 weeks in advance—specify the exact dates of your intended stay and how much you are willing to spend. For same-day booking, be there between 10 a.m. and 6 pm. (In high season it's risky to arrive at the last minute with no shelter fixed.) Its location: *Europa-Center, 1000 Berlin 30*; ☎ *21234.*

The Internationaler Studentischer Austauschdienst • (*ARTU, Hardenberstr. 9*; ☎ *3100040*) offers the A-to-Z of Berlin's student services. Believe it or not, the cable address is "STUDSERVICE BERLIN."

Amerika Haus (*Hardenbergstr. 22*; ☎ *8197661*), just up the street, is another beehive of helpful facilities and gossip. An information service, a workshop, music and film departments, a library and a lounge are at your disposal. In the absence of a Berlin Student Union, this United States Information Service complex is also a congenial hub for striking up acquaintances.

WHERE TO EAT

LEAST $

Sperlingsgasse • *Lietzenburger Str. (across from the Arosa Hotel).* The name means "Sparrow Alley." The idea is to recreate a portion of Old Berlin along a gaslit, cobblestone lane lined with boutiques and dining or snacking parlors. The lineup includes the **Spatzennest Schnapsdrossel**, the **Bierbrunnen Mikri-Gonia**, a popular sausage and burger stand (extra-low prices), the **Raabe Diele** (a beer hall that resembles a bakery; pea soup and goulash for about $3), the **Spitze** (artists' hangout), the **Pizzeria**, the **Habel Weinstube** (winehouse), plus the **Kolibri**, the **Spatzen Cafe** and the **Zwitscher Stubchen**. Prices don't hurt a bit in any of them.

Joe's am Kudamm • *Kurfurstendamm 225 (200 yards from Kaiser-Wilhelm Memorial Church).* A baronial beer hall. Heavy wooden beams and columns. Small bar, routine sidewalk cafe. Slow but cordial service. Open noon to midnight all week. Anywhere from $6 to $10 will buy a substantial meal.

Schultheiss Brauha • *Across from the Hotel Bristol-Kempinski.* A sparkling midtowner in 3 segments: Schnitzelhaus, Stehkneipe and Futterklappe. All good and reasonably priced.

Heinz Holl • *Damaschkestr. 26.* 3 varieties of steak in a 6-table dining room. The beef will set you back about $15. Hurricane lamps provide a cozy glow. You're buying a lot of atmosphere, but it's worth it.

Alt-Berliner Schneckenhaus *Ku-damm 37;* ☎ *8835937.* Tucked into the rear of its building, it is quieter than most of the bustling street-fronters along this main drag. Candle-lit ambience; outstanding German wines. Lovers love it.

Promina • *Uhlandstr. 162.* Good; swift service.

Hardy an der Oper • *Zauritzweg 9.* Turn-of-the-century-style curtain call for opera fans. Limited but amusing late-night menu. Noted for its wine.

Nolle • *Nollendorfplatz U-bahn Station.* This converted subway car makes an amusing pub. Moderate prices and quality food.

Berlin Museum • There's a pub here, too, which is open during museum hours (11 a.m.–6 p.m.) except Mon. Like the one above, it serves typical Berlin tavern snacks and beverages at low cost.

Grille • *Kurfurstendamm 202.* Features a stable decor. Specialties run from sandwiches to pepper steaks; the surprise entry on the tip sheet— "Feuerzangenbowle"—is for parties of 6 or more only.

Tai-tung • *Budapester Str. 50.* Good place to get tung-taied to Chinese food.

Dubrovnik • *Budapester Str. 50.* Yugoslavian and Balkan specialties at low prices. Deservedly popular.

CHAINS

Huhner Hugo • Excellent for value; branches at *Brandenburgischestr. 33* and *Kurfurstendamm 212.*

Hardtke • *Meinekestr. 27 a & b.* Recessed by a courtyard; $7 lunch special; normal outlay at $9. The side-by-side branches are separate operations.

Trattoria Roma • *Uhlandstr. 120.* Purveys pasta with appetizing gusto. Quiet; sound cookery. About $7 for a satisfactory meal.

DEPARTMENT STORE DINING

The top floor at the big **Kaufhaus des Westens** (**KaDeWe**) has different food sections, each with a bar: German, French, seafood, pastries, bread, beer, cheeses, etc.; all crowded but serving fresh delicacies, sandwiches and more.

EXCURSION

Kleine Orangerie • If you visit Charlottenburg Castle (refer to "What to See and Do") you may have an excellent breakfast or lunch at the Kleine Orangerie facing the palace's orchard, inside the grounds. There's both restaurant and cafeteria; brunch on Sun. runs from 10 a.m. to 2 p.m.; portions are colossal and very good for the money. Roast beef sandwich on a garlic loaf costs about $6 and is a meal in itself; strudel with hot vanilla cream sauce ($5) is a delicious topper. Tables outside for fair weather.

MORE $$

Hecker's Deele • *Grolmanstr. 35;* ☎ *88901.* A handsome corner of Westphalia with corresponding specialties plus other German cuisine. At 8 p.m. the cozy Kutscher-Stube opens for intimate dining. Smoked sausages, farmers' platters, chops, ham, wursts, dumplings and all the treasures of the rustic larder available for approximately $6 per heaping serving. Excellent for atmosphere, price and flavor at lunch or dinner.

Herzogliches Brauhaus Tegernsee *(a.k.a. "Tegernseer Tonnchen")* • *Mommsenstr. 34;* ☎ *3233827.* Bavarian-style country cooking. Named after the "brewer's small barrel"; decor follows this theme.

Kopenhagen • *Kurfurstendamn 203.* Valhalla for Danophiles. Denmark under glass—a glazed sidewalk cafe and cozy interior area presided over by a stained glass Little Mermaid. 129 items on the menu from open sandwiches to full meals. Naturally, prices vary widely.

Europa-Center • In this skyscraper near the Kaiser-Wilhelm Memorial Church are the modernistic **Tiffany's**, the **Deli-France** for quick *morceaux*, the Japanese **Daitokai**, **Alt Nurnberg**, the Chinese **Jade**; the **Pasta & Pizza**, plus several more fast food places.

Funkturm • *Messedamm 11.* Berlin's self-service answer to the Eiffel Tower. At a height of 150 feet, the panorama alone makes it worth a visit.

Barbecue • *Kurfurstendamm 176.* Reasonable tariffs for meats; we prefer it to the Argentinian-style Churrasco, also on the Ku-damm.

NIGHTLIFE

Berlin offers the gamut of after-dark attractions for pockets of every size.

Go in • *Bleibtreustr. 17.* Folksy, with a literary program and song daily (8 p.m.). Wonderfully Germanic.

Berliner Liedermacher • *Damaschkestr. 21.* is similar; location near the Kurfurstendamm makes it convenient. Both are kneipen (a cozy sort of tavern).

Subway • *Kurfurstendamm 105.* Recreates a U-bahn mood on weekends, also Wednesdays. Disco.

Sektor • *Hasenheide 13.* Does its disco neon tricks on a glass and metal footing. Lots of room; music daily from 8 p.m.

Spatz • *Kurfurstenstr. 30.* Features a downstairs locale and a tavern mood. Good food and cheerful.

Big Eden • *Kurfurstendamm 202.* Often employs topless disc jockettes in this gigantic emporia.

Riverboat • *Hohenzollerndamm 174-177.* Offers everything from "*musique à gogo*" to "*danse maritime*"; students and musicologists crowd every table between the smokestack and the paddle wheel. As strange as it may seem, Berlin goes Irish—after sunset.

Pubs: The **Pub** (*Eisenacher Str. 6*), the **Irish Inn** (*Damaschkestr. 28*) and the **Irish Harp Pub** (*Giesebrechtstr. 15*) all lilt to Gaelic melody and nostalgia. Here are only 3 of the crop, so if you wish to search out more, join the chorus of "When Irish Eyes Are Glanzend," and ask direction to the next pub.

Eierschale "*Eggshell,*" • *Podbielskiallee 50.* An international students' hangout that sometimes features live music by the Spree-City-Stompers. Sun.-Thurs. from 7 p.m. to midnight, with cover charges $2 (graduates) or $1 (undergraduates); on Fri. and Sat. it closes about 2 a.m. and levies are slightly higher. Expect to be asked to show your ISI Card; if you're under 18, also expect to be kicked out at 10 p.m. or so.

Nashville Country Club • *Breitenbachplatz 8.* Nearby in location and in mood. Live and recorded Dixieland is the call of the tune. Berlin is well-known for its interest in aberrant sex shows.

Chez Nous • *Marburger Str. 14.* The classic address for transvestite programs (performances at 8:30 p.m. and 11 p.m.; also at 1 a.m. on Fri. and Sat.),

Dollywood • *Welserstr. 24, corner of Fuggerstr.* Often the choice of Berliners. Open late but nearly always jammed; weekends you might have to wait an hour or so in line to get in. Diverting, if human freak shows appeal; rather gross otherwise.

GAMBLING

Casino • State-licensed and found in the Europa Center is open from 3 p.m. to 3 a.m. for roulette and until 5 a.m. for Black Jack. Entrance and minimum play each are about $6. Well run and honest. A second one has opened on Alexanderplatz; it occupies the penthouse of the **Stadt Berlin Hotel**. Bring your passport to both.

WHAT TO SEE AND DO

Highlights of special interest include: the remains of **The Wall** (Checkpoint Charlie displays a remnant); the refreshed and proud **Brandenburg Gate**; the **Soviet War Memorial**—a monument containing stones from the former Reich's Chancellery, the two first T-34 tanks to enter the city and masses of wax flowers; the Freedom Bell at **Schoneberg Town Hall**, which rings for 3 minutes daily at noon; the **Kaiser-Wilhelm Memorial Church** (*Gedachtnis Kirche*), around the war ruins of which, after years of debate, a modern building designed by Professor Egon Eiermann was raised; popular organ recitals and a brief meditation service at 6 p.m. Mon.-Fri. This, incidentally, is not the Dom, the city's historic cathedral which has finally been reopened after decades of repair. **Charlottenburg Castle**, bearing the baroque architectural tradition of the Prussian kingdom; the **Museum of Pre-and-Proto-history** and the **Egyptian Museum** housing the 3000-year-old bust of the Egyptian Queen Nefertiti; **Ernst-Reuter-Platz**, named for the great burgomaster—a 41-jet fountain gives jazz-ballet effect amid rising modern skyscrapers in one of Europe's largest traffic circles; the **Ethnological Museum**, a fantasy-land of man and his earth, includes perhaps the finest exhibitions anywhere of African and Island cultures, plus the **Art Gallery**, also at Dahlem, with 600 valuable paintings from the 13th to the 18th centuries; the **Academy of Arts**, built with $2,000,000 contributed by Berlin-born Philadelphian Henry H. Reichhold, houses the creative arts (theater, studios and halls); the **Hansa Quarter**, site of the '57 International Building Exhibition transformed into a 1600-apartment residential section by 54 architects from all over the globe; the 1936 **Olympic Stadium**, scene of Jesse Owens' triumph; the Zoo, largest in Europe, with its 10,900 critters in the aquarium and pens (some of which are housed in the excellent Children's Zoo); **Potsdamer Platz**, formerly the apex of the prewar capital which became a desolate area and is now rising from the dust; **Museum Fur Verkehr und Technik** (*Trebbiner Str. 9*), a delightful antique car museum—some real gems here (check as to the opening); the **Arts and Handicrafts Museum** at Tiergarten, near Philharmonie and the new hall for chamber music designed by architect Hans Scharoun. Well worth hearing is the **Berliner Philharmonic Orchestra** in its dazzling concert hall also designed by Hans Scharoun. Next door is the **National Gallery** in its modern home on Potsdamer Str. (free; closed Mon.). If your visit corresponds with the dates of the city's **Performing Arts Festival**, don't miss these outstanding cultural events at the **Deutsche Oper Berlin**. There are 18 playhouses in the city. There's also a wax museum and chamber of horrors called the **Panoptikum** located at the Ku'damm Eck. The summer timetables of the 4 major sightseeing bus operators list 40 tours plus separate excursions through the undivided city, bus-cum-boat parlays and a nightclub round. In addition, steamer trips on the Spree and Havel rivers and the

lakes around the metropolis are yours at reasonable prices—including moonlight cruises with dancing on Fri. and Sat. All tours are automatically bilingual (English) if there are any non-Germans in the group. Berlin is a huge city, now comprising almost 1000 sq. kms. Dozens of parks, lakes, castles and beaches are all within 45-minute reach. Here, in order of popularity, are the most interesting excursions.

The **Grunewald** ("Green Forest"), a smaller Bois de Boulogne, is a vast park with restaurants, the 430-foot Grunewald observation tower, a 4-1/2-century-old royal hunting lodge recast as an art and hunting museum, miles of lakeside vistas and—in warm weather—lovers lazing on its grass. Perched on a 250-foot hill, the tower offers a magnificent view of the Havel and Wannsee, the flora and the faces staring up from an open-air refreshment terrace below. The lodge has a beautiful spiral staircase, a scattering of Old Dutch masters and, during the season, an idyllic series of courtyard concerts.

The **Pfaueninsel** ("Peacock Island"), a seahorse-shaped islet in the Havel, with the ruins of an Italian castle (built, they quip, to resemble the ruins of an Italian castle), groves of California pines, technicolored Asian ginkgoes and majestic Lebanese cedars. Also there's a dairy, a hunter's shelter, a memorial to Queen Luise and dozens of strutting peacocks. Take the S-Bahn to Wannsee Station and stroll the beautiful footpath through the woods from Konigstrasse. When the sun shines, it is a glorious outing.

The Tegel Schloss and **See**. A U-Bahn links Wedding and Tegel; this charming estate and its mirror-smooth lake are easily accessible. About 40 minutes out; colorful and historic forest inn (the city's oldest, built in 1660); rambling country house constructed in the 1700s and still owned by the current Humboldt family. Although the mansion tour can be a trifle tedious (antiques, sculpture, heirlooms), the nearby 2-1/2-mile lake is lovely. Skippers at the docks will ferry you out to the rock-and-grass islands; scenic walkways; lakeside restaurants; jammed on weekends. If you can take or leave museums and monuments, the nautical side alone might make the journey worthwhile. The Schloss is open Sundays only from May to September.

The **Wannsee** bathing beach is confined to a 1/2-mile stretch of sand; on Sundays in July and August you'll find 30,000 Berliners trying to cool off here. Euphemistically, it is called the "Lido of Berlin." The shores of the Tegel and the smaller lakes also teem in season.

A morning's spin to Potsdam by motorcoach can be highly engaging. This includes a visit to Sans Souci. Dresden (interesting despite its destruction), Meissen and Leipzig also can be absorbed on a 2-day swing; the lovely Spreewald loop is of 1-day duration. All are relatively inexpensive; it's fascinating to see the change in these formerly eastern zones.

For the latest data on all of the above, consult the official **Tourist Office** (*Europa-Center*, ☎ *21234*) or inquire at the Information desk at the Budapester Strasse entrance of Europa-Center (☎ *262-6031*); the latter now has 40 specialists equipped to answer any questions on recreational, artistic, or commercial topics. There are branches at Tegel Airport, Brandenburg Gate and at the Hauptbahnhof.

SPORTS

HORSEBACK RIDING

In lovely **Grunewald**, saddle up at **Zeitschule Wallenhauer** (*Auerbacher- Str. 10*; ☎ *8911522*).

For children, the **Volkspark Jungfernheide** is an escape valve: swimming pools, sports grounds, running tracks, lawns, an open-air theater—a plethora of distractions on a sunny day.

TENNIS

The **Tennis Club Rot-Weiss** ("Red-White," *Oberhaardter Weg 47;* ☎ *8262207*) is the finest. For $17 you may play on the same clay surfaces employed for the international tournaments. Officially, a member should invite you, but try phoning and you may be offered hospitality.

WHERE TO SHOP

EYEGLASSES

Sohnges, (*Kurfurstendamm 139 and 210 and Reichsstr. 83; Munich headquarters, Briennerstr. 7*) is one of the 2 or 3 top optical houses in the world.

CUTLERY

J. A. Henckels (*Kurfurstendamm 33*) since 1731 has backed its famous trademark of "The Twins" as a guarantee of Germany's finest products in the field. Other Henckels branches are in **Dusseldorf**, **Frankfurt**, **Hamburg**, **Cologne**, **Munich**, **Dortmund**, **Copenhagen** and **Brussels**. The best-stocked hunting ground for gifts in the $2-$20 bracket is the Kaufhaus des Westens ("KaDeWe"), Berlin's largest department store.

FLEA MARKET

At *Strasse des 17 Juni*, you'll find all the hustle and bustle. Forget about antiques, but there's a lot of newer dross to pick through. Get off at the *Zoologischer Garten* stop of either the U-Bahn or S-Bahn and stroll through the Tiergarten. Open Sat.-Sun. 10 a.m.-5 p.m. There are said to be excellent buys of all descriptions in pawnshop windows along Bleibtreustrasse. While sometimes these unclaimed pledges are real finds, all too often they are someone's unwanted junk priced up to the hilt.

PORCELAIN

Staatliche Porzellan-Manufaktur Berlin offers enormous savings on their 2nd and 3rd quality firings at the factory (*Wegelystr. 1*). Forget about *Mini-City* in the Europa Center. We found the stock poor and the prices high.

BONN

This close neighbor of Cologne is undergoing a period of great change. Almost half of the federal administration has now moved to Berlin, with more shifting every month. Its population was more than doubled by its absorption of 10 adjoining communities, pushing up the head count to 300,000. It boasts **Poppelsdorf Palace**, the **Rhenish Land Museum**, the versatile **Zoological Research Institute and Museum** and Beethoven as its most famous son. There's a frenetic and impersonal atmosphere. The traffic jams of former times have been somewhat reduced by ring roads and bridges, thank goodness. But rain still falls on its unfortunate inhabitants 162 days per year! Staying in Cologne would be more enjoyable, we think, but if you do overnight, try the **Central**, the **Weiland**, or the **Schwan**, each with breakfast only; the **Continental** at the station is more expensive.

BREMEN

Germany's 2nd-largest seaport is a typical *Hanse* (medieval merchants' union) city. Fine Ratskeller with more than 600 different German wines, 8-century-old marketplace, 600-year-old City Hall and a history of being a free state since 1646, plus being the capital of Bundesland. **Zur Post** is a charming family-style hotel; the **SchaperSiedenburg** is more distinctive and unique in character.

COBLENZ AND COCHEM

The Roman-built **Moselle Valley** route from the Luxembourg border to Coblenz, where the Moseller joins the Rhine, remains one of the most pleasant drives or river cruises of Europe; its wine hamlets such as Cochem are enchanting. So is the **Rhine Valley**, when you're allowed to ignore its traffic-choked segments; you may also cover it in either direction between Coblenz and Wiesbaden/ Mainz on the renowned steamer excursions. **Boppard**, 12 minutes by train from Coblenz, is a nice quiet starting point that is on the ferry line. The viewful **Gunther** (☎ *06742-2335*) is a very pleasant inexpensive garni hotel. The **Hotel Lillie** serves good food and local wine. Driving is the most fun. If you like medieval castles, **Marksburg**, near **Braubach**, will probably intrigue you most.

COLOGNE

Overnight it became the Romanesque capital of Germany: A dozen churches, neglected for centuries, have been restored and opened to the public. **St. Pantaleon**, was consecrated a thousand years ago! This ancient apex, which invented *eau de Cologne* around 1791, took a terrible beating in the war. The area surrounding the **Cathedral** was leveled for blocks—but this magnificent structure, the largest Gothic building in the world, miraculously escaped destruction. It takes about 20 minutes to climb the 509 steps to the belfry's filigreed spire for a Nearer-My-God-To-Thee view of the Rhineland. Don't fail to see the dramatically designed **Museum Ludwig**, which architects and art historians are praising as a landmark of our time. It contains a chocolate tycoon's (Peter Ludwig) art donations. You must also visit the famous Wallraf-Richartz treasures (**Museum** of the same name) from the Middle Ages to the last century. For serious music there's the splendid 2000-seat Concert Hall—lined in American oak—which is home for the Kolner Philharmonie. A 6-lane bridge spanning the Rhine provides the final link between the city and the Ruhr-Frankfurt autobahn— as an alternate, of course, to the more exciting 6-1/2-minute swing on the aerial ropeway (altitude 165 feet!). The Cologne-Bonn Airport makes it handy to air travelers. A roof over your head? Inquire at the city's Tourist Office; they can find you a hotel or inexpensive rooming house if you decide to linger—and probably you will. If you are just pausing, have lunch at the **Fruh** (behind the Dom Hotel) or at the **Paffgen** (also central). But whatever you do, don't miss the awesome **Romisch-Germanisches Museum** in midcity (on the site of Roman occupation, with excellent early glass collections), the breathtaking nearby Cathedral, the Dionysus Mosaic, the stunning theater-opera house, the playhouse and the old segments that remain more or less behind and below the Museum. The **Museum of East Asian Art** offers superb collections of Chinese, Japanese and Korean works. Then you have the **Kunsthalle**, the **Rautenstrauch-Joest** (African and Melanesian items) and the **Diozesan Museums** (later Gothic, small and select). For overnighting, here are my choices: **Brandenburger Hof** (*Brandenburgerstr. 2-4*; ☎ *122889*), **Thielen** (*Brandenburgerstr. 1-7*; ☎ *12- 3333*), **Rossner** (*Jakordenstr. 19*; ☎ *122703*), **Stapelhauschen** (*Fischmarkt 1-3*; ☎ *212193*) and **An der Philharmonie** (*Grosse Neugasse 36*; ☎ *21-0105*).

DUSSELDORF

Here is the nation's center of *haute couture* and Germany's wealthiest city on a per capita basis, running a close second to Frankfurt as a hub of finance. The main street, called "Ko," runs along a lovely waterway; skies are not polluted since industry lives elsewhere; the Old Town ("Altstadt") froths with beer halls and fine antique

Rhine-Westphalian architecture. It's a cultural city with links to Goethe and Heine, an engaging **Museum Complex** at Ehrenhof, a fine **Opera House** and **Theatre**; naturalists will love the **Aquazoo** and **Lobbecke Museum**. Hotel accommodation plentiful but geared to upper brackets; good restaurants, **Benrath Castle**, scads of churches and art galleries, the **Kunst Museum**, with a glass collection that is worth a special trip, a 4-story apartment-style bordello with 228 "tenants" and 8000 "visitors" a day, cosmopolitan citizens and handsome environs, one of which includes the $5,000,000 **Minidomm**, elf-size scaledowns of world-famous wonders from Gothic cathedrals to Kennedy Airport (open Easter till Nov. 1 from 9 a.m.-5 p.m.; between Dusseldorf and Mulheim). The **City Museum of Inland Navigation** is in the restored tower of a former castle. Since hotels are pretty costly in this heartland of commerce, we'd recommend day-and-nighttime excursions or bunking in a boardinghouse. The Domo (*Scheurenstr. 4*; ☎ *211/374001*), about 2 blocks from the Central Station, is said to have friendly owners and offer exceptional value. At mealtimes try such old-timers as the 17th-century **Zum Schiffchen** (*Hafenstr. 5*), with its selection of wines at moderate prices, or the less expensive **Schumacher Brewery** (*Oststr. 123*), where you can quaff the house brews; **Im Goldenen Kessel** (*Boelkerstr. 44*) also is said to be substantial for the reasonable outlay.

FRANKFURT AM MAIN

A center of trade for nearly a millennium, this is a shrewd, hardworking city that also now boasts dramatic architecture and an abundance of cultural activities, including 40 museums, the major ones found along theMain-side Museum Bank.

Insider Tip

The municpal museums are free on Wednesday (They include museums on Fine Art, Historical, Applied Arts, Ethnology, Ancient Sculpture andFilm. Just head for the Römer, cross the bridge and along the Main river. On Saturday don't miss the fleas market on Saturday along the river front from 8am to 6pm or the Sachsen hausen Market on Diesterwegplatz on Friday 8am to 6pm.

From medieval to modern times, commerce trade fairs have been a staple stock in trade. As the principal junction of Germany's rail, river and road networks and the site of its largest and busiest airport, this birthplace of Goethe is an ideal starting point for excursions to the more rustic and romantic heartlands. As a finance hub, it is sometimes called "Bankfurt" or "Mainhattan," a jibe at its preoccupations but nonetheless the source of its well-endowed institutions of enlightenment.

DIRECTORY

U.S. Consulate General • *Siesmayerstr. 21;* ☎ *740071.*

American Express • *Steinweg 5;* ☎ *21051.*

Barber • Those in the station area are the least expensive.

Hairdresser • Friseursalon Behrens, *Schillerstr. 28;* ☎ *282339.*

Dry Cleaning and Pressing • Gebr. Rover, ☎ *251718*, with 40-plus outlets.

Suit Rental • Amor ,*Zeil 43;* ☎ *284271*, or Kurt Weingart, *Eiserne Hand 7;* ☎ *556639.*

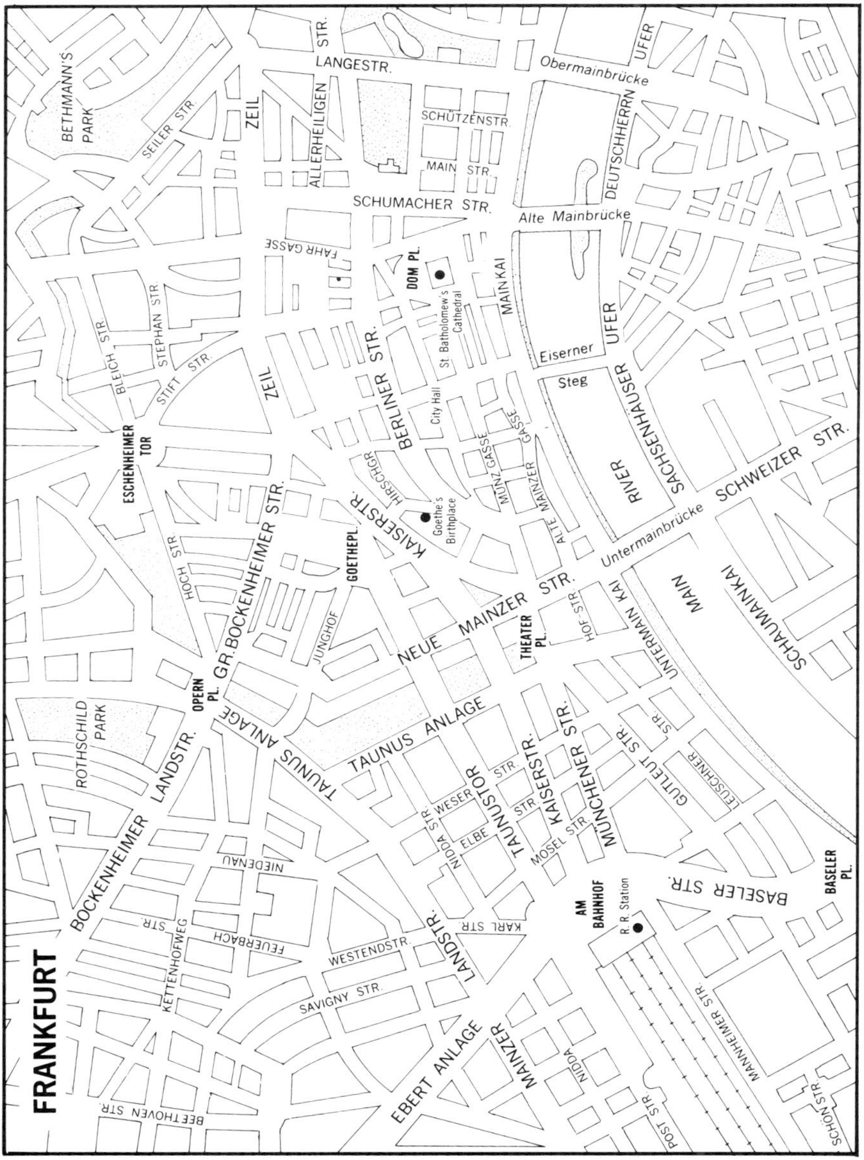
FRANKFURT
BETHMANN'S PARK
SEILER STR.
ZEIL
LANGESTR.
STR.
ALLERHEILIGEN
SCHÜTZENSTR.
MAIN STR.
SCHUMACHER STR.
Obermainbrücke
UFER
DEUTSCHHERRN
Alte Mainbrücke
FAHR GASSE
DOM PL.
St. Batholomew's Cathedral
MAINKAI
Eiserner Steg
UFER
STEPHAN STR.
BLEICH STR.
STIFT STR.
BERLINER STR.
City Hall
MÜNZ GASSE
GASSE
ESCHENHEIMER TOR
SACHSENHAUSER
RIVER
SCHWEIZER STR.
HIRSCHGR.
KAISERSTR.
Goethe's Birthplace
MAINZER
ALTE
Untermainbrücke
HOCH STR.
GR. BOCKENHEIMER STR.
GOETHEPL.
NEUE MAINZER STR.
HOF STR.
KAI
UNTERMAIN
MAIN
SCHAUMAINKAI
JUNGHOF
THEATER PL.
OPERN PL.
ROTHSCHILD PARK
TAUNUS ANLAGE
LANDSTR.
TAUNUSTOR
STR.
KAISERSTR.
MÜNCHENER STR.
STR.
GUTLEUT STR.
LEUSCHNER
WESER STR.
NIDDA STR.
ELBE
MOSEL STR.
BOCKENHEIMER
NIEDENAU
BASELER STR.
BASELER PL.
AM BAHNHOF
R. R. Station
KARL STR.
FEUERBACH
STR.
KETTENHOFWEG
WESTENDSTR.
LANDSTR.
SAVIGNY STR.
EBERT ANLAGE
MAINZER
NIDDA
MANNHEIMER STR.
POST STR.
SCHÖN STR.
BEETHOVEN STR.

English-Speaking Doctor • Dr. Gunter Meiler, *Cronstettenstr. 10;* ☎ *592595.*

English-Speaking Dentist • Dr. William W. Simkins, *Reuterweg 93;* ☎ *554353.*

Police • Central Headquarters, *Friedrich-Ebert-Anlage 9-11;* ☎ *755-1* or, in emergency, ☎ *110.*

Favorite Pawnshops • Leihhaus Elbestrasse, *Elbestr. 29;* ☎ *234230 and* Leihhaus am Eschenheimer Turm, *Schillerstr. 30.*

HOW TO GET AROUND

Use the subway whenever you can. After you've mastered the route map and transfer points, you can easily (and cheaply) reach the main targets in and around town. The Hauptwache will be your best starting block, but the Bahnhof is also useful.

Additionally, 40 bus routes, 14 streetcar lines and 7 subway connections continue to service the city and suburbs. The fare is $1.30 DM, rising to $2.70 DM during rush hours, whether or not you transfer.

To save stacks of D-Marks, the train connection between the airport and town is swift and efficient. Look for signs to the "Bahnhof" and buy a ticket from a machine; check the track number to the city. The 12-minute trip saves money—$3.60 DM vs. $29 DM by taxi. (During rush hours, the rail fare is bumped to $4.60 DM.) You might wish to purchase the 24-hour ticket ($8 DM; half-price for children) for unlimited travel; the airport route is included.

WHERE TO STAY

Hotels here are much more oriented to the business traveler than to the tourist. Listed below are the "best" establishments I found in their respective price categories. If they're not to your taste, consult the **Tourist Information Office**, *in Hauptbahnhof, North Side.* Strangely, Frankfurt seems to be different from other German cities. Here it is accepted practice to bargain for lower hotel rates with the desk clerk. But do it before you check in rather than when you are checking out.

LEAST $

Goldener Stern • *Karlsruher Str. 8;* ☎ *233309.* Bills itself as a hotel for families and "traveling businessmen." No lobby. Standard singles (starting at $20) claustrophobically narrow; doubles (beginning at $38) not much broader; only 1 bath. For a lone bunk, try #24; if doubling up, try #21.

Haus Hubner • *Westendstr. 23;* ☎ *746044.* Fresh and uplifting. Space for 60 with a high proportion of singles; #617, a large double with bath, particularly pleasant. Its Karlstube is an attractive dining nook.

City • *Sömmeringstr. 23;* ☎ *593197.* 27 rooms. Though slightly high in price, it is very centrally situated and well managed. All units with bath or shower, phone and some with color TV; 25% discount for stays of one week.

Vera • *Mainzer Landstr. 118;* ☎ *745023.* Will do in a pinch.

YOUTH HOSTELS

The 500-bed **Haus der Jugend** *Deutschherrnufer 12;* ☎ *619058.* Europe's largest—and one of the very finest of the finest of the organization's several hundred branches. Bright, clean and comfortable. Generous meals at reasonable prices. An excellent value.

MORE $$

Pension Uebe • *Gruneburgweg 3;* ☎ *591209.* 29 rooms. About 10 minutes by foot from the center. On the 3rd, 4th and 5th floors of a commercial building. Bright and cheerful with big, big sleeping quarters—especially the doubles. Clean and carpeted. Twin occupancy from $62 for the first 4 nights, then $2.50 less; singles at half-fare, with the same 4-day gimmick; breakfast included; showers $3.50.

An der Messe • *Westendstr. 102;* ☎ *747979.* 88 rooms with bath and shower, radio and refrigerator. From $99 for singles to $138 for doubles, inclusive of service, tax and breakfast; 30-car garage and proximity to fairgrounds make it convenient for motorists.

Munchner Hof • *Munchener Str. 46 (in the station area);* ☎ *230066.* 80 no-personality rooms with bath or shower. Quiet accommodations in the rear. OK.

Am Kurfürstenplatz • *Am Kurfuerstenplatz 38;* ☎ *777816.* Midtown calm on a small square about 5 minutes from the university. Such rustic touches as lanterns in the breakfast lounge and a meal gong. 36 good-size chambers; 5 public baths; wall-to-wall carpets; kindly personnel. Moderate levies.

Niedenau • *Niedenau 5;* ☎ *722536.* Only 8 rooms, 4 with bath. Modern, cozy and commendable.

Wurttemberger Hof • *Karlstr. 14 (near the station);* ☎ *23310667.* Large units. No luxury, but dependable.

Hotel-Pension West • *Grafstr. 81;* ☎ *778011.* On 2 floors of an ancient house across from the university. Chipper and chummy with kitchen and breakfast den. Spacious twins and singles.

Palmenhof • *Bockenheimer Landstr. 89-91;* ☎ *7530060.* Far from elegant, but old- fashioned and engaging. Outdoor parking with a bit of luck. Convenient tram connections. 75 ample bedchambers. 15 with showers. Maximum single around $55; top double about $90 (excluding breakfast).

Wiesbaden • *Baseler Str. 52;* ☎ *232347.* 66 rooms. Passably comfortable but somewhat cramped crannies. No frills, no private baths. Garage. Kind folks. Relatively low rates.

Union • *Munchener Str. 52;* ☎ *231254.* In an unsavory area well within auditory range of the railway. 93 cheap, clean and unexciting chambers. Adequate, but not advised for the demure.

Nord • *Eckenheimer Landstr. 166;* ☎ *553109.* For emergencies only.

EVEN MORE $$$

Jaguar • *Theobald-Christ-Str. 17-19 (appropriately near the zoo);* ☎ *439301.* 37 small but well-laid-out units, nearly all with bath or shower. Crystal chandeliers and wall-to-wall "jaguar fur" carpets. All in all, fairly sleek.

Luxor • *Allerheiligentor 2-4;* ☎ *293067.* Larger rooms in modern tone but duller decor. 100 rooms with bath and W.C.; some doubles with sofa. All-inclusive prices of $50 for 1, $80 for 2. Not bad.

Westend • *Westendstr. 15;* ☎ *746702.* Singularly business-oriented aura. Conference facilities. 40 utilitarian chambers with phones, many of them singles. Pretty costly.

Schwille • *Grosse Bockenheimer Str. 50;* ☎ *920100.* 83 rooms. A worthy rest stop.

Sophienhotel Schwille • *Sophienstr. 36 (near the university);* ☎ *702034.* Newer and ultramodern; 50 "efficiency" compartments; 35 private baths.

Admiral • *Hölderlin Str. 25 (near the Zoo station);* ☎ *448021.* Rooms with full baths. Adequate shelter for the outlay.

Republik • *Dusseldorfer Str. 20;* ☎ *251337.* So internationally minded, its rooms are named for 42 countries instead of being numbered. A house rule in 16 languages warns not to forget to deposit your clef, llave, chiave, sleutel, Schlussel, nyckel, nogle, klucz, kljuc, kulcs, klyuch, klidi, mouftah, mafteach, kagi, or key.

Hotel am Zoo • *Alfred-Brehm-Platz 6 (opposite the Zoo);* ☎ *490771.* 140 rooms. Clean and not unpleasant. Rates highish, but the quality's there.

Excelsior • *Mannheimer Str. 7-9;* ☎ *2560801.* No less than 394 rooms buzzing with package tours that have given it quite a workout

Camping: Two fine sites are the **Niederrad** grounds (at *Bruchfeldstrasse 72;* ☎ *672262; 46 rooms*) and the **Heddernheim** (*Sandelmuhle 35;* ☎ *570332*). Both offer a wide gamut of facilities (snack bars, showers and foodstuffs for sale). Contact the **Deutscher Camping Club**, *Mandlstr. 28, 8 Munich 23* for a pamphlet about campsites throughout the Federal Republic,

SUGGESTIONS FOR STUDENTS

The University Quarter is along Senckenberganlage in the West End. Subways U-6 and U-7 go to Bockenheimer Warte, a medieval watchtower on its north side (employed in ancient times as an early warning system for the city). The big Fair Grounds (Messegelande) cut across the southern boundary.

LODGINGS

If you're a summer visitor, you may be in luck; scads of normally student-filled boardinghouses rent their empty rooms between semesters. These are usually cozy and always inexpensive.

Studentenwerk • (*Jugelstr. 1;* ☎ *7983051* or *7983054*) may have beds available in the months of Aug. and Sept. Other billets are:

Dietrich-Bonhoffer-Haus • *Lessingstrasse 2;* ☎ *729061.*

Alfred-Delp-Haus • *Beethovenstrasse 28;* ☎ *748077.*

Friedrich-Dessauer-Haus • *Friedrich-Wilhelm-von-Steuben-Strasse 90;* ☎ *782089*

Studentenwohnheim Deutschordenshaus • *Bruckenstrasse 3;* ☎ *617053*).

CLUBS

Mackie-Messer-Disko-Club • *Zeppelin-Allee 2.* Where the liveliest action takes place. Call ☎ *751138* for the lowdown on membership, usually easy to obtain.

STUDENT AID

German National Tourist Association • *Beethovenstr. 69;* ☎ *75720.* There are no special agencies that cater solely to the traveling collegian—but you can usually find help here.

WHERE TO EAT

LEAST $

Grub Alley (slang for *Fressgass* or, more politely, *Grosse Bockenheimer Strasse*) • Here you can feed on local specialties: *real* frankfurters, Bethmannchen marzipan and smoked meats. There are dozens of snackeries and plenty of activity.

Panorama • *Henninger Tower.* One of 2 dining circles atop a 410-foot barley storage silo. One revolution per 45 minutes to take in the Hessian landscape. Henninger beer on tap.

Hauptwache • *Hauptwache Platz.* 2-tier cafe that is more interesting for its historic significance than for its gastronomy. Coffee and cake are sufficient.

Hess Backhaus • *Leipzigerstr. 5.* A superb midcity choice offering cheese-covered hot pretzels, local stangen (about $1.50), sandwiches (roughly $4) and fabulous rolls and sweets, including Dampfnudel ($2.50). Stand-up service at an outstanding fast foodery.

SACHSENHAUSEN

The Old Town across the river offers jovial apple-wine taverns usually rollicking with fiddle and harmonica melodies; low-cost dishes such as *Handkas mit Musik* (cheese with oil, onion and spices), salami, wursts and open sandwiches. **Grauer Bock** and **Klaane Sachsenhauser** are exemplary spots for little bites for little money. They are great fun.

Zum Germalten Haus • *Schweizerstr. 67;* ☎ *614559.* Serves many choices of the regional cuisine—and in portions that challenge the stoutest appetites. (Look at plates on other tables for ideas on what to select.) Boisterous fraternal atmosphere, full of good cheer; interesting paintings and murals depicting Old Frankfurt. Prices very low for the high-quality rewards. You and your buddies in humanity furnish the entertainment.

Neuer Fundus • *Theatre Platz.* For a coffee, a bite, or a full meal. Very well situated and pleasant for lingering.

THE RÖMER DISTRICT

A plaza and heartbeat of ancient and modern Frankfurt; where the Romans settled. You'll find numerous cafes and beer salons.

Alt Limpurg • libating beer and apple-wine, dates back to 1405. The nearby

Braustubli • nearby is touristy but fun.

Schirn • is dark, cozy and loaded with singles after nightfall; music is taped. This broad esplanade and the spokes radiating from it contain at least a dozen more nooks. Half the fun is finding the one that suits you.

Asia • *Gallusanlage 2 (at the corner of Kaiserstr.);* ☎ *253989.* Excellent for oriental food.

Waerland-Stuben • *Steinweg 10;* ☎ *283189.* Tops for vegetarian meals. Open 11 a.m.–7:30 p.m. and 11 a.m.–3 p.m. on Sat.

CHAINS

Wienerwald • For chicken-on-a-spit. Biggest poultry buy just over $3, including all the trimmings. Branches at *Holzgraben 31*, *Opel Rondell*, *Morfelder Landstr. 235 (across the river in Sachsenhausen)*, *Rennbahnstrasse 5*, *Tituscorso*, *Kaiserstrasse 75* and *Rothschildallee 32.*

Schultz's • Pans out southern fried chicken, but a soggy sampling seemed to have lost something in the translation. A so-called *Frisch und Golden* 2-piece snack box with French fries and coleslaw about $4.50. Branches at *Hansaallee 34*, *Schweizerstr. 76*, *Eckenheimer Landstr. 341*, *Borsigallee 22* and *Konigsteiner Str. 61.*

SNACKS AND PIZZA

Pizzeria Party near the Niedenau Hotel dispenses Italian piemanship, as does the **Dante** on the Römerplatz. The nearby **Bonaparte** is recommended for light bites.

PASTRY

Lochner • Found in the passage under the Hauptwache, griddles tasty waffles at about $1 apiece.

STUDENTS

University Mensa • *on the campus, at Bockenheimer Landstr. 133.* Mensa hips up low-cost cafeteria cookery any time but summertime.

MORE $$

Bruckenkeller • *Schutzenstr. 6; ☎ 284238.* Oozing with atmosphere for about $36 per diner. Medieval-type cellar with strolling accordion, violin and guitar trio. 20 candlelit tables in 3 tiers and perhaps 50 more in the inner sancta. 80-item menu and 200,000-bottle wine subcellar.

Zum Storch • *Saalgasse 3-5 (facing the beautiful Domplatz); ☎ 284988.* Tables set off in cozy alcoves. Candle and lantern light. Splendid cuisine at startlingly low prices. The herring, Schweinshaxe and venison were superb; likewise the reception and service. A great place and a great value.

Frankfurter Stubb • *In the cellar of the Frankfurter Hof.* A novelty stop specializing in 19th-century Hessian dishes. A team of experts authenticated every single detail from culinary selections to decoration in each of the 11 underground rooms. Results are impressive and so is the service. Count on an outlay of at least $19 per person; an unusual and memorable evening.

NIGHTLIFE

Afterdark diversions run from innocent, interesting, naughty, to downright wicked in this hub. Locally the joints are known as "*Nepp*" (a loose translation of "clip," which has now been adopted universally throughout Germany)—so take it from there as to what you can expect.

For simple music and good-natured togetherness, the low-cost jazz clubs are most fun (that is, if you've already been to the wine restaurants in the Old Town).

Jazz-Kneipe • *Berlinersstr. 70; ☎ 287173.* Transports you to Basin St. on the first bar. The notes are noteworthy, the drinks are cheap, the house is packed and smiles abound. Snacks available. A splendid, red-hot, midcity address.

Sinkkasten • *Bronnerstr. 5; ☎ 280385.* Also a lively one. You don't have to buy a drink, but membership costs are a few dollars for a month. This is followed by the modernistic

Jazz Keller • *Kleine Bockenheimerstr. 18a; ☎ 288537.* The tall, thin timber-and-stucco building.

Jazz-Haus • On the same street at #12 (look for the cornet hanging over the door)

Jazz Life • *Kleine Rittergasse 22-26; ☎ 626346.* High-spirited entertainment.

St. John's Inn • *Grosser Hirschgraben 20.* An elegant *wunder-bar* for a festive nightcap. Salubrious drinking at the wraparound bar in comfortable booths, or beside the grand piano. Crackling hearth in winter. Drinks about $7.50; snacks available; dart board; open 5:30 p.m. to 2 a.m. Saw no dancers, just chitchat.

Dauth Schneider • *Neuer Wall 7.* For traditional German beer-and-song, this is a merry one. About 10 minutes from the center (cross the Obermainbrucke and walk 3 blocks along Dreieichstr.); lovely recessed summer garden with 16 tables; small kitchen for light suppers. Fun atmosphere heightened by harmonica, arm-locking and group swaying; inexpensive ($1 per large glass of Apfelwein, $2 for Johannisbeerwein, $2.50 for a rich but Kauf Kopf of beer). Don't go before 7 p.m.

Zum Fichtekranzi • *Next corner, at Wallstr. 5.* Another folk center. Decor a Prussian mural; same prices and same service hustle as the Dauth. Closed on Mon.

Lorsbacher Tal • *Grosse Rittergasse 49-51.* This place lines 2 sides of a beguiling summer courtyard. Surprisingly tranquil midtown site; 9 tree-shaded tables; no music.

Insider Tip

The "car-girl" profession got its start here. This term sprang from the notorious Rosemary Nitribitt murder in Frankfurt, which became the inspiration for 3 movies, several books and countless magazine pieces in almost every language. These are the prostitutes who solicit from Mercedes and other expensive automobiles; their fees often go as high as 400 marks per rider.

Of the selected streets where madchen ply their trade, Mosel, Elbestr. and Taunusstrasse are the busiest. Most of the intimacy occurs, however, in the so-called sex clubs on these same avenues as well as along Kaiserstr., where such names as the Love Inn, Contact Hof and other obvious handles advertise the wares. In the marts where Third World gentlemen deal for goods, items begin at 30 DM, sprinting on up to 100 DM if the chap wears shoes. AIDS, of course, is part of the scenery. Many local newspapers or periodicals provide photos, measurements, hours, phone numbers and special talents.

WHAT TO SEE AND DO

Any visit to Frankfurt should start with a visit to the **Tourist Information Office** (*Im Hauptbahnhof, North Side, near track 23,* ☎ *2123-8849 or 8850 or 8851; Mon.–Sat. 8 a.m.–10 p.m., Sun. 9:30 a.m.–8 p.m.).* The helpful (but harried) staff will pinpoint your targets with maps, suggest dozens of alternates and provide pamphlets. Be certain to get a copy of the *Frankfurter Woche*, with tips on galleries, concerts and cabarets. There is no shortage of publications on what to do in Frankfurt Look for *Fritz* (free at the tourist office) *Kultur Frankfurt* (2DM) or *Journal Frankfurt* (2.80DM) the best magazine that rates restaurants and nightclubs available in English or German at most Kiosks in the train station. There is also an Tourist Information Office as you enter the Römer. All museums open on Tues. and then Thurs. through Sun. 10 a.m.–5 p.m., Wed. 10 a.m.–8 p.m., closed Mon., free except for The Städel.

The Römer (City Hall) • exhibits its fabulous Kaisersaal (coronation feast room of 10 Teuton emperors) from 9 a.m.–5 p.m. all week and from 10 a.m.–4 p.m. on Sun., Apr.-Sept. Hours from Oct. through Mar. are 9 a.m.–4:30 p.m.; admission DM 1. Frankfurt's compelling museum cluster on the Main River bank includes 11 choices—from cinema and communications to folk art and sculpture, to ethnology, architecture, furnishings and interior design, Jewish culture and classical and modern art, of course. All are within walking distance and most are free. This was a recent winner of the Temple Fielding Travel Award.

St. Bartholomew's Cathedral • Locally called the "Dom," magnificent tower site of the aforementioned crownings; marvelous frieze of its namesake's life cycle, (daily 9 a.m.–12:30 p.m. and 3–6 p.m., Fri. 9 a.m.–10:30 a.m.).

Goethe's birthplace • *Grosser Hirschgraben 23*; museum and house; everything from his law books to Frau Rat's Room (admission charge of DM 3; half-price for students, Mon.–Sat. 9 a.m.–4 p.m., sun. 10 a.m.–1 p.m.).

The Städel Kunstinstitut • *Schaumain Kai 63; DM 6.* One of those in the Main Bank district, it's strong on excellent 19th and 20th-century works, with examples by Van Gogh, Degas, Manet, Monet, Rodin, Millet, Cézanne and others, but versatile in other periods, too; $2 for adults and $1 for children, (Tues.-Sun. 10 a.m.-5 p.m.; closed on Mon.).

The Museum of Modern Art • *Schaumain Kai 17.* Known to local wags as the "Slice of Cake" because of its daring architecture, designed by Richard Meier, located near the Römer and the Dom.

The Zoo • The largest in West Germany and one of Europe's best; 3200 animals of 600 species; Exotarium with polar, tropical, jungle and sea environments; monkey feeding time at 3:45 p.m. (open between 8 a.m. and sunset; take Tram #18, U6 or U7 and Bus #40; 8 a.m.–6 p.m. daily; 9.5 DM admission; half price on the last Sat. of the month).

The Palmengarten • *On Bockenheimer Landstr*, tropical park with a lake and strolling lovers (open 9 a.m. until dusk; idyllic).

The Opera House (Alte Oper) • *Opera Platz.* Built in 1880, a dazzler.

The Eschenheimer Turm (A 15th-century defense tower) and highest defensive tower in Germany, one of 42.

The Stadtwald • an enchanting forest are popular.

WHERE TO SHOP

Kaiserstrasse and Goethestrasse are the best shopping streets, despite the handful of hole-in-the-wall tourist traps larded with junk souvenirs in the former. Most of the department stores and production-belt establishments are on Rossmarkt and Zeil. The Römer (*City Hall Sq.*) has been given new life.

The Flea Market • is on the south side of the river near the Flosserbrucke in the Schlachthof area; it operates every Saturday from 8 a.m.-3 p.m. in winter and till 4 p.m. in summer.

J. A. Henckels • (*Rossmarkt 11 and Kaiserstr. 20*) with their famous trademark of "The Twins" has Germany's finest cutlery.

Foto Hobby • (*Rossmarket 23*), (cameras and optical devices). It has it all, but has won fame as the leading Leica center in Europe. Excellent buys.

Confections • (*Bethmannchen*) is the globe-shaped marzipan named for a local banking family of the last century. The 3 almond halves typify the decoration. It can be found in any bake shop and makes a fine take-home gift.

FREIBURG

This is a beautifully situated university town on the southern limb of the Black Forest. What a view from the 3700-foot Schauinsland skyhook! Lots of absorbing architecture such as the Munster and the Turm; a fine collection of medieval art at the Augustiner Museum; lots of scholarly pursuits; lots of good wine; lots of nice people. Much less expensive than **Baden-Baden** if you wish to roam the *Schwarzwald*. **Am Rathaus**, **Barbara** and **Schwarz-Walder Hof** offer reasonable accommodation; breakfast is the only meal.

HAMBURG

With approximately 1.6-million population, here is Germany's first seaport and second largest city. Its 890-foot-tall TV spindle has a rotating restaurant. Dine in the famous **Ratsweinkeller**, stroll through **Planten un Blomen Park**, shop along **Alster Lake**, visit one of Germany's largest collections of fine paintings at the **Art Gallery** (50 showrooms!), take a whirl through that rowdy **Reeperbahn** night district, ride a steamer to **Blankenese** on the Elbe River, or to the island of **Helgoland**, tour the port by boat (about $6), browse among the antique cars at **Hiller's Auto Museum** (*Kurt-Schumacher-Allee 42*) with vehicles dating back to an 1895 Landry, or see **Hagenbeck's zoo** with its Troparium to display its apes, snakes, crocodiles and other animals in natural surroundings. The Tourist Office also offers tandem harbor-and-city excursions. If you are down by the port, you may wish to take a peek into the 1869 warehouse containing the city's **Museum of Erotic Art**, a town which can speak with authority on the subject. It's located on *Bernhard Nocht Strasse*. In the center, **Alte Wache** and the more expensive **Kronprinz** are convenient choices for midtown shelter. **Alsterhof** and **Baseler Hof** also are reliable. **Deichstrasse** is famous for its fish restaurants. Also have a look at the **Fischereihafen** *(Grosse Elbstrasse 143; ☎ 381816)*, next to the fish market (especially active Sun. mornings).

HANOVER

This attractive mercantile mart boasts a marvelous jam-free street system and is a handy springboard for exploring the **Niedersachs** region. It is the capital of Lower Saxony and is now more than 750 years old. See the **New City Hall**, **Market Church** and walk the **Red Line**. In the **State Opera** and the **Herrenhausen Park and Palace** you'll find first-quality music and theater. Going north, at **Hodenhagen**, there's a **wildlife park** with numerous residents of Serengeti shivering under the weak German sun.

HEIDELBERG

Immortalized by Sigmund Romberg in his *Student Prince*, Heidelberg boasts a captivating location astride a riverbank; the world's largest wine barrel (58,000 gallons); the **Karzer Prison** where obstreperous 15th-century students of its celebrated university were jailed; undergraduate dueling clubs (now revived); the awesome railway station and the 127-foot TV tower (observation platform open to the public). Inexpensive rooms available at the **Kohler**, the **Reichpost**, or the **Regina**. **Alt Heidelberg** and **Zum Ritter** are more costly. If you are only passing through, take a light meal, wine or coffee at **Schinderhannes** (*Theatrestr.*), named for a highwayman of Mainz fame. It's a colorful spot. Otherwise there are dozens of options along the busy Hauptstrasse and the tributary pedestrian zones for tasty tidbits. The **Museum Restaurant** is terrific for full meals, good service and Old World atmosphere. As a center of education it benefits greatly from resident cultural programs as well as visiting theater and musical presentations (both outdoor and indoor); jazz, art exhibits and lectures abound, so look at the Heidelber Aktuell publication as soon as you arrive to learn what's going on. And that will be plenty. Heidelberg itself is guilty of nothing except an excess of beauty and historic charm; this means that in summer you may have to share it with thousands of other outlanders. At all other seasons, however, it is tranquil and enchanting.

LUBECK

This "Queen of the Hanse" is so rich in monuments, antiquities, paintings, waterways, harbors and antique salt-storage houses that it's a great favorite of serious-minded voyagers. The meadows of Mecklenburg lie east of the former frontier between the two Germanys. Thomas Mann was born here, observed life here and wrote *Buddenbrooks* as a manifestation of its citizens. (Some still haven't forgiven the bounder.) See the museum within the **Holstein Gate**, the **Marienkirche**, **Jakobikirche**, **mansions**, the **Rathaus** and a wonderful warren of streets. **Hotels Lysie**, **Jensen** and **Kaiserhof** are not too costly; some houses accept boarders within their distinctive antique walls and the rates are very low. **Travemunde**, the neighboring Baltic resort, offers a gambling casino and plenty of excitement in summer. For only a few marks you can hop aboard a motorlaunch and witness history afloat in a 50-minute minicruise. Check in at Obertrave-Holstentor at Lubeck. **Kiel**, nearby, was the marine host for the sailing contests of the Olympics. Worth a visit, particularly by salty types.

MAINZ

Across the Rhine from **Wiesbaden**; the principal attraction of this humdrum center is a unique **cathedral**—one of Europe's most imposing mishmashes of Romanesque, Gothic and baroque architecture. In 1440, **Johann Gutenberg** slapped the ink on the first movable type here and now there's a printing museum in his honor.

MUNICH

This is the capital of evergreen Bavaria and one of Europe's most captivating cities. The people are noted for their hospitality and gaiety. The setting is ideal—only 30 miles north of the Alps—which makes it perfect as a base for further travels into the most scenic regions of the Continent. Large areas are given over to pedestrian malls; history is everywhere; prices are among the most attractive in Germany despite its burgeoning economy.

DIRECTORY

U.S. Consulate • *Koniginstr. 5*; ☎ *28880.*

American Express • *Promenadeplatz 6*; ☎ *290900.*

Barber • *Bachmaier Schutzenstr. 11*; ☎ *591882.*

Hairdresser • Holl , *Friedrichstr. 1.*

Dry Cleaning and Pressing • Wurth, *Rindermarkt 17.*

English-Speaking Doctor • Dr. F. Fruhwein, *Briennerstr. 11*; ☎ *223523*, or Dr. Werner Ludwig, *Ungererstr. 6*; ☎ *394492.*

English-Speaking Dentist • Georg Bauer, *Maximilianstr. 6*; ☎ *295680.*

Police • Central Station, *Ettstr. 2*; ☎ *2141.* Accident patrols, ☎ *110* for English-speaking dispatcher.

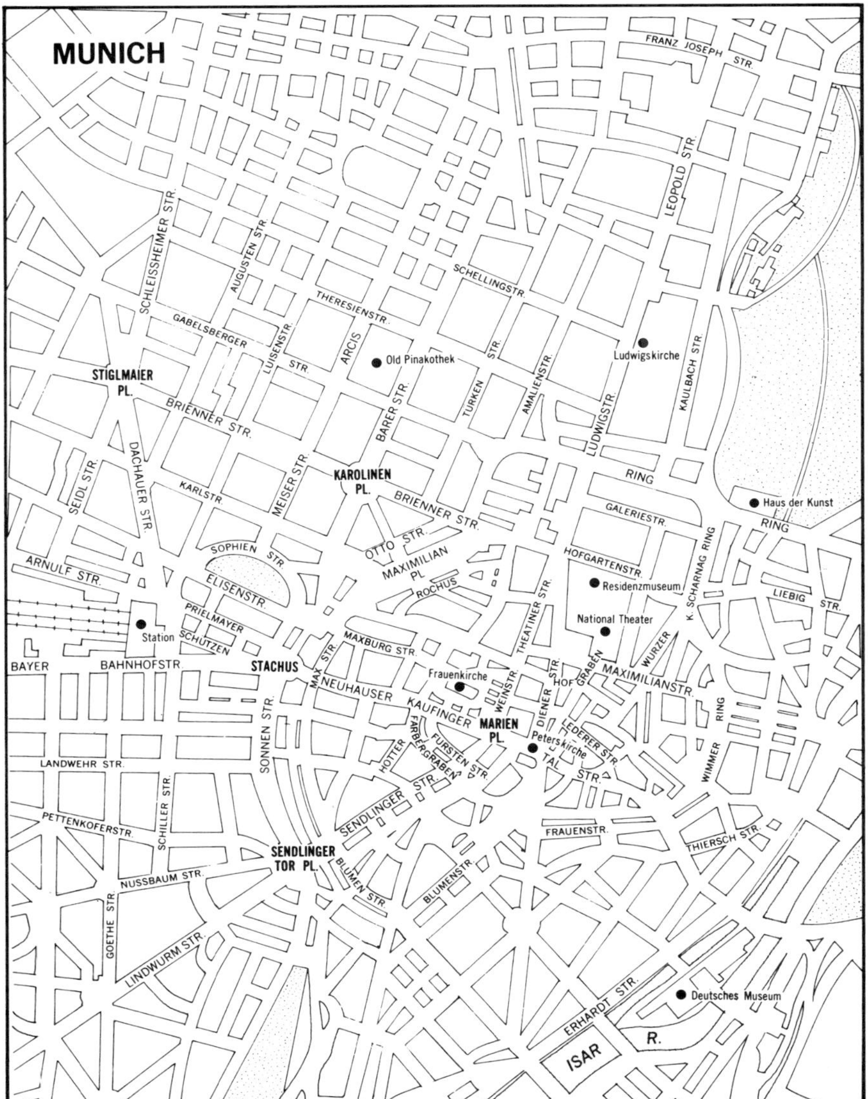
MUNICH
FRANZ JOSEPH STR.
LEOPOLD STR.
SCHLEISSHEIMER STR.
AUGUSTEN STR.
SCHELLINGSTR.
THERESIENSTR.
GABELSBERGER STR.
LUISENSTR.
ARCIS STR.
Old Pinakothek
Ludwigskirche
KAULBACH STR.
STIGLMAIER PL.
BRIENNER STR.
BARER STR.
TURKEN STR.
AMALIENSTR.
LUDWIGSTR.
DACHAUER STR.
SEIDL STR.
KARLSTR.
MEISER STR.
KAROLINEN PL.
RING
Haus der Kunst
GALERIESTR.
OTTO STR.
MAXIMILIAN PL.
SOPHIEN STR.
ARNULF STR.
ELISENSTR.
ROCHUS
HOFGARTENSTR.
Residenzmuseum
K. SCHARNAG RING
LIEBIG STR.
PRIELMAYER
Station
SCHÜTZEN
MAXBURG STR.
THEATINER STR.
National Theater
WURZER
BAYER
BAHNHOFSTR.
STACHUS
MAX STR.
NEUHAUSER
Frauenkirche
WEINSTR.
HOF GRABEN
MAXIMILIANSTR.
KAUFINGER
MARIEN PL.
DIENER STR.
Peterskirche
LEDERER STR.
SONNEN STR.
FÄRBERGRABEN
HOTTER
FÜRSTEN STR.
TAL STR.
WIMMER
LANDWEHR STR.
SCHILLER STR.
SENDLINGER STR.
PETTENKOFERSTR.
FRAUENSTR.
THIERSCH STR.
SENDLINGER TOR PL.
BLUMEN STR.
BLUMENSTR.
NUSSBAUM STR.
GOETHE STR.
LINDWURM STR.
Deutsches Museum
ERHARDT STR.
ISAR R.

HOW TO GET AROUND

In town, use the main railway station (Hauptbahnhof) as your home base for bus or tram travel. For $10 DM, you can enjoy 24 hours of unlimited midtown transportation; for twice this outlay, you can cover the entire metropolitan network aboard all city vehicles for the same period—quite a bargain! Take Bus #41 or #12 streetcar to the Schloss Nymphenburg; for the Haus der Kunst and gallery area, use bus #55 and get off at Koniginstr.; U #3, U #6, or U #2 for sorties into Schwabing (disembark at the fork formed by Ungererstr. and Leopoldstr.); and tram #18 to the Deutsches Museum (Ludwig's Bridge). The newly and vastly expanded subway system is a swift and efficient means of getting from point-to-point if seeing the terrain is not too important to you. For the full range of targets and routes, pick up *Rendezvous with Munich*, the excellent brochure that tells it all, station-to-station.

Heading for town from the wonderfully revamped airport you have the S-bahn option or the bus. Skip past the porters (one mark—per piece for your cargo) and grab a baggage cart that will cost you a single mark.

MOTORCYCLES, SCOOTERS

Motorrad-Spaett KG (*Rudesheimer Str. 9*; ☎ *579370*). For new models, of course, it is a buyer's market. Most of the German makes are superb.

CAR HIRE

If your budget allows occasional auto rental, an agency that has always given unfailingly efficient service is **Auto Sixt** (*Seitzstr. 11*; ☎ *223333*)—a Munich-based company with a fleet (Germany's largest) of self-drive or chauffeur-driven vehicles. Europe-wide pickup and delivery.

WHERE TO STAY

LEAST $

Hotel-Pension Erika • *Landwehrstr. 8;* ☎ *554327.* 30 clean bedchambers; singles, $28 or so, plus $2.50 for private shower and W.C. Only breakfast served. Reserve ahead.

Pension Schubert • *2 Schubertstr. (near Kaiser-Ludwig Platz);* ☎ *535087.* Noted for its hospitality. Twin billings start at $46 (with sausage and eggs for breakfast). Very central and handy to U-Bahn connections.

Pension Haydn • *9 Haydnstr.;* ☎ *531119.* Another musical number with a fine location; superior comfort; $40 tabs; warm-hearted conducting by proprietor Kathuda.

YOUTH HOSTELS

Wendl-Dietrich-Str. 20 ☎ *131156* and **Burg Schwaneck** (groups only) in suburban *Pullach* (☎ *7930644*). Reasonable prices.

Haus International *Elisabethstr. 87*; ☎ *120060.* Has 420 beds in a modern mood. Difficult to find space, though.

Jugend-hotel *Goethestr. 9*; ☎ *555891.* Offers 25 beds for girls only.

MORE $$

Europaischer Hof • *Bayerstr. 31;* ☎ *551510.* With its own chapel in case you're feeling romantic—or reverent. Hospital-style hygiene. Each unit with phone, radio and crucifix. Twin rate: $65 to $77 (with bath $93 to $150); singles, $36 to $46. Exceptional.

Pension Diana • *Altheimer Eck 15;* ☎ *2603107.* Very central. Entrance unkempt, but clean inside; 18 twins at about $53 (including shower); $8 for extra bed. Six smart singles at $36; 1 tub and 2 toilets; loads of one-faucet sinks. Even if you add $1.50 for breakfast and $2 to use the bathtub, it delivers reasonable comfort for your marks.

Thalkirchner Apartments • *Thalkirchner Str. 72;* ☎ *521681.* Located near the city's South Gate. All units with phone, radio and color TV; stocked kitchenette; separate W.C.; bath or shower. Readers say its brightest asset, however, is its amiable proprietress, Frau Anita Gross, whose hospitality and helpfulness to travelers are peerless.

Am Hofgarten • *Wurzerstr. 9;* ☎ *229004.* Side-street tranquillity and a 5-car garage; 4 accommodations with separate tub; 7 with shower cabinets in room; washbasins and telephones throughout. 10 singles from $38; 9 doubles from $62. OK.

Pension Utzelmann • *Pettenkoferstr. 6;* ☎ *594889.* Only 11 units. Singles $23 and doubles from $50. Cozy if you can get in.

Pension Dollman • *Thierschstr. 49 (near the Isar River and the Maximilianeum);* ☎ *238080.* Stark appointments; singles $76-83 and doubles $86-105. Spotless. Reserve very early. Good investment.

Adler • *Ledererstr. 8 (near the Hofbrauhaus beer hall);* ☎ *223991/2.* 20 twins from $77, 10 singles from $56 and 3 triples from $83. No private plumbing. Stark.

Helvetia • *Schillerstr. 6;* ☎ *554745.* 40 bathless units and 3 with baths. Singles from $33, twosomes from $57. Strictly emergency shelter.

Senefelder • *Senefelderstr. 4 (directly across from the station);* ☎ *551540.* While 63 of its austere units have a bath or shower, the remaining 33 share one public bath. Singles from $38 and doubles from $70. Neatness is not one of its virtues.

Pension Hungaria • *Brienner Str. 42;* ☎ *521558.* A short stroll from the station and the Lenbachvilla, on a noisy corner of Augustenstr. Wide variety of accommodations. Rates from $34-$48. Just so-so.

EVEN MORE $$$

Intercity • *Bahnhofplatz;* ☎ *558571.* Best buy by a wide margin. Smack inside the main station; 184 snappy-clean rooms, over half with bath or shower; all with radios, double doors and sound-absorbent windows. Doubles from $95 per couple; singles from $57. Professional, alert and friendly staff.

Arabella Central • *Schwanthalerstr. 111;* ☎ *510830.* On a quiet, viewful knoll; not too central. Cozy breakfast room. All 63 units with private balcony; frigobar; radio console; orange divans often used as extra bed. Twin rates from $130. Costly, but very well run.

Excelsior • *Schutzenstr. 11;* ☎ *551370.* Far more luxurious than its neighbors; 135 large and spotless bedchambers, 85 with bath. Singles $92-$140; doubles $125-$178.

Austrotel • *Arnulfstr. 2;* ☎ *53860.* Well scrubbed; 18-story commercial building; sometimes noisy on street side; 90 baths; higher altitudes advised for tranquillity and view. All-inclusive single tabs from $122 and doubles from $165.

Adria • *Liebigstr. 8A;* ☎ *293081.* 54 rooms; all but 12 with bath or shower; several with bars and tiny refrigerators; usually spacious singles. #106, a charming double with sitting area, the most expensive at around $128; normal twins from

$83 up; solos from $79. No dining salon (but the **Trift Stuberl**, *at the corner of St. Anna Pl. and Triftstr.* is intimate, cheap and excellent). Hospitable and comfortable.

Schweiz-Gebhardt • *Goethestr. 26;* ☎ *539585.* Offers about 45 fully bathed billets, each named for a city in Switzerland; most with TV; some with typewriters (obviously Goethe is expected to return); all with "Massage Boy" beds, radio, safe and Helvetian photographs. Singles from $53; doubles $73-$158.

Amba • *Arnulfstr. 20 (next to the station);* ☎ *592921.* 90 original units plus 40-room addition. Rates: singles $60; doubles $120. Much package- tour traffic. Clean, comfortable, well situated. Should provide ample return for your money.

Drei Lowen *("Three Lions")* • *Schillerstr. 8;* ☎ *551040.* Well regarded locally. Two attractive dining rooms. Cheery accommodations; most with private bath; sound-proofed windows. Singles from $80 and doubles from $118. Kind personnel.

Daniel • *Sonnenstr. 5 am Karlsplatz Stachus;* ☎ *554945.* Centrally located; 74 rooms with showers; 20 fronting the traffic. Singles from $45; doubles $66 and up. Not bad.

Hahn • *Landsbergerstr. 117;* ☎ *5027037.* 40 appealing rooms (singles from $56; doubles from $99) and inviting Bavarian restaurant. Moderate and good.

Tourotel • *Domagkstr. 26;* ☎ *360010.* 50 singles ($77), 86 doubles ($110) and 94 studios, all with bath and shower, W.C., phone, electric alarm clock, air conditioning and radio. Also, a restaurant, beer stand, bar, gym, swimming pool, sauna, shopping facilities, barber, hairdresser, plus "space for 100 cars and buses"! Though reachable by U-Bahn 6, really too far out for all but motorists.

Arosa • *Am Farbergraben (with entrance at Hotterstr. 2);* ☎ *267087.* In a former commercial building; 75 clean, office-like rooms; singles from $66 and doubles from $93.

Mark • *Senefelderstr. 12;* ☎ *559820.* 104 tiny chambers with W.C.s, most with bath or shower. High-priced ($60-$100) for what it offers.

Platzl • *Munzstr. 8-9 (opposite the tumultuous Hofbrauhaus);* ☎ *237030.* Totally renewed and with excellent facilities. Prices have risen accordingly. The beer hall neighbor is its chief disadvantage (unless you're thirsty).

Modern • *Schillerstr. 16;* ☎ *594771.* 50 tiny units ($44-$108) that are neat; fine if you don't have much luggage.

CAMPING

The **Thalkirchen** site (*2.3 miles southwest of the center*) is located near the Hellabrunn Zoo grounds. If you're car-less, Bus #57 from Send-linger- Tor-Platz will deposit you within minutes of its gates—about 10 minutes on weekends and twice that on weekdays to the nearest bus or train stop. Modern facilities (showers, washing space and glassed-in restaurant); nearby Gaststatte and swimming pool; economical overnight fees. Consult the national headquarters of the **German Camping Forum** (*Mandlstr. 28*), a service organized by consumers and tradesmen, for other suggestions.

SUGGESTIONS FOR STUDENTS

Foreign scholars usually head first for Schwabing, a sprawling section that starts about 10 blocks north of the Hauptbahnhof, extends along Leopoldstrasse's baseline and then moseys beside the Englischer Garten. Although it is almost anonymous in daylight, at eventide Schwabing becomes bustling and alive.

OVERNIGHTS

During the August to mid-October vacation, the student boarding- houses accept foreign visitors. (Most close, incidentally, around Christmas for a break of several days.) They're called *Studentenwohnheime* and they're sprinkled throughout the area. Many offer pension plans. Nonacademic travelers are also eligible, but demand is so high that preference goes to the earliest knock at the door.

YMCA • *Landwehrstr. 13;* ☎ *5521410.* Reliable.

Haus International • *Elisabethstr. 87;* ☎ *120-060.* Near Olympic Village, also is a worthy bet. Certainly the nearby facilities are tempting for athletic types.

Sleeping Tent/Youth Camp am Kapuzinerholzl • *Franz-Schrank-Str. 8;* ☎ *1414300.* Run by the city of Munich (Jugendamt) and by the Kreisjugendring, its open from end of June through August. Sleeps 400 in a large tent; canteen, toilets, showers and information bureau and a second recreation tent. Just over $4 per person includes blankets, air mattresses and hot tea in the morning. Streetcar stop Botanischer Garten for trams #17 and #21.

NIGHTLIFE

Schwabing plays host for just about everything—punk-rock bands, Herzegovinian quartets, you name it. Go late.

SPECIAL PROBLEMS

Pop in at the **Information Center for Overseas Professors and Students** (*Leopoldstr. 15;* ☎ *346721*), the **Internationaler Studentenclub** (*Adelheidstr. 15*) or the **Carl-Duisberg-Gesellschaft** (*Schwanthalerstr. 91;* ☎ *5309207*). Finally, the **Youth Information Center** (*Paul-Heyse-Str. 22;* ☎ *51410660*) near the station, is a meeting place in which students can obtain discount tickets and fraternize. It's open from 11 a.m.-7 p.m. on weekdays and to 5 p.m. on Saturday; closed Sunday. Here you will find lists on low-cost lodgings, dining spots and student nightspots. The city also maintains a chain of clearly marked Information Booths that dispense maps and directions.

WHERE TO EAT

LEAST $

Gaststatte Leopold • *Leopoldstr. 50 (in the heart of Schwabing);* ☎ *399433.* Amiable, inviting place with rough wooden floors and posture-perfect chairs. Middle-priced menu of savory food. Lunch about $7, dinner from $10. Hard to beat.

Ratskeller • *City Hall;* ☎ *220313.* A special Old World elan permeates separate halls. Dine in the blue-ceiling segment in winter and the open courtyard in summer. Excellent values and flavors among its enormous selection of regional dishes; try the cool herring in cream sauce and the deep-fried mushrooms; gargantuan portions. Worth a visit.

Mowenpick Markthallen • *Neuhauser Str. 11 (across from the Michaelskirche;* ☎ *2603001).* Double-time service; 2 main dining areas. Lunch about $6; a la carte choices with soup from $4–7. Spotless throughout. A solid link in a chain.

Schnell Imbiss • *Schillerstr. 3.* Hustles you in and out between 8:30 a.m. and 3 a.m. daily. Soup-schnitzel-beer (or soft drink) standard at about $5. If you eat at one of the *ImBiss'* standup stalls next door (Rindsbratwurst, $1.50; half-chicken, $3.50) and then return for a drink and the music, you'll spend about $6.

Nurnberger Bratwurstglockl • *Frauenplatz 9.* Wood-paneled tavern with long tables; wursts crackling over the roaring fire in the kitchen. Sausages served (Nurnberg style) on a pewter plate. Other choices include sauerbraten and goulash. The *pfannkuchen* (large, jelly-filled pancake) was a delectable dessert. Inexpensive and fun.

Bratwurst Friedl • In the very center of the town's pedestrian sector, also splendid for the fingerling sausages, stadtwurst (roasted, grilled, or boiled), deep- fried mushrooms, salads and, of course, tankards of excellent beer.

Asado • *Tal 76.* Midtown and charming. The pork and dumplings were delicious at $5; helpings were heaping.

Brauhaus • *Tal 10.* **Augustiner Keller** *near the station.* **Hofbraukeller** *Wiener Platz.* All 3 are sound values. It's hard to spend more than $8 per person at any.

Franziskaner *Residenzstr. 9.* **Lowenbraukeller**, *Nymphenburger Str. 2.* Two beer halls with lots of local color. The last is a mammoth structure plus garden where 3000 can eat, drink and revel at the same time. Popular antics on the ground floor; more sedate dining upstairs.

Hofbrauhaus • An oompah band usually accompanies the serious quaffing at ground level (about 1300 gallons flow daily down loyal gullets); upstairs salons quieter; food excellent value.

Mathaser Beer City • Near the main station. Jealously claims title to the highest beer consumption under any one roof in the world. Daily concerts in the main section from 10:30 a.m.–4 p.m. and from 4:30-midnight with a bigger band. Upper split-level for the view; open-air garden on top during warm months. Zestful every day except Dec. 24, when it rests.

Weinstadl • *Burgstr. 5.* Prefer wine to beer? Try this modest Old City tavern, virtually unchanged for more than 5 centuries. Munich's oldest house; town scribes worked at long wooden tables. Main floor plus cellar. Nothing fancy and nothing pretended. Main courses from $5 to $9; enormous variety of wines available by the glass; try the Obatzter, a housemade specialty.

Cornelius Schuler Buffeterial • *Bayerstr. 13* Soup $1.50; *schnitzel* about $5; cafeteria offerings at attractive prices. Cordial service; L-shaped counter.

SNACKS

Rischart is a must for watching the famous glockenspiel performances from sidewalk tables. Pastries are bellringers, too. **Vinzenz Murr** *(Rosenstr. 7)* and **Mayer Murr** *(Augustenstr. P).* are actually butcher shops, but these and their affiliates dot the city offering stand-up counters with top-quality, low-cost snacks to eat on the spot or to take out. Open during normal shopping hours.

STREET STANDS

Bahnhof within the main train station. There are about 30 huts, bins, kiosks and stands purveying wursts, sandwiches, croissants, pizzas, dairy products, or anything to be gobbled on the run—and soooo cheaply! Milk bar and beer taps also pump day and night. For interior dining, there's the low-cost **Schaffler Saal**, plus a cafeteria and picnic bars. **Rialto Ice Cream Bar** *(Leopoldstr. 62)*. 13 flavors starting at about 75¢.

DO-IT-YOURSELF

The **Deutscher** supermarket (and flocks of others) are bargain bonanzas. Head for their 2-mark vending machines for wines, cheeses, sausages and breads.

STUDENTS

The **University Cafeteria** *(Leopoldstr. 15)* specializes in low-cost comestibles. Fall-winter-spring only.

MORE $$

Goldene Stadt • *Oberanger 44*. Four adjoining rooms with a family ambience that blends sophistication with a gentle, informal sense of ease. Slavic and local dishes. Top off your repast with an order of Barack in a stovepipe glass; $30 should cover a substantial feast. Terrific.

Zum Metzgerwirt • *Nordliche Auffahrtsallee 69*. Perfect for visitors to the magnificent Schloss Nymphenburg. (There's a Palmhaven snackery on the inner estate.) A family-style tavern with 2 cozy chambers. Huge portions of traditional Bavarian cookery. Rates from $5–$8 per platter. A solid value.

Olympia Tower • A 951-foot TV spike looming over Olympic Park and one of the great sightseeing sites of Bavaria. On a clear day you can see the Alps (65 miles away) from its upper tiers. Entrance fee circa $2.50. Ground- floor

Atrium-Restaurant • Ascent via the fastest elevator in Europe (23 feet per second) to a revolving 3-speed, 32-table panoramic dining ring; stationary snack bar; upper-level observation deck, plus a children's platform still higher (low but thick safety-conscious walls). Cuisine is typical and even savory in a few simple choices. Main dishes about $9; desserts about $3. Take the U 3 from Marienplatz or the U 2 ("U" is for "subway") from Hbf.

HIKING AND DINING

At nearby **Schleissheim**, the **Wald-restaurant Bergl** is set amid dozens of forest trails for working up an appetite or working off a gluttony. Quieter midweek than weekends.

NIGHTLIFE

Munich has a glittering variety of nightspots, but after midnight avoid the main station area, which bristles with troublemakers.

Starting with the strip parlors—somehow an addiction for certain elements all over Germany—the undies fly best usually in the Maximiliansplatz and tributary streets.

Ba-ba-lu • *Ainmillerstr. 1*, offers an electrified and electrifying top-volume combo; popular bar; no cabaret. Other playpens are:

Domicile • *Leopoldstr. 19)*

Sunset • *Leopoldstr. 69*, which is is quite popular and

Der Neue Wende Kreis • *Herzogstr. 81)* a cozy Schwabing dance and romance haven.

Allotria • *Oskar von Miller, Ring 3*, is an old-fashioned Dixieland jazz saloon with beer, sandwiches, sausages, soups and soft beverages. Afterward, up the street drop into

Charivari • *Turkenstr. 92.* Just up the street for late night crowds, Charivari resembles a Greenwich Village coffee house; a troubadour softly frets over his Spanish guitar. (One source of illumination was a lantern hung inside a horse collar.)

BEDTIME SNACKS

Bavarians cling to the custom that Weisswurste, the renowned white sausage, must be consumed "before the noon bells ring." Everyone ritualistically winds up the night's romp by stuffing his own case with this specialty. Scores of places sell it.

WHAT TO SEE AND DO

The galleries listed below are free on Sunday; on weekdays, you'll pay $3.50 DM or so.

The jewel of Munich is the **Old Pinakothek**, crammed with 700 masterpieces by Rembrandt, Durer, Rubens, El Greco, Titian, Raphael and other immortals or mortals. Go from 9 a.m.-4:30 p.m. The **New Pinakothek** offers such delights as one of Van Gogh's "Sunflowers," Cezanne's "Railway Cutting," and Manet's "Breakfast in the Studio." Wassily Kandinsky's pioneer abstract art is at the **Lenbachvilla** (Municipal Gallery, 10 a.m.-6 p.m.), which also contains a Paul Klee room and a selection from the Blaue Reiter school. The **Residenzmuseum** is a trove of portraits, busts and priceless collections of antique porcelain. Many rooms in renaissance, rococo and neoclassical styles and the baroque Cuvillies Theater are within its depths. The adjoining Schatzkammer (Treasury) features 10 chambers glittering with masterpieces by goldsmiths and lapidaries from the Middle Ages to the baroque period. Gates remain open from 10 a.m.–5 p.m. on weekdays and from 10 a.m.–1 p.m. on Sunday.

Next to the combined Berlins, Munich boasts the greatest concentration of live theater anywhere in the nation. Nearly every night, 12,000 seats are up for grabs by music, ballet, opera, drama, comedy and cabaret (political) devotees. Our favorites: Strauss by the **Bavarian State Opera** in the **National Theater** and Mozart in the rococo-opulent **Cuvillies Theater**. Bold and Brechtian, the **Kammerspiele** (Municipal Playhouse) is insatiably experimental. This one and the staid **Bavarian State Theater** (housed in the Residenz Theater) are the 2 biggest in the city. In addition, the **Gartnerplatz Theater** (light opera) has amusing performances.

Aficionados of architecture will discover the **Frauenkirche** (massive, late-Gothic brick cathedral finished in 1488 by Jorg Ganghofer, containing the tomb of Emperor Ludwig, the Bavarian), the **Peterskirche** (first brick laid 1181; the tower 14th century; baroque conversion started 1756), the **Michaelskirche** (Renaissance richness, with Gerhard's 1590 bronze statue of the Archangel), the **Ludwigskirche** (Friedrich von Gartner's 1829-1843 neoclassical triumph) and **St. Matthew's Church** (launched in 1952; lines of ship at anchor; intriguing).

The **Deutsches Museum**. Superlatives for this massive Isar River fortress always fall short of the mark. It commenced operation in 1907, on the premise that every possible technical and natural-scientific advance must be chronicled either by models or by the real thing. During a circuit of 16 miles, you can stroll past the 2700-year-old run from a Teutonic plank road, circle what is claimed as the oldest ship known to man, check your mileage on one of the earliest slide rules, clamber around WW I and II prop planes and jet fighters and then settle back into an easy chair for lunch. This complex also contains the wonderful **Zeiss Planetarium**, plus the **Technical Forum** and the fabulous **IMAX** film presentations, which stretch two-dimensional viewing into the third dimension. Give it at least one full day.

Schloss Nymphenburg, Munich's minor Versailles, took 2 centuries to assemble. Bavarian princes and electors were its habitants as late as 1918; the Wittelsbachs, Bavaria's longtime leading family, use it in summer. Now its spacious and beautiful grounds are awash with concert crowds, strollers, sitters and lovers from 9 a.m.–5 p.m. in the summer and from 10 a.m.–4 p.m. in winter.

ODDITIES

Try the **Beer Museum** (in the Municipal Museum) and "**Valentin-Museum**," (a museum of "blooming nonsense"). The latter delights practical jokers. No first-timer should miss the 11 a.m. performance of the world- famous **Glockenspiel**.

Pick a spot on the 5th and 6th floors respectively of the Cafe Glockenspiel and The Hoch-Cafe Peterhof, across from the Town Hall setting of this group of bells and animated figures. Go early if you plan to take photographs so that you can cop a table by the window. The hours (usually at 11, 12 and 5 in summer and 11 only in winter) are posted at the base of the tower.

Two sprees you probably won't want to miss, if you're anywhere near Germany when they're running, are the fabled

OCTOBERFEST

Oktoberfest (late September through early October) and **Fasching** (Nov. 11—11:11 hrs. on the 11th day of the 11th month, but most exciting around Jan. 7.) A local maxim states that the former is for *Bier* und *Wurst* and the latter is for *Sex* und *Sekt* (German champagne).

Less festive but also heady is the **Strong Beer Festival**, known locally as **Starkbier-zeit** and observed during Lent. The suffix "or" (Imperator, Patronator, Salvator and more) refers to this extra-potent brew. Because Salvator is the most famous, visit their own beer hall at Hochstr. 77 for a pre-Easter sampling.

CONCERTS

One of Europe's most romantic musical treats is the **Nymphenburg Palace Concert** series in June and July. The site is west of the city, but inquire locally because the restoration program for the Festival Hall may still be under way. In the city there is an active chamber music schedule in June. The **Opera Festival** takes the spotlight in July and August. Consult the local papers or a hotel concierge for details on performances, but expect difficulty getting seats.

OLYMPIC PARK

The scene of the 1972 Olympics, open to everyone, has become a recreation center that goes full tilt. You may use the pool, tennis courts, ice rink and other facilities for a small fee.

MOVIES

Although all films are automatically dubbed into German, selected original-language reelers are shown every Thursday at **Theatiner Filmkunst** or each evening in summer at **Hollywood** (*Schwanthalerstr. 2*). Consult the local newspapers for films and schedules.

MARKETS

Kettles, clothes, candlesticks—you name it—can be picked up cheap IF you hit it right at the **Auer Dult**, a flea market that has been going on in one form or another here since the 12th century. It is held 3 times a year (one week at the end of April, one at the end of July and one in mid-October) at Mariahilfplatz. Last, on any workday morning and until 6 p.m., the bustling stalls at the **Viktualienmarkt** are worth a look; closed Saturday afternoon and all day Sunday; it is near Marienplatz and the Rathaus. In December, magically the Marienplatz turns into the principal Christmas supply center for Bavaria.

PUBLICATIONS

Munich Weekly can be helpful, as can the monthly pamphlet imaginatively titled **Munchen**. At 9:15 a.m. weekdays the **Bayerischer Rundfunk** transmits the news in English (on the third channel). Reading matter can be found in reasonable supply at **Anglia English Bookshop** (*Schellingstr. 3*).

EXCURSIONS

Full-day forays into the countryside south and southeast of Munich are enormously popular. You can speed down the autobahn (or proceed by rail) to **Garmisch**, an alp-ringed resort on Germany's highest mountain; ride to **Neuschwanstein**, the fairy-tale castle that is a super-opulent monument to its incurably insane builder; make a pilgrimage to **Oberammergau**, the Passion Play capital; or zigzag up to **Berchtesgaden**, where the city's renowned salt mines vie with Hitler's Eagle's Nest. Take a day, a lunch and plenty of film. The bus tours from Munich provide transportation and a guide (but no lunch) for around $68 DM. By train, it's cheaper to Garmisch, but more expensive to Berchtesgaden.

WHERE TO SHOPIN MUNICH

BAVARIAN SPECIALTIES AND CLOTHING

You'll find a decent selection at **Wallach** (*Residenzstrasse 3*).

CAMERAS AND ACCESSORIES

Kohlroser • *Maffeistr. 14*, is a photographer's Nirvana. The staff here is absolutely the top in the fields of photography and optics—in a nation that has always dominated these sciences. Replete to the rafters with every kind of equipment, including dozens of low-priced bargains; 2-day service for Ektachrome processing.

CUTLERY AND SOUVENIRS

Bestecke & Praesente • *Karlsplatz 25*, cuts, snips, shears, carves, drills— but never bores. For kitchen, garden, tableside, hunting, or just for any old cut-ups, here is the blade maker. Many other items, too, which make fine take-home gifts.

MUSICAL INSTRUMENTS

Lindberg • *Kaufingerstr. 8*, can outfit a marching band in minutes—but he'll take hours, if necessary, to help you choose the musical instrument you want.

OUTDOOR MARKET

One of Germany's finest is on **Viktualienplatz**. Here everything from flowers to flounders is for sale—including some of the most scrumptious cheeses. It's open during the usual store hours and closed Saturday afternoon and all day Sunday

RAINY-DAY BROWSING

In the huge underground shopping center, directly beneath the **Stachus** (the main square), dozens and dozens of firms display their wares.

SPORTING GOODS

Sport-Scheck • *Sendlingerstr. 85*, is an amazing emporium that can supply you with the essentials and accessories for almost any diversion or athletic pursuit. An interior stone wall, 6 stories high, is used for testing your nerves as well as the climbing equipment (great fun for onlookers) and an ingenious ramp can prove the gripping power of hiking boots. Don't miss this one.

WOOD CARVING

Karl Storr • *Kaufingerstr. 25*, specializes in hand-carved religious items. To locate this address, go to the Dom in Frauenplatz, look to the right of the main entrance of the church and you'll see it at Liebfrauenstr. Some (not all) of the fine articles here have reverential prices.

SHOPPING ZONES

Briennerstrasse, **Theatinerstrasse** and **Maximilianstrasse** are the toniest. **Kaufingerstrasse** is only for pedestrians. Most large department stores are located between **Marienplatz** and **Karlsplatz**. **Leopoldstrasse** (and the entire Schwabing district) has seen better days, in our opinion.

NURNBERG

A charming example of the once-moated medieval metropolis, its walls, towers and ancient landmarks have been almost completely restored (one tower stands 1000 feet tall beaming TV pictures to all the nearby ground- lings); nevertheless, the impressive **Kaiserburg** (Imperial Palace) dominates the local landscape; the **Germanisches Nationalmuseum** is one of the finest classical repositories of art in the north of Europe; the **Meistersingerhalle** is handsome. Durer's 5-century-old dwelling and the St. Lorenz and St. Sebaldus churches are the most popular sights. At St. Lorenz, be sure to see the altarpiece carvings (the suspended polychrome garlands) and the stained glass. When you are in the delightfully presented **Konigstor** enclave, you will note how new construction has been restrained so that the ancient spires still dominate. Here you'll stand in the **Arsenal Courtyard** and browse along the **Craftsmen's Alley** (*Handwerkerhof*), displaying pewter, glass, woodwork, ceramics, also with cafes and nooks for sipping wine. For overnighting, the **Drei Raben** and **Prinzregent** are solid moneysavers. **Drei Linden** and **Victoria** are alternatives.

OBERAMMERGAU

In 1633, Europe was ravished by the Black Plague. After 85 villagers of the secluded mountain hamlet of Oberammergau had perished, the elders of the community assembled before the altar of St. Rocco's Church and vowed that if more ravages could be spared, each 10th year thereafter they would present a play of thanksgiving that would enact the life and sufferings of Jesus. In miraculous fashion, the disease instantly waned. Not a single person fell ill thereafter. Since then, the grateful citizenry and their descendants have scrupulously adhered to their pledge and presented plays in years ending on 10.

The leading candidate among its hotels is still the ancient **Alois Lang**. Quiet situation enhanced by a no-tour-group policy (rare in this frenetic hive); 51 rooms; all units with private balcony and most with bath; carpeting throughout. Its 3 dining rooms serve up savory cuisine. The **Wolf** offers more charm in its bedchambers (especially the top-floor Bavarian rooms), but its central situation and busy-busy public areas give it a somewhat commercial feel. Flowers and colorful touches everywhere; prices lower than the leader; very good value. **Alte Post** comes up with cheery accommodations but a very low bath count. **Bold** plays host to battalions of G.I.s during ski season. **Wittelsbach** turns over more tourists, it seems, than does Mr. Cook. In neighboring *Ettal*, also in Oberbayern, the barnish **Ludwig der Bayer** has a big name locally, but it's too institutional. We dislike this one with or without a Passio.

RUDESHEIM

Cattle car tourism has despoiled it as a worthwhile stopover; even as a lunching choice, I'd skip it. Here the ancient vineyards tumble down the Rhine banks and the antique half-timbered houses tilt toward each other along the narrow medieval lanes. Across the river from **Bingen** and 30 kms. downstream from **Wiesbaden**, this gaudy, overdone beer-soaked mecca is best seen (if at all) during the fringe seasons when the human outpourings from the coaches and cruisers are in less evidence. Messrs. Kodak, Agfa and Leica have provided spectacular castle ruins, the **Mechanical Music**

Cabinet with self-motivated instruments (open Easter until late October) and the **Broemserburg Wine Museum** with its fine interior collections and its splendid exterior panoramas. Clearly, the 3-1/2 million tourists who funnel through this settlement of 10,000 souls realize they are being injected into a maelstrom of package gawking. If you have your own transportation and feel like splurging on a truly memorable luncheon pause, drive to the riverside Krone at nearby **Assmannhausen** or sip wine and snack at the fabulous ancient **Eberbach Cloister** (*kloster*) in the vinelands above. In this tranquil setting, Burgundian monks created the matrix for quality (cabinet) German vintage.

STUTTGART

This industrial hub takes pride in its pleasant location, mineral springs, eye-popping 692-foot **Fernsehturm** (TV tower) restaurant, **German Antiques Fair**, a world-famous ballet company and the dramatically modern **Liederhalle** for concerts. Apart from Picasso and numerous staples of expressionism, you'll discover the largest collection of Otto Dix' German expressionist paintings at **Galerie der Stadt Stuttgart**.

Museums are excellent—and they are free; then there are the **Wilhelma Zoo** and **Botanical Gardens** and such important **factories** as Daimler- Benz, Porsche, Kodak-Germany and Bosch-Germany. There's an attractive, leafy 2-mile **promenade** from the Schlossplatz down to the Neckar. At yuletide the city prides itself on displaying the largest **Christmas Market** in Germany, a festival it has been celebrating in a similar fashion for three centuries. For overnighting check first with the **Stuttgart Tourist Board** (*Lautenschlagerstr. 3*), which puts together weekend packages at amazingly low prices (breakfasts, sightseeing and discount vouchers included).

THE ROMANTIC ROAD

This fascinating route was a vital and thriving lifeline during the Middle Ages, when a military link between fortresses was imperative for survival. The word "Hof" (suffixed to the names of so many modern German hotels) derives from the walled and safe "courtyard" where travelers could rest while passing from stronghold to stronghold. Initially, they slept in their carriages or under their horses. Soon drink was provided. Later food was served. Finally overnight shelters were constructed. When the wars ended, the transportation lanes were shifted and these great installations became superannuated.

Wurzburg, about 60 miles southeast toward Nurnberg, offers a spectacular beginning for your pilgrimage. The Franks founded it in the 7th century and Irish monks gave it a Christian essence about 100 years later. Today its most noteworthy features emphasize the power and riches of its once great economy and religious orders. The **Prince-Bishops' Palace** is a sightseeing must; the chapel is dazzling with gold applique on marble; Tiepolo's paintings adorn the walls; the adjoining Castle is awesome for its majestic chambers. Visit to **Marienberg Fortress** with its treasury of priceless Riemenschneider woodcarvings, costumes, pewter and paintings of a like category, including Cranach's Adam and Eve. The **Cathedral** is a glorious manifestation of Romanesque style as is the **Neumuenster**, a basilica that was begun in the 11th century. There are approximately 20 other sightseeing alternatives of considerable interest spread throughout the town. Most of them can be visited with determined footwork if you have a pedestrian nature, the midtown area being convenient and attractive for walking. Should your spirits flag, adequate regional restoratives can be found at the **Buergerspital**, which is a working wine house with roots planted in the early 14th century. The **Ratshaus** offers a multitude of dining segments including a beer cellar, the Shield Hall and the colorful Old Wurzburg room. Another amusing choice is the dining salon of the **Hotel Am Markt**, with its fantastic view of the Falcon House and ecclesiastical buildings. If you linger, the **Franziskaner** is a fine breakfast-only inn (which contradicts itself by providing the very attractive Klosterschanke restaurant). **Central** and **Schonleber** are good as are the **Hammerlien**, **Strauss** and **Zum Ochsen**. **Ambergerand Walfish** are higher priced hotels. Even though the authentic Way begins in the Wurzburg environs, you might wish to get further along your route and spend your first night in either **Mainz** or **Wiesbaden**; accommodations are numerous and inexpensive in both hubs. In the latter, the famous **Kaiser Friedrich Baths** are worth seeing.

Rothenburg ob der Tauber is one of the wonderlands of Europe, standing above the Tauber, which today is a nearly dried-up fiction. The streets are cobbled, the cottages and buildings lean toward each other and painted signs and guided windlasses glisten in the sunlight while bells chime hauntingly through the evening hours. Craftsmen work at the windows of their ateliers, creating delightful wax figures, textiles, or spice cakes. And what better place on earth to have 12 months of Christmas? The unique **Kathe Wohlfahrt's Christkindlmarkt** (*Herrngasse 2*) is a bewildering sight on an August day or any time of the year. Inside there is Christmas music, trees are alight, angels sing carols from loggias and if you count them you will probably notice as many as 50,000 different items in the inventory—a fairyland of toys, decorations and gift ideas that provoke thoughts of everyone back home. While there are many historic things to see here or elsewhere on the Romantic Road, this particular emporium is unique in the world. Incidentally, if you show this book to Mr. Wohlfahrt or any other key personnel, they will give you a Christmas ornament as a memento of your visit. For overnighting, try the **Tilman Riemenschneider**, the **Baren**, or the (of course) **Romantik Hotel Markusturm**. Move on through **Feuchtwangen** to the walled city of **Dinkelsbuhl**, which is a glorious antique gem set among lakes. The painted houses ramble among 20 towers and gateways. **Gasthof zur Sonne** is a wonderful stopping place. Its pastel green facade tumbles with flowers from each window and there is a bewitching sun terrace facing the street. The neighboring **Eisenkrug** is also excellent for economizing; it offers a restaurant, wine cellar and cafe. **Deutsches Haus**, oozing with antiquity, is proud of its dining room illuminated with painted legends and heraldry on the wooden beams. You might wish to try the regional specialty here of snail soup. **Goldene Rose**, in the same upper bracket, also prides itself on its darkwood dining segment, which is steeped in history; reception is up one flight.

Nordlingen is not for lingering and **Donauworth** also is hardly worthwhile; both should be daylight pauses only. In **Augsburg**, **Pension Anita** is a good buy, followed by the **Dom**, the **Post** and the neighboring **Ost** (just the Post offers meals, while the others serve breakfast only). The city itself is rather large, known for its **Fuggerei** (named for a powerful local dynasty) and the **Rotes Tor**, for open-air opera and Mozart summer festivals. In **Landsberg**, the pleasant **Goggl** has augmented its basic allure, with a handsome timbered interior, gay textiles and much improved gastronomy. In **Regensburg** (off "The Romantic Road" but in the same district), the tiny **Avia** is more intimate than the nicely restored and restyled **Parkhotel Maximilian**; this pair is more costly than guest houses such as the **Weidenhof**, the **Straubinger Hof**, or the fancier **Karmeliten. Rottenbuch**, **Wies**, **Steingaden** and world-renowned **Schwangau** are thrilling for rubbernecking. **Hirsch** in nearby **Fussen**, boasts 50 rooms, a listless restaurant and a cozy country-style Stube for beer, wine and trencherman fare. **Sonne** should be the budget choice for overnighting here. If you are heading this way for the purpose of seeing the Neuschwanstein and Hohenschwangau castles, opt for either the road-hugged, tiny **Lisl und Jagerhaus** or the **Muller** at the base of the path leading up to the summits. The latter with some chambers attractively finished in pinewood; snack bar; tavern; not bad if you can sweet-talk private plumbing from the reception people.

The Muller is sited beside the horse-carriage station, where you can rent a buggy for the arduous ascent of the mountain. Not incidentally, the concession has been in the same family since the days when here sat the royal throne of Bavaria. Since cars can't maneuver the path and since slick infighting has staved off construction of a road to the castles—perhaps for the preservation of peace and quiet—the rates seem inordinately high; the charges fluctuated mysteriously; if you don't want to walk up, it's best to pool with 5 other visitors for sharing the bill. It is a glorious area you will never forget. To reverse this itinerary, Munich is the place to begin.

THE GRIMMS' FAIRY TALE ROUTE

This fairy trail might be considered to augment the above tour. It starts at either **Bremen** (a glorious old-fashioned port) or **Hanau** (mantled in history) and passes **Kassel**, where the imaginative Grimm brothers were first inspired to bind together their everlasting collection of yarns. The forests, dales and antique villages with their tilting cottages and brooding clocktowers are the stuff of storybook pastimes. Honeymooners will swoon over ancient **Trendelburg Castle**, where from the Tower (now a bridal suite) Rapunzel, while locked in and denied food, let down her tresses to collect a gift parcel. Try to see **Lowenburg**, the Hansel and Gretel House, the Pied Piper town of **Hameln**, Sleeping Beauty's castle at **Sababurg, Homberg** in the Schwalm region, ancient **Fritzlar** and romantic **Marburg**, to name only a few of the antique delights in this wondrous route, which is nearly 400 miles in length. In general you will be following the meanders of the Weser River, an area rich in history, royalty and beauty. This circuit by car should occupy about two days—at a minimum.

FOR MORE INFORMATION ON GERMANY

USA German National Tourist Office, *747 Third Ave., New York, NY 10017;* ☎ *(212) 308-3300; 11766 Wilshire Blvd., Suite 750, Los Angeles, CA 90025;* ☎ *(310) 575-9799;*

CANADA *175 Bloor St. E., N. Tower, Suite 604, Toronto;* ☎ *(416) 968-1570.*

INSIDER TIP

"Reunification" and rebuilding are the primary concerns for western and eastern Germans at this instant. Hence, what you may find in this freshly updated chapter could be slightly different by the time its ink is dry. Always ask locally—especially in East-West frontier regions—about changes that may affect your travel plans. The Berlin area is the most fluid since the shattering and removal of the Wall and its re-creation as the once and future capital of a united nation. At present about half of the federal administration has moved from Bonn, with more shifting every month. Now for a few specifics.

(1) **Lufthansa**, *the German national airline, also cooperates throughout the world with the German National Tourist Board, so look for its listing in your phone directory.*

(2) In Germany the **German National Tourist Board** *is located at* Beethovenstrasse 69 in Frankfurt. *It publishes color-illustrated booklets in English covering every region of the Federal Republic. It can also provide a list of all subordinate offices throughout the nation.*

(3) Local authorities operate numerous information centers. Their offices are recognizable by a red plaque with a white "I".

(4) At least 50 feudal palaces and castles have been converted into hotels all over the nation. For details write to **Gast im Schloss**, Geschaftsstelle, Vor der Burg, Postfach, D-3526 Trendelburg 1, Germany.

GREECE

Parthenon

From Homer to Henry Miller, Greece has fed the fertile imagination and the sensitive soul. Author Mary Stewart once told me, "If you can't love a Greek, you can't love." It's a stirring nation whose people still seem motivated by some historic and mystical folk-memory.

On the **Acropolis**, a towering rock plateau that looms over the whitewashed capital, the stately **Parthenon** was built in honor of the patron goddess Athena. To its east lies the **Temple of Zeus**, to its south the **Dionysus Theatre**. Hugging the slopes, the historic residential quarter has long since given way to the **Plaka**, whose narrow, winding streets conceal orthodox churches reminiscent of Byzantium; shops; and ranks of tavernas where thousands of Greeks gather each night to drink, hold hands, sing, dance, and hear it on the grapevine. It's in this night scene that you're likely to catch the haunting sound of *bouzoukis*, mandolins, and guitars.

Cross the Corinth Canal into Peloponnesus to find **Mycenae** and the impressive site excavated by Schliemann in the 1880s. Cradled in the shadow of the rolling hills is the murdered Agamemnon's citadel, his grave, once filled with gold and treasure, now proudly preserved in Athens' **Archaeological Museum**. (Incidentally, Schliemann's mansion on Panepistimiou St. near **Constitution Square** in central Athens has been restored to its former glory and is today a fascinating numismatic museum.)

About 100 miles north of Athens rises legendary **Mount Parnassus**, where ancients regularly consulted the Oracle of Delphi, as well as the nearby **Temple of Apollo**. Spotting monuments such as these may be comfortably done in the low season when the weather's not so torrid and when your money goes farther.

There's fine swimming around the entire mainland from April to mid-October and a take-your-pick of dazzling sandy, uncrowded beaches. Fishing and skin diving in clean, clear water and excellent sailing in the Aegean are major attractions—and not expensive ones to pursue.

And then there are the **Greek Islands**. Call them a dream, a fantasy, or what you will, but the 1400 or so isles remain an illusion for most people. Scattered throughout the Mediterranean, Aegean, and Ionian seas, these isolated outposts vary immensely, yet all of them seem too intriguing to miss. Most Greek islands are perfect as economy holiday destinations. If they are well developed, there is always a great variety of opportunity for low-cost shelter. If they are only rock dots, the adventurous can easily find a bed in a monastery or a tiny room in a peasant's house. The welcome mat is out and the invitation is genuine. Mary Stewart was right.

TIPS ON GREECE

ACCOMMODATIONS

Scores of trailer grounds and tent sites have been set up in various rural areas—if you're interested, be sure to check with the **Automobile and Touring Club of Greece** (*6 Amerikis St., Athens*), the previously mentioned **GNTO**, or local Tourist Police who can be helpful and who almost always speak English or several European languages.

Travelers with permits from the Ministry of Northern Greece are welcomed at the monastery on Mount Athos, where kindly monks will bunk and sometimes feed any deserving male for a pittance. (Contact the Directorate of Civil Affairs, *Platia Dimitriou in Thessa-*

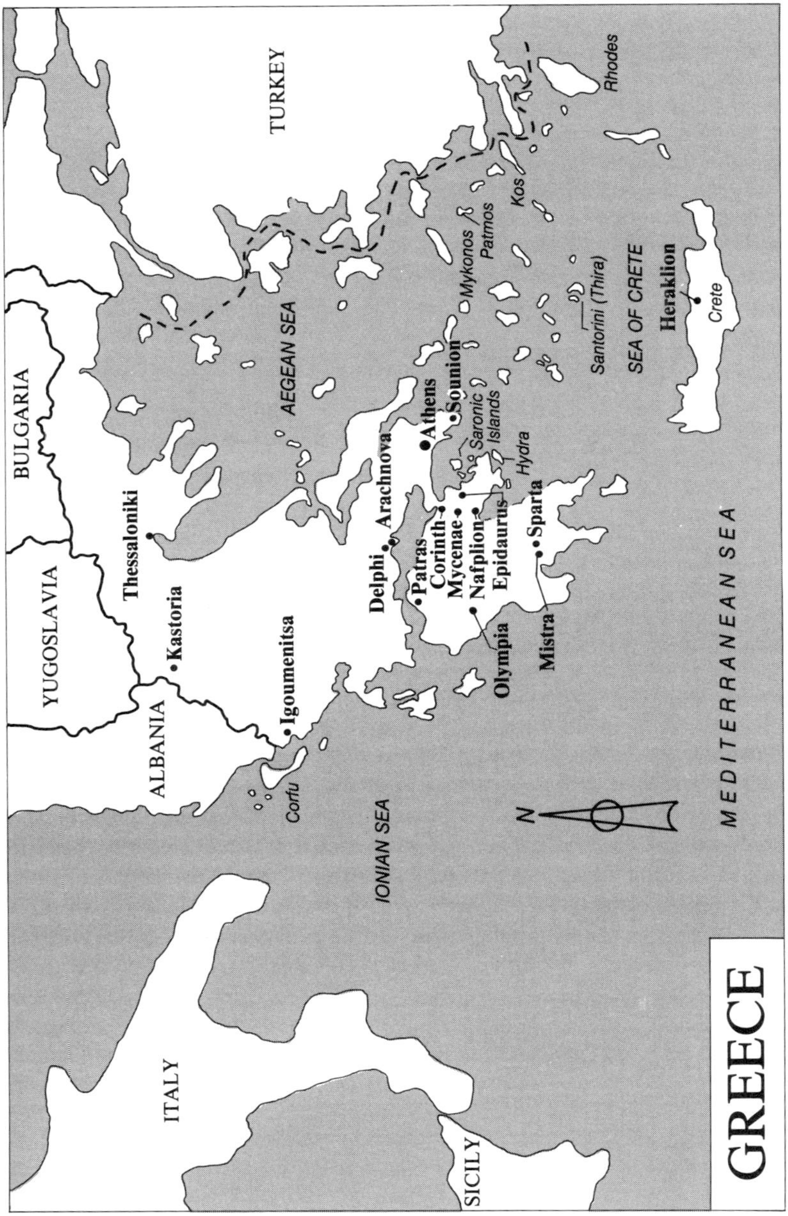
GREECE
TURKEY
BULGARIA
YUGOSLAVIA
ALBANIA
ITALY
SICILY
AEGEAN SEA
IONIAN SEA
SEA OF CRETE
MEDITERRANEAN SEA
Thessaloniki
Kastoria
Igoumenitsa
Corfu
Delphi
Arachnova
Athens
Sounion
Patras
Corinth
Mycenae
Nafplion
Epidaurus
Sparta
Mistra
Olympia
Saronic Islands
Hydra
Mykonos
Patmos
Kos
Rhodes
Santorini (Thira)
Heraklion
Crete
N

loniki, ☎ *031-270092.*) Other similar hermitages throughout the land admit pilgrims without this special document.

Hotel prices are still not high in the cities, although taxes and Common Market entry are pushing up the totals. On lesser-known islands you can still find a clean room for two for $20 per night. Often the owners will come to meet your boat or bus. You can also find these digs through the Tourist Police, local shopkeepers, or taverna tenders. Also there's a trend in the islands for large hotels to install grocery stores so that visitors can effect even greater economies during their holiday visits.

FOOD

When Greeks try to cook like the French, the results are usually disappointing, if not disastrous. When they cook like Greeks, they turn out interesting fare.

Delicious classic preparations are *dolmades* (grape leaves stuffed with meat, rice, onion, and seasonings); *souvlakia* (a succulent facsimile of shishkebab, consisting of lamb, tomatoes, and peppers roasted on a spit); *moussaka* (chopped meat with baked potato, baked pumpkin, veal, eggplant, tomato sauce, cheese, eggs, and spices); the magnificent red mullet, finest in the seven seas; *kalamaraki* (tenderized squid); octopus (so delicate that it tastes like chicken-lobster); and the local *langouste* (clawless crayfish). There's a large choice of other specialties. Incidentally, Greek ice cream can be excellent.

While pizza is the rage now, first try a Greek *Peinerli*, a "sandwich" of crisp dough shaped like a Viking ship and containing your choice of fillers: cheese and tomato sauce, chopped meat and cheese, chopped meat and egg, ham and cheese, ham and egg, sausage and egg, fried egg and ground meat only, all huge, and all within the span of $4.50-5.50. When it comes piping hot to the table, mix the fillers on the "deck" so that they soak into the underside of the crust. **Y Pighi Eleftheriatis** ("The Source") at Drosia, 14 miles northeast of Athens, is the original creator and king of this dish—a lovely drive for lunch on a benign day and 102% worth the trip!

Not recommended is a little number called *Kokoretsi* (sometimes spelled Cocoretzi), which is a mushy intestine stuffed with liver, *very* fresh kidneys and innards, half-baked by an apathetic fire.

If you like yogurt and are tired of the usually disappointing Greek breakfasts, look for the ambrosial Total brand; it's marvelous mixed with sliced fresh fruit.

Meal hours are generally 7-10 a.m. for breakfast, 1:30-3 p.m. for lunch, and 9-11 p.m. for dinner. As in Egypt, Spain, or Portugal, the later the hour, the larger the crowd.

Caution: Water from the tap is safe in Athens, Rhodes, Delphi, Olympia, Corfu, and Crete; although conditions are improving, the timid should stick to bottled varieties. Fruits, melons, and vegetables that grow in the ground should always be washed. In the large centers, restaurateurs generally do this before serving such foods. Don't worry in the good places in Athens, but when you buy them yourself or eat them in villages this precaution must be taken.

Whenever you tackle the flavorful little Greek clams called Thalassina, always squeeze a drop of lemon juice over each one before downing it; if it doesn't wiggle when the juice hits it, leave it alone!

In many Greek tavernas and restaurants it is customary to walk into the kitchen area and point out the dishes you desire. That's why the chef's work is often performed near the entrance; guests then can select before seating. Fresh fish usually are kept in ice lockers or stainless steel wardrobe drawers.

DRINKS

Brandy is the national hard drink; Metaxa, sharply sweet, is the most popular; Camba, far dryer and smoother, is the closest contender. Ouzo is the national aperitif; it is a thaumaturgist's cross between French Pernod, Javanese arrack, and Turkish raki, with a faint licorice flavor. Order Sans Rival brand (its superiority to all others is notable); mix it with water plus lots of ice. No Greek whiskey is made, but Greek vermouth is quite drinkable. So is Greek beer, which is mighty refreshing on a hot summer's day. Heineken and Amstel, the Dutch beers, are now available, too, plus a few German lagers.

Order your wines aretsinato ("without resin") or your mouth will pucker so much that you'll think you've eaten a basketful of unripe persimmons. In Homeric times, the Greeks smeared the linings of their wine barrels with pine sap, a crude preservative. Over the centuries, the people grew to like the turpentine flavor, and today's vintages are therefore deliberately resinated. But to the neophyte, they taste like a blend of nail polish remover and deck enamel. Greek wine is properly poured from a brass mug; nowadays you'll also find it served in aluminum replicas. In tavernas, the protocol is to half-fill your cup, especially when quaffing the resinated ones. If you specify that you want aretsinato, they'll always find an unprocessed bottle of the same brand for you.

Among dry-to-medium white wines, Elissar, Cava Kamba, Palini, St. Helena, Demestica, King, Tsantalis, and Minos are especially favored. Cava Boutari and Caviros reds (Burgundy-type) are heavyish but sound; both are good complements to extra spicy or garlicky dishes. Montenero is another popular cup. Mavrodaphni and Samos are sweet to very sweet. Outside this select group, Hellenic wines are without exception second-rate according to American and European tastes.

Soft drinks? Fresh citrus juices, particularly orange, are splendid; they're harder to find in summer because fall is the harvest season.

GETTING AROUND

TRAINS AND BUSES

Greece is a member of the money-saving Eurailpass system. The international expresses through Yugoslavia to Zurich, Paris, Ostend, Germany, or other European points are comfortable. There is good diesel railcoach service from Athens to Corinth, Olympia, Nauplia (Nafplion), or Tripolis, and from Athens to Levadhia, Larissa, or Salonika (Thessaloniki). The roadbed to the Peloponnesus is narrow-gauge and obviously rooted in a firm foundation of Jell-O. A second-class Touring Card allows unlimited train travel in Greece for 10, 20, or 30 days. Information and tickets at *1 Karolou St., Athens*, (☎ *5222491*) or *6 Sina St.*, (☎ *3624402.*) Domestic buses serve Delphi, Corinth, Marathon, Larissa, Levadhia, Patras, and a host of others. For about $38, there's a 14-hour trek to the island of Corfu. Prices are considerably higher on the tourist-catered excursions. As one example of possible savings, however, the 4-hour run to Argolis or Delphi costs about $60 by tour bus, including lunch; thrice-daily domestic service cuts this a mere $6 or so. Since there is no central terminus, ask the National Tourist Organization Information Office for copies of the English-language schedules; the departure points are scattered.

FERRIES TO AND FROM GREECE

Ships are quite good. The 4500-ton **Neptunia** sails to and from Brindisi via the Corinth Canal to Piraeus (Athens). There are special 30% reductions for students; auto-club members also receive discounts. The same line operates the **Poseidonia**, the **Appia**, and the sleek **Egnatia** on runs between Brindisi (Italy) and Patras. Stops at Corfu and Igoumenitsa; facilities range from airplane-type seats to deluxe cabins for both day and overnight sojourns; drive-on-drive-off gangways; swimming pool and restaurant; runs every day of the week during summer, 6 days during fringe periods, and 3 days per week in winter. Information and reservations obtainable from **Hellenic Mediterranean Lines** (*Pam Am Building, West Mezzanine, 200 Park Ave. New York, NY 10017*; ☎ *(212) 697-4220*). A quality cruiser (anchorages include Marseille, Genoa, Ancona, Naples, Piraeus, Cyprus, and Haifa) has also been hitched up. With the clean, fast vessels now at the voyager's disposal—plus a piggyback railway service for automobiles through Italy, a sleeper-bus hookup between Naples and Brindisi in summer, and a fine highway waiting at the threshold to Greece—this Aegean nation is easy to reach.

Interisland boats are frequent, informal, and low priced for spontaneous in-season island hopping. In an effort to encourage tourism to some remote isles, the country will provide free transportation to and from them if only you will go. Ask the National Tourist Organization to identify them, as well as for up-to-the-minute time schedules.

MOTORING

Greece's roads are not her greatest selling point. They are often rutted, washed out, snow blocked, or mud drenched; occasionally they give the impression of vanishing entirely. Don't start any motoring journey after dark. The countryside is so desolate that if a breakdown occurs, you can be stranded until dawn. Trucks begin their long hauls in the evening; their headlights can be blinding and they clog the major highways all through the night.

If you plan to motor extensively in this land, it is recommended that you join ELPA, the Greek Automobile and Touring Club. There is a registration fee of roughly $50 plus a charge of about $50 per year. This organization is similar to the American AAA. Among other services, it gives road assistance, legal advice if needed, and discounts on various gas coupons.

The traffic in the capital's narrow streets and its environs is simply indescribable. There is no way to believe it, except to see it.

CAR HIRE

There are several major self-drive companies in Athens. All feature competitive rates, but all are expensive by international standards.

Hellascars, at *148 Syngrou Ave.*, comes up with a variety of wheels, from VWs to station wagons to microbuses. **Hertz** is located at *12 Syngrou Ave.*, opposite the Temple of Jupiter. A fleet of drive-yourself small-to-medium-size vehicles is available. Delivery may be made anywhere in the metropolitan area for a small fee. Minimum age is 21. **Avis**, at *48 Queen Amalias Ave.* and the International Airport, offers similar cars. The minimum age for the renter is 25. Auto rental isn't cheap—but of course no cars are manufactured in Greece, and the import duties are responsible. On the islands, rates are even higher due to the short season. Japanese minis and jeep-type vehicles are prevalent. Scooters (mopeds) often are available, but think twice if you are going into mountains, because they are usually underpowered and worn out. Sharing a car may be more economical.

GASOLINE

When you ask for x gallons, the pump jockey will want a seemingly outrageous sum, even by today's mind-boggling prices. But don't squawk; he has just squeezed in British gallons, each one nearly a fifth larger than the U.S. measure.

SPORTS

MOUNTAINEERING AND SKIING

Snow skiing is of dubious worth to dedicated alpine enthusiasts, but facilities are developing steadily. **Mount Olympus** wears a white cap usually from mid-December to end-April, and **Mount Parnassus** can sometimes be skied even in May. The school at the latter is run by the National Tourist Organization. We've counted a dozen additional sites, most with one or two ski lifts each. For full details on other sites and training, contact the **Hellenic Federation of Mountaineering and Skiing**, *7 Karageorghi Servias St., Athens 126;* ☎ *3234555.*

FISHING

Because of the obvious abundance of sea fishery, river and lake angling receive low priority. Trout live at **Lake Tavropou** (*Karditsa*), **Kale Ladonos** (*Tripolis*), and in many cold running streams, especially in Epirus; you may not hook them legally between November 1 and February 15. Carp, eel, blenny, and sardines reside in the lakes of Thessaloniki, Ioannina, and Macedonia.

SIGHTSEEING

Learn traditional Greek dances in Rhodes. Courses start every Sun. from June 5-Sept. 25; regional styles are varied each week so you can expand your skills all through the summer. Weekly fee is about $80 for 30 hours of classes. For full information: Traditional Dance Center, *12 Massalias St., Athens 144;* ☎ *3609087, 2510801; or Old Town Theater, Rhodes;* ☎ *(0241) 29085, 20157.*

SHOPPING

SHOPPING HOURS

Not at all uniform: Mon. and Wed. from 8:30 a.m.-4:30 p.m., Tues., Thurs., Fri., 8:30 a.m.-2 p.m. and 5 p.m.-8 p.m. Please check locally about Sat. schedules. *The Plaka* area of Athens is a local exception; stores here don't miss a beat, staying open daily till 9 p.m.

THINGS NOT TO BUY

Ready-made dresses or suits (improving through the rash of Italian-style boutiques) and some Greek blouses. (The Hellenic figure has narrow shoulders and an ample bosom.)

WHERE TO GO

ARACHOVA

About 5 miles from Delphi on the road up from Athens is one of Greece's important rug-making hamlets. Antique shops and stalls line its streets. For whatever you buy, be sure to haggle, and expect most of your bluffs to be outbluffed. (The cliche "as shrewd as a rug merchant" is true!)

OSIOS LUKAS

Take a detour on the way to Arachova to admire the striking mosaic tiles in the 11th-century Byzantine monastery. This is not a spot for overnighting and barely a stop for snacking.

ATHENS

Don't believe the travel brochures, but you should experience a satiating feast of marvels anyway. For first-timers with visions of tranquil temples and romantic ruins, the initial impact of down-to-earth Athens with its endless concrete, ceaseless bumper-to-bumper traffic, eye-singeing pollution, and raucous noise can come as both an unexpected and unaesthetic jolt. When this happens, just look up at the elegant Parthenon rising far above the urban tangle. Its awesome presence never fails to mitigate the harsh intrusion of man's contemporary blight.

It's a capital both ancient and modern, with hardly any middle ground. The Golden Age of Pericles occurred in the 5th century B.C. when Attica was the matrix of civilization. Out of this grew the exquisite Acropolis, the plays of Sophocles and Euripides, orations of Demosthenes, the wisdom of Socrates and Plato, and seemingly the wealth of every thought process and concept that continues in modern form in western culture. Then, with the rise of Constantinople in the 4th century A.D., the Middle Ages passed Athens by. For almost 15 centuries Athens was overpowered and overshadowed by the Roman and Ottoman empires. In 1834, Athens was revived as the capital of a greatly reduced but proudly independent Greece.

DIRECTORY

U.S. Embassy • *91 Vassilissis Sophias Ave.*; ☎ *7212951* or *9+ 7218400-1.*

American Express • *Constitution Sq., 2 Ermou St.*; ☎ *3244975.*

Laundromat • Rex, *182 Syngrou Ave.*; ☎ *9564561.*

Barber and Hairdresser • Ioannidis, *3 Karageogi Servias St.*; ☎ *3223413*, and Ritsa Paul *Mitropoleos 16*; ☎ *3222189*; For ladies only. All hair salons closed Wed. afternoons.

Dry Cleaning and Pressing • Yavrilati Brothers, *67 Panepistimiou Ave.*

English-Speaking Doctor • Dr. G. Anastasopoulos, *14 Righillis St.*; ☎ *710964.*

English-Speaking Dentist • Dr. S. Kanellakis, *16 Voukourestiou St.*; ☎ *3621963*, or Dr. James C. Yantsios, *52 Vassilisis Sophias Ave.*; ☎ *720800.*

Police • *7 Syngrou Ave.*; ☎ *9214392* or *9239224.*

Favorite Pawnshop • Government Pawnshop, *40 Academias St.*; ☎ *3610457.*

HOW TO GET AROUND

BUSES

More than 41 bus routes crisscross the shrines of nearly every Athenian tourist attraction in sight. A ride costs 50 Drs.; you can buy individual tickets or books of ten; a limited tram circuit (50 Drs.) functions from midnight until 6 a.m. For surface forays, Constitution Square is the best place to board. Take Trolley #1, #12, to "Moussion" for the National Archaeological Museum, and to "Righilis" for the Byzantine Museum; take Bus #230 to the Acropolis for the Theater of Dionysus, the Herodes Atticus Theater, and to "Thissiion" for the Stoa of Attalus. You can walk from the point of origin to the Benaki Museum (2 blocks), the Museum of War Souvenirs (about 150 yards), the Zappion Gardens (same 150 yards), Hadrian's Arch and Temple of Zeus (about 200 yards), and the Tomb of the Unknown Soldier (in the Square). Ghennadios Library? Flag down Bus #023 at either Kolonaki Square or Kaningos Square; your destination is "Evangelismos." Subway trains meander throughout the central precincts and even out to Piraeus in 30 minutes, for a trifling outlay. Embark on these at Omonia Square. Should you care to forego this underground route on a balmy day, every green bus on Philellinon Street goes to the Ancient Theater of Piraeus; get off at the Navy Museum.

TAXIS

These are low priced but are generally full or off duty; if neither, they frequently stop to pick up other fares going your way. The rate (and it changes frequently) is 200 Drs. on the meter at the start; luggage is extra; fares are doubled from 1 to 5 a.m. Minimum fare is 280 Drs. Taxis are even more important than ever now that car traffic in the center is restricted (in order to reduce pollution). Private autos with even-number license plates may enter the center on specified days, odd-number ones on the alternate days. But taxis may roam all the time.

AIRPORTS

Athens has two airports: the Olympic, or west, one for all Olympic Airways flights; and the International, or east airport, for other international services and charter. A convenient bus from the latter to central Constitution Square costs about a dollar (200 Drs.).

WHERE TO STAY

If going to Athens for a week or more, visitors, especially those traveling with families, may want to consider apartment rentals, covered at the end of this section. These have resisted the inflation spiral a bit better than other capital hostels. Singles may be difficult to book because hoteliers often shove 2 beds into a micro-accommodation during high season. Get your reservation confirmed in writing whenever you can. After September you can probably haggle room rents down by as much as 20% off the summer rate. Since the heat builds up early in the season, April and May can be pleasant fringe months—and without the crowds.

LEAST $

Pension Thission • *2 Aghias Marinas; ☎ 3467634 or 3467655.* Sidewalk cafe pastry shop. Refreshing roof garden/bar with breathtaking panorama of Acropolis and Mount Lycabettus. Only 20 rooms; 2 boasting air conditioning; all with balcony and sitz bath. Clean, neat, and simple. Reserve early.

Theoxenia • *6 Gladstonos St.; ☎ 3600250.* 60 rooms, all with showers, and many featuring balconies. Rates very reasonable for value received.

Lydia • *121 Liossion St. (near the Larissa station on Bus Route #5); ☎ 8219980.* 35 units. May be worth the long haul from Constitution Square if your room is on one of the 2 newer top floors. These units have balconies, showers, and better amenities; 12 have Parthenon view. Good people, good welcome, and good value. Book first.

Keramikos • *30 Keramicou St.; ☎ 5247631.* 30 minuscule rooms, each with a tiny tub. Bar and cafeteria. Not bad.

Swiss Home • *7 Alkmanos St.; ☎ 710235.* 18 units at attractive prices. Proprietor speaks English; his wife and their 2 children also very hospitable.

Nestor • *58 Ag. Konstantinou St.; ☎ 5235576.* 54 rooms with bath or shower.

Apollon • *Deligheorghi 14; ☎ 5245211.* Better, though groups usually take up all of its 70 dens—each with shower or bath and radio, some with carpeting. Rear units quietest. Functional dining salon. Fair.

Epidauros • *14 Koumoundourou St.; ☎ 5230421*, and **Athinea**, *9 Vilara St.; ☎ 5234648.* Both in the shadow of Omonia Square and under the same man-

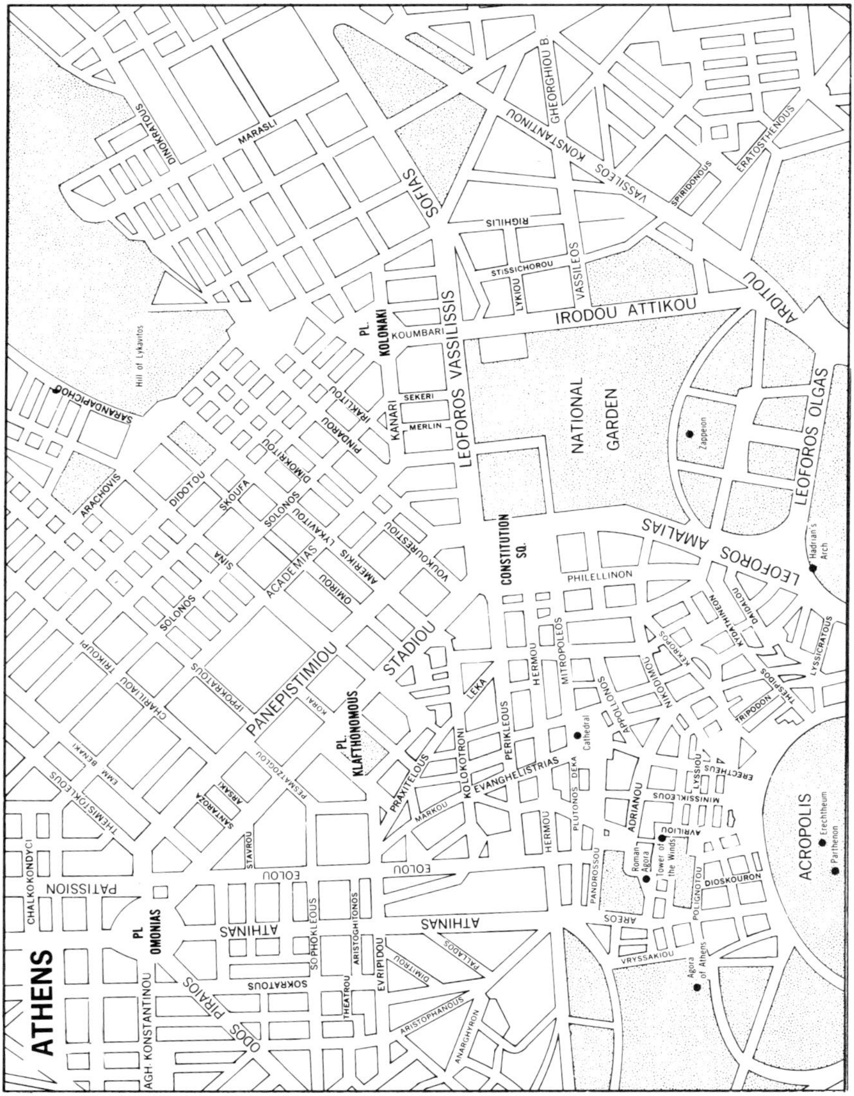
ATHENS
PL OMONIAS
PL. KLAFTHONOMOUS
PL. KOLONAKI
CONSTITUTION SQ.
NATIONAL GARDEN
ACROPOLIS
Erechtheum
Parthenon
Hill of Lykavitos
Zappeion
Hadrian's Arch
Cathedral
Roman Agora
Tower of the Winds
Agora of Athens
LEOFOROS VASSILISSIS SOFIAS
LEOFOROS AMALIAS
LEOFOROS OLGAS
VASSILEOS KONSTANTINOU
VASSILEOS GHEORGHIOU B.
IRODOU ATTIKOU
ARDITOU
ERATOSTHENOUS
SPIRIDONOUS
RIGHILIS
STISSICHOROU
LYKIOU
KOUMBARI
SEKERI
MERLIN
KANARI
IRAKLITOU
PINDAROU
DIMOKRITOU
SOLONOS
SKOUFA
DIDOTOU
SINA
ARACHOVIS
SARANDAPICHOU
MARASLI
DINOKRATOUS
LYKAVITOU
AMERIKIS
VOUKOURESTIOU
ACADEMIAS
OMIROU
TRIKOUPI
CHARILAOU
IPPOKRATOUS
PANEPISTIMIOU
STADIOU
KORAI
EMM BENAKI
THEMISTOKLEOUS
ARSAKI
SANTAROZA
PESMATZOGLOU
STAVROU
EOLOU
PATISSION
CHALKOKONDYCI
AGH. KONSTANTINOU
ATHINAS
SOPHOKLEOUS
ARISTOGHITONOS
SOKRATOUS
PIRAIOS ODOS
THEATROU
EVRIPIDOU
DIMITROU
PALLADOS
ARISTOPHANOUS
ANARGHYRON
PRAXITELOUS
MARKOU
KOLOKOTRONI
LEKA
PERIKLEOUS
EVANGHELISTRIAS
HERMOU
MITROPOLEOS
PHILELLINON
PLUTONOS DEKA
APPOLLONOS
NIKODIMOU
KEKROPOS
KYDATHINEON
DAIDALOU
LYSSICRATOUS
THESPIDOS
TRIPODON
ERECTHEUS
LYSSIOU
MINISSIKLEOUS
ADRIANOU
AVRILIOU
PANDROSSOU
DIOSKOURON
POLIGNOTOU
AREOS
VRYSSAKIOU

agement; 89 rooms between them, about 3/4 with bath or shower and private balcony. Clean, but somewhat scuffed.

Achilles • *21 Lekka St. (near Constitution Square); ☎ 3223197.* Not to be confused with the Achillion described elsewhere, because this one is more modest. Reasonable rentals. Breakfast available; 23 of its 32 doubles expandable to 3rd-person alcove demisuites at a 20% hike in tariff.

Hermes • *19 Apollonos St.; ☎ 3235514.* Handy to Constitution Square. Bar, luncheon restaurant, and cafeteria. Colorful roof garden for warmweather dining looking at Acropolis; half-board required.

Nefeli • *16 Hyperidou St.* A good bet for visitors who enjoy the Plaka district (the Chelsea or Greenwich Village of Athens). Tandem rates of close to $45. Special, chiefly for its amiable location.

Omonia • *☎ 5237210.* 275 rooms on cacophonous square of the same name. Flashy public areas; restaurant and bars overlooking the action. Private terrace, bare walls, tiny storage areas, lamps with firefly wattage. The prices fit.

Amaryllis • *45 Veranzerou St.; ☎ 5238738.* 60 rooms, all with private plumbing.

Cleo's Guest House • *18 Apollonos St.; ☎ 3235640.* An abundantly kind boardinghouse with fine service.

Acropolis House • *Kodrou 6; ☎ 3222344.* Not unlike Cleo's. Top floor boasts a neckstraining view of the Acropolis.

Hostel Pnica • *51 Apostolou Pavlou St.; ☎ 3468859.* Faces a park near the Parthenon. Two of its 10 simple doubles with private plumbing.

Aristides and **Semiramis** • *50 Sokratous St.; ☎ 522388 and 18 Aristotelous St.; ☎ 5223046.* Both grim and cheerless.

Marina • *13 Voulgari St.; ☎ 5237832.* 81 dreary units, but rates are low.

Pythagorion • *28 Ag. Konstantinou St.; ☎ 5242811.* Fresh and appealing for its category; 106 pillows.

Athens House • *4 Aristotelous St.; ☎ 5240539.* A friendly traveler says this is a good buy and that the multilingual proprietor is a kind host. On earlier inspection I found the site noisy for light sleepers.

Paradise Hostel • *Mezonos and Akominatou Sts.* (*100 yards from the railroad station*); *☎ 5220084.* Haven't checked it out. Rooms of 2-5 beds ranging from $8.50 per person, inclusive of kitchen privileges and a hot shower day or night.

YMCA • *28 Omirou St.; ☎ 3626970.* Charges about $7.50 per single.

XEN (YWCA) • *11 Amerikis St.; ☎ 3624291.* An especially good bet. Central location. Spacious lounge. Low-cost public cafeteria. Overnights start at about $9.50 for dorm bed, to $21 for a single, breakfasts included. Although enforcement has been lax, there's a rule against accepting anyone over 25.

The price is the main factor for this homely trio. Way down on the list for all three. **Alma**, *(5 Dorou St.; ☎ 5240858).* A full house—114. **Asty** *(2 Pireous St.; ☎ 5230424).* Can accommodate 224 visitors. **Florida** *(25 Menandour St.; ☎ 5239712).* Space for 127 guests.

PRIVATE HOMES

The **Tourist Police** (*headquarters at Syngrou Ave. 7; ☎ 9239224*) place foreign visitors (voluntarily) in Athenian homes during the high season. If necessary, you can count on these officials for adequate shelter.

MORE $$

Lycabette • *6 Valaoritou St.; ☎ 3633514.* Convenient side-street entrance near Constitution Square. Most accommodations with shower and balcony; radios. Lounge. A reader complained of faulty air conditioning, so be sure to ask if it works in the room you are given—and don't let them charge you for it if it doesn't. Basically, this is a worthy stop.

Athenian Inn • *22 Haritos St. in Kolonaki; ☎ 7238097.* Offers 63 kips at the foot of Lycabettus in a well-regarded district. Prices are midrange while facilities are higher than many others in this category.

Arethusa • *6-8 Mitropoleos (near Constitution Square); ☎ 3229438.* Offers viewful roof garden, mezzanine cafeteria, and 85 quiet panel-windowed bedchambers with radio, carpet, and air conditioning. Ask for a unit ending in "01" or "08"—in the same moderate price range as the standard twins, but providing an extra dividend in scenery and space.

Stanley • *1-5 Odysseos St., Karaiskaki Square; ☎ 5241611.* Group-oriented. Drive-you-crazy traffic noise. New wing grafted to 350-unit original. Bar, tearoom, and restaurant; barber and hairdresser; garage; rooftop pool. Pretty fair bedrooms, no view, baths somewhat raw. Big-bed singles from $28; duos for $45 with the day's first meal; add 25% for air conditioning.

Alfa • *17 Chalkokondyli St.; ☎ 5243584.* Lounge and cafeteria. All 100 rooms with tub or shower; some ample and attractive, others not; five 8th-floor units with private balcony. Tour parties pour in during summer. Satisfactory.

Plaka • *7 Kapmikares St.; ☎ 3222096.* Restaurant and rooftop Taverna Plaka. All 70 chambers with bath or shower; some with terraces; rear units with beautiful view of Acropolis; 5th and 6th floors best.

St. George Lycabettus • *2 Kleomenous (Platia Dexamenis); ☎ 7290710.* Good view of the Acropolis from the rooftop restaurant/bar; quiet neighborhood. Doubles now soaring to $75-plus!

Athens Gate • *10 Syngrou Ave.; ☎ 9238302/9.* Again, a roof garden overlooking Acropolis. Doubles up to a thundering $85. This and the above are examples of inflation pioneers in the capital—more than doubling their rates in a few short seasons.

Omiros • *15 Apollonos St.; ☎ 3235486.* In fun Plaka precinct. Cheery lounge; snack bar; restaurant; small summer roof garden overlooking the cityscape. All accommodations sport bath or shower and small terraces. Ask for double #505. A nice spirit.

Tempi • *29 Eolou St.; ☎ 3213175.* Another good value in the Plaka. The Kanakis family who runs it has made many American friends.

Sirene • *15 Lagoumitzi St.; ☎ 9229310.* 103 units on ear-shattering approach route to airport. Commercial zone developing into a hotel district. Roof restaurant and pool; lobby diner. Clean, airy rooms with wide windows.

Atlantic • *60 Solomon St.;* ☎ *5235361.* 144 cramped rooms, all with bath or shower.

Candia • *40 Diligianni St.;* ☎ *5246112.* Renewal not long ago providing uplifted space for 254 persons.

Achillion • *32 Aghiou Konstantinou;* ☎ *5225618.* 63 balconied units; 14 back chambers quieter. Clean and rather appealing.

Jason • *Nikiforou 3-5;* ☎ *5248031.* Dull bar and lounge. Lower floors with splendid view of a wretched dumpyard; levels 6, 7, and 8 far better for vistas. Provides a few 6-person rooms.

Eretria • *12 Chalkokondyli St., Kaningos Square;* ☎ *3635311.* Signs of wear in fusty lobby, bar, and lounge. Central air conditioning. Sitz baths almost throughout.

Arcadia • *46 Marnis St.;* ☎ *5226571.* Not too far from Omonia Square. Clean but spartan. Small lounge-bar. About 65% of its 100 rooms with private plumbing. Medium-low rates.

Minoa • *12 Karolou St.;* ☎ *5234622.* Frequently prebooked to the rafters with Club Mediterranée members, but you may register if there's space. Bistro de Paris restaurant; 7th-floor roof garden. 50 rooms, all with bath or shower and balcony; each named for a village with a Club outpost.

Stadion • *38 Vas. Konstantinous Ave.;* ☎ *7226054.* Total of 70 average-size but charmless units. Strictly for shelter.

Myrto House • *40 Nikis St.;* ☎ *3234560.* Equally blah.

Solomos • *72 Solomou St.;* ☎ *5231435.* Boasts a lobby-lounge, small bar-let and the following: "Cool air—when available—at no extra charge." (Do you think that means in winter?)

Titania • *52 Panepistimiou Ave.;* ☎ *3609611/9.* An aesthetically sterile candidate with 333 rooms, handy central location, and parking. Steep tariffs.

Dorian Inn • *15 Pireos St.;* ☎ *5239782.* Inn-vites you to 150 air-conditioned rooms and pool. Preponderance of tour groups.

EVEN MORE $$$

King Minos • *1 Pireos St.;* ☎ *5231111.* Conveniently yet somewhat noisily sited near Omonia Square. Lounge, bar, hairdresser and barbershop. King-size bedchambers. Full air conditioning. Marble baths with colored tubs and W.C.s. A superb value.

Electra • *5 Hermou St. Constitution Square;* ☎ *3223222.* Extensive renovations here (as in the entire Electra chain in recent months), good air conditioning, 180 capacity, 100% tub ratio, fine restaurant, cafeteria plus snack bar. Recommended.

Electra Palace • *Nikodimou St. 18;* ☎ *3241401.* Electra's younger sister, but almost the same size; Plaka district address; swimming pool.

Golden Age • *57 Michalakopoulos St.;* ☎ *740861.*

Parthenon • *6 Makri St.;* ☎ *9234594.*

Ermeion • *66 Ermou St.;* ☎ *3212753.* Only a short stroll from Constitution Square and Monesteraki.

Esperia Palace • *22 Stadiou St.; ☎ 3238000.* Restaurant, cafeteria, and little bar; 185 rooms with veranda and private bath; several air-cooled; squat-down tubs numerous. Bid for an upper to take advantage of the vista and to avoid traffic din.

Astor • *16 Karageorgi Servias St. (near Constitution Square); ☎ 3255555.* 133 air-conditioned chambers. Bar and rooftop restaurant. Efficiency bedrooms with radio, doubles feature private balcony, a plethora of ultra-tiny baths with 2-step tubs, 3 suites. Solid and worthy.

Galaxy • *22 Academias Ave.; ☎ 3632831.* Bar, snack counter, and restaurant. Air conditioning. 108-room capacity. Good value.

APARTMENTS

Except where noted, no restaurant facilities.

Riva • *114 Michalacopoulou St.* (*in the Hilton district*); *☎ 7706611.* Offers the brightest amenities of all—often better, in fact, than facilities at the leading deluxe hostelries at double the price for a fraction of the space. Snackery and bar; 7 rooms and 60 apartments with air conditioning, maid service, music consoles, and homey touches. Nice kitchens, full range of utensils provided free of charge, ceramic-tile baths, plenty of storage area; quiet. No minimum stay required. Most apartments comprise a foyer, a lounge or salon, and top level 1 or 2 bedrooms. Prices? 2-bedroom spreads with salon about $115 per day; sleeping unit for $90; normal twin-bedded hotel rooms for about $75. Rates reduced for stays of more than 15 days. Garage and probably by now a restaurant.

Ariane • *22 Timoleondos Vassou St.* (*near the American Embassy*); *☎ 6466361.* 25 units in a quiet residential zone. Easy parking. Shopping nearby. Ample furnishings, air conditioning, modern kitchens, good closet space, and immaculate baths. One-room accommodations (for a couple) at $63; $81 for parlor and balcony; 1 large suite with a pair of bedchambers and twin terraces for almost $100; 20% winter discount. Excellent.

The Embassy • *down the street at #15; ☎ 6421152.* Older, but still comfortable. No air conditioning; daily maid service; babysitting nannies. Modest but adequate appointments at reasonable rates. Deservedly popular with U.S. Foreign Service personnel.

Kolonaki Flats • *7 Kapsali St.; ☎ 713759.* Quiet site. First and second floors with larger units and kitchenettes; fourth level devoted to studios. Its $85 twins are great values.

CAMPING

Campers find **ELPA** a great help for caravan data. The initials stand for the Automobile and Touring Club of Greece (*6 Amerikis St.*; *☎ 77916 15*). **Dafni**, the lone entry in the Athens area, is 6-1/4 miles along the road to *Delphi.* The **NTOG** (mentioned at the very beginning of this chapter) can give you lists of parking sites nationwide, or ask at the **Greek Camping Association** (*102 Solonos St., Athens; ☎ 3621560*).

SUGGESTIONS FOR STUDENTS

Two Athens precincts that buzz with collegians are **Neapolis** and **Exarcheia**. Each is near Constitution Square and the University complex at Odos Panepistimiou.

LODGINGS

The **YMCA** and the **YWCA** are both covered under "Where to Stay—Least $." At their low cost, they are great when compared with some of the other digs in this capital. Look for their XAN or XEN signs.

Pension Zina • *23 Appollos St.* Also offers special accommodations for students; they pay about $9 per bunk.

Hotel Carolina • *57 Kolokotroni St.* A double without breakfast rents for $23. The people here are exceptionally kind.

Athens Youth Hostel • *57 Kypselis St.* ☎ *8225860.* The only hostel recognized by the International Youth Hostel Organization. International student I.D. required. Reservations should be made in advance. Beds about $4.50 a night.

Pagration • *75 Damareos;* ☎ *7519530.* You'll pay slightly less and it's open all year. No student ID card necessary; hot showers, washing machine, no curfew; a family operation.

Athens Connection • *20 Ioulianou St.* Housed in a 6-story building with single, double, or triple rooms, private or common facilities, a 6 a.m.-noon breakfast term, an all-day bar, luggage and safe storage, plus assistance in making travel bookings. We've heard praise, and it sounds ideal, but we've never seen it personally.

DISCOUNTS

The Student Section of **Viking Travel Co.**, (*3 Philellinon St.;* ☎ *3229383*) can stretch your cash assets by offering 10-40% reductions on surface transport to Italy, Turkey, Israel, and other Mideast points, special rail and air package plans, and a galaxy of domestic bus and boat tours to scholars only. Popular and reliable. Another operator, **Transexpress** (*28 Nikis St.;* ☎ *3224255,* FAX *216633*), specializes in youth transportation.

WHERE TO EAT

LEAST $

Delphi • *13 Nikis St. (Just off Constitution Sq.).* Continues to earn well-deserved success. Delicious national specialties; 60 crowded tables humming from noon-1 a.m.

Brothers • *Viktorias Sq.* A Corfu import. Pick your own repast before sitting down. Fish plates especially fresh and well presented.

Xinou • *4 Geronta St.* One of the top Plaka stops. Tumbledown to the eye; 3 wandering musicians play exquisite folk melodies while wearing Buster Keaton expressions. Almost exclusively Greek clientele. The drill here is to snag a table early, pick your platters on an all-share-a-bite basis, and enjoy a feast. Guests mill freely in the open kitchens among the owners, cooks, waiters, and cousins. Inexpensive and definitely recommended. Since it serves the best cookery (of its type) in Athens, you'd best reserve because there's seldom a seat free any time of the year.

Syntrivani tou Syntagmatos • *5 Philellinon St.* 61 tables in a labyrinth of straw-lined corridors; covered wooden veranda, gravel patio, garden. Full meals in the $13 neighborhood. Simple and worthy.

Meteora • *Xenofonos 10.* Sterile and basic decor; 18 tables at ground level; 20 more on upper balconette. Spotless, modern kitchen. Specialties: shrimp with rice in casserole or veal shish kebab. Their boast, "Enjoy Home Cooking."

Galleria • *Panepistimiou 52.* Very inexpensive and very good for hot and cold snacks, pastries, pizza, and ice cream. The location is in the finest shopping tenderloin.

TAVERNAS

For a change of atmosphere and diet, pay a visit to a typical taverna. The previously mentioned **Xinou** could be considered in this category, too. It is unusual and a sound value. These famous institutions, most of which operate during the colder months only, feature rotisserie-type grills, hearty menus, wine from huge barrels, folk music that is often deafening, and informal family-style hospitality. Within the city (not the environs), most do not serve lunch; evening is the time to go.

Barba Statis • *19 Kydathineon St.; ☎ 3225084.* Bright, open kitchen; 8 couples can be shoehorned in for dinner. Fair cookery. Sensible tariffs with specialties in the $9 range. Open for lunch and until 1 a.m.

Kritiku • *24 Mmissikleous St.* 4 rooms that offer an escape from the traditional sidewalk cracklings of shish kebab (souvlaki). More kebab joints than you can shake a shish at on this street.

Riga • Does its summer thing *in Plaka on Kyrissou St.*; in winter *at the junction of Adrianou* and *Yperidou streets.* Worth the chase in any season.

SNACKS OR LIGHT MEALS

Try the souvlakia stands at the end of Mitropoleos St., heading into Monastiraki. The coffee-bar trade is percolating vigorously.

Brazilian • *Stoa Kalliga Arcade at 4 Karageorgi Servias St.* It's one of the best. At street-level counter, canapes and other light bites for $4; upstairs a cheery triangular food bar, plus nearly a score of tables; open all week from 8 a.m.-11 p.m.

Diomia • *5 Diomias St.* Continues its deserved popularity. On a summer night it is relaxing to sit at the open-air cafe in Plaka's lovely

Kapnikareas Square • This is a definitive Greek experience for after-dinner people-watching.

Elysee • *1 Mitropoleos St.* A 24-hour contender, but lacks charm—and air conditioning. Sidewalk seating at 10 tables in an arcade; indifferent cookery except for the pastry-work.

Pizza Riviera • *61 Ipirou; ☎ 8816873.* First-rate pizza for about $6. Family atmosphere.

Floca • *16 Emmanuel Benaki St.* Whips up attractive self-service offerings, plus soda-fountain-style specialties; good.

Atheneon • *In the Esperia Hotel (Stadiou St. at Ed. Low St.).* Substantial and worthy.

Grill • *At the Delphi Hotel (1 Aghiou Konstantinou Sq.).* Also substantial and worthy.

Don't forget the tictacs, those sizzling little stands clustered around *Omonia* and *Constitution Squares*; their freshly flamed, $2.50 souvlakia is terrific.

MORE $$

Vassilena • *Corner of Etolikon and Vitolion Sts., port of Piraeus.* An amazing grocery shop-restaurant, 20 minutes from the heart of Athens. No menu; 1-price, no-choice parade of perhaps 20 dishes that will take you 2-1/2 hours to consume. On last visit, this was only part of the meal: raw clams, herring, headcheese, milk cheese, shrimp, octopus, dolmades, whiting, lobster, batter-fried shrimp, garlic-treated Vienna sausages, red mullet, tarama salad, moussaka, and oranges—not to mention lemon soup as the next-to-last course. Price of this gargantuan repast? Only around $18 (without wine) per person! Lunch and dinner served but Never on Sunday. Only about 14 tables.

Facyo • *5 Efroniou St.* A bit more expensive but a delight in almost every way. About 18 tables decked by an ornate, colorful, ancient-style Macedonian ceiling. Choose appetizers from refrigerated cases (Turkish dried sardines, garlic yogurt, dolmades, redfish roe mousse, and lots more); hot dishes in adjoining segment.

Corfou • *6 Kriezotou St.* (*a step from the King's Palace Hotel*). Simple, spotless, reasonable, and enormously popular. Rustic front area; more refined rear; rush-rush atmosphere.

EVEN MORE $$$

Dionyssos • *43 Rovertou Galli;* ☎ *9233182.* Almost as important as the Parthenon to the tourist trade. Pleasant to watch the sound-and-light spectacle on the Acropolis as you dine! Best view from upstairs terrace; below for snacks and libations. Captains frequently hard sell costly dishes. Nearly always jammed evenings, so reserve well in advance. Open from 8 a.m. to 2 a.m.

To Steki • *1 Trias St.;* ☎ *8218048.* A perennial favorite. Choose in typical Greek fashion from the food counter. But if you don't make your desires known, a huge, multicourse, delicious fixed meal will appear for about $36, including local wine. One of the best of its type.

Yerofinika • *10 Pindarou St.;* ☎ *3622719.* Approach through a narrow alley. Diet-busting dishes, including desserts that deserve commendation.

Nine Plus Nine • *Platia Stadiou.* Dinner only in one segment; disco in the other; order table in advance.

Steak Room • *6 Aeginitou St.*; ☎ *7217445.* Many American patrons; 25 tables. Most expensive cuts sell for around $18, including green salad, baked potato, or French fries. A bit of Americana: ice water appears automatically.

NIGHTLIFE

Ever try a *bouzouki*? The official restraint has been lifted on the devilmay-care custom...when excitement reaches a climax. Today this simple and inexpensive merriment of yore has become a startlingly expensive pastime. First, the customer has no trouble in spending up to $40 per person for the dinner. Second, the crockery and the small baskets of flowers that are thrown are purchased by the piece—the cost of the latter averaging from $10 to an uncanny $40 per unit (for only cheap bus station crockery)!

If you go, sit well away from the stage or protect your eyes from flying fragments. The heavy action generally starts after midnight.

Fantis • *In the Plaka district.* Fair, but we can't really forgive the management for spoofing up the evening with electronic musical assists. Our meal was routine-to-poor. One dancer carried a table clenched between his teeth—more tender, we'll wager, than our beefsteak.

Dilina • *At distant Glyfada.* Ranks in the top league at the moment.

Kalokerinos • *10 Kekropos St.* Not a favorite of ours.

Mostrou • *Mnissikleous St.* A cabaret also in the Plaka district, which pulls at the strings of many an Athenian heart with its own show backed by folk music.

As is the case with most nightspots, they rise and fall rapidly—frequently disappearing altogether before the print in this book is dry. Athenian nighteries seem to be particularly fickle, so for your up-to-the-instant convenience and fun we're going to list the top bouzouki players and singers currently in vogue. If you can pinpoint where they are at the moment of your visit (with the help of some local tip-sheet or your concierge), you could derive heaps of musical lore in a short time. They are: *Doukissa, Alexiou, Argyrakis, Miropanos, Sakellariou, Parios, Bithikotsis, Hadji, Poulopoulos, Voskopoulos, Marinella, Moscholiou, Kokotas, Mitsakis, Tsitsanis, and Zabetas*—and they're generally considered to be the Carusos of the troupe.

Rebetika, the hard-edged yet haunting "blues" of the Greek underworld, is enjoying a revival in Athens; it's played on the bouzouki and the baglama.

Pigi Tou Rebetikou • *Agia Glykeria 11, Galatsi;* ☎ *2921820.* Best known *rebetika* center.

Taximi • *Isavron 29, Exarcheia;* ☎ *3639919.*

Quasimodo • *Tsakalof 13, Kolonaki;* ☎ *3618339.*

Harama • *Skopeftirion, Kaiseriani;* ☎ *7664869.*

The continuing popularity of taverns has caused a major nightclub debacle. **Galaxy** is one of the front-runners. Big time entertainment nightly; high but value-filled tabs; nearly always crowded. Be sure to reserve ahead. **Fantasia** is a lesser light. **Copacabana**, now at *4 Kallirois St.*, produces the biggest floor of all. Sort of a Levantine version of any gin mill or bump-and-grind emporium one might find in any big city. The geography changes, but the game's the same. **Athinea** offers winter-only dancing at *6 Venizelou Ave.*; in summer it gallops to an enchanting open-air site at the racecourse. No cover charge; no cabaret; passable vittles; dinner reservations mandatory.

DISCOTHEQUES

Platters spin at the **Galaxy** *of the Hilton.* **Nine Muses**, the previously mentioned **Nine Plus Nine**, and the **Stardust** wrap up the disc'n'dance scene. **Take Five** is a disco-diner; very popular with hungry night owls.

WHAT TO SEE AND DO

Highlights among the classic attractions in or near Athens include the **National Archaeological Museum** (priceless ancient treasures); the **Benaki Museum** (more modern Greek and Levantine displays); the interesting **Museum of War Souvenirs**; the **Byzantine Museum**; the **Ghennadios Library** (Byzantine books, manuscripts, and art objects)—plus such world-famous ruins as the **Acropolis** with its **Parthenon**. This landmark is under such serious siege from air pollution, spike heels, and jet vibrations that a project is under way to halt the 20th-century corrosion; some measures include prohibiting cars and tourist buses from parking in the area, shuttering factories, gas, and electricity plants in the vicinity, and using low-sulfur content fuels in nearby apartments. A number of sculptures have been placed in the Acropolis Museum, while replicas have been substituted on the building itself. Over the next 10 years, the Parthenon will be disassembled and renewed—an undertaking unprecedented in the annals of archaeological restoration.

You should also try to see **Hadrian's Arch of Triumph**, the **Temple of Zeus**, the **Theater of Dionysus**, the **Stoa of Attalus**, the **Goulandris Natural History Museum**, and the **National Picture Gallery**. Museums generally snooze one day a week, most often Monday or Tuesday. Entry is usually about $3.

Son et Lumière ("Sound and Light") spectacles are presented 3 times nightly between Apr. 15 and Oct. 15 at the Acropolis. More than 1500 varicolored floodlights play over the site for 45 minutes, accompanied by a musical score and a dialogue in English, French, or German. (Find out the time in advance for your language preference.) Not scheduled on full-moon evenings; seating on the *Hill of Pnyx*. Summertime concerts by the **Athens State Orchestra** or ancient drama performances in the **Herodes Atticus Theater** at the base of the Acropolis are wonderful. The combination of romantic antiquities and starlit nights is unforgettable. If you're a June-Sept. visitor, don't miss the **Epidarus Drama Festival**—Greek theater at its purest, featuring the top stars of the nation.

The **Zappion Gardens** are renowned for their art shows, held at intervals throughout the year.

Folk dancing (*Dora Stratou*) takes place under the stars nightly, weather permitting, from June-Sept., at the theater on the west flank of the Philoppapus Hill, across the Acropolis. In the Plaka, incidentally, there is an engaging display of costumes and tapestry at the **Folklore Museum** (*19 Kidnarthineon St.*). Also in this district try to visit **Anafiotika**, an island culture recreated in loving and living detail on the north face of the Acropolis.

The cable railway on **Mount Lycabettus** whisks sightseers from Plutarchou and Aristippou streets through a 225-yard tunnel to its crown in 10 minutes (for pennies). At the top: a restaurant and snack bar.

CONCERTS

The glistening new **Athens Concert Hall** stands proudly on Vassilissis Sophias Ave., opposite the U.S. Embassy, an edifice of white masonry and tinted glass. Major performers and orchestras already are appearing here. Tickets begin at about $10, depending on the artist or group. During high summer, the previously mentioned **Herodes Atticus Theatre** hosts the capital's popular music and drama festival. In the past, performers have been selected so that almost all the virtuosi have been Greek, but lately names such as Bolshoi and Covent Garden have been luring international audiences. Check the season's program beforehand and pick up your tickets in advance at the Syntagma Square bureau.

MOVIES

The **Attikon** and the **Apollon** show in English; the trouble is neither is open in summer. But the city's drive-ins are; your concierge can tell you what's playing, as can the newspapers. Many show in English.

MARKETS

The famous old **Varvakion Market** has been razed. Now in the neighborhood of *Athinas, Armodion*, and *Aristoyiton* streets, you will find most of the meat, fish, fruit, and vegetable stalls that have been temporarily displaced by the demolition and reconstruction.

SPORTS

Wonderful swimming, fishing, and skin diving from late Apr. (summer comes early) to late Sept. In the area are *Voula* and *Vouliagmeni* (favored); also lovely and less than 1 hour away are *Varkiza, Agios Andreas, Rafina, Kavouri*, and *Glyfada*. Most charge minimal fees for lockers, chairs, umbrellas, and sometimes, fresh-water showers. Vouliagmeni has water-skiing. The **National Swimming Pool** near the Olympic Stadium is open only 4 hours daily (12:30–4:30 p.m. weekdays; 9 a.m.–2 p.m. Sun.). Tennis and golf also can be found around the capital.

PUBLICATIONS

This Week in Athens, *The Week in Athens*, and the monthly edition of *The Athenian* are invaluable source material on local events.

WHERE TO SHOP

ART REPRODUCTIONS

Both the **Benaki Museum** and the **National Archaeological Museum** have shops that sell moderately priced replicas of some of the best works in their collections.

COPPER ARTICLES

Take a stroll along **Ifestou St**. for the darnedest assortment of copper utensils and bric-a-brac you've probably ever seen.

FLEA MARKET

Pandrossou St. is the beginning of the Athens equivalent—known as **Monastiraki**—grand fun for the bargain hunter and antique hound, if they hit it at the right moment. Operative daily from 9 a.m.-1:30 p.m. and 5-8 p.m.; weekends from 8 a.m.-2 p.m. This lane feeds into Ifestou St.

HANDICRAFTS

These or the other regional souvenirs are the first thing trippers see—and usually seek. Scads of cheapjack joints brassily overcrowd the center of the city. **Attalos** (*3 Stadiou St.*) is a calm haven in this agitated sea and there's a plenitude of high-quality objects to gratify you. An interesting handicraft candidate is the **National Welfare Fund** *(24A Voukourestiou St. plus Boutique in Hilton)*. The excellently wrought tulip-design needlepoint work can be had as a throw-cushion cover. Then there's the permanent exhibition of **Greek Folk Art and Handicrafts** *(9 Mitropoleos St.)*, which is certainly worth a visit.

MUSIC

Music Box *(2 Nikis St. and 52 Panepistimou St.)* is a sure-fire bet for the latest and most popular bouzouki recordings. Cassettes cost around $5.

RUGS

Karamichos-Mazarakis *(31-33 Voulis St.)* for at least 400 years—probably a thousand!—has been the leading creator of Greece's *flokati*—gorgeous, fluffy, 100% virgin wool floor coverings. These gems of the textile world get better with wear. They are loomed only by hand and are the finest in the world, in our opinion. Don't miss their Mykonos branch on Harbor Road at the port if you're island hopping.

SHOPPING ZONES

The **Constitution (Syntagma) Sq**. area and the **Plaka** district.

CORFU

A little charmer measuring 48 by 20-1/2 miles and boasting 150,000 residents—1/5 of them in the city proper. Albania—you can't swim over without a visa—is only a half mile away. (The strife in this former Communist bastion is so pronounced, don't even think about going.) Corfu island has more than 5 million olive trees, but olive oil, the only industry that challenges tourism, has finally lost its lead against the mushrooming facilities for the traveler. Here is a floral paradise—the principal garden spot of Greece—chiefly because of the rich soil and high rainfall. The gentle atmosphere is scented by wildly rampant natural blossoms—wisteria, jasmine, dahlias, camellias, and mimosa. The airport has been enlarged; Olympic wings in with Boeings; a few jets swoop in on international runs; BA has a link with London.

The Italy-Greece car ferries run from 3 to 7 days per week, depending upon the time of year. Smaller craft make daily runs to and from the Greek mainland. **Corfu**, its capital and main port, has no commercial fishing interests whatever. The best swimming is at the Yacht Club. **Dassia** (4 miles) splashes up next. **Paleocastritsa** (40 minutes) is packed with bathers. **Ermones** is pebbly. **Sidari** has sand, but it's an hour's drive. **Kanoni** (2 miles) is rocky and not too appealing. **Mon Repos**, in the town itself, isn't worth the effort.

WHERE TO STAY

Corcyra Beach Hotel • *Perches bright and white on a slope above Gouvia Bay (5 miles from Corfu town).* 20 bedchambers in the central complex; more than 100 individual bungalows; swimming pool plus 2 private beaches. Simple, clean, worth every drachma.

The Kanoni • *One mile south of Corfu.* A horizontal slab containing a rather poor restaurant-by-pool, 150 bedchambers (mostly twins) with balconies, air conditioning; telephones, and baths; service office rushed and rude.

Astir-Corfu • *On the noisy main street of the port.* Not too appealing.

Swiss and **Splendid** • They are both small, with no private plumbing.

The Messonghi • An unimaginative edifice wrapped round 462 sterile rooms; boringly traditional lobby; fair beach.

Delfinia • Neighboring the above, it has 4-stories, is fair in amenities but full of groups.

Oasis • Crassly commercial but boasts a good location.

Grand • *10 miles west of the capital.* Its brochure (top-heavy with photos of girls surfing elsewhere) plumps for 210 air-cooled rooms, suites, and apartments, each with its own bath, phone, and radio.

Palace • *At Kondokali.* It's first-class and young.

Chandris • *At Dassia.* Offers both hotel and bungalow accommodations.

Across the island, you'll find the **Mega** and the **Costa** in *Ypsos* and 2 small ones at *Zephysos.*

AUTHOR'S OBSERVATION

Cabs are metered. Make a flat rate in hiring cars. Bikes and scooters are very cheap to rent.

NIGHTLIFE

The Hilton's Casino offers a shaft of moonlight to the otherwise dreary after dark situation. Within this fun-loving oasis you'll find roulette, baccarat, and boule. Gaming rooms open from 5 p.m. to 4 a.m. **Dichtia** features bands, dancing, and alfresco revels in summer. **Rignatela**, a regional haven, is along the route to the Miramare Beach. **Taverna Avra** takes its name from its hometown facing Ulysses Island, the spot where the Homeric hero trysted for 12 years.

SHOPPING

Look for handicrafts at **The National Welfare Organization** (*8 Kapodistriou St.*), traditional jewelry at **Spilia Oro** (*Nik. Theotoki 119*), unusual hand-painted dresses, skirts, and T-shirts at **Aris** (*74 Nikiforou Theotoki St.*), and for catchy tunes and haunting laments try **Irene Kefalinos Music House** (*nearby to Aris*).

CORINTH

Do find time to ascend the 1900-foot **Acropolis** at *Acrocorinth* for the view of the Peloponnesian mountains, Parnassus, and the Corinthian and Saronic gulfs. The remains of the 6th-century B.C. **Temple of Apollo** and the **Baths of Aphrodite** in Ancient Corinth easily take 2nd and 3rd prizes. Because a large part of the city was leveled by earthquakes, most of the buildings of the anno domini period look uneasily pseudomodern.

CRETE

Except for Athens and its three neighboring one-day excursion targets of **Delphi**, the **Apollo Coast Road to Cape Sounion** and the **Peloponnesus**, here is certainly the greatest magnet for foreign visitors to the nation. Scandinavians, Germans, and British are the vanguard of the invaders, in that order. Although individual voyagers swarm here in profusion, they are overwhelmingly outnumbered by tour groups.

Here are some thumbnail gleanings:

Geography • This largest of the Greek islands is vaguely shaped like a deer's torso. It is 160 miles long but never more than 36 miles wide. Variegated terrain ranges from beaches and plains to rolling foothills to the rugged mountains of up to more than 8000 feet forming its central spine. On the same latitude as Tripoli in North Africa.

Population • About 460,000.

Climate • So beneficient that you can safely squeeze in an extra month on either end of the normal European tourist season.

Industry • Olive oil, wine, nuts, citrus fruit, dairying, and small mineral workings; raisins are a prime export.

Culture • Western civilization was born here about 3000 B.C. when the Minoans migrated from Asia Minor. Through causes still unknown to archaeologists or historians, this great power mysteriously vanished 1600 years later—possibly due to the tidal waves caused by the eruption of Santorini's volcano. Since then Crete has been occupied by the Dorian Greeks, the Romans, the Genoese, the Venetians, the Turks, England, France, Russia, Italy, Germany, and other rulers. The Venetian influence is strongly evident today.

Connections • Between an assortment of ports on Crete and various points on the mainland or other islands, there are several daily Olympic flights plus more than a dozen ferries, the majority of them in "B" and "C" grades with 3 or 4 classes. Early reservations strongly advised.

Wines • In hot weather you'll probably like Dilanda Minos, a delightful, very palatable, and deliciously cooling white.

WHAT TO SEE AND DO

IRAKLION

("Heraklion" in English, with its name changed from Candia in 1823), the capital and principal port with 100,000 residents is the hub—sleazy, strident, and graceless. Because tourism is just too good in this sellers' market (there are 70 travel agencies and 85 rent-a-car offices), with very rare exceptions facilities are dismayingly crummy. Almost all vacationers regard it as a jump-off point for greener pastures.

IERAPETRA

Ierapetra in the Lassithi county has a Roman and Venetian heritage; there's a fortress and plenty of sun late into the autumn.

Worthwhile sightseeing targets are limited to the absolutely splendid **Archaeological Museum**, **the Historical Museum**, and the nearby world-famous ruins of the **Palace of Knossos**.

PHAESTOS

Phaestos is second only to Knossos in Minoan culture; try to see it. Also in the Mesara Plain is the Bronze Age palace of **Aghia Triada**. The site at *Samaria Gorge* is chiefly Byzantine and dotted with ancient chapels. The northeast coast of the island seems to be the most engaging.

HANIA

"Canae" in English, 85 miles due west and about one-half the size of Iraklion, is the island's second city. Except for a far lesser flood of foreign visitors, in atmosphere and facilities it rather closely resembles its larger sister. The listless **Kydon** is its only Class A hostelry. Among the 7 Class B entries, the little **Doma** is the overall leader in attractiveness.

AGIA NIKOLAOS

"St. Nicholas" in English (and often spelled "Ayios Nikolaos" in Greek) is a port town 44 miles east of Iraklion. Although its overnight accommodations are spartan, try the **Minos Palace**, **the Minos Beach**, or the **Coral**.

Best place to eat is the **Cretan Restaurant**; next come **Rififi** (for view) and **Limni**. **Argo** makes a fair pizza. Normally there is a lovely air of languor here, particularly on sun-drenched days.

As doubtless you have gathered, wise pilgrims flee the twin cities as fast as they can to settle into a beach colony. A string of huge, totally self-sustaining resort factories have sprung up. Perhaps 95% of their patronage is conducted tours. Most operate in season only. Curiously but incorrectly, the majority of them seem to have used the same interior decorators, including the pervasive Cretan-style theme. Common to most are such features as air conditioning, 1 or more swimming pools with snack bars, cocktail bars, one or more big restaurants with buffet lunches, a taverna, a coffee shop, a TV and card room, a hairdresser, a news kiosk, one or more boutiques, piped music, a disco, a sauna, tennis courts, minigolf, sailboats, pedalboats, riding, bowling alleys, table tennis, billiards, a children's playground, "bungalows," and other facilities that give them the scope of all-inclusive minivillages built for pleasure. Not at all incidentally, it is important to realize the difference between bungalows and "bungalows." The former are individual or semi-individual detached structures of which you will find only a few here. The latter are tiered clusters of rooms, often in 2-storied buildings, which accommodate 20 or 30 parties in what are actually annexes. These are normally more expensive than the lodgings within the main edifice. Don't expect to find high cuisine, vintage wines, or the soaring butterfly colors of summer gossamer gowns anywhere; total informality reigns 24 hours per day.

There are 2 deluxe settlements that are head, collar, and shoulders above the rest. These are the **Elounda Beach** and the **Astir Palace Elounda**. Among the lower-priced group, the **Creta Maris** is tops.

The construction pattern of **Kernos Beach**, also near **Malia**, is diametrically opposed to standard planning, with its center of activities adjoining the beach rather than the reception area. Be sure to visit the ruins at Malia's outskirts—in some ways more exciting than Knossos.

Minos Beach, a 44-mile drive, is on the skirt of a bay within walking distance of Ag. Nikolaos. Inaugurated in '61 as the granddaddy of them all, the years have taken such a toll it no longer merits its deluxe official rating. Beautiful setting; seedy lobby; 106 twin-bedded bungalows with showers and porches; 2 beaches; clean and threadbare. This once-fine house has lapsed into a weary old shoe. No wonder that instead of trying to revive it, its owners have recently opened the opulent 300-bed **Yarizina** across the bay.

On the north coastal road between Iraklion and Hania, the only operation worth a mention is the giant **Capsis Beach**, about 45 minutes from the former. A long and variegated cluster of "bungalows" descends from a gentle hillside to the huge, V-shaped nexus that is on a narrow peninsula with sea scenes on both sides. Almost every imaginable amenity described earlier can be found here.

To sum up the big picture, it is easy to understand how the natural wonders and the man-made allures of this fifth largest island in the Mediterranean have so quickly made Crete the rage among bargain-seeking pilgrims to this ancient and gracious nation.

WHERE TO STAY

With one exception, the hotels run the gamut from production belt mediocrity to wretched.

Galaxy • *67 Dimocratias Ave.* A U-shaped, 4-story building on stilts surrounding a polyangular pool. Two roof gardens; dining room; coffee bar; big pastry shop; total of 144 rooms with shower and 28 with bath, all simply decorated, small, functional, and with individual terrace.

Xenia • *Midcity.* Marginally modernistic, not too costly, and bristling with packaged tours.

Atlantis • A depressing machine without a trace of spirit or flair. Lobby stark and unattractive; rooftop pool (we'd be surprised if you'd want to use it); cynically impersonal staff; rooms and balconies clean, no more than technically adequate in furnishings, with atrociously thin walls. Add the noise from the traffic, the children's tennis court directly opposite, and loud-voiced neighbors—wow!

Astoria Capsis • *On the main square.* The 150-unit goes it one better in its air conditioning. Otherwise we found it even more dreary.

El Greco • 90-room, C-grade just off a small square a few blocks from the sea-front, serves breakfast only. Small, amiable lobby backed by a little garden; friendly barlet adjoining. An unusually satisfactory family operation in the low-priced category.

WHERE TO SHOP

Tourist junk is rampant. **Zacharopoulos** in the *Knossos Palace* is worth exploring for jewelry and handicrafts. **Helen Kastrinojianni**, opposite the *Iraklion Museum*, also features local handiwork plus attractive woven fabrics. **Midas**, on *Freedom Square*, stocks some gold and silver table pieces and picture frames of excellent quality. **Ariane**, on *Dikeosinu St.* and at the Astoria Hotel, displays a selection of *bijoutie* and shells.

DELPHI

This magnet, 105 miles from Athens, is the most classic sightseeing target of the nation. It draws countless thousands of excursionists—and well it should, but were it not for the teeming mobs that overswam it, few travel rewards in Greece could be richer.

AUTHOR'S OBSERVATION

Among hotels we'd choose the Amalia ($57 for doubles) or the Xenia (similar prices). We hear that the Hotel Europa is a good budget stop.

HOW TO GET AROUND

Aside from do-it-yourself bus service, **CHAT** (*4 Stadiou St.; ☎ 3222886*) offers a coach tour for around $45; the ride is 4 hours each way. Key Tours, the cooperative enterprise of Athens travel agencies, also provides similarly priced packages. There are magnificent vistas along this road; the driver will pause frequently for your picture-taking. The highway itself is not the best. Many little tavernas along the way serve dolmades, cheese, and other regional favorites.

WHAT TO SEE AND DO

The **Oracle**, **museum**, and **theater** are in the near suburbs of **Delphi**. Don't miss these or **Ossios Loukas**, the Byzantine monastery with world-famous and dazzling mosaics.

Levadhia 1-1/4 hours out, comes up with a striking panorama of Mt. Parnassus and the Thebes Plain. Its principal restaurant is unattractive, but there are several snack bars that serve some of the most delicious shish-kebabs we've ever curled our tongues around. (Don't forget the dash of salt-and-oregano mixture and a liberal splatter of lemon juice!) For sunnyday lunching, we like the charming little establishment at *Falling Water*, on the edge of town. Scads of rug shops in this center, none of which seemed especially intriguing. In fact, prices seemed higher along this route and quality lower than in Athens for similar items.

EPIDAURUS

Do as the ancients did by making a pilgrimage to the **Shrine of Aesculapius**. While there, your other targets of special interest are the museum and the **Epidaurus Theatre**, which looks as if the last performance ended only last night.

KASTORIA

Built on the Lake of Kastoria (Orestias), which runs far to the north, almost to the Albanian frontier. A number of its churches date back to the 11th century. Except for the dedicated archaeologist, antiquarian, or perhaps a scholarly monk, the distance from Athens outweighs the rewards.

MYCENAE

Here the **Lion Gate** and the **Tombs of the Kings** are the big attractions. This playground of Agamemnon reached its high point in the 13th century B.C. The marvelous excavations are a compulsory lure to any student of antiquity. There are good bed-and-breakfast facilities in the vicinity where the prices are surprisingly low. Of restaurants, try **George Kolizetos's place**; he's a master of the skillets.

MYKONOS

This dazzling white islet in the Cyclades is tourist conscious—but not spoiled. Aside from its archaeological attractions and its 300 tiny churches (you may see 3 individual chapels side-by-side-by-side), it is most famous for its pet pelicans—Peter and 2 or 3 cronies. Long ago the original bird, who flew in from the unknown, was credited as the talisman who relieved the islanders' financial woes. Mykonos folk believe they will prosper as long as a pelican is in residence to freeload on the community. Not too long ago a party of blackhearted scoundrels from a neighboring island snuck in and birdnapped Pete. Before this fowl deed was undone, the inhabitants were on the edge of the bloodiest Armageddon since Paris kidnapped Helen.

Area: 32.5 square miles. Population: about 10,000. Terrain: largely rocky. Climate: usually windy but sunny. Industries: fisheries and tourism.

BEACHES

Excellent, especially along **Plati Yialos Bay** in the direction of *Psarou.* The swimming is wonderful. If you want a remote strand, try **Kalafatis**. **Eleni Boni** rents rooms high above the town with magnificent sunset views; about $20 per double. Things to see? Practically nothing—and nearly everything. It is a town to stroll through. And at sunset, the world ends at *Little Venice*, an incredibly romantic jumble of houses and seascape where lovers gather at gloaming. Since the roads are poor and they go almost nowhere, it stands to reason that there is practically no motor traffic. Greek Easter is nothing short of spectacular here. Don't be alarmed when you see the outdoor services at midnight, boys tippling in the belfries ready to haul on the bell cords, skyrockets going off, and the magnificently robed priest calling out "Christ is Risen!" while parishioners try to toss lighted firecrackers under his skirts. (Most of the explosives, not all, are wrapped in rope to prevent injury.) Then come processions, incense, plenty of imbibing throughout the holiday weekend, and so much lamb to eat that you'll think your hide is coming up in white fleecy tufts.

WHERE TO STAY

No changes here. Since officials are worried about insufficient water supplies, an embargo was imposed on new construction. Thus what was, is—and probably will be for a long time to come.

The Xenia • *On a promontory overlooking a bay.* A picket line of windmills, and the white-on-white townlet of Mykonos. Comfortable, motel-like accommodations; abundant and sometimes even appetizing cookery; extremely nice people run it. Our top choice for convenience and pleasure.

Kouneni • *In midvillage.* An old-fashioned homestead with vine-clad patios, it is ideal for nostalgics and near to everything.

Mykonos Beach Bungalows • A white-washed and dazzling clutch of simple buildings and hospitable people. The views from here are spectacular.

The Leto • Owned by the same company, *nibbles at the edge of the main tour boat and fishing harbor,* so bathing here is not the best. Its uninspired decor leaves us cold.

The Aphrodite • *About a 30-minute bus jog across to the desolate end of the island.* Maintains a romantic lonely vigil over some of the most breathtaking sea-and-landscapes in the Cyclades. Two beaches enfolding twin coves; 110 so-called bungalows which, in fact, are joined in one stair-step structure; all with bath and balcony facing the waves; swimming pool; tennis; ample recreation hubs for the groups to which it seems to cater; careless service, as might be expected in so remote a clime. The solitude is the thing here—good or bad.

The hotels will likely require that you have breakfast and one other meal. We pecked with the pet pelicans at both **Alefkandra** and **Fouskis**. Though the regional cookery was good at both, we prefer the former because of its sea view and beguiling, sail-covered open plaza. **Filippi** and **Edem** are more expensive, but the mood evoked at both is worth almost any price; neither, however, is prohibitive in cost. Every turn in the lane seems to have a cafe, a snack corner, or a pastry parlor, so never fear starvation.

NIGHTLIFE

The very air lilts with Greek music wafting with forlorn softness from the myriad bars. The best places to weep or fall in love with its infatuating melodies are at the **Mykonos**—rush ceiling (the only thing hurried about it), dancing, and someone normally on hand to give informal instruction in the bouzouki. Next come the **Montparnasse** (go to the back room for more meaningful hand-holding), the **7 Seas** (near the harbor and strong on atmosphere), and **Maltemi**. **Castro**, which can be gay. (There's quite a large gay colony on the island; the older establishment is resentful of the effect this may be having on the native youth.) The **Remezzo** leads the discotheque file. It specializes in fluid sedations for the more sedate set, plus heavy breathing, sighs, and sips on its incredibly beautiful harborside patio. The **9 Muses** is much more of a swinger; it's recommendable for old married couples who are enjoying their 2nd-week anniversary. Because lots more await, the fun is to wander and discover.

EXCURSIONS BY SEA

The most popular is the 1/2-hour voyage on stout fishing launches over to the small island of **Delos** with its extensive ruins, mosaics, and famous stone lions. Quickie trips can be had for very low fares, leaving at 9 a.m. from the main harbor and returning from the rocky uninhabited archaeological sites by lunchtime.

AUTHOR'S OBSERVATION

Walking, drinking ouzo in the port, and viewing the Archaeological Museum plus the Mykonos Folklore Museum overlooking the dock, are pleasant ways to spend the day.

WHERE TO SHOP

Panos turns lovely handwoven textiles into bags, ponchos, shawls, tablemats, cushions, and coverlets; meet **Joan Kousathanas**. **Kouros** (*Matoyianni St.*) has attractive ceramics and icon copies. **Karamichos-Mazarakis** *(Harbor Rd.)* are the experts for flokati and other Greek rugs. Prices are low by U.S. standards, and the merchants are not averse to engaging in the fine Greek pastime of bargaining.

Mykonos is special, offering the rare mixture of rewards that so many vacationers seek but seldom find in combination: sun, sea, and relative solitude.

NAUPLIA

Also called Nafplion, was the first capital after independence. This scenic center, with its 18th-century **Venetian Palamidi Fortress**, overlooks the mountains of Arcadia. Take a short boat ride to the **fortress isle of Bourdzi** in the bay and visit the headland at **Akronafplia**. Here's a good springboard for excursions to the ruins of **Tiryns** and **Epidauros**.

Turn over almost any rock in this region and you're likely to find a temple, an amphitheater, or a scientist with his nose to the limestone. Although it's a l-o-n-g haul for a 1-day excursion from Athens, legions of foreign travelers take it in stride. Wise planners start very early, comb the principal inland sightseeing classics during the morning, have a late lunch and possibly a short siesta, and then return via the new and spectacular coastal highway. This lovely little port is the most southerly settlement of importance on what is technically the Greek mainland. (Actually this province is an island that is connected only by a single bridge at Corinth.) The **Amalia** is said to be superb. Both of the **Xenia Hotels**, one somewhat newer than the other, are sited high on a hill that blesses them with glorious panoramas over the harbor and sea. The lower one, with sound cuisine and comfortable rooms, is Class A. The upper one, in the luxury category, is more striking and elaborate, with an even more dramatic view; 55 bedchambers in its main building and 54 "bungalows" in 2 connecting double-story annexes. All of the interiors are air-conditioned. The exhilarating indoor-outdoor restaurant is 2 levels below the entrance. They are excellent and not too, too costly for overnighting.

OLYMPIA

Once it was thronged by visitors from every cranny of the ancient world who came to participate in or to view the original Olympic games. Now you'll encounter only a small town of about 700 inhabitants, but there is a first-class hotel—the 150-room **Amalia** with bath and shower for every unit, air conditioning, and a swimming pool. While the Stadium is, of course, the main focal point, the ruins of the **Temple of Zeus** and the Museum (which houses the famed *Hermes* by Praxiteles and the *Victory of Paeonius*) are other powerful magnets.

PATRAS

You're most likely to catch this rather uninteresting port only in passing, since virtually its only role of importance is to act as the fulcrum between the routes by land or by sea to and from western Greece.

RHODES

Largest of the Dodecanese Islands, this "Isle of Roses" is one of the happiest tourist targets in the Mediterranean or Aegean areas. Its 54-by-27-mile ocarina-shaped frame lies just 16 miles off the Turkish coast. Its capital of the same name comes with a medieval core, cobblestones, up-to-the-minute discos, and casual seaside dining. Extensive restoration of the fortifications and dwellings within the walled city will continue for some years. Despite rampant tourism, the people continue to be overwhelmingly kind. Best season? Late spring or early fall (Summer can be very hot and winter unpredictable.)

WHERE TO STAY

If you don't mind risking rain or wind, prices from Nov.-Apr. have been slashed 50% to spur off-season tourism. A Class-A accommodation might total $25 to $30 with breakfast, even during peak months. It's a buyers' market.

Rodos Bay • *Sited 2 miles out toward the airport on a mountain perch fronting the beach.* At 11 stories, the loftiest building on the island (allegedly 30 feet higher than the vanished Colossus). Rooftop saltwater pool; bar and restaurant. 25 relatively spartan alpine bungalows; 35 split-level suites; 175 bedchambers with white stucco walls, air conditioning, telephones, baths, or showers.

Belvedere • *Midtown site.* 165 rooms, all with bath or shower; fronts with terraces looking seaward; backs overlooking a truck route. Tennis court and swimming pool.

Mediterranean • *Midcity.* Bathers' tunnel under the road for easy beach access.

Ibiscus • Continually updated by dedicated management; fresh grill, air conditioning in places.

Oceanis • *Sited a few miles from the city.* Inviting swimming pool; handsome public rooms; air conditioning; well-appointed bedchambers. If you prefer a noncentral address (across the highway from the breakers), this is better than the Ibiscus.

Metropolitan Capsis • Roof garden, pool, sauna, and gym. Seaview rooms with air conditioning.

Golden Beach • *Peers furtively at Mt. Filerimos across a narrow strand of sand.* Complemented by enough athletic paraphernalia to sponsor its own Olympic games. Bath, telephone, and radio for every registrant.

Chevaliers Palace • A modern castle that can be fun in a hoked-up way, decoratively speaking.

Imperial • Almost viewless.

Plaza • Pleasant.

Spartalis • Eschews the obligatory pension policy; 3rd floor claims the finest rooms; not all accommodations have bath or shower.

Olympic • *One block from the sea.* 46 small rooms; front units with terraces; tiny baths.

Cairo Palace • 111 rooms with baths or showers. Restaurant.

Soleil • 93 rooms, 41 baths, one newer wing. Garden restaurant.

WHERE TO EAT

The pension requirement of many hotels between July 1 and Sept. 30, has killed the restaurant industry. Independent dining spots are shockingly bad, in fact.

Kon Tiki • *At the extension of a marina.* It runs the tightest ship.

Alexis and **Oscar's** • According to a local wag (no pun), the first—located on Socrates St.—is marked by a dog fountain. "Do not let this dissuade you; it's recommended for fish," he states.

Deluca • *Near Hotel des Roses.* Offers wretched regional fare in less than hospital-clean conditions.

Farm House • *A 3-minute walk from the Grand Hotel Asitr Palace.* Sea-vista terrace in summer; open kitchen hearthside in winter. Inexpensive, simple, good. Recommendable.

Fotis • *Off Socrates St., in the Old Quarter.* Serves fresh seafood. Worth a visit.

Casa Castellana • Despite its Spanish moniker, specializes in steaks.

Elli • So-so for snacks.

TAVERNAS

Baboulas ("Ghost") is haunted by burly sailor lads and assorted toughies. **The Yachting Club** sails in with alfresco service; forthright, unglamorous cuisine; fine view. **The Park Rodini**, *2 miles from the center*, comes up with music occasionally; agreeable for dancing; not too bad for a late bite. Several cafes line the New Market; all on the dull side.

NIGHTLIFE

Nearly all of the deluxe and first-class hotels have nightclubs that function from time to time. **The Miramare** spotlights dancing in the bar. **Akteon**, harborside near the Colossus site, has dancing but no cabaret.

WHAT TO SEE AND DO

The site of one of the Seven Wonders of the World, the **Colossus of Rhodes**, which, it is said, once straddled the harbor and was destroyed by an earthquake in 224 B.C.; a 1-hour tour of the ramparts and defenses of the Old Town (a must for every visitor), built by the Crusaders; the magnificent medieval walled city of the **Knights Hospitalers of St. John of Jerusalem** (today the Knights of Malta), with its castles, palaces, and fairy-tale ruins; the **Archaeological Museum** and the **Palace of the Grand Masters**; **the Thermal Springs of Callithea**, 6 miles out, with Moorish architecture, a grotto restaurant, a spring house, 3 kinds of beneficial waters, and a discouraging array of 120 toilets; the splendid cellar **Aquarium**, with an amazing variety of rays, moray eels, turtles, brilliant starfish, and local sea denizens in a series of tanks; the **Valley of Butterflies** at *Petaloudes*, 15 miles out, where clouds of pinkish-gray beauties rise by the thousands as you walk along the little cascades (season only). You may pedal about the capital on a rented bike for very low rates. Finally, try not to miss the drive out to *Lindos*, an hour from your metropolitan doorstep. This ancient, lime-washed, seacoast village is nestled in a rugged meander of an age-old ravine. Park your car in the town square and take the 20-minute hike up the footpath to the cliff-high fortress and the quietly eroding sandstone **Acropolis**. The awe-inspiring vistas of the sapphire water, the cubistic white-on-white jumble of houses, the fishing harbor, the still lagoon in a bracelet of volcanic rock, and the far-ranging sweep of a golden sandy beach, are breathtaking. If you pack a picnic lunch, nibble and daydream on the flower-covered slopes below the ramparts; you will be much happier than if you had dined at the handful of rawboned tavernas in the town. On the way down, take the path leading to the small but gemlike **Byzantine chapel**. Be sure to give a moderate tip to the 212-year-old woman who explains in perfect Greek just what every statue, painting, niche, and curlicue means. If you don't camp on the cliffs or down by the sea, the **Pallas** and **Electra** boardinghouses are about the only pads available.

SANTORINI

The beauty here is incredible. Santorini not only yields its name to the chief island but to the profoundly deep, dark basin composed of 5 surrounding Cycladic isles that form the caldera or "kettle." It is regrettable that so many visitors see this white-washed poem only briefly when the cruise ships are in port—a criminal loss for anyone who has traveled so far and who will be denied the inner secrets of one of the Hellenic world's most breathtaking attractions.

Phoenicians and Dorians settled as early as 2000 B.C., probably one of the first Minoan colonies. In 1520 B.C. a shattering volcanic eruption totally destroyed the civilization, simultaneously creating yet another legend to add to the string of Lost Atlantis myths. In recent times, archaeologists discovered **Akrotiri**, a Bronze Age town of approximately 30,000 inhabitants. But since there were no human remains or precious artifacts such as jewels or gold, it is presumed that the citizens had been forewarned. In my view, Akrotiri must be considered one of the most important finds of Western civilization, tying together many of the mysteries of our earliest ancestry. In **Thira** you will see reproductions of the magnificent frescoes that have been swept away to the **Athens Museum**—as much an affront to Minoan culture as the limp excuses England has made for appropriating the Elgin Marbles. To a sensitive American, this would be as offensive as finding our own Miss Liberty one day guarding the entrance to Yokohama harbor. Here is a splendid excavation of monumental importance that should be preserved for the people who occupy its historical presence and where the art should haunt the memory of earlier periods and inspire visitors and residents alike.

Most arrivals are brought in by lighter from the ships and make the halfhour climb by foot or by burro to the upper village; the cable car ride takes only minutes. Viewful terrace restaurants along the higher shelf are ornamented by displays of drying octopus and squid; lamb and fish also generally are available. The better choices for mealtiming include **Lichnari**, **Leonidas**, and (of course) a **Zorba's**. Additionally, **Babis** and **Fantasia** are recommendable. So is **Camille Stafani**, but it doesn't overlook the sea. Be sure to sample the soft, mellow Santorini Lava red wine, a product of the volcanic ash.

If there is time, one must experience sunset from the promontory village of **Oia**, one of the most soulfully romantic settings to be found anywhere. There are cafes and restaurants along the clifftop (the **Kyklos** is best). Other sightseeing targets might include the black sand beach of **Kamari** and the **Monastiri**, which peeps impishly from between the legs of towering communication spires on the 2000-foot mountain that soars above the valley and shore.

The top hotel in the capital is the small and viewful Atlantis; otherwise, most of the shelter is in boarding houses and pensions.

Shoppers will find themselves in a cliff-high paradise. On the steps spiraling down to the port, don't miss Robos for hand-woven dresses, floppy shirts, rugs, vests, and bedspreads. Ladies will go bonkers-in-Greek for the **Aris** handpainted dresses; the colors are zesty and ideal for summer. An address will do no good; it's in the high town. Jewelry is always an area of caution, but **Greco Gold** (also in midvillage) appears to be the most reputable and have the highest quality stocks. Ask for Yanis or Stefanos Keramidas.

ANTIQUES

Go to **Athanasios Papatheodorou**, not far from the Atlantis Hotel. It's bursting with beautiful items, especially the *akrokeramo* (decorative finials). If you're still not magenta from walking up and down the mountain lanes, go to step 566 where you'll find **E. Youkas**, the specialist for carpets and wall hangings and pillow covers. All are hand loomed and surprisingly inexpensive.

By all means try to arrange your visit to include more than the few hours the ships' anchorages provide.

SARONIC ISLANDS

Because of the close proximity to Athens and the convenience, high speed, and low cost of transportation, you can enjoy a shoestring cruise that will also permit you to disembark at 4 of the most beautiful islands in Greek waters. The Saronic Gulf is formed in a J running south and west from Piraeus; its isles are accessible from this primary Greek port by both conventional ferries as well as hydrofoils (called Flying Dolphins) that zip along at 30-36 knots. If you don't have time to cruise to Rhodes, Crete, Corfu, or island cultures of the Mediterranean, Cyclades, or Aegean, by all means try to book onto these handy water jitneys for one of the greatest experiences to be had on ship and shore.

Aegina, closest to Piraeus, offers splendid beaches and a history that goes back to Neolithic times. The temple of **Aphaia Athena** is the dominant architectural target from the 5th century B.C. Other ruins include a theater and stadium.

Excellent bathing at **Agia Marina** (8 miles from the port) and lovely scenery at the fishing village of **Perdika**. For overnighting, **Danae** is satisfactory followed by the bungalows of **Nausika** or the **Pension Pavlou**.

Poros is really one marvelous whitewashed dream with yacht moorings strung along a lane of open cafes and wind-tossed patios. Across the strait is the mainland town of **Galatas**.

There is not much to do except hold hands, stroll, and fall into blissful Hellenic reverie. For romancers on limited budgets it is a paradise. Another **Pavlou** serves for shelter; the **Neon Aegli** is the largest hostelry, followed by the **Poros**.

The main thing here is to try to find an accommodation overlooking the water and the boats that pass through the channel. For shopping notions, speak to Stacy Soloyanis at **Apollon**, beside the Fountain Square.

Hydra is at the very bottom of the "J." Certainly the busy port which stairsteps up the steep mountain chalice is one of the most frequently photographed frames of scenery to be found anywhere in Homeric waters. Fishing as well as recreation vessels create a cheerful atmosphere of activity; all town life fringes the harbor under awnings or in the shade of the pastel buildings. The prestigious **School of Fine Arts** is located in **Villa Tombazi**.

The mansions sprinkled around the bowl reflect the 19th-century heyday when fleets sailed in and gave the island the nickname of "Little England." While its topography is rock, good beaches exist at Kaminia, Molos, Palamida, and Bisti on the western flank, as well as on the Miramare strand at Mandraki. Both **Miranda** and **Miramare** (Mandraki) control the top hotel ranking, while **Hydrousa**, **Delfini**, **Cavos**, and **Amaryllis** provide reasonable comfort in a lower category.

Spetses is the most distant from the capital—approximately 2 hours by hydrofoil. There is no special archaeology here, but islanders are proud of *Bouboulina*, their heroine sea captain who led her small fleet against the mighty Turkish armada and defeated them with such a trouncing that the Turks never again returned. Minuscule water taxis take bathers to nearby private beaches for small sums and retrieve them at appointed times. No cars function after 3 p.m.—only charming horsedrawn fiacres. One *must* is to have an exotic cocktail at sunset on the roof of the **Hotel Ilios** (*Soleil*). The **Spetses** is modern; **Possidonion** is old-fashioned but in a good position; Kasteli offers hotel and bungalow accommodation. **Roumanis** and **Myrtoon** are also worth considering in a lower bracket.

In all of these a limited pension plan is possible at your hotel, but I would by far recommend that you dine along the port frontages where dozens of attractive tavernas serve precisely the same thing in far more bewitching surroundings.

For reservations, travel arrangements, or a helping hand, Ioanna Nicolareisis has offered to assist readers of this book. She is the attractive young manager of **Dapia Tours** in the middle of the town of Spetses; (☎ *0298-72040*).

SKIATHOS

A dot-size island, almost due north from Athens and due south from Salonika, best known for its mica-deposit **Golden Beach**. Its principal village is utterly enchanting—and utterly undisturbed except on boat days, which occur chiefly over the weekends (but even this excitement doesn't ruffle the aboriginals). Luxury living took a grand leap forward when the **Skiathos Palace** was unveiled. **Xenia**, right on the other tip of the beach's crescent, is under the same management. These houses cater almost exclusively to package tours. However, this island is still relatively undeveloped. There's nothing to shop for, and no places of refreshment except the coffee bars along the quay (or, of course, your hotel); be sure to sample *loukamades*, a honeyed doughnut, at the last cafe on the harbor before the stairs leading to the restaurant. The island's beauty is captivating, its serenity celestial.

SOUNION

If you're here at sunrise or sunset, you might be sufficiently lucky to be blessed with one of the most inspiring moments of your lifetime. The gleaming white marble of the **Temple of Poseidon** has been the first vision of the Cape seen by mariners navigating from the Eastern markets, the Dardanelles, and the Aegean archipelago. Lonely and silent, its beauty is—well, "awesome" just doesn't half describe it.

SPARTA

Above the plains of the modern town, the **Temples of Athena** and **Artemis**, as well as the **Circus**, rise against the snow-banked crags of Taiyetos. You may also inspect a worthwhile museum in midvillage, a number of Byzantine churches and palaces, and a fortress built by the Franks. Only about 3 miles away are the magnificent Byzantine ruins of **Mistras**.

FOR MORE INFORMATION ON GREECE

USA

National Tourist Organization of Greece • *645 Fifth Ave., New York, NY 10022,* ☎ *(212) 421-5777.*

Greek National Tourist Organization • Once abroad, you may find help at the Information Office of the Greek National Tourist Organization, *2 Amerikis St., Athens.*

Hellenic Tours • For travel arrangements, Hellenic Tours, *23/25 Ermou St., Athens*, is one of the most ethical companies on the scene.

INSIDER TIP

When you land on an island or wish to overnight in a village, go to the local police station (if there is no Tourist Police Office). They will find you a room at very reasonable rates.

IRELAND

Cross the Celtic Sea to Ireland—a wholly enchanting experience amid a wealth of natural beauty. There are ramshackle, bustling coastal towns, broad tranquil loughs, and ethereal mountains wreathed in a tawny mist as soft as the sound of the Irish brogue.

The Emerald Isle lives up to its name, to be sure, and has a special appeal to nature lovers and sportsmen alike. Seventy salmon rivers course through its verdant countryside, and there's plenty of inexpensive fishing everywhere. (There's also very expensive angling at some select pools.) In spring, when the mayfly is up, it's said that half of Ireland heads for the hills where the brown trout leap in the numerous lakes of the west and north midlands. Course or stream fishing, too, is an evergreen attraction with pike, bream, perch, and rudd waiting to be hooked in streams and cascades set in such idyllic surroundings.

The Irish are great horse lovers; racing, breeding, hunting, polo, and riding are major pastimes. The **Royal Dublin Society's Horse Show**, held in August, is a must for those who enjoy show jumping, dressage, horsemanship, and simply the color of these natural pageants. The costs are low and the rewards are 18 hands high.

The hoot and cry of a lusty fox hunt—like it or not—is something you might inadvertently experience as you rove the grassy hills. Although Ireland's famous son, Oscar Wilde, described it as "The unspeakable in pursuit of the uneatable," the blood sport remains popular throughout much of the island.

Contrary to neighboring rumor, the Scots do not have a monopoly on golf; Ireland loves its links. There are more than 200 courses throughout the tiny country, some with worldwide reputations;

Dublin has almost three dozen courses. Any duffer can always be assured of a game. Greens fees are minuscule by North American standards, and clubs can be rented cheaply at most courses.

But, of course, for the sightseer generally, Ireland is every bit the sparkling gem it purports to be; a trip through it is both fascinating and relaxing. Since distances are short, you can pack a lot of action into a little time. Stay close to the coast for the most attractive scenery. Set your wheels in motion in Dublin, heading south amid the gracious Wicklow Hills, through Arklow and historic Wexford, founded by hardy Norse voyagers and later favored by Oliver Cromwell; he occupied the town and made it his residence in 1649. John Barry, founder of the U.S. Navy, was born nearby; his statue stands in the crescent overlooking Wexford's busy harbor. Westering on to Waterford, visit the home of the famous crystalware and Sir Walter Raleigh's home at Myrtle Grove; there's a fine Elizabethan gabled house, where he sat at an upper window and penned his epistles to his "Faerie Queen." Arriving in Cork, Ireland's second city, call at **Blarney Castle**, where many visitors dangle upside-down to kiss the famous stone and win "the gift of the gab."

From Cork there are several different routes, but don't miss Glengarriff with its subtropical vegetation and oddly Mediterranean scenery set on Bantry Bay. Take a boat trip out to Garinish Island, about one mile out in the bay; it's a paradise of azaleas, camelias, and rhododendrons, where Shaw wrote *Saint Joan*. The nation has world-famous gardens, some of them on private estates which often are open to public view. In the following sections, I'll mention the better choices for your travels. Visitors to the southwest must include the "**Ring of Kerry**" tour. The magnificent vistas to be seen from **Macgillicuddy's Reeks** (the highest mountain range in Ireland) are never to be forgotten: an eagle's eye view of corries, rivers, and lakes, surrounded by red sandstone rising up sheer from the water's edge to the slopes of the densely forested hills. The beauty of **Killarney** has been lauded by many writers, including Wordsworth, Tennyson, and Thackeray. Make your own evaluation while sporting around in a horse-drawn jaunting car, a feature of "Heaven's Reflex" set in Erin's most captivating corner. An excellent choice of hotels makes Killarney an ideal base. Ireland is a tableau of splendor, from rugged northern Rosapenna through southern Skibbereen,—with twinkling, eloquent romantics as your hosts.

TIPS ON IRELAND

FOOD

Irish cuisine is superb—especially the grills, roast beef, steaks, shellfish, salmon, or traditional dishes such as corned beef and cabbage. Try to have these rather than continental fare. Emphasis is on fresh-

IRELAND
ATLANTIC OCEAN
N. IRELAND
Belfast
Ballynahinch
Newry
Boudoran
Sligo
Ballina
Castlebar
Westport
Carrickmacross
Dundalk
IRISH SEA
Clifden
Cong
Oughterard
Cashel Bay
Galway
Athlone
Mulingar
Dublin
Ballyvaughn
Wicklow
Shannon
Limerick
Kilkenny
Adare
Tipperary
Cashel
Cahir
Wexford
Tralee
Waterford
Killarney
Glenbeigh
Waterville
Cork
Bantry
N
ATLANTIC OCEAN

ness and natural flavor and not on complex composition and costly nouvelle-isms. The harvest from the sea is especially rewarding.

In the counties (not cities, generally), the man of the sod prefers his roast beef stone dead; if you like yours rare, specifically ask to have it "underdone" when you order. Milk is rich and plentiful; soda fountains (called "cafes" or "milk bars") list such exotic items as Banana Split Joy and Chocolate Kiss Shake. Instead of heading for the fancier restaurants, you can often find solid inexpensive cooking in modest taverns and pubs. The following Dublin section lists many, but every village in the nation also boasts a few for a pint and a bite.

DRINKS

A taste of Irish whiskey is a must for drinkers. No potatoes at all; it's triple distilled from barley. (Scotch is merely twice distilled!) Put $2.50 on the bar, ask for "a half one," and up will come this unique, potent, and healing libation.

A consortium called Irish Distillers now produces all of this category of spirits in the country, despite the continuing competition among individual brands: John Jameson's (Holinshed's "Sovereign Liquor At Its Finest"), John Power's ("Enjoy That Gold Label"), and D. E. Williams at Tullamore ("Give Every Man His Dew"). Cork's, makers of Paddy ("Will 'oo have a Paddy?"), means your host is a true-blue Cork man. Bushmill's Black Label, a long aged premium offering, is extra-full-bodied. Many people regard it as the best of all.

Generally speaking, however, the average Irish toper is not a natural consumer of hard booze. He is a devotee of stout—a dark, very rich, very special beer. This dedication is so important that the price of the pint is chronically a dominant issue in political elections.

Guinness stout comes both in bottle and on draught, and is produced from barley, hops, water, and yeast. The pedigree yeast used in brewing the world-famous Irish stout today is derived from the original strain used by the first Arthur Guinness who founded the brewery in 1759. He took a 9000-year lease that has only another 8766 years to go before it expires! This well-known Dublin landmark on the south bank of the River Liffey at St. James's Gate stands on 60 acres; it's the largest brewery in Europe and biggest exporter in the world. Visitors are welcome any time between 10 a.m. and 3 p.m. from Mon.-Fri. (bank holidays excepted) to see a film on its operation and to sample the product. Murphy's stout is particularly popular in the southern part of the country, and has been issuing from the Lady's Well Brewery in Cork since 1885. It's quite smooth and a bit lighter and sweeter than Guinness. Many North Americans take both these diluted with beer or ale; Black Velvet (50% champagne and 50% stout) holds vast appeal.

Beer flows in Niagaras, of course. The Harp brand can be found universally, but you'll probably have to ask for an extra-cold one. Otherwise it will be served to you at skin temperature.

Wine is not one of Ireland's stronger points; away from the main centers, it is often limited in selection, secondary in quality, and poor in handling and presentation. Due to the heavy influx today of German visitors and residents, the white grape is now beginning to appear in greater quantity.

Irish coffee (also known as Gaelic coffee) is one of the pleasantest beverages possible to sample. To make it, add a jigger of Irish whisky to 2/3 of a glass of steaming black coffee; add sugar to taste; float thick, rich cream on the top. Many people substitute this drink for a sweet (usually called a "pudding") after their meal.

For your after-dinner liqueur, Irish Mist is to Ireland what Drambuie is to Scotland. An increasingly popular liqueur is Bailey's Irish Cream, a blend of the nation's traditional elixir and dairy juice. Two more brands of the same ilk are Carolans and Waterford Cream. They are sweet, rich, and bristling with calories.

Don't drive a car if you have consumed an influencing degree of alcohol. As in the United Kingdom, the police crack down mercilessly by applying the roadside "Breathalyser" test to anyone they suspect. Offenders face fines, loss of driver's licenses, and possibly jail terms.

GETTING AROUND

BOAT

Crossing from the United Kingdom to Ireland on a **Sealink** vessel is pleasant and efficient. Cost of a berth is only a smidgen above the price of the fare. British Rail-Sealink provides several car ferry sailings daily on the *St. Columba* and the *St. David*, which cover the Holyhead (Wales)/Dun Laoghaire route; also on the *Stena Normandica* sailing between Fishguard (Wales) and Rosslare (County Wexford). Another service joins Liverpool with Belfast, and Larne (N. Ireland) with Stranraer (Scotland). All details (including special midweek fares) may be obtained from Britrail Travel International Inc., *630 3rd Ave., New York, NY 10017;* ☎ *212-599-5400,* FAX *620419.*

B & I Line has daily sailings on two luxury car ferries (the *Connacht* and the *Leinster*) between Liverpool and Dublin and Holyhead and Dublin; on the *Innisfallen* between Pembroke (Wales) and Rosslare. All details (including special bargain fares) may be obtained from B & I Line General Agent, Lynott Tours Inc., *350 Fifth Ave., Suite 2619, New York, NY 10118;* ☎ *212-760-0101,* FAX *668715.*

Irish Ferries operate a direct car ferry between Le Havre and Rosslare (5 times per week) and also between Cherbourg (twice weekly) and Rosslare from April to September. If you have a Eurailpass, you can ride free as a deck passenger.

AIR CONNECTIONS

Aer Lingus and **Ryan Air** leave from 9 British and 13 continental points; there are also services between Shannon Airport and Dublin, Cork to Dublin, and Dublin to Belfast. On all of these, make advance reservations or get to the embarkation point very early. You might also check the British schedules of British Airways, Virgin, and Dan Air as an added convenience.

TRAINS

Ireland is a member of the Eurailpass network, offering unlimited mileage first-class (Super Standard) tickets and second-class (Standard) space for Eurail Youth pass holders. The Irish tracks link up with the European systems via Irish Ferries, operating ships between Rosslare and Cherbourg and Le Havre. Among the blue-ribbon runs, the Enterprise Express and the Dublin-Cork Express are outstanding. A recent breakfast consisted of the following: piping hot scones, ham finger sandwiches, fluffy cake, generous servings of coffee, and other temptations; the head attendant could not have been nicer.

BUSES

Long-distance runs—and some of the newer short-haul links—are modern and speedy. But when you climb aboard the average rural Irish bus, prepare yourself for An Experience. The community friendliness and banter are wonderful.

The **C.I.E.** *(35 Lower Abbey St., Dublin; ☎ 300777)* is a big-time organization with large and comfortable vehicles. It offers a wide choice of full- and half-day tours. Departures are made from the **Central Bus Station**; children under 15 go half-fare; top targets include: Wexford (John F. Kennedy's ancestral home), Glendalough and Avoca, the Liffey Valley and Blessington Lakes, Doonaree, the Boyne Valley, and the Carlingford Peninsula. Information may be obtained from the Dublin office, or, before departure from the U.S., contact C.I.E., *122 East 42nd St., New York, NY 10168*; ☎ *212-972-5600.* Travelers are so fond of these C.I.E. excursions (particularly the bus trips) that they're sold out long in advance; please make the earliest possible reservation to nail down your space. Once in Dublin you'll find C.I.E. at *35 Lower Abbey St.*; ☎ *1-300777.*

MOTORING

Irish roads have patchy surfaces—and watch that cow, wagon, or flock of sheep around every 2nd or 5th curve! It's a wonderful country to drive in if you're not in a frenetic rush. Road network of 55,000 miles, and one of the lowest car-density ratios across the Atlantic; well-marked highways; only a light sprinkling of advertising billboards. The mountains, lakes, fields, and beaches are all there for you.

Always remember that confounding traffic-flow pattern: The left is right, and the right is wrong! And, as a pedestrian, look both ways always before crossing the streets.

The use of seat belts is compulsory for the front-seat passenger and driver. If the front-seat passenger is a child under 12 and under 4 feet 11 inches, he or she must have a suitable means of safety restraint. If the child is under 17 years and over 4 feet 11 inches, he or she must have a safety belt. The penalties for nonuse are quite severe.

CAR HIRE

There are several excellent firms. **Murrays Europcar**, with one of the largest fleets, has offices in Dublin and Cork; Dublin, Cork, and Shannon airports; Galway; and Rosslare, County Wexford. **Hertz** also has an extensive fleet spread between the Dublin headquarters and branches in Cork, and at Dublin, Shannon, and Cork airports. Rates vary according to the vehicle and the season; local delivery and pickup (usually within a distance of five miles) are free. Recently the government reduced VAT on rentals from 23% to 10%.

BICYCLES

Raleigh Rent-a-Bike has approximately 100 branches around the country that rent ordinary bicycles by the day (about $10) or week (S48). Deposits are required; insurance is automatic; an extra charge is made if you leave your cycle with another representative in the chain. There are 15 outlets in Dublin, including **Charley's** (*Ballybough Rd.*).

SPORTS

We've already mentioned the popularity and low cost of golf, but did you ever see a hurling match? It resembles a hardy blend of hockey and lacrosse. Reputed to be the fastest form of mayhem afield, it is a spectacular sport played with "camans" or "hurleys" (hip-high lengths of ash with a broad base). The small leather-covered ball may be struck on the ground or in the air and travels at such speed that it is sometimes hard for the spectator to follow its flight. Especially pulsing are the interprovincial and all-Ireland finals, which produce great local excitement—and even a few survivors.

BICYCLING

Combine 3 days in Dublin or Cork with a 7-day "Go as you Please" bed-and-breakfast bicycle tour for about $300; without the 3-day "appetizer," about $240. Contact the **O'Mara Travel Company Ltd.**, *12/14 College Green, Dublin 2*; ☎ *773886.*

Bike-and-hostel holidays are offered at the varying rates per age group: Information from **An Oige**, *39 Mountjoy Square, Dublin 1*; ☎ *36311.*

HORSES

You might like to try a 2- or 3-week riding course that touches all equestrian bases. Approximately $475 for the former; $625 for the latter. Accommodation with families in the Dublin area. Contact **Adventure Holidays**, *St. Paul's Summer School, St. Paul's College, Sybil Hill, Raheny, Dublin 5;* ☎ *316666/323535.*

From June 1 to July 15, a 7-day horse riding program is offered in County Wexford. Tuition at around $150; living with a local family an additional $80 or so, or at **Horetown House**, *Foulksmills, Co. Wexford;* ☎ *(051) 63633/63706.*

A nomad at heart? How about roaming the Irish countryside in a horse-drawn caravan? Generally equipped with 4 bunks (seats during the day), stove, pots, pans, table service, linens, pillows, and bags of oats for the nag. After a briefing on the care and feeding of your bangtail, you're on your own to tour at an average of about 9 miles a day. High-season, 1-week summer rates from $400 to $800. Overnights for the horses about $13. Contact **Slattery's Travel Agency**, *Tralee, Co. Kerry;* ☎ *(066) 21722;* **Dieter Clissmann Horse-Drawn Caravan Holidays**, *Carrigmore, Glenealy, Co. Wicklow;* ☎ *(0404) 8188.*

WATERSPORTS

For from $226 to $373, both aspiring and accomplished sailors can take a course near Cork with food and housing at the sailing center: **Baltimore Sailing School**, *The Pier, Baltimore, Co. Cork;* ☎ *(028) 20141.*

Sailing instruction and cruises available through **Glenans Irish Sailing Centres**, *28 Merrion Sq., Dublin 2;* ☎ *611481.* The price depends on duration, season, and the vessel, but will include tuition, food, and lodging.

The International Sailing Centre offers 1- or 2-week instruction packages on sailing or sailing/wind surfing. Prices: 1 week for $250. Contact address: *5 East Beach, Cobh, Co. Cork;* ☎ *(021) 811237/504311.* Further information from the Secretary, **The Irish Association for Sail Training**, c/o *Irish Federation of Marine Industries, Confederation House, Kildare Street, Dublin 2;* ☎ *779801.*

Want to try Wicklow's white-water rivers in a canoe? About $40 buys a weekend course; $173 a week inclusive of lodging and meals. Facts from Tiglin Adventure Centre. (See Paragraph 1 under "Adventure Holiday.")

Canoe rentals from $20 to $31 daily or $61 to $103 weekly from **Irish Canoe Hire**, *25 Adelaide St., Dun Laoghaire;* ☎ *800251.* Cull more details from the Development Officer, *Irish Canoe Union, 4/5 Eustace Street, Dublin 2;* ☎ *719690.*

If you merely want pool swimming on a hot day in the capital, dive in at Markievicz *(Townsed St.)*, Sean McDermott *(also in the center)*, or Rathmines *(south side)*.

FISHING

For both sea and freshwater angling, Ireland has few rivals. Its Gulf Stream coast provides a choice of 50 different species. For in-depth details, write Mr. Hugh O'Rorke, **Irish Federation of Sea Anglers**, *67 Windsor Dr., Monkstown, Co. Dublin.* Freshwater fly casters can hook brown trout, sea trout, and salmon; spinning and hookbait enthusiasts pull in pike, perch, bream, rudd, trench, roach, and dace in over 600,000 acres of cultivated waters. Write the Angling Division at the **Irish Tourist Board** for further details or send $1 plus return postage to the Literature Dept., Irish Tourist Board P.O. Box 1083, Dublin 8 for the publication *Ireland—Freshwater Course Angling.*

HANG GLIDING

To arrange this, write to **Irish Hang-Gliding Association**, *5 Blonkurk Gardens, Drumcondra, Dublin 9.*

SIGHTSEEING

RIVER CRUISES

Captain your own vessel on the Shannon, the Erne, the Grand Canal, or the River Barrow. Brief instruction in handling given before you set sail. Most boats have from 2-8 berths and rent for about $500-2500, depending on season and on-board amenities. Almost a dozen companies ply the Shannon. Cheaper among them are **Shannon Castle Line**, *Dolphin Works, Ringsend, Dublin 4;* ☎ *600964/600588;* **SGS (Marine) Limited**, *Ballykeeran, Athlone, Co. Westmeath;* ☎ *(0902) 85163;* and **Atlantis Marine Limited**, *Bob Parks Marine Centre, Killaloe, Co. Clare; Whitegate, Co. Clare 242.*

ADVENTURE HOLIDAY

A week of activities dictated by weather/wind/tide conditions; anything from rock climbing to windsurfing to mountain camping. Full-board accommodation in 4-bed rooms. All equipment included in the $200-or-so fee. For information on this and other adventure programs: **Tiglin Adventure Centre**, *near Ashford, Co. Wicklow;* ☎ *(0404) 4169.*

HOME AWAY FROM HOME

Stay with an Irish family and take part in their daily activities through **Experiment in International Living**, *Byrnesgrove Centre, Ballyragget, Co. Kilkenny;* ☎ *(056) 41127.*

IRISH STUDIES

Interested in Celtic Ireland? Contemporary Ireland? Irish crafts or literature? Programs offered year-round at the **Centre for Irish Study Tours**, *14 the Green, Cypress Downs, Dublin 6.*

WHERE TO GO

BANTRY

The extreme southwest (Bantry-Ballylicky-Kenmare and around the legendary "Ring of Kerry" to Killarney) is beautiful and worth seeing. A loop along the L-54 coastal road up to Ballyvaughan is even more breathtaking. There are glorious seascapes and landscapes in wild and unforgettably impressive terrain. The Georgian **Bantry House** is surrounded by Italian landscaping, statuary, and emerald (Irish, of course) lawns. Be sure to see the exhibit here based on the French warship that sank and was recently discovered in Bantry Bay. Bed and breakfast accommodations are available, ☎ *027-50047*; craft items; snack center.

While in Killarney, don't miss the extraordinary excursion up the mountain to "Ladies' View" and "Moll's Gap." You'll also enjoy a turn through the **Muckross House Folk Museum** in town. One of the nation's best rock gardens borders Lough Leane and is rich in azaleas, rhododendrons, and water plants. If you have a car or take a conducted bus tour, you may jaunt by cart, pony trap, or pony back, up, in, out, and around, to the upper lake. Here a filling picnic lunch may await. Your return may be made by big comfortable rowboats, with 4 brawny oarsmen pulling you down the 14-mile channel through 3 lakes. This is a 6-hour trip. The easy way is by self-drive automobile.

In Tralee, County Kerry, "Siamsa" is the **National Folk Theatre**, where the traditions of the countryside—the thatching, weaving, butter churning, and story telling—are brought alive through mime, music, song, and dance.

CASHEL

It's not a long way to **Tipperary**—from here. You'll need only about 20 minutes by car to penetrate the heart of the famous county that gave its name to this martial song. While the castle and the cathedral of this lovely old town are its principal sights, they are almost outweighed by its old-fashioned atmosphere. Take time to explore; your rewards will be enormous; the entire area is thick with Gaelic antiquities.

CORK

Cork City is Ireland's 2nd most important town. It's on the River Lee, way down south. Cork Airport serves increasing tourist traffic to the southern counties. One side of the riverbank is chiefly industrial; the other is residential. A nice homey nest with a cozy bar and slipper comfort rooms is the **Arbutus Lodge** on the hill that backs the town. The food is as inviting as the gentle folk who serve it.

Nearby, the backwater havens of Courtmacsherry, Unionhall, Schull and the fishing port of Kinsale are picture-postcard material of the quiet seaside life.

Perhaps the most famous single tourist landmark is **Blarney Castle**, 6 miles from the center of Cork (*75 miles from Shannon, 160 miles from Dublin*). If you kiss the stone—true love never comes cheap—you'll have to pay a fee at the entrance.

If you are in search of gardens, visit the **Castle at Timoleague** with its ancient friary and proud old trees. At Castletownroche you'll discover the 18th-century **Annes Grove** hugging the green above the River Awbeg. The walls contain a treasury of botany. If you have a small group, ☎ *022-26145* and they can prepare a lunch for you.

DINGLE

Dingle is heaven on the shore for scenery—squat croft cottages, wisps of white chimney smoke, lonely cliffs, foam, sea, and wheeling gulls. If you're doing the Ring of Kerry auto-loop, take an extra day to enjoy this neighboring bay and promontory.

DUBLIN

Dublin is big-city Ireland—packed with interest and evocative of a unique character. Long before the Danes settled here in A.D. 852, "Dubhlinn" or "Dark Pool"

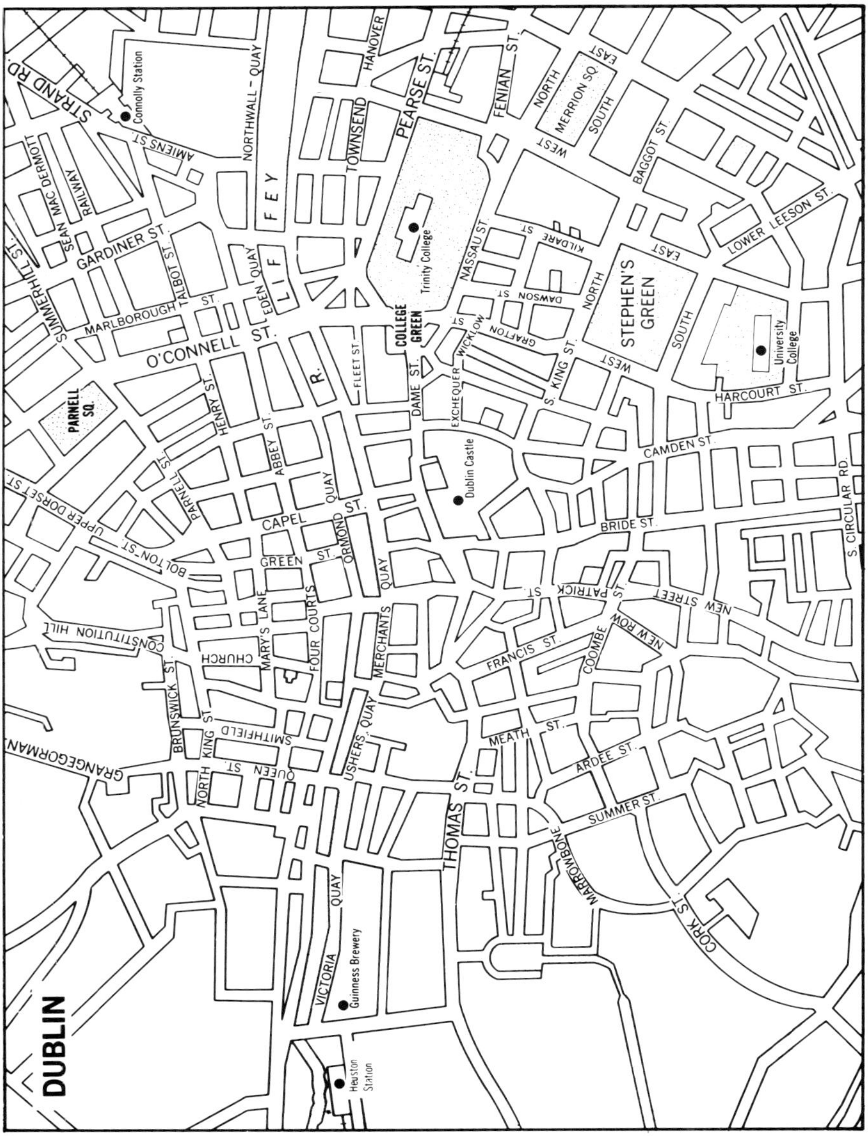
DUBLIN
STRAND RD.
Connolly Station
AMIENS ST.
NORTHWALL - QUAY
HANOVER
TOWNSEND
PEARSE ST.
FENIAN ST.
NORTH
MERRION SQ.
SOUTH
EAST
WEST
BAGGOT ST.
LOWER LEESON ST.
SUMMERHILL ST.
SEAN MAC DERMOTT
RAILWAY
GARDINER ST.
TALBOT ST.
MARLBOROUGH ST.
EDEN QUAY
L I F F E Y
R.
Trinity College
NASSAU ST.
KILDARE ST.
DAWSON ST.
STEPHEN'S GREEN
NORTH
SOUTH
EAST
WEST
University College
O'CONNELL ST.
COLLEGE GREEN
FLEET ST.
WICKLOW ST.
GRAFTON ST.
PARNELL SQ.
HENRY ST.
DAME ST.
EXCHEQUER
S. KING ST.
HARCOURT ST.
ABBEY ST.
Dublin Castle
CAMDEN ST.
PARNELL ST.
UPPER DORSET ST.
QUAY
CAPEL ST.
ORMOND
BRIDE ST.
S. CIRCULAR RD.
BOLTON ST.
GREEN ST.
QUAY
PATRICK ST.
NEW STREET
CONSTITUTION HILL
MARY'S LANE
FOUR COURTS
MERCHANTS
NEW ROW
CHURCH
FRANCIS ST.
COOMBE
BRUNSWICK ST.
NORTH KING ST.
SMITHFIELD
USHERS QUAY
MEATH ST.
GRANGEGORMAN
QUEEN ST.
ARDEE ST.
THOMAS ST.
SUMMER ST.
MARROWBONE
CORK ST.
VICTORIA QUAY
Guinness Brewery
Heuston Station

was mentioned as a place of note by Ptolemy. The official appellation, *Baile Atha Cliath* ("Town of the Hurdle Ford") recalls a time when it was only a crossing point on the Liffey River, south of the ancient Celtic capital at Tara. Today the Liffey, still following its course to Dublin Bay, passes through the heart of the city under 10 lovely bridges. Both shopping and sightseeing are enjoyable and relaxed in this town of casual pace. There are wide streets and elegant squares bound by many wonderful examples of 18th-century Georgian architecture. Dublin has been the backdrop (often controversial) of a staggering roster of poets, authors, and playwrights—Yeats, Joyce, and Synge, as examples—who drew their inspiration from the capital. The Abbey Theatre, the Gate, and the Gaiety all bear witness to the Dubliners' pride in their unique literary culture.

So take your time. Tune into its ease and its hospitality. Sink a pint of rich dark Guinness; listen to the skirl of the Irish pipes or a tenor recalling the ballads of former times. The fun and romance of the entire nation come into focus here.

DIRECTORY

U.S. Embassy • *42 Elgin Rd., Ballsbridge;* ☎ *688777.*

American Express • *116 Grafton St.;* ☎ *772874.*

Dry Cleaning, Pressing and **Laundromat** • Check Yellow Pages (called "Golden Pages" by the hyperbolizing Irish) for the one nearest your hotel.

Barber and Hairdresser • Peter Mark, *Grafton St.;* ☎ *714399.*

Suit Rental • Check Yellow Pages.

English-Speaking Doctor and Dentist • You might try dialing ☎ *999* in an emergency; the operator can find medical help at all hours. Otherwise, hotels can advise for routine matters. The **Dublin Dental Hospital** is *at Lincoln Place;* ☎ *794311* and can handle aches from 9-11 a.m. and 2-4 p.m.

Police • Central Office, *Pearse St.;*☎ *778141.*

Favorite Pawnshop • John Brereton, *108 Capel St.;* ☎ *726759.*

HOW TO GET AROUND

DART

Refers to **Dublin Area Rapid Transport** and, while nothing in Ireland is too rushed, this system will move you along at a smart pace. It runs between Howth and Bray, through the city center and along the coast. Study the route map when you arrive and DART to your destination.

Use the **bus** stops on O'Connell, Abbey, and Fleet streets as your principal starting points. You can ride to the Gate Theatre and the Municipal Gallery on Lines #11, #12, #13, #16, #16A, #22, or #22A (ask to be let off at Parnell Sq.); to St. Stephen's Green on Lines #10, #11, #13, #14, #14A, #15, #15A, #15B, or #20B; to G. B. Shaw's House on Lines #19 and #22; to Phoenix Park on Lines #10, #14, #23 or #25; to Guinness's on Line #21; to St. Michan's on Lines #34 or #34a; and to the Joyce Museum on Line #8. Inquiries fielded at the CIE office (*59 Upper O'Connell St.;* ☎ *787777*). Fares are low.

To and from Dublin Airport, hop aboard or off at the **Central Bus Station** (*Store St.*). Departures about every 20 minutes; fare about $5. Bus #41 rolls toward the tarmac at 30-minute intervals from Lower Abbey St. for about half the price. A taxi run will cost around $16 to $20.

WHERE TO STAY

Many Irish hostelries will not hold a reservation after 6 p.m. unless specifically advised ahead of time.

Finding a room during the **May Spring Show** or **August Horse Show** is difficult. Nail down that booking in writing.

Today more than 70% of bedrooms come with private bath, so specify your preference when you reserve.

Babysitting for tourists has become a nationwide cartel. The Irish Tourist Board issues a book (*Guest Accommodation*), indicating availability of this service up to midnight at a rate of about £1 per hour. Since most hostelries already offer a 10–50% discount for children under 10, this is a built-in bonus.

LEAST $

A bonanza! Here is your chance to get at the grass roots of the ould sod, to mix at the breakfast table, and to enjoy the company of kindly Irish landladies who have time to chat with their houseful of 8 or 10 guests. Should you arrive without reservations, be sure to telephone before setting out. Most of these are a long, costly taxi-hop from the center, and many simply can't squeeze you in if you haven't booked in advance. Officially classified as "Town Homes" for having a minimum of 3 bedrooms, they expect you to pay approximately $22 per person.

Avalon House • *55 Aungler St.; ☎ 750001*, FAX *75-0303*. For a good start, the people here are tuned in to the needs of budget travelers.

Suncroft • *110 Sandford Rd., Ranelagh; ☎ 971375*. Mrs. S. McKenna's is a 4-room, red-brick residence. Beautifully kept; double-glaze windows; central heating; hot and cold water in all accommodations. Bed and breakfast about $20. The homemade brown bread is a marvel.

Mrs. A. Haire's • *73-74 Dollymount Park, Clontarf; ☎ 332690.*

St. Aidan's • *150 Clonliffe Rd. Drumcondra; ☎ 376750.*

Cill Fiontain • *56 Castle Ave., Clontarf; ☎ 336402*. All are reliable for neatness, cleanliness, and low prices. Mrs. Creagh and Mrs. Murnane are the respective proprietresses at the latter two.

HOSTELS

The **Irish Youth Hostel Association** oversees several choices.

Morehampton House • *78 Morehampton Rd.; ☎ 680325*. Near Herbert Park in the Donnybrook precinct, regular bus service on lines #10, #46a, or #64a takes you to this quiet situation; bunks for 86 persons. From Apr. to Sept., there is another facility at *39 Mountjoy Sq., Dublin 1* (this group's headquarters, *☎ 745734*) with dormitory space for both sexes. In July and Aug., luggage may be deposited from noon to 5 p.m. at both hostels. Tabs per night run around $8 (over 21 years), $5 (18-21 years). In July and Aug. there is a temporary hostel at **Scoil Lorcain**, **Monkstown** *(near Dun Laoghaire Pier)*.

Mrs. B McDonagh • *59 St. Lawrence Rd., Clontarf; ☎ 333597*. Self-catering apartments with cooking facilities, off-street car parking, and good bus connections to the center (#'s 28, 29, 31 and 54). The area is residential; rates at a reasonable $11 per night.

YWCA Hostel • *Radcliffe Hall, St. John's Road, Sandymount; (☎ 694521).* You'll find 54 rooms (22 with bath). Bed and breakfast for $15, but add another $2 for room with private bath.

For summer visitors to the Dublin area, suburban **Dun Laoghaire** (*a half-hour ride from the capital*) is a seaside haven that attracts longer stayers. I also recommend the following:

Mrs. M. Basquille's • *23 Mellifont Ave.; ☎ 805351.* This hostel is extra-cheerful.

Innisfree • *31 Northumberland Ave.; ☎ 805598.* Mrs. Quinton's freshly updated spot welcomes guests into a happy kindred atmosphere. Room and breakfast approximately $20 in these family-operated houses.

MORE $$

Pretty good when you can locate one, but far too few in the central precincts. Most of the lodgings simple, clean, and located in the nearby suburbs. The Irish Tourist Board has graded these guesthouses with letter designations, "A" being the top category; all must have a minimum of 5 bedrooms.

Mount Herbert • *Herbert Rd., Ballsbridge; ☎ 684321.* Near the rugby stadium and Herbert Park's tennis courts. Bus #52 rolls almost to the entrance; #2 and #3 halt nearby, making downtown very accessible. 88 spacious units; sauna; solarium; TV; pleasant dining room. $33 per person without private bath; $34 with (including a hearty Irish breakfast).

Egan's House • *7/9 Iona Park; ☎ 303611.* Egan's spotless 23 rooms, all with bath, color TV, and phone. Appealing wine bar; relaxed restaurant; lounges with open fires. Quiet, homey situation near Botanic Gardens. A specialty of the house is its afternoon tea with homemade brown bread and scones; tea kettle in every bedroom.

Iona House • *At #5 on the same street; ☎ 306217.* Contains 14 rooms, 12 with shower and W.C.; radios, color TV, and phone in every one. Coffee shop. 50% reduction for children bunking with parents. Bid for a view of the small garden area.

St. Jude's Guest House • *17 Pembroke Park—beside the American Embassy; ☎ 680483.* Lies several miles north of city center in an excellent residential zone. Solid values—a cause not lost by its proprietor—in the $30 range for twosomes, including breakfast.

Ariel • *52 Lansdowne Rd., Ballsbridge; ☎ 685512.* Another suburbanite. Can be reached by buses #5 through #8. U.S. Embassy and Lands-downe Road rugby ground are neighbors.

EVEN MORE $$$

Montrose Hotel • *About 15 minutes from the center in residential Stillorgan; ☎ 693311.* About $65 buys a reasonably comfortable double. Every unit with TV, central heat, radio, and direct-dial phone. Belfield Grill; Robert Room Restaurant for table d'hôte and à la carte; huge bar; health studio; hairdresser.

Tara Tower • *Merrion Rd.; ☎ 694666.* Charm downstairs, simplicity above in its 84 rooms with bath. Lounge; coffee house. Ask for a unit with a huge picture window on the bay. Rates similar to the Montrose.

Kellys • *36 South Great George's St.;* ☎ *779277.* A homey family spot run by Tom and Paula Lynam. Irish breakfast is reason enough to bunk in with these hospitable people. About 80% of the units with shower or bath.

Ashling • *Parkgate St., About 1-1/4 miles from the center, near Heuston Station and beside Phoenix Park;* ☎ *772324.* Restaurant, grill, salad bar, and sandwich nook. All 56 units with bath, phone, radio, color TV. $57 per person for bed and full Irish breakfast.

North Star • *Amiens St., Opposite Connolly Station (the main hub for points north and west); beside the Airport Bus Terminal; convenient to car ferries;* ☎ *363136.* 40 satisfactory rooms and ideal as a springboard for further travels.

CAMPING

At the moment the only official sites in the Dublin area are **Shankill Caravan Park**, Shankill (*near Bray*); ☎ *2820011*, open Easter to Oct. 31, and at nearby Rush the **North Beach Caravan and Camping Park**. Otherwise, in this most hospitable of countries, almost any farmer's field will do. Just ask permission, because they're accustomed to such requests; usually you'll be waved in with a warm welcome.

The **Ryan Tours/Hotel** group has established an excellent travel skein for visitors to the U.K. and Ireland. With offices in New York, London, and Dublin, one can arrange package trips (fly/drive or car ferry) to numerous centers of interest at surprisingly low cost. You can also book on an individual basis through Ryan.

Another ingenious twist—this one more specialized—is the **Rent-AnIrish-Cottage Program**. Each of these cottages is complete with half-door (that may not sound complete but you also get the other half), traditional furnishings, all-electric kitchen, living room with open peat-burning hearth, central heating, and modern conveniences. Ask your travel agent to get the basics from the **Irish Hotel/Guest Houses and Farm Houses Association** or from the **Country Homes Association**.

SUGGESTIONS FOR STUDENTS

The major student arena encompasses Grafton Street, Temple Bar, and St. Stephen's Green. Here you'll find the heaviest concentration of Trinity Collegians, several low-cost restaurants, and the Royal Irish Academy.

For special lodgings, get in touch with the **National University** *(49 Merrion Sq.;* ☎ *767246).*

STUDENTS' NIGHTLIFE

At Belmont Villas in suburban Donnybrook, **St. Mary's Tennis Club** has a tiny combo that singes the thatch on its little cottage-style clubhouse on Sat. only; $4.50 entry fee; 85¢ soft drinks; open every night in summer. Arrive with a date if you can because you'd be lucky to find one here; a bit of fast talking normally skirts the casual membership requirements. Recommended.

WHERE TO EAT

LEAST $

Arnotts • *Henry St.* Offers a titanic Irish breakfast for £2 and a wide selection of snacks and full meals to follow if hunger ever returns.

Le Savoir Faire • *Grafton St.* In the center-city Switzer's department store, it is pence for pence one of the tops in town. Offers such refinements as smoked salmon, crab salad, and orange mousse. Open only for breakfast and lunch. Enthusiastically recommended.

Birch Tray • Cafeteria in the same store, less expensive and recommended.

Nico's • *33 Dame St.* Pleasant for lunch. Piano music after dusk. 26-choice, 4-course fixed lunch menu. Veal and pasta specialties, plus steaks, chops, fish, and fowl. Fair wine list. À la carte dinners in the $17 bracket. Quite good.

Jules • *15 Lower Baggot St.* A recently refurbished complex comprising restaurant, wine bar, disco (Thurs. through Sun.), and snooker rooms.

Stag's Head • *1 Dame Ct.* Between 12:30 and 2:30 p.m. offers all the corned beef, roast beef, and vegetables you can eat for perhaps $11. Cellar snack haven and bar. Service informal but kind. Go for lunch only.

Murphy Doodles • *18 Suffolk St.* Have some tacos, a quiche, chili, a tasty delicatessen choice, or some other multinational selection. Inexpensive and varied. Also fun, but hardly living up to its fine Irish handle.

SNACKS

Munchies • *Wicklow St. and Baggot St.* Represents the coming of the sandwich bar to Dublin. Good, too.

Marks Brothers • *7 South Great George St.* More of the same plus soup and lively animation.

Wynns • *Abbey St.* Takes special pride in its snack-lunch section.

Bewley's Cafes • *10 Westmoreland St., 13 S. Great Georges St., and 78 Grafton St.* Actually, the name is a misnomer as they are daytime coffee shops excelling in their own breads, rolls, and top-grade-but-low-cost cookery.

Bad Ass Cafe • *9/11 Crown Alley.* You may cook your own steaks here, but not your own pizza.

Jonathan's • *Irish Life Mall, Middle Abbey St.*

ILAC Centre • *Henry St.*

Golden Grill • *O'Connell St.*

PUBS

The pub lunch is burgeoning in popularity. Eminently practical because the fare is light and the service fast.

On a nationwide basis they operate from 10:30 a.m.–11:30 p.m. in summer. In Dublin, Waterford, Limerick, and Cork, pubs close from 2:30 p.m.–4 p.m.—irreverently known as the "Holy Hour." Sunday hours nationwide are 12:30 p.m.–2 p.m. and 4–11 p.m. Public service in the entire country is bone-dry on Christmas Day and Good Friday. St. Patrick's Day now has same opening hours as a normal Sun.

As in England, the venerable color, serenity, and neighborliness of Irish pubs are undergoing a change, but there are still some fine traditional ones about. The newer types are called "Singing Pubs." Younger people frequent this mutation while the middle-aged and the elderly maintain their loyalty to the traditional-style establishments. I recently overheard an old-timer puff into one of the latter from the cold muttering, "It's a lazy wind. It won't blow around you so it blows through you." At another spot I listened to one Irishman grousing about his enemy, "He's so thirsty, he'd drink porter out of a sore leg."

MODERN PUBS

Slattery's Terenure House • *Terenure Rd. 3 sections in a large building.* The first floor lounge is a bar; the second a spartan bar for the serious male toper; the third its piéce de résistance, an upstairs cabaret-bar (small admission charge), which holds 400. Electric organ and lone singers or small groups. Sound system switched to maximum. Open Thurs. through Sun.

William Searson • *42 Upper Baggot St.* Contemporary complex of three bars with lounges: two modern, and the public bar in fake turn-of-the-century. Could be a cocktail lounge in any American city.

CLASSIC PUBS

The Bailey • *Duke St.* For decades, nay centuries, one of the city's most celebrated haunts of the literati. Ground-floor bar; upstairs restaurant; air of conviviality manifestly inviting; so is the splendid quality of its foodstuffs, with many fresh fish specialties and an emphasis on French-style cooking. Richly recommended for blue-ribbon pubbery.

Davy Byrnes • *Duke St.* Draws more than its share of Earnest Young Authors.

Patrick Conway • *Parnell St.* With its dark panels and semi-partitions, this pub is authentically old-school Hibernian. Ham cooked in red wine plus the ubiquitous steak-and-kidney pie, its best-known specialties. Typical charm in somewhat faded surroundings.

Neary's • *Chatham St.* Friendly and unpretentious. With a tiny cocktail bar on one side,tavern style.

McDaid's • *Harry St. off Grafton St.* This one remains popular. A recent facelifting does not detract from its familiar mood.

MORE $$

Beaufield Mews • *Woodlands Ave. (in nearby Stillorgan).* A quiet haven. Softly illuminated converted stable. 5-course menu nightly for about $24. Open 7 to 10 p.m., but never for lunch, Sun., Mon., bank holidays, or Christmas and Easter weeks. Very attractive.

Powerscourt • *S. William St.* A terrific midtown redevelopment under one vast warehouse roof—Dublin's answer to London's rejuvenated Covent Garden. With boutiques, indoor plazas, crafts, and artisan ware—and, of course, restaurants. Here are the names of some of the top entries:

Oisin's • *31 Upper Camden St.; ☎ 753433.* Runs higher in price than I'd usually recommend ($35–40) for a 5-course feast, but here there are real value and splendid opportunity to savor genuine Irish cookery that is both historic and rare. Cockle soup, coddle, poteen-fired sausage, rich stews, soda bread; mix it up with live, soft Irish music, and you'll have an evening to remember. The approach, too, is genteel, not blatantly folkloric. Better to save up for this big night out and carry away a pleasant recollection.

Pink Bicycle • Amusing cafeteria on upper ring of the atrium. Tables on balcony as well as inside; most animated viewing at outer tier. Colorful food presentation; a full meal for a maximum of $5.

Blazing Salads • The vegetable world is appetizing and abundant, both from sea and shore.

Periwinkle • Ground-floor lunch counter (plus a few tables), with some of the best, most attractive and cheapest high-quality light bites in Dublin. Seafood and shellfish bar. Handsome wood interior. Splendid as a shopper's repose.

Mary Rose • In the center of the courtyard, slightly raised on podium with great parasols over tables. Appetizing meal for close to $9. Middle of the action.

Hanky-Pancakes • Serving, you guessed it. Also waffles. Usually packed with flap-jack fans.

Casper's Drink & Food Emporium • *Wicklow St.* Across from Switzers, on Grafton St., and down a few steps to a delightfully dark, intimate, clean tavern. Tables plus counter service; polished woodwork; Tiffany-style lamps. Lunch for $7; fuller repast for about $18. Lamb excellent (in 5 ways); pork, fish salads, veal, quiches all superb. Irish Coffee that does credit to the Emerald Isle. Open daily noon to midnight. Superb.

Gallagher's Boxty House • *20-21 Temple.* Bar does all of its cooking in the Irish fashion; the mood, too, is decidedly nationalistic.

NIGHTLIFE

Jurys Irish Cabaret (*Ballsbridge*) is a traditional must, especially for first timers who have a rather hefty $52 to spare. With the substantial dinner (beginning at 7:30 p.m.) comes lively entertainment by an Irish cabaret of regional dancers, singers, and harpists (8:20 p.m. start). Offered nightly (except Mon.) in season. Be sure to reserve in advance! Others of note for this type of cabaret include the 2-hour extravaganza at the **Burlington Hotel** and the **Braemor Rooms** (*Churchtown*)—with dancing after the show to a resident trio. Both pipe Mon. through Sat.; figure meal and revels to cost $49 and $41, respectively, per person. At a lower rate and wonderfully Irish in tone and casual in presentation, is the **Abbey Tavern** out at Howth. It's been going along successfully for years, and I love it for its easygoing communal approach. Public transportation runs out here. Phone before going; ☎ *322006.*

DANCING

At this writing, most popular are: **Samantha's** (*facing Ely Place*), **Joys** (*Baggot St.*), and **Papillon Disco** (*Kildare St.*). **The Wildebeest** (*Johnson's Court*) is wild for rock and jazz. **Bad Bob's Backstage Bar** (*35-37 E. Essex St.*) goes for country and folk music; **Brazen Head** (*Bridge St.*) and **An Beal Bocht** (*Charlemont St.*) are traditional folk depots. But since they open and close with the speed of a strobe light, check upon arrival to be sure they are still swinging. Admission to most costs around $8, a bit higher on weekends. Many serve a light supper as part of the entry price.

WHAT TO SEE AND DO

A few of the many: The **Abbey Theatre**, which embraces the smaller **Peacock Theatre**, the **Gate Theatre**, the **Hugh Lane Municipal Gallery of Modern Art**, the **National Gallery**, **St. Stephen's Green**, **Georgian Merrion Square**, **Phoenix Park**, **Guinness's**, the **James Joyce Museum** (sited in the Martello Tower in suburban Sandycove, where the master lived), and the most engaging **Dublin Writers Museum**. **Malahide Castle**, the **"Crusader's Corpse"** in St. Michan's Church, the **Book of Kells** in Trinity College, the **Douglas Hyde Gallery** (also at Trinity), **Newbridge House**, the **Viking Center**, and scores more.

There's also the world-famous **Dublin Horse Show**, held every August. The catches are: hotel rates during the pageant soar, and finding space is a major problem.

Your best sightseeing tools? A copy of *Dublin, Ireland*; a current edition of *Events of the Week*; the **Tourist Trail**, a signposted walking tour of Dublin; and the *Dublin Ordnance Survey Street Plan*, indexed and marked in great detail. All available at the Tourist Information Office (*14 Upper O'Connell St.*).

THEATER, ET AL.

This is the lifeblood of Irish culture—some of the finest acting and best productions you may experience in all your theater-going years. Yet the prices are astonishingly low. The best seats cost only around $17, and many good locations will be half that. If you don't wish to stand in line or risk getting turned away, go to Switzers Department Store, which handles bookings for a multitude of events but, of course, adds on its commission. HMV record stores also purvey the ducats.

MARKETS

Fruit and fish sellers gather on **Mary's Lane** weekdays from 8 a.m. to 5 p.m.; they go home at noon on Saturday.

Moore St. remains the most famous spot for foodstuffs, but due to area development, some of the peddlers have moved indoors in the region.

Iveagh Market (*Francis St.*) features old clothes (Tues. through Sat.).

GARDENS

The **National Botanic** exhibits at **Glasnevin** go back 2 centuries; the institute itself is surrounded by wonderful displays.

Howth Castle, however, is more romantic for its panorama of the capital. Try to catch it in spring when the rhododendrons are preening.

WATERSKIING

The **Dublin/Balscadden Power Boat and Ski Club**, 30 minutes from Dublin on the #42 bus to Malahide, will tow you for about $11 per run. Local boats also available.

Tara Street Swimming Bath is the best downtown pool.

WHERE TO SHOP

Shopping hours are generally from 9 a.m. to 5:30 p.m., Mon.–Sat. In some parts of the country, stores shutter at 1 p.m. on Wed. or Thurs.

AUTHOR'S OBSERVATION

All goods shipped to the States are exempt from the hefty 21% VAT (Value-Added Tax). Ask about the rebate scheme, which should give you back about 17.35% of your costs, recently set up at airports.

ARAN ISLAND HANDICRAFTS

Cleo (*18 Kildare St.*) has handicrafts in profusion at decent tariffs. The handknits and weavings for both sexes draw inspiration from Ireland's past.

DEPARTMENT STORES

It's a toss-up between **Brown Thomas** and **Switzers** (*both on Grafton St.*). The former is smaller and more elegant than the latter.

Arnott's (*Grafton St. and Henry St.*) and **Clery's** (*O'Connell St.*) are down a peg or two.

GENEALOGISTS

Heraldic Artists Ltd. (*3 Nassau St.*) is our choice in a field where commercialism is rife. They'll research your ancestors or supply you with extensive material so you can trace them yourself. They design wall plaques with coats of arms, parchments with details pertaining to a name, scrolls, family trees, and other decorative devices. Over 1/2 million names in their extensive files.

HANDWOVEN, HAND-KNIT, OR HAND-FASHIONED WEARABLES

Both the **Blarney Woollen Mills** (*21-23 Nassau St.*) and the **Dublin Woollen Co.**, (*41 Lr. Ormond Quay, Ha'Penny Bridge*) can wrap you from bonnet to sock-toe in the fairest woolies—perfect for crisp, cool, weather.

IRISH HARPS AND BAGPIPES

Waltons (*2-5 North Frederick St.*) is worth a visit by anyone with music in his heart. Harps run the scale from $500–2500, including packing and shipping to New York. Sheet music and recordings are also available.

IRISH PRODUCTS (GENERAL)

House of Ireland (*37/38 Nassau St.*) says it all in its name. Whether you are looking for a doll collection, a Celtic cross, a bedspread, or a distinctive item to wear right now, don't miss this wonderland of Erin.

OUTDOOR ACCESSORIES

H. Johnston Ltd. (*11 Wicklow St.*) is a traditional center with a fine collection of blackthorn walking sticks, sticks for race-watching, and umbrellas.

SOUVENIRS

As such they are either very good or horrid. There has been, however, a marked improvement in recent years with many new shops opening all over the nation selling items of high quality, as well as craft workshops that welcome the public. The **Kilkenny Shop** (*Nassau St.*) is good. You'll find a tasteful collection of carefully selected knitwear, woven articles, porcelain stoneware, glass, copper, brass, and jewelry, to name just a few. **Fergus O'Farrell** (*60 Dawson St.*) has an interesting, high-quality potpourri, with many handmade items. It is far superior to the usual junk traps. **Powerscourt Town House Centre** (*Clarendon St.*) is a covered courtyard with several levels bursting with shops, boutiques, and eating places; great if the weather is bad. At **Tower Design Centre** (*Pearse St.*) visitors may watch artisans at work. **St. Stephen's Green Centre** is another conglomeration; similar rewards if you graze in this green. Out at the **Guinness brewery** (a mile from town) you can purchase any number of gimmicks stamped with the brand name and quench your thirst with a free sample of their most famous concoction on draft.

TWEEDS

Kevin and Howlin, Ltd. (*31 Nassau St.*) is our choice for menswear. The selection of ready-made jackets is extensive, and they have women's sizes as well. You will find the subtle shades of this Irish landscape in the carefully composed handloomed Donegals. Look at the dashing and timeless walking hats, too, which will last through many decades of storm or chill.

SHOPPING ZONES

Grafton St., **Nassau St.**, **Kildare St.**, **Royal Hibernian Way**, **Westbury Mall**, and **Dawson St.** are more fashionable areas than Henry St., Mary St., Talbot St., and South Great George's St.

GALWAY

Since tourism began in Ireland, **Galway** and its seaside suburb of Salthill have been the traditional gateways to the wild and glorious western counties of **Galway** and **Mayo** and the islands off this coast. The region offers spectacular geography, a fascinating breed of people, and beauty that is even more pristine—containing the widely renowned area of Connemara, a land of stone walls, mountains, lakes, woods, and magnificent secluded beaches. It is bordered on the east by sleepy Lough Corrib, which boasts an island for every day of the year. In Mayo you'll discover magnificent **Clew Bay**, an area covering 50 square miles of sheltered rock-dotted waters, under

Croagh Patrick's stony head; there are splendid seascapes and landscapes on all sides. Ferries make the Aran run in only 90 minutes nowadays (only 35 minutes from Rossaveal). You can enjoy a lot of scenery and add a beautiful dimension to your Irish experience for very little in cost.

KENMARE, KERRY AND KILLARNEY

Since all of these are links in the aforementioned Ring-of-Kerry run, please see "Bantry."

LIMERICK

Ireland's 3rd city is so inextricably woven into the skein of international air travel that it is covered in the next paragraph.

SHANNON INTERNATIONAL AIRPORT

Shannon is the airport and Limerick is the town. Transit passengers generally have time to catch a bite in the airport's outstanding Lindbergh Room restaurant, to polish off a quickie at its friendly bar (amazingly low prices), and, if not bound for Dublin or domestic points, to load up with duty-free purchases.

Within easy reach of the airport are the 3 medieval banqueting castles: **Bunratty**, **Knappogue**, and **Dunguaire**, the last 2 open only for summer pilgrims. During the colorful 15th-century banquet in the Great Hall of Bunratty Castle, a "Lord and Lady" are elected. Now this monument, with its Irish village complex, cottages, a forge, a candle maker, weaver, potter, and a souvenir and crafts shop to the rear, is open the calendar 'round. Also a number of interesting castles, prehistoric lake dwellings, ring forts, and museums reflecting the natural history and culture of the area can be taken in on day tours by coach from Limerick City. Pop into the tourist office at the Granary for details.

Another attraction in the area is the **Craggaunowen Project**, where replicas of the lake dwellings and forts of the early Christian Irish have been constructed. The leather Brendan boat in which Tim Severin and his crew sailed the Atlantic is also housed at Craggaunowen.

THE RIVER SHANNON

Cabin boats are available for self-operated cruises of the Shannon River where you can get away from it all by enjoying the peace, quiet, and scenery of one of the world's most unpolluted and beautiful freshwater streams where all commercial traffic is banned.

WATERFORD

Fourth city in Ireland, situated on the **River Suir** about 18 miles from where it joins the sea, it was a great meeting place of historical paths. Today the byways and side streets of the old town center provide a microcosm of Irish history. The town, of course, is world-famous for the beauty of its shimmering crystal; best known landmark is Reginald's Tower (erected in 1003), a massive stone Viking fortress, still in good condition. Though heavily restored, it serves as Waterford's **Civic Museum** where items from the corporation archives are on display.

WEXFORD

Nestled where the River Slaney enters Wexford Harbor, an ancient place of narrow winding lanes, it is also active in commerce. For walking tours, Wexford has a more historic atmosphere than most Irish cities. Much of the old Norse arrangement survives in the low alleys leading from the main street to the quays. Some of Ireland's finest beaches and resorts are within easy reach of Wexford town, and the area from here to Rosslare is one of the driest and sunniest in Ireland.

WICKLOW

An hour's drive south of the capital, Wicklow is known as the Garden of Ireland by virtue of its unique combination of woodland, mountain, lake, and glen. Stately homes and gardens such as **Russborough** and **Powerscourt**, **Avondale** and **Mount Usher** attract thousands. The seaside resorts of **Bray**, **Greystones**, **Arklow**, and **Wicklow Town** itself are highly popular. Inland, historic Glendalough and the immortal **Vale of Avoca**, with its Meeting of the Waters, are best visited by following the scenic routes outlined on the *Wicklow—Garden of Ireland Map* available at Tourist Information offices.

FOR MORE INFORMATION ON IRELAND

USA • *757 Third Ave., New York, NY 10017;* ☎ *(212) 418-0800.*

CANADA • *10 King St. East, Toronto, M5C 1C3;* ☎ *(416) 364-1301.*

INSIDER TIP

The master organization is called Bord Failte Eireann. The Information Office in Dublin is located at Baggot St. Bridge, while Dublin tourism help can be found at both the airport, as well as at 14 Upper O'Connell St. *For a small charge, it can also find accommodation for you almost anywhere in the nation.*

ITALY

Cathedral of Florence

Here's a four-in-one country—if you also count the independent entities of *The Vatican*, *San Marino*, and the *Sovereign Military Order of Malta*. In all four there are 57 million residents and (seemingly) 57-million-and-one differing opinions on any subject at any given instant. If any citizen disagrees with another, a strike is called. Never mind, the Italians prove day after day that good times exist even in states of chaos.

For the tourist, it is the epitome of what a foreign destination should be. Apart from a natural gift for hospitality, Italian real estate contains about as much variety and natural beauty as any pair of eyes could absorb. The ranges of its northern alpine semicircle, with its pristine lakes and popular ski resorts, give way to the rich Po Valley. On either side of the boot, there is a sea yielding marvelous coastal resorts. The Tuscan landscape, with Florence as its capital, rolling Umbria, Perugia, Assisi—hilltowns of the Middle Ages—are vivid reminders of Giotto, Botticelli, Cimabue, Masaccio, Piero della Francesca, and Donatello. Works by Da Vinci and Michelangelo appear even in relatively minor sites along the way.

Through the Marche, the savage and mountainous Abruzzo to Latium and the Eternal City. Down through Campania to the sleepy mezzogiorno—Naples, Capri (jewel of the Tyrrhenian Sea) to Pompeii with its well-preserved forum, baths, and mosaics, plus the neighboring villages surrounding Herculaneum where exciting archaeological finds are being unearthed almost hourly. Calabria's rugged terrain leads you down—and very inexpensively—to the toe toward Sicily, where Mount Etna grumbles in perpetual moodiness. There's a feeling here of suspension in another distant era. Olive and lemon groves speckle the rough hillsides; shepherds take biblical poses among their herds of sheep and goats. Italy—with its blood-red Ferraris, Armani stylings, and Olivetti high-tech, as well as its crumbling monuments from before the time of Romulus and Remus—is both timely and timeless.

TIPS ON ITALY

ACCOMMODATIONS

It's magic! Simply by a stroke of Italian legislation, all pensioni (pensions or boarding houses) all over the land have become "hotels." Therefore don't be misguided in your search for modestly priced shelter. What's in a name? You'll have to look under the roof to find out.

To the many supplements added to the hotel bill, cashiers will slap on the ever-present IVA, or added value tax, which tacks on 4% or 19% (depending on the category) and ups meals by 9%. So don't always trust the "official" prices; too often, they are only the start. Always insist that you are quoted the total rate, including service, taxes, and all supplements. Italian law (frequently abused) requires that the basic rate, plus all charges for service and taxes, be posted in every room. Don't always believe the published version. If the room clerk likes you, he might accept your request for a discount.

In some of the rural or smaller urban hostelries, late arrivals can often talk down the price by as much as 50%.

FOOD

Discounting the North, where rice is king, the average Italian exists on bread and pasta. From the basic ingredient—wheat flour—spring dozens of variations from agnellotti to ziti. Many are served in gargantuan portions; after a dinner plate of this "appetizer," the visitor

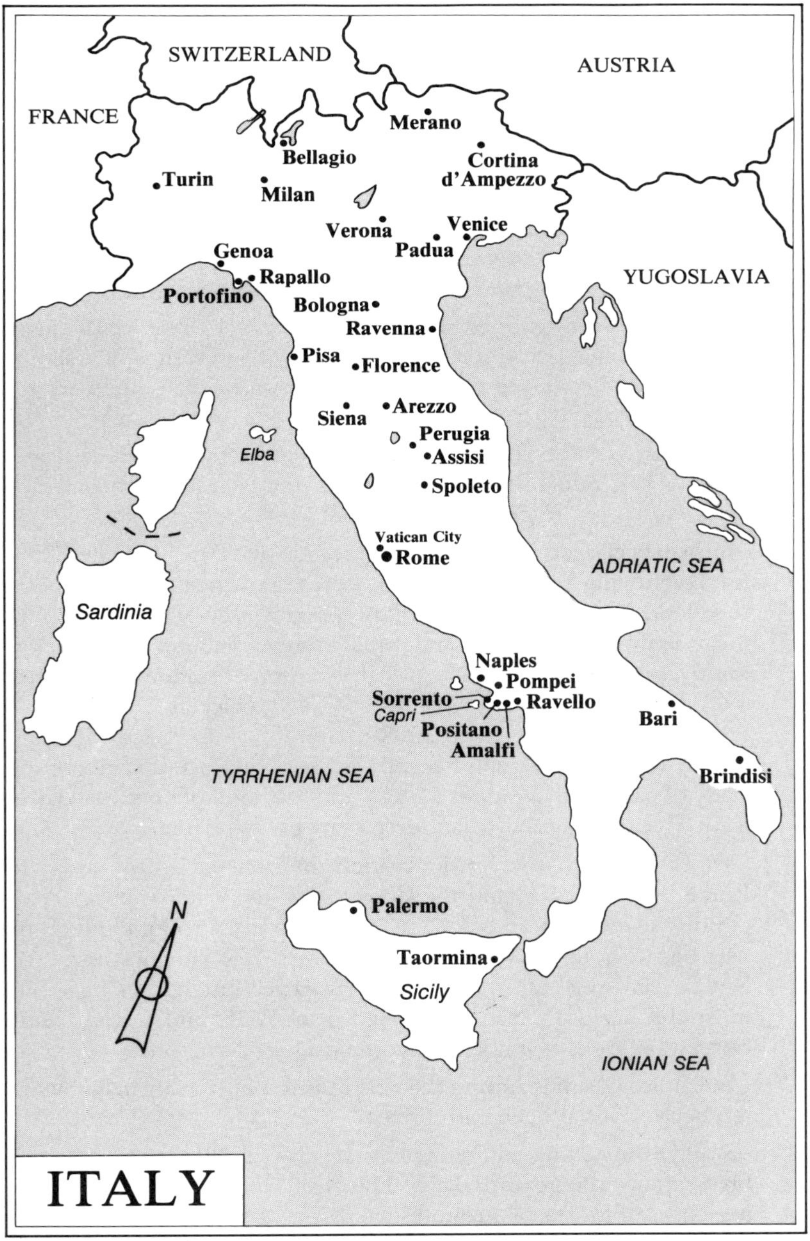
SWITZERLAND
AUSTRIA
FRANCE
Merano
Bellagio
Cortina d'Ampezzo
Turin
Milan
Verona
Venice
Padua
Genoa
Rapallo
Portofino
YUGOSLAVIA
Bologna
Ravenna
Pisa
Florence
Arezzo
Siena
Elba
Perugia
Assisi
Spoleto
Vatican City
Rome
ADRIATIC SEA
Sardinia
Naples
Pompei
Sorrento
Ravello
Capri
Bari
Positano
Amalfi
TYRRHENIAN SEA
Brindisi
Palermo
N
Taormina
Sicily
IONIAN SEA
ITALY

seldom can find room for the meat, potatoes, vegetables, salad, and dessert that follow. In most places you can order a half ("mezza") portion of spaghetti, fettuccine, ravioli, and other simple pastas, but you must request this and later check your bill to see that you have not been charged the full rate.

Risotto appears in innumerable versions. The basis is towel-rubbed rice, simmered in an iron skillet in bouillon or chicken broth until the kernels are dark and tasty. With this are mixed mushrooms, peppers, onions, saffron, butter, and cheese; veal, chicken, pork, lobster, beef, or other ingredients can then be added. Risotto alla Milanese is perhaps the most famous; you might prefer the one with chunks of chicken, asparagus, browned onions, tomatoes, and peas.

Prosciutto, dark spicy local ham served in wafer-thin slices, is an excellent cocktail appetizer. It's wonderful with fresh figs or a slice of melon—but be sure to order it crudo (raw), or they might serve it cotto (cooked).

Antipasti (salami, cheese, prosciutto, celery, egg, artichoke hearts, black olives, pimento, and other spicy foods) are the Italian hors d'oeuvres. They're generally quite oily.

Other specialties worth trying are Scampi alla Griglia (grilled crawfish resembling large grilled shrimp), sea crab cocktail (eat the delicate "coral" separately), Cannelloni (pasta stuffed with pate or other meats and baked in cheese and tomato sauce), Minestrone (delicious multivegetable soup with regional variations of added pasta, rice, etc.), Pollo alla Diavola (called "deviled chicken," but actually broiled with herbs), Scaloppine San Giorgio (veal stuffed with ham, cheese, and mushrooms), Pansoti con Salsa di Noci (a Genoese specialty of pasta with a walnut filling), and that king of desserts, Gateau Saint-Honore, purely Italian, despite its French name.

Water? Stick to the bottled variety in rural or village areas (in Rome, Milan, Turin, and the larger cities, tap water is pure). Most popular sparkling brands are San Pellegrino and Crodo; Fiuggi is the best bet without gas (said to be the remedy for kidney stones); the almost-flat Sangemini is sold in pharmacies but not in bars. The most chic sip is Ty Nant, imported from Wales and served from a bottle that looks as if it should contain Dom Perignon.

Italian ice cream is among the best in Europe. It's safe in all big cities, because it has been pasteurized.

Scandals involving adulterated comestibles regularly raise the eyebrows, if not the ire, of Italians. This year, the danger of your receiving cheese bloated by ground banana peels, butter processed from donkey fats, or other more nauseous concoctions is relatively small —all but nonexistent if you adhere to the addresses suggested in this book.

Key to Italian classifications: Below the expensive or medium-price restaurants comes the trattoria, which is generally less costly, unfancy, and good. Pizzerias are often limited to pasta selections, but they can become more ambitious and serve wider choices; pizza bianca is the least expensive variety—a snack with no tomato sauce to add the distinctive color. Cheapest of all are the tavola caldas ("hot tables").

DRINKS

Grappa, vermouth, and brandy are the national hard drinks. Grappa, popular in the north, is a raw, harsh, high-proof beverage made from the leftovers of the ordinary distillation process. By the terms of a Franco-Italian treaty, the brandy may no longer be called "cognac" but, of course, it is; Vecchia Romagna and Rene Briand are pleasant brands. To anyone used to Gordon's or Beefeater, local gin can be a magic carpet to the Al Capone days. Cocktails get worse, province by province, as you progress from the Swiss border to Sicily. Local whiskies also are poor, but some of the liqueurs (notably Strega and Aurum) are extremely palatable. If you like licorice flavoring, try Sambuca (anisette) served con mosche (with "flies," which are floating coffee beans).

In Italy, about 55% of the soil is dedicated to the grape. The varieties are numerous and rewarding. It is not unusual for foreigners to believe that chianti is inexpensive. Some of these in the top levels are among the nation's finest and they can be costly. Tavola types (printed on the label) should indicate that they are reasonably priced.

Vinofeiters, who turned out 300 million gallons annually of adulterated or false wines, used to be a big headache, but now many of them are wearing pinstripes in Italian jails. The controls have been significantly strengthened. Ingredients had run the gamut from water, sugar, denatured alcohol, apple juice, potato juice, turnip juice, dried fig paste, curry, glycerine, or other chemical and coloring products—many of which were barred by law from human consumption. It sounds like a lot of trouble for a small profit, but the manufacturing costs were estimated at 1/5 those of the true grape essence.

Today the government has a classification system similar to France's appellation controlee. If you stick to the officially classified labels only, you'll know what's inside the bottle. If limited to 3 wines in Italy—1 red, 1 white, and 1 rose—here's a short list:

- For the red—Valpolicella (Bolla)
- For the white—Soave Bertani
- For the rose—Bolla

Bardolino (a red from Verona), **Verdicchio** (a white from the Adriatic slopes), and **Rosatello** (a rose) are excellent alternatives; some prefer them. The **Lambrusco** from *Emilia* and the **Recioto** from *Verona* are sparkling reds also worthy of attention. Chianti is available everywhere; Antinori is an excellent label in this category. All but one of the Italian roses, including **Bertolli** and **Rosatello**, are downright poor when compared with the products of southern France. The exception is Bolla, made by peeling the grapes before fermentation. Barolo is my favorite on a winter day when its red richness is warming. You might disagree and choose something lighter, like Barbera, for instance. Sparkling **Asti Spumante** is an approximate facsimile of champagne; the dry types are okay but the sweet ones are cloying.

Try either a **Carpano** "Punt e Mes" (characteristic bitter vermouth) or a **Cinzano** with soda, ice, and lemon peel on a hot day; they're national favorites. Or ask for an "Americano"—sweet vermouth, bitter Campari, a dash of soda, and a lemon peel.

Soft drinks? Fruit sodas, mainly orange and lemon, plus the Cinzano company's canned colas, are plentiful. For plain juice, the citrus standbys are good; you'll also find an assortment of apple juices and apricot blends.

The best tonic in the world for overeating, flatulence, gas pains—practically any minor stomach ailment—is an Italian bitter called Fernet Branca. The taste is horrible, but the effect is atomic.

GETTING AROUND

TRAINS

The **Italian National Railway** system is so heavily used that much of the equipment is being grossly—even dangerously—overworked. Prices, although lately increased, are among the lowest in Europe. The new high-speed trains are receiving a bad press. They are not too sure-footed in snow and when they are hissing along at full cry you may have to take a motion-sickness remedy for the rock-n-roll.

The quality of the restaurant-car cuisine is improving but remains less inspiring than the vistas you will see as you zip across the lovely countryside. Have a sandwich at your seat; if you don't make your own, some snacks and drinks are usually sold in the aisles. On long-distance express conditions are usually comfortable. You'll probably get there on time (barring extenuating circumstances, such as Italy's ubiquitous strikes).

The cheapest sleeping accommodation is called the *Carrozze Cuccette*, ordinary coaches fixed up with bunks. Reserve well in advance; your kip will come with pillow and blanket; no linen.

You may save money by buying an 8-, 15-, 21- or 30-day Italian Tourist Ticket, a "circular" ticket (a minimum of 600 miles within 60 days), or a "family" ticket (minimum of 4).

BUSES

For selected point-to-point hops, as well as for guided touring, the leader is **SITA**. Most of its fleet is made up of 40-seaters with a bar, a public-address system, individual reading lights, 2 drivers, a hostess, and the last word in cruising luxury. Tickets are valid for 60 days; stopovers are unlimited. You are seldom deposited at a station or terminal; wherever local laws permit, they'll go straight to your hotel.

MOTORING

At this writing, gasoline is roughly double the back-home price; the superhighway speed limit is 75 mph. For years Italian traffic has been a national nightmare—and disgrace. Not only has it become unbearably choked in key areas, but the laws have been so lax that hot-shot driving seems to be the rule of the road. If you join in, a speeding ticket might nick you for $200.

The pride of Italy's civil engineers is the 4-lane road-ribbon slashing 469 miles down the Peninsula from *Milan* to *Naples*. It is called *L'Autostrada del Sole* ("Turnpike of the Sun"). Milan and Naples are separated by 9 hours of freeway driving. A further spur from Naples to *Reggio Calabria* also is open. Incidentally, be sure not to miss the modern restaurants operated by Autogrill—packaged food products—particularly on the northern stretches.

The 142-mile toll road from *Verona* to the *Brenner Pass* is useful. This 4-lane, divided-traffic trunk, skirting all major centers, includes 15 miles of tunnels. There's a shortcut from the *Aosta Valley* to *Chamonix* (France) via the *Mont Blanc Tunnel.*

The highway code requires placement of a red triangular warning device 50 yards down the road whenever you park or change a tire. You may buy this marker, but if you prefer to rent one, the Auto Club office at the frontier will issue a receipt, which makes payment refundable when you surrender the marker on departure.

RENT-A-SCOOT

Go to Via della Purificazione in the capital or ☎ *465485* for the scoop.

CAR HIRE

The CIT, now offering a variety of the most popular European makes, is a good source. In Florence, **Auto-Travel** (*Via Santa Reparata 12/E*; ☎ *483537*) and **Maggiore** (*Via Maso Finiguerra 11*; ☎ *210238*) are satisfactory. If you should meet any snags, contact the **Automobile Club d'Italia** (*Via Marsala 8*; ☎ *4998*) or the **Automobile Club d'Italia** (*Via Cristoforo Colombo 261*; ☎ *5106*), both in Rome.

SPORTS

CYCLING

Tour Tuscany on a two-wheeler. About $350 provides bike, lodging (hotel or farmhouse), breakfast, and guide for 11 days throughout Aug. and Sept. Full details from **"Ciao & Basta,"** *Costa de Magnoli, 24*; ☎ *50129 Firenze*; ☎ *(055) 263985.* For further programs: **Federazione Ciclistica Italiana**, *Piazza Stazione, 2, Florence*; ☎ *283926.*

HIKING

Climb the Apuan Alps; $260 covers lodging (hotel in Florence, refuges on the road), packed lunches, beverages enroute, and guide for 8 days. Also Aug. and Sept. Ciao & Basta can fill you in. For Tuscan outings, write to **C.A.I.**, *Via Proconsolo, 10, Florence*; ☎ *216580.*

HORSES

For information on equestrian holidays, contact **Associazione Nazionale per il Turismo Equestre** (ANTE), *13, Largo Messico, Rome*; ☎ *864053.*

Florence features two tracks: **Ippodromo delle Mulina** (trotters), *Viale del Pegaso*; ☎ *411130/411107*; and **Ippodromo** "Le Cascine" (flat racing), *Piazzale delle Cascine*; ☎ *360056/360598.*

WATERSPORTS

Drop a line for fishing in Florence to **F.I.P.S.** (*Federazione Ital. Pesca Sportiva*), *Via dei Neri, 6, Florence*; ☎ *214073.*

CANOEING

Societa Canottieri Firenze, **Lungarno dei Medici**, *8, Florence*; ☎ *282130*; or **Societa Canottieri Comunali**, *Lungarno Ferrucci, 6, Florence*; ☎ *6812151.*

WINDSURFING

Contact **Classe Windsurfer**, *Via Puccini 9, Rome*; ☎ *8442410* or ☎ *855213.*

WINTER SPORTS

The Alps, of course, are the best. Prices are well below U.S. levels in scores of breathtaking alpine venues. The Dolomite range is also a paradise. Most popular targets within a few hours of the capital are the 6,336-foot **Campo Imperatore**, the 5,400-foot **Mount Catino**, the 4,942-foot **Mount Terminillo**, the 4,125-foot **Ovindoli**, the 3,972-foot **Mount Livata**, and the 3,708-foot **Roccaraso**. Near Florence, slopes of **Abetone** and of **Vallombrosa** are the most popular.

HANG GLIDING

To overfly Florence, contact the **Delta Club Firenze**, *Via Montebello, 45, Florence*; ☎ *2579849.*

SIGHTSEEING

LANGUAGE STUDIES

Spend 2 weeks, 4 weeks, or 3 months conjugating in Florence. The first course covers 60 hours for about $200; the second, 40 for $175; the third, 120 for about $325. Stay with a family (bed and breakfast very low in cost; half board from $16), in a boarding house (B & B $35), or in an apartment. More info from **Centro Lorenzo de'Medici**, *Piazza Delle Pallottole, 1, 50122 Firenze*; ☎ *(055) 283142.*

Two- and four-week courses also available most of the year at **Centro di Lingua e Culture Italiana Fiorenza**, *Via S. Spirito 14, 50125*

Firenze; ☎ *(055) 298274*. Cost? $200 and $285, respectively. Assistance with lodgings in private homes, pensions, hotels, or apartments.

For full-term courses covering Italian language and culture, it's **Centro di Cultura per Stranieri**, **Universita degli Studi di Firenze**, *Via Vittorio Emanuele, 64, 50134 Firenze*; ☎ *(055) 472139*. 6-week summer course shortest and cheapest at about $150; 10-week terms at $180. List of lodgings available.

For language and culture studies in Florence, Siena, or Rome, write **Centro Linguistico Italiano Dante Alighieri**, *Via de'Bardi 2, Firenze*; ☎ *(055) 284955*; 4-week programs available from $70 to $275.

COOKING

Four weeks of culinary culture at the above Centro comes to about $150. To whet your appetite further, contact **Cooking in Florence**, *Giuliano Bugialli, Via Pilastri, 52, Frienze*; ☎ *675132*; or **Italian Academy of Cooking**, *16, Via Lorenzo da Brindisi, Rome*; ☎ *5111557*; or **Fattoria di Bacchereto**, *Carmignano presso Prato*; ☎ *(055) 8712191*.

WINE TASTING

For courses in the Prato area, get details from the **Associazione Italiana Sommeliers**, *Sezione de Prato, c/o Unione Commercianti di Prato, Via Santa Trinita 27, Prato*; ☎ *26247*. In Florence, **Associazione Italiana Sommeliers**, *c/o Dino Casini; Via Ghibellina, 51/r, Firenze*; ☎ *241378*.

ARTS & CRAFTS

Interested in art history, ceramics, decoration, or antiques? Month-long courses from $100 to $230; lodging an additional $25 to $47 daily, depending on single or double occupancy in private home, pension, hotel, or mini-apartment. A similar range of courses plus painting available at **Instituto per l'Arte e il Restauro**, *Palazzo Spinelli, Borgo S. Croce, 10, 50122 Firenze*; ☎ *(055) 244808*.

One-eight-month courses in ceramics, sculpture, painting, and restoration of antiques are offered at the **International School of Ceramics**, *Via di Monterinaldi, 45 "Bolognese Nuova," Firenze*; ☎ *400233*.

For ceramics and pottery study in Prato, contact **Fornace della Fattoria di Bachereto**, *Carmignano presso Prato*; ☎ *(055) 8712191*.

ART APPRECIATION

Write to **Associazione Pratese Amici dei Musei e dei Beni Ambientali**, *Villa Rucellai, Via di Canneto, 16, Prato*; ☎ *460392*.

FARM HOLIDAYS

When in Prato, look up **Club Sucini**, *Sant'Ippolito di Vernio presso Prato*; ☎ *957593*, or in Florence: **Agriturist**, *Via Proconsolo, 10, Firenze*; ☎ *287838*.

HOME EXCHANGES

Try Tuscan-based **Scambio Casa**, *Costa dei Magnoli, 24, Firenze*; ☎ *263985.*

LOCAL RACKETS

Simply as background, you might like to know that a social and economic research institute (CENSIS) reckons that Italy's crime represents 12% of the gross national product, that perhaps a million of its 57 million inhabitants may be involved in the sport, and that 75% of the sins go unpunished.

In any hole-in-the-wall shop that sells nonproprietary goods, never take the first price; offer them about half what they ask, and bargain from there. The larger and more chichi establishments are fairly well regulated; the "quaint" places are the ones geared to take advantage of tourists.

Restaurant checks are sometimes padded; smaller hotels will make "mistakes" on telephone calls you never made. A growing blight is the rigged tabulating machines at the cashiers' desks of hotels, including various large and so-called respectable houses. Your statement will be meticulously itemized, often correctly—but the total will be hundreds or thousands of lire too high. Add up every tab, wherever you go in Italy—and check your change everywhere, especially at Fiumicino Airport.

Every major tourist center in the nation is plagued by armies of "steerers" who take commissions on customers brought to shops. One common ploy is to introduce themselves as a "Count," a "Countess," or a similar phony title.

Be careful of tortoiseshell objects, which are prohibited in the U.S. in any case. There is a plastic imitation in many supposedly reputable shops. The test is this: When held up to the light, portions of the plastic are nearly transparent, while the genuine article is always uniformly opaque. Neither material burns, although unscrupulous merchants will tell you that plastic is inflammable—and then apply a match to "prove" that you're getting the real shell.

Pickpockets are not uncommon. Whenever you walk through an Italian train to the dining car, keep one arm over your wallet. Watch yourself in trams, buses, elevators, train stations, airports, and all other crammed places.

Along the same line, Italian talent for doing almost anything aboard a motorscooter has reached a new peak in purse-snatching. The 2-wheeled bandit zips up, hooks the handbag from the lady's arm, and scampers away through traffic. Another ploy is to stop the scooter or car to ask a foreigner a question—but in a low voice. When the helpful dupe leans forward or comes nearer, the thief snatches a necklace, watch, or purse and romps over the horizon (often on a stolen vehicle or on one that has the license plates covered).

It's probably not as good an idea as it seems to buy a used car in Italy these days. A motor mafia has been so effective in stealing, repainting, and renumbering automobiles that there are now agents from whom you can order the type of car you desire and it will roll up on delivery a few days (or nights) later. This, of course, implies that your own car might get snatched and later appear in the underground market, since foreign vehicles may be tougher to trace. Much of the conversion work, incidentally, takes place in the catacombs.

Another mischief gives nightmares to motorists. When thieves see a parked car loaded with luggage, they ice-pick one tire. The owner removes his possessions to lighten it and get at the spare. Quick as a flash, he has one less piece of baggage—and it's always the little one—the jewel box, the briefcase, or the handbag with the traveler's checks in it.

Many filling station attendants will tell you you need oil when you don't. Wait a couple of minutes with the motor turned off for the oil to settle, then make sure that he shoves the dip-stick down the full distance. Examine the mark yourself, and watch the attendant very carefully so he won't wipe a false line onto the rod.

Cartons of "black-market" cigarettes might be offered at seemingly irresistible low prices. Open the parcel first. If you don't, later you may find yourself the new owner of a package of tightly packed, exquisitely blended Sicilian sand.

Make your deal with Venetian gondoliers in advance. It will be expensive in any case. Walking is convenient in this city if you have a map. Public transportation is relatively cheap, much less than by gondola (which only should be used as a sightseeing lark).

WHERE TO GO

AMALFI

An important maritime republic during the Middle Ages. Today dozens of daily bus tours from Naples pause here for refreshment on the spectacular coastal drive between *Salerno* and *Sorrento*. Small, rambling village; handsome hotels and adequate boarding houses (although they charge too much in high season); enchanting coastal land—and seascapes. The **Cavalieri** is reasonable in price for shelter; so are the **Luna** and the **Miramalfi**.

AREZZO

A Tuscan town of about 90,000 souls only 55 miles from Florence, but often missed by tourists lured to Italy's "main attractions." The **Old Town** is on a hillside, alive with Renaissance lanes and modern activity; on the lower fringe, the **San Francesco Church** boasts the frescoes of *Piero della Francesca*; about midway up, the belfried 11th-century **Santa Maria della Pieve**, a Romanesque stalwart; and just behind it **Piazza Grande**, where the **Saracen Joust** takes place the first Sunday in Sept. There's also an antique market the first Sun. of each month (except Sept.). An easy run from Florence if that's where you're staying—and well worth the effort. If you wish to overnight, try the **Drago** on Via Fleming.

ASSISI

A wonderful little town. Take time to admire the renowned **Basilica of St. Francis**, absorb its Gothic architecture, and drink in the view of the plains below. If you'd like a scholarly and pleasant guide to their home, the brothers at the **San Damiano Convent** (☎ *812273*) are superb; no charge, of course—just alms to the church, which are voluntary. (Otherwise the commercial guides also know their belfry ropes perfectly well.) **Hotel Giotto** has been renovated; reasonably priced; it's near the Basilica. **Umbra** would be an alternative choice or **Olivera Inn** (6 miles out) if you have wheels. You might also consider **At. Anthony's Guest House** (*10 Via G. Alessi*; ☎ *812542*) run by Graymoor Sisters, a religious order based in NY. Meals served in a 12th-century vault; 20 rooms in the villa at roughly $24 per soul including breakfast. Open May to late autumn. Very rewarding for scholars, sightseers, or peace lovers.

BARI

Founded by the Illyrians and civilized by the Greeks, it is the chief port and commercial mart on Italy's heel; next to Naples, the most important peninsular city in the south. **The crypt of St. Nicholas**, patron saint of gift-giving and the inspiration of Santa Claus, is here (his symbol of 3 brass balls was later purloined by pawnbrokers). Leading attraction is the famous **Levant Fair** (10 days around mid-Sept); otherwise offers fair swimming, antiquities, and an excellent springboard for visiting nearby **Alberobello**, the **Castellana Caves**, **Castel del Monte**, and **Trani**. The hotels are awful and expensive for the low value. **7 Mari** is passable; **Leon d'Oro** is only so-so.

BOLOGNA

This major city (nearly 1/2 million citizens) has retained its antique presence despite the frenzy of commerce and modern traffic. Seat of the oldest university in the world (the word "university" was invented here) and the richest cuisine of the nation. Lots of foreign students in educational residence; more than 20 miles of arcaded walks; leaning towers, splendid palaces designed by such masters as *Tibaldi* and *Vignola*; 10 museums with treasures from Etruscan to modern times; **National Gallery** with works by 56 great painters, including Raphael's "St. Cecilia"; villa and mausoleum of **Guglielmo Marconi**. "Baloney" originated in Bologna; to sample the original article, ask for *Mortadella*. You can find good shelter at the **Due Torri**, the **Roma**, or the **Re Enzo** (6 miles out); **San Donato** is central, but a smidgen more costly.

BRINDISI

This southeastern seacoast village vibrates in a 10-month season to the noise of thousands of motorized trippers bound for Greece via the car and passenger ferries. We loathe it. Details on the ships and the conditions may be found under "Greece." Rather than overnighting here, try to time your arrival to correspond with your ship's departure. Be careful with all possessions here.

CAMOGLI

Here's a lovely unsung coastal town near *Genoa* (Recco exit on the autostrada) that offers a beach of black volcanic sand, ancient chapel towers, tiers of fishermen's houses in ocher, buff, pink, and persimmon, and dozens of boats nibbling at snug harbors. Adequate shelter at **Pensione La Camogliese** with its seaside restaurant (same view as at the neighboring and costly **Cenobio dei Dogi**); additional rooms at the **Riviera** and **Seleno** hotels. Excellent dining at **Rosa, Vento Ariel**, and **Gatto Nero**, all on the frontage. Be sure to take a skiff over to **San Fruttuoso**, an isolated pocket of beauty that you'll never forget.

CAPRI

Thoroughly bewitching from April until mid-October. In summer, it can become crowded with day-excursionists from the mainland. Saturation point is reached around Aug. 15, the midsummer holiday of **Ferragosto**. Off season it is lovely—an environmentalist's dream, in fact. At that time, prices are quite reasonable at boarding houses surrounding the main piazza at Capri and even cheaper up at *Anacapri*, 20 minutes higher. **Blue Grotto**; funicular from main port to main village; chairlift to mountain peak; from May 1 to Sept. 30, private cars banned from the tiny isle (fines for disobeying this rule can hop from $80 to $800); taxis and buses available throughout the year; one small, so-so beach at *Marina Piccola*; hydrofoil service (40 minutes) from Naples to Capri in half the time of the less expensive—but much more crowded—regular service. **Hotel Floridiana** is reasonable; the **Luna's** prices are a bit higher, but the situation is agreeable; **Flora** is also worthy. In spring or fall, you might love it; in summer, *Elba* (to the north) is less hyperactive but not a patch on Capri for beauty and cheer.

AUTHOR'S OBSERVATION

Try The Sea Gull, off the main piazza, for gifts and fabulous ceramics or Carthusia (2 stores in Capri and one up at Anacapri) for locally blended perfumes. Anacapri has wonderful Mariorita for chic and casual wearables.

ELBA

Virgil called this "The Generous Island." This was Napoleon's home prior to his famous 100 days. To travelers in search of tranquillity rather than frenzy, it already has replaced Capri; the vanguard carry the banners of Sweden and Germany to its shores. Simple, primitive, unspoiled; glorious mountains, shimmering olive-toned landscape, breathtaking beaches; only 8 small towns, a dozen small villages, and a scattering of hamlets on this 30-mile home of 32,000 people; hotels, restaurants, and nightlife limited but adequate; 30-minute hydrofoil service between *Piombino* and *Portoferraio* 15 times per day, plus numerous regular ferry crossings; daily high season link with *Leghorn* (Livorno) via the *Isle of Capraia;* excursions (100 minutes) to Corsica from mid-June onward; scenic route, reminiscent of the Amalfi Drive, touching 10 enchanting little hamlets. Health addicts can oink in therapeutic mud baths at the **Terme of San Giovanni**. For the panorama of a lifetime, take the **rope-railway** ("cabinovia") from Marciana to the 3100-foot peak of **Monte Capanne**. Nearby is the uninhabited rock known as **Monte Cristo**, the islet where the "Count" found his buried treasure. At *Marciana* you can stay at the **Del Golfo**. At *Marina di Campo*, try **Dei Coralli**, near the beach, or the less costly **Iselba**. **The Garden** is satisfactory in *Portoferraio.*

FLORENCE

Here is Italy's capital of refinement, often considered the intellectual and artistic keystone of the nation. Lovers of fine painting, architecture, and churches will surely rate this one of the most rewarding targets on the Continent. What's more, these manmade treasures are handsomely set off by a captivating natural setting on the Arno River at the foot of the Apennines, the nation's mountainous spinal column. A powerful republic in medieval times, Florence dominated kingdoms as it later dominated the Renaissance with its flair for art and commerce. From 1847 to 1861, Robert and Elizabeth Barrett Browning lived their poetic romance here, dedicating their time to each other and their talents to the cause of Italian independence. It is a convenient city, either for long stays or as a springboard for viewing the rich regions of Tuscany and Umbria. Hotels are varied and cuisine is excellent. The people are among the most gracious in the land.

DIRECTORY

U.S. Consulate • *Lungarno Amerigo Vespucci 38*; ☎ *2398276.*

Laundromat • Lavamatic, *Via 27 Aprile 1.*

Dry Cleaning and Pressing • Lavanderia Tacconi, Fosca, *Via del Parione 14*; ☎ *272384.*

Suit Rental • Sartoria Teatrale, *Piazza del Duomo 2*; ☎ *292384.*

English-Speaking Doctor • Dr. John Fenwick, *Borgognissanti 21*; ☎ *211821.*

English-Speaking Dentist • Dr. Francesco D'Inzeo, *Via Tornabuoni 1*; ☎ *298471.*

Police • Central Station, *Via Zara 2*; ☎ *483201*; Emergency, ☎ *113.*

Favorite Pawnshop • My lire lasted longer in this city, so I didn't look.

HOW TO GET AROUND

Sights are so close, you'll stroll to most of them; for crosstowning, 37 streetcar and bus lines thread through the major piazzas; the **Local Tourist Office** (*Azienda Promozione Turistica*) (Via Mansoni 16, ground floor) can give you all necessary details on local sightseeing, as well as on other Florentine matters.

WHERE TO STAY

LEAST $

Azzi • ☎ *213806*

Marini • ☎ *284824*

Merlini • ☎ *212848 Via Faenza 56.* Located 1, 2, and 3 flights up, respectively, in a former monastery. All run by sweet old ladies; all ooze tranquillity. Combined total of 30 units; terrace-equipped #9 in the Marini perhaps the best pick; bright accommodation in the top-floor Merlini; summer breakfasting outdoors also a plus in the last. Prices in all peak at about $25 per person in twins; a smidgen higher in singles; less in triples.

Marcella • A worthy alternative.

Adam • *Via Monalda 1;* ☎ *210369.* Exceptional quality at a reasonable price. Quiet location.

Nizza • *Via del Giglio 5;* ☎ *269897.* About $25 per overnighter; no breakfast available; $2.75 extra per bath; ask for a quiet accommodation if one is available, because during high season the car traffic can be a menace to sleep.

Varsavia • *Via de'Panzani 5;* ☎ *215615.* For emergency use only.

YMCA and YWCA • You'll find an office within the S. Maria Novelle main rail terminus.

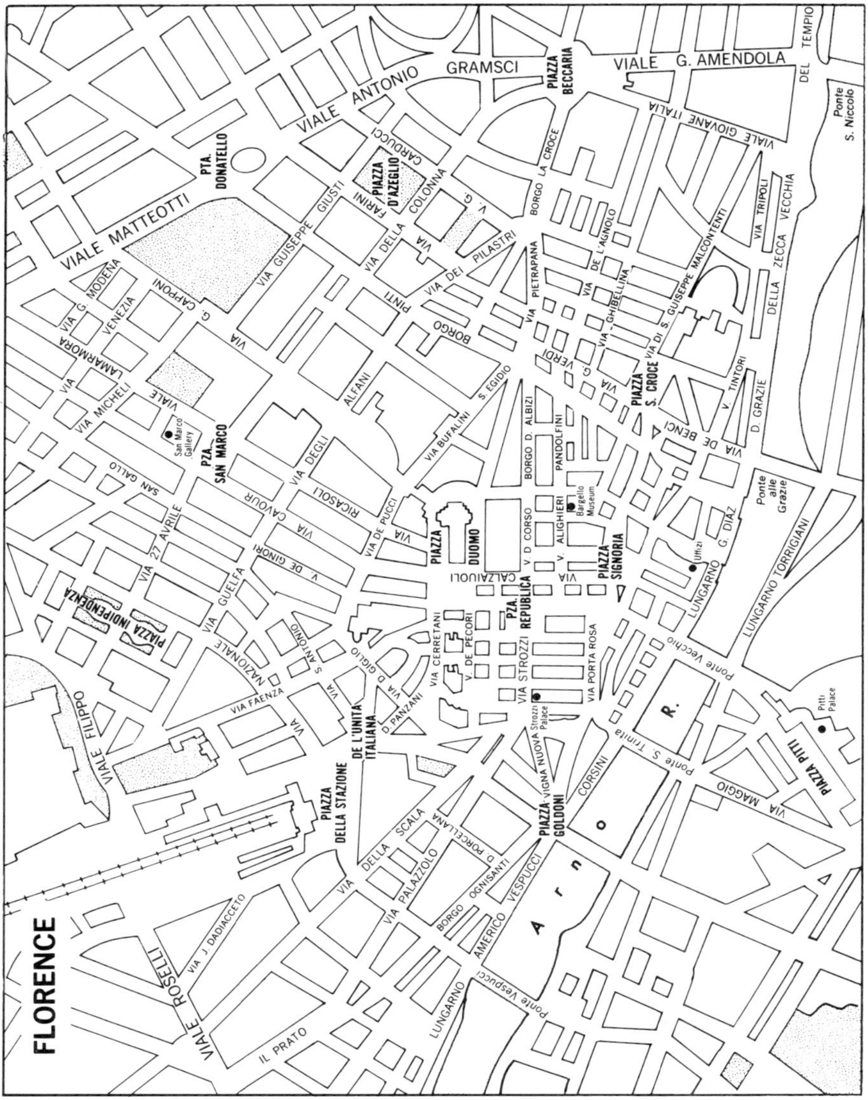
FLORENCE
VIALE ANTONIO GRAMSCI
PIAZZA BECCARIA
VIALE G. AMENDOLA
DEL TEMPIO
Ponte S. Niccolo
VIALE GIOVANE ITALIA
CARDUCCI
PIAZZA D'AZEGLIO
FARINI
V. COLONNA
PTA. DONATELLO
VIALE MATTEOTTI
VIA GIUSEPPE GIUSTI
VIA DELLA COLONNA
BORGO LA CROCE
VIA TRIPOLI
ZECCA VECCHIA
DELLA
VIA MALCONTENTI
VIA DI S. GUISEPPE
VIA DE L'AGNOLO
VIA GHIBELLINA
VIA PIETRAPANA
VIA DEI PILASTRI
PINTI
BORGO
VIA G. MODENA
VENEZIA
CAPPONI
VIA G.
LAMARMORA
VIA MICHELI
VIALE
VIA
San Marco Gallery
PZA. SAN MARCO
SAN GALLO
ALFANI
S. EGIDIO
VIA BUFALINI
VIA DEGLI
VIA G. VERDI
PIAZZA S. CROCE
V. TINTORI
D. GRAZIE
VIA DE BENCI
BORGO D. ALBIZI
PANDOLFINI
Bargello Museum
V. ALIGHIERI
V. D CORSO
VIA CAVOUR
RICASOLI
VIA DE PUCCI
PIAZZA DUOMO
CALZAIUOLI
PIAZZA SIGNORIA
Uffizi
G. DIAZ
Ponte alle Grazie
LUNGARNO TORRIGIANI
LUNGARNO
VIA 27 AVRILE
V. DE GINORI
VIA GUELFA
PIAZZA INDIPENDENZA
NAZIONALE
S. ANTONINO
VIA FAENZA
VIA D. GIGLIO
VIA CERRETANI
V. DE PECORI
PZA. REPUBLICA
VIA STROZZI
VIA PORTA ROSA
Ponte Vecchio
Pitti Palace
PIAZZA PITTI
VIA MAGGIO
Ponte S. Trinita
Strozzi Palace
VIGNA NUOVA
CORSINI
PIAZZA GOLDONI
D. PANZANI
DE L'UNITA ITALIANA
PIAZZA DELLA STAZIONE
VIALE FILIPPO
D. PORCELLANA
VIA DELLA SCALA
VIA PALAZZOLO
BORGO OGNISANTI
AMERICO VESPUCCI
Ponte Vespucci
LUNGARNO
Arno R.
VIA J. DADIACCETO
VIALE ROSELLI
IL PRATO

Ostello della Gioventu • *Viale Righi 2-4;* ☎ *601451.* A lackluster imitation of larger and better efforts elsewhere. Suburban site. Dormitory accommodations at about $18 per night. Midnight curfew inconvenient.

MORE $$

Centrale • *Via dei Conti 3;* ☎ *215216.* As the name suggests, it's central. Appealing dining room; superior food; 20 viewless, silent bedchambers, 7 with tub and WC, 3 with shower; comfortable beds. Figure $55 or so per head with breakfast; about $20 extra for half pension. Reserve in advance.

Silla • *Via dei Renai 5;* ☎ *2342888.* Near piazzale Michelangelo. Good parking outside. Amiable restaurant; outdoor terrace with panorama. Quarters vary widely in size, position, and quality; some singles celllike. Traveling with the family? Ask for #3, #33, or #34. Lacks the intimate charm of the Centrale, but patio and vista make up for a lot.

Alba • *Via della Scala 22 (near the station);* ☎ *211469.* Melange of periods and decors. 40 simple rooms of livable size; tub-equipped #22 the best double.

La Residenza • *Via Tornabuoni 8;* ☎ *284197.* In the middle of the action. An array of salons, anterooms, bar, garden, 25 clean havens; 13 baths or showers.

Morandi • *Alla Crocetta, Via Laura 50;* ☎ *2344797.* Very close to the Dom, remarkably quiet for such a central location. Large, airy rooms kept neat and fresh by an English lady, Mrs. Doyle, and her family.

Consigli • *Lungarno Amerigo Vespucci 50;* ☎ *214172.* Arno-sited near the U.S. Consulate, a hellaciously long haul from the sights. Half pension at $46 per person. Passable.

Boston • *Via Guelfa 68;* ☎ *496747.* Began life in 16th century. Very central. A light sleeper? Ask for a garden room.

Ausonia & Rimini • *Via Nazionale 24;* ☎ *496547.* Was updated recently and has helpful staff. Very handy to major sites. Singles at close to $35; twins about $48; breakfast included.

Mona Lisa • *Borgo Pinti 27;* ☎ *2479751.* Now going up rather steeply in price.

Albion • *Via del Prato 22r;* ☎ *214171.*

Argentina • *Via Curtatone 12;* ☎ *215408.* All very agreeable. Sound value for your lira. The last one a long way from midtown.

Cristallo • *Via Cavour 29;* ☎ *215375.* Recently improved and now very pleasant for the outlay.

Bandini • *Piazza Santo Spirito 9;* ☎ *215308.* Eye-popping sweep of the city; 10 comfortable accommodations; 1 private bath, which even the Supreme Pontiff might have trouble securing.

Atlantic Palace • *Via Nazionale 12;* ☎ *213031*

Macchiavelli • *Next door;* ☎ *216622*

Nuovo Italia • *Around the corner;* ☎ *268430.* A trio oriented for package tour travel; the first is the best now that it has been upgraded extensively. All suitable for an overnight.

EVEN MORE $$$

Hermitage • *Vicolo Marzio 1; ☎ 287216.* So central it almost buttresses both the Ponte Vecchio and the Uffizi Gallery. Handsome roof garden; riverside parlor. Attractive dining area with excellent cookery; 18 clean, quiet, attractive quarters; 14 tubs or showers. Room, bath, and 2 meals for $85 per person; subtract about $2 each for accommodations without private plumbing.

Rita Maior • *Via della Mattonaia 43; ☎ 2477990.* A 20-minute ride from the center. Proximity to a playground makes it ideal for families. Garden dining area; trattoria-style pastaria. Half the 35 units have shower. Partial to double #48, while #62 offers more solitude in back. Dual tabs close to $110; extra beds $5 more. A solid bargain.

Ariston • *Via Fiesolana 40; ☎ 2476693.* Centrally sited near the piazza Santa Croce, yet it is relatively quiet. All 29 rooms with private bath and phone. Well recommended by travelers. Ask for Mario Parisio.

Berchielli • *Lungarno Acciaioli 14; ☎ 264061.* A lovely palazzo on the River Arno that was carefully—nay, lovingly—restored. The atmosphere has gone from old- to new-fashioned, which may shock loyalists who have stopped here for its special homegrown flavor. Still, it's very good.

Porta Rossa • *Via Porta Rossa 19; ☎ 287551.* Also unique; born in the 14th century, it is Florence's oldest hotel. Midcity location with an observation tower that looks straight into the eye of Tuscan history.

Quisisana • *Lungarno Archibusieri 4; ☎ 216692.* On the 3rd and 4th levels of a building that once stabled Medici horses. Formal dining room. Especially fond of #40, a gracious chamber with bath down a 1/2-flight of stairs. Although #33 has only a curtain-covered sink and shower, it boasts an exceptional view of the Ponte Vecchio from verdant terrace.

Beacci Tornabuoni • *Via de'Tornabuoni 3 (near piazza Santa Trinita); ☎ 212645.* Occupies 3 stories atop a midcity art gallery. Beguiling Old World ambience. Lounge; roof terrace for breakfasting; small restaurant with commendable food; 29 accommodations, 21 baths; some with balky plumbing; a few noisy and poor.

Aprile • For a change of pace, a poetic report (eat your heart out, Mr. Chaucer):

Thirty-eight units hath Aprile,
Faintly commercial in appeale.
Bar and courtyard always active,
Two dining rooms, lounge goodly attractive.
Of baths, we count one more than 20;
Prices? Well, now, That's A-plenty.
Sixty-five ($) for one, a C-note in tandem.
Concierge Antonio is the Grand Panjandrum.
Via della Scala 6 is where you'll go—
And it's only a toot from the train depot.
Or lazy folks can just telephone, by heaven,
To number two, one, six, two, and three seven.
If the midtowne Aprile's not your scenic sonnet,
Marche on so you Maye try Colombo's bonnet!

Columbus • *Lungarno Cristoforo Colombo 22A;* ☎ *677251, 2 and 3.* Remote situation. Dining salon plus breakfast and snack corner; bar; 105 airconditioned bedchambers, all with bath or shower; those ending with "13" biggest. Very good if you don't mind the distance from midcity.

Mediterraneo • *Lungarno del Tempio 42-44 (at the foot of Ponte S. Nicolo);* ☎ *660241.* Also a fair punt up the Arno. Twin dining rooms for the house's 60% tour traffic; bar; shops. Rooms functional; telephones, baths, and showers; $95 per double (less meals, which are not mandatory).

Claridge • *Piazza Piave 3;* ☎ *268533* and **Ville Sull'Arno lungarno** *C. Colombo 1;* ☎ *670971.* Two excellent tranquil havens. The first a stately, fully renovated town house with the aura of a fine Italian period piece. The second, more modern but also comfortable, hugging the vernal Arno shore.

Bretagna • *Lungarno Corsini 6;* ☎ *218618.* Pleasant nest of 20 rooms in a 13th-century building abutting the Arno. Elegant dining den. Rooms #3 and #21 with baths the choice doubles; #34 the only one facing the river.

Hotel River • *Lungarno della Zecca Vecchia 18;* ☎ *2343529.* Overlooks Arno, as name hints. A mediocre dining room and 46 poor bedchambers.

Arianna • *Via di Barbano 12r;* ☎ *496742.* A substantial value.

San Giorgio & Olimpic • *Via Sant'Antonino 3;* ☎ *284344.* Suffers from acute groupitis. About $55 per head (extra for food) buys acceptable space.

Pendini • *Via Strozzi 2, 4th floor (facing piazza della Republica);* ☎ *211170.* A sound bet.

Basilea • *Via Guelfa 41;* ☎ *214587.* Perhaps worth noting in an emergency.

Regency Umbria • *Piazza Massimo d'Azeglio 3;* ☎ *245247.* Good, but a long way from sightseeing targets. Steepish prices.

Augustus & Dei Congressi • *Piazza dell'Oro;* ☎ *283054.* One block from the Ponte Vecchio. All 70 rooms with terraces, telephones, air conditioning, and baths.

Continental and **Lungarno** • *Lungarno Acciaiuoli 2;* ☎ *282392 and Borgo San Jacopo 14;* ☎ *264211.* Their prices sting from Italy's dizzy inflation spiral.

Fiesole • This is a lovely hill town known for its wine that's about 25 minutes from Florence by Bus #7.

Villa San Girolamo • *12 Via Vecchia Fiesolana;* ☎ *59141.* The famous Blue Nuns run the terraced, garden-girt 50-room. The vistas of Florence and the Tuscan landscape are breathtaking. Figure about $60 per twin occupancy.

CAMPING

Cross the Arno to the wooded slopes below piazzale Michelangelo. Sylvan setting unmolested by traffic; facilities improving; not expensive.

SUGGESTIONS FOR STUDENTS

Piazza San Marco is the most popular rallying point for collegians.

OVERNIGHTS

Casa dello Studente, (*Calamandrei, Viale Morgagni 51;* ☎ *43891*), a comfortable 59-room hostelry, becomes a student boardinghouse during the summer. Tumultuous location; no restaurant; bright bedchambers with fresh wardrobes and pleasant furnishings, but no carpets. Singles at circa $15 and doubles at near $23;

add $2 for an extra bed; washing and ironing facilities available. House rules? A 1:30 a.m.-7:30 a.m. curfew. A ban on washing or cooking in your quarters; "hall loitering"; card playing; boudoir-hopping. Finally, to rub your nose deeper: an 11 p.m. "silence" rule. Operative (if you can call it that) from mid-July through Sept.; females accepted between July 25 and Sept. 15 only, wedding certificates required for all couples. Despite this endless parade of silly "do's" and "don'ts," it has above-average comfort. If you can tolerate the curbs, you might even like the place.

LANGUAGE STUDY

For language study, we hear praise for **ABC Scuola di Lingua e Cultura Italiana** (*Borgo Pinti 38*; ☎ *055-2479220*), which also has a summer program on Elba for combining learning with leisure. They can arrange accommodation.

WHERE TO EAT

LEAST $

Angiolino's • *Via Santo Spirito 36R;* ☎ *2398976.* Two-room entry with 18 tables and limited selection; excellent preparation of spaghetti, chicken, and fish. Closed Sun. and Mon. Amusing, despite occasionally gruff waiters.

Rosticceria S. Piero • *Via Matteo Palmieri 34.* Economical and substantial. A rustic, family-run tavern. Highly recommended in this category.

Buca di San Giovanni • *Piazza San Giovanni 8;* ☎ *287612.* U-shaped cellar across from the San Giovanni Baptistery and Santa Maria del Fiore Cathedral. Hors d'oeuvre table; rushed but efficient service; popular with local families. Reasonably priced Tourist Menu (had to ask for it) yielded macaroni with meat sauce, scaloppini milanese, a 1/2-bottle of house wine, and an orange. Open till 1 a.m. Closed Sun. and Mon.

Da 5 Amici • *Via de'Cimatori 30R;* ☎ *296672.* Another family-style trattoria; 23 tables often frequented by friends of the original "5." Closed Mon.

La Nuova Campana • *Via Borgo San Lorenzo 24R (a few steps from Piazza San Giovanni)* ☎ *21-1326.* Spaghetti for about $4; meat dishes around $6.50; pizza from $4. Closed Wed.

Il Fagiano • *("The Pheasant") Via de'Neri 57.* Less glitter but better food. Two rooms, 1 with a fireplace. No-nonsense ambience. Sparkling. About $14 for the average meal. Closed Mon.

Orcagna • *Piazza della Signoria 1R;* ☎ *292488.* More alluring candidate at more substantial tariffs. Sound cookery. Worth a try, but never on Sundays.

Giannino • *Via Borgo San Lorenzo 37R.* Cooks with loving care. Tuscan motif. Pianist. Steak costly; ask for the Tourist Menus. Closed Fri.

La Nandina • *Piazza Santa Trinita 3.* Invites guests to sit beside the stoves. Simple, comely stop with wholesome nutrients; cheerful attention. Around $14 should fill you up. Very pleasant. Closed Sun.

Giglio Rosso • *Via Panzani 5 (below the Varsavia Hotel).* Popular with tourists. Blue plates in $14 class, including gratuity.

Montecatini • *Via dei Leoni 6R.* Renews millions of calories expended by culture lovers who visit the Uffizi. Often crowded at lunch. Better for light bites than heavier fare. Closed Wed.

Battistero • *Via Ricasoli 5R.* Often overrun by bus excursionists. A handy few yards from the Duomo. All meals a la carte. Average $10 per serving. Closed Mon.

Fior di Loto • *Via dei Servi 35R;* ☎ *2398235.* Your tummy shouting for a change of pace? Here is the prime Chinese restaurant in Florence. Perhaps 60 tables. Spotless. Prices push it beyond economy level if you order several dishes, but salvation may be had in the absence of olive oil. Closed Mon.

Sergio • *Via dei Servi 42-44R.* Occupies a 2-century-old house 100 yards from the Duomo. Summer-only veranda; small bar. Better for drinking than serious dining.

Antica Trattoria e Fiaschetteria dei Quattro Leoni • *Via dei Vellutini 1R.* Hard to find. Corner entrance near the Pitti Palace, around block from the Ponte Vecchio. Bare features; ample supply of fresh bread and fruits. Cordial personnel. Low prices.

SNACKS

La Borsa • *Via por S. Maria 55R;* ☎ *216109.* Sit under the shade of an ancient tower, have a fruit bowl or sandwich, and gaze directly at some of Tuscany's grandest sights, only 50 yards from the Uffizi. Resting on Sun.

SELF-SERVICE

Old Bridge • *Beside the Ponte Vecchio on Via dei Bardi.* Combines sound and savory cooking with a lovely panorama of the river.

Grand Italia • *Near station.* A worthy midtown alternative.

Marchetti • *106 Calzaioli.* Offers a counter and a few tables; pizza by the piece; good fresh salads. Near to the Duomo so worth remembering.

La Lampara • *Via Nazionale 36R;* ☎ *215-164.* Great for pizza. Take-away counter plus sit-down section. Extra-nice staff and hospitable atmosphere. Pies for about $4. Open late, but ovens cool on Tues.

Motta • *Via Martelli 2.* Part of a global chain that offers top quality.

Paskowski Extra Bar • *Piazza della Republica 6.* Closed Mon.

Metro Buffet • *Piazza dell'Olio.*

Scudieri piazza • *S. Giovanni.* Closed Wed.

Pino's • *Via Guicciardini 66R.* Closed Sun.

All worthwhile contenders for pasta and light fare.

STUDENTS

The Mensa Universitaria, *Via San Gallo 25A*, overlooks a quiet courtyard. Basic regional cookery; 3-course lunch or dinner about $4; special meal hours for outlanders (1:45 p.m.–2:30 p.m., and 8:45 p.m.–9:30 p.m.); closed Aug. to mid-Sept. **Casa D. Studente**, *p. Calamandrei*, another sound bet for low-cost meals. Also refer back to the Rosticceria S. Piero, a favorite with local scholars.

MORE $$

Icche C'E C'E • *Via Magalotti 11 rosso;* ☎ *26-2867.* In local parlance: "What is, is." And it is good! Hanging lamps over tables; framed wine labels. Try crostini and antipasti, the fusili with basil and tomato, the treneta al pesto, and finish with caprino goat cheese. The house wine (out of a barrel) is recommendable.

La Loggia • *Piazzale Michelangelo 1;* ☎ *2342832.* Alfresco lunching or dining at municipally owned, century-old former art gallery. Hillside site; 180° panorama of city. About 90 tables; small glassed-in restaurant for winter. Decidedly good cuisine; professional service. Enchanting and rather costly; closed on Wed.

Otello • *Across from the station on Via Irt. Oricellari 36R;* ☎ *215819.* Great for giant-size appetites. Masses of antipasti on rolling carts; tonnage servings of everything from spit-roasted tordi (thrushes) to hocks to sweets. Even peppermills are 5 feet tall! Sit in the hut-style room. Tariffs within reason; Tues. is the day off.

Cibreo • *Via dei Macci 118R;* ☎ *2341100.* Just the reverse of Otello: quiet, designed more for Florentines than for tourists and no heroics in decor. Superb cuisine with no fireworks. Closed Sun. and Mon.

Osteria Natalino • *Via Borgo degli Albizi 17R;* ☎ *263404.* Just outside Florence at the piazza di S. Pier Maggiore. Popular with neighborhood residents because of its simple atmosphere and fine Tuscan cookery. Private tables up front and communal types out back. Quick waiters. Open noon to 3 p.m. and 7 to 11 p.m.; closed Sun.

Osteria del Cinghiale Bianco • *Borgo San Jacopo 43R;* ☎ *215706.* Cozy, crowded, and fun. Raw stone and intimate lighting; flowers for cheer; cookery that will please and nourish. Closed Tues. and Wed.

Paoli • *Via Tavolini 12R;* ☎ *216215.* Old World and country-quaint. Fettucine and cannelloni excellent; also Rognoncino Trifolato and rather expensive Scampi alla Marinara. About $50 for 2 including wine, cappuccino, tip, tax, and cover. Closed Tues.

Bordino • *Via Stracciatella 9/R;* ☎ *213048.* Refined cuisine a beautiful match for the atmosphere. Great value and variety. Closed Sun.

La Bussola • *Via Porta Rossa 58R;* ☎ *293376.* Florentine version of an all-night deli (substitute lasagna for lox, prosciutto for pastrami, and crema caramella for cheesecake). Lasagna alla Ferrarese and Scaloppa alla Parmigiana outstanding for price. Closed Mon.

Queen Victoria • *Via Por Santa Maria 32R.* Once a fin-de-siecle pub with a Florentine twist, now a popular snack bar with superb pastas, salads, blue-plate specials, and fruit. Closed Mon.

Orologio • *About 20 yards away.* Similar but smaller.

Leo in Santa Croce • *Via Torta 7R;* ☎ *270829.* Might better have been dubbed Disneyland East. Mighty gimmicky in its Viking, Jack and the Beanstalk, and King Arthur motifs.

Quattro Stagioni • *Via Maggio 61R;* ☎ *218906.* Passes its "Four Seasons" much more sedately. The owner is the chef, and after cooking at some of the best restaurants in town, he is now doing his own thing—and doing it well. He never does it on Sun., however.

Cantinetta Antinori • *Piazza Antinori 3;* ☎ *292234.* An expression of good taste by one of the most respected chianti producers in Italy. Accompanying great wines that bear its labels are soups, light meals, and cheese. Delicious and not expensive for what you get. (Antinori is not trying to gain from restauration, only seeking to create an inviting and fashionable showcase for sampling its vintages; it has succeeded nobly.) Shuttered Sat. and Sun.

NIGHTLIFE

Piano bars are not expensive and Florence offers stylish ones. **Loggia Tornaquinci** (*Via Tornabuoni 6*), **Full Up** (*Via della Vigna Vecchia 21*), and **Bistrot** (*Piazza Pitti 9*) all are in the mood business. **Tabasco** (*Piazza S. Cecilia 3*) is said to be gay.

Discotheques are given a good play in Florence. **Space Electronic** (*Via Palazzuolo 37*) has the highest wattage. **Tiffany** (*Lungarno Colombo 23*), Rockafe (*Borgo Albizi 66*), and **Yab Yum** (*Via Sassetti 5*) are swingers in the night. Expect psychedelic embellishments; strobe lights, pop and op art, luminescent paint work. Officially a "membership" operation, meaning you'll probably be admitted if you're wearing pockets.

WHAT TO SEE AND DO

Visiting hours vary. Weekdays (except for Mon., when they are closed) the main museums operate from 9 a.m. to 2 p.m. Admission to most is between $2 and $8. Sunday closing hour set at 1 p.m. An experiment to keep some museums open until 11 p.m. may be continued, so ask locally for details. Since the terrorist blast at the Uffizi, stricter security measures are being applied and opening hours may vary. Before setting out for the day ask your hotel receptionist to phone the museum to confirm the schedule.

The Uffizi, (*Piazza degli Uffizi*) contains examples of nearly every great Florentine painter. Normally open 9 a.m.-7 p.m. (normally closed Mon. as are all state museums). Hefty door charge for these marvelous treasures. The gallery is fully functional.

Next in line, the **Pitti Palace**, across the Arno, proudly boasts the graceful **Boboli Gardens**, the royal apartments, a modern art gallery, a "traditional" collection (the Raphaels and Titians are outstanding), and the charming *Forte di Belvedere*, which displays art exhibitions.

Then you might consider: the renovated **San Marco Museum** (*Piazza San Marco*), a Fra Angelico shrine; **Galleria dell' Accademia** (*Via Ricasoli 60*), with Michelangelo's "David"; **Museo Archeologico** (*Piazza Santissima Annunziata 9*), overflowing with Etruscan art and crafts; the **Bargello Museum** (*Via del Proconsolo 4*), housing a national trove of Florentine sculpture crowned by Donatello's version of "David"; **Medici Chapel**, (*off the Piazza Madonna*); **Giotto's historic Bell Tower**, (*Piazza del Duomo*); the **Strozzi Palace**, (*Piazza Strozzi*), with its magnificent courtyard; and **Casa Guidi**, Robert and Elizabeth Barrett Browning's home.

AMUSEMENT PARK

Luna Park is located at the Cascine Park. Sometimes it closes, but almost surely it is functioning on weekends. Very popular.

MOVIES

Cinema Astro (*Piazza San Simone, only 2 blocks from the piazza Santa Croce*) has performances in English.

MARKETS

The big one is the **Centrale** on the Borgo San Lorenzo; morning is the time. An interesting fruit and vegetable patch at **Piazza Santo Spirito** functions until around noon every day but Sun. Among the line of pushcarts along the **Via dell'Ariento** (near the Medici Chapels), Stall #13 has eyecatching bulky fishermen's pullovers and cardigans and other sweaters. Vendor suggests you buy them a size small, because these mixtures of wool and synthetic yarns stretch. This market is closed on Sun. The straw market (**Mercato del Porcellino**), open daily until 8 p.m. at the Loggia del Mercato Nuovo also features leather goods. The Flea Market (**Mercato delle Pulci**) at **Piazza dei Ciompi** near the Loggia del Pesce was the fish market of the 16th century; closed Sun.; not special.

EXCURSIONS

Fiesole, a 1/2-hour to the north, 50¢ bus ride (#7 leaves from piazza Stazione and piazza Duomo every 20 minutes), is an ideal destination. Ancient Etruscan *villaggio* enchanting for its views of the cypress and olivefilled Tuscan landscape, with all of Florence and a good swatch of the Arno as your backdrop.

CHIANTI COUNTRY

There's a splendid run to be had through Italy's prestige vinelands, only 1/2 hour from Florence. Go south to *San Casciano*, the home of Machiavelli, then to the market center of *Greve* with its arcades and flowered balconies. (You might enjoy lunch at the Hotel Verrazzano or a snack at the Lepanto Cafe). *Siena* is only 20 miles farther, through beautiful vineyards, if you wish to carry on the journey. An attractive overnight stop is *Albergo il Colombaio* at *Castellina* (☎ *0577-740444*) in the midst of harvest zone.

WHERE TO SHOP

ART REPRODUCTIONS

Alinari Brothers Ltd. (*Palazzo Rucellai, Via della Vigna Nuova*) has everybody licked on prints, paintings, picture frames, books, etchings, and related lines.

BELTS

Infinity (*Borgo SS Apostoli 18R*) will wrap your middle in any style you like; from American West to swashbuckle to high-fashion to high-tech. These people know the worth of a well-dressed girth. Great fun.

BOOKS

Try **BM** (*Borgo Ognissanti 4R*), which carries a volume-load of English language titles. Owner Batazzi is slave to his well-stocked shelves.

CERAMICS

Galleria Machiavelli (*Via Por S. Maria 39R*) has a great array of decorative plates, vases, jugs, ashtrays, pitchers, serving dishes, and fruit and vegetable arrangements. The traditional bird motif is particularly joyful.

EXTRAORDINARY GIFTS

Balatresi (*Lungarno Acciaioli 22R*) creates eye-popping alabaster eggs, fruit, decorative owls, and unusual boxes. In the celebrated brown onyx of Tuscany, they offer trays, boxes, vases, and animals. Also importantly featured are magnificent pieces in hard stones such as malachite, lapis lazuli, and rodonite, as well as exquisite enamelware. Safe shipment assured to anywhere in the world. Honest, friendly, fascinatingly different. **Ducci** (*Lungarno Corsini 24R*) also goes in for carvings, but chiefly in wood; very unusual household and office items, plus trays and Alinari boxes bearing famous art reproductions.

GLOVES

Madova (*Via Guiccardini 1R*) and **Chris Gloves** (*Por Santa Maria 42R*) carry moderately priced models.

LEATHER GOODS

John F (*Lungarno Corsini 2*) affords you the luxury of fine leather for reasonable tariffs. Everything from apparel to briefcases is available.

FLORENTINE PAPER AND STATIONERY GOODS

IL Papiro (*Via Cavour 55R, Piazza Duomo 24R, and Lungarno Acciaiuoli 42R*) specializes in *papier a cuve*, a decorative technique that produces distinctive sheets in subtle hues and abstract design. It is said to have been perfected in 17th-century France and is also known as "marbleized paper." They sell individual sheets as well as notebooks, boxes, and desk appurtenances covered in it. If you can't find what you're looking for there, then try **Giulio Giannini & Figlio** (*Piazza Pitti 36-37R*) or **Bottega Artigiana del Libro** (*Lungarno Corsini 38-40R*).

MEMENTOS IN SILVER

Sacchi (*Lungarno Acciaiuoli 82R*) begins with economical silver cameos, runs through a zoo of shining animals, to lovely picture frames and on to stratospheric levels for collectors of the craft.

SHOES (LADIES)

One of the best bets is **Lily of Florence** (*Via Guicciardini 2R*). All U.S. sizes; reasonable prices.

The **Straw Market** (*along the loggia del Mercato Nuovo*) is loaded with crude souvenirs of every description. Most of them cost a song.

SHOPPING STREETS

Via Tornabuoni is the Fifth Avenue, and **Via Calzaiuoli**, **Via Strozzi**, **Via Vigna Nuova**, and **Via Por Santa Maria** are the equivalents of 34th Street. **Ponte Vecchio**, the dramatic little shop-lined bridge, is limited to gold and silver jewelry, coral, embroideries, blouses, and specialty items. The **Lungarno Acciaioli** and **Lungarno Corsini**, which run along the north bank of the Arno up from the Ponte Vecchio, have a variety of stores. The San Lorenzo **"Central" Market** and the **Mercato del Porcellino** (*Piazza del Mercato Nuovo*) are also good for casual hunting.

Shopping hours: 9 a.m.–1 p.m., and 3:30–7:30 p.m., plus Mon. morning closings in winter (changed to Sat. afternoons in summer) and Feast Days (there are plenty of the latter).

AUTHOR'S OBSERVATION

Since any guide you use usually gets a 10% rakeoff on your purchases, go alone and tell the storekeeper "I've been sent by no one, I'm paying cash, and I expect the usual 10% discount!" And if you buy a hefty amount in any one store, always bargain!

GENOA

(Genova) Fifth in size; perhaps the least publicized and visited center in the country. This decaying port became an air-harbor, as well, when it constructed a huge platform over the water named Christopher Columbus Airport—1992 marked the 500th anniversary of the discovery of America by a local navigator. It's one of Europe's most modern termini, part of a renewal program that will finally touch all districts of the city. Its proudest button for this season is the $100 million Teatro Carlo Felice. Something was done about highway routes to the south; long tunnels hewn at unbelievable cost now make the approach easier. The **Crespi**, the **Nuova Astoria**, and the nicely revamped **Eliseo** are adequate as local inns. The last is in the medium-price Jolly chain of which the **Plaza** is yet another link.

MESSINA

This strait port has a fair shake of new or improved accommodations, lavish portions of squalor, ravenous wolf packs of mosquitoes, and a chronic shortage of mosquito netting. A gem of a city—to miss.

MILAN

Italy's 2nd city, with 1-3/4 million people, the financial and industrial center of the nation. Urbanity and sophistication at their highest next to Rome; one of the most advanced cities in Europe, intellectually and technically—and, according to late surveys, also one of the most expensive. It's in the heart of Lombardy (so close to Switzerland that St. Moritz seems to be the weekend retreat of nearly every rich Milanese skier); Como, Maggiore, and other Italian lakes are close by. The **Duomo**, most famous landmark on the upper half of the Peninsula, concentrates 2300 statues and some of the world's finest stained glass in 2 treasure-filled acres. The **Brera Gallery** sets off its paintings with a unique display technique. The **Poldi Pezzoli Gallery**, tiny but choice, is the cultural contribution of an unselfish private citizen; Botticelli's "Virgin" and a priceless collection of porcelains are found here. The air-conditioned Rinascente Department Store is one of the most modern establishments of its kind in Europe. Then, of course, there are Leonardo da Vinci's slowly fading "**Last Supper**," **La Scala Opera** (don't miss its museum, open daily at specified times and during all performance intermissions), the **Museum of Modern Design** in the Sforza Castle, and a host of other high points within the huge Sforza complex: ancient art, oriental, Egyptian, applied arts, and musical instruments. The **International Samples Fair** in mid-Apr. attracts exhibitors from 83 countries and is visited by more than 4 million. Looking for diversion? The **Sinigallia** flea market, Via Calatafimi, operates on Sat. Two airports: Malpensa and Linate. Lots of factories including nearly 3000 U.S. firms; some slums, of course, but scads of interesting things, too. Primarily commercial; un-Latin feeling of hustle and bustle; with 1 million cars clogging the streets, tourism rates minor importance.

If you do pause here, the **De la Ville**, the station-area **Andreola**, and the neighboring **Splendido** are substantial overnight choices. **Casa Svizzera** (*Via San Raffaele 3*) is in the second category. The **Rosa** has been renewed; prices match first-class rewards. **Galilee** is fresh and appealing. Both very central; but everything so costly in this city, only a short visit is advised.

Now for a gathering of *trattorias*, each distinctive in its manner, and tops in its particular category: Don't be put off by the entrance at the **Cucina delle Langhe** (*Corso Como 6*), a discouraging approach to the truly outstanding Pied-montese tables within; hardy, genuine cooking at honest prices. **Osteria dei Binari** (*Via Tortona 1*) also features cookery from the Piedmont as well as *emiliano* preparations. Artists, journalists, and jet-setters now occupy the places where a century ago travelers paused to change horses. Popular, but never on Sundays or midday either. **Osteria Via Pre** (*Via Casale 4*) presents such an unabashedly phony fishhouse interior that you can easily forgive the decorator—if only out of a sense of humor. You could overlook a lot more once you have dived into the typically Genovese dishes, felt satisfaction with every morsel, and received a bill so low that you might blink with wonder. Closed Mon.; very commendable for value. **Torre Di Pisa** (*Via Mercato 26*) inclines one block from the Brera Academy, which used to be the center of Milan's redlight district. Today the area is respectable, the "Tower of Pisa" having become a popular rendezvous for advertising people and fashion models. There is a smattering of up-market bohemia here that seems to attract many swinging singles. And, oh yes, the food? That's okay, too. **Alfredo-Gran San Bernardo** (*Via Borghese 14*) specializes in, of all things, Milanese dishes. Plain to look at, but easy to take otherwise. An outstanding meal, perfectly served, will lighten your budget by perhaps $30. The last 2 shuttered on Sun. **Albric** (*Via Albricci 3*) is also a worthwhile bet in the medium category. A family place with warm attention. Closed Sun. and Aug. **Molo 13** (*Via Rubens 13*) is in the fairgrounds district; specialties of Sardinia, especially fish. No biz on Wed. Don't miss a turn at the colorful and amusing **Taverna del Gran Sasso** (*piazzale Principessa Clotilde 8*), with its decor of rustic kitchenware and abundant foodstuffs. Serafino is a solid bet that costs even less.

MONTECATINI

Only 25 miles from Florence, catches much of the overflow when Florentine hotels are overbooked. A lovely spa chiefly known to Europeans who have appreciated it for centuries. The waters are famous for their supposedly beneficial effects on the liver. Within the immediate area are over 300 square miles of parks and gardens that tend to keep things cool during the hottest months; more than 250 hotels or pensions; many attractions.

NAPLES

Personal affection for this 3rd largest city is tempered with irritation and pity. With exquisite natural assets, Naples could be *the* gemstone in the Tyrrhenian tiara. Instead, gangsters (called *Camorra* locally) have almost paralyzed it. The taxi drivers, porters, boatmen, almost the entire skein of personnel who greet the tourist have gotten in on the act. Recently as many as 60,000 merchants demonstrated against the "protection" and other rackets run by Mafialike families. Probably they will remain powerless to effect a change, but the effort is a noble one. Attractions include **Vesuvius**, one of the world's most magnificent bays, the **Royal Palace** (museum and apartments), **Capodimonte's** picture gallery, the **Castel Nuovo** (Anjou Castle) and the former **monastery of San Martino**, the **San Carlo Opera House**, 499 churches, songs such as "O Sole Mio" and "Funiculi Funicula"—a score of wonders, if one could only see them in peace. For excursions to Pompeii, Capri, Ischia, Sorrento, Amalfi, and other places, it is a necessary transportation point. If you overnight, the Britannique was restyled and updated not too long ago; **Fontane al Mare** is an inexpensive seafronter; **Cavour** is in the station area; greatly improved since its revamping. For dining, the most colorful shacks are on the fish row of the port called Santa Lucia. It's fun even for strolling and very near to the center of town. Try **Transatlantico** or **Ciro**. Incidentally, though pizza was born in *Napoli*, the local creation is a far, far distant cousin of the thick, rich pies we are used to in North America. Don't think you are being cheated; these are meant to be anemic. **La Cantinella** and the nearby **Rosolino** (*both on Via N. Sauro*) are reliable choices. In Posollipo, try **Villa Antica**. (Postscript: The latest gesture of endearment for tourists leaving the Naples exit of the Autostrada is for a car to dart in front of the vehicle. When both are stopped, a larrikin on a motorbike whizzes by, reaches into the foreign car for a purse or anything of value, and flashes away. Roll up your windows and lock all doors, as well as the trunk.)

PALERMO

Although Italy's 6th city and Sicily's largest center, the lion's share of commerce is concentrated around **Catania**, on the east coast. Labeled by its promoters "The Golden Shell," some aspects are pleasant, but vacationing facilities are so limited it's not worth a special journey. If you are on "hold" here, opt for the **Citta del Mare Hotel Village**, 20 miles west of Palermo along the coast. More of an entertainment enclave than a straight hostelry, this option is for vacation-bound travelers rather than transients. **Locandas Lungarini** and the **Primavera** (*both at Via Lungarini*) are okay for money-saving stops in the city. **Sole** (*Corso v. Emanuele 291*) is more substantial. Overnight car-ferry connections with Naples (and other more distant points) are excellent aboard the vessels of the Tirrenia line; clean, comfortable ships that can save 2 full days of driving over desolate hills of southern Italy.

PERUGIA

Like neighboring Assisi, it draws a flood of excursionists. An ancient hill town, site of the University for Foreigners. The **Collegio del Cambio** has some fine frescoes, the **National Gallery** has some famous paintings, and the panorama of the valley is lovely. Best to visit during the fringe seasons when tourism is relatively light. If you pause, the **Excelsior Lilli** is okay in the center; the **Park** is only a few minutes outside of town by car.

PISA

Has the legendary 8-century-old **Leaning Tower**, the **Square of Miracles**, plus the venerable **Duomo**, baptistery, and exquisite Gothic church by Nicola Pisano. The Tower, incidentally, is not only leaning these days; it's bending so precipitously that they've conducted a worldwide contest for the proper prop-up solution to save it. (The engineers seem to have settled on a plan to sink 6 wells—3 on the town's outskirts of 394 ft. depth and 3 of 197 ft. near the Tower—to equalize the pressure of the water table.) Because of recent "cultural terrorism" closed-circuit television is on vigil all of the time; the enchantment of the district around the Cathedral is closed to the public between 11 p.m. and 7 a.m. June (*Giugno Pisano*) is best, when **Il Gioco del Ponte** (*tug-of-war on the bridge*) and other pageantry bring it alive. The **Arno** is very central as a hotel choice, while the Royal Victoria is by the river (with heavy group patronage).

POMPEII

Usually it is seen on brief excursions from Naples. On a short visit it's impossible to take in a large number of structures. If you have time for only one site, Pompeii emphatically is the most comprehensive and thrilling. Three other ancient cities in the Bay of Naples area: **Cumae** (*11 miles northwest of Pozzuoli*); **Paestum** (*30 miles southeast of Salerno*); and **Herculaneum** (a.k.a. "Ercolano," *7 miles northwest of Pompeii*). The last is better-preserved than Pompeii and restoration is proceeding. This site was covered by mud rather than ash; hence, the details are intact. The first features the foundations of two acropolis temples and the trapezoidal tunnel where, according to tradition, Sybil delivered her oracles. Paestum has 3 temples, perhaps the best-preserved Greek sacred structures in the world.

PORTOFINO

This "Superb Port" has one of Europe's most romantic natural settings —a tiny, cliff-lined harbor of unsurpassing charm and intimacy, over which broods a castle; several very pleasant pensions are tucked into the backwaters of the harbor; hotels are extraordinarily expensive here. It's about 25 miles by road from Genoa. Spring and fall are the best times to go; in summer it's often crowded and on weekends it can take hours (literally) to find a parking spot.

POSITANO

In the opinion of many, the star attraction of the Amalfi Drive and of the entire area near Naples. The houses of this highly paintable village climb straight up the mountainside. If planning an overnight in this region, it's a sensible stop. Increasingly popular.

RAPALLO

Only a short hop from Genoa, it's on the sea but cupped in a chalice of mountains. Pleasant weather, summer or winter. Typically crowded during holiday periods. Try to book at either the **Grand Hotel & Europa** or at the **Grande Italia E Lido**.

RAVELLO

Perched above Amalfi, and more attractive; one of the best targets on the peninsula. Its **Villa Rufolo** gardens are famed (here Wagner was purportedly inspired to compose Parsifal) and its wines well regarded by Italian connoisseurs. Hotels are sky-high here, so consider Amalfi as your stopover.

RAVENNA

Situated halfway between Venice and Ancona, this gem is a culture-seeker's paradise—historically and artistically, one of the outstanding smaller sites of the Western world. No other city can compete with its wealth of Byzantine architecture or its unique mosaics. Ecclesiastical treasures; **Dante's tomb**; **Theodoric's tomb**; a scholar's heaven. Giant ENI rubber-and-fertilizer plant; indifferent hotels (**Centrale Byron** is fair); 6 miles from the sea, on the Corsini Canal.

RIMINI

On the Adriatic coast east of Florence, it might be called the Atlantic City of Italy. Impressive asphalt "boardwalk" parallels sea; broad beaches for 15 miles through neighboring "Rimini Riviera" (Riccione, Cattolica, Miramare, Viserba, Viserbella, Torre Pedrera, Igea Marina, and Bellaria). Strictly a resort, May-Sept. only; jump-off spot for easy excursions to Ravenna and San Marino; fair restaurants and nightclubs; the **Malatestian Temple** is the most remarkable attraction; prices cheap, in general. There are scores and scores of hotels, but you might try the **Napoleon** or the **Kursaal** for starters, which are not expensive.

ROME

Set among its seven legendary hills, it is Eternal. The pillars of the Caesars still pinpoint the pastel blue heaven. Great avenues—now filled with invading tourists—still mark the paths of returning victorious legions. Without a skyscraper to be seen, the splendid dome of St. Peter's still dominates a metropolis that has only spread out with time, not up. The grace and harmony of several eras are well met, not offending each other because the Romani throughout history have always loved their hill-bound capital and preserved its splendor. Now, however, they are covering the russet, ocher, and antique buff of its buildings with white paint or sandblasting away much of its ancient facade. It's in an effort to restore the Rome of the 18th century. Small, intimate streets where dwelled the literary and artistic colossi of the Quattrocento lead into grand piazzas, still resplendent with the memory of martial power throughout the known world—a civilization that went out from Rome and left its indelible stamp 3000 years afterward. There are the romantic (after all, the word was born here) gardens of the spectacularly rich and tasteful Borghese dynasty. There are statues and fountains at almost every street corner. There are sidewalk cafes in endless profusion. There's the preposterous memorial to Vittorio Emanuele (within sight of the glorious Forum) looking like a gigantic antique white marble typewriter. There are enough churches to serve all of Christianity for millennia to come. There are voluble, happy people and animation. There is a hidden kiss, a child kicking a soccer ball in the street—everywhere the eternity that is Rome.

DIRECTORY

U.S. Embassy • *Via Vittorio Veneto 121*; ☎ *46746741.*

American Express • *Piazza di Spagna 38*; ☎ *688751* or *689741.*

Barber and Hairdresser • Peppino, *Via Mario de' Fiori 82, corner of Via Bologna* for men; Armando & Nino, *Piazza di Spagna 54*; ☎ *673718*, for ladies.

Dry Cleaning and Pressing • Berlioz, *Piazza Barberini 19*; ☎ *462331*, or Presto Kleen, *Via Sicilia 156*; ☎ *478684.*

Suit Rental: Misano • *Via Nazionale 88*; ☎ *462005.*

English-Speaking Doctors • Dr. Salvatore Mannino, Office: *Via Lisbona 9*; ☎ *8448712*; Home ☎ *3274562*; Dr. Frank Silvestri, *Via Ludovisi 36*; ☎ *485706*; and Dr. A. K. Ovadia, ☎ *6793457.*

English-Speaking Dentist • Dr. A. K. Ovadia, *Piazza di Spagna 72*; ☎ *673457.*

Police • Questura di Roma, Uffico Stranieri, *Via S. Vitale 15*; ☎ *4686.*

Favorite Pawnshop • Monte di Pieta (*P. Pieta*) is the largest in the world.]

AUTHOR'S OBSERVATION

One of the most helpful touring organizations in the world is located in Italy. It's called Compagnia Italiana Turismo (CIT) with 50 offices in Italy and 49 in foreign cities. The Rome headquarters are located in Piazza della Republica. Address any inquiries to Dr. Cesare Della Pietra, General Manager. For escorted tours or group arrangements, CIT is peerless.

HOW TO GET AROUND

Public transport within the capital is efficient, physically overtaxed, and inexpensive. You'll pay peanuts per ride on any of the 58 bus and trolley bus lines or the 14 streetcar routes. The price also is miniature on Line A of the subway system, which extends from Cinecitta to Via Ottaviano (near St. Peter's). Some of the more important stops in the center include Termini, piazza della Republica, and piazza di Spagna. Line B approximately doubles your opportunities and even scampers out of midtown to EUR and the popular beach region of Ostia. Check the route maps or any platform or Termini Station.

AIRPORT TO TOWN

You'll be soaked up to $40 or so if you take a taxi the 19 miles between Leonardo da Vinci (Fiumicino) Airport and the capital. For about $7 the special train will transport you to Stazione Ostiense. In addition, some airlines run their own services; check on this when reconfirming your flight arrangements.

TAXIS

Like everywhere else, a few hacks navigate only by the Great Circle Route, but most are honest. The meter starts ticking at around one buck and adds that much again for every mile; there's a surcharge at night.

MOTORING

If you're heading for Rome in the evening, buy gas before leaving the Autostrada; under a city ordinance, all gas stations in the capital close at 7 p.m.

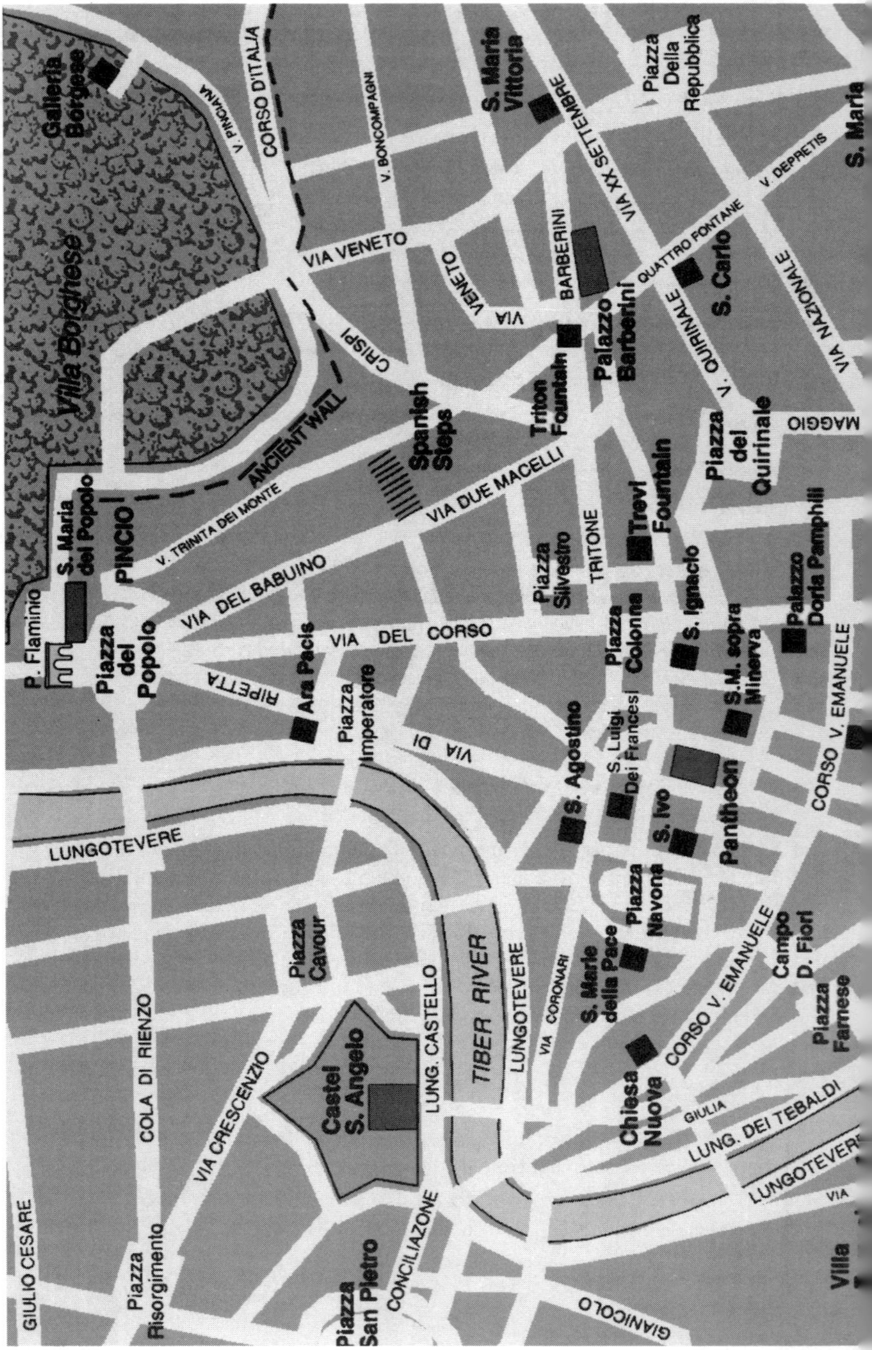
Galleria Borgese
Villa Borghese
V. PINCIANA
CORSO D'ITALIA
V. BONCOMPAGNI
S. Maria Vittoria
Piazza Della Repubblica
VIA VENETO
VIA VENETO
BARBERINI
VIA XX SETTEMBRE
V. DEPRETIS
S. Maria
QUATTRO FONTANE
S. Carlo
V. QUIRINALE
VIA NAZIONALE
CRISPI
ANCIENT WALL
Spanish Steps
Triton Fountain
Palazzo Barberini
Piazza del Quirinale
MAGGIO
Trevi Fountain
V. TRINITA DEI MONTE
VIA DUE MACELLI
PINCIO
S. Maria del Popolo
P. Flaminio
Piazza del Popolo
VIA DEL BABUINO
Piazza Silvestro
TRITONE
S. Ignacio
Palazzo Doria Pamphili
VIA DEL CORSO
Piazza Colonna
Ara Pacis
RIPETTA
Piazza Imperatore
VIA DI
S. Agostino
S. Luigi Dei Francesi
S.M. sopra Minerva
CORSO V. EMANUELE
Pantheon
S. Ivo
Piazza Navona
LUNGOTEVERE
Piazza Cavour
TIBER RIVER
LUNGOTEVERE
VIA CORONARI
S. Marie della Pace
Campo D. Fiori
CORSO V. EMANUELE
Piazza Farnese
LUNG. CASTELLO
COLA DI RIENZO
VIA CRESCENZIO
Castel S. Angelo
Chiesa Nuova
GIULIA
LUNG. DEI TEBALDI
LUNGOTEVERE
VIA
GIULIO CESARE
Piazza Risorgimento
CONCILIAZONE
Piazza San Pietro
GIANICOLO
Villa

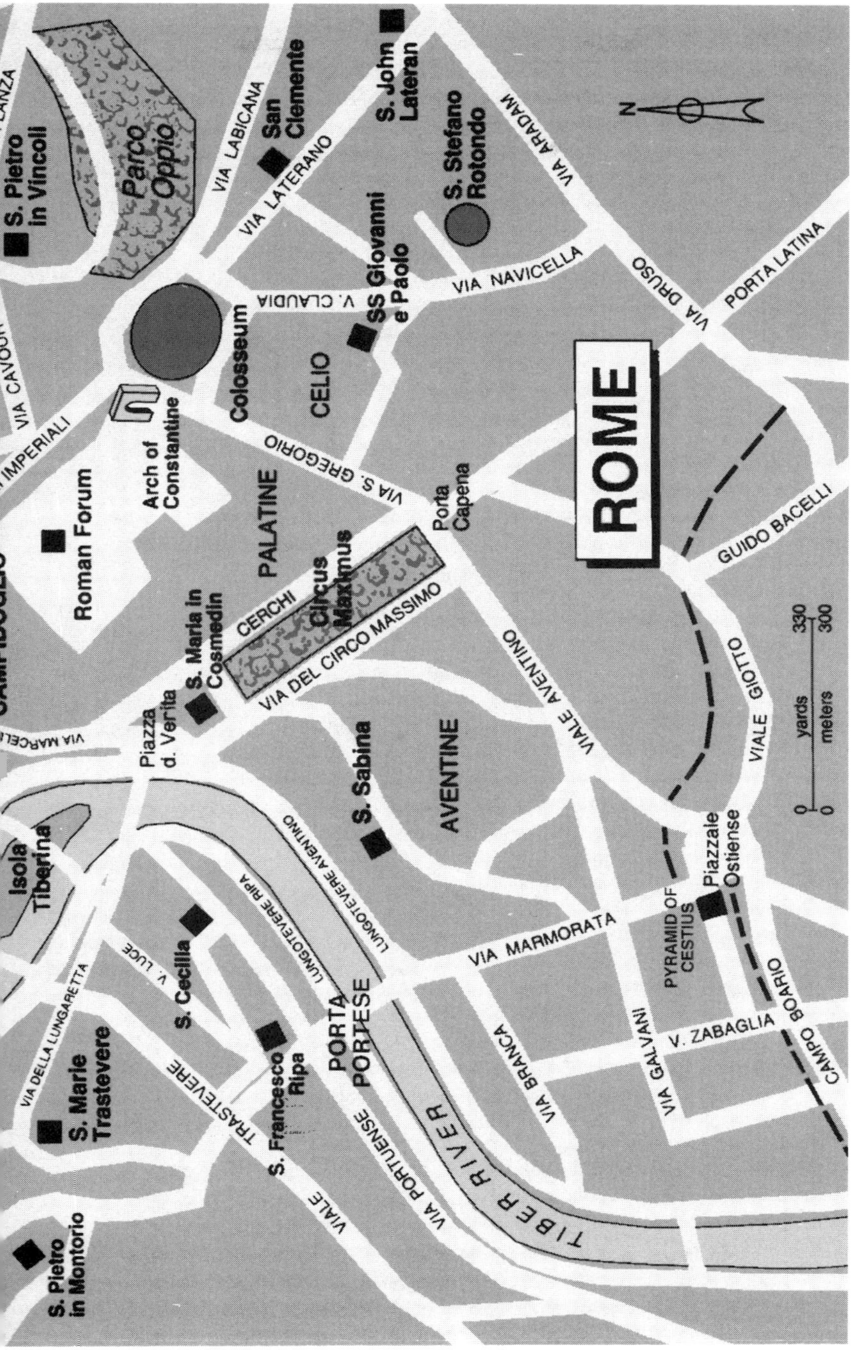
ROME
Colosseum
Arch of Constantine
Roman Forum
PALATINE
CELIO
AVENTINE
Circus Maximus
S. Pietro in Vincoli
Parco Oppio
San Clemente
S. John Lateran
S. Stefano Rotondo
SS Giovanni e Paolo
S. Maria In Cosmedin
Piazza d. Verita
S. Sabina
Porta Capena
Isola Tiberina
S. Cecilia
S. Francesco Ripa
S. Marie Trastevere
S. Pietro in Montorio
PORTA PORTESE
Piazzale Ostiense
PYRAMID OF CESTIUS
TIBER RIVER
VIA LABICANA
VIA LATERANO
VIA CAVOUR
V. CLAUDIA
VIA NAVICELLA
VIA ARADAM
VIA DRUSO
PORTA LATINA
VIA S. GREGORIO
CERCHI
VIA DEL CIRCO MASSIMO
VIALE AVENTINO
GUIDO BACELLI
VIALE GIOTTO
VIA MARMORATA
VIA GALVANI
V. ZABAGLIA
CAMPO BOARIO
VIA BRANCA
LUNGOTEVERE AVENTINO
LUNGOTEVERE RIPA
V. LUCE
VIA DELLA LUNGARETTA
VIALE TRASTEVERE
VIA PORTUENSE
VIA MARCELLO
yards
meters
0
330
300

CAR HIRE

Surprisingly expensive. The giant **CIT** chain ("Compagnia Italiana Turismo") offers a selection of European cars. Midtown depot handily located at *Via Antonio Bosio 21*; friendly, courteous staff; recommended—but to the better-heeled only.

Hertz may be found at *Via Sallustiana 28* (☎ *542941*). **Avis** has its main office at *Piazza Esquilino 1/C* (☎ *4701216*) with several other branches elsewhere in town. Both are competitive in price.

WHERE TO STAY

LEAST $

In this division, prices hover around $65 for a double with breakfast. Be sure your quotation specifies if it is a per-person rate, or a room rate, and what other supplements are included.

Erdarelli • *Via Due Macelli 28*; *6791265* and **Pierina**, *annex, Via Due Macelli 47*; ☎ *6791522*. Very good but noisy (street leads to piazza di Spagna); try for rear (some have balconies); demi pension required in summer. Erdarelli, with 28 bedchambers, 20 baths or showers, 3 refurbished floors, and dining room, is preferable. Reserve early.

Venezia • *Via Varese 18*; ☎ *4457101*. A brief stroll from the station. Belies discouraging facade; 60 small, cheerful rooms; about 25% with bath or shower. Singles for $48; doubles at $65, including breakfast.

Esedra • *Piazza della Republica 47*; ☎ *4883912*. Shares building with Terminus (see later) and the Eureka (below). Breakfast nook with fireplace. Pleasant vistas from front units; light sleepers in the rear. Per-person charge $30, including breakfast and service; supplement for a bath.

Eureka • *Piazza della Republica 47*; ☎ *4825806*. Also on the 3rd floor. Doubles around $58, inclusive. Better—but at these tabs, no big discovery.

Canova • *Via Urbana 10/A*; ☎ *4740633*. Hard to find near minuscule Piazza de San Lorenzo in Lucina, just off Corso; 8 convertible twins plus 1 single.

San Pietro • *Via Cardinale Cassetta 9*; ☎ *630876*. Hard-to-find Vatican-area address. Spotless. Reserve early here.

Fontana • *Piazza di Trevi 96*; ☎ *6786113*. Overlooks Trevi. In old-style edifice with corresponding character. No kitchen; no breakfast. Some doubles in the $35 area. Book #19 or #20 (both with bath and Trevi views).

Del Popolo • *Via degli Apuli 41*; ☎ *490558*. Out-of-the-way setting reached by Bus #11. Administered by Salvation Army. Complete facilities, including bar, restaurant, and summer garden. Women admitted between June 1 and Sept. 30 only. Around $14 per night. Eminently practical.

Ausonia • *Piazza di Spagna 35*; ☎ *6795745*. In courtyard beside American Express. Extremely clean, comfortable, well-kept, but going wild in its prices. Why the staff should be so grumpy surprises me.

Albergo Piazza di Spagna • *Via Mario de' Fiori 16*; ☎ *6793061*. Though perfect location for shoppers or sightseers, a disappointment. A bit better are **Pensione Galli Via Milazzo 20**. and, on the second floor, **Maria Carezza**.

La Villetta • *Via Ettore Perrone 1 (near the station)*; ☎ *7592759*. A substantial house in a convenient district.

HOSTELS

To help the city absorb the high-season tide, religious institutes welcome boarders of all faiths and ages. Here are 5 top entries, which enforce a mandatory full-pension plan and prefer groups.

Domus Pacis • *Via Torre Rossa 4;* ☎ *620143, across the Tiber near the American Academy.*

Domus Maximi • *Via Santa Prisca 11B;* ☎ *5746135, situated in the Aventino quarter, two minutes from the piazza Albania.*

Domus Mariae • Resting up to 500 noggins per night—most of them under the command of tour-leading proconsuls.

Suore del Rosario • *Via della Circonvallazione Tuscolana 40;* ☎ *745373, within the Cinecitta precinct.*

Suore Preziosine • *Via Santa Maria Mediatrice 8;* ☎ *631759.* Taxes, meals, service, and all other amenities should run from $19 to $28 per person.

MORE $$

Texas and Seven Hills • *Via Firenze 47;* ☎ *4742107.* Joint enterprise on the 3rd through 6th floors of old *palazzo*; 40 dim chambers, 30 baths or showers; suite arrangements for families. Units with plumbing average $47 per person. Special dining at nearby La Toscanella. Seven Hills fallow is winter. Cocktail hour a pleasant dividend.

Suisse • *Via Gregoriana 56;* ☎ *6783649.* Centrally sited. Homey ambience; 5th-floor terrace dining; 39 rooms; penthouse view of Spanish Steps; 10 baths, 8 public; #35 large triple with plumbing. Soothing rates for the required demi pension in season.

Scalinata di Spagna • *Piazza Trinita dei Monti 17;* ☎ *6793006.* Alluring location at the top of Spanish Steps. Fabulous view from roof, used for sunbathing and breakfasting in summer. Redecoration continuous.

Sicilia Daria • *Via Sicilia 24;* ☎ *4821913.* On the 5th floor of business building; good enthusiastic ownership. Kitsch on the walls; amusing furnishings; 54 rooms, all with baths or showers. Superb maintenance.

Nardizzi Americana • *Via Firenze 38;* ☎ *4880368.* Fine location 2 blocks from Piazza della Republica. Extensive updatings; all units with shower and private w.c.; very warmhearted management. Elfin dining chamber. Some of its dozen rooms overlook garden of Palace of Presidential Guards. A good stop that is always improving.

Augustea • *Via Nazionale 251;* ☎ *4883589/483852.* Amiable little restaurant. Clean bedrooms, demi pension required. Twins from $35 per person; singles at $33. Cozy.

Home in Rome • *Via Corsica 4;* ☎ *865598.* Residentially sited, offering 18 regular accommodations and 4 rent-by-the-month flats. Dining nook with tiny adjoining bar. Nearby swimming (summer) for $1.50 daily. Clean rooms vary in size and desirability; all but 2 with private bath; #6 a good large double with balcony, couch, and coffee table.

Villa Florence • *Via Nomentana 28;* ☎ *4403036.* Converted manse set far back from the busy thoroughfare. Private garage. Garden, lounge, 10-table restaurant; 24 dated rooms without baths; doubles #15 or #10 with balconettes; #11 a good single with veranda. Rear carriage-house flat a charming choice for families.

Trinita dei Monti • *Via Sistina 91 (close to the Spanish Steps)*; ☎ *6797206*. Maintains high standards in superb but noisy situation. Nice but unfancy; 16 really expansive rooms with 8 private and 3 public baths. Very decent digs.

Tefi • *Via di S. Basilio 53*; ☎ *4881283*. Comes recommended by a reader who was impressed by the unusual high value here for the money (about $36 per person in a twin). Some singles also available. Proprietor Podiò Fabrisio is a most willing and able host, according to our correspondent.

Merano • *Via Veneto 155*; ☎ *4821808*. Ultracentral and tranquil; 24 rooms, 7 showers, and 1 private tub. Moderate tariffs. Half pension available.

Condotti • *Via Mario de'Fiori 37*; ☎ *6794661*. Kindly management; 21 twins with baths or showers. Small bar.

Sistina • *Via Sistina 136*; ☎ *6799347*. Fresh appointments nearly throughout; basement bar; 29 lodgings, all but 6 with bath; 19 with a nice view of the neighborhood church.

Canada • *Via Vicenza 58*; ☎ *4457770*. Ample cheer; air conditioning on request; direct-dial phones; sound comfort at rates that are not too buckling.

Elite • *Via Crispi 49 (a block east of the Spanish Steps)*; ☎ *6783083*. Singles with spongy beds, sitz baths, telephone showers, and protruding hotwater heaters; doubles better, but with similar bathrooms. Perky restaurant.

Tiffany • *Viale Manzoni 22 (near the Lateran Palace)*; ☎ *7316476*. In a midtown residential district; 19 rooms; 13 showers. Quite nice.

Terminus • *Piazza della Republica 47*; ☎ *4881505*. Shares quarters with earlier-mentioned Esedra and Eureka. Lounge and dining salon; 20 good size bedchambers (including some lofty ceilings); #39, on the square, particularly pleasant. Kind staff.

Valle • *Via Cavour 134*; ☎ *4815736*. Resides conveniently though raucously on the street cutting between the Station and the Forum. Many groups. Cost-conscious interiors; adequately clean; 31 rooms, 10 with cramped bathrooms. Reasonable rates. On the same street, at #33, the Genoa is a worthy alternative.

Villa Le Terraze • *Via Morgagni 5*; ☎ *858525*. Converted private dwelling at noisy noncentral location.

Consul • *Via Aurelia 727*. Also not in midtown, quite pleasant for living comforts.

Concordia • *Via Capo le Case 14*; ☎ *6795693*. Somewhat overpriced.

Sant'Anna • *134 Borgo Pio*; ☎ *6541602*. Near the Vatican; quite agreeable; and so are the prices in this special area of Rome. (Not everyone wants to be so far from the commercial districts.)

EVEN MORE $$$

Valadier • *Via della Fontanella 15*; ☎ *3610559*. Beautiful in an ornate, gilt-edged fashion; richly outfitted lounge in old European style; wooden bar; Renoir restaurant. Very smart. Slightly more cozy in tone is a house run by the same skillful administration: **Diplomatic** *Via Vittoria Colonna 28*; ☎ *6542084*, with patio and salon dining, clean-line appointments; greater simplicity than the above, but still worth the investment.

Britannia • *Via Napoli 64*; ☎ *4883153*. Extremely central, near rail station; soundproofed rooms, air-conditioned. Fantastic modern decor; beautiful materials of synthesized woods, tweedy textiles, greenery, and polished marble. American bar plus frigo-bar in room; radio. Outstanding value for such spirited modernity.

Raphael • *Largo Febo 2*; ☎ *650881*. A close neighbor to the piazza Navona. Original art in rooms; lobby filled with museum pieces from antique sled to pre-Columbian pottery; Picasso ceramics in bar; Berocal multiples in downstairs restaurant; 90 units with air conditioning and baths. A tasteful collectors' choice.

Panama • *Via Salaria 336*; ☎ *862558*. Superb despite noncentral siting. Take Bus #35 from the station, or motor in on N-4 from north. Tranquil and cozy. Ample parking. Large front rooms, some with panoramic windows; few chambers with small balconies; rear units overlooking garden; most with private bath. Becoming quite expensive, but also chic and attractive.

Fiamma • *Via Gaeta 61* (*across piazza dei Cinquecento from station and airline terminal*); ☎ *4818436*. Quality-for-money; 65 rooms; bar; lounge; no restaurant. Rooms #209, #309, #409, and #423 comfortable large doubles. Breakfast $5.50; air conditioning in some doubles at $5 per day.

Siena • *Via Andrea delle Fratte 33*; ☎ *6796121*. Freshly updated; all units with bath; color TV; tiny bedrooms but king-size prices. Its central position kicks up the costs.

Carriage • *Via delle Carrozze 36* (*on a side street off the piazza de Spagna*); ☎ *6793152*. Full-bath accommodations (25) with good furnishings and radios. Smallish #46 and #47 open onto viewful rooftop terrace. Bar.

Lloyd • *Via Alessandria 110* (*near the Pia Gate*); ☎ *8540432*. Amiable and good; 60 rooms, spacious and colorful; frigo-bars; bath or shower. Doubles with bath $130, singles $90.

Nord-Nuova Roma • *Via Amendola 3*; ☎ *4885441*. Routine dining room; better-than-average service and food. Good twins with tub or shower. Groups by the busload in season. Very sound bet.

Degli Aranci • *Via Barnaba Oriani 11*; ☎ *870202*. In pleasant residential district about 1-1/2 miles north of piazza del Popolo. Dining veranda; 35 baths or showers for 45 units; best come with private balconies; twins about $110 inclusive.

Columbus • *Via della Conciliazione 33* (*almost in the shadow of St. Peter's*); ☎ *6865435*. Vatican-owned. Converted convent; 107 rooms, 60 with bath. Try for #345 or #221. Breakfast optional and extra. Suggested solely to the ecclesiastically inclined due to individual and tour group pilgrimages.

Atlante • *Via Vitelleschi 34*; ☎ *6872300* and **Garden Atlante** *Via Crescenzio 78*; ☎ *3598884*. Roughly in the same area, between St. Peter's and Castel St. Angelo. Both are fresh, boldly and colorfully decorated, and both offer free airport pickup; air-conditioned; color TV; bath and shower; shared management. Very cheerful.

Madison • *Via Marsala 60 (hard by the Terminal Station)*; ☎ *4454344*. Lounge; dining salon and terrace; 102 rooms, several with modern baths.

Pace Elvezia • *Bordered on 2 sides by Via IV Novembre with main entrance at #104*; ☎ *6795105*. Tranquil haven in a traffic-choked street. Lounges and restaurant; 64 spacious, old-style bedrooms; #90, with arched windows and small balcony, appealing.

Colosseum • *Via Sforza 10 (on a back street near the Colosseum)*; ☎ *4827228*. Overdecorated rooms, all 50 with shower or tub; panorama from higher units. Baronial breakfast hall. Singles better than dwarfish twins.

Oxford • *Via Boncompagni 89*; ☎ *4828952*. Near heartland of Via Veneto. Pleasant, quiet surroundings, nevertheless.

Sorrento • *Via Nazionale 251*; ☎ *4882444*. On 5 floors of main-artery commercial building. Some units seemed worth $50-per-person; some didn't. Front rooms excessively noisy. Inspection before selection strongly advised.

D'Inghilterra • *Via Bocca di Leone 14*; ☎ *672161*. Antiques abound. Deluxe comforts at first-class tariffs. Coffee shop, air conditioning, color TV. All units with bath; some delightfully posh suites.

CAMPING

Flaminio and **Nomentano** • *Located Via Flaminia Nuova*; ☎ *3332604 and Via Nomentana*; ☎ *6100296*. On historic pikes and well situated in the outskirts.

Roma Camping • ☎ *6223018*. 5 miles to the east, just off the Aurelia Consular Road.

SUGGESTIONS FOR STUDENTS

Apart from the thousands of Vatican-visiting scholars (many of whom you will see in clerical garb), this metropolis boasts no less than 36 colleges, academies, institutes, and graduate schools *administered solely for foreigners*! The hub is the University of Rome, founded by Papal edict in the 13th century and now incorporated into a *citta* (city) of its own.

The **Rome Provinciale Tourist Board** (*Via Parigi 11*; ☎ *4881851*) an endless font of information and assistance with regard to student lodgings, transportation, tours, museums, concerts, sports, expositions and similar pastimes. Branches at Fiumicino Airport and the Termini Rail Station. Open 8 a.m. to 7 p.m.

LODGING

Casa dello Studente (*Via Cesare de Lollis 24*; ☎ *490243*) sprawls inside the Citta Universitaria. A huge hangar that literally bulges with so many beds that over 1000 persons could probably be squeezed into its accommodations. Bustling cafeteria-style dining room, also open to accredited nonresidents; complete sports facilities nearby; no curfew; *operative July 21 to Sept. 20*. Potentially the finest stopover in its class, because of its excellent location and enormous capacity.

The 165-unit **CIVIS Student Hostel** (*Via Ministero Affari Esteri 56*; ☎ *3962951*) occupies a special category. This modern bargain hostelry is *closed* between June 15 and Sept. 1, thus making it available only for low-season vacationers. Rates approximately $30 per double. Rewards greater for longer visits than for overnighting.

You might also try **Ostello del Foro Italico** (*Viale delle Olimpiadi 61*; ☎ *3964709*), which is an approved youth hostel with 350 beds and possibly some of the best guidance facilities in town.

DINING

The dining room at the aforementioned **Casa dello Studente** (*Via Cesare de Lollis 24*) offers fixed-price dinners for patrons with the proper collegiate I.D. cards—plus meal tickets from the **Centro Italiano Relazioni Culturali con l'Estero**.

STUDENT DISCOUNTS

The Relazione Universitarie (*Via Palestro 11*; ☎ *4755265*) can provide reservation aids, sightseeing tips, cut-rate air and rail travel, and 20% reductions on bus excursions. Can also help arrange housing in a private home for perhaps $10 per night per person. Operative 9 a.m.–1 p.m. and 2–6 p.m. weekdays; closed Sat. afternoons and Sun.

PROBLEMS, PERSONAL OR GENERAL

Pop in at either the city's Department of Youth, Sport, Turismo, and Cinema (*Piazza Campitelli 7*; ☎ *661*), where the efficient staff will handle your queries, or at the **Clerici Vagantes** (*Via Savoia 46*; ☎ *857950*), where Signore DeMeo serves with courtesy, wisdom, and good humor. Incidentally, if you're an artist, be sure to consult the **Associazione Artistica Internazionale** (*Largo Corrado Ricci 44*; ☎ *688445*) for details on current exhibitions, trade chitchat, or housing bargains.

WHERE TO EAT

LEAST $

Pizzerias (like the fast-food *tavola caldas*) are almost always inexpensive and usually offer more than their namesake for nourishment. Three superior choices:

Antica Pizzeria er Buco • *Via del Lavatore 91.*

Leoncino • *On the street of its name, which spurs from the busy Via del Corso.* Closed Wed.

La Berninetta • *Via Cavallini 14.* Shuttered on Mon.

l'Archetto • *Via dell'Archetto 26*; ☎ *6789064 and Via Agostino Bertami 6 in Trastevere.* A spaghetteria and pizzeria. Delicious prosciutto and funghi, crostini, and 15 other dishes. Hanging lamps; fun atmosphere at good prices. Closed Mon.

Scoglio di Frisio • *Via Merulana 256*; ☎ *734619.* Always terrific. Cave motif. Fish specialties; try spaghetti with clam sauce, filet of sole with peas, mushrooms and olives (ask for "alla Frisio"). Bustling with families, foreign residents, and sightseers. Neopolitan music with table-to-table singing at intervals. Dinner only; closed Sun.

L'Albanese • *Via dei Serpenti 148*; ☎ *470777.* Immaculately clean. Similar to hundreds of others, but friendly, quiet, and very good. Closed on Sun. Pizzeria open evenings.

Da Mario • *Via della Vite 55 (just off the piazza di Spagna)*; ☎ *6783818.* A busy hive. Tuscan cookery. Sawdust, raffia, and mended tablecloths. Lots of happy locals. Savory fare at bargain levels. Also off on Sun.

Mario's Hostaria • *Piazza del Grillo 9*; ☎ *6793725.* Excellent $16 dinners with wine. Ask for owners Mario or Giovanni.

Bolognese • *Piazza del Popolo*; ☎ *3611426.* Genial clientele enjoying colossal portions of regional dishes. Hearty meal and wine about $32 for 2. Convenient to nearby antique and art galleries.

Da Nello • *Via Principe Amedeo 7H* (*Near the station*). About 20 tables. Reasonable fixed-price menu. Solid cookery, ample portions, and the price is right, if you don't order à la carte.

Trattoria Pizzeria Sciarra • *Piazza dell'Oratorio 75*; ☎ *679076*. Close to Trevi Fountain. Substantial food. Very low prices. Quick-service *Tavola Calda* inside; outdoor terrace. Especially fine fettuccine.

Giovanni • *Via Filippo Turati 36*; ☎ *737750*. Bills itself *trattoria* and *bottiglieria*, meaning both food and wine play important roles. Not related to the restaurant farther along; under "More $$."

Al Girarrosto di Eva • *At #7*. Next choice lining this same Via Filippo Turati. Indoor or outdoor dining. For food only; forget atmosphere.

Al Fagianetto • *At #2* ☎ *7314338*. More urbane trappings; still lower prices. Pleasant terrace; 20 tables. Closed Thurs.

Menghi • *Via Flaminia 57*. Dishes out home-style fare. Horrible service (which bothers nobody). Order à la carte because tourist menu is limited.

Della Campana • *Vicolo della Campana 18*; ☎ *655273*. No frills but high quality. Menu varied. A marvelous buy in pleasant surroundings.

La Toscanella • *Via Modena 54* (*one block from Piazza della Republica*); ☎ *461289*. Simple, neighborhood cafe with flavor. Good, substantial, traditional cookery; doesn't strain the budget.

Taverna degli Artisti • *Via Margutta 54* (*near Piazza del Popolo*). Pleasant evening spot with small combo. While not notoriously expensive, bill can creep up if you're not careful.

Taverna Trilussa • *Via del Politeama 23*; ☎ *588918*. Family rendezvous offering Roman fare. Prefer larger of the 2 rooms. Occasional guitar; spaghetti and fettuccine savory bets. Sambuca often awarded free. Happy, honest tavern.

Tavernelle • *Via Panisperna 48*; ☎ *4740724*. Popular at lunch. Minestrone, tortellini, spaghetti, and fettuccine alla Bolognese heavy favorites. Robust, inexpensive house wines complement cuisine perfectly. Closed Mon.

Grande Italia • *Piazza della Republica*. Bar on street floor. Lasagna, pizza Napoletana, and antipasto are appetizing; tourist menus guarantee more variety at not unreasonable tabs. Open for breakfast. Closed Sun.

Pierdonati • *Next to the Columbus Hotel*; ☎ *6543557*. Pasta dishes excellent. A meal with house wine averages $17. Closed Tues. and Aug.

Mario's • *53 Via Moro*. Exceptional cuisine at unbeatable prices—but remoteness and so-so service are detractions.

L'Eau Vive • *85 Via Monterone* (*between Pantheon and Piazza Navona*); ☎ *6541095*. Entrance left of 16th-century Palazzo Lante della Rovere. Best-known unit of an international chain combining French food with religious inspiration. Waitresses members of the Women Missionary Workers of the Immaculate Conception. Good selection of seafood; tempting desserts. Also fine French wines. Occupies 1st and 2nd floor of the palace. Three-course tourist menu at lunch may be as little as $9. A la carte with wine about twice that. Open Mon. through Sat. for lunch and dinner. Reservations advised.

IN THE PIAZZA SFORZA CESARINI

In summer, the plaza becomes an outdoor fiesta catered by two restaurants and a coffee and ice cream parlor. Boundaries unclear; **Polese** by far the better of the pair (*at the head of the square*; ☎ *6561709*). About $13 buys a full-course dinner. Since ice cream is better at **Gino Bella** on the corner, move a few yards for dessert.

GERMAN

Birreria San Marcovia • *Via Nazionale.* May hit the spot after a week or so of pasta and vino. Lowenbrau on draft.

CAFETERIAS

Italy Italy • *Piazza Barberini. Seats 1250 in a snack bar, a cafeteria, 2 restaurants.* In concept, efficiency, and output (but not in cuisine), one of the closest imitations of a U.S.-type operation in the nation. All prices standardized throughout this behemoth, with a 12% charge added only when the customer is served at a table. Open late; closed Tues. (but this could alter).

Best Burger • Does a burger flip at *#15 on Via Barberini.*

California • *Via Bissolati 54.* Does a similar act. Vast self-service facility plus additional options; snacks plus American-style coffee, if desired.

Falconi's • *Piazza dei Cinquecento 47*; ☎ *464291.* Perhaps the most popular straight cafeteria in the capital—unquestionably more so for its convenience than for its fare. Key site near the station; basement premises; average array of national dishes in the $6 range.

Pan-Pan • *Piazza Don Sturzo 21.* Roughly $8 per sitting, including wine and service.

Imperiale • *Via Flaminia 11.* Routine in decor and concept; dishes well prepared, appetizingly presented, but too often tepid or downright cold.

Big Mac? If necessary, look in Piazza di Spagna. Meet the Pope? **Boso** (*Via dei Serpenti 23*) is where Karol Wojtyla used to sip his morning cappuccino when he was a theology student at Angelicum College.

TAKEOUT MEALS

One of the most satisfactory is **Pizzeria Girarrosto** (*Via Leopardi 44-66*). Two specialties are whole chicken spitted and grilled to your order and the pizza. You'll find no tables and no chairs—only a streamlined metal-and-glass counter. Dependable, fast, and good.

FRUIT

Take summer refreshment at any of the capital's numerous watermelon stands. About 50¢ per generous slice.

MORE $$

Biblioteca del Valle • *Largo del Teatro Valle 9.* Tops for local color and physical charm in the $28-38 category. Cellar "library" of wines. Restaurant on one side; less costly pizza parlor on the other with music and dancing.

Girarrosto Toscano • *Via Campania 29* (*off Via Veneto, facing Borghese Garden's battlements*); ☎ *493759.* Open grill. Prosciutto and salami hors d'oeuvres could be a meal in themselves; meat-filled tortellini heavenly; so was inch-thick Florentine steak (priced according to weight—the steak's, not yours). Closed Wed.

Giovanni • *Via Marche 64* (*again off Via Veneto, near the U.S. Embassy*); ☎ *493576.* Another rewarding choice. Packed at lunchtime. Fettuccine with meat sauce and veal scaloppine especially good. Meal for one perhaps $28. Heartily recommended.

Abruzzi • *Just off piazza Santi Apostoli at Via del Vaccarbi*; ☎ *6793897*. About as homely and nondescript as a restaurant can be with its crazy-paved stone floor, part-tile walls, and shelvings with no special order. The cooking, however, is among the best we've found for the outlay in all of Italy. Saturday is the day of rest.

Corsetti • *In Trastevere, at piazza San Cosimato 27*; ☎ *585300*. Excellent seafood. Appealing *ambiente*. Roughly $26 without wine—a mite expensive for what you get. Recommended as a borderline bargain.

Al Chianti • *Via Ancona 17*; ☎ *861083*. Sometimes called "Ernesto & Mario." Tuscan flavor; 14 tables. Exceptional viands lose some savor under highpressure rush of the service.

Taverna Giulia • *23 Vicolo dell'Oro*; ☎ *6869768*. Genoan specialties. Pasta al pesto recommended. Selection so enormous that your bill depends on your appetite. Closed Sun. and Aug. Outstanding.

Piperno • *9 Monte de'Cenci*; ☎ *6540629*. Interesting area of ancient Jewish ghetto. Ethnic specialties such as *carciofi alla guidea* (fried artichokes); also *filetti di baccala con fritto vegetariano* (cod filets with fried vegetables). A curiosity; closed Sun. evenings, Mon. and Aug.

Gigetto • *Via del Portio d'Ottavia 2/a*; ☎ *6861105*. Another old standby in this neighborhood for this ethnic cuisine. On this same street at #1E you'll find *Uno al Portico d'Ottavia*, which is strictly kosher.

Al Moro • *Vicolo delle Bollette 13*. A block below the Trevi in 3 rooms of unmemorable style. Cookery that will answer any hunger; easy atmosphere.

Da Pancrazio • *Piazza de Biscione, across from piazza Navona*; ☎ *6561246*. Also modest to the eye, fulfilling for the tummy, and easy on the budget. Closed Wed.

NIGHTLIFE

Apart from 2 or 3 venerable landmarks, the Roman nightclub has little staying power. Inexplicably, the Latin entrepreneur bows out of the nightscape as summer approaches.

Solution? Save some of your cultural sightseeing for eventide; many of the more famous monuments, palaces, and plazas are illuminated after dark. Several museums take turns in staying open late, when and if the staffs agree. You'll keep cooler, avoid jostling crowds, and spend less. For hours and other details, check *This Week in Rome*.

As in so many other capitals, every legitimate nightclub is expensive. Discotheque-style action is something else. But for the Big Time circuit, be prepared to spend a bundle.

Strangely, most of the music haunts bear American names: **Mississippi Jazz Club** (*Borgo Angelico 16*), **Billie Holiday Jazz Club** (*Via Orti di Trastevere 43*), and **St. Louis Music City** (*Via del Cardello 13a*) are only a few. After these come **Ziegfield** (*Via dei Piceni 28*), **Music Inn** (*Largo dei Fiorentini 3*), and **Dorian Gray** (*Piazza Trilussa 41*). The bands move around a lot, so you'll have to ask locally who's playing and where.

New Sing-Song • *Vicolo Rossini 6, corner campo Marzio and Prefetti;* ☎ *6873651.* More like an extended piano bar. Street-level entry off Parliament Sq. Seven different chambers, crannies, alcoves and nooks; waiters in Beaujolais-red jackets with wide black lapels; dancing here and there; snacks served in winter only. No entry fee, but the cheapest beverage, beer, is $3.75 at the bar and $5 at the tables. Animated and amusing—but expensive.

Il Pipistrello • "The Bat," *Via Emilia 27, about 2 blocks from the American Embassy.* A lively, crowded cellar. Piano player pounds the ivories standing up; Scotch about $6 at the bar; usually jammed from 9 p.m. to 4 a.m.; cozy, friendly, and good for its clangorous type.

Foro Italico Tennis Bar • *Near the Olympic Stadium.* Might be your answer if you're in the dancing mood. After sunset, this trim little clubhouse retires its rackets and table-tennis paddles for night activities. Foreigners welcomed; music; drinks dispensed at competitive levels. Because tournaments can preempt the festivities, ☎ *393308* for reassurance that it is open to the public.

DISCOTHEQUES

Piper 80 • *Via Tagliamento 9.* The leading edge of factory-style musical mania.

Stelle and **New Life** • *Via C. Beccaria 22 and Via XX Settembre 92.* Also far from sleepy havens.

M Uno • Remains the leader for local cafe society types, but it is rather costly.

Revolution • *Via dei Bentivoglio 15.* Turns on the New Dance and special effects.

747 • *Viale Kennedy 131.* Lands with a cargo of disco-thunder.

Life 85 • *Via Trionfale 130/a.* Specializes in revivals (musical, that is, not religious).

Hysteria • *Via Giovannelli 3.* Rants in a funky and soul-felt fashion. There are at least 4-dozen more choices each night in Rome, so ask locally for the flavor that suits your taste.

CAFES

The ubiquitous cafes are an important part of the Roman scene, since professional and social lines are often drawn on the customer's choice of establishment. Some time ago, the resident Beautiful People vetoed the Via Veneto. At this writing (subject to change), while the sightseers still gape from wicker or wire chairs along this street, the *real* Mr. Bigs—film stars, artists, and fashion *doyens*—sip their cocktails quietly in the **Cafe Rosati** or the **Cafe Canova** . For a $2 cup of coffee, you can join the set.

Grande Italia offers a live band after dark. After 7 p.m., whenever you sit down (not stand at a counter), the almost confiscatory Italian amusement tax skyrockets your coffee to the neighborhood of $2.

AFTER THEATER

For late light bites, try the friendly little **Bar dell'Epoca** (*Piazzale di Porta Pia 122-123*).

BEER HALLS

They are experiencing a heady growth. Try the froth at **Piazza Santi Apostoli**, where there are several. **Birreria Tempera**, *on adjoining Via di San Marcello*, comes in for toasts of praise.

WHAT TO SEE AND DO

There are myriad fares and sightseeing programs for visitors. Apply at the ATAC (transport company) kiosks in numerous localities around the town. Examples: rail station, Largo Argentina, piazza San Silvestro.

City-circling streetcars, labeled #30, give a roundhouse survey of the metropolis, so that you may select the areas that offer the greatest appeal for further explorations. The Colosseum is a convenient starting point. Other stops include the piazzale Flaminio, porta Pinciana, the station, Basilica Santa Maria Maggiore, porta San Paolo, Monte Savello, Ponte Vittorio, and piazza Cavour. The city also offers metropolitan bus service, of course. Board through the middle door (not fore or aft) and immediately buy a ticket. One reader climbed in the front entrance, sat down and was promptly fined $10 by a company monitor.

Bus tours are big business—but, unfortunately, even the reputable SITA program here leaves a great deal to be desired. For about $18 and upward, you may ride for a maximum of 4 hours—but cover only a small fraction of the capital's major targets. Standard landmarks include **St. Peter's**, the adjoining **Vatican Museum**, **Lateran Palace** (16th-century papal apartment open to the public), the 1900-year-old **Pantheon**, the **Capitoline Hill** ("Campidoglio"), the **Roman Forum**, the **Colosseum**, **Trajan's Column**, **Piazza Navona**, and the **Spanish Steps**. The **Sistine Chapel** is closed on Sat. afternoon and Sun. Vatican City is covered more extensively further on. Incidentally, the porticoes and colonnades of the Roman Forum (Foro Romano) have finally been refurbished after years of work. Entrance is on Via IV Novembre where modern sculpture is often exhibited.

Art lovers usually see the following: the **Borghese Gallery** (fabulous family art collection housed in a beautiful park estate), the **Museo Nazionale Romano delle Terme** (the "Venus of Cyrene" and parts of Hadrian's Arch are among its many highlights), the **Palazzo Venezia** (medieval fortress restored in Renaissance style, with Mussolini's famous balcony appended), the **Palazzo Farnese** (Michelangelo's superb architecture is the current French Embassy, but today, unfortunately, you're only allowed to enjoy the facade, the **Capuccini Chapel** (with walls and furniture of human bones), the **Villa Giulia Museum** (renowned Etruscan art-and-handicraft assemblage, which is closed Mon.), the **Capitoline Museum** (inaugurated in a.d. 1471 and claimed as the world's oldest), the massive 1800-year-old **Castel Sant'-Angelo**, once a fortified refuge for the Popes and connected to the Vatican Via a secret passage, the scores of beautiful squares and fountains, including **Barberini**, **Colosseo** (Arch of Constantine), **Civilta Italica** (ultramodern and stunning), **Fontana di Trevi**, **Quirinale**, **Trinita dei Monti**, **Pincio**, **Colonna**, **Popolo**, and the banks of the **Tiber**, and the imposing marble palace of sports, artificial lake, and terraced grounds of the **Foro Italico**—the Olympic Village.

More than 250 halls of culture, historical sites, and galleries are open to you year-round with a low-cost pass that is available through Alitalia and the Italian Line. In addition, the season ticket for entry to all State exhibits will probably be reissued this year. To be sure, check with the Tourist Office (see below).

CATACOMBS

The Catacombs, beside the oldest segment of the Appian Way, involve a long and tedious ride. In normal traffic, the St. Sebastian and St. Calixtus tombs are 25 minutes from the center. Any of the 3 satisfy that necromantic yen equally well. Often the tours (conducted by multilingual monks) are indisputably creepy, so they continue to be very popular among visitors. Locked up noon-2:30 p.m. daily.

AUTHOR'S OBSERVATION

A clutch of Dutch nuns offer no-cost informative Roman circuits with English explanations usually on Tues., Thurs., and Sat. with slide lectures often on Fri. (tea at 5 p.m., before the slides). Information and reservations at Foyer Unitas at 30 Via di S. Maria dell Anima (facing Piazza Navona); ☎ 6865951.

OPERA

During July and Aug., outdoor opera is performed within the crumbling walls of the **Baths of Caracalla**. Spectacular staging; prices vary with opus and seating. **Opera House** offers opera and concerts from Nov. to June.

Consult with the **Tourist Information Office** at *Via Parigi 11* (☎ *4881851*) or the branch in the main station (☎ *4871270*). They bristle with maps, pamphlets, and sound advice. Here's a tip learned the hard way: Always set out at around 10 a.m. or 5 p.m. Otherwise, the 4 daily rush-hour mobs will shred you and your itinerary into vermicelli.

CONCERTS

Scores of virtuosos and chamber ensembles play in the recital halls almost the year-round. These include **Accademia di Santa Cecilia**, **Filarmonica Romana**, **Oratorio del Gonfalone**, and quite a few others. The important ones are listed in *Carnet di Roma*, available at the Tourist Office.

FESTIVALS

The happy-go-lucky Roman Summer in July and Aug. is also haphazard. Programs not always announced, and when they are, not always followed, so check newspapers or call the Rome Tourist Office (☎ *488748* or *4881851*) for daily details.

RIVER EXCURSION

From Marconi Bridge to Ostia, principal port of ancient Rome. Also takes in a seaside village; 9 a.m.-5 p.m.; $5 adults; $3.60 children, students, and elderly. Box lunch provided for a little over $5. Details available through *Ente Provinciale per il Turismo* (*Via Parigi 5*).

AMUSEMENT PARK

Luna Park (*Via delle Tre Fontane, EUR*) is too far from the center for travelers without cars. The Borghese Gardens are lovely for midcity strolling.

MOVIES

The **Pasquino** (*Vicolo del Piede 19*) reels out English films for rather high prices.

MARKETS

At the **Mercati Generali** (*Via Ostiense*), Rome's general market, almost anything can be haggled over daily (not on Sun.) 8 a.m.-1 p.m. The **Piazza Vittorio Market** smaller and more limited. Trastevere has its flea market Sun. mornings at **Porta Portese**; a smaller one operates daily at Via Sannio near St. John Lateran. Visiting the food market at **Campo dei Fiori**, near piazza Navonna, Mon.-Sat. from 9:30 a.m., is a great way to get a feeling for the everyday life of a Roman housewife.

PUBLICATIONS

The previously mentioned *Carnet di Roma* is a handy tipsheet for music, theater, dining, and nightlife. If you read Italian, then journals such as *Il Tempo*, *Repubblica* (especially Saturday's *Trovaroma* section), and *Messaggero* are reliable.

Finally, if you plan to tour further afield, don't be gulled by some of the local concierges who are commission-hungry enough to push the 1-day Rome-Naples-Sorrento-Rome sightseeing excursions. Usually they depart at 7 a.m. and return at midnight, when the poor limp fish are spooned out of the vehicles. During this 17-hour marathon, only perhaps 3-1/2 hours are passed on terra firma. Result: Victims absorb almost nothing of the character of the stopovers and are zombies during the debilitating hangover that lingers. For a more rewarding glimpse of these southern attractions, hop a *rapido* (train) for Naples and check into a hotel. Take a round-trip afternoon bus excursion to Vesuvius and Sorrento. Reasonably early the next morning, board a hydrofoil (preferred) or conventional ship to Capri and/or Ischia; on certain days there are direct sea connections between these 2 island resorts. Then, in the late afternoon, return to Rome by rail.

WHERE TO SHOP

DEPARTMENT STORE

La Rinascente • *Piazza Colonna-Piazza Fiume.* Offers scads of small items for gifts or memorabilia. Good, but not special.

FASHIONS FOR THE YOUNG

Piper Market • *Piazza Euclide 5.* Has a help-yourself policy; 6 loudspeakers spurring sales with American music; a first-hand review of Rome's "with it" couture—always bearing a distinctive Italian flavor. The average spread is from $10 to $35.

LEATHER WEARABLES

Skin • *Via Due Macelli 87/88 and Via Capo le Case 41-44.* Now pushing the big names. The product itself is not cheap, but you'll be receiving top Italian quality, styling, and durability. Though costly, Skin's skins are well under U.S. levels for fashions you can't even find back home. Hidebound in the most modish way. For even better bargains and lower prices, visit Skin's sister operation, Renard.

Renard • *Via Due Macelli 53.* You'll find ready-to-wear jackets, pants, and lambskin coats here.

Bizan • *Same street at #49/51.* The leather ready-to-wear garments are augmented by silks and wool, as well as accessories to match.

XL • *Via Due Macelli 59-A.* The accent is definitely on youth. Printed leather and suede, lots of studs for ornamentation—the latest trends seen here first.

OPTICAL WEAR

No trip to Italy would be complete without the ultimate in their famous suntime accessories. (Italians even wear them at night.) **Ottica Bileci** (*Via Due Macelli 83*) is smack in the middle of the Spanish Steps shopping fulcrum. The latest in frames, glass, plastics, or even their own contact lenses can be found. Prices aren't for movie stars, either—even though the styles look like they should be.

PAPER

Papirus (*Via Capo Le Case 55a*) can supply every delicate desire in stationery—your personality reflected in the pattern, color, or texture you choose for yourself or as a gift. This art is unique; you'll recognize the marbleized technique immediately.

AUTHOR'S OBSERVATION

Postage stamps that will later rise in value? The Vatican City post office is your local target.

PRINTS

Fine Arts G. Panatta • *Via F. Crespi, 117.* Moderate prices; browse through the print and drawing collection. Small store, but a wide range of subjects; some might be perfect as a memory of Rome.

Alinari • *Via del Babuino 98.* For artistic painted boxes and panels. The prices for these splendid gift items are unbelievably low—while the quality is extraordinarily high.

RELIGIOUS ARTICLES

Al Pellegrino Cattolico • *Via di Porta Angelica 83.* Across from St. Peter's, has a complete stock for the devout. They will have your rosaries blessed by the Pope and delivered to your hotel, at no extra fee.

SHOES

Magli • A nationwide chain, offers stylings and selections that are inexpensive and smart. Most bargain hunters like the Magli touch. The branch at *Via Vittorio Veneto 74* has been the most convenient location.

Tradate • *Via del Corso.* Also a good bet.

Cardinali • *Via di Propaganda Fide.* Near the Spanish Steps, a favorite with costconscious locals. Along Via dei Giubbonari and Via Arenula near the Ghetto there are more than 20 stores.

SILKS

Silks and other fine materials by the meter? **Galtrucco** (*Via del Tritone 14*) has just about everything. It is the traditional pacemaker of its field. A bonanza.

TIES

Giofer • *Via Frattina 118.* Stocks every cravat any man could imagine.

Roxy • *Via Frattina 115.* Nearby and a like-minded operation.

BARGAIN-BUYING AREAS

Via Nazionale • A long street in midcity that is lined with nice shops in the popular-price bracket. The styles are chic, but the levies are among the most reasonable in all of Italy; keen competition does it.

Via Cola di Rienzo • Across the river from Piazza del Popolo. Haggle *hard*! If you're flying in or out, check at Fiumicino Airport; a duty-free shop operates here, but generally we find no savings in apparel; best bargains are in cigarettes, alcoholic beverages, electronic and camera equipment.

AUTHOR'S OBSERVATION

Shopping hours? Since the siesta custom is observed, almost all of the stores are open from 9-9:30 a.m. to 1 p.m. and from 3:30 to 7:30 p.m. (4 to 8 p.m. in summer), although some work steadily from 10 a.m. to 6 p.m. In winter, stores close all day Sun. and Mon. mornings. In summer, stores shutter Sat. afternoons instead of Mon. mornings.

SAN GIMIGNANO

A lovely hill town known for its medieval towers—14 punctuating the Tuscan heaven. (Once there were 72.) Containing only 5000 souls who engage largely in wine production, it is far quieter than Florence, yet less than an hour away via the turnpike. There are memories of Ghibellines, Guelphs, Dante, and great family feuds so common to that era. Try not to miss it. **Leon Bianco** is a well-situated small hotel with moderate prices. **Cisterna**, on the same central square, is a bit more expensive, and the restaurant is one of the best and most scenic in the midtown.

SAN MARINO

San Marino, the world's oldest and smallest republic, is in the Apennines, entirely surrounded by Italian soil, 20 minutes by car from Rimini and the Adriatic Sea via the Autostrada. Though landlocked, San Marino has arranged a toehold of Adriatic beach at Riccione—15 miles by your car's odometer, but almost 2 hours distant on a busy Sun. afternoon in Aug. The Casino, closed as a gambling hall, functions as an occasional dance center or sports arena. In July don't miss the colorful national crossbow championship. Spring is usually the time for the Formula I Grand Prix road race—with Ferrari always the favorite son. Overnight in Rimini for the best value.

SAN REMO

Lying 9 miles from the French border toward Nice, this scenic coastal strip is a beauty spot on the extended limbs of the Côte d'Azur. Those resplendent trappings of leisure—race track, golf course, and luxury hotels—are quite attractive for nabobs who don't mind paying today's prices for yesterday's fancies. The top drawing card is still the annual Song Festival (late Jan.). **Ospedaletti**, 3 miles away, is startlingly cheaper; try the **Rocce del Campo** as a hotel choice.

SARDINIA

Most alluring is the savage, sea-lapped **Costa Smeralda**, 30 miles of wild, lonely, ponete-blown coves. Along this littoral—more extensive, incidentally, than the entire Belgian seaboard—are at least 80 powder-white beaches. It's a land of twisted cork trees, soughing pines, and glistening juniper, with a boscage of rosemary that scents the wind. Angular mountains of granite and basalt. Vales dotted with nuraghi (prehistoric fortress-shaped structures). Speech is a Low Latin, with dialect overtones of ancient Genoese, Libyan, Phoenician, Spanish, and Carthaginian. The inlets and quiet corners along the Costa Smeralda are far too numerous to mention; a typical one has been described accurately as "a Pacific bay on a Brittany coast." There are several hotels of varying categories, co-crowned by the magnificent **Cala di Volpe** and the equally luxurious cottage-style **Pitrizza**. These 2 are astronomically expensive, but the **Porto Cervo**, in the port of the same name, is medium priced and excellent. Nearby are many reasonable lodging houses. **Olbia** is the hub of local commerce, so it has a fair number of small hotels, pensions, and hostels. Cuisine? Much of it is about as exciting as a hangnail. The local fare, based ponderously on pasta, is even worse.

Inexpensive car-ferry tours chug to the park-size islet of **La Maddalena**, Garibaldi's rock-dotted place of exile on **Caprera** (his house is a museum), plying to and from nearby **Palau** all through the day.

Connections with the Continent are good. The easiest way is aboard the sleek turboprop airline, Alisarda, which calls regularly at Rome, Nice, and Milan. **Olbia** has a paved airstrip; from here, it's a 1/2-hour drive by hotel taxi to the Costa Smeralda along a modern and lovely seaway. Alitalia zips in from Milan and Rome to **Alghero** and **Cagliari**. British Airways has a London link with Alghero. Passenger and car ferries stream 4 times a day in summer from the port of Rome (Civitavecchia) to Olbia and the adjoining **Golfo Aranci**. A loop with Genoa is also possible aboard the Canguro Rosso (Red Kangaroo). Genoese luggers drop anchor at Olbia and **Porto Torres**.

In the south, 80 miles from Cagliari, **Forte Hotel Village** is composed of 600 2-bedroom cottages of inviting style, plus the 114-room conventional **Hotel Castello**, all glued together in such a way as to provide an appealing sports-entertainment-dining package.

SIENA

A mesmeric passage to the Renaissance; probably the only city in Italy to retain so much ancient charm. As an illustration, filmmakers found Verona's complexion had changed so radically over the years that they used Siena to shoot *Romeo and Juliet*. Cars are barred in high season from the center, where most of the historic buildings are situated. The **Duomo**, the **Town Hall**, the **Pinacoteca**, and the **Music Academy** are musts; the capper is the spectacular **Palio** ("the world's craziest horse race"), a pageant climaxed by hell-for-leather riding in the huge piazza del Campo; this event is held twice annually on the Festivals of the Madonna, July 2 and Aug. 16. **Piccolo Hotel Il Palio** is on Piazza del Sale. The **Duomo** and the **Vico Alto** are a bit more expensive. **Bernini** and **Lea** are good moneysavers. The restaurants around the central piazza are touristic. Forgive them for they know well what they do. Okay, if you insist, try **Al Mangia**, **Alla Speranza**, or **Osteria Le Logge**.

SORRENTO

A cliff-high tourist center with many coach tours passing in summer. The beauty of the sea, gardens, and rugged hills is impressive, especially if you can see them in the fringe seasons; some excellent hotels, pensions, and restaurants, but in high season they are almost all socked in by package trippers. You'll have to hunt for your lodgings here, but try first at the **Bellevue-Syrene**, the **Cristina**, or the **Caravel**.

TAORMINA

Garden spot of Sicily on a headland almost 1000 feet above the outer Straits of Messina (above the bathing beach, too, which is good to know in advance). Mount Etna, the volcano of Ulysses and still active, thrusts its snow-capped cone through the clouds to the rear. Highlight of the city's social glitter is its annual **Taormina Arte Festival** from mid-July to mid-Sept. Italy's most important event in the motion picture industry, plus music and theater presentations. In the town itself, the **Diodoro Jolly** is an attractive and viewful medium-priced hotel. The **Bristol** is older in style and good value. Many younger folk prefer to stay at **Mazzaro Beach**, directly below, to which there is a funicular. Easter is the climax of the season; midsummers are very hot; midwinter climate is sometimes grossly overrated. Alitalia flies from Rome to Catania in an hour; another direct bus connection to Taormina takes another hour.

TURIN

In this serene metropolis in the Piedmont near the French border (readily discernible in the local dialect), about 30,000 natives work in the huge Fiat autoworks, so it's not surprising to find—apart from almost constant air pollution—a fascinating **Museum of the Automobile**, containing 370 vintage models. Citizens are equally proud of their city's art treasures, **Egyptology Museum** (second most important in the world), **Cinema Museum**, former **Royal Palace**, **Palazzo Madama** (see the Spring Room), and **Palazzo del Lavoro**. Based on a strong Francophile influence, here is a way of life which, like Milan's, differs from that of the rest of Italy. Hotels are costly due to the business traffic; try the **Victoria** or the **President**, which are reasonable but still on the high side. **Stazione E Genova** is handy to the Porta Nova station. In summer, it would be best to find accommodation with air conditioning, more for breathing than for comfort. Hence, the costs will rise.

VATICAN CITY

Standing on the side of a hill on the west bank of the Tiber, it is separated from Rome and Italy only by a wall. The Pope is absolute monarch, with full legislative, executive, and judicial powers.

Dominating the City is the **Church of St. Peter**, largest in the world and sited in the smallest independent state in the world. Close by is the **Apostolic Palace**, home of His Holiness and site of the famous Vatican Museum. It is the biggest residential castle in existence, with 1400 rooms that cover some 13-1/2 acres. Within are the City Governor's Palace, a post office, a tribunal, a mosaic factory, a barracks, an observatory, a railway station, a power plant, a newspaper, a pharmacy, food shops, TV station, and the super-radio station over which the Pope broadcasts messages to 6 continents. Sampietrini is the name given to those who maintain the Basilica but do not live here. The dome, Michelangelo's work, is almost as high as the tallest Egyptian pyramid; from doorway to altar, you could tuck in the towers of New York's Waldorf-Astoria, with room to spare. In the museums, chapels, and libraries of the Vatican you'll find Raphaels, Michelangelos, Peruginos, Botticellis, tapestries, liturgical vessels, priceless manuscripts. An elevator will whisk you to the base of the dome; from there you can climb the winding stairs to the pinnacle for a splendid view of the meandering Tiber and Rome. Then take the walk around the inside upper periphery, put an ear close to the wall, and listen to people talking hundreds of feet away. St. Peter's alone is worth a special trip from America. (Note: the Sistine Chapel, with its stunningly cleaned ceiling that throws new light on ancient art, is closed on Sat. afternoon and Sun.)

GUIDES

Available outside the Cathedral or inside the Vatican Museum—but only engage official ones. Most speak English.

CAMERAS

Photographic equipment (including flash) is now allowed within the Basilica.

AUDIENCE WITH THE POPE

Best way to arrange this is through a letter from your bishop to the Prefettura della Casa Pontifica in Vatican City. Small group or individual meetings are becoming more and more difficult to arrange, though His Holiness grants a few almost daily. Apply as soon as you arrive in Rome. We're also told that the Paulist Fathers at the Church of St. Susanna are extremely helpful in this respect.

On Wed., an enormous audience is held in St. Peter's; tickets are readily available, provided you don't require reserved seats. There are 3 classes: The first 2 permit you to sit in grandstand structures flanking the main altar, while the 3rd is simply admission for standing room. For tickets to this (as well as to the excavations beneath St. Peter's), apply to the same source mentioned above. Thousands flock to these gatherings, so get there early! For special audiences (Baciamano), ladies should wear dresses, high necklines, long sleeves, and veils (now optional, but more courteous); men should appear in business suits and ties. Dress requirements for the Wed. services are nearly as rigid, although they are constantly violated by scores of unknowing travelers. The Papal address is condensed and translated in English, French, German, and Spanish. The big assemblages are scheduled from Oct. to July, moving to the summer residence in Castel Gandolfo from July to late Sept. Transportation to St.

Peter's is provided at nominal cost; hotel pickup and round trip are available through CIT, American Express, and Thomas Cook, also for relatively few lire.

Women should wear long sleeves when visiting any Catholic house of worship. The Vatican bars miniskirts and hotpants at St. Peter's Basilica unless you agree to wear a plastic raincoat (lent you by the attendants).

VENICE

Venice is a ravishing architectural absurdity. Built on a complex of 118 islands, its crumbling edifices, relics of a globally powerful and prosperous era between the 11th and 15th centuries, inch their inevitable way into the Adriatic. Millions of tree-trunks driven into the swampy lagoon could not secure a firm foundation for the great city, but its labyrinth of 150 canals with almost 400 bridges still swarms with water-borne traffic, as stately black gondolas and sleek varnished motor launches ply among piers and marble palaces. It fascinated Byron, Goethe, Rilke, Shelley, and Wagner. The same pre-Renaissance grandeur that inspired them is visible to you today. The Doge's Palace, the Basilica in St. Mark's Square, the Bridge of Sighs recall the Golden Age when Venice was the center of world banking, when the Republic controlled the eastern Mediterranean, and when Marco Polo sailed from its harbor to open the Oriental trade routes.

DIRECTORY

U.S. Consulate • *Milan*; ☎ *02-65281.*

American Express • *San Marco, Piscina San Moise*; ☎ *5200844.*

CIT Office • *San Marco 48*; ☎ *5223487.*

Laundromat • Westinghouse, *Frari 2604, Castello 5190, or Calle della Mandola.*

Barber • Hotel Diurno, *San Marco, Calle Ascensione*; ☎ *5231357.*

Hairdresser • Carol's, *Via XXII Marco*; ☎ *5229944.*

Dry Cleaning and Pressing • Pulitura a Secco, *Calle Specchieri 629.*

English-speaking Doctor • Dr. Salvatore Saccardo, *Via XXII Marzo 2337 Calle delle Ostreghe*; ☎ *55221370.*

English-speaking Dentist • Prof. Antonio Beltrame, *1343/b San Marco-AScensione.*

Police • Central Station, *Fondamenta San Lorenzo, Castello*; ☎ *5220406*; Police Emergency, ☎ *113.*

HOW TO GET AROUND

The visitor can count on the *Vaporetto* #1 (a circular route around the city), about 400 gondoliers, and about 150 launch operators. The fastest waterbus is the *diretto* variety, known as Line #2; at about a quarter a ride, it's always an express. The least expensive is the *vaporetto* (Line #1; about $1 per spin) covering all stations on the Grand Canal. The *circolare* (boat #5) chugs out to Giudecca or Murano. Embarkations may be made at any of 16 main landings. Use Dock #12 for the Fine Arts Academy and the Guggenheim Collection; Dock #10 for Scuola di San Rocco; Dock #15 for San Marco. If you plan to stay awhile, ask about the "daily ticket" for extensive travel around the waterways.

TO OR FROM THE AIRPORT

Don't be herded onto a private motor launch (around $55). Take a bus that leaves piazzale Roma for Marco Polo Airport about one hour before each flight. Cost per person is about $2, *and have the exact change, because they won't return any.* Also public boat connections (motoscafi) to and from S. Marco and the airport. The ride takes about 3/4-hour and runs about $7.50. Check times locally.

If you can handle your luggage, do not take a water taxi from the rail station. Instead, find the public *motoscafo/vaporetto* stop with convenient transportation to all canal-side hotels. Difference in price? For a taxi you are likely to shell out at least 28,000 lira. The most you will pay by using public transportation is 2500 lira per person (add the same amount for each piece of luggage.)

PARKING

Since cars are banned from the center, you will be compelled to stow your vehicle. There are 3 major choices: **Tronchetto**, a parking island in itself (*to your right as you motor in on the Ponte della Liberta*), **Autorimessa Comunale** (*Piazzale Roma*), or **Garage San Marco**. Fees are expensive.

One way to beat the traffic and the excessive tariffs is to store it in one of suburban **Mestre's** garages on the mainland. Pilferage and break-ins are not uncommon.

WHERE TO STAY

LEAST $

Hostelries with rock-bottom prices are usually in the suburbs.

Rossi • *Cannaregio 262*; ☎ *715164.* A passable exception to the above rule. Near Lista di Spagna boardwalk and Santa Lucia station. Roughly $35 a double.

Falier • *Calle Falier 126, S. Croce*; ☎ *28882.* Salizzada San Pantalon precinct. Dormitory space recently converted to double rooms. Competitive rates.

Battiston • *Lista di Spagna 191A*; ☎ *700355.* Recently refashioned, but when we last saw it, it was clean, comfortable, and balconied. About $33 per double.

Pensione Accademia-Villa Maravegie • *Dorsoduro 1058*; ☎ *5237846.* Grand Canal location. Terrace and garden. Dining room and bar. Maintenance standards not the best.

Ostello Venezia • On island of Giudecca, *10 minutes by motor launch from piazza San Marco.* Popular choice and worth the inconvenience of location.

Albergo Diurno • *San Marco Calle Ascensione 1266*; ☎ *5285567.* Air-conditioned. Seems geared for the quick-turnover client rather than the lingerer.

MORE $$

Gardena • *Santa Croce 239*; ☎ *5235549.* Near Santa Lucia rail terminus. Cross ponte Scalzi going toward piazzale Roma and watch for its sign on the left; 30 immaculate, fresh-looking rooms. Dining salon. Maximum doubles about $120, including private bath; standard twins only a bit less; singles in the $80 range; taxes and service included.

Flora • *San Marco 2283A*; ☎ *705844.* Down an alley off the famous piazza, but not far enough to avoid the noise when the city is jammed. Best feature, its quiet garden. Breakfast only; other meals available at 2 associated nearby restaurants; 40 rooms, adequate but not opulent; most with bath or shower. Units #37 and #38 face the ground-floor courtyard; #3 and #15 also choice. Singles at $60; doubles at nearly $100, including morning meal, service, and taxes. *May be closed any time between Nov. 15 and Feb. 15.*

Torino • *Ponte delle Ostreghe 2356*; ☎ *705222.* Dates back to A.D. 1500. Since then, its 55 rooms have had a fairly good rejuvenation.

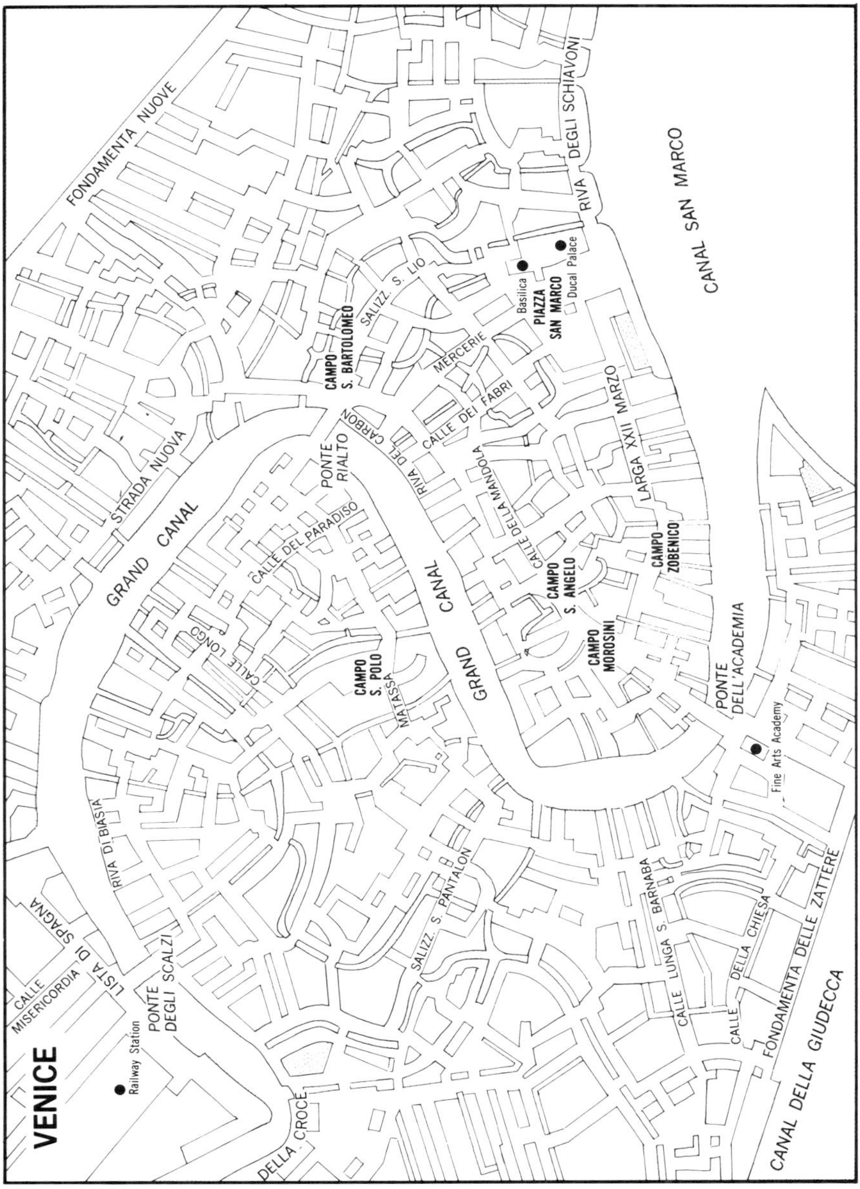
VENICE
Railway Station
PONTE DEGLI SCALZI
LISTA DI SPAGNA
CALLE MISERICORDIA
DELLA CROCE
RIVA DI BIASIA
GRAND CANAL
STRADA NUOVA
FONDAMENTA NUOVE
CALLE LONGO
CALLE DEL PARADISO
CAMPO S. POLO
MATASSA
SALIZZ. S. PANTALON
PONTE RIALTO
CAMPO S. BARTOLOMEO
SALIZZ. S. LIO
RIVA DEL CARBON
CALLE DEI FABRI
MERCERIE
Basilica
PIAZZA SAN MARCO
Ducal Palace
RIVA DEGLI SCHIAVONI
CANAL SAN MARCO
CALLE DELLA MANDOLA
CAMPO S. ANGELO
CAMPO MOROSINI
CAMPO ZOBENICO
LARGA XXII MARZO
PONTE DELL'ACADEMIA
Fine Arts Academy
CALLE LUNGA S. BARNABA
CALLE DELLA CHIESA
FONDAMENTA DELLE ZATTERE
CANAL DELLA GIUDECCA

Bel Sito • *S. Marco 2517, S. Maria Del Giglio*; ☎ *5223365.* Well sited, friendly, and quiet.

Montecarlo • *Calle Specchieri 464*; ☎ *707144.* Handy though noisy situation near the main piazza; 45 rooms, all but 10 with private bath or shower. Many large, high-ceilinged units (a scattering with air conditioning); poorly illuminated.

Carpaccio • *S. Polo 2765*; ☎ *5235946.* Marvelous view of the Grand Canal; relatively remote location; lovely old building; 17 incongruously contemporary accommodations; most with bath or shower. Counting breakfast and surcharges, twins go from about $95.

Ateneo • *San Fantin 1876*; ☎ *5200588.* Short walk to St. Mark's Square; 23 rooms, 10 tubs, 5 showers. OK for the outlay.

American Hotel • *San Vio 628, Dorsoduro*; ☎ *704733.* Overlooks the San Vio Canal and the Grand Canal. Tranquil; 30 bedrooms, 20 with bath or shower; about 1/2 with tiny balconies; #5 and #16 the choicest. Reasonably priced.

Pension La Calcina • *Zattere 780, Dorsoduro*; ☎ *706466.* John Ruskin's former residence; 32 bedchambers, about a dozen in front with baths facing the island of Giudecca. Historic surroundings with homey atmosphere.

Albergo S. Lucia • *Lista de Spagna Calle Misericordia 358 (near the station)*; ☎ *715180.* Clean but almost bathless 50-room domain. Low prices for reasonable value.

Hotel de l'Alboro • *San Marco 2894B*; ☎ *706977.* Same ownership as the Hotel Ala (see below). Near the #9 vaporetto stop. Only 16 well-used rooms.

San Maurizio • *San Marco 2624*; ☎ *89712.* Under the same aegis, too small to bother with.

Hotel S. Cassiano • *Ca'Favretto S. Croce-Calle della Rosa 2232*; ☎ *5223051.* 15th-century Gothic palace. Dining room overlooks the waterway; canal-side bar. Quite inviting.

Massimo-Felix • *Calle dei Febbri 981, S. Marco*; ☎ *5236722.* Fair. Varying opinions from readers; some positive, some negative.

Gallini • *Calle della Verona 3673 (close to the Opera)*; ☎ *5236371.* Well run and properly maintained. The location couldn't be better.

Locanda Silva • *Fondam, Rimedio 4423, Castello*; ☎ *5227643.* Stuffed into a side street 5 minutes from San Marco; 25 bathless chambers; sound beds; very clean. Kind staff.

Atlantico • *Castello 4416*; ☎ *709244.* Central situation. Attractive clientele. Routine tariffs.

Casa de'Stefani • *Santa Barnaba 2786*; ☎ *5223337.* Convenient to the Academy Quarter; 2 meals and 2 beds at $48 per person.

EVEN MORE $$$

La Fenice • *San Marco 1936 (adjoining the theater of the same name)*; ☎ *5232333.* Above the well-known La Fenice restaurant; no connection between the two. Magnet for theatrical performers. Lounge and bar but no dining; 68 rooms and 64 baths (some of the sitz type); some individual air-conditioned units. Twins in the $100 range. Still a honey.

Hotel Ala • *Campo Santa Maria del Giglio, S. Marco 2494*; ☎ *708333*. Neighbor of deluxe Gritti Palace; close to the Grand Canal. Attractive restaurant; 77 chambers with 90% bath count.

Patria Tre Rose • *Calle dei Fabbri 905, S. Marco*; ☎ *5222490, 5228567*. Occupies busy site just below St. Mark's belltower. Dining room (out of service Nov.–Mar.); bar and tiny lounge; breakfast roof garden; 31 restful, colorful accommodations; 13 with private plumbing; some with balconies. *Closed Nov. and Dec.*

Concordia • *San Marco 367*; ☎ *706866*. Close to St. Mark's Cathedral. Restaurant and nearly half its 60 units face piazza. Demi-pension obligatory during peak months. Kitchen closed Nov. to mid-March.

Pension Seguso • *Zattere 779, Dorsoduro*; ☎ *5222340*. Beautiful vista of Giudecca Canal. Alfresco terrace; antique-studded lounge; breakfast den; dining room. Chambers (1/2 with bath) boast Old World features; carved ceilings, massive oaken beds, wardrobes, and oriental rugs; #23 double plus bath and balcony, with panorama; #41, bigger but no balcony, also viewful.

Boston • *Piazza San Marco, Ponte dei Dai 848*; ☎ *5287665/6*. Breakfast parlor and lounge; 45 accommodations, 2/3 with either bath (some sitz) or shower; #404 and #405 only units with balcony above tiny canal; #406 probably best for grand size; no singles with plumbing available in summer. Closed Nov. 15-Mar. 15.

Cavalletto • *Calle Cavalletto 1107*; ☎ *5200955*. Commercial; outfitted for groups. Dining room and bar fresh; full-length balcony facing canal; 78 out of 81 smallish accommodations have private plumbing. Best corner doubles: #16, #36, #56. Fairly steep in price.

Carlton Executive • *Santa Croce 578 (near the railway station)*; ☎ *718488*. Garden restaurant, well-stocked bar, air conditioning; 197 beds, 84 full-length baths. Entirely refurbished and very well run.

CAMPING

Nearly 40 sites. Three suburbs particularly well endowed.

Punta Sabbioni • At the tip of a long peninsula, quiet and boasts relatively fast ferry access to the piazzale Roma.

Marina • ☎ *966146*. The most spacious.

Miramare • ☎ *966150*. Smaller but of the first magnitude; facilities are numerous.

SUGGESTIONS FOR STUDENTS

Venice's Dorsoduro (literally "hardback") suburb swarms with international scholars in season. The University of Ca'Foscari (calle San Toma) and the Institute of Architecture (calle Tolentini) are the hubs.

LODGINGS

Foresterie • The appellation for hostels that welcome collegiate boarders.

Hostel Venezia • *Fondam. Zitelle 87*; ☎ *5238211*. Tops the list. Splendid position on La Giudecca; panoramas of San Marco and a never-to-be-forgotten sunset; dining hall pans out noodles or soup, hamburger, French fries, and an apple for $10 or so. Upper precincts with 480 beds in 40-to-a-dorm sets (170 allocated to women); clean; total of 11 baths; tiptop vistas from the high perches; about

$5.75 per night; *10 p.m. curfew*; closed in Dec. Take the *#5 vaporetto* from the train station and have your camera handy.

Domus Civica • *Salizzada San Rocco 3082*; ☎ *721103*. Women only.

DINING

Mensa Universitaria (*Corte Marcona 3879*) and the **Foresteria Universitaria** (*Calle larga Ca'Foscari 3861*) are excellent choices. Both operate from noon to 2 p.m. and 7 to 9 p.m.; full meals start around $3; *student cards are not always required.*

DISCOUNTS

C.T.S. can be helpful; it's at *Ponte Ca'Foscari*; ☎ *705660*.

WHERE TO EAT

LEAST $

"Tavole Calde""Hot tables" are always cheap and often appetizing. Try any of the following quintet:

Chat Qui Rit • *S. Marco 1131*; ☎ *5229086*. Closed Sat.

Toscana • *P. le Venezia*; ☎ *5285281*. Closed Tues.

Da Colpo • *Campo S. Provolo 5719*; ☎ *5221506*. Closed Mon.

Al Teatro Goldoni • *S. Marco 4747*; ☎ *5222466*. Closed Wed.

S. Bartolomeo • *S. Marco 5423*; ☎ *5223569*. Closed Mon.

Self-Service Rialto • *S. Marco 4173*; ☎ *5237709*. If you want a slightly different twist, eat here.

A la Vecia Cavana • *Rio Terra S.S. Apostoli*; ☎ *5287106*. Borders a canal. Try the Sardine Saor (a local starter), the antipasto of fish, the Scampi alla Cavana (on a wooden skewer), the eel in tomato sauce, the polenta on a shingle, the grilled salad, and the white wine of Verona.

Antica Locanda Montin • *San Trovaso, Fondamenta Eremite 1147*; ☎ *5227151*. (*Not far from either the Ca' Rezzonico or Accademia vaporetto landings*). Another strong contender. Bar and inviting garden. Figure about $18 per person. Strongly suggested.

GHETTO NUOVO AND GHETTO VECCHIO

Filled with amusing and inexpensive dining spots. Several excellent candidates: **Ai Cugnai**, **Ai Padovani**, and **Al Chef** (*the latter two on Campo San Barnaba*). For pizza, **Da Gianni** and **Al Faro**. For fuller meals, **Trattoria Tre Gobbi**; indoor and outdoor dining.

Al Teatro • *Campo S. Fantin 1917* (*by the Teatro La Fenice*); ☎ *5237214*. Always top pizzeria in town; 16 types available only during mealtimes when the stoves are hot. Costliest concoction: split-and-spitted chicken for about $6.

Trattoria da Bruno • *Salizzada S. Lio, Calle del Paradiso 5731*. Favored by locals. Substantial fare. Worth a stop if you're near the Rialto.

Trattoria da Raffaele • *San Marco 2347* (*beside the Rio della Ostreghe*). Aperitifs canal-side; dining inside. Fast, friendly service. Extra meat sauce on pasta upon request—without charge. Go evenings, not for lunch. Quite good.

Acciugheta • *Castello 4357*; ☎ *5224292*. One of the best for the price, with a declarative accent on regional cuisine. Closed Wed.

Citta di Vittorio • *San Marco 1591.* At this location even sundried clamshells can be bewitching; but after the view the cookery is superb as well, as you will discover. As with most reliable fish houses, it doesn't work on Mondays (since there's no netting done on Sundays).

Trattoria Rosa Rossa • *Calle della Mandola 3709.* Undiscovered by foreigners. About $12 for 3-course meal of the day (gratuities included). Heaping spaghetti Special; meat choices from $8. Solid fare at low prices.

Bella Venezia • *Cannaregio 129.* Caressed by soft breezes off Lista di Spagna. Highly popular with everyone from displaced drugstore cowboys to local academicians. Homespun cookery in the $8 range. Fun.

Rosticceria Gislon • *Calle Bissa 5423.* For quick snacks.

Tre Gobbi • *Cannaregio 148* and **Tre Spiedi** *same street at #5906.* A pair of tres that often play to a full house. The quality for such a low kitty is understandable. The first closes Tues. and the latter on Mon.

MORE $$

Harry's Bar • *San Marco 1323;* ☎ *5236797.* Well, every American has got to know about it. Here's where Mr. Hemingway's Colonel whiled away so many brooding hours. Intimate, friendly, sophisticated, cheerful—and world famous. Limited but excellent menu at thunderingly high prices—so be warned before sentiment sets in.

Trattoria La Colomba • *Frezzeria 1665;* ☎ *5223817* and **Al Graspo de Ua**, *Campo San Bartolomeo 5094.* Offer nearly parallel attractions in genuine Italian cookery. No summer terrace at latter, but more charm. Both in the $35 price range.

Centrale • *Calle Specchieri 425.* Bills itself as "Tipical" Venetian. Workaday front section plus charming courtyard option. Inconsistent cookery. Set meal at $14, but expect to pay 1/3 more.

Trattoria Antica Carbonera • *Calle Bembo 4648;* ☎ *52254798.* Down Grand Canal from Rialto; $12 dining (wine extra); a worthy target.

Da Nane Corte Dell'Orso • *San Bartolomeo 5495 (near the Rialto Bridge);* ☎ *5224673.* Sit outside in sunny weather. Peek into kitchen. Seafood selections uniformly savory. Better than average.

Piccolo Martini • *Calle Frezzeria 1501 (a block from San Marco);* ☎ *5285136.* Cheerful and charming. Bar and 8 tables. Flavorful antipasto, spaghetti, and lasagne. Big meal for nearly $26. Closed Mon.

Madonna *(Rialto 594;* ☎ *5223824),* **Poste Vecchie** *(Pescheria 1608;* ☎ *721822)* and **Letizia** *(Rialto 692;* ☎ *5229526)* are 3 choices *near Rialto Bridge* to stretch your lire admirably. The first so popular it's tough to get in. The second, simple, clean, and completely regional; fixed menu at $18 or so; good selection; no fuss or rush. The third is satisfactory but not sensational.

NIGHTLIFE

If the stars are out, Venice glows with strollers and lovers. But in bad weather, there are a few possibilities:

Birreria alla Grotta • *San Marco 400, a 50-yard stroll from St. Mark's Square.* A 24-carat tourist joint—so unabashedly so, in fact, that this is an asset. The walls and ceilings contain phony stalactites and other gimmickry. Patrons often join in community songfests of pop and opera. Prices cheap, and the crowd is a melange of everybody.

Caffe Florian • *Piazza San Marco 56.* Lures the cognac-and-coffee crowd. Sprawling sidewalk tables accommodating perhaps 150; gay piano-harmonica-violin lilts; indoor Victorian bar; 20% surcharge on all drinks for music. Delightful in season, but you pay plenty for the prime patch of real estate.

Blue Moon • *Piazzale Bucintoro.* In the Lido has a smoky and frenetic atmosphere; small combo; $2 entry fee; dinner-of-sorts for about $9.50; closed in low season. Beloved by sailors and young people.

El Souk • *Accademia 1056.* Draws a student clientele. Brick and wood decor with small bar near entrance; ringed by booths; lots of signatures and graffiti; monaural phono; honest drinks at about $5. Sign over the door sets the tone of the establishment: "If You Don't Have Nothing To Do, Don't Do It Here."

Ai Musicanti • *Ponte Canonica 4309.* Also called Taverna del'700, serves up operatic arias, folksongs, and gondolier serenades from 9 p.m. to 1 a.m. Capacity 300; air conditioning; entry plus a quaff of spumante for about $13. Food served only at midday.

WHAT TO SEE AND DO

St. Mark's Square, the palaces, the Grand Canal, the galleries, the smaller campi, the mosaics in the churches—the list is endless.The best place to start? Opt for the **Ducal Palace**. Open every day from 8:30 a.m.-7 p.m. in summer and 9 a.m.-4 p.m. in winter; admission is about $3.50.

A **gondola ride**. Better stick to the city waterbuses, which are inexpensive, or take a walking tour around town. A gondola loop of 1 hour now costs about $50 for 5 people and that is jacked up 25% after 7 p.m. Other supplements too, tacked on by these ultraslippery operators, so always nail down an agreed price before you step aboard. Public transport is very reasonable.

St. Mark's Basilica is the next choice. Go any time from 10 a.m. until sunset; no charges save for entry into the Golden Altarpiece Treasure and the upper level. The mosaics, chapels, treasure, crypt, and presbytery are only a few of its highlights. The buckling stone floor is a microcosmic example of what's been happening to all of Venice. This year you will probably see the famous Golden Quadriga (4 steeds) back in place on their familiar balcony. These will be replicas, cast in Milan from the originals, which suffered from Venetian pollution. If some portions of the basilica happen to be closed, see the Sacristan, who might unlock them for you.

AUTHOR'S OBSERVATION

To prevent theft of the art treasures, about 50 churches have been kept locked except during services. The times for these rituals are usually posted on the main doors of the house of worship. Morning prayer is generally 6-8 a.m. on weekdays or 7 a.m. to 1 p.m. Sundays. Check hours for vespers, evening mass, or devotions which often occur Saturdays. God proposes, Man disposes, in unholy Venice!

GALLERIES

The **Fine Arts Academy**, across the ponte dell'Accademia, is indisputably the city's richest treasury of the Masters. Paintings by Titian, Veronese, Tintoretto, the Bellinis, Tiepolo, and many others; operative from 9 a.m. to 2 p.m., closed at 1 p.m. on Sun.; $3.50 entry. (Tip: to revivify yourself, stroll to the Giudecca Canal and have a coffee or a drink on the terrace in front of the house in which John Ruskin lived and worked, now the Pension La Calcina.)

The renowned **Guggenheim Collection** is assembled in one of the city's least attractive buildings and, apart from a few major pieces of exceptionally fine modern sculpture, I find the two-dimensional graphics tedious. Obviously, millions of trippers disagree. Operative April to Oct. daily except Tues. from noon to 6 p.m.; Sat. closing at 9 p.m.

The **Scuola di San Rocco** (*Salizzada San Rocco*) has over 50 Tintorettos. Summer hours from 9 a.m. to 1 p.m. and 3 p.m. to 6:30 p.m.; limited winter showings from 10 a.m. to 1 p.m.; admission roughly $3.50. The adjoining **Friars' Church** (*Frari*) has Titian's "The Assumption" and "The Madonna of Ca' Pesaro." The architectural concepts of this structure are interesting, too. Hours 9 a.m.–noon and 2:30–5:30 p.m.; small entry fee.

Palazzo Grassi is a conversion of an 18th-century palace into a modern art exhibition center. Fiat is backing it, having employed architect Gae Aulenti to effect the transformation.

NEAR VENICE

Within the lagoon, the prime targets are the smaller islands: **Burano** (lace), **Murano** (glassware), **Torcello** (fine Byzantine churches); Stra is a small town on the mainland facing the Brenta River. On the **Burchiello** loop you'll visit Villa Pisani, at Stra, with its legendary frescoes. This little vessel plies the Brenta Canal from Padova to Venice (and reverse) from March 25 to Oct. 27. It's a pleasant full-day excursion. If you prefer only glimpses, special CIT cruisers make short tours three times a week. For more leisurely sightseeing, the *vaporetti* depart from the Fondamenta Nuove (end of rio dei Gesuiti). These casual, point-to-point voyages should be among the most enchanting of your Venetian byway and seaway explorations.

The **Lido**, a separate settlement a few minutes' run by powerboat, offers a galaxy of summer attractions, capped by its famed beaches and Casino. An inexpensive express *vaporetto* excursion plus a short stroll to the Adriatic shore.

MARKETS

The **Rialto** is so fascinating that no one should miss it. The earlier in the morning, the better.

WHERE TO SHOP

ARTS AND CRAFTS

Union of Venetian Artistic Artisans (*Calle Larga San Marco 412/413*, please check this address since they might have moved) is located right behind the piazza San Marco and is exactly what its name implies. It's the logical place to start to fill your shopping bags.

GLASSWARE

Pauly & Co. (*Ponte dei Consorzi Piazza San Marco*) is world famous and worthy of a special buying mission. Don't miss a tour through this unique pleasure dome.

LACE AND LINEN

Jesurum (*Ponte Canonica 4310*) is expensive in the main, but you can still find gift choices—towels, napkins, pin cushions, and such, which are special and not so costly.

LEATHER

Luigi Vogini is at each of the four corners of S. Marco-Ascensione and, once again, while it is known for rich pickin's, the billfolds, bags, and accessories for men and women are exceptional and not too hard on that old wallet or purse you're retiring.

PHOTOGRAPHS, PRINTS, BOOKS

Osvaldo Bohm (*S. Moise 1349/50*) is a specialist on matters Venetian.

PRIMITIVE JEWELRY

Paolo Scarpa (*Merceria S. Salvador-S. Marco 4850*) is a "discovery"—a one-of-a-kind creator who has combed Africa and Asia for the most unusual adornments. Unique pieces begin at $100.

Venice teems with guides, concierges, gondoliers, and other fast operators hungry for commissions on your purchases. The usual bite is 20-25% on glass, and 15% on lace. As in Florence, don't even tell the concierge of your hotel where you're going, because he might tell the merchant that he sent you, and claim his rakeoff on your money.

To counter fringe operators, the Chamber of Commerce and the legitimate old-line merchants set up the **Venetian Crafts Association** to guarantee both product quality and business ethics among its members; look for the Association's 4-leaf-clover symbol displayed by all its participants.

Shopping Hours: Generally 9 a.m.–12:30 p.m., and 3–7:30 p.m. Closed all day Sun. and Mon. mornings in winter, but in summer they never seem to lock their doors.

VERONA

The city of Romeo and Juliet provides a whirl of ancient byways, tiny piazzas, hill and valley vistas, an open market, superb opera at the open arena in summer or in its modern hall in winter.

Lingering is a pleasure in this quiet town. In ascending order in terms of cost, the renewed **San Pietro** is nice, but out of the center; the **Giulietta & Romeo** and the **Milano** are both good pensions; the **Accademia**, the **San Luca**, the **Italia**, and the **Colomba d'Oro** all provide excellent value. The **Grand** asks more money, but its comfort is acknowledged. For inexpensive dining **Armando**, **Greppia**, and **Ciopeta** can be recommended. In the expensive division, **Verona Antica**, **12 Apostoli**, and **Marconi** are excellent. In between these extremes, **Torcoloti**, **Al Bragozzo** (for fish), and **Ca' de L'ebreo** are substantial choices for regional cooking.

FOR MORE INFORMATION ON ITALY

USA • Italian Government Travel Office, *630 Fifth Ave., New York, NY 10020*, ☎ *(212) 245-4961*, (also known as "ENIT"); *500 N. Michigan Ave., Chicago, IL 60611*, ☎ *(312) 644-0990*; *360 Post St., San Francisco, CA 94108*, ☎ *(415) 392-5266.*

CANADA • *1 Place Ville Marie, Suite 2414, Montreal, Quebec, HEB 3M9*, ☎ *(514) 866-7667.*

LUXEMBOURG

Here's the world's only remaining Grand Duchy, a postage-stamp country that conjures up images of swashbucklers vaulting over battlements under a hail of arrows. Throughout most of its 1000-year history, it has been looked upon as a military prize, spending 9 of its 10 centuries as a fortress of one sort or another—a tableau of turrets, crossbows, gold braid, armor, and more castles than you can shake a pike at (74 at last tally).

The peaceful 20th-century landscape further embraces ambling rivers, undulant meadows, deep forests, and unbelievably ancient hamlets with such storybook names as Munshausen, Clemency, Heiderscheidergrund, Pontpierre, and Pintsch, which reflect the three languages spoken by its 380,000 inhabitants—German, French, and a jaw-breaking indigenous dialect called Letzebuergesch.

In its feisty younger days it traded parry and thrust with Burgundy, Spain, Austria, France, and Germany. In early statehood it joined Belgium in rebellion against the Netherlands, only to lose its major part, the present Luxembourg Province, to Belgium nine years later. In its political maturity it teamed up with both Belgium and Holland to form the Benelux Economic Union, the forerunner of the European Common Market. The punishing and heroic war years are dramatically illustrated at the Diekirch Historical Museum, about 30 minutes north of the capital.

Though smaller than Rhode Island, Luxembourg is enormously sophisticated. Within its 999 square miles, everybody seems to get rich on steel mills (7th largest production in the world but declining overall), banks (more than 180), holding companies (some 5000), and on a thriving trade fostered by favorable tax regulations and discreet money management—the latter somewhat to the annoyance (read jealousy), but often to the furtive convenience, of its EC brothers. It also boasts an active gold exchange.

TIPS ON LUXEMBOURG

MONEY

Within the Grand Duchy, the Luxembourgian franc and the Belgian franc are valued equally. The Luxfranc is interchangeable with the currencies of the U.S., Great Britain, France, West Germany, and Italy. When you leave, however, make sure you've converted all your local notes into Belgian ones because they are not generally accepted in other lands.

As for prices, they tend to be high, and that includes lodgings. No need to dread the levels of Brussels, but don't bank on bargain travel, as you might in rural Spain or Greece. For $10-$15, you can consume (and even digest) a meal that might cost twice as much in the Belgian capital.

FOOD

The skilled chefs of Luxembourg combine the saucy lightness of their French counterparts with the stick-to-the-ribs heartiness of their German neighbors on the other side of the Moselle. National specialties include *black pudding and sausages*, *thinly sliced Ardennes ham* served hot or cold, *jellied suckling pig*, *smoked pork with broad beans*, *calf's liver dumplings*, *hare*, *trout*, *crawfish*, *pike*, and a galaxy of pastries. You also should try **Letzebuerger Kachke's** for breakfast or with cocktails if you're in the market for a size-48 pucker. This cooked and aged cottage cheese is a source of deep national pride; it's also the chief reason for the burgeoning sale of breath-sweeteners here. No one who tastes it for the first time is apathetic. You'll either love it or loathe it, but one thing is certain: A mouthful back home would guarantee at least 6 free seats on the rush-hour bus.

SPORTS

CYCLING

Special trails exist in the *Vianden*, *Luxembourg*, *Echternach*, and *Diekirch* areas; bicycle rental available.

HIKING

Over 3000 miles of marked trails throughout the country. Nearly every Sat., Sun., or holiday, walking tours totaling 5-25 miles are organized by **Federation Luxembourgeoise des Marches Populaires**, *L-2018 Luxembourg, P.O. Box 794.*

HORSES

The mounted Tour of Luxembourg and **Tour of the Valley of the Seven Castles** are offered by the **Secretariat de la Federation Luxembourgeoise des Sports Equestres**, *90 route de Thionville, Luxem-*

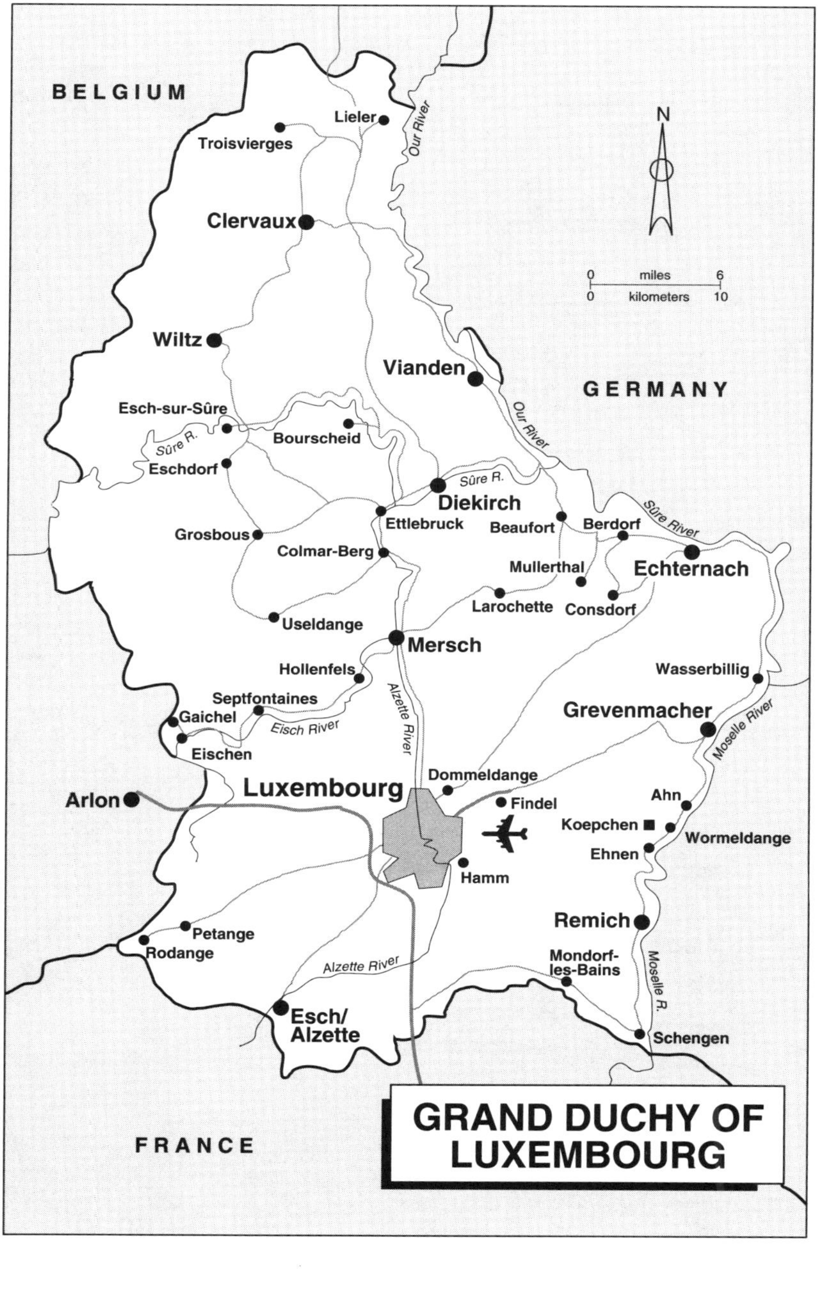
BELGIUM
GERMANY
FRANCE
N
0 miles 6
0 kilometers 10
Lieler
Troisvierges
Our River
Clervaux
Wiltz
Vianden
Esch-sur-Sûre
Bourscheid
Sûre R.
Eschdorf
Our River
Sûre R.
Diekirch
Ettlebruck
Beaufort
Berdorf
Sûre River
Grosbous
Colmar-Berg
Mullerthal
Echternach
Larochette
Consdorf
Useldange
Mersch
Hollenfels
Wasserbillig
Septfontaines
Grevenmacher
Gaichel
Eisch River
Alzette River
Moselle River
Eischen
Dommeldange
Arlon
Luxembourg
Findel
Ahn
Koepchen
Wormeldange
Ehnen
Hamm
Remich
Petange
Rodange
Mondorf-les-Bains
Alzette River
Moselle R.
Esch/Alzette
Schengen
GRAND DUCHY OF LUXEMBOURG

bourg, which also provides information on the country's various riding schools.

WATERSPORTS—CANOEING

On the waters of the upper *Sure River.*

FISHING

Regulations are complex. For details write **Administration des Eaux et Forets**, *P.O. Box 411, 2014-Luxembourg.*

Want to mosey along the Moselle? For such a cruise, touch base with **Navigation Touristique de la Moselle**, *Grevenmacher, 32 route de Thionville, P.O. Box 33;* ☎ *758275.*

SIGHTSEEING

WINE TASTING

Numerous wine and champagne cellars along the **Moselle** produce dry, fruity wines. Most are open to the public for visits and samples. You'll find wine museums at *Ehnen* and *Bech-Kleinmacher.*

FESTIVALS

Annual classical music and theater festivals are held in *Luxembourg City, Echternach*, and *Wiltz* from March to Aug.

WHERE TO GO

LUXEMBOURG CITY

You've heard of a one-horse town; well, this is a one-town country—the capital being the only city of any appreciable size. Since castles are to Luxembourg as coals are to Newcastle, it's not surprising that the name Luxembourg derives from Lucilinburhuc, the "Little Castle" of the Count of Ardennes. It's equally unsurprising that the city began life as a bastion on nearly impregnable terrain—as did the strongholds of *Vianden*, *Beaufort*, and *Bourscheid.*

DIRECTORY

U.S. Embassy • *22 boulevard Emmanuel-Servais;* ☎ *40123.*

Laundromat • Washerette, *6 rue Bender;* ☎ *483207.*

Dry Cleaning • Tout a Neuf, *45 avenue de la Liberte;* ☎ *40166.*

English-Speaking Doctor • Dr. Carlos Harf, *34 Phillippe II;* ☎ *23773 or 319244.*

English-Speaking Dentist • Dr. Jean Klepper, *49 boulevard Royal;* ☎ *21174.*

Police • *58 rue Glesener;* ☎ *409401;* emergencies*:* ☎ *012.*

Favorite Pawnshop • Wait for Brussels, since there is none in such a Grand little Duchy.

WHERE TO STAY

In keeping with the quirky nature of this country, hotel listings must, perforce, break cadence. Expense accounters may find suitable shelter, but cheaper lodgings are as scarce as wells in Death Valley. There are only 35 officially sanctioned inns in this fortress city. The vast majority, however mean or obscure, tap the trade for shockingly high tariffs since so many visitors have come to commune with their money or investments at the local banks. From these, we have tried to cull the best value for your money. Addresses out of the high-rent district can be counted on one

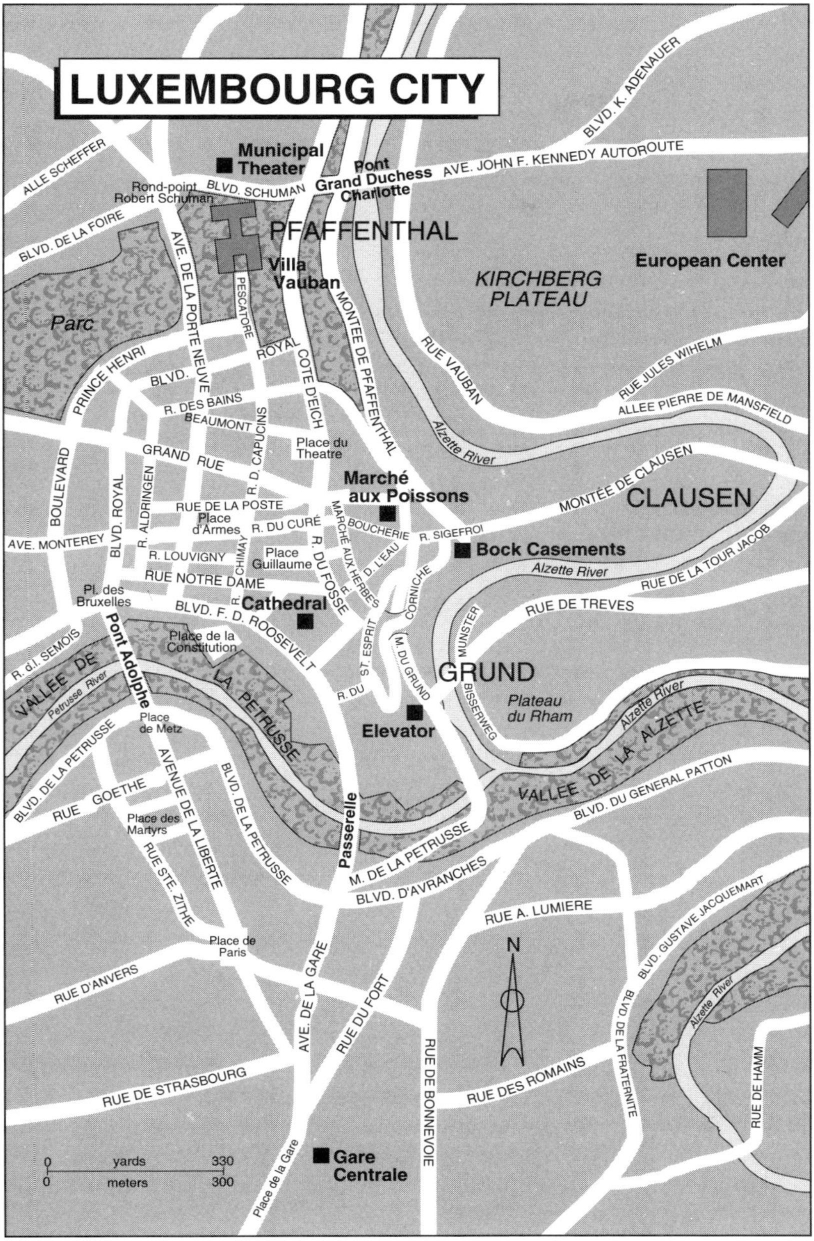
LUXEMBOURG CITY
Municipal Theater
Pont Grand Duchess Charlotte
Rond-point Robert Schuman
BLVD. SCHUMAN
AVE. JOHN F. KENNEDY AUTOROUTE
BLVD. K. ADENAUER
ALLE SCHEFFER
BLVD. DE LA FOIRE
PFAFFENTHAL
Villa Vauban
European Center
KIRCHBERG PLATEAU
Parc
AVE. DE LA PORTE NEUVE
PESCATORE
MONTEE DE PFAFFENTHAL
RUE VAUBAN
RUE JULES WIHELM
ALLEE PIERRE DE MANSFIELD
Alzette River
PRINCE HENRI
BLVD. ROYAL
COTE D'EICH
R. DES BAINS
BEAUMONT
R. D. CAPUCINS
Place du Theatre
GRAND RUE
BOULEVARD
BLVD. ROYAL
R. ALDRINGEN
Marché aux Poissons
MONTÉE DE CLAUSEN
CLAUSEN
RUE DE LA POSTE
Place d'Armes
R. DU CURÉ
MARCHÉ AUX HERBES
BOUCHERIE
R. SIGEFROI
Bock Casements
AVE. MONTEREY
R. LOUVIGNY
CHIMAY
Place Guillaume
R. DU FOSSE
R. D. L'EAU
CORNICHE
Alzette River
RUE DE LA TOUR JACOB
RUE NOTRE DAME
Pl. des Bruxelles
R. Cathedral
BLVD. F. D. ROOSEVELT
RUE DE TREVES
MUNSTER
R. d.l. SEMOIS
Pont Adolphe
Place de la Constitution
ST. ESPRIT
M. DU GRUND
GRUND
VALLEE DE LA PETRUSSE
Petrusse River
R. DU
BISSERWEG
Plateau du Rham
Alzette River
VALLEE DE LA ALZETTE
Elevator
Place de Metz
BLVD. DE LA PETRUSSE
AVENUE DE LA LIBERTE
BLVD. DE LA PETRUSSE
BLVD. DU GENERAL PATTON
RUE GOETHE
Place des Martyrs
Passerelle
M. DE LA PETRUSSE
RUE STE. ZITHE
BLVD. D'AVRANCHES
RUE A. LUMIERE
BLVD. GUSTAVE JACQUEMART
Place de Paris
N
RUE D'ANVERS
AVE. DE LA GARE
RUE DU FORT
BLVD. DE LA FRATERNITE
Alzette River
RUE DE BONNEVOIE
RUE DES ROMAINS
RUE DE HAMM
RUE DE STRASBOURG
0 yards 330
0 meters 300
Place de la Gare
Gare Centrale

hand; they are uniformly small and inconvenient to reach. Your best bargains, incidentally, are likely to be found on weekends when business travelers scat back to their homelands, leaving the hostelries empty. This would be the best time for sightseeing the whole of this pocket-size duchy.

In the luxury category, with prices similar to those of top-liners in other capitals, are the **Intercontinental**, **Le Royal** and the midcity, traditional **Cravat**; the **President** has been fancied up so that its tariffs are now pretty lofty. The Intercontinental, incidentally, is outside of the center at Europa Park; hence, a car would be useful. All of the above are mentioned only for your convenience, since selection overall is so limited.

Pullman • Also not exactly an economy stop, offers a novel money-saving program: If you wing in on *Icelandair* (and you booked to another destination), the 3-day "Stopover Program" will pick you up at the airport, deliver you to the Pullman (or the 150-unit **Aerogolf-Sheraton**, *Route de Treves;* ☎ *34571*, also in the package), serve you all your meals, provide private-bath accommodation, turn on a citywide sightseeing tour, and toss in return transportation to the airport—all for the price of the room alone! To get in on this bargain, see your travel agent or Icelandair. Otherwise, this and the costlier Aerogolf-Sheraton are awfully expensive.

Francais • *14 place d'Armes;* ☎ *474534.* Good restaurant; 23 units; typical front double with huge bed, tiny shower, radio, and engaging view of the pedestrians in the plaza; priced at around $48.

Senator • *38 rue Joseph Junck;* ☎ *492351.* Very central; 29 units; $48 for 2, $40 for 1 (with bath).

Alfa • *16 place de la Gare (opposite the station);* ☎ *490011.* 100 units. Courteous staff.

Empire • *34 place de la Gare (hard by the tracks);* ☎ *485252.* 30 clean and reasonable rooms with a 50% shower count. Restaurant; double rate $65.

Schintgen • *6 rue Notre-Dame;* ☎ *22844.* 35 attractive rooms which rent for about $55 per twosome.

City • *1 rue Strasbourg;* ☎ *484608.* Faces the noisy place de la Gare; restyled and prices peaking at $75 per twin.

Airfield • You can try getting tucked into one of its 10 yawning hangars. Taxi fare to town around $15 plus tip, but you won't have to dash for your plane at checkout time.

Parc Hotel • On the Echternach highway at Dommeldange. Good reports on this entry, but $80 doubles put it in sky-high range.

Youth Hostel • *2 rue du Fort Olisy;* ☎ *26889.* Offers central heating, hot showers, and full meals. Under 26? Pay about $8.50 per bed. Over? $12. Breakfast $2.25 additional; dinner and dessert $7.75.

WHERE TO EAT

LEAST $

It's a rich little nation. Consequently many people dine at home or at the fancier hotels and restaurants. Your best bet for a snack or inexpensive meal is in the downtown station area.

Ems Cafe Brasserie • *30 place de la Gare.* A station stop with piped melodies. Hamburger with egg and potatoes about $8.75. Goulash runs $1 more.

Buffet de la Gare • Left of the main terminal doors. Self-service and reasonable solid fare.

MORE $$

Speltz • *rue Chimay 8.* Like its name, Gallic in tone, pleasant, and reliable, except Sunday nights and Mondays, when it closes.

Caesar • *18 avenue Monterey.* As brassy as Julius, more of a brasserie; fun and usually animated, with prices around $23.

Cravat Hotel • Has a rotisserie that serves beautiful, though costly, cuisine. Its more modest cafe features regional dishes at reasonable prices.

WHAT TO SEE AND DO

The city is so small that almost everything will be within walking distance of your hotel. For starters, slip into your most comfortable shoes and take the 2-hour walking tour that begins at the **place d'Armes** (site of the tourist office); this takes in the **place de la Constitution**, an eye-popping view of the **Petrusse Valley** and **Adolphe Bridge**, a lovely promenade along the **Walls of the Corniche**, the **Castle Bridge**, and the impressive **Bock Casemates**. This is the Grand Duchy at its grandest.

During the summer months, there are folklore exhibits 2 to 4 times a week, concerts, theater performed in dungeons, wine-tasting festivals, and plenty of tunnel-snooping. For information on these, and scores more, go to the **Tourist Information Office** (*place d'Armes;* ☎ *222809 and 227565*) where kindly, helpful staffers will open the heart of their nation for you.

Autocars Sales-Lentz (☎ *501050*) operates modern buses that fan out on 3- and 5-hour excursions to the **Ardennes**, **La Petite Suisse** and the renowned **Castle at Vianden**, **La Petite Suisse** and the **Moselle Valley**, and a 3-hour jaunt around the city and its environs. If you take one of the northern loops to *Vianden* and *Beaufort*, you'll pass Luxembourg's famous bronze statue of **General George S. Patton** and one of his tanks. Both face the wartime foe from the Saar.

For saving money, buses are best. Taxis are dependable but not very plentiful; virtually no place of interest is more than 2 ticks of the meter from anyplace else. Between **Hertz** (*25 avenue de la Liberte;* ☎ *485485*) and **Avis** (*2 place de la Gare,* ☎ *489595*), you'll find a fair array of small and medium-size cars for rent. **Budget Rent-a-Car** is represented at the airport (Findel), ☎ *433412.*

FOR MORE INFORMATION ON LUXEMBOURG

USA • **Luxembourg Tourist Information Office**, *801 Second Ave., New York, NY 10017,* ☎ *(212) 370-9850.*

THE NETHERLANDS

Centraal Station, Amsterdam

The cliches, of course, are wooden shoes, windmills, flowers, cheese, beer, and canals. It's a flat little kingdom, a considerable chunk of it below sea level. At the coastal fringes reclamation goes on apace, and, by dint of ceaseless work and spectacular engineering know-how, the persevering Dutch have won back nine-tenths of the land that since A.D. 1200 had been disappearing into Davy Jones' locker. Whole new villages have been created and thousands of acres of fertile soil added to the nation's resources.

One advantage of being a lowland: it's easy to move around. Many robust citizens, including the royals, take to their bicycles for short runs, errands, or outings. But for longer trips the public transport systems are cheap, clean, and efficient, the roads superb. English is spoken extensively here, so communication with the helpful Hollanders is pleasant (usually jovial) and easy. Accommodations generally are as crisp and clean as an alderman's collar, as fresh and inviting as a tulip patch—and not very expensive since the Dutch are used to hosting millions of visitors from every financial strata. The national cuisine is notable: herring, smoked eels, oysters, and hotpots vie with exotic Indonesian rijsttafel and Oriental fare to be sampled in scores of interesting ethnic restaurants.

One of the finest trips in the Netherlands (which Americans familiarly call *Holland*) is a jaunt around the Zuiderzee (now called "Ysselmeer"), a mistily beautiful gulf tamed by an 18-1/2-mile-long dam and dotted with quaint fishing villages among its polders. The wild island of Texel preserves a rare spoonbill colony; apart from walking, cycling, or watching the marsh birds, you can ride horseback, sail, or fish here, too.

In spring and summer, Holland is a horticultural heaven with its dazzling bulb fields and early-morning flower auctions as sights to see. In an area slightly southwest of Amsterdam, you can visit some of the country's finest fields in bloom. Then there are the redolent cheese markets of Gouda, Purmerend, and, especially, Alkmaar, where dairy farmers stack their products on the ground. When the cheeses are sold, porters in traditional costumes carry them away on wooden litters. Halfway between Amsterdam and Alkmaar is Beverwijk, an exotic town on Sundays when the Oosterse Markt (Oriental Market) takes over. There are so many Islamic people—hear the imam's call?—that Holland graciously provides a showcase of ethnic minorities thriving in their own milieu. In Oudewater, supposed ladies and gentlemen can be weighed on a 16th-century "witch scale" to determine whether or not they are evil. Giethoorn has no streets at all—just canals. Farmers herd their cattle by boat, and weddings or funerals float serenely or eerily by; at Kinderdijk, near Rotterdam, you'll find an unforgettable squadron of windmills, nearly 20 in all.

The Gothic and Renaissance facades and tree-lined canals of Delft impart a thoroughly old-world atmosphere to a city famous for its porcelain.

Now Het Loo, the Royal Dutch residence at Apeldoorn, has been restored, and its baroque splendors of house and gardens can be shared with you. This "Versailles of Holland" is a wonderful excursion target.

Holland is a parade-in-duplicate, an ever-changing pageant of new scenes so often reflected in its shining canals and still ponds.

NETHERLANDS
NORTH SEA
N
Edam
Volendam
Haarlem
Zandvoort
Amsterdam
Aalsmeer
Wassenar
Schevenigen
The Hague
Utrecht
Woerden
Oudewater
Gouda
Rotterdam
Zwolle
Laren
Arnhem
GERMANY
BELGIUM

TIPS ON HOLLAND

FOOD

The Dutch relish their food; their cuisine at its best is delicate, savory, and full of unexpected nuances. At its worst, however, it's turgid, greasy, overly rich, and heavy.

Under ideal circumstances, breakfast offers a choice of various breads, butter, cheese (always), tea or coffee, a boiled egg, and meat. The famous "Dutch Coffee Table" (sometimes a warm dish, then cold meats, cheese, fruits, and beverage) is the national lunch. Many people have a light afternoon tea, and dinner is always the heaviest meal of the day.

Typical Dutch dishes are also typically American: steak with French fries and salad, asparagus with egg and butter sauce, boiled beef. More exotic are minced beef (*rolpens*) with fried apples and, in winter, curly cabbage and sausage, and hotchpotch (*hutspot*).

Dutch pea soup (*erwtensoep*) is wonderful. It's loaded with spicy sausages and pork fat; thick, rich, and inert as infantry pancakes—but good!

Some specialties are herring (try *Hollandse Nieuwe*—"new" herring with onions—best in May and June, as an appetizer), smoked eels (excellent) and other fish; cheese (seek out the scrumptious Kernheimer type); Deventer gingerbread, currant bread, and small sugared fritters (*poffertjes*); mouth-melting chocolate (Droste and Van Houten are the best); a special caramel candy (*Haagse Hopjes*); and an unusual egg-flip concoction (*Advocaat*).

The best bet of all—something no American should miss—is the world-famous *rijsttafel* (pronounced rye-staffel, and translated as rice table). This, for want of a more descriptive phrase, was the ceremonial feast of the Dutch colonists in Indonesia. The cuisine is like nothing most of us have ever sampled—vaguely Chinese, but with such major departures that it is unique in the annals of dining. A big rijsttafel might consist of more than a score of separate platters. Starve yourself all day; permit yourself only the order of *Sateh Babi* (spit-roasted pork on a stick in a delicious hot sauce) with your cocktails; when you sit down to face the dizzy array, put 2 spoonfuls of rice in the center of your plate and limit yourself to one small taste of everything. Otherwise you're licked from the start. Highest recommendation of all for any visitor.

Skip lobster, oysters, and salmon in Holland; they're horribly expensive.

If you're hungry at an odd hour of the day, try an *Uitsmijter sandwich* (translated as "bouncer"). It's one of the 3 national types: roast beef, ham, or veal (take your choice) with lots of trimmings and fried eggs on top. Wonderful as a bedtime snack, too, if you have a stomach like a Bessemer converter.

There's really no need to patronize Holland's deluxe restaurants. In the most modest establishments, the cooking is quite good, nearly always abundant, and the price probably will run $11 to $20 for a substantial meal. Cafes and cafeterias are even cheaper, of course, and you'll find them everywhere.

In about 400 restaurants throughout the land you'll find a **Tourist Menu**—a 3-course meal for about $10. Eating places participating in this plan will display an emblem of a fork with a camera dangling from one of its tines and the words *Tourist Menu* in bold letters.

DRINKS

A bonanza. Those good Heineken and Amstel beers are about $1.70 per mug. Dutch gin (they call it *jenever*) has a uniquely volatile, aromatic, and slightly bitter flavor. The *Oude Klare* is a dryer and more sophisticated type than the stronger, more highly flavored *Jonge*. Drink it from a shot glass. (Incidentally, if proper form is followed, it will be served, instead, in a "tulip" glass—and your first sip must be slurped while the glass rests on the bar!) Never attempt to make a martini of it; it simply isn't made for any kind of mixing.

The liqueurs are interesting; over 40 varieties are now on the shelves. Ask for Bols or Hoppe products; they are always dependable, while some imitations are not.

Soft drinks? In addition to all the familiar sweet beverages, there is also a wide assortment of fruit beverages; one brand we like is the Hero group.

When the round is on, you say: "Let's have a *borrel*!" It's the universal Dutch invitation. Since brewers are usually given exclusive contracts, most Dutch restaurants sell only one brand of beer.

GETTING AROUND

TRAINS

Fast service, accurate schedules, high frequency. During rush hours you may have to stand up all the way, but how long can that be in a country about the size of Maryland? Ride first class because distances are short, the price difference is trivial, and second can be murderously overcrowded.

Electric trains run from Amsterdam to The Hague every quarter hour, and more often during the traffic peaks; some of them have coffee bars. There are also hourly night runs linking major hubs with Schiphol.

Watch out for the inland 1-day excursion ticket because the return half expires as soon as the last train on the timetable of that night pulls out. The free booklet *Touring Holland by Rail* available at the sales window of any station, has further information.

The best bet for serious riders (unless you have your Eurailpass) is the *7-day Rover ticket* that is valid all over the **Netherlands Railways network**. Use it as often and as much as you like—for about $78 in first or $59 in second class. It is available at all Dutch railway stations. (Bring a passport photo.) While you're at it, find out about the "Strip Tickets" (which have nothing to do with local cabarets); they also can be used on buses, trams, and metros all over the country. Place the "distance" stub in a stamping device at the rear or front of trams and at the front of buses, or ask the driver to do it.

BUSES

Routes and heavy timetables take you to nearly every city. Most of the vehicles are relatively new. They are comfortable for short distances, but we do not recommend them for long hauls. Cross-country coaches are cheaper but require a lot of changing and considerably more time than trains. Ask the **Amsterdam Tourist Office** (*Central Station;* ☎ *6266444*) to supply details.

MOTORING

Once you arrive, the **ANWB** (Royal Dutch Touring Club) offers a variety of services, including road, walking, cycling, waterway, and air maps. ANWB provides signposts throughout the land and a patrol service. For assistance, day or night call ☎ *06-0800* on special roadside telephones along major highways.

CAR HIRE

A flock of rental agencies is at your disposal here; their Amsterdam addresses: **Hertz** (*Overtoom 333;* ☎ *6122441*), **Avis** (*Nassaukade 380;* ☎ *6836061*), **EuropCar** (*Overtoom 51;* ☎ *6832123*), **K & L** (*Van Ostadestr. 232;* ☎ *6717066*), and **Budget-Rent-a-Car** (*Overtoom 121;* ☎ *6126066*). Despite slight differences in base rates, the per-kilometer charges, delivery costs, collection costs, and insurance extras quoted by all these firms add up within pennies of each other.

TAX-FREE CAR PURCHASE

ShipSide, a U.S.-Dutch, tax-free automobile showroom and selling agency, is in operation at **Schiphol**, Amsterdam's International Airport. Upon debarkation, any nonresident may take his pick any day of the week from its selection of foreign-made cars and drive away within 30 minutes. Some models, however, are so popular that factory schedules cannot meet public demands, either in delivery dates or options. Make known your preference (especially in the more expensive makes) by beginning your correspondence early, because the cars on hand are often either the stocks of mass-volume producers or fancier vehicles. This fleet has been provided in advance with ownership cards, license plates, and all other documentation except your International Driver's License. Its catalogue may be had from *50 Chestnut Ridge Rd., Montvale, NJ 07645* or from any KLM office.

CAMPERS

A company called **Braitman en Woudenberg** (*Droogbak 4, 1013 GE; ☎ 6221168*) tells us that it can supply VW vehicles (Wesfalias) and vans from its headquarters near the Central Station in Amsterdam. Rates (varying with the dollar exchange) run about $500-800 per week—cooking gear supplied and free pillows and sleeping bags, too, if you wish; purchase and buy-back programs available. Ask for Mr. Kluver.

HITCHHIKING ON BARGES

(Shhhhh! Officially it's forbidden.) Nevertheless, inland sailors expect to accommodate more than 1000 thumbers this year—and most of them love the company! Rotterdam is the Dutch apex, because this is the jump-off point for the Rhine journey that can extend all the way to Basel, Switzerland. (Heidelberg, Germany, is the most popular launching pad.) Some skippers may quite properly ask for a small daily contribution for food; others scorn money. You may be asked to produce your *International Student Identity Card.* Hints: Be well groomed and clean in appearance, regardless of the simplicity of your clothes. Women, don't try to look sexy or flirt; the captain may decide you will distract the crew and leave you on the quay. If you don't like a barge, or if the people are unpleasant, merely disembark at the next river lock or port and catch a new ride on a better one with a more congenial group.

SPORTS

CYCLING

In the Low Countries, it's money saving, unstrenuous, and cheap. Rentals? Several Amsterdam agencies rent bikes from $5 a day to $24 per week. Contact **Koenders** (*Stationsplein 33*) in the Centraal railroad station (*☎ 6248391*). Another agency perfect for pedaling around the large Amsterdamse Bos is **Fiets-O-Fiets** (*Amstelveenseweg 880-900; ☎ 6445473*).

Two-wheeled tours–Ask the **Netherlands Board of Tourism** for its informative brochure *Cycling in Holland.* Or contact **Ena's Bike Tours** (*Dr. M.L. Kingstraat 4, 1121 CP Landsmeer; ☎ 020-6923584*); daily departures at 10 a.m. from the cycle depot, Amstel Station, Amsterdam for guided cycling to windmills or a cheese farm, and 7-1/2-hours of pedal-pushing beside the canals and byways of scenic Holland; day tour around 50 guilders; June to Oct. Other informative addresses: **Koninklijke Nederlandse Toeristen Bond ANWB**, *Wassenaarseweg 220, 2596 EC The Hague; ☎ 070-3147147* and **Stichting Fiets**, *Europaplein 2, 1078 GZ, Amsterdam; ☎ 020-5491212.* You might also try **Discovery** (*Meerhuizenstraat 1/3; ☎ 6647400*), which is said to provide excellent service through

Director Bernie Dunn, a transplanted American who loves his work and likes his clients. His "waterland" tours are splendid communions with nature right in the Amsterdam district. (Not that it ever rains in the Lowlands, but Bernie also provides ponchos.)

WATERSPORTS

For canoeing: **Nederlandse Kanobond** *P.O. Box 1160, 3800 BD Amersfoort;* ☎ *033-6223411.*

For cruising, windsurfing, and sailing: **Koninklijk Nederlands Watersport Verbond**, *Postbus 87, 3980 CB Bunnik;* ☎ *03405-70524.* **Holland History Sails**, *Herengracht 49, 1398 AC Muiden;* ☎ *02942-3927.* **Nederlandse Vereniging van Sportvissersfederaties** *Postbus 288, 3800 AG Amersfoort;* ☎ *033-634924.* To get the angle on fishing.

HORSES

Find a mount and a trail through **Stichting Nederlandse Hippische Sportbond**, *Postbus 456, 3740 AL Baarn;* ☎ *02154-21841.*

HORIZONTAL MOUNTAIN CLIMBING

It's done at **Pieterburen** across the mud flats of the Wadden Sea in Groningen. At low tide you could trudge up to Denmark in these bird-rich shallows, but I doubt that you'd get that far too quickly. The sport is called "wadlopen" locally and the VVV can point you to the guides who know every sandbar and mussel shoal in the province. Quite a mud lark, but wear your oldest shoes.

SIGHTSEEING

BLOSSOM TIME

If the season is right, you can build a petal-pushing tour around Dutch gardens. Famous **Keukenhof at Lisse** (open late March through May) is the largest flower patch on this globe. It's an hour from Amsterdam. At nearby *Vogelenzang* tulips are on parade April through May and from July through September at **Frans Roozen Nursery**, which has a proud 1000 varieties of bulbs. Then there's **Het Loo Palace**, near *Apeldoorn* (which you can reach by train from Amsterdam), **Castle Middachten** at *De Steeg*, **Castel de Haar** (*Utrecht area*), and evergreen **Aalsmeer** (see "Where to Go").

WINE TASTING

Wijnkelders Robbers & Van den Hoogen, *Velperweg 23, 6824 BC Arnhem;* ☎ *085-455912*, will tell you where, how, and how much. What? You never heard of Dutch wine?

FESTIVALS

In June the Holland Festival features concerts, opera, ballet, and much more culture, mainly in Amsterdam, but also in The Hague. For program details contact **Holland Festival**, *Kleine Gartmanplantsoen 21, 1017 RP Amsterdam;* ☎ *020-6276566.* During July, jazz lovers can attend the **North Sea Jazz** festival in The Hague. Contact *P.O. Box 87840, 2508-DE The Hague;* ☎ *070-3502034.*

HOME EXCHANGE

Lodging logistics looked after by **Intervac**, *Paasberg 25, 6862 CB Oosterbeek;* ☎ *085-341187.*

SHOPPING

Shopping hours are complicated as all get-out. Normally shops open Tues.–Sat. from 9 a.m. till 5:30–6 p.m. On Mon. they start from around 11 a.m. or they might not open at all. Some establishments close for lunch, and the rest are shuttered for a morning, an afternoon, or a whole day. Each store will usually have a notice about its hours. Many spots have late-night shopping on Thurs. or Fri. evenings. In holiday and seaside resorts most shops open also in the evenings and during weekends. Since there are so many other variables, be sure to check before leaving your hotel. For export items totaling more than 300 guilders per store, there's a 17-1/2% VAT rebate minus a service charge. Discuss this at the shop where you make the purchase.

THINGS NOT TO BUY

Increasingly, Dutch products are developing a uniformity that speaks of the success of the European Economic Community. Hence, standards on many items are similar to those elsewhere within the brotherhood. There's hardly a need to warn you about souvenir junk. Watch Delftware—counterfeits are peddled nationwide.

WHERE TO GO

AALSMEER

Only 10 miles from Amsterdam, a tiny town is the permanent flower center, both physically and commercially. Hundreds of thousands of blooms from the surrounding countryside pour in to be sorted, selected, and sold at auction in a gigantic wholesale market—in the mornings only! There are exquisite colors and varieties, many brand-new to the North American amateur gardener. It is a lovely spectacle that may be viewed any day from 7:30 to 11:30 a.m. except Sat. and Sun.; Mon. and Tues. are best; Fri. is the worst.

ALKMAAR

Try this one on any Fri. morning between mid-Apr. and mid-Sept.; a happy tour if the weather is benign. A huge cheese market runs full blast from 10 a.m. until noon; we recommend that you arrive early. It is novel, lively, and surprisingly odorless. There's another at **Purmerend** from 11 a.m. to 1 p.m, every Thurs. during July and Aug.

AMSTERDAM

Recently, Amsterdam telephone numbers were promoted to seven digits. Add a "6" in front of all listings that you come across employing the old numeration.

In this aquarian metropolis, it is easy to find plenty of good, reasonably priced accommodations, fine restaurants, low-cost sandwich shops, an intriguing nightlife, and a wealth of things to see and do.

Since Amsterdam's concentric skein of canals covers virtually the whole city, you could begin your visit with a cruise aboard one of the glass-topped launches that ply the smaller canals as well as the broader waterways and main harbor. Thousands of impressive merchant houses still border the 50 miles of tree-lined channels.

Amsterdam was not conceived for the automobile; streets are geared to the pedestrian and cyclist. But to relieve aching feet or for longer distances, the tram network is fast, cheap, and ubiquitous.

Art galleries? Amsterdam practically invented them. See the **Rijksmuseum**, **the Stedelijk**, the **Van Gogh Museum**, and **Rembrandt's house**, where many of the master's etchings and sketches are kept. While you are in this world center of the diamond industry, you might like to see how gems are cut—right in the center of town.

An excellent bird's-eye view of the whole city can be had from the tower of the graceful 14th-century **Old Church** in *Oudekerksplein*. You'll be able to pinpoint landmarks both ancient and modern in this one-time medieval fishing village that grew up to be one of Europe's key commercial, financial, and cultural centers.

DIRECTORY

U.S. Consulate • *Museumplein 19*; ☎ *6790321.*

American Express • *Damrak 66*; ☎ *6262042.*

Laundromats • At *Oude Doelenstr. 12* and *Haarlemmerdijk 16 hs.*

Dry Cleaning & Pressing • Palthenette, *Vijzelstraat 57*; ☎ *6230337.*

English-Speaking Doctor and Dentist • ☎ *6642111* ("Central Medical Service").

Police • *Elandsgracht 117, corner Marnixstr.*; ☎ *5599111.*

Amsterdam Tourist Information Office • *opposite the Centraal Railway Station*; ☎ *6266444.* A secondary VVV Office has opened on *Leidsestraat 106*, in order to better serve tourists at this opposite end of town.

Favorite Pawnshop • *Stadskredietbank, Oude Zijds Voorburgwal 300*; ☎ *6222421.*

HOW TO GET AROUND

Amsterdam's public transit is almost unrivaled on the Continent. First, pay a small sum at the **GVB** (Amsterdam Municipal Transport System) booth in the square fronting Centraal Station for an invaluable route map. Free folders with instructions on transportation schemes are also available there. ☎ *6272727* for further information (8 a.m.–11 p.m.).

If you are en route to or from the airport, public transportation (now possible on a new rail route, too) is, of course, cheapest. The rail link takes 20 minutes to reach Centraal Station and costs $2.50. Tram #5 leaves Centraal Station and stops at South Station where you can board a train bound for the tarmac. Via this system your overall outlay is about $2 for 45 minutes of travel; trains leave every quarter hour.

To get you started ... from Centraal Station Square: take the subway or tram to Rembrandt's house, the Waag, and the Portuguese Synagogue; hop Tram #4 or #9 to the Rembrandtplein. Board Tram #1 or #2 nearby—crossing the Singell Flower Market first—at the foot of Nieuwezijds Voorburgwal for the Royal Palace, the Beguinage, the Leidseplein, and the Rijksmuseum, and Tram #2 or #5 for the Stedelijk Museum and the Concert Hall.

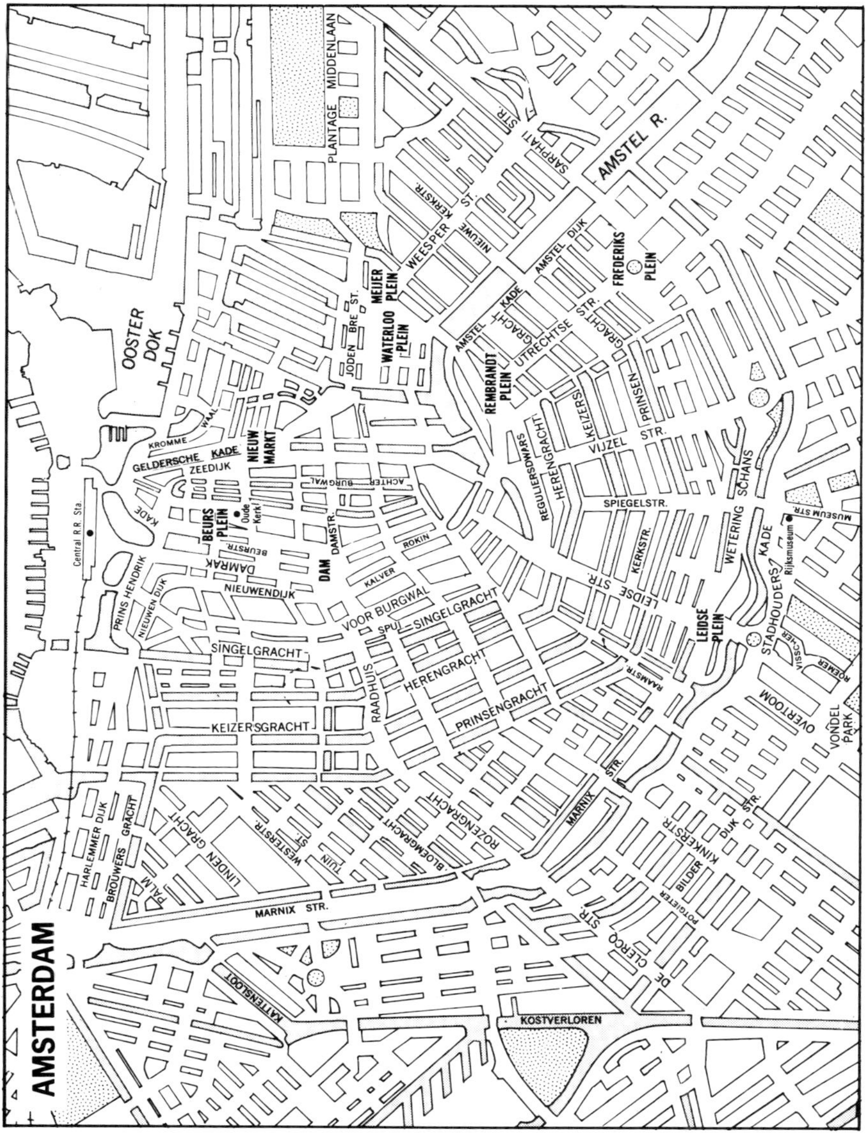
AMSTERDAM
PLANTAGE MIDDENLAAN
SARPHATI STR.
AMSTEL R.
NIEUWE KERKSTR.
WEESPER ST.
AMSTEL DIJK
FREDERIKS PLEIN
MEIJER PLEIN
WATERLOO PLEIN
JODEN BRE ST.
OOSTER DOK
AMSTEL KADE
REMBRANDT PLEIN
UTRECHTSE STR.
GRACHT
PRINSEN GRACHT
KEIZERS
VIJZEL STR.
HERENGRACHT
REGULIERSDWARS
SPIEGELSTR.
WETERING SCHANS
KADE
MUSEUM STR.
Rijksmuseum
KROMME WAAL
GELDERSCHE KADE
NIEUW MARKT
ZEEDIJK
ACHTER BURGWAL
KADE
BEURS PLEIN
Oude Kerk
Central R.R. Sta.
BEURSTR.
DAMRAK
DAMSTR.
ROKIN
DAM
KALVER
KERKSTR.
LEIDSE STR.
PRINS HENDRIK
NIEUWEN DIJK
NIEUWENDIJK
VOOR BURGWAL
SPUI
SINGELGRACHT
LEIDSE PLEIN
STADHOUDERS
VISSCHER
ROEMER
SINGELGRACHT
RAADHUIS
HERENGRACHT
RAAMSTR.
OVERTOOM
VONDEL PARK
PRINSENGRACHT
KEIZERSGRACHT
MARNIX STR.
HARLEMMER DIJK
BROUWERS GRACHT
LINDEN GRACHT
WESTERSTR.
TUIN ST.
BLOEMGRACHT
ROZENGRACHT
KINKERSTR.
BILDER DIJK STR.
PALM
MARNIX STR.
POTGIETER
DE CLERCQ STR.
KATTENSLOOT
KOSTVERLOREN

Capsule hints: (1) Dutch words on the platform signs are *van* (from), *over* (via), and *naar* (to). (2) Normal service ceases about midnight; your day pass or 2–3-day ticket is valid on special night bus

PEDAL POWER

This time it's not a bike but a *pedalo*—4 seats on floating pontoons. It's a novel way to explore Amsterdam's wonders. Rent them at **Vester Church**, in front of the *Rijksmuseum, Schreierstoren,* and *Central Station.* It costs about $8 per hour—cheap when divided 4 ways. Another agency is **Canal Bike**, with moorings at the *Leidsplein* (between the Marriott and American hotels), on *Prinsengracht* (near Anne Frank House), on *Keizersgracht*, and between the **Rijksmuseum** and **Heineken Brewery**. You receive a coupon for a free drink if you park for lunch or dinner at the Lido. It's a special treat to pedal your course around the canals at night when buildings and bridges glitter under illumination.

WHERE TO STAY

LEAST $

Adolesce • *Nieuwe Keizersgracht 26;* ☎ *6263959.* Claims an 80% North American occupancy in the 16–25 age group. Take subway or tram #9 from the Central Station to Waterlooplein; 18 doubles, all with basins; only 4 public showers for a full house of 120. Breakfast included in your overnight price; rising to a loftier bracket but certainly worth the outlay.

Seven Bridges • *Reguliersgracht 31;* ☎ *6231329.* Recently revamped. Quiet site where $40 per head buys bed and breakfast. Recommended.

Van Onna • *Bloemgracht 102;* ☎ *6265801.* Presents 9 rooms; singles at $25 and doubles at double that. Intimate breakfast room. #11 on the front and #16 on the rear are prime put-ups.

Abdelaziz • *Noorderbreek 46;* ☎ *29085321.* From the family name of Nouri and Colette who have only 2 large rooms and extra-large hearts. Their home is out at Landsmeer in Amsterdam North, about 15 minutes (bus #91) from Central Station in a residential district. The homespun mode of living may be a welcome change from hotel accommodation. Phone to see if there's space.

MORE $$

De Munck • *Achtergracht 3;* ☎ *6236283.* Blissfully quiet midtowner near major canals. Proud of a legacy that goes back to 1727. Some units with shower and W.C. Dual occupancy from $55. Cozy; excellent value.

Canal House • *Keizersgracht 148;* ☎ *6225182.* Offers 27 comfortable accommodations in a 17th-century structure with room for trios and quartets. Chandeliered lounge and garden-view breakfast area. Teahouse in the back, bar up front. Within walking distance of many important sites. Pleasant summer and winter and moving up steadily in quality.

Fantasia • *Nwe. Keizersgracht 16;* ☎ *6248858.* Another canal house. From 1733. Pleasant young couple own and run it. Very clean; all rooms with shower. Reliable and inviting.

Casa Cara • *Emmastraat 24;* ☎ *6623135.* Not far from Concert Hall in a quiet neighborhood. Mood and sparkle similar to Fantasia's. Most units with shower and W.C. Good investment.

Wiechmann • *Prinsengracht 328;* ☎ *6263321.* At the juncture of Prinsen and Looiers canals. Breakfast room and small bar; 63 pillows; a few front rooms with balcony or bay window overlooking *gracht*; some familysize and 18 double units with bath or shower (tubs are enormous); singles dry; no personal W.C.s. Locked at 11 p.m. but keys provided. Per person rates start at $75 for singles with basin and end in the $100 bracket for doubles, multiple rooms, and better solitary digs; breakfast included.

Parkzicht • *Roemer Visscherstr. 33 (near the Leidseplein);* ☎ *6181954.* Patio and dining lounge. Run by the friendly Cornelissen family. Unit #6 is my pick; #5, with its h-u-g-e bed, not far behind. Sumptuous breakfasts. Clean.

Van Gelder • *Damrak 34;* ☎ *6247879.* Modest oasis across the quay from sightseeing boats. Bar. Triples offer a spacious double and a single bed, antiquated twin sinks, a table, and cupboards. Location the prime drawing card.

Hotel de Lantaerne • *Leidsegracht 111-117;* ☎ *6232221.* On the corner of 2 waterways. Basement breakfastry. Newly outfitted accommodations. Now recommended.

Ronnie • *Raadhuisstr. 41b;* ☎ *6242821.* Here are 15 pads mounted over a stamp shop on a noisy thoroughfare. Breakfast nook. Clean. Huge windows a minus when they look down on the buses and trams, all of which connect with the railway station (a plus).

Ambassade • *Herengracht 341;* ☎ *6262333.* Comprises 5 former merchants' homes on a charming, quiet waterway. Public rooms with French period pieces. Room service; 105 beds. Very good and now in a higher category, but still an excellent value.

Hospice San Luchesio • *Waldeck Pyrmontlaan 9;* ☎ *6716861.* Established in 1961 by Third Order of St. Francis for Roman Catholic and Protestant clergymen, their families, and members of religious organizations. Tram #2 leads from center city to this clean, spartan, 25-unit refuge. Botanical garden, chapel. 2 toilets on each level, but a shower in every chamber. Figure $21 per pilgrim, including breakfast.

The Owl • *Roemer Visscherstr. 1-3;* ☎ *6189484.* 65 nests. Doubles close to $70.

Falcon Plaza • *Valkenburgerstraat 72;* ☎ *6382991.* Has been redone in a cozy way. Good value now. P.S.: If you enjoy Chinese food, it's near the gigantic floating restaurant called the Sea Palace. (You and 600 others can enjoy a big oriental repast at a reasonable outlay.)

Belga • ☎ *6249080.* Smart and smoothly run by the warm-hearted Vreugd family. Very clean. Some units with shower and W.C. Competitive rates.

Hotel Kap • *Den Texstraat 5B;* ☎ *6245908.* Excellent for families. Here's why: 5 4-bedded rooms; rates around $45 a pillow.

Roemer Visscher • *Roemer Visscherstraat 10 (plus a Vondelstr. annex for studio apartments);* ☎ *6125511.* With 24-hour coffee shop/restaurant. 50 rooms, most with Murphy beds that create almost a daytime living room. Telephones, bath, and TV. A few blocks from Museum Square.

EVEN MORE $$$

Die Port van Cleve • *Nieuwe Zijds Voorburgwal 178;* ☎ *6244860.* Occupies 5 floors above the restaurant of the same name in a convenient midcity location. Clean and bright. Topside singles offer pleasant views; other less inspiring small units down in the depths. Per-person rates now reaching into the skies, $75 or so. Excellent for seekers of Dutch-style charm.

Amsterdam Classic • *Gravenstraat 14-16;* ☎ *6233761.* If the tariffs for Die Port van Cleve are too hefty—and they've skyrocketed lately—just across the way is this fine typically Dutch house, formerly a distillery and very near Dam Square and the Royal Palace. All 33 rooms with shower and W.C., color TV, radio; spacious and clean; prices 30% below the above hotel. Very hospitable people, too.

Barbizon Centre • *Stadhouderskade 7-9 (opposite Leidseplein and almost in wings of Municipal Theater);* ☎ *6851351.* Bar, lounge, and restaurant with menus at about $18. Well over 100 rooms, all with bath. All its quiet chambers have been refurbished; I prefer those on the 6th floor. Several units feature studio beds convertible to triples. Heavily group-oriented. Highly recommended but getting expensive.

Museum Hotel • *Next to the National Gallery.* Attracts many students and tour groups. Simple, clean rooms; prices cheaper than the Barbizon at roughly $120 per duo. For reservations write **AMS Booking Center**, *P.C. Hooftstraat 2, P.O. Box 50564, 1007 DB.*

Delphi • *Apollolaan 101-105;* ☎ *6795152.* A 50-room delight Suburban-sited near Hilton. Inviting breakfast nook. Doubles $125 range; basin-equipped singles about $80 (at times disturbingly converted to twosomes when the crush is on). Very nice.

Zandbergen • *Willemsparkweg 205;* ☎ *6769321.* Located in Amsterdam's southern district. Each comfortable unit with bath and TV. Singles at $55 and tandems up to $80 with breakfast. Pleasant air of intimacy.

Wijnnobel • *Vossiusstraat 9;* ☎ *6622298.* Borders Vondelpark and Leidseplein. A family place. No private baths. Tariffs at $50 for a double room. I like its unpretentious manner and excellent location.

Schiller Karena • *Rembrandtplein 26/36;* ☎ *6231660.* One convenient block from Amstel River; 80 showers or baths per 200 occupants. Smallish but comfortable singles; more spacious doubles. Dining room renovated.

Casa 400 • *James Wattstr. 75 (near the Amstel Station);* ☎ *6651171.* 400 rooms with shower, toilet, and radio. Rates from $46-58 per head, including breakfast. Still a bargain in this bloated economy. Open June to Oct.

Marianne • *Nicolaas Maesstr. 107;* ☎ *6797972.* Priced to the point where it must compete with more luxurious hotels. Though friendly and nice, inconvenient location works against it. No restaurant. All units with W.C. and shower.

Mercure • *Noorderstr. 46;* ☎ *6220328.* A slick simulation of the 17th century. Super neat and super booked. Dining salon and bar. Ample amenities. In season, the individual traveler might score a billet. Recommended.

Toren • *Keizersgracht 164;* ☎ *6226033.* Short walk from Dam Square's Royal Palace and the Anne Frank House: 44 chambers in a 1618 structure. Small dining room with fireplace; cozy bar. I like back rooms facing the garden best. Recommended.

Hotel Aalborg • *Sarphatipark 106-108;* ☎ *6799057.* Near the colorful Albert Cuyp open-air market. Good shelter for 70. All rooms with bath. Singles about $60; doubles up to $70.

Hotel Interland • *Vossiusstr. 46 (across from Vondelpark);* ☎ *6622344.* The graciousness and hospitality of owner-manager Martin van der Zalm is impressive. Partially revised townhouse provides value and comfort. Quiet area, yet very central. Unfortunately, our latest information indicates Interland is slipping; we consequently list 3 substitutes as follows:

Asterisk • *Den Texstraat 14-16;* ☎ *6262396.* Most rooms with shower or bath; singles $40, doubles $60 or so.

De Gouden Kettingh • *Keizersgracht 268;* ☎ *6248287.* Cozy and clean; singles $55, doubles $55–75. Bar for guests.

Barbarcan • *Plantage Muidergracht 86;* ☎ *6236241.* Near the zoo; 34 beds. Only a few rooms with showers.

CAMPING

Produce your passport at any of three well-tended grounds and you'll be waved in without a club card.

The Amsterdamse Bos • *Kleine Noorddijk 1, Amstelveen;* ☎ *6416868.* 2-1/2 miles from Schiphol Airport.

Vliegenbos • *Meeuwenlaan 138, Amsterdam-Noord;* ☎ *6368855.* Drawing many young campers, across the River IJ. Each offers trailer space plus toilet and washing facilities; rates run about $2 per person, $1.50 per automobile, and on a similar level for other facilities.

Euro Camping "De Badhoeve" • *Uitdammerdijk 10, Amsterdam/Kinselmeer;* ☎ *02904-294.* Open all year with plenty of space for tents and trailers.

Gaasper • ☎ *020-6967326.* On the lake of the same name; the parkland surroundings are lovely. It's about 20 minutes from Amsterdam.

As for the vehicle in your travels, you might consider multinational **Continental Campers Inc.** (*1194 Walnut St., P.O. Box 306, Newton, MA 02161;* ☎ *964-5090*). Their variety is too vast to spread out on this printed campground, but the devout will find ample leads from this source. See beginning of this chapter ("Getting Around") for remarks on a similar outfit in Amsterdam.

SUGGESTIONS FOR STUDENTS

Don't waste time looking for the student quarter. All the 19,000-plus scholars at Amsterdam University (*Spui 21*) and the Free Reformed University (*De Boelelaan 1115*) live somewhere else in the city.

The Hans Brinker Hotel • *Kerkstraat 136;* ☎ *6220687.* Offers 256 kips in doubles, triples, quadropads, and dorms. The breakfast room looks out on a walled garden with tables and umbrellas in spring and summer. Barflies can sip and rap amid jukebox, piano, taped tunes, pinball machines, and at least 300 ice skates (minus runners) that dangle from the ceiling like sausages in a butcher shop. Most chambers share showers. Rates of $13.50–17 a head including breakfast, service, and taxes—a small price to pay for its decent personnel and high standards of sanitation.

OTHER CHOICES

Here are several bonus entries:

Eben Haezer • *Bloemstraat 179;* ☎ *6244717.* 230 beds, 6 baths, and dormitory accommodation for $7.

Sleep In • *Maritskade 28;* ☎ *6947444.* A 700-bed building (30 showers, luggage room, meals), stocked with adventuresome, fun-loving youngsters. Figure about $5 per night. (Sleeping bags, of course, are *de rigueur.*) Open all year.

Shelter • *Barndesteeg 21;* ☎ *6253230.* Just that; 188 barrack bunks for about $7.50.

RESTAURANTS

Mensa Atrium • *02 Achterburgwal 237.* Cheap and substantial. Closed Sat. and Sun.; lunch from $4, dinner about $5; 50¢ more for nonstudents.

COFFEE BAR

Witch #1 • *Eerste Bloemdwarsst. 1.* Located in the oldest part of town, serves toasted "sandwitches" and "Witchburgers" for the solids; java and jowling for the fluids. Curious off-beatery.

Otherwise, visiting collegians will find that their confreres head for the entertainment areas listed below: the Leidseplein, the Rembrandtsplein, and Thorbeckeplein.

DISCOUNTS, TRAVEL TIPS, GENERAL INFORMATION

The **NBBS** (*Dam 17;* ☎ *6237686*) can steer you to guilder-saving establishments and handle your booking and transportation needs.

The General Association of Amsterdam Students (*ASVA, Spinhuissteegl;* ☎ *6225771*) is also a fast-moving outfit for finding rooms at short notice and issuing reduced-rate theater tickets to collegiate ID-card bearers.

WHERE TO EAT

LEAST $

Heineken Hoek • *Smack on Leidseplein.* Interior recently refreshed. Outside tables, too. Daily special platters unbelievably low in cost, abundant in quantity, and reasonably high in quality. One of the better buys. Top recommendation for its category.

Dialoog • *Conveniently sited next to the Anne Frank House.* Offers a fresh ambience, crisp salads, a variety of sandwiches, soups, pastries, and (are you ready?) bagels and brownies. If the lowly sandwich can be rated imaginative, it reaches a kind of zenith here. Thanks to the Brooklyn readers who "discovered" it.

De Groene Lanteerne • *Haarlemmerst. 43;* ☎ *6241952.* Claims to be world's narrowest restaurant—not hard to believe at 3 strides wide. Cozy hearth. Superb menus at $22 but rising steadily. Many à la carte selections. Generous helpings. After dinner it might be a tight squeeze getting out!

Tong-Ah • *Korte Leidsedwarsstr. 119-121;* ☎ *6234829.* Oriental fare in a no-nonsense atmosphere. Nice staff and ample selection with classics such as savory chop suey and sweet-and-sour pork. Open noon-11 p.m. daily. You'll get your guilder's worth here.

De Orient • *van Baerlestraat 21;* ☎ *6734958.* One of the best of this city's many Indonesian restaurants. On Wednesday evenings it offers a buffet table for all-you-can-eat repasts. Attractive and well priced.

Oud Holland • *N. Z. Voorburgwal 105;* ☎ *6246848.* This restaurant will delight your senses with local comestibles for an amazingly low outlay. The name means "Old Holland" and that's what it purveys (along with superb dishes) in its finest sense. Cheaper than Dorrius (next category) and very close in quality.

Restaurant 't Heertje • *Herenstraat 16;* ☎ *6258127.* Reportedly offers fresh, solid Dutch fare. Economical "main meal" menu runs $10-17 per person, including 5 different vegetables, salad, and potatoes. À la carte appetizers also available. Sounds good. Open 5 to 11 p.m. Closed Wednesday.

Isola Bella • *Thorbeckeplein 7-9.* Minestrone confirmed that oil and water don't mix. Saltimbocca best of a poor and varied selection. Hope never to return to that restroom—ever.

Kow Loon • *Single 498.* Whips up so-called Oriental fare; 10% discount for students.

Golden Temple • *Utrechtsestraat 126.* Vegetarian garden where men in turbans offer delicious creations from behind the busy cafeteria counter.

Poentjak Pas • *Nassaukade 366;* ☎ *6180906.* Also produces the mysteries of Indonesia, at values that are exceptional. Any day but Mon.

CHAINS

McDonald's • *Muntplein 9, Albert Cuypstraat 75, and Nieuwendijk 212.* Inevitably on the scene. But why not take your fast food in Dutch style?

EET Cafes and **Sing-Singel** • *Prinsengracht 193 and Singel 101.* Trendsetters for good low-cost meals (15-25 guilders). Try Bak.

SNACKS

An unusual and entertaining adventure is to nibble your way through the colorful **Open Air Market** (*Waterlooplein*). Actually, if your appetite is up to it, you may easily put together the ingredients for a full lunch. Many of the cheeses are in such heavy local demand that they are never exported. Sausages come in all shapes and sizes. Each baker offers his own fresh-from-the-oven specialty. One extra treat is the Frisian Sugar Bread, with cinnamon and sugar cubes blended into its dough. Closed Sun. Another one—this for the kids—is called **David & Goliath**, in the Historical Museum complex of buildings in midtown. Although the food is tiptop, the main attraction is the 30-foot statue of Goliath glaring down at tots who don't finish their spinach. Great at any age.

HERRING

The nation is famous for these dainties, of course. You'll find a wonderful street stand for them at the junction of *Albert Cuyp and Ferdinand Bolstraat.* More formal fishing at **Haringhuis Jan Hendriks**, *Oude Doelenstraat 18.*

PASTRY

Pott *(Voetboogst 22-24)* is good and inexpensive. **Delice** *(on Leidsestraat)* is not one of my favorites. (Did you know, incidentally, that confectionery advertising is restricted on radio and TV here in the interest of healthier teeth? Sweets ads must appear after 8 p.m. and can't focus on anyone under 14 years of age. This in a country where pot-market quotations are readily available in public squares and grass is openly sold and used on Main St.)

Sandwich shops (*broodjeswinkels*) are common throughout the city. The fun is that you design your own combination by choosing from the voluminous arrays of cheeses, meats, fish, and other tidbits. Just point at this, that, this, this, and that. *Broodjes* are either eaten on the spot or on the run. **Broodje van Kootje** seems to have cornered the market simply by being located on every market corner. **Good** at *Leidseplein 20* and at *Spui 28*; excellent money-savers. **Upstairs**, *Grimburgwal 2*, is up a steep flight of you-guessed-it. Pancakes come with 20 choices of fruit-spread, including ginger, apricot, apple-and-raisin, pineapple, strawberry, and blueberry at $2-3 a pile. **Van Dobben**, *Korte Reguliersdwarsstr 5*, speeds you along with a bewildering array of sandwiches and a large selection of American soft drinks. Simple, inexpensive, and worth a try.

MORE $$

Die Port van Cleve • *Nieuwe Zijds Voorburgwal 178 (almost behind the Royal Palace); ☎ 6244860.* Bodega on one side, cafeteria-like chamber on the other. Traditional dining room upstairs. The specialty is beefsteak. Since it opened in 1870, these have been numbered in sequence; yours is likely to be tagged about 6,600,000—if it ends in triple zeros, all your wine is on the house.

Bistro le Provencal • *Weteringschans 91 (facing the Rijksmuseum); ☎ 6239619.* Features French food; 13 tables decked in candles and roses. Operative noon-2 p.m. and 5:30 p.m.-midnight. Shuttered Sun., Mon., and holidays. Highly praiseworthy.

Sea Palace • *Oosterdokskade 8; ☎ 6264777.* A huge floating pagoda near Central Station with space for 700 diners. I know that it sounds hopelessly touristic, but the value is good and the concept is special. Similar to the famous Hong Kong establishment which originated the jumbo idea.

Five Flies • *Spuistr. 294; ☎ 6248369.* Holland's most famous restaurant for almost a generation had been hit by Flit, and we could not recommend it for years to discerning travelers. Now, however, it seems to be a bit more lively. Beguiling decor and spectacular showmanship still snare the tourists.

Haesje Claes • *Spuistraat 275; ☎ 6249998.* Vaguely across the street from the Five Flies, but has a more authentic air about it. Friendly service; large servings of Dutch cookery; set menu of about $18 plus a vast selection of special dishes. Go more for meat than for seafood. The antique setting plus the warmth of the staff are truly winning.

TAVERNS

De Admiraal • *Herengracht 319; ☎ 6254334.* Has the trappings of an ancient distillery with storage bins for wine. Kegs and giant ceramic jugs surround the walls. Excellent beverages from a signature brewer (Gulpener); superb snacks to accompany your sipping or full meals. Here you'll find the atmosphere of Holland's best "brown cafes."

Bols Taverne-Creperie • *Rozengracht 106; ☎ 6245752.* A must for atmosphere, premeal nibbles, and liquid refreshment. Spirited fun since 1575. Try a cheese platter, or a sausage plate, or a crepe, or a steak, or anything—but do try something! Open Mon.-Sat. closed Sun.

Hans en Grietje • *27 Spiegelgracht; ☎ 6246782.* Not far from the Rijksmuseum and open since 1640. Brick and timber bar; beamed ceiling; amiable and lively crowd. A pair of excellent pubs that every true pub crawler should try.

Rum Runners • *Prinsengracht 277; ☎ 6274079.* As mentioned, Amsterdam has a taste for the exotic. This newcomer (as if you hadn't guessed from its unchaste title) offers a speakeasy character laced with Caribbean cocktails and cookery. Often there's live music, too. Very central location.

NIGHTLIFE

The metropolis swings with everything from Oak Rooms to Times Square tourist traps to neighborhood taverns to honky-tonks. Sip Scotch in expensive, dressy membership clubs, or drink beer while nervously clutching your wallet in one of the most wide-open bordello districts in Europe. Liberal statutes have served as a cordial invitation to drug users (the city provides a narcotics quality control service), sidewalk politicians, and free-love proponents, as well as the sexually uninhibited of all callings. With the tightening up of legal loopholes in England, France, and Germany, Holland has become a temporary haven for both the gay and the way-out sets.

You'll find two main centers of after-dark action: With notable exceptions, the more chichi establishments are clustered around the **Leidseplein**; the **Rembrandtplein** area is more earthy, particularly where it joins the **Thorbeckeplein**. One of the most popular straight fun spots is the zesty dance-and-drink circle of the **Marriott Hotel**. Disco and live music packs 'em in all evening on weekends; wide spread of tasty tidbits; splendid as a pop-in candidate or as a haunt for passing the entire evening. Highly recommended to merrymakers of any budgetary status.

NIGHTCLUBS AND DISCOTHEQUES

The Lido • *Max Euweplein 64, facing Leidseplein.* The brightest button in town tonight. It is a multimillion dollar effort that is full every session.

Juliana's • *Apollolaan 138-140.* For members, but for a nominal fee anyone can enter; very trendy it is.

Mazzo • *Rozengracht 114.* Has a split personality: excellent video shows ongoing except when live groups play.

BARS

Bamboo • *Lange Leidsedwarsstr. 6h just off the Leidseplein.* A melange of Zambesian masks, Surinamese mariachis, and a honky-tonk pianist. Swarms of happy visitors enjoy good fun at low prices.

Carrousel • *Thorbeckeplein 20.* Has 3 musicians, medium-high drinks, goofy dolls on the walls, and topless waitresses. (One wag remarked that they are really not topless, only partially dressed.) Worn surroundings but the modest show is usually amusing—when it's not too heavily narrated in vernacular Dutch.

Continental Bodega • *Lijnbaansgracht 245.* The best place for sherry and nibbles between noon and 8:30 p.m.; popular among those who have got to be seen on the scene.

Mulliner's • *Just down the gracht at #266.* The hospitality is genuine and the mood far better than the above.

Castell • Generally haunted by men.

Hoppe • *Spui 18.* Has a smoky, woody atmosphere that draws a collegiate crowd until 1 a.m. Congenial.

Le Maxim • *Leidsekruisstr. 35.* Has lost its star pianist; still it's got something. Very civilized; very rewarding; closed Mon.; otherwise open late.

Cafe Reynders • *Leidseplein 6.* Provides a smattering of Little Bohemia.

PUBS

The Britannia, *Korte Leidsedwarsstr. 24.* Affectionately known as "the Brit" to scores of English-speaking residents of the capital, is the friendliest and most authentic import from across the channel. If you don't strike up an immediate conversation at the bar, you can always start off by "taking chalks" at the dartboard. No-nonsense, standup mien; draft Heineken; British-type beer available. **The Old Bell**, *Rembrandtplein 46 and Van Diemenstr. 8*, in sharp contrast, is more pricey and more stuffy; the emphasis on table service. Dutch artists often air their tonsils in impromptu song.

DIXIELAND JAZZ

Joseph Lam's Jazzclub • *van Diemenstraat 242;* ☎ *6228086.* Thumps up classical Delta City notes on Fri., Sat., and Sun. It's a fun place.

WHAT TO SEE AND DO

The first thing any visitor should do is to take a boat ride (*rondvaart*) around the city—especially during the **Festival** when everything's ablaze with special illumination from sunset to midnight. For about $5 you can travel for an hour on the most interesting canals. Along *the Rokin, the Nassaukade,* and *the Damrak* you'll find 4 or 5 lines, all controlled by the municipality. The **Kooij fleet** is not my favorite; **Holland International** would be my 1st choice. Boats leave at regular intervals; all have glass roofs. You'll see everything from the Blue Bridge to the *Brouwersgracht* (Brewer's Canal—you see, you're learning Dutch already) to the red-light district.

AUTHOR'S OBSERVATION

Museums in Amsterdam were about to change their opening hours and days when we had to close this chapter–and there was the rumor they might be available on Mondays–so the wisest thing would be to check with the Amsterdam Tourist Office first.

Rembrandt's House • *Jodenbreestraat 4-6.* A block northeast of Waterlooplein is more than a repository of the artist's memorabilia. Within these 4 floors you will view at least 100 of the master's etchings, his etching press, and scores of his plates. Open from 10 a.m. to 5 p.m. and from 1 to 5 p.m. on Sun. and holidays; $2 admission to a great collection.

Amsterdam Historical Museum • *Kalverstr. 92.* Chock-full of international art treasures. Don't miss the statue of David and Goliath in the restaurant—great for the kiddies. Open daily 11 a.m.–5 p.m.

The Magnificent Rijksmuseum • *Stadhouderskade 42, at the north end of the Museumplein.* This museum should be a main target. Everyone goes to see the Rembrandts, but there are hundreds of other immortal works from the primitive to the premodern. Exquisite prints, perfect for framing, are on sale. The hours are 10 a.m.–5 p.m., except Sun. and holidays, when it doesn't open until 1 p.m.; closed Mon. There's also an inexpensive restaurant. Entrance fee about $3.

Rijksmuseum Vincent Van Gogh • *Paulus Potterstr. 7-11.* Devoted to the works of Van Gogh and his friends and contemporaries, Gauguin, Manet, and Toulouse-Lautrec. Open 10 a.m.–5 p.m. Tues.-Sat.; Sun. and holidays 1–5 p.m.; Mon. closed.

Stedelijk • *"Municipal Museum," Paulus Potterstr. 13.* Offers a modern art panoply from Picasso to Chagall, Monet, Miró, Degas, Cézanne, Braque, Mondrian, Matisse, and Toulouse-Lautrec. The most illustrious American painter represented: Willem de Kooning. Operative daily, 11 a.m.–5 p.m. Admission about $3.50.

INSIDER TIP

There is a new budget ticket for the museums; this covers 170 of them and is a good bargain. Ask at the VVV Office or at museums.

The 4-story Anne Frank House • *Prinsengracht 263.* The martyred child wrote her 2-year diary here before being discovered and killed by the Nazis. The house is in deep financial trouble. The Anne Frank Foundation, launched in 1960 to keep the house open as a permanent monument to the dangers of political extremism, has applied a support fee for admission of $3. We believe that this symbol of courage in the face of inhumanity is worth an hour of your time and as many loose guilders as you can contribute.

Madame Tussaud's • *Dam 20.* Fashioned in the image of the famous London wax museum. Open daily 10 a.m.–5:30 p.m

Royal Palace • Built as the town hall in 1662; perched on exactly 13,659 pilings; famous for van Helt Stockade's allegoric ceiling paintings; open weekdays June through Aug.; please check for exact hours.

Nieuwe Kerk • Late Gothic church with wooden vaults and uniquely clustered columns; open every day but the sabbath from 11 a.m. to 4 p.m. and on Sun. 1–3 p.m., but shuttered Jan. and Feb.

Oude Kerk • Consecrated in 1306; Iron Chapel that houses timeworn municipal documents; steeple carrillon, open Apr. through Sept., Mon.–Sat. 10 a.m.-4 p.m.

The Waag • Completed in 1488; merchant's weights-and-measures house until 1819; circular floor plan.

Portuguese Synagogue • Early 17th-century structure; a haven for refugees from the Inquisition.

The Stock Exchange • Built in 1903; the earliest employment of structural iron.

The Beguinage • *End of Begijnensteeg, off Kalverstraat.* A courtyard quadrangle of 17th- and 18th-century homes; known and enjoyed by far too few of us outlanders.

The Mint Tower • *Muntplein 3 blocks to the south.* The nation's coin presses were hidden in its octagonal base after the French captured Utrecht in 1672.

CONCERTS

The historic **Concertgebouw Orchestra** remains one of the world's best; it performs in the building to which it gives its name. Other halls include the new high-tech $73-million **Het Muziektheater** (Music Theater), for opera and ballet, the **Muzieklyceum**, the **Bachzaal**, and **Waake Kerk**; ensemble gatherings often occur in major churches, the **Stedelijk** and the **Amstelkring Museum**. The **Ysbreker** is the best for modern composers.

MOVIES

All foreign movies appear in original versions with Dutch subtitles. Because the Dutch are such avid film fans, the selection is wide. Nuisance: after perhaps every other reel, the house lights blink on and hordes head for the lobby. These several intermissions are declared by the canny managements as thirst and hunger quenchers; almost every theater has its own snack and soup bar. Final tip: While in Amsterdam, try to go to the fabulous **Tuschinski Cinema** (*Reguliersbreestr. 26*). It is something out of another era. We refuse to spoil the fun or your surprise by describing it here, but do make an effort to catch it!

MARKETS

There's a big one called **Waterlooplein** (but actually located on *Valkenburgerstraat*). The best day is Sat. The antique mart functions from May through Sept. at *Nieuwmarkt*. Others are **Albert Cuypstraat**, **Dapperstraat**, **Mosveld**, **Lindengracht**, **Vespuccistraat**, and **Plein '40-'45**.

Flowers toss their heads along the **Singel** (Mon.-Sat.), clothing on Mon. morning at the **Noordermarket/Westermarkt**, stamps and coins on Wed. and Sat. afternoons at **Nieuwezijds Voorburgwal**, and birds (Sat. morn) at **Noordermarkt/Westerstr**, Amstelveld.

PUBLICATIONS

The VVV produces a handy tip sheet, available in its several offices and at most hotels. There are guidebooks in the bookstores, kiosks, and market stands, plus U.S. and British newspapers for current events.

WHERE TO SHOP

Diamonds, Delftware, handicrafts, maritime gear, and bric-a-brac are your best buys. Top shopping streets are P.C. Hooftstraat, van Baerlestraat, and Rokin. Kalverstraat and Leidsestraat have deteriorated alarmingly. The famous **Amstelveen Shopping Center** is 20 minutes from Schiphol Airport.

DELFTWARE, RUSSIAN LACQUERED BOXES, • EUROPEAN CRYSTAL, AND CHINA

Both **Focke & Meltzer**, *P.C. Hooftstraat*, *Okura Hotel*, and **Hogendoorn & Kaufman**, *Rokin 124*, are purveyors for collectors of special pieces while run-of-the-factory products at popular prices can be seen at **Delftware Old-New "Renasciamento"** and **Galleria d'Arte** (*Prinsengracht 170*). The latter has as many items as letters in its name.

DIAMONDS

They are a terrific bargain. Unless you're an expert, however, do your buying only at **Bonebakker** (*Rokin 88-90*), an excellent and reliable old-line house to be trusted. All sizes, cuts, and prices; polishing of stones done on the premises; prices strictly standard. Absolute tops.

HANDICRAFTS

Galerie-Atelier Voetboog, (*Voetboogstraat 16, off the Spui*) is a joint effort of more than 40 artists. Each day several are on hand so that visitors may watch them at work. Hand-painted silk, jewelry, drawings, ceramics, and textiles abound; open Tues.–Sat. 11 a.m.–5 p.m.

MARITIME GEAR

Andries de Jong Ship Shop, (*Muntplein 8*) is an outstanding chandler, especially noted for its lamps, maps, and useful seagoers' fare.

MARKET

Don't forget the **Waterlooplein Flea Market**, near the new semicircular Music Theater, Mon.–Sat. 10 a.m.–4 p.m.

AUTHOR'S OBSERVATION

Departing passengers at Schiphol Airport with destinations outside the Benelux countries may save on various luxury items (liquors, tobacco, perfumes, binoculars, tape recorders, watches, toys, and computers) at its Tax Free Shopping Center, largest and with the most competitive prices on the Continent. One recurring problem is that stocks are sometimes depleted.

GOUDA

It's pronounced "How-da," not "Good-da"; most travelers find it a convenient follow-up to Aalsmeer. A lovely plaza with contrasting red-and-white shutters and golden trim surrounds the Town Hall. **The cheese market** functions here on Thursday mornings from late June through Aug.; it also displays antique handicrafts. Then push on to either **Woerden** or **Oudewater**. The tiny canalside path that ambles through the latter village and moseys on to Utrecht provides a charming sample of the rural Netherlands. Utrecht has her diversions, but we prefer to skim along east to **Soesterberg** for lunch, before viewing the **Royal Palace of Princess Juliana and Prince Bernhard** at nearby **Soestdijk**.

HAARLEM

Haarlem's attractions number chiefly three. First, the **Frans Hals Museum**, which not only shows his portraits of the militia and governors, but those of his contemporaries, and scores of 17th- and 18th-century artifacts. Open 11 a.m.–5 p.m. and Sun. and bank holidays 1–5 p.m. Then take a 10-minute walk through the district flanking **Nieuw Heiligland**, a street in the oldest part of town. A working and socializing byway for the area's craftsmen, it offers visitors a rare peek at another side of Holland. Nearby you'll find the fabulous **Roozen Nursery** which from April through most of May is a glorious show of tulips. Finally, there's **Zandvoort beach**—a wide bathing strand with its own casino. It's so close to Amsterdam that you'll probably not wish to overnight here.

THE HAGUE

The Dutch seat of government, considerably smaller than Amsterdam or Rotterdam, offers many excellent museums and many square miles of beautiful ancient Dutch architecture. One building which decidedly is not antique is the **Omniversum**, the world's first public space theater, with a dome 76-feet in diameter, the globe's largest sound system, and enough computers and projectors to send you off into a time warp. Astronomers have nicknamed it the planetarium's planetarium. At the Spui, there is a fine concert and ballet hall in contemporary style. Then, near to The Hague, you have the lively beach resort of **Scheveningen** with its casino at the Kurhaus (entry 9 Fl.) and a fairy-tale wonder for kids and adults alike: **Madurodam**, the most amazing miniature city in existence. This modernday Lilliput, condensed into approximately 4 acres, employing 2-1/4 miles of railway track and illuminated by 50,000 lights, is a complete community of castles, churches, homes, shops, docks, airport—everything imaginable. Its thousands of details are a perfect 1/25th of their normal scale. Almost 1 million visitors promenade its 2-mile circuit annually. Open from late March until Jan. with longer hours in summer months (9 a.m.–11 p.m.); 11 Fl. for adults, 9 Fl. for 65 and older, 6 Fl. for 2–12-year-olds. The Hague is once again the court capital now that Queen Beatrix makes her residence in the **Palace Huis ten Bosch**; **Noordeinde Palace** is now used for ceremonies and as a working palace for Queen Beatrix. If you wish to sample Eurasia, then go in spring to the **Pasar Malam Besar**, eleven days and nights of exotic festivities honoring the food, dance, music and aromas of the nation's eastern colonies. It draws more than 100,000 admirers, usually in late June.

ROTTERDAM

The mighty port, slightly more than an hour from Amsterdam, is proud of its glorious river views and its excellent harbor installations. Since Amsterdam probably will be your base—and a very rewarding one at that—you can easily visit this city on a day excursion. (Even nighttime concertgoers can be back shortly after midnight.) Try the VVV (**Rotterdam Tourist Office) Sightseeing Tour**, operated by historic tram and boats: departures at 1:15 p.m. from Centraal Station Apr.–Sept.; about $11 per person. It takes 2-1/4 hours and fans out from the VVV office; this is the best. Or take one of the well-known **Spido cruises of the fabulous docks**—1-1/4 hours for $6.50, with frequent departures in both summer and winter from the *Willemsplein Landing Stage*. **The Blijdorp Zoo**, perhaps the most modern in Europe, is wonderful for any age group. Then you might visit **Boymans' van Beuningen Museum** (very important collection, with Bosch, selected 17th-century landscape artists, a few Rembrandts and Van Goghs, and many modernists). **The Maritime Museum Prins Hendrik** records the lifeline of this salty metropolis. To cap this array, the **de Doelen concert hall** at the Kruiskade is fascinating for music lovers and audiophiles. It is the most massive on the Continent, offering some of the finest classical and experimental programs on the European scene each season.

SPAKENBURG

You'd be missing a paramount joy if an authentic old Dutch village were to be bypassed on your itinerary. But before offering any positive suggestions on this subject, here's a negative one: The once-classic tourist meccas of **Marken** and **Volendam** are not recommended in summer; in winter they're okay. The government has been laboring valiantly (but with little success) to root out the sham. Skip these traps and go to **Spakenburg** instead. Here's a hamlet where the folk dress and charm are far more genuine; only a 60-minute drive from Amsterdam. Or push beyond Zwolle to **Giethoorn** (called "The Dutch Venice") and **Staphorst**, which is straight from an old print. (Traditional dress has disappeared in Giethoorn but is still worn in Staphorst and nearby **Rouveen**.) These are even more alluring than Spakenburg, especially during the summer. In all, be sure to obtain prior permission if you wish to photograph any of the inhabitants. Hours when regional costumes are customarily worn are at church meeting times on Sunday: 9:30–10:30 a.m., 5–6 p.m., and 7–8 p.m. They are the real stuff, not hammy theatrical displays—but they are fading, sad to say. Already a few residents are practicing the cornball trickery that spoiled Marken and Volendam forever.

UTRECHT

This business beehive commands the geographic center; it's one of the oldest cities in the land. Well-maintained but commercial hotels; busy restaurants; up-to-the-minute facilities. A railway junction, a hub for religious life, science, communications, trade—some Dutch prefer it to its larger sisters. Americans often don't because many find it somber and dull. Famous industrial fair in March and September; among museums, the **Catharyne Convent**, the **Barrel Organ**, **the Central**, with ancient and modern works, and the **Railway exhibits** are the best-known of its approximately 15 candidates; in addition, 8 castle museums are within Utrecht Province. The cathedral is magnificent (you can climb to its peak); the **Vismarkt** (fish market) is so unusual no one should miss it. And speaking of sea denizens, there's a wonderful **Dolfinarium** northeast at coastal *Harderwijk*, where the lovely critters perform tricks; nearby is the 4-H clubber's dream at the **Flevohof** agricultural exhibit. **Avifauna** at *Alphen* is a delight for viewing swans, rare geese, wood ducks, plus other ornamental waterfowl that occupy a Rhineside park. For overnighting, in nearby *Zeist*, the **'tKerckebosch** (*Arnhemse Bovenweg 31*) is a hotel in a resurrected church. **Cafe de Paris** (*Drieharingenstraat 16, in the Old Town*) is now owned by one of the renowned **Fagel brothers**; try its superb (costly) Gallic entrecote. The canalside **Velasquez** (*Oude Gracht 115*) oozes with cellar-type charm. **Tantes Bistro** (Aunt's Bistro) at *Oude Gracht Werf 61*, is proud of its delicious eels stew specialty. Cozy ambience and moderate cost.

THE ZUIDERZEE

Finally, the most rewarding trip in Holland—one of the most stimulating and delightful holidays in the North—is the circuit of the Zuiderzee (the official name is now the "IJsselmeer") with a stopoff at the wild and beautiful island of *Texel*.

The Zuiderzee (Ysselmeer) is a gigantic salt lake that indents the center of Holland's coastline all the way down to Amsterdam. It has been blocked off from the ocean by a remarkable 18-1/2-mile dam that has permitted the full reclamation of hundreds of thousands of acres of tillable, valuable land.

If you're driving your own automobile, you can make this circle in one day of very hard driving. If you can spare 2 days, you must still skip Texel. But if you can stretch the journey to 3 or 4 days, you are in for a trip you'll never forget. Here's the real heart of Holland.

FOR MORE INFORMATION ON THE NETHERLANDS

The Netherlands Board of Tourism • *355 Lexington Ave. (21st Floor), New York, NY 10017, ☎ (212) 370-7360; • 90 New Montgomery St., Suite 305, San Francisco, CA 94106, ☎ (415) 543-6772; • 225 N. Michigan Ave., Suite 326, Chicago, IL, ☎ (312) 819-0300.*

INSIDER TIP

(1) Working with the NBT are more than 400 local offices called VVV, one bureau for every Dutch hamlet that can show the census takers a population of more than 2 human beings, 3 dogs, and 5 cows. They are wonderful!

INSIDER TIP

(2) Be sure to ask your travel agent about a national coupon system which includes admission to more than 350 galleries and exhibits nationwide. Last year it was called the Museum Pass, but at this writing they were changing the name and some details.

(3) In Amsterdam, VVV is located opposite the Central Station and at Leidsestraat 106. *In Rotterdam it's at* Coolsingel 67 *and another booth at the Central Station. The Hague is served by an office out at neighboring Scheveningen,* Gevers Deynootweg 126; *there is another booth at the Central Station.*

NORWAY

Stavanger

If you budget very carefully, you can wander all over one of the most unsung beauty spots of Europe—a country that is often forbidding to thrifty vacationers due to Scandinavia's reputation for wickedly high costs. Still, it can be seen and enjoyed when you know how to put extra stretch into your travel dollar. The Norse kingdom at the top of Europe is long and narrow, covering vast distances, a rangy land of fjords, mountains, forests—with waterfalls in summer and snowfalls in winter. It can embezzle the Midnight Sun, appropriate the Arctic Circle, and lay partial claim to nomadic Samis and their reindeer herds. Natural beauty is a birthright; there's a shortfall of sophistication; cities are good enough—good enough to work in, but even Norwegians get out into their mesmeric countryside whenever they can. In the capital, the citizens are so rural-minded that they have built parks throughout its midriff and ringed its periphery with forested ski trails where after office hours they exercise away the sedentary day life. While you are in the Norseland, try to keep moving. After a cheerful get-acquainted call, move away from Oslo, which is beguiling but not typical; go west to the salty shipping center of Bergen and up through the 50,000 salt-and-pepper islands that flank the majestic fjords; go north to Finnmark on the edge of Lapland, or if you have a car, to the Peer Gynt mountain country. Named for the mythical folk hero of Ibsen's poetic drama and Grieg's opera, this is one of the few remaining, lightly trodden, touristic areas of western Europe. It is so pristine in fact, that you can safely quench your thirst from any pool or stream.

One of the best bets for the first-timer is an exciting fjord tour by coach and steamer; stops are made at delightful hotels, and in addition to fantastic scenery, there are all sorts of fascinating special events the ordinary traveler misses—including a mush out to the edge of Norway's largest ice-field, lunch at an ancient farm, and much more. Some of the globe's most alluring seaside and countryside are waiting for you.

TIPS ON NORWAY

FOOD

Norwegian food follows the Nordic tradition of color, variety, and delicacy. Although the accent is on fish—hundreds of preparations—that doesn't mean they don't know a good beefsteak when they see one. They usually avoid fish on Mondays. By law, nets cannot be put out on Sunday; the Saturday catch, while preserved perfectly on ice, meets with singular unenthusiasm. If you are on a budget there are scores of street stands for fish bait, sausages, pastries, and true Nordic snack fare of ultrahigh standards. (The minimum requirement for *wursts*—called *polsers* here—as one example, is much greater than U.S. norms for fast foods.) And certainly you won't have to fall back on the proliferating pizza joints for an inexpensive filler when you feel hungry.

Besides the savory ocean harvests, Norwegian specialties are *ptarmigan* (mountain grouse), *flatbread* (crispy, wafer-thin crackers), *multer* (delicious mountain cloudberry jam), *tyttebaer* (a cranberry with a difference, called the "lingon" berry in Sweden), cheeses of the Port du Salut type (not the goat's milk cheese that tastes like caramel), or Jarlsberg, *kreps* (small, freshwater crayfish), reindeer steak (dark red, fine flavor), whale steak (ugh!), and the ubiquitous and pleasant Norwegian "sandwich" that will haunt you wherever you go. The historic luxury breakfast consists of smoked salmon, herring

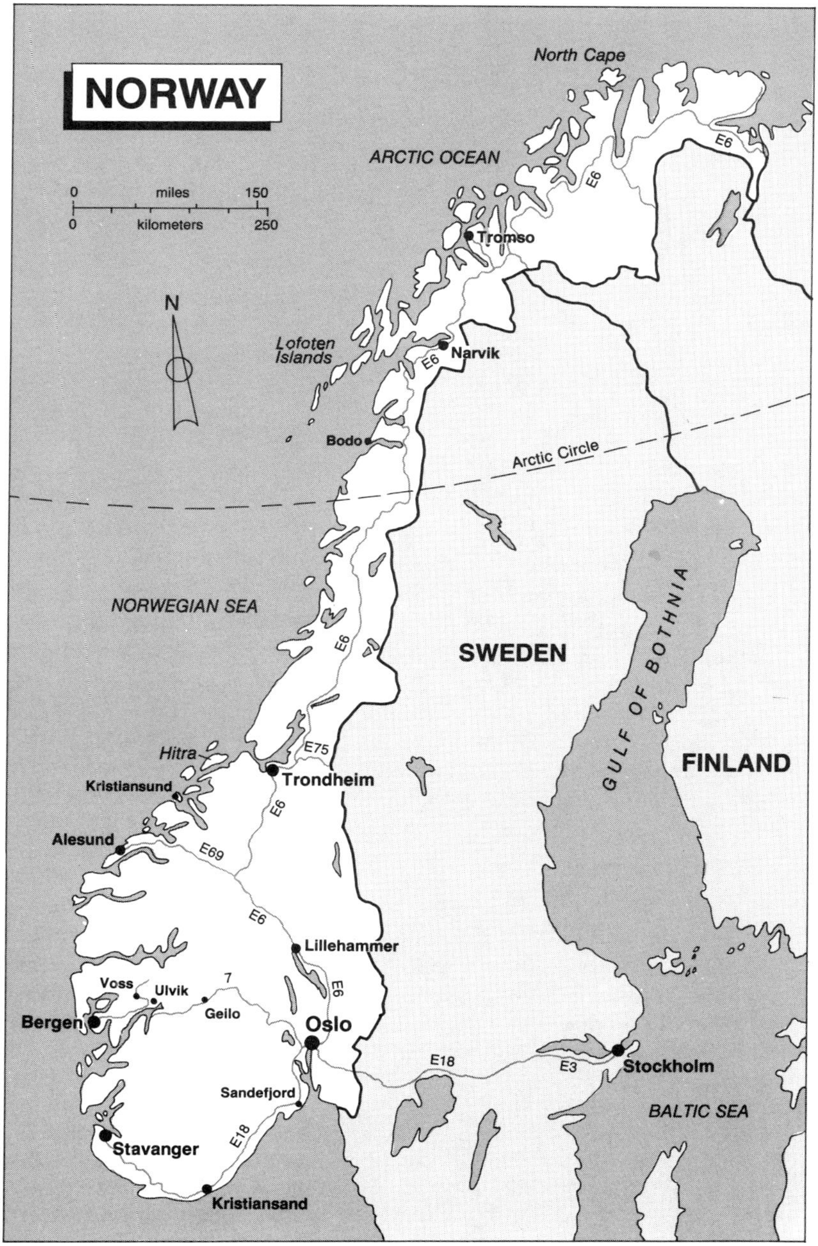
NORWAY
North Cape
ARCTIC OCEAN
0 miles 150
0 kilometers 250
E6
Tromso
N
Lofoten Islands
Narvik
Bodo
Arctic Circle
NORWEGIAN SEA
SWEDEN
GULF OF BOTHNIA
FINLAND
Hitra
E75
Trondheim
Kristiansund
Alesund
E69
Lillehammer
Voss
Ulvik
7
Geilo
Bergen
Oslo
E18
E3
Stockholm
Sandefjord
BALTIC SEA
Stavanger
Kristiansand

with onions, cheeses, and other hardy delicacies served open-style—with a boiled egg and coffee on the side.

Norway is a coffee-drinking nation; the tea is mediocre. It is also the biggest cheese-eating country; per capita, each Oslo citizen (man, woman, and infant in arms) packs away nearly 25 lbs. per year.

In the flossy restaurants, luxury meals are expensive in the extreme.

DRINKS

There's a governmental beverage control in Norway called the *Vinmonopolet.* The law tells you how, where, when, and what you can swallow; and also as in the U.S., the regulations contradict themselves backward, forward, and sideways. Here are the rules concerning drinking in public places: Beer can be served all day and all evening but only from noon on Sundays. Naturally, many restaurants are licensed for beer and wine, while larger places generally serve all beverages. Spirits may be dispensed from 3 p.m. to midnight or 1 a.m. None may be purchased on Sundays or on May 17 (Constitution Day). Tourist hotels begin pouring at 1 p.m.

The prices are intoxicating. A 4-centiliter portion (far from generous) of normal Scotch, bourbon, vodka, or gin runs around $5 to $6.50; aquavit is slightly less; long drinks pour from $7.50 to $8.50; cognacs and other liqueurs run $5. As for wines, avoid them. Inferior Bordeaux commands up to $35 per bottle in hotels or restaurants, ranging up to $65 for better grades; Burgundies go for $40 to $80 and champagnes from $45 to $75. Sherry, such as Tio Pepe or La Ina, costs about $6 a glass. It's a great place for anyone who's on the wagon. If you must have your tipple, buy your own bottle at one of the government stores (Vinmonopolet), which operate weekdays 10 a.m.-5 p.m. (an hour later on Thurs.); Saturday opening is at 9 a.m., closing at 1 p.m. Buy all liquor for weekend consumption or for any day-off-the-beaten-track excursions before leaving Oslo; otherwise you're liable to be limited to beer and wine.

Linje Akevit or aquavit is the pride of Norwegian distillers. *Linje* means *line*, in this case the Equator, and every bottle of this brand has been mellowed on a ship that has crossed the Equator. The action of the sea supposedly softens and matures the aquavit. Always drink it with beer; this "keeps away the red nose," Norwegians say. (The Danes say the opposite!) A brand called Brennevin 60% has one of the highest proofs of any spirit in the world—120. (The strongest proprietary Scotch, in comparison, is 86.)

The most popular local liqueur is St. Halvard, a Benedictine type worth trying. Claret is the national favorite in wines, and the stocks are now very good. Beer drinkers should order the export (or "gold") type; the lighter ones are thin.

Soft drinks? You'll find Pepsi and Coke going strong almost everywhere, at $1.20 in the shops (per bottle) or $2.20 in restaurants. *Solo* is the local effervescent orange drink; *Sino* is its nonfizz tablemate; both are nearly the same in price, as are the popular lemon beverages.

GETTING AROUND

TRAINS

Trains are very good in either first or second class, and fares are low. You can ride 796 miles straight up to Bodo in the Land of the Midnight Sun. There's excellent service, streamlined cars, clean compartments, polite conductors; diner service is gradually being replaced by cafeteria cars—which is good news for the budgeteer.

MOTORING

Fast overnight passenger-auto ferry service between Oslo and Kiel (Germany) is available. The 19-hour voyage cuts 3 hours from the fastest train ride and at least 1 day from the best driving time. Accommodations include deluxe suites, single cabins, double cabins (many of which are more attractive than various transatlantic offerings), a sleeperette section with airplane-type reclining seats and appealing lounges and public quarters. Immaculately clean; good cuisine; dancing in summer; tempting bargains aboard in tax-free shopping. Year-round service with daily sailings (both directions) from May through Sept. and 2 in winter. There's also a link between Oslo and Copenhagen. The lovely, fast *Queen of Scandinavia*, another car-carrying vessel with excellent modern amenities, has been joined by guess who: the *King of Scandinavia*. Drive-on, drive-off ferries also operate across the North Sea between Newcastle and Bergen-Stavanger, and connecting Kristiansand, Amsterdam, and Harwich. For further information, communicate with your travel agent, the **Bergen Steamship Co., Inc.**, *505 Fifth Ave., NY 10017*, the **Fred Olsen Steamship Co.** *of Kristiansand*, or the **Color Line**, *P.O. Box 1422 Vika 0115, Oslo.*

Driving in Norway has its rigors. The roads per se are safe, but their extreme narrowness and their curves between the mountains and the fjords constitute a prickly mental hazard. Since much of the time your maximum average is 35 mph, Norwegian official sources consider 175 miles a stiff haul for one day. Incidentally, in summer or winter, in daylight or at night, headlights are compulsory. (Nordics joke that a Volvo is born with its lights on and dies when they go out.)

CAR HIRE

Anyone under 21 should ask the people at **Scandinavia** (*Fredensborgveien 33;* ☎ *202150*) about their terms for younger drivers. **Hertz** and **Avis** are also in town.

SPORTS

HIKING AND CLIMBING

The **Norwegian Mountain Touring Association**, believed to be the oldest hiking club in the world, owns 50 huts, and shares 150 others with affiliated organizations through the 3 principal centers for piton and alpenstock experts: **Jotunheimen** (the highest), the **Rondane** area, and the **Hardanger Plateau**. The first is for summer, the second for families; both are a 4-1/2-hour train ride northwest of Oslo; the third is favored for winter.

Another important nexus: the **Norwegian Alpine Center**, *Hemsedal*, is 120 miles from the capital. Elementary and advanced courses are offered in rock-climbing and rescue. For further information, contact the Norwegian Tourist Board, *655 Third Ave., New York, NY 10017.*

WINTER SPORTS

If you like competition, try to catch the 15-kilometer **International Monolith Ski Race**, *Frogner Park* (January) or the **Holmenkollen Ski Festival** (March), one of the most thrilling in the nation.

Skiing alone? Try **Norefjell**, 3 hours by bus from the University; it has a hotel, cottages, and a scattering of guesthouses; plenty of rental equipment. There are 14 centers not too far from the capital. For further details, phone the **Norway Information Center** at ☎ *830050* or the Skiing Association at ☎ *141690.*

BOATING

Ask (for Oslo waters) at the above-mentioned Norway Information Center.

ARCHERY TO WHALEBONE WHITTLING

Contact the above-mentioned Norwegian Tourist Board.

SHOPPING

In most cities, hours are from 9 a.m.–5 p.m. (summer hours can be shorter); 9 a.m.–1 or 2 p.m. on Sat. Norway closes tight the week before Easter, for a 5-day national vacation—plus at least 7 other official holidays.

THINGS NOT TO BUY

Very little. Textiles still seem 2nd line, in general; leather goods are expensive and not worth it. Stick to the arts and crafts, and you won't go wrong.

A useful tax-free system affords you the opportunity of getting an immediate rebate of the 16.67% VAT (net 10%-15% after service charge deductions) by cashing the Tax-free Shopping Cheque merchants provide. (Plan to spend a minimum of $300 NOK per store to be eligible.) Look for the red, white, and blue tax-free sticker in the shop window; always have your passport with you; do not use the goods while in the country; export them within a month; have them ready to show at all departure points (airports, ships, ports, borders) along with the properly filled-in documentation and the money is yours! This serves for credit card purchases as well.

WHERE TO GO

AALESUND

If you can squeeze the time, board one of the low-cost Coastal Expressway steamers from Bergen—there are 3 excellent ones. Run along the country's stunning West Coast among several thousand greystone skerries, darting into and out of the Gulf Stream nearly all the way up to the top of the world. Aalesund will be one of your handsomer ports of call on the voyage. It rests on an assemblage of camelback islands. When your ship pauses in its lee for the usual 2-1/2-hour docking, make an excursion to the summit of **Aksla Mountain**. Though only 625 feet high, the restaurant at its penthouse level affords a breathtaking view of the strikingly intricate waterways below.

BERGEN

This salty capital of the West Coast is more than 900 years old. Not only do the cruises begin here for the North Cape but larger liners chug over to the British Isles from her deep-fjord port. It is a great springboard for seeing the West—a 1-day excursion to Flam, the famous Troll Tours, or the 2-day run to Oslo are highly rewarding sidelights. The Bergen basin swings after sunset—whether Sol sets at midnight or 3 p.m. The medieval charm will captivate you by day and enchant you by night. There's a magnificent panorama from the funicular to **Floyen**. There's a fish market where you can select your dinner while it is still swimming; there are turreted bastions, crazy little houses built before 1800, the **Bryggen Archaeological Museum**, the **Edvard Grieg shrine** at his home called Troldhaugen, **Grieg Concert Hall**, the **Aquarium**, the intriguing **Maritime Museum**, good restaurants, and good comfort. Petroleum, trade, and harbor activities keep most of the people busy; don't believe the legend that "it always rains in Bergen"—it is only 99% true, and then only in 10- or 15-minute spells.

For aid in securing more data as well as accommodations in this city, go to the **Information Office of Tourism** on Torgalmenningen Square. It can recommend shelter for roughly 150NK-250 per night per person. You can expect significantly lower rates in the summer and even better bargains when you ask for "Last Minute Prices." Other suggestions include the **Hotel Park Pension** (*Harald Harfagresgt. 35;* ☎ *320960*), which is quiet and pleasant; the **Toms** (*C. Sundtsgate 52;* ☎ *232335*), which offers substantial rewards for $65 per single and $90 for two. The **Neptun** (*Walckendorffsgate 8;* ☎ *901000*) is considerably more costly but very good indeed. The 40-room **Augustin** (*C. Sundtsgt. 24;* ☎ *230025*) is central, fresh, and cheerful; we like it for the price. The **SAS Royal** (for business travelers; ☎ *543000*) is priced up in the SAS skies, but remember to ask for a cut rate if you are here in summer. Tip-top quality.

For dining, you may want to sample the **Bryggen Tracteursted**, located in an artisans' enclave that dates back to 1702. The area itself is fascinating for those who are interested in crafts. Restaurant upstairs (at **Fiskekroken** you can select your own fish at the neighboring market and hand it to the chef to prepare) or pub downstairs serving beer, wine, sandwiches, and waffles. The up-one-flight **Bryggeloftet** (*Bryggen 6*) is a popular harbor stop that has remained intact since it opened its doors in 1909.

Suspended ship models; tapestried chairs and banquettes; cozy, relaxed, and smoky in an agreeable way. Also good are **Jeppes Kro** (*Vagsalmenning 6*), which resides on four floors of a harborside building, and the brightly refreshed shopping and dining spots located at the bus station. (You'll even discover a Chinese fast foodery here!) If you want to pick up your own delicatessen and create your own picnic, do your shopping at the food boutique of **Sundt's** department store.

For shopping we like **Prydkunst EB Hjertholm** (*Olav Kyrresgt 7*) for imaginative creations and **Bergens Glasmagasin** (*Olav Kyrresgate 9*) for its highly transparent talents—in glass, of course.

Best shopping areas include Strandgaten, Torgalmenningen, Marken and the above-mentioned Bryggen, especially noted for its artisan workshops. Opening hours are Mon., Tues., Wed. and Fri., 9 a.m. to 4:30 p.m., Thurs. 9 a.m.–7 p.m. and Sat. 9 a.m.–2 p.m. The two big shopping centers—**Galleriet** (*Torgalmenningen*) and **Bystasjonen** (*main Bus Station*) remain open weekdays until 8 p.m. and Sat. until 4 p.m.

Bergen is a colorful seaport well worth the time to enjoy.

FREDRIKSTAD

Here's a tale of two cities—the new town and the ancient fortress-hamlet now devoted to the **Plus works**, an art and artisan colony that in itself is worth a jaunt to Scandinavia. For the more curious who are not satisfied by window shopping, the interesting ateliers within these four-century-old walls are open to the public.

FROGNERSETEREN

A tramway scrambles 1460 feet up to the brow of this mountain aerie. At sea level the grand spread of the **Oslofjord** provides a hypnotizing spectacle of maritime activity and the mortals who creep along its shores. Since it is only 30 minutes by train from midtown Oslo, this perch provides a magnificent observation platform for rushing through your film allowance a week ahead of schedule. You can get snacks at either of 2 restaurants here, and walk mountainside paths.

GAMVIK

What! Never heard of it? It's pretty remote; east of the Northcape and 4-1/2 hours' flying time from Oslo. **The Hotel 71°** is the most northerly kip in the world, with 32 beds, ample comfort, and the Arctic Ocean at your doorstep. We'd advise reserving in advance.

GEILO

On the main railway line halfway between Oslo and Bergen, it offers one main street, a handful of cozy hotels snuggling above the valley, excellent food on virtually every table, modest prices, and an intimate spirit of holiday frolic. The ski runs are not as long as they are in the midriff of the Continent, and the cold (yet super dry) air may be too brittle for all except the hardiest outdoor types. But, as a let's-get-away-from-the-rabble resort, this tiny gem is hard to beat. There's a unique beauty, too, that is different from the Alps—and a great part of the fun is skiing among the hospitable Scandinavians. The local Tourist Office can arrange accommodation or rental of any tack or gear for any sport—from hunting on foot, on skis, or aboard a gasoline-pepped Snow Cat, to pony trekking in the forests, to trout fishing at any of the 40 nearby lakes or streams. Both the Ro and the Geilo Pension provide excellent shelter. There's also a Youth Hostel in the vale. For a relaxing pause to refresh sagging spirits through unspoiled natural treasures, we'd be hard put to think of any better spot.

KRISTIANSAND and KRISTIANSUND

Kristiansand is on the lower tip of the nation; it is a thriving ferry point for Denmark, England, and Holland. Kristiansund straddles 3 islands with connecting bridges. This center is a fishing port and the striking-out point for climbing tours to the *Nordmore Alps*. Lovely to look at, it does not offer much action except in gelid February when vocalists warm up their adenoids for the annual Opera Festival.

NOREFJELL

This popular target is about 3 hours from Oslo by bus. In winter the ski powder mounts up to 5400 feet—on the peak, of course. In summer it is an environmentalist's dream come true. Nature buffs adore it anytime. And, since the ride is so scenic, getting there is at least half the fun, too.

OSLO

Here is Scandinavia's most expansive and oldest capital—crowding a thousand years and still spry, fresh faced, and engaging. Over half of its 175 square miles is woodland, encompassing a mountain that was the nucleus of a Winter Olympics. In latitude it is on a par with Seward, Alaska and Canada's Hudson Bay, but its temperatures mimic those of Massachusetts.

Situated on gentle slopes on the Oslo Fjord (linking the town to the sea), the city's 1/2 million inhabitants enjoy their mostly modern and largely unpolluted environs from a setting that is almost suburban. There's a feeling that it is a village that is still growing, but in a casual, easygoing way; there's a distinct maritime flavor throughout. Moreover, Oslo is perhaps the most underrated art center of modern Europe.

DIRECTORY

U.S. Embassy • *Drammensveien 18;* ☎ *22-448550.*

American Express • c/o Winge Travel Agency, *Karl Johansgate 33;* ☎ *22-419500.* This is the place to cash your checks.

Dry Cleaning and Pressing• Garderobe Service, *Grensen 8;* ☎ *22-429571*, also for shoe repair.

Laundromat • Majorstua Myntvaskeri, *Vibesgt. 15;* ☎ *22-694317.*

Barber • Continental Hotel Frisor, *Stortingsgaten 26;* ☎ *22-412282.*

Hairdresser • Grand Martins, in the Grand Hotel, *Karl Johansgate 31;* ☎ *22-421120.*

Suit Rental • Festantrekkbyrået, *Nygate 2B;* ☎ *22-171284.*

English-Speaking Doctor • Emergency treatment at Oslo Legevakt, *Storgaten 40;* ☎ *22-117070*, and Oslo Akutten, *Nedre Vollgt. 8;* ☎ *22-412440;* 8 a.m.–8 p.m. Mon.–Fri.; 9 a.m.–3 p.m. Sat.; noon–8 p.m. Sun..

English-Speaking Dentists • Dentists' "watch" from 8–11 p.m. weekdays, and from 11 a.m.–2 p.m. Sat.–Sun. and holidays, at Toyensenter, *Kolstadgt. 18;* ☎ *22-674846.*

Police • Criminal, *Gronlandsleiret 44;* ☎ *22-669050*, and ☎ *002* for emergency.

GETTING AROUND

BUSES AND STREETCARS

Apart from the rush-hour unpleasantness (8–9 a.m. and 3–5:30 p.m.), here's the nation's finest network.

Use Grensen and Stortingsgata as your starting points. Take the #2 tram to Frogner Park and the Vigeland Sculptures (dismount at Kirkeveien); take the underground (#s 3, 4, 5, or 6) to the Munch Museum. The #30 bus (or summer ferry from Radhusplassen) hauls in the full catch of nautical attractions at Bygdoy (Viking Ship Hall, Kon-Tiki Museum, etc.).

VIKING BIKING

Try a 6-hour tour every Wed. going to the lovely Nordmarka forests. They begin at Vestbanen, adjoining the Norway Information Center. The company is called **Den Rustne Eike**; ☎ *836359*. Deadline for registry is 6 p.m. on Tues. They also rent bicycles for general use.

WHERE TO STAY

LEAST $

The **Oslo Tourist Board** branch in the Central Railway Station open from 8 a.m. to 11 p.m. throughout the year) can best make arrangements for you in this category. Most dwelling space is in the 150NK-250 range (for singles and doubles respectively), plus a few kroner for the Lord Mayor's services.

Holtekilen Sommerhotell • *Michelets vei 55, Stabekk;* ☎ *533853.* Noncentral location. Converted schoolhouse lodgings. Singles at $40 and doubles $58. Friendly and worthy. Open June through late Aug.

West Side • *Observatoriegt 13;* ☎ *607255.* Offers breakfast as its only meal. Other attributes make up for the limited nutrients.

Linde • *Thomas Heftyesgt. 41;* ☎ *553782.* A pension lodging and a good one for budget hunters. Intimate and reliable.

YOUTH HOSTELS

Oslo Youth Hostel Haraldsheim (*Haraldsheimveien 4;* ☎ *22-155043*) is on a hillside; about $30 buys bed and breakfast; 280 pallets in several dorms; try to nail down your booking by mail if possible; staffers harried with reservation problems at peak periods. **Youth Hostel Pan** is also said to be good, but I have not seen it personally.

Other rural hostels reportedly also stretch your $25 to cover bed and board with no extras. Write to **Interscan** (*Kungsholmsgatan 10, Stockholm, Sweden*) for details on its money-saving booking plan that incorporates 21 Norwegian, 22 Danish, and 27 Swedish independent hotels. A "bonus passport" costs about $20 and entitles you to numerous bargains. Obtain this from **Scandinavian National Travel Office** in New York. At the same time ask about the Hotelcamp program, a federation of 38 establishments in southern Norway offering twin rates for about $35 per night. The snag is that reservations can only be made within 4 days of arrival.

MORE $$

At press time, singles in this group command roughly $45; doubles begin at $65.

St. Hanshaugens Hospits • *Geitmyrsveien 31 (across from the park);* ☎ *468428.* Warm, woolly bedroom decor in its 26 doubles and 7 singles. Recommended as a summer-only residence. Take Bus #17.

Hotell-Pensjon Hall • *Fritznersgt. 21;* ☎ *557726.* Okay, but little else. No private baths; singles $80, doubles start at $98.

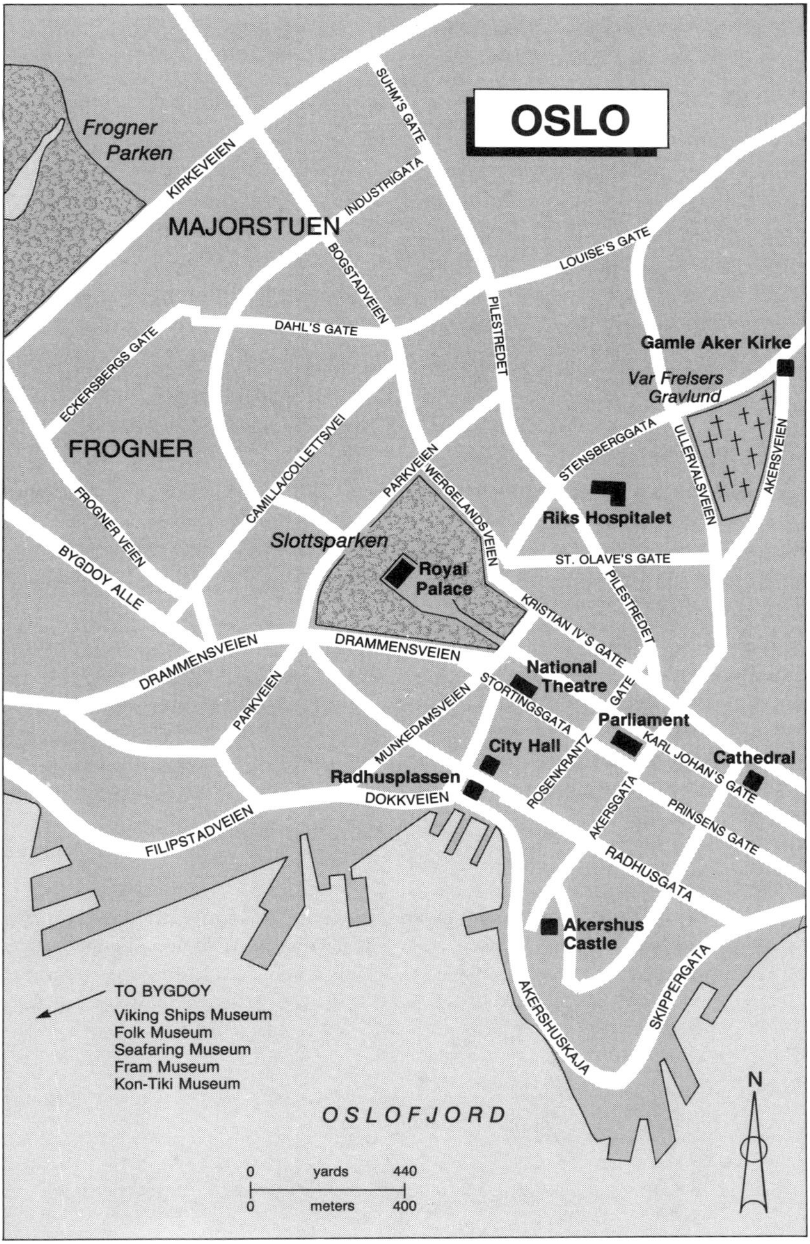
OSLO
Frogner Parken
KIRKEVEIEN
SUHM'S GATE
INDUSTRIGATA
MAJORSTUEN
BOGSTADVEIEN
LOUISE'S GATE
DAHL'S GATE
PILESTREDET
ECKERSBERGS GATE
Gamle Aker Kirke
Var Frelsers Gravlund
FROGNER
CAMILLA/COLLETTSVEI
PARKVEIEN
WERGELANDSVEIEN
STENSBERGGATA
ULLERVALSVEIEN
AKERSVEIEN
Riks Hospitalet
FROGNER VEIEN
BYGDOY ALLE
Slottsparken
Royal Palace
ST. OLAVE'S GATE
KRISTIAN IV'S GATE
PILESTREDET
DRAMMENSVEIEN
DRAMMENSVEIEN
National Theatre
STORTINGSGATA
GATE
PARKVEIEN
MUNKEDAMSVEIEN
Parliament
City Hall
ROSENKRANTZ
KARL JOHAN'S GATE
Cathedral
Radhusplassen
DOKKVEIEN
AKERSGATA
PRINSENS GATE
FILIPSTADVEIEN
RADHUSGATA
Akershus Castle
SKIPPERGATA
AKERSHUSKAJA
TO BYGDOY
Viking Ships Museum
Folk Museum
Seafaring Museum
Fram Museum
Kon-Tiki Museum
OSLOFJORD
N
0 yards 440
0 meters 400

City • *Skippergt. 19 (near Central Railway Station);* ☎ *422429.* Prices moving up here, too. Singles now $80-90; doubles $86-120.

EVEN MORE $$$

In this category you'll shell out from $110 for a single and from $145 for a double.

IMI • *Staffeldtsgt. 4 (about 100 yards from SAS bus terminal and palace grounds);* ☎ *205330.* Alcohol-free; well furnished. Homey throughout. Several suites available. Solo kips $100 in the median range; doubles $130 for starters. A good bet.

Cecil • *Stortingsgt 8;* ☎ *427000.* A handsome newcomer to the midtown area; 100 of its 112 units are what are termed "single/combi" rooms which stretch to accommodate two persons. While the price for a loner seems high, the twin rate in these is very reasonable. Atrium breakfast venue on the second floor; basement parking.

Rica Victoria • *Rosenkrantzgt. 13;* ☎ *429940.* A postmodern gem, also in the heart of the city, and again with atrium-style architecture. Warm interior, especially the restaurant and bar; comfortable bedrooms in traditional tones. Similar prices to Cecil.

Gabelshus • *Gabelsgate 16;* ☎ *22-552260.* Converted Norwegian manor about 5 minutes from center. Residential setting with tiptoe tranquillity. Elegant dining; 45 spacious rooms, all with bath or shower; about a dozen neat studio units. Favorites are #206 and #207 opening onto huge balconies. Singles from $135 and doubles from $180.

Saga • *Eilert Sundtsgt. 39;* ☎ *22-430485.* Quiet residential area between Palace Park and Frogner Park, minutes from the center by nearby tram; 35 totally refashioned rooms with either bath or shower; many doubles convert to triples; family units as well. Singles from $120 and doubles from $140.

Ritz Hotell • *Fr. Stangsgt. 3;* ☎ *22-443960.* Stately white townhouse adjoining Embassy Row, 5 minutes by tram from center. Lovely dining salon; 48 rooms, some with conventional twins, some with head-to-head convertibles, some with 3 beds; 19 showers or tubs; #213 an especially nice double. High on both aesthetics and value.

Pan Course (Youth Hostel) and Conference Center • *Sognsveien 218 (across from the Kringsja Station);* ☎ *22-187080.* Two gigantic edifices. Lounges; large restaurant, cafeteria, and bar; sauna. Bank, post office, hairdresser, supermarket, and souvenir shop in adjoining building. Lake swimming; 700 studio-type bedchambers with either private or shared bathrooms, all with showers. Units with private baths larger, with refrigerators and balconies.

Anker • *Storgt 55;* ☎ *22-114005.* Open year-round. Space for 55; all rooms with private bath. Singles $90 and doubles $120.

West • *Skovveien 15;* ☎ *22-554030.* Runs a fine show. All 44 units with shower. Breakfast only. Attractive lounge. Prices have increased to $120 per single and $145 per double.

Norum • *Bygdoy Alle 53;* ☎ *22-447990.* Especially geared for traveling families. About 10 minutes from center; tram and bus nearby; 58 large, old-fashioned units, 42 with bath or shower. Singles from $145 and doubles from $180.

Bondeheimen • *Rosenkrantz 8;* ☎ *22-429530.* Occupies 4th–6th floors of office building; cafeteria on ground floor. Immaculate, spacious accommodations; small beds; 32 singles ($130–140); 21 doubles ($140–150), also triple occupancy; most with shower and toilet.

Norrona • *Grensen 19;* ☎ *22-426400.* Worth the outlay in this expensive hotel economy; 13 convertible singles ($97); 19 doubles ($125); 7 private baths. Drinks dispenser on tap. Clean, well maintained. Like it.

Rica Triangel • *Holbergs plass 1 (directly behind the airport bus terminal);* ☎ *208855.* Alcohol-free. Overlooks square near Royal Palace. Most 53 expandable singles and 30 twins relatively spacious.

Gyldenlove • *Bogstadveien 20;* ☎ *22-601090.* Some units with bunk beds, some with frigo-bars. Steepish tariffs for middling value (singles $110 and doubles $140), but acceptable if others are full.

Helsfyr • *Stromsveien 108;* ☎ *22-657000.* Handiest for motorists; 15 minutes north of town; first-class house with full bath count, bar, restaurant, and stube. Singles $145 and doubles at $185.

Rica Oslofjord • *Sandviksveien 184;* ☎ *67-545700.* At the waterside closer to Fornebu Airport than to town. Facilities are excellent if you prefer this outskirting location.

CAMPING

The **Bogstad** site, 15 minutes from the center (☎ *22-507680*), is a fine example of the tent cities kept by the Norwegian automobile clubs. Secluded setting in a pleasant wood; 20 chalets (without shower and W.C.) for 4 or 5 usually booked long in advance; 16 new chalets with shower and toilet, plus TV, but without linens; space for perhaps 1000 tents with plotside parking; cozy canteen adjoining the reception center; washrooms, showers, ironing areas, and service stations; open all year. **Ekeberg** camp (about 10 minutes from downtown on a hill overlooking the capital; ☎ *22-198568*). is another comfortable choice. Near a riding school, domestic animal zoo, kiddie pool, and sports fields, all concentrated within a "nature park."

Throughout this land, you are likely to see signs for "Hytter," referring to sites for huts, cabins, tents, or trailers. Huts usually offer 4 bunk beds (generally no linen or sleeping bags), a table, and perhaps some chairs; shower and sauna facilities often in the center of the compound. Cabin rental is usually a superb value.

SUGGESTIONS FOR STUDENTS

The University of Oslo's campus, at Blindern, 10 minutes out, is active year-round; the International Summer School usually fills it during high season. Board the Sognsvannsbanen tram (#3); it drops you within seconds of its center.

This sparkling suburban complex buzzes with a grill and a cafeteria, a drugstore, a TV lounge, a bookshop, a barber and hairdressing salon, a grocery shop, a bank, a post office, and a student travel bureau.

OVERNIGHTS

Write to the **Univers Reiser A.S.** (*University Center, Blindern, Oslo, Norway*) at your earliest opportunity. If you just plain *arrive*, however, call them at ☎ *453200* between 8:30 a.m. and 4 p.m.—and cross your fingers. These people can also arrange low-cost excursions on planes, trains, and ships. Courteous service; exhaustive supply of timetables and travel lore; 100% dependable.

DINING

University City Grill and Cafeteria (*in Blindern, opposite the Administration Building*) requires that you show your student ID card. If your credentials are absent—or out of date—a school sweatshirt or varsity jacket might get you in at peak periods. Inexpensive hot meals; closing at 5:30 p.m. each day. One of the best of its type in Europe.

DISCOUNTS

The **Norsk Students' Union** (*Lokkeveien 7;* ☎ *556020/21*) will check your ID card, give you facts, figures, food chits, and information on price reductions in various night spots.

Bargains? Be sure to consult the Blindern bulletin boards of the **Norwegian Students' Association**.

AFTER DARK

At **Alaska** (*Slemdalsveien 7*), at Majorstuen, Europe's largest beer tanks have been installed alongside the grill and discotheque. Very popular with the teen groups and used mainly for concerts.

In suburban Bygdoy, the **Norske Studenters Roklubb** draws young Americans for English cider and talking till dawn—except in July when it doesn't function.

SPECIAL PROBLEMS

Ask for help at the **University's Office for Students Abroad** (*Blindern Administration Building;* ☎ *455050*) or talk with Mrs. Martha Sivesind at the **Univers Reiser A.S.** (*Lavbygget Building;* ☎ *453200*).

WHERE TO EAT

LEAST $

First a snack: **Wenche's Lunch Shop**, *Kongensgt. 7.* Near the City Hall (*entrance on Radhusgt.*), just a dash from the sightseeing-boat piers. Have sandwiches or salad baskets made up, choose a soft drink, and enjoy a picnic cruise from the open deck of the little cruiser. This one has only take-away food, but is it good!

Cafe Avec • *Tordenskioldsgt 12.* Another splendid "sand-witchery"; also superb waffles. There are a few seats, but mainly it's for the take-away traffic.

Baker Brygge • Located in a vast complex of boutiques for all budgets, this place explodes with ethnic nutrients purveyed at stalls inside: **Chopsticks** for Chinese, **Upper Crust** for pastry, **Porten** for Nordic nibbles, a bagel shop or brownies or pecan pie, Mexican, Near Eastern...Whew! In summer there's a huge open terrace facing the boats where light refreshment is available while you gobble with your chums. A great spot.

Chagall • *Situated on Karl Johansgate, the main square.* Newly refashioned in old Victorianisms; deejay on Wed., Fri., and Sat.; with-it music; counter and table service. **Sostrene Larsen** restaurant, downstairs, serves light fare at reasonable prices.

Egon • *Karl Johansgt. 37.* More sedate than Chagall and more serious about its cookery. Big windows overlook the square; decor as mixed as its menu.

Studenten Joh Albrecht • *Karl Johansgt. at #45.* Chiefly for young people and very chummy. There's a brewer's copper kettle in front. A popular gathering spot.

The Scotsman • *Karl Johansgate 17.* Pipes up with a bagful of vittles. The local Laird is Olav Thon. Live folk and country music from 7:30 p.m.

Baron and Baroness • *Stortingsgaten 10.* Offers some food with its piano-bar and disco motif. A bit schizo but fun.

Stortorvets Gjaestgiveri • *Grensen 1.* A 17th-century charmer offering 20th-century cookery. Main dishes in the $12 bracket. Country and folk singing several days a week; jazz on Fri. and Sat.

Henie-Onstad Museum • Cafeteria here can be combined with a lakeside excursion (Turn to "What to See and Do").

Kafé Celsius • *Radhusgt. 19.* A charmer located in a building that dates from 1626. Bar, hearthside dining, and gallery; courtyard garden; beautifully sited near the historic Akershus Fortress.

Coco Chalet Coffee Shop & Pie House • *Øvre Slottsgt. 8.* Yum-yum-yum all the way home. A quiet mood, ideal for lunch or a snack in the evening and with a mellow ambience.

CHAINS

Kaffistovas, inexpensive cafeterias, dot the capital. Try Rommegrot, a specialty at the *Rosenkrantzgate 8* outlet. Its cookbook buzzes until 6 p.m. weekdays, 3:30 p.m. Sat.

OTHER QUICKIES

Basarhallene features a cheerful outdoor cafe called **Cappuccino** beside the fountain of the cathedral gallery. In summer this scenic bit of real estate is ideal for a Pitta Basar, mango tarts, and coffee.

Bygdoystuene • *At the Folk Museum—Museumsveien.* Shares Bygdoy site with National Open-Air Folk Museum. Operative 7 days a week, May–Sept.; early June to mid-Aug. closing at 5 p.m. Copious servings; main dishes in $12 range; soup around $3; also sandwiches (the Dagwood Granddaddy a gustatory giant). On Sun. only, a belt-busting blue-plate dinner for perhaps $13.

MORE $$

Your bill should hover in the neighborhood of $35 per person.

Najaden • *In the Maritime Museum, on the island of Bygdoy;* ☎ *22-438180.* Picture windows on the fjord and legendary polar ship *Fram.* Major meal (euphemistically called "lunch" by foreigners) served 11 a.m.–7 p.m.; starts at perhaps $27 table d'hôte (but leave a $4 cushion for tempting extras). Summer dining till midnight. Men must wear jackets after 7 p.m. Reserve ahead; go by ferry (10 minutes from Town Hall).

Don Quixote • *On the street to the island called Bygdoy Allee.* Not Spanish as the name suggests, but international. Large windows overlook the avenue; lantern illumination; excellent service and agreeable cuisine. It has the advantage of being open on Sundays.

Ludvik • *Torggata 16.* Built into a kooky bathhouse—the ceiling hung with bloomers, golf clubs, a motorcycle, sled, rocking horse, propeller, and assorted kitsch. The joint is really only a pub, sometimes with live music; the atmosphere is young, alive, and jovial. A good place to see Oslo à la mode.

Vika area • Near the concert hall. A number of small new restaurants such as the **Rica Plaza** (with dancing) and **The Cheese Inn** (*Vikaterrassen, Ruselokkveien 3*)—an attractive pair. The district is worth investigating.

Brasseriet • *In the Hotel Scandinavia.* Excellent value for light meals. Occasional line waiting to enter. Open 6:30–11 p.m. **Charly's Cafe**, in the same building, is vibrant at times, with good value always.

Lipp • *Roald Amundsensgate 2;* ☎ *22-414400.* In Hotel Continental along with neighboring **Leo's Loft** and **Steamen**. First-rate Swiss chef (the filet mignon béarnaise sandwich a delight). Fair selection of wines; beer on tap. Highly recommended.

Djengis Khan • A Mongolian barbecue hut in the colorful Stroget shopping mall. Hardly the reason for coming to Norway.

Holberg's Årstidene • *In the Hotel Scandinavia.* Named for the playwright and one of the city's more exclusive hubs. Steaks superb; theater theme by famous designer Bjorn Wiinblad. Jacket and tie required.

Restaurant Larsen • *Sorkedalsveien 1 (near Frogner Park);* ☎ *22-606492.* Downstairs cafeteria, cozier upstairs restaurant. Cheerful. Open until midnight 5 times a week.

Blom • *Karl Johansgt. 41;* ☎ *22-427300.* This wonderfully decorated and warmly appealing famous old haunt is a refashioned wine store catering to artists and writers; Norwegian specialties well presented; varied sandwich table from 11 a.m. to 2 p.m.; closed Sun. Rollicking and very properly priced for the value and atmosphere.

NIGHTLIFE

Leo's Loft, *in the Hotel Continental*, is the hottest haven by far. It resembles a sail loft, but only in appearance. Though managed by the deluxe hotel interests, it is very economically priced and evokes a zesty mood, the reasons for its continuing success.

Rockefeller Music Hall (*Torggt.*) is a youthful retreat with live music, concerts, a bar, and an exciting rock cinema. Always zinging.

Frolich (*Drammensveien 20*) offers live music and a live atmosphere. **Comeback** (*Rosenkrantzgt. 11*) is a jovial eatery with disco-antics. Of a similar nature is **Barock** (*Universitetsgt. 26*).

Jazz? Try **Stortorvets** (*Grensen 1*) Fri. evenings and Sat. afternoons, or the **Oslo Jazzhus** (*Toftesgt 69*) Thurs., Fri., and Sat. nights. The **New Orleans Workshop** (*Jegerhallen, Akersgt. 40*) is another good beat.

The discotheque at **Frascati Restaurant** (*Stortingsgata 20*) is one of the most popular nightspots in town. There's another disco-center in the **Scandinavia Hotel** called **Galaxy Night Club**. Singles usually make the scene at any club or hotel lounge in the city without gravitating to any special address or district.

The **Bonanza** (*downstairs in the Grand Hotel, Karl Johansgate 31*) is a convivial whitewashed cellar with Indian plumes and Wild West tack; the entertainment is amusing. Closing hour is 2 a.m. Not advised for its costly fare, but recommended for a casual evening of drinking and dancing.

Dizzy (*Universitetsgt. 26*), is a restaurant-cum-discotheque, but adding live music and sporadic shows.

BEDTIME SNACKS

Sjakk Matt, *Haakon VII*, is new and zesty. So are **Last Train** *(Karl Johansgt.)* **Lipp** and the **Continental's Steamen Fortuna**. **Pigalle Restaurant** (*Gronlandsleiret 15, near the East Railway Station*) is open for sandwiches until 3 a.m. Still can't sleep?

Then try **Nichol & Son** (*Roald Amundsensgt. 1*), another fun place, or **Three Brodre** (Brothers—*a pedestrian lane off Karl Johansgt.*) with its library bar at ground level and Victorian elegance upstairs in the Old World dining salon.

WHAT TO SEE AND DO

The **Viking Ship Hall** (*Huk Av. 35, Bygdoy*) contains an incredible collection dating back as far as 1100 years, including a Viking oceangoing warship, coastal cargo vessels, a patrician pleasure craft, and a Norwegian queen's ornate ninth-century sleigh. Door charge of about $2; open 10 a.m.–6 p.m. from May through Aug., 11 a.m.–5 p.m. in Sept., to 4 p.m. in Oct., and 3 p.m. from Nov. through Mar. (If you drive down to **Tonsberg** you can see the 1100-year-old longship that finally has been restored; it is located at the **Vestfold Museum**.)

The **Kon-Tiki Museum** (*Bygdoynes*) is the berth-place of anthropologist Thor Heyerdahl's world-famous raft. The renowned balsa-and-hemp craft has been cleverly set into a theatrical "sea," in order to demonstrate its crude but cunning navigational system. Dramatic artifacts of the explorer's long passage also are on display, including rough-hewn native dugouts, Easter Island stone gods, a cave dwelling, fierce tribal weapons, and a virtual zoo of oceanic denizens. The **Ra II** also can be admired in this museum. Entry $2; open 10:30 a.m.–4 p.m. from Nov. to Mar.; 10:30 a.m.–5 p.m. from Apr. 16 to May; 10 a.m.–6 p.m. from May 18 to Aug.; 10:30 a.m.–5 p.m. Sept.–Oct. Bus #30 is the one to catch or a ferry from Pier 3 near City Hall.

The **Fram** is one of the hardiest scientific vessels of all time—the ship that tackled 3 turn-of-the-century forays to both Poles and the North Canadian ice wastes. She is moored inside a cathedral-like boathouse, and she may be inspected at times that vary with the season and the time of the sunset. Ask locally or ☎ *22-438370*; her kindly custodians may be persuaded to open up for your exclusive viewing during periods when it might otherwise be closed. Same transportation as above. Entrance fee about $3.

The **Norwegian Maritime Museum** is jammed with gear from whaling, cargo, and working boats—capped by a model of a fishing station. Opening hours range between 10–10:30 a.m. and closings between 4–8 p.m., depending on both days and months; hence, be sure to inquire for the particular day you plan your visit. Entry costs about $3.

The nearby **Norwegian Folk Museum** (*Museumsveien 10*) boasts the nation's finest collection of architectural antiquities. It also features a **Museum of Peasant Art** filled with wonderful whimsy, Sami (or Lapp) items, and costumes from all districts. The grounds contain 170 structures culled from the countryside and carted here for splinter by splinter reconstructions. Best on the lot is the 860-year-old, serpent-crowned Viking stave church. (Only 25 are left in Norway today; there once were 300.) Ibsen's study is here; there's a restaurant, plus a cafe in a tiny cottage. Open 11 a.m.-5 p.m. from May 15 through Sept. 15; rest of year, noon-4 p.m.; on Sun. it opens at 11 a.m.; admission about $5.50. A fabulous full-day, lowcost outing.

More fair weather outings? Take the electric train (Line #15) up the 1460-foot **Frognerseteren**.

The **Ski Museum**, a 20-minute ride by rail, jealously guards its 1923 title as the world's first. But that's just a preliminary superlative. You can either check your posture against the crouch of a 2034 B.C. stone figure, or compare your boot size with the 2500-year-old athlete's footprint on a board fished from the Norwegian bogs.

Opening times: 10 a.m.–3 p.m. (Mon.–Fri.) and 11 a.m.–4 p.m. (Sat.-Sun.) from Oct. to April. Summer months it opens as early as 9 a.m. and closes as late as 10 p.m., depending on the length of the day—so ask locally for exact hours. Entry about $4.

The **Munch Museum** (*Toyengate 53*), 5 minutes from the center, is based on 300 of this famed artist's lifetime output of 1000 paintings and twice as many graphic plates. White-brick and natural-wood interior; labyrinth of research and exhibition rooms; small lecture hall; reasonably priced restaurant; take Line 3, 4, 5, or 6 to Toyen; closed Mon.; entry about $1.50.

Head to **Frogner Park** for a look at Gustav Vigeland's haunting cycle of bigger-than-life sculptures. This controversial 74-acre testament in stone has been called "an artistic triumph" and "a colossal fraud." Whether you like it or loathe it, we guarantee that you will be spellbound. While you're here, the nearby **Vigeland Museum** (*Nobelsgate 32*) might prove an interesting bonus. Take Tram #2 or Bus #20 to Frogner plass. Open until 6 p.m. in summer.

Living history? The medieval **Akershus** (*Festningsplass*) and the modern **Radhuset** (*Radhusplassen, entrance from Fridtjof Nansens Plass*), both also central, are 2 of the city's proudest architectural cousins. The former is the nation's 700-year-old castle-cum-state house, bustling with royalty, parliamentarians and the continual pomp of receptions, dinners, and other governmental circumstance. Open 10 a.m.–4 p.m. (Mon.–Sat.); 12:30 p.m. opening on Sun.; its battlements provide remarkable views of the inner harbor. The latter is the City Hall. Its towers house a delightful 38-bell carillon, a 15-foot astronomical chronometer, and—best of all—a mammoth timepiece whose 25-foot hour hand (illuminated nightly) outstretches every other clock in Europe.

Finally, the **Henie-Onstad Art Center** at *Hovikodden (8 miles from Oslo; take Bus #151, 153, 161, 162, 252, or 261)* combines a multitude of treasures with dining facilities. In addition to the superb paintings and sculpture lovingly collected by Sonja Henie, the late ice star, concerts frequently are given in the giant recording studio, and there are ballet and folk-dancing performances at the outdoor amphitheater. You can stoke up in a cafeteria with well-cooked, inexpensive selections served inside and on a huge open-air terrace. The hours are at the whim of the rising and the setting of the sun. The entrance fee is about $3 for adults and half-price for the juniors. Check for the specific activities when you're in town.

CONCERTS

Oslo is extraordinarily musical; there's something doing almost every day. The city pops its buttons over its multimillion-note **Concert Hall** called the **Spectrum** (which also can present ice hockey and house conventions, or provide theater, opera, and ballet). Open-air performances grace the forecourt of the **Vigeland Museum** (*Nobelsgate 32*) in summer on Sun. at 1 p.m. and on Wed. at 7 p.m. The presentations inside the cathedral on Wed. at 7:30 p.m. are equally notable. The **Munch Museum** schedules frequent recitals. *On the island of Bygdoy*, the **Norwegian Folk Museum** mounts a hoedown each Sun. at 5 p.m. from mid-May until midSept. at its open-air theater; these same folk, incidentally, jig at 8 p.m. at the restaurant during weekdays.

MOVIES

Original versions are shown everywhere; if they are foreign, they're given Norwegian subtitles, though films for children are often dubbed into Norwegian. Many American and English films play each week.

MARKETS

Several good ones. The **Youngstorget** and the **Stortorget** lean heavily toward botanical items, while **Aker Brygge** boasts a very special maritime atmosphere. Best time for all is in the early morning. You might also like to browse among Oslo's **Cathedral Bazaars**, ateliers housed in the crescent adjoining the capital's main site of worship. Textiles, antiques, ceramics, and silver are inside; a flower market blossoms outside.

SWIMMING

In sunnier months, Oslo's **Frogner Bad** (*off Kirkeveien, Frognerveien 67, entrance Middlethuns gate, subway to Majorstua*) is a balmy poolside oasis; attendants at this massive outdoor aquatic playpen flip the heaters up to 70°F. Pleasant setting near the Vigeland statues; only pennies to rent a suit and towel; operative May 20 to mid-Sept. In winter, the **Vestkantbadet** (*Sommerogaten 1*), near the U.S. Embassy in Oslo, will bathe you either Finnish or Roman style. Indoor pool, normal bathhouse amenities, and sunray treatments also available; clean, not costly, and recommendable. Men: Mon., Wed., Fri.; Women: Tues., Thurs., Sat.

TENNIS

At the **Frogner Park** in Oslo, but be sure to book in advance in the summer season. Visitors of tournament caliber can often squeeze into the seedings during the June and Aug.-Sept. competitions.

PUBLICATIONS

The English printout of *What's On in Oslo* is an extremely handy pocket guide.

WHERE TO SHOP

Aker Brygge (*facing the port*) is the name of an exciting complex of shops, food stands, boutiques, and restaurants. The full panoply of retail items is here—and it's just plain fun to browse among the hundreds of choices. Whatever it is, you'll probably find it here.

ARTS AND CRAFTS

Norway Designs (*Stortingsgaten 28—across from the Hotel Continental*), down one flight, brings together the best of the nation, focusing on pottery and ceramic sculpture, impressive wrought-iron candelabra, jewelry, hand-carved replicas of Viking motifs, shawls, throw rugs, wool (plus patterns for knitting)—even egg warmers. **Den Norske Husflidsforening**, commonly called "Husfliden" (*Mollergatan 4*) adds furniture, fabrics, looms, weaving materials and rugs to its kaleidoscopic inventory. **Heimen** (*Arbeidergt—corner Kr. IV's gt.*) specializes in textiles, hand-knits, and national costumes.

DEPARTMENT STORES

Steen & Strom (*Kongensgate 23*) is reputable and versatile. So is **Christiania Glasmagasin** (*Stortorvet 10*).

ENAMELWARE

In exquisite enameling, **David-Andersen** (*Karl Johansgate 20*) is considered by experts to be the leading house in the country. Their irresistible, moderately priced, enameled demitasse spoons, collection of 11th-century Viking jewelry facsimiles, and many other items are equally tempting. Recently expanded; fully air-conditioned. Tops for gifts—to friends or to yourself.

SWEATERS

William Schmidt & Co. (*Karl Johansgate 41*) has everybody in the capital licked in wearables and souvenirs with authentic Nordic flavor. The most popular sellers are the wonderful hand-knitted sweaters and pullovers in Old Norwegian patterns.

INSIDER TIP

Finally, we implore *that you not miss the* **Shopping Bazaar** *known locally as* **Basarhallene**. *The butchers' stalls in the historic brick firehouse behind the cathedral* (Kirkegate near Stortorget) *have been rebuilt into little shops which are absolutely enchanting.*

Shopping zones? **Karl Johansgate** *plus the side streets off it are the heartbeat of the capital. Previously mentioned* **Aker Brygge** *is like a shopping village within the city. Lower price tags can be found along Markveien and Thorvald Meyersgate.*

PEER GYNT MOUNTAIN COUNTRY

One of the few remaining little-known, lightly trod, breathtakingly beautiful touristic magnets in western Europe. Scenic glory and tranquillity are the keynotes of what its dwellers have long called "Our Friendly Wilderness." Within this triangle of 2200 square miles, with its apexes at *Rondane*, *Jotunheimen*, and directly above *Lillehammer*, you may drive for an hour without encountering another car or seeing a single billboard. It is so pristine, in fact, that you may safely quench your thirst from any pool, brook, stream, lake, or other body of water in the entire region!

The name springs from Ibsen's most acclaimed poetic drama, Grieg's opera, and the ballet that followed—one of which, incidentally, is presented hourly somewhere in the world 365 days per year. They evolve around the picaresque international adventures of this mythical Norwegian folk hero. Before starting, the playwright tracked down the grave of farmer Per (one *e*) Gynt, the crumbling headstone of which attracts legions of pilgrims to the serene little cemetery in Vinstra.

This grid of diverse ranges and 5 valleys is about 3-1/2 hours north of Oslo by train or car. Bus excursions are made from both of the capital's airports and from landings of ferries from abroad. Because of the shortage of taxis, through prior arrangements, hotel cars meet guests at the nearest station.

The winter season from Dec. through Apr. draws the majority of visitors to the slopes for downhill and cross-country skiing. Conversely, the less costly summer season from the end of May to Oct. 1 shows greater popularity in the glades. During the latter you may enjoy the lovely skeins of carefully marked and supervised walking trails, fishing, excursions, various sports including tennis (no golf)—but mostly relaxing to commune with nature at its sublime peak.

All lodgings are quoted on the full pension plan. There are five deluxe hotels and one combined deluxe-economy hotel which, while operated independently, are closely linked in an exchange program that permits their clients to lunch, dine, or participate in their other facilities without extra charge. They are fully licensed to serve drinks. This fraternity has its own travel agency, **Gudbrandsdalsreiser** (*2640 Vinstra*) that can reserve rooms and set up itineraries—even walking tours if you're feeling energetic.

WHERE TO STAY

FEFOR Best Western • *2640 Vinstra.* The most economical establishment in this group draws our top ranking. Mountainside site over lake; ski lift and more than 100 miles of marked trails, skating rink, curling, tennis, minigolf, outdoor pool, fishing, riding, squash, gymnasium, saunas, and dancing nightly; delicious country-style cuisine with marvelous breakfast buffet; well-maintained 1902 structure with Robert Scott mementos from his training here for South Pole expedition; old-fashioned public rooms with good fireplaces; essentially small bedchambers, some with showers, with the best in the new wing; basic quarters for basic outlays in the rear. There's also a chalet village with spacious self-service facilities.

Gola Hoifjellshotell • *P.O. 2646 Gola;* ☎ *062-98109.* Owned by the Norwegian-American Line, offers double-barreled amenities. Cozy main building with greenery, fine tapestries, antiques, and 30 well-furnished units (try for No. 107); 10-room chalet wing in birch with its own brand of charm; 4 individual yesteryear and 25 double-party guest cottages, each simply and practically equipped for 6 persons with cooking gear, refrigerator, shower, toilet, electric clothes dryer, fireplace, and wall-to-wall carpets; riding, tennis, sailboats, fishing, minigolf, 3 neighboring ski lifts, and cross-country ski tracks prepared by machine; closed Oct., Nov. and May. A happy oasis, especially for families with children in its cottages.

Wadahl • *P.O. 2645 Harpefoss.* A magnet for young and young-in-heart Norwegians, Danes, Germans, and others who seek a folksy vacation. Sprawly public area of no special distinction; large, plasticized dining room; cigarette, candy, drink, and slot machines seemingly everywhere; handsome new indoor pool to supplement the outdoor installation; tennis, riding, fishing, rowboats, ski lift, machine-readied slalom slope; lively atmosphere.

Golaseter Fjellkro • *P.O. 2645 Harpefoss.* Serious economizers may garner a welcome bonus if they reside here on the hilltop directly above the gates of the Wadahl. It's only a short walk to the sports, dining, and dancing activities at this much more elaborate and expensive hostelry, which quickly can become the seat of the action. The 90-unit pension, with 3-5 beds and running water only in each room, is simplistic; there's a reception desk combined with a self-service restaurant and coffee bar, plus a tiny lounge and a bodega-disco. No wonder it is chosen by so many money-saving groups, with the price at about $55 for 2 people, including breakfast!

Kampesaeter Fjellstue • *P.O. 2643 Skabu,* ☎ *062-95525.* Offers a very plain but ingratiating rustic atmosphere and a panorama that is fantastic. Attractively extended dining room; nighttime stube that r-o-c-k-s in season; 90 rooms and 4 guest cottages; furnishings somewhat tacky; riding in summer. There's a convivial feeling here à la comfortable clothes and old shoes.

Sodorp Gjestgivergard • *In the valley village of Vinstra.* Architecturally a Norwegian chalet, is almost a straightforward American-style motel in its interior. A pleasant young couple named Austerheim attained their life's dream when they opened it in '76; he does the cooking—and well. Large dance hall with live music twice weekly; 27 rooms with convertible beds, showers, and no frills; dignified Lord Mayor's Room for conferences; lunch stop for bus groups; open all year. This first meeting place for the small community is a clean and cheerful mixing ground.

Gausdal Hoyfjellshotell • *2622 Soingvoll,* ☎ *062-28500.* A member of the deluxe groupment with correspondingly deluxe rates. In our opinion, however, it is most certainly not worth its standard investment. Except when the chartered tours pour in for the noontime meal, the ambience is notably relaxed—but so is the upkeep. The most felicitous feature is its indoor pool with its adjoining solarium. The accommodations—125 of them and 4 with balconies—are adequately large but very far from inspired. The food makes up in quantity for what it lacks in quality. The general manager and the staff we encountered were the souls of graciousness and kindness—but we had the feeling that here is a hard-used hotel factory that copes impersonally with its large turnover. Perhaps you might disagree.

Espedalen Fjellstue • *2627 Svatsum*l; ☎ *062-99912.* 50 beds for sportspeople; no private showers or toilets; starting point for the canoe-camping excursion.

Vinsterlia • *In Skabu.* 18-room pension; operated by British musician Ronald Franklin and his actress-wife; music school out of season.

Ruten Fjellstue • *In Espedal.* Stunning sweep of countryside; chalet-type construction; showers or washbasins; steam bath; dancing; ski lessons; full pension $55. Closed when we tried to inspect them.

AUTHOR'S OBSERVATION

Send all of your queries for brochures, any other information, and/or reservations to dynamic, dedicated Hans Petter Kleiven (Nedre Gate 2, 2640 Vinstra), chief of the Tourist Traffic Assn. for the entire area.

SANDEFJORD

Until recently this minnow-size port was the home of the Norwegian whaling fleet. While only 2 hours by rail from the capital, it's light years away in atmosphere. The **Whaling Museum** is the main sightseeing target.

STAVANGER

Except for a housing shortage that has rocketed residential rental and sales prices beyond the troposphere, a skyscape dotted by sleek new high-rise buildings, and fatter costs of living, little has been changed in this old, bucolic, and lovely fishing port in its emergence as a key petroleum center. (It remains, in fact, the capital of the national sardine industry.) The oil strike pattern (now somewhat in recession everywhere) of hard-boozing boomers, honky-tonk joints with B-girls, con artists, pitchmen, grifters, and venal merchants does not exist—and never has since the first black gold was discovered off its shores. The same Norwegian orderliness and the same fetchingly open simplicity prevail. Nor has it become a resort, despite the fact that 10 of the country's 18 miles of beaches are in this area. It is a characteristically charming town where most of the 96,000 residents still smile in their encounters with other members of humanity. Incidentally, the people pronounce their town as "Stah-VAN-grr." A "Siddis" is a person from here.

If you plan to overnight, check first at the **tourist office** in the **Culture House** (*Solvberget*), where the helpful staffers will try to find you reasonably priced space in private homes. (Hotel rates can be shocking.) Our suggestions otherwise run as follows: The **Stavanger Sommerhotell Molkeho-len** (*Madla;* ☎ *554800*), open June 1 through Aug. 21, with space for 250 plus some minisuites with kitchen; then the passably hospitable **Rogalandsheimen** (*Musegt. 18;* ☎ *520188*); the **Commandor** (*Valberggt. 9;* ☎ *528000*), near the water, is an amalgam of 6 elderly houses containing a total of 38 bedrooms and no private baths, where singles cost $35 and doubles range from $40 to $60; and the central austere, 110-bed **Grand** (*Klubbgaten 3*; ☎ *33020*). The quayside **Victoria** (*Skansegt. 1*; ☎ *520526*), oldest in the port, offers clean dwelling space. This one and the sleek **SAS Royal** are pretty costly.

For dining, **Skipperstuen** *in the Commandor*, with red-checked tablecloths, is a tavern producing Norwegian-style breakfasts plus hamburgers and chili dogs later in the day. **Dickens Pub** (*Skagenkaien 6*), across from the Market, is good for pizza and beer.

For nightlife, **Scandic** is small, intimate, and smoky. Finally, the **Hotel Alstor** operates a big, brassy dance-bar in its basement.

SUNDVOLLEN

From **King's View** on **Kleivstua** you can pretend you're the Liege of The Mountain. Way, way down there among the forested fastnesses, those sparkling bits of sapphire are the **Tyrifjorden Lake** linkage. The hotel here was built in 1780 as a ski-mail station.

TRONDHEIM

Founded in A.D. 997 by Norwegian King Olav Tryggvason, this city of 135,000 inhabitants is up the coast from Bergen, nestled in the wrinkles of hundreds of rock-dots and inlets. The **cathedral**, dating from about 1100, is the finest of its kind in Scandinavia. Try to see the **Ringve Museum of Musical History**, a bit outside of town; all guides are students who can demonstrate each instrument. The **Folk Museum** at *Sverresborg* is comprised of 50 different buildings from the region. Pick up at the **tourist information** at Market Place an inexpensive sightseeing brochure with maps and walking tours around the city. While there, inquire about the various **bus or boat excursions** to the islands of **Hitra** or **Froya**, which depart from the Railway Station quay. (Price roughly $23; 2 hours each way; pensions available for lingerers.) Geographically you'll find Trondheim's setting delightful. It's on a fjord; the old name is Nidaros, which means "Mouth of the River Nid"—and that's just what it is.

For overnighting, check with the tourist office for accommodation in **private homes**. In these the cost will be about 150NK-250—and cleanliness is virtually guaranteed. The cheapest hotel space runs close to $100 per double, including breakfast, and the quality of these facilities is so poor that we cannot recommend any individual address.

For students, the **Trondheim Youth Hostel** offers good shelter. **Dronningen** (*26 Dronningensgate*) is opposite the oldest wooden building in Norway. Spiral staircase but no elevator; 32 rooms, few private toilets; bed and breakfast only. The stone-faced **Gildevangen** doesn't inspire us with raptures of innkeeping joy, but its 58 units plus the cafeteria/dining salon serve a basic old-fashioned function.

VOSS

This birthplace of Knute Rockne presented the University of Notre Dame a handsome memorial honoring the immortal coach in '62. Pilgrims to this burgeoning village will find a cableway and several ski lifts; the trails for walking or slicing down the soft white hills are among the loveliest we've ever seen (be sure to go to the very top first). Impressive ancient church in the town square; fine headquarters for fjord motoring excursions or skiing patrols into the nearby wilderness; excellent apres-ski activities, too.

FOR MORE INFORMATION ON NORWAY

Norwegian Tourist Board • *655 Third Ave., New York, NY 10017,* ☎ *(212) 949-2333, FAX (212) 983-5260.*

INSIDER TIP

(1) In the Norwegian capital, the Oslo Tourist Information Office is located at City Hall (Radhuset) with a division at the Central Station.

(2) As you are almost bound to spend part of your visit in the capital, be sure to purchase the low-cost, money-saving **Oslo Card** *at City Hall. A splendid guidebook goes with it, describing the free or cut-rate bargains in transportation, dining, museum entry, shopping, and scores of other benefits. It's one of the best buys in the North!*

(3) If you travel in the summer, when Norway is at its most enchanting, you can often realize savings of up to 50% on hotel bills since this is the nation's low season. Therefore, always request a seasonal reduction, and you'll probably receive one. PS: Weekends are usually much cheaper than weekdays.

PORTUGAL

For the tourist, this is still the best buy in today's Europe. Portugal has changed little in terms of sightseeing prizes, remaining one of the continent's friendliest and most colorful countries. Once a grand colonial power, 16th-century Portugal ruled an empire more than 100 times its size. Today it nominally administers only Macao, an island of 6 square miles close to Hong Kong. This formerly potent nation of great navigators and explorers in Renaissance times has lost its worldly status in the contemporary era, but it is the least spoiled and least expensive of all the countries covered in this book.

Touring around this minuscule republic is delightfully different. Its mountainous northern reaches are wild and wooded. Ox-drawn carts trudge tortuous roads to tiny farms that checker the terraced slopes, and at harvest time in the fall, peasants gather their grapes into wicker baskets that they carry on their backs down steep mountain tracks. The color-filled and festive port-wine harvests are something you may not want to miss. Those interested in sea-bathing, fishing, or boating head for the Atlantic coast—rugged with cliffs and graced by golden sands.

Sample port wines in the entrepots of Vila Nova de Gaia near Porto, or observe a wide slice of birdlife in the marshes and lagoons that surround Aveiro, as the local seaweed-gatherers drift by, poling the tangles into flat boats. Visit the hilltop city of Fatima (Portugal's Lourdes), where yearly pilgrimages culminate in a moving candlelit procession in celebration of the miraculous vision of the Virgin Mary, said to have appeared there in 1917.

Lisbon, the capital, is simultaneously a bright and crumbling mixture of the traditional and the contemporary, the elegant and the down-at-heel, rightly famous for its abundant and varied seafood and its lively native atmosphere. South of Lisbon the country is fascinating in its isolation; vivid sunlight etches harsh outlines of pastel houses in remote Moorish villages surrounded by corktree forests and wind-blown boscage.

Sagres is at the southwesterly tip of Europe and the fabulous Algarve Coast, Portugal's salubrious suntrap; resorts here vie with the finest on any of the five continents. The glamorous beaches of Albufeira contrast sharply with the brisk, businesslike vitality of nearby Portimao, an old Arabic fishing port, with its bustling, noisy market and its outlandishly painted fleet.

The warmth of the Portuguese people and their folklore are expressed in the soulful melodies of their unique *fado* love songs, which will enchant you wherever you go.

TIPS ON PORTUGAL

ACCOMMODATIONS

Portuguese terminology for innkeeping may seem strange to the first time visitor. The next section describes pousadas. Hotels exist everywhere, of course. *Estalagem* and *albergaria* are privately run hostelries of varying standards; *residencias* offer shelter and breakfast but no other meals. During this period of economic crisis, Portuguese hoteliers are often talking to shadows on the wall, so it is commonplace to bargain for lower prices than the rack rates for rooms.

PORTUGAL'S POUSADA SYSTEM

If you want to see the real Portugal, the above-mentioned pousada system is ideal, though not the travel bargain it used to be. This splendid network was conceived and developed by the government and is now administered by the **National Tourist Company** (**ENATUR**). The highest you will pay during low-season is $150 for top-grade (CH) twin accommodation, including breakfast. Most other pousadas charge around $85. High season prices range between $95 and $200 depending on category; meals cost between $25 and $40, varying on number of courses and pousada standards. There are 4 categories: "CH" top, "C superior," "C," and "B."

Pousada—means "a place to rest." Each of these charming, colorful, cozy, comfortable country inns has a 4-fold purpose: To provide this "place to rest," the natural bounty of its selected land, the riches and curiosities of its regional cookery, and reasonable tariffs for high quality.

The 30 links (plus another 2 on Madeira) in the chain offer meticulous cleanliness, a friendly welcome, and the authentic flavor of the particular province in which each is located. While a scattering of these refuges are on the plain side, most compare favorably with the better first-class—and even deluxe—private establishments.

ATLANTIC OCEAN
A Coruña
Costa Verde
Oviedo
ASTURIAS
Santiago de Compostella
Costa del Rias
GALICIA
Pontevedra
Vigo
Bayona
León
Rio Miño
Viana do Castelo
Braga
Bom Jesus
Bragança
Guimarães
CASTILL
Vila Real
Oporto
Penafiel
Rio Douro
Rio Duero
Toro
Vall
Aveiro
Viseu
Salamanca
Coimbra
Guarda
Figueira da Foz
Ávila
El Escoria
Pombal
Batalha
Leiria
Nazaré
Fátima
Alcobaça
Castelo Branco
Tomar
Óbidos
S
P
Alcântara
Cáceres
Trujillo
Guadalupe
Marvão
Rio Tajo
Sintra
Lisbon
Elvas
Mérida
Rio Guadiana
CAST
Setubal
Évora
EXTREMADURA
Badajoz
Beja
PORTUGAL
Córdoba
Rio Guadalquivir
ALGARVE
Huelva
Sevilla
Sagres
Lagos
Faro
ANDAL
Granad
Costa de la Luz
Ronda
Cádiz
Málaga
Gibraltar
MOROCCO
PORTUGAL

Naturally, we don't have space here to describe each of these candidates. For your convenience, however, the following chart offers basic information on all of them.

POUSADAS		
Name and Address	**Units**	**Category**
do Castelo 2510 Obidos (Estremadura) ☎ 062-959105	9	CH
do Infante 8650 Sagres (Algarve) ☎ 082-64222, 64223	23	C
dos Loios 7000 Evora (Alto Alentejo) ☎ 066-24051	32	CH
Palmela (in Palmela Castle) 2950 Palmela ☎ 01-2351226	27	CH
da Rainha Santa Isabel 7100 Estremoz (Alto Alentejo) ☎ 068-22618	23	CH
da Ria Bico do Muranzel, Torreira 3870 Murtosa (Beira Litoral) ☎ 034-48332	19	C
Sra. das Neves 6350 Almeida ☎ 071-54290, 54283	21	C
do Mestre Afonso Domingues 2440 Batalha (Estremadura) ☎ 044-96260	21	C
de São Filipe 2900 Setubal ☎ 065-523844	14	CH
de Santa Barbara 3400 Oliveira do Hospital ☎ 038-52252	16	C
de Santa Catarina 5210 Miranda do Douro (Tras-Os-Montes) ☎ 073-42255	12	C
de Santa Clara 7665 Santa Clara-a-Velha (Baixo Alentejo) ☎ 083-98250	6	B

POUSADAS Name and Address	Units	Category
de Santa Luzia 7330 Elvas (Alto Alentejo) ☎ 068-629194	16	C
de Santa Maria 7330 Marvao (Alto Alentejo) ☎ 045-93201	13	C Superior
de Santo Antonio 3750 Agueda (Beira Litoral) ☎ 034-521230	12	C
de São Bartolomeu 5300 Branganca (Tras-Os-Montes) ☎ 073-22493	17	B
de São Bento 4850 Canicada (Minho) ☎ 053-647190	30	C Superior
de São Bras 8150 S. Bras de Alportel (Algarve) ☎ 089-842305	23	C
de São Gens 7830 Serpa (Baixo Alentejo) ☎ 084-90327	18	C
de São Goncalo 4600 Amarante (Douro Litoral) ☎ 055-461113	15	B
de São Jeronimo 3475 Caramulo ☎ 032-861291	6	B
de São Lourenco 6260 Manteigas (Beira Alta) ☎ 075-98150)	22	C Superior
de São Pedro 2300 Tomar ☎ 049-381175	15	B
de São Teotonio 4930 Valenca do Minho (Minho) ☎ 051-824020	15	C Superior
Nossa Senhora da Oliveira 4801 Guimares (Minho) ☎ 053-514157	16	C
de Santa Marinha de Costa 4800 Guimares (Minho) ☎ 053-514453	55	CH

POUSADAS		
Name and Address	**Units**	**Category**
de Vale do Gaio **7595 Torrao** **☎ 065-66100**	**7**	**B**
de D. Dinis **4920 Vila Nova de Cerveira (Minho)** **☎ 051-795601)**	**29**	**CH**
do Barao de Forrester **5070 Alijo (Tras-os-Montes)** **☎ 059-95467**	**11**	**B**
de São Tiago **7540 Santiago do Cacem (Baixo Alentejo)** **☎ 069-22459**	**7**	**B**

FOOD

Portuguese cuisine is neither fiery nor doughy. The French influence is pronounced, not the Spanish; the eye is as important as the palate. In some dining spots, mostly regional ones, olive oil and garlic are heavily used. Remember 3 phrases: *sem azeite* ("without oil"), *com manteiga* ("with butter"), and *sem alho* ("without garlic"). Coffee is the pillar of almost everyone's diet. Some travelers prefer *Carioca* style, which comprises equal parts of coffee and hot water; others like it *com leite*, that is coffee and milk, 50-50; after a heavy meal, try *bica* (espresso) with lots of sugar.

Fish appears nearly daily in the diet. Big, fat, fresh (and redolent) sardines are the best buy. Since many top restaurants won't prepare them because of the smell, smaller taverns will. (In Lisbon, try them at the Feira Popular, close to the small bullring called **Campo Pequeno**.) Cod is an ever-lovin' favorite for the Portuguese, a festival dish and a staple anytime. There are more different ways to prepare it than there are citizens.

Cheese? *Serpa*, snappy and tangy, is outstanding. *Queijo fresco*, used as a butter substitute, is good, too. In winter, try the creamy *Queijo da Serra*. Water in Lisbon, *Estoril* and *Oporto*, is sweet and potable, but do not trust it anywhere on your rural forays; always ask for bottled varieties. *Agua de Luso* is the best-known brand, though our favorite is *Pedras Salgadas.*

The 10% service charge and the 3% tourist tax in Portuguese restaurants are included in your bill, but you may wish to leave a tip of 5% or so if the attention has been exceptional.

DRINKS

Port is the major national wine. Of the 5 types, Vintage, which takes 20 years to reach its prime, is the best. Crusted, never dated, is also excellent. Ruby and Tawny (favorites of most travelers) are blends of up to 40 wines. White, which is light and pleasant, is the only one served before a meal. The rest are consumed at the end with the cheese.

Madeira, though not as fashionable as it used to be, is as fine as it ever was. This is the only wine that thrives on motion, and it has the longest life of any. The 3 best types are Bual, Sercial (dry, characteristic flavor), and Malmsey (on the sweet side). The Blandy brand is always surefire.

The table wines are most often no better than fair—although a few are delicious. Leading candidates are Clarete, Ferreirinha (a very fine red), Quinta da Aguieira (excellent in red and white), Ermida (a delicate white), Vinho Verde Alvarinho (a refreshing young white that lends a cool magic to any lunchtime), Gatao (available in small bottles; a white fruity, soft elixir that is "alive"), and Bucaco (supply rather severely restricted). Otherwise, there are Dao Cerejeira (red and quite dry), Dao Terra Atlas (red), Grandjo (very sweet white), and the white Monopolio Constantino, which are also beloved locally. Among the rosé wines, the famous, slightly sweet Mateus leads the list. As for naturally sparkling choices, you might find Caves da Raposeira "Bruto" to be the most acceptable local substitute for champagne; it is cloyingly sweet. Last, there's always the wine of the country, in "open" servings referred to as vinho da casa.

Portuguese brandy has its special attractions. Constantino is frequently seen, but try to find a black-label, 5-star Maciera if you are looking for exceptional rewards for a low price.

Ginginha, the cherry liqueur first invented and distilled by local monks, is worth a try.

Tuborg, Carlsberg and Sagres have lately become the ranking beers. Super Bock is heading up, too. Imperial is always pumped from a tap. It's pretty good.

If you're a soft drink fan, sample those wonderful orangeades, which are at their peak in winter (harder to find in summer). The Compal firm produces peach, orange, grape, tomato, apricot, pear, and other fruit juices. Smashing quality.

GETTING AROUND

TAXIS

The Portuguese taxi driver is a wild one. The tariffs are moving up, but are still moderate for the plethora of thrills!

TRAINS

There are 4 stations in the capital. If you're arriving from Spain you'll slide in at **Santa Apolonia**, on the river somewhat east of the center. Others include the **Sul e Sueste** (*Praca do Comercio*) for connections to the south and southeast of the country, and the "**Rossio**"

(*Praca Dom Pedro IV*). The train for Estoril leaves from **Cais do Sodre** (regular departures until about midnight).

There are now many diesel locomotives and diesel "autocoach" cars. You may have lunch or dinner for about $16, or breakfast for $5. Several domestic rural runs still use woodburners, which often carry neither drinking water nor restaurant cars. Carry your own supply of food and drink on these, just in case.

BUSES

A network of express buses covering practically the entire country has been set up in the last few years. About 90% are operated by state-owned **Rodoviaria Nacional**, headquartered on *Avenida Casal Ribeiro, 8B, 5th floor*; ☎ *545439*. Three private companies complete the circuit: **Avic Turismo**, *Av. Defensones de Chaves 99*; ☎ *767227*; twice-daily service between Lisbon, Oporto, and the main towns along the seaboard of Minho province; one-way Lisbon-Moncao (the longest route—about 320 miles) costs approximately $16, **Turilis Viagens e Turismo**, *Campo Pequeno 42-E, Lisbon*; ☎ *7970309*; operates more or less the same routes at the same rates, and **Mundial Turismo**, *Avenida Antonio August de Aguiar 90-A, Lisbon*; ☎ *575740*; runs deluxe service between Lisbon-Oporto and Lisbon-Algarve; one way about $16.

MOTORING

Be sure to get the brochures on all of the government pousadas and privately run estalagens that interest you from either your hotel concierge or the tourist office before departure. As we stated earlier, most are far superior to any hotel within miles.

CAR HIRE

In Lisbon you'll find at least a dozen agencies in the self-drive market race. Giant operators such as **Europcar/Contauto** (☎ *535115*), **Hertz** (*Av. 5 de Outubre 10*, ☎ *579027*) and **Avis** (*Av. Praia da Vitoria 12-C*, ☎ *561177*) have moved in; their reputations are secure. Respected competitors include **Emintauto** (*Rua Ferreira Lapa 42*), **Cael** (*Rua Pereiro 2A*; ☎ *651396*), and **Guerin** (*Av. Alvares Cabral 45-B-C*; ☎ *689174*). Motorcycles are difficult to rent, so don't bother looking.

SPORTS

HORSES

Care to visit an outstanding stud farm? Head for fascinating **Estacao Zootecnica Nacional** at *Fonte-Boa*, about 2 hours' drive from Lisbon. The director takes pride in his 1500 prize animals; magnificent among them, the Alter and Lusitano strains are Portuguese in origin.

BULLFIGHTING

Different from the Spanish version: the magnificently attired and mounted *cavaleiro* replaces the pedestrian *matador*; and the bull is not killed! Season: Apr.-Sept., usually at 10 p.m. Thurs. in Lisbon; occasionally on Sun. Inquire locally elsewhere. Get your concierge to buy tickets or ask the tourist office for assistance.

SOCCER

European football fans will find magnificent stadiums (especially in Lisbon), where first-division matches may be watched for a mere $7 (best seats $26-55).

SHOPPING

Shopping hours vary slightly. You may be sure of one thing, though: Everybody puts up the shutters for lunch, either from noon–2 p.m. or 1–3 p.m. In compensation, they don't close until 7 p.m. Check locally as to Sat. closing. Banks operate weekdays from 8:30 a.m. to 3 p.m.

THINGS NOT TO BUY

Don't buy anything American, because it costs 2 or 3 times what it does in the States. And antiques are distinctly for the expert in Portugal. Street peddlers hawk "Omega" and other brands of Swiss watches. Pure fake, of course.

WHERE TO GO

ALCOBACA

Located on the Lisbon-Oporto road about 75 miles from the capital, this Gothic ecclesiastical complex has overtones of the classic French abbey. Begun in A.D. 1178, it contains architecture of the 12th-14th centuries.

Pensão Mosteiro (*Av. Joao de deus 1; ☎ 42183*) offers adequate accommodation. So does **Pensão Restaurante Coracoes Unidos**, a bit larger; $40 for double with bath and $30 without; meals served for $12 and you can take either half or full board. Dine at either **Trindade** or **Bau**.

ALGARVE

Sometimes called the Algarve Coast, this southernmost region of the nation experienced a real estate boom that began about a dozen years ago. Things quieted down for a while, but once again touristic activity is vital and thriving. From **Sagres** to **Vila Real de Santo Antonio** (Spanish frontier), the motorist will find some of Europe's finest beaches. When the weather is right, it can be one of the most rewarding targets on the European Continent. The prices (though reasonable by European standards) are the highest in Portugal.

Here's a list of pensions and restaurants where you won't pay more than $38-55 for a double room and $16-28 for a full meal (including a half bottle of wine).

Albufeira: **Pensão Vila Bela** (*Rua Coronel Aguas 15; ☎ 089-512101*), **Restaurant O Dias** (*Praca Miguel Bombarda*). Armacao de pera: **Pensão Hani** (*Rua Rainha Santa 4; ☎ 082-312230*). Faro: **Pensão O Farao** (*Largo da Madalena 4; ☎ 089-823350*), **Restaurante Dois Irmaos** (*Largo Terreiro do Bispo 18*). Lagos: **Pensão Lagosmar** (*Rua Dr. Faria e Sousa 13; ☎ 63523*), **Restaurante Porta Velha—Casa dos Grelhados** (*Rua Candido dos Reis 12-1°*). Montegordo: **Pensão Paiva** (*Rua Pedro Alvares Cabral; ☎ 081-444187*). Portimao: **Pensão Afonso III** (*Rua Herois *do Ultramar 1;* ☎ *24282)*, **Restaurante O Bicho** *(Largo Gil Eanes 12)*. Praia da Rocha: **Pensão Solar do Pinguim** *(Av. Antonio Feu;* ☎ *24308)*, **Restaurante Safari** *(Rua Antonio Feu)*. S. Bras de Alportel: **Pensão Santo Antonio** *(Poco dos Ferreiros;* ☎ *42175)*. Quarteira: **Restaurante Atlantico** *(Av. Infante de Sagres 91)*. Sagres: **Restaurante A Tasca**. Silves: **Restaurante Ladeira** *(Ladeira de S. Pedro)*. Tavira: **Restaurante Imperial** *(Rua Jose Pires Pedinha 22)*. Vila Real de Sto. Antonio: **Restaurante Edmundo** *(Av. da Republica 55)*.

At the following hotels, prices for double occupancy during high season range between $75 and $95:

Albufeira: **Hotel Baltum** (*Av. 25 de Abril;* ☎ *089-589103*). Faro: **Hotel Albacor** (*Rua Brites de Almeida 25;* ☎ *22093*). Lagos: **Hotel São Cristovao** (*Rossio de S. Joao;* ☎ *63051*). Quarteira: **Hotel Apartamento Atis** (*Av. Projectada e paralela a Infante Sagres;* ☎ *089-389771*). Sagres: **Hotel da Baleeira** (☎ *64212*). Tavira: **Hotel-Apartamento Eurotel** (*Quinta das Oliveiras;* ☎ *22041*).

ALMEIDA

This place, situated 35 miles northeast of Guarda and a mere 9 miles from the Spanish border, offers a luxurious new pousada. It boasts 22 comfortable rooms, a restaurant, and the facilities of a modern hostelry.

ARRAIOLOS

This village—not too far from **Estremoz**—is famed for its distinctive carpets, which in their modern concept resemble those of our own southwestern Indians. Its buildings are quaintly painted blue and white. Despite those scant attractions, it is a waste of time as a sightseeing target. You may eat for about $15 at **Aguias D'Ouro**, on the main square. Otherwise, there's the excellent **Pousada da Rainha Santa Isabel** in Estremoz, where they'll charge $26 for one course or $35 for two dishes.

BARCELOS

Only 20 miles north of **Oporto**, Barcelos is famous for its 13th-century polychrome cockerel—legendary symbol of Portugal. Every Thursday there is an almost bewildering display of varied handicrafts (especially ceramics) in its busy open market. **Albergaria Condes de Barcelos** and **Pensão D. Nuno** provide adequate shelter at a reasonable cost. Dine at **Restaurante Arantes** (*Avda. da Liberdade 33*).

BATALHA

Numerous pilgrims to Portugal make the trip principally to see and worship in the **cathedral at Batalha**, the finest Gothic structure on the Iberian Peninsula. It is north of the capital and not far from *Fatima* and *Nazare*, both of which should be on any itinerary. A fine stop is at **Batalha's Pousada Do Mestre Afonso Domingues**, next to the cathedral. **Pensão Gladius** (*on Praca Mousinho de Albuquerque;* ☎ *044-96760*) offers 10 bedrooms with bath for almost one-fourth ($40 for a double) of what you would pay at the pousada.

BRAGA

This historic shrine, rich with churches, paintings, monuments, and tombs, lies inland some 44 miles from the northern frontier. **Pensão Grande Residencia Avenida** is a substantial haven of 22 rooms, 9 with private bath. There are about 8 other more modest inns; and at the other end of the scale, the 132-unit **Turismo** steals the first-class thunder from the local skies. Its 2 latest additions, **Caranda** and **Residencial S. Marcos** are clean and functional. Otherwise, **Hotel Joao XXI** and **Pensão Grande Residencia Avenida** should provide adequate shelter. Dine at either **O Ignacio**

(*Campo das Hortas 4*) or **Restaurante Avenida** (*Av. Central 13-1*). Quite a journey from Lisbon, but well worth it for adventurers and students of Portuguese culture.

BUCACO

About 60 miles north of **Batalha**, 12 miles east of **Sangalhos**, these are spectacular woodlands. The king's hunting lodge has been converted into a grandiose, ultrarococo, and inexpensive hotel. To save money, overnight at the above-mentioned **Estalagem Sangalhos** at Sangalhos, in the Bairrada area, and make day trips to the ultraposh **Hotel Palacio** here. Advance reservations are a must at both places. Otherwise, drive to *Luso*, 6 miles away, where adequate accommodation may be found at either **Pensão Alegre** ($38 for a double) or **Pensão Regional**, which charges 20% less.

CASCAIS

This bathing resort is a suburb of the capital, roughly a half-hour's drive west along Portugal's **Costa do Sol**. It has long been a favorite residence of royalty in exile. It lies immediately next to **Estoril**, but there is an older feeling to it, a closer association with the sea and the fishing industry. Prices may be even a smidgen lower than in Estoril, but the difference will be small. For overnighting, **Pensão Casa Lena**, **Pensão Palma**, **Albergaria Valbom**, **Nau**, **Equador**, **Baia**, **Nuno Filipe**, and **Estalagem Do Farol** are substantial for the modest prices, while **Residencial Na. Sra. Das Preces** asks slightly more, provides more (including fado almost every evening), and could be too animated for seekers of tranquillity after dusk. Bullfights are staged here almost every Sun. during July, Aug., and Sept. Try **Costa Azul** (*Rua S.J. de Carvalho 3*) or **Primavera** (*Praca Costa Pinto 6*) for savory local cuisine.

COIMBRA

Coimbra, the fourth city, is ancient, beautiful, and serene. It spreads itself lazily over one big hill, rising from the banks of the **Mondego River** (the longest that has its source in Portugal) to a dominant clock tower at its cap. The nation's largest university, with more than 12,000 students, is here; its 150,000-volume library alone is worth a special trip for bibliophiles. The famous fado "April in Portugal" was composed as a tribute to this two-tiered town of the "miracle of the roses": When Queen Isabel was about to offer bread to the poor, legend has it that it was transformed into blossoms. Don't miss the **Portugal dos Pequenitos** (Children's Portugal), a park where you'll find miniature reproductions of regional buildings. **The Estalagem** in nearby *Santa Luzia*, the **Astoria** (*Av. Navarro*), the **Avenida** (*Av. Emilio Navarro 37*), and the **Residencial Larbelo** (*Largo da Portagem 33*) offer unpretentious accommodation. Try the air-conditioned **D. Pedro** for decent fare or the modest **Ze Manuel, Pinto de Ouro** (*Av. Joao das Regras 68*) or **Restaurante Democratica** (*Trav. da Rua Nova 7*) for home cooking. (In any case, save the artistic Penacova toothpicks for a better occasion.) Archaeology fans should focus on the **Roman remains of Conimbriga** (9 miles south). Marvelous mosaic floors (some of which can still be seen), imposing temples, and a forum were unearthed at this formerly sumptuous settlement, rediscovered in 1930.

ESTORIL

This resort just west of **Cascais** offers a wide public beach, lovely gardens, and a number of inexpensive sidewalk cafes, plus a casino. Passports are required if you wish to assault the gaming rooms; the entrance fee is $3.50 for all rooms or $1.50 to enter the hall for slot machines only; while minimum bets vary with the games and the tables, they're slightly higher than in the Las Vegas hotel parlors or in London's glittery digs. Estoril now draws autumn and winter tourists to augment its traditional spring and summer following. Hotels **Inglaterra**, **Londres**, **Zenith**, **Paris**, and **Lido** are my favorites in the $100-125 range for double occupancy, while **Pensão Chique do Estoril** (*Av. Marginal 62*) and **Pensão Pica-Pau** (*Rua D. Afonso Henriques 2*) cost 40% less. Try **O Petisco** (*Av. Biarritz 3*) or **Sinaleiro** (*Av. Saboia 35*) for inexpensive dining.

ESTREMOZ

This fascinating city is easily accessible from Lisbon by car over excellent highways (which will also enable you to see *Evora* in the same day's excursion). Take time for at least a meal or a night (though a double room may cost over $175 in high season) at the palatial **Pousada da Rainha Santa Isabel** (☎ *22618*). Overlooking the whitewashed stucco houses amid the awesome beauty of an era that will never return to Portugal, it is a living museum of aristocratic antiques, furnishings, paintings, and other art. The food and the service are superlative for a provincial haven. You'll find much cheaper accommodation at either **Pensão Residencia Carvalho** or **Pensão Mateus**.

Dine at **Aguias d'Ouro** for a reasonable $17 full meal. While here, try to make a side trip farther east to **Borba** and **Vila Vicosa**, spending the morning viewing the **Palace of the duke de Braganca**, kept precisely as when the penultimate Portuguese king, Dom Carlos, resided here. If more time is available, make the 24-mile run over to **Elvas** and try the delicious 3-course fixed price (about $30) lunch at the **Pousada Santa Luzia**, near the Spanish frontier.

EVORA

Here's a sleepy little town near the Spanish border, with the **Temple of Diana**, quaint monasteries, and antiquities dating back to the Romans. Evora is one of the keystones of Portuguese history. For overnighting, refer to the preceding special section on "Portugal's Pousada System." The **Pousada dos Loios** is worth a trip in itself, but again, summer price for a double will come to $180 easily. My second choice is **Albergaria Vitoria** on *Rua Diana da Lis*, outside the walls. This 48-unit inn (all doubles with bath at $80) provides modern comforts and excellent attention. Less expensive candidates are **Hotel Planicie**, **Pensão Giraldo**, **Pensão O Eborense**, **Pensão Riviera**, or **Santa Clara**. **Restaurante Giao** (*Rua da Republica 81*) is a good bet for dining.

FATIMA

Atop a mountain range called **Serra d'Aire** this is the scene of the celebrated religious miracle—where the Virgin Mary is said to have appeared before 3 peasant children on repeated occasions during 1917. The site is about 90 miles from Lisbon; take the route to **Vila Franca de Xira**, on to **Alenquer**, to **Rio Maior** on the new road, and thence to **Batalha** and **Fatima**. Or if you don't have a car and don't like the frequent and easily available bus excursions (ask your hotel concierge about these), you may take the train, which will deposit you within 15 miles of your goal at a station now named **Fatima**; run up the rest of the way by taxi. **The Sud-Express** (Paris-Lisbon) also stops daily at this point and is met by shuttle buses. When traveling locally by rail, it's wise to pack a lunch and something to drink. Still another option for drivers who wish to get there fast is simply to take the new **Lisbon-Oporto highway**, which passes close to Fatima (watch for the exit). You may stay at the **Beato Nuno** (operated by the Carmelite Fathers; 8 rooms with bath, 60 with shower, 65 roomettes; many altars; English-speaking priest always on duty). **The Hotel Pax**, the **Pensão Floresta**, the **Pensão Zeca**, the **Estalagem Os Tres Pastorinhos**, the **Hotel Santa Maria**, the **Hotel Cinquentenario**, the **Hotel Regina**, the **Pensão Beato Nuno**, and **Hotel de Fatima** (which now has 250 beds, 2 restaurants, and a conference room) pull down high rates. The 20 or so small pensions of the hamlet are adequate for brief low-cost shelter; among these, **Pensão Casa das Irmas Dominicanas** with 60 rooms is our favorite. **Restaurante Catarino** serves adequate food. You'll undoubtedly witness a lot of commercialism that thrives at the outer fringes. The magnificent new church and mammoth esplanade will ultimately resemble the great plaza of Rome's St. Peters.

GUIMARAES

"*Aqui nasceu Portugal*" (Portugal was born here) can be read in big characters on an ancient wall in the main square of this enchanting village. Here, 32 miles north of *Oporto*, was the nation's first capital and the birthplace of its first king, *Alfonso Henriques*. Its castle (main tower built after the Norman invasion in A.D. 996) is regarded as the foremost monument of this nation; while the 15th-century **Palace of the Dukes of Braganca** reveals the influence of various styles imported from northern Europe. Its collegiate **Church of Our Lady of the Olive Tree** (of incredible beauty) served as seat to the former Royal Chapter. In fact, a stroll through the town is a time warp into the Middle Ages. Or you can travel further back into history, by visiting the archaeological digs of pre-Roman ruins at **Briteiros**. **Santuario da Penha** (Sanctuary of the Rock) is situated 1800 ft. above sea level. **Pousada de Santa Marinha da Costa**, with its 55 rooms ($180 for a double), is the country's largest pousada. It boasts 3 restaurants and first-class services. You also may overnight at the recently inaugurated **Albergaria das Palmeiras** boasting 23 doubles, **Pensão S. Mamede**, the 16-room **Pousada Santa Maria da Oliveira** ($125 double occupancy) or the 63-room, modern, tall, functional **Fundador Dom Pedro**. **Nicolino** is recommendable for its amiable staff, good food, and low prices; ditto for **Jordao** on Avenida Afonso Henriques. Across the charming main square, unpretentious **Cervejaria Martins** will serve you a trencherman's beefsteak, fried egg, rice, tomato, ham, chips, and one beer for the princely sum of $8. **Vira-Bar** is more sophisticated and, naturally, more expensive.

LISBON

Since A.D. 1260, this has been continental Europe's westernmost capital. A profusion of burnt-orange roofs climb the hills, rising in tiers from the busy harbor. Like the nostalgic discoveries cluttered in Grandma's attic, Lisbon's architectural delights are a little worse for wear and years of neglect—but are nevertheless warm and wonderful.

Perhaps the city's prime asset, however, is its proximity to both the sea and the mountains. Estoril and Cascais are only half an hour away; lush and lovely Sintra is about 45 minutes. With train and bus connections among these points so frequent and convenient, it is conceivable that you could do some capital sightseeing in the morning, spend a few bronzing hours on the beach in the afternoon, and enjoy a quiet, relaxing dinner with fado of a summer evening amidst the cooling breezes of the castle-crowned hills.

DIRECTORY

U.S. Embassy • *Av. das Forcas Armada*; ☎ *7266600.*

American Library • *Av. Duque de Loule 22-B*; ☎ *570102.*

American Express • *Star, Av. Sidonio Pais 4-A;* ☎ *3559871.*

Laundromat • Lavimpa, *Av. Estados Unidos 105A* and seven other branches throughout the city; they also have a one-hour dry cleaning service.

Barber and Hairdresser • Barbearia Eduardo VII, *Av. Sidonio Pais 2,* for men; Cabeleireiro Eva, *Praca Marques de Pombal 1,* for ladies. Organizacoes Lucia Piloto also is reputable, with 5 shops in Lisbon.

Dry Cleaning and Pressing • Tinturaria Portugalia, *Rua Alfredo da Silva 10.*

Suit Rental • Guarda Roupa Paiva, *Parque Mayer,* ☎ *3428883.*

HOW TO GET AROUND

Clean, safe, comparatively modern, and inexpensive. Buses and trams are the cheapest and the most fun. Many of the former are big, solid doubledeckers. Both charge on a zone basis, but the average ride costs under 35¢ if you buy a 10-ticket coupon book beforehand. Tickets will be obliterated on one or two ends depending on number of zones. Some of the streetcars traverse the steepest portions of the seven hills, always with their upper carriages perfectly on the level. The 21-station subway is another bargain. Be sure to pick up a transit map and timetables at the **Santa Justa elevator** (*midtown at the corner of Rua Santa Justa and Rua Aurea*). By itself, this rococo landmark qualifies as a bizarre experience.

A one-week **Tourist Ticket**, valid on all forms of public transport in the city (including the 4 funicular elevators), costs about $13; $10 if you prefer a 4-day one. Also available at the Santa Justa elevator.

WHERE TO STAY

LEAST $

Pensão Do Sul • *Praca Dom Pedro IV 59; Av. Almirante Reis 34 and 28; central switchboard:* ☎ *848088 or 847259.* Pick of the litter: Almirante Reis 34 annex with 36 bedrooms, 27 baths, and newer furnishings. Doubles the best buy. Bathrooms cramped. Everything spotless. Singles about $30-36, doubles about $33-44; bed and breakfast. No pension plan available.

Mansao Santa Rita • *Av. Antonio Augusto Aguiar 21;* ☎ *547109.* A 16-room *residencia* squeezed into the 6th floor of a creaky office building. Double occupancy $55-65.

Residencia Lisbonense • *Rua Pinheiro Chagas, 3rd floor;* ☎ *544628.* Offers 22 basic rooms with bath and 8 with running water. Dry singles $28, wet $36, with breakfast into the bargain. Doubles with bath, top out at $52. Some units with 3 beds.

Grande Pensão Alcobia • *Poco de Borratem 15;* ☎ *865171.*

Pensão Canada • *Av. Defensores de Chaves;* ☎ *538159.*

Pensão Alicante • *Av. Duque de Loule 20-2;* ☎ *530514.*

Pensão D. Sancho I • *Av. da Liberdade 202-3;* ☎ *548648.*

Pensão Astoria • *Rua Braamcamp 10-2;* ☎ *41317.*

Pensão Dublin • *Rua de Santa Marta 45-2;* ☎ *555489.*

MORE $$

You'll average from $55-80 per day for a double room, generally with bath. Pension or demipension arrangements (the inclusion of one or all of your main meals) will cost an extra $18-33 for two per day.

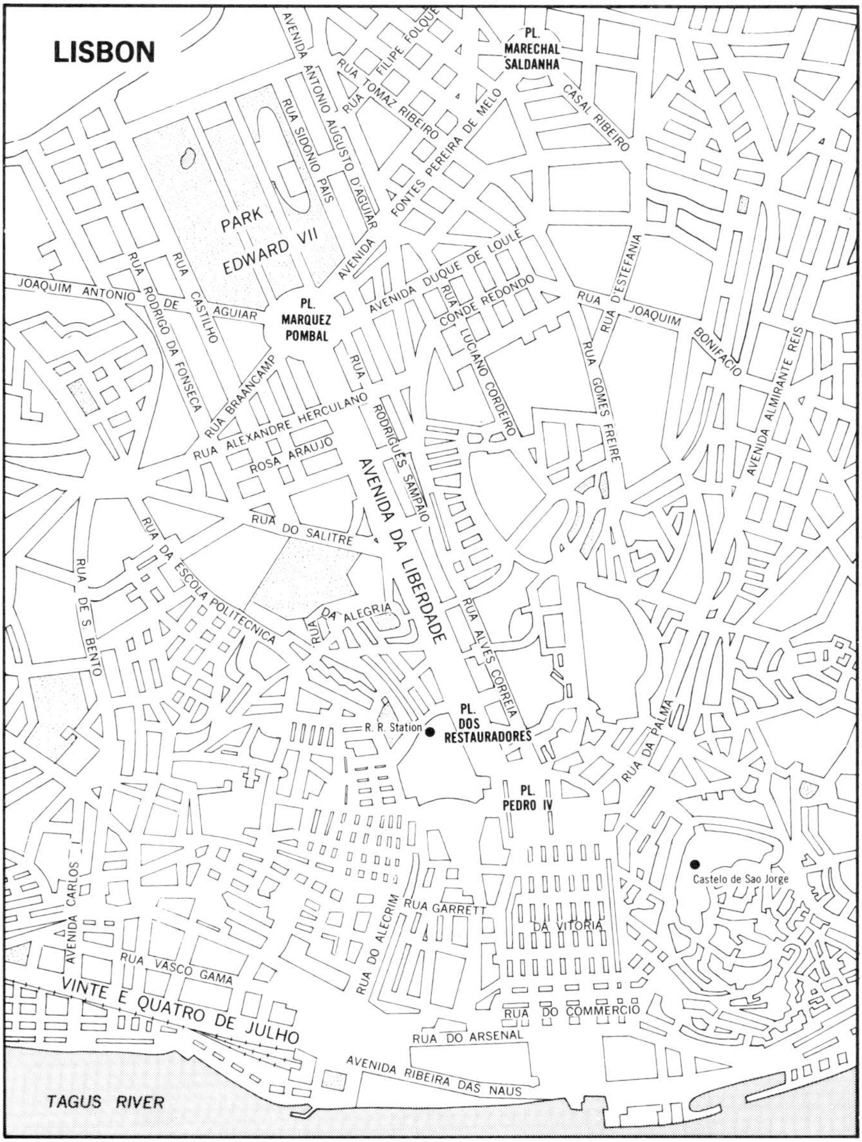
LISBON
PARK EDWARD VII
PL. MARQUEZ POMBAL
PL. MARECHAL SALDANHA
PL. DOS RESTAURADORES
PL. PEDRO IV
R. R. Station
Castelo de Sao Jorge
TAGUS RIVER
AVENIDA ANTONIO AUGUSTO D'AGUIAR
RUA FILIPE FOLQUE
RUA TOMAZ RIBEIRO
RUA SIDONIO PAIS
FONTES PEREIRA DE MELO
CASAL RIBEIRO
AVENIDA DUQUE DE LOULE
RUA CONDE REDONDO
RUA D'ESTEFANIA
RUA JOAQUIM BONIFACIO
AVENIDA ALMIRANTE REIS
JOAQUIM ANTONIO DE AGUIAR
RUA RODRIGO DA FONSECA
RUA CASTILHO
RUA BRAANCAMP
RUA ALEXANDRE HERCULANO
ROSA ARAUJO
RUA LUCIANO CORDEIRO
RUA GOMES FREIRE
RUA RODRIGUES SAMPAIO
AVENIDA DA LIBERDADE
RUA DO SALITRE
RUA DA ESCOLA POLITECNICA
RUA DE S. BENTO
RUA DA ALEGRIA
RUA ALVES CORREIA
RUA DA PALMA
AVENIDA CARLOS
RUA DO ALECRIM
RUA GARRETT
DA VITORIA
RUA VASCO GAMA
VINTE E QUATRO DE JULHO
RUA DO COMMERCIO
RUA DO ARSENAL
AVENIDA RIBEIRA DAS NAUS

Impala • *Rua Filipe Folque 49;* ☎ *528914, 25, or 28.* Almost entirely "suites," with small bath, shower, midget fridge, barette, and kitchenette. Cost of $125 per apartment for 1-4 persons year-round.

do Reno • *Av. Duque de Avila 195, at the São Sebastiao subway stop;* ☎ *548181.* Room-and-breakfast rates of $66 for singles, $75 for doubles. All 50 twin chambers with bath, telephone, and radio; 6 singles. Satisfactory.

Excelsior • *Rua Rodrigues Sampaio 172;* ☎ *537151* and **Principe**, *Av. Duque de Avila 199;* ☎ *536151.* Both specialize in groups. The former serves breakfast only. Main advantages: 100% private bath count, 100% air conditioning, and piped music. Around $85 a double. The latter (same building as the do Reno) levies $80-100 for its twin accommodations; its commodious triples are the best bet. Food charges reasonable: about $19.

Capitol • *Rua Eca de Queiros 24;* ☎ *536811 to 15.* On a bylane 1-1/2 blocks from the Praca Marques de Pombal. TV lounge; basement bar; adequate restaurant. 7th-floor units air-conditioned at no extra charge. All 58 rooms with bath and telephone. Cramped bathrooms. Double with breakfast costs $120; $170 with one major meal. Meals: $24. Not bad.

Residencia America • *Rua Tomas Ribeiro 47, 7th floor, across from the Sheraton Shopping Center;* ☎ *557974.* Under same management. Lounge, restaurant, bar. Most of its 56 units with private bath; 1-3 beds per unit. Excellent value.

Residencia Capital • *Rua Elias Garcia 87.* Not to be confused with the next listing.

Capitol Dom Afonso Henriques • *Rua Barao Sabrosa 204.*

Pax, *Rua Jose Estevao 20;* ☎ *561861*, **Imperador**, *Av. 5 de Outubro 55;* ☎ *51557*, and **Pensão Residencia Roma**, *Travessa da Gloria 22-A;* ☎ *3460557.* Not to be confused with newer Hotel Roma are all likable contenders.

Hotel Roma • *Av. de Roma 33;* ☎ *767761.* A splendid value, but no heart. Offers pool, gym, 3 restaurants, 2 bars, and a movie. 265 air-conditioned rooms.

Miraparque • *Av. Sidonio Pais 12;* ☎ *578070.* Handsomely converted apartment building that operates pension style; 100 sparkly, full-bathed accommodations; good dimensions. Doubles at $90 with breakfast and $180 full pension. Favorite of journalists and visiting diplomatic corps.

Internacional • *Rue da Betesga 3, in the center, near Rossio Square;* ☎ *346401.* Noisy. Slightly seedy; 60 units; 50% bath ratio. Service seemed so mediocre and foot-dragging, it bordered on high comedy.

Dinastia I • *Rua Dom Joao V7;* ☎ *685420.* 32 gaunt, cheerless twins in a noncentral situation. Found lax control and miserable housekeeping at highish prices (for Portugal).

Nazare • *Av. Antonio Augusto de Aguiar 25, 4th and 5th floors;* ☎ *542016.* Convenient downtown location; 32 rooms with bath. Winning bar and lounges; no dining room. Some huge doubles. Singles near $40; twin occupancy around $65.

Metropole • *Praca Dom Pedro IV 30;* ☎ *3469164.* Offers good situation for museum and shopping enthusiasts. Adequate amenities. Reasonable tabs.

Hotel D. Afonso Henriques • *Rua Criostovao Falcao 8;* ☎ *8146574.*

Hotel Vip • *Rua Fernao Lopes 25; ☎ 3521923.*

Hotel Suico Atlantico • *Rua da Gloria 13; ☎ 3461713.*

Hotel Apartamento Cidade Nova • *Avda. Gomes Pereira 29; ☎ 707382.*

EVEN MORE $$$

Dom Carlos • *Av. Duque de Loule 121, only 2 short blocks off Av. de Liberdade; ☎ 539071.* Bar-lounge and breakfast room. Full air conditioning. All singles, twins, and suites with radio, phone, and diminutive but adequate bathroom.

Flamingo • *Rua Castilho 41, just off Eduardo VII Park; ☎ 532191.* Prettiest upstairs. Restaurant with excellent food. All rooms with bath and telephone; #51, a favorite double.

Diplomatico • *Rua Castilho 74; ☎ 562041.* Near the Flamingo. Dining salon and pub; 90 quiet, air-conditioned quarters; private baths and radios. Top 3 levels offer breathtaking picture of Lisbon and River Tagus.

Lisboa • *Rua Barata Salgueiro 5, just off Avenida da Liberdade; ☎ 554131.* 55 units plus 6 luxurious suites. Private parking; piano bar; fully air-conditioned; amenities galore but no restaurant. Singles $150-200; doubles $180-240. A new and already popular hotel.

Holiday Inn Lisbon • *Avenida Antonio Jose de Almeida 28-A; ☎ 7935222.* Another recent addition. It boasts 169 rooms and 8 suites (Presidential one is a cost overrun). Restaurant; bar; several conference facilities; air-conditioned throughout; outdoor pool plus health club. High tariffs ($250 singles and $300 doubles) in this uptown contender.

Eduardo VII • *Av. Fontes Pereira de Melo 5; ☎ 530141.* Occupies a busy situation. Rooftop bar and restaurant. All 95 pads with private bath.

Rex • *Rua Castilho 169; ☎ 682161.* Nobly revamped and an excellent location.

Jorge V • *Rua Mouzinho da Silveira 3; ☎ 562525.* Lovely neighborhood. TV lounge. 45 radio, telephone, and shower-equipped rooms. Partial to #604, a cheery double with large closet and marble bath.

Principe Real • *Rua de Alegria 53; ☎ 3460116.* Conveniently near Av. de Liberdade, the Botanical Garden, Eduardo VII Park, and downtown Lisbon. Neat doubles $170 and singles $140; 2 dozen large rooms, all with private baths.

CAMPING

The **Parque de Campismo de Monsanto** (*☎ 720061*), about 10 minutes toward *Estoril* along the *Auto-Estrada do Oeste*, is recommended; low-cost cafeteria, small shops, a swimming pool, and proximity to the beaches of Estoril. Glorious sylvan setting; facilities rudimentary; Oct.-April 75¢, May-Sept. $3 per person per night. Ask either the **Portuguese Camping Federation** (*Rua Voz de Operario 1 r/c; ☎ 862350*) or the **Lisbon Camping Club** (*Rua da Misericordia 137; ☎ 3463626*) for directions to this and to other camping sites.

SUGGESTIONS FOR STUDENTS

Here are the 3 biggest concentrations of collegians: **Cidade Universitaria**, a sprawling campus in a pleasant arbored setting near the Hipodromo and Campo Grande (perhaps 15 minutes from the center, by Buses #31, #35, #38); **Instituto Superior Tecnico**, off a continuation of *Av. Duque de Avila* (Bus #20 or #22 from Praca Marques de Pombal), and **Escola Politecnica**, beside the *Jardim Botanico* (Botanical Gardens), and on the *Rua da Escola Politecnica*.

LODGINGS AND MEALS

Try **Forte Catalazete** at *Oeiras* (☎ *3559081*), adjacent to the **Motel Continental**, which recently was enlarged and now belongs to the **Portuguese Association of Youth Hostels** *(at 137 Avenida Dugue d'Avila, 1000 Lisbon)*. It has 92 beds in total and 4 double rooms, bar, kitchen, TV room, conference facilities, and is open the year-round. As low as $8 per person with breakfast; lunch or dinner only $6 and about $10 during high season. A real bargain. Two other candidates are **Turicoop-Turismo Social e Juvenil** (*Rua Pascoal de Melo 15-1;* ☎ *531804*) and **Turismo Juvenil** (*Praca de Londres 9-B;* ☎ *8484957*).

YOUTH HOSTELS

There are 17 located in the capital, Alcoutim (*Algarve*), Areia Branca, Braga, Catalazete, Coimbra, Leiria, Penhas da Saude (*Serra da Estrela*), Portalegre, Portimao, Oporto, Sintra, São Martinho (*Alcobaca road*), São Pedro de Moel (open May 1-Sept. 30), Vila Nova de Cerveira, Vila Real de Santo Antonio, and Vilarinho das Furnas (*National Park of Peneda-Geres*). The Lisbon one was revamped recently; it is located at *Rua Andrade Corvo 46*; ☎ *571054*. Overall rates are quite similar to those of Catalazete.

Youth Hostels may only be utilized by members. Applications must be submitted to **American Youth Hostels, Inc., Nat. Admin. Office**, *1332 "I" Street, NW, 8th Floor, Washington, DC 20005*. Bookings in Portugal are handled by the **Associacao Portuguesa de Pousadas de Inventude**, *46 Rua Andrade Corve, 1000 Portugal;* ☎ *571054.*

WHERE TO EAT

LEAST $

Solmar • *Rua das Portas da Santo Antao 108, around the corner from the Pan Am office.* Unprepossessing facade; cheerful interior. House specialties: crabs and fish (seasonal) taken alive from their own aquarium. Average meal pushing $35. Avoid the expensive lobster or shrimp.

Principe do Calhariz • *Calcada do Combro 28, about 3 blocks west of Praca Luis de Camoes.* Saloon atmosphere. Normal portions about $10; smaller rations $8. Room dominated by large TV.

Sagitario • *Between Jeronimos Monastery and Coach Museum.* The latter closed Mon., but check first. A solid bet for sightseers. Several snack bars along this same row—none good, but all clean enough for a nibble. While out here, don't miss the Galeotas Room of the Marine Museum, containing early airplanes as well as boats.

Churrasqueira • *Campo Grande, somewhat distant from downtown.* In a park. Reminiscent of a bustling butcher shop that decided to go into the restaurant business—and succeeded in a big way. Indoor and outdoor dining, a tearoom, and a cozy nook. Low prices; giant veal chop a bargain in bovinity. Open noon to midnight every day.

Marisqueira Popular • *Rua dos Correeiros 207, near Rossio.* Amiable service; 18 simple tables in one small room. Popular chicken and vegetable soup only 75¢; Pescada Cosida $8; full meal $12. Gregarious, to say the least.

Casa Lira de Ouro • *Rua Nova de S. Mamede 12, near Pensão São Jorge.* Features spit-roasted chicken ($13). Long bar; 18 tables. Good local wines and brandies. Brighter and better scrubbed than most of its ilk. Never order lobster ($44 per catch). Operative till 2 a.m. daily.

Churrasco • *Rua das Portas de Santo Antao 83, near Rossio.* Also specializes in grilling fowl. Stays open an hour later and is equally attractive. Cozy bar for predinner nips.

Arameiro • *Travessa de Santo Antao 21.* Chicken specialty. Bright, clean, air-conditioned. Fixed-price menu a modest $13; great success.

Novo Dia • *Rua Antao de Almada 4-C.* Very good. A splendid location in Largo de São Domingos, just behind the Rossio.

Celta • *Rua Gomes Freire 148-C and D.* Also rewarding, yet more atmospheric.

Tulipa • *Rua Conde Redondo 17.* Specializes in snacks.

Here's a list of 10 choices where they won't charge you more than $14-18 for a full meal including a half bottle of wine:

Xico Carreira • *Parque Mayer; ☎ 3463805.*

Tio Pepe • *Calcada do Sacramento 36; ☎ 3469308.*

Bonjardim • *Trav. de Santo Antao 12; ☎ 3424389.*

As Velha • *Rua da Conceicao da Gloria 19; ☎ 3422490.*

Cervejaria da Trindade • *Rua Nova da Trindade 20; ☎ 3423506.*

Adega Progreso • *Rua dos Sapateiros 203; ☎ 3428382.*

Porto de Abrigo • *Rua dos Remolares 16; ☎ 3460873.*

Joao do Grao • *Rua dos Correeiros 222; ☎ 3424757.*

Cafreal • *Rua das Portas de Santo Antao 71; ☎ 3468447.*

Estrela • *Rua dos Sapateiros 111; ☎ 3428237.*

SNACKS

In this country, the term signifies only that service is more rapid than average. One of the smartest snack bars in Lisbon is in the ultraritzy Hotel Ritz, while the Hotel Roma has one of the most modern in the nation.

Among those still thriving is the **Derbi** (*Rua das Portas de Santo Antao*), which is okay. The self-service **Noite e Dia** (*Av. Duque de Loule 51-A*) is a honey of a value; highly recommended. **Benard** (*Rua Garrett 104, off the Rua do Carmo*) is a handy coffeehouse for that break in the shopping routine. The drugless drugstore, **Apolo 70** (*Avenida Julio Dinis, 10-A,D,E*), the **Torio** (*Rua Tomas Ribeiro 38*), and the **Paquito** (*Visconde Valbom*) all feature quick-bite fare, cleanliness, and low prices. **Monumental** (*Rua Castilho, near the Hotel Flamingo*) and **Caprilia** (*Rua Braamcamp*) rate highly for value.

Bairro Alto (*High Quarter*) low-cost. Ancient Lisbon also can be found in *Bairro Alto* which, together with *Alfama* and *Mouraria*, is one of the capital's most typical sectors. Right at the heart of the city, it was founded in 1513, soon developing into the zone for nobility. Following nature's usual course in the last century, it was converted into a residential area of the working class. Its narrow cobblestone lanes, its *varinas* (fishmongers), and laden carts create a market atmosphere. It also has a nightlife that focuses on fado, a few streetwalkers, inexpensive restaurants, *tascas* (snack havens), and numerous small bars. This "short list" comprises what, in our opinion, are the better choices along with their specialties.

TASCAS

Baralto • *Rua Diario de Noticias 31.* Cod *minho* style ($9-16).

Primavera • *Trav. da Espera 34.* Filets of hake Primavera ($10-16).

O Fidalgo • *Rua da Barroca 27.* Grilled cod and broad beans ($10-15).

Tasca Do Manel • *Rua da Barroca 24.* Eels stewed with bread ($10-15).

O Capuchinho • *Rua da Rosa 71.* Cod "na Canoa" ($9-10).

Adega Das Merces • *Trav. das Merces 2.* Boiled meat with macaroni and vegetables ($9-12).

RESTAURANTS

Bota Alta • *Trav. da Quaimada 37.* Royal cod ($11-17).

Mata Bicho • *Rua Gremio Lusitano 18.* Rabbit Algarve style ($13-20).

Cocheira Alentejana • *Trav. Poco da Cidade 19.* Roast suckling pig ($13-18).

Farta Brutos • *Trav. da Espera 16.* Many local dishes ($15-22).

El Ultimo Tango • *Rua Diario de Noticias 62.* Frogfish Florence style ($15-21).

MORE $$

Arraial • *Rua Conde Sabugosa 13-A.* Colorful and zesty. Fast, friendly service by costumed waiters. Huge portions. Heavy use of olive oil, so if your system growls, stick to simple grills. Not central, but worth the cab fare. Open daily for lunch and dinner.

Eduardo VII • *Atop hotel of same name.* An old reliable. English bar; open terrace; view of gently sloping city and river beyond; a meal of hors d'oeuvres or soup; fish, veal, or smoked beef; and serpa cheese, coffee, and a mellow port should cost you around $44. Appetizer cart held 27 choices. Open for lunch and 7:30-10 p.m.

Faz Figura • *Rua do Paraiso 15-B.* Resides high in Alfama district overlooking harbor cranes and shipping channel of the Tagus. Posh, clublike atmosphere. Indoor and outdoor dining. The shrimp cocktail (a splurge) was delicious; steak Portuguese cooked in casserole with boiled potatoes and smoked ham; tiny Squid Gratine lovely.

Estalagem do Cavalo Branco • *Av. do Almirante Gago Coutinho 146;* ☎ *8486121.* You eat what's put before you; food is excellent, the price low. On my last visit, I was served whitefish in hot cheese sauce surrounded by crisp cauliflower and fried potatoes.

A Quinta • ("The Farm"). Near the Santa Justa outdoor elevator in the heart of town. Adequate portions in the $15 range. Wondrous rooftop view of harbor. Choices include Hungarian goulash, steak-and-kidney pie, corned beef, and fluffy omelets.

Delfim • *Rua Nova de S. Mamede 23.* Low-priced and rewarding. Unpretentious white-and-blue-tile decor. We suggest fried pork with clams, grilled turbot with tartar sauce, and the house dessert. National cuisine and ambience; friendly staff. Excellent for its category.

Antonio • *Rua Tomas Ribeiro 63, in shadow of Sheraton.* Of two rooms, we prefer one farther back. Always busy; Portuguese come for excellent piscatorial preparations. You might appreciate the house specialty called *Acorda*, resembling a marriage of a souffle and a damp omelet; made with whipped bread, egg, clams, shrimp, and black olives. A huge lunch for 2 with wine will cost about $50.

Lorde • *Rua Victor Cordon 14-A.* Large chimney, miniature bar, and 10 intimate tables in an oak-paneled room. Bar girls are not uncommon; high prices are.

A Gondola • *Av. de Berna 64.* Under the airport's flight path. Italian dishes; delightful enclosed garden.

Bodegon • *In the Hotel Fenix, Praca Marques de Pombal.* Popular with locals and tour group leaders. On hot days stick to the appetizing cold-plate lunch.

Cortador • ("Butcher Shop"), *Ave. de Berna 36* (a.k.a. "Oh Lacerda!"). Used to be a favorite, but has become too commercial with too sharp an eye for the tourist trade.

NIGHTLIFE

Lisbon has few conventional nightclubs. The world-famous *fado* restaurants are their one-of-a-kind replacement. Here is the birthplace and home of the heartrending folk music so beloved by the people. The word means "fate," and therein lies the essence of its mood. Within the "taverns" (for want of a better term), young girls in aprons or potbellied characters in sweaters will suddenly burst forth in these stylized, haunting laments. Informal atmosphere; adequate food; songs that will never leave you; generally (but not always) inexpensive. Reserve early everywhere.

Incidentally, a hopped-up version, the so-called *pop fado*, is a monstrous travesty.

Lisboa a Noite • *Rua das Gaveas 69.* For *classic fado*, our number one choice. The $21 minimum (including service and all taxes) might seem expensive until you consider the fine musical cast that guarantees its continuing quality. Whitewashed den under arches; open tile-lined kitchen at one end; guitars and copperware on the walls. Solid local fare; fado renditions every 20 minutes or so after 11 p.m.; the soul-buffeting voice of Fernanda Maria in the wee hours.

Senhor Vinho • *Rua do Meio-a-Lapa.* My second choice.

Timpanas • *Near the harbor in Alcantara district.* Popular, inexpensive, and good.

A Severa • *Rua das Gaveas 57.* Near Lisboa a Noite packs many groups into its small room; a merry ambience in which perhaps 70% of the clients are fellow tourists; 38 tables; streetlamp lighting; attentive table watching. The least you can spend here is about $22; if you plan on dining, the average cost of a meal with wine is $58–72 per person.

Luso • *Travessa da Queimada 10.* Much more institutional. Shows from 10 p.m. to 2 a.m. These revels occur in a 17th-century building that has been eviscerated and refitted. For a finale, the troupe invited onlookers to join the corn-fed hoedown. Within 20 minutes, out came semi-dry photos of each wide-eyed participant.

Other popular and less expensive stops:

Parreirinha de Alfama • *Beco do Espirito Santo 1* and **Machado**, *Rua do Norte 91.* Perhaps the most famous.

O Forcado • *Rua da Rosa 221.* Purveys by the nightful.

Ad Lib • *Rua Barata Salgueiro.* Not too expensive, and the music is excellent.

Cova da Onca • *Av. de Liberdade 248-B.* Meaning "The Jaguar's Cave"

Hipopotamo • *Av. Antonio Augusto de Aguiar, 3-A.*

Beat Club, • *Rua Conde de Sabugosa, 11-D.*

A Cave • *Av. Antonio Augusto de Aguiar 88* and **Club 81**, *Rua Silva Carvalho 81.*

A Lareira • *Praca Aqueduto das aguas Livres, 8-I.* Resides in a single room flooded by red light; bar, jukebox, and tables strung partially around the dance floor; an $8 weekday minimum that sneaks up to $10 on weekends. Go late.

WHAT TO SEE AND DO

In Lisbon, the **Coach Museum** (one of the unique collections of vehicles in the world; open 10 a.m.–6:30 p.m. from June through Sept., closing at 5 p.m. otherwise; closed Mon.); the 2000-year-old **Castelo de São Jorge** (open 8 a.m. to sunset); and the **Alfama** (the old quarter of the city adjoining the castle and the cathedral). See the **Popular Museum** and a slice of life left over from the days of Columbus. A magnificent collection of national and foreign attire from the 4th through the 18th century can be found at the **National Costume Museum** (*Museu Nacional de Traje*), **Largo Julio Castilho**, **Parque do Monteiro-Mor**, **Lumiar**. **The Museu de Marinha** (*Praca do Imperio 2*) exhibits naval uniforms, arms, and equipment. **Museu Gulbenkian**, reopened in its home on Av. Berna, is an impressive cultural landmark; filled with art, furniture, and rare craft items from this great and wealthy collector's homes. The **Museu Nacional de Arte Antiga** (Museum of Ancient Art), at *Rua das Janelas Verdes 95*, displays a superb collection of paintings, pottery, porcelain, and other manifestations of Portuguese antiquity. The **Museu Nacional do Azulejo** (Tile Museum), at *Rua da Madre de Deu 4*, is a marvel; it glistens with what should be considered Europe's most impressive show of colored glazed tiles. If you want to make the rounds in a delightfully unusual way, the **Star Travel Agency** (*Av. Sidonio Pais 4-A*) operates tours that crisscross the city in trolley cars decked out in turn-of-the-century finery. Multilingual guides; daytime and evening excursions; low tariffs; great fun, especially for first-time visitors. **Cityrama** also runs tours.

Sintra is an easy excursion destination; refer to our alphabetical listing for details. If possible, go on the second or fourth Sunday of any month to see São Pedro's colorful market.

For a shorter outing, **Estoril** is also covered in our separate report. Half an hour by car or fine train ($2) from the center of Lisbon.

You might enjoy the drive from Lisbon to **Setubal**. This sardine-factory center is also a pleasant ride from town. Don't miss the **Church of Jesus**, in which the pillars are twisted to resemble fishermen's ropes.

The **strand of Caparica**, the wooded bay of **Portinho d'Arrabida**, and the rustic harbor of **Sesimbra** (**Espadarte** is a good moderately priced lunch stop), are all within a 30-mile radius south of the capital. Sand, beach, simplicity, low price tags.

CONCERTS

The musical season takes off at the **Gulbenkian** in the fall; concerts are held in many churches, too, as well as in the halls referred to below for ballet; from early winter to early summer, opera is performed at the **S. Carlos**. Ballet is offered by the **Gulbenkian Foundation**, **São Luis Municipal Theater, Coliseu dos Recreios**, and the **National Ballet Group** during fall, winter, and spring for as low as $4. Of special interest is the **Lisbon Players group**, which is composed of English-speaking thespians who perform sporadically at **Estrela Hall** in the British Hospital.

AMUSEMENT PARK

None as such. For a substitute, at Campo Grande the **Feira Popular** ("People's Fair") whirls with regularity during the summer months. Two other proud landmarks are the **Botanical Gardens** on *Rua da Escola Politecnica* and the interesting **Estufa Fria** in the *Parque Eduardo VII* opposite the Ritz Hotel.

MOVIES

All films are shown in their original versions, so simply check any of the periodicals below; the reported titles are in Portuguese and the best seats cost less than $4.

MARKETS

The **Mercado da Ribeira** is the big one; it's down by the **Estoril Railway Station** at *Cais do Sodre*; no action on Sun. On Tues. and Sat. the **Lisbon Flea Market** begins early in the mornings, but it's hardly worth setting your alarm clock for. A better bet for low-grade antiques and whatnots is the bazaar at **S. Pedro de Sintra**, which functions every 2nd and 4th Sun. of each month.

PUBLICATIONS

What's On in Lisbon is invaluable for information on activities in or near the capital. The *Anglo-Portuguese News* tells it all in our tongue. *Your Companion in Portugal* is such a reliable brochure that every traveler since Vasco da Gama seems to have used it. Lisbon's City Hall organizes a vast program of events every year (published in March) at very low admission costs, so we suggest you pick up your free copies from any of the numerous tourist offices (identifiable by the sign "Turismo").

EASY WARM-WEATHER EXCURSIONS

Floresta Do Ginjal, • *Ginjal 7, Cacilhas;* ☎ *2750087.* Offers the best view of Lisbon on the far side of the Tagus. Drive or bus over the 25th of April Bridge or, far better, buy a ferry ticket and take the 10-minute voyage with a robust assembly of workers, farmers, fishermen, children, assorted commuters, and horse-drawn wagons. These ply to and fro every 10 minutes until 9:30 p.m., after which they run every half hour till morning. Turn right sharply at the landing and follow the dock past a string of competitors. This 3-stage restaurant can hold 500 at a time. Windows overlook the masts of Portugal's North Atlantic fishing fleet. The English, French, and Portuguese menu is filled with $9-14 dishes; service is jolly, gracious, and efficient. An appetizer, consisting of fish cake, potato salad, sardines, salami, ripe olives, curried rice, ham, and cockles was great. The entree was perfectly grilled red mullets, mixed salad, and pineapple. Open every day for lunch and dinner. Good for both food and scenery.

Goncalves • *Only 20 yards away from Floresta do Ginjal;* ☎ *2750062.* Becoming very popular.

Restaurante Policia • *Rua Marques Sa de bandeira 112.* Small bar; 26 tables on two levels; Portuguese meal (mostly fish) about $18. Open noon–3 p.m. and 7–9:30 p.m. The name has no connection with the law.

Galeto • *Av. da Republica*, and **Solar Boemio**, *Rua dos Gorreeiros 125-129.* Are two above-average choices; vittles served with genuine warmth and charm.

O Paco • *Av. de Berne*, and **Antonio**, *Rua Tomas Ribeiro.* Another worthy pair.

WHERE TO SHOP

CERAMICS AND PORCELAINS

Vista Alegre, (*Largo do Chiado 18*) is justifiably the nation's leader. **Sant'Anna**, (*Rua do Alecrim 91A*) carries many reproductions of antique tiles, plates and ashtrays. **Viuva Lamengo** (*Largodo Intendente Pina Manique 25*) has a large, inexpensive inventory, but it isn't overly thrilling to us.

EMBROIDERIES, ORGANDIES, AND TAPESTRIES

Madeira Superbia (*Av. Duque de Loule 75A and also at Rua Augusta 231*, plus branches at the *Hotel Ritz*, and in *Estoril* and *Faro*) is the house, in our opinion. Every piece of its richly wrought stock comes directly from its venerable studios and "factory" in the island capital of *Funchal*. Among the low-priced lures awaiting your inspection are lovely breakfast sets (1 mat and 2 napkins), floral needlepoint chair covers, and squares for cushions. You'll also find tempting rugs, pictures, and evening bags; lots more.

GOLD AND SILVER JEWELRY

Gold is the best bet in the country. By law 19-1/4 carats is the minimum weight that can be sold over the counter. Of the many respectable shops in Lisbon, the most reliable and interesting is **W. A. Sarmento**, *Rua Auera 251* (bottom of the Santa Justa elevator). There is a large display of alluring, intricately filigreed earrings, brooches, cufflinks, and similar items, most in handworked, gold-plated silver—at prices lower than you'd think. Ask for friendly and helpful Mr. Arthur Sarmento, who speaks flawless English.

HANDICRAFTS

Centro de Artesanato, (*Rua Castilho 61*) is fair for routine gifts. Also try **Casa Quintao** *(Rua Ivens 30)*, known for its Beiriz and Arraiolos rugs. Art from the Azores is represented at **Casa Regional da Ilha Verde** (*Rua Paiva de Andrade 4*).

SHOPPING CENTERS

Centro Comercial das Amoreiras, (*Avenida Duarte Pacheco*) is mammoth—the largest in the land. It incorporates 309 shops, plus restaurants and an exhibition hall. **The Imariz complex**, across from the Sheraton, is tiny by comparison.

SHOPPING ZONES

The **"Chiado" district**, which includes Nova do Almada, Rua Garrett, and Rua do Carmo; **Rua da Escola Politecnica** and its extensions (best for antique hunting); and the **"Baixa" section**, whose streets run from Rossio Sq. to the Tagus River. The newest additions to the scene are the **Bairro Alto** and the **Praca das Flores**.

The 17% tax (IVA) is easily refunded through the Tax Free for Tourists program. (By the way, on Madeira this bite is only 12%. Gold objects costing more than $98 are reduced by a generous 19%, making them quite a bargain.) Ask the shopkeeper to issue a Tax Free Cheque if you've bought at least 11,000 escudos worth of goods. By following the simple procedures, you can obtain an immediate refund at the Lisbon airport or have it mailed to you either as a deduction on your credit card or as a direct check.

NAZARE

About 3 hours out from the capital is a colorful little fishing village and Portuguese summer resort of whitewashed houses, tourist-conscious fisherfolk, and narrow streets that all run down to the sea. Legend ties the famous local tartan costumes to a crew of Scotsmen shipwrecked here centuries ago, while a more recent version talks of Wellington's troops, who stopped here during the Napoleonic wars. You may buy this unique handwoven cloth along the beach. Wonderful swimming; fishing from sardine to fighting carapau; boats at reasonable rates. There's a funicular (when it works!) to the **Sitio**, or Upper Town, where you'll find a lighthouse, a church, and a glorious view.

WHERE TO STAY

The **Hotel Nazare**, the **Hotel Dom Fuas**, the **Hotel Mare**, and the **Hotel Da Praia** are passable. In addition, the following pensãos charge from $50 to $75 for a double during high season: **Ribamar**, ☎ *46158*; **Madeira**, ☎ *46180*, located on beach front; **Central**, ☎ *46510*; **Beira Mar**, ☎ *46458*; and the **Laranjo**. The first-class **Hotel da Praia** is on *Avenida Vieira Guimaraes*. Eat in your hotel instead of in the tourist traps along the shore; exceptional independent restaurants, however, are: **Mar Bravo** and **Beira-Mar**, both near the beach.

OBIDOS

This totally walled city is an easy excursion from Lisbon or a worthwhile overnight stay if you can secure accommodation in the **Pousada do Castelo** (☎ *95105*). The hostelry contains a mere 6 rooms, half of them with private bath, but it is so overwhelming in its beauty that we urge you to spend some time here if you can. This installation is built into the fortress tower—at the same time both intimate and grand. A visitor has the feeling that he is part of the court of a noble household. In the lower village, also within the crenellated walls, is the **Estalagem do Convento**, which has attractive accommodations. **Albergaria Rainha Santa Isabel**, **Pensão Martim de Freitas**, and **Albergaria Josefa de Obidos** are convenient too. A mildly athletic tourist can circumnavigate the entire village walking on the wide tops of the walls. In the hamlet itself, there are numerous bars, several churches, and the inevitable souvenir shops. As a possible alternative to the above stopping places, you may find space in the recently revamped and expanded 41-room **Hotel da Torre-Motel**, 2 miles out of town toward Santarem, or at **Casa de Hospedes Madeira**. **D. Joao V**, **Alcaide**, and **Lidador** are discreet local restaurants. Try not to miss this fascinating jewel.

OPORTO

There's plenty of activity in this gateway to the sea. The town is built on a dome-shaped hill; exits of a fine 2-tier bridge hit the riverbank at both top and bottom levels. Local color abounds too; life is far simpler than it is in the capital. Don't fail to visit the wine lodges at **Vila Nova da Gaia**, across the Douro. Of approximately 30 installations, we suggest the old and prestigious **Ferreira caves**, where a team of 8 multilingual guides will show you the cellars and explain the process of wine making. Phone **Mr. Fernando Xavier** (☎ *300866*) in advance; readers of this guide will be shown "old bin," the cooper section, and be privileged to sample the prize wines. Ferreira very likely will offer a house souvenir or, if you prefer, a rebate on a 45-minute **Three Bridges Cruise** along the river (April to Oct., except Sat. afternoons and Sun.)

The **cathedral** (begun in the early 12th century) and the **Soares dos Reis Museum** in the Carrancas Palace (its cavernous hulk stuffed with gold artifacts and paintings) are musts for viewing.

WHERE TO STAY

Pensão Avis, (*Av. Rodrigo de Freitas 451;* ☎ *320772*), **Pensão Universal**, (*Av. dos Aliados 38-1;* ☎ *2006758*), and **Pensão Lis**, *(Rua de Antero do Quental 659;* ☎ *492305*) are my choices in the $50 per double range, whereas **Hotel Peninsular**, (*Rua Sa da Bandeira 21;* ☎ *2003012*), **Hotel Nave**, (*Av. Fernao de Magalhaes 247;* ☎ *576131*), and **Hotel Malaposta**, (*Rua da Conceicao 80;* ☎ *2014352*) will charge almost double. Restaurants? For less than $17 you may enjoy a full meal with wine at **Abadia** (*Trav. Passos Manuel, 22*), **Imperial** (*Praca da Liberdade 125*), **Solar da Conga** (*Rua do Bonjardim 294*), or **São Pedro** (*Rua do Bonjardim 300*).

Oporto is ideal as a base of operations; excursions through the wine country to **Bom Jesus**, to **Braga**, to **Guimaraes**, and to dozens of fascinating villages such as those in the **Minho Province**, the seaside resort of **Ofir**, or **Barcelos**, are recommended either as visiting targets or overnighting oases. Especially popular in autumn, when the grapes are in harvest.

PALMELA

Situated 25 miles south of Lisbon in the midst of a wine-growing district, this ancient village is renowned for its 8th-century Moorish castle, peaking 700 feet high on the summit of the **Arrabida**. Within its fortified walls, **Pousada de Palmela** will delight your senses with its mysterious blend of austerity, coziness, and serenity; 27 impeccable rooms; magnificent salons; a well-regarded restaurant. Otherwise, you'll find decent fare at either **Perola da Serra** or **Retiro Azul**. Try not to miss this enchanting hamlet.

SESIMBRA

Portugal's main resort for sea angling (especially swordfish) is located only 45 minutes from Lisbon via the gloriously panoramic bridge. **The Hotel Do Mar** nestles 75 yards above the sea and this still unspoiled fishing village. Vaguely Hawaiian-style construction; buildings stagger up a hillside for successively better vistas of the bay; entrance at top with access to 4 tiers of rooms and terraces; glassy crown composed of a 2-section restaurant with a sweeping view. The shoreside **Espadarte** offers 80 modest rooms with private baths or showers—some with balcony. Its restaurant—quite naturally—specializes in sea fare. About 3 miles away, **Estalagem dos Zimbros** has the advantage of being closest to the imposing Cabo Espichel. It has 35 clean bedchambers, a swimming pool, and 2 tennis courts. **Angelus**, **Ribamar**, and **Pedra Alta** are simple eateries.

SINTRA

Sintra is about a half-hour from Lisbon by car and perhaps 15 minutes more by train or bus. If you can arrange it, go on the second or fourth Sunday of any month and take in the colorful market of São Pedro, a Sintra staple. Drive out through Estoril, then take the spectacularly beautiful mountain road through a national forest preserve. Tuck in the marvelous beach of **Guincho** and take a look at **Cascais**.

When you near your goal, climb up through gardens and flowering camellia trees to the mammoth fairy-tale castle perched on a high peak. **Pena** was the summer home of the last kings of Portugal; its splendor is stunning, with an overlay of whimsy and extravagance. The grounds here and at nearby **Monserrate** are exquisite. Entry fees are insignificant. The road leads down past the old Moorish castle atop a neighboring crest to the little town in the valley. Some of the finest *quintas* (country estates) of Portugal are here. Don't miss the **Royal Palace of Sintra**, until 1910 a royal redoubt built on the ruins of a Moorish fortress by King João I in the 14th century and now housing a museum of historical interest.

You'll find adequate accommodation (about $47 per double) at **Pensão Sintra** (☎ *9230738*) or 20% less at **Pensão Nova Sintra** (☎ *9230220*) but no rooms with bath here. You may also try **Hotel Central** (☎ *9230963*), $95 per double in high season, and **Hotel das Arribas** (☎ *9292145*). The latter has been converted into an aparthotel; $68 for two during high season; add $17 per guest (up to 5). No restaurant. Try either **dos Arcos** (*Rua Serpa Pinto 4*) or **Alcobaca** (*Rua das Padarias 7*) for local fare.

FOR MORE INFORMATION ON PORTUGAL

USA • **Portuguese National Tourist Office**, *590 Fifth Ave., New York, N.Y. 10036-4704,* ☎ *(212) 354-4403.* • You may also obtain information from the Portuguese embassies or other governmental agencies.

INSIDER TIP

(1) It's worth noting that State-operated pousadas or inns exist all over Portugal. (This organization, **ENATUR***, won our "Temple Fielding Travel Award" not long ago.) These are rest houses often located in palaces or historic buildings; prices today have shot skyward and are not far from normal commercial levels. The places, however, are exceptional. Information can be obtained from the* **Portuguese National Tourist Offices** *in New York or in Lisbon from the* **Director General for Tourism** *(*executive offices at Av. Antonio Augusto de Aguiar 86, with Travel Information facilities at Praca dos Restauradores 27*).*

(2) The Portuguese State Tourist Office has developed what they call "Turismo no Espaco Rural" (countryside tourism), now divided into **Turismo de Habitaçao** *(manor houses, residential homes, and buildings of special architectural value and exquisite decoration; $60-100 singles and $80-125 doubles, although prices go up by 30% in about a dozen of these houses, especially in the Sintra region),* **Turismo Rural** *(rustic homes that match their region's environment but are located within towns or nearby; $32-60 singles and $40-65 doubles), and* **Agroturismo** *(farmhouses in agricultural areas where guests may participate in farming chores or other forms of rustic animation; singles $40-70 and doubles $50-110). Some of these manors ("solares") date back to the 15th century; many are located off the beaten paths throughout the country. I suggest the Costa Verde (Green Coast) region in the north, especially Guimaraes, Viana do Castelo, and* Ponte de Lima. *Contact* **Mrs. Maria do Ceu** *(*at TURIHAB Posto de Turismo in the town of Ponte de Lima, ☎ 058-942335; FAX 32618 PTPL*). For most of the other regions, communicate with* **Mrs. Ines Pinheiro** *(*at Torre D2-3A, 12th floor, Alto da Pampilheira, 2750 Cascais; ☎ 4867958 and 2844464; FAX 43304 PITSAP*). Also you may contact* **Mrs. Joaquina Alvim at PRIVETUR** *(*Travessa de Cima dos Quarteis, 24-2-A, 1200 Lisbon*;* ☎ 654953 and 2868232*).*

SCOTLAND

Scotland is a small country but an immensely varied one. There are heather-covered moors, towering granite mountains, misty valleys and glens, lochs, rivers, islands, and sea. Its history bristles with tales of fearsome tribes and brave patriots. James VI of Scotland—simultaneously ruling England—first united the crowns of these two long-antagonistic kingdoms. (Our Jamestown was named for him; so was the King James version of the Bible.) Today, in its Presbyterian faith and French-inspired body of laws, Scotland exercises a degree of cherished autonomy. Folkways and traditions are pronounced. Brawny, kilted giants toss the *caber* (a twelve-foot-long pine trunk), and lassies dance the highland fling over crossed swords to the skirl of the pipers. Championship long-horned cattle are bred for show; canny sheep dogs respond to masters who whistle their complicated commands. The Royal Highland Gathering of the Clans at Braemar each September is the most famous of these purely Scottish events.

Robert Bruce's realm is a living museum of antiquities, with 2ndcentury Roman camps, an assortment of more than 150 castles, museums, craft villages, and some monuments dating to the Iron Age. You can visit the birthplaces of Robert Burns, Thomas Carlyle, and Andrew Carnegie; moreover, you can scout out your very own Caledonian ancestry at Edinburgh's Register House.

Many people prize Scotland for its unparalleled fishing, some for its limitless and inexpensive golf, and some even come to ski in offbeat winter resorts. But its greatest lure is its serene natural beauty. The Highlands are among the most glorious holiday areas in the world. Split across the center by Loch Ness and Loch Lochy, they twinkle and spire over more than half the country's terrain. Grouse, deer, salmon, trout, ptarmigan, and hare abound. So do tourists, but still it's a country where you can travel for hours and not encounter another human being. There's a purity that few other nations can match. Try to see beyond the limits of its cities and villages—the places where the Scots go when the world is too much with them.

TIPS ON SCOTLAND

MONEY

In practice (but not in theory), all of Great Britain's currencies are mutually interchangeable. Nevertheless, it's sometimes difficult to convert Scottish paper money to English currency, especially in the London area.

FOOD

The Scots possess excellent raw materials for their kitchens. Grilled meats and seafare respond favorably to chefdom, but frequently vegetables seem to be no more than culinary afterthoughts. The pastry is superb.

Specialties—*Haggis* (see "Haggis Ceremony"); *Scotch broth*; *Cocky-Leeky* or *Cock-a-Leekie* (chicken and leek soup); roasted or stewed Scottish *grouse* or *ptarmigan*; fresh Scottish *trout*, *salmon*, *haddock*, *cod*, or *sole*; *Arbroath Smokies*; *Scottish kippers*; *fried Scottish herring in oatmeal batter*, or *grilled Scottish herring with mustard sauce*; *Scottish Findon Haddock* (finnan haddie) *with poached egg*; *scones*; *Scottish pancakes*; *oatcake*; *shortbread*; *Scottish heather honey*; *Black Pudding* (oatmeal, blood, and seasonings); *White Pudding* (oatmeal base); *Black Bun or Parkin* (chewy with raisins and ginger); *marmalade*; many, many more.

Meal hours: lunch, 12:30–2 p.m.; tea, 3:30–5 p.m.; dinner, 7–9 p.m. or later in summer, but 6–8 p.m. in winter. Chinese and Italian restaurants usually operate until midnight, providing almost the only after-theater fare on any Main Street.

No visitor can ever say that he knows the real Scotland until he has gone through the **Haggis Ceremony**. This national festival dish of oatmeal, assorted chopped meats, and spices must be specially prepared, but that's easy: just call any good hotel or restaurant a day ahead and order a Haggis with your dinner the following night, in place of the fish course. Be sure to order hot mashed turnips on the side, and be doubly careful not to forget what the Scots call the "gravy"—straight Scotch whisky sipped between bites, the only liquid that complements this fascinating dish.

When a Scot doesn't eat at home or at a friend's house, he almost automatically heads for a hotel. As a consequence, the Scottish restaurant, while improving, is not yet up to continental standards.

SCOTLAND
Nairn
Inverness
Grantown-on-Spey
Loch Ness
Aberdeen
Braemar
Fort William
Pitlochry
Dunkeld
Dundee
Iona
Oban
Perth
NORTH SEA
ATLANTIC OCEAN
St. Andrews
Dunblane
Stirling
Glasgow
Edinburgh
Peebles
Prestwick
N
N. IRELAND
ENGLAND

DRINKS

For nearly 500 years, distillers all over the civilized world have tried to imitate Scotch whisky. One major effort was made by the giant Spritfabriker Company of thirsty, dollar-short, postwar Denmark, when vast supplies of Scottish machinery, peat, barley, and hundreds of tons of pure Scottish glen water were loaded aboard ships and transported to Aalborg. But even with identical ingredients and identical methods—for reasons that are still unclear—no foreign-produced product has ever come near the original.

Scotch is classified into 5 types—4 geographical (Highland, Lowland, Islays, and Campbeltowns) and the fifth chemical (grain spirits for processing). North Americans overwhelmingly prefer the Highland category because its peat-fire-dried malt adds the distinctive smoky tang to which their palates are accustomed. Malt itself is a pure elixir and unblended.

After it is matured in casks for at least 3 years (usually 4 or 5), secret blending formulae are applied by each producer. The Scotch we drink in the States usually contains from 17 to 45 different whiskies.

Ironically, it's sometimes a chore to find one's familiar brands by the bottle in the nation of their birth. Too much is exported.

Drambuie, that Isle of Skye nectar, is the national liqueur. Its base of course, is Scotch. For saving his life during his attempt to regain the throne, Bonnie Prince Charlie gave the Laird of Mackinnon the recipe, and it has been guarded as carefully as the crown jewels since 1745. Glayva is the second-string national liqueur.

Scottish brewers build brass knuckles into many of their products. "Prestonpan's 12-Guinea Ale" (delicately referred to, when ordered, as "a wee heavy" or "a dump") is one of the strongest ales made; it's dark, thinnish, sweetish. The cost is from $1.10 to perhaps $1.50, depending on the source.

McEwan's, the most popular export ale, and Younger's, the leading beer, are served on draft in the better pubs.

Incidentally, Scotland's bars now open on Sundays.

COUNTRY VS. TOWN

There's not much point in devoting a lot of time to any hub but Edinburgh or the growing cultural nexus of Glasgow, so afterward head for Scotland's glorious countryside.

The variety is astonishing. Within an area roughly the size of West Virginia, you'll find fjords, glens, moors, mountains, flatlands, prairies, heaths, bogs, woodlands, rills, Alpine lakes, and Gulf Stream-nourished palm trees (island of Arran).

The lower end of *Loch Lomond* buzzes with excursion coaches, trailers, and campers in season. *Balloch*, at the southern tip, is euphemistically called the "Henley of Scotland." Hundreds of small pleasure craft are either at anchor or skimming the waves. During the milder months, twice-daily steamer sailings across the Loch originate from here. A few miles north, past the hamlets of Luss and Arden, the Highlands make their abrupt rise—a startling contrast, with glorious scenery. It's a 2-1/2 to 3-hour trip each way, and you'd probably love it. If only for the record, this region shouldn't be missed.

The motorcoach loop to *Inverness* (about $20), back to *Fort William* (3 hours), and on to *Glasgow* (5 hours) is a breathtaking bargain. Round-trip bus excursions from Inverness, encompassing the enchanting *Isle of Skye*, operate on selected days between May and Sept. If you pause on Skye, the **Skeabost Inn** is a lovely stop. It's at *Portree*; while the prices are not very low, the value is indeed very high. A fine oasis for lingering.

GETTING AROUND

TRAINS

Since Scotland is crosshatched by branches of the British Railways system, see "Trains" in the section on England. You might also ask your travel agent about more localized rail transport, which includes bus and steamer travel in the Highlands and among the islands.

MOTORING

The roads are good almost everywhere. Many are so narrow and twisty that you won't make much time—but who cares, in this scenic Valhalla? The surfaces, by-lanes included, are generally excellent, and even in the most remote areas of the nation, you'll always find a gas station within a 30-mile radius.

CAR HIRE

We've never found a self-drive agency in Edinburgh that gave us as much satisfaction as **Cameron & Campbell Ltd**. of Glasgow. This does not mean you won't find excellent, 100% reputable firms in the capital because you will. It is likely that pickup and delivery could be arranged in Edinburgh for a small extra fee; a note to the Cameron & Campbell headquarters (*1900 Great Western Rd., Glasgow W.3*) would answer this question. A Stateside or international license is usually mandatory; some firms require that the driver be 25 or older. **Go Blue Banana**—that's the name of an innovative minibus service that covers more than 500 scenic miles around Scotland. It visits 20 youth hostels every two days so that you can sightsee, sleep and move on to the next destination for an all-inclusive $70 of unlimited travel (nonsmoking, incidentally). The Banana may be plucked from May 15 to Oct. 31 by phoning ☎ *31-2282281*. Of course, you may sleep elsewhere, but the plan is sensational in concept.

EXCURSIONS

The most rewarding cross section of landscape, history, beauty, and charm on the Scottish map for the visitor in a hurry? Here's a 48-

hour itinerary that allows you to split the nation in half, to sample every type of terrain, and to view the major sights.

Edinburgh, of course, is the beginning and end of your journey. **Inverness**, capital of the Highlands, is your midway stop. Start off at 8:30 a.m. for **Stirling**, and get the **Firth of Forth** lowlands behind you as quickly as you can. At nearby **Doune**, there's an unthinkably ancient fortress-castle plus a sports and racing car collection of the 20s and 30s. But perhaps you'd rather push on to **Gleneagles**, Scotland's most fabulous hotel, for a coffee break; this baronial country golfing estate is something special. Then proceed to the Dewar's White Label town, **Perth**, for lunch, before cutting northwest along the river valley through **Pitlochry**, **Blair Atholl**, along glorious **Glengarry**, through **Drumochter Pass** and the **Forest of Atholl** down to **Dalwhinnie** and onward. (During the early May to Sept. period, the **Pitlochry Festival Theatre**, founded by the late John Stewart, draws culture-hungry crowds to its competent performances. Five plays ranging, say, from Shakespeare to Chekhov to Jean Anouilh to Noel Coward are presented Mon. through Sat.) By teatime, **Carrbridge** should loom up and the simple, fishing-and-sporting **Carrbridge Hotel** should refresh you with light high tea for about $6 per person. You might want to take in the **Landmark Visitor Centre**, which capsules Highland history and lore within one building and the surrounding grounds. It has its own restaurant plus shops. One hour after you're road-bound again, you'll be in **Inverness**.

The 2nd day you take a totally different route, and it's even more spectacular. Start no later than 8 a.m. After leaving the "*Ceud Mile Failte!*" sign (Gaelic for "100,000 Welcomes!") behind at the city limits of *Inverness*, loaf along the **Caledonian Canal** until it opens into **Loch Ness**; then parallel the 29 miles of lakeside. **Loch Lochy** is next—and then, 7 miles before **Spean Bridge**, you'll pass the famed **Commando Memorial.** Now it's time for coffee in the **Milton Hotel** in **Fort William**. Nearby is Scotland's highest peak, *Ben Nevis.* Then swoop across the magnificent **Rannoch Moor** and **Black Mount** to stop for lunch in **Tyndrum**. After the turnoff at **Crainlarich**, there's an interesting ride down **Glen Falloch** to the northern tip of Loch Lomond, and you will view in its entirety this lake, all the way down to its termination at **Balloch**. Tea at **Drymen** and home to Edinburgh, in time for dinner.

Less than 400 miles, round trip—with about 4000 miles' worth of scenery! Both are stiff daily hauls, so dawdle longer if you can, but if you can't, within these 48 hours you'll get a greater kaleidoscope of Scotland than most travelers get in a week.

SPORTS

CYCLING

For 6-day guided tours through **Campbell Country**, the **Castles of Grampian**, the **North-West Highland** and **Outer Hebrides**, or following the Retreat of **Bonnie Prince Charlie**, write **Highland Guides**, *Aviemore, Inverness-shire;* ☎ *Aviemore 810729.*

HIKING

Take the highroad or the lowroad to the Highlands; 1 week to 1 month full-board packages from about $300. **Holiday Fellowship**, *142/144 Great North Way, London NW4 1EG;* ☎ *2033381.*

MOUNTAINEERING

Try snow- and ice-climbing coupled with ice ax and crampon techniques; rock climbing and cross-country skiing are thrown in for good measure; 1-week courses from Feb. to Apr. About $200 covers course, full board, lodging, and equipment. Bring 6 pairs of woolen socks. Taskmasters are **Loch Rannoch Scottish School of Adventure**, *Bunrannoch Hotel, Kinloch Rannoch, Pitlochry, Tayside;* ☎ *(08822) 325.*

HORSES

Pony trekking and riding facilities are so prevalent that you're on your own to request the equestrian particulars from the following sampling:

Hayfield Riding School (Aberdeen) Ltd., *Hazlehead Park; Aberdeen* ☎ *35703;*

Cairnhouse Pony Trekking Center, *Cairnhouse, Isle of Arran;* ☎ *Blackwaterfoot 256;*

Tower Farm Riding Stables, *85 Liberton Drive EH16 6NS, Edinburgh;* ☎ *(031) 664-3375;*

Inverness-shire Great Glen Riding Center, *Torlunday, Fort William;* ☎ *Fort William 3015.*

SKIING

If you can't get to the Alps, you might try the frigid Cairngorms, the highest range in the British Isles. A 5-day, all-inclusive package runs around $250. January to May. Write to **Cairngorm Hotel**, *Aviemore;* ☎ *(0479) 810233.*

Nearby **Insh Hall** (*Kincraig, by Kingussie, Inverness-shire;* ☎ *Kincraig 272*) offers a similar 5-day package at similar prices; children slightly less.

Or you can head for the **Spittal** at **Glenshee** and **Glencoe**, or the newly groomed area called **The Lecht** (*11 miles west of Strathdon*).

If Vail, Aspen, or St. Anton are your yardsticks, however, Scottish skiing won't measure up.

WATERSPORTS

There are terrific sailing holidays for all ages, including tuition and on-board accommodation from roughly $240 per person per week. Contact **Fingal Yachts Ltd.**, *Ardfern, by Lochgilphead, Argyll;*

☎ *Barbreck (08525) 283.* In addition to tuition, **North Channel Yachts** (*Stroul Bay, Clynder, Dunbartonshire;* ☎ *Clynder (043683) 430*) offers bareboat charters; 1-week courses run about $450, including VAT; charters from $90 to $170 per person.

Dayboat courses from $120 per week (excluding VAT and accommodation) and residential courses from $230 available at **Lochearn & Coastal Sailing School** (*Dalvreck House, Crieff, Perthshire;* ☎ *Crieff (0764) 2292*) Apr. to Sept.

How about a week of camping and canoeing your way in a double kayak from the foot of Ben Nevis through Loch Ness to Inverness? (You might even meet Nessie.) Cost? About $230. **Great Glen Canoe Expeditions**, *Insh Hall, Kincraig, Fort William PH21 1NO;* ☎ *(05404) 272.* July and Aug. only.

A weekend trout fishing course, or a 4-day, midweek trout fishing holiday, available at the **Tontine Hotel** (*High Street, Peebles;* ☎ *(0721) 20892*). Former from April to May at about $150, including lodging and meals; latter from Apr.–Sept. for about $200, all-inclusive.

From May to Oct. you can try a 5-day fly-fishing course at **The Post House** (*Aviemore Centre, Aviemore PH22 1PH;* ☎ *(0479) 810771*); $300 per person covers tuition, tackle, bed, breakfast, and dinner; children under 14 sharing parents' room only about $125.

HANG GLIDING

Soar through 2- to 4-day basic and advanced courses from $65 to $130, without accommodation (which can be arranged). **Cairnwell Hang-Gliding School**, *By Braemar, Aberdeenshire AB3 5XS;* ☎ *Braemar 628.*

SPORTS SMORGASBORD

If you're a member of a Youth Hostels Association or prepared to join, you can enjoy bargain holiday activities ranging from rock climbing to wildlife safaris. For full course details, contact **Scottish Youth Hostels Association, National Office**, *7 Glebe Crescent, Stirling FK8 2JA;* ☎ *Stirling (STD 0786) 2821.*

Finally, to map out any sports program to its finest detail, turn to the **Scottish Sports Council**, *1/3 St. Colme St., Edinburgh;* ☎ *2258411.*

SIGHTSEEING

FESTIVALS

The enriching 4- and 8-day package tours to the annual **Edinburgh Festival of Music and Drama** in August are available through **Tours and Travel Promotions** (*25 Brunstane Dr., Edinburgh EH15 2NF;* ☎ *6695344*). About $120 for the former and $200 for the latter includes transport pass, ticket for Tattoo, bed, breakfast, and VAT.

If planning to go it alone, write first to the **Scotland and Edinburgh Information Centre**—Tourist Accommodation Service (*Waverley Market*; ☎ *5572727*)—since masses of people book a year ahead. "Postal bookings" best placed during the first half of May through **Festival Office** (*21 Market St.*; ☎ *2264001*). Counter bookings begin in July. Both on a first-come-first-served basis.

Castles and Gardens: **The National Trust for Scotland** has more than 90 properties containing 90,000 acres of oohhs and aahhs—some of the finest historic structures in the proud heritage of the country. Fortresses such as **Castles Fraser**, **Drum**, **and Craigievar** (all near Aberdeen), **Falkland** (Fife), **Culzean** (Ayr) and **Hill of Tarvit** (Cupar) are just a few of the outstanding examples. The gardens are equally fascinating as are the "Little Houses" such as the Bachelors' Club where Burns debated with his friends. The destinations are too numerous to list here, but you can obtain a brochure from this fine organization by writing *5 Charlotte Sq., Edinburgh EH2 4DU* (☎ *031-226-5922*). The free publication would be invaluable in helping you plan your rovings.

SHOPPING

Store hours: Usually 9 or 9:30 a.m.–5:30 p.m. Mon.-Sat. and as late as 8 p.m. on Thurs. On Sundays you'll find a few functioning on Princes St. plus those at Waverley Market Shopping Center. Concerning Purchase Tax rebates, please refer back to the "England" chapter since the system is identical.

LOCAL RACKETS

So startlingly rare in this honest, decent, God-fearing land that when even a mild one pops up, the citizenry explodes. I still smile at the memory of the red-hot newspaper hassle, some years ago, which raged about the "revolting spectacle" of certain "disreputable-looking characters" along the Trossachs highways who were fast-talking tourists out of an occasional buck. "Dressed in a caricature of Highland clothing," one horrified critic stormed, "and playing the bagpipes badly, these individuals behave like Eastern mendicants!" This violent reaction against such minor chiseling is your guarantee of the high moral integrity of the Scots.

WHERE TO GO

ABERDEEN

This northcoaster successfully blends medieval mellowness with the activity of a frenetic seaside resort. The excitement and bustle have been heightened of late by the offshore oil fever that has refashioned Aberdeen into less of a tourist center and more of a staging center for the petroleum industry. Burgeoning living costs, of course, have resulted. A **Holiday Inn** greets arrivals at the busy airport. The **Bucks-**

burn Moat House also takes advantage of the boom; this is a reasonably priced establishment, but much cheaper digs can be found among the plethora of boardinghouses that line the main approach roads. The town itself is situated on the banks of the Don and the Dee rivers. Between the mouths of these streams, a 2-mile sandy beach has been dedicated to holidaymakers—perfect for Polar Bear Club bathers. Outstanding university, 15 lovely parks, spectacular **Rubislaw granite quarry**, venerable **St. Machar's Cathedral**. **The Fish Market** is one of the most interesting in the United Kingdom.

BALLATER

This captivating townlet might be called the gemstone of the castle belt. Down the pike a few miles is the queen's own **Balmoral** where the gardens are open to public inspection (when she is not in residence). A bit farther is magnificent **Craigievar**, which was lived in until very recently and was left totally intact and furnished when the owners shifted to other digs so that everyone could share the beauty of their ancestral estate. Of course, **Braemar Castle** is next door and is viewable; the lecture tour here is superb. In the same region is **Crathes Castle and Gardens**, **Drum Castle**, and engaging **Banchory Museum**. There's the Z-plan **Castle Fraser** with its extensive **Castles of Mar exhibition**. This area is so sylvan and so enchanting that unless you had compelling reasons for settling in nearby busy, dusty Aberdeen, we would overwhelmingly urge you to bunk in one of the cozy lodging houses on the fringes of this town.

DUNDEE

The subject of many a fine limerick, this jam and jute hub commands a majestic site over the **Firth of Tay**. The bay-spanning bridge makes the links of **St. Andrews** convenient. (The courses, incidentally, are open to the public and cost very little for greens fees; the problem is obtaining a starting time in summer months when they often are booked solid a year in advance.)

EDINBURGH

This dramatic and stately city is dominated by the imposing **Edinburgh Castle**, always a fortress, once the home of Mary, Queen of Scots, and the birthplace of James I. At a height of nearly 270 feet, the battlements offer a spectacular view of the city and a patchwork of countryside that sweeps to the coast.

The Royal Mile runs down Castle Hill through a medieval Old Town packed with historic wonders, to **Holyrood Palace** where the queen resides when in the city. It continues on to the **High Kirk**, with its crown-shaped spire, fascinating museums, and enchanting 16th- and 17thcentury houses that line the narrow lanes.

Elegant Princes Street offers the top stores and beautiful gardens. Neighboring George Street forms another key shopping nexus for antiques, tartans, woolens, crafts, and authentic Highland regalia that are chiefly obtainable in this unique country.

Edinburgh is an evergreen mecca for golfers: eighteen 18-hole circuits within the city limits, plus five 9-hole rounds. Fees for play and club rentals are laughably low in comparison with North American levels.

The keynote annual event is the exciting **Edinburgh Festival** with the **Military Tattoo**, a spotlit spectacle with precision marching to regimental pipe-bands in traditional dress uniform, which takes place each night in the Esplanade of Edinburgh Castle, and presents a nostalgic and moving display of Scotland's capital city at its

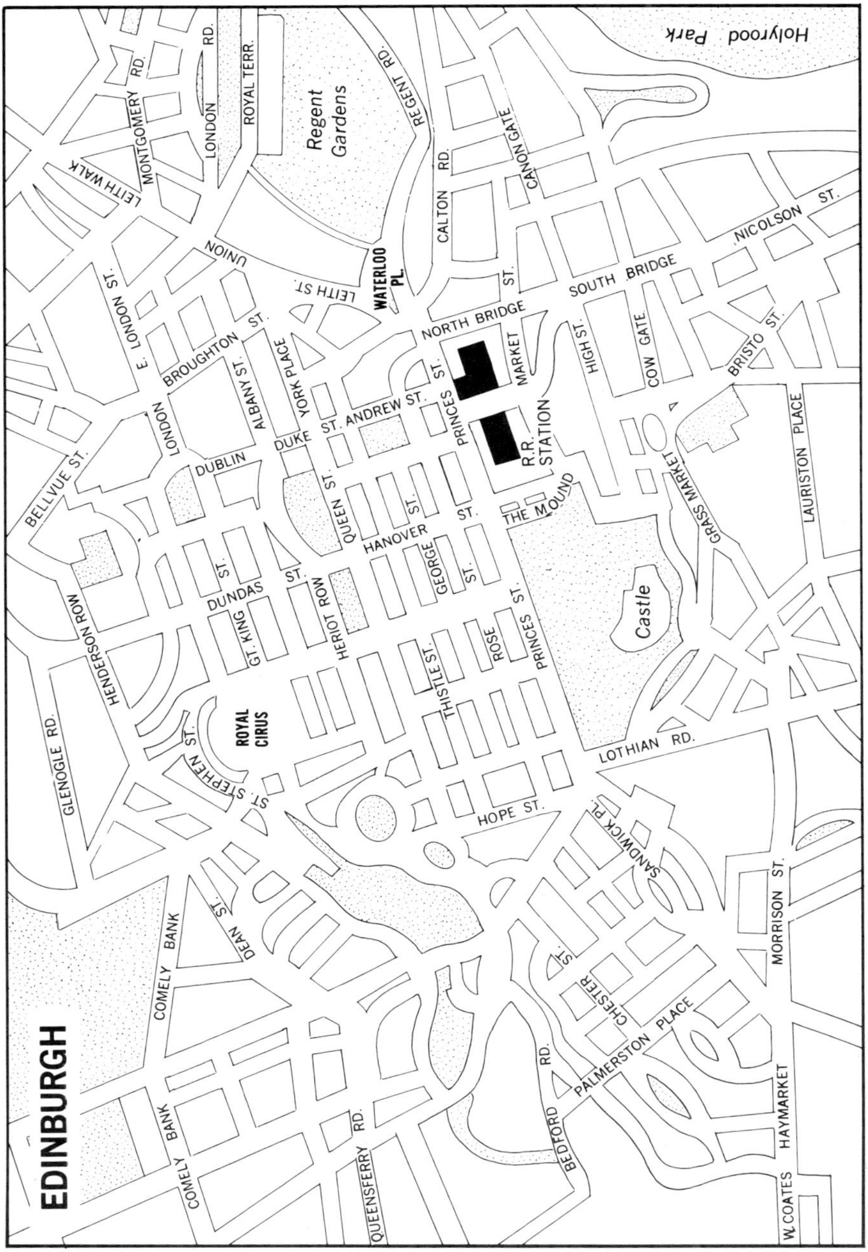
EDINBURGH
Holyrood Park
Regent Gardens
Castle
ROYAL CIRUS
WATERLOO PL.
R.R. STATION
LEITH WALK
MONTGOMERY RD.
LONDON RD.
ROYAL TERR.
REGENT RD.
CALTON RD.
CANON GATE
UNION
LEITH ST.
NORTH BRIDGE
SOUTH BRIDGE
NICOLSON ST.
E. LONDON ST.
BROUGHTON ST.
ALBANY ST.
YORK PLACE
ST. ANDREW ST.
PRINCES ST.
MARKET ST.
HIGH ST.
COW GATE
BRISTO ST.
LONDON
DUBLIN
DUKE
QUEEN ST.
HANOVER ST.
THE MOUND
GRASS MARKET
LAURISTON PLACE
BELLVUE ST.
HENDERSON ROW
DUNDAS ST.
HERIOT ROW
GEORGE ST.
GT. KING ST.
THISTLE ST.
ROSE ST.
PRINCES ST.
GLENOGLE RD.
ST. STEPHEN ST.
LOTHIAN RD.
HOPE ST.
SANDWICK PL.
MORRISON ST.
COMELY BANK
DEAN ST.
CHESTER ST.
PALMERSTON PLACE
BEDFORD RD.
QUEENSFERRY RD.
HAYMARKET
W. COATES

regal best. If you arrive at this time of year, be sure your bookings are confirmed in writing.

DIRECTORY

U.S. Consulate • *3 Regent Terrace;* ☎ *5568315.*

American Express • *139 Princes St.;* ☎ *2257881.*

Laundromat • *82 Dalry Road, 54 Elm Row, 342 Leith Walk, 13 S. Clerk St.* and *Broughton St.*

Barber and Hairdresser (combined) • Steiner's, *Waverly Market;* ☎ *5567788.*

Dry Cleaning and Pressing • Pullars, *23 Frederick St.* and *46 Shandwick Place.*

Suit Rental • Dormie Hire Service, *46 Frederick St.;* ☎ *2252625.*

Doctor • University Health Service (*Bristo St.*) is for students only. In emergency cases, all local hospitals are available. Otherwise, consult your hotel concierge or the General Practitioner in the district in which you are staying.

Dentist • Dental Hospital, *31 Chambers St.;* ☎ *2259511.*

Police • Central Station, *Fettes Ave.;* ☎ *3113131* or ☎ *999*, the general emergency number.

Favorite Pawnshops • Duncanson, *10 St. Stephen St.;* ☎ *2254830* and Equitable, *106-108 Lauriston Pl.;* ☎ *229-4448.*

HOW TO GET AROUND

Ride buses whenever possible. There's a spur to nearly every major attraction. The Corporation Transport Map is an inexpensive and indispensable key to the network. Fares are only a few pennies per mile. Weekly passes are available at the Ticket Centre on Waverly Bridge. Edinburgh is a great city for strolling.

Most sights are concentrated in the center, so you'll probably prefer to walk.

WHERE TO STAY

LEAST $

While capacity is somewhat restricted, you can expect to pay very little for lodgings. A double without bath averages perhaps $17 per person. For space reasons, the selection below is limited to a representative cross section. **The Accommodation Bureau** (*Waverley Market;* ☎ *5572727 or 5571700*) can give the names, addresses, and tariffs of scores more.

SYHA Youth Hostel • *17-18 Eglinton Crescent;* ☎ *3371120.* With shop, cooking facilities, sheet hire and £2.50 dinners. Open 7 a.m.–11 a.m. and 2 p.m.–2 a.m. Buses 26 or 31 from the tourist office. Or another at *7-8 Bruntsfield Crescent;* ☎ *4472994* with similar services but no evening meals. Buses 11 or 16 from Scott Monument. Prices at both vary with age category, but average about £6–7 per night.

Independent Hostel • *Blackfriars St.;* ☎ *5573984.* This one also offers the self-catering possibility.

Belford Youth Hostel • *6-8 Douglas Gardens;* ☎ *2256209.* Are you an ardent churchgoer? Well, now you can even sleep in one. This is a converted (sic) 19th-century house of worship where you may snooze beneath a five-story, high-vaulted ceiling. There are some more private areas for confessions among families or couples. Tithings of £7 per nocturnal passage.

Ben Doran Guest House • *11 Mayfield Gardens.* An 8-room candidate in Newington district, a 10-minute bus ride from Princess St. Rates start at $17 per visitor.

Rimswell House • *33 Mayfield Gardens.* 20 rooms, again 10 bus-minutes from Princes St. Fine comfort but at slightly higher rates.

Lanrick Guest House • *8 Murrayfield Gardens,* (*near the Murrayfield Rugby Stadium*). Proprietress Pretsel gives her small domain great attention. Dwelling space from $16.

Craigelachie • *21 Murrayfield Ave.* It's recommendable for comfort and for the district. Handy public transportation.

Ross • *2 Murrayfield Ave.* Mr. and Mrs. Benjamin come up with 9 bedrooms in a residential patch convenient to city transport.

The Avenue • *4 Murrayfield Ave.* The Benjamin's neighbor, Mrs. Maxwell, manages her 9 rooms with consummate care.

Kiloran Guest House • *17 Leamington Terrace;* ☎ *2291789.* 8 units, 1 full bath, 2 showers and W.C.

Millfield Guest House • *12 Marchhall Rd.;* ☎ *6674428.* Adjoins Holyrood Park. Take buses 2, 14, 21, 33, or 49. Also close to Royal Commonwealth pool and saunas. Rates run up about $17 per person; possibly less in shared accommodations. Good breakfast; lounge for tea. Take your latchkey and use it as your own home.

Claymore • *6 Royal Terrace.* One of the best values in its category and even better than before since its recent doorstep-to-rooftop renovation. The location is a big advantage for sightseers.

Mrs. E. Morrison • *6 Drum Brae Walk;* ☎ *339-5779.* Hospitality is the word. Neat as a dram of pure Highland malt.

Tankard House • *40 East Claremont St.* Friendly, clean, and well-priced for careful budgets. Tariffs $15 to $21 per person, bed and breakfast. Excellent location, too.

Christian Alliance • Formerly called the Central YWCA, *14 Coates Crescent.* ☎ *2253608.* It's lean but livable; requires advance booking. A solid roof—but for the shelter of women only.

MORE $$

Scores of "bed and breakfast" signs dot the residential areas. Householders sometimes rent out all but 1 room (theirs) in their homes. Many contain only 2 or 3 bedchambers. In this category you should pay about $20 per person. These accommodations are quite comfortable.

Raeburn House • *112 Raeburn Pl.;* ☎ *3322348.* Located near Edinburgh Academy's playing fields, in a Georgian building dating from 1809, 10 minutes from center by #24 or #29 bus. TV lounge; cocktail nook; cheery breakfast room. Six doubles or twins, 1 family unit; none has privy or shower, but public facilities sparkle; basins and heaters in all quarters. All trade at close to $23, including a hearty breakfast.

Royal Terrace • *17-20 Royal Terrace;* ☎ *5573222.* A happy find; 100 chambers carved out of 2 Georgian mansions. Dining room. Cordial management asking a royal sum for your company. Nevertheless, the rewards are 4-star. Be sure to confirm your reservation far in advance.

St. Valery • *36 Coates Gardens;* ☎ *3371893.* 9 rooms in a hospitable atmosphere. Dining salon. Hearty breakfasts. Doubles, twins and singles with average at roughly $21 per noggin. Buses #12, 26, 28, and 31 connect with center. Again, worth a try, space permitting.

Eglinton • *29 Eglinton Crescent;* ☎ *3372641.* A 13-room enterprise; lively dining nook; bar; prices slightly higher than the above entry. A happy house.

Beresford • *32 Coates Gardens;* ☎ *3376121.* Reappears this year as a refashioned house of about 9 rooms. Viable low rates for solid value.

Northumberland • *33 Craigmillar Park;* ☎ *6676971.* 18 rooms and 14 showers. 1st floor back views, country scenery from midtown address. Other popular features: a car park, an attractive bar, and ample 4-course meals.

EVEN MORE $$$

Ellersly House • *Ellersly Rd. (about 2 miles from center);* ☎ *3376888.* Garden and croquet green enhance this converted private home. Ambience of dignified charm and quiet relaxation. Stately dining room; 54 sleeping units with bath and shower; 4 suites. Two large car parks.

Mount Royal • *53 Princes St.;* ☎ *2257161.* Often praised for panorama from lounge, bar, dining room and front units; 161 units, most with private plumbing. Rear accommodations less viewful but quieter. Solid.

Gordon Bruce • *14-16 South Learmonth Gardens;* ☎ *3323232.* Owned by a Mr. Taylor who provides 49 rooms with private facilities. On a quiet square within an easy walk of the center. Private bath or shower with each room. Color TV. Lounge and restaurant.

Ailsa Craig • *24 Royal Terrace;* ☎ *5566055.* Similar but smaller; located on a tranquil Georgian lane. Easy walk to the center; 18 bedrooms, most with private bath, TV and teamakers. Figure about £20 per noggin including breakfast.

Post House • ☎ *3348221.* Among the most appealing modern addresses in the nation, about a 15-minute drive from the center on Corstorphine Rd.; view across rolling meadows toward Pentland Hills. Excellent restaurant. Bar. Superb comfort. Very fond of it, but it's not cheap.

Royal Scot • ☎ *3349191.* A little farther out on the same pike. Also handy to the airport (frequent shuttle service). Cheerful appeal and extra-cordial staff. Leisure and fitness facilities.

King James • *St. James Centre;* ☎ *5560111.* Back in town; somewhat commercial. A courtly assembly of lunching, lounging, and dining facilities. Smallish accommodations, comfortably furnished.

SUGGESTIONS FOR STUDENTS

Collegians inhabit 5 separate precincts in Edinburgh—Newington, Grange, Marchmont, Churchill, and Stockbridge—near the 4-century-old University. Nicolson Square and Chambers Street are two major reference points on the South Bridge campus map.

LOW-COST DINING

For scholars at Potter Row try *5 Bristo Sq.*, where each portion of fuel costs about $2.75. Moreover, it can be swallowed, digested, and even enjoyed.

STUDENT TOURING

Edinburgh University Students Travel Assoc. • *3 Bristo St.;* ☎ *6682221.* Knows nearly all the questions and answers. Their specialty is moving students around.

SYHA • *161 Warrender Park Rd.;* ☎ *2998660.* Another efficient source. They have tempting night bus-rail-and-hostel programs that are excellent if your wanderlust is lusting for new terrain.

The University Union • *Teviot Row 8;* ☎ *6672091.* Another oracle for visiting scholars. Its bulletin boards are revised twice weekly to keep you abreast of trading-post bargains and other useful information.

WHERE TO EAT

LEAST $

Henderson's Salad Table • *94 Hanover St.* Under a fruit and vegetable market. A delight. Cafeteria-style service. More than 16 salad platters. Low prices. Open 8 a.m.-11 p.m. Closed Sun.

Waverley Market • *Huddles down on the low side of Princes St.* A modern enclave teeming with interesting corners, snack bars, and browsing grounds. On a clear day, it is pleasant to sit outside on the public benches and enjoy a midtown picnic in the park.

Rutland No. 1 • *Corner of Rutland and Princes St.* Food and furnishings in the mood of a wine bar. Very chummy atmosphere.

Kushis Lothian • *16 Drummond St.* Provides exceptional value for your Scottish Sterling.

CHAINS

The battle of the buns continues between **Big Mac** and the burly **Burger King**. Alas, the Scots have not adapted their flavors to the fast-food concept. The nearest example was a "haggis roll," served up at a jernt called Joe's Haggis Bar. Joe was a nice Pakistani and his take-away snack wasn't bad. Still, whenever I tell a Scottish friend about this acceptable inexpensive treat, they back away from me as if the very idea might be contagious.

MORE $$

Blah Blah! Café • *63 Dalry Rd.;* ☎ *3132139.* A useful address almost opposite Haymarket Station and convenient to many bed-and-breakfast establishments. It opens for breakfast at 7 a.m. and ends the day with à la carte offerings from 6 p.m.–11 p.m. A house specialty is the haggis-topped Steak Prince Charlie for $8.50. Nice staff and pleasant art deco surroundings.

Vito's • *55A Frederick St.* Bright touch of Tuscany in the heart of the city. (Prefer this Vito to original one at 109 Fountainbridge.) Two small rooms plus bar and lounge. Amiable Italian waiters. Muscular seasonings in abundant selection of Latin dishes. Different and uplifting.

George Hotel • The dining room is excellent for a set meal of roast beef, Yorkshire pudding, a colossal baked potato, and a tossed salad. Great value in wonderful surroundings.

Doric Tavern • *15-16 Market St.;* ☎ *2251084.* A friendly nest of 9 tables in cozy, informal aura. Superior food.

Cousteau's • *Hill St. Lane North.* As you might have guessed, it's a breath of sea-fresh air. Swim fins and giant diving mask outside suggest nonexistent link with the famous French naturalist. Excellent mussels; splendid grilled fish. The showstopper is a spectacularly attractive cold seafood platter served in a rugged scoop of cork bark almost a foot long. Expensive by local standards, but very reasonable when measured by international rates for such quality. Closed Sun.

Cramond Inn • *Where River Almond meets Firth of Forth;* ☎ *3362035.* A long-favored little gem; 5 miles (20 minutes by #41 bus) from midcity; 300-year-old village tavern with adjoining pub. Pleasant bar seats; peat fireplace; handsome lounge. Specialties include steak and kidney pie, chicken-ham pie, Welsh rarebit, lobster, crab (in season), duck, and smoked salmon. Cramond bottled-and-labeled Burgundies, Bordeaux, and Champagnes; outstanding wine list. Caution: 8 tables and 25 persons are the limit, so be sure to phone and reserve before you go.

NIGHTLIFE

There's a decided touristic aura to the ever-popular (and not-so-cheap) "Scottish Nights" of folksong-and-dance. These almost always take place at the leading hotels only in the summer months and begin at 7-7:30 p.m., ending between 10:30-11 p.m. Usually dinner is available or required. If you arrive for the show only, the cost is about $15; with dinner and no wine approximately twice as much. You might check the schedules at the **George Hotel**, **Prestonfield House**, **Learmonth**, **King James** and **Royal Mile Banquets** (*9 Victoria St.*). **The Jacobean Banquet** given throughout the year at **Dalhousie Courte** is traditional, too, but in a more stately manner. For the last, a bus leaves from Waterloo Place (beside the Post Office) at 5:45 p.m., fare included. Royal Mile Banquets functions around the calendar.

DISCOTHEQUES

Discotheques are budding like daisy patches. On your nightwalk you might bounce into:

Buster Brown's • *25 Market St.* A fun-filled mood.

Amphitheatre • *Lothian Rd.* Specializes in light shows; modern tone; proper dress suggested. (Remember, this is Scotland.)

Red Hot Pepper Club • *3 Semple St.* Ripe for frolicing.

The Network • *3 West Tollcross.* The latter a high-energy nightery sometimes with shows.

Calton Studios • *26 Calton Rd.* Usually gets into high gear long after midnight and snoozes shortly before dawn.

PUBS

As in London and Dublin, the public house of yore is rapidly being replaced by a hybrid that is part saloon and part discotheque. The oldest and best examples, physically unchanged for decades, are rich with color, flavor, and charm. A few of the newer editions sparkle, too. The routine neighborhood corner-tavern examples, on the other hand, are most often painfully plain and colorless.

The Abbotsford • *3 Rose St.* Transports you to mellow Victorian days. Lunch here or nibble its snacks from noon to 2:30 p.m. and 5–11 p.m. Upstairs you can tuck into traditional Scottish fare.

The Traverse Theatre • *Castle Terrace.* Mixed crowd; active bar; good food; art, plays and films shown at regular intervals.

The Tankard • *49 Rose St.* For those who enjoy Gotham's famous P. J. Clarke's. That means darkness, good cheer, flavorful light bites, and the trappings of a popular, chic tavern.

Other pubs include the atmospheric **Victoria & Albert** (*12 Frederick St.*), **Scott's Bar** (*Rose St.*), **Bianco** (*Hope St.*), **The Beehive** (*Grassmarket*), and the often gay **Laughing Duck** (*24 Howe St.*).

WHAT TO SEE AND DO

First stop: the **Tourist Information Centre** at Waverley Market. Smiling staffers will load your arms with pamphlets and brochures while answering your queries. They'll also help to arrange your motorcoach excursions and book your accommodation. They further offer an advance reservations service. Very useful and kind.

Edinburgh Castle is the battlement from which to start your trip. At least 2/3 of the city's most important history took place along the so-called **Royal Mile**—nearly a straight line from the castle to **Holyrood Palace**. Here lie the **shrine** (within the castle), the **High Kirk** (**St. Giles' Cathedral**), **John Knox's House**, the **Canongate Tollbooth**, **Queen Mary's Bath House**, and a half-dozen other landmarks. Coin-activated telescopes also permit you to spy on the **Scott Monument**, the **Royal Scottish Academy**, the **Scottish-American War Memorial**, and the smart shops along Princes Street.

The National Gallery, on "The Mound," is a treasure house lined with fine paintings. Among them are El Greco's *St. Jerome*, Tiepolo's *Finding of Moses*, Rembrandt's *Hendrikje Stoffels*, and Gauguin's *Jacob Wrestling with the Angel*. The modern art holdings are on Belford Rd., where you can view Picasso, Moore, Hockney, Lichtenstein, and lots of others of the 20th century. Both open between 10 a.m. and 5 p.m.; on Sun., go at 2 p.m. Admission free to either gallery. For the latter, take bus 13 from George St.

The best way to inspect the **Auld Toon** is from the castle's esplanade. A low-priced conducted tour beginning at **Waverly Bridge** (including an open-top bus) meanders through its narrow streets to Holyrood Palace. En route you will spot a number of fascinating ancient courtyards with adjacent hideaways that have sheltered centuries of famous Scotsmen and Scotswomen from the hurly-burly of the city's main thoroughfare.

Craigmillar Castle, in a district now known for its breweries, offers another striking panorama of the cityscape. Entrance fee 60 pence with half price for children; open 9:30 a.m.-5 p.m. during summer. Sat. only. Historic and worthy. Take bus 33, 82, 83, or 89.

Energetic travelers might relish the hike from the Holyrood grounds to **Salisbury Crags, Samson's Ribs**, and **Duddingston Village**.

The Royal Botanic Gardens (*Inverleith*) draw nature lovers and culture voyeurs. Pampered grounds with a magnificent heather backdrop. Free admission. There's a nice restaurant here.

Finally, **Arthur's Seat** affords still another fine perspective of this lovely metropolis.

CONCERTS

Of course, there's the world-famous, splendid **Edinburgh Festival**. See earlier "Special-Interest Holidays" for more details on this late-summer attraction. Also for halcyon time, check out the **West Princes St. Gardens** for alfresco dancing, fife pipings, talent shows, and early evening fun. All year 'round there are performances at **Usher Hall** and **Queen's Hall**.

MARKETS

Antiques seem to proliferate on *Thistle*, *Dundas*, and *Victoria* Streets, also at *Grassmarket* and *Candlemaker Row*. The Sunday **Ingliston Market** from 10 a.m. to 4 p.m. is the largest open-air fiesta of its type in Europe. Antiques fairs draw thousands to the **Roxburghe Hotel** and assembly rooms.

PUBLICATIONS

All major U.K. newspapers are available. Locally, we're rather partial to *The Scotsman*. The Sabbath issue of *Scotland on Sunday* is very well edited and designed to keep you busy all week. Get *The List* for schedules of concerts, films, exhibitions, all music and theatre.

WHERE TO SHOP

BRASS RUBBINGS

The Scottish Stone & Brass Rubbing Centre, (*Trinity Apse, Charmers Close, High St.*) provides an inexpensive way to plagiarize nicely.

HANDICRAFTS

Living Craft Centre, (*12 High St; opposite John Knox's House*) carries the regional gamut of baskets, pottery, knitwear, jewelry, printed textiles, and stone carvings. You can also watch a kilt being stitched together or a bagpipe under construction.

JEWELRY, GOLD AND SILVER

Hamilton & Inches, (*87 George St.*) the leading jeweler, features striking gold and silver Luckenbooth brooches and pendants with their distinctive entwined hearts; skean dhus (daggers); 40 different solid silver clan brooches; kilt pins, some set with smoky quartz, amethyst, or citrines. Tempting displays of Edinburgh thistle glass are another feature.

PRINTS

Collectors seeking old prints of Edinburgh often have good luck at **John Nelson** (*Victoria St.*) or **Grant's** (*George IV Bridge*).

TARTANS AND TWEEDS

Geoffrey (**Tailor**), right beside the John Knox House (*57-59 High Street*), is well liked by locals. **Kinloch Anderson** (*Commercial St. corner Dock St., Leith*) has been in business since 1868. They'll even pay your taxi fare if you claim the refund upon arrival. Their workmanship is superb, and they number many royals among their loyal customers.

SHOPPING ZONES

Princes St., George St., Royal Mile, and Grassmarket. Then there are the Waverley Market, St. James Centre, and Stockbridge (for curios).

FORT WILLIAM

The 4406-foot hump of Britain's highest mountain, Ben Nevis, peers from the mists above upon this lochside settlement. Since the bastion of old was a focal point for military activity, you'll find many castles and museums tucked away in the area. The town and its fringes are loaded with inexpensive boarding houses and if you wish to overnight, just look for the "Room Free" signs in the front windows. Otherwise, **Tourist Board at Cameron Centre** (*Cameron Sq.*) can point you in the direction of appropriate lodging for your budget.

GLASGOW

The dynamic metropolis was recently honored as the *Cultural Capital of Europe*; opera, ballet, and musical performances were commissioned especially for the celebrations. With 3/4 million inhabitants, here is the traditional commercial capital of Scotland, which is now moving forward in the arts and tourism. Shipbuilding and engineering have given way to the dynamic new electronics and burgeoning service industries. The famous cathedral dates back to 1197 and the University to 1450. The **Kelvingrove Art Gallery**, **City Chambers**, **Hunterian Museum**, **Provand's Lordship 1471 house, Botanic Gardens**, and **Zoo** are among the city's attractions; there are 50 public parks. The center of the city has undergone a vast and impressive modernization, cleaning, and a cultural uplift that has become a deserved badge of pride. Hotels are now abundant and quite good; a tough, rigidly enforced antismoke campaign has dispelled the one-time franchise on smog; handsome antiquities have been steamed, sandblasted, and brought back to life. **Pollok Park** features a young but already worldfamous museum 3 miles out from the center: **The Burrell Collection** contains the accumulated art treasures of shipping magnate Sir William Burrell; among them, *Egyptian pottery*, *Chinese porcelain* and *jade*, *Oriental carpets*, *European armor*, *Greek* and *Roman sculpture*, and a dazzling collection of paintings including works by Rembrandt, Cézanne, and Degas. This has been hailed as one of Europe's finest repositories and alone is worth a trip to Scotland. Your ears as well as your eyes will be well served; there's the new and magnificent **Glasgow Royal Concert Hall**, which invites the world's finest orchestras and virtuosi to perform here. On a lighter side, the **Museum of Transport** is a delight. For example, did you know Scotland was once an important car manufacturer, producing such marques as the *Argyll*, *Albion*, and *Arrol-Johnston*? If you overnight, guest-houses such as the **Charing Cross** (*310 Renfrew St.*), **McLays** (*same street at #268*), and the **Victorian House**, (*214 Renfrew St.*) are reasonable stops.

INVERNESS

Many use it as their principal base while looping the Highlands. There are good hotels, adequate restaurants, but such an air of organization and tour dedication that I'd prefer to seek the tranquility of the wonderful neighboring countryside and villages.

IONA

A short cruise in the Inner Hebrides? Here, facing the New World, is the rock dot where St. Columba landed and began to Christianize the north of Britain in the sixth century. A 1-3/4-hour whisk via hydrofoil from **Oban**, skirting the vast, lonely, and hauntingly beautiful island of **Mull**. (You can also hop to Mull on a ferry, take an overland transfer, and cross to Iona at the western extremity.) Within easy walking distance of the small dock are the ancient **Abbey**, the **Nunnery**, a coffee shop and, naturally, a golf course. Of the 2 tiny hotels, we prefer the **Columba** to the **Argyle**, but both afford reasonable comfort and restful vistas of the Sound and Fionnphort on the Ross banks. Shoppers can visit charming "**Fiona of Iona**," mistress of Iona Scottish Crafts, where woolens, jewelry, and pottery of the isles are purveyed.

OBAN

Here is one of our favorites. It's so salty you can almost taste the kippers on your lips for days after you leave. The vistas of the **Firth of Lorn** and the blue glaze, which lusters Mull and beyond to Iona (see above), and the Hebrides are inviting to anyone who is venturesome. A marvelous port and takeoff point for faraway harbors.

PERTH

A shipping center on the Tay, at the fringes of the Highlands. Okay for an overnight but not worth a longer pause.

ST. ANDREWS

The great seaside golf courses—five spectacular ones here—are heaven-in-clover. American greens' fees are outrageous by comparison, but you might have difficulty obtaining a starting time unless you book ahead, especially on the famed *Old Course*. (The other four, incidentally, are superb and offer similar landscaping.) Don't worry about clubs because you can rent them. And don't worry about clothes. One wintry Sunday I played a round with a marmalade mogul who had come directly from church; he teed off in his heavy overcoat, fedora hat, and street shoes. Anything goes—and you should too. The next best form of entertainment is shopping at the fantastic **St. Andrews Woolen Mill** which is right beside the Old Course Pilmour Links. Bargains galore in knitwear. A must. For pausing, the **Argyle** in town is economical, but if you have several partners or a family (and also a car), the **9 pine lodges** at *Kincaple* (3 miles out) are excellent for foursomes. Weekly rates are amazingly low, and by doing your own cooking, you'll save bundles on food.

ST. FILLANS

This waterside hamlet is a dream, and the **Four Seasons Hotel** certainly must occupy one of the most eye-catching patches of Perthshire open to the tourist. *Loch Earn*, worthy of a volume of poetry, is at your doorstep. Nice people, good food, abundant comfort, moderate prices for the grand rewards.

STIRLING

Not too far from Perth, either in miles or in mood—so our evaluations are thme (see above).

FOR MORE INFORMATION ON SCOTLAND

For **USA** and **CANADA** see "England."

The **Scottish Tourist Board** (*23 Ravelston Terrace, Edinburgh*) is your source for any kind of travel aid.

For pamphlets and guidance on what to see, from Edinburgh's Royal Mile to Sule Skerry, or from salmon fishing to hang gliding or skiing, phone or write **STB's Information Desk**, *P.O. Box 705, Edinburgh,* ☎ *031-3322433.*

For special requests concerning places to hunt, golf, fish, ride, sail, or you-name-it, write to Mrs. J. Ball, **Tours and Travel Promotions**, *25 Brunstane Drive, Edinburgh, EH15 2NF,* ☎ *031-6695344*, FAX *72165.*

Enquire at the **STB** concerning the discount cards for visitors.

SPAIN
INCLUDING MALLORCA

Bullfighting season runs from March to mid-October.

Old World Spain seems to have recovered from the 500th anniversary party celebrating the discovery of the New World. The Olympics in Barcelona and Expo in Seville left many proud monuments and new facilities for future generations. Spain itself today has become a land of discovery. For the first-time visitor, the face of Iberia is like that of an ornate clock: the numerals on the perimeter are noteworthy, and Madrid, in the center, is the heart of the movement. Starting at "XII" you have Santander with a history going back to the Cantabrians and a might which reflected the power of ancient Rome. Moving east, there is San Sebastian at the edges of the Pyrenees like a jewel couched in green velvet facing the wind-tossed Bay of Biscay. Then down to mountainous Pamplona, the pulse beat of Navarra where, each year at the Feria de San Fermin, brave souls still expose themselves to the "running of the bulls." The hands sweep through the throbbing tourist sectors of the Costa Brava to Barcelona, pride of Catalonia, which boasts the Cathedral and room where Queen Isabella celebrated Columbus's triumphant return from the Americas. Then comes the gaiety of Valencia with its Fallas and the ever present smell of citrus groves and roses. Granada and the fabulous Alhambra strike "VI," one of the most rewarding movements in the passage of your time abroad. There's the slow and easy, sunlit Costa del Sol for lazing, golf, and aquatic sports—not to mention the continuous nighttime activities for which the area is famous. Into Andalucia and sun-baked Seville with its Moorish antecedents, neighboring Cordoba standing in the shimmering heat, up to lovely Salamanca, to the rugged Atlantic fjords of Vigo and finally to the stately antique grace of Santiago where so many other crusades have ended. There are many important "minutes" in between and fascinating, fairy-tale towns in the interior—yes, even castles in Spain—but if time is pressing, the "clockwise route" probably includes the greatest variety in this vast and variable peninsula.

As the second largest country in Europe, traditionally sunny Spain is also becoming the number-one travel destination on the Continent. Visited annually by a tourist contingent larger than its own population of 40 million, Spain—except for certain coastal zones—still is not overcrowded. The peseta-dollar exchange ratio is not what it was in early years—so tell us something new—but you do receive reasonable value compared with other travel destinations.

As we remarked above, Spain has much to offer apart from the fun-in-the-sun for which it is known to the multitudes of European visitors who crowd its beaches every summer. Along the northeastern frontier, the lofty ranges of the Pyrenees reveal grandiose snowfields and some truly splendid ski resorts that cost perhaps half of winter holidaying in the Swiss Alps—good enough for the avid sporting interests of the Spanish royal family. Below the mountains on the Catalonian seaboard, Barcelona provides some unforgettable attractions: the extraordinary Templo Expiatorio de la Sagrada Familia by Antonio Gaudi, master of a uniquely personal and bizarre architectural style; the Miro Museum; and the Picasso Gallery, which houses more than 2000 of his works, are typical of the many important features of this artistic and intellectual city. Embark here or anywhere south of this Columbian port for the bewitching Balearic Islands: the triangle of Mallorca, Menorca, and Ibiza.

Explore Andalucia, home of flamenco music and some of the world's most astonishing unknown guitar greats, to be heard in local

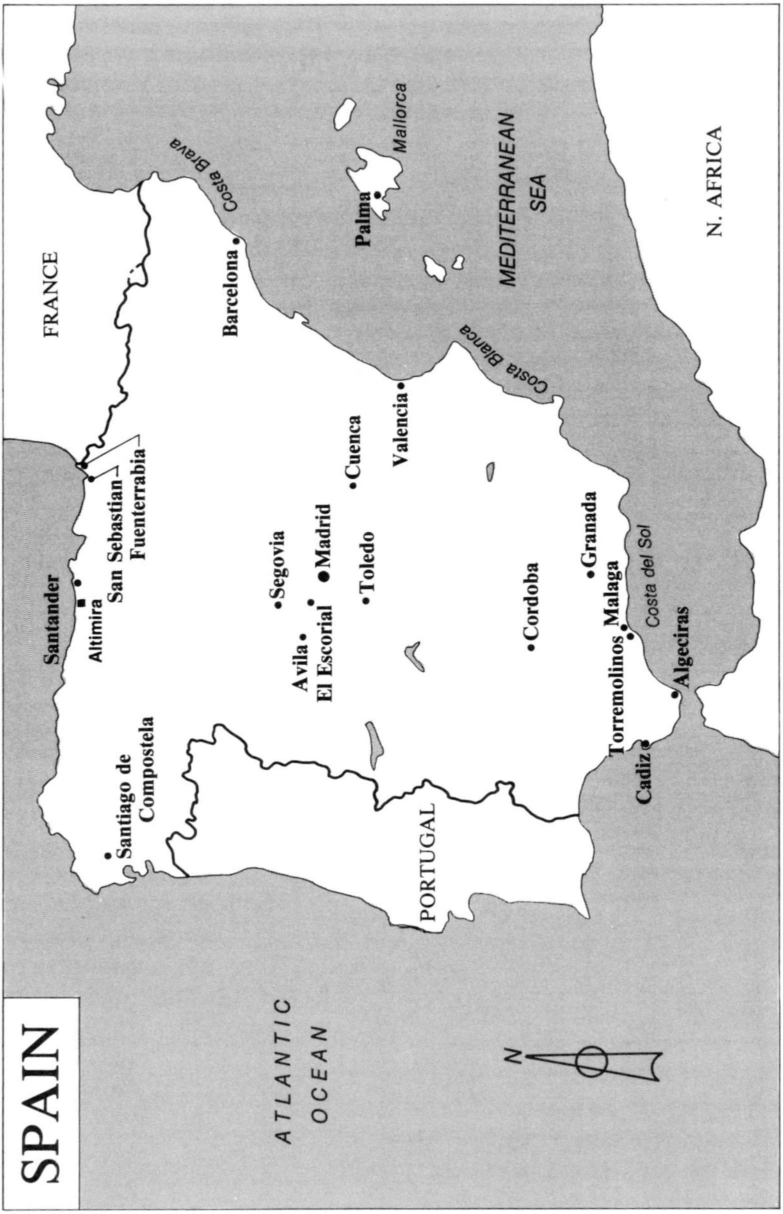
SPAIN
FRANCE
Costa Brava
Mallorca
MEDITERRANEAN SEA
N. AFRICA
Palma
Barcelona
Valencia
Costa Blanca
Cuenca
San Sebastian
Fuenterrabia
Santander
Altimira
Segovia
Madrid
Toledo
Avila
El Escorial
Cordoba
Granada
Malaga
Costa del Sol
Torremolinos
Algeciras
Cadiz
Santiago de Compostela
PORTUGAL
ATLANTIC OCEAN
N

bars and cafes. Madrid, seat of the Spanish government, is Europe's most elevated capital. There's a nobility and elegance here that typifies the unique atmosphere of this fascinating nation.

TIPS ON SPAIN

WHERE TO STAY

Tariffs remain reasonable by continental standards despite significant inflation and new taxes in Spain. If you are suspicious when checking in, ask to see the official rate card at the front desk; it is required that your daily scale be tacked up in the room itself. Some 160 Youth Hostels throughout the country offer safe, clean, and sometimes even spectacular accommodations (one is in a windmill). Costs run between $8-10 overnight, $6-8 meals, $8-13 bed and breakfast, $12-16 half-board, and $16-22 full-board. For further information and a complete listing, write to **Albergues Juveniles**, *Calle Jose Ortega y Gasset 71, Madrid-28006* (☎ *347-7700*; FAX *402-2194*). For students, a number of organizations offer accommodation and boarding possibilities during the summer months. Prices range from $22 to $28, including meals. The following centers (all in Madrid) may be of use to you: **Colegio Mayor Nebrija** (☎ *2432007*), **Colegio Mayor Diego Covarrubias** (☎ *2439000*), **Colegio Mayor Jimenez Cisneros** (☎ *2437800*), **Colegio Mayor Miguel Antonio Caro-Pabellon**, and **Colegio Mayor Santa Teresa de Jesus** (☎ *5491750*).

SPAIN'S PARADOR SYSTEM

They may no longer be cheap, but where else can you choose between sleeping in a baroque bedchamber once used as a prison, living on a huge rock almost completely circled by a river, climbing the battlements of a castle, sipping cocktails under eucalyptus trees while gazing at a Moorish fortress and the coast of Africa, or nestling next to caves that were inhabited 12,000 years before the birth of Christ?

Since 1928, the farsighted Ministry of Industry, Commerce and Tourism has been restoring and constructing a nationwide chain of inns forged mainly from remodeled 13th-16th-century palaces, monasteries, manor houses, and defensive bastions, plus several newer links fashioned to blend with the styles of their locales. They span not only the history of the country, but also its varied topography: from the green, rainy Basque country, to steel-hardened Castile, to the towering Pyrenees, and down to the golden beaches along the Costa del Sol.

There are 86 paradores. Every unit is immaculately clean and provided with baths and showers, telephones, and central heating; all have around-the-clock service. Most have a garage, richly decorated public areas, air conditioning, and a swimming pool or two; others go still further by offering golf, tennis, skiing, hunting, or fishing facilities. In addition, the system also operates 3 Hosterias (lodges) in remote climes and 4 conventional hotels. These, too, are excellent for their types.

Because the personnel in these inns are drawn locally, the service is often more willing than professional. However, it is nearly always openhearted.

Despite current expansions, the capacity of the paradores intentionally is kept quite small; many have fewer than 50 bedchambers. This limitation ensures that thundering hordes of sightseers will never trample you in the corridor outside your room. The disadvantage, however, is that with over 40 million visitors annually roaming over the Spanish landscape, these stops—even at their higher cost today—are in enormous demand throughout the year. It is, therefore, imperative to reserve as far as possible in advance. **Marketing Ahead** (*433 Fifth Ave., New York, NY 10016;* ☎ *212-686-9213*; FAX *212-686-0271*) is the American representative for the entire system and will handle all bookings. The U.S. headquarters of the **Spanish National Tourist Office** in New York (*665 Fifth Ave.*; ☎ *212-759-8822*) or its branches in Chicago and Beverly Hills will gladly supply a mass of information about the chain.

Once you arrive in Spain you can make your bookings at the **Paradores Madrid headquarters**, *Velazquez 18*, ☎ *91-435-9700*; FAX *44607 RRPP*; FAX *435-9869*.

The chart below provides some pertinent facts to help you plan your itinerary.

A SELECTION OF PARADORES		
Name and Address	**Units**	**Doubles**
Conde de Gondomar **Bayona (Pontevedra)** **(☎ 355000)**	**124**	**$145**
Conde de Orgaz **Toledo** **(☎ 221850-54)**	**76**	**$145**
Condestable Davalos **Ubeda (Jaen)** **(☎ 750345)**	**31**	**$145**
Condes de Alba y Aliste **Zamora** **(☎ 514497)**	**27**	**$130**
Costa de la Luz **Ayamonte (Huelva)** **(☎ 320700, 320726)**	**54**	**$135**

A SELECTION OF PARADORES		
Name and Address	**Units**	**Doubles**
Cristobal Colon **Mazagon (Huelva)** **(☎ 376000)**	**43**	**$145**
De Bailen **Bailen (Jaen)** **(☎ 670100)**	**86**	**$ 95**
Malaga Del Golf **Torremolinos** **(☎ 381255)**	**60**	**$145**
El Emperador **Hondarribia (Guipuzcoa)** **(☎ 642140)**	**16**	**$145**
Enrique II **Ciudad Rodrigo** **(Salamanca)** **(☎ 460150)**	**27**	**$120**
Fuerteventura **Puerto del Rosario** **Fuerteventura (Las Palmas)** **(☎ 851150)**	**50**	**$105**
Malaga Gibralfaro **Malaga** **(☎ 221903)**	**12**	**$125**
Gil Blas **Santillana del Mar** **(Santander)** **(☎ 818000)**	**56**	**$150**
Gredos **Navarredonda (Avila)** **(☎ 348048)**	**77**	**$105**
Hernan Cortes **Zafra (Badajoz)** **(☎ 550200)**	**45**	**$140**
La Arruzafa **Cordoba** **(☎ 275900)**	**94**	**$160**
Luis Vives **El Saler (Valencia)** **(☎ 1611186)**	**58**	**$145**
Marques de Villena **Alarcon (Cuenca)** **(☎ 331350)**	**13**	**$140**
Monte Perdido **Bielsa (Huesca)** **(☎ 501011)**	**24**	**$105**

A SELECTION OF PARADORES		
Name and Address	**Units**	**Doubles**
Monterrey **Verin (Orense)** **(☎ 410075)**	**23**	**$100**
Nerja **Nerja (Malaga)** **(☎ 520050)**	**73**	**$140**
Raimundo de Borgona **Avila** **(☎ 211340)**	**62**	**$120**
Reyes Catolicos **Mojacar (Almeria)** **(☎ 478250)**	**98**	**$115**
Rey Fernando II de Leon **Benavente (Zamora)** **(☎ 630300)**	**30**	**$115**
Ribadeo **Ribadeo (Lugo)** **(☎ 110825)**	**47**	**$115**
San Francisco **Granada** **(☎ 221440)**	**39**	**$250**
Valle de Aran **Viella (Lerida)** **(☎ 640100)**	**135**	**$100**
Via de la Plata **Merida (Badajoz)** **(☎ 313800)**	**82**	**$115**
Virrey Toledo **Oropesa (Toledo)** **(☎ 430000)**	**44**	**$105**

Other paradores are **Del Adelantado** (Cazorla, Jaen), **Del Albarino** (Cambados, Pontevedra), **Antonio Machado** (Soria), **Alcazar del Rey Don Pedro** (Carmona, 20 miles from Seville), **Canadas de Teide** (La Orotava, Santa Cruz de Tenerife), **Carlos V** (Jarandilla de la Vera, Caceres), **Casa del Baron** (Pontevedra), **La Concordia** (Alcaniz, Teruel), **Costa Blanca** (Javea, Alicante), **Costa Brava** (Aiguablava-Bagur, Gerona), **Hosteria Cruz de Tejeda** (Tejeda, Gran Canaria), **Ferrol** (Ferrol, La Coruna), **Conde de la Gomera** (San Sebastian de la Gomera, Santa Cruz de Tenerife), **Puerto Lumbreras** (Murcia), **La Mancha** (Albacete), **Molino Viejo** (Gijon, Asturias), **Don Pedro de Estopinan** (Melilla), **Principe de Viana** (Olite, Navarra), **Puebla de Sanabria** (Puebla de Sanabria, Zamora), **San Telmo** (Tuy, Pontevedra), **Santa Cruz de la Palma** (Santa Cruz de la Palma, Santa Cruz de Tenerife), **Santo Domingo de la Calzada** (Santo Domingo de la

Calzada, La Rioja), **Teruel** (Teruel), **Vich** (Vich, Barcelona), **Tordesillas** (Tordesillas, Valladolid), **Casa del Corregidor** (Arcos de la Frontera, Cadiz), **Trujillo** (Trujillo, Caceres), **La Muralla** (Ceuta), **Zurbaran** (Guadalupe, Caceres), **San Marcos** (Leon), **Caceres,** and **Reyes Catolicos** (Santiago de Compostela, Coruna)

FOOD

Regional specialties are interesting and their variety enormous. Almost every 50 miles of distance produces another strictly local culinary creation. If food interests you, read a Spanish cookbook before your trip and make notes on the dishes from the districts you plan to visit. Within the (above) parador system, the cuisine of each hostel reflects the gastronomy of the province where it resides. It's a fine way to broaden your education and your girth simultaneously.

In Spain (unlike in Mexico) tortilla is the word for omelet, with another noun added to specify its type. Salads, fruits, and fresh vegetables are safe wherever you go. So are most dairy products today, including ice cream.

Aside from straight meat and poultry, here are some popular dishes: *langosta* (the clawless local "lobster," which is wickedly expensive), *paella* (world-famous Valencia specialty of rice, peppers, shellfish, chicken, saffron, etc., served in a huge frying pan, usually inexpensive), *lenguado* (sole), *perdiz* (small whole partridge, rich and savory), and *centollo* (tender, flavorful crab from the Bay of Biscay).

Roast lamb (*cordero asado*) and roast suckling pig (*cochinillo*) are generally the finest meats. Beef, though improving, is usually (but not always) mediocre; it's seldom "topped" with grain, and it's slaughtered either too young or too old.

Spanish hams, like those from Jabugo, Trevelez, and Tervell, deserve their worldwide admiration.

Exquisite fruit of all varieties, including the world's best oranges (winter only); honey with the fragrance of rosemary, marjoram, and orange blossoms; almond nougat, marzipan, and tons of confections. As for cheeses, the better types include the *Tetilla* (soft and greasy), *Cabrales* (fermented and piquant), *Burgos* (all cream), *Asturias* (smoke-cured), and *Manchego.* The last, which has been molded in matting and preserved in oil, is a particular favorite.

Spanish meal hours are as follows: Breakfast at your option. Lunch from about 1–3:30 p.m.—so it might be 4:30 p.m. before you stagger away from the table to your siesta. Dinner at about 8:30—but 10 p.m. is more usual, which means the meal sometimes ends after midnight.

DRINKS

Sherry, the national wine, comes in 7 major types; it is always bottled blended rather than "straight." Call it Jerez and drink it usually before meals, sometimes chilled (but never with ice). The name is usually credited to an English corruption of the town from which it comes, but other scholars maintain that Jerez de la Frontera was formerly known as *Scxherisch* during the four-century-long Moorish occupation. And even prior to that, the Phoenicians called it *Xera* and the Romans wrote *Ceret* on their maps. Through the revolving *solera* system of mixing, the old and the new vintages are combined to produce a product that is always standard. Years ago, a small inner circle of British pukka sahibs made super-dry sherry a mark of social elegance in England; this foible, based on snobbism far more than on actual taste, quickly spread to America. (Though Tio Pepe is the best-known brand of this type, there are many fine cheaper labels available all over Spain.) During my residence in Spain, I have been weaned away from the Manzanillas, Finos, and other salty, acrid varieties, and now prefer Long Life (or any similar Oloroso blend)—old, soft, and golden, with just enough dryness and richness of body to give true delight. If you enjoy the sweet variety, Domecq's Celebration Cream and Valdespino's Jerez Dulce are full-bodied, smooth, and surprisingly low in cost.

Spanish red table wines are perhaps the most underrated—and soothingly priced!—of any in Europe. You'll pay about 75¢ per glass if you ask for *corriente* in either *tinto* (red) or *blanco* (white). Countless gallons flow over the border each year to be sold as "French" types in France and elsewhere. Most of these reds resemble Burgundies rather than Bordeaux, in their heaviness and fullness (though we can't guarantee that Iberian pressings do not appear in the leading Bordeaux); the whites, not as fine, are most often sweet or oily; rosés, especially Las Campanas and Senorio de Sarria brands, can be softer than French types and at a fraction of the French prices.

If forced to pick out one-of-a-kind for expensive daily consumption, we'd take *Marques de Riscal* for red, *Monopol* for white, *Cepa de Oro* for Chablis, and *Codorniu N.P.U.* for Spanish "champagne." Vina Pomal and Federico Paternina "Ollauri" also used to be superior rubies in their "Reserva" class, but their quality has fallen off. In general, if you are in taverns or bars, order the house wine (*vino de la casa*); it's what the boss drinks and the price will be right.

During the summer, restaurants mix up the cooling, refreshing wine punch called *Sangria*. Choose your own base (red, white, or champagne); it will be served in a pitcher with orange and lemon slices, Seltzer, sugar, and usually a tiny glass of cognac for flavor. It's available anywhere at any mealtime. Dubonnet and Campari are also popular in warm weather.

Scotch and bourbon are expensive and available everywhere thirst exists. Several years ago, the Iberian highlanders from Segovia succeeded in producing a first-cousin facsimile of Scotch. It is called DYC (pronounced as in Tracy) and its price is at least half that of

Scottish export varieties. If DYC doesn't please you (and quite possibly it won't), switch to Fundador *coñac* for your highball. You'll pay perhaps $1.50 per glass or around $10 per bottle in the average bar or grocery shop. The Spaniards like Carlos I, Gonzalez Byass Lepanto, Terry 1900, and similar rich, nutty, and heavy distillates.

Liqueurs—just name your favorite, and chances are good they'll have it. Any big bar stocks at least 30 or 40 different varieties, and they are about one-third the back-home price.

Beer—San Miguel has taken over the leadership among domestic labels. This Philippines-based company bottles it in Lerida on their true Pilsner formula; available nearly everywhere; light, creamy, and refreshing. Foreign beers such as Heineken, Tuborg, and others are either imported (expensive) or are brewed locally under license (lower in cost).

For soft drinks, Coca-Cola is omnipresent, even in the smallest villages; Tab, the low-cal cola, is now being marketed; 7-Up is found almost everywhere now (otherwise, ask for "Gaseosa," a reasonable Iberian facsimile); ginger ale and Schweppes tonic water and bitter lemon (other brands are fierce) can both be had nearly everywhere; lemonade (*limonada*) and orangeade (*naranjada*) are wonderful in winter but not so good in summer; *horchata*, a very sweet milky summer beverage made from a native root, has an almond flavor that is highly pleasing. Kas is a refreshing nonalcoholic bitter.

Finally, drink bottled water always, even though the tap water is usually sweet and potable. If you like it without bubbles, ask for *agua mineral sin gas* (Solares and Font Vella are two good brands); if you wish bubbles, any *agua mineral con gas* such as San Narciso or Vichy Catalan will do.

GETTING AROUND

TRAINS

Spanish railways have been improving notably in the quality of the cars, but service is another matter that probably won't thrill you. In the Madrid-Cadiz-Madrid sleepers, the Wagon-Lits' comfort standard matches that of almost any European country. There are still many rough patches in the roadbeds, but now there are some smooth ones, too.

Border-to-major-city and major-city-to-major-city schedules are also quite comfortable—if you pick the best expresses. **AVE** (an acronym for "high speed" but also meaning "bird" in Spanish) is the meteoric rapid service between Madrid and Seville, a $5.2-billion rail route that is darkly controversial in Iberia. It covers the 300-mile stretch in about 3 hours, but trackage does not allow it to roll over the 8000 additional miles of the nation's network. The older but speedy **Talgo** plies between Irun and Madrid as well as La Coruna,

Malaga, Cordoba, Granada, Seville, Murcia, Santander, Bilbao, and the capital—and, across the border, with Lisbon, Paris and Geneva. Another section makes the Barcelona-Madrid connection in 9 hours. A few other diesels (e.g., the **Cataluna-Galicia** cross-country service and the Madrid-Granada-Almeria links) are about as good as you'll find outside Switzerland. You may put your car aboard a piggyback-and-sleeper special between Madrid and Malaga's "Sun Coast." New rolling stock with bar-cafeteria facilities is being added to various schedules between the capital and Seville, Cadiz, Malaga, Alicante, and Valencia. But away from these, dining cars are rare; equipment is dirty, slow, and overcrowded; and arrivals are seldom on time. Fortunately, there has been a decrease in railroad accidents within the recent past in Spain, but most lines are antiquated and single-track, leading to numerous traffic delays. Station restaurants are almost always unappetizing and unsatisfactory.

The Tarjeta Turistica (tourist card) allows unlimited mileage for approximately $140 one week, ($200 for two weeks or $260 for three weeks) on second class. (First class costs 40% more.) Your hotel concierge or **RENFE** (Spanish Railways; ☎ *(91) 5630202*) will supply additional information.

TAXIS

Fares are inching up to match fuel and other dollar-based inflation, but still a bargain compared with U.S. rates. Avarice seems to be the inevitable handmaiden of upward economic movement nationwide. Many cars now have fancy digital meters on which there are 4 buttons the driver presses: #3 is used within the major city limits. As soon as these are passed, he presses #2, which ups the rate; #1 is for Sundays and holidays only, and #4, at this writing, is a dummy. Result: Exactly the same distance costs 25% more than it should on a purely distance basis.

SUBWAYS

In the capital, you can often avoid the hassle with hacks by opting for this fast, clean, and efficient public transport. It will set you back all of 135 pesetas per ride. A time-saver and a money-saver in an increasingly traffic-choked metropolis.

BUSES

Juliatours, **Pullmantur** and **Trapsatour** offer a bewildering, extensive repertory of minibus excursions.

According to the latest information, there are 10 fixed all-inclusive deluxe tours, 2 so-called Slow Motion tours, scores of optional-combination itineraries, and a galaxy of city or suburban sightseeing junkets. Here are typical ones: A week-long Andalusian tour from Madrid to Granada-Torremolinos-Seville-Cordoba and back to Madrid; a 5-day version of practically the same itinerary; a 9-day Iberian swing encompassing the capital at both ends and covering Salamanca, Viseu, Fatima, Lisbon, Seville, Antequera, and Granada; a

castle sweep of 3 days' duration in the Madrid region; a Moroccan "Caravan" departing from Tangier for 7 days of nomading from Rabat to Casablanca, Marrakesh, Meknes, Fez, Xauen, Tetuan, and returning to Tangier. Vehicles are 29-, 34-, or 40-seaters with radio, individual lights, public-address system, reclining chairs, 2 drivers, and a multilingual interpreter-guide; those on southern routes are now air-conditioned. Tickets are issued for full or partial journeys, but preference is for applicants who want the whole thing. Baggage is limited to 66 lbs.

These are comprehensive tours, of course, so naturally the prices are higher than for simple transportation. If you pick your own destination and travel by bus, you will probably save 20% or so, but your meals and independent hotel bookings might eat up that difference easily unless you are really determined to economize. Doing it on your own does provide more freedom, but for saving money it's a dubious option.

MOTORING

If your car is medium-size, large, or a peppy one, get Super wherever you can (unleaded gas is increasingly available too); it is advertised as containing a rating of 97 octane, but its performance is a lot closer to 80. The majority of stations are closed on Sundays and fiestas, so be sure your tank doesn't run dry then. (If you read Spanish, a sign is posted at the closed stations on holidays describing where the nearest open one is located.) *Autopistas* (turnpikes) are excellent but not very extensive. The secondary links often are efficiently graded, beautifully banked, cleverly engineered, well marked, and basically safe, but generously endowed with potholes, wrinkles, and bumps. Information about road conditions (often optimistic) may be had by phoning the **Tele-Ruta** (☎ *5352222*).

TRAFFIC

Inhabited areas can be a jumble of trucks, cars, motor scooters, bicycles, and daring pedestrians. One crowning rule must never be forgotten: The vehicle to the right ALWAYS has the right of way, except at a few scattered junctions with triangular signs reading "*Ceda el Paso*" ("Yield"). Even if you're flashing around a traffic circle via a main road, that little guy from the dirt path on your right has the privilege of horning in in front of you—and he will damn well expect you to hit the brakes, if necessary.

CAR RENTAL

Avis seems to live up to its promise of trying harder. There are numerous desks in town and every hotel can obtain a car for you. (If you take the trouble to phone for yourself, however, you may save the 20% commission usually given to the agent who simply rings up the central office.) **Hertz** (Edificio Espana) boasts quite a few stations and scores of independents have sprung up (**Budget**, **Inter-rent**, **Eu-**

ropecar, etc.). **Nizo**, the local Volkswagen rental office, is at *Vallehermoso 34, Madrid.*

MOTOR SCOOTER HIRE AND PURCHASE

Antonio Castro (*Conde Duque 13*) specializes in rentals at medium-to-high tariffs. Quite a few other companies are licensed to sell everything from Lambrettas to Guzzis to Mobylettes. Among the better-known suppliers are **Motors Villar** (*Juan de Dios 7*), **Motor City** (*Plaza de Zorrilla 4*), **Moto Guzzi** (*Julian Camarillo 9*), and **Canto** (*Princesa 26*). All in Madrid.

SPORTS

BULLFIGHTING

Technically, it's not a sport but a cruel yet historic pageant, a blood rite that is not recommended to anyone with a love for animals. Draw a top matador and you'll witness a Spanish tradition at its peak; draw a second-rater or a novice or a weak bull (more and more likely these days), and you're liable to watch sickening butchery. This distinction is vital. Season runs Mar. to mid-Oct. Don't purchase the most expensive seat in the shade (*sombra*) if you're squeamish and likely to leave after the first kill (there are 6 bulls); *barrera* is first row; *contrabarrera* is second row; *tendido* is rest of seats till *gradas* and *andanada* at the very top (under shelter); as you know *sol* means on sunny side while *sombra* gets you on the shade. Tickets run from perhaps $10 to $60 and cannot be purchased far in advance.

SKIING

A selection of resorts in the **Pyrenees** offers week-long instruction. Per-person price runs from $135 bed-and-breakfast to $450 full board. Here are some popular places to contact for the fine points: **Oficina de Informacion y Reservas**, **Candanchu**; ☎ *(974) 373192/373194*; **Oficina de Turismo de Baqueira-Beret,** *Apartado 60-Viella, Valle de Aran*; ☎ *(973) 645025/645050*; and **Tuca Val D'Aran**, **Viella**, *Valle de Aran, Lerida*; ☎ *(973) 640855*. In the famous **Rioja** wine region a 1-week, half-board ski-instruction package costs from $150 to $400. Contact **Valdezcaray**, **Travesia Tenorio 8**, *Ezcaray (La Rioja)*; ☎ *(941) 354275*. Warning: When warm winds blow, your winter holiday can melt away before your ski tips.

New Granada, Sol-y-Nieve in the Sierra Nevada is lovely if you like skiing in warm snow. Prices at all are a fraction of those at other continental sports centers. More information from the **Federacion Espanola de Deportes de Invierno**, *Calle Claudio Coello 32, Madrid-1*, ☎ *2758943.*

HORSES

On weekends or daily from July through the rest of the summer see the Sierra de Gredos on horseback; 4- and 8-hour guided tours leave from the **Parador Nacional de Gredos**; respective prices about $45 and $80. For information in Madrid ☎ *4166592* or ☎ *2534881*; or contact **Parador Nacional de Gredos**, *Navarredonda de Gredos (Avila)*; ☎ *(918) 348048.*

SAILING

The tack to take is the **Federacion Espanola de Vela**, *Calle Juan Vigon 23, Madrid 28003*; ☎ *52335305/52338408.*

SIGHTSEEING

LANGUAGES

Spanish courses offered at summer youth residences in Santander, Avila, Mallorca (Catalan), Caceres, and Ciudad Real. For details, write **Instituto de la Juventud y Promocion Comunitaria**, *71 Calle Jose Ortega y Gasset, Madrid-28006.*

WORKING HOLIDAYS

You can obtain firsthand experience in archaeology, ecology, or similar disciplines through the Ministry of Culture that runs work camps on an exchange basis. Information available through **International Educational Exchange**, *202 E. 42nd Street, New York, NY 10017*; ☎ *(212) 661-1414.*

CASINOS

Spain permits gambling in 17 provinces (with 22 casinos so far). Naturally, tourist zones are favored, so if you are gamboling around Iberia this year looking for games of chance, check whether your area has opened a casino. About a half hour out of Madrid, there's a fine one with shuttle bus service to the city. Ask any tourist office for the schedule. As the government monitors all activities related to gambling, you can be pretty sure you will get a fair shake or shuffle.

SHOPPING

Shopping hours: generally from 9:30–10 a.m. to 1:30 p.m. and then from 4:30 to 8 p.m. The law allows shops, if they wish, to remain open during the siesta hours, so check locally. Major department stores do so in any case. The Value-Added tax, or IVA, as it is known locally, is set at 15%. Talk to the shopkeeper about getting the rebate on any single item you purchased that cost more than 15,000 pesetas. The mechanisms for such discounts are in place, but staffs haven't had much practice in refunding schemes.

THINGS NOT TO BUY

Spanish shawls. The only real Spanish shawls are antiques from China. This has become a tourist racket; prices are outrageous. Beware also of the metal on the cheaper varieties of handbags or costume jewelry; it might tarnish all too soon.

LOCAL RACKETS

Rare—but watch any transaction in some of the gypsy quarters or open markets. You can count on magnificent honesty from most Spaniards, but hucksters anywhere in the world live by trickery.

So-called discounted "Ronson" and "Omega" lighters, "Parker" pens, and other "branded" items are now being hawked by sidewalk sharpies in the cafes of the larger cities. It's all sucker bait, counterfeited in illicit Tangier factories—and guaranteed not to work.

Sometimes the taximeter racket can be annoying (especially with airport cabs). Either they'll "forget" to zero the counter from the last haul, so that you'll pay the previous passenger's ride as well as your own, or "forget" to haul down the flag at all, so that at the end you can be snared with an "estimated" fare. The capital is not unique as a victim of this occasional disease, and some hotel doormen are in cahoots with drivers.

Keep an eye peeled for purse snatchers and pickpockets in the subway, buses, interior parking buildings (especially in elevators), and crowded areas. They've sharply increased lately.

WHERE TO GO

ALGECIRAS

Here's the traditional gateway to Gibraltar, now reopened from mainland Spain. In temperament, we'd call it a smaller "Cadiz". The dreary shipping atmosphere of the town itself, which used to depress most voyagers, has vanished to be replaced by the feeling of excitement associated with a staging area for exotic journeys still further afield. Transmediterranea's hydrofoil link to **Ceuta** and **Tangier** (1-1/2 hours) enhances holiday rewards. North Africa is a terrific easy-to-reach target. Good budget hotels are the **Anglo-Hispano**, the **Alarde**, the **Al-Mar**, and the **Octavio**.

The **Reina Cristina** is more costly. As to restaurants, **Iris** (*San Bernardo 1*) and **Marea Baja** (*Trafalgar 2*) are our favorites; meals range between $18 and $60, depending on your appetite and budget.

ALTAMIRA

The glorious *stone age caves* that had been closed to the public since 1977 are open again to very limited-number groups. You'll be awed by more than 150 clearly polychromatic drawings of hunters' prey dating back over 20 millennia. See "Santander" for further information on this region.

AVILA

Many people put this one on their excursion list from the capital since it is just under 70 miles northwest of Madrid. From a distance, it's a fairy-tale city with 86 towers and a medieval wall rising starkly from the landscape; inside it reflects the austerity of its clerical inhabitants and the dour society of that era. Avila veal is known for its refinement and is prized nationwide by tablesiders. **Meson del Rastro** (*Plaza del Rastro 1*) and **Piquio** (*Estrada 4*) are two good examples. If you don't mind $120 for one-night accommodations, then the **Parador Raimundo de Borgona** would be an ideal choice.

BARCELONA

Set on a rich plain between two rivers and two towering mountains, its convenient situation makes it a natural springboard for travel either way along the Spanish coast, up to the high hills, over to the Balearic Islands, or across the sea to the Riviera, Italy, and North Africa. Hotels are increasing both in number and quality; restaurants are good; nightlife bubbles with the enthusiasm of these energetic people. Catalans feel a very special identity with their metropolis (home of the 1992 Olympics), which produces so much of the nation's wealth. Although its cultural attractions are numerous (with contrasting wonders from the unthinkably ancient cathedral (adjoining where Columbus returned from his New World voyage), to the unfinished *Sagrada Familia* by Gaudi, to the artist-endowed **Picasso Museum**, to **La Ciudad Condal amusement park**), it is a huge commercial port. For overnighting, **L'Alguer** (*Pasaje Pedro Rodriguez 20*) is conveniently located within walking distance from Montjuic center and the university district; its tranquil street may be hard to find even for your taxi driver. Homey ambience; 33 unpretentious rooms with bath and telephone ($40 singles and $65 doubles); central heating. Proprietor Sabater will not only welcome you wholeheartedly but proudly explain his Catalan heritage while offering you a local Montserrat liqueur in his cozy lounge. **Regencia Colon**, **Mitre**, and **Regente** are substantial medium-price hotels. The **Regina** and the **Royal** are very central, practical, and worthy. **Balmoral** is more residential; **Manila** is good but more costly. For dining, **Casa Bofarull-Los Caracoles** is famous and moderate in cost; it has a phenomenal atmosphere. **Carballeira** (*Reina Cristina 3*) is recommended. Also agreeable is **El Pa Torrat** (*Santalo 68*) for regional cooking till late at night or **Tramonti** (*Diagonal 501*) if you prefer true Italian dishes.

CADIZ

Cadiz, perhaps the oldest inhabited city in western civilization, might be too commercial for your taste. It's an important port and industrial center, but has its romantic side, too. I'm drawn first to its 18th-century baroque cathedral. Art lovers are immediately attracted to Goya's paintings at **Santa Cueva church** or admire the **Murillos at San Felipe Neri church**. The **Museum of Art and Archaeology** is another must; here you'll admire the **Phoenician sarcophaguses** so characteristic of this metropolis. For overnighting, **Atlantico** (*Parque Genoves 9*), **Francia y Paris** (*Plaza Calvo Sotelo 2*), **Regio** (*Ana de Viya 11*), **Regio II** (*Lopez Pinto 79*), and **Isecotel** (*Paseo Maritimo*) should provide adequate shelter. By far the leading restaurant in the community is **El Faro** (*San Felix 15*), where a tantalizing variety of seafare may be savored—in fact, most of it is provided daily by local anglers! **El Anteojo** (*Alameda de Apodaca 22*) and **Meson del Duque** (*Paseo Maritimo 12*) follow suit.

CORDOBA

This ancient bastion beguiles us more on each successive visit, yet it's practically changeless. Its colossal **Mezquita** (1000-year-old mosque that is now the cathedral) is one of the showplaces of the nation; its *Romero de Torres collection* (the 20th-century eccentric who painted prostitutes as saints) is intriguing; its narrow streets in the Old Town and Jewish quarter have color and charm. About 5 miles out, the fabulous ruins of the **Medina Azahara** are breathtaking; this palace (almost a mile long and more than 1/2-mile wide) was built at the same time as the Mezquita, by the *Caliph of Cordoba*. The nearby **Monasterio San Jeronimo** (vintage 1405), with its enchanting primitive cloister, is also worth a visit; try to talk your way into its privately owned precincts. Also worth seeing is the **Palacio de Viana**, with its 11 patios and superb art collections. Best stop for kilometers is the **Parador de la Arruzafa** (see "A Selection of Paradres" section); moreover, you can dine here inexpensively and very well. **Residencia Maimonides** (*Torrijos 4*), **El Califa** (*Lope de Hoces 14*), and **Los Gallos** (*Avda. Medina Azahana 7*) also are recommended. **El Churrasco** (*Romero

16) and **Ciros** (*Paseo de la Victoria 19*) serve excellent local fare while **Costa Sol** (*Plaza Costa Sol 2*) specializes in fresh sea catches.

COSTA BLANCA

The "White Coast," the fancy touristic name for the coastline of Alicante between **Valencia** and **Murcia**, has been popularized to handle the overflow from the crowded **Costa Brava**. According to a recent survey, **Benidorm** is the number one destination for the British. (An English Benidormitory perhaps?) The Dutch descend here in such strength that one zone in the Alicante area is jestingly called "*Coveta Fuma*" (roughly translated, "Smoked Herring"). Burgeoning facilities make it a group lodestone for the Spanish economy. For overnighting in Benidorm, I suggest seafront **Costablanca** (*Av. Alcoy*) or **Don Pancho** (*Avda. del Mediterraneo*), while **La Palmera** (*Carretera Diputacion*) will pamper your gustatory senses with savory regional cuisine.

COSTA BRAVA

The "Rugged Coast," that stretch of mountains, cliffs, and bays between Barcelona and the French border, has been despoiled by too many bodies for too little space. With only a few exceptions, the hotels in almost every price bracket are miserable. **Tossa** and **Lloret de Mar**, as two of many examples, are aburst with cracker boxes thrown up helter-skelter. In addition, only a handful of hotels are situated on scenic sites. Some sections of the "Rugged Coast" are more panoramic and breathtaking than the Amalfi Drive. Many roads are still narrow and serpentine, resulting in gigantic traffic snarls during the holiday months. Point-to-point travel, therefore, is a pain in the neck (except via the Cruceros excursion fleet, with frequent sailings, convenient termini, and pleasant scenery). My choice in the Costa Brava is **Rosas** (85 miles north of Barcelona) with its lovely bay and nearby beaches. Both **Almadraba Park** and **Canyelles Platja** will provide adequate lodging. **La Llar** (road to Figueras, C-260) offers exquisite cuisine in a family atmosphere; a modestly priced five-course menu attracts gourmets from all over the region; very good for a splurge but also excellent for à la carte.

COSTA CALIDA

The "Warm Coast," the sun-toasted province between *Alicante* and *Andalusia*, extends along 140 miles of pearl-white strands, snug little coves, and hidden inlets. Highway and air connections are excellent. Recreational facilities, including a casino and golf links, center around the 94-square mile **Mar Menor**, so-called because it is embraced by the elongated, 300- to 2000-foot-wide flatland called **La Manga** ("The Sleeve"). This sea and landscape phenomenon means you can choose between calm lake waters and occasionally rough Mediterranean sea bathing. Top hotel choices run from the **Cavanna** to **Doble Mar Casino** to **Galua-sol**. **Borsalino** serves decent French-style cooking while **Dos mares** specializes in regional fare; try the latter's *cordero al ajo* (lamb with garlic). In **Murcia** (the capital) itself, there's reasonable shelter at **Siete Coronas Melia**, **Conde de Floridablanca**, and **Fontoria**. For a meal, don't miss **El Rincon de Pepe**, famed for its fish pies, stuffed peppers, and sinfully fattening desserts.

COSTA DEL SOL

The "Sunny Coast," with *Torremolinos*, *Marbella*, and other resort settlements strung along the 106-mile strip of seacoast on the Algeciras-Estepona-Malaga road, is simultaneously youthful, aristocratic, and Bohemian. One thing it is not is dull.

Rampant construction from deluxe to budget level has transformed hamlets, villages, and entire areas into an Iberian version of a Florida land boom. With so many hostelries writhing for attention, the newest trend is the low-cost apartment dwelling for 1-week-or-longer residence. This can save you quite a bit of money. The region provides a melange of superior-to-poor hotels, restaurants, and other attractions, including fair-to-middling beaches. (All beaches in Spain are public, so use any strand you like.) Definitely worth a visit. Torremolinos is covered in more detail below.

If you are looking for the old quiet "Costa" of yore, try *Almunecar*, an hour's drive east of Malaga. The **Hostal Tropical**, *A. Europa 3*; ☎ *633458* is only a few steps from the beach and the cost is merely $36 per night for two. Then stroll down the esplanade, have a drink and free tapas at a thatch-roofed bar, and consider retirement for life on this hospitable Mediterranean shore.

CUENCA

This is a renowned center of modern art, about 100 miles east of Madrid; a journey here should be an excursion in itself. The charm of this town is due to its quaint old cliff dwellings that have been restored by the artist residents. Be sure to visit the museum, composed of several contiguous "hanging houses." **Torremangana** is the leading hotel, followed by **Alfonso VIII**, **Cueva del Fraile** ("Monk's Cave") and **Xucar**. Try **El Figon de Pedro** for excellent regional cuisine or **Meson Casas Colgadas** for a breathtaking view.

GRANADA

Located 90 miles northeast of Torremolinos along a road leading into the Sierra Nevada. **The Alhambra** is a fabulous reward at the end of this curving, scenic trail. The $8 combination ticket, valid for 2 days, entitles you to wander through all of the majestic precincts of the 700-year-old Moorish palace and the nearby terraced gardens of the **Generalife**. Take time to linger among its flora, pools, arcades, mosaic wonderland, and fountains (the Lion Fountain is world famous, of course); you'll find an architectural symphony that shouldn't be missed.

Overnighters may head for the few hostelries on the hill. Inside the castle wall, the state-sponsored **Parador San Francisco** (☎ *221493*) offers splendid and atmospheric accommodations with prices ranging up to $170 or so per double; this beauty has become so popular that reservations must be made at least 6 months in advance. Lesser charmers at much lesser tariffs are the simple and friendly **Hostal America**, within the walls of the Alhambra, **Residencia Macia**, **Alixares del Generalife**, and **Residencia Ana Maria**. **Carmen de San Miguel** (*Torres Bermejas 3*) and **Pilar del Toro** (*Hospital de Santa Ane 12*) serve exquisite local meals.

JEREZ DE LA FRONTERA

Welcome to the home of sherry and Iberian-style cognac. The word "sherry" evolved from attempts by 18th-century British dockworkers to pronounce Jerez. The local spirit world revolves around these palatable products to the exclusion of all other interests. Tour one of the major *bodegas* (Gonzalez Byass, Pedro Domecq, Harvey's, Sandemann, or Williams & Humbert), which extend all the way down to the oceanside village of Puerto de Santa Maria. All are open from 10 a.m. to 1 p.m. on weekdays, all are free, and all will load you with such samples of their wares that you'll be as stiff as a plank by noon; advance booking mandatory, though. Charming little country town with lots of color. For overnighting, **Aloha** (*Km 637, Madrid Road*) or **Capele** are decent choices. **Torres** and **Coloso** are less expensive. Try either **El Bosque** (*A. Domecq 26*) or **Gaitan** (*Gaitan 33*) for savory regional fare.

MADRID

Right in the heart of Spain, on its lofty central plateau, without so much as a proper river, Madrid was little more than a minor fortress town until the 14th century. In 1561 it became the capital. Today it is very much a walking, talking city that is fast leaving behind the mañana syndrome and the afternoon siesta to join the antic split-second activity of the 80s. While it used to be inexpensive, today it is even more costly than New York for the visitor who wishes to live and dine in upper-bracket standards. Fortunately though, it hasn't left behind its traditional charm and sophistication. Madrid's interesting cafes and restaurants buzz with urban vitality; its nightlife runs late even if it sleeps less tomorrow morning.

The city's prides include the famous **Prado**, one of the foremost art museums in the world, and the vast **Royal Palace**, overflowing with priceless antiques and boasting a throne-room ceiling by *Tiepolo.* (Juan Carlos resides in the more modest Zarzuela Palace.) Keen-eyed bargain spotters can also seek out the **Rastro**, the rambling flea market in the **Plaza de Cascorro**. Even if you don't find your treasure of a lifetime, it probably won't cost you a single peseta to mingle with the crowds of shoppers, browsers, and, alas, pickpockets in this exhilarating district. There are scores of lovely fountains and squares, the latest one in the *Salamanca* quarter, designed by Salvador Dali.

The shopping in the conventional areas of the metropolis is among the best in Europe. Moreover, there are dozens of excursion targets for inexpensive sightseeing in the immediate vicinity.

DIRECTORY

U.S. Embassy • *Serrano 75*; ☎ *5763400.*

American Express • *Plaza de las Cortes 2*; ☎ *4295775.*

Barber • Cachon, *Carrera de San Jeronimo 5*, Peluqueria de Caballeros, *Princesa 70, Carranza 32, or Cruz 10*, Canamero, *Fuencarral 112*, or Pardo, *Buenavista 41.*

Hairdressers • Hermanos Blanco, *Noviciado 7, Almirante 15, or Principe de Vergara 82*, Eduardo, *Gran Via.* Peluqueria Florida, *Puerta del Sol 12, 1 flight up*, Sanlorien, *Paseo de la Castellana 4*, Peluqueria Rufi, *Gravina 1*, or Peluqueria Besy, *Glorieta Bilbao 4.*

Laundry • La Emperatriz, *Plaza del Peru 7*; ☎ *2593430*, Lavanderia Madrid, *Virgen de la Fuencisla 12*; ☎ *3261202*, and Lavomatique, *Basilica 20*; ☎ *5344315.*

Dry Cleaning and Pressing • Amaya, *Plaza Republica Ecuador 3*, Los Americanos, *Alberto Aguilera 70*, Nuria, *General Sanjuro 22*, or Royal, *Victor Pradera 36.*

Medical Emergencies • ☎ *061.*

Suit Rental • Casa Jimenez, *Preciados 42*; ☎ *2480526.* Gerardo, *Principe de Vergara 25*; ☎ *5761294*, and Gil Arranz, *Jose Ortega y Gasset 45*; ☎ *4028355.*

Police • Central Station, *Amador de los Rios 7*; ☎ *5371000* or ☎ *091* for real emergencies.

Pawnshop • Caja de Ahorros y Monte de Piedad de Madrid, *Plaza Celenque 2.* Pawnshops in Spain are banks!

HOW TO GET AROUND

At Madrid's Barajas Airport, you'll find the terminal bus just outside the point where you pick up your baggage or clear Customs. It's about a $2.75, 20-minute cruise to the debarkation center at Plaza Colon. The same trip by taxi runs about $14.

TAXIS

Within the city, cab fares are no longer as cheap as they used to be, although they are still among the least expensive on the Continent. Four important supplements over the meter reading are charged: one for a railroad station call, another for each suitcase, one for the bullring, and a special boost on holidays and after midnight. Few rides will cost you more than $5; Madrilenos usually tip 10-15%; with conspicuous exceptions, most drivers are honest and reckless. In daylight, look for the red line around the chassis; after dark, wave at the cars with tiny green windshield lights.

MADRID'S SUBWAY

Service is efficient, cheap, and as easy to follow as Paris' Metro. Plunk down your 135 pesetas, grab your receipt, and go through the turnstile. Transfers available on all of its 9 lines. **Puerta del Sol** is the hub of the system; obtain a map of the network there. Get off the train at "Atocha" for the Prado, "Opera" for the Royal Palace, "Retiro" (and then take Bus #1) for the Lazaro Galdiano Museum, "Florida" Goya's Tomb, and "Ventas" for the Bullfighting Museum.

CITY BUSES

Buses are abundant. You can save even more by purchasing the special ten-ride "*abono*" ticket.

TRAINS

There are 3 passenger stations: **Norte** (*Paseo de Onesimo Redondo, near the Royal Palace*) with services for northern Spain and a few French destinations, **Atocha** (*Glorieta de Carlos V, near the Prado*) for western and southern Spain, and **Chamartin** *(Agustin de Foxa)* for eastern Spain and France.

WHERE TO STAY

LEAST $

Several provide reasonable rewards for around $25 or less. Demipension is customarily required during peak-travel months.

Maravillas, **Marichelo**, and **Posada del Dragon** • *Malasana 23;* ☎ *4484000*; *Fernando el Catolico 9*; ☎ *4483438* and *Cava Baja 14*; ☎ *2653225*; FAX *2652875*. These three are real bargains. Each has personality and provides great value for your pesetas.

Hostal La Macarena • *Cava de San Miguel 8*; ☎ *3659221*. Recommended for the young and gregarious. Hard-to-find site near Plaza Cuchilleros, 1 flight up. Lounge and dining room; 20 rooms. Per-person rates with breakfast about $17. Popular, so reserve early.

Valencia and **Continental** • *Gran Via 44;* ☎ *5221115; same address,* ☎ *5214640.* Almost duplicates in layout and basic amenities. Only a few of the former's 30 cells glimmer with bright touches. The latter seemed warmer in staff attitudes.

Don Juan and **Chocolate** • *I, Recoletos 18*; ☎ *2755000* and *Joaquin Maria Lopez 29*; ☎ *5491058*. Adequate at this price range ($22 for a single).

MORE $$

Primary charges per person in doubles with bath and 2 meals average $48-80; $42-62 without food. Many occupy space in commercial structures which may lock the main door after midnight.

California • *Gran Via 38;* ☎ *5224703*. A warm welcome awaits 1 flight up. Bar and lounge. Restaurant; 27 simple, attractive, ample quarters, all with bath and tele-

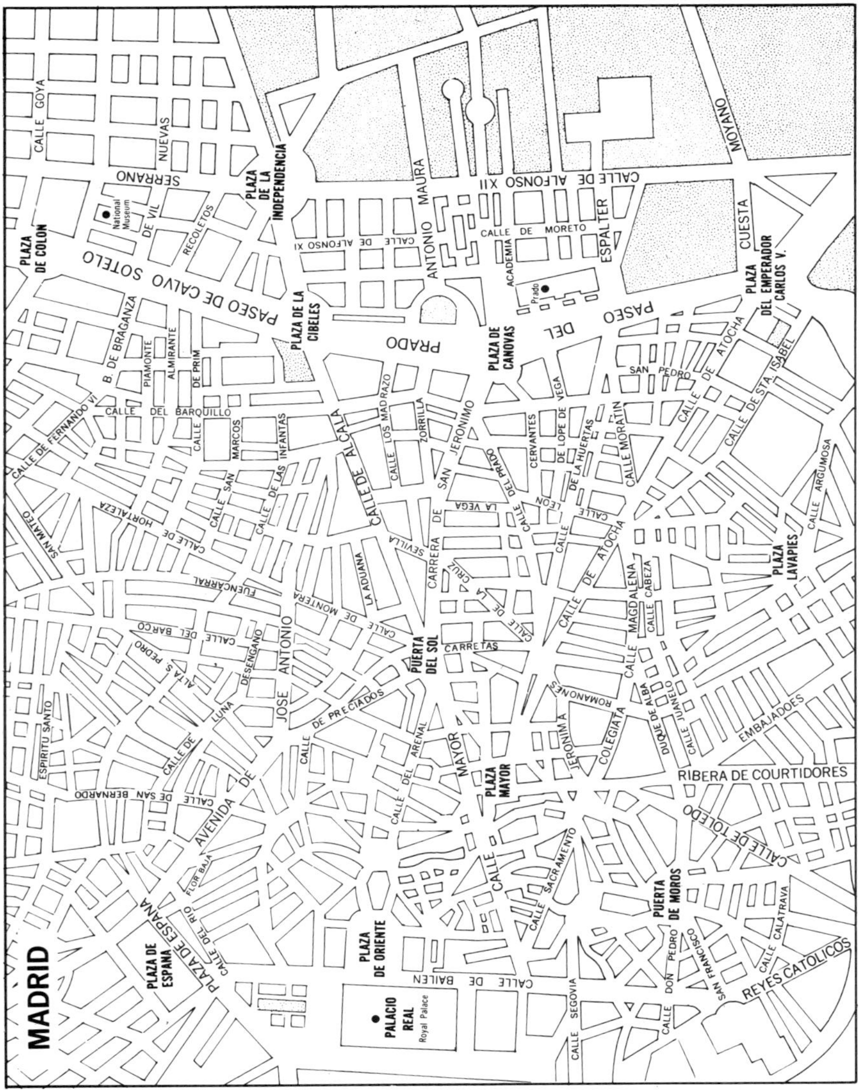
MADRID
CALLE GOYA
NUEVAS
SERRANO
National Museum
DE VIL
RECOLETOS
PLAZA DE LA INDEPENDENCIA
PLAZA DE COLON
PASEO DE CALVO SOTELO
B. DE BRAGANZA
PIAMONTE
ALMIRANTE
DE PRIM
PLAZA DE LA CIBELES
CALLE DE ALFONSO XI
ANTONIO MAURA
CALLE DE ALFONSO XII
CALLE DE MORETO
ACADEMIA
ESPALTER
Prado
MOYANO
CUESTA
PLAZA DEL EMPERADOR CARLOS V.
PASEO DEL PRADO
PLAZA DE CANOVAS
SAN PEDRO
CALLE DE ATOCHA
CALLE DE STA. ISABEL
CALLE DEL BARQUILLO
CALLE DE FERNANDO VI
CALLE
MARCOS
INFANTAS
CALLE DE LAS
CALLE SAN
CALLE LOS MADRAZO
ZORRILLA
CALLE DE ALCALA
SAN JERONIMO
CERVANTES
DE LOPE DE VEGA
DE LAS HUERTAS
CALLE MORATIN
CALLE ARGUMOSA
CALLE DE HORTALEZA
SAN MATEO
CALLE DEL PRADO
LA VEGA
CALLE LEON
CALLE
CARRERA DE SAN JERONIMO
SEVILLA
LA ADUANA
CRUZ
CALLE DE LA
CALLE DE ATOCHA
MAGDALENA
CALLE CABEZA
PLAZA LAVAPIES
FUENCARRAL
CALLE DE MONTERA
CALLE DEL BARCO
ALTA S. PEDRO
DESENGAÑO
JOSE ANTONIO
PUERTA DEL SOL
CARRETAS
CALLE
ROMANONES
DUQUE DE ALBA
CALLE JUANELO
EMBAJADORES
ESPIRITU SANTO
CALLE DE LUNA
CALLE DE PRECIADOS
CALLE DEL ARENAL
MAYOR
PLAZA MAYOR
JERONIMA
COLEGIATA
RIBERA DE COURTIDORES
CALLE DE SAN BERNARDO
AVENIDA DE
CALLE DE TOLEDO
FLOR BAJA
CALLE SACRAMENTO
CALLE
PUERTA DE MOROS
CALLE CALATRAVA
PLAZA DE ESPAÑA
CALLE DEL RIO
PLAZA DE ORIENTE
CALLE DE BAILEN
CALLE SEGOVIA
CALLE DON PEDRO
SAN FRANCISCO
REYES CATOLICOS
PALACIO REAL
Royal Palace

phones; #201 a gigantic terraced unit that sleeps 4 or 5. High-ish tariffs ($65 per double and $44 per single) but good value.

Opera • *Cuesta Santo Domingo 2;* ☎ *5412800.* Kind staff. Reasonably priced rooms considering the view. All 99 of them spacious and air-conditioned. Restaurant and cafeteria. Singles $45 and doubles $62. In general, sound.

Residencia San Antonio de la Florida • *Paseo de la Florida 13;* ☎ *2471400.* Fresh and inviting, fronts North Station; 96 rooms, all with bath and tiny private balcony overlooking the Casa Campo National Park. Air-conditioned. Bar, breakfast room, cafeteria, snack bar, and restaurant. Garage, too. Twins $70, singles $44. Outstanding value.

Anaco • *Tres Cruces 3;* ☎ *5224604.* We especially recommend balconied top-floor rooms. Doubles $80; singles $52.

Hotel Residencia Madrid • *Carretas 10;* ☎ *5216520.* Its 76 unpretentious rooms, all with shower, are accompanied by a small bar and 2 salons; front ones noisy; some 3-bed combos utilize 2 chambers. Doubles $70; singles $53.

Miami • *Gran Via 44;* ☎ *5211464* and **Alibel** *same address;* ☎ *2323500.* The first, on the 8th floor, most agreeable—if the elevator is working. Only 10 spotless balconied rooms with bath for $42. The second has 16 uninspired though acceptable bedchambers.

Negresco • *Mesonero Romanos 12;* ☎ *5226530.* Many undersize rooms overstuffed with bulky furniture; bath and showers absorb precious bedroom space; some mattresses very poor. No singles; doubles $44. Breakfast only. Only passably clean; emergency shelter.

Mediodia • *Plaza del Emperador Carlos Quinto 8 (across from Atocha Station);* ☎ *2273060.* Has also seen happier times. Glaring bare-bulb illumination. Cracked plaster in abundance. Doubles $53; singles $35. Bed-chambers so-so.

Gaos • *Mesonero Romanos 14;* ☎ *5316305.* Next to Negresco. Nice twins with small sitting rooms; other accommodations not so hot.

EVEN MORE $$$

This group will levy between $65 and $135 per person in a twin with tub, and perhaps up to $110 single.

Pintor-Goya • *Goya 79 next to Retiro Park and fashionable Calle Serrano shopping;* ☎ *5254521.* TV corner, bar, barber, hairdresser. Air-conditioned. Total of 176 chambers with bath; best doubles, with large terraces, on top 2 floors; good beds; radios. $120 for standard twins and $80 for singles. So-called American breakfast $14. Highly recommended.

Hotel Residencia Florida Norte • *Paseo de la Florida 5;* ☎ *5428300.* Almost as good. (Not to be confused with Residencia San Antonio de la Florida.) Salon, bar, cafeteria, and futuristic subterranean restaurant. TV lounge, gift shop, hairdresser and barbershop. 100-slot garage. All 338 units with air conditioning and taped music; all but smallest singles have independent sitting area and ample dimensions. Doubles $115; singles $85. Heavily patronized by groups.

Emperatriz • *Lopez de Hoyos 4;* ☎ *5761910.* Tranquil, noncentral location beside the tree-lined Paseo de la Castellana. Light, clean, and chipper. Restaurant and bar. Bathrooms with double basins, telephones, and superefficient shower heads. Always loaded to rafters in high season, so reserve early.

Mayorazgo • *Flor Baja 3;* ☎ *2472600.* In midcity on a tiny, hard-to-find street off noisy Gran Via. Semicozy snack bar/cafeteria, gelid restaurant. Excessively modernistic with some period pieces. A few thoughtful extras and functional plumbing. Recommended.

Chamartin • *Chamartin Station;* ☎ *7337011.* An abundance of almost 400 rooms plus several restaurants and snack facilities, shops, 4 cinemas, a skating rink, and a disco. Whew! Reservations: *6 E. 46th St., NYC;* ☎ *(212) 661-4540 or* ☎ *(800) 223-1588.*

Serrano • *Marques de Villamejor 8, off Calle de Serrano, near U.S. Embassy;* ☎ *4355200.* No restaurant, but cozy pub with snacks. Spotless contemporary chambers. All doubles ($115) with frigobar. Eager, kindly staff.

Arosa • *Calle de la Salud 21;* ☎ *5321600.* Entrance beside shop windows stuffed with souvenirs on one of this avenue's busiest corners. Nevertheless, half the hotel offers a quiet side. Spacious TV salon. All 126 large, fully carpeted quarters with bath or shower, air conditioning, radio, phone, and piped music. Doubles $130; singles $95.

Reyes Catolicos • *Angel 18;* ☎ *2658600.* Arosa's 38-room sidekick is just as alluring and may even offer more intimacy and flair. La Grillade restaurant famous for its beef, but rather expensive. Doubles $85; singles $53.

Principe Pio • *Paseo de Onesimo Redondo 16, next to the North Station;* ☎ *2478000.* Only a short stroll from the Palacio Real. Bar and routine basement restaurant; 160 rooms with air conditioning, wall-to-wall carpets, taped music. Mighty fetching for tariffs of $70 for solitaries and $100 for companions. Very agreeable.

Residencia Agumar • *Reina Cristina 11-13;* ☎ *526900.* Sited on a noisy street close to Retiro Park. Plain bar, cafeteria/snack dispensary, pink and purple disco. 250 rooms (45 singles at $95) complete with clean but elfin baths and radios. Bid for rear accommodation. Seems glaringly obvious it was especially designed for tours.

Lope de Vega • *Gran Via 59, 9th floor;* ☎ *2477000.* In a dreary commercial building; 50 bedchambers enhance the graceful Old World ambience of its public rooms.

Mercator • *Atocha 123, near the Prado;* ☎ *4290500.* Renovated on a regular cycle. Snack bar and garage; 90 units, all with private bath, simple furnishings; some with terrace. Prefer units with wooden floors. Tariffs around $60 for singles, climb to $80 for twins. Modern wing best.

Paris • *Alcala 2;* ☎ *5216496* and **Lar**, *Valverde 16;* ☎ *5216592.* Both satisfactory if you draw one of their refreshened rooms (Doubles $72; singles $55).

Prado • *Prado 11.* Very central. Comfortable accommodation. Nice people. Quite a buy as a sleeper.

Ingles • *Echegaray 12.* Limp amenities shine in comparison with its back-street environment. District well known for multitude of *tapas* (snack) stands and bars. Doubles $65; singles $48.

Conde Duque • *Plaza Conde de Valle Suchil 5;* ☎ *4477000* and **Hotel Tirol**, *Marques de Urquijo 4;* ☎ *2481900.* The former with American-style restaurant and bar; the latter with nearby shops, theaters, dining, and dancing spots; both adequate but more expensive than the rest for $160 twin rates (breakfast extra).

CAMPING

The **Alameda de Osuna** grounds, toward the airport along the Barajas highway about 10 minutes by car, is the best close-in bet. Its big disadvantage is the noise created by the buses and trucks that stream by almost continuously.

SUGGESTIONS FOR STUDENTS

Madrid's University City ("Ciudad Universitaria") is one of the handsomest and best-planned campuses near the heart of any European capital; has 100,000 students, a soccer field, a rugby stadium, a track, and jai-alai courts.

OVERNIGHTS

Try the dormitory residences during the July-Sept. interregnum. Most are huddled into the triangle formed by Calle Princesa, Calle Alberto Aguilera, and Calle San Bernardo. Leading contenders:

Colegio Mayor Jose Miguel Guitarte • *Amaniel 2;* ☎ *5212990.* About $14 per day including full board;

Santa Maria de la Almudena • *Paseo Juan XX111;* ☎ *5347207.* For young women exclusively, similarly low prices.

Special problems...The **Oficina de Informacion Juvenil Sol** (*located in Puerta del Sol's subway station, main hall;* ☎ *5219511*) offers to solve almost any puzzle.

WHERE TO EAT

LEAST $

Nuevo Barco • *Barco 8.* Top choice on a street teeming with similar restaurants; 24 small tables in medium-size quarters. Short on atmosphere but long on hygiene. Agreeable cooking of Castilian specialties, stews, and classic platters. Open 1–4 p.m. and 8:30–11:30 p.m.

Pagasarri • *Barco 7;* ☎ *5326889.* Lures hordes at midday. Average meal $12. Hardly a temple of gastronomy, but if Nuevo Barco is full, a sturdy alternate.

Casa Felix • *39 av. Breton de Herreros;* ☎ *4412479.* Ground-level bar; decorative grillroom upstairs. Busy at lunch. Loyal returnees for trout and steaks; $50 can feed 2 amply, with wine; rushed service.

El Cuchi • *Cuchilleros 3;* ☎ *2664424.* Conveniently sited off Plaza Mayor. Friendly staff and generous portions of savory Mexican and local cuisine. A real charmer. It's inexpensive too at $20 for full meal.

El Bulevar • *Alberto Aguilera 17;* ☎ *2410447.* Located near the university enclave. Clean, bright, air-conditioned, and nearly always jumping. Most dishes about $8; tourist menu $16. Substantial wine list. Amiable waiters.

Aymar • *Reyes 10, near the Plaza Hotel.* An amusing but cramped backyard tavern. Tapas section adjacent to tiny bar. Compact 5-table dining circle. Crab Supreme and paella play starring roles.

El Pajar • *("The Barn") Calle de Luna 3, 3 blocks off Gran Via;* ☎ *5224801.* Two exceptionally clean salons. Tourist menu (tucked down on right of carte), offered soup, chicken, salad, and wine for close to $18; it was delicious. A smiling waiter and music topped off a delightful experience.

Prost • *Edificio Multicentro Orense 6;* ☎ *4552894.* It's a *cerveceria*, a beer tavern, serving light bites and frothing with atmosphere. If you're not too hungry and are looking for a German peg to hang a cozy mood on, search no further.

MEXICAN FARE

El Charro • *San Leonardo 3;* ☎ *2475439.* On a narrow street behind the Plaza Hotel; a tiny, 7-table nook; in warm weather a front garden seats perhaps 3 dozen. Large menu ranging from a $9 enchilada dish, up to the $17 platter containing guacamole salad, nachos, stuffed jalapeno, 2 chicken *enchiladas con mole*, rice, 2 tamales in corn husks, beans, tortillas, and Mexican sweet custard. Carte de jour set at $11. Poorly mixed tequila margaritas; take-out orders available; open noon–4 p.m. and 8 p.m. to midnight.

Mexico Lindo • *Somewhat far out at Plaza del Equador 4;* ☎ *2594833.* Okay if you are overcome by an irrepressible craving from somewhere south of the border. Otherwise, only fair. Average $15.

Luarques • *Ventura de la Vega, 16;* ☎ *4296174 or 4296175.* What it lacks in decor it makes up for with its *chuleta de ternera* (veal chop) *especial de la casa*; succulent, tasty, and tender. And only about $19 a standard meal. The wait for a table at lunch and dinner tells it all. A solid value.

Alfredo's Barbacoa • *Lagasca 5;* ☎ *5766271.* Appetite for reasonably priced Americana. Barbecued spare ribs? Juicy hamburger? The dude in the western duds and Texas sombrero is the gringo to see. Open 1 p.m.–1 a.m. Fun.

Domine Cabra • *Huertas 54;* ☎ *4294365.* Relaxed, romantic atmosphere; looks like it should be more expensive than it really is; $18-or-so will satisfy both hunger and thirst very pleasantly in the midst of a nocturnal "hot spot" where friendships might be struck up after dinner.

SNACKS OR SELF-SERVICE

Jufer • *Gran Via 26.* A small midtowner with a flag-draped entrance, has 11 stools along the counter and wall, a drinking bar, high-velocity service, and plenty of smiles. Best bets are bacon and eggs, veal dinners, soups, and thirst-throttling orangeades.

Navazo • *Plaza Mayor 35.* More elaborate; jammed and hectic at mealtimes. Sidewalk patio, open-rafter ceiling; stool-or-table interior dining; all meals about $6 extra at latter.

Cerveceria Santa Barbara • *Plaza Sta. Barbara 8.* Comes up with splendid shellfish or other appetizers to whet your thirst for what might be Madrid's best homebrewed beer. Long marble bar; 2 rows of wooden tables. Worthy.

Uncle Sham, perhaps? Lots of imitators. The genuine article and very popular with Spaniards:

McDonald's • *2 outlets on the Gran Via and numerous shops in other parts of town.* There is also a sizable contingent of both **Burger Kings** and **Wendy's**. **Pizza Hut** has opened its doors at *Plaza Santa Barbara 8* (Metro Alonso Martinez).

California chain • *Headquarters at Goya 47; immensely popular.* Madrid's largest. Specializes in so-called American short-order and soda fountain items. Branches: *General Martinez Campos 28, Salud 21, Plaza Callao 7, Goya 21, and Gran Via 49.*

The 6-link Nebraska chain • More of the same. Sampled *Gran Via 32*; received decent steak inundated with vegetables. Open daily 7 a.m.-2 a.m.

Manilas • *Gran Via 41, Carmen 4,* and *Montera 23.* Also in the center, also American imitators, and also singularly lacking in New World know-how.

Hollywood's • Your best bet. For milkshakes and burgers as good as back home (or better). Most popular branch: *Calle Magallanes next to Washington Irving Library.*

Kentucky Fried Chicken • Coops at *Hurtado de Mendoza 13, Gran Via, and Raimundo Fdez. Villaverde 21.*

A TIP ON TAPAS

Tapas are light bites, almost always consumed while standing at a bar or counter; *tascas* are the nooks where you go to eat them. The early evening tavern-hopping circuit—a Madrid tradition—is one of the most colorful and fun-filled adventures you can have. Dozens of these tascas are concentrated within a radius of 4 or 5 blocks. The game, played by hundreds of local residents nightly from 7 to 10 p.m. is to stroll from place to place, stopping just long enough in each one to nibble—not gorge on!—its outstanding appetizers. **Calle de Manuel Fernandez Gonzalez** is more or less the main throughway.

Each stop banners its own specialties. **Los Bocadillos**, (*Marques de Urquijo 1*) offers assorted snacks in an easy ambiance at good prices. **La Casona**, which can pack in 400 nibblers, is noted for its potatoes and mushrooms. **La Chuleta** (*Echegaray 20*) draws ham and *mariscos (shellfish)* fans; **Museo del Jamon**, only ham; **La Casa del Abuelo** (*Nunez de Arce 5*), only shrimp. **La Trucha** (*Nunez de Arce 6*) is renowned for its *bacalao* (cod), steeping casseroles of baby shrimp, oysters, and *verbena* (a sampling of smoked fish hors d'oeuvres). **Posada del Enano** (Dwarf's Inn) features *boquerones* (a very special anchovy); **O'Pote** has no beer but offers delicious *vieiras* (scallops); **Motivos** is proud of its *chanquetes* (marvelous sea minnows); **Espuela** has *pinchos morunos* (mini-shish kebabs); **Taberna Toscana** brings out other tempters such as a fresh mixed salad with tuna; **Los Corsarios** (*Calle de Barbieri 7*) swings with young people; **Mallorca** covers the field with a vast assortment; cellar-sited **Cuevas Sesamo** is where we usually throw in the towel, with the reviving *Sol y Sombra* (half anise and half Spanish coñac). Drink either the house wine or common sherry ($1.50 to $3 per serving); beer is too filling in full bottles, but they have half bottles or serve it in wineglass portions. Many more places may be explored in these alleys. They are very inexpensive.

MORE $$

Botin • *Cuchilleros 17;* ☎ *2664217.* To savor the true feeling of Spain, make the 2-minute stroll from the Plaza Mayor. Reserve for evening dining at this shrine, famous the world over for its bullfighting guests, roast suckling pig, and roast lamb. Hemingway gave the place considerable attention. Much cooking still done in original oven, vintage 1725! If splurging, order *Cordero Asado* (lamb) or *Cochinillo Asado* (pig). A colorful *bodega* (wine cellar) has additional tables. Definitely worth a visit.

Casa Paco • *Puerta Cerrada 11.* Close by. Of the two floors, we prefer the second. Always bustling, if not hectic. Steak, the main feature, usually ordered by weight; the *Cebon de Buey* cut is scrumptious; seafood platters also good. If the meat is not done quite well enough for you, slice off a slab and touch it to your heavy, oven-hot porcelain dish and it'll be brown in a jiffy! Average meal $38. Authentic and enjoyable peasant-style cooking.

Giardino • *Jorge Juan 39; ☎ 5760874.* Many succulent choices on short menu. *Besugo à la bilbaina* (baked sea bream with red peppers), veal brochette, and custard with almonds provided an Eden of culinary delights.

Meson de San Javier • *Calle del Conde 3; ☎ 2480925.* Typical, ingratiating little bodega in 16th-century building on a tiny, hard-to-find street. From Puerta Cerrada walk down Calle Segovia, turn right on Calle Cordon, and left into Calle del Conde. Baby chicken stuffed with ham and roasted in butter at about $9 is about the most expensive dish. Reserve in advance.

Edelweiss • *Jovellanos 7, near American Express.* German meal with beer for around $22. Herring in sour cream and onions (Arenque Cream); bratwurst with potato salad and sauerkraut; pumpernickel; also many non-Teutonic selections. No-nonsense decor; indifferent service. Go very early or very late, as it's always overfull at meal hours and doesn't accept reservations.

Caves of Luis Candelas • *Cuchilleros 1, just off Plaza Mayor.* This place has gone overboard for the tourist, tarnishing its authentic flavor. Inexpensive 3-choice tourist menu; fair bet, if you don't mind battling the throngs.

NIGHTLIFE

Madrid at night is full of *marcha* (action); most of the places below are open the year-round; some function summer only.

For flamenco:

Corral de la Moreria • *2 Moreria 17.* Means "Corral of the Moorish Quarter"—and for most first-timers, it lives up to its name; about 10 performers on last visit, all much more attractive than those in other flamenco parlors (dynamic Lucero Tena is best); corner bar; capacity for about 80 viewers; popular for dinner; food miles from great, but at least edible; initial drinks from $16; later drinks in the $11 range. Tops for zing and fire, although sometimes short on artistry and polish.

Casa Pastas • *Canizares 10.* Quite popular, too.

Zambra • *Velazquez 8.* This nightspot has made a comeback after several years of retirement. Locals agree it is good again, but it is one of the most expensive nightspots in town.

Cafe de Chinitas • *Torija 7.* Today resembles an elegant Spanish salon, but the original cafe was a far more modest Malaguenian *tablao* of the 1850s. Clean, fresh atmosphere; insignificant bar; chairs, tables, and other trimmings carrying out the Andalusian motif. Enthusiastic flamenco ensemble; performances well conceived but not too spontaneous; excellent costumery; top guitarists and singers; honest drinks; no groups. Rewarding in its special way just as the Corral is.

Torres Bermejas • *Mesonero Romanos 15.* Comes on strong in decorative skills. Underground cavern with gold-coffered ceiling; walls brightened by Moorish tiles; tiny loggia beside the stage; 30 tight-fit tables. Entrance fee of about $13, honest whiskey for $9; beer for $6; service eager but often untutored; numerous package groups tumbling in. Performers not too professional. (Flamenco can often be enhanced by this, since its essence is spontaneity.)

If you have the urge to get up and dance, then hasten yourself over to: **Al Andalus**, *(Capitan Haya 19)*, **El Porton** *(Lopez de Hoyos 9)*, or **Ole Sevilla** (*Marques de Leganes, corner San Bernardo*), where you may stamp your heels, click castanets, whirl, and clap.

DISCOTHEQUES

Under official statute, supposedly nobody younger than 18 is admitted to any of these. We doubt that it's strictly enforced.

Abre Vilma, **Alre**, **Vaqueira** and **Max** • *Paseo Habana 41*; *Cea Bermudez*; *Islas Filipinas*; and *Aduana 21*. These are the hottest discos of the moment.

El Callejon • *Nunez de Balboa 63.* Incorporates a giant video screen.

Jaccara • *Principe de Vergara 90.* Features modern music concerts every fortnight.

La Boite • *Plaza de las Comendadoras.* Greets customers with a white brick facade and globe sconces; silvered walls; gilded mirrors; danceable music; steep tabs. Sophisticated.

Bocaccio • *Central Colon.* Huge, even for a big-city disco; turnof-the-century decor on ground level; more with-it substrata for dancing (just follow the decibels); attractive patrons; expensive but unadulterated drinks. Popular; more central than La Boite and in some ways better.

Kitsch, **Hanoi** and **Archy** • *32 Galileo*; *81 Hortaleza*; *11 Marques de Riscal.* All three are very central and popular.

Tartufo • *Victor Hugo at Gran Via.* A tasteful standby. Clubby upstairs atmosphere; only 3 intimate tables flanking a working fireplace; lower-level rectangular den with smallish dance floor and excellent lighting displays; couples-only admission policy; good drinks.

Long Play • *Plaza Vazquez de Mella 2.* Run by Diego Martin, the best-known deejay in town; other than that, we found it standard, except for the drinks, which were too small.

Pacha • *Metro Tribunal.* $13 admission covers first drink; successive drinks at about $9; attracts all ages but more popular with the younger set.

Keeper • ☎ *4481353.* Another zinger in the Arapiles area. Because of its popularity, you must reserve a table in advance. $10 gets you in and slakes your first thirst.

Calle Alberto Alcocer • This place sports several discos. Tops among them is **Mau-Mau** (Hotel Eurobuilding) and **Pina**; admission to both about $13; being more sophisticated, men are expected to be in tie and jacket.

Among other fun-for-everybody establishments:

El Biombo • *Chino Isabel La Catolica 6.* One of the leaders; balcony with handsome bar and a few tables at street level; main seating area and dance floor 1 flight down. Sizzling orchestra of 14-16 musicians; cabaret not an extravaganza but excellent in quality; $13 minimum. Closed July and Aug. Clean, pleasant, and decent.

Bali Hai • *Flor Alta 8;* ☎ *5312550.* Presents Polynesian and Eastern food. Color-illustrated drink card; a choice of exotic beverages sipped from coconut shells; raffia and bamboo decor suggestive of a Malayan long house; high-backed Malacca chairs; waiters in glossy fruit-salad-hued jackets; superb combo for dancing. The samplings of Micronesian, Chinese, Japanese, and Indian tidbits were savory—and the bill averaged $19 per person. Entry fee demanded. Recommended for romancers.

JAZZ

Cafe Central • *Across from the Hotel Victoria, at Plaza del Angel 10.* Offers live performances starting about 10:30 p.m.; drinks slightly high from this hour on; relaxed, informal atmosphere; usually packed.

Whisky Jazz Club • *Diego de Leon 7; ☎ 2611165/2615145.* Live music nightly; 3 split-level tiers: bar at the bottom, jazz combo at midlevel, balcony atop. About $8 entrance and $10 drinks. Go late.

Cafe Berlin • *Jacometrezzo 4.* Another of my favorites, for jazz in a sophisticated setting.

BARS FOR FUN

Oliver Club • *Conde Xiquena 3.* Strictly for sipping, gossiping, and/or hand holding. Its piano lilts are sometimes discreet and sometimes shrill. Owned by director-actor Adolfo Marsillac, it attracts many Spanish film and theatrical stars to see and be seen. Very pleasant; standard prices, too.

Cuevas Sesamo • *Principe 7.* Bangs out a mean honky-tonk piano. Two cave-style chambers reverberate to impromptu choruses; walls emblazoned with strained humor (e.g., "Geometricians Banned"); one bottle of wine satisfies your quartet's minimum obligation; $4 per glass if you're alone. The action continues until 2 a.m.

Brasserie • *General Oraa 5.* Chic for cocktails, but dinner is expensive.

Castellana Terraza • *Castellana 8* and **Sky Garden** atop *Edificio Espana*, on Plaza of same name are top choices among Madrilenos. For alfresco sipping, when it's hot only.

LATIN AMERICAN

Oba-Oba • *Off Plaza Callao.* Pumps out live Brazilian sounds in its compact basement; for a $8 minimum you can dance; though the decor is blah, the Latin beats are top-flight.

Barrio Latino • Two branches: *Segovia 19* and *Tetuan 27.* Much more sophisticated than Oba-Oba at twice the price; live-band and cabaret-style performances. Go late.

IR DE COPAS (BAR HOPPING)

For drinks and socializing, Madrid has distinctive *zonas* characterized by different ambientes and clientele. Here's a sampling:

The area around **Calle Huertas** is full of music cafes, lively pubs and bars; favorites are **La Fidula** (classical musical performances), **El Hecho**, **La Trocha, La Fontaneria** (cleverly decorated in a plumbing motif), and **Ombu** (featuring a hypnotist-magician Tues. at 11 p.m.); there are many more, so explore.

The area in and around **Plaza Santa Barbara** (Metro Alonso Martinez) offers 3 lively watering holes: **Pub Santa Barbara** and **Cafe Universal** (both in Calle Fernando VI) and **Cafe Paris** (usually packed on weekends).

Malasana is the bohemian, slightly seedy, part of town; folk and classical music at **La Manuela**; South American melodies at the tiny **Blanqueada**; pubs all around the *Plaza dos de Mayo* (where much of Madrid's drug dealings take place).

Calle Orense in the newer northern end of town vibrates with all manner of pubs, bars, discos, and music clubs too numerous to mention here; most places attract a young crowd. Intimate hand holding with a belle epoque aura at **El Mundo de Guermantes**, *San Hermenegildo 22; ☎ 4471101*, a cafetin offering sophisticated cocktails and soft classical music; clientele informal and romantic. **Universal**, *Fernando VI 8*, is a favorite of artists and scholars.

Students and young folk habitually gather in the little mesones, or 18th-century bars, in the Old Town for singing, guitar music, and conversation. One recent discovery was the **Meson Torre Narigues**, *Factor 8*, around the corner from *Calle Mayor 86.* Two tiny rooms on the ground floor; one in the basement, where the stones date from A.D. 880; rough-hewn decor; farm implements; friendly welcome by proprietor Pedro Lopez, who might lend you his guitar if you play. Open nightly until 3 a.m.; cool in summer; relaxing any time of year. Similar mesones, such as **Las Rejas** and **Meson del Segoviano**, are along *Calle Cuchilleros* and *Calle Cava Baja*, near the southwest corner of *Plaza Mayor.* **Meson Castilla (#26)** and **Los Gatos Blancos (#21)** are better bets, in my opinion; both are a few steps beyond **Segoviano** on *Cava Baja.*

WHAT TO SEE AND DO

First stop for any art lover is, all too obviously, the **Prado**. With its staggering treasures of *El Greco, Velazquez, Goya, Ribera, Murillo, Botticelli, da Vinci, Tintoretto, Rubens, Fra Angelico, Van Dyck, Raphael, Bosch,* and dozens of others, this is considered by many to be the number 1 art gallery of the world. The fabulous **Thyssen Collection** is on display in nearby **Villahermosa Palace** now that the Spanish government has bought the 800-plus works for $350 million—an absolute "Steal" since some estimates consider the value nearer to $2 billion. Picasso's impassioned "Guernica" has just been moved over to the **Queen Sofia Art Center** from the neighboring **Cason del Buen Retiro**. Open from 9 a.m. to 7 p.m. Mon. to Sat.; Sun. 9 a.m.–2 p.m.; closed Mon.; admission about $4. Its 2200 works by 440 artists criss-cross at least 6 centuries and 5 different major schools. Thus, you will need a bare minimum of a full day. Purchasing a guide (available in English), for $4 (a book, that is) is almost essential. You may want to have a look through the excellent reproductions on sale, too. A worthwhile side trip from the Prado is the **Museo de la Real Academia de Bellas Artes de San Fernando**, containing 1500 paintings and 800 sculptures; among them are *El Greco, Murillos, Goyas, Riberas, Rubens, and Velazquez.* It vies with the Prado as the tops; try to see its 14 Goyas (among them 2 self-portraits) on view in their original setting. If you are a Picasso addict, the 50-mile romp northeast of Madrid to *Buitrago* will reward you with the **Museo Picasso**, showing 48 works given to Pablo's friend and barber (he needed one?), Eugenio Arias.

The Royal Palace (*Plaza de Oriente*) has one of Europe's finest collections of furniture, tapestries, carpets, oils, arms, and armor. Open weekdays 9:30 a.m.–5 p.m.; Sun. 9 a.m.–2 p.m. (Oct.–March); closes an hour later rest of months; admission about $5. **Generalissimo Francisco Franco's 16th-century palace** outside the town limits at El Pardo has been opened to the public by King Juan Carlos. Admission about $4 for a guided tour of 32 rooms; inquire in Madrid concerning the days and hours it welcomes visitors.

The National Museum of Archaeology (*Serrano 13*) has gathered together an assemblage of prehistoric, interim period, and Middle Ages objects, as well as ceramics from many eras, and now features a subterranean reproduction of the cave drawings at Altamira. Open between 9:30 a.m. and 8:30 p.m. weekdays; 9:30 a.m.–1:30 p.m. Sun. and holidays; closed Mon. Admission $2.50.

At the **Convent of the Barefoot Carmelites** (*Plaza de las Descalzas Reales*) you may view paintings, sculptures, and tapestries from 10:30 a.m. to 12:30 p.m. and 4 p.m.–5:30 p.m. Tues., Wed., Thurs. and Sat.; 10:30 a.m.–12:30 p.m. Fri. Closed Mon. Admission is $3.50.

The Museum of Contemporary Art (*Juan de Herrera 2*), is now devoted to exhibitions so, it's more an art gallery. Closed Mondays.**The Lazaro Galdiano Museum** (*Serrano 122*) is a showcase for oils and sketches of Iberian, primitive Flemish, Italian, French, and English genre. Also boasts exquisite examples of the ceramic, enamel, ivory, wood carving, coin, jewelry, and furniture-making realms. Mornings only; $2 to ramble through its 30 rooms; delightful. **The Queen Sofia Art Center** (*Santa Isabel 52*) was initially a modern exhibition center, but it was later converted into a museum of modern art and now displays works from Miro and Picasso, including the famous **Guernica**. Closed Tues. **The Wax Museum**, *in the Plaza Colon*, displays tableaux that include *Cortes, the Conquistadores, Cervantes, Romeo and Juliet, El Cordobes and his bulls, Einstein, Rasputin*, Wild West movie sets, your favorite hatchet murderer, and scores more; these are backgrounded with appropriate music. Hours are 10:30 a.m.–2 p.m. and 4 to 9 p.m. Entrance $4; children $2.

Goya's Tomb, now becoming a shrine, rests in the *Church of San Antonio de la Florida*. The cupola's frescoes are early works by the master. It was being revamped at our manuscript deadline, so please check new visiting hours with your concierge. **The Museo Taurino** ("Bullfighting Museum," *Plaza de Toros*) is practically a compulsory stop for any aficionado. Its portraits, posters, and costumes constitute an unequaled homage to the heroes and the heritage of bullfighting. Open 10 a.m.–3 p.m., Tues.–Fri.

The Madrid Zoo (*Casa de Campo*) is beautifully laid out and great fun. Features Chulin, the only baby panda born and surviving in captivity; check with your concierge for the hours.

Bus excursions hit 5 popular suburban targets. Check with your concierge or the **Tourist Information Office** (*Duque de Medinacelli 2, ☎ 4294951 and 5 other branches around the capital*) for schedules and exact details. **A.T.E.S.A.** is now a minibus and auto rental giant—but **Julia**, **Pullmantur** and **Trapsatur** will provide excellent service; full-day routing fares depend on the destinations. Here are the leaders:

El Escorial, 31 miles out, boasts Philip II's gigantic castle-monastery of the same name. Its kilometers of rooms are filled with paintings, books, royal tombs, and royal antiquities—all laid out, incidentally, in a 400,000-square-foot model of the smaller torture grid used in the *martyrdom of St. Lawrence*. Time permitting, stop for a quaff at **La Cueva**, an 18th-century inn turned *mesontaverna*; authentic and rustic; be sure to take a peek at the innermost courtyard. **Valle de los Caidos** ("Valley of the Fallen"), Generalissimo Franco's monument to casualties of the Spanish Civil War, now serves as his own tomb (behind the altar). It is so colossal in scope that it might be straight from the time of the Pharaohs. A mountain of rock, topped by a cross 500 feet high and 300 feet across the arms (elevator inside), has been converted into a gigantic basilica and great nave; you'll find the **8 Tapestries of the Apocalypse**, an *800-foot crypt, a carved transept, a cloister, a monastery, an ecclesiastical study center, and a hostel*. It is approximately 30 miles from the capital. Various agencies' buses fan out to both the Valley and neighboring *El Escorial* in a $45-or-so excursion that includes lunch. Toledo, Segovia, and **La Granja** are the other popular targets.

CONCERTS

Free outdoor musicales are often presented during summer in **Retiro Park. The Madrid Auditorium**, inaugurated in 1988, is where the prestigious performances are given; the least expensive seats are always sold first. Operetta fanciers should not miss the world-famous **Zarzuela** if there's action here during their visit.

AMUSEMENT PARK

Traditionally, weekenders stroll or paddle around in midcity **Retiro Park**, where there seem to be endless ways to pass the time by doing absolutely nothing. Although the **Casa de Campo** is newer, it is thriving as an Iberian version of Coney Island in miniature. Ask your concierge for details.

MOVIES

Though original-language films are being increasingly screened, most are still dubbed.

MARKETS

The Rastro (*near Calle Ribera de Curtidores*) displays myriads of flea market-type castoffs every Sunday and holiday from 10 a.m. to 2 p.m. This is the "Thieves' Market"—and it teems with pickpockets. If any object should catch your fancy, bargain hard! **The Stamp and Coin Market** (northeast corner of the Plaza Mayor) assembles on Sunday mornings only. Here local hobbyists buy, sell, or exchange old, new, rare, and all varieties of their commodity. But these characters are so shrewd that unless you're an expert and unless you speak Spanish with complete fluency, it might be much wiser to look rather than swap.

PUBLICATIONS

For national and regional fiesta listings, the handsome **Tourist Calendar** is available at any of Spain's official information branches in New York, Chicago, Los Angeles, Miami, and Toronto.

WHERE TO SHOP

Best bets are *botas* (wine bags), Toledo ware, selected (not all) leather goods, Perlas Majorica, decorative bric-a-brac, colognes, straw work, and casual shoes and boots.

ARTISANWARE

Artespana, (*Ramon de la Cruz 33, Hermosilla 14, and Centro Comercial Madrid 2 La Vaguada*) is a brilliant showcase for Spain's finest craftsmen utilizing clay, leather, copper, bronze, wood, cane, raffia, straw, glass, and textiles to create definitive Iberian products. **Mercado de la Puerta de Toledo** (Toledo Gate Market) is a covered exhibition center for antiques, jewelry, and assorted Spanish items. The selection is better than at the nearby **Rastro**.

DEPARTMENT STORES

Galerias Preciados, (*Plaza del Callao 1, 2 blocks above Puerta del Sol*, and 4 other branches) and **El Corte Ingles**, (*Preciados 3* plus 4 other addressses) are leading lights.

EMBROIDERY

Casa Bonet of Mallorca (*Av. Tous y Maroto 46*), Madrid (*Nunez de Balboa 76*), and Marbella (*Plaza de la Victoria 3*), the world's mightiest name in embroidered linens and needlework, stitches exquisite handworked pieces such as handkerchiefs and cocktail napkins at very low prices. Ask for English-speaking Mr. Bonet in the Tous y Maroto center, and Miss Pilar in Madrid—and don't miss Casa Bonet!

GALLERY

Kreisler is the name to remember. **Galeria Kreisler** (*Hermosilla 8)* features exceptional traditional Spanish art. **Jorge Kreisler** (*Calle de Prim 13*) offers avant-garde Spanish collections ranging from the oils, graphics, and sculptures of such masters as Miro, Picasso, and Juan Gris, to those of virtually every artist of note within Iberia, to those of the younger group who show exceptional promise as future investments.

GLOVES

Samaniego (*Principe 19*) has all lengths; some silk-lined; handcrafting at no extra cost—if you can wait the usual week for delivery.

PERFUMES

H. Alvarez Gomez, (*Paseo de Castellana 41, Sevilla 2, and Serrano 14*) stocks every cosmetic product and bottled scent available locally. Since several French perfumers make cologne in Spain—*Guerlain*, for example—the prices are good.

SHOES

Now all qualities are produced at astoundingly low tabs. The "casuals" especially are most often superb. **Bravo-Calzados de Lujo** (*Serrano 42, Hermosilla 12, Gran Via 31 and 68, Goya 43, Princesa 58*, plus branches in many other cities) will make you wish you were a centipede. There are handbags, accessories, and leather clothing as well.

MALAGA

This busy wine port throbs with 550,000 residents. Although here is the nexus of this sunny coast, its bustling commerical tone makes it more of a vacation springboard for the outlying resorts than a sightseeing goal. What to explore? The **Renaissance Cathedral** (10:30 a.m.–1 p.m. and 3:30–6 p.m.); the **Alcazaba**, ancient palace of the Arab kings (10 a.m.–1 p.m. and 4–7 p.m. in winter; 5–8 p.m. in summer); **Archeological Museum** (inside the Alcazaba); **Castle of Gibralfaro,** begun by the Phoenicians but finished by the Arabs; **Fine Arts Museum** (*Calle San Agustin 6*; 10 a.m.–1 p.m. and 5–8 p.m. in winter; 11 a.m.–1 p.m. and 5–8 p.m. in summer); and the partly excavated **Roman Amphitheater** (next door to the Alcazaba). Besides the scenic, small **Parador Nacional de Gibralfano**, the **Bahia Malaga** (*Somera 8*) **Casa Curro** (*Sancha de Lara 7*), and **Los Naranjos** (*Sancha 35*) are worthy contenders. Try **Antonio Martin** (*Paseo Martimo*), **Casa Pedro** (*Playa de El Palo, Quitapenas 112*), or **Refectorum** (*Cervantes 8*) for moderately priced seafood and other regional specialties.

MALLORCA AND BALEARICS

Mallorca, roughly 60 miles by 50 miles at its widest points, was a recent recipient of the **Temple Fielding Travel Award**, an honor recognizing the island's massive effort to upgrade the level of tourism. It is the major land mass of the archipelago and the capital of the Balearic Islands (Menorca, Ibiza, Formentera, Cabrera, and scores of rock-dots). Lying almost exactly 100 miles southeast of Barcelona, it is 25 minutes by air or 8 to 9 hours by steamer. It has 5000-foot mountains, lush plains, magnificent beaches, benevolent climate, colorful background, comparatively reasonable prices, and 5 million tourists per year—nearly as many as all of Greece! Hotels and boardinghouses number in the thousands (literally), so there is no trouble finding lodging in any price range except during the peak weeks of midsummer. (May–June and September–October are the most agreeable periods in any case.)

July–August is high season, with practically flawless weather. Spring and fall are lovely; November-December and March-April are chancy—sometimes glorious, sometimes awful; parts, but only parts, of January and February are very raw, chilly, and unpleasant. The legendary false spring called *Las Calmas de Enero* ("The Calms of January"), similar to Indian Summer, blankets the land for 2 to 3 weeks in heavenly weather. This title is incorrect, because sometimes it falls in February; but whenever it comes, the spellbinding perfume and blossoming of nearly 100 million almond trees in petals of pink or white are reasons enough to visit the island off season. There's good swimming from late spring to middle fall only. There's good walking all year-round, whether in the hills to mountaintop refuges or on the cultural tours of the capital, which go back to prehistoric structures, through the Roman and Arabic periods to the union with Aragon and to modern Mallorca, with its invasions by tourists. It is also a favorite flyway for birdwatchers.

Mallorca has the profile of a goat's head: *Palma*, the capital, is at the mouth, *Soller* is near the eye, and Formentor is on one of the horns. Palma, its only large center, has approximately 375,000 inhabitants, most of the good restaurants, hotels, nightclubs, shops, most of the frenzy. At peak season (not so noticeably in the spring or fall), the capital is packed; strike out during July and August for the tiny villages, to find the real charm of the island.

Adequate accommodation in Palma proper may be found at **Palas Atenea Sol**, (*Paseo Maritimo 29*) or **Playa de Palma Sol** if you prefer beach and sea view. **Celler Sa Premsa** (*Plaza Obispo Berenguer de Palou 8*) serves unpretentious Mallorquin cuisine while **Fonda del Puerto** (*Paseo Sagrera 5*) specializes in sea fare. We suggest you visit **Cala D'Or** (40 miles from the capital) and try to stay at **Cala Gran** or the **Tucan**. For local specialties, dine at **Es Clos** or **La Cala**. Further north, **Puerto Pollensa** is another gem. This former fishing village now boasts white-sand beaches and one of the most magnificent bays in the Mediterranean. The **Residencia Sis Pins** is our choice for overnighting and there's a plethora of snack bars, restaurants, and grills.

MINORCA (OR MENORCA)

Minorca is quite different. It is smaller, of course, flatter and more wind-blown. **Mahon**, its capital and chief port (the largest natural harbor in the whole Mediterranean and the reason Nelson chose it for his fleet), sprawls over the surrounding low hills. The leading hotel is the **Port Mahon**, followed by the **El Paso**, which is inexpensive and adequate.

Ciudadela, at the northwest tip, has a Moorish quality and is more ingratiating. Top stops here are the **Almirante Farragut** and the **Cala Blanca**.

IBIZA

The avant-garde seem to settle mainly in the capital, Ibiza (town), also the main port. Due to the infusion of creative young people, it is now gaining prominence as a fashion hub for casual women's wear. A famous local brand is called **Ad Lib**, an abbreviation for *ad libitum*, of course. This is also the springboard for day excursions to tiny **Formentera**, an inlet within sight of Ibiza that has served as a magnet for hippies and nudists throughout the Mediterranean. Across Ibiza from the capital is the more group-oriented settlement of **San Antonio**, which offers better beach facilities, but lacks the youthful flair, costumerie, and eccentricities of the main town and neighboring Formentera. Plenty of inexpensive accommodations available in all of these centers; good cuisine, however, is becoming more expensive here than on Mallorca.

SALAMANCA

This town, capital of the province of the same name, has been called "the little Rome" because of its numerous buildings in golden colored stone. As a center of Spanish culture for more than 7 centuries, its university is one of the oldest in Europe. **Gran Hotel** and **Monterey** can provide excellent double accommodation with bath for about $75 per night; **Regio** is perhaps 20% cheaper; **Alfonso X** is a substantial middle-range candidate. The town offers extensive accommodation in low-cost boardinghouses and hostelries. Regional dishes worth trying are the *suckling pig toston*, *farinatos*, and *bollo maimon* at **El Meson** (*Poeta Iglesias 10*) or **Rio de la Plata** (*Plaza del Peso 1*). Salamanca itself is a feast.

SAN SEBASTIAN

Originally the Roman port of *Easo*, it has been Spain's most jam packed bathing resort for centuries. Winning setting, with its semicircular bay flanked by twin mountains and backed by green hills; practically no ancient buildings or antiquities of note. Golf and horse racing at *Lasarte*; tennis at *Ondarreta*; plenty of jai alai, yachting, and other sports; site of one of Europe's four most important annual film festivals. *La Concha* (The Seashell), the world-famous beach, is imposingly attractive. It is a Basque center politically and sociologically, so occasionally you still might detect signs of unrest. The **Niza** and the **Monte Igueldo** offer convenient accommodation. If you feel like spending $38 on an "assorted sampling" of the top regional cuisine, go to **Arzak** (Alto de Miracruz 2) and ask for the chef's *menu de degustacion*.

SANTANDER

This gracious northern town used to be the favorite high-season resort of Spanish royalty. Together with a scenic bay and numerous beaches, it is also known for its **Menendez Pelayo International** summer courses for foreigners. Both the university and the students' residence are located within **La Magdalena's Royal Palace**. Its music and dance festival also lures numerous visitors. For accommodation, try the ultracommercial **Bahia**, which counts 179 tiny cubicles with baths. **Maria Isabel** would be our next choice followed by the **Santemar**. Further out, at *Santillana del Mar*, the **Parador Gil Blas** is a sweet medieval complex in a wonderfully intimate dairying hamlet. Don't miss this touch of arcadia if you are within 100 miles of the village. **Los Infantes** is in the same settlement, blending Old World decor with modern times. Simple but nice. At *Fuente De*, along the route of the Picos de Europa mountains, there's the 4-star **Parador Nacional del Rio Deva**.

If you care for marine fare, I suggest you anchor at either **Bar del Puerto** or **La Sardina**, where you'll savor some of the best dishes of *Cantabria* at reasonable prices. But if you want to go tilting at windmills, try **El Molino** at *Puente Arce*, barely 7 miles away. Here you'll enjoy a quiet feast in a baroque country mansion with fresh, even daringly imaginative, cuisine. It's more expensive, too.

SANTIAGO DE COMPOSTELA

A dream, an ecstasy for the eyes. It used to be so remote that most pilgrims, except those from the ancient journeys, seemed to have missed it. That is changing, however; Iberia Airlines has made this a Spanish gateway with a flight from New York. **Labacolla Airport**, serving the *Galicia* region, has been expanded and improved. There's a casino for further gambols. There are numerous inexpensive boardinghouses in the byways surrounding the central cathedral, but if you can afford about $175 per couple for a night at the **Hotel de los Reyes Catolicos**, do book into this monarchial palace. It is nothing short of magnificent architecturally. The **Peregrino**

(*Rosalia de Castro*), **Santiago Apostol** (*road to the airport*), and **Hostal Vilas** (*Avda. Romero Donallo 9*) provide adequate shelter at more reasonable prices. Try **Las Huertas** (*Las Huertas 16*), **La Tacita de Oro** (*General Franco 31*), and **Don Gaiferos** (*Rua Nova 23*) for local cuisine.

SEGOVIA

Under 50 miles from the capital, it couldn't be more Castilian in flavor, with moats, castles, a marvelous Roman aqueduct, and the renowned **Zuloaga Museum of Ceramics** (which most travelers especially enjoy). The internationally famous **Meson de Candido** and **Jose Maria** restaurants are best. **Casa Amado**, **Cesar**, and **Meson Duque** also are excellent. For overnighting, we suggest the **Acueducto**, **Los Linajes**, or **Puerta de Segovia.** The **Parador** is excellent of course, but costly.

A popular excursion from Madrid is the **Segovia-La Granja tour**. If you're on your own, you can easily pause for an inspection of the "Valley of the Fallen" (see Madrid's "What to See and Do"), only an 8-mile round-trip detour from the direct route. Then continue on via the modern toll road that tunnels 1-1/2 miles under the Guadarrama Mountain Range. Storybook La Granja is the "Spanish Versailles," with fountains, gardens, summer palace, and the nation's finest tapestry collection.

SEVILLE

Just plain glorious with its wealth of archaeology and art. It has now recovered from the 1992 Expo (Columbus Day five centuries down the line). Nine bridges were added to its riverfront as well as a new rail station. The Expo still exists in part (about one-third of it in the *Cartuja*) with 35 attractions, some of them new and even futuristic. (This adopted theme park is closed Mon.) Churches, convents, tombs, museums, and galleries on practically every block; orange trees line the winding streets, and in the parks are snow-white pigeons that will light on the head, shoulders, and arms of any traveler who'll spend 3¢ for birdseed. The **Feria**, held soon after Holy Week, is the biggest, most frenzied, and most colorful traditional celebration in Spain. This event alone is worth a special trip to Europe—but reserve your space months in advance, because every pallet in the district is sought after by the hordes of outside visitors. To see the sights in Old World style, climb into a horse-drawn carriage of the cathedral; about $22 for one hour. For accommodation, try **Los Lebreros**, **Nuevo Lar**, **Pasarela**, or **Colon**. **Casa Senra** (*Becquer 4*), **La Albahaca** (*Plaza de Santa Cruz 12*), **La Juderia** (*Cano y Cueto 13*), and **Maitres** (*Republica Argentina 54*) serve regional dishes at reasonable prices.

TOLEDO

It is 44 miles south of Madrid and has often been called "the most perfect and brilliant record of genuine Spanish civilization." The setting is magnificent, the beautifully restored **Alcazar** is a tremendously moving emotional experience, the cathedral is a treasure house of art, **El Greco's house** is interesting. (His best works have gone elsewhere.) An effort is being made by some merchants to hold the prices for like merchandise down to Madrid levels. If you are in doubt, save your souvenir shopping for the capital. The **Parador Conde de Orgaz** is one of the most splendid (and expensive!) links in the nationwide chain for dining or overnighting. The **Hostal del Cardenal**, at the old city gates, also is glorious if you can get in and if you feel like paying superheated price tags. Otherwise, **Alfonso VI** should provide convenient accommodation at a more reasonable cost level. Castillian dishes can be savored at any of the following restaurants:

La Tarasca, (*Hombre de Palo 6*), **Adolfo**, (*Granada 6*), or **Casa Aurelio**, (*Plaza Ayuntamiento 8*).

TORREMOLINOS

Young people from a galaxy of nations bedroll here. On any balmy afternoon the town's tiny, outgrown main plaza might be the most sociable hub on the **Costa del Sol** for the under-25 and gregarious, while night action concentrates on the Montemar district. With its plethora of pubs, discos, snack bars, and hastily built concrete hotels crowded along the beach, it has lost much of the romance and charm one might expect after reading Michener's *The Drifters*. But if you seek action, noise, sunshine, and the possibility of spontaneous "friendships," you'll probably like what's here. Youngsters will certainly enjoy the artificial sea and gigantic waves at **Atlantis Aquapark**.

DIRECTORY

U.S. Consulate • None. In Fuengirola: *Edificio El Ancla, Ramon y Cajal s/n*; ☎ *(95) 2474891.*

Laundry • Lavanderia Miramar (*Plaza de Andalucia*).

Dry Cleaning • Tintoreria Costa del Sol, *Calle Cauce next to Restaurant Bodegon.* ☎ *2380320*; 1-1/2-hour service.

Barber • Peluqueria Oscar, *on the balcony over Pasaje Particular San Jose*, or Longchamp, *La Nogalera Stall #309.*

Hairdresser • One in almost every large hotel or apartment complex. Also, Lionel of London, *Calle San Miguel.* Very inexpensive almost everywhere.

Newspapers and Books in English • International Library, *Barrio Andalucia in the Nogalera complex.*

English-speaking Doctor • Dr. Seara, Clinica Los Naranjos, *off Plaza Costa del Sol*; ☎ *2380828* or ☎ *2851421.*

English-speaking Dentist • Dr. P. Citales, *Villa Ykines, Avda. P. de Mallorca 42*; ☎ *2383775* and ☎ *2380826.*

Police • Sical s/n; ☎ *2389999.*

Post Office • *Plaza de Andalucia.* Open 9 a.m. to 1 p.m. and 2:30 to 7 p.m..

Tobacco Shop • Registered depot at Calle San Miguel 27.

Day Nursery • Villa Isabel ,*Ramos Puente 1.*

Tourist Office • *Edificio La Nogalera* 516; ☎ *2381578.*

Favorite Pawnshop • None—that we could find.

WHERE TO STAY

LEAST $

Plata • *Pasaje Pizaro 1;* ☎ *2375734.* Contains 40 rooms, 2 restaurants, a discotheque, a TV salon, jam-packed special-events program, and frenetic atmosphere. Battle-scarred doubles unadorned but well scrubbed; twins for $30 with full plumbing; $22 shower only.

Los Arcos • *Av. Carlota Alexandre 110;* ☎ *2380822.* It's seen better days. Shelter and little more.

Minerva • *Cruz 10;* ☎ *2382084.* **Loro Rojo**, *Avda Imperial 4;* ☎ *2375445*, and **La Palmera,** *Avda Palma de Mallorca 37.* Would be my next candidates in the $30-per-twin category.

MORE $$

Since most of these are downtown, bid for an inside room. You'll pay between $35 and $60 per twin; add $10 per person per meal.

Isabel • *Playa del Lido;* ☎ *2381744.* Close to seaside, a short stroll south of town. Cheerful restaurant; alfresco dining terrace; discotheque. A mere 40 units, mostly doubles with seaview terraces, some corner triples; large twin-basin bathrooms; frigobars. Doubles $60, singles $45, including breakfast. A spacious, ultraclean haven, exceptional in its category.

Piscis • *Av. del Lido;* ☎ *2381745/6.* Nearby, on a foothill near the water. A laborious trudge up to the bluff to town. Attractive lounge, bar, and restaurant; boutique; beauty shop. Of 36 doubles, half face street and water, other half overlook garden and pool from sunny balconies. Comfortable beds; clean baths; 3 meals for about $50. Fair.

Hostal Europa • *Via Imperial 32;* ☎ *2388022.* Seems like an American motel; 22 neat, unadorned bedchambers at $60 per double, including bath, service, taxes, and breakfast; no shower curtains. Full air conditioning, unusual in this price range.

El Pozo • ("The Well") *Calle Casablanca 2;* ☎ *2380622.* 31 rooms; handful of noisy streetfront verandas. Doubles with tubs $40, breakfast $9. Given a dour reception. Only so-so.

La Roca • *Km. 228, Carretera de Cadiz, Benalmadena;* ☎ *2441740.* Far from center. Veddy, veddy British in both feeling and clientele. Twins with bath and terrace for $80; some suites for $60. Often chockablock with tours.

Blason • *Avenida de los Manantiales I;* ☎ *2386655.* Has midtown location to speak for it—which it does, hour after hour, night after sleepless night.

EVEN MORE $$$

In this bracket, tariffs hover between $70 and $120 per double with bath or shower but without meals. Nearly all are in adjoining districts such as Benalmadena or La Cariheula—names that mean nothing to anyone except the local Chamber of Commerce, since Torremolinos is composed of former settlements gobbled up in the touristic boom.

Alay • *Km. 229, Carretera de Cadiz, Benalmadena;* ☎ *2441440.* Well planned, well-executed, eye-pleasant, multilevel, 264-room hotel-plus-apartment complex officially rated first class. Its own ribbon of sandy beach; 2 freshwater pools (one heated in winter); discotheque; bars; cafeteria; boutiques; game nook. Rather small studio doubles or conventionals about $90 a day; a few singles for about $70. Excellent. More about apartments in following special section.

Tropicana • *Tropico 6, Montemav;* ☎ *2386600.* Recently renovated but keeps its unique personality. Polynesian-style poolside dining. Lures romancers and Trader Vic-torians. Beach bar with dance circle; garden sun deck. Waterfront dotted with chairs, parasols, and small craft. Most units with terraces. Doubles from $95.

Parador del Golf • *Road to Malaga/Churriana, Apartado 324;* ☎ *2381255.* Displays 60 units located along main road toward Malaga near airport flight path.

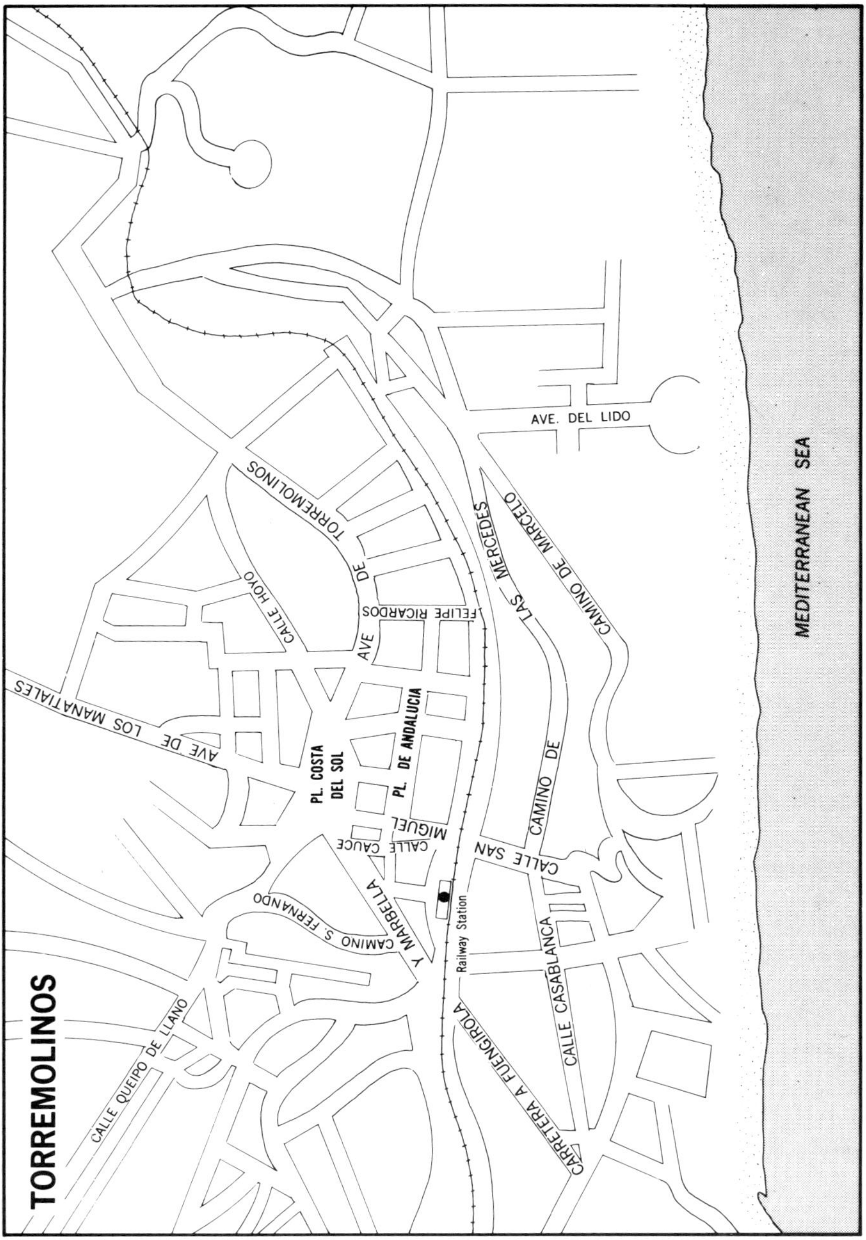
TORREMOLINOS
MEDITERRANEAN SEA
AVE. DEL LIDO
CAMINO DE MARCELO
CAMINO DE LAS MERCEDES
AVE DE TORREMOLINOS
CALLE HOYO
FELIPE RICARDOS
AVE DE LOS MANANTIALES
PL. COSTA DEL SOL
PL. DE ANDALUCIA
CALLE SAN MIGUEL
CALLE CAUCE
CAMINO S. FERNANDO
CARRETERA A FUENGIROLA Y MARBELLA
Railway Station
CALLE CASABLANCA
CALLE QUEIPO DE LLANO

Occupies center of a well-kept, 18-hole golf course. Attractive pool, terraces, and lounges. Outdoor dining May-Sept. Private shoreline. Motel atmosphere with do-it-yourself service standards; doubles from $130.

San Antonio • *La Luna 23, La Carihuela.* ☎ *2386611.* A relatively small hotel (80 rooms) with good accommodation value for your money (doubles at $70).

APARTMENTS

La Nogalera • ☎ *2381500.* Gigantic 5-building conglomerate. Borrows best features of luxury hotels and combines them with residential-style living. Offers playgrounds, 2 pools, a restaurant, room service, bar, telephones, automatic laundry, and shops. Working fireplaces; fully equipped kitchens; private terraces with sun furniture; exceptionally good baths; 2-person apartments for $45 or $60 if it's a threesome during high season.

Apartamentos Alay • *Km. 229, Carretera de Cadiz;* ☎ *2441440.* Adjoining Hotel Alay; 156 immaculate, air-conditioned 1- and 2-bedroom billets for 3-5 people. Biggest goes for about $120 per day; full hotel facilities included.

Eurosol • *Playa Montemar;* ☎ *2380085.* Satellite city composed of 17 sterile edifices; 5 of these gargantuan beachside dominos lease apartments on a temporary basis; house 2-9 transients. In the hottest months, figure about $40 per person; 15 days minimum.

Bonanza • *Km. 225, Carretera de Cadiz;* ☎ *2441749.* Charges only $50 for 3-person apartment. Steep, hilly hike from the breakers; pool. Some lower rooms noisy. No phones or air conditioning; dim or seductive lighting (depending on your point of view—or your companion); makeshift kitchen facilities.

WHERE TO EAT

LEAST $

La Concha • *Calle del Bulto 45, La Carihuela;* ☎ *2381017.* Although usually quieter, evokes atmosphere similar to neighboring Casa Antonio. (See next subsection.) Large hearth and sea-view picture window. Specialty is seafood. Insist on tourist menu because à la carte is costly. Always crowded; deservedly popular.

El Faro • *Calle Cauce;* ☎ *2381315.* Main restaurant superior to annex and more jovial. Small windows provide welcome ventilation; a cozy cordiality pervades the scene. Sherry consomme, paella, and a tart at $25, plus tip.

Casa Prudencio • *Calle Carmen 45, La Carihuela;* ☎ *2381452.* Same mood as Casa Antonio. (See "MORE $$".) Fewer edible choices run from omelets to fish. Set meal around $18. Liked by the locals.

La Pulcinela • *Calle Cauce 8.* Pizza oven at entrance. Outdoor dining in summer. Pasta available 7 p.m. to 12:30 a.m.

El Porron • *Calle Cauce;* ☎ *2381085.* a.k.a. Al Pollo Dorado ("Golden Chicken"). Provides takeout and delivery service. Roasted hen about $10.

ORIENTAL FARE

Hong Kong • *Plaza Costa del Sol.* Directly above Piper's discotheque and **Mi Bohio** Probably best. Dining room flanked by sedate bar. Air conditioning. Crisp egg rolls, tasty *nasi goreng*, and spiced sweet-and-sour pork.

Canton • *Calle San Miguel.* Seemed less rewarding.

SNACKS

Los Mariscos • A crowded open-air stand on the main plaza, boasts delicious shellfish and couscous.

El Goloso • In the little passage at the side of Bar Central, grills hot dogs and hamburgers that almost promise a galloping case of heartburn; don't miss the $6 Crepes Grand Marnier flipped up by its singing, slinging, acrobatic "chefs."

The Beachcomber • *La Nogalera.* Produced Euro-version flapjacks with maple syrup for $7.

Quitapenas • *Calle San Miguel 34.* Offers tapas on 2 tiers.

MORE $$

Hotel Tropicana • *Km. 229.5, Carretera de Cadiz;* ☎ *2380110.* Leads off for international fare. South Seas decor; $28 dinner better than adequate.

Cucho's • *Behind the Central Market.* Comes recommended by a helpful reader who has lived in the area since Moorish times. He extols the "exquisite leg of lamb with mint sauce and the tender, delicious pepper steak."

Casa Antonio • *Paseo Maritimo, Playa de Bajandillo;* ☎ *2383060.* A noisy, jam-packed, French-style auberge near the Tropicana. One meal of hot baby clams in sauce and another of a crisp fish-fry specialty of the coast (Fritura Malaguena) with beverages came to almost $43. Don't sit near the glass and wrought-iron door that bangs annoyingly with each departing customer. Colorful and pretty good.

Casa Guaquin • *Carmen 37;* ☎ *2384530.* Praised for its seafood and scenic terrace overlooking Carihuela Beach. Attentive service. Warmly recommended.

Excursion point • Try **El Campanario** in the *Sitio de Calahonda development near Mijas.* You can have a swim, a riding lesson, or play a few sets of tennis. The 15-table restaurant is stronger on gastronomy than aesthetics.

NIGHTLIFE

Torremolinos lives for sunset. Important: In most spots pay for your drinks and snacks the moment they are served.

The best value is at **Taberna Flamenca Pepe Lopez** (*below Plaza Gamba Alegre*), which presents a better-than-average flamenco show in its smoky underground domain. Seating and bar space for about 200; no fire exits visible to us; straw and bamboo ceiling vaults; dimly illuminated tables; hanging yokes, pans, and farm implements; some views blocked by pillars; stand-up tabs from $8 for whiskey to twice that for table service. Mass-production entertainment and atmosphere, but fair enough for the outlay.

At **Mi Bohio**, *Calle Palomas, near Plaza Costa del Sol,* a vaguely South American aura predominates. "Stars" formed by pinholes in the night-blue ceiling; broom-straw porticos over the bandstand proscenium; dado of split timbers; banquettes circling the interior. Easy atmosphere.

DISCOTHEQUES

In summer, Torremolinos swings best. Off season, the action slows to a toddle. **Long-Play**, *Av. Montemar 75,* is tops, even slicker than its Madrid operation. Intimate, well-illuminated room with a brown-felt hide; ample dance oval; long plays and tapes at reasonable volume levels; attractive clientele along its L-shape bar or at its tables. **Piper's Club Plaza**, *Costa de Sol,* is one of the wildest. Two entrances to a multilevel subterranean cavern; 3 bars; several dance floors and ramp-style platforms; spiral walkways lined with felt benches; red-and-blue checkerboard ceiling and used auto parts. Water cascades from stone ledges into scattered free-form pools, some of which contain free-form go-go girls who gyrate on their own private islands. Loud, distortion-free sound system; strobes, spots, flick-filters; up-to-the-instant disc music; 250-person design capacity; twice as many usually in attendance. The door fee of about $12 includes a first drink. **Cleopatra**, next door, is a small dancing den with a revolving and reflecting "eye" chandelier; paneled, padded bar flanked by a huge sun disk; waiters in Egyptian tunics; hieroglyphics, sphinxes, and other touches tastefully arranged. Uncut drinks for about $13 the first time and less thereafter, provided you drink at the bar. We like it.

BARS FOR FUN

The **Blue Note** is the only spot we can recommend along the Begona Passage. You'll find a bar on one side, leather-covered banquettes on the other, and a translucent illuminated dance floor in the center. Inexpensive for exposure to such a charming piano-bar. **Bier Keller**, *Calle San Miguel*, contrives bargain-basement Bavarian Gemutlichkeit. Long wooden benches; drippy candles in Weisswein bottles; German beer-hall music; the management sometimes sponsors bingo games and beer-drinking contests. **Kontiki**, *Calle Los Perros*, **La Carihuela** is on a lane between the Las Palomas Hotel and the sea; modest adornments; inexpensive.

The Cowboy Bar is in the Mansion Club, on the main trail to Malaga. Chief Honcho is amiable John Pierce, (proprietor), an American who knows more about this area than the mayor's wife. A pool table for sporting types; country 'n' western music for us layabouts. Mighty pleasin' it is, too. The Royal Pub does it English style, with pianer music in the evenings. Both are popular for the thirsty.

WHAT TO SEE AND DO

Who comes to Torremolinos for museums, art galleries, or Moorish architecture? Thus, if you seek culture rather than sun, surf, and the tinkling of ice cubes, drop the entire Costa del Sol from your planning. With a car the best targets are easily reached. If not, there are frequent bus excursions—many run daily—to the most important destinations:

Fuengirola, (11 miles west along the coast road) is a fresher Torremolinos with greater open spaces and an earlier bedtime. The bus ride is about $3. Its two highlights are the ruins of **10th-century Sohail Castle** and the attractive shoreline promenade. **Mijas** (10 miles northwest of Torremolinos and 5-1/2 miles north of Fuengirola) is one of the most charming and peaceful Andalusian villages in the area—but only when the tour buses are not rumbling in. Perched 1400 feet up the cool, green sierra, its rambling collection of buildings shelter 8000 inhabitants. "Burro Taxis" are available at *La Cuerva del Burro*, a few steps off the *Plaza de la Paz*; they cost $6 for a stroll. The pine-scented valley and coastal vistas are best viewed from the **Santuario de la Virgen de la Pena chapel**, at the top of the village. If you're lunching here, try **El Mirlo Blanco**, ("The White Blackbird"); $26 or so should round you out with substantial Basque specialties. A regular bus from Torremolinos costs about $5 one way. Conducted tours also depart for Mijas at 3:45 p.m., returning via Fuengirola at about 8 p.m.; all-inclusive fare is around $18. Worth a visit.

Nerja, (on the coast 40 miles west via Highway #340), an attractive village, has become better known since its limestone caverns were discovered in 1959. Despite cloying colored illumination and the self-conscious classical background music, the formations themselves are very lovely; neither the prehistoric paintings nor the primitive burial grounds are currently open to public view. By Carlsbad standards, the grotto is a pigmy; much of your enjoyment on the 30-minute tour will depend upon your guide; the entrance fee is about $4 ($1.50 children). This long, all-inclusive group tour from and to Torremolinos costs about $42 per head. Interesting, but not compelling.

Other worthy side trips from Torremolinos include *Granada, Ronda, Marbella, Seville, Cordoba, and Tangier.* All are available in organized excursion packages; the last can also be reached independently via the 5-hour ferry across the straits from Malaga.

VALENCIA

An ancient port with a special charm. Its lifeline, water, is held in such reverence that the 1000-year-old Arab ceremony of electing a tribunal to regulate the flow to the orchards is still practiced and still recognized under the Spanish legal system. (You can see the judges in session every Thursday outside the cathedral door.) Few points of antiquarian interest. But the high spots of the year are the famous **Fallas fiesta**, on *St. Joseph's Day (Mar. 19)*, the **July Fair**, and the magnificent **Battle of the Flowers** (*July 31*). Try to arrange sleeping accommodations beforehand. If you arrive without a booking, many rooming houses can offer basic shelter. It's worth the discomfort. If money's no object, the **Rey D. Jaime** is easily tops in the city. Try **El Chef** (*Jorge Juan 15*) for inexpensive regional cuisine, the economic **Txoko** (*Calle Gorgos 12*) for savory Basque creations, or **El Plat** (*Conde Altea 41*) for a different rice dish every day.

FOR MORE INFORMATION ON SPAIN

USA • Spanish National Tourist Office, *665 Fifth Avenue, New York, NY 10022,* ☎ *(212) 759-8822*; FAX *(212) 759-8822*; *845 North Michigan Ave., Chicago, IL 60611,* ☎ *(312) 642-1992*; FAX *(312) 642-9817*; *8383 Wilshire Blvd., Suite 960, Beverly Hills, CA 90211,* ☎ *(213) 658-7188*; FAX *(213) 658-1061*; *1221 Brickwell Ave. Miami, FL 33131,* ☎ *(305) 358-1992*; FAX *(305) 358-8223.*

CANADA • *102 Bloor St. West, 14th floor, Toronto, Ontario M5S 1M8,* ☎ *(416) 961-3131*; FAX *(416) 961-1992.*

SWEDEN

Stockholm, The Royal Palace

Sweden earns more than its normal quota of superlatives for such a small nation of such minuscule population. Its beauty can be overwhelming even though much of it is flatter than Ohio. Lakes, rivulets, and seascapes abound. It is the most introverted, difficult, and complex of the Scandinavian countries, but it is also the biggest, richest, and most innovative. In addition, it enjoys one of the highest standards of living in the world—higher, in fact, than the U.S.—with an outstanding panoply of social services that smoothes life's paths for its 8 million inhabitants.

Through much of the 20th century, the Social Democrats have been the dominant political party, providing this constitutional monarchy with some of the most progressive social legislation in the western community. Much of its prosperity, of course, can be attributed to its complete neutrality during both world wars.

During the Viking era, Swedish influence was felt from the Black Sea as far west as Ireland, and in the Middle Ages it was culturally and militarily linked with Norway and Denmark. Later, its colonial force crossed the Atlantic to establish New Sweden, now Delaware.

Stockholm is the natural starting point for your Swedish rounds. Take a low-cost commercial steamer through the glorious archipelago of 24,000 islands and skerries with their sunny beaches, tranquil pastures, and cobalt bays. Voyage out to insular Gotland wandering through the walled capital Visby, an ancient fortified town of timber dwellings and toylike boutiques. There are Viking remains and even traces of Minoan, Greek, and Roman occupation, as well as scores of medieval country churches. Malmo, in the southern province of Skane, is the heart of the Chateaux Country—a district abounding in orchards and fields of flowers. At Loderup you can visit **Dag Hammarskjold's farmhouse**. Northward at Vaxjo in Smaland, watch glassblowers practice their world-famous art. Incidentally, minutely flawed masterpieces can be bought for incredibly low prices at the famous studios of **Boda**, **Kosta**, and **Orrefors**. Take a 3-hour train ride to Ostergotland, which is Sweden in a capsule—forests, rolling terrain, camel-back mountains, and lovely lakes. North of the Arctic Circle where Norrland merges indistinguishably with Lapland, the sun never disappears during June and July. Meanwhile, throughout the rest of the Land of the Midnight Sun it never quite darkens. Fields are rich in golden wheat—one-tenth of the people are tillers. The Gulf Stream creates more warmth than you might expect. It is a fascinating land of jewel-like beauty and aquarian grace.

TIPS ON SWEDEN

WHERE TO STAY

Good news! The tax on hotel rooms has been cut almost in half. Alas, the reduction does not include food, but it helps the visitor to some degree.

A number of hotel chains offer splendid low-cost programs in summer. Be sure to inquire about these of the **Swedish Tourist Board** (see opening remarks) before your departure from home. Also ask them or your travel agent for details on this and other Swedish discount programs for car-rental, rail, bus, air, and ferry transportation plans.

Scandic is the leading operator of motels in Sweden. Naturally it would be folly to make a blanket judgment covering so many motels (now numbering more than 70), but we've liked the ones we've inspected. Prices are in the medium range and below the average out-

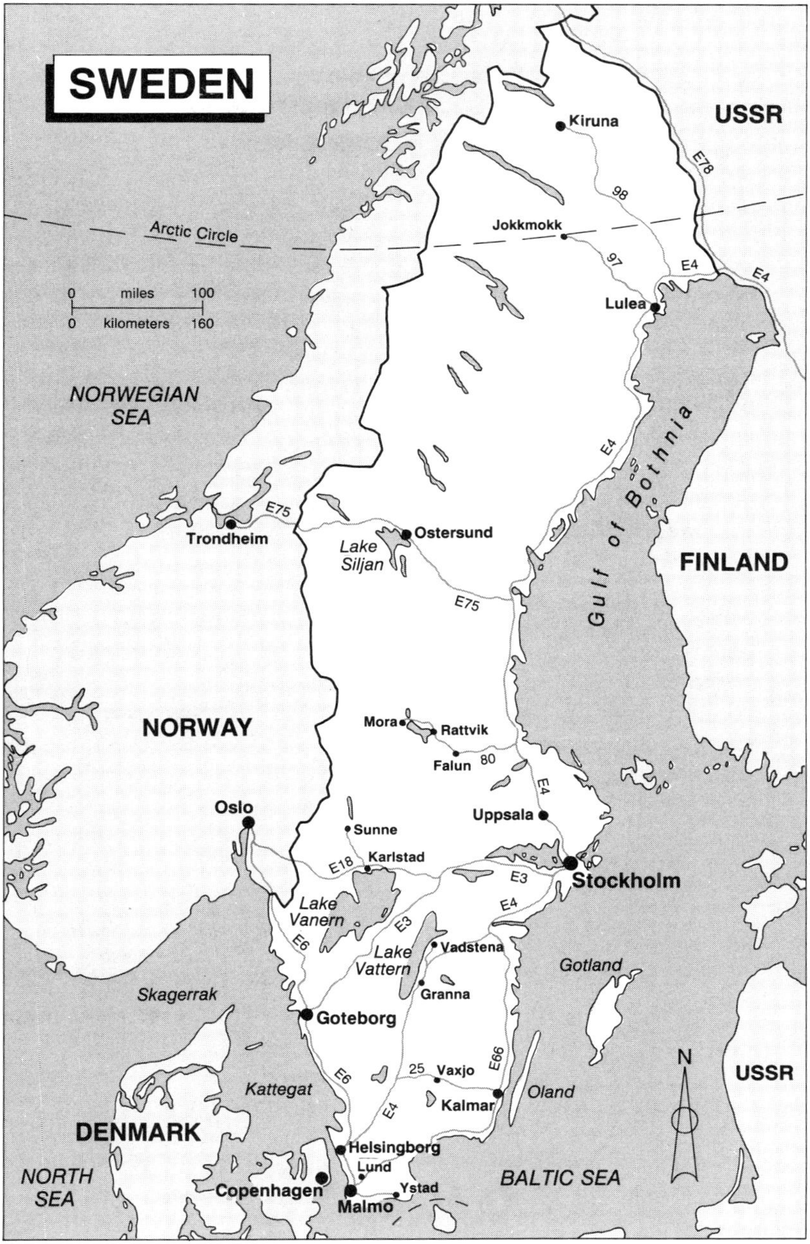
SWEDEN
USSR
Kiruna
E78
98
Arctic Circle
Jokkmokk
97
E4
E4
Lulea
0 miles 100
0 kilometers 160
NORWEGIAN
SEA
E4
Gulf of Bothnia
E75
Trondheim
Ostersund
Lake
Siljan
FINLAND
E75
NORWAY
Mora
Rattvik
Falun
80
E4
Oslo
Uppsala
Sunne
Karlstad
E18
Stockholm
E3
Lake
Vanern
E4
E3
E6
Lake
Vattern
Vadstena
Gotland
Granna
Skagerrak
Goteborg
E66
N
25
Vaxjo
USSR
E6
Kattegat
Oland
Kalmar
E4
DENMARK
Helsingborg
Lund
NORTH
SEA
Copenhagen
Ystad
BALTIC SEA
Malmo

lay for a nice room in Stockholm. The group offers a special *Hotel Cheque* that provides bargain rates, so ask your travel agent before leaving the U.S.A. Children under 12 (in age not in volume) may stay free in the parents' room, including free extra beds and breakfasts. **Best Western, Romantik** and **Reso** have similar plans as well as an organization called **Countryside Sweden**.

There's also a **Bed & Breakfast confederation** of 200 hotels in 125 localities offering bargains in 3 different price groupings. The **SARA** chain (100 hotels in Scandinavia) comes on strong with a very generous Bonus Pass that can strike off as much as 50% from the normal rate. **Sweden Hotels** (145 independent members) is another confederation which offers significant bargains. Check the money-saving plans because the groups are excellent.

LOG CABIN RENTAL

Outdoor enthusiasts, with 96,000 lakes, endless miles of forest, a 2000-mile coastline, and scads of internal watercourses offered them within the nation, often find joy in this type of vacation relaxation. Cabins in the resorts on both the west and east coasts rent from $170 to $240 per week, depending on how cozy you want to be. See the **Swedish National Tourist Office** or any of its mother country affiliates for help in arrangements.

YOUTH HOSTELS

They are predominantly in rural areas and the far north, where extensive tourist facilities are otherwise unavailable. Generally they incorporate separate dorms for separate genders, washrooms, and a common room for meals, letter-writing, and evening recreation. (A few even have accommodations for families.) On the average—and this is average, not specific—a bed with pillow is $8 to $11 (for members; $4 more for nonmembers) per night, sheets are $2 extra (you may bring your own). If no food service exists, free kitchen facilities are normally available. These are listed under the category of "self-catering" establishments; there are other facilities for camping, caravaning, hostel-exchanges between international participants are further elastic if you take the trouble to ask. All are constructed to encourage you to come and to save you money, especially in the summer months. For information write to the **Swedish Touring Club**, *Box 25, Drottninggatan 31, S-11120 Stockholm.*

CURRENCY WARNING

Try not to change money at **Arlanda Airport's** banking facility. (This is Stockholm's International terminus.) Wait until you arrive at a city bank where the rate is more reasonable. I received the best return at branches of the well-regarded Handelsbanken.

FOOD

As throughout Scandinavia, it is fairly expensive. Even if you are in Sweden for a brief period, however, you should try a smorgasbord, going full blast at **Operakallaren**, and **Stallmastaregarden** restaurants in Stockholm. Elsewhere in the capital, this can be found at the **Grand Hotel** (on the Veranda), at **Ulriksdals Wardshus**, at **Solliden in Skansen** (noon to 4 p.m.), and at several scattered oases. Some city restaurants offer its items individually on small plates, tailored to the customer's girth and pocketbook; these are known as *assietter*. Cardinal rule with smorgasbord: Eat all fish on the first plate, meats on the second, and hot appetizers on the third (optional). Never mix your fish and your meat, under any circumstances.

Then there is *stromming*, the dwarf Baltic herring that is the ping-pong ball of the national kitchen. The Swedish cook boils, fries, pickles, pounds, and minces it, makes croquettes, fishburgers, and canapes of it—serves it in every conceivable fashion except raw. One popular presentation is two fillets, back to back, with parsley between—a herring sandwich, in effect. There is also plenty of the inevitable (and delicious) smoked eel. But the very best, in our opinion, is the juicy, delicately sweet salmon trout.

There are no special meal hours in Sweden. Most people lunch from 12 to 2 p.m., dine from 5 to 8 p.m. and later "sup" on light snacks—but restaurant kitchens are open continuously during the day and evening. Your large repast (whether lunch or dinner) will cost you plenty (especially if you entertain any ideas of cocktails, wine, or even local snaps), with the average perhaps $10 to $20, and this perhaps with beer. Be prepared for a bricklayer's breakfast.

DRINKS

Through government-controlled package outlets called *Systembolag* (green and yellow signs), almost any major hard beverage is available—but at a cost that can be numbing from the neck upward.

Although you may buy unlimited amounts of whatever you choose from 9:30 a.m. to 6 p.m. on weekdays, the Swedish parliament voted to ban all sales in monopoly stores over the weekend. This is being effected as part of the government's drive to curb drunkenness. (Weak beer, called pilsner or lattol, will still be purveyed in supermarkets.) Restaurants serve wine and spirits from noon until closing time or on Sundays until 1 p.m. (You've got to be quick on the Lord's Day.)

Aquavit is the national drink. It is also called "snaps," "brannvin," and "aqua vitae." The base is potatoes or grain. Drink it well chilled with smorgasbord (not with the entree or by itself), gulp the potion in 2 or 3 swallows (don't sip), and chase it quickly with beer. The best brand, to our taste, is Skane; Ahus is closest to Denmark's Aalborg. Swedes prefer others, such as Overste (slightly spiced, slightly sweet) or O.P. (aroma of cumin). Absolut, which we call vodka, is also termed as snaps in Sweden.

Swedish Punch is a sweet beverage. The ingredients are Java arrack and a special distillation of rum; float Remy Martin or some other good French cognac on the top of the glass and you'll find a drink fit for the gods. Expensive but worth it.

Beer—your best bargain in alcohol throughout the Nordic lands—comes in the following three grades (based on their alcoholic content): Starkol (4.5%), Folkol (2.8%), and Lattol (1.8%). One Swedish wag quips that the first leaves you in no doubt as to whether you are drinking beer, and the last in some doubt as to whether you're drinking water. Pripps and Spendrup are the most popular brands for middle-of-the-road (figuratively speaking, of course) drinkers. The latter in export version (brown with gold lettering) is one of the best beers I've ever enjoyed.

For nonalcoholic imbibers, American-made colas are available. Among regional products, there is an excellent "lemonade" called *Sockerdricka*—a cross between the British ginger beer and the American ginger ale, with nonpotent additions. There's a fruit beverage called *Pommac;* a pleasant, fresh orange beverage called *Lift*; and a watery, insipid combination of fruit syrup and water called *Saft* issued in various flavors. *Grappo* is grapefruit juice, tart and refreshing.

GETTING AROUND

You can now roam the nation a bit more economically than last year. The government has just cut the Value-Added Tax on some tourist-related services from 21% to 12%. Thus, domestic air fares, rail tickets, and even ski lifts will be a smidgen cheaper.

TRAINS

Superior. There's a continuous program to hitch up new "comfort" cars with double-deck domes and posh up-to-date amenities. First-class smoking compartments often come equipped with twin banquettes of 3 seats each, plus a table flanked by 2 sink-in adjustable armchairs—all in the same roomy, handsome, and practical salon area. Other compartments (including second class) are conventional but also relaxing and well-designed. Many runs feature half-coach snack bars instead of full-fledged dining cars. They're immaculately clean; the limited menus come in 3 languages; soft drinks, wine, export beer, tea, and coffee are the only beverages.

Almost without exception, the service is fast, frequent, and on time.

The Swedish Railways, known as "**SJ**" (Statens Jarnvagar), operate 95% of the nation's railroads, 20% of its buses, and some of its highway motor freight, plus a network of travel offices. If you want to see a lot, SJ offers several Nordic roundabout plans, and Sweden, of course, participates in the money-saving Eurailpass program described in the opening chapters. All fares are low. Sleepers are very cheap.

The small charge for reserving your seat in advance applies on all routine daylight trains; on the Intercity (the 80-mph express that makes the Stockholm-Goteborg run in a shade over 4-1/2 hours and is the fastest in Scandinavia) and other long-range runs such as to Malmo and Copenhagen from the Swedish capital, the levy is applicable in either direction.

Round-trip tickets are valid for a month; one-way must be used within 10 days. For information on the capital's **Tourist Card**, which provides 3 separate plans for traveling in and around the capital on bus, subway, and ferry, please refer to "How to Get Around" in the Stockholm section. It is a potent money saver if you plan to roam a lot.

MOTORING

The price of gasoline in Sweden is a bit less than in some other European nations, but it's still like French perfume after U.S. levies. Many stations are self-service, which means you can fill up at all hours of the night from automatic pumps (provided you have the appropriate money). Distances between cities are rather long, so you should consider opting for public transportation if you can't defray the expense of motoring with several others aboard.

CAR HIRE

In Stockholm **Hertz** (*Master Samuelsgatan 67; ☎ 240720*) comes up with Volkswagens, Opels, Saabs, Fiats, Volvos, and Fords. It also has on hand several models specially equipped with ski racks, snow tires, and a ski holiday pack. **Avis** (*Sveavagen 61; ☎ 349910*) has similar products and prices. Both are reliable—but also very costly, we think, for the values. Ask your travel agent about the "*Rent-a-Car Cheque*" system, which for a set daily sum provides about 200 free miles and insurance; you pay for gas, of course. Both Avis, Hertz, and **Inter Rent** participate in the program. Other fine companies, for which you'll find outlets throughout the nation, include **Europcar** and **Budget/OK**. Very good weekend rates; also inquire at train stations (but these must be returned to the point of initial delivery).

MOTORCYCLES AND SCOOTERS

No rentals. For bikes, see the Swedish Touring Club; they even put together packages for cyclists.

SPORTS

SKIING

Stockholm alone has more than 250 miles of marked trails (many for cross-country skiing). Instruction in some centers free. The 55-mile annual **Vasa cross-country race** in *Dalarna* is very popular; it's always run the first Sunday in March. For full data and directions, drop into any of the Stockholm Information Service's inquiry bureaus listed in "What to See and Do."

CYCLING

Four- and seven-day tours in Oland are very reasonable, but the exact charge varies with the seasons, and on your elected meal plan and point of origin. These radial tours return to the same lodging every night. Contact **Olands Turistforening**, *Box 115, S-387 00 Borgholm; ☎ (0485) 12340.*

Four- to eleven-day pedaling packages in **Gotland** offer campground, full-board hotel, or no-meal youth hostel accommodations. Prices climb from close to $100; they can include boat trip from mainland to Gotland and back. Details from **Gotlandsresor**, *Box 2081, 621 02 Visby; ☎ (0498) 19010.*

For additional information on other tours and specifics on other cycling activities, write **Cykelframjandet**, *Box 3070, S-103 61 Stockholm.*

HIKING

The **Sodermanland Hiking Trail**, southwest of Stockholm, is a clearly marked 300-mile nature trail through unspoiled countryside; camping places at 10-mile intervals; recommended; a tent, rainwear, food, swimming costume, stove, and all the usual camping accoutrements. Further info from **Friluftsframjandet**, *Box 110, S-64200 Flen; ☎ (0157) 137 61.*

For details on other hiking possibilities, contact the travel bureau of the **Swedish Touring Club**, *Drottninggatan 31, Box 25, S-101 20 Stockholm; ☎ (08) 7903200.*

WATERSPORTS

For the lowdown on canoeing capers, contact **Svenska Kanotforbundet**, *Idrottens Hus, 123 87 Farsta; ☎ (08) 7136357/7136372* (Mon.–Fri. 10 a.m.–2 p.m.).

All saltwater fishing is free right up to the shore, but police permission must be obtained by foreign visitors for stream or lake angling; apply to the local police station or the **Fisher Board** (Fiskeristyrelsen) in *Gothenburg (Box 2565, S-403 17).*

SIGHTSEEING

BIRDWATCHING

In late spring and summer, **Oland** is best; in autumn, **Falsterbo** and **Ottenby**.

BADHUS BATHING

Sample a Swedish public bath; loll as nature made you in a big bathtub while the attendant applies a large brush. Have heard of very low-cost baths at **Vanadisbadet** (open only in summer), but haven't personally exposed hide nor hair to their Swedish steel wool. If you survive, let us know how it went.

SHOPPING

Standard shops are normally open from 10 a.m. to 6 p.m. Mon.–Fri. and from 10 a.m. to 4 p.m. on Sat. in winter, but 2 p.m. in summer. Closing times for department stores may vary; Mon., Thurs., or Fri., 7 p.m.; Tues. and Wed., 6 p.m.

THINGS NOT TO BUY

The quality of Swedish products is renowned. In integrity of merchandise, you won't get stung. Price is the major consideration.

WHERE TO GO

GOTEBORG

(Gothenburg in English.) Pronounced "YOTE-ah-borg," by its residents, this hub is nearly 4 centuries old. This ancient seat, Sweden's busiest port, is a combination of industrial energy and thriving cultural activity. There are many historic canals here, and the Gota River ends the famous Gota inland waterway that winds cross-country to Stockholm. Several hotels are available. Dining spots are now more engaging than before. There are ample tourist facilities. The city is an interesting one, and the inland boat ride across the peninsula is a relaxing and pleasant journey. You can fly back to Stockholm by fast, frequent SAS service. If you overnight, the most economical stops are **Forum** (*Brahegatan 9;* ☎ *031/840080*), **Allen** (*Parkgatan 10;* ☎ *031/101450*), and **ME:S Pensionat** (*Chalmersgatan 27A*; ☎ *031/101450*). **Ostkupan** (*Mejerigatan 2*; ☎ *031/401050*) is a youth hostel.

Eggers, more costly, is very charming. Food costs are high in fancier midtown establishments patronized by expense accounters in the center of commerce, but most offer a daily special that is reasonable. Also a set menu can usually be found at midday for about $6.50.

Fiskekrogen is one of the better bets for seafood; **Atta Glas** is on a boat moored midcity; **White Corner** is a choice for beefeaters.

HELSINGBORG

With barely a squint you can see Helsingor (Elsinore) across the Oresund on Danish soil. It has always been a busy corridor between the 2 nations, nestling in sea-bathed history in Skane, one of the oldest districts of Sweden. The **Town Hall**, the 13th-century **St. Mary Church**, the **Karnan Tower**, and a host of leftover architecture from the 12th to the present century are interesting cultural attractions.

LAPLAND

This far-northern reach of the world, topped by Norway's Finnmark, is so remote that many travelers will find it too expensive in terms of time and money. Since the Lapps totally ignore national boundaries, be prepared to follow the herds if you wish to see these extraordinarily independent folk. See "Finland" for more details.

MALMO

It's right on the southern tip closest to Denmark and Germany. This is the jumping-off point for excursions to the Swedish chateaux country; there are over 100 fine ones from the 16th and 17th centuries. Several major hotels, one outstanding restaurant in a restored house, plenty of shops, plenty of bustle; 6 miles of quays, Sweden's biggest man-made harbor, and one of Scandinavia's largest and most modern theaters are here. SAS runs shuttles daily to and from Copenhagen; immaculate and comfortable ferryboats make the crossing in 1-1/2 hours, and 30 hydrofoil services per day in both directions nip the time to a mere 45 minutes. Good stops include the **Scandinavia**, **St. Jorgen**, and the **Scandic**; excellent dining and rich color are available at the ancient midcity **Kockska Krogen**.

MARIEFRED

Better known for its revered **Gripsholm Castle**, with its deer park, than for its fine lake bathing and excellent camp sites. The castle walls enfold Gustav III's court theater, a mammoth art collection, and magnificently restored chambers. Your steamer ride from the capital takes perhaps 4 hours: a delightful trip—especially if into an overnight jaunt.

ORREFORS

Here is the "Kingdom of Crystal." Fewer than 1000 souls inhabit this forest community between Vaxjo Kalmar. A world-famous glass center, just off the main east-coast highway between Denmark and Stockholm (220 miles north of Helsingborg), is an especially interesting little detour for mofprists. You may watch master glass-blowers turn out exquisite products at any or all of 16 glassworks in the district. The main attractions are at Orrefors and Kosta-Boda. All have exhibitions and museums, and it is possible to buy handmade glass at very moderate prices.

OSTERGOTLAND

About 2 hours by train from Stockholm are rolling fields, sweeping forests, glorious lakes, and smaller mountains in one panoramic package. The high point for most visitors is the excursion on either the Gota or the Kinda canals.

These waterborne journeys are enthralling if you like your thoroughfares paved with H2O. You may also play golf, sail, hike, bicycle, fish for salmon or char, go to the horse races or country fairs, or loaf at your leisure. Although the essence of rurality, it is often busy and always healthily robust.

SALTSJOBADEN

The celebrated beach resort, 25 minutes by train from the center of Stockholm. Plan to lunch at either the Grand Hotel (for the affluent) or at one of the proliferating food bars (for thinner wallets). If you are young, adventurous, and want to skirt the crowds at this popular hub, detrain at the station nearest Erstaviksbadet, a wooded beach with fewer excursionists and wonderful swimming.

SANDHAMN

The largest national yachting center, with perhaps the best bathing of all. Departures take place from Stockholm by boat at 10 a.m., steaming back by about 10 p.m. It's a 3-1/2-hour ride each way—but definitely worth it when the gentle Swedish sun is shining. Package loops including a boat trip, room, breakfast are available for about $65. The only hotel is a charming country place (with bunk beds) associated with the Royal Yacht Club. Prices are at crew level. In summer, the long hours of light can be deceptive. Anywhere in the archipelago be sure you are at the boat landing in plenty of time for departure. Many visitors miss the later voyages simply because it still seems like noon in the late afternoon.

LAKE SILJAN

The **charmfields** of Dalarna in the Darlecarlia province on its shores are an enchanting segment of the globe. Prices are much lower than in the capital. There are good but too few accommodations in Tallberg, Rattvik, and further around the lake at Morastrand; be sure to reserve in advance during the warm months. Don't expect bright lights and action because in this glorious pastoral setting they don't even have sidewalks to roll up at night. Ideal for shedding the problems of today's crazy world.

SKOKLOSTER

Dominating a large lake about 3/4 of the way toward Uppsala from Stockholm, here is one of the most magnificent palaces in the hemisphere. Built in the mid-17th century for Field Marshal Carl Gustaf Wrangel—the gorgeous interiors bear witness to the splendor of Sweden's Golden Age as a major power. If you're wheeling toward the University City, it's more than worth the short detour.

STOCKHOLM

This 700-year-old city built on 14 islands is glistening, efficient, and beautiful to the eye. Spires, stately palaces, graceful bridges, boats, and green parks abound. Somewhat larger than Washington, it has 800,000 residents, 3 railroad stations, a subway system that is a triumph of contemporary artistic and engineering endeavor, excellent hotels, restaurants, and shops.

A leisurely cruise around Stockholm's waterways and islands provides a wondrous and inexpensive overall impression of this fresh, clean metropolis; eagle-eye panoramas can be had from the 400-foot **Kaknas TV Tower**, Scandinavia's loftiest edifice, or from the pinnacle of City Hall. The latter is a masterpiece of early 20th-century civic architecture incorporating the ornate Golden Hall; the Blue Hall is the annual site of the Nobel Prize banquet.

The Old Town is dubbed "The City Between the Bridges"—an area of twisting waterside alleys, linked by flights of crooked steps, lined with artists' studios and curious wee boutiques. About a fifth of this medieval enclave is occupied by the Royal Palace, a sumptuous antique treasury of artifacts from centuries past. More recent monarchs reside at baroque Drottningholm on the island of Lovon; the tasteful interiors, elegant gardens, and 18th-century **Court Theatre** make this a fascinating, easy, and inexpensive excursion quest from midcity.

DIRECTORY

U.S. Embassy • *Strandvagen 101*; ☎ *630520.*

American Express Travel Representative • *Birger Jarlsgatan 1.*

Barbers • *Hotorgshallen.*

Hairdresser • Bjorn Axen at *NK.* Also the beauty salon at the *NK Department Store* or the *Hotel Continental* (fast service and, from time to time, a cut rate).

Dry Cleaning and Pressing • Sturebadstvatten, *Gallerian at Sturebadet Grev Turegatan 9.*

Suit Rental • Hans Allde, *Birger Jarlsgatan 58.*

English-Speaking Doctor or Dentist (or other emergencies) • ☎ *900000.*

Police • Headquarters, *Agnegatan 37;* ☎ *7693000.*

Favorite Pawnshop • SKAPA, *Drottningholmsvagen 25 or Norrtulls-gatan 6.*

HOW TO GET AROUND

Be sure to buy the broad-view, low-cost **Stockholm Card**, which opens a vast realm of sights, admissions, favors, and transportation to you. Prices are set so low that if you plan to do an average amount of sightseeing, you will come out well ahead in your budget.

Prime targets? Take the subway to Brommaplan and the bus from there to Drottningholm Palace, or board a ferry from the Stadshusbron, near the main railway station; Bus #47 speeds you to Djurgarden, Skansen, and the warship Wasa; Bus #41 deposits you at the Royal Mint; the National and Modern Art museums may be reached on foot from the Opera.

DO-IT-YOURSELF TOUR

Buses #54 and #62 circle most of the top attractions in the center of the city. Avoid taxis, especially to or from Arlanda Airport ($5 by bus vs. $30 by cab). Not only are they shockingly expensive, but you can seldom find one when you need it. In an emergency, the radio-taxi phone number is ☎ *150000.* One taxi company (ask locally if you are interested) offers halfprice fares to women after midnight. The object is to provide a reasonably priced alternative to late-night rides on the subway for lone travelers.

WHERE TO STAY

The **Stockholm Information Service** (*Sverigehuset, Kungstradgarden;* ☎ *7892000*) staffs a hotel booking office in the Central Railway Station the year-round. These helpful and knowledgeable specialists will tuck you into a hotel or a hostel. The fee is in the $3 range—surely nominal when weighed against the time and the scouting headaches saved. Two other organizations render similar services.

Allrum • *Wallingatan 34, S-111 24 Stockholm;* ☎ *08-213789.* Minimum of 5 nights.

Hotelltjanst AB • *Vasagatan 15-17, S-111 20 Stockholm;* ☎ *08-104437.* Minimum of 2 nights.

LEAST $

Since low-cost sleeping space in the capital is so scarce, if you have not prepared your way through any of the aforementioned pre-arrival plans, the youth hostels are compassionate and do not demand formal affiliation of their guests.

af Chapman • ☎ *6795015.* A sailing ship moored within a 15-minute walk (no public transportation) of the center might be the answer if you're young, hearty, and nautical of mind. Pleasant dining room. Small but tidy cabins; tiered berths, corner desks, 3-drawer wardrobes; separate showers but no baths. The segregated-by-gender section sleeps 130; youth hostel members pay $8 to 11 per night, nonmembers about $4 more; sheets (paper ones) are $3 and last about 3 nights; huge breakfast for $5. Open Apr. 1 to Dec. 15.

Anno 1647 • *Mariagrand 3*; ☎ *6440480.* Stays open year-round; offers 42 rooms.

Columbus • *Tjarhovsgatan 11*; ☎ *441717.* Open year-round.

Skeppsholmen • *Opposite the Chapman;* ☎ *6795017.*

Zinken • *Zinkensvag 20*; ☎ *6582900.*

Gustaf af Klint • *Stadsgardskajen 153*; ☎ *6404077.* The rates run from $6 to $12 per night.

MORE $$

Although some lodgings at this level can be found in bigger hostelries, simply not enough exist. As a result, this listing contains many small hostelries and rooming houses.

Jerum • *Studentbacken 21;* ☎ *166109* and **Domus** *Korsbarsvagen 1*; ☎ *160195.* Heavily patronized by young people. The former, about 10 minutes from the

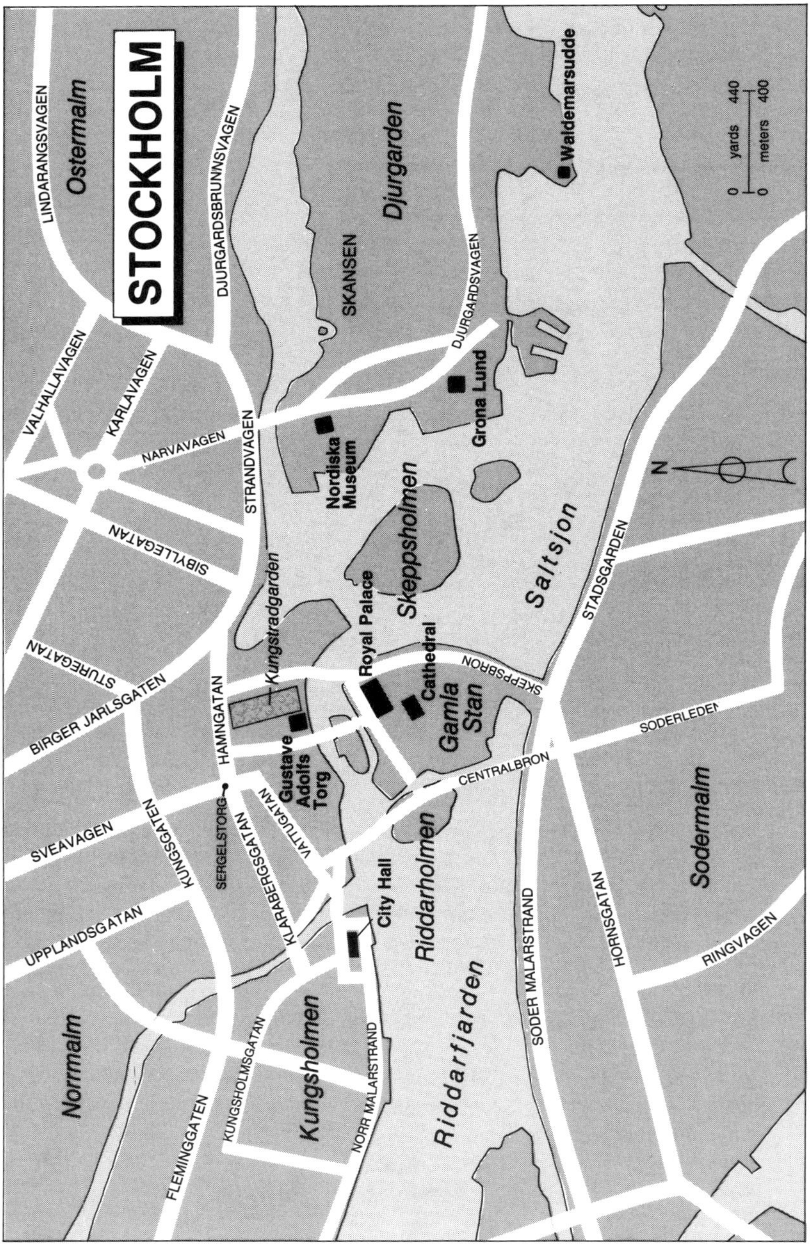
STOCKHOLM
Ostermalm
LINDARANGSVAGEN
DJURGARDSBRUNNSVAGEN
Djurgarden
SKANSEN
Waldemarsudde
0 yards 440
0 meters 400
DJURGARDSVAGEN
Grona Lund
Nordiska Museum
VALHALLAVAGEN
KARLAVAGEN
NARVAVAGEN
STRANDVAGEN
SIBYLLEGATAN
Skeppsholmen
N
Saltsjon
Kungstradgarden
Royal Palace
Cathedral
STUREGATAN
BIRGER JARLSGATEN
HAMNGATAN
SKEPPSBRON
Gamla Stan
STADSGARDEN
SODERLEDEN
Gustave Adolfs Torg
CENTRALBRON
SVEAVAGEN
SERGELSTORG
KLARABERGSGATAN
VATTUGATAN
Riddarholmen
KUNGSGATEN
City Hall
Sodermalm
UPPLANDSGATAN
SODER MALARSTRAND
HORNSGATAN
RINGVAGEN
Riddarfjarden
NORR MALARSTRAND
KUNGSHOLMSGATAN
Kungsholmen
Normalm
FLEMINGGATEN

center, has modern TV lounge and cafeteria with substantial food at blue-plate prices; 120 units, all with showers, toilets, telephones, double doors, and an overall feeling of comfort despite severe space limitations. Rates: $42--$55 alone and about 15% more for twins, including breakfast, service and taxes. Operated midJune to end of August only. The latter, 10 minutes out by bus #50, is smaller but its prices are higher in winter; in summer they are similar. Both recommended.

City • *Slojdgatan 7, Hotorget;* ☎ *222240.* Smartly refreshened vintage structure. Cozy restaurant-bar. Garage nearby; 147 billets, among them many fine, spacious 2-person units; lovely updatings that could warrant a luxury rating, but prices remain reasonable; no alcohol served.

Kung Karl • *Birger Jarlsgatan 23;* ☎ *6113110.* Offers 87 rooms, 80 private toilets.

Flyghotellet Brommaplan • *Brommaplan;* ☎ *262620.* Small, neat, tranquil. A short walk to subway station, putting it about 15 minutes from midcity.

Kom • *Dobelnsgatan 17-19;* ☎ *235630.* Intimate, inexpensive, worth the outlay.

Queen's • *Drottninggatan 71-A;* ☎ *249460.* Offers 17 passable accommodations if everything else is booked.

EVEN MORE $$$

Adlon • *Vasagatan 42;* ☎ *245400.* Reasonable shelter; a 5-minute walk from center; 58 chambers, large proportion of singles; except on 6th floor, small tub or shower in each room. Prices: $50 singles without bath and pushing $70 for two.

Reso Hotel Bromma • *Near domestic airport;* ☎ *252920.* Basic but adequate. Comprises 141 units; mostly sit-down (not stretch-out) baths. A combination of nitty-gritty amenities and far-out location detracts from its appeal.

Flamingo • *Hotellgatan 11 (in suburban Solna);* ☎ *830800.* Might be termed a supermarket hostelry. Load your luggage onto grocery cart in lobby and wheel it to your bin; no reception staff to show you the way. Restaurant, grill, bar, cocktail lounge clean, hypermodern.

Karelia • *Birger Jarlsgatan 35;* ☎ *247660.* Getting long in the tooth. Fair, at best.

MOTELS

Due to the distances from the center, no nonmotorist should consider staying in them. Virtually standard facilities include austere modern decor, restaurant, bar, cafeteria, shop, and functional quarters with small bath, shower, radio, and TV. Some also have a sauna; studio twins are in the $75 range. On the fringes there are some good choices if you have a car; rates go down in summer. These include the **Star** (☎ *920100*), the **Welcome** (☎ *760-2520*), and the **Sollentuna**.

CAMPING

A bonanza for summer travelers. Our favorites are the **Bredang** site (☎ *977071*), easily reached by subway, and the **Angby** grounds (☎ *370420*), across the sound from Drottningholm Palace, adjacent to one of Stockholm's lakeside beaches. Both clean and well tended; plenty of toilets and showers. Other names to remember are **Farstanas** (☎ *0755-50215*), **Flaten** (☎ *773-0100*), and **Ostnora** (☎ *0750-40016*).

SUGGESTIONS FOR STUDENTS

The founding fathers must have shot arrows in 111 directions when they decided to situate the buildings of the University. Seemingly, you'll stumble across them in almost every area you go. The **International Youth Center** (*Valhallavagen 142;* ☎ *634389*) welcomes all foreign undergraduates with dances, movies, lectures, sightseeing tours, picnics, and other events during 2 months of the summer vacation. Go here for detailed advice on sleeping space and dining.

SPECIAL LODGINGS

In season, tighter than the skin on a Swedish sausage.

Try the **Youth Hostel** aboard the sailing ship *af Chapman* (mentioned earlier). **Skeppsholmen**, near the af Chapman, is open year-round; rates about $13 per night; ☎ *6795017.*

Botkyrka (*Eriksbergsskolan* ☎ *075362105*) and **Huddinge** (*Sundby gard* ☎ *7469480*) are further choices along with **Dalaro** (☎ *0750-51602*) and a unique hideaway called **Longholmen** (☎ *668-0510*), which in earlier times had been a prison. (With good behavior you'll be out in three days!)

WHERE TO EAT

The restaurants of Sweden have entered an extremely difficult period due to the rocketed cost of labor. Within a very recent span, the combined salaries, social security levies, and taxes jumped murderously. The VAT (Value-Added Tax, which has nothing to do with value but only to do with tax) leapt in one instant from 12.9% to 25%! A newspaper reported that a Stockholm restaurant answered this by offering a "half-price lunch" of soup, chicken, and dessert of approximately $10, plus a beer for $2.65. Lines of people waited in the street to get in on the bargain. We have been able to turn up only a handful of establishments that offer sound fare at reasonable prices.

LEAST $

Station Restaurants • To start your day off happily and economically, tuck into the all-youcan-eat breakfast buffet (also available at the stations of Goteborg and Malmo). About $7 for this savanna spread of eggs, cereal, anchovies, herring, bread, rolls, orange juice, butter, cheese, jams, tea, coffee, hot chocolate, milk and—whew, well, see for yourself! Will save you wads of kroner in this costly capital. Groaning-board repast (from 11 a.m. to midnight) close to $13 for 16 cold dishes and 2 hot choices—and, again, you may go back for refills.

Covered Markets • Try the dozens of opportunities for snacks, hot plates, tacos, vegetarian foods, kebabs, and other fast-fare at **Hotorgshallen** and **Ostermalmshallen**. **Kungshallen** (near the first) also is ample for browsing.

NK Department Store • The fourth-floor cafe is superb for quality and selection. Good prices, too, for such high standards.

PUB Department Store • *Underground near Hotorget station.* Its cafeteria offers a similar approach to NK, but not as appealing in our view; prices, however, are lower.

Daily News • *Swedenhouse, Hamngatan 27.* One of the most pleasant restaurants in the city—and right in the heart of the shopping district. Order the meal of the day for best value. The place is big but active all day long, and on several levels.

Roda Rummet • *Norra Bantorget.* Stays open late, catering to taxi drivers with hardy fare.

La Cle • *Hamngatan* and nearby **Wienerkonditoriet** *Biblioteksgatan.* Also a late night spot with hearty fare.

Sturekatten • *Riddargatan 4.* A bakery featuring patio pleasantries and tearoom tasties. Unless you're chronically skinny, tie one hand behind your back!

Kaffegillets Storstuga • *Trangsund 4.* Of the same genre. Help-yourself beverage counter opposite pastry-and-sandwich display; warm dishes; rathskeller for weary students; 5 p.m. closing during warm months. A fun stop in the Old Town.

Little Kobenhavn • *Opposite the NK.* Specializes in Danish food. Moderate tabs.

Birger Bar • *Smalands gatan opposite Collage.* Good to remember if you have a small appetite since half portions may be ordered. Italian dishes chiefly.

Pizzeria Piazza-Opera • *Gustav Adolfstorg 20.* Provides a quasi-Peninsula *appoggiatura* to the far-north cityscape. Open until midnight. Acceptable.

Capri • *Nybrogatan.* Big on pasta and Latin foodstuffs.

GARDEN DINING

Try the moderately priced outdoor cafeteria at **Djurgardsbrunns Wardshus**, (*Norra Djurgarden Djurgardsbrunn*). Nice clientele. Rewarding. At *Kungstradgarden Park*, summer beckons many to the **Blanche Cafe**. You'll also want to experience **Rosendals Tradgardar** in *Djurgarden*, about 10 minutes by foot from the former home of Prince Eugen, now an art museum called **Waldemarsudde**. Snacks and pastries are served in greenhouses where much of the organic food is grown. Tables and parasols dot the lawn or you can munch at tables under the glass roofs. There's also a market for the purchase of natural products. Take bus #47 to the end of the line; it's a short stroll from here. Many families go on weekends.

At *Skansen* (see farther along), **Stora Gungan** is a 2-room hut in the Old Town Quarter with waitresses in costume. The spectacular "herring board" consists of a half-dozen fish choices plus sour cream, chives, bread, rolls, dill, tomatoes, lettuce, Jansen's Temptation (potato and anchovy hot specialty), Swedish meatballs, lingonberry preserves, and—whew—they also have *pytti panna* or spaghetti for close to $7.50. Open until 4 p.m. but rests on Mon.

Yet another good bet: **Brunnspaviljongen**.

SNACK BARS

First, try **Cassi Grill-Bar** (*Narvavagen 30*) by the Karlaplan Circle. **Annorlunda** (*Malmskillnadgatan 50*) is a crisp and appetizing salad bar. **Ortagarden** (*Nybrogatan 31*) does a similar thing for vegetable lovers, but it also offers a hot buffet. Then there's **Ciro Bar** (*Sibyllegatan 34*). **Torg Café** (*Ostermalms Torg 2*) and **Konditori Relax** (*Sveavagen 102*) have the same management and similar top quality quiche, soup, and salad bar selections. While at the former, be sure to visit the nearby **Ostermalms Hallen**, a fascinating vast food hall. The two sit-down restaurants among the busy stalls are excellent. Just seeing this market is a lifetime event!

STANDUP COUNTERS

Miramar (*on Strandvagen*) is currently the most popular; **Sturekatten** (*Riddargatan 4*) whips up pastries for a coffee break.

Bla Porten (*Djurgardsvagen*) offers a buffet of fruit, breads, and tempting sweets. **Smuggler** (*Museum of Modern Art*) is crisp with salad choices.

PUBS

Two are unusually inviting. **Tudor Arms** (*Grevgatan 31*) is done in half-timber and white stucco. A young throng parades through every evening for steak-and-kidney pie, roast beef, and other publican specialties. "Time" is called at 9:20 or 9:30 p.m.

Engelen (*Kornhamstorg 59B*) can be fun and funny, too. The pill-size **Kolingen** (*downstairs*) is a discotheque that just happens to include a sauna.

Prinsen • *Master Samuelsgatan 4.* A weird but successful blend of Victorian pub and New Orleans honky-tonk. Open grill; 3 dining enclaves. Massive selection; excellent sandwiches in the $3.50 to $5.50 range.

Cattelin • *Storkyrkobrinken 9.* Traditional standby. Simple, friendly atmosphere; 5 seating areas. Seafood annex. Dish of the day perhaps $6.50; will cost you around $18 to fill your midriff. Open all year. Service can be inconsistent.

Stortorgskallaren ("Cellar by the Market") • *On Great Square, in Old Town.* Radiates intimacy with 24 candlelit tables. At street level, a bar and 2 small dining rooms for overflow trade. Tariffs in the medium category. Unelaborate, agreeable, and devilishly hard to pronounce.

Godthem Inn • *Rosendalsvagen 9, in Deer Park.* Lures Skansen-bound revelers with 3 tiers of "environmental dining." Ground floor features resident strings and small adjoining bar; second stratum done in orange and aqua and padded chairs; top layer bustles with service and tariffs in inverse proportion to the altitude. Your expenditure at the summit should total between $10-14 per appetite. Amusing.

Timjan • *Riddargatan 8.* In a midtown precinct. Swedish-style bistro elan. Main dishes $11 bracket; "Grandmother's Pie," at about $7, a favorite snack.

MORE $$

Vau de Ville • *Corner of Hamngatan and Norrlandsgatan.* A midtown, bistro-cum-brasserie that has wowed Stockholm with its French repasts. Fast service; baguette sandwiches or full meals; the pivotal point of the city.

Martini • *Nearby at Norrmalmstorg 4; ☎ 679-8220.* A fun place that is always busy—even on Sundays from 1 p.m. to 10:30. Three areas for sitting: ground floor, lower level (dark), and outdoor covered terrace (best). Bistro personality with a twist of Italian. Bravo!

Eleonora • *Nybrogatan 53; ☎ 634500.* Adjoining the Mornington Hotel, this represents the city's leading edge in modern food and matching decor. Tables illuminated by rail lights and spots; folk art and paintings on walls; silver candlesticks and flowers. Dishes such as leek-marinated salmon or quenelles, fried reindeer steak, avocado with crevettes; summer menu of 2 choices for about $13; bottled wine worth the difference over the open house varieties. Distinctive and pleasant.

Ostergok • *Kommedorsgatan 46.* Three completely separated restaurants side by side by side. The piscatorial segment on a street corner is the quintessence of simplicity. Directly adjoining, a cozy, taverny establishment for grills and other meats. Menus available in both Swedish and English. Price levels in this duet virtually identical. Reserve in advance and pay no attention to the pizzeria that forms yet another portion of this *menage a trois*; the cooking is a scandal on the good name of Italy.

Coco & Carmen • *Banergatan 7; ☎ 609954.* An artsy lunch snuggery in midtown. Wooden floors, potted plants; noteworthy pâtés, mousses, and salads; about $17 for a light meal without beverage.

Grand Hotel • Glass-wrapped bar-terrace features a lavish smorgasbord. Elegant ambience; beautiful view of harbor. Eye-popping variety; delicious preparation. About $32 for all you can eat. Advance bookings here also urged, especially evenings.

Gourmatique • *Old Town.* As bad as the name sounds, the place itself is attractive. Windows overlooking the antiquity of viking empire; soft lighting plus brass candlesticks; mulberry-tone tablecloths; good solid Nordic cookery as well as international choices. The prices are appealing, too.

CHINESE FARE

Contrary to the virtually universal low-cost policy in other western cities, it is startlingly expensive. The most plush is **Jasmine** (*Kornhamnstorg 55*). The **Shanghai** (*Sveavagen 47*) provides a large selection of Oriental dishes. We particularly enjoyed the chicken with mushrooms and bamboo shoots at the **Mai Fa** (*Drottninggatan 71*). Other possible candidates for chopsticking are the **Hong King** (*Kungsholmsstrand 23, near the harbor*), **China** (*Rorstrandsgatan 9-A*), **Ming Yuan** (*Smalandsgatan 22*) and **China Garden** (*Karlavagen 15*). Nearly all of these are open continuously from 11:30 a.m. to 11 p.m.

NIGHTLIFE

Large conventional nightspots are almost prohibitively expensive.

Victoria • *Kungstradgarden;* ☎ *101085.* A paradox: a conservative, quiet, solid businessmen's restaurant at lunch that turns into the most raucous, crowded, merry singles center in Sweden from 5 p.m. onward. Its 3 good-size rooms plus warm-weather terrace are so jammed with celebrants (or would-bes) that to be certain of entry, reservations are normally mandatory to pass the waiting line at the door. All sexual tastes and persuasions should find exactly the partner they seek virtually up to its 3 a.m. closing. Snacks to full meals are always available. The fastest action is at the bar.

Stampen • *Stora Nygatan 7.* Good for Dixieland. The ceiling and walls are hung with whimsical junk items: An upside-down Christmas tree, a bib-andtucker, a baby carriage, and—behind the bar—a forlorn stuffed dog. Beer only at around $4.50 per mug; small, crowded, and friendly.

Tre backar • *Tegnergatan 12* . Provides live music several nights per week.

Kaos Lilla • *Nygatan 21.* Goes more to modern notes and bars.

Golden Days • *Kungsgatan 29.* Throbs with British piano and banjo pickin's on the merry mock-stern of a ship.

The Sturehof • *Stureplan 2.* A Scotch-house tavern type, is such a whopping success that it's nearly always jammed with young fans. Again, nothing stronger than beer or wine is available.

The Kolingen • *Kornhamnstorg 59.* Below the Engelen restaurant, is garlanded by strings of colored bulbs. Entrance for $7; dancing to "traditional jazz"; one secluded cuddling corner.

King Creol • *Kungsgatan.* Stunned the local populace by introducing strip tease to this staid metropolis. In its brassy precincts the lonely male should find a plethora of feminine companionship.

Among other popular places are **Baldakinen** and **Baldakinens Pelarsal** (*both at Barnhusgatan 12-14*), plus the previously mentioned **Daily News** which has a late edition after the evening meal. **Collage** (*Smalandsgatan 2*) is an evergreen disco for those in their mid-twenties. **Down Town** (*Norrlandsgatan 6*) and **Alexandra** (*Birger Jarlsgatan 29*), are also in this league.

WHAT TO SEE AND DO

Drottningholm Palace • The royal residence of the king and his family, is particularly impressive and the most beautiful of royal homes, with Gobelin tapestries scattered around as freely as bathroom rugs. The adjoining **Court Theater**, untouched since 1766, is still very much in use; several times per week beginning in May, performances "De l'Epoque" are featured. See it if you can; 20 minutes by bus, or 50 minutes by frequent steamers.

Djurgarden • *The former Royal Deer Park.* Shouldn't be missed. It's the island home of world-famous **Skansen**: A magnificent open-air museum with authentic farms, a zoo, a Lapp camp, Nordic antiques, and great natural beauty. Open any day in May, June, July, or Aug. at each hour from 10 a.m. to 6 p.m. Dial ☎ *670020* for up-to-the-minute developments on everything from the concerts to the folk dancing to the performances by international artists to the teenage dance fests to the feeding time of the animals. There's a Tivolilike park, too, for rides and entertainment for youngsters. You may also take the ferry boat from Nybroplan or from Slussen. It is 7 minutes from the city by Bus #47.

CITY SIGHTSEEING

Skepp O Hoj • Rents both at the Djurgardsbrons bridgehead. Moreover, there's a lovely little floating tearoom gazebo and across the canal you can rent little sailing smacks and power boats. We prefer canoes, however, and a picnic along the banks. Both are inexpensive.

Other packaged motorcoach excursions include the 2 **"Grand City" Tours** and the **Chateau Tour** to Uppsala and Sigtuna. Outings by motorboat include the **Grand Scene Tour Under the Bridges**, the **Royal Canal Tour**, the **Archipelago Tour**, and a **Summer Evening Tour**.

Prices vary from $4 to $7.50 for capital sightseeing and $10 to $16 for the longer or more highly adorned circuits. Most of them are operated in summer only. Tickets may be purchased at the **Tourist Information counter** (*Sweden House, Hamng 27*) at any travel bureau, and at all leading hotels. Or contact **Tourist Sightseeing** (*Skeppsbron 20, Box 2253;* ☎ *240470*) for their selection of prearranged tours. Silja or Viking Lines steamers depart from the capital for the semi-autonomous **Aland Islands**, halfway to Finland. The 13-hour round trip costs about $20 and you can fill up on tax-free stores aboard, provided you stay out of Sweden 24 hours; sights galore and a pretty fair smorgasbord on some of the ferries. Inquire locally for details.

Excursion Shop Swedenhouse • *Kungstradgarden, Box 7542;* ☎ *7892000.* Offers some offbeat excursions; e.g., a bicycle tour of Uto Island or a flight over Stockholm. Rates are often quite low for the unusual nature of the trips.

A marvel is the 17th-century warship *Wasa*, which was salvaged intact from the 110-foot depths of Stockholm Harbor. Divers with powerful water-jets pumped 6 tunnels beneath her hull, through which several thousand feet of 6-inch steel cables were threaded to hoist her out of the mud and up to the surface—one of the most complicated and dangerous undersea projects ever undertaken. She's in a remarkable state of preservation for her 3-1/2 centuries—mostly due to the cold waters in which she laid. The **Wasamuseet** is continuing to grow as more discoveries are displayed.

Culture seekers will find scores of other rewarding targets in the capital: there are more than 50 museums; the booklet *Stockholm This Week* describes all of them. For special exhibitions which change periodically, check the *Svenska Dagbladet* on Fridays or the *Dagens Nyheter* on Saturdays; in addition to these newspapers, *Stockholm This Week* also covers the same ground. Before starting the chase, however, acquaint yourself with the low-cost, all-inclusive bus and subway bonanza available at SLs, Pressbyran's. This **SL Card** is somewhat different from the **Stockholm Card**.

The latter offers one version for the city's core and the other ranging out to the suburbs. It includes a ferry ride to Djurgarden. Determine which covers your needs best before you buy.

Here's a sampling for erudition: The **Moderna Museum** (*Skeppsholmen Island*) with masterworks by Munch, Matisse, Kandinsky, Calder, Picasso, plus Swedish abstracts; open 11 a.m.–9 p.m. daily. **Gustav III's Antikmuseum**, in the royal palace, with the king's fascinating appanage of Italian sculpture; very low admission fee; varying hours and limited winter showings; ask any tourist office branch for the exact exhibit times during your sojourn. The **National Museum**, in Sodra Blasieholmshammen, with the gamut of paintings, engravings, sculpture, sketches, and handcrafts comprising the national art treasury; foreign masters include Rembrandt, Rubens, Renoir, Manet, Cezanne, Bonnard, Braque, and other titans; free on Tues.; $2.50 otherwise; open from 11 a.m. to 4 p.m. every day, plus from 7 to 9 p.m. on Tues., the **Antiquities** and **Royal Mint**, corner of Narvavagen and Linnegatan, with ore-lore dating back to prehistoric times; $1 admission. Closes at the same time as the National on all days of the week, and the **Far Eastern Antiquities Museum** *at Skeppsholmen*, which contains one of the finest collections of Chinese art in the West.

Kaknastornet TV Tower • The tallest building in Scandinavia, 10 minutes by Bus #69 from the city's center (Karlaplan). An acrophobe's prayer and $1 will get you to the observation deck, open in summer from 9 a.m. to midnight.

Stockholm Information Service • Sponsors "**Miss Tourist**"; a telephone voice in English will give you facts on local events of interest. The program is changed daily. Just dial ☎ *221840.*

Your metropolitan oracle is the **Stockholm Information Service** *(Sweden House, Hamng 27*). It operates inquiry bureaus at the **Hotelcentralen** (*Central Station*), and from mid-May through mid-Sept. at the city hall.

CONCERTS

The midsummer performances under the sky at **Djurgarden** are marvels. They are also given in front of the **Maritime Museum**. Check the Tourist Center or the local papers for what's on and when. Opera and concert seasons begin in late Aug. or early Sept. at the **Royal Opera** (*Gustaf Adolfs Torg.*) and at the **City Concert Hall** (*Hotorget*), respectively. Movies: Original-language versions run with Swedish subtitles.

MARKETS

Hotorget is the public market in the center of the city. Here, by early Sept., you'll find vegetables, flowers, practically every kind of North Atlantic fish from minnows to whales—scads of things. Morning is the best time.

PUBLICATIONS

Stockholm This Week should be THE handbook for anyone who doesn't read Swedish. Available at tourist information offices and at most hotels.

WHERE TO SHOP

Glass handcrafts, ceramics, chocolate, and lovely household items, prints, and textiles are among popular items. The merchandise is a knockout; so, unfortunately, are most of the prices. Never bargain in Sweden. The merchants have bigger bank accounts than you or we have, and they couldn't care less if you "leave it lay." Jensen silver and Royal Copenhagen porcelain are heavily represented locally, but they sell for less in Denmark.

DEPARTMENT STORES

NK is the leader in Sweden for quality and variety. It was revamped last year and its individual boutique approach to merchandising met with instant success.

Ahlens, large and extremely modern, is good.

PUB, a cooperative, is lower-level and less interesting.

EVENING OR SUNDAY BUYING

The **Hotorget Station** (subway) and **Central Station** (basement) feature a cluster of merchandisers open until 10 p.m. daily, plus Sun. afternoons and evenings.

GLASS

The outstanding specialist for Orrefors, Kosta, and other Swedish beauties is **Svenskt Glas** (*Birger Jarlsgatan 8*). It's a small, exquisite Tiffanystyle establishment that has supplied the royal families of Sweden, Denmark, and England for more than 60 years. Engraved, pure crystal, art glass; colored multilayered, one-of-a-kind pieces; bar glasses, ashtrays, tableware, monogrammed ware, the works.

SWEDISH HANDCRAFTS

Svensk Hemslojd (*Sveavagen 44*) is an association founded in 1899 to preserve ancient Swedish handcraft skills by centralizing and marketing the best work of the best artisans and to encourage new techniques and new refinements. Every table, brass and iron, tea cozy, basket, apron, woodcarving, or other objet d'art (there are hundreds!) on these spacious, colorful, L-shape premises reflects the overwhelming success of these policies. Most employees are at home in our language. Look for the distinctive wooden Dalarna horse hanging over the entrance.

De Fyras Bod, "The Four Shop" (*Birger Jarlsgatan 12*), and **Konsthantverkarna** (*Master Samuelsgatan 2*) are also excellent for handicraft items.

Gunnarson (*Drottninggatan 77*) displays intriguing adventures in woodcarving.

HOME FURNISHINGS AND GIFTS

Svenskt Tenn (*Strandvagen 5*) has been a fixture in Stockholm for six decades. While their specialty is pewter handmade to their own designs, they also have furniture, cheerful hand-printed textiles, lamps (see the pleated shades that repeat fabric patterns), and hundreds of other objects.

ICELANDIC WOOL CLOTHING

Islands (*Jarntorget 83 in Old Town*) carries a wide selection of Alfoss ice wool stylings.

LAPPWEAR AND CRAFTS

If you are not mushing to the far north, then hike over to **Nordkalott Shopen** (*Norrbackagatan 48. You'll have to take the T-bahn to St. Eriksplan or Bus #47 to Karlbergsvagen*) to discover a full range of boots, clothing, jewelry, and carvings from the top of the world. If up in the Old Town, visit **Sameslojden** (*Sjalagardsgatan 19*).

SHOPPING CENTERS

The 5-block **Gallerian** even houses an English **Marks & Spencer**, the leading UK department store chain; across the street is **PK**, also very substantial.

Hotorgscity ("Haymarket") is near the concert hall. Architecture of tomorrow; central patio for refreshments; some (not all) top merchants represented here.

Sture Gallerian (*Grev Turegatan*) is an amusing shop-eat-swim complex in what were the Turkish Baths.

There is a 25% VAT (Value-Added Tax) on all purchases, but tourists are entitled to about a 15% cash refund. To take advantage of this savings, buy at the tax-free shops (there are over 13,000 of them!) displaying the blue and yellow tax-free sticker, carry your passport with you, and ask for a taxfree receipt or check with each purchase. (You must spend at least 101 SEK to be eligible for the rebate.) All packages must be intact on departure, complete with all exterior marks of identification, and submitted for inspection upon request at the tax-free service counter. Be sure to allow plenty of time at the airport because summertime lines at these desks can be long.

LAKE STORSJON

Intrigued by an unusual hunting expedition? Then head north to Lake Storsjon and search for the Swedish brother of the Loch Ness Monster, which was sighted again a few years ago by four workmen. King Oscar I long ago commissioned an official hunting party, and his ancient beastsnaring equipment can still be seen in the Ostersund City Museum. Accounts vary about this uncaught but oft-seen fellow. Some say he's black, others say he's brown. Some measure his length at 15 feet, some swear on the Bible that he's not an inch under 70 feet. But ALL agree on one observation: he wears a *very* sinister smile.

UPPSALA

It is so ancient that even New Uppsala is an antique. Old Uppsala goes back to the time of the Sveas, forebears of the Swedes of today. They were ruled by the Yngling Dynasty (not Asians as the name might suggest, but fellow noblemen) who defended a mighty realm and interred their kings in a trio of mounds which has drawn tourists since A.D. 500. The newer burg, site of one of the most venerable universities in Europe, was born prior to the Middle Ages. When Christianity came to town, it routed the heathens and established its own following. The nation's archbishop still considers Uppsala not only his own pulpit but also the seat of every Godfearing lay brother or sister in the land.

VAXHOLM

A quaint town, formerly a fishing village, about an hour out of the capital by bus or steamer. Situated along a narrow strait thronged with yachts, sailing vessels, motorboats, steamers, and ferries. The most interesting attractions are the 16th-century fortress, the town, the shops, and the lovely woodlands. A few small restaurants may be found. There is swimming at **Erikso** nearby.

VISBY

The chief town on the island of Gotland, due south of Stockholm and within easy reach of the capital. A walled city, it was a trading power of the Baltic, a link in the ancient Hanseatic League; it remains rich with medieval buildings and churches of the 12th and 13th centuries.

FOR MORE INFORMATION ON SWEDEN

USA Swedish Tourist Board • *655 Third Ave., 18th floor, New York, NY 10017*; ☎ *(212) 949-2333.*

Stockholm Information Service • Headquarters at Sweden House (Kungstradgarden), plus a summer tourist bureau at City Hall and a hotel booking office year-round at Central Railway Station.

The Swedish Tourist Board • Located at Sweden House, deals mainly with people in the communications world and officially is not open to the public; however, in an emergency it can offer advice and assistance in a limited fashion.

Youth Hostels • Comprising more than 270 shelters, farmhouses, and historic buildings, function chiefly during the summer months. For details write to *Svenska Turistforeningen* (Swedish Touring Club), *Box 25, S-10120 Stockholm*. Hitchhiking, incidentally, is sternly discouraged in Sweden.

Radio Stockholm • Broadcasts world news and local events for tourists Mon.–Fri. from 6 p.m.–7 p.m. from late June through Aug.

SWITZERLAND

Lucerne, Switzerland

With standards as high as their snow-tipped Alps, the Swiss command a special mandate on quality. It's a neat little nation where cleanliness is not only next to godliness but sometimes seems to be a notch above it. The cities are perfection itself; even the humblest farmhouses in the back-of-beyond are bowered with carefully pruned vines and bedecked with bright flower boxes; fields are so well groomed you'd think they were primping for a calendar photographer to preserve them everlastingly on film. For the tourist it's Valhalla, Nirvana, and Disneyland rolled into one. More than 60% of the nation is alpine, peaking at over 15,000 feet atop the glorious glacier-clad Dufourspitze in the Monte Rosa chain, only a few hours from downtown Geneva. The average height of those Helvetian mountains is well over a mile from the sea's surface and between the Alps and the Jura in the northwest lie the central plains of wildflowers and economic bliss—the powerhouse zone of Swiss industry that has made it one of the richest countries on earth.

But while it is the home of international banking, the repository of wealth, and the soul of stability, Switzerland need not be expensive. It suffers somewhat from an exaggerated press that has often focused on the luminaries who relax in Gstaad, St. Moritz, or those who confer with their gnomes at Zurich banks and visit their trust funds in cool green vaults. In fact, there are scores of value-plus boardinghouses, hotels, and inns where the sheets are crisp and sparkling, where the breakfast trays are heaped with croissants and buttered rolls, hot coffee and fruits from the abundant Swiss orchards—at prices that are astonishingly low. Many times we have gone skiing from lovely little chalet hotels where room and full board (delicious, too) came to roughly $50 per day per couple, while next door a glittering palatial hotel with the same vista, smaller balconies, and the same breakfast charged almost ten times the price we were paying. Both establishments were fine in their respective fashions, but you don't have to spend fortunes in Switzerland to enjoy its myriad pleasures.

Traveling around the country by bus or train is yet another delight. The national railroad network is 100% electrified and runs with the precision of a Swiss watch. There are several excellent money-saving ticket options by train or bus that are well worth checking out with your travel agent or the Swiss National Tourist Office.

Summer bristles with folk fairs, music and film fests, jazz concerts, cultural exhibits, and a multitude of gala events in historic, idyllic settings; in the mellow fall, the grape harvests provoke colorful wine festivals and seasonal celebration.

Any time and in almost any place in this southern niche of heaven, a special joy can be found—and, best of all, at an affordable price.

TIPS ON SWITZERLAND

FOOD

Switzerland has superb cuisine; it's not all chocolate and cheese, as many visitors suppose. The Swiss borrow from their four distinct culinary neighbors, but they also produce a prodigious kitchen of their own.

If you are traveling widely and want to save Alps of greenbacks, be sure to patronize any of Switzerland's 73 railway station restaurants. The standards are demanding, the quality is dependable, and the price for value just cannot be beaten. (As a comical note on this theme, we once met an American airline pilot from the Midwest

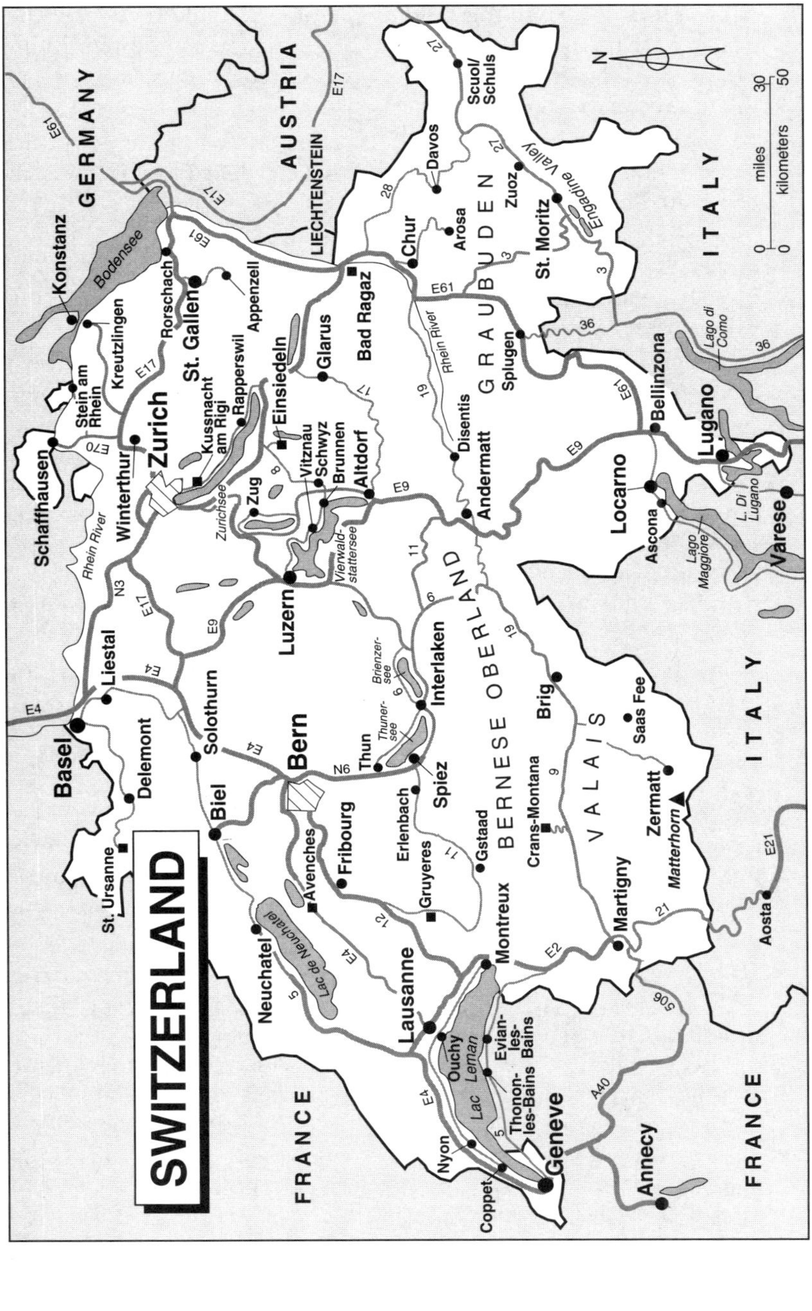
SWITZERLAND
GERMANY
AUSTRIA
LIECHTENSTEIN
FRANCE
ITALY
Konstanz
Bodensee
Kreutzlingen
Rorschach
St. Gallen
Appenzell
Stein am Rhein
Schaffhausen
Rhein River
Winterthur
Zurich
Kussnacht am Rigi
Rapperswil
Einsiedeln
Glarus
Bad Ragaz
Chur
Davos
Arosa
Scuol/ Schuls
Zuoz
St. Moritz
Engadine Valley
GRAUBUDEN
Splugen
Disentis
Andermatt
Bellinzona
Lugano
Lago di Como
Locarno
Ascona
Lago Maggiore
L. Di Lugano
Varese
Zug
Zurichsee
Vitznau
Schwyz
Brunnen
Altdorf
Vierwald-stattersee
Luzern
Basel
Liestal
Delemont
Solothurn
Bern
Biel
St. Ursanne
Thun
Thuner-see
Brienzer-see
Interlaken
Spiez
Erlenbach
Fribourg
Avenches
Gruyeres
Gstaad
BERNESE OBERLAND
Crans-Montana
Brig
Saas Fee
Zermatt
Matterhorn
VALAIS
Martigny
Montreux
Neuchatel
Lac de Neuchatel
Lausanne
Ouchy
Lac Leman
Evian-les-Bains
Thonon-les-Bains
Nyon
Coppet
Geneve
Annecy
Aosta
N
miles 0 30
kilometers 0 50
E61
E17
E70
E4
E9
E2
E21
N3
N6
A40
506

who—while going up to the mountains to ski—annually would change trains at a certain village because the station restaurant was so outstanding. We asked this bold navigator if he could remember the name of the town. "Oh, sure," he replied. "It was signposted 'BUFFET.' ") So always keep an eye out for Buffet, Switzerland—one of the top recommendations in this book.

Fondue and *raclette* usually are served in stuben or stubli, special rustic rooms within larger restaurants where the strong aromas can be isolated from other diners.

As for cheeses, every canton seems to have at least one. Go to a grocery store (such as the **Migros** Chain) and look over the stock. Usually an attendant will let you sample slivers. Then the ordering will be easier in restaurants.

Sausage is a national specialty and each region also has its own types. The big, fat Zurich version, a bologna with a Napoleonic complex, is one of the most succulent. Even more famous is the St. Gall Bratwurst. Order sausage with fluffy, hashed-brown potatoes called *Rosti*, and you're in for a treat. Out of the lakes, try perch or omble. Other typical offerings of this region include *Geschnetzeltes nach Zurcher Art* (thin-sliced veal with a cream sauce), *Zurcher Leberspiessli* (liver strips with sage seasoning, spit-roasted and served with beans), or *Ratsherrentopf* (mixed grill on a bed of rice or noodles).

Fine beef that is air-dried in the snow-tipped mountains for months, and then sliced in tissue paper-thin slabs, with freshly ground pepper then added to taste, is a specialty of the Valais and Graubunden. It is known variously as *Bundnerfleisch*, *Viande Sechee*, and *Viande Sechee des Grisons.*

DRINKS

Everything in the way of hard drink is available at prices that may freeze your tongue to the roof of your mouth. (The best economy is to buy your supply in a tax-free shop and set up a pharmacy in your own hotel room.)

Swiss wines? A very good buy, usually. They have a unique character: a freshness, a slight effervescence, a distinct tang. Most of them should be ordered young. (The wine, that is, not necessarily the buyer.) Request it in pitchers and take the pressing of the canton you are visiting. It will be much cheaper than bottled varieties and usually quite agreeable, especially the whites.

Try Fendant white and Dole red. You'll always be reasonably safe if you order either of these. Personally, we prefer the Cortaillod of Neuchatel to the Dole, but that's merely a matter of taste. Other satisfactory types, at random, are Oeil de Perdrix (Neuchatel, Valais, and Geneva areas), Maienfelder, Alstatter, and Churer-Schiller (St. Gall and Graubunden), Mont d'Or, Dezaley, and St. Saphorin (La-vaux), Torrente-Chateau la Tour (Valais), and Cru de Champreveyres or the sparkling whites of Bienne or Neuchatel.

Swiss beer is cheap and plentiful—but rather weak. The type made in the Valais is the exception. *Cardinal*, however, is probably the most popular lager type.

For teetotalers, the noncarbonated, natural white or red grape juice called *Grapillon* is wonderfully refreshing; about a big fat buck, and be sure that it's served icy cold. *Apfelsaft* is a pleasant and soft apple cider; the milk-based *Rivella* product is still taking the country by storm.

Kirsch, made from the juice of compressed cherry pits, is the national hard drink. *Pflumli* and *grappa* are often used to reduce the chill-factor of ski slopes.

Absinthe has long been banned by the government, but it is bootlegged all over the land. You'll find it in almost every rural inn or tavern—but the proprietor must trust you before he'll serve you, just as in the U.S. speakeasy days.

SUGGESTIONS FOR STUDENTS

Look (and book) into the superb Swiss hostels which are all over the land. Even if you are a non-student you may use them; all you must do is show membership in the **International Youth Hostel Assoc.** The Swiss **Student Travel Office** (*Backerstr. 52, Zurich*) arranges excursions and charter flights. London, Copenhagen, Stockholm, Prague, Moscow, and Tel Aviv were among the previous destinations that might or might not be repeated this year. Zurich or Basel are the jump-off points. They also offer climbing and hiking tours in the Alps, reduced 1-way student railway journeys, as well as ship sailings. For any of them, reserve in advance. That's the only way you'll get a ticket—and at these rates, they're worth an all-out effort. Incidentally in high season, travelers under the age of 26 are given preference; otherwise there is no age restriction or favoritism.

GETTING AROUND

TRAINS

Excellent. **Trains** are well scrubbed, wonderfully serviced, punctual, and amazingly speedy, even through the Alps. One of the fastest runs is made by the noon flier from Geneva to Zurich. Incidentally, both of these major cities have rail links from their respective international airports into town. Eurailpass, in any of its several forms, applies in Switzerland.

The food in the dining cars is excellent. Breakfast (ham and eggs—the works) costs around $8; lunch and dinner are about $15 and the selection is wide so that you can just have snacks if you wish. Service is polite, fast, and efficient except on crowded mainliners (e.g., Zurich-Geneva), when you may have to stand up for your sandwich and drink instead of disturbing an empty table that has been set up for a full meal. Good News! This year you may book onto a **Cheese Express** and dip into a fabulous fondue or raclette while the Swiss scenery aids digestion. The bad news is that the hospitable Swiss have added a **McDonalds Dining Car** to their benighted rail network. Is that why you traveled to Helvetia?

There are several classifications—and knowing what each does is important. First is the ordinary variety, full fare for 1-way trips. Validity in this point-to-point category is 6 months.

Second is the round-trip ("Return Rail") class, of up to 20% saving on the cost of 2 single rides. Validity varies between a day and a month depending on the distance traveled.

Third is the Swiss Pass. It can be issued in 3-day, 8-day, 15-day, or 1-month versions that allow you to travel at will around the country on rails, by steamer, on postal motorcoaches, or up and down numerous cableways. It also says "go" for travel on streetcars and buses in 30 Swiss cities. The savings can be tremendous for anyone who plans to move around a lot. The 3-day version (Flexi-Pass) is valid for 15 days, nonconsecutive. There are also benefits for transporting your car by rail, which can save needless hours of driving over passes or on snow-clad roads. Available at some rail depots or some branches of the Swiss National Tourist Office.

Fourth is the **Swiss Card** (and the Half-Fare Card) of a month's duration. These will take you to most of the principal tourist targets. For a modest lump sum, you receive a 50% discount and unlimited round-trip travel (train, bus, and boat).

Fifth is the Party type. Groups of at least 6 persons get a significant reduction, with a free "conductor" ticket for parties of 15 or more.

Children under 6 years of age ride as guests of the conductor; children from 6 to 16 (!) pay half-fare. With a Family Card (20SF), Mom and Pop who have valid tickets can take the kids along free (up to 16 years).

EXCURSION BUSES

Good to excellent. Many of the cross-country motorcoaches are air conditioned and equipped with wide-angle windows. You can also take the Postal Buses, which have an inbred advantage over trains: they travel over the high mountains and scenic passes through many villages while trains stay chiefly in the valleys.

MOTORING

The **Mont Blanc** (entirely in France but useful for a Swiss connection) and Great St. Bernard tunnels are both godsends. The former, a 2-lane, 15-minute run, cuts the winter Geneva-Turin distance from 500 to 170 miles. You'll be charged up to $28, depending upon the size of your vehicle. The latter is priced at a more modest $15 or so. The tunnel (10.1 miles) through the **St. Gotthard Pass** brings the Mediterranean countries about 2 hours closer to northern Europe. This connects with another all-weather subalpine autoroute and with Helvetia's longest bridge, running beside the beautiful Lake Lucerne—the whole package costing its citizens about 3/4-billion dollars! A lot of time can be saved by transporting your car right through the high ranges on rail flatcars. One of the most convenient in the north/south vector is the Loetschberg tunnel, but study your maps for others. You can sit inside your car as you ride.

PRIORITY ON MOUNTAIN ROADS

Priority is not given to the car on the outside here, but to the one headed uphill. The only exception is the postal bus, which always has the right of way when it blows its musical horn.

Watch your speedometer! Radar traps snoop all over the landscape. A violation of as little as 10 kilometers per hour (6 mph) over the limit can sock you with a 50-franc fine—payable on the spot. In general, the police are polite, correct—but oh so tough.

CAR HIRE

Europcar offers up-to-the-minute automobiles of all categories, both self-drive and chauffeur-driven; International Tour Organization for itinerary-planning, hotel reservations, theater and festival tickets, sightseeing excursions, and other services across Europe; interesting "Helvetian Hideaway" plan (in conjunction with Swissair) for 2 days of low-cost exploring.

Avis and **Hertz** also function in major towns or at airport locations.

BICYCLE RENTALS

Under the national railroads' program, you can easily hire one at any Swiss station and return it at any other. The cost is low.

SPORTS

SKIING

Both Alpine and cross-country activities dominate the winter, of course, but summer schussing is also an attraction at many resorts (some of which are described later in this chapter).

St. Cergue is about a half hour from the center of Geneva; **Zermatt** now has the highest glacier skiing in Europe. See St. Moritz and Zermatt under separate listings.

Other winter sports? Most cities and resorts now have ice rinks where you may rent skates (about $11); very often there's curling, too. Hockey and ice shows are additional features.

MOUNTAINEERING

For information on mountaineering centers, write the **Swiss National Tourist Office**.

Springtime's famous **Haute Route** comprises climbing, walking, and ski-touring in 6-day packages (April to June) along Europe's highest ridges. A week of guidance, most food, lodging in huts, lifts, and other transportation costs about $350; a good skier in top condition can make it, albeit with a certain amount of huff-and-puff. Write or phone the capable Dipl. Berg-Skifuhrer Franz Schwery, c/o Zermatt (☎ *028/672880*) for details of this unforgettable and magical experience. Franz is tough, smart, and fun to be with, too.

For serious rope and crampon work in the Zermatt area, count on a minimum of $150 per day for guide services; a few destinations are marked down to $90. (Never take an unofficial guide—that's akin to accepting cut-rate brain surgery!) Climbing equipment rentable. Details from Kurdirektor Amade Perrig at the Zermatt Tourist Office. Book your guide only through him; fees standardized.

A custom-made curtain raiser for both novices and more advanced cliffhangers? The **Riffelhorn**. Ride up the funicular from Zermatt to Riffelberg; then go by foot 1000 feet up a hogback. The **Matterhorn**, **Monte Rosa**, and a breathtaking panorama spread in front of you; peep over the rim for a glimpse of the glacier thousands of feet straight down. Perfectly safe and perfectly easy with a good guide. Take your lunch.

The Matterhorn can be climbed by nonprofessionals in good physical condition. Although still far from a cakewalk, the most hazardous portions were eliminated long ago. Extremely difficult faces remain for experts only. Dozens of lesser peaks in the same range await the amateur, but never try any without proper equipment and a guide.

HIKING

150 huts scattered throughout the Alps sleep a total of 6592. Installed by the Swiss Alpine Club, they are yours for the asking. Even in fine weather the taller mountains (over 3000 meters) are not without dangers; go prepared for the worst conditions even on short climbs, because the Alps have rapidly changing conditions. If you simply want to walk around the top of the Swiss world, most lifts will take you up in summer and bring you back to the valley if you don't care to hike down a path. In any case, take stout, rubber-toothed, ankle-high shoes; tennis and jogging shoes are too flimsy.

FISHING

Out of this aquatic world! Lake trout (20-pound fellows) periodically work their way up the tumbling mountain rivers; also salmon, rainbows, pike, graylings, and lazy fat perch in profusion. Take a fly without wings, one that looks a little starved, because the Palmer type doesn't work; or take worms and a bamboo pole. But always check first with the regional tourist office or you might be the critter that gets hooked. Permits are easy to obtain.

SIGHTSEEING

The **Gypsy Wagon Adventure** can provide a splendid slice of Helvetian trailblazing most sights unavailable to the conventional wanderer. The National Tourist Office tells it all, or ask any good travel agent to give you a brochure.

SPAS

In most of Switzerland's 22 spas you can combine a cure with daily excursions, shopping trips, museum visits, or pleasant smalltown strolls. For a complete list of the resorts, contact the **Swiss National Tourist Office** (*608 Fifth Ave., New York, NY 10020*; ☎ *(212) 757-5944*). Or, of course, the Swiss bureau in your area. (See "For More Information" at the end of this chapter.)

The SNTO can fill you in on a rainbow of special-interest activities and packages. To name a few: ballooning, chocolate yumyum tours, cycling, gourmandizing and cooking, golf, anti-stress programs, jazz, photography, riverrafting, stagecoach trips, tennis and summer skiing.

SHOPPING

Shopping hours are so varied that there's no good rule of thumb. Stores open anytime from 8 to 8:30 a.m.; some fold up for lunch from 12 or 12:30 p.m. to 1:30 or 2 p.m., while some stay open all day; most (not all) close at 6:30 p.m. on weekdays and midday or 5 p.m. on Sat.

Buying a watch? Fielding's *Shopping Europe* rates the watches of leading Swiss manufacturers and suggests guidelines every potential customer should know. Sorry, but space here is too limited to tackle this complex area, even in condensation.

WHERE TO GO

APPENZELL

Here is one of the oldest free cities in Europe, with a birth certificate going back to the 11th century. Today it is basically a dairy and textile center that sits dozing on the left bank of the Sitter River. As you approach it from St. Gall or Vaduz (Liechtenstein), it appears to be two-dimensional—precisely in the graphic form that their painters render with such charming manneristic style. Swiss evenings (outside of this canton) ripple with laughter over these people who are said to be the shortest in the nation. Though jokes abound, we have never found any difference in these hardy, musical, and delightful human beings. Don't be surprised if you see cattlemen or even soldiers wearing a single gold earring because this is a custom carried on into the present era. The main church is a glorious study in baroque art with painted panels, gilded altars, and ornate niches. There are scores of walks in the hills all mapped out for you; if you want to take a horse-drawn carriage (10 SF for 30 min. per person and half price for children), you'll find them in front of the Hotel Santis any summer day.

For overnighting, a good inexpensive bet is the **Taube**, a large brown chalet with white trim, and a preponderance of flower boxes under the windows and on the walls. For the **Alpenblick** you'll probably need a car, but the savings will make it worthwhile. In the village other choices include the smart **Adler** (breakfast only and very good), the **Lowen** (a bit commercial), the **Appenzell** (fine value), the Hecht (so-so), and the excellent but costly Santis.

For dining, the **Gasthaus Hof** reveals a rustic interior in bleached wood; there is also a pleasant garden restaurant. Inexpensive local dishes are offered. The **Wirtshaus Rossli** sports a weathered brown wood exterior with white curtains billowing from the windows and fringed with huge geranium plants. A fountain gurgles at the entry. The selection here is very slight, but the cold dishes may be just what you are looking for on a summer day. **Barli**, again flower-lined, offers a few tables in a tiny house down by riverside. Wonderfully fresh trout are caught from the Sitter at its doorstep. The **Linde**, the **Sonne**, and the **Drei Konige** are fair bets for light meals. If you have a sweet tooth, try the **Appenzell Biber** or the **Biberli**, which are filled, spiced pastry containing honey and almond paste. This is an eccentric little land that adores its independence. If you happen to be in the area on the last Sunday in Apr., don't miss the *landsgemeinde*, which is the cantonal democratic assembly held in the town square. Ancient costumes are worn during the colorful ceremony.

AROSA

Located in a fairly low vale 68 miles north of St. Moritz, this year-round playground is primarily a family place—drawing many native Swiss, Germans, Dutch, Belgians, and an increasing number of Britons. Ample ski slopes, cross-country trails, sports programs with qualified leaders, ski lifts, aerial cableways, and chair hoists; glorious 2-hour excursion up to 7600 feet over the famous **Arlenwald Circle** by horse-drawn sleigh; active ski school with more than 100 instructors; summer 9-hole golf course, horseback riding, tennis, fishing, gliding, rowing, alpine bathing "beach"; frequent rail connections with Lucerne or Zurich. You'll enjoy a stay at the **Merkur**, the **Central**, the **Excelsior**, or the **Valsana**, although they are all more expensive than the scores of excellent boardinghouses sprinkled over the town. The information center in midvillage can tell you each day where space is available.

ASCONA

This scenic city of **Ticino** (the Italian-speaking district) and its associated resort of Losone nestle on the sunny banks of **Lake Maggiore**. All watersports are available, plus golf, horseback riding, and tennis. But best of all for strong-legged adventurers are the fascinating walks that can be made from here. For lazybones, the main activity is sipping ices on the lakefront piazza. For shopping in lovely boutiques, viewing art galleries, and browsing, the cultural center is ideal.

Casa Moscia (☎ *351268*) is the name of the local youth hostel. Reasonable breakfast-only accommodation can be found at the **Piazza** (☎ *351181*) or the **Schiff** (☎ *352533*); both overlook the lake.

Elvezia (☎ *351514*) is another happy low-cost choice, offering the pleasant **da Ivo** restaurant with Italian specialties. During the summer months there are frequent musical presentations such as the New Orleans Festa, classic music weeks, and the jovial Muppets Festival. The soft textures of Italy are evident everywhere.

BASEL

A cultural dowager—a mere 2000 years old—who is so cosmopolitan that she shares her roots with both France and Germany, Basel is also a major financial center. The confluence of these social and economic wellsprings provides the city with a unique richness that discriminating voyagers appreciate. The **Kunstmuseum**, as one outstanding example, offers such variety, not to mention quality, that by itself warrants a visit to this warm-hearted metropolis; its many antiquities, its Holbein collection plus 28 other museums (most are free on Sun. and close on Mon.), its university (which was in operation before Columbus weighed anchor), its zoo, its extraordinary chemical plants, and its skyline on the Rhine are additional lures for adventures. Past the Lane of 11,000 Virgins, where stands the **Three Kings Hotel** (the nation's oldest), you'll find **The Bird's Claw** (engine-free ferry that spans the river as many as 300 times a day; cost: about 65¢). Ride to **Little Basel** to see the narrowest house and the smallest brewery, appropriate for this miniature sector. The **Carnival** in Feb. or Mar. or the **Swiss Industries Fair** in March are extraordinarily interesting; the former challenges anything that Hollywood could produce. The entire Old Town is turned over to pedestrian traffic, 24-hour revelry, parades, fests, and costly displays of costumery. If anyone would accuse the Swiss of being inhibited, they should first witness Carnival in Basel. If you plan to linger, the **Alfa** is reasonably priced. The **Admiral** is slightly higher in cost. Both, however, are good value for accommodation.

BERNE

The capital of Switzerland, one of the few undestroyed medieval cities of Europe, is charming. The Aare River divides it twice, in a horseshoe, and the turreted buildings on its banks look like an illustration from Grimm's Fairy Tales. The world's oldest and largest horological puppet show every hour in its historic **Clock Tower**, famous 15th-century **Bear Pits** housing the city's traditional mascots, excellent hotels (many low-cost pensions can be suggested by the Tourist Office in the station), fine little shops, covered sidewalks, winding streets dotted with beautiful polychrome antique sculpture and fountains, are in an almost rural atmosphere. The **Bristol** and the **Alfa** are very attractive hotels in the center; rates are reasonable. The **City** is a superb buy, too, in the moderate category.

CRANS-MONTANA

Though it started off only recently as an ultra-exclusive redoubt for European industrial captains, stars, and second-chalet Swiss, it now offers a broad enough innkeeping base for all usufructuares, regardless of social or financial status. From a resident population of around 5000 in the sleepy offseason, the crescent of hills that has lengthened on both ends of town can accommodate some 35,000 visitors. To cope with the high-season traffic jams, the citizens cleverly provided free transportation on bus shuttles—smart, convenient, and a perfect economic problem solver for all. This lately "discovered" Valais perch, 5000 feet above sea level, deserves a social ranking a few rungs below St. Moritz (best for skiing) and Gstaad. The excellent shops bear the names of stalwarts including Hermes, Dior, Pucci, and the like—but only a few yards away you can buy a wurst for 70¢ or stroll in the very same sun that reddens the face of Robert Redford. Virtually every major resort amenity available, including wonderful golf in summer. For a skiing holiday the **Etoile** is handy to the lifts. The **Regina** is very reasonably priced. **Des Melezes** and the **Serenella** are additional choices. Dine within your hotel pension plan because independent restaurants are quite expensive. If you are careful, prices will be in line with those of many far less glittery havens.

GENEVA

At the fringe of this graceful, peace-loving city, the lake is fantastically blue, except for the sparkling white plume of the world's tallest fountain—the **Jet d'Eau**.

The atmosphere is Gallic, the buildings are handsome, the gardens are bursting with color. The Old Town still thrives although it is structured by scenery out of the

Middle Ages. In Aug. the city is at its busiest and most festive. On the first of the month, the fete nationale is celebrated with bonfires. The next big bash comes at midmonth with the **Fetes de Geneve**—3 days and nights of street-revelry, confetti battles, parades, ballet, jazz concerts, folklore displays, the St. Hubert Auto Rallye, and numerous symphony concerts. All this is topped off by a gigantic fireworks display over the lake.

DIRECTORY

U.S. Embassy • *in Berne, the capital;* ☎ *031-437011.*

American Express • *7 rue du Mont-Blanc;* ☎ *7317600.*

Laundromat • Blanchisserie du Lac, *19 rue de Monthoux.*

American Mission • *3 av. de la Paix;* ☎ *7387613.*

Lost and Found • *7 rue des Glacis de Rive;* ☎ *7876000.*

Barber and Hairdresser • Williams at Cornavin station, ☎ *7317529.*

Dry Cleaning and Pressing • Netto, *2 Place Cornavin.*

Suit Rental • Balestra, *20 av. du Mail;* ☎ *284140.*

English-Speaking Doctor • Dr. P. Alphonse, *1 Ch. de l'Escalade;* ☎ *462108.*

English-Speaking Dentist • A. Tempia, Medecin-Dentiste, *46 boulevard des Tranchees;* ☎ *467540.*

Police • Central Headquarters, *19 boulevard Carl-Vogt;* ☎ *275111* or *117.*

Favorite Pawnshop • Caisse de Prets sur Gage, *5 rue des Glacis de Rive;* ☎ *7367525.*

HOW TO GET AROUND

Local public transit is swift, inexpensive, and spotlessly clean. Most of it originates on the place Cornavin, in front of the main railway station. From here, take Bus #8 or F to the Palais des Nations; Bus #1 to the Museum of Art and History (get off at Malagnou); Bus #5 or Trolleybus #3 to the University Library (disembark at place Neuve), or to the Palais Eynard (trolley stop in front); Bus #1 to the Museum of Old Musical Instruments (place Sturm is closest).

Please refer to what we've already suggested in connection with the Swiss Pass. The TPG (Transports Publiques Genevois) offers a 1-day pass valid on all buses, trams, and trolley-buses for close to $4; children charged about $2.50. Out-of-towners also gain reductions on downtown and suburban runs by purchasing a multiride card. These come in several forms available from machines along the TPG routes. When your card is inserted into a slot, consider yourself automated for travel.BIKES AND MOTORSCOOTER RENTAL AND PURCHASE

Most of the models you'll see on Geneva's streets are Italian. Don't be tempted to buy one here if you can make your purchase across the border. Bikes can be rented for $6.50 per 12-hour stint from the railroad station center.

CAR HIRE

If it's Swiss-managed it will be reliable. Try **Hertz** (*60 rue de Berne;* ☎ *7311200*); **Avis** (*44 rue de Lausanne;* ☎ *7319000*), which offers a bargain with its smallest range of cars; and **Budget** (*37 rue de Lausanne;* ☎ *7325252*), which is dependable. **Alsa** agency, we are told by local friends, offers very low rates. (*22 rue des Paquis;* ☎ *7329090*). In any case, if you book the vehicle yourself, you can usually qualify

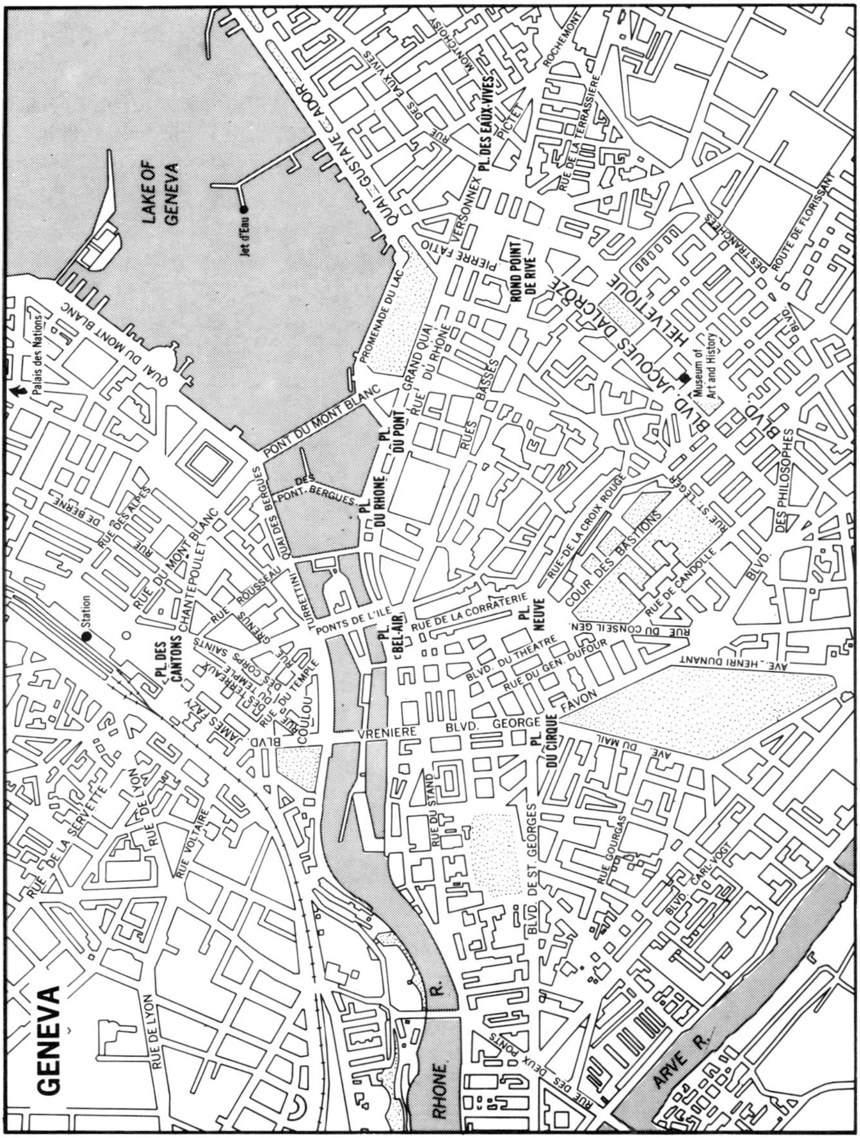
GENEVA
LAKE OF GENEVA
Jet d'Eau
Palais des Nations
QUAI DU MONT BLANC
QUAI GUSTAVE ADOR
RUE DES EAUX VIVES
MONTCHOISY
PL. DES EAUX-VIVES
PICTET
ROCHEMONT
RUE DE LA TERRASSIERE
VERSONNEX
PIERRE FATIO
ROND POINT DE RIVE
PROMENADE DU LAC
GRAND QUAI
QUAI DU RHONE
RUES BASSES
BLVD. JACQUES DALCROZE
HELVETIQUE
Museum of Art and History
DES TRANCHEES
ROUTE DE FLORISSANT
BLVD. DES PHILOSOPHES
PONT DU MONT BLANC
PL. DU PONT
PL. DU RHONE
PONT DES BERGUES
QUAI DES BERGUES
RUE DE BERNE
RUE DES ALPES
RUE DU MONT BLANC
CHANTEPOULET
RUE ROUSSEAU
GRENUS
TURRETTINI
PONTS DE L'ILE
PL. BEL-AIR
RUE DE LA CORRATERIE
PL. NEUVE
RUE DE LA CROIX ROUGE
COUR DES BASTIONS
RUE ST. LEGER
RUE DE CANDOLLE
RUE DU CONSEIL GEN.
BLVD. DU THEATRE
RUE DU GEN. DUFOUR
AVE. HENRI DUNANT
Station
PL. DES CANTONS
RUE DES CORPS SAINTS
RUE DU TEMPLE
DES TERREAUX DU TEMPLE
BLVD. JAMES FAZY
COULOU
VRENIERE
BLVD. GEORGE FAVON
PL. DU CIRQUE
AVE. DU MAIL
RUE DU STAND
BLVD. DE ST. GEORGES
RUE GOURGAS
BLVD. CARL VOGT
RUE DE LYON
RUE DE LA SERVETTE
RUE VOLTAIRE
RHONE R.
RUE DES DEUX PONTS
ARVE R.

for a hefty 20% discount (which would otherwise go into the pocket of your hotel concierge if he made the phone call for you).

WHERE TO STAY

LEAST $

In the following hotels the prices have hardly budged. The dollar value, however, related to the rock-hard Swiss franc, changes with frequency. Switzerland suffers from minuscule inflation worries; U.S. and Canadian dollars reflect variances in our economies since they are less constant than Switzerland's tidy management policies.

Paquis-Fleuri • *23 rue des Paquis;* ☎ *7313453.* A stunning choice with 12 glistening rooms and a quiet courtyard. No private baths, but all units have phones. American-style breakfasts.

Pension des Tourelles • *2 boulevard James-Fazy;* ☎ *7324423.* 23 large, clean rooms, several with balcony and river views. Rates of 50–60 SF, 70–90 SF, and 90–110 SF for singles, doubles, and triples, respectively. Good value, when you consider that these charges include breakfast and extras.

Grenil • *7 av. St. Clotilde;* ☎ *283055.* Run by YM-YWCA. Big, clean, modern, and inexpensive. Individual or dorm accommodations. Meals available. Convenient and roundly recommended. Especially appropriate for the young.

Cloche • *6 rue de la Cloche;* ☎ *7329481.* It's clean and well situated for sightseers and shoppers.

Central • *2 rue de la Rotisserie;* ☎ *214594* or *3114594.* Superior-grade family hotel for about 40 guests; rooms available with up to 5 beds; normal twin with bath about $33. Exceptional value.

Du Lac • *15 rue des Eaux-Vives;* ☎ *7354580.* Similar size and feeling of intimacy; prices roughly the same; bedchambers with radio and telephone. As sound as a Swiss franc, frankly speaking.

MORE $$

Montbrillant • *2 rue Montbrillant;* ☎ *7337784.* By the station and lately refashioned inside and out. Inexpensive restaurant; small bar for clients. Doubles start around $66 and all have private bath. Book rear to avoid track noises. Very helpful staff. Each departing guest usually receives a personalized bon voyage note plus a Swiss chocolate.

Luserna • *12 av. Luserna;* ☎ *441600* or *344-1600.* In Servette Quarter. Handy for motorists. Tidy suburban edifice; 30 agreeable rooms; 3 fresh attic charmers with skylights. Dual tariff of $42 or so. Run by Walter family.

Beau-Site • *3 place du Cirque;* ☎ *281008* or *328-1008.* Classic atmosphere and immaculately clean. Nicely renovated. Recommended.

Pension Saint-Victor • *1 rue Le Fort;* ☎ *461718.* Quiet semisuburban site on a traffic circle; 12 spacious, freshly scrubbed singles and only 1 antiquated but comfortable double. Nearly always full to capacity with long-term residents.

EVEN MORE $$$

The price level here rises to as much as $40 per noggin for a double and up to $60 for a single.

Grand Pre • *35 rue du Grand-Pre;* ☎ *7339150.* One of the best buys on the Geneva scene; 85 tasteful units—singles in front, doubles in back; only 6 singles without bath or shower. A crisp, happy atmosphere. Skilled staff. Abundant rewards. Easy access to midtown or the airport.

De Berne • *26 rue de Berne;* ☎ *7316000.* Extensively restyled; lobby and bar inviting with woody touches; soundproof windows; air conditioning; efficient and snap-crackle clean. Professional management. Midtown location.

Hotel d'Alleves • *13 passage Kleberg;* ☎ *7321530.* 40 large, individually decorated rooms, all with bath or shower; 5 penthouse duplexes. Most units with phone, radio, TV, and scale. Wide variance in rates, so check your choice of accommodation first thing. Popular Le Mazot restaurant; $9.50 noon menu.

Hotel du Midi • *place Chevelu;* ☎ *7317800.* Dining salon, snack bar, and cafe (for wines, raclettes, or fondues); 82 spiffed-up accommodations, all with tub, telephone shower, heated towel racks, small refrigerator, safe, scale, clock-radio-phone console, doublepane windows, and sewing kit.

Lido • *8 rue de Chantepoulet;* ☎ *7315530.* Smaller, more economical option near station. No meals. Nearly all 32 cozy rooms with private plumbing. TV on request. Reserve one of the 15 rear lodgings. Cordial management. Recommended.

Excelsior • *34 rue Rousseau;* ☎ *7320945.* Writing salon; breakfast nook; bar/snack-bar combo. 50 colorful chambers with radios and telephones throughout. Top-floor spreads with balconettes. Column composed of #15, #25, #35, #45, and #55 boast 2 bathrooms each—one with shower, toilet, and basin, and the other with tub, bidet, and sink. Highly commendable.

CAMPING

There are several sites in the Geneva canton. You'll probably need a map and perhaps some specific instructions on how to find them from the **Touring Club of Switzerland** (*9 rue Pierre-Fatio;* ☎ *7358000*). The list is as follows:

Pointe a la Bise • *1222 Vesenaz;* ☎ *7521296; bus E from R. Point de Rive.*

d'Hermance • *Chem des Glerrets;* ☎ *7511483; bus E from R. Point de Rive.*

Du Val d'Allondon • *Route des Granges;* ☎ *7531515; direction Chatelaine-Peissy.*

Sylvabelle • *10 Chem. de Conches; bus #8 or 88 from R. Point de Rive.* This would be my last chioice.

All charge about $2 per person, a franc less for a tent or trailer, and still less for parking your car. Be sure your sleeping bag is warm.

SUGGESTIONS FOR STUDENTS

There are hordes of foreign students in Geneva. The main campus, on the *rue de Candolle*, is where you'll meet most of your confreres. This old and beautiful section forms the southwestern edge of the *promenade des Bastions.* University institutes are scattered throughout the city.

From June to mid-July, classes will still be in session; therefore, special lodgings for you will be tight. Your best bets are: the **Cite Universitaire** (*46 av. de Miremont*) with bunks from $6 to $14, the **Centre Protestant** (*2 av. du Mail*), the **Centre Catholique** (*30 rue de Candolle*), and the excellent **Auberge de Jeunesse** (*rue Rothschild 28-30;* ☎ *7326260*). There are about 2 dozen additional houses or dorms to which the tourist office can direct you, but the above four are good for starters. All will do their damnedest to try to squeeze you in. Most charge about $7 per night.

DINING

Restaurant Universitaire (*rue Hugo-de-Senger 4*) open 10 a.m.–3 p.m.; closed weekends; **Cite Universitaire** (*above address*) 7 a.m.–10 p.m.; **Universitaire Internationale** (*rue de Paquis 63*) 7:15 a.m.–8:30 p.m.; closed weekends; **Le Zofage** (*rue de Voisins 6*) 7 a.m.–midnight.

STUDENT AID

Infor Jeunes (*rue Verdaine 13; ☎ 3114422*) is your best source; functioning Mon.–Fri. from 10 a.m. to 6 p.m.; with phone answering service until 10 p.m.

WHERE TO EAT

LEAST $

Before jumping behind a napkin, perhaps you'd enjoy an informal stroll along the *rue des Etuves* where tiny cafes compete to lure the best accordionists in the district. You can drink and snack your way from one serenade to another. It's proper, incidentally, to leave a tip of a franc or so for the star musician.

Au Pied du Cochon • *4 place du Bourg de Four; ☎ 7204797.* Specializes in pig's feet. Turn-of-the-century atmosphere. Boisterous crowd of students and coffee-house types. Huge portions of "trotters" come in 4 different styles at around $6.50; succulent when simmered in Madeira; other meat dishes also available. Onion soup is a low-cost appetite quencher.

Vedia-Rive • *rue du Rhone 65; ☎ 7355211.* Produces good pizzas in amiable surroundings. Low-cost plats du jour; short orders available. Personality of a large modernized tavern. Cozy and recommendable for light or ravenous appetites.

Casanova • *3 quai du Mont Blanc; ☎ 7322566* and **La Cascade**, *19 quai des Bergues; ☎ 7322566.* Italian, French, and Swiss cuisine; $7 lunch plates; cheerful service. Both with outdoor dining in balmy weather. Lake vista at former; Rhone view at latter. A very worthy pair.

Cafe de Paris • *26 rue du Mont Blanc; ☎ 7328450.* Serves but one thing—and it's possibly the most popular restaurant in Geneva: Steak with Cafe de Paris sauce, French fries, and salad for about $13; pitchers of wine. Packed always, and absolutely delicious.

Relais de l'Entrecote • *49 rue du Rhone.* A close facsimile offering same fare and excellent sweets. Slightly cheaper and more attractive. The atmosphere is more to our taste.

Cafe Restaurant de la Pointe • *6 rue Villereuse; ☎ 7367680.* Specializes in Steak au Poivre. Inexpensive and piquant.

Bistro du Boucher • *15 av. Pictet-de-Rochemont (in the Old Quarter); ☎ 7365636.* Folklore-ish ambience. Handsome presentation; sound food. Heavy local trade but increasingly popular with foreigners.

Au Viet-Nam • *rue de Monthoux 56; ☎ 7325849.* Happy, unpretentious nook offering Vietnamese and Chinese comestibles; (former are lighter, crisper, and drier than the latter); 10 plain tables up front and 6 rearward. Staples include meatballs in soy sauce, sweet-and-sour meatballs, pork and onions, chicken and bean sprouts (all $7), and Imperial (egg) Rolls ($2.25 each). Superior value. Closed Thurs. and Fri. until 7 p.m. and the month of July.

PIZZAS

Siesta • *7 rue Versonnex; ☎ 7359696.* Close to the center; *plats du jour* about $6.50. Strongly recommended.

Navy Club • *31 place Bourg de Four, in the Old Town.*

L'Age d'Or • *11 rue Cornavin;* ☎ *7313093.*

PUBS

Britannia • *6 place Cornavin;* ☎ *7325960.* Diagonally opposite the station, dispenses suds, salads, and more solid staples daily. Sidewalk tables; dartboard. Entrecote, French fries, asparagus, stewed tomatoes, and salad at $10 were right for the price.

Coutance Bar • *16 rue de Coutance;* ☎ *7327445.* Presents spotless maintenance, delicious Entrecote, and sensible limits of $10-or-so for full-course dining; packed at meal hours and worth trying.

Mr. Pickwick • *80 rue de Lausanne;* ☎ *7316797.*

Duke of Wellington • *3 rue Etienne-Dumont.*

COINTRIN AIRPORT

Counter-and-table service at the same altitude as public observation deck. Average plates about $9. **Restaurant Le Plein Ciel**, **Le Cercle Bar**, and **Le Rotisserie** One flight above are more elegant. Same runway vista for about twice the price. At Cointrin Station you'll find **Aux Bonnes Choses** pizza and plat du jour, **and La Marmite**, and brasserie.

SNACKS

When economic paralysis sets in, trot over to *22 rue du Mont-Blanc* for a Big Mac and a milkshake; not very Swiss and you can easily find a fondue for a similar outlay, but sometimes ethnicity calls.

During shopping hours try **Manora** on the ground floor of Placette Department Store. Plats du jour served at 3 fixed-price levels. **Couic-Self-Service** in same emporium has plates at $2.75; fare is good. Also a stand-up **Ski Bar** for light bites in the Sports Department.

SELF-SERVICE OR CAFETERIA DINING

Migros grocery and department stores all over the nation often have snack bars with wonderful food at low prices. There are several in Geneva (35 on last count), so ask locally. If you are packing a picnic, these are the best for price and quality all over Switzerland.

MORE $$

Olivier de Provence • *13 rue Jacques-Dalphin.* Outstanding family-run enterprise; 14 tables with candle illumination and kitchen chairs. Savory calves' liver and big-casseroled potatoes au gratin the top attraction here. Advance reservations necessary. Popular, and rightly so.

Movenpick • The various links of this well-known chain offer a wide gamut of price levels. Complex on *rue du Cendrier* serves excellent roast beef and Yorkshire pudding. Upstairs Beef Club divided into dining trio plus bar. Outstanding grills; a variety of cuts and prices. Spitted chickens $8; 7 p.m. Tues. smorgasbord $12. Huge dessert menu. Open noon–2:30 p.m. and 7-midnight. Ground-floor Pep Center provides hot plates, cold plates, and pastry from 12 to 12. The place de la Fusterie branch also going strong. Embraces a lounge, cafe, terrace, small bar, rotisserie, and the de la Mouette, which has become so fashionable that many of the local elite give dinner parties here. Operative partially or wholly from 7 a.m. to 1 p.m., depending on the dining area. In the less expensive sections (not Beef Club or Mouette), a full meal costs about $14.

Movenpick has yet another pair of entries in this city (plus dozens all over the nation). They are uniformly reliable and attractive.

Edelweiss • *2 place de la Navigation.* A handsome "alpine chalet" constructed inside the building. Outfitted with every tourist gimmick in the 10,000-page Typical Helvetian Decorator's Handbook. Presentation so unabashed it comes off remarkably well. Menu selection spare, but portions generous. Above-average quality for a dine-and-dance restaurant. Twin-meal bill plus entertainment and combo music could peak at close to $65. Decidedly worth seeing and trying if you're in a mood to splurge.

Cafe de la Mairie • *20 place du Marche in Carouge.* Whomps up tasty fish and meat platters in several fashions; exceptional *lapin a la moutarde* (rabbit in mustard sauce) and *polenta* for about $14. I was impressed by the ambitious menu.

Auberge Communale de Confignon • *6 place de l'Eglise;* ☎ *7571944.* On hill overlooking city; about 10 minutes out by car or perhaps 15 minutes via bus #2. Fast, friendly service. Superb food—especially meat. Samples: *Quenelles de Brochet* (1 order for 2 is enough); *Coquille St. Jacques* (also a large portion); huge *Cote de Boeuf* served with tarragon butter; delicious Souffle de Brochet; excellent wines. Locals highly praise several chicken selections, *Carre d'Agneau,* and game in season. Uninhibited ordering could raise your tab to at least $30 per person. Although you won't find this one loaded with tourists, reserve in advance; savvy Genevois pour in nightly; in summer try to book on terrace for inspiring view.

Roberto's • *10 rue Pierre-Fatio.* Turns out lip-smacking Swiss and Italian cookery with main dishes and *plats du jour* at $13; specialties from about $10; Roberto's pastas are famous for their freshness; excellent tortellini in cream sauce. Deadline for lunch orders at 2 p.m.; for dinner at 10:15 p.m. Sometimes haughty service. Closed Sat. night and Sun.

Les Armures • *1 Puits St.-Pierre.* Half dozen rooms on 3 floors. I favor downstairs Oubliettes. Cozy dungeon bar. Reasonable price tags. Chef does great racelette ($2.40 per plate, minimum 3 portions); fondue $9.50; mountain-dried beef thinly sliced $10.25; Assiette Maison $11. Half-liter of "open" wine $7.50. A recent meal better than ever. Open 8 a.m.-1 a.m.

NIGHTLIFE

Geneva is expensive any time of day—and more so at night—because it is filled with bankers and their visiting clients, expense-account executives, and UN diplomats whose treasury ministers sign the chits. Some of these—and especially the last group, who are spending taxpayers' money—can very easily waltz through $1000 per evening.

Midnight Rambler • *21 Grand-Rue.* Up in the Old Town (which is lovely itself for midnight rambles and browsing along the cobbled streets at the windows of antique shops). Dancing begins at 9 p.m.; closed Mon.

Grillon • *5 place de la Fusterie* or *12 passage Malbuisson.* Has a wide following—from agile young people to portly money managers and their svelte escorts. Entrance one flight up; dance floor. Eye-stabbing spectrum of colored lights; bouncy-to-corny orchestra; beer at a heady $3 per glass; whisky about $5. T'aint much, but it's something.

La Clemence • A place more interested in purposeful drinking. Amiable crowds and smoky ceilings; 7-table terrace for fair-weather persuasions; no dancing; no food; inexpensive drinks. Locals sometimes call this house *La Cloche* (The Bell), because its tower rang out the pardons of prisoners in the Middle Ages. Closed Sun.

Griffin's Club • *36 boulevard Helvetique.* Officially a private club and consequently appeals more to a limited audience of uppercrust residents or frequent visitors. Pleasant, subterranean hideaway; dining-room service from 8 p.m. to 3 or 4 a.m.; rustic but slick banquettes and low executive chairs. Fashionable and costly.

Le Petit Palais • *6 rue Tour-de-Boel.* A split-level cave with 2 alternating combos and a crowded dance *piste.* Good service; well ventilated; whiskey for $8; open until 3 a.m.

Pussy Cat Saloon • *15 Glacis de Rive.* Sharing its main portal with Le Club 58, features shows at 10 p.m. and midnightly. Edwardian decor; good strip in the style of Paris' Crazy Horse; $5 entrance on weekends.

Club 58 • A disco haunt that is hyperactive—for Switzerland, that is.

Au Byblos • *3 rue de la Boulangerie.* Popular with youngsters. Drinks about $6.50; a bit higher on weekends; ragged Levis almost *de rigueur* in this no-alcohol spot.

Harry's New York Bar • *8 rue Confederation.* Chiefly for leisurely toping in the predictable pattern that Harry's evoke. Superb salads, pasta, ham-and-cheeseburgers; clubby atmosphere and nice service. The prices are very reasonable.

Brasserie Lipp • On an upper tier above Harry's and cleverly integrated into the Old Town via a patio. Windows overlook a terrace with greenery from a Belle Epoch salon. Next door in the same Confederation complex is a Creperie for delicious low-cost snacks.

A Mortimer • *2 Bourg-de-Four.* Fun in a similar casual tone.

New Mylord • *84 rue du Rhone.* Has made a successful comeback after a dark age.

PRESLEEP SNACKS

Mazot (*16 rue du Cendrier*) is especially popular with the after-theater set. Movenpick outlets encourage self-service lines that bustle with yawning locals until the sinfully late Swiss hour of 12:30.

WHAT TO SEE AND DO

There are quite a few sights you shouldn't miss, plus one you can't miss.

The latter is the **Jet d'Eau**—a 110-gallon-per-second water spout that drenches the wings of unwary angels who hover less than 410 feet above the lake. Visible from miles around practically every day between Apr. and Sept.

The first "must" is the **Palais des Nations**, former home of the League of Nations and the current UN headquarters in Europe. Magnificent arbored setting beside Lake Leman; open to the public daily from April to October (except Sat. and Sun.) from 10 a.m. to noon and 2 p.m. to 4 p.m.; closed during the Christmas holidays; multilingual guides; hundreds of interior and garden attractions; $5 general admission, $3 for military personnel, free for children.

The venerable **Museum of Art and History** (*rue Charles-Galland*) offers a section devoted to the history and development of Swiss timepieces. Another segment has a large collection of Van Goghs, Dufys, Chagalls, Rouaults, and Gauguins, plus examples of Rodin. Best of all, it won't cost you 1 centime. Gates open from 10 a.m. to 5 p.m. all week except Mon.

The nearby **Petit Palais Museum** (*2 Terrasse St.-Victor*) is evoking critical acclaim. The 17th-century townhouse contains works from 1890 until the present. It focuses in depth on certain periods. There are not just a few, but scores of paintings from a given year or decade that recreate the ambience of the art world at that given time. Entrance fee around $6 or $3 for students.

If you are a historian, the **Reformation Wall** and the **Town Hall** provide plenty of atmosphere and understanding of the local Swiss political ferment.

St. Peter's Cathedral contributes a religious element, the basis of the reform movement anyway.

Scholars might enjoy looking through the papers of Jean-Jacques Rousseau in the **Public** and **University Library** (*promenade des Bastions*); no charge; 9 a.m.–noon and 2–5 p.m.; Sat. mornings only and closed on Sun.; toddling over to the **Museum of Old Musical Instruments** (*23 rue Lefort, at side of Russian Cathedral*); 85¢ admission; or sifting through the memorabilia at the **Voltaire Museum and Institute** (*25 rue des Delices*). These form a minor part of this city's treasure chest; to really dig into the gold, pick up the brochure at the Tourist Office titled *Discover Geneva*, which lists 42 targets plus the details on admission charges, hours, and which banker's wife commissioned what block of sculpture at which time of day on May 6, 1559.

Daily motorcoach tours cover these landmarks—as well as other sights—for about $17 per person. Departures from the main bus terminal on *place Dorciere*. Guides speak English, French, and Spanish (sometimes, sad to say, all at once). Make certain yours speaks intelligibly before stepping aboard. ☎ *7314140* to discover when your own language group is scheduled to rendezvous.

In Aug. Geneva is at its busiest. For openers, on the first, the fete nationale is celebrated with bonfires. The next big jubilee comes during the mid-month Fetes de Geneve—3 days and nights of open-air dancing and drinking on the quays, confetti battles, weekend afternoon parades, ballet, music, and folkway performances imported from other continents, capped by a gigantic fireworks display over the lake. Spliced into the 31-day revelries are outdoor jazz concerts, the Hunters' Fanfare, and numerous symphonies.

SWIMMING

Geneva's **municipal pool** costs $4.50 per dunker. Plenty of water skiing on the lake. Ask the Geneva Tourist Office where and how to arrange a tow.

CONCERTS

For big names and big orchestras, **Victoria Hal** seems to stay about the busiest of the musical centers in the city. Leading soloists perform regularly at the **Conservatoire**.

The **Grand Theatre** houses a ballet company, an opera troupe, a choir, and the famous Orchestre de la Suisse Romande; the only problem is obtaining a ticket to any performance. Last, if you have youngsters in tow, they would probably enjoy the **Theatre des Marionnettes de Geneve**.

MOVIES

While basically they appear in their original language versions, in some cases the language of the region (French in this area) is dubbed in instead. The local newspapers normally indicate which type is being shown at what particular hour. If in doubt, any good concierge will check this out for you.

PUBLICATIONS

La Semaine a Geneve (*The Week* in Geneva) tells it all. This series is also produced for all major centers in the nation. It lists the standard tourist attractions plus outstanding events.

These are merely drops in the bucket. Ask the **Geneva Tourist Office** (*Gare Cornavin;* ☎ *7385200;* FAX *412679*) for their brochures, maps, pamphlets, and flyers. They can also fix hotel reservations and excursion tickets.

WHAT AND WHERE TO BUY

Main shopping street? The long stretch named at various points *rue de la Confederation*, *rue de Marche*, *rue de Croix d'Or*, and *rue de Rive* is the hub. The *rue du Rhone* is also worth stalking.

SWISS ARMY KNIVES

Coutellerie du Mont Blanc (*rue du Mont Blanc 7*) is the leading edge for all sorts of cutlery. They will even engrave your name on a knife for free.

SWISS CHOCOLATES

Any **Migros** grocery store sells their own brand of chocolates at phenomenally low prices for such quality. We would even defy you to discern the difference between this grocer's labeling and, let's say, the much, much more expensive Lindt & Sprungli chockies. What a saving!

GOLD COINS FOR BRACELETS

The larger banks sell many kinds of gold coins from many lands, some for collection and some for investment. Be especially wary of $20 U.S. gold pieces; some rascals mint beautiful new ones—with plastic cores! Before buying, be certain to have all gold coinage weighed and be sure you receive the same coins that were put on the scales.

SWISS HAND-EMBROIDERIES

Langenthal (*rue du Rhone 13*) tops 'em all for delicacy. Many gift items such as funny pot-holders and pincushions (heart-shape) are very low in price.

FLEA MARKET

Many bargains (if you know your target items well) at **Plaine de Plainpalais**. The mornings of Wed. and Sat. are active, but oft-times it remains busy into the afternoons. Some of the city's leading antique dealers now operate in this area.

ONE OF THE BIGGEST DRUGSTORES IN THE WORLD

Pharmacie Principale (*Confederation Centre*). Everything from dried pimpernel flowers to turtle oil to maternity garments to miniature chamois to bikinis. If you look hard enough, you'll also find toiletries and medicine!

DEPARTMENT STORES

Le Grand Passage and **Placette** take top billing. **Hennes** and **Mauritz** (H & M) (*41 and 40 rue du Marche*) is a clothing emporium with stunning bargains for both sexes.

GRINDELWALD

Thirteen miles up the valley from Interlaken, you'll discover this tiny toenail on the foothills of the magnificent Bernese Oberlands. Europe's longest gondola will set you atop the point called

First for a fantastic view of the spires above and the Lilliput below. A rack-railway scrambles up the 2-mile-high **Jungfraujoch** to the loftiest station in the Alps. Flanking this is the infamous "North Wall" of the **Eiger**, that formidable barrier of stone and ice that has taken the lives of so many climbers. The Jungfrau is next door. It is easy to visit the Grindelwald Glacier and its gorge. In town there is swimming, skating, and curling at the Sport Arena. For ordinary hiking it is one of the better choices in the nation because the valley itself is low enough to exhibit greenery and flowers. Higher valleys above the tree line often resemble moonscape once the snows have melted and only the rock shows through. For its great beauty, one of the leading excursions on the Swiss map. The **Hirschen** is pretty good for accommodation, and it has the assets of being smack in the center and low in cost. **Alpine**, also central, is a solid bet and the **Weisses Kreuz** is almost adjoining the rail depot. For more tranquil digs, try the Silberhorn. If you really want to pamper yourself, go to the lovely refashioned **Belvedere** and the caring hospitality of the Hauser family.

INTERLAKEN

A perennial favorite, due largely to the Flower Clock, the Castle, the 12th-century Castle Church, the legendary view of the Jungfrau from the hotels lining the **Hoheweg**, the **Music Festival**, and medieval **Unterseen**. The funicular up the **Harder Kulm**, the **Ibex Preserve**, and the circle trip to the Jungfraujoch (Lauterbrunnen and Kleine Scheidegg) are musts, and the Schilthorn plus Piz Gloria (via Murren) are spellbinding too. Have lunch in the revolving top-of-the-world restaurant, which is the manmade finial of the piz (Romansh for "peak"). Cruise on the lakes of **Thun** and **Brienz** (the latter village known for its woodcarving); **Thun**, **Spiez**, and **Oberhofen** bristle with Middle Age castles. The drive from **Montreux** to **Lucerne** via **Interlaken** threads along the shores of 5 lakes and through innumerable alpine vistas. The area fairly oozes with things to do and see. For overnighting, you'll probably never forget the **Gasthof Hirschen** at neighboring **Matten** on the edge of town; the architecture is *chalet Suisse* and as charming as can be imagined. Rates are reasonable, food is good, there's garden dining in summer, and the people (Peter and Marian GrafSterchi) are kind. (☎ *036-221545*)

LAUSANNE

About 40 minutes from Geneva, this academic enclave is the second key center for holidays in French Switzerland. Unusually beguiling climate, with a record of 1912 hours of sunshine per year. Its university and schools are world famous. It offers good sports, entertainment, and food, along with the world's shortest subway and a rather somnolent lakeside aura. Also the **Olympic Museum** (*avenue Ruchonnet 18*); free admission; variable opening hours so inquire locally before setting out. For shelter, excellent values can be had at **Maisons Pour Etudiants** (*64 av. de Rhodanie*; ☎ *6178154* and at 3 ch. des Falaises), **Centre Universitaire Catholique** (*29-31 boulevard de Grancy*; ☎ *276066*), at **Foyer Unioniste de Lausanne**, **Le Cazard** (*15 rue Pre-du-Marche*; ☎ *205261*), **Foyer la Croisee** (*15 av. Marc-Dufour*; ☎ *204231*) and at the **Youth Hostel** (*1 ch. du Muguet*; ☎ *265782*). The **Pension Bienvenue** (*2 rue du Simplon*; ☎ *262986*) reserves its bienvenues for ladies only. Quality hotels include the **Alpha-Palmiers** (*congress center*; ☎ *230131*), the **City** (*rue Caroline 5*; ☎ *202141*) and, for longer stays, the **Agora** (*av. Rond-Point 9*; ☎ *6171211*). The new **Movenpick-Radisson** offers 365 superb units and upscale prices; nevertheless, it's good value for francs. For more details, zoom in on the **Lausanne Tourist and Convention Bureau**, (*2 av. de Rhodanie, CH-1006*; ☎ *021-6177321*). One of its newsy brochures lists almost 50 choices of lodging houses or pensions for clean, reliable accommodation. Ask about the special bargains in transportation available for the city and region.

LEYSIN

Here in the Alpes Vaudoises is a fully developed, high-pulse winter sports and summer mecca. It is 13 miles by road or 4 by rail from the lake-level junction of Aigle.

Admirably situated on a sun-catching slope, with a glorious panorama below; 2 teleferics to the tips of the **Berneuse** and **Mayen**; a score of very simple hotels provide all the basics for base-rock rates; restaurants similar in concept; heavy patronage by Swiss and English *en famille*; a varied ski-lift capacity can handle almost 12,000 passengers per hour; there's a vast **Sports Hall** and ice rink, swimming pool—even an American football field!

LOCARNO

Young sprogs might find it a bit too sleepy for long-term loafing, but it's a natural stop for the motorist to or from Italy. It's serene and tranquil, with a lovely setting on the shores of **Lake Maggiore**; the Ticinese here are among the most warmhearted and hospitable people of Switzerland. One of the scariest (absolutely safe!) cable-car ascents in the Alps; **International Film Festival** every Aug.; quiet, friendly atmosphere. While top-line hotels cater to the carriage trade, the **Mirafiori** and the centrally sited **Beau Rivage** are exceptional values with fine views and are within easy walking distance of the waterfront activity.

LUCERNE

Here is one of the most beautifully situated towns of Switzerland. Lake Lucerne, also called Lake of the Four Forest Cantons (*Vierwaldstattersee*), is surrounded by mountains, most notably the Rigi and Pilatus. What could be more fetching to the tourist's eye than the reflected Alps in the snow-pure waters, the medieval town walls, the tiered spires, and the covered bridges? Located where the Reuss River cascades from the lake, Lucerne originally grew around the 8th-century monastery of St. Leodegar and became an important trade center on the St. Gotthard route. If you are looking for postcard scenery, look no further. If, however, you are looking for a different Lucerne, find the iron pole in front of the rail station, which can point you to 27 other foreign manifestations of this Helvetian city. Examples: Lucerne, Brazil (5630.4 miles), Lucerne, Wyoming (4400.9 miles), and Lucerne, Maine (3137.1 miles).

DIRECTORY

U.S. Consulate • Zurich, *Zollikerstr. 141*; ☎ *01/552566*, is the nearest.

Barber and Hairdresser • Live For Hair, *Museggstr. 4*; ☎ *511228*; Louis Klauser, *Hofstr. 1*; ☎ *513566.*

American Express • *Schweizerhofquai 4*; ☎ *501177.*

Dry Cleaning and Pressing • Exacta, *Alpenstr. 5.*

693Suit Rental • Beth Spani, *Bundesplatz 1*; ☎ *232305.*

English-Speaking Doctor • Check the list at the Tourist Office.

English-Speaking Dentist • Dr. H. P. Brunner, *Pilatusstr. 5*; ☎ *233545*, or Dr. Felix Epelbaum, *Murbacherstr. 19*; ☎ *233322.*

Police • Central Station, *Obergrundstr. 1*; ☎ *217711.*

Favorite Pawnshop • Pfandleihanstalt Lucerne, *Munzgasse 5*; ☎ *234939.*

HOW TO GET AROUND

Within the town, walk or ride a bike to see and enjoy more. Because distances are rarely taxing, jaunts are so rewarding that the Tourist Office has mapped out special walking tours. Pick up its Little City Guide, outlining these itineraries.

All **trolley cars** and **buses** can be boarded at Station Square. In many cases you can purchase tickets from automatic vending machines before boarding. Cars on these routes carry no conductors; drivers will refuse your silver. To save time, read the English-language instructions posted at the stops.

WHERE TO STAY

LEAST $

This city is so frustratingly tight that we offer the following possibilities: make Lucerne a day-trip excursion point from your headquarters in Zurich or elsewhere in eastern Switzerland; check the opportunities at the Youth Hostel Am Rotsee ; bid for a bungalow at the local camping site (see "Camping"); or (4) if you do decide to linger in this lovely town, let the **Tourist Office** (☎ *041-517171*) try to wedge you into one of the pensions they claim is always available. If they can pry up a suitable booking, Lucerne is ideal as a springboard because it is so central to everything Swiss.

Youth Hostel • *Am Rotsee Sedelstr. 24;* ☎ *368800.* Beds down as many as 200. Take Bus #1 from Station Square, get off at the Schlossberg stop, then make the 15-minute hike.

Villa Maria • *Haldenstr. 36;* ☎ *041-312119.* A pension about a mile from the center in a residential area near a lakefront promenade. Three stories with about a dozen rooms. Very reliable, but not in winter when Maria snoozes.

Pro Filia • *Zahringerstr. 24;* ☎ *224280* and **Panorama** *Kapuziner Weg 9;* ☎ *362298.* Two value-packed pensions to keep on your travel list.

MORE $$

Johanniter • *Bundesplatz 18;* ☎ *231855.* A short stroll from the station. Nicely cozy pine-paneled stube for Swiss-style meals and wine sipping; another tavern with lamps hanging over tables; yet another more formal dining room; comfortable bedchambers, some with bleached open-beam rafters; hospitable people. In low season, a double goes for $38 per person with a huge breakfast buffet, all service and taxes included. Proprietor Gerhard Fahrni is very helpful.

Baslertor • *Pfistergasse 17;* ☎ *220918.* Small but growing. Now has a garden-terrace-swimming pool combo, Joe's Grill with a wide choice of platters. Capacity 75. Shows a lot of zest and a genuine talent for raising its prices.

Waldstatterhof • *Zentralstr. 4;* ☎ *235493.* Another station hotel. No alcohol served on the premises. 9 baths for about 100 people. Spacious rooms. Demi-pension from $23 to $41. Capably but austerely managed by the Association of Swiss Women.

SSR House • *12 St. Karliquai 12;* ☎ *512474.* A broad selection of 2- and 4-person bedrooms with space for 90. All units with hot and cold water; showers on each floor. Spacious dining salon; reading nooks; garden. Some parking. Figure $19-25 per head for bed and bread in the morning. Recommended.

Krone • *Weinmarket 12;* ☎ *516251.* Bans alcohol, locks up at midnight; requires key deposit. On a lovely square in the Old Town. Popular self-service restaurant with fresh produce, salads, Birchermuesli, fruit, hamburgers, and hot dogs. Wide-angled bedchambers, down-the-hall bath.

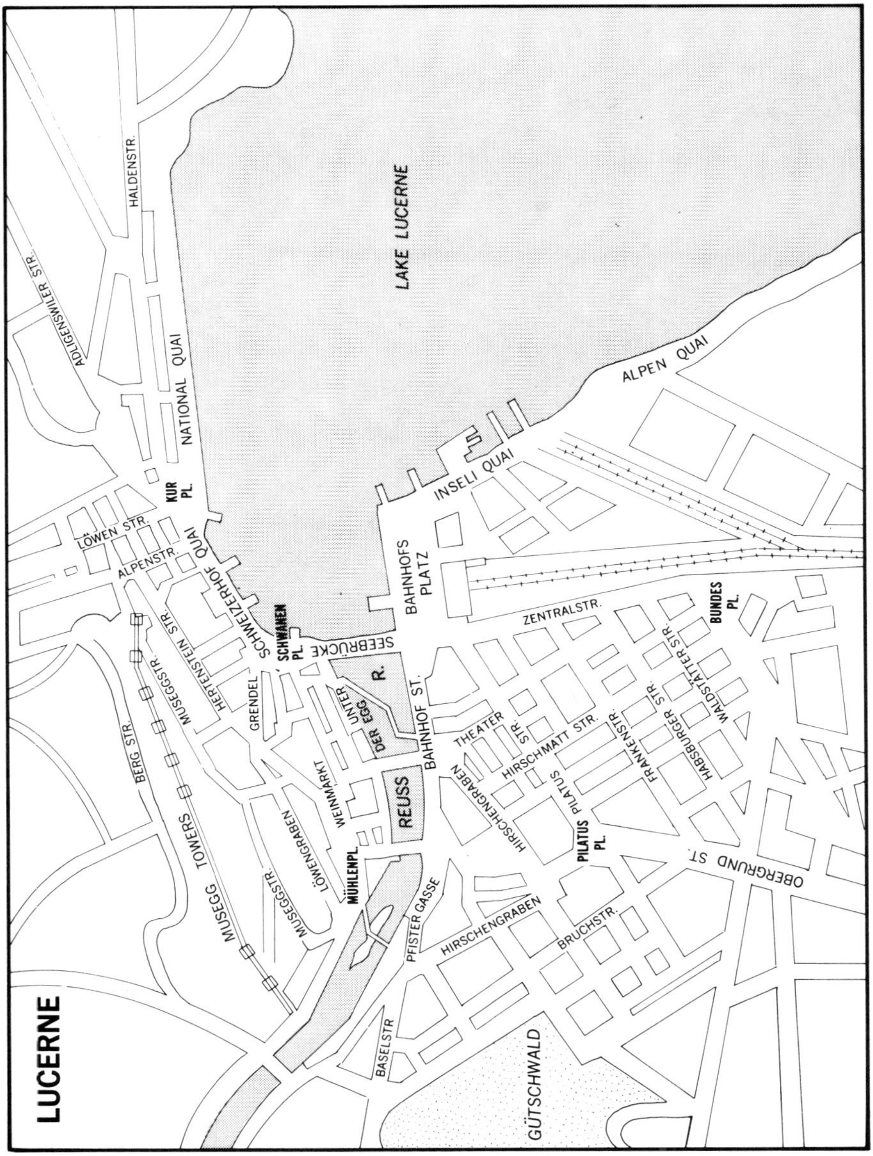
LUCERNE
LAKE LUCERNE
HALDENSTR.
ADLIGENSWILER STR.
NATIONAL QUAI
KUR PL.
LÖWEN STR.
ALPENSTR.
SCHWEIZERHOF QUAI
SCHWANEN PL.
SEEBRÜCKE
HERTENSTEIN STR.
MUSEGGSTR.
BERG STR.
GRENDEL
UNTER DER EGG
R.
REUSS
WEINMARKT
LÖWENGRABEN
MUSEGGSTR.
MUSEGG TOWERS
MÜHLENPL.
BAHNHOFS PLATZ
BAHNHOF ST.
INSELI QUAI
ALPEN QUAI
ZENTRALSTR.
BUNDES PL.
THEATER STR.
HIRSCHENGRABEN
HIRSCHMATT STR.
PILATUS
PILATUS PL.
FRANKENSTR.
HABSBURGER STR.
WALDSTÄTTER STR.
OBERGRUND ST.
PFISTER GASSE
HIRSCHENGRABEN
BRUCHSTR.
BASELSTR
GÜTSCHWALD

Kolping • *Friedenstr. 8;* ☎ *512351.* Group-oriented. Now with air-conditioned restaurant (economy prices), renovated rooms, and plenty of quiet due to side-street location. Tabs from $23 per head ($3 bath supplement), including breakfast. Not inspirational, but certainly fair value.

Drei Konige • *Lakeside, 20 minutes out at Kussnacht am Rigi.* Appealing.

Balm • *Also on exit route.* So quiet that the name fits perfectly.

EVEN MORE $$$

This tourist mecca contains only 80 hostelries, and all of them—luxury houses included—are filled to their minarets during high season; they are often empty in the low-to-no-season.

Luzernerhof • *Alpenstr. 3;* ☎ *514646.* This 70-room hotel and its 12-unit annex are honeys. Sited only one block from the lake. Lounge-bar. Spacious bedchambers all boast bath or shower, silent valets, sound-resistant windows, "safe" drawers, and radios; $80 buys a standard double to include service, taxes, breakfast, and a warm smile from the caring staff. Local gourmets ardently frequent its superb restaurant where prices are startlingly low for the quality.

Goldener Stern • *Burgerstr. 35;* ☎ *230891.* Enjoys a handy situation on Franziskanerplatz. Snack nook and dining salon. Very clean and not too expensive for its bracket. Its brochure reads, "With our 15 bedrooms, we belong to the category of the 'small' hotels." That says a lot in Switzerland.

CAMPING

Even tentless wanderers might wish to consider this facility.

Camp Lido Lucerne • *Lidostr. 6008.* An unusually well-equipped way station on the outskirts, features furnished bungalows, hot showers, a car wash, a shopping center, and other lures. Take bus #2; look for a large sign indicating a right-hand turnoff. Minimum reservation of 5 nights; unfilled bookings cancelled after 6 p.m. during June, July, and Aug.; gates shut at 10 p.m.; open Mar.-Oct. Cottages and caravans with 4 beds rent for about $15. Tent and trailer sites $3 per night; a microscopic reduction for card holders and a 50% discount for anyone 16 or younger.

SUGGESTIONS FOR STUDENTS

Bad news: no student quarter in Lucerne. There is, however, a student bunkhouse called the **Touristenhotel**, just a 5-minute walk from the station. Bed and full board costs $18-21 per person. Book through the following (got a good stout pencil?): **Schweizerischer Studentenreisebedienst (SSR)**, *Baeckerstrasse 40, P.O. Box 3244, CH-8023 Zurich, Switzerland.* For low-cost dining, we recommend either of the self-service restaurants in the grocery emporia of **Migros** and **Coop** on *Hertensteinstr.*

WHERE TO EAT

LEAST $

Lapin • *Museggstr. 2.* House prides: 4 types of sausage. Bratwurst and Rosti potatoes qualify as Helvetian soul food. Fixed-price platters begin at $7.50. The ladles are Alp-size. Counter service available. Unrivaled.

Stadtkeller • *Sternenplatz 3.* Almost more Swiss than the Swiss. Swiss music; Swiss food; Swiss flag-throwing; Swiss alpenhorn tooting. Very crowded and noisy in season. Necessary to reserve in advance.

William Tell • This floating restaurant moored at lakeside in midcity functions from Easter until autumn.

Wilden Mann • *Bahnhofstr. 30.* Serves 15th-century atmosphere along with regional dishes, French food, and snacks. Located in a charming hotel in Old Town. Historical and cozy and becoming more expensive.

OTHER NOTATIONS

Bell Delicatessen • *Next to the Post Office at Seebrucke.* Can make up superb picnics for takeout; a quartered roast chicken in gelee is a meal in itself and very reasonably priced.

Movenpick • Has several outlets for snacks and light meals.

McCheaper • *Weinmarkt 12.* A wee-Mac Swiss version of our American chain.

ITALIAN FOOD

Spaghetti Factory • *Hertensteinstr. 5.* One of the best in the moderately priced category. The decor transmits the light-hearted approach in dining—and a light touch, too, in billing. A jovial place.

COFFEE AND PASTRY

The **Ruedi** and the riverside **Spreuerbrucke** have special personalities. Both feature bewitching waterfront terraces.

MORE $$

Old Swiss House • *Lowenplatz 4.* First choice for a refined and colorful meal. Overdone Swiss decor. Excellent cuisine, kind service, and a warm welcome. Prices substantial, but light luncheon menus easier to swallow financially. Reservations mandatory in season. Quality way, way above the average. Open daily 10 a.m.-midnight.

Luzernerhof Hotel • The dining room of this aforementioned hotel offers unfancy but delicious wares. Chef loads his menus with honest creations: vegetables are vegetables; gravies are gravies; there's no trickery. Attractive. Reasonable outlay.

NIGHTLIFE

Outside of the few bright spots covered below, Lucerne's darkling hours are devoted to decorous repose.

Hazyland • *Haldenstr. 21.* Features its own disk jockey. It swings. You will, too.

Kursaal-Casino • *Haldenstr. 6.* Has been given a pep-up inside and out. A new nightclub was added. Boule the only game offered; the stakes are laughably low (as they are throughout Switzerland). Entrance about $3, half of which is credited to your bar tab; drinks for a minimum of about $5; nightly folklore performances.

Dupont Bar • *Unter der Egg 10.* Has improved slightly—but that's not saying much.

Mr. Pickwick's Rathausquai • Leans to pubbery, as the name implies.

Kakadu Hirschenplatz • Was really romping; the flashier set were getting their kicks by blowing the paper envelopes off their drinking straws. The chalet-style

Alpengarten • *Felsental 1.* Somewhat out of town via Bus #2, attracts a more mature patronage.

Soundrace • *Zentralstr. 45.* For a youthful following **Flora**, *Seidenhofstr. 3,* features dancing and a sedate crowd.

WHAT TO SEE AND DO

For a valley-wide wrap-up, treat yourself to a visual feast from atop Mount Pilatus, which rises 7000 feet above sea level. From here the city, river, and lake spread out in a breathtaking panorama. Take Trolley #1 to Kriens and then board the aerial cable car for an unforgettable ride up the steep mountain face.

Back down to earth, there are at least 4 prime targets for most first-timers:

Chapel Bridge, a red-roofed wooden span built over the Reuss in 1333, is the best preserved portion of the municipality's once-elaborate system of fortifications. For a graphic course in local history, stroll its lengths; partitions consists of 112 17th-century paintings depicting Lucerne's past.

Glacier Gardens and its museum have frozen the clock even further back in time. Ice Age relics, cradled for eons in the Gotthard flows, on view daily from 8 a.m. to 6 p.m. from May to Sept.; cutoff hours are shortened in winter; the glacier sleeps Mon. Admission about $2.

Swiss Transport Museum provides Europe's most comprehensive exhibit of the development of air, land, and sea travel. Many vehicles in working order, including engines that can be set in motion at the push of a button. For the hungry, there are 3 restaurants; one in a restored lake steamer; another self-service. Climb aboard between 9 a.m. and 6 p.m. (in low season, operative from 10 a.m.-4 p.m).

Lion Monument was described by Mark Twain as "the most mournful and moving piece of stone in the world." The majestic beast perpetually dies in memory of the Swiss Guards who fell in Paris at the beginning of the French Revolution. Though pierced to the heart by a lance, he still holds his paw protectively over the shield of the Bourbon kings. During the summer, evening chamber-music concerts are given just beneath his whiskers. He is gloriously sculpted, in a glorious setting.

Switzerland's only **Planetarium** twinkles in the Transport Museum.

OTHER LANDMARKS

Simply too many to list in this limited space, so inquire at the **Lucerne Tourist Office** (*Frankenstr. 1*; ☎ *517171*). These people will provide brochures, directions, and suggestions.

CONCERTS

If you're in town between mid-Aug. and early Sept., don't miss the **Music Festival**. Annually since 1938, world-renowned conductors, orchestras, choirs, and soloists have jousted for encores at this cultural conclave. For tickets and information, write P.O. Box CH-6002, Lucerne.

MARKETS

Lucerne is a strolling city. Markets both ancient and modern are available on both banks. Of the many, we are most drawn to the **Kornmarkt**. While you are at it, saunter along the river promenade; since it is free of car traffic, the sights, sounds, and daydreams can be magic.

WHERE TO SHOP

Bader is the top stop for a Swiss watch—not only for its wide variety but also for the personal service. You should try to see Bader-Huus in the famous (and previously mentioned) Kornmarkt, a lovely match of 16th-century architecture and 20th-century timepieces. A second shop is located at Pilatusstrasse, near the station. Both offer great savings.

SOUVENIRS

Casagrande (*Kapellgasse 24, branches Hertensteinstr. 35 and Schwanenplatz 6*) offers embroidery, clocks, carvings, ceramics, Swiss Army knives—the works! And all top quality at the best prices available in the nation.

LUGANO

Lugano hugs the lovely edge of the lake that shares its name, just around the corner from Locarno, which nestles on the Maggiore lakeside; both are backstopped by mountains. In season, the sun-flecked shore teems with holidaymakers. In fringe periods its Convention Center buzzes contentedly. The weather is superb. One of its biggest drawing cards is the gambling casino of **Campione d'Italia** ("Sample of Italy"), almost directly across the lake by frequent ferry service—an isolated chunk of Italian territory, 1.8 square miles in area. The steamer excursion to **Gandria** is also popular in summer. About 120 hotels or pensions, mostly geared to thrifty travelers who appreciate sound value; a youth hostel called **Ostello della Gioventu** (*Lugano-Crocifisso at via Cantonale 13,* ☎ *562728*); a good medium-price hotel is the **Continental**, sited in its own viewful park, funiculars, chair lifts, and cable cars galore. You also probably would be content in **Kocher's Washington**, **Walter au Lac**, **Ceresio**, **Canva Riviera au Lac**, or **Beha**. For reasonable dining, try the Ticino cellar **La Tinera** in the pedestrian area (*behind Credito Svizzero*), **Olympia** (*main square*), or **Steib** in the excitingly fresh shopping center called **Quatiere Maghetti**. You should see the **Santa Maria degli Angioli Church** and its Luini frescoes as well as the **Cathedral San Lorenzo** with its early Renaissance facade.

MONTREUX

On the quiet eastern bank of Lake Geneva, Montreux was once a main station on the Grand Tour. Until recently it clung to an elegance that had faded. Now it's bouncing back through forward-looking and lively luring of the European traveler. Conventions inevitably headquarter here and now visitors are being received in a host of restored Victorian hostelries—even in a daring modernistic Hyatt! The **Casino** was given a milliondollar hypo in redecoration and additions. Huge, stunning, glass-wrapped nightclub, with cabaret and galas; handsome dining room and bar; French theater; waterfall and discotheque; provincial-style restaurant adjoining; vast, sweeping terrace, magnificent in season. The casino (smallish bets only) was staked by the municipality, local merchants, tourist taxes, and other sources. Very much worth a look. So are the dramatically medieval Castle of Chillon, the lakeside promenades and roads, the heated pool, the **Golden Rose Television Festival** (May), the **Jazz Festival** (July), and the annual **Music Festival** here and in neighboring Vevey (end-Aug. to early Oct.). In springtime the hills are alive with the sounds of the **International Choral Festival**, a lovely occasion and one you'll remember. The **Great St. Bernard Tunnel** (coupling Germany's autobahn and Italy's Autostrada) continues to make it a crossroads stopover during peak periods. A good way to soar above all that is to take the loop up to Rochers de Naye.

During off season the **Helvetie** offers rates of close to $75 per duo. The **Splendid** keeps its tariffs low year-round. Many guest houses stay open throughout the calendar and these are superb economy stops.

MUNSTER

Just a village in the *Valais*—but it may be the one you've always been looking for. The art is from the Middle Ages, the scenery from the Great Architect. Tiny barns, cozy boardinghouses, walks by the rivulet, conifers up to the skyline—the Alps in capsule form. You can reach it by car from Visp or via the Furka-Oberalp Rail line. Spellbinding for walking in summer and for cross-country skiing in winter.

RAPPERSWIL

This ancient town on the eastern shore of the Zurichsee could be called the gemstone of the Swiss Gold Coast. Lake steamers nibble at its quays, gulls wheel overhead, coots squawk in the eddies, plane trees shade its promenades—and up on the ramparts looms an imposing castle-museum that certainly should be visited (especially by travelers of Polish heritage, since the links to that nation are touchingly sentimental). The winsome little **Hotel Freihof** or the amiable **Hirschen** will grill you a lake fish or tuck you in comfortably for the night in puffy-pillowed comfort at startlingly low rates; the **Schwanen** will do it fancier for a little more. Numerous hostelries and inviting dining nookeries line the waterfront. Best to amble in this "City of Roses" and settle where pure whimsy takes you. If you are headquartering in Zurich or elsewhere along the lake, the steamers call in at this port throughout the day. Transportation on ships is included in travel programs described earlier in this chapter.

ST. GALL

The **Monastery of St. Gallen** was the cultural focal point of Central European culture throughout medieval times. The settlement itself began in 612 as a hermitage. Gallus, a monk, was its founding padre. The **Abbey Library** contains monographs of Charlemagne's reign, plus paintings of the period. Now that the city is so heavily into commerce—linen, embroidery, and cotton being the fabric of its modern success story—a visit to the **Textile Museum** is a complement to the historic tableau. In this eastern cantonal capital are numerous inns and boardinghouses, both in the town as well as in the surrounding hills. And while here, try the local grilled sausages—yum! (What a tasty way to save money.) A rewarding springboard you'll probably like more for its Old Town than for its routine newer segments. The **Jaegerhof** is a small hotel with relatively small prices. The is an alternative choice.

ST. MORITZ

Let's face it, St. Moritz is *the* Imperial Majesty of alpine resorts. Concurrently, a high season holiday here could easily sunder a king's ransom. There is lots of loose prattle about how cheap it can be during the "shoulder" months. Don't believe it. You'll quickly discover that those "shoulders" are not very broad once you scan its Graubunden calendar and try to fit in your full vacation's share of schussing. Unless you happen to be in a membership venture (Club Mediterranee, as one example), the independent fun seeker might find it too costly for any carefully calculated budget.

Languard for more daring spenders, presents the same view as the famous Palace; fresh clean rooms; huge breakfasts; nice people; very central. The **Eden** also features a prize-winning lake view. **Meierei** looks straight down the length of the lake; a wonderful house with superior cooking, but it's a 15-minute walk to the center.

Waldhaus am See is another scenic choice that oozes personality. Because they are not directly beside the lifts, the last two make superb summer residences for walkers.

Chesa Sur L'En, also a bit out, is unique architecturally, a period piece of Italian ornate carpentry and luxury. Though once a patrician villa for a rich eccentric, the rates are very reasonable and the Schwarzenbach family are marvelous hosts. The setting, too, is enchanting among the firs. For dining, most hotels have pension plans.

Corvatsch is cheery for Italian dishes, **Veltliner Keller** is more traditional and good, while the **Albana** plays to a rather sophisticated audience at its cellar grill. In summer it can be pure rapture-of-the-heights; due to this very tranquillity, however, a few days, during the warm months, suffice for most visitors. Try to make the excursion to **Roseggletscher** (with its fantastic farmhouse restaurant); get the horsedrawn carriage (or sled) at **Pontresina Station**. It's a day full of scenery you'll never forget. Or take the evening cable up to **Muottas Muragl** for the wondrous sunset dinner (transport is deducted from your meal price). For strollers, hike the lakeside path toward **Maloja**, where you can eat at the **Bellavista** or take the 50-minute route to **Isola** and have some of the world's best risotto at the outdoor tables of the **Pension Lagrev** before returning to **Sils-Maria**.

Throughout the lovely **Grisons**—or "Heidiland"—the lesser-known hamlets and villages offer fabulous holiday scenery, abundant comfort, and prices that you can handle. In the same canton, **Davos**, another major tourist center, is far less expensive; moreover, the skiing is phenomenal. Nearby **Klosters** might also have been custom-made for top skiers. These friendly neighbors share the famous **Parsenn**, one of the longest ski runs in the world. Klosters may be a bit more economical. Stay at the **Bundnerhof**, the **Garni Malein**, the **Casanna**, or the **Arve**; top pensions are the **Soldanella**, **Minerva**, or the **Silvapina** at *Dorf.*

Bahnhofli (also at Dorf) is a fine budget dining spot. In Klosters, we also like **Gotschna-Stubli**, **Pizzeria Vereina**, and **Coop**. *Samedan*, only 10 minutes from St. Moritz but far more economical, offers the pleasant **Hotel Bernina**; lifts to Celerina and the Bernina Pass are quite handy. **Kleine Scheidegg** is proud of its wooded slopes and headily aromatic air. Intrepid Class-AAA climbers occasionally play Russian Roulette on the brooding Eiger at the hamlet's doorstep. **Kandersteg** strikes us as being cold, with a mystical suggestion of lonely savage crags and towering spires; in addition, it seems to be excessively avalanche-prone. **Wengen** we happen to love. As in **Zermatt**, cars are verboten. This provides a jingle-bells atmosphere. Even though Murren turns on a remarkably similar personality, we somehow prefer little Wengen for its more special ambience. **Champery**—born with a chill factor all its own—hugs an Alp that swoops down into France near sparkling **Avoriaz**. Although the town hunches at the nadir of a gelid valley, once you attain the upper slopes, you'll find plenty of warm sun and rolling terrain. Prices come in at the bottom end of Helvetian standards. **Verbier** is a classic family-style resort, especially with Scandinavians. No huge hotels; many little ones, however, plus an abundance of private chalets, contribute to its intimacy. The open-bowl situation admits a galaxy of sunlight; makes the residents sunny, too.

SAAS FEE

Just the opposite of Verbier, in our judgment. This high, cold, and jagged cranny is better suited to ultraserious sportsmen, ski-mountaineers, and similar types of masochists. The nightlife is great—as long as you don't stay up later than 8 p.m. Culturally, however, it is one of Switzerland's more interesting corners and architecturally speaking, it is comely, too.

Flims embraces 3 separate areas into one pay-all-ski-all network. Most hostelries face the sun and are of recent vintage. So are a predominance of the visiting Flimstars.

ADDITIONAL SKI CENTERS

The list seems endless—Adelboden, Lenzerheide, Pontresina, Savognin, Lenk, Andermatt, Engelberg, Valbella and it is. Those spotlighted here currently welcome the greatest influx of stems, sterns, and parallels. Most U.S. ski-bashers who have slalomed around the Alps once, return to the States with size-48 smiles on their well-tanned faces. In any of the above towns, go to the Tourist Information Centers, which have lists of all accommodations available at any price level; they even know the status of occupancy, will provide a map, and might even make a phone call for you to reserve your room.

VILLARS

Just off the main artery to Italy, not far from Montreux, it is situated at 4265 feet, above the Rhone Plain, and enjoys a mild climate sheltered from the north winds. Throughout the summer, tennis, swimming, mountain-golf (18 holes), fishing, horseback riding, and minigolf are available. In winter, it offers 28 miles of cross-country ski runs, over 175 miles of alpine paths, 29 ski lifts, 2 mountain railways, and 3 cable cars, chairlifts, plus the experience of 60 Swiss Ski School instructors. Around the calendar you'll find a Sports Center with Fitness Club, Sauna, and Solarium, and a covered artificial ice rink for skating, curling, and hockey; indoor tennis and squash; there's also bowling. Admission to most of these is cheaper for holders of a visitor's card. All categories of hotels for all categories of wallets. Nightlife is varied and plentiful.

La Renardiere has only 22 rooms, but a heart of gold. The **Curling** (near the ice rink) is a worthy hotel choice. This extremely pleasant and richly scenic mecca is one of the oldest resorts of the land.

WINTERTHUR

An industrial hub but with a degree of flavor and art. There are narrow streets and ancient buildings, many inexpensive places to overnight, the 11th-century **Hegi Castle** with regional cultural displays, the **Oscar Reinhart Museum** and the **Foundation** (both filled with splendid paintings), a **clock museum**, the **Swiss Technical Museum** called "Technorama," the 18th-century **Heimatmuseum** with craft items, and, to relax in midtour, the seven-century-old **Schloss Wuelflingen**, a charming mansion that is now a roadside inn. By train this city is only a half hour from Zurich if you want to make a day excursion.

ZERMATT

A glance is not enough. Travelers for centuries have arrived to view or ascend the spellbinding Mattherhorn or to link their souls into the beautiful Monte Rosa chain. In winter, skiing is the great preoccupation; the hills are dotted with wonderful little huts for meals or wine stops. In summer the slopes are devoted to hikers and nature-loving at its supreme best. Toy barns are opened to allow the cattle to roam freely. The air is almost shockingly pure to metropolitan nostrils, since cars and motor traffic always have been forbidden in the area. It was for this and other related reasons pertaining to my concern for the environment that Zermatt recently won our annual **Temple Fielding Award**. Few places in the "civilized" world can touch it.

DIRECTORY

Laundromat • Look for it in the Center.

Barber and Ladies' Hairdresser • Center.

Children's Hotel and Day Nursery • Kindergarten Pumuckel (*next door to the Hotel La Ginabelle*; ☎ *673545*) or at Kinderparadies at the Hotel Nicoletta (☎ *661151*). Ages up to 8; day care from $10; half day at about $7; full board at $10. Ask at the Tourist Office about nanny service.

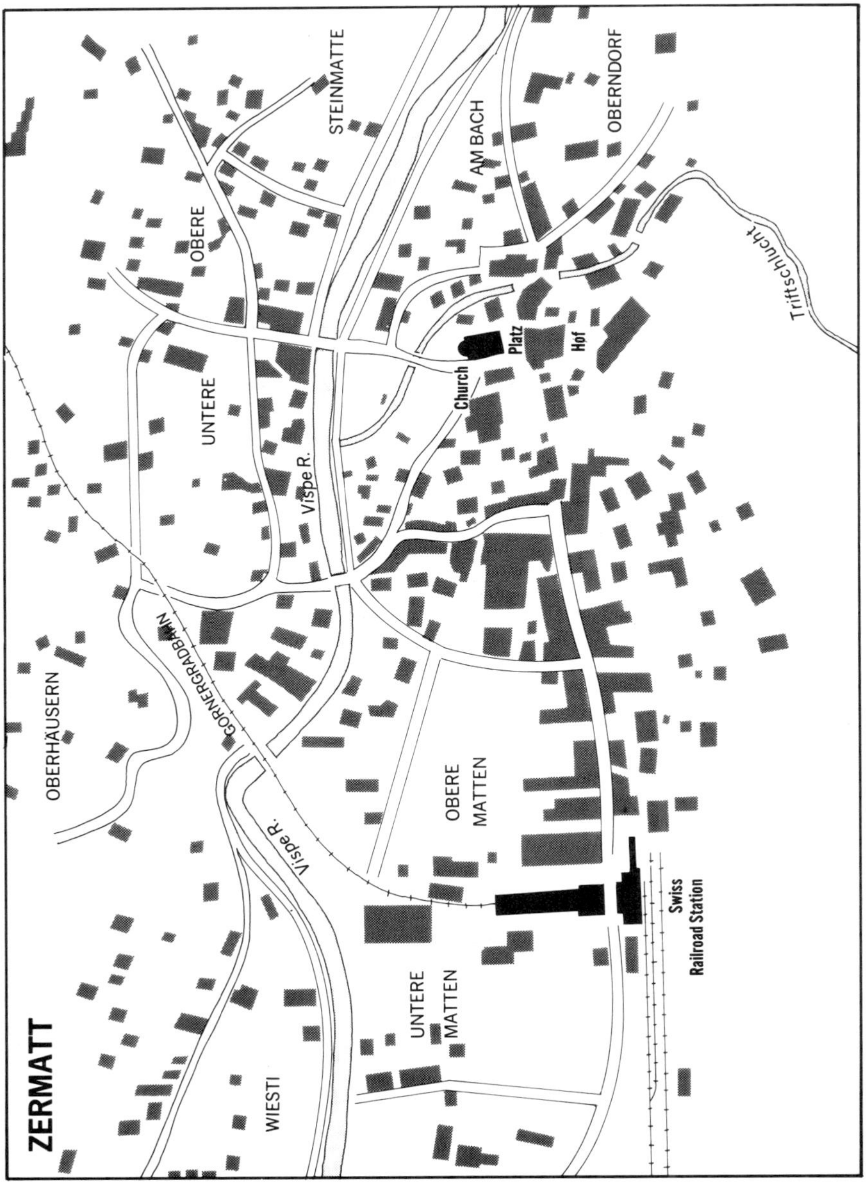
ZERMATT
STEINMATTE
OBERNDORF
AM BACH
OBERE
UNTERE
Vispe R.
Church
Platz
Hof
Triftschlucht
OBERHÄUSERN
GORNERGRADBAHN
Vispe R.
OBERE
MATTEN
Swiss
Railroad Station
UNTERE
MATTEN
WIESTI

Doctors • The village has but five; if anything grave develops, the nearest medical establishment is Regionalspital St. Maria *in Visp*.

There is helicopter service available directly to its roof. If you have any hesitancy about local facilities—the pharmacists and medical personnel are splendid for most purposes—get in touch immediately with Dr. Betti Huhnholz (*21 Bahnhofstr., Visp*; ☎ *464443*). She speaks English perfectly and is the soul of humanity. We have used her services personally, and she has our full confidence as a general practitioner.

Official Ambulance Service • ☎ *673486*.

Air Zermatt Heliport • ☎ *673486/87*.

Police • ☎ *117*.

Favorite Pawnshop • Doesn't exist.

HOW TO GET AROUND

In and around the village you have 3 choices—walking, solar-electric buses, or the **horse-drawn taxis**. The latter are gaily painted wheeled carriages in summer or gleaming brass and-leather-tacked sleighs during the snow months. They greet you at the station to trot you to your hotel. Although every corner of town is easily accessible by foot, your luggage and skis or other gear will undoubtedly necessitate this jingle-bell romp to your lodgings. Since several can ride together, tariffs are often shared. Also a sort of sled-wagon with cheaper rates for a load of about a dozen. Quiet **Electrocar taxis** (5 seats) plus the above buses also effect haulage if you prefer modern transport.

TRAINS

From such centers as **Geneva** (4 hours), **Zurich** (5 hours), **Berne** (3-1/4 hours), and **Milan** (4 hours), you'll probably change at **Brig** for the Zermatt link. Some mainliners go to **Visp**, the alternative transfer point. This narrow-gauge journey takes slightly over 1 hour on the express or as long as 92 minutes on the milk runs. While there are 19 departures up and 16 down per day, only 6 up and 4 down are nonstop.

Air-Zermatt (☎ *673487/86*) helicopter joyrides cost about $150 for a 20-minute uplift. The Matterhorn round trip is, however, an investment for a lifetime experience. For emergencies, it could literally be a lifesaver. Since the medical facilities of this isolated village are painfully limited, its charter facilities as an airborne ambulance may be mandatory if a critical climbing or skiing injury should occur. The nearest hospital (St. Maria) is down at Visp. Personally we found it to be excellent; Dr. Peter Z'Brun, its chief, is one of the nation's leading orthopedic surgeons. Otherwise, further afield, there are the medical centers of Berne or Lausanne.

MOTORING TO ZERMATT

You can, but in winter be prepared with chains or snow tires. Your car should be parked in the open lot at nearby Taesch (shuttle trains every quarter hour to Zermatt); be sure your antifreeze is adjusted to -30°C in snowtimes. Otherwise, leave it at the heated filling station garages at Taesch or in the lower valley at Visp and take the train. Heated garage space down here costs from $5 to $7.25 for 24 hours; in winter this is money well spent. Outdoors, the rates are under $3.50 per day; perfectly okay if your car is protected by antifreeze. (About -30°C should be enough in midwinter.) There are numerous parking establishments in both settlements.

WHERE TO STAY

Because of the unique nature of this village, we divide the stopovers listed into 2 different groups: the lodgings that operate on the full pension or the demipension plan of 3 or 2 compulsory meals and the "Hotels Garni" of compulsory breakfast only, with other meals occasionally offered on an optional basis. In our lead-off pack, naturally, the quotations may look higher at first glance, but when you work out the cost of dining continually in expensive restaurants or buying meals at the seasonal ski station centers and mountain huts, the first plan often sums up at a cheaper rate over a full holiday span.

During Christmas and the later high ski season (Feb.-March), far-in-advance reservations are an absolute MUST. Hapless gypsies who skid into town unannounced may seek advice from the **Zermatt Tourist Office** (☎ *661181*) *near the main station.* Almost adjoining the station there's a travel agency that maintains an information board indicating which hotels have vacancies.

FULL OR HALF PENSION

Alex • ☎ *671726.* Now open year 'round for skiers or hikers—and always for romantics—it is easily the top choice, despite higher-than-average tariffs. Quiet panoramic perch off a narrow lane just 1 block from the station. Snack corner and cozily rustic bar—the most popular in Zermatt. Heated indoor pool that goes semi-outdoor in summer; 2 saunas; massage parlor; squash courts plus tennis hall; outdoor tennis court. Main-level dining-and-breakfast room made from transplanted Swiss barns. Famous cellar Taverne Chez Alex delightfully regional. Per-person rates run from $70 and waaaay-up, depending on accommodation and season—but include a large breakfast and a gourmet dinner. Alex Perren, a 4th-generation mountain-guide-turned-host, will go all out for your welcome and comfort—if he's got space for you. His smiling wife and helpmate, Gisela, is a beautiful bonus; young Alex, their son, looks like a Hollywood star who somehow fell into the hotel business. Very popular with North Americans.

Pollux • ☎ *671946.* On main village drag. Filled with fun lovers because of its penchant for live music, dancing, and revelry. Several dining and sipping corners. Overall prices in line with the ample rewards.

Welschen Pension • ☎ *671979.* Offers far more homespun chalet warmth than some other higher-priced hotels in the valley. Hostess Ruth Inderbiner is the personification of Swiss hospitality, as are other members of her family. Scenic, practical situation near base of Sunnegga-Blauherd underground funicular. Salon with fireplace. Dining room windows frame Matterhorn; 12 rooms with alpine decor, 8 with bath or shower; a handful more in the family annex. Full pension with bath, $70 per person; without bath, $60.

Hotel Dom • ☎ *671371.* 50 units between river and main street. Geared for the gregarious. Lounge and restaurant; 15 units in newer wing. Balconies on sunny southern exposure. Bed, bath, and three squares from $50 to $60; with washbasin only about 35% less.

Touring • ☎ *671177.* Across river and tranquil. No private baths but basins throughout. Full pension about $45; modified American Plan reductions of $2.50. A friendly, better-than-adequate retreat.

Julen • ☎ *672481.* Large dining hall; open-air terrace for summer; 35 rooms; 10 pine-clad units with private plumbing; most with balcony. Snowbird rates from $55-or-so; summer tabs from $35; $2.50 off sans lunch.

Alpina • ☎ *671050.* In tiny alley near heartbeat of town; 25 somewhat fusty rooms, 10 with bath; waterless models from $30 per guest; tub-equipped shelters for $36; $2.75 off for demipension.

Ferienhaus Silvana • ☎ *672012.* Hunkers halfway up the Schwarzee slopes at Furri cable-car stop. Basic dorm-style doubles and triples rent for $22 per person, including full pension. But skiers will find it tends to limit them to a single mountain, and it's a helluva hike after the lift closes.

HOTELS GARNI

Antika, **Allalin**, **Matterhornblick** and **Beau Rivage** • ☎ *672151*; ☎ *671631*; ☎ *671010*; ☎ *671884.* Four charmers located in the same large chalet edifice. Wonderfully central with an enchanting view of the Matterhorn from the rear. The first offers the kind attentions of the Julen-Ragotti family, plus sauna and fitness room. Accommodations are rustic bliss. Same family runs the superb Stockhorn Restaurant just 150 yards away. The second entry similar in tone and providing approximately same facilities with a touch more luxury. The latter two tend more toward modernity. Good solid houses, but a bit cooler in aspect. All, however, are excellent as money-savers.

Eden & Rex • ☎ *672655/671005.* A winsome Siamese twinsome; 2 bed-and-breakfast addresses joined in the middle at an indoor pool. Chalet annex; sauna; mutual administration. Upstairs boasts unusually spacious accommodations, most with verandas and all with alpine vistas. Rates from $45 with bath, $35 dry. If you don't mind stepping out to dine (the Old Zermatt is close by), it's a delightful year-round haven.

Jagerhof • ☎ *673714.* Quite a haul from center; 33 attractive units, all with private bath and toilet; $40 per person. Clean, airy, and cheerfully informal. Good people run it.

Romantica • ☎ *671505.* As its name suggests, located in a romantic hillside setting above main street. Bar-lounge and breakfast nook; 12 neat rooms in main structure, 9 with bath and nearly all with balconies. Also 2 fetching pastoral cottages.

Bergfreund ("Mountain Friend") • ☎ *672567.* Across river, closer to lifts, and cheaper; 12 bathless bedchambers. $34 per person. Simple, but more than worth the investment.

Malva • ☎ *673033.* Next door. Restaurant overlooking stream and quaint old town cemetery. Fixed-price dinners about $11; à la carte versions higher. All units have balconies and southern view; corner rooms largest and most pleasant; singles small and dark. Bathless winter rates at $20 per head; with tub or shower from $25. Livable, even lovable.

Cima • ☎ *672337.* Overlooks Ski School rendezvous area not far from the Gornergrat Station. Light, airy breakfast room; 11 plain doubles with balconies and 3 so-so singles. Bed and breakfast about $30 per person.

Stockhorn • ☎ *671747.* Better known for its restaurant than its 14 bedchambers. Basic shelter available for $34 in snowtimes and $20 in off months.

Tannenhof • ☎ *673188.* Pleasant. During inspection couldn't find a soul who spoke anything but Schwyzerdutsch. Tariffs from $35, *Schatzie.*

Pension Perren • ☎ *673502.* Garni wing seems fresher than main house. But then we have never been fond of its original all-meals section, which seems overpriced for rewards.

LEAST $

Bahnhof • ☎ *672460.* Near the station, barnlike. Run for eons by descendants of late, great guide, Alohas Biner. The present Biner, a charming lady, adds to overall appeal of this budget hideaway. Just 15 ultra-low-cost rooms with zero amenities; 12 shelters sleeping 3 to 4 each. Small, dorm bedding squad of 6; larger one for platoon of 13. Communal mess hall with facilities for do-it-yourself breakfasts (extra charge). Per-head rates from $18 to $27. A chummy, we're-all-inthis-together bond among clientele. Clean. Chiefly for climbers; in summer nearly everyone is up and out or out and up before sunrise.

Belle Rive • *Near the Eden & Rex.* Breakfast only. Reliable.

Orion • *On the route to Trocknersteg*; another reasonable buy.

YOUTH HOSTEL

Jugendherberge • ☎ *672320.* Farther up the valley than the Jagerhof, provides 200 bunks for about $8.50 per night. Cooking permitted. Closed Nov.

CAMPING

There's a privately owned site in the vicinity operated in conjunction with the **Swiss Camping Association**. This is at the entrance to the village near the heliport. It offers toilet and washroom facilities and small canteens; rates are about $2.50 per night. Open June 15 through Sept. 10 only.

WHERE TO EAT

Skiers, climbers, or strollers seldom return to town for lunch. When the pangs hit, most head for one of the 38 cafeterias, snack bars, or other restaurants up on the slopes. (Hardly anyone skis all the way down to town for lunch.) A full ration of cafeteria production-line nutrients might cost around $9. If you are willing to spend this much, then the best atmosphere is in the cozy log huts tucked away along the ski runs. (Some are indicated by a wineglass shown on the plan of the mountains.) Smart economizers fill their backpacks or beltpacks with a cold lunch or with raw materials purchased at grocery shops. Unless they carry a thermos (a nuisance), they supplement this with hot soup, coffee, *gluhwein* (hot wine), or similar beverages available on the mountain. Picnics, however, are not welcome (or permitted) inside the mountain restaurants.

Dress in all restaurants is informal. Modish sweaters and ski-pants predominate. Coats and ties seldom seen except in the Zermatterhof or Mont Cervin Hotels.

LEAST $

Le Vieux Vallais • *Next to town's only moviehouse.* Belongs to Hotel Elite. Multitier main chamber and counter from which to watch the pizza-making. Second room to side. Overlooks Ski School and departure point for the Gornergrat train. Savory pasta with all trimmings, about a half dozen grilled items, and other selections. Recommended.

Bahnhof Restaurant • *In the station.* Offers plain but solid vittles in simple surroundings. Fixed meal about $8 to include meat, potatoes, green vegetables, and a salad; wagon choices from $3. Substantial.

Cafe du Pont • *Next to bridge at upper end of village.* It's genuine Zermatt in old style. In cafe portion, cable workmen sip *pflumli* and play endless games of *jass* (with cards). Intimately dark stubli for fondue and raclette plus other simple dishes. Tiny hayloft offers a few more seats. Here the prestige of Swiss timepieces has no meaning whatsoever.

Stockhorn • Hutlike—an intimate and yet sophisticated rustic retreat. Ground floor for grills done on the popping wood fire plus other meals; cellar features raclette, fondue, and snacks. Staff in local costumes.

Gitan • *In Hotel Darioli.* Whomps up appetizing grills in charm-laden nookery. Excellent attention by friendly personnel.

Old Zermatt • Candlelit tables in Couronne Hotel.

Weisshorn • Very atmospheric, as is the regional cookery.

Stadel • Means "tiny barn" and that's the mood; beyond that the dining choices are solidly alpine.

Simi's • Excellent but remote.

Pollux's Arvenstube • A hotel on the main drag with a large popular restaurant. All packed to the rafters just after the lifts close down.

MORE $$

Taverne Chez Alex • *In the cellar of the previously described Hotel Alex.* Our pick of entire Valais mountains or meadows for 3 reasons: culinary quality, value, and aesthetic alpine appeal. Fixed dinner offering 6 courses at reasonable price for gourmet quality; high-cost à la carte choices unnecessary here. We are hooked on the place and its friendly people.

Spycher • Back-o'-town eatery with bar at rear. Lodge decor. Overheated as only the Swiss can overheat a restaurant (it's an art—as is the garrote). Dinner now nudging $45.

Spaghetti Factory • *In the Hotel de la Poste.* Gears up for slaphappy nutritional industry nightly in cheerful surroundings. Not for the sedate.

NIGHTLIFE

For its size, Zermatt can turn on a bonanza of after-dark revelry. Many hotels swing long after the normal bewitching hours. So do the bars. So do a bevy of typical alpine hideaways.

The winter crowd is young, vigorous, and fun-loving. Most are skiers first and night owls second—but they manage! Informal aprês-ski attire is acceptable almost everywhere. For just drinking and camaraderie at glacier-bottom prices, try the **Slalom**, the **Darioli**, and the **Stockhorn** hotel bars.

The Alex now offers the best disco atmosphere in town, cleverly integrated into the bar and lounge areas, which feature 2 dance platforms. Better find a cozy corner by midnight because everyone pops in at sometime or other.

The **Zermatterhof** has the poshest citylike tone in town. Huge, busy salon; files of tables and chairs; deft waiters; dancing to a small combo; mixed crowd of all ages; many spectators. One of the few spots where men usually (not always) wear suits or sport jackets and ties.

Rendezvous Bar, a network of chambers in the venerable Hotel Mont Cervin, is the most sought-after spot in town. If you want a table, you'd better get there by 11:30 p.m. No minimum; quite good.

Le Village, *in the Hotel de la Poste*, is the oldest discotheque in the valley. There's a $3 door charge. Barnlike lower chamber; once you recover night vision, wood, stucco, and shingles visible everywhere; jammed dance circle; balustraded loft; active

Broken Ski Bars; drinks about $4; up-to-tomorrow musical selections; conversation possible for lip-readers only.

The midtown **Walliserkanne**, adjoining but not associated with the Hotel Wallis-erhof, is far more provincial in tone. Groups of tables among the low-banister partitions; waitresses dressed in dirndls; spiral staircase to its upper level or down to a handsome swing-a-ding-ding grotto. Normally crowded, smoky, and convivial.

Brighter lights and higher spirits regularly sparkle at the previously described **Hotel Pollux**, which like the above two, is on the main street of the village. Active bar with jiggers and jigging; disco plus group dancing on occasion; lively, fun-filled participants and spectators.

APRES-SKI SPOTS

When the magic hour arrives, the **Old Zermatt**, adjoining the Couronne Hotel, explodes. Habitués try to squeeze 20 of their jovial number around tables suitable for 10. Stucco and wood decor; open fire; bar up a couple of steps; barrel-keg seats; glug wine (gluhwein), hot buttered rum, raclette, and special orders of the day. Watch your change here; in this bedlam, mistakes are easily made (and somehow they were never in our favor). For the gregarious.

For the most elegant cocktailers, the hours from 6 to dinner time are usually devoted to the piano bar at the **Mont Cervin Hotel**. Our choice, however, is the sweater company around the **Alex Hotel Bar**. One of the happiest corners in Europe, whether you sit at the counter on its ram's-head stools, lean against the stone oven baking out your aches of the day, or cuddle in a sequestered nook or in the larger salon behind the bar room itself. Ask George, the wildest barman alive, to fix you one of his specials—guaranteed to improve your mood, your skiing, and your lovelife. Something for everyone here.

The Stockhorn would be another candidate for a romantic Zermatt snuggery, especially downstairs in the stubli.

The Walliserkanne is well known. Thickly atmospheric; pulses at tea-dancing time and after dinner. A spoiler for us was its waddle of snippish waitresses with too much work and too few manners.

Elsie's Place is in an ancient building; scads of college pennants and other oddments stuck here and there; 6 tables; small semicircular bar; knotty walls; friendly. Elsie's prides: Irish coffee (delicious, but an expensive $6), ham and eggs, hot dogs, other light snacks, and every beverage imaginable. The packages of biscuits, nuts, and crackers placed on the tables are not on the house. Except in May, Oct., and Nov., goes full blast from 10 a.m. to midnight, 7 days a week. A Zermatt fixture that was "discovered" before the Matterhorn.

For pastry and coffee, **Zellner**, above a small delicacy shop on the main street, does it best of all. Nice view of the town, too.

WHAT TO SEE AND DO

The incomparable **Matterhorn**, dubbed the "Lion of Zermatt" by Karl Baedeker a century ago and called *Mont Cervin* by the French, overwhelms the village backdrop in massive, beautiful, and ever-present dominance. Visible nearly everywhere you go—seemingly so close you can reach out to touch it.

The town itself is still a delight, despite now-swarming hordes of holiday-makers. A soft white mantle and glistening icicles decorate its patchwork of brown chalets in winter; in summer, you can count more than 3000 species of butterflies fluttering among the abundant wild blossoms.

The **Alpine Museum**, near the post office, contains relics of the tragic 1865 expedition that first scaled the Matterhorn. Edward Whymper, who led the party of seven, was one of the three who survived when the rope sundered and hurled the others 4000 feet onto the glacier below. In addition to this frayed line and other ancient climbing equipment, early models of skis and related items are shown. Winter openings daily from 10 p.m. to noon and from 4 to 6 p.m. Summer hours longer. Admission $1.50 per person.

The small **Anglican Church** and adjoining cemetery lie behind the museum; almost entirely given over to the remains of British climbers who lost their lives.

Several events dot the Aug. calendar. On the 5th, the **Kapellenfest**, a religious holiday, centers its activities on the chapel at Schwarzee, which was built following the prayerful promise of a lost climbing party after all of its members had been rescued. On the 15th, there is a costumed open-air **folklore festival**.

During the first half of the month, the **Academy of Music Festival** offers public concerts.

No holiday-maker, whatever the season, should fail to try at least one mountain railway, funicular, teleferic, or chair-lift ride up the surrounding slopes or peaks. The 50-minute rack-and-pinion ascent to the **Gornergrat** is the most comfortable—as well as the most reassuring to acrophobes, since its cog wheels are always firmly connected to terra firma. Other rides provide scenic splendors virtually unequaled in the western world.

Several mildly active walking tours embrace the tiny hamlets and other sites in the foothills. Prize destinations include **Winkelmatten**, **Zum See**, **Blatten**, and **Furi**; **Zmutt**, a wonderfully isolated, ancient hilltop settlement, has an enchanting antique chapel; scores of other forest paths abound. Information on these casual explorations may be had from the Tourist Office near the station. Ask for the excellent Zermatt Aerial Map, (about $1.20), which outlines these and other excursions. Serious climbers also find this chart useful.

SPORTS

Skiing is a winter and summer attraction here, the latter being practiced high along the **Plateau Rosa** and over the frozen **Theodul Glacier**.

During the cold months, there are no less than 40 ski runs for every grade of skier and 36 major lifts and tows (1 train, an underground cable railway, 11 cable cars, 3 cabin lifts, 2 open chairlifts, 18 T-bar or pomalifts, plus several training tows for beginners). An exciting zone spanning the permanent whipped-cream meadows of the Little Matterhorn is groomed for gliding in a region 12,500 feet above sea level! It's an easy run and best suited for warm-day skiing. You can find sitzmarks along 150 miles of officially maintained courses (including down to Cervinia), nearly all above the tree line. Although expert off-trail adventurers can shatter new powder over an infinity of white, guides are strongly advised for anyone unfamiliar with the valleys, glaciers, ravines, covered barbed wire fences, and avalanche zones. This is especially true for heli-ski enthusiasts.

Here's the geography of the 3 major lift systems: **Blauherd** in the east, often the best in winter, will put you above 10,000 feet high onto the **Unter Rothorn**, **Gornergrat**, the middle mountain, where a combination of train and cable hitch reaches the 11,100-foot level on Stockhorn, and **Schwarzsee** in the south, where several links almost bring you to the Italian frontier at **Plateau Rosa** or at **Theodulpass**, the 10,900-foot mark. Side note: If you take your passport and extra money, you may cross the border and ski down into **Cervinia** on an additional daily ticket, which has been made available.

At this writing, winter all-lift tickets are sold in consecutive 1-to-21-day, and 1-month segments. You may also buy 1-to-21-day billets on the lifts serving any one of the 3 areas. Easy riders on short stays may prefer to invest in the coupon booklets.

The **Ski School** (☎ *675444*) operates daily except Sun. year round; in winter, morning and afternoon 2-hour sessions are held. Sample tuition at press time: 1 day at 60 SF, 3 consecutive days at 140 SF, and 6 consecutive days at 195 SF; private instruction is a lofty 140 SF per 1/2-day and these are available 7 days per week. Children are given a very slight reduction, but lunch and a beverage are included. Its practice tows are gratis for beginners only.

At dale level, the ice skating rink near the station is open from 9:30 a.m. to 4 p.m. during the winter months. Ski rentals slide up to near $38 per week for the latest models with the finest and newest safety bindings; they are insured against breakage usually, but not against theft. (You can purchase theft insurance separately. You can also buy skiing insurance for yourself—and this you should do if you are not adequately covered by your own policy.) Cross-country hickories with "rat-trap" bindings also are available. Skates with boots may be rented for $15 per week or $20 per fortnight. Curling is also a popular cold weather sport. The outdoor lanes are at the ice rink; indoor ones at the **Arca Hotel**. Don't forget our previous mention of Ski-touring with Franz Schwery, described under "Sports" at the beginning of this chapter; the High Route is passable from April through June.

A privately owned **minigolf course** is adjacent to the **Christiana** and **Dufour hotels**. Electric projection golf is linked to Julen Sport, a shop overlooking the hockey rink.

WHERE TO SHOP

PHARMACY

You'll need one for sun- or windburn, sore muscles, and other mountain woes. **Testa Grigia** is it; everyone here can answer your needs in English, too.

SOUVENIRS

Wega, across from the post office, down by the station, and in the new Schweizerhof Hotel, offers a large collection of sundries including photo supplies, postcards, stationery, books, wood carvings, copper pots, dried flowers, baskets, and similar mementos.

Boutique Sylvia displays more artistic wares; some not regional, others not even Swiss.

For ski pants, parkas, sweaters, après-ski paraphernalia, climbing and other sports equipment, browsing through the racks and shelves at **Glacier Sport** (main street) and **Julen Sport** (facing the hockey rink) is a pleasant pastime. Both rent ski equipment as well as sell it.

EMBROIDERY

Langenthal, on the main street about 50 yards from the train station, is the linen and needlework name everyone knows in discerning Switzerland. Lots of gift items and take-home treasures at excellent prices.

Shopping hours: Generally from 8 a.m. until noon and from 2 until 7 p.m. Sun. shopping from 8 a.m. until 9:30 a.m. and 4 p.m. until 6:30 p.m. During the summer, however, it's nonstop from 8 a.m.–7 p.m. weekdays and 8–9:30 a.m. and 3:30–6:30 p.m. Sun.

ZURICH

Zurich is the largest and most business-oriented metropolis in Helvetia; industry, commerce, and culture are centered here. You'll find the leading banks and insurance companies; biggest shops, markets, excellent hotels, restaurants, and amusements. A speedy rail service now zips between the international airport and midtown in a mere ten minutes. From the tops of the encircling hills, the city is a stunning sight. Villas and gardens stretch down to the silvery inland sea, with snow-capped peaks as the background. Make Zurich and Geneva your excursion centers, as everything worth seeing in the nation can be covered from these two bases. If you can, plan to be in Zurich in June; the month-long Festival here of classical music and exhibitions is one of the most famous on the Continent.

DIRECTORY

U.S. Consulate • *Zollikerstr. 141*; ☎ *552566.*

American Express • *Bahnhofstr. 20*; ☎ *2118370.*

Dry Cleaning and Pressing • Terlinden, *Lowenstr. 29*; ☎ *2110811.*

English-Speaking Doctor • Dr. Harry Korrodi, *Rainweg 7, Kusnacht*; ☎ *9105256.*

English-Speaking Dentist • Dr. Heinrich Mooser, *Bederstr. 105;* ☎ *2022464*, or Dr. Max Schniter, *Bederstr. 42* ☎ *327712.*

Police • Amsthaus I, *Witikonerstr. 202*; ☎ *532337*; Emergency: ☎ *117.*

Favorite Pawnshop • Pfandleihkasse der Zurcher Kantonalbank, *Zurlindenstr. 105*; ☎ *4611933.*

HOW TO GET AROUND

Clean, smooth running, well planned, punctual—and inexpensive. The main railway station (Bahnhofplatz) is also the terminus for most city buses and streetcars.

For the Urania Observatory, board Tram #7 or #10, #11, or #13; for Kronenhalle, Tram #4 or #11; for the Rietberg, Tram #7 or #10; for the Haus zum Rechberg, Tram #3 or Bus #31; for the historical buildings on the Limmatquai, Tram #4 or #15; and for the miniature railway, Tram #6 to Zurichbergstrasse. The Swiss National Museum is behind the north side of the Bahnhof. Ask the Tourist Office for its clear little city map, which also outlines all the principal runs.

Fares are based on zones; except for Bus #68, which is roughly $4 to or from the airport, you'll pay about 80¢ for the first five stages. You may purchase the money-saving day ticket, which is valid for unlimited travel on all public service vehicles for 24 hours: only $3.50.

At all train stations, snag a luggage cart instead of a porter; you'll save 1 franc per bag.

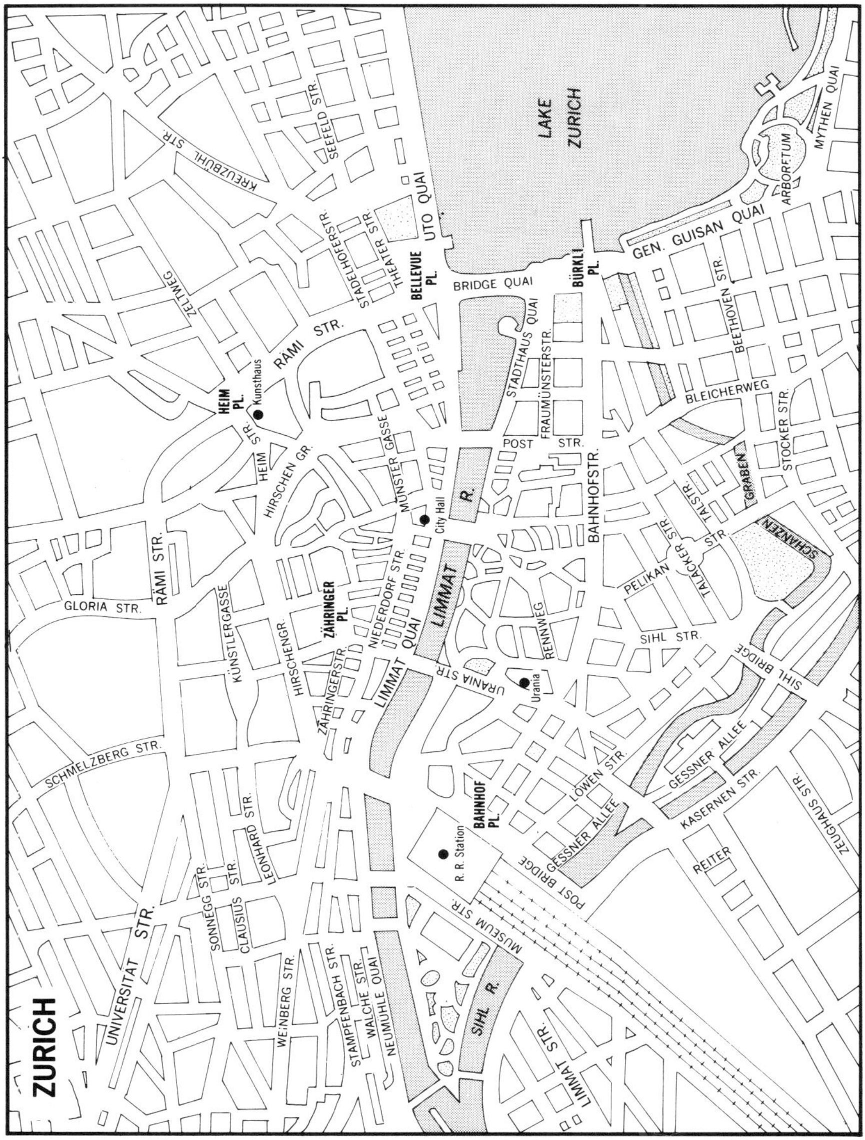
ZURICH
LAKE ZURICH
UTO QUAI
BELLEVUE PL.
BRIDGE QUAI
BÜRKLI PL.
GEN. GUISAN QUAI
ARBORETUM
MYTHEN QUAI
SEEFELD STR.
KREUZBÜHL STR.
STADELHOFERSTR.
THEATER STR.
ZELTWEG
RÄMI STR.
HEIM PL.
Kunsthaus
HEIM STR.
HIRSCHEN GR.
MÜNSTER GASSE
City Hall
R.
LIMMAT
LIMMAT QUAI
NIEDERDORF STR.
ZÄHRINGER PL.
ZÄHRINGERSTR.
HIRSCHENGR.
KÜNSTLERGASSE
GLORIA STR.
RÄMI STR.
SCHMELZBERG STR.
LEONHARD STR.
SONNEGG STR.
CLAUSIUS STR.
UNIVERSITÄT STR.
WEINBERG STR.
STAMPFENBACH STR.
WALCHE STR.
NEUMÜHLE QUAI
SIHL R.
MUSEUM STR.
LIMMAT STR.
R. R. Station
BAHNHOF PL.
POST BRIDGE
GESSNER ALLEE
LÖWEN STR.
URANIA STR.
Urania
RENNWEG
SIHL STR.
PELIKAN STR.
TALACKER STR.
TAL STR.
GRABEN
SCHANZEN
STOCKER STR.
BLEICHERWEG
BEETHOVEN STR.
BAHNHOFSTR.
POST STR.
FRAUMÜNSTERSTR.
STADTHAUS QUAI
SIHL BRIDGE
KASERNEN STR.
ZEUGHAUS STR.
REITER

MOTORSCOOTER HIRE

Local informants say that **F. Hauser** (*Baslerstr. 117*; ☎ *641643*) is the leading agency. Shiny, well-tended, 1- or 2-seat Vespas powered by frisky 50-c.c. to 200-c.c. engines; prices vary with size of vehicle and length of rental.

WHERE TO STAY

If you have any problem upon arrival, the **Tourist Office** at the main station is an excellent travelers' aid; phone ☎ *2114000.*

LEAST $

Schaefli • *Badergasse 6*; ☎ *2514144.* In an alley of the Old Quarter. Active restaurant with live pop music in the evenings. Spacious bedchambers, a few with balconies, no private plumbing, sinks in every room; very few public showers. Singles at $29; per person doubles averaging $25 and triplets at $17. Optional breakfast for $2.50

Martahaus • *Zahringerstr. 36*; ☎ *2514550.* Zurich's leading YWCA. For women, the best buy in town. Handy site across the Limmat from the station. Bedrooms functional. $28 for lodging. 11:30 p.m. lockout.

YMCA • *Sihlstr. 33*; ☎ *2213673.* Only a block from Bahnhofstrasse's smart shops. Perfectly clean. Friendly. About $20 per person.

HOSTEL

Zurich Youth Hostel in suburbs (*Mutschellenstr. 114-116*; ☎ *4823544*). Clean and comfortable; 320 bunks; emergency accommodation for 100 more. Game room, snackery, cafeteria, showers, and clothes-washing nook. Twins $18 in summer, a bit more in winter; 8-person units $6 less; 2-day minimum stay Apr.–end of Oct. Closing hour 10 p.m., with fines imposed until 1 a.m. lockup. Tram #7 from station takes 20 minutes, while walking takes an hour. North American guests without Youth Hostel cards pay $18 per night more than confreres from elsewhere. One of the finest overnighteries of its type in Europe.

Regina *(Hohlstr. 18*; ☎ *2426550)* **Justinushelm** *(Freudenbergstr. 146*; ☎ *3613806*) and **Seefeld** *(Seehofstr. 11*; ☎ *2522570*). Three additional inexpensive, value-packed choices. Excellent small hotels.

MORE $$$

Pension • *St. Josef 64 Hirschengraben*; ☎ *2512757.* Five minutes by foot from station. Beautifully maintained modern Catholic house. Singles at $32, doubles at $63 with bath. Lunch available for $8, light supper for $10. Excellent value.

Poly • *Universitatstr. 63*; ☎ *3629440.* For conventional hotel-style comfort closer in, a cheerful choice. Cozy TV parlor. Pleasant indoor-outdoor restaurant (no alcohol); 15 singles, 24 doubles. All units bright, spotless, and spacious. Most with terraces and good views, some without personal WC. Best picks: #17 twin and #21 single. Lodging with shower $30 for 1, $25 each for 2, or $20 per triplet in trios. Breakfast included at these rates; other meals dispensed at low fixed prices and a la carte. Advance reservations required.

Bristol • *Stampfenbachstr. 34*; ☎ *470700.* Also a "garni" (only breakfast available). Has been totally renovated and appears as a fresh candidate this season. A good choice nowadays and nights.

Limmathaus • *Limmatstr. 118*; ☎ *2715240.* Trams #4 and #13 from the station take about 5 minutes; 55 rooms near National Museum. Institutionlike dining;

menus from $6. Numerous rules for residents. Accommodations good but dated. Clean and commercial.

Vorderer • *Sternen Bellevueplatz*; ☎ *2514949*. On Lake Zurich. Rooming-house demeanor. Street-level Boulevard Restaurant; more formal 2nd-tier dining room. Singles $34 and doubles $48. Careful maintenance.

Hinterer • *Sternen Freieckgasse 7*; ☎ *2513268*. Borders Old Town. Provides ample comfort at $25-$35 per unit. Central address that's interesting.

Italia • *Zeughaustr. 61*; ☎ *2410555*. Nearby with kind reception; rustic-style restaurant. Doubles and triples better bargains than cramped singles. Recommended more for warmth than physical facilities.

Rothus ("Red House") • *Marktgasse 17*; ☎ *2521530*. 53 rooms in the midst of the Old Quarter. Restaurant and bar. Decent but routine sleeping areas.

Seidenhof • *Sihlstr. 7-9*; ☎ *2116544*. A temperance entry in midcity. Beautifully outfitted in sleek modern tones; outstanding comfort; twins in $60 range. Excellent restaurant and snack facility.

Limmathof • *Limmatquai 142*; ☎ *474220*. Continues to offer restricted dimensions, old-fangled plumbing, and old-hat furnishings, but visitors like the staff and homespun comforts such as they are. (Not to be confused with the Limmathaus.)

EVEN MORE $$$

Tiefenau • *Steinwiesstrasse 8-10*; ☎ *2512409*; *U.S./res.* ☎ *(800) 221-8138/9*. Elegance itself, in fine European tradition; many antiques, Persian carpets, crystal chandeliers; handsome cottage-front Au Gourmet restaurant with garden terrace for warm months; tree-lined residential street, but handy to midtown. Gracious hosting. Twin with bath, buffet breakfast, and extras about $175.

Neues Schloss • *Stockerstrasse 17*; ☎ *2016550*. Midtown location; professional management by dynastic Swiss hotel family (Seiler); becoming known nationally for its outstanding restaurant, which is cozy and small. Interior charm belies a disappointing facade. Similar tariffs as Tiefenau.

Arc Royal Comfort Inn • *Leonhardstr. 6*; ☎ *2616710*. Atop steep Weinbergstrasse, near rail terminal and Limmatquai. Bright, airy, breakfast-only den. Roof garden; 8-car garage; 55 chambers—half singles, half doubles—with shower, WC, radio, and phone. Emphasis on function rather than frills (puffy comforters, not blankets, a wonderful exception); $80 and $115 for singles and doubles. Excellent.

Franziskaner • *Niederdorfstr. 1*; ☎ *2510120*. Former private mansion facing fountain and statue of Rudolf Stussi. (As you undoubtedly remember, he was Zurich's Burgermeister from 1430 to 1443.) Fine candlelit dining den. Kembel Bar. Attractive quiet bedchambers; #35, a double overlooking Herr Stussi's bronze cranium, rents for about $75; singles with breakfast $110; Homey.

CAMPING

The Seebucht site in suburban Wollishofen (See *Str. 557*; ☎ *4821612*) has bivouacs with showers, drinking water, toilets, and an especially pleasant rural vista of the hills and the flowing Mythenquai. Since every square inch of turf is usually staked out during high season, it's wiser to telephone before making the trek: about a 15-minute walk from the nearest commuter train stop. It can also be reached by bus. It functions from May through Sept. only. The **Tourist Office** in the Main Station has data, booklets, etc., on the different campsites located within the boundaries of Zurich; facilities and operative periods vary, so it's a good idea to ask for a briefing as soon as you arrive. The Tourist Office is open every day from 8 a.m. until late in the evening.

SUGGESTIONS FOR STUDENTS

The right bank of the Limmat River nourishes the student quarter. Here you'll find the venerable 150-year-old University of Zurich, the famed Swiss Federal Institute of Technology, the **Swiss Student Travel Office**, called SSR (*Leonhardstr. 10*; ☎ *2423000*), and the **International Student Club**, near the Bahnhofstr., left bank of the Limmat. Main streets are Ramistrasse and—appropriately—Universitatstrasse. Seilbahn cable cars scoot into the Institute's backyard from Central Square.

DINING

For students only, the University Cafeteria (*Kunstlergasse 12*) and the Studentheim an der ETH (*Clausiusstr. 21*) lead the pack. Both offer fair cooking, rapid service, sensible tabs of $4 or so for the works. Other good stops for students or the general public are:

Migros Cafeterias (*Sihlbrucke, Loewenstr. 31; Stadelhofen, Falken Str. 19-21; or Limmatplatz 4-6*); **Wellenberg** (*Niederdorfstr. 7*).

NIGHTLIFE

The International Student Club operates a discotheque. Jammed; jovial; drinks not expensive; go about 10 p.m. except on Wed. when it's closed. The infamous "needle park," known as Platz Spitz to the drugs sub-culture, has reopened after a year's clean-up; it now bristles with private security guards.

STUDENT AID

The expert team at the SSTO fields most questions. They'll swamp you with data. In summertime they run a special Student Reception Service—the first one in Switzerland—which not only dishes up every type of travel information about the city and nation, but also offers fondue fests, dancing parties, community sings in a well-known cellar, photo-sightseeing of Zurich, and many other delights. Ask for their cut-rate tickets to local theaters and movie houses (programs frequently in English).

WHERE TO EAT

Meal hours are about the same as they are at home. Most restaurants serve lunch from noon to 2 p.m. and dinner from 6 to 10 p.m. But hotels usually hold back the evening fare until 7 p.m. or later.

LEAST $

Blockhaus • *Schifflande 4 (off Bellevueplatz and Limmatquai);* ☎ *2521453.* Swiss country-inn motif. Wood, wood, everywhere. Soft illumination; piped music. Savory 3-course lunch at $12; fondue a house specialty at $7. Rustic grace, reasonably prompt attention, and praiseworthy foodstuffs.

Bierhalle Kropf • *In Gassen 16;* ☎ *2211805.* One of the oldest restaurants in the land. Great for personality and 19th-century froufrou. Fumbling but friendly service. Simple, delectable meals at rock-bottom prices for such quality (and for high-priced Switzerland). If you like pot-au-feu, here's the best you may find for many a mile. We love it and its authentic antiquity.

Le Dezaley • *Romergasse 7;* ☎ *2516129.* Tucked into narrow side street near Grossmunster. Small, open patio to rear. Swiss cookery at fair prices. Call for reservations. Closed Sun.

Bodega Espanola • *Munstergasse 15*; ☎ *2512310*. Basic but joyful atmosphere. Roving singers in Bilbao costumery. Coal stove between its two dining rooms; Iberian staff. Simple, savory, 7-item menu of Spanish specialties about $8. Make it dinner if you can, because it's livelier.

Restaurant Gleich • *Seefeldstr. 9*; ☎ *2513203*. Vends vegetarian vittles in two chambers. Larger dining area in old style; potted plants (nonedible) near ceiling and others dividing share-and-share-alike tables; fruit juice bar and pastry counter. Mile-long menu; set meals, salads, and entrees. Very popular and extraordinarily good.

Bauschanzli • *Stadthausquai 13*; ☎ *2112862*. Wonderful alfresco spot for a summer day. On an island in the Limmat, reached by a footbridge near Baur au Lac Hotel. Large lunch teller (fixed-price platter) $5; freshwater fish $9 per catch. *Bodenseefelchen* is especially tasty. If you order it, ask your waiter to give you one from "German water" because locals joke that these are bigger. (The Bodensee is simultaneously in Germany, Austria, and Switzerland). Jazz concerts Sun.; swans, gulls, and Mother Nature every day.

Zum Gelben • *Schnabel Zinnengasse 9 (beside the Munsterhof)*; ☎ *2110620*. One of few places in Switzerland where you're likely to find acceptably (but not fully) authentic Chinese cookery (Cantonese). Midcity address difficult to find; 19 tables in two tiny rooms. Tantalizing array of 135 dishes. Generous solo repast came close to $12.

California Asylstrasse • *125*; ☎ *535680*. As simple as American apple pie—also brownies, cheesecake, and like forms of stateside cookery. Corn, chili, T-bones for two, fantastic salads, even California wines! Splendid for homesick tummies.

Mere Catherine • *Up tiny lane off Ruden Platz at Nagelihof 3*; ☎ *2622250*. French in mood—one of best in nation. Animated; timber and stucco; mezzanine globe sconces; several set menus and excellent; also a la carte. Cheapest meal was salad, chicken in roquefort sauce, and green noodles; veal dishes quite appealing too. Varies choices daily. What doesn't vary is the huge slice of pub atmosphere.

Zeughauskeller • *Bahnhofstr. 28-A*; ☎ *211265*. Big regional menu; tubs of pallid Swiss beer. Simple, fairly inexpensive, unelaborate—a good value.

Kantorei • *Spiegelgasse 33*; ☎ *2619962*. Passable beef burgers, quiche and fondue-for-two. Fair for fare but not for flair. Closed Sun.

Malatesta • *Niederdorfstr. 15*; ☎ *2514274*. Small bar and restaurant in Old Quarter. Chianti-style decor. Service so excruciatingly awkward, you might climb the wall.

Alexander Hotel • *Niederdorfstr. 40 (in the Old Quarter)*; ☎ *2518203*. Features streetside counter serving terrific sausages and cheese tartlets. Prices delightfully low; treats hot and flavorful.

CHAINS

Movenpick now has 8 outlets in this city (others in Geneva, Berne, and Lucerne). The most popular example is in *Dreikonighaus at Beethovenstr. 32*; here, as in the Geneva operations, you'll find everything from standup facilities to the Deluxe Baron de la Mouette Rotisserie-Grill. In the eat-and-run section, the customer's exact time of arrival is printed on his order form; 2 huge clocks are visible, and if more than 12 minutes pass between the time the order is given and served, the meal is on the house. (It doesn't happen often!) Another link is the **Silberkugel Hauptbahnhof** (*Bahnhofplatz 14*, directly opposite the railroad station), which has counters for sitting down, counters for standing up, and counters for outgoing orders. With its sandwiches set at such low tabs, it is followed by the crowd. The most elegant entry is the **Pfauen** beside the Schauspielhaus (Theater). The ground floor has a counter section, tables, and food displays; the restaurant upstairs is captivatingly decorated in art nouveau themes. Other Movenpick branches are at *Dreikonigstr. 21* (called Claridenhof), *Paradeplatz*, *Sihlporte* (this one closes Sun.), and in the *Bahnhofplatz subway*.

Migros has a devoted following. It's a proliferating family of supermarket cafeterias in all the major Swiss burgs. Zurich has several. Perhaps the most popular is the Sihlbrucke operation, 10 minutes from the station. Self-service lineup of sliced meats, salads, steam-heated main courses, bread, desserts, and beverages; snacks from $2.75; hot meal from $5.75. A boon if hunger strikes near a suburban outlet.

Feldschlosschen • *Bahnhofstr. 81*; ☎ *2115034*. A very attractive brewer's entrant. Sidewalk cafe for aperitifs; 2-tiered dining inside; charming terrace. Straight from travel posters, and fun.

"Bahnhofbuffet SBB" • Excellent second-class restaurant in main station. Don't wander into glossier first-class precincts unless traveling on expense account.

BARGAIN-BASEMENT BISTROS

Olivenbaum • *Stadelhoferstr. 10*. Leads a sober pack of nonalcoholic, no-tips restaurants.

Rutli • *Asylstr. 110*. A stolid contender in this category. At lunchtime, Frohsinn 4 spots in town.

Karli • *Kirchgasse 14*. Popular with a wide cross section of Zurich's citizenry, plus a fair sprinkling of tourists. Both offer quick, well-presented, ready-made meals (not self-service) at close to $5.50.

SNACKS AND LIGHT BITES

No sweet-toothed traveler should dream of missing the tiny **Schober** on an aisle (*Napfgasse 4*) of Munstergasse in the ancient Niederdorf sector of Old Zurich. The private house (reminiscent of Demel in Vienna) was given to the city; the pastries are marvelous, served on marble-top tables; 2 tiers for nibbling, one having a small garden behind glass. Even if you only order a coffee, try to see it.

STANDUP COUNTERS

Try **Gans** (*Niederdorfstr. 88*) or **Zum vorderen Sternen** (*Bellevueplatz, in the hotel Vorderer Sternen*); both offer fair griddle work, plus greased-lightning service. Just the thing when pinched for time, centimes—or both. Even cheaper?

Marinello is a kiosk on the Gemusebrucke surrounded by vegetable stands; it purveys wursts, ham and eggs, donuts, and pastries for economy tabs.

Cafe Odeon on the banks of Limmat Zurich landmark since 1911. Mata Hari, Lenin, and Mussolini among its frequenters, as were Joyce, Einstein, Thomas Mann, Franz Lehar, Temple Fielding, and numerous others. Turn-of-the-century decor.

MORE $$

Kronenhalle • *Ramistr. 4*. Often comes up with praiseworthy cookery. Service standards awful, but nobody seems to care. Magnificent collection of paintings by world's leading impressionists; brasserie ambience. Rendezvous of journalists and people in the arts. One of the coziest and most beguiling bars in Helvetia directly adjoins.

Haus zum Ruden • *Limmatquai 42.* Built 1295, restored in 1936, and refreshed (but not altered) quite recently. Preserves charm of traditional Guild House. The cookery, however, has gone from hardy fare to nouvelle in the French style. Drop by earlier if you want to reserve a table overlooking the river. Other guild (zunfthaus) choices might include

Zur Waag and **Zur Schmiden** • *Just off the Bahnhofstr. in its own plaza and Marktgasse 20, Niederdorf.* These are distinctive and honored institutions in this city. While not cheap, they do offer superb value.

Monchhof • *Seestr. 30, in neighboring suburb of Kilchberg, about 5 minutes around lake from center.* For attractiveness in agrestic tones, few places of any price category can match it. A reformed lakeside residence offering Edwardian-style pub at ground level and two stunning dining rooms on two tiers above. Windows overlooking both gardens and waterfront; delicious nouvelle cuisine at close to $50 for two with wine and extras. In other establishments of similar stature, the tab could easily be double that amount.

Lindenhofkeller • *Pfalzgasse 4;* ☎ *2117071.* Quiet, elegant rotisserie with brass chandeliers, copper pans on walls, and some of the finest veal to be swallowed anywhere—especially with cream-cognac sauce and morilles (local mushroom). Order regional wine to hold price level within reason.

NIGHTLIFE

Not very much is available since many Zurchers switch off early.

Financial note ... Nightspots charge small or zero admission fees from Sun. through Thurs. On weekends, when you must compete with hordes of hometown swingers, you'll generally pay from $2 on Fri. or from $3 on Sat.

Casa Bar • *Munstergasse 30.* Our leading suggestion. From teatime until 7 p.m.-or-so, light piano music is the drawing card; from about 8 p.m. on, the house throbs with live, big-beat Dixieland. Nondescript decor; packed with sitting and standing bodies; no dancing; poorly ventilated; beer for $1.80; hard drinks for about $4.

Polygon • *Marktgasse 17.* Offers a pretty-polly variety show; otherwise birds of a feather gather at the bar or dance with night owls.

Other options include the **Oepfelchammer** (*Rindermarkt 12*) mostly for students, the **Weisser Wind** (*Oberdorfstr. 20*) with good food in the early evening and good cheer later, and **Select** (*Limmatquai 16*).

TOPLESS BARS

Until recently the Zurich city fathers thought that a topless saloon was an outdoor cafe; they now know differently. None that we saw was much better or worse than the others; if you're bent on suds without duds, they're bustin' out all over the cathedral area off Limmatquai.

DISCOTHEQUES

The Queen Anne • *Club Dufourstrasse 43.* The first in the city open to the general public. Prime situation, only a few steps from the Eden au Lac and Bellerive au Lac Hotels; startingly fancy for this metropolis.

Boite de Nuit • Pleasant in a quiet way. Musical shows nightly; elegant clientele; very a la mode at the moment; perhaps a little too expensive.

PUBS

Of the pair currently in the city, we far prefer the **Oliver Twist** (*Rindermarkt 6, with another entrance on Leuengasse*). Two rooms separated by two bars; several tables and cozy booths; flintlock muskets and coach lamps; piped-in mood music; no-tipping policy. "Sailor's Size" beer steins for $2; pizzas for $3.50; sandwiches for $2; fish 'n' chips for $3.25; so-called apple pie for $1.50. Informal and friendly.

The Carlton Pub in the Carlton Elite Hotel (*Bahnhofstr. 41*), on the other hand, is 1/8th pub and 7/8ths gussied-up hotel bar.

WHAT TO SEE AND DO

From the tops of the encircling hills, the city itself is a stunning sight. Villas and gardens stretch down to the silvery inland sea, with majestic snow-capped mountains always in the background. A TV-observation tower atop the 2860-foot **Uetliberg** puts the entire panorama in focus; three restaurants are available; trains depart from Selnau Station and reach the summit in 30 minutes; round trip is $3.50.

Lindenhof Hill, site of the old Roman fort just opposite the Limmatquai, offers pleasant gardens in a central location. The nearby **Urania Observatory** (*Uraniastr. 9*) provides interesting scientific interpretations of the Zurich nightlife. Go late: 8:30 p.m.–11 p.m. (Apr.–Sept.) or 8 p.m. to 10 p.m. (Oct. to Mar.). Heavenly bodies, courtesy of Leitz.

The **Rietberg** (*Gablerstr. 15*) had (and perhaps still has) the nation's largest and best cache of Asian and African treasures. When last here, the coveted Von der Heydt Collection was on view every day except Mon. (10 a.m.–noon, 2–6 p.m.) Priceless! Admission $1.50; Sun. and Wed. entrance is gratis.

The **Kunsthaus** (*Heimplatz*) guards the city's most fabulous modern Swiss and foreign art collection. No admission charge on Sun. and Wed. afternoons; about $1.50 other times; one of the world's finest.

If you're a Chagall fan, pop into the **Fraumunster Church**, which is oh-so-proud of its stained-glass apse by the Russian master. It's right in the middle of the city.

FOR THE KIDS

They'll relish the **Toy Museum** (*Fortunagasse 15*). Bet you will, too.

If you go for rococo, **Haus zum Rechberg** (*Hirschengraben 40*) is the icing on the local wedding cake. Proud burghers single it out as the finest patrician house of many. In order to preserve its freshness, entry is permitted only on Wed. and Sat. from 2 to 6 p.m. (plus twice a month on the first and third Sun. from 10 a.m. to noon). Other historic buildings: Zimmerleuten at #40, Ruden at #42, and Saffran at #54—all on the Limmatquai in midtown; Meise at #20 and Waag at #8, both on the Munsterhof; Schneidern at Stussihofstatt 3, and Schmiden at Marktgasse 20. Each offers something special to that special sightseer.

BOATING

Many craft for rent along the quays; hourly tariffs in the $5 range. Proprietors Hans Hitz and Walter Jenzer skipper the Utoquai sailings.

J. Sulger (*at Hafen Enge*) and **F. H. Wiss** (*on Seefeldquai*) farther out so less besieged in season. **F. A. Konig** (*Limmatquai, near Restaurant Terrasse*) and **Walter Leeman** (*Burkliplatz, off Bahnhofstr.*) more convenient locations.

Water skiing available from **Bellevueplatz** and **Marina Jelmoli** on the *Stadthausquai.*

ODDITY

The free, municipal collection of cacti—yes, cacti!—is Europe's most complete. Breezy site across from **Belvoir Park** at *Mythenquai 88*; open daily from 8 to 11:30 a.m. and 1:30 to 4:30 p.m. and Sun. from 10 a.m. to noon and 2 to 5 p.m.

SURFING IN ZURICH

You may chuckle at the curl, but an electric wave machine at the **Dolder Grand Hotel's Wellenbad** swells local hearts. It's high above the town—a pool and sunning space; $2.50 admission. About 20 minutes from the center (tram #6 then #5). Open 9 a.m.–8 p.m. all week long.

Finally, the **Miniatur-Eisenbahnanlage** is a toy-size railroad near the zoo. Towns, hamlets, castles, mountains, automatic railways, remote-control steamers, and other real-life objects reproduced in exact dimensions and detail, on a scale of 1 to 25.

WHAT AND WHERE TO BUY

Our first and last errands on Swiss soil are to load up twice on what we consider some of the finest chocolates in the world—Lindt's. **Lindt & Sprungli** are traditionally Switzerland's number-one craftsmen of their art. The vast selection ranges from 50¢ to $25. No candies containing alcohol are passed by U.S. Customs.

SWISS HAND-EMBROIDERIES

Langenthal (*Strehlgasse 29*) has needled its expert way into the finest homes in the world. You'd be surprised to see how reasonable the costs are for linens and other household goods.

HANDCRAFTS

If you want honest-to-goodness regional craftsmanship instead of souvenir-stand junk, **Schweizer Heimatwerk** is tops. Among their many shops, five convenient locations include: *Rudolf-Brun-Brucke* (headquarters); National Bank Building (*Bahnhofstr. 2*); *Rennweg 14* (a few steps away from the main shop) in the main railway station; plus the *Transit Halls A and B in Zurich Airport.* Manageress Brassel in the Rudolf-Brun-Brucke center or Manageress Butler in the Bank Building will take care of you. When you have examined this most exciting harvest of exclusively Swiss treasures, have you finished your adventure in this basic purlieu? Let's hope not—and here's why:

Spindel ("Spindle," *St. Peterstrasse 11 off Bahnhofstrasse 31*) is another offshoot of this organization and within its 3-story structure is one of the best commercial assemblages of international hand-wrought arts and crafts from every European nation. Italian, French, and German hand-loomed materials and hand-printed aprons; English, French, Sardinian, Danish, and Czech traditional and modern ceramics; Portuguese, French, and Italian pewters; wonderful array of Finnish toys; Icelandic and Norwegian homespun knitwear; many, many other transcontinental as well as Swiss delights. See Manageress Akhrif-Hartung.

DEPARTMENT STORE

Jelmoli (*Bahnhofstrasse/Seidengasse 1*) is the largest in the nation and you'll find everything imaginable—even spaetzli makers in the kitchenware department.

Globus is another fine choice.

The main shopping street is *Bahnhofstrasse*; secondary targets abound along *Limmatquai*, *Rennweg*, and *Sihlstrasse*.

FOR MORE INFORMATION ON SWITZERLAND

Eastern USA • Swiss National Tourist Office, *608 Fifth Ave., New York, NY 10020*; ☎ *(212) 757-5944.*

Western USA • *222 N. Sepulveda Blvd. (Suite 1570), El Segundo, CA 90245;* ☎ *(310) 3355980* and *260 Stockton St., San Francisco, CA 94108;* ☎ *(415) 362-2260.*

Mid-western USA • *150 N. Michigan Ave., Chicago, Il. 60601;* ☎ *(312) 630-5840.*

CANADA • *154 University Ave. (Suite 610), Toronto, Ont. M5H 3Y9;* ☎ *(416) 971-9734.*

INSIDER TIP

In Zurich for everyday travel questions you can rely on the **Tourist Office** *at* 15 Bahnhofplatz. *Almost every turn in the Swiss road that can claim more than five people, six cows, and a house cat, also has a tourist information office.*

INDEX

G

J

K

L

Y

Z

PHOTO CREDITS

Student Travel	Norwegian Tourist Board
Belgium	H. Constance Hill
Denmark	Danish Tourist Board
Finland	Finnish Tourist Board
France	French Government Tourist Office
Germany	German National Tourist Office
Greece	Greek National Tourist Organization
Italy	Italian Government Tourist Board
Netherlands	H. Constance Hill
Norway	Norwegian Tourist Board
Spain	Robert Young Pelton/Westlight
Sweden	Swedish Tourist Board
Switzerland	Swiss National Tourist Office

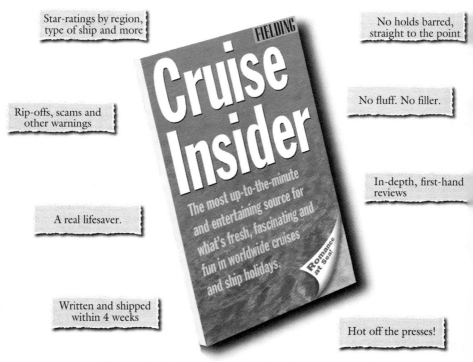

Favorite People, Places & Experiences

ADDRESS:	NOTES:
Name Address Telephone	
Name Address Telephone	
Name Address Telephone	
Name Address Telephone	
Name Address Telephone	
Name Address Telephone	
Name Address Telephone	

Favorite People, Places & Experiences

ADDRESS:	NOTES:
Name Address Telephone	
Name Address Telephone	
Name Address Telephone	
Name Address Telephone	
Name Address Telephone	
Name Address Telephone	
Name Address Telephone	

Favorite People, Places & Experiences

ADDRESS:	NOTES:
Name **Address** **Telephone**	
Name **Address** **Telephone**	
Name **Address** **Telephone**	
Name **Address** **Telephone**	
Name **Address** **Telephone**	
Name **Address** **Telephone**	
Name **Address** **Telephone**	

Favorite People, Places & Experiences

ADDRESS:	NOTES:
Name Address Telephone	
Name Address Telephone	
Name Address Telephone	
Name Address Telephone	
Name Address Telephone	
Name Address Telephone	
Name Address Telephone	

Favorite People, Places & Experiences

ADDRESS:	NOTES:
Name **Address** **Telephone**	
Name **Address** **Telephone**	
Name **Address** **Telephone**	
Name **Address** **Telephone**	
Name **Address** **Telephone**	
Name **Address** **Telephone**	
Name **Address** **Telephone**	

Favorite People, Places & Experiences

ADDRESS:	NOTES:
Name Address Telephone	
Name Address Telephone	
Name Address Telephone	
Name Address Telephone	
Name Address Telephone	
Name Address Telephone	
Name Address Telephone	

Favorite People, Places & Experiences

ADDRESS:	NOTES:
Name **Address** **Telephone**	
Name **Address** **Telephone**	
Name **Address** **Telephone**	
Name **Address** **Telephone**	
Name **Address** **Telephone**	
Name **Address** **Telephone**	
Name **Address** **Telephone**	

Favorite People, Places & Experiences

ADDRESS:	NOTES:
Name Address Telephone	
Name Address Telephone	
Name Address Telephone	
Name Address Telephone	
Name Address Telephone	
Name Address Telephone	
Name Address Telephone	

Favorite People, Places & Experiences

ADDRESS:	NOTES:

Name

Address

Telephone

Name

Address

Telephone

Name

Address

Telephone

Name

Address

Telephone

Name

Address

Telephone

Name

Address

Telephone

Name

Address

Telephone

Favorite People, Places & Experiences

ADDRESS:	NOTES:
Name	
Address	
Telephone	
Name	
Address	
Telephone	
Name	
Address	
Telephone	
Name	
Address	
Telephone	
Name	
Address	
Telephone	
Name	
Address	
Telephone	
Name	
Address	
Telephone	

Favorite People, Places & Experiences

ADDRESS:	NOTES:
Name Address Telephone	
Name Address Telephone	
Name Address Telephone	
Name Address Telephone	
Name Address Telephone	
Name Address Telephone	
Name Address Telephone	

Favorite People, Places & Experiences

ADDRESS:	NOTES:
Name Address Telephone	
Name Address Telephone	
Name Address Telephone	
Name Address Telephone	
Name Address Telephone	
Name Address Telephone	
Name Address Telephone	

Favorite People, Places & Experiences

ADDRESS:	NOTES:
Name Address Telephone	
Name Address Telephone	
Name Address Telephone	
Name Address Telephone	
Name Address Telephone	
Name Address Telephone	
Name Address Telephone	

Favorite People, Places & Experiences

ADDRESS:	NOTES:
Name Address Telephone	
Name Address Telephone	
Name Address Telephone	
Name Address Telephone	
Name Address Telephone	
Name Address Telephone	
Name Address Telephone	

Favorite People, Places & Experiences

ADDRESS:	NOTES:
Name Address Telephone	
Name Address Telephone	
Name Address Telephone	
Name Address Telephone	
Name Address Telephone	
Name Address Telephone	
Name Address Telephone	